1956	1958	1960	1962	1964	1966	1968	1970	1971	1972	1973	1974	1975	1976	1977
271.9	296.6	332.3	363.8	411.7	481.8	558.7	648.9	702.4	770.7	852.5	932.4	1,030.3	1,149.8	1,278.4
72.0	64.5	78.9	88.1	102.1	131.3	141.2	152.4	178.2	207.6	244.5	249.4	230.2	292.0	361.3
91.8	106.5	113.8	132.2	145.1	174.3	212.8	237.1	251.0	270.1	287.9	322.4	361.1	384.5	415.3
2.3	0.4	2.4	2.4	5.5	1.9	−1.3	1.2	−3.0	−8.0	0.6	−3.1	13.6	−2.3	−23.7
438.0	467.9	527.4	586.5	664.4	789.3	911.5	1,039.7	1,128.6	1,240.4	1,385.5	1,501.0	1,635.2	1,823.9	2,031.4
47.3	52.7	57.0	61.0	66.6	85.6	90.9	109.1	118.9	130.9	142.9	164.8	193.0	208.9	231.6
390.7	415.2	470.4	525.5	597.8	712.7	820.6	930.6	1,009.7	1,109.5	1,242.6	1,336.2	1,444.2	1,615.0	1,799.8
−2.5	−2.7	−3.2	−4.3	−5.0	−5.2	−6.2	−6.4	−7.7	−8.7	−12.7	−15.7	−13.3	−17.2	−20.7
34.5	40.6	46.1	52.7	60.7	71.2	83.2	99.5	113.5	117.8	127.9	140.0	155.3	175.8	184.7
358.7	377.3	427.5	477.1	542.1	646.7	743.6	837.5	903.9	1,000.4	1,127.4	1,211.9	1,302.2	1,456.4	1,635.8
10.0	11.4	16.4	19.1	22.4	31.3	38.7	46.4	51.2	59.2	75.5	85.2	89.3	101.3	113.1
22.0	19.0	22.7	24.0	28.0	33.7	39.4	34.4	37.7	41.9	49.3	51.8	50.9	64.2	73.0
14.1	11.9	16.3	22.6	28.6	37.6	33.6	23.0	32.4	41.1	44.8	29.5	49.1	57.3	73.1
27.4	35.0	40.6	46.5	52.7	62.3	82.6	107.4	122.5	136.1	156.6	180.2	218.8	241.8	260.5
340.0	370.0	412.7	457.9	515.8	606.4	714.5	841.1	905.1	994.3	1,113.4	1,225.6	1,331.7	1,475.4	1,637.1
37.2	39.2	46.5	52.3	52.8	67.3	88.3	104.6	103.4	125.7	134.4	153.3	150.3	175.5	201.1
302.8	330.8	366.2	405.6	463.0	539.1	626.2	736.5	801.7	868.6	979.0	1,072.3	1,181.4	1,299.9	1,436.0

1956	1958	1960	1962	1964	1966	1968	1970	1971	1972	1973	1974	1975	1976	1977
2,141.1	2,162.8	2,376.7	2,578.9	2,846.5	3,227.5	3,466.1	3,578.0	3,697.7	3,898.4	4,123.4	4,099.0	4,084.4	4,311.7	4,511.8
2.0	−1.0	2.5	6.0	5.8	6.6	4.8	0.2	3.3	5.4	5.8	−0.6	−0.4	5.6	4.6
8,930	8,922	9,210	9,666	10,456	11,417	12,196	12,823	13,218	13,692	14,496	14,268	14,393	14,873	15,256
27.2	28.9	29.6	30.2	31.0	32.4	34.8	38.8	40.5	41.8	44.4	49.3	53.8	56.9	60.6
1.5	2.8	1.7	1.0	1.3	2.9	4.2	5.7	4.4	3.2	6.2	11.0	9.1	5.8	6.5
27.4	26.0	29.7	32.4	36.6	43.9	47.3	47.9	48.5	53.2	57.5	57.2	52.0	56.0	60.1
136.0	138.4	140.7	147.8	160.3	172.0	197.4	214.3	228.2	249.1	262.7	274.0	286.8	305.9	330.5
3.77	3.83	4.82	4.50	4.50	5.63	6.30	7.91	5.72	5.25	8.03	10.81	7.86	6.84	6.83
168.9	174.9	180.7	186.5	191.9	196.6	200.7	205.1	207.7	209.9	211.9	213.9	216.0	218.0	220.2
66.6	67.6	69.6	70.6	73.1	75.8	78.7	82.8	84.4	87.0	89.4	91.9	93.8	96.2	99.0
2.8	4.6	3.9	3.9	3.8	2.9	2.8	4.1	5.0	4.9	4.4	5.2	7.9	7.4	7.0
4.1	6.8	5.5	5.5	5.2	3.8	3.6	4.9	5.9	5.6	4.9	5.6	8.5	7.7	7.1
43.4	46.0	48.8	52.9	57.5	62.0	65.4	67.0	69.9	72.2	74.5	73.2	75.8	78.5	79.8
0.1	2.9	1.9	4.6	4.6	4.1	3.1	2.0	4.4	3.3	3.2	−1.7	3.5	3.6	1.6
2.7	0.8	2.8	3.4	6.8	3.0	0.6	2.3	−1.4	−5.8	7.1	2.0	18.1	4.3	−14.3
272.7	279.7	290.5	302.9	316.1	328.5	368.7	380.9	408.2	435.9	466.3	483.9	541.9	629.0	706.4

(Continued)

Economics

Principles, Problems, and Policies

SIXTEENTH EDITION

Economics
Principles, Problems, and Policies

Campbell R. McConnell
University of Nebraska

Stanley L. Brue
Pacific Lutheran University

 **McGraw-Hill
Irwin**

Boston   Burr Ridge, IL   Dubuque, IA   Madison, WI   New York   San Francisco   St. Louis
Bangkok   Bogotá   Caracas   Kuala Lumpur   Lisbon   London   Madrid   Mexico City
Milan   Montreal   New Delhi   Santiago   Seoul   Singapore   Sydney   Taipei   Toronto

To **Mem** and to **Terri** and **Craig**

McGraw-Hill
Irwin

ECONOMICS: PRINCIPLES, PROBLEMS, AND POLICIES

Published by McGraw-Hill/Irwin, a business unit of The McGraw-Hill Companies, Inc., 1221 Avenue of the Americas, New York, NY, 10020. Copyright © 2005, 2002, 1999, 1996, 1993, 1990, 1987, 1984, 1981, 1978, 1975, 1972, 1969, 1966, 1963, 1960 by The McGraw-Hill Companies, Inc. All rights reserved. No part of this publication may be reproduced or distributed in any form or by any means, or stored in a database or retrieval system, without the prior written consent of The McGraw-Hill Companies, Inc., including, but not limited to, in any network or other electronic storage or transmission, or broadcast for distance learning.

Some ancillaries, including electronic and print components, may not be available to customers outside the United States.

This book is printed on acid-free paper.

domestic   1 2 3 4 5 6 7 8 9 0 VNH/VNH 0 9 8 7 6 5 4
international   1 2 3 4 5 6 7 8 9 0 VNH/VNH 0 9 8 7 6 5 4

ISBN 0-07-281935-9

Publisher: *Gary Burke*
Executive sponsoring editor: *Lucille Sutton*
Developmental editor: *Erin Strathmann*
Editorial assistant: *Rebecca Hicks*
Editorial coordinator: *Karen Minnich*
Marketing manager: *Martin D. Quinn*
Lead developer, Media technology: *Anthony Sherman*
Senior project manager: *Jean Lou Hess*
Senior production supervisor: *Rose Hepburn*
Director of design BR: *Keith J. McPherson*
Photo research coordinator: *Judy Kausal*
Photo research: *Robin Sand*
Lead supplement producer: *Becky Szura*
Senior digital content specialist: *Brian Nacik*
Cover design: *Michael Warrell, Design Solutions*
Interior design: *Michael Warrell, Design Solutions*
Typeface: *10/12 Jansen*
Cover, part/chapter opening image photographer: © *Photonica Toshiya Kumakura*
Compositor: *GTS Companies, York, PA Campus*
Printer: *Von Hoffmann Corporation*

Library of Congress Cataloging-in-Publication Data

McConnell, Campbell R.
     Economics : principles, problems, and policies / Campbell R. McConnell, Stanley L. Brue.—16th ed.
          p. cm.
     Various multi-media supplements are available to supplement the text.
     Includes index.
     ISBN 0-07-281935-9 (alk. paper)—ISBN 0-07-111212-X (international : alk. paper)
     1. Economics. I. Brue, Stanley L., 1945–   II. Title.
HB171.5.M47 2005
330—dc22

                                                2003061502

INTERNATIONAL EDITION ISBN 0-07-111212-X
Copyright © 2005. Exclusive rights by The McGraw-Hill Companies, Inc. for manufacture and export. This book cannot be re-exported from the country to which it is sold by McGraw-Hill. The International Edition is not available in North America.

www.mhhe.com

Campbell R. McConnell earned his Ph.D. from the University of Iowa after receiving degrees from Cornell College and the University of Illinois. He taught at the University of Nebraska–Lincoln from 1953 until his retirement in 1990. He is also coauthor of *Contemporary Labor Economics*, sixth edition (McGraw-Hill/Irwin), and has edited readers for the principles and labor economics courses. He is a recipient of both the University of Nebraska Distinguished Teaching Award and the James A. Lake Academic Freedom Award and is past president of the Midwest Economics Association. Professor McConnell was awarded an honorary Doctor of Laws degree from Cornell College in 1973 and received its Distinguished Achievement Award in 1994. His primary areas of interest are labor economics and economic education. He has an extensive collection of jazz recordings and enjoys reading jazz history.

Stanley L. Brue did his undergraduate work at Augustana College (South Dakota) and received its Distinguished Achievement Award in 1991. He received his Ph.D. from the University of Nebraska–Lincoln. He is a professor at Pacific Lutheran University, where he has been honored as a recipient of the Burlington Northern Faculty Achievement Award. Professor Brue has also received the national Leavey Award for excellence in economic education. He has served as national president and chair of the Board of Trustees of Omicron Delta Epsilon International Economics Honorary. He is coauthor of *Economic Scenes*, fifth edition (Prentice-Hall), and *Contemporary Labor Economics*, sixth edition (McGraw-Hill/Irwin), and author of *The Evolution of Economic Thought*, sixth edition (South-Western). For relaxation, he enjoys international travel, attending sporting events, and skiing with family and friends.

LIST OF KEY GRAPHS

We have always had three main goals for *Economics* (and its companion editions, *Macroeconomics* and *Microeconomics*), the nation's best-selling textbook. Those goals remain and are spelled out under "Fundamental Objectives" below, but the sixteenth edition embodies a new and exciting development that deserves your earliest attention: The sixteenth edition is accompanied by and integrated with a phenomenal new enhancement, *DiscoverEcon* with Paul Solman Videos*, that brings to economics education an entirely new level of excellence and excitement not possible in earlier editions. This new program, which consists of video tutorials by Paul Solman, the noted Economics Correspondent (Public Television), interactive exercises, and testing (supported by a powerful classroom management system allowing the reporting of results by students to instructors), promises to set a new standard in the ease and excellence of economics instruction.

Our users have always known those things that a book does best. And the sixteenth edition recognizes that

*Developed by Gerald Nelson at the University of Illinois, Urbana-Champaign.

principle. *DiscoverEcon with Paul Solman Videos* is not a book replacement program. It is an exciting extension of this edition that will allow students to hear real lectures on key concepts anywhere and anytime they have access to a computer. Those same students will be able to build and practice economic skills, and report the results to their instructors online. The method for this has been kept simple while the message has been kept foremost. Economics matters.

We are particularly pleased that recent editions have gained market share in the face of formidable new entries. An estimated 13 million students worldwide have now used this book. *Economics* has been adapted into Australian and Canadian editions and translated into Italian, Russian, Chinese, French, Spanish, Portuguese, and other languages. It continues to be used in Russia and other Russian-speaking countries.

Fundamental Objectives

We have three main goals for *Economics:*
* Help the beginning student master the principles essential for understanding the economizing problem, specific economic issues, and the policy alternatives.
* Help the student understand and apply the economic perspective and reason accurately and objectively about economic matters.

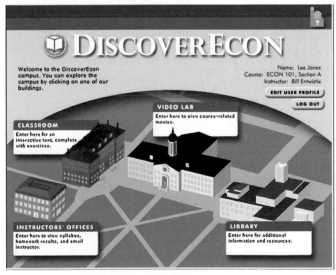

Web link: www.mcconnell16.com/discoverecon

- Promote a lasting student interest in economics and the economy.

What's New and Improved?

One of the benefits of writing a text that has met the market test is the opportunity to revise—to delete the outdated and install the new, to rewrite misleading or ambiguous statements, to introduce more relevant illustrations, to improve the organizational structure, and to enhance the learning aids. A chapter-by-chapter list of changes is available at our website, www.mcconnell16.com. The more significant changes include the following.

Two-Path Macro

We have extensively reorganized and revised Chapters 9, 10, and 11 to provide two alternative paths through the macro. We know that nearly all instructors like to cover somewhere in their macro course the basic relationships between income and consumption, the real interest rate and investment, and changes in spending and changes in output (the multiplier, conceptually presented). So now all these topics are found in Chapter 9, "Basic Macroeconomic Relationships." The instructor can then proceed from Chapter 9 directly to either Chapter 10 "The Aggregate Expenditures Model" or Chapter 11, "Aggregate Demand and Aggregate Supply." This organization is logical and allows those instructors who prefer not to teach the equilibrium AE model to skip it without loss of continuity. As before, the remainder of the macro is AD-AS based.

CONSIDER THIS . . .

A Matter of Degrees: Is College Worth the Cost?

Teachers and parents constantly encourage able students to attend college. Yet Microsoft cofounder Bill Gates and talk show host Oprah Winfrey* both dropped out of college, and baseball star Alex Rodriguez never even bothered to enroll. Is it wrong to emphasize college, or did Gates, Winfrey, and Rodriguez make good choices?

Deciding to go to college involves weighing future benefits and present costs. The future benefits are higher expected-lifetime earnings. The present costs include *direct costs*, such as tuition and books, and the *indirect costs* (or *opportunity costs*) of forgoing income that could be earned as a full-time worker with a high school diploma. Students attend college because they expect the long-run benefits of a degree to exceed the short-term costs.

Unlike most students, Gates faced huge opportunity costs for staying in college. He had a vision for his company, and starting work young helped ensure Microsoft's success. Similarly, Winfrey landed a spot in local television news when she was a teenager, eventually producing and starring in the *Oprah Winfrey Show* when she was 32 years old. Getting a degree in her twenties might have interrupted the string of successes that made her famous talk show possible. And Rodriguez knew that professional athletes have short careers. Therefore, going to college directly after high school would have taken away four years of his peak earning potential.

So Gates, Winfrey, and Rodriguez understood opportunity costs and made good choices. But it's important to note that their experiences are not typical. College graduates usually earn about 50 percent more during their lifetimes than persons with just high school diplomas. For most students, "Go to college, stay in college, and earn a degree" is very sound advice.

*Winfrey eventually went back to school and earned a degree from Tennessee State University when she was in her thirties.

© Stefan Zaklin/Getty Images

Consider This Vignettes

New to the book are 32 analogies, examples, or stories that help drive home central economic ideas in a student-oriented, real-world manner. For instance, the idea of trade secrets is described with the story of "catgut" and violin strings, while the income of street entertainers is shown to suffer from the fact that they provide a type of public good. These brief vignettes, each accompanied by a photo, illustrate key points in a lively, colorful, and easy-to-remember way.

Contemporary Discussions and Examples

The sixteenth edition contains discussions of many new or extended topics. Here are a few:
- The economics of the war on terrorism
- China's rapidly emerging economy
- Corporate financial and accounting misconduct
- Explosion of demand for DVD players, DVDs, and digital cameras
- New marginal income tax brackets
- Expansion of the European Union
- Consumption impacts of mortgage refinancing
- The recession of 2001 and the sluggish recovery of 2002 and early 2003
- Bush tax cuts, expansionary fiscal policy, and soaring Federal budget deficits
- Fed-engineered interest-rate cuts
- The debate over artful monetary management versus inflation targeting
- The continuing productivity surge
- Minimum efficient scale applications (commercial aircraft versus redi-mix concrete plants)
- Effects of rising insurance costs on the cost curves of individual firms
- Strategic behavior as an entry barrier
- The 10 most rapidly expanding, and the 10 most rapidly declining, U.S. occupations
- Diverging profit paths of Wal-Mart and Kmart
- Global warming issues
- Alternative antitrust philosophies
- The Microsoft antitrust case
- Subsidies under the Farm Act of 2002
- The Gini ratio as a measure of income inequality
- Prescription drug coverage and other health care issues
- Large U.S. trade deficits

Revised Demand and Supply Chapter and Elasticity Chapter

We have moved the discussion of price floors and price ceilings in Chapter 20 of the previous edition to Chapter 3 on demand and supply. Chapter 20 ("Elasticity of Demand and Supply") now has a tighter focus and also has room for new elasticity-of-supply applications that relate to antiques versus reproductions and to the volatile price of gold.

Three Bonus Web Chapters, Including a Second Supply and Demand Chapter

Three chapters are available for free use at our website, www.mcconnell16.com. The first of these, "Applications and Extensions of Supply and Demand Analysis" (3Web), is entirely new and provides real-world examples of changes in supply and demand, shortages and surpluses arising from preset prices, and overconsumption of non-priced goods (or resources). For instructors who want to extend the supply and demand analysis of Chapter 3, this chapter also explains consumer surplus, producer surplus, and efficiency losses. The other two web chapters, "The Economics of Developing Countries" (39Web) and "Transition Economies: Russia and China" (40Web), are also available for instructors and students who have a special interest in those topics. The three web chapters have the same design, color, and features as regular book chapters, are readable in Adobe Acrobat format, and can be printed if desired. All are supported by the *Study Guide*, Test Banks, and other supplements to the book.

New Web Button Content

We continue to link the book through web buttons to pedagogical features found at our website. Two types of icons appear throughout the book, indicating that additional content on a subject can be found online. Button types include:

 This symbol directs students to **Interactive Graphs.** Developed under the supervision of Norris Peterson of Pacific Lutheran University, this interactive feature depicts major graphs and instructs students to shift the curves, observe the outcomes, and derive relevant generalizations. Ten new Interactive Graphs have been added to the twenty in the previous edition.

Production Possibilities Curve

The data presented in a production possibilities table can also be shown graphically. We use a simple two-dimensional graph, arbitrarily representing the output of capital goods (here, robots) on the vertical axis and the output of consumer goods (here, pizzas) on the horizontal axis, as shown in **Figure 2.1 (Key Graph).** Following the procedure given in the appendix to Chapter 1, we can graph a **production possibilities curve**

2.1 Production possibilities curve

curve is a production *frontier* because it sh attainable outputs. To obtain the various pizza and robots that fall *on* the product curve, society must achieve both full empl ductive efficiency. Points lying *inside* (to curve are also attainable, but they reflect therefore are not as desirable as points on inside the curve imply that the economy c of both robots and pizzas if it achieved f and productive efficiency. Points lying *outs* of) the production possibilities curve, like

 This symbol directs students to **Origins of the Idea.** These brief histories were written by Randy Grant of Linfield College and, with the new entries, examine the origins of 70 major ideas identified in the book. Students will find it interesting to learn about the economists who first developed such ideas as opportunity costs, equilibrium price, the multiplier, comparative advantage, and elasticity.

GLOBAL PERSPECTIVE 5.1

The World's 10 Largest Corporations
Five of the world's ten largest corporations, based on dollar revenue in 2002, were headquartered in the United States.

- Wal-Mart (USA) $247 billion
- General Motors (USA) $187 billion
- Exxon Mobil (USA) $182 billion
- Shell (Britain/Netherlands) $179 billion
- BP (Britain) $179 billion
- Ford Motor (USA) $164 billion
- DaimlerChrysler (Germany) $141 billion
- Toyota (Japan) $132 billion
- General Electric (USA) $132 billion
- Mitsubishi (Japan) $109 billion

Source: Fortune, www.fortune.com.

New Last Words and Global Perspectives

New *Last Word* topics are September 11 and the war on terrorism (Chapter 2); efficiency gains from generic drugs (Chapter 3Web); the long-run fiscal imbalance in the Social Security system (Chapter 18); pricing based on differences in group demand elasticity (Chapter 20); the controversy over CEO pay (Chapter 28); and the WTO protests (Chapter 37). In addition, a few Last Words have been relocated to match reorganized content.

New *Global Perspective* pieces include a list of the world's 10 largest corporations (Chapter 5), the top 12 globalized nations (Chapter 6), the full-employment budget deficits or surpluses in selected nations (Chapter 12), and U.S. goods and services trade deficits with selected nations (Chapter 38).

LAST WORD September 11, 2001, and the War on T

Production Possibilities Analysis Provides Insights on the Economic Effects of the Terrorist Attacks on the United States and the U.S. Government Response at Home, in Afghanistan, and in Iraq.

The horrific destruction of buildings in New York (World Trade Center) and Virginia (Pentagon) resulting from the September 11, 2001, terrorist attacks not only caused tremendous loss of life but also reduced U.S. production capacity. In production possibilities analysis, this outcome is illustrated as an inward shift of the economy's production possibilities curve. But this shift was relatively slight because the attacks destroyed only a small fraction of the nation's labor and capital. In fact, the loss of capital (about $16 billion) was similar to the losses the United States experienced in major natural disasters such as hurricanes and earthquakes. The loss of nearly 3000 lives, however, was greater than in those occurrences. These deaths reduced future output and earnings by an estimated $3 billion to $4 billion.*

Production possibilities analysis also is helpful in assessing the costs and benefits of waging the war on terrorism, in-cluding

framework is a useful way of approaching choice ficiency requires that society expand producti goods until MB   MC.

The events of September 11, 2001, and the they posed increased the perceived marginal b goods. If we label the horizontal axis in Figure 2. fense goods," rightward sh curve, you w optimal qua goods rises. In cerns relating 11, the United more of its r fense. But the also reminds too much or as too little. T should not e goods beyond MB   MC. If i sacrificing civi greater value goods obtaine

It is too so whether the t and the div sources to military action and homeland defense growth of U.S. production capacity. On the one h curity measures throughout the economy may d away from capacity-expanding capital to capital th ects existing capital. (Governm required lug

Distinguishing Features

Comprehensive Explanations at an Appropriate Level *Economics* is comprehensive, analytical, and challenging yet fully accessible to a wide range of students. Its thoroughness and accessibility enable instructors to select topics for special classroom emphasis with confidence that students can read and comprehend independently other assigned material in the book. Where needed, an extra sentence of explanation is provided. Brevity at the expense of clarity is false economy.

Fundamentals of the Market System Many economies throughout the world are making difficult transitions from planning to markets. Our detailed description of the institutions and operation of the *market system* in Chapter 4 is even more relevant than before. We pay particular attention to property rights, entrepreneurship, freedom of enterprise and choice, competition, and the role of profits because these concepts are often misunderstood by beginning students.

Early Integration of International Economics We give the principles and institutions of the global economy early treatment. Chapter 6 examines the growth of world trade, the major participants in world trade, specialization and comparative advantage (without the more difficult graphs), the foreign exchange market, tariffs and subsidies, and various trade agreements. This strong introduction to international economics permits "globalization" of later discussions in both the macro and the micro chapters.

Early and Extensive Treatment of Government Government is an integral component of modern capitalism. This book introduces the economic functions of government early and accords them systematic treatment in Chapter 5. Chapter 30 examines government and market failure in further detail, and Chapter 31 looks at salient facets of public choice theory and taxation. Both the macro and the micro sections of the text include issue- and policy-oriented chapters.

Step-by-Step Approach to Macro We believe that it is a mistake to yank the student back and forth between elaborate macro models. So we systematically present macroeconomics by:
- Examining the National Income and Product Accounts and previewing economic growth, unemployment, and inflation

- Discussing three key macro relationships
- Presenting the aggregate expenditures model (AE model) in a single chapter
- Developing the aggregate demand–aggregate supply model (AD-AS model)
- Using the AD-AS model to discuss fiscal policy
- Introducing monetary considerations into the AD-AS model
- Using the AD-AS model to discuss monetary policy
- Extending the AD-AS model to include both short-run and long-run aggregate supply
- Applying the "extended AD-AS model" to macroeconomic instability, economic growth, and disagreements on macro theory and policy.

Emphasis on Technological Change and Economic Growth This edition continues to emphasize economic growth. Chapter 2 uses the production possibilities curve to show the basic ingredients of growth. Chapter 8 explains how growth is measured and presents the facts of growth. Chapter 17 discusses the causes of growth, looks at productivity growth and the New Economy, and addresses some of the controversies surrounding economic growth. Chapter 26 provides an explicit and cohesive discussion of the microeconomics of technological advance, including topics such as invention, innovation, and diffusion; start-up firms; R&D decision making; market structure and R&D effort; and creative destruction. Chapter 39Web focuses on the developing countries and the growth obstacles they confront. Chapter 40Web examines growth in China and Russia.

Stress on the Theory of the Firm We have given much attention to microeconomics in general and to the theory of the firm in particular, for two reasons: First, the concepts of microeconomics are difficult for most beginning students; abbreviated expositions usually compound these difficulties by raising more questions than they answer. Second, we wanted to couple analysis of the various market structures with a discussion of the impact of each market arrangement on price, output levels, resource allocation, and the rate of technological advance.

Focus on Economic Policy and Issues For many students, the macro chapters on fiscal policy, monetary policy, and public debt and the micro chapters on antitrust, agriculture, income inequality, labor issues, and health care are where the action is. We guide that action along logical lines through the application of appropriate analytical tools. In the micro, we favor inclusiveness; instructors can effectively choose two or three chapters from Part 9.

Integrated Text and Website *Economics* and its website are highly integrated through in-text web buttons, web-based end-of-chapter questions, bonus web chapters, multiple-choice self-tests at the website, web newspaper articles, web math notes, and other features. Our website is part and parcel of our student learning package, customized to the book.

Organizational Alternatives

Although instructors generally agree as to the content of principles of economics courses, they often differ as to how to arrange the material. *Economics* includes 10 parts, and that provides considerable organizational flexibility. We chose to move from macroeconomics to microeconomics because that is the course sequence at the majority of colleges and universities. The introductory material of Part 1, however, can be followed immediately by the microanalysis of Parts 6 and 7. Similarly, the two-path macro enables covering the full aggregate expenditures model or advancing directly from the basic macro relationships chapter to the AD-AS model.

Some instructors will prefer to intersperse the microeconomics of Parts 6 to 8 with the problems chapters of Part 9. Chapter 33 on agriculture may follow Chapter 23 on pure competition; Chapter 32 on antitrust and regulation may follow Chapters 24 to 26 on imperfect competition models and technological advance. Chapter 35 on labor market issues (unions, discrimination, and immigration) may follow Chapter 28 on wages; and Chapter 34 on income inequality may follow Chapters 28 and 29 on distributive shares of national income.

Instructors who teach the typical two-semester course and feel comfortable with the book's organization will find that, by putting Parts 1 to 5 in the first semester and Parts 6 to 10 in the second, the material is divided logically between the two semesters. For those instructors who choose to emphasize international economics, Parts 1 to 5 and 10 may be treated the first semester, and Parts 6 to 9 the second.

Those teaching a one-semester course will discern several possible chapter groupings. At the end of the Table of Contents we suggest outlines for three one-semester courses, emphasizing macroeconomics, microeconomics, or a survey of micro and macro theory, and two one-quarter-course options.

Pedagogical Aids

Economics is highly student-oriented. The "To the Student" statement at the beginning of Part 1 details the book's many pedagogical aids. The sixteenth edition is also accompanied by a variety of high-quality supplements that help students master the subject and help instructors implement customized courses.

Supplements for Students

- **Study Guide** William Walstad of the University of Nebraska at Lincoln, who is one of the world's leading experts on economic education, has prepared the sixteenth edition of the *Study Guide*, which many students find indispensable. Each chapter contains an introductory statement, a checklist of behavioral objectives, an outline, a list of important terms, fill-in questions, problems and projects, objective questions, and discussion questions. The answers to *Economics'* end-of-chapter Key Questions appear at the end of the *Study Guide*, along with the text's glossary.

  The *Guide* comprises a superb "portable tutor" for the principles student. Separate *Study Guides* are available for the macro and micro paperback editions of the text.

- **DiscoverEcon with Paul Solman Videos** (www.mcconnell16.com/discoverecon) A DVD and software program, this student online tutorial plus videos is new with the sixteenth edition of McConnell and Brue. It contains a fully updated and enhanced version of DiscoverEcon, developed by Gerald C. Nelson at the University of Illinois–Urbana–Champaign, with topical reviews, exercises, interactive graphs, multiple-choice test questions, and the option for e-submission of test and essay results to the instructor. It provides links to related videos for key topics on an accompanying DVD. Paul Solman, economics correspondent for *The Lehrer News Hour*, is the creator of the video component, which consists of 30 video segments ranging from 7 to 10 minutes in length. They explain the key economic ideas such as economic growth, elasticity, and production possibilities in a memorable, accessible way. All of these resources are closely linked to the text by chapter and page references.

- **Website** (www.mcconnell16.com) Highly visible "Web buttons" in the text alert students to points in the book where they can springboard to the site to learn more. There also are weekly news updates, an interactive glossary, and self-grading tests—all specific to *Economics*. For the math-minded student, there

From a Chapter 2 video, Production Possibilities.

is a "Want To See the Math?" section, written by Professor Norris Peterson, where they can explore the mathematical details of the concepts in the text. There are also three optional bonus web chapters, as previously discussed.

Supplements for Instructors

- **Online Course Management with DiscoverEcon with Paul Solman Videos** With the new DiscoverEcon with Paul Solman Videos, instructors can assign the DiscoverEcon software exercises as homework, track student participation and progress, and give immediate feedback on student essays. The new syllabus development tool makes it possible to build an online syllabus with direct linking to DiscoverEcon exercises, special websites and the Solman videos. In addition to the DiscoverEcon interactive exercises that give every student a unique problem set, the software now contains ALL end-of-chapter questions, with a newly designed graph tool that lets students construct graphs to answer questions and include them with the essay answers. Essay grading is dramatically simplified with the new instructor website that shows the student answer and a recommended answer written by Stan Brue.
- **Instructor's Manual** Randy Grant of Linfield College has revised and updated the *Instructor's Resource Manual*. It includes chapter summaries, listings of "what's new" in each chapter, teaching tips and suggestions, learning objectives, chapter outlines, data and visual aid sources with suggestions for classroom use, and questions and problems.

  Available again in this edition is an MS-WORD version of the *Manual*. Instructors can print out portions of the *Manual*'s contents, complete with their own additions and alterations, for use as student handouts or in whatever ways they wish. This capability includes printing out answers to the end-of-chapter questions.
- **Instructor's Resource CD-ROM** This CD contains everything the instructor needs, including Power-Point slides, transparencies of the text graphs and charts, Test Bank I, and the *Instructor's Manual*.
- **Three Test Banks** Test Bank I contains about 6300 multiple-choice and true-false questions, most of which were written by the text authors. Test Bank II also contains around 6300 multiple-choice and true-false questions, written by William Walstad. All Test Bank II questions are categorized according to level of difficulty: easy, moderate, or difficult. Finally, Test Bank III contains more than 600 pages of short-answer questions and problems created in the style of the book's end-of-chapter questions. Test Bank III can be used to construct student assignments or design essay and problem exams. Suggested answers to the essay and problem questions are included.

  For all test items in Test Banks I and II, the kind of question is identified (for example, D = definition, C = complex, etc.) as are the numbers of the text's pages that are the basis for each. Also, each chapter in Test Banks I and II has an outline or table of contents that groups questions by topics. In all, more than 12,500 questions give instructors maximum testing flexibility while ensuring the fullest possible text correlation.

  Test Banks I and II are available in computerized Brownstone Diploma versions, as well as in MS Word. Diploma systems can produce high-quality graphs from the test banks and feature the ability to generate multiple tests, with versions "scrambled" to be distinctive. This software will meet the various needs of the widest spectrum of computer users. *Essays and Problems* is available in printed and MS Word formats.
- **Color transparencies** There are more than 200 new full-color transparencies for the sixteenth edition. They encompass all the figures appearing in *Economics*. Additionally, the figures and tables from the text are found on the Instructor's Resource CD-ROM.

A Note about the Cover

The sixteenth-edition cover includes a photograph of a roof detail of a building in the Cyclades, a group of Greek islands in the Aegean Sea. The location of the building is especially appropriate, given that the modern word "economics" comes from the Greek *oikonomikos*, meaning "household management."

The photo highlights Greek architecture, which combines reliance on precision of order and the ability to break away from strict geometrical precision to create a more pleasing whole. That is exactly what we have tried to accomplish with *Economics*. Our goal is to present the principles of economics in a precise, orderly, step-by-step way. There is great beauty, logic, and power in economic models—a fact that we emphasize throughout the book. But an overemphasis on economic theory in the introductory course renders the subject flat and boring and does students a great disservice. Time and again *Economics* breaks away from the models by examining real-world examples and institutional detail. These necessary departures occur not only within the main flow of the text but also in special applications chapters, the new Consider This pieces, the Last Word minireadings, and the supporting web content. All this adds up, we think, to a more pleasing whole—in this case, a more realistic introduction to economics and the economy.

Acknowledgments

We give special thanks to Norris Peterson of Pacific Lutheran University and Randy Grant of Linfield College, who teamed up to create the "button" content on our website. We again thank James Reese of the University of South Carolina at Spartanburg, who wrote the original Internet exercises. Although many of those questions have been replaced or modified in the typical course of revision, several remain virtually unchanged. We also thank Robert Jensen of Pacific Lutheran University for his meticulous help in proofreading the entire manuscript and C. Norman Hollingsworth at Georgia Perimeter College for his ever-popular and creative PowerPoint slides. Finally, we thank William Walstad and Tom Barbiero (the coauthor of our Canadian edition) for their helpful ideas and insights.

We are greatly indebted to an all-star group of professionals at McGraw-Hill—in particular Gary Burke, Lucille Sutton, Erin Strathmann, Jean Lou Hess, Keith McPherson, Martin Quinn, Karen Minnich, and Rebecca Hicks—for their publishing and marketing expertise.

We thank Jacques Cournoyer for his vivid Last Word illustrations and Robin Sand for her selection of the Consider This photos. Michael Warrell provided the vibrant cover.

The sixteenth edition has benefited from a number of perceptive reviews. The contributors, listed at the end of the Preface, were a rich source of suggestions for this revision. To each of you, and others we may have inadvertently overlooked, thank you for your considerable help in improving *Economics*.

Stanley L. Brue
Campbell R. McConnell

CONTRIBUTORS

Reviewers

Christie Agioutanti, *Baruch College, CUNY*
Basil Al-Hashimi, *Maricopa Community College*
Ayman Amer, *Mount Mercy College*
John Atkins, *Pensacola Junior College*
John Baffoe-Bonnie, *Pennsylvania State University*
Asatar Bair, *Riverside Community College*
Paul Ballantyne, *University of Colorado at Colorado Springs*
Carl Bauer, *Oakton Community College*
John Bethune, *Barton College*
John E. Bowen, *Park University*
Louis Bravman, *Pennsylvania State University*
Joyce Bremer, *Oakton Community College*
Stacey Brook, *University of Sioux Falls*
Bruce Brown, *California State Polytechnic University at Pomona*
John S. Cameron, *Southwest State University*
Robert J. Carlsson, *University of South Carolina*
David Chen, *North Carolina A&T State University*
Betsy Jane Clary, *College of Charleston*
Al Culver, *California State University at Chico*
Dale DeBoer, *Colorado University at Colorado Springs*
Al DeCook, *Broward Community College*
Brian de Uriarte, *Middlesex County College*
Kevin Duncan, *University of Southern Colorado*
Clara Ford, *Northern Virginia Community College*
Michael Forney, *Austin Community College*
Dina Franceshi, *Fairfield University*
David G. Garraty, *Virginia Wesleyan College*
Shailendra Gajanan, *University of Pittsburgh*
Alejandro Gallegos, *Winona State University*
David Gay, *University of Arkansas*
Kirk Gifford, *Brigham Young University, Idaho*
Stephen W. Griffin, *Tarrant County College, South Campus*
Jay Goodman, *University of Southern Colorado*
Shiv Gupta, *University of Findlay*
Paul Harris, *Camden County College*
Charles Hawkins, *Lamar University*
Mark Healy, *William Rainey Harper College*
Victor B. Heltzer, *Middlesex County College*
Michael Heslop, *Northern Virginia Community College*
Charles Hiatt, *Central Florida Community College*
Rick Hirschi, *Brigham Young University, Idaho*
William Hogan, *University of Massachusetts, Dartmouth*
Reza Hoshmand, *Daniel Webster College*
Andy Howard, *Rio Hondo Community College*
Ahmed Ispahani, *University of La Verne*
David J. Jobson, *Keystone College*
George H. Jones, *University of Wisconsin, Rock County*
Wayne Jordan, *Central Florida Community College*
Veronica Z. Kalich, *Baldwin-Wallace College*

Tim Kane, *University of Texas at Tyler*
William C. Kerby, *California State University at Sacramento*
Alan Kessler, *Providence College*
Alfred Konuwa, *Butte College*
Barry Kotlove, *Edmonds Community College*
Kate Krause, *University of New Mexico*
Felix B. Kwan, *Maryville University*
Gary A. Latanich, *Arkansas State University*
Rudy Ledesma, *Marian College*
John Lovett, *Texas Christian University*
Drew E. Mattson, *Anoka-Ramsey Community College*
Larry T. McRae, *Appalachian State University*
Masoud Moallem, *Rockford College*
Barbara A. Moore, *University of Central Florida*
Antoni Moskwa, *Allegheny College*
Panos Mourdoukoutas, *Long Island University*
Annette Najjar, *Lindenwood University*
David J. O'Hara, *Metropolitan State University, Minneapolis*
Alexandre Padilla, *Metropolitan State College of Denver*
Ginger A. Parker, *Miami-Dade Community College, Kendall*
Bruce Pietrykowski, *University of Michigan, Dearborn*
Santiago Pinto, *West Virginia University*
Joe Pomykala, *Towson University*
Robert D. Potter, *University of Central Florida*
Arthur Raymond, *Muhlenberg College*
Javier Reyes, *Texas A&M University*
Barbara Ross-Pfeiffer, *Kapi'olani Community College*
Henry Ryder, *Glouchester County College*
William Sander, *DePaul University*
M. Anne Schulte, *Des Moines Area Community College*
Jerry Schwartz, *Broward Community College*
Esther-Mirjam Sent, *University of Notre Dame*
Calvin Shipley, *Henderson State University School of Business*
Chuck Sicotte, *Rock Valley College*
Dorothy Siden, *Salem State College*
Carl Simkonis, *Northern Kentucky University*
Garvin Smith, *Daytona Beach Community College*
Donna Thompson, *Brookdale Community College*
Debra Way, *University of Cincinnati at Clermont*
W. Parker Wheatley, *Carleton College*
Thomas G. Wier, *Northeastern State University*
Krissa Wrigley, *Boise State University*
Sheng Yang, *Wayland Baptist University*

User Survey Respondents

Phil Adelman, *DeVry University*
Len Anyanwu, *Union County College*
Mark Bebensee, *The Citadel*
Emil B. Berendt, *Friends University*
George Bohler, *Florida Community College at Jacksonville*

Barbara Brown, *Pace University*
Francine Butler, *Grand View College*
Regina Cassady, *Valencia Community College*
Henry F. Check Jr., *Pennsylvania State University, Lehigh Valley*
Rebecca Cline, *Middle Georgia College*
Fred Close Jr., *Cochise College*
Norman Cure, *Macomb Community College*
Richard Dempsy, *Ohio State University, Lima*
Manfred Dix, *Tulane University*
Gene Elander, *Plymouth State College*
Erick Elder, *University of Arkansas at Little Rock*
Chris Erickson, *New Mexico State University*
Loretta Fairchild, *Nebraska Wesleyan University*
Lawrence Frateschi, *College of DuPage*
Alfred Friedberg, *Mohawk Valley Community College*
S. N. Gajanan, *University of Pittsburgh*
Alejandro Gallegos, *Winona State University*
Maria Gamba, *University of Findlay, Ohio*
William Gardner, *Pennsylvania State University, Fayette*
Julie Granthen, *Oakland Community College, Michigan*
Philip J. Grossman, *South Carolina State University*
Terry Gustafson, *California State University at Chico*
Lydia Harris, *Goucher College*
Mark Healy, *William Rainey Harper College*
Patricia Hermann, *Coastal Bend College*
Thomas Hiestand, *Concordia College*
Elizabeth Hill, *Pennsylvania State University, Mont Alto*
Tracy Hofer, *University of Wisconsin, Stevens Point*
Naphtali Hoffman, *Elmira College*
Jack Hou, *California State University at Long Beach*

David Jobson, *Keystone College*
Paul A. Joray, *Indiana University, South Bend*
Frederick Jungman, *Northwest Oklahoma State University*
Lawrence Kendra, *Cuyahoga Community College*
John Kinworthy, *Concordia University*
Harry Kolendranos, *Daville Community College, Virginia*
Bozena Leven, *The College of New Jersey*
Michael McCully, *High Point University*
Jerome L. McElroy, *St. Mary's College, Indiana*
Meghan Millea, *Mississippi State University*
Carl Montano, *Lamar University*
Wayne Morra, *Arcadia University*
Allan Olsen, *Elgin Community College*
Mitch Redlo, *Monroe Community College*
Charles A. Reichheld III, *Cuyahoga Community College*
Virginia Reilly, *Ocean County College*
Kathryn Roberts, *Chipola Junior College*
Michael Romzy, *Waynesburg College*
Sarah Rook, *University of South Carolina, Spartanburg*
Barbara Ross-Pfeiffer, *Kapi'olani Community College*
Laurence Shute, *California State Polytechnic University at Pomona*
John Sinisi, *Pennsylvania State University, Schuylkill*
Tom Soos, *Pennsylvania State University, McKeesport Campus*
Donna Thompson, *Brookdale Community College*
Lee Van Scyoc, *University of Wisconsin, Oshkosh*
Thomas Wier, *Northeastern State University*
Eugene Williams, *McMurray University*
Gwen Williams, *Alvernia College*
Wendy Wood, *Bevill State Community College*

BRIEF CONTENTS

PART TEN

International Economics and the World Economy

CONTENTS

PART TWO
Macroeconomic Measurement and Basic Concepts

PART THREE
Macroeconomic Models and Fiscal Policy

24   Pure Monopoly   438

25   Monopolistic Competition and Oligopoly   460

26   Technology, R&D, and Efficiency   484

Suggested One-Semester and One-Quarter Course Outlines

(Core Chapters Are Indicated by "c"; Optional Chapters by "o")

Chapter	One-Semester Course			One-Quarter Course	
	Macro Emphasis	Micro Emphasis	Macro-Micro Survey	Macro Emphasis	Micro Emphasis
1	c	c	c	c	c
2	c	c	c	c	c
3	c	c	c	c	c
3 Web		o	o		o
4	c	c	c	c	c
5	c	c		c	c
6	c	c		c	c
7	c		c	c	
8	c		c	c	
9	c		c	c	
10	c		c	c	
11	c		c	c	
12	c		c	c	
13	c		c	c	
14	c		c	c	
15	c		c	c	
16	c		o	o	
17	c		o	o	
18	c		o		
19	c		o		
20		c	c		c
21		c			
22		c	c		c
23		c	c		c
24		c	c		c
25		c	o		c
26		c	o		c
27		c			c
28		c			c
29		c			c
30		o			o
31		o			
32		o[1]			
33		o[2]			
34		o[3]			
35		o[4]			
36		o			
37	o	o			
38	o	o			
39 Web	o				
40 Web	o				

[1] If used, Chapter 32 may follow Chapter 26.
[2] If used, Chapter 33 may follow Chapter 23.
[3] If used, Chapter 34 may follow Chapter 28 or 29.
[4] If used, Chapter 35 may follow Chapter 28.

Economics

Principles, Problems, and Policies

Part I | An Introduction to Economics and the Economy

To the Student

This book and its ancillaries contain a number of features designed to help you learn economics:

- **Web buttons**   A glance through the book will reveal many pages that contain symbols in the columns. These "buttons" are designed to direct you to the text's Internet site: www.mcconnell16.com. The ⬜ button stands for "Interactive Graphs." Brief exercises ask you to interact with the graphs, for example, by clicking on a specific curve and dragging it to a new location. These exercises will enhance your understanding of the underlying concepts. The 🔑 button stands for "Origin of the Idea." These pieces trace the particular idea to the person or persons who first developed it.

    After reading a chapter, thumb back through it to note the symbols and the number that follows them. On the home page of our Internet site select Student Center and find the web-button content. We think you will find this interactivity between the text and the Internet highly engaging and helpful.

- **Other Internet aids**   Our Internet site contains many other aids. In the "Student Center" you will find self-testing multiple-choice quizzes, links to relevant news articles, a student discussion room, and much more. For those of you with very strong mathematics backgrounds, be sure to note the "See the Math" section on the website. There, you will find nearly 50 notes that develop the algebra and, in some cases, the calculus that underlie the economic concepts.

- **Appendix on graphs**   Be assured, however, that you will need only basic math skills to do well in the principles course. In particular, you will need to be comfortable with graphical analysis and a few quantitative concepts. The appendix to Chapter 1 reviews graphing, slopes of curves, and linear equations. Be sure not to skip it.

- **Reviews**   Each chapter contains two or three Quick Reviews and an end-of-chapter summary. These reviews will help you focus on essential ideas and study for exams.

- **Key terms and Key Graphs**   Key terms are set in boldface type within the chapters, listed at the end of each chapter, and defined in the Glossary at the end of the book. Graphs with special relevance are labeled Key Graphs, and each includes a multiple-choice Quick Quiz. Your instructor may not emphasize all these figures, but you should pay special attention to those that are discussed in class; you can be certain that there will be exam questions on them.

- **Consider This and Last Word boxes**   Many chapters include a Consider This box. These brief pieces provide analogies, examples, and stories that help you understand and remember central economic ideas. Each chapter concludes with a Last Word minireading. Some of them are revealing applications of economic concepts; others are short case studies. While it is tempting to ignore in-text boxes, don't. Most are fun to read, and all will improve your grasp of economics.

- **Questions**   A comprehensive list of questions is located at the end of each chapter. Answering these questions will enhance your understanding. Several of the questions are designated as Key Questions and are answered in the *Study Guide* and also at our Internet site. End-of-chapter "Web-Based Questions" ask you to find information at specified websites. If you encounter "dead links" or outdated directions, check the Student Center at the text's website for posted updates.

- **Study Guide and Multimedia**   We enthusiastically recommend the *Study Guide* accompanying this text. This "portable tutor" contains not only a broad sampling of various kinds of questions but a host of useful learning aids. *Multimedia Discover Econ with Paul Solman*—a website and DVD that comes with the book—provides computer tutorials and videos that also will be helpful to your study.

Our overriding goal is to help you understand and apply economics. With your effort, our effort, and the effort of your instructor, you will be able to comprehend a whole range of economic, social, and political problems that otherwise would have remained puzzling and perplexing.

Good luck with your study of economics. We think it will be well worth your effort.

1 | *The Nature and Method of Economics*

People's economic wants are numerous and varied. Biologically, humans need only air, water, food, clothing, and shelter. But in contemporary society we also seek the many goods and services that provide a comfortable or affluent standard of living. Fortunately, society is blessed with productive resources—labor and managerial talent, tools and machinery, land and mineral deposits—that are used to produce goods and services. This production satisfies many of our economic wants and occurs through the organizational mechanism called the *economic system* or, more simply, the *economy*.

The blunt reality, however, is that our economic wants far exceed the productive capacity of our limited or scarce resources. So the complete satisfaction of society's economic wants is impossible. This unyielding truth underlies our definition of **economics**: *It is the social science concerned with the efficient use of scarce resources to achieve the maximum satisfaction of economic wants.*

1.1 Origin of term "economics"

Numerous problems and issues are rooted in the challenge of using limited resources efficiently. Although it would be tempting to plunge into them, that sort of analysis must wait. In this chapter, we need to discuss some important preliminaries.

The Economic Perspective

Economists view things through a unique perspective. This **economic perspective** or *economic way of thinking* has several critical and closely interrelated features.

Scarcity and Choice

From our definition of economics, it is easy to see why economists view the world through the lens of scarcity.

Since human and property resources are scarce (limited), it follows that the goods and services we produce must also be limited. Scarcity limits our options and necessitates that we make choices. Because we "can't have it all," we must decide what we will have, and what we must forgo.

At the core of economics is the idea that "there is no free lunch." You may get treated to lunch, making it "free" to you, but there is a cost to someone—ultimately to society. Scarce inputs of land, equipment, farm labor, the labor of cooks and waiters, and managerial talent are required.

CONSIDER THIS . . .

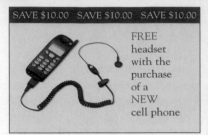

SAVE $10.00   SAVE $10.00   SAVE $10.00

FREE
headset
with the
purchase
of a
NEW
cell phone

© Photodisc/Getty Images

Free for All?

Free products are seemingly everywhere. Sellers offer free software, cell phones, and checking accounts. Dentists give out free toothbrushes. At state visitor centers, there are free brochures and maps.

Does the presence of so many free products contradict the economist's assertion "There is no free lunch"? No! Resources are used to produce each of these products, and because those resources have alternative uses, society gives up something else to get the "free" good. Where resources are used to produce goods or services, there is no free lunch.

So why are these goods offered for free? In a word: marketing! Firms sometimes offer free products to entice people to try them, hoping they will then purchase those goods later. The free software may eventually entice you to buy the producer's upgraded software. In other instances, the free brochures contain advertising for shops and restaurants, and that free e-mail program is filled with ads. In still other cases, the product is only free in conjunction with a larger purchase. To get the free bottle of soda, you must buy the large pizza. To get the free cell phone, you need to sign up for a year's worth of cell phone service.

So "free" products may or may not be truly free to individuals. They are never free to society.

Rational behavior means that the same person may make different choices under different circumstances. For example, Jones may decide to buy cans of Coca-Cola in bulk at a warehouse store rather than a convenience store, where they are much more expensive. That will leave him with extra money to buy something else that provides satisfaction. Yet, while on a Saturday drive, he may stop at a convenience store to buy a single can of Coca-Cola. Both actions are rational.

Rational behavior also means that choices will vary greatly among individuals. High school graduate Alvarez may decide to attend college to major in business. Baker may opt to take a job at a warehouse and buy a new car. Chin may accept a signing bonus and join the Navy. All three choices reflect the pursuit of self-interest and are rational, but they are based on differing preferences and circumstances.

Of course, rational decisions may change as costs and benefits change. Jones may switch to Pepsi when it is on sale. And, after taking a few business courses, Alvarez may decide to change her major to biology.

It is clear that rational self-interest is not the same as selfishness. People make personal sacrifices to help family members or friends, and they contribute to charities because they derive pleasure from doing so. Parents help pay for their children's education for the same reason. These self-interested, but unselfish, acts help maximize the givers' satisfaction as much as any personal purchase of goods or services. Self-interest behavior is simply behavior that enables a person to achieve personal satisfaction, however it may be derived.

Marginalism: Benefits and Costs

The economic perspective focuses largely on **marginal analysis**—comparisons of *marginal benefits* and *marginal costs*. (Used this way, "marginal" means "extra," "additional," or "a change in.") Most choices or decisions involve changes in the status quo (the existing state of affairs). Should you attend school for another year or not? Should you study an extra hour for an exam? Should you add fries to your fast-food order? Similarly, should a business expand or reduce its output? Should government increase or decrease its funding for a missile defense system?

Each option involves marginal benefits and, because of scarce resources, marginal costs. In making choices rationally, the decision maker must compare those two amounts. Example: You and your fiancé are shopping for an engagement ring. Should you buy a $\frac{1}{4}$-carat diamond, a $\frac{1}{2}$-carat diamond, a $\frac{3}{4}$-carat diamond, or a larger one? The marginal cost of the larger-size diamond is the added expense beyond the cost of the smaller-size diamond. The

Because these resources could be used in alternative production activities, they and the other goods and services they could have produced are sacrificed in making the lunch available. Economists call these sacrifices *opportunity costs*. To get more of one thing, you forgo the opportunity of getting something else. So the cost of that which you get is the value of that which is sacrificed to obtain it. We will say much more about opportunity costs in Chapter 2.

Rational Behavior

Economics assumes that human behavior reflects "rational self-interest." Individuals look for and pursue opportunities to increase their **utility**—that is, pleasure, happiness, or satisfaction. They allocate their time, energy, and money to maximize their well-being. Because they weigh costs and benefits, their decisions are "rational" or "purposeful," not "random."

1.2
Utility

marginal benefit is the greater lifetime pleasure (utility) from the larger-size stone. If the marginal benefit of the larger diamond exceeds its marginal cost, you should buy the larger stone. But if the marginal cost is more than the marginal benefit, you should buy the smaller diamond instead.

In a world of scarcity, the decision to obtain the marginal benefit associated with some specific option always includes the marginal cost of forgoing something else. The money spent on the larger-size diamond means forgoing something else. Again, there is no free lunch!

One surprising implication of decisions based on marginal analysis is that there can be too much of a good thing. Although certain goods and services such as education, health care, and homeland defense seem inherently desirable, we can in fact produce too much of them. "Too much" occurs when we obtain additional amounts of them even though their marginal costs (the value of the forgone options) exceed their marginal benefits. Then we are sacrificing alternative goods and services that are more valuable *at the margin*—the place where we consider the very last units of each. For example, society can produce too much health care, and you can buy too large a diamond. **(Key Question 4)**

1.3 Marginal analysis

This chapter's Last Word provides an everyday application of the economic perspective.

Why Study Economics?

Is studying economics worth your time and effort? More than half a century ago John Maynard Keynes (1883–1946), one of the most influential economists of the 1900s, said:

> The ideas of economists and political philosophers, both when they are right and when they are wrong, are more powerful than is commonly understood. Indeed the world is ruled by little else. Practical men, who believe themselves to be quite exempt from any intellectual influences, are usually the slaves of some defunct economist.

Most of the ideologies of the modern world have been shaped by prominent economists of the past—Adam Smith, David Ricardo, John Stuart Mill, Karl Marx, and John Maynard Keynes. And current world leaders routinely solicit the advice and policy suggestions of today's economists.

For example, the president of the United States benefits from the recommendations of his Council of Economic Advisers. The broad range of economic issues facing political leaders is suggested by the contents of the annual *Economic Report of the President*. Areas covered typically include unemployment, inflation, economic growth, taxation, poverty, international trade, health care, pollution, regulation, and education, among others. And the Federal Reserve (the U.S. central bank) relies heavily on economic analysis in shaping its monetary policies.

Economics for Citizenship

A basic understanding of economics is essential for well-informed citizenship. Most of today's political problems have important economic aspects: How aggressive should we be in pursuing the war on terrorism at home and abroad? How can we ensure that corporate executives act in the long-run interest of their shareholders and not just themselves? What level of taxes should we have? How can we make the social security retirement program financially secure? How can we increase the rate of economic growth? How can we reduce poverty?

As voters, we can influence the decisions of our elected officials in responding to such questions. But intelligence at the polls requires a basic working knowledge of economics. And a sound grasp of economics is even more helpful to the politicians themselves.

Professional and Personal Applications

Economics lays great stress on precise, systematic analysis. Thus, studying economics invariably helps students improve their analytical skills, which are in great demand in the workplace. Also, the study of economics helps people make sense of the everyday activity they observe around them. How is it that so many different people, in so many different places, doing so many different things, produce the goods and services we want to buy? Economics provides an answer.

Economics is also vital to business. An understanding of the basics of economic decision making and the operation of the economic system enables business managers and executives to increase profit. The executive who understands when to use new technology, when to merge with another firm, when to expand employment, and so on, will outperform the executive who is less deft at such decision making. The manager who understands the causes and consequences of recessions (downturns in the overall economy) or inflation (rising prices) can make more intelligent business decisions during those periods.

Economics helps consumers and workers make better buying and employment decisions. How can you spend your limited money income to maximize your satisfaction?

How can you hedge against the reduction in the dollar's purchasing power that accompanies inflation? Is it more economical to buy or lease a car? Should you use a credit card or pay cash? Which occupations pay well; which are most immune to unemployment?

Similarly, an understanding of economics makes for better financial decisions. Someone who understands the relationship between budget deficits or surpluses and interest rates, between foreign exchange rates and exports, between interest rates and bond prices, is in a better position to successfully allocate personal savings. So, too, is someone who understands the business implications of emerging new technologies.

In spite of these practical benefits, however, you should know that economics is *mainly* an academic, not a vocational, subject. Unlike accounting, advertising, corporate finance, and marketing, economics is not primarily a how-to-make-money area of study. Knowledge of economics and mastery of the economic perspective will help you run a business or manage your personal finances, but that is not the subject's primary objective. Instead, economics ultimately examines problems and decisions from the *social*, rather than the *personal*, point of view. The production, exchange, and consumption of goods and services are discussed from the viewpoint of society's best interest, not strictly from the standpoint of one's own pocketbook.

QUICK REVIEW 1.1

- Economics is concerned with obtaining maximum satisfaction through the efficient use of scarce resources.
- The economic perspective stresses (a) resource scarcity and the necessity of making choices, (b) the assumption of rational behavior, and (c) comparisons of marginal benefit and marginal cost.
- Your study of economics will help you as a voting citizen as well as benefit you professionally and personally.

Economic Methodology

Like the physical and life sciences, as well as other social sciences, economics relies on the **scientific method.** It consists of a number of elements:

- The observation of facts (real-world data).
- Based on those facts, the formulation of a possible explanation of cause and effect (hypothesis).

- The testing of this explanation by comparing the outcomes of specific events to the outcome predicted by the hypothesis.
- The acceptance, rejection, or modification of the hypothesis, based on these comparisons.
- The continued testing of the hypothesis against the facts. As favorable results accumulate, the hypothesis evolves into a *theory*. A very well tested and widely accepted theory is referred to as a *law* or *principle*. Combinations of such laws or principles are incorporated into *models*—simplified representations of how something works, such as a market or segment of the economy.

Laws, principles, and models enable the economist, like the natural scientist, to understand and explain reality and to predict the various outcomes of particular actions. But as we will soon see, economic laws and principles are usually less certain than the laws of physics or chemistry.

Theoretical Economics

Economists develop models of the behavior of individuals (consumers, workers) and institutions (businesses, governments) engaged in the production, exchange, and consumption of goods and services. They start by gathering facts about economic activities and economic outcomes. Because the world is cluttered with innumerable interrelated facts, economists, like all scientists, must select the useful information. They must determine which facts are relevant to the problem under consideration. But even when this sorting process is complete, the relevant information may at first seem random and unrelated.

The economist draws on the facts to establish cause-effect hypotheses about economic behavior. Then the hypotheses are tested against real-world observation and data. Through this process, the economist tries to discover hypotheses that rise to the level of theories and principles (or laws)—well-tested and widely accepted generalizations about how individuals and institutions behave. The process of deriving theories and principles is called **theoretical economics** (see the lower box in Figure 1.1). *The role of economic theorizing is to systematically arrange facts, interpret them, and generalize from them.* Theories and principles bring order and meaning to facts by arranging them in cause-and-effect order.

Observe that the arrow from "theories" to "facts" in Figure 1.1 moves in both directions. Some understanding of factual, real-world evidence is required to formulate meaningful hypotheses. And hypotheses are tested through gathering and organizing factual data to see if the hypotheses can be verified.

FIGURE I.I

The relationship between facts, theories, and policies in economics. *Theoretical economics* involves establishing economic theories by gathering, systematically arranging, and generalizing from facts. Good economic theories are tested for validity against facts. Economists use these theories—the most reliable of which are called *laws* or *principles*—to explain and analyze the economy. *Policy economics* entails using the economic laws and principles to formulate economic policies.

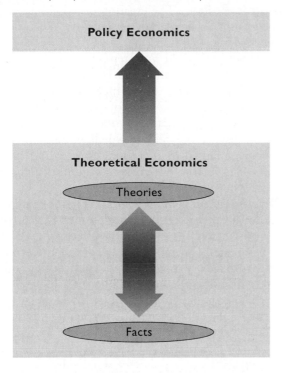

Economic theories and **principles** *are statements about economic behavior or the economy that enable prediction of the probable effects of certain actions.* Good theories are those that do a good job of explaining and predicting. They are supported by facts concerning how individuals and institutions actually behave in producing, exchanging, and consuming goods and services. But these facts may change in time, so economists must continually check theories against the shifting economic environment.

Theories, laws, and principles are highly useful in analyzing economic behavior and understanding how the economy operates. They are the ingredients of *analytical economics*—the ascertaining of cause and effect, of action and outcome, within the economic system.

Several other points relating to economic principles are important to know.

Terminology Economists speak of "hypotheses," "theories," "laws," and "principles." Some of these terms

overlap, but they usually reflect a gradation of confidence in the generalizations. A hypothesis needs initial testing; a theory has been tested but needs more testing; a law or principle is a theory that has provided strong predictive accuracy, over and over. The terms "economic laws" and "principles" are useful even though they imply a degree of exactness, universal application, and even moral rightness that is rare in any social science. The word "theory" is often used in economics even though many people incorrectly believe theories have nothing to do with real-world applications. Economists often use the term "model," which combines principles into a simplified representation of reality.

In this book, custom or convenience will govern the use of "theory," "law," "principle," and "model." Thus, to describe the relationship between the price of a product and the amount of it purchased, we will use the term *law of demand*, rather than theory or principle of demand, simply because this is the custom. We will refer to the *circular flow model*, not the circular flow law, because the concept combines several ideas into a single representation.

Generalizations As we have already mentioned, economic theories, principles, and laws are **generalizations** relating to economic behavior or to the economy itself. They are imprecise because economic facts are usually diverse; no two individuals or institutions act in exactly the same way. *Economic principles are expressed as the tendencies of typical or average consumers, workers, or business firms.* For example, when economists say that consumer spending rises when personal income increases, they are well aware that some households may save *all* of an increase in their incomes. But, on average, and for the full economy, spending goes up when income increases. Similarly, economists say that consumers buy more of a particular product when its price falls. Some consumers may increase their purchases by a large amount, others by a small amount, and a few not at all. This "price-quantity" principle, however, holds for the typical consumer and for consumers as a group.

Other-Things-Equal Assumption Like other scientists, economists use the *ceteris paribus* or **other-things-equal assumption** to construct their generalizations. They assume that all other variables except those under immediate consideration are held constant for a particular analysis. For example, consider the relationship between the price of Pepsi and the amount of it purchased. It helps to assume that, of all the factors that might influence the amount of Pepsi

1.4
Ceteris paribus

purchased (for example, the price of Pepsi, the price of Coca-Cola, and consumer incomes and preferences), only the price of Pepsi varies. The economist can then focus on the "price of Pepsi–purchases of Pepsi" relationship without being confused by changes in other variables.

Natural scientists such as chemists or physicists can usually conduct controlled experiments where "all other things" are in fact held constant (or virtually so). They can test with great precision the assumed relationship between two variables. For example, they might examine the height from which an object is dropped and the length of time it takes to hit the ground. But economics is not a laboratory science. Economists test their theories using real-world data, which are generated by the actual operation of the economy. In this rather bewildering environment, "other things" *do* change. Despite the development of complex statistical techniques designed to hold other things equal, control is less than perfect. As a result, economic principles are less certain and less precise than those of laboratory sciences. That also means they are more open to debate than many scientific theories (for example, the law of gravity).

Abstractions   Economic principles, or theories, are *abstractions*—simplifications that omit irrelevant facts and circumstances. Economic models do *not* mirror the full complexity of the real world. The very process of sorting out and analyzing facts involves simplification and removal of clutter. Unfortunately, this "abstraction" leads some people to consider economic theory impractical and unrealistic. That is nonsense! Economic theories are practical precisely because they are abstractions. The full scope of economic reality itself is too complex and bewildering to be understood as a whole. Economists simplify—that is, develop theories and build models—to give meaning to an otherwise overwhelming and confusing maze of facts. Theorizing for this purpose is highly practical.

Graphical Expression   Many of the economic models in this book are expressed graphically; the most important are labeled Key Graphs. Be sure to read the appendix to this chapter as a review of graphs.

Policy Economics

Policy economics recognizes that theories and data can be used to formulate *policies*—courses of action based on economic principles and intended to resolve a specific economic problem or further an economic goal. Economic theories are the foundation of economic policy, as shown in the upper part of Figure 1.1. Economic policy normally is applied to problems after they arise. However, if eco-

nomic analysis can predict some undesirable event such as unemployment, inflation, or an increase in poverty, then it may be possible to avoid or moderate that event through economic policy. For example, you may read in the newspaper that the Federal Reserve has reduced interest rates to increase private spending and prevent a recession.

Economic Policy   The creation of policies to achieve specific goals is no simple matter. Here are the basic steps in policymaking:

- *State the goal.*   The first step is to make a clear statement of the economic goal. If we say that we want "full employment," do we mean that everyone between, say, 16 and 65 years of age should have a job? Or do we mean that everyone who *wants* to work should have a job? Should we allow for some unemployment caused by inevitable changes in the structure of industry and workers voluntarily changing jobs? The goal must be specific.

- *Determine the policy options.*   The next step is to formulate alternative policies designed to achieve the goal and determine the possible effects of each policy. This requires a detailed assessment of the economic impact, benefits, costs, and political feasibility of the alternative policies. For example, to achieve full employment, should government use fiscal policy (which involves changing government spending and taxes), monetary policy (which entails altering interest rates), an education and training policy that enhances worker employability, or a policy of wage subsidies to firms that hire disadvantaged workers?

- *Implement and evaluate the policy that was selected.* After implementing the policy, we need to evaluate how well it worked. Only through unbiased evaluation can we improve on economic policy. Did a specific change in taxes or the money supply alter the level of employment to the extent predicted? Did deregulation of a particular industry (for example, electricity) yield the predicted beneficial results? If not, why not? What were the harmful side effects, if any? How might the policy be altered to make it work better? **(Key Question 8)**

Economic Goals   If economic policies are designed to achieve certain economic goals, then we need to recognize a number of goals that are widely accepted in the United States and many other countries. They include:

- *Economic growth*   Produce more and better goods and services, or, more simply, develop a higher standard of living.

- *Full employment* Provide suitable jobs for all citizens who are willing and able to work.
- *Economic efficiency* Achieve the maximum fulfillment of wants using the available productive resources.
- *Price-level stability* Avoid large upswings and downswings in the general price level; that is, avoid inflation and deflation.
- *Economic freedom* Guarantee that businesses, workers, and consumers have a high degree of freedom in their economic activities.
- *Equitable distribution of income* Ensure that no group of citizens faces poverty while most others enjoy abundance.
- *Economic security* Provide for those who are chronically ill, disabled, laid off, aged, or otherwise unable to earn minimal levels of income.
- *Balance of trade* Seek a reasonable overall balance with the rest of the world in international trade and financial transactions.

Although most of us might accept these goals as generally stated, we might also disagree substantially on their specific meanings. What are "large" changes in the price level? What is a "high degree" of economic freedom? What is an "equitable" distribution of income? How can we measure precisely such abstract goals as "economic freedom"? These objectives are often the subject of spirited public debate.

Also, some of these goals are complementary; when one is achieved, some other one will also be realized. For example, achieving full employment means eliminating unemployment, which is a basic cause of inequitable income distribution. But other goals may conflict or even be mutually exclusive. They may entail **tradeoffs,** meaning that to achieve one we must sacrifice another. For example, efforts to reduce income inequality may weaken incentives to work, invest, innovate, and take business risks, all of which promote economic growth. Taxing high-income people heavily and transferring the tax revenues to low-income people is one way to equalize the distribution of income. But then the incentives to high-income individuals may diminish because higher taxes reduce their rewards for working. Similarly, low-income individuals may be less motivated to work when government stands ready to subsidize them.

When goals conflict, society must establish ways to prioritize the objectives it seeks. If more economic freedom is accompanied by less economic security and more economic security allows less economic freedom, society must assess the tradeoffs and decide on the optimal (best) balance between them.

QUICK REVIEW 1.2

- Economists use the scientific method to establish theories, laws, and principles. Economic theories (laws, principles, or models) are generalizations relating to the economic behavior of individuals and institutions; good theories are grounded in facts.
- Theoretical economics involves formulating theories (or laws and principles) and using them to understand and explain economic behavior and the economy; policy economics involves using the theories to fix economic problems or promote economic goals.
- Policymaking requires a clear statement of goals, a thorough assessment of options, and an unbiased evaluation of results.
- Some of society's economic goals are complementary, while others conflict; where conflicts exist, tradeoffs arise.

Macroeconomics and Microeconomics

Economists derive and apply principles about economic behavior at two levels.

Macroeconomics

Macroeconomics examines either the economy as a whole or its basic subdivisions or aggregates, such as the government, household, and business sectors. An **aggregate** is a collection of specific economic units treated as if they were one unit. Therefore, we might lump together the millions of consumers in the U.S. economy and treat them as if they were one huge unit called "consumers."

In using aggregates, macroeconomics seeks to obtain an overview, or general outline, of the structure of the economy and the relationships of its major aggregates. Macroeconomics speaks of such economic measures as *total* output, *total* employment, *total* income, *aggregate* expenditures, and the *general* level of prices in analyzing various economic problems. No or very little attention is given to specific units making up the various aggregates. Macroeconomics examines the beach, not the sand, rocks, and shells.

Microeconomics

Microeconomics looks at specific economic units. At this level of analysis, the economist observes the details of an economic unit, or very small segment of the economy, under a figurative microscope. In microeconomics we talk of an individual industry, firm, or household. We measure the price of a *specific* product, the number of workers employed by a *single* firm, the revenue or income of a *particular* firm or household, or the expenditures of a *specific* firm, government entity, or family. In microeconomics, we examine the sand, rocks, and shells, not the beach.

The macro-micro distinction does not mean that economics is so highly compartmentalized that every topic can be readily labeled as either macro or micro; many topics and subdivisions of economics are rooted in both. Example: While the problem of unemployment is usually treated as a macroeconomic topic (because unemployment relates to *aggregate* spending), economists recognize that the decisions made by *individual* workers in searching for jobs and the way *specific* product and labor markets operate are also critical in determining the unemployment rate. **(Key Question 10)**

Positive and Normative Economics

Both macroeconomics and microeconomics involve facts, theories, and policies. Each contains elements of *positive* economics and *normative* economics. **Positive economics** focuses on facts and cause-and-effect relationships. It includes description, theory development, and theory testing (theoretical economics). Positive economics avoids value judgments, tries to establish scientific statements about economic behavior, and deals with what the economy is actually like. Such scientific-based analysis is critical to good policy analysis.

Policy economics, on the other hand, involves **normative economics,** which incorporates value judgments about what the economy should be like or what particular policy actions should be recommended to achieve a desirable goal. Normative economics looks at the desirability of certain aspects of the economy. It underlies expressions of support for particular economic policies.

Positive economics concerns *what is,* while normative economics embodies subjective feelings about *what ought to be.* Examples: Positive statement: "The unemployment rate in several European nations is higher than that in the United States." Normative statement: "European nations ought to undertake policies to reduce their unemployment rates." A second positive statement: "Other things equal, if tuition is substantially increased, college enrollment will fall." Normative statement: "College tuition should be lowered so that more students can obtain an education." Whenever words such as "ought" or "should"

appear in a sentence, there is a strong chance you are encountering a normative statement.

Most of the disagreement among economists involves normative, value-based policy questions. Of course, there is often some disagreement about which theories or models best represent the economy and its parts. But economists agree on a full range of economic principles. Most economic controversy thus reflects differing opinions or value judgments about what society should be like. **(Key Question 11)**

QUICK REVIEW 1.3

- Macroeconomics examines the economy as a whole; microeconomics focuses on specific units of the economy.
- Positive economics deals with factual statements ("what is"); normative economics involves value judgments ("what ought to be"). Theoretical economics is "positive"; policy economics is "normative."

Pitfalls to Sound Reasoning

Because they affect us so personally, we often have difficulty thinking accurately and objectively about economic issues. Here are some common pitfalls to avoid in successfully applying the economic perspective.

Biases

Most people bring a bundle of biases and preconceptions to the field of economics. For example, some might think that corporate profits are excessive or that lending money is always superior to borrowing money. Others might believe that government is necessarily less efficient than businesses or that more government regulation is always better than less. Biases cloud thinking and interfere with objective analysis. All of us must be willing to shed biases and preconceptions that are not supported by facts.

Loaded Terminology

The economic terminology used in newspapers and broadcast media is sometimes emotionally biased, or loaded. The writer or spokesperson may have a cause to promote or an ax to grind and may slant comments accordingly. High profits may be labeled "obscene," low wages may be called "exploitive," or self-interested behavior may be "greed." Government workers may be referred to as "mindless bureaucrats," and those favoring stronger government regulations may be called "socialists." To objectively analyze economic issues, you must be prepared to reject or discount such terminology.

Definitions

Some of the terms used in economics have precise technical definitions that are quite different from those implied by their common usage. This is generally not a problem if everyone understands these definitions and uses them consistently. For example, "investment" to the average citizen means the purchase of stocks and bonds in security markets, as when someone "invests" in Microsoft stock or government bonds. But to the economist, "investment" means the purchase of newly created real capital assets such as machinery and equipment or the construction of a new factory building. It does not mean the purely financial transaction of swapping cash for securities.

Fallacy of Composition

Another pitfall in economic thinking is the assumption that what is true for one individual or part of a whole is necessarily true for a group of individuals or the whole. This is a logical fallacy called the **fallacy of composition;** the assumption is *not* correct. A statement that is valid for an individual or part is *not* necessarily valid for the larger group or whole.

Consider the following example from outside of economics: You are at a football game and the home team makes an outstanding play. In the excitement, you leap to your feet to get a better view. A valid statement: "If you, *an individual*, stand, your view of the game is improved." But is this also true for the group—for everyone watching the play? Not necessarily. If *everyone* stands to watch the play, probably nobody—including you—will have a better view than when all remain seated.

A second example comes from economics: An *individual* farmer who reaps a particularly large crop is likely to realize a sharp gain in income. But this statement cannot be generalized to farmers as a *group*. The individual farmer's large or "bumper" crop will not noticeably influence (reduce) crop prices because each farmer produces a negligible fraction of the total farm output. But for *all* farmers as a group, prices decline when total output increases. Thus, if all farmers reap bumper crops, the total output of farm products will rise, depressing crop prices. If the price declines are relatively large, total farm income might actually *fall*.

Recall our earlier distinction between macroeconomics and microeconomics: *The fallacy of composition reminds us that generalizations valid at one of these levels of analysis may or may not be valid at the other.*

Causation Fallacies

Causation is sometimes difficult to identify in economics. Two important fallacies often interfere with economic thinking.

Post Hoc Fallacy   You must think very carefully before concluding that because event A precedes event B, A is the cause of B. This kind of faulty reasoning is known as the *post hoc, ergo propter hoc*, or **"after this, therefore because of this," fallacy.**

Example: Suppose that early each spring the medicine man of a tribe performs a special dance. A week or so later the trees and grass turn green. Can we safely conclude that event A, the medicine man's dance, has caused event B, the landscape's turning green? Obviously not. The rooster crows before dawn, but that does not mean the rooster is responsible for the sunrise!

A professional football team hires a new coach and the team's record improves. Is the new coach the cause? Maybe. But perhaps the presence of more experienced and talented players or an easier schedule is the true cause.

Correlation versus Causation   Do not confuse correlation, or connection, with causation. Correlation between two events or two sets of data indicates only that they are associated in some systematic and dependable way. For example, we may find that when variable X increases, Y also increases. But this correlation does not necessarily mean that there is causation—that an increase in X is the cause of an increase in Y. The relationship could be purely coincidental or dependent on some other factor, Z, not included in the analysis.

Here is an economic example: Economists have found a positive correlation between education and income. In general, people with more education earn higher incomes than those with less education. Common sense suggests education is the cause and higher incomes are the effect; more education implies a more knowledgeable and productive worker, and such workers receive larger salaries.

But causation could also partly run the other way. People with higher incomes could buy more education, just as they buy more furniture and steaks. Or is part of the relationship explainable in still other ways? Are

How Can the Economic Perspective Help Us Understand the Behavior of Fast-Food Consumers?

The economic perspective is useful in analyzing the behavior of fast-food customers. These consumers are at the restaurant because they expect the marginal benefit from the food they buy to match or exceed its marginal cost. When customers enter the restaurant, they go to the shortest line, believing that that line will minimize their time cost of obtaining food. They are acting purposefully; time is limited, and people prefer using it in some way other than standing in line.

If one fast-food line is temporarily shorter than other lines, some people will move to that line. These movers apparently view the time saving associated with the shorter line as exceeding the cost of moving from their present line. The line switching tends to equalize line lengths. No further movement of customers between lines occurs once all lines are about equal.

Fast-food customers face another cost-benefit decision when a clerk opens a new station at the counter. Should they move to the new station or stay put? Those who shift to the new line decide that the time saving from the move exceeds the extra cost of physically moving. In so deciding, customers must also consider just how quickly they can get to the new station compared with others who may be contemplating the same move. (Those who hesitate in this situation are lost!)

Customers at the fast-food establishment do not have perfect information when they select lines. For example, they do not first survey those in the lines to determine what they are ordering before deciding which line to enter. There are two reasons for this. First, most customers would tell them "It's none of your business," and therefore no information would be forthcoming. Second, even if they could obtain the information, the amount of time necessary to get it (a cost) would most certainly exceed any time saving associated with finding the best line (the benefit). Because information is costly to obtain, fast-food patrons select lines without perfect information. Thus, not all decisions turn out as expected. For example, you might enter a short line and find someone in front of you is ordering hamburgers and fries for 40 people in the Greyhound bus parked out back (and the employee is a trainee)! Nevertheless, at the time you made your decision, you thought it was optimal.

Imperfect information also explains why some people who arrive at a fast-food restaurant and observe long lines decide to leave. These people conclude that the marginal cost (monetary plus time costs) of obtaining the fast food is too large relative to the marginal benefit. They would not have come to the restaurant in the first place had they known the lines would be so long. But getting that information by, say, employing an advance scout with a cellular phone would cost more than the perceived benefit.

Finally, customers must decide what food to order when they arrive at the counter. In making their choices, they again compare marginal costs and marginal benefits in attempting to obtain the greatest personal satisfaction or well-being for their expenditure.

Economists believe that what is true for the behavior of customers at fast-food restaurants is true for economic behavior in general. Faced with an array of choices, consumers, workers, and businesses rationally compare marginal costs and marginal benefits in making decisions.

---

education and income correlated because the characteristics required to succeed in education—ability and motivation—are the same ones required to be a productive and highly paid worker? If so, then people with those traits will probably obtain more education *and* earn higher incomes. But greater education will not be the sole cause of the higher income. **(Key Question 12)**

A Look Ahead

The ideas in this chapter will come into much sharper focus as you advance through Part 1, where we develop specific economic principles and models. Specifically, in Chapter 2 we build a model of the production choices facing an economy. In Chapter 3 and its companion Bonus Internet Chapter 3 Web, we develop and apply laws of demand and supply that will help you understand how prices and quantities of goods and services are established in markets. In Chapter 4 we combine all markets in the economy to see how the *market system* works. And in Chapters 5 and 6 we examine important sectors (components) of the economy, specifically, the private sector, the government sector, and the international sector.

SUMMARY

1. Economics is the study of the efficient use of scarce resources in the production of goods and services to achieve the maximum satisfaction of economic wants.

2. The economic perspective includes three elements: scarcity and choice, rational behavior, and marginalism. It sees individuals and institutions making rational decisions based on comparisons of marginal costs and marginal benefits.

3. Knowledge of economics contributes to effective citizenship and provides useful insights for politicians, consumers, and workers.

4. Economists employ the scientific method, in which they form and test hypotheses of cause-and-effect relationships to generate theories, laws, and principles. Economists often combine theories into representations called models.

5. Generalizations stated by economists are called principles, theories, laws, or models. The derivation of these principles is the object of theoretical economics. Good theories explain real-world relationships and predict real-world outcomes.

6. Because economic principles are valuable predictors, they are the bases for economic policy, which is designed to identify and solve problems to the greatest extent possible and at the least possible cost. This type of application of economics is called policy economics.

7. Our society accepts certain shared economic goals, including economic growth, full employment, economic efficiency, price-level stability, economic freedom, equity in the distribution of income, economic security, and a reasonable balance in international trade and finance. Some of these goals are complementary; others entail tradeoffs.

8. Macroeconomics looks at the economy as a whole or its major aggregates; microeconomics examines specific economic units or institutions.

9. Positive statements state facts ("what is"); normative statements express value judgments ("what ought to be").

10. In studying economics, we encounter such pitfalls as biases and preconceptions, unfamiliar or confusing terminology, the fallacy of composition, and the difficulty of establishing clear cause-effect relationships.

TERMS AND CONCEPTS

economics

economic perspective

utility

marginal analysis

scientific method

theoretical economics

principles

generalizations

other-things-equal assumption

policy economics

tradeoffs

macroeconomics

aggregate

microeconomics

positive economics

normative economics

fallacy of composition

"after this, therefore because of this," fallacy

STUDY QUESTIONS

1. "Buy 2, get 1 free." Explain why the "1 free" is free to the buyer but not to society.

2. What is meant by the term "utility" and how does it relate to the economic perspective?

3. Cite three examples of recent decisions that you made in which you, at least implicitly, weighed marginal costs and marginal benefits.

4. *Key Question* Use the economic perspective to explain why someone who is normally a light eater at a standard restaurant may become somewhat of a glutton at a buffet-style restaurant that charges a single price for all you can eat.

5. What is the scientific method, and how does it relate to theoretical economics? What is the difference between a hypothesis and an economic law or principle?

6. Why is it significant that economics is not a laboratory science? What problems may be involved in deriving and applying economic principles?

7. Explain the following statements:
   a. Good economic policy requires good economic theory.
   b. Generalization and abstraction are nearly synonymous.
   c. Facts serve to sort out good and bad hypotheses.
   d. The *other-things-equal assumption* helps isolate key economic relationships.

8. *Key Question* Explain in detail the interrelationships between economic facts, theory, and policy. Critically evaluate this statement: "The trouble with economic theory is that it is not practical. It is detached from the real world."

9. To what extent do you accept the eight economic goals stated and described in this chapter? What priorities do you assign to them?

10. *Key Question* Indicate whether each of the following statements applies to microeconomics or macroeconomics:

    a. The unemployment rate in the United States was 5.8 percent in March 2003.

    b. The Alpo dog-food plant in Bowser, Iowa, laid off 15 workers last month.

    c. An unexpected freeze in central Florida reduced the citrus crop and caused the price of oranges to rise.

    d. U.S. output, adjusted for inflation, grew by 2.4 percent in 2002.

    e. Last week Wells Fargo Bank lowered its interest rate on business loans by one-half of 1 percentage point.

    f. The consumer price index rose by 1.6 percent in 2002.

11. *Key Question* Identify each of the following as either a positive or a normative statement:

    a. The high temperature today was 89 degrees.

    b. It was too hot today.

    c. Other things equal, higher interest rates reduce the total amount of borrowing.

    d. Interest rates are too high.

12. *Key Question* Explain and give an example of (*a*) the fallacy of composition, and (*b*) the "after this, therefore because of this," fallacy. Why are cause-and-effect relationships difficult to isolate in economics?

13. Suppose studies show that students who study more hours receive higher grades. Does this relationship guarantee that any particular student who studies longer will get higher grades?

14. Studies indicate that married men on average earn more income than unmarried men of the same age. Why must we be cautious in concluding that marriage is the *cause* and higher income is the *effect*?

15. (*Last Word*) Use the economic perspective to explain the behavior of the *workers* (rather than the customers) observed at a fast-food restaurant. Why are these workers there, rather than, say, cruising around in their cars? Why do they work so diligently? Why do so many of them quit these jobs once they have graduated high school?

16. *Web-Based Question: Three economic goals—are they being achieved?* Three major economic goals are economic growth (rises in real GDP), full employment (less than 5 percent unemployment), and price-level stability (less than 2 percent inflation annually as measured by the consumer price index, or CPI). The White House statistical website, www.whitehouse.gov/fsbr/esbr.html, provides links to economic information produced by a number of federal agencies. Visit the separate links for Employment, Output, and Prices to assess whether the United States is currently meeting each of these three goals.

17. *Web-Based Question: Normative economics—Republicans versus Democrats* Visit both the Republicans' www.rnc.org/ and the Democrats' www.democrats.org/ websites. Identify an economic issue that both parties address, and compare and contrast their views on that issue. Generally speaking, how much of the disagreement is based on normative economics compared to positive economics? Give an example of loaded terminology from each site.

Graphs and Their Meaning

If you glance quickly through this text, you will find many graphs. Some seem simple, while others seem more formidable. All are included to help you visualize and understand economic relationships. Physicists and chemists sometimes illustrate their theories by building arrangements of multicolored wooden balls, representing protons, neutrons, and electrons, which are held in proper relation to one another by wires or sticks. Economists most often use graphs to illustrate their models. By understanding these "pictures," you can more readily comprehend economic relationships. Most of our principles or models explain relationships between just two sets of economic facts, which can be conveniently represented with two-dimensional graphs.

Construction of a Graph

A *graph* is a visual representation of the relationship between two variables. Table 1 is a hypothetical illustration showing the relationship between income and consumption for the economy as a whole. Without even studying economics, we would expect intuitively that people would buy more goods and services when their incomes go up. Thus we are not surprised to find in Table 1 that total consumption in the economy increases as total income increases.

The information in Table 1 is expressed graphically in Figure 1. Here is how it is done: We want to show visually or graphically how consumption changes as income changes. Since income is the determining factor, we

FIGURE 1

Graphing the direct relationship between consumption and income. Two sets of data that are positively or directly related, such as consumption and income, graph as an upsloping line.

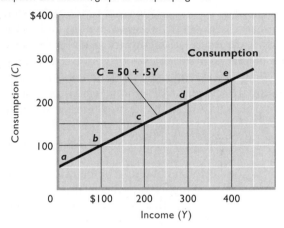

represent it on the **horizontal axis** of the graph, as is customary. And because consumption depends on income, we represent it on the **vertical axis** of the graph, as is also customary. Actually, what we are doing is representing the *independent variable* on the horizontal axis and the *dependent variable* on the vertical axis.

Now we arrange the vertical and horizontal scales of the graph to reflect the ranges of values of consumption and income, and we mark the scales in convenient increments. As you can see, the values marked on the scales cover all the values in Table 1. The increments on both scales are $100 for approximately each $\frac{1}{2}$ inch.

Because the graph has two dimensions, each point within it represents an income value and its associated consumption value. To find a point that represents one of the five income-consumption combinations in Table 1, we draw perpendiculars from the appropriate values on the vertical and horizontal axes. For example, to plot point *c* (the $200 income–$150 consumption point), we draw perpendiculars up from the horizontal (income) axis at $200 and across from the vertical (consumption) axis at $150. These perpendiculars intersect at point *c*, which represents this particular income-consumption combination.

TABLE 1

The Relationship between Income and Consumption

Income per Week	Consumption per Week	Point
$ 0	$ 50	a
100	100	b
200	150	c
300	200	d
400	250	e

15

You should verify that the other income-consumption combinations shown in Table 1 are properly located in Figure 1. Finally, by assuming that the same general relationship between income and consumption prevails for all other incomes, we draw a line or smooth curve to connect these points. That line or curve represents the income-consumption relationship.

If the graph is a straight line, as in Figure 1, we say the relationship is *linear*.

Direct and Inverse Relationships

The line in Figure 1 slopes upward to the right, so it depicts a direct relationship between income and consumption. By a **direct relationship** (or positive relationship) we mean that two variables—in this case, consumption and income—change in the *same* direction. An increase in consumption is associated with an increase in income; a decrease in consumption accompanies a decrease in income. When two sets of data are positively or directly related, they always graph as an *upsloping* line, as in Figure 1.

In contrast, two sets of data may be inversely related. Consider Table 2, which shows the relationship between the price of basketball tickets and game attendance at Gigantic State University (GSU). Here we have an **inverse relationship** (or negative relationship) because the two variables change in *opposite* directions. When ticket prices decrease, attendance increases. When ticket prices increase, attendance decreases. The six data points in Table 2 are plotted in Figure 2. Observe that an inverse relationship always graphs as a *downsloping* line.

Dependent and Independent Variables

Although it is not always easy, economists seek to determine which variable is the "cause" and which is the

FIGURE 2

Graphing the inverse relationship between ticket prices and game attendance. Two sets of data that are negatively or inversely related, such as ticket price and the attendance at basketball games, graph as a downsloping line.

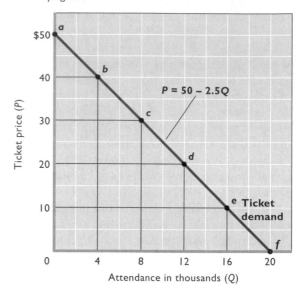

$P = 50 - 2.5Q$

"effect." Or, more formally, they seek the independent variable and the dependent variable. The **independent variable** is the cause or source; it is the variable that changes first. The **dependent variable** is the effect or outcome; it is the variable that changes because of the change in the independent variable. As noted in our income-consumption example, income generally is the independent variable and consumption the dependent variable. Income causes consumption to be what it is rather than the other way around. Similarly, ticket prices (set in advance of the season) determine attendance at GSU basketball games; attendance at games does not determine the ticket prices for those games. Ticket price is the independent variable, and the quantity of tickets purchased is the dependent variable.

You may recall from your high school courses that mathematicians always put the independent variable (cause) on the horizontal axis and the dependent variable (effect) on the vertical axis. Economists are less tidy; their graphing of independent and dependent variables is more arbitrary. Their conventional graphing of the income-consumption relationship is consistent with mathematical presentation, but economists put price and cost data on the vertical axis. Hence, economists' graphing of GSU's ticket price–attendance data conflicts with normal mathematical procedure.

TABLE 2

The Relationship between Ticket Prices and Attendance

Ticket Price	Attendance, Thousands	Point
$50	0	a
40	4	b
30	8	c
20	12	d
10	16	e
0	20	f

Other Things Equal

Our simple two-variable graphs purposely ignore many other factors that might affect the amount of consumption occurring at each income level or the number of people who attend GSU basketball games at each possible ticket price. When economists plot the relationship between any two variables, they employ the *ceteris paribus* (other-things-equal) assumption. Thus, in Figure 1 all factors other than income that might affect the amount of consumption are presumed to be constant or unchanged. Similarly, in Figure 2 all factors other than ticket price that might influence attendance at GSU basketball games are assumed constant. In reality, "other things" are not equal; they often change, and when they do, the relationship represented in our two tables and graphs will change. Specifically, the lines we have plotted would shift to new locations.

Consider a stock market "crash." The dramatic drop in the value of stocks might cause people to feel less wealthy and therefore less willing to consume at each level of income. The result might be a downward shift of the consumption line. To see this, you should plot a new consumption line in Figure 1, assuming that consumption is, say, $20 less at each income level. Note that the relationship remains direct; the line merely shifts downward to reflect less consumption spending at each income level.

Similarly, factors other than ticket prices might affect GSU game attendance. If GSU loses most of its games, attendance at GSU games might be less at each ticket price. To see this, redraw Figure 2, assuming that 2000 fewer fans attend GSU games at each ticket price. (**Key Appendix Question 2**)

Slope of a Line

Lines can be described in terms of their slopes. The **slope of a straight line** is the ratio of the vertical change (the rise or drop) to the horizontal change (the run) between any two points of the line.

Positive Slope   Between point b and point c in Figure 1 the rise or vertical change (the change in consumption) is +$50 and the run or horizontal change (the change in income) is +$100. Therefore:

$$\text{Slope} = \frac{\text{vertical change}}{\text{horizontal change}} = \frac{+50}{+100} = \frac{1}{2} = .5$$

Note that our slope of $\frac{1}{2}$ or .5 is positive because consumption and income change in the same direction; that is, consumption and income are directly or positively related.

The slope of .5 tells us there will be a $1 increase in consumption for every $2 increase in income. Similarly, it indicates that for every $2 decrease in income there will be a $1 decrease in consumption.

Negative Slope   Between any two of the identified points in Figure 2, say, point c and point d, the vertical change is −10 (the drop) and the horizontal change is +4 (the run). Therefore:

$$\text{Slope} = \frac{\text{vertical change}}{\text{horizontal change}} = \frac{-10}{+4}$$

$$= -2\frac{1}{2} = -2.5$$

This slope is negative because ticket price and attendance have an inverse relationship.

Note that on the horizontal axis attendance is stated in thousands of people. So the slope of −10/+4 or −2.5 means that lowering the price by $10 will increase attendance by 4000 people. This is the same as saying that a $2.50 price reduction will increase attendance by 1000 persons.

Slopes and Measurement Units   The slope of a line will be affected by the choice of units for either variable. If, in our ticket price illustration, we had chosen to measure attendance in individual people, our horizontal change would have been 4000 and the slope would have been

$$\text{Slope} = \frac{-10}{+4000} = \frac{-1}{+400} = -.0025$$

The slope depends on the way the relevant variables are measured.

Slopes and Marginal Analysis   Recall that economics is largely concerned with changes from the status quo. The concept of slope is important in economics because it reflects marginal changes—those involving 1 more (or 1 less) unit. For example, in Figure 1 the .5 slope shows that $.50 of extra or marginal consumption is associated with each $1 change in income. In this example, people collectively will consume $.50 of any $1 increase in their incomes and reduce their consumption by $.50 for each $1 decline in income.

Infinite and Zero Slopes   Many variables are unrelated or independent of one another. For example, the quantity of wristwatches purchased is not related to the price of bananas. In Figure 3a we represent the price of bananas on the vertical axis and the quantity of watches

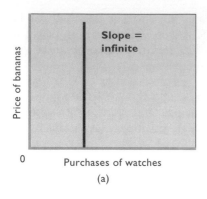

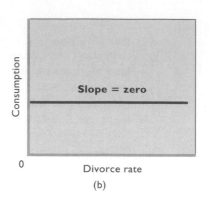

FIGURE 3

Infinite and zero slopes.   (a) A line parallel to the vertical axis has an infinite slope. Here, purchases of watches remain the same no matter what happens to the price of bananas. (b) A line parallel to the horizontal axis has a slope of zero. Here, consumption remains the same no matter what happens to the divorce rate. In both (a) and (b), the two variables are totally unrelated to one another.

demanded on the horizontal axis. The graph of their relationship is the line parallel to the vertical axis, indicating that the same quantity of watches is purchased no matter what the price of bananas. The slope of such a line is *infinite*.

Similarly, aggregate consumption is completely unrelated to the nation's divorce rate. In Figure 3b we put consumption on the vertical axis and the divorce rate on the horizontal axis. The line parallel to the horizontal axis represents this lack of relatedness. This line has a slope of *zero*.

Vertical Intercept

A line can be located on a graph (without plotting points) if we know its slope and its vertical intercept. The **vertical intercept** of a line is the point where the line meets the vertical axis. In Figure 1 the intercept is $50. This intercept means that if current income were zero, consumers would still spend $50. They might do this through borrowing or by selling some of their assets. Similarly, the $50 vertical intercept in Figure 2 shows that at a $50 ticket price, GSU's basketball team would be playing in an empty arena.

Equation of a Linear Relationship

If we know the vertical intercept and slope, we can describe a line succinctly in equation form. In its general form, the equation of a straight line is

$$y = a + bx$$

where y = dependent variable
a = vertical intercept
b = slope of line
x = independent variable

For our income-consumption example, if C represents consumption (the dependent variable) and Y represents in-

come (the independent variable), we can write $C = a + bY$. By substituting the known values of the intercept and the slope, we get

$$C = 50 + .5Y$$

This equation also allows us to determine the amount of consumption C at any specific level of income. You should use it to confirm that at the $250 income level, consumption is $175.

When economists reverse mathematical convention by putting the independent variable on the vertical axis and the dependent variable on the horizontal axis, then y stands for the independent variable, rather than the dependent variable in the general form. We noted previously that this case is relevant for our GSU ticket price–attendance data. If P represents the ticket price (independent variable) and Q represents attendance (dependent variable), their relationship is given by

$$P = 50 - 2.5Q$$

where the vertical intercept is 50 and the negative slope is $-2\frac{1}{2}$ or -2.5. Knowing the value of P lets us solve for Q, our dependent variable. You should use this equation to predict GSU ticket sales when the ticket price is $15. **(Key Appendix Question 3)**

Slope of a Nonlinear Curve

We now move from the simple world of linear relationships (straight lines) to the more complex world of nonlinear relationships. The slope of a straight line is the same at all its points. The slope of a line representing a nonlinear relationship changes from one point to another. Such lines are referred to as *curves*. (It is also permissible to refer to a straight line as a "curve.")

Consider the downsloping curve in Figure 4. Its slope is negative throughout, but the curve flattens as we move down along it. Thus, its slope constantly changes; the curve has a different slope at each point.

To measure the slope at a specific point, we draw a straight line tangent to the curve at that point. A line is *tangent* at a point if it touches, but does not intersect, the curve at that point. Thus line *aa* is tangent to the curve in Figure 4 at point *A*. The slope of the curve at that point is equal to the slope of the tangent line. Specifically, the total vertical change (drop) in the tangent line *aa* is −20 and the total horizontal change (run) is +5.

Because the slope of the tangent line *aa* is −20/+5, or −4, the slope of the curve at point *A* is also −4.

1.1 Curves and slopes

Line *bb* in Figure 4 is tangent to the curve at point *B*. Following the same procedure, we find the slope at *B* to be −5/+15, or −$\frac{1}{3}$. Thus, in this flatter part of the curve, the slope is less negative.

(Key Appendix Question 7)

FIGURE 4

Determining the slopes of curves. The slope of a nonlinear curve changes from point to point on the curve. The slope at any point (say, *B*) can be determined by drawing a straight line that is tangent to that point (line *bb*) and calculating the slope of that line.

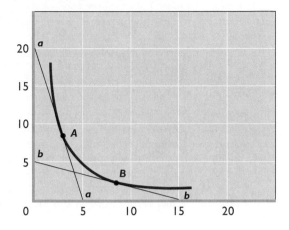

APPENDIX SUMMARY

1. Graphs are a convenient and revealing way to represent economic relationships.

2. Two variables are positively or directly related when their values change in the same direction. The line (curve) representing two directly related variables slopes upward.

3. Two variables are negatively or inversely related when their values change in opposite directions. The curve representing two inversely related variables slopes downward.

4. The value of the dependent variable (the "effect") is determined by the value of the independent variable (the "cause").

5. When the "other factors" that might affect a two-variable relationship are allowed to change, the graph of the relationship will likely shift to a new location.

6. The slope of a straight line is the ratio of the vertical change to the horizontal change between any two points. The slope of an upsloping line is positive; the slope of a downsloping line is negative.

7. The slope of a line or curve depends on the units used in measuring the variables. It is especially relevant for economics because it measures marginal changes.

8. The slope of a horizontal line is zero; the slope of a vertical line is infinite.

9. The vertical intercept and slope of a line determine its location; they are used in expressing the line—and the relationship between the two variables—as an equation.

10. The slope of a curve at any point is determined by calculating the slope of a straight line tangent to the curve at that point.

APPENDIX TERMS AND CONCEPTS

horizontal axis

vertical axis

direct relationship

inverse relationship

independent variable

dependent variable

slope of a straight line

vertical intercept

APPENDIX STUDY QUESTIONS

1. Briefly explain the use of graphs as a way to represent economic relationships. What is an inverse relationship? How does it graph? What is a direct relationship? How does it graph? Graph and explain the relationships you would expect to find between (*a*) the number of inches of rainfall per month and the sale of umbrellas, (*b*) the amount of tuition and the level of enrollment at a university, and (*c*) the popularity of an entertainer and the price of her concert tickets.

In each case cite and explain how variables other than those specifically mentioned might upset the expected relationship. Is your graph in part *b*, above, consistent with the fact that, historically, enrollments and tuition have both increased? If not, explain any difference.

2. *Key Appendix Question* Indicate how each of the following might affect the data shown in Table 2 and Figure 2 of this appendix:

   a. GSU's athletic director schedules higher-quality opponents.

   b. An NBA team locates in the city where GSU plays.

   c. GSU contracts to have all its home games televised.

3. *Key Appendix Question* The following table contains data on the relationship between saving and income. Rearrange these data into a meaningful order and graph them on the accompanying grid. What is the slope of the line? The vertical intercept? Interpret the meaning of both the slope and the intercept. Write the equation that represents this line. What would you predict saving to be at the $12,500 level of income?

Income per Year	Saving per Year
$15,000	$1,000
0	−500
10,000	500
5,000	0
20,000	1,500

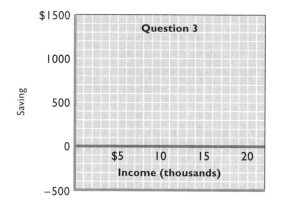

4. Construct a table from the data shown on the graph below. Which is the dependent variable and which the independent variable? Summarize the data in equation form.

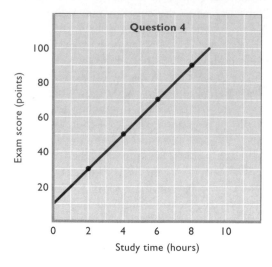

5. Suppose that when the interest rate on loans is 16 percent, businesses find it unprofitable to invest in machinery and equipment. However, when the interest rate is 14 percent, $5 billion worth of investment is profitable. At 12 percent interest, a total of $10 billion of investment is profitable. Similarly, total investment increases by $5 billion for each successive 2-percentage-point decline in the interest rate. Describe the relevant relationship between the interest rate and investment in words, in a table, on a graph, and as an equation. Put the interest rate on the vertical axis and investment on the horizontal axis. In your equation use the form $i = a + bI$, where i is the interest rate, a is the vertical intercept, b is the slope of the line (which is negative), and I is the level of investment. Comment on the advantages and disadvantages of the verbal, tabular, graphical, and equation forms of description.

6. Suppose that $C = a + bY$, where C = consumption, a = consumption at zero income, b = slope, and Y = income.

   a. Are C and Y positively related or are they negatively related?

   b. If graphed, would the curve for this equation slope upward or slope downward?

   c. Are the variables C and Y inversely related or directly related?

   d. What is the value of C if $a = 10$, $b = .50$, and $Y = 200$?

   e. What is the value of Y if $C = 100$, $a = 10$, and $b = .25$?

7. **Key Appendix Question** The accompanying graph shows curve *XX'* and tangents at points *A*, *B*, and *C*. Calculate the slope of the curve at these three points.

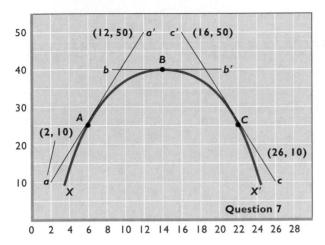

Question 7

8. In the accompanying graph, is the slope of curve *AA'* positive or negative? Does the slope increase or decrease as we move along the curve from *A* to *A'*? Answer the same two questions for curve *BB'*.

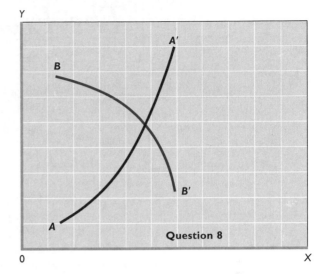

Question 8

2 | *The Economizing Problem*

You make decisions every day that capture the essence of economics. Suppose you have $50 and are deciding how to spend it. Should you buy a new pair of jeans? Two or three compact discs? A ticket for a concert? Should you forgo work while you are attending college and concentrate solely on your coursework and grades? Is that an option for you, given the high cost of college? If you decide to work, should it be full-time or part-time? Should you work on campus at lower pay or off campus at higher pay? What are the implications of your employment for your course grades?

Money and time are both scarce, and making decisions in the context of scarcity always means there are costs. If you choose the jeans, the cost is the forgone CDs or concert. If you work full-time, the cost might be greater stress, poorer performance in your classes, or an extra year or two in college.

This chapter examines the fundamentals of economics—scarcity, choices, and costs. We first examine the *economizing problem,* focusing closely on *wants* and *resources.* Next, we develop two economic models: (1) a *production possibilities model* that incorporates and illustrates several key ideas, and (2) a simple *circular flow model* that identifies the major groups of decision makers and major markets in the economy.

The Foundation of Economics

Two fundamental facts together constitute the **economizing problem** and provide a foundation for economics:
- Society's economic wants—that is, the economic wants of its citizens and institutions—are virtually unlimited and insatiable.
- Economic resources—the means of producing goods and services—are limited or scarce.

All that follows depends directly on these two facts.

Unlimited Wants

What do we mean by "economic wants"? We mean, first, the desires of consumers to obtain and use various goods and services that provide pleasure or satisfaction, or what economists call "utility." These wants extend over a wide range of products, from *necessities* (food, shelter, clothing) to *luxuries* (perfumes, yachts, race cars). Some wants such as basic food, clothing, and shelter have biological roots. Other wants, for example, the specific kinds of food, clothing, and shelter we seek, are rooted in the conventions and customs of society.

Over time, wants change and tend to multiply, fueled by new products. Not long ago, we did not want DVD players, Internet service, digital cameras, lattes, or pagers because they simply did not exist. Also, the satisfaction of certain wants tends to trigger others: the acquisition of a Neon or Civic has been known to whet the appetite for a Porsche or a Mercedes.

Services, as well as products, satisfy our wants. Car repair work, the removal of an inflamed appendix, legal and accounting advice, and haircuts all satisfy human wants. Actually, we buy many goods, such as automobiles and washing machines, for the services they render. The differences between goods and services are often smaller than they appear to be.

Businesses and units of government also strive to satisfy economic goals. Businesses want factories, machinery, trucks, warehouses, and phone systems to help them achieve their production goals. Government, reflecting the collective wants of its citizens or goals of its own, seeks highways, schools, and military equipment.

All these wants are *insatiable*, or *unlimited*, meaning that our desires for goods and services cannot be completely satisfied. Our desires for a *particular* good or service can be satisfied; over a short period of time we can surely get enough toothpaste or pasta. And one appendectomy is plenty. But goods *in general* are another story. We do not, and presumably cannot, get enough. Suppose all members of society were asked to list the goods and services they would buy if they had unlimited income. That list would probably never end.

In short, individuals and institutions have innumerable unfilled wants. *The objective of all economic activity is to fulfill wants.*

Scarce Resources

The second fundamental fact is that *economic resources are limited or scarce.* By **economic resources** we mean all natural, human, and manufactured resources that go into the production of goods and services. That includes all the factory and farm buildings and all the equipment, tools, and machinery used to produce manufactured goods and agricultural products; all transportation and communication facilities; all types of labor; and land and mineral resources. Economists classify all these resources as either *property* resources (land, raw materials, and capital) or *human* resources (labor and entrepreneurial ability).

Resource Categories   Let's look at four specific categories of economic resources.

Land   **Land** means much more to the economist than it does to most people. To the economist land includes all natural resources—all "gifts of nature"—that are used in the production process, such as arable land, forests, mineral and oil deposits, and water resources.

Capital   **Capital** (or *capital goods* or *investment goods*) includes all manufactured aids used in producing consumer goods and services. Included are all tools, machinery, equipment, factory, storage, transportation, and distribution facilities. The process of producing and purchasing capital goods is known as **investment.**

Capital goods differ from *consumer goods* because consumer goods satisfy wants directly, while capital goods do so indirectly by aiding the production of consumer goods. Note that the term "capital" as used by economists refers *not* to money but to *real capital* such as tools, machinery, and other productive equipment. Money produces nothing; it is *not* an economic resource. So-called money capital or financial capital is simply a means for purchasing real capital.

Labor   **Labor** is a broad term for all the physical and mental talents of individuals available and usable in producing goods and services. The services of a logger, retail clerk, machinist, teacher, professional football player, and nuclear physicist all fall under the general heading "labor."

Entrepreneurial Ability   Finally, there is the special human resource, distinct from labor, that we label **entrepreneurial ability.** The entrepreneur performs several functions:

- The entrepreneur *takes the initiative* in combining the resources of land, capital, and labor to produce a good or a service. Both a sparkplug and a catalyst, the entrepreneur is the driving force behind production and the agent who combines the other resources in what is hoped will be a successful business venture.
- The entrepreneur *makes the strategic business decisions* that set the course of an enterprise.
- The entrepreneur is an *innovator.* He or she commercializes new products, new production techniques, or even new forms of business organization.
- The entrepreneur is a *risk bearer.* The entrepreneur in a market system has no guarantee of profit. The reward for the entrepreneur's time, efforts, and abilities

may be profits *or* losses. The entrepreneur risks not only his or her invested funds but those of associates and stockholders as well.

Because these four resources—land, labor, capital, and entrepreneurial ability—are combined to *produce* goods and services, they are called the **factors of production. (Key Question 4)**

Resource Payments   The income received from supplying raw materials and capital equipment (the property resources) is called *rental income* and *interest income*, respectively. The income accruing to those who supply labor is called *wages*, which include salaries and all wage and salary supplements such as bonuses, commissions, and royalties. Entrepreneurial income is called *profits*, which may be negative—that is, losses.

Relative Scarcity   The four types of economic resources, or factors of production, or *inputs*, have one significant characteristic in common: *They are scarce or limited in supply.* Our planet contains only finite, and therefore limited, amounts of arable land, mineral deposits, capital equipment, and labor. Their scarcity constrains productive activity and output. In the United States, one of the most affluent nations, output per person was limited to roughly $36,000 in 2002. In the poorest nations, annual output per person may be as low as $300 or $400.

Economics: Employment and Efficiency

The economizing problem is at the heart of the definition of economics stated in Chapter 1: *Economics is the social science concerned with the problem of using scarce resources to attain the maximum fulfillment of society's unlimited wants.* Economics is concerned with "doing the best with what we have."

Economics is thus the social science that examines efficiency—the best use of scarce resources. Society wants to use its limited resources efficiently; it desires to produce as many goods and services as possible from its available resources, thereby maximizing total satisfaction.

Full Employment: Using Available Resources

To realize the best use of scarce resources, a society must achieve both full employment and full production. By **full employment** we mean the use of all available resources. No workers should be out of work if they are willing and able to work. Nor should capital equipment or arable land sit idle.

But note that we say all *available* resources should be employed. Each society has certain customs and practices that determine what resources are available for employment and what resources are not. For example, in most countries legislation and custom provide that children and the very aged should not be employed. Similarly, to maintain productivity, farmland should be allowed to lie fallow periodically. And we should conserve some resources—fishing stocks and forest, for instance—for use by future generations.

Full Production: Using Resources Efficiently

The employment of all available resources is not enough, however. To achieve efficiency, society must also realize full production. By **full production** we mean that all employed resources must be used so that they provide the maximum possible satisfaction of our economic wants. If we fail to realize full production, economists say our resources are *underemployed.*

Full production implies two kinds of efficiency—productive and allocative efficiency. **Productive efficiency** is the production of *any particular mix of goods and services in the least costly way.* When we produce, say, compact discs at the lowest achievable unit cost, we are expending the smallest amount of resources to produce CDs and are therefore making available the largest amount of resources to produce other desired products. Suppose society has only $100 worth of resources available. If we can produce a CD for only $5 of those resources, then $95 will be available to produce other goods. This is clearly better than producing the CD for $10 and having only $90 of resources available for alternative uses.

In contrast, **allocative efficiency** is the least-cost production of *that particular mix of goods and services most wanted by society.* For example, society wants resources allocated to compact discs, not to 45-rpm records. We want personal computers (PCs), not manual typewriters. Furthermore, we do not want to devote *all* our resources to producing CDs and PCs; we want to assign some of them to producing automobiles and office buildings. Allocative efficiency requires that an economy produce the "right" mix of goods and services, with each item being produced at the lowest-possible unit cost. This means apportioning limited resources among firms and industries in such a way that society obtains the combination of goods and services it wants the most. **(Key Question 5)**

Production Possibilities Table

Because resources are scarce, a full-employment, full-production economy cannot have an unlimited output of goods and services. Consequently, people must choose which goods and services to produce and which to forgo. The necessity and consequences of those choices can best be understood through a *production possibilities model*. We examine the model first as a table and then as a graph.

Assumptions   We begin our discussion of the production possibilities model with simplifying assumptions:

- *Full employment and productive efficiency*   The economy is employing all its available resources (full employment) and is producing goods and services at least cost (productive efficiency).
- *Fixed resources*   The available supplies of the factors of production are fixed in both quantity and quality. Nevertheless, they can be reallocated, within limits, among different uses; for example, land can be used either for factory sites or for food production.
- *Fixed technology*   The state of technology—the methods used to produce output—does not change during our analysis. This assumption and the previous one imply that we are looking at an economy at a certain point in time or over a very short period of time.
- *Two goods*   The economy is producing only two goods: pizzas and industrial robots. Pizzas symbolize **consumer goods,** products that satisfy our wants *directly;* industrial robots symbolize **capital goods,** products that satisfy our wants *indirectly* by making possible more efficient production of consumer goods.

The Need for Choice   Given our assumptions, we see that society must choose among alternatives. Fixed resources mean limited outputs of pizza and robots. And since all available resources are fully employed, to increase

TABLE 2.1

Production Possibilities of Pizzas and Robots with Full Employment and Productive Efficiency

Type of Product	Production Alternatives				
	A	B	C	D	E
Pizzas (in hundred thousands)	0	1	2	3	4
Robots (in thousands)	10	9	7	4	0

the production of robots we must shift resources away from the production of pizzas. The reverse is also true: To increase the production of pizzas, we must shift resources away from the production of robots. There is no such thing as a free pizza. This, recall, is the essence of the economizing problem.

A **production possibilities table** lists the different combinations of two products that can be produced with a specific set of resources (and with full employment *and* productive efficiency). Table 2.1 is such a table for a pizza-robot economy; the data are, of course, hypothetical. At alternative A, this economy would be devoting all its available resources to the production of robots (capital goods); at alternative E, all resources would go to pizza production (consumer goods). Those alternatives are unrealistic extremes; an economy typically produces both capital goods and consumer goods, as in B, C, and D. As we move from alternative A to E, we increase the production of pizza at the expense of robot production.

Because consumer goods satisfy our wants directly, any movement toward E looks tempting. In producing more pizzas, society increases the current satisfaction of its wants. But there is a cost: More pizzas mean fewer robots. This shift of resources to consumer goods catches up with society over time as the stock of capital goods dwindles—or at least ceases to expand at the current rate—with the result that some potential for greater future production is lost. By moving toward alternative E, society chooses "more now" at the expense of "much more later."

By moving toward A, society chooses to forgo current consumption, thereby freeing up resources that can be used to increase the production of capital goods. By building up its stock of capital this way, society will have greater future production and, therefore, greater future consumption. By moving toward A, society is choosing "more later" at the cost of "less now."

Generalization: *At any point in time, an economy achieving full employment and productive efficiency must sacrifice some of one good to obtain more of another good. Scarce resources prohibit such an economy from having more of both goods.*

KEY GRAPH

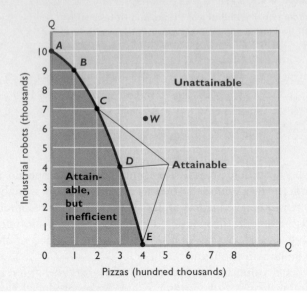

FIGURE 2.1

The production possibilities curve. Each point *on* the production possibilities curve represents some maximum combination of two products that can be produced if resources are fully and efficiently employed. When operating on the curve, more robots means fewer pizzas, and vice versa. Limited resources and a fixed technology make any combination of robots and pizzas lying outside the curve (such as at W) unattainable. Points inside the curve are attainable, but they indicate that full employment and productive efficiency are not being realized.

QUICK QUIZ 2.1

1. Production possibilities curve *ABCDE* is bowed out from the origin (concave to the origin) because:
   a. the marginal benefit of pizzas declines as more pizzas are consumed.
   b. the curve gets steeper as we move from *E* to *A*.
   c. it reflects the law of increasing opportunity costs.
   d. resources are scarce.

2. The marginal opportunity cost of the second unit of pizza is:
   a. 2 units of robots.
   b. 3 units of robots.
   c. 7 units of robots.
   d. 9 units of robots.

3. The total opportunity cost of 7 units of robots is:
   a. 1 unit of pizza.
   b. 2 units of pizza.
   c. 3 units of pizza.
   d. 4 units of pizza.

4. All points on this production possibilities curve necessarily represent:
   a. allocative efficiency.
   b. less than full use of resources.
   c. unattainable levels of output.
   d. productive efficiency.

Answers: 1. c; 2. a; 3. b; 4. d

Production Possibilities Curve

2.1
Production possibilities curve

The data presented in a production possibilities table can also be shown graphically. We use a simple two-dimensional graph, arbitrarily representing the output of capital goods (here, robots) on the vertical axis and the output of consumer goods (here, pizzas) on the horizontal axis, as shown in **Figure 2.1 (Key Graph).** Following the procedure given in the appendix to Chapter 1, we can graph a **production possibilities curve.**

Each point on the production possibilities curve represents some maximum output of the two products. The curve is a production *frontier* because it shows the limit of attainable outputs. To obtain the various combinations of pizza and robots that fall *on* the production possibilities curve, society must achieve both full employment and productive efficiency. Points lying *inside* (to the left of) the curve are also attainable, but they reflect inefficiency and therefore are not as desirable as points on the curve. Points inside the curve imply that the economy could have more of both robots and pizzas if it achieved full employment and productive efficiency. Points lying *outside* (to the right of) the production possibilities curve, like point *W*, would represent a greater output than the output at any point on the curve. Such points, however, are unattainable with the current supplies of resources and technology.

Law of Increasing Opportunity Cost

Because resources are scarce relative to the virtually unlimited wants they can be used to satisfy, people must choose among alternatives. More pizzas mean fewer robots. The amount of other products that must be forgone or sacrificed to obtain 1 unit of a specific good is called the **opportunity cost** of that good. In our case, the number of robots that must be given up to get another unit of pizza is the *opportunity cost*, or simply the *cost*, of that unit of pizza.

2.1
Opportunity
cost

In moving from alternative A to alternative B in Table 2.1, we find that the cost of 1 additional unit of pizza is 1 less unit of robots. But as we pursue the concept of cost through the additional production possibilities— B to C, C to D, and D to E—an important economic principle is revealed: The opportunity cost of each additional unit of pizza is greater than the opportunity cost of the preceding one. When we move from A to B, just 1 unit of robots is sacrificed for 1 more unit of pizza; but in going from B to C we sacrifice 2 additional units of robots for 1 more unit of pizza; then 3 more of robots for 1 more of pizza; and finally 4 for 1. Conversely, confirm that as we move from E to A, the cost of an additional robot is $\frac{1}{4}$, $\frac{1}{3}$, $\frac{1}{2}$, and 1 unit of pizza, respectively, for the four successive moves.

Note these points about these opportunity costs:

- Here opportunity costs are being measured in *real* terms, that is, in actual goods rather than in money terms.
- We are discussing *marginal* (meaning "extra") opportunity costs, rather than cumulative or total opportunity costs. For example, the marginal opportunity cost of the third unit of pizza in Table 2.1 is 3 units of robots (=7 − 4). But the *total* opportunity cost of 3 units of pizza is 6 units of robots (=1 unit of robots for the first unit of pizza *plus* 2 units of robots for the second unit of pizza *plus* 3 units of robots for the third unit of pizza).

Our example illustrates the **law of increasing opportunity costs:** The more of a product that is produced, the greater is its opportunity cost ("marginal" being implied).

Shape of the Curve

The law of increasing opportunity costs is reflected in the shape of the production possibilities curve: The curve is bowed out from the origin of the graph. Figure 2.1 shows that when the economy moves from *A* to *E*, it must give up successively larger amounts of robots (1, 2, 3, and 4) to acquire equal increments of pizza (1, 1, 1, and 1). This is shown in the slope of the production possibilities curve, which becomes steeper as we move from *A* to *E*. A curve that gets steeper as we move down it is "concave to the origin."

Economic Rationale

What is the economic rationale for the law of increasing opportunity costs? Why does the sacrifice of robots increase as we produce more pizzas? The answer is that *economic resources are not completely adaptable to alternative uses.* Many resources are better at producing one good than at producing others. Fertile farmland is highly suited to producing the ingredients needed to make pizzas, while land rich in mineral deposits is highly suited to producing the materials needed to make robots. As we step up pizza production, resources that are less and less adaptable to making pizzas must be "pushed" into pizza production. If we start at *A* and move to *B*, we can shift the resources whose productivity of pizzas is greatest in relation to their productivity of robots. But as we move from *B* to *C*, *C* to *D*, and so on, resources highly productive of pizzas become increasingly scarce. To get more pizzas, resources whose productivity of robots is great in relation to their productivity of pizzas will be needed. It will take more and more of such resources, and hence greater sacrifices of robots, to achieve each increase of 1 unit in the production of pizzas. This lack of perfect flexibility, or interchangeability, on the part of resources is the cause of increasing opportunity costs. **(Key Question 6)**

Allocative Efficiency Revisited

So far, we have assumed full employment and productive efficiency, both of which are necessary to realize *any point* on an economy's production possibilities curve. We now turn to allocative efficiency, which requires that the economy produce at the most valued, or *optimal*, point on the production possibilities curve. Of all the attainable combinations of pizzas and robots on the curve in Figure 2.1, which is best? That is, what specific quantities of resources should be allocated to pizzas and what specific quantities to robots in order to maximize satisfaction?

Our discussion of the *economic perspective* in Chapter 1 puts us on the right track. Recall that economic decisions center on comparisons of marginal benefits and marginal costs. Any economic activity—for example, production or consumption—should be expanded as long as marginal benefit exceeds marginal cost and should be reduced if marginal cost exceeds marginal benefit. The optimal amount of the activity occurs where MB = MC.

Consider pizzas. We already know from the law of increasing opportunity costs that the marginal cost (MC) of

FIGURE 2.2

Allocative efficiency: MB = MC. Allocative efficiency requires the expansion of a good's output until its marginal benefit (MB) and marginal cost (MC) are equal. No resources beyond that point should get allocated to the product. Here, allocative efficiency occurs when 200,000 pizzas are produced.

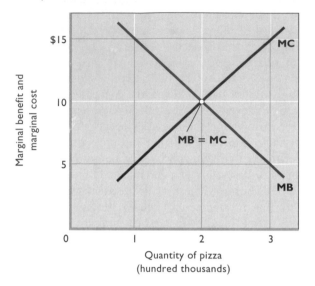

additional units of pizzas will rise as more units are produced. This can be shown by an upsloping MC curve, as in Figure 2.2. We also know that we obtain extra or marginal benefits (MB) from additional units of pizzas. However, although economic wants in the aggregate are insatiable, studies reveal that the second unit of a particular product yields less additional utility or benefit to a person than the first. And a third provides even less MB than the second. So it is for society as a whole. We therefore can portray the marginal benefits from pizzas with a downsloping MB curve, as in Figure 2.2. Although total benefits rise when society consumes more pizza, marginal benefits decline.

The optimal quantity of pizza production is indicated by the intersection of the MB and MC curves: 200,000 units in Figure 2.2. Why is this the optimal quantity? If only 100,000 pizzas were produced, the marginal benefit of pizza would exceed its marginal cost. In money terms, MB might be $15, while MC is only $5. This suggests that society would be *underallocating* resources to pizza production and that more of it should be produced.

How do we know? Because society values an additional pizza as being worth $15, while the alternative products that those resources could produce are worth only $5. Society benefits—it is better off in the sense of having a higher-valued output to enjoy—whenever it can gain something worth $15 by forgoing something worth only $5.

Society would use its resources more efficiently by allocating more resources to pizza. Each additional pizza up to 200,000 would provide such a gain, indicating that allocative efficiency would be improved by that production. But when MB = MC, the benefits of producing pizzas or alternative products with the available resources are equal. Allocative efficiency is achieved where MB = MC.

The production of 300,000 pizzas would represent an *overallocation* of resources to pizza production. Here the MC of pizza is $15 and its MB is only $5. This means that 1 unit of pizza is worth only $5 to society, while the alternative products that those resources could otherwise produce are valued at $15. By producing 1 less unit, society loses a pizza worth $5. But by reallocating the freed resources, it gains other products worth $15. When society gains something worth $15 by forgoing something worth only $5, it is better off. In Figure 2.2, such net gains can be realized until pizza production has been reduced to 200,000.

Generalization: *Resources are being efficiently allocated to any product when the marginal benefit and marginal cost of its output are equal (MB = MC).* Suppose that by applying the above analysis to robots, we find their optimal (MB = MC) output is 7000. This would mean that alternative C on our production possibilities curve—200,000 pizzas and 7000 robots—would result in allocative efficiency for our hypothetical economy. **(Key Question 9)**

QUICK REVIEW 2.2

• The production possibilities curve illustrates four concepts: (a) *scarcity* of resources is implied by the area of unattainable combinations of output lying outside the production possibilities curve; (b) *choice* among outputs is reflected in the variety of attainable combinations of goods lying along the curve; (c) *opportunity cost* is illustrated by the downward slope of the curve; (d) the law of *increasing opportunity costs* is implied by the concavity of the curve.

• Full employment and productive efficiency must be realized in order for the economy to operate on its production possibilities curve.

• A comparison of marginal benefits and marginal costs is needed to determine allocative efficiency—the best or optimal output mix on the curve.

Unemployment, Growth, and the Future

Let's now discard the first three assumptions underlying the production possibilities curve and see what happens.

Unemployment and Productive Inefficiency

The first assumption was that our economy was achieving full employment and productive efficiency. Our analysis and conclusions change if some resources are idle (unemployment) or if least-cost production is not realized. The five alternatives in Table 2.1 represent maximum outputs; they illustrate the combinations of robots and pizzas that can be produced when the economy is operating at full capacity—with full employment and productive efficiency. With unemployment or inefficient production, the economy would produce less than each alternative shown in the table.

Graphically, we represent situations of unemployment or productive inefficiency by points *inside* the original production possibilities curve (reproduced in Figure 2.3). Point *U* is one such point. Here the economy is falling short of the various maximum combinations of pizzas and robots represented by the points *on* the production possibilities curve. The arrows in Figure 2.3 indicate three possible paths back to full-employment and least-cost production. A move toward full employment and productive efficiency would yield a greater output of one or both products.

FIGURE 2.3

Unemployment, productive inefficiency, and the production possibilities curve. Any point inside the production possibilities curve, such as *U*, represents unemployment or a failure to achieve productive efficiency. The arrows indicate that, by realizing full employment and productive efficiency, the economy could operate on the curve. This means it could produce more of one or both products than it is producing at point *U*.

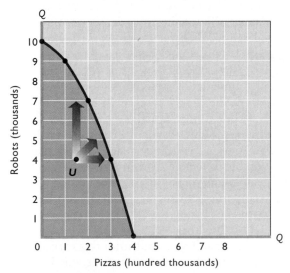

TABLE 2.2

Production Possibilities of Pizza and Robots with Full Employment and Productive Efficiency

	Production Alternatives				
Type of Product	**A′**	**B′**	**C′**	**D′**	**E′**
Pizzas (in hundred thousands)	0	2	4	6	8
Robots (in thousands)	14	12	9	5	0

A Growing Economy

When we drop the assumption that the quantity and quality of resources and technology are fixed, the production possibilities curve shifts positions—that is, the potential maximum output of the economy changes.

Increases in Resource Supplies Although resource supplies are fixed at any specific moment, they can and do change over time. For example, a nation's growing population will bring about increases in the supplies of labor and entrepreneurial ability. Also, labor quality usually improves over time. Historically, the economy's stock of capital has increased at a significant, though unsteady, rate. And although we are depleting some of our energy and mineral resources, new sources are being discovered. The development of irrigation programs, for example, adds to the supply of arable land.

The net result of these increased supplies of the factors of production is the ability to produce more of both pizzas and robots. Thus 20 years from now, the production possibilities in Table 2.2 may supersede those shown in Table 2.1. The greater abundance of resources will result in a greater potential output of one or both products at each alternative. Society will have achieved economic growth in the form of expanded potential output.

But such a favorable change in the production possibilities data does not *guarantee* that the economy will actually operate at a point on its new production possibilities curve. Some 137 million jobs will give the United States full employment now (2003), but 10 or 20 years from now its labor force will be larger, and 137 million jobs will not be sufficient for full employment. The production possibilities curve may shift, but at the future date the economy may fail to produce at a point on that new curve.

Advances in Technology Our second assumption is that we have constant, unchanging technology. In reality, though, technology has progressed dramatically over time.

An advancing technology brings both new and better goods *and* improved ways of producing them. For now, let's think of technological advance as being only improvements in the methods of production, for example, the introduction of computerized systems to manage inventories and schedule production. These advances alter our previous discussion of the economizing problem by improving productive efficiency, thereby allowing society to produce more goods with fixed resources. As with increases in resource supplies, technological advances make possible the production of more robots *and* more pizzas.

Thus, when either supplies of resources increase or an improvement in technology occurs, the production possibilities curve in Figure 2.3 shifts outward and to the right, as illustrated by curve $A'B'C'D'E'$ in Figure 2.4. Such an outward shift of the production possibilities curve represents growth of economic capacity or, simply, **economic growth:** *the ability to produce a larger total output.* This growth is the result of (1) increases in supplies of resources, (2) improvements in resource quality, and (3) technological advances.

The consequence of growth is that our full-employment economy can enjoy a greater output of both robots and pizzas. *While a static, no-growth economy must sacrifice some of one product in order to get more of another, a dynamic, growing economy can have larger quantities of both products.*

Economic growth does not ordinarily mean proportionate increases in a nation's capacity to produce all its products. Note in Figure 2.4 that, at the maximums, the economy can produce twice as many pizzas as before but only 40 percent more robots. To reinforce your understanding of this concept, sketch in two new production possibilities curves: one showing the situation where a better technique for producing robots has been developed while the technology for producing pizzas is unchanged, and the other illustrating an improved technology for pizzas while the technology for producing robots remains constant.

Present Choices and Future Possibilities An economy's current choice of positions on its production possibilities curve helps determine the future location of that curve. Let's designate the two axes of the production possibilities curve as *goods for the future* and *goods for the present*, as in Figure 2.5. Goods for the future are such things as capital goods, research and education, and preventive medicine. They increase the quantity and quality of property resources, enlarge the stock of technological information, and improve the quality of human resources. As we have already seen, goods for the future, like industrial robots, are the ingredients of economic growth. Goods for the present are pure consumer goods, such as pizza, clothing, and soft drinks.

Now suppose there are two economies, Alta and Zorn, which are initially identical in every respect except one: Alta's current choice of positions on its production possibilities curve strongly favors present goods over future goods. Point *A* in Figure 2.5a indicates that choice. It is located quite far down the curve to the right, indicating a high priority for goods for the present, at the expense of fewer goods for the future. Zorn, in contrast, makes a current choice that stresses larger amounts of future goods and smaller amounts of present goods, as shown by point *Z* in Figure 2.5b.

Now, other things equal, we can expect the future production possibilities curve of Zorn to be farther to the right than Alta's curve. By currently choosing an output more favorable to technological advances and to increases in the quantity and quality of resources, Zorn will achieve greater economic growth than Alta. In terms of capital goods, Zorn is choosing to make larger current additions to its "national factory"—to invest more of its current output—than Alta. The payoff from this choice for Zorn is more rapid growth—greater future production capacity.

FIGURE 2.4

Economic growth and the production possibilities curve. The increase in supplies of resources, the improvements in resource quality, and the technological advances that occur in a dynamic economy move the production possibilities curve outward and to the right, allowing the economy to have larger quantities of both types of goods.

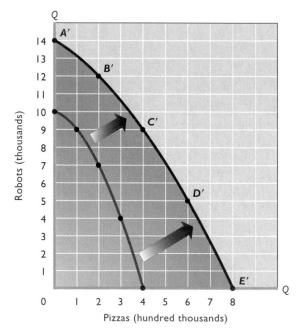

FIGURE 2.5

An economy's present choice of positions on its production possibilities curve helps determine the curve's future location.   A nation's current choice favoring "present goods," as made by Alta in (a), will cause a modest outward shift of the curve in the future. A nation's current choice favoring "future goods," as made by Zorn in (b), will result in a greater outward shift of the curve in the future.

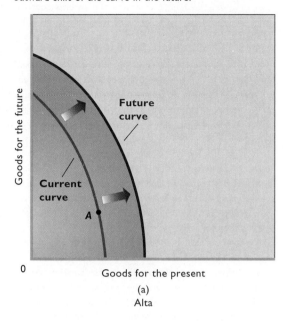

(a)
Alta

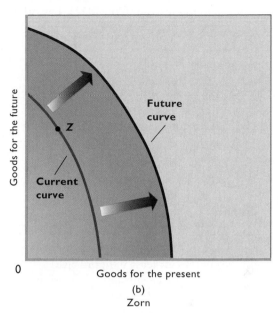

(b)
Zorn

**2.2
Present
choices and
future
possibilities**

The opportunity cost is fewer consumer goods in the present for Zorn to enjoy. Is Zorn's choice thus "better" than Alta's? That, we cannot say. The different outcomes simply reflect different preferences and priorities in the two countries. **(Key Questions 10 and 11)**

A Qualification: International Trade

Production possibilities analysis implies that an individual nation is limited to the combinations of output indicated by its production possibilities curve. *But we must modify this principle when international specialization and trade exist.*

You will see in later chapters that an economy can circumvent, through international specialization and trade, the output limits imposed by its domestic production possibilities curve. *International specialization* means directing domestic resources to output that a nation is highly efficient at producing. *International trade* involves the exchange of these goods for goods produced abroad. Specialization and trade enable a nation to get more of a desired good at less sacrifice of some other good. Rather than sacrifice 3 units of robots to get a third unit of pizza,

as in Table 2.1, a nation might be able to obtain the third unit of pizza by trading only 2 units of robots for it. Specialization and trade have the same effect as having more and better resources or discovering improved production techniques; both increase the quantities of capital and consumer goods available to society. The output gains from greater international specialization and trade are the equivalent of economic growth.

QUICK REVIEW 2.3

- Unemployment and the failure to achieve productive efficiency cause an economy to operate at a point inside its production possibilities curve.

- Increases in resource supplies, improvements in resource quality, and technological advance cause economic growth, which is depicted as an outward shift of the production possibilities curve.

- An economy's present choice of capital and consumer goods helps determine the future location of its production possibilities curve.

- International specialization and trade enable a nation to obtain more goods than its production possibilities curve indicates.

Examples and Applications

There are many possible applications and examples relating to the production possibilities model. This chapter's Last Word, on September 11, 2001, and the war on terrorism, is one such application. Consider a few others.

Unemployment and Productive Inefficiency
In the depths of the Great Depression of the 1930s, the United States operated well inside its production possibilities curve. At one point, one-quarter of U.S. workers were unemployed and one-third of U.S. production capacity was idle. The United States has suffered a number of much milder downturns since then, the latest occurring in 2001. In that year total production fell, unemployment increased, and the economy operated inside its production possibilities curve.

Almost all nations have experienced widespread unemployment and unused production capacity at one time or another. Since 1995, for example, several nations including Argentina, Japan, Mexico, Germany, and South Korea have had economic downturns that placed them inside their production possibilities curves, at least temporarily.

Economies that experience substantial discrimination based on race, ethnicity, and gender do not achieve productive efficiency, and thus they operate inside their production possibilities curves. Because discrimination prevents those discriminated against from obtaining jobs that best use their skills, society has less output than otherwise. Eliminating discrimination would move such an economy from a point inside its production possibilities curve toward a point on its curve.

Similarly, economies in which labor usage and production methods are based on custom, heredity, and caste, rather than on efficiency, operate well inside their production possibilities curves.

Tradeoffs and Opportunity Costs
Many issues illustrate the tradeoffs and opportunity costs indicated by movements along a particular production possibilities curve. (Any two categories of "output" can be placed on the axes of production possibilities curves.) Should scenic land be used for logging and mining or be preserved as wilderness? If the land is used for logging and mining, the opportunity cost is the forgone benefits of wilderness. If the land is used for wilderness, the opportunity cost is the lost value of the wood and minerals that society forgoes.

Should society devote more resources to the criminal justice system (police, courts, and prisons) or to education (teachers, books, and schools)? If society devotes more resources to the criminal justice system, other things equal, the opportunity cost is forgone improvements in education. If more resources are allocated to education, the opportunity cost is the forgone benefits from an

---

© Stefan Zaklin/Getty Images

A Matter of Degrees: Is College Worth the Cost?
Teachers and parents constantly encourage able students to attend college. Yet Microsoft cofounder Bill Gates and talk show host Oprah Winfrey* both dropped out of college, and baseball star Alex Rodriguez never even bothered to enroll. Is it wrong to emphasize college, or did Gates, Winfrey, and Rodriguez make good choices?

Deciding to go to college involves weighing future benefits and present costs. The future benefits are higher expected-lifetime earnings. The present costs include *direct costs,* such as tuition and books, and the *indirect costs* (or *opportunity costs*) of forgoing income that could be earned as a full-time worker with a high school diploma. Students attend college because they expect the long-run benefits of a degree to exceed the short-term costs.

Unlike most students, Gates faced huge opportunity costs for staying in college. He had a vision for his company, and starting work young helped ensure Microsoft's success. Similarly, Winfrey landed a spot in local television news when she was a teenager, eventually producing and starring in the *Oprah Winfrey Show* when she was 32 years old. Getting a degree in her twenties might have interrupted the string of successes that made her famous talk show possible. And Rodriguez knew that professional athletes have short careers. Therefore, going to college directly after high school would have taken away four years of his peak earning potential.

So Gates, Winfrey, and Rodriguez understood opportunity costs and made good choices. But it's important to note that their experiences are not typical. College graduates usually earn about 50 percent more during their lifetimes than persons with just high school diplomas. For most students, "Go to college, stay in college, and earn a degree" is very sound advice.

*Winfrey eventually went back to school and earned a degree from Tennessee State University when she was in her thirties.

---

improved criminal justice system. If we decide to devote more resources to both, what other goods and services do we forgo? Health care? Homeland defense?

Shifts in Production Possibilities Curves
We have seen that more resources, better-quality resources, and improved technology shift a nation's production possibilities curve outward. An example of more resources is the large increase in the number of employed women in the United States in the past 40 years. Sixty percent of adult American women work full-time or part-time in paid jobs today, compared to only 40 percent in 1965.

Over recent decades, women have greatly increased their productivity in the workplace, mostly by becoming better educated and professionally trained. As a result, they can earn higher wages. Because those higher wages have increased the opportunity cost—the forgone wage earnings—of staying at home, women have substituted employment in the labor market for the now more "expensive" traditional home activities. This substitution has been particularly pronounced among married women. Along with other factors such as changing attitudes and expanded job access, the rising earnings of women have produced a substantial increase in the number of women workers in the United States. This increase in the quantity of available resources has helped push the U.S. production possibilities curve outward.

An example of improved technology is the recent spurt of new technologies relating to computers, communications, and biotechnology. Technological advances have dropped the prices of computers and greatly enhanced their speed. Cellular phones and the Internet have increased communications capacity, enhancing production and improving the efficiency of markets. Advances in biotechnology, specifically genetic engineering, have resulted in important agricultural and medical discoveries. Many economists believe these new technologies are so significant that they are contributing to faster-than-normal U.S. economic growth (faster rightward shifts of the nation's production possibilities curve).

Economic Systems

Every society needs to develop an **economic system**—*a particular set of institutional arrangements and a coordinating mechanism*—to respond to the economizing problem. Economic systems differ as to (1) who owns the factors of production and (2) the method used to coordinate and direct economic activity. There are two general types of economic systems: the market system and the command system.

The Market System

The private ownership of resources and the use of markets and prices to coordinate and direct economic activity characterize the **market system,** or **capitalism.** In that system each participant acts in his or her own self-interest; each individual or business seeks to maximize its satisfaction or profit through its own decisions regarding consumption or production. The system allows for the private ownership of capital, communicates through prices, and coordinates economic activity through *markets*—places where buyers and sellers come together. Goods and services are produced and resources are supplied by whoever is willing and able to do so. The result is competition among independently acting buyers and sellers of each

product and resource. Thus, economic decision making is widely dispersed.

In *pure* capitalism—or *laissez-faire* capitalism—government's role would be limited to protecting private property and establishing an environment appropriate to the operation of the market system. The term "laissez-faire" means "let it be," that is, keep government from interfering with the economy. The idea is that such interference will disturb the efficient working of the market system.

2.2 Laissez-faire

But in the capitalism practiced in the United States and most other countries, government plays a substantial role in the economy. It not only provides the rules for economic activity but also promotes economic stability and growth, provides certain goods and services that would otherwise be underproduced or not produced at all, and modifies the distribution of income. The government, however, is not the dominant economic force in deciding what to produce, how to produce it, and who will get it. That force is the market.

The Command System

The alternative to the market system is the **command system,** also known as *socialism* or *communism.* In that system, government owns most property resources and economic decision making occurs through a central economic plan. A central planning board appointed by the government makes nearly all the major decisions concerning the use of resources, the composition and distribution of output, and the organization of production. The government owns most of the business firms, which produce according to government directives. The central planning board determines production goals for each enterprise and specifies the amount of resources to be allocated to each enterprise so that it can reach its production goals. The division of output between capital and consumer goods is centrally decided, and capital goods are allocated among industries on the basis of the central planning board's long-term priorities.

A *pure* command economy would rely exclusively on a central plan to allocate the government-owned property resources. But, in reality, even the preeminent command economy—the Soviet Union—tolerated some private ownership and incorporated some markets before its demise in 1992. Recent reforms in Russia and most of the eastern European nations have to one degree or another transformed their command economies to capitalistic, market-oriented systems. China's reforms have not gone as far, but they have reduced the reliance on central planning. Although there is still extensive government ownership of

KEY GRAPH

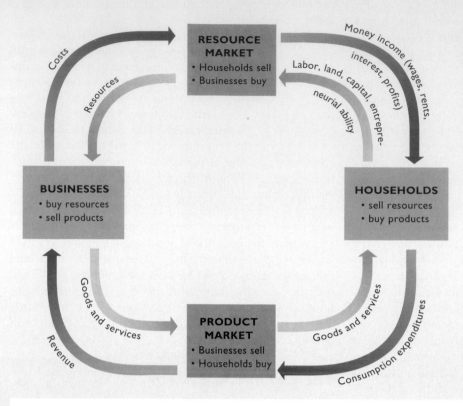

FIGURE 2.6

The circular flow diagram. Resources flow from households to businesses through the resource market, and products flow from businesses to households through the product market. Opposite these real flows are monetary flows. Households receive income from businesses (their costs) through the resource market, and businesses receive revenue from households (their expenditures) through the product market.

In the diagram (Figure 2.6):

RESOURCE MARKET
• Households sell
• Businesses buy

BUSINESSES
• buy resources
• sell products

HOUSEHOLDS
• sell resources
• buy products

PRODUCT MARKET
• Businesses sell
• Households buy

Labels around the flows: Costs, Resources, Money income (wages, rents, interest, profits), Labor, land, capital, entrepreneurial ability, Goods and services, Revenue, Goods and services, Consumption expenditures.

QUICK QUIZ 2.6

1. The resource market is the place where:
   a. households sell products and businesses buy products.
   b. businesses sell resources and households sell products.
   c. households sell resources and businesses buy resources (or the services of resources).
   d. businesses sell resources and households buy resources (or the services of resources).

2. Which of the following would be determined in the product market?
   a. a manager's salary.
   b. the price of equipment used in a bottling plant.
   c. the price of 80 acres of farmland.
   d. the price of a new pair of athletic shoes.

3. In this circular flow diagram:
   a. money flows counterclockwise.
   b. resources flow counterclockwise.
   c. goods and services flow clockwise.
   d. households are on the selling side of the product market.

4. In this circular flow diagram:
   a. households spend income in the product market.
   b. firms sell resources to households.
   c. households receive income through the product market.
   d. households produce goods.

Answers: 1. c; 2. d; 3. b; 4. a

---

resources and capital in China, the nation has increasingly relied on free markets to organize and coordinate its economy. North Korea and Cuba are the last remaining examples of largely centrally planned economies.

The Circular Flow Model

Because nearly all the major nations now use the market system, we need to gain a good understanding of how this system operates. Our goal in the remainder of this chapter is to identify the market economy's decision makers and major markets. In Chapter 3 we will explain how prices are established in individual markets. Then in Chapter 4 we will detail the characteristics of the market system and explain how the system addresses the economizing problem.

As shown in **Figure 2.6 (Key Graph),** the market economy has two groups of decision makers: *households* and *businesses*. (We will add government as a third decision

Production Possibilities Analysis Provides Insights on the Economic Effects of the Terrorist Attacks on the United States and the U.S. Government Response at Home, in Afghanistan, and in Iraq.

The horrific destruction of buildings in New York (World Trade Center) and Virginia (Pentagon) resulting from the September 11, 2001, terrorist attacks not only caused tremendous loss of life but also reduced U.S. production capacity. In production possibilities analysis, this outcome is illustrated as an inward shift of the economy's production possibilities curve. But this shift was relatively slight because the attacks destroyed only a small fraction of the nation's labor and capital. In fact, the loss of capital (about $16 billion) was similar to the losses the United States experienced in major natural disasters such as hurricanes and earthquakes. The loss of nearly 3000 lives, however, was greater than in those occurrences. These deaths reduced future output and earnings by an estimated $3 billion to $4 billion.*

Production possibilities analysis also is helpful in assessing the costs and benefits of waging the war on terrorism, including the wars in Afghanistan and Iraq. The Defense Department estimated that the costs of homeland security and the war on terrorism in Afghanistan were $30 billion in 2002. First estimates of the cost of the war in Iraq are $62 billion and reconstruction may cost even more.

If we categorize all of U.S. production as either "defense goods" (= military goods + homeland defense goods) or "civilian goods," we can measure them on the axes of a production possibilities diagram such as that shown in Figure 2.1 (page 26). The opportunity cost of using more resources for defense goods is the civilian goods sacrificed. In a fully employed economy, more defense goods are achieved at the opportunity cost of fewer civilian goods—health care, education, pollution control, personal computers, houses, and so on. The cost of waging war is the other goods forgone.[†] The benefits are the gains from protecting against future loss of American lives, assets, income, and well-being.

Society must assess the marginal benefit (MB) and marginal cost (MC) of additional defense goods to determine their optimal amounts—where to locate on the defense goods–civilian goods production possibilities curve. Although estimating marginal benefits and marginal costs is an imprecise art, the MB-MC framework is a useful way of approaching choices. Allocative efficiency requires that society expand production of defense goods until MB = MC.

The events of September 11, 2001, and the future threats they posed increased the perceived marginal benefits of defense goods. If we label the horizontal axis in Figure 2.2 (page 28) "defense goods," and draw in a rightward shift of the MB curve, you will see that the optimal quantity of defense goods rises. In view of the concerns relating to September 11, the United States allocated more of its resources to defense. But the MB-MC analysis also reminds us we can spend too much on defense, as well as too little. The United States should not expand defense goods beyond the point where MB = MC. If it does, it will be sacrificing civilian goods of greater value than the defense goods obtained.

It is too soon to evaluate whether the terrorist attacks and the diversion of resources to military action and homeland defense will slow the growth of U.S. production capacity. On the one hand, added security measures throughout the economy may divert resources away from capacity-expanding capital to capital that simply protects existing capital. (Government-required luggage screening machines will cost $4 billion alone!) More troublesome might be a significant shift of economic resources from business capital to military operations and reconstruction abroad. Also, research and development (R&D) spending could shift toward the war on terrorism and away from private sector innovations that expand production capacity. If the war on terrorism impedes the accumulation of private capital and reduces technological advance, the long-run growth rate of the U.S. economy will diminish. That is, the production possibilities curve will not shift as far outward as it would otherwise. On the other hand, military R&D sometimes produces technological advances—such as the global positioning system (GPS)—that have extensive application in the private sector.

---

*It is important to realize that insurance coverage on buildings and individuals does not reduce the loss to the economy. The insurance payments do not bring back the destroyed resources. Their replacement requires new resources, which have alternative, forgone, uses.

[†]Because the U.S. economy was not fully employed in 2001, 2002, and 2003, the tradeoff between defense goods and civilian goods was not as severe as it otherwise would have been. A portion of the added defense goods resulted from reemploying resources, rather than diverting resources away from civilian goods.

maker in Chapter 5.) It also has two broad markets: the *resource market* and the *product market.*

The upper half of the diagram represents the **resource market:** *the place where resources or the services of resource suppliers are bought and sold.* In the resource market, households sell resources and businesses buy them. Households (that is, people) own all economic resources either directly as workers or entrepreneurs or indirectly through their ownership of business corporations. They sell their resources to businesses, which buy them because they are necessary for producing goods and services. The funds that businesses pay for resources are costs to businesses but are flows of wage, rent, interest, and profit income to the households. Resources therefore flow from households to businesses, and money flows from businesses to households.

Next consider the lower part of the diagram, which represents the **product market:** *the place where goods and services produced by businesses are bought and sold.* In the product market, businesses combine the resources they have obtained to produce and sell goods and services. Households use the income they have received from the sale of resources to buy goods and services. The monetary flow of consumer spending on goods and services yields sales revenues for businesses.

The **circular flow model** suggests a complex, interrelated web of decision making and economic activity involving businesses and households. Businesses and households are both buyers and sellers. Businesses buy resources and sell products. Households buy products and sell resources. As shown in Figure 2.6, there is a counterclockwise *real flow* of economic resources and finished goods and services, and a clockwise *money flow* of income and consumption expenditures. These flows are simultaneous and repetitive.

2.3
Circular flow diagram

SUMMARY

1. Economics is grounded on two basic facts: (a) Economic wants are virtually unlimited; (b) economic resources are scarce.

2. Economic resources may be classified as property resources—raw materials and capital—or as human resources—labor and entrepreneurial ability. These resources constitute the factors of production.

3. Economics is concerned with the problem of using or managing scarce resources to produce the goods and services that satisfy the economic wants of society. Both full employment and the efficient use of available resources are essential to maximize want satisfaction.

4. Efficient use of resources consists of productive efficiency (producing all output combinations in the least costly way) and allocative efficiency (producing the specific output mix most desired by society).

5. An economy that is achieving full employment and productive efficiency—one that is operating on its production possibilities curve—must sacrifice the output of some types of goods and services in order to increase the production of others. Because resources are not equally productive in all possible uses, shifting resources from one use to another brings the law of increasing opportunity costs into play. The production of additional units of one product requires the sacrifice of *increasing* amounts of the other product.

6. Allocative efficiency means operating at the optimal point on the production possibilities curve. That point represents the highest-valued mix of goods and is determined by expanding the production of each good until its marginal benefit (MB) equals its marginal cost (MC).

7. Over time, technological advances and increases in the quantity and quality of resources enable the economy to produce more of all goods and services—that is, to experience economic growth. Society's choice as to the mix of consumer goods and capital goods in current output is a major determinant of the future location of the production possibilities curve and thus of economic growth.

8. The market system and the command system are the two broad types of economic systems used to address the economizing problem. In the market system (or capitalism) private individuals own most resources and markets coordinate most economic activity. In the command system (or socialism or communism), government owns most resources and central planners coordinate most economic activity.

9. The circular flow model locates the product and resource markets and shows the major real and money flows between businesses and households. Businesses are on the buying side of the resource market and the selling side of the product market. Households are on the selling side of the resource market and the buying side of the product market.

TERMS AND CONCEPTS

economizing problem	land	investment	entrepreneurial ability
economic resources	capital	labor	factors of production

full employment	production possibilities table	economic system	product market
full production	production possibilities curve	market system	circular flow model
productive efficiency	opportunity cost	capitalism	
allocative efficiency	law of increasing	command system	
consumer goods	opportunity costs	resource market	
capital goods	economic growth		

STUDY QUESTIONS

1. Critically analyze: "Wants aren't unlimited. I can prove it. I get all the coffee I want to drink every morning at breakfast." Explain: "Wants change as we move from childhood to adulthood, but they do not diminish."

2. What are economic resources? What categories do economists use to classify them? Why are resources also called *factors of production?* Explain: "If resources were unlimited and freely available, there would be no subject called *economics.*"

3. Why isn't money considered a capital resource in economics? Why is entrepreneurial ability considered a category of economic resource, distinct from labor? What are the major functions of the entrepreneur?

4. *Key Question* Classify the following Microsoft resources as labor, land, capital, or entrepreneurial ability: code writers for software; Bill Gates; production facility for Windows CD-ROMs; "campus" on which Microsoft buildings sit; grounds crew at Microsoft campus; Microsoft corporate jet.

5. *Key Question* Distinguish between full employment and full production as they relate to production possibilities analysis. Distinguish between productive efficiency and allocative efficiency. Give an illustration of achieving productive efficiency, but not allocative efficiency.

6. *Key Question* Here is a production possibilities table for war goods and civilian goods:

| | Production Alternatives | | | | |
Type of Production	A	B	C	D	E
Automobiles	0	2	4	6	8
Missiles	30	27	21	12	0

   a. Show these data graphically. Upon what specific assumptions is this production possibilities curve based?

   b. If the economy is at point *C*, what is the cost of one more automobile? One more missile? Explain how the production possibilities curve reflects the law of increasing opportunity costs.

   c. What must the economy do to operate at some point on the production possibilities curve?

7. What is the opportunity cost of attending college? In 2002 nearly 80 percent of college-educated Americans held jobs, whereas only about 40 percent of those who did not finish high school held jobs. How might this difference relate to opportunity costs?

8. Suppose you arrive at a store expecting to pay $100 for an item but learn that a store 2 miles away is charging $50 for it. Would you drive there and buy it? How does your decision benefit you? What is the opportunity cost of your decision? Now suppose you arrive at a store expecting to pay $6000 for an item but discover that it costs $5950 at the other store. Do you make the same decision as before? Perhaps surprisingly, you should! Explain why.

9. *Key Question* Specify and explain the shapes of the marginal-benefit and marginal-cost curves. How are these curves used to determine the optimal allocation of resources to a particular product? If current output is such that marginal cost exceeds marginal benefit, should more or fewer resources be allocated to this product? Explain.

10. *Key Question* Label point *G inside* the production possibilities curve you drew in question 6. What does it indicate? Label point *H outside* the curve. What does that point indicate? What must occur before the economy can attain the level of production shown by point *H?*

11. *Key Question* Referring again to question 6, suppose improvement occurs in the technology of producing missiles but not in the technology of producing automobiles. Draw the new production possibilities curve. Now assume that a technological advance occurs in producing automobiles but not in producing missiles. Draw the new production possibilities curve. Now draw a production possibilities curve that reflects technological improvement in the production of both products.

12. Explain how, if at all, each of the following events affects the location of the production possibilities curve:

   a. Standardized examination scores of high school and college students decline.

   b. The unemployment rate falls from 9 to 6 percent of the labor force.

   c. Education spending is reduced to allow government to spend more on health care.

   d. A new technique improves the efficiency of extracting copper from ore.

13. Explain: "Affluence tomorrow requires sacrifice today."

14. Suppose that, on the basis of a nation's production possibilities curve, an economy must sacrifice 10,000 pizzas domestically to get the 1 additional industrial robot it desires but that it can get the robot from another country in exchange for 9000 pizzas. Relate this information to the following statement: "Through international specialization and trade, a nation can reduce its opportunity cost of obtaining goods and thus 'move outside its production possibilities curve.'"

15. Contrast how a market system and a command economy try to cope with economic scarcity.

16. Distinguish between the resource market and the product market in the circular flow model. In what way are businesses and households both *sellers and buyers* in this model? What are the flows in the circular flow model?

17. (*Last Word*) Draw a production possibilities curve that has capital goods on one axis and consumer goods on the other. In the figure, demonstrate the effect of the destruction of the World Trade Center and loss of lives on production possibilities. Draw another production possibilities curve that has defense goods and civilian goods on the two axes. In the figure, demonstrate an increased use of resources for defense goods in a fully employed economy. Referring to your diagram, identify the opportunity cost of the added defense goods. Why did the United States willingly incur this type of opportunity cost following September 11, 2001?

18. *Web-Based Question: More labor resources—what is the evidence for the United States and France?* Go to the Bureau of Labor Statistics' website at www.bls.gov/ and select Get Detailed Statistics. Look for Labor Force Statistics from the CPS and click the Most Requested Statistics icon. Find U.S. civilian employment data for the last 10 years. How many more workers were there at the end of the 10-year period than at the beginning? Next, return to the Detailed Statistics page. Use the Most Requested Statistics icon next to Foreign Labor Statistics (it's under Productivity and Technology) to find total employment growth in France over the last 10 years. In which of the two countries did "more labor resources" have the greatest impact in shifting the nation's production possibilities curve outward over the 10-year period?

19. *Web-Based Question: Relative size of the military— who's incurring the largest opportunity cost?* Go to the Central Intelligence Agency's website, www.odci.gov/cia/publications/factbook/index.html, to determine the amount of military expenditures and military expenditures as a percentage of GDP for each of the following five nations: Brazil, Japan, North Korea, Russia, and the United States. Which one is bearing the greatest opportunity cost?

3 | *Individual Markets: Demand and Supply*

According to an old joke, if you teach a parrot to say "demand and supply," you have an economist. There is an element of truth in this quip. The tools of demand and supply can take us far in understanding both specific economic issues and how the entire economy works.

3.1 Demand and supply

With our circular flow model in Chapter 2, we identified the participants in the product market and resource market. We asserted that prices are determined by the "interaction" between buyers and sellers in those markets. In this chapter we examine that interaction in detail and explain how prices and output quantities are determined.

Markets

Recall from Chapter 2 that a **market** is *an institution or mechanism that brings together buyers ("demanders") and sellers ("suppliers") of particular goods, services, or resources.* Markets exist in many forms. The corner gas station, e-commerce sites, the local music store, a farmer's roadside stand—all are familiar markets. The New York Stock Exchange and the Chicago Board of Trade are markets where buyers and sellers of stocks and bonds and farm commodities from all over the world communicate with one another to buy and sell. Auctioneers bring together potential buyers and sellers of art, livestock, used farm equipment, and, sometimes, real estate. In labor markets, the quarterback and his agent bargain with the owner of an NFL team. A graduating finance major interviews with Citicorp or Wells Fargo at the university placement office.

All situations that link potential buyers with potential sellers are markets. Some markets are local, while others are national or international. Some are highly personal, involving face-to-face contact between demander and supplier; others are impersonal, with buyer and seller never seeing or knowing each other.

To keep things simple, we will focus in this chapter on markets consisting of large numbers of independently acting buyers and sellers of standardized products. These are the highly competitive markets such as a central grain exchange, a stock market, or a market for foreign currencies in which the price is "discovered" through the interacting decisions of buyers and sellers. They are *not* the markets in which one or a handful of producers "set" prices, such as the markets for commercial airplanes or operating software for personal computers.

Demand

Demand is *a schedule or a curve that shows the various amounts of a product that consumers are willing and able to purchase at each of a series of possible prices during a specified period of time.*[1] Demand shows the quantities of a product that will be purchased at various possible prices, *other things equal*. Demand can easily be shown in table form. Table 3.1 is a hypothetical **demand schedule** for a *single consumer* purchasing bushels of corn.

Table 3.1 reveals the relationship between the various prices of corn and the quantity of corn a particular consumer would be willing and able to purchase at each of these prices. We say "willing and able" because willingness alone is not effective in the market. You may be willing to buy a digital camera, but if that willingness is not backed by the necessary dollars, it will not be effective and, therefore, will not be reflected in the market. In Table 3.1, if the price of corn were $5 per bushel, our consumer would be willing and able to buy 10 bushels per week; if it were $4, the consumer would be willing and able to buy 20 bushels per week; and so forth.

Table 3.1 does not tell us which of the five possible prices will actually exist in the corn market. That depends on demand and supply. Demand is simply a statement of a buyer's plans, or intentions, with respect to the purchase of a product.

To be meaningful, the quantities demanded at each price must relate to a specific period—a day, a week, a month. Saying "A consumer will buy 10 bushels of corn at $5 per bushel" is meaningless. Saying "A consumer will buy 10 bushels of corn per week at $5 per bushel" is meaningful. Unless a specific time period is stated, we do not know whether the demand for a product is large or small.

TABLE 3.1

An Individual Buyer's Demand for Corn

Price per Bushel	Quantity Demanded per Week
$5	10
4	20
3	35
2	55
1	80

---

[1]This definition obviously is worded to apply to product markets. To adjust it to apply to resource markets, substitute the word "resource" for "product" and the word "businesses" for "consumers."

Law of Demand

A fundamental characteristic of demand is this: *All else equal, as price falls, the quantity demanded rises, and as price rises, the quantity demanded falls.* In short, there is a negative or *inverse* relationship between price and quantity demanded. Economists call this inverse relationship the **law of demand.**

3.2
Law of demand

The other-things-equal assumption is critical here. Many factors other than the price of the product being considered affect the amount purchased. The quantity of Nikes purchased will depend not only on the price of Nikes but also on the prices of such substitutes as Reeboks, Adidas, and New Balances. The law of demand in this case says that fewer Nikes will be purchased if the price of Nikes rises *and if the prices of Reeboks, Adidas, and New Balances all remain constant.* In short, if the *relative price* of Nikes rises, fewer Nikes will be bought. However, if the price of Nikes and the prices of all other competing shoes increase by some amount—say, $5—consumers might buy more, less, or the same amount of Nikes.

Why the inverse relationship between price and quantity demanded? Let's look at three explanations, beginning with the simplest one:

- The law of demand is consistent with common sense. People ordinarily *do* buy more of a product at a low price than at a high price. Price is an obstacle that deters consumers from buying. The higher that obstacle, the less of a product they will buy; the lower the price obstacle, the more they will buy. The fact that businesses have "sales" is evidence of their belief in the law of demand.

- In any specific time period, each buyer of a product will derive less satisfaction (or benefit, or utility) from each successive unit of the product consumed. The second Big Mac will yield less satisfaction to the consumer than the first, and the third still less than the second. That is, consumption is subject to **diminishing marginal utility.** And because successive units of a particular product yield less and less marginal utility, consumers will buy additional units only if the price of those units is progressively reduced.

3.3
Diminishing marginal utility

- We can also explain the law of demand in terms of income and substitution effects. The **income effect** indicates that a lower price increases the purchasing power of a buyer's money income, enabling the buyer

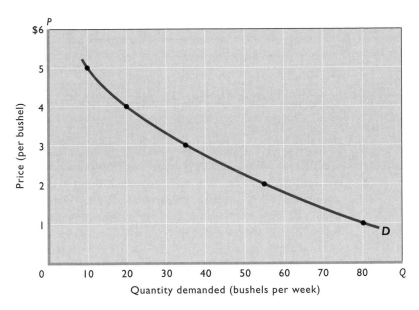

FIGURE 3.1

An individual buyer's demand for corn. Because price and quantity demanded are inversely related, an individual's demand schedule graphs as a downsloping curve such as *D*. Specifically, the law of demand says that, other things equal, consumers will buy more of a product as its price declines. Here and in later figures, *P* stands for price, and *Q* stands for quantity (either demanded or supplied).

to purchase more of the product than she or he could buy before. A higher price has the opposite effect. The **substitution effect** suggests that at a lower price buyers have the incentive to substitute what is now a less expensive product for similar products that are now *relatively* more expensive. The product whose price has fallen is now "a better deal" relative to the other products.

For example, a decline in the price of chicken will increase the purchasing power of consumer incomes, enabling people to buy more chicken (the income effect). At

3.4
Income and
substitution
effects

a lower price, chicken is relatively more attractive and consumers tend to substitute it for pork, lamb, beef, and fish (the substitution effect). The income and substitution effects combine to make consumers able and willing to buy more of a product at a low price than at a high price.

The Demand Curve

The inverse relationship between price and quantity demanded for any product can be represented on a simple graph, in which, by convention, we measure *quantity demanded* on the horizontal axis and *price* on the vertical axis. In Figure 3.1 we have plotted the five price-quantity data points listed in Table 3.1 and connected the points with a smooth curve, labeled *D*. Such a curve is called a **demand curve.** Its downward slope reflects the law of demand—people buy more of a product, service, or re-

source as its price falls. The relationship between price and quantity demanded is inverse.

Table 3.1 and Figure 3.1 contain exactly the same data and reflect the same relationship between price and quantity demanded. But the graph shows that relationship more simply and clearly than a table or a description in words.

Market Demand

So far, we have concentrated on just one consumer. But competition requires that more than one buyer be present in each market. By adding the quantities demanded by all consumers at each of the various possible prices, we can get from *individual* demand to *market* demand. If there are just three buyers in the market, as represented in Table 3.2, it is relatively easy to determine the total quantity demanded at each price. Figure 3.2 shows the graphical

TABLE 3.2

Market Demand for Corn, Three Buyers

Price per Bushel	First Buyer		Second Buyer		Third Buyer		Total Quantity Demanded per Week
$5	10	+	12	+	8	=	30
4	20	+	23	+	17	=	60
3	35	+	39	+	26	=	100
2	55	+	60	+	39	=	154
1	80	+	87	+	54	=	221

FIGURE 3.2

Market demand for corn, three buyers.   We establish the market demand curve *D* by adding horizontally the individual demand curves (*D*₁, *D*₂, and *D*₃) of all the consumers in the market. At the price of $3, for example, the three individual curves yield a total quantity demanded of 100 bushels.

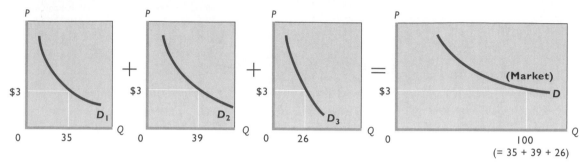

summing procedure: At each price we add the individual quantities demanded to obtain the total quantity demanded at that price; we then plot the price and the total quantity demanded as one point on the market demand curve.

Competition, of course, ordinarily entails many more than three buyers of a product. To avoid hundreds or thousands or millions of additions, we suppose that all the buyers in a market are willing and able to buy the same amounts at each of the possible prices. Then we just multiply those amounts by the number of buyers to obtain the market

demand. This is the way we arrived at curve D_1 in Figure 3.3, for a market with 200 corn buyers whose demand is that shown in Table 3.1. Table 3.3 shows the calculations.

In constructing a demand curve such as D_1 in Figure 3.3, economists assume that price is the most important influence on the amount of any product purchased. But economists know that other factors can and do affect purchases. These factors, called **determinants of demand,** are assumed to be constant when a demand curve like D_1 is drawn. They are the "other things equal" in the

FIGURE 3.3

Changes in the demand for corn.   A change in one or more of the determinants of demand causes a change in demand. An increase in demand is shown as a shift of the demand curve to the right, as from D_1 to D_2. A decrease in demand is shown as a shift of the demand curve to the left, as from D_1 to D_3. These changes in demand are to be distinguished from a change in quantity demanded, which is caused by a change in the price of the product, as shown by a movement from, say, point *a* to point *b* on fixed demand curve D_1.

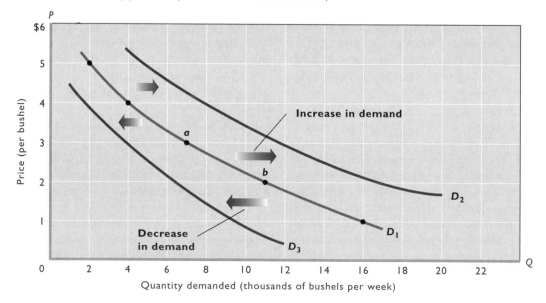

TABLE 3.3
Market Demand for Corn, 200 Buyers

(1) Price per Bushel	(2) Quantity Demanded per Week, Single Buyer		(3) Number of Buyers in the Market		(4) Total Quantity Demanded per Week
$5	10	×	200	=	2,000
4	20	×	200	=	4,000
3	35	×	200	=	7,000
2	55	×	200	=	11,000
1	80	×	200	=	16,000

relationship between price and quantity demanded. When any of these determinants changes, the demand curve will shift to the right or left. For this reason, determinants of demand are sometimes referred to as *demand shifters*.

The basic determinants of demand are (1) consumers' tastes (preferences), (2) the number of consumers in the market, (3) consumers' incomes, (4) the prices of related goods, and (5) consumer expectations about future prices and incomes.

Change in Demand

A change in one or more of the determinants of demand will change the demand data (the demand schedule) in Table 3.3 and therefore the location of the demand curve in Figure 3.3. A change in the demand schedule or, graphically, a shift in the demand curve is called a *change in demand*.

If consumers desire to buy more corn at each possible price than is reflected in column 4 in Table 3.3, that *increase in demand* is shown as a shift of the demand curve to the right, say, from D_1 to D_2. Conversely, a *decrease in demand* occurs when consumers buy less corn at each possible price than is indicated in column 4, Table 3.3. The leftward shift of the demand curve from D_1 to D_3 in Figure 3.3 shows that situation.

Now let's see how changes in each determinant affect demand.

Tastes A favorable change in consumer tastes (preferences) for a product—a change that makes the product more desirable—means that more of it will be demanded at each price. Demand will increase; the demand curve will shift rightward. An unfavorable change in consumer preferences will decrease demand, shifting the demand curve to the left.

New products may affect consumer tastes; for example, the introduction of compact discs greatly decreased the demand for cassette tapes. Consumers' concern over the health hazards of cholesterol and obesity have increased the demand for broccoli, low-calorie beverages, and fresh fruit while decreasing the demand for beef, veal, eggs, and whole milk. Over the past several years, the demand for coffee drinks, bottled water, and sports utility vehicles has greatly increased, driven by a change in tastes. So, too, has the demand for DVDs and digital cameras.

Number of Buyers An increase in the number of buyers in a market increases demand. A decrease in the number of buyers in a market decreases demand. For example, improvements in communications have given financial markets international range and have thus increased the demand for stocks and bonds. And the baby boom after the Second World War increased demand for diapers, baby lotion, and the services of obstetricians. When the baby boomers reached their twenties in the 1970s, the demand for housing increased. Conversely, the aging of the baby boomers in the 1980s and 1990s was a factor in the relative slump in the demand for housing in those decades. Also, an increase in life expectancy has increased the demand for medical care, retirement communities, and nursing homes. And international trade agreements have reduced foreign trade barriers to American farm commodities, thus increasing the demand for those products.

Income How changes in income affect demand is a more complex matter. For most products, a rise in income causes an increase in demand. Consumers typically buy more steaks, furniture, and electronic equipment as their incomes increase. Conversely, the demand for such products declines as their incomes fall. Products whose demand varies *directly* with money income are called *superior goods*, or **normal goods.**

Although most products are normal goods, there are some exceptions. As incomes increase beyond some point, the demand for used clothing, retread tires, and third-hand automobiles may decrease, because the higher incomes enable consumers to buy new versions of those products. Rising incomes may also decrease the demand for soy-enhanced hamburger. Similarly, rising incomes may cause the demand for charcoal grills to decline as wealthier consumers switch to gas grills. Goods whose demand varies *inversely* with money income are called **inferior goods.**

Prices of Related Goods A change in the price of a related good may either increase or decrease the demand for a product, depending on whether the related good is a substitute or a complement:

- A **substitute good** is one that can be used in place of another good.
- A **complementary good** is one that is used together with another good.

Substitutes   Beef and chicken are examples of substitute goods or, simply, *substitutes*. When the price of beef rises, consumers buy less beef, increasing the demand for chicken. Conversely, as the price of beef falls, consumers buy more beef, decreasing the demand for chicken. *When two products are substitutes, the price of one and the demand for the other move in the same direction.* So it is with pairs such as Nikes and Reeboks, Colgate and Crest, Toyotas and Hondas, and Coke and Pepsi. So-called *substitution in consumption* occurs when the price of one good rises relative to the price of a similar good.

Complements   Complementary goods (or, simply, *complements*) are goods that are used together and are usually demanded together. If the price of gasoline falls and, as a result, you drive your car more often, the extra driving increases your demand for motor oil. Thus, gas and motor oil are jointly demanded; they are complements. So it is with ham and eggs, tuition and textbooks, movies and popcorn, cameras and film. *When two products are complements, the price of one good and the demand for the other good move in opposite directions.*

Unrelated Goods   The vast majority of goods that are not related to one another are called *independent goods*. Examples are butter and golf balls, potatoes and automobiles, and bananas and wristwatches. A change in the price of one has little or no effect on the demand for the other.

Expectations   Changes in consumer expectations may shift demand. A newly formed expectation of higher future prices may cause consumers to buy now in order to "beat" the anticipated price rises, thus increasing current demand. For example, when freezing weather destroys much of Florida's citrus crop, consumers may reason that the price of orange juice will rise. They may stock up on orange juice by purchasing large quantities now. In contrast, a newly formed expectation of falling prices or falling income may decrease current demand for products.

Similarly, a change in expectations relating to future product availability may affect current demand. In late December 1999 there was a substantial increase in the demand for gasoline. Reason? Motorists became concerned that the Y2K computer problem might disrupt fuel pumps or credit card systems.

Finally, a change in expectations concerning future income may prompt consumers to change their current spending. For example, first-round NFL draft choices may splurge on new luxury cars in anticipation of a lucrative professional football contract. Or workers who become fearful of losing their jobs may reduce their demand for, say, vacation travel.

In summary, an *increase* in demand—the decision by consumers to buy larger quantities of a product at each possible price—may be caused by:

- A favorable change in consumer tastes.
- An increase in the number of buyers.
- Rising incomes if the product is a normal good.
- Falling incomes if the product is an inferior good.
- An increase in the price of a substitute good.
- A decrease in the price of a complementary good.
- A new consumer expectation that either prices or income will be higher in the future.

You should "reverse" these generalizations to explain a *decrease* in demand. Table 3.4 provides additional illustrations of the determinants of demand. **(Key Question 2)**

Changes in Quantity Demanded

A *change in demand* must not be confused with a *change in quantity demanded*. A **change in demand** is a shift of the

TABLE 3.4

Determinants of Demand: Factors That Shift the Demand Curve

Determinant	Examples
Change in buyer tastes	Physical fitness rises in popularity, increasing the demand for jogging shoes and bicycles; patriotism rises, increasing the demand for flags.
Change in number of buyers	A decline in the birthrate reduces the demand for children's toys.
Change in income	A rise in incomes increases the demand for normal goods such as donuts, sports tickets, and necklaces while reducing the demand for inferior goods such as cabbage, turnips, and inexpensive wine.
Change in the prices of related goods	A reduction in airfares reduces the demand for bus transportation (substitute goods); a decline in the price of DVD players increases the demand for DVD movies (complementary goods).
Change in expectations	Inclement weather in South America creates an expectation of higher future prices of coffee beans, thereby increasing today's demand for coffee beans.

demand curve to the right (an increase in demand) or to the left (a decrease in demand). It occurs because the consumer's state of mind about purchasing the product has been altered in response to a change in one or more of the determinants of demand. Recall that "demand" is a schedule or a curve; therefore, a "change in demand" means a change in the schedule and a shift of the curve.

In contrast, a **change in quantity demanded** is a movement from one point to another point—from one price-quantity combination to another—on a fixed demand schedule or demand curve. The cause of such a change is an increase or decrease in the price of the product under consideration. In Table 3.3, for example, a decline in the price of corn from $5 to $4 will increase the quantity of corn demanded from 2000 to 4000 bushels.

In Figure 3.3 the shift of the demand curve D_1 to either D_2 or D_3 is a change in demand. But the movement from point a to point b on curve D_1 represents a change in quantity demanded: *Demand has not changed; it is the entire curve, and it remains fixed in place.*

QUICK REVIEW 3.1

- A market is any arrangement that facilitates the purchase and sale of goods, services, or resources.
- Demand is a schedule or a curve showing the amount of a product that buyers are willing and able to purchase, in a particular time period, at each possible price in a series of prices.
- The law of demand states that, other things equal, the quantity of a good purchased varies inversely with its price.
- The demand curve shifts because of changes in (a) consumer tastes, (b) the number of buyers in the market, (c) consumer income, (d) the prices of substitute or complementary goods, and (e) consumer expectations.
- A change in demand is a shift of the demand curve; a change in quantity demanded is a movement from one point to another on a fixed demand curve.

Supply

Supply is *a schedule or curve showing the amounts of a product that producers are willing and able to make available for sale at each of a series of possible prices during a specific period.*[2] Table 3.5 is a hypothetical **supply schedule** for a single producer of corn. It shows the quantities of corn that will be supplied at various prices, other things equal.

[2]This definition is worded to apply to product markets. To adjust it to apply to resource markets, substitute "resource" for "product" and "owners" for "producers."

TABLE 3.5

An Individual Producer's Supply of Corn

Price per Bushel	Quantity Supplied per Week
$5	60
4	50
3	35
2	20
1	5

Law of Supply

Table 3.5 shows a positive or direct relationship that prevails between price and quantity supplied. *As price rises, the quantity supplied rises; as price falls, the quantity supplied falls.* This relationship is called the **law of supply.** A supply schedule tells us that firms will produce and offer for sale more of their product at a high price than at a low price. This, again, is basically common sense.

Price is an obstacle from the standpoint of the consumer, who is on the paying end. The higher the price, the less the consumer will buy. But the supplier is on the receiving end of the product's price. To a supplier, price represents *revenue*, which serves as an incentive to produce and sell a product. The higher the price, the greater this incentive and the greater the quantity supplied.

Consider a farmer who can shift resources among alternative products. As price moves up, as shown in Table 3.5, the farmer finds it profitable to take land out of wheat, oats, and soybean production and put it into corn. And the higher corn prices enable the farmer to cover the increased costs associated with more intensive cultivation and the use of more seed, fertilizer, and pesticides. The overall result is more corn.

Now consider a manufacturer. Beyond some quantity of production, manufacturers usually encounter increasing *marginal cost*—the added cost of producing one more unit of output. Certain productive resources—in particular, the firm's plant and machinery—cannot be expanded quickly, so the firm uses more of other resources, such as labor, to produce more output. But as labor becomes more abundant relative to the fixed plant and equipment, the additional workers have relatively less space and access to equipment. For example, the added workers may have to wait to gain access to machines. As a result, each added worker produces less added output, and the marginal cost of successive units of output rises accordingly. The firm will not produce the more costly units unless it receives a higher price for them. Again, price and quantity supplied are directly related.

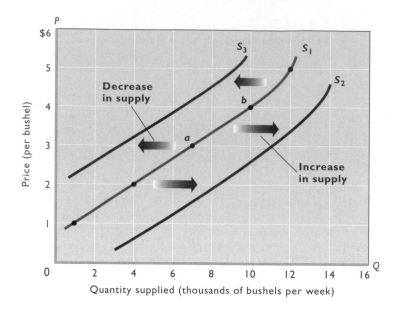

FIGURE 3.4

Changes in the supply of corn. A change in one or more of the determinants of supply causes a change in supply. An increase in supply is shown as a rightward shift of the supply curve, as from S_1 to S_2. A decrease in supply is depicted as a leftward shift of the curve, as from S_1 to S_3. In contrast, a change in the *quantity supplied* is caused by a change in the product's price and is shown by a movement from one point to another, as from *a* to *b*, on a fixed supply curve.

The Supply Curve

As with demand, it is convenient to represent supply graphically. In Figure 3.4, curve S_1 is a graph of the market supply data given in Table 3.6. Those data assume there are 200 suppliers in the market, each willing and able to supply corn according to Table 3.5. We obtain the market **supply curve** by horizontally adding the supply curves of the individual producers. Note that the axes in Figure 3.4 are the same as those used in our graph of market demand (Figure 3.3), except for the change from "quantity demanded" to "quantity supplied" on the horizontal axis.

Determinants of Supply

In constructing a supply curve, we assume that price is the most significant influence on the quantity supplied of any

product. But other factors (the "other things equal") can and do affect supply. The supply curve is drawn on the assumption that these other things are fixed and do not change. If one of them does change, a *change in supply* will occur, meaning that the entire supply curve will shift.

The basic **determinants of supply** are (1) resource prices, (2) technology, (3) taxes and subsidies, (4) prices of other goods, (5) price expectations, and (6) the number of sellers in the market. A change in any one or more of these determinants of supply, or *supply shifters*, will move the supply curve for a product either right or left. A shift to the *right*, as from S_1 to S_2 in Figure 3.4, signifies an *increase* in supply: Producers supply larger quantities of the product at each possible price. A shift to the *left*, as from S_1 to S_3, indicates a *decrease* in supply: Producers offer less output at each price.

Changes in Supply

Let's consider how changes in each of the determinants affect supply. The key idea is that costs are a major factor underlying supply curves; anything that affects costs (other than changes in output itself) usually shifts the supply curve.

Resource Prices The prices of the resources used in the production process help determine the costs of production incurred by firms. Higher *resource* prices raise production costs and, assuming a particular *product* price, squeeze profits. That reduction in profits reduces the incentive for firms to supply output at each product price. For example, an increase in the prices of iron ore and coke will increase the cost of producing steel and reduce its supply.

TABLE 3.6

Market Supply of Corn, 200 Producers

(1) Price per Bushel	(2) Quantity Supplied per Week, Single Producer		(3) Number of Sellers in the Market		(4) Total Quantity Supplied per Week
$5	60	×	200	=	12,000
4	50	×	200	=	10,000
3	35	×	200	=	7,000
2	20	×	200	=	4,000
1	5	×	200	=	1,000

In contrast, lower *resource* prices reduce production costs and increase profits. So when resource prices fall, firms supply greater output at each product price. For example, a decrease in the prices of sand, gravel, and limestone will increase the supply of concrete.

Technology Improvements in technology (techniques of production) enable firms to produce units of output with fewer resources. Because resources are costly, using fewer of them lowers production costs and increases supply. Example: Technological advances in producing flat-panel computer monitors have greatly reduced their cost. Thus, manufacturers will now offer more such monitors than previously at the various prices; the supply of flat-panel monitors has increased.

Taxes and Subsidies Businesses treat most taxes as costs. An increase in sales or property taxes will increase production costs and reduce supply. In contrast, subsidies are "taxes in reverse." If the government subsidizes the production of a good, it in effect lowers the producers' costs and increases supply.

Prices of Other Goods Firms that produce a particular product, say, soccer balls, can sometimes use their plant and equipment to produce alternative goods, say, basketballs and volleyballs. The higher prices of these "other goods" may entice soccer ball producers to switch production to those other goods in order to increase profits. This *substitution in production* results in a decline in the supply of soccer balls. Alternatively, when the prices of basketballs and volleyballs decline relative to the price of soccer balls, producers of those goods may decide to produce more soccer balls instead, increasing their supply.

Price Expectations Changes in expectations about the future price of a product may affect the producer's current willingness to supply that product. It is difficult, however, to generalize about how a new expectation of higher prices affects the present supply of a product. Farmers anticipating a higher wheat price in the future might withhold some of their current wheat harvest from the market, thereby causing a decrease in the current supply of wheat. In contrast, in many types of manufacturing industries, newly formed expectations that price will increase may induce firms to add another shift of workers or to expand their production facilities, causing current supply to increase.

Number of Sellers Other things equal, the larger the number of suppliers, the greater the market supply. As more firms enter an industry, the supply curve shifts to the right. Conversely, the smaller the number of firms in the

TABLE 3.7

Determinants of Supply: Factors That Shift the Supply Curve

Determinant	Examples
Change in resource prices	A decrease in the price of microchips increases the supply of computers; an increase in the price of crude oil reduces the supply of gasoline.
Change in technology	The development of more effective wireless technology increases the supply of cell phones.
Changes in taxes and subsidies	An increase in the excise tax on cigarettes reduces the supply of cigarettes; a decline in subsidies to state universities reduces the supply of higher education.
Change in prices of other goods	An increase in the price of cucumbers decreases the supply of watermelons.
Change in expectations	An expectation of a substantial rise in future log prices decreases the supply of logs today.
Change in number of suppliers	An increase in the number of tatoo parlors increases the supply of tatoos; the formation of women's professional basketball leagues increases the supply of women's professional basketball games.

industry, the less the market supply. This means that as firms leave an industry, the supply curve shifts to the left. Example: The United States and Canada have imposed restrictions on haddock fishing to replenish dwindling stocks. As part of that policy, the Federal government has bought the boats of some of the haddock fishers as a way of putting them out of business and decreasing the catch. The result has been a decline in the market supply of haddock.

Table 3.7 is a checklist of the determinants of supply, along with further illustrations. **(Key Question 5)**

Changes in Quantity Supplied

The distinction between a *change in supply* and a *change in quantity supplied* parallels the distinction between a change in demand and a change in quantity demanded. Because supply is a schedule or curve, a **change in supply** means a change in the schedule and a shift of the curve. An increase in supply shifts the curve to the right; a decrease in supply shifts it to the left. The cause of a change in supply is a change in one or more of the determinants of supply.

In contrast, a **change in quantity supplied** is a movement from one point to another on a fixed supply curve. The cause of such a movement is a change in the price of the specific product being considered. In Table 3.6, a decline in the price of corn from $5 to $4 decreases the quantity of corn supplied per week from 12,000 to 10,000 bushels. This is a change in quantity supplied, not a change in supply. *Supply is the full schedule of prices and quantities shown, and this schedule does not change when price changes.*

> ### QUICK REVIEW 3.2
>
> * A supply schedule or curve shows that, other things equal, the quantity of a good supplied varies directly with its price.
> * The supply curve shifts because of changes in (a) resource prices, (b) technology, (c) taxes or subsidies, (d) prices of other goods, (e) expectations of future prices, and (f) the number of suppliers.
> * A change in supply is a shift of the supply curve; a change in quantity supplied is a movement from one point to another on a fixed supply curve.

Supply and Demand: Market Equilibrium

We can now bring together supply and demand to see how the buying decisions of households and the selling decisions of businesses interact to determine the price of a product and the quantity actually bought and sold. In Table 3.8, columns 1 and 2 repeat the market supply of corn (from Table 3.6), and columns 2 and 3 repeat the market demand for corn (from Table 3.3). We assume that this is a competitive market—neither buyers nor sellers can set the price.

Surpluses

We have limited our example to only five possible prices. Of these, which will actually prevail as the market price for corn? We can find an answer through trial and error. For no particular reason, let's start with $5. We see immediately that this cannot be the prevailing market price. At the $5 price, producers are willing to produce and offer for sale 12,000 bushels of corn, but buyers are willing to buy only 2000 bushels. The $5 price encourages farmers to produce lots of corn but discourages most consumers from buying it. The result is a 10,000-bushel **surplus** or *excess supply* of corn. This surplus, shown in column 4 of Table 3.8, is the excess of quantity supplied over quantity demanded at $5. Corn farmers would find themselves with 10,000 unsold bushels of output.

A price of $5, even if it existed temporarily in the corn market, could not persist over a period of time. The very large surplus of corn would prompt competing sellers to lower the price to encourage buyers to take the surplus off their hands.

Suppose the price goes down to $4. The lower price encourages consumers to buy more corn and, at the same time, induces farmers to offer less of it for sale. The surplus diminishes to 6000 bushels. Nevertheless, since there is still a surplus, competition among sellers will once again reduce the price. Clearly, then, the prices of $5 and $4 will not survive because they are "too high." The market price of corn must be less than $4.

Shortages

Let's jump now to $1 as the possible market price of corn. Observe in column 4 of Table 3.8 that at this price, quantity demanded exceeds quantity supplied by 15,000 units. The $1 price discourages farmers from devoting resources to corn production and encourages consumers to attempt to buy more than is available. The result is a 15,000-bushel **shortage** of, or *excess demand* for, corn. The $1 price cannot persist as the market price. Many consumers who want to buy at this price will not get corn. They will express a willingness to pay more than $1 to get some of the available output. Competition among these buyers will drive up the price to something greater than $1.

Suppose the competition among buyers boosts the price to $2. This higher price will reduce, but will not eliminate, the shortage of corn. For $2, farmers devote more resources to corn production, and some buyers who were willing to pay $1 per bushel will not want to buy corn at $2. But a shortage of 7000 bushels still exists at $2. This shortage will push the market price above $2.

Equilibrium Price and Quantity

By trial and error we have eliminated every price but $3. At $3, *and only at that price*, the quantity of corn that

TABLE 3.8

Market Supply of and Demand for Corn

(1) Total Quantity Supplied per Week	(2) Price per Bushel	(3) Total Quantity Demanded per Week	(4) Surplus (+) or Shortage (−)*
12,000	$5	2,000	+10,000 ↓
10,000	4	4,000	+6,000 ↓
7,000	**3**	**7,000**	**0**
4,000	2	11,000	−7,000 ↑
1,000	1	16,000	−15,000 ↑

*Arrows indicate the effect on price.

KEY GRAPH

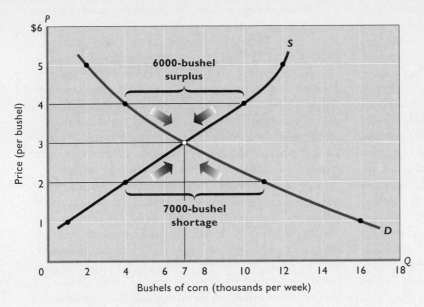

FIGURE 3.5

Equilibrium price and quantity. The intersection of the downsloping demand curve D and the upsloping supply curve S indicates the equilibrium price and quantity, here $3 and 7000 bushels of corn. The shortages of corn at below-equilibrium prices (for example, 7000 bushels at $2) drive up price. The higher prices increase the quantity supplied and reduce the quantity demanded until equilibrium is achieved. The surpluses caused by above-equilibrium prices (for example, 6000 bushels at $4) push price down. As price drops, the quantity demanded rises and the quantity supplied falls until equilibrium is established. At the equilibrium price and quantity, there are neither shortages nor surpluses of corn.

QUICK QUIZ 3.5

1. Demand curve D is downsloping because:
   a. producers offer less of a product for sale as the price of the product falls.
   b. lower prices of a product create income and substitution effects that lead consumers to purchase more of it.
   c. the larger the number of buyers in a market, the lower the product price.
   d. price and quantity demanded are directly (positively) related.

2. Supply curve S:
   a. reflects an inverse (negative) relationship between price and quantity supplied.
   b. reflects a direct (positive) relationship between price and quantity supplied.
   c. depicts the collective behavior of buyers in this market.
   d. shows that producers will offer more of a product for sale at a low product price than at a high product price.

3. At the $3 price:
   a. quantity supplied exceeds quantity demanded.
   b. quantity demanded exceeds quantity supplied.
   c. the product is abundant and a surplus exists.
   d. there is no pressure on price to rise or fall.

4. At price $5 in this market:
   a. there will be a shortage of 10,000 units.
   b. there will be a surplus of 10,000 units.
   c. quantity demanded will be 12,000 units.
   d. quantity demanded will equal quantity supplied.

Answers: 1. b; 2. b; 3. d; 4. b

farmers are willing to produce and supply is identical with the quantity consumers are willing and able to buy. There is neither a shortage nor a surplus of corn at $3.

With no shortage or surplus, there is no reason for the $3 price of corn to change. Economists call this price the *market-clearing* or **equilibrium price,** "equilibrium" meaning "in balance" or "at rest." At $3, quantity supplied and quantity demanded are in balance at the **equilibrium quantity** of 7000 bushels. So $3 is the only stable price of corn under the supply and demand conditions shown in Table 3.8.

The price of corn, or of any other product bought and sold in competitive markets, will be established where the supply decisions of producers and the demand decisions of buyers are mutually consistent. Such decisions are consistent only at the equilibrium price (here, $3) and equilibrium quantity (here, 7000 bushels). At any higher price, suppliers want to sell more than consumers want to buy and a surplus results; at any lower price, consumers want to buy more than producers make available for sale and a shortage results. Such discrepancies between the supply and demand intentions of sellers and buyers then prompt price changes that bring the two sets of intentions into accord.

A graphical analysis of supply and demand should yield the same conclusions. **Figure 3.5 (Key Graph)** shows the market supply and demand curves for corn on the same graph. (The horizontal axis now measures both quantity demanded and quantity supplied.)

Graphically, the intersection of the supply curve and the demand curve for a product indicates the market equilibrium. Here, equilibrium price and quantity are $3 per bushel and 7000 bushels. At any above-equilibrium price, quantity supplied exceeds quantity demanded. This surplus of corn causes price reductions by sellers who are eager to rid themselves of their surplus. The falling price causes less corn to be offered and simultaneously encourages consumers to buy more. The market moves to its equilibrium.

Any price below the equilibrium price creates a shortage; quantity demanded then exceeds quantity supplied. Buyers try to obtain the product by offering to pay more for it; this drives the price upward toward its equilibrium level. The rising price simultaneously causes producers to increase the quantity

3.1
**Supply
and
demand**

© Photodisc/Getty Images

CONSIDER THIS . . .

The Cutting Edge

In viewing demand and supply curves such as those shown in Figure 3.5, you might wonder if demand is more important than supply in determining equilibrium price and quantity or if supply is more important than demand. The answer is that in competitive markets demand and supply are equally important.

Economist Alfred Marshall (1842–1924) used a vivid analogy to make this point. He likened demand and supply to two blades of a scissors. Which blade of the scissors cuts the paper? To be sure, if the lower blade is held in place and the upper blade is closed down upon it, one could argue that the upper blade has cut the paper. But would the paper have been cut without the lower blade? And if the upper blade is held in place and the lower blade is closed up against it, one could argue that the lower blade has cut the paper. But would the paper have been cut without the upper blade?

The answer to these questions is that it is the interaction of the two blades of the scissors that cuts the paper. Both are necessary and both are important. So it is with demand and supply in competitive markets. Demand (which reflects utility) and supply (which reflects costs) jointly determine equilibrium price and quantity. Without a demand curve, there is no equilibrium price and quantity. But the same is true for supply. Without it, no equilibrium price and quantity exist. Equilibrium price and quantity result from the *interaction* of demand and supply, and each is *equally* important.

supplied and prompts many buyers to leave the market, thus eliminating the shortage. Again the market moves to its equilibrium.

Rationing Function of Prices

The ability of the competitive forces of supply and demand to establish a price at which selling and buying decisions are consistent is called the **rationing function of prices.** In our case, the equilibrium price of $3 clears the market, leaving no burdensome surplus for sellers and no inconvenient shortage for potential buyers. And it is the combination of freely made individual decisions that sets this market-clearing price. In effect, the market outcome says that all buyers who are willing and able to pay $3 for a bushel of corn will obtain it; all buyers who cannot or will not pay $3 will go without corn. Similarly, all producers who are willing and able to offer corn for sale at $3 a bushel will sell it; all producers who cannot or will not sell for $3 per bushel will not sell their product. **(Key Question 7)**

Changes in Supply, Demand, and Equilibrium

We know that demand might change because of fluctuations in consumer tastes or incomes, changes in consumer expectations, or variations in the prices of related goods. Supply might change in response to changes in resource prices, technology, or taxes. What effects will such changes in supply and demand have on equilibrium price and quantity?

Changes in Demand Suppose that supply is constant and demand increases, as shown in Figure 3.6a. As a result, the new intersection of the supply and demand curves is at higher values on both the price and the quantity axes. Clearly, an increase in demand raises both equilibrium price and equilibrium quantity. Conversely, a decrease in demand, such as that shown in Figure 3.6b, reduces both equilibrium price and equilibrium quantity. (The value of graphical analysis is now apparent: We need not fumble with columns of figures to determine the outcomes; we need only compare the new and the old points of intersection on the graph.)

Changes in Supply Now suppose that demand is constant but supply increases, as in Figure 3.6c. The new intersection of supply and demand is located at a lower equilibrium price but at a higher equilibrium quantity. An increase in supply reduces equilibrium price but increases equilibrium quantity. In contrast, if supply decreases, as in Figure 3.6d, the equilibrium price rises while the equilibrium quantity declines.

FIGURE 3.6

Changes in demand and supply and the effects on price and quantity.   The increase in demand from D_1 to D_2 in (a) increases both equilibrium price and equilibrium quantity. The decrease in demand from D_1 to D_2 in (b) decreases both equilibrium price and equilibrium quantity. The increase in supply from S_1 to S_2 in (c) decreases equilibrium price and increases equilibrium quantity. The decline in supply from S_1 to S_2 in (d) increases equilibrium price and decreases equilibrium quantity. The boxes in the top right corners summarize the respective changes and outcomes. The upward arrows in the boxes signify increases in demand (D), supply (S), equilibrium price (P), and equilibrium quantity (Q); the downward arrows signify decreases in these items.

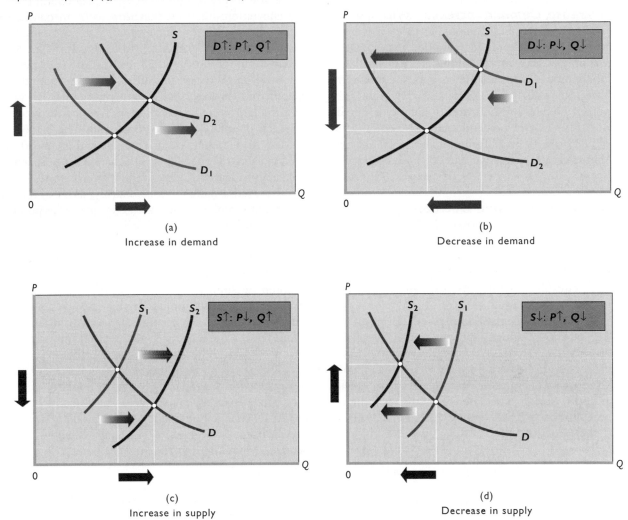

(a)
Increase in demand

(b)
Decrease in demand

(c)
Increase in supply

(d)
Decrease in supply

Complex Cases   When both supply and demand change, the effect is a combination of the individual effects.

Supply Increase; Demand Decrease   What effect will a supply increase and a demand decrease have on equilibrium price? Both changes decrease price, so the net result is a price drop greater than that resulting from either change alone.

What about equilibrium quantity? Here the effects of the changes in supply and demand are opposed: the increase in supply increases equilibrium quantity, but the decrease in demand reduces it. The direction of the change in quantity depends on the relative sizes of the changes in supply and demand. If the increase in supply is larger than the decrease in demand, the equilibrium quantity will increase. But if the decrease in demand is greater than the increase in supply, the equilibrium quantity will decrease.

Supply Decrease; Demand Increase   A decrease in supply and an increase in demand both increase price. Their combined effect is an increase in equilibrium price greater than that caused by either change separately. But their effect on equilibrium quantity is again indeterminate, depending on the relative sizes of the changes in supply and demand. If the decrease in supply is larger than the increase in demand, the equilibrium quantity will decrease. In contrast, if the increase in demand is greater than the decrease in supply, the equilibrium quantity will increase.

Supply Increase; Demand Increase What if supply and demand both increase? A supply increase drops equilibrium price, while a demand increase boosts it. If the increase in supply is greater than the increase in demand, the equilibrium price will fall. If the opposite holds, the equilibrium price will rise.

The effect on equilibrium quantity is certain: The increases in supply and in demand each raise equilibrium quantity. Therefore, the equilibrium quantity will increase by an amount greater than that caused by either change alone.

Supply Decrease; Demand Decrease What about decreases in both supply and demand? If the decrease in supply is greater than the decrease in demand, equilibrium price will rise. If the reverse is true, equilibrium price will fall. Because decreases in supply and in demand each reduce equilibrium quantity, we can be sure that equilibrium quantity will fall.

Table 3.9 summarizes these four cases. To understand them fully, you should draw supply and demand diagrams for each case to confirm the effects listed in Table 3.9.

Special cases arise when a decrease in demand and a decrease in supply, or an increase in demand and an increase in supply, exactly cancel out. In both cases, the net effect on equilibrium price will be zero; price will not change. **(Key Question 8)**

A Reminder: "Other Things Equal"

We must stress once again that specific demand and supply curves (such as those in Figure 3.6) show relationships

between prices and quantities demanded and supplied, *other things equal*. The downsloping demand curves tell us that price and quantity demanded are inversely related, other things equal. The upsloping supply curves imply that price and quantity supplied are directly related, other things equal.

If you forget the other-things-equal assumption, you can encounter situations that *seem* to be in conflict with these basic principles. For example, suppose salsa manufacturers sell 1 million bottles of salsa at $4 a bottle in 1 year; 2 million bottles at $5 in the next year; and 3 million at $6 in the year thereafter. Price and quantity purchased vary directly, and these data seem to be at odds with the law of demand. But there is no conflict here; the data do not refute the law of demand. The catch is that the law of demand's other-things-equal assumption has been violated over the 3 years in the example. Specifically, because of changing tastes and rising incomes, the demand for salsa has increased sharply, as in Figure 3.6a. The result is higher prices *and* larger quantities purchased.

Another example: The price of coffee occasionally has shot upward at the same time that the quantity of coffee produced has declined. These events seemingly contradict the direct relationship between price and quantity denoted by supply. The catch again is that the other-things-equal assumption underlying the upsloping supply curve was violated. Poor coffee harvests decreased supply, as in Figure 3.6d, increasing the equilibrium price of coffee and reducing the equilibrium quantity.

These examples emphasize the importance of our earlier distinction between a change in quantity demanded (or supplied) and a change in demand (supply). In Figure 3.6a a change in demand causes a change in the quantity supplied. In Figure 3.6d a change in supply causes a change in quantity demanded.

Application: Government-Set Prices

Prices in most markets are free to rise or fall to their equilibrium levels, no matter how high or low those levels might be. However, government sometimes concludes that supply and demand will produce prices that are unfairly high for buyers or unfairly low for sellers. So government may place legal limits on how high or low a price or prices may go. Is that a good idea?

Price Ceilings and Shortages

A **price ceiling** sets the maximum legal price a seller may charge for a product or service. A price at or below the

TABLE 3.9

Effects of Changes in Both Supply and Demand

Change in Supply	Change in Demand	Effect on Equilibrium Price	Effect on Equilibrium Quantity
1. Increase	Decrease	Decrease	Indeterminate
2. Decrease	Increase	Increase	Indeterminate
3. Increase	Increase	Indeterminate	Increase
4. Decrease	Decrease	Indeterminate	Decrease

ceiling is legal; a price above it is not. The rationale for establishing price ceilings (or ceiling prices) on specific products is that they purportedly enable consumers to obtain some "essential" good or service that they could not afford at the equilibrium price. Examples are rent controls and usury laws, which specify maximum "prices" in the forms of rent and interest that can be charged to borrowers. Also, the government has at times imposed price ceilings either on all products or on a very wide range of products—so-called price controls—to try to restrain inflation. Price controls were invoked during the Second World War, during the Korean conflict, and in the 1970s.

Graphical Analysis

We can easily show the effects of price ceilings graphically. Suppose that rapidly rising world income boosts the purchase of automobiles and shifts the demand for gasoline to the right so that the equilibrium or market price reaches $2.50 per gallon, shown as P_0 in Figure 3.7. The rapidly rising price of gasoline greatly burdens low- and moderate-income households, which pressure government to "do something." To keep gasoline affordable for these households, the government imposes a ceiling price P_c of $2 per gallon. To impact the market, a price ceiling must be below the equilibrium price. A ceiling price of $3, for example, would have had no immediate effect on the gasoline market.

What are the effects of this $2 ceiling price? The rationing ability of the free market is rendered ineffective. Because the ceiling price P_c is below the market-clearing price P_0, there is a lasting shortage of gasoline. The quantity of gasoline demanded at P_c is Q_d and the quantity supplied is only Q_s; a persistent excess demand or shortage of amount $Q_d - Q_s$ occurs.

The important point is that the price ceiling P_c prevents the usual market adjustment in which competition among buyers bids up price, inducing more production and rationing some buyers out of the market. That process would continue until the shortage disappeared at the equilibrium price and quantity, P_0 and Q_0.

By preventing these market adjustments from occurring, the price ceiling poses problems born of the market disequilibrium.

Rationing Problem

How will the available supply Q_s be apportioned among buyers who want the greater amount Q_d? Should gasoline be distributed on a first-come, first-served basis, that is, to those willing and able to get in line the soonest and stay in line? Or should gas stations distribute it on the basis of favoritism? Since an unregulated shortage does not lead to an equitable distribution of gasoline, the government must establish some formal system for rationing it to consumers. One option is to issue ration coupons, which authorize bearers to purchase a fixed amount of gasoline per month. The rationing system would entail first the printing of coupons for Q_s gallons of gasoline and then the equitable distribution of the coupons among consumers so that the wealthy family of four and the poor family of four both receive the same number of coupons.

Black Markets

But ration coupons would not prevent a second problem from arising. The demand curve in Figure 3.7 reveals that many buyers are willing to pay more than the ceiling price P_c. And, of course, it is more profitable for gasoline stations to sell at prices above the ceiling. Thus, despite a sizable enforcement bureaucracy that would have to accompany the price controls, *black markets* in which gasoline is illegally bought and sold at prices above the legal limits will flourish. Counterfeiting of ration coupons will also be a problem. And since the price of gasoline is now "set by government," there might be political pressure on government to set the price even lower.

Rent Controls

About 200 cities in the United States, including New York City, Boston, and San Francisco, have at one time or another enacted rent controls: maximum rents established by law (or, more recently, have set maximum rent increases for existing tenants). Such laws are well intended. Their goals are to protect low-income families from escalating rents caused by perceived housing shortages and to make housing more affordable to the poor.

FIGURE 3.7

A price ceiling results in a persistent shortage. A price ceiling is a maximum legal price such as P_c that is below the equilibrium price. It results in a persistent product shortage, here shown by the distance between Q_d and Q_s.

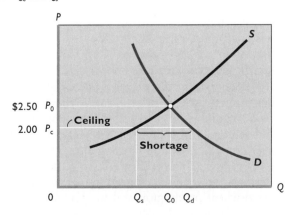

What have been the actual economic effects? On the demand side, it is true that as long as rents are below equilibrium, more families are willing to consume rental housing; the quantity of rental housing demanded increases at the lower price. The main problem occurs on the supply side. Price controls make it less attractive for landlords to offer housing on the rental market. In the short run, owners may sell their rental units or convert them to condominiums. In the long run, low rents make it unprofitable for owners to repair or renovate their rental units. (Rent controls are one cause of the many abandoned apartment buildings found in larger cities.) Also, insurance companies, pension funds, and other potential new investors in housing will find it more profitable to invest in office buildings, shopping malls, or motels, where rents are not controlled.

In brief, rent controls distort market signals and thus resources are misallocated: Too few resources are allocated to rental housing, and too many to alternative uses. Ironically, although rent controls are often legislated to lessen the effects of perceived housing shortages, controls in fact are a primary cause of such shortages. For that reason, most American cities have either abandoned or are in the process of abandoning rent controls.

Price Floors and Surpluses

A **price floor** is a minimum price fixed by the government. A price at or above the price floor is legal; a price below it is not. Price floors above equilibrium prices are usually invoked when society feels that the free functioning of the market system has not provided a sufficient income for certain groups of resource suppliers or producers. Supported prices for agricultural products and current minimum wages are two examples of price (or wage) floors. Let's look at the former.

Suppose the equilibrium price for wheat is $2 per bushel and, because of that low price, many farmers have extremely low incomes. The government decides to help out by establishing a legal price floor or price support of $3 per bushel.

What will be the effects? At any price above the equilibrium price, quantity supplied will exceed quantity demanded—that is, there will be a persistent excess supply or surplus of the product. Farmers will be willing to produce and offer for sale more than private buyers are willing to purchase at the price floor. As we saw with a price ceiling, an imposed legal price disrupts the rationing ability of the free market.

Graphical Analysis   Figure 3.8 illustrates the effect of a price floor graphically. Suppose that S and D are the

FIGURE 3.8

A price floor results in a persistent surplus.   A price floor is a minimum legal price such as P_f, which results in a persistent product surplus, here shown by the horizontal distance between Q_s and Q_d.

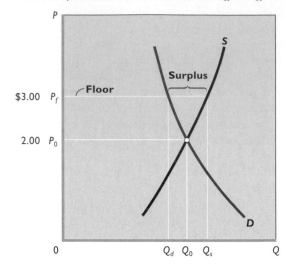

supply and demand curves for wheat. Equilibrium price and quantity are P_0 and Q_0, respectively. If the government imposes a price floor of P_f, farmers will produce Q_s but private buyers will purchase only Q_d. The surplus is the excess of Q_s over Q_d.

The government may cope with the surplus resulting from a price floor in two ways:

- It can restrict supply (for example, by instituting acreage allotments by which farmers agree to take a certain amount of land out of production) or increase demand (for example, by researching new uses for the product involved). These actions may reduce the difference between the equilibrium price and the price floor and that way reduce the size of the resulting surplus.
- If these efforts are not wholly successful, then the government must purchase the surplus output at the $3 price (thereby subsidizing farmers) and store or otherwise dispose of it.

Additional Consequences   Price floors such as P_f in Figure 3.8 not only disrupt the rationing ability of prices but distort resource allocation. Without the price floor, the $2 equilibrium price of wheat would cause financial losses and force high-cost wheat producers to plant other crops or abandon farming altogether. But the $3 price floor allows them to continue to grow wheat and remain farmers. So society devotes too many of its scarce resources to wheat production and too few to producing

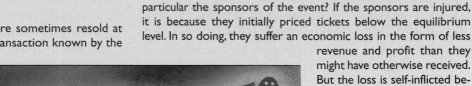

Some Market Transactions Get a Bad Name That Is Not Warranted.

Tickets to athletic and artistic events are sometimes resold at higher-than-original prices—a market transaction known by the term "scalping." For example, the original buyer may resell a $50 ticket to a college bowl game for $200, $250, or more. The media often denounce scalpers for "ripping off" buyers by charging "exorbitant" prices. Scalping and extortion are synonymous in some people's minds.

But is scalping really sinful? We must first recognize that such ticket resales are voluntary transactions. Both buyer and seller expect to gain from the exchange. Otherwise, it would not occur! The seller must value the $200 more than seeing the event, and the buyer must value seeing the event more than the $200. So there are no losers or victims here: Both buyer and seller benefit from the transaction. The "scalping" market simply redistributes assets (game or concert tickets) from those who value them less to those who value them more.

Does scalping impose losses or injury on other parties, in particular the sponsors of the event? If the sponsors are injured, it is because they initially priced tickets below the equilibrium level. In so doing, they suffer an economic loss in the form of less revenue and profit than they might have otherwise received. But the loss is self-inflicted because of their pricing error. That mistake is quite separate and distinct from the fact that some tickets are later resold at a higher price.

What about spectators? Does scalping deteriorate the enthusiasm of the audience? Usually not! People who have the greatest interest in the event will pay the scalper's high prices. Ticket scalping also benefits the teams and performing artists, because they will appear before more dedicated audiences—ones that are more likely to buy souvenir items or CDs.

So is ticket scalping undesirable? Not on economic grounds. Both seller and buyer of a "scalped" ticket benefit, and a more interested audience results. Event sponsors may sacrifice revenue and profits, but that stems from their own misjudgment of the equilibrium price.

---

other, more valuable, goods and services. It fails to achieve allocative efficiency.

That's not all. Consumers of wheat-based products pay higher prices because of the price floor. Taxpayers pay higher taxes to finance the government's purchase of the surplus. Also, the price floor causes potential environmental damage by encouraging wheat farmers to bring hilly, erosion-prone "marginal land" into production. The higher price also prompts imports of wheat. But, since such imports would increase the quantity of wheat supplied and thus undermine the price floor, the government needs to erect tariffs (taxes on imports) to keep the foreign wheat out. Such tariffs usually prompt other countries to retaliate with their own tariffs against U.S. agricultural or manufacturing exports.

It is easy to see why economists "raise the caution flag" when politicians advocate imposing price ceilings or price floors. In both cases, good intentions typically lead to bad economic outcomes. **Key Question 13**

3.2 Price floors and ceilings

SUMMARY

1. A market is any institution or arrangement that brings together buyers and sellers of a product, service, or resource.

2. Demand is a schedule or curve representing the willingness of buyers in a specific period to purchase a particular product at each of various prices. The law of demand implies that consumers will buy more of a product at a low price than at a high price. So, other things equal, the relationship between price and quantity demanded is negative or inverse and is graphed as a downsloping curve. Market demand curves are found by adding horizontally the demand curves of the many individual consumers in the market.

3. Changes in one or more of the determinants of demand (consumer tastes, the number of buyers in the market, the money incomes of consumers, the prices of related goods, and price expectations) shift the market demand curve. A shift to the right is an increase in demand; a shift to the left is a decrease in demand. A change in demand is different from a change in the quantity demanded, the latter being a movement from one point to another point on a fixed demand curve because of a change in the product's price.

4. Supply is a schedule or curve showing the amounts of a product that producers are willing to offer in the market at each possible price during a specific period. The law of supply states that, other things equal, producers will offer more of a product at a high price than at a low price. Thus, the relationship between price and quantity supplied is positive or direct, and supply is graphed as an upsloping curve. The market supply curve is the horizontal summation of the supply curves of the individual producers of the product.

5. Changes in one or more of the determinants of supply (resource prices, production techniques, taxes or subsidies, the prices of other goods, price expectations, or the number of sellers in the market) shift the supply curve of a product. A shift to the right is an increase in supply; a shift to the left is a decrease in supply. In contrast, a change in the price of the product being considered causes a change in the quantity supplied, which is shown as a movement from one point to another point on a fixed supply curve.

6. The equilibrium price and quantity are established at the intersection of the supply and demand curves. The interaction of market demand and market supply adjusts the price to the point at which the quantities demanded and supplied are equal. This is the equilibrium price. The corresponding quantity is the equilibrium quantity.

7. The ability of market forces to synchronize selling and buying decisions to eliminate potential surpluses and shortages is known as the rationing function of prices.

8. A change in either demand or supply changes the equilibrium price and quantity. Increases in demand raise both equilibrium price and equilibrium quantity; decreases in demand lower both equilibrium price and equilibrium quantity. Increases in supply lower equilibrium price and raise equilibrium quantity; decreases in supply raise equilibrium price and lower equilibrium quantity.

9. Simultaneous changes in demand and supply affect equilibrium price and quantity in various ways, depending on their direction and relative magnitudes.

10. A price ceiling is a maximum price set by government and is designed to help consumers. A price floor is a minimum price set by government and is designed to aid producers.

11. Legally fixed prices stifle the rationing function of prices and distort the allocation of resources. Effective price ceilings produce persistent product shortages, and if an equitable distribution of the product is sought, government must ration the product to consumers. Price floors lead to persistent product surpluses; the government must either purchase the product or eliminate the surplus by imposing restrictions on production or increasing private demand.

TERMS AND CONCEPTS

market	determinants of demand	supply	surplus
demand	normal goods	supply schedule	shortage
demand schedule	inferior goods	law of supply	equilibrium price
law of demand	substitute good	supply curve	equilibrium quantity
diminishing marginal utility	complementary good	determinants of supply	rationing function of prices
income effect	change in demand	change in supply	price ceiling
substitution effect	change in quantity demanded	change in quantity supplied	price floor
demand curve			

STUDY QUESTIONS

1. Explain the law of demand. Why does a demand curve slope downward? What are the determinants of demand? What happens to the demand curve when each of these determinants changes? Distinguish between a change in demand and a change in the quantity demanded, noting the cause(s) of each.

2. *Key Question* What effect will each of the following have on the demand for product B?
   a. Product B becomes more fashionable.
   b. The price of substitute product C falls.
   c. Income declines and product B is an inferior good.
   d. Consumers anticipate that the price of B will be lower in the near future.
   e. The price of complementary product D falls.

3. Assess the effects of the terrorist attacks of September 11, 2001, and the war on terrorism on the demand for the following items in the United States: airline tickets, gasoline, hotel rooms, American flags, books about Afghanistan, and Arabic interpreters.

4. Explain the law of supply. Why does the supply curve slope upward? What are the determinants of supply? What happens to the supply curve when each of these determinants changes? Distinguish between a change in supply and a change in the quantity supplied, noting the cause(s) of each.

5. *Key Question* What effect will each of the following have on the supply of product B?
   a. A technological advance in the methods of producing product B.
   b. A decline in the number of firms in industry B.
   c. An increase in the prices of resources required in the production of B.
   d. The expectation that the equilibrium price of B will be lower in the future than it is currently.
   e. A decline in the price of product A, a good whose production requires substantially the same techniques and resources as does the production of B.
   f. The levying of a specific sales tax on B.
   g. The granting of a 50-cent-per-unit subsidy for each unit of B produced.

6. "In the corn market, demand often exceeds supply and supply sometimes exceeds demand." "The price of corn rises and falls in response to changes in supply and demand." In which of these two statements are the terms "supply" and "demand" used correctly? Explain.

7. *Key Question* Suppose the total demand for wheat and the total supply of wheat per month in the Kansas City grain market are as shown in the next column:
   a. What is the equilibrium price? What is the equilibrium quantity? Fill in the surplus-shortage column and use it to explain why your answers are correct.

Thousands of Bushels Demanded	Price per Bushel	Thousands of Bushels Supplied	Surplus (+) or Shortage (−)
85	$3.40	72	_____
80	3.70	73	_____
75	4.00	75	_____
70	4.30	77	_____
65	4.60	79	_____
60	4.90	81	_____

   b. Graph the demand for wheat and the supply of wheat. Be sure to label the axes of your graph correctly. Label equilibrium price P and equilibrium quantity Q.
   c. Why will $3.40 not be the equilibrium price in this market? Why not $4.90? "Surpluses drive prices up; shortages drive them down." Do you agree?

8. *Key Question* How will each of the following changes in demand and/or supply affect equilibrium price and equilibrium quantity in a competitive market; that is, do price and quantity rise, fall, or remain unchanged, or are the answers indeterminate because they depend on the magnitudes of the shifts? Use supply and demand diagrams to verify your answers.
   a. Supply decreases and demand is constant.
   b. Demand decreases and supply is constant.
   c. Supply increases and demand is constant.
   d. Demand increases and supply increases.
   e. Demand increases and supply is constant.
   f. Supply increases and demand decreases.
   g. Demand increases and supply decreases.
   h. Demand decreases and supply decreases.

9. In 2001 an outbreak of foot-and-mouth disease in Europe led to the burning of millions of cattle carcasses. What impact do you think this had on the supply of cattle hides, hide prices, the supply of leather goods, and the price of leather goods?

10. Explain: "Even though parking meters may yield little or no net revenue, they should nevertheless be retained because of the rationing function they perform."

11. Use two market diagrams to explain how an increase in state subsidies to public colleges might affect tuition and enrollments in both public and private colleges.

12. Critically evaluate: "In comparing the two equilibrium positions in Figure 3.6a, I note that a larger amount is actually purchased at a higher price. This refutes the law of demand."

13. *Key Question* Refer to the table in question 7. Suppose that the government establishes a price ceiling of $3.70 for wheat. What might prompt the government to establish this price ceiling? Explain carefully the main effects. Demonstrate your answer graphically. Next, suppose that

the government establishes a price floor of $4.60 for wheat. What will be the main effects of this price floor? Demonstrate your answer graphically.

14. What do economists mean when they say that "price floors and ceilings stifle the rationing function of prices and distort resource allocation"?

15. *Advanced Analysis* Assume that demand for a commodity is represented by the equation $P = 10 - .2Q_d$ and supply by the equation $P = 2 + .2Q_s$, where Q_d and Q_s are quantity demanded and quantity supplied, respectively, and P is price. Using the equilibrium condition $Q_s = Q_d$, solve the equations to determine equilibrium price. Now determine equilibrium quantity. Graph the two equations to substantiate your answers.

16. *(Last Word)* Discuss the economic aspects of ticket scalping, specifying gainers and losers.

17. *Web-Based Question: Farm commodity prices—supply and demand in action* The U.S. Department of Agriculture, www.usda.gov/nass, publishes charts on the prices of farm products. Go to the USDA home page and select Charts and Maps and then Agricultural Prices. Choose three farm products of your choice and determine whether their prices

(as measured by "prices received by farmers") have generally increased, decreased, or stayed the same over the past 3 years. In which of the three cases, if any, do you think that supply has increased more rapidly than demand? In which of the three cases, if any, do you think that demand has increased more rapidly than supply? Explain your reasoning.

18. *Web-Based Question: Changes in demand—baby diapers and retirement villages* Other things equal, an increase in the number of buyers for a product or service will increase demand. Baby diapers and retirement villages are two products designed for different population groups. The U.S. Census Bureau website, www.census.gov/ipc/www/idbpyr.html, provides population pyramids (graphs that show the distribution of population by age and sex) for countries for the current year, 2025, and 2050. View the population pyramids for Mexico, Japan, and the United States. Which country do you think will have the greatest percentage increase in demand for baby diapers in the year 2050? For retirement villages? Which country do you think will have the greatest absolute increase in demand for baby diapers? For retirement villages?

3
WEB

Applications and Extensions of Supply and Demand Analysis

Chapter 3W is a companion chapter to Chapter 3 of the textbook. This chapter, located at the book's website, www.mcconnell16, contains a number of applications of supply and demand. Depending on time and preferences, your instructor may assign all, part, or none of this chapter.

Chapter 3W Contents:

4 | *The Market System*

Suppose that you were assigned to compile a list of all the individual goods and services available at a large regional shopping mall, including the different brands and variations of each type of product. We think you would agree that this task would be daunting and the list would be long! And yet, even though a single shopping mall contains a remarkable quantity and variety of goods, it is only a minuscule part of the national economy.

Who decided that the particular goods and services available at the mall and in the broader economy should be produced? How did the producers determine which technology and types of resources to use in producing these particular goods? Who will obtain these products? What accounts for the new and improved products among these goods?

In Chapter 3 we saw how equilibrium prices and quantities are established in *individual* product and resource markets. We now widen our focus to take in *all* product markets and resource markets—*capitalism,* also called the *private-enterprise system* or simply the *market system.* In this chapter we examine the characteristics of the market system and how that system answers questions such as those posed above.

Characteristics of the Market System

The market system, as practiced in industrially advanced economies, has several notable characteristics. Let's examine them in some detail.

Private Property

In a market system, private individuals and firms, not the government, own most of the property resources (land and capital). In fact, it is this extensive private ownership of capital that gives capitalism its name. This right of private property, coupled with the freedom to negotiate binding legal contracts, enables individuals and businesses to obtain, use, and dispose of property resources as they see fit. The right to bequeath—the right of property owners to designate who will receive their property when they die—sustains the institution of private property.

Property rights encourage investment, innovation, exchange, maintenance of property, and economic growth. Why would anyone stock a store, build a factory, or clear land for farming if someone else, or the government itself, could take that property for his or her own benefit?

Property rights also extend to intellectual property through patents, copyrights, and trademarks. Such long-term protection encourages people to write books, music, and computer programs and to invent new products and production processes without fear that others will steal them and the rewards they may bring.

Property rights also facilitate exchange. The title to an automobile or the deed to a cattle ranch assures the buyer that the seller is the legitimate owner. Moreover, property rights encourage owners to maintain or improve their property so as to preserve or increase its value. Finally, property rights enable people to use their time and resources to produce more goods and services, rather than using them to protect and retain the property they have already produced or acquired.

Freedom of Enterprise and Choice

Closely related to private ownership of property is freedom of enterprise and choice. The market system requires that various economic units make certain choices, which are expressed and implemented in the economy's markets:

- **Freedom of enterprise** ensures that entrepreneurs and private businesses are free to obtain and use economic resources to produce their choice of goods and services and to sell them in their chosen markets.
- **Freedom of choice** enables owners to employ or dispose of their property and money as they see fit. It also allows workers to enter any line of work for which they are qualified. Finally, it ensures that consumers are free to buy the goods and services that best satisfy their wants.

These choices are free only within broad legal limitations, of course. Illegal choices such as selling human organs or buying illicit drugs are punished through fines and imprisonment. (Global Perspective 4.1 reveals that the degree of economic freedom varies greatly from nation to nation.)

Self-Interest

In the market system, **self-interest** is the motivating force of all the various economic units as they express their free choices. Self-interest means that each economic unit tries to do what is best for itself. Entrepreneurs try to maximize profit or minimize loss. Property owners try to get the highest price for the sale or rent of their resources. Workers try to maximize their utility (satisfaction) by finding jobs that offer the best combination of wages, hours, fringe benefits, and working conditions. Consumers

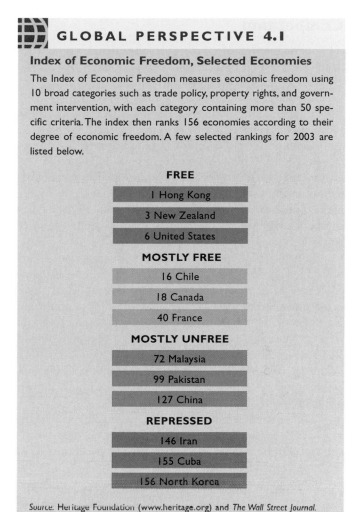

GLOBAL PERSPECTIVE 4.1

Index of Economic Freedom, Selected Economies

The Index of Economic Freedom measures economic freedom using 10 broad categories such as trade policy, property rights, and government intervention, with each category containing more than 50 specific criteria. The index then ranks 156 economies according to their degree of economic freedom. A few selected rankings for 2003 are listed below.

FREE
- 1 Hong Kong
- 3 New Zealand
- 6 United States

MOSTLY FREE
- 16 Chile
- 18 Canada
- 40 France

MOSTLY UNFREE
- 72 Malaysia
- 99 Pakistan
- 127 China

REPRESSED
- 146 Iran
- 155 Cuba
- 156 North Korea

Source: Heritage Foundation (www.heritage.org) and *The Wall Street Journal*.

try to obtain the products they want at the lowest possible price and apportion their expenditures to maximize their utility. The motive of self-interest gives direction and consistency to what might otherwise be a chaotic economy.

Recall that the pursuit of self-interest is not the same as selfishness. Self-interest involves maximizing some benefit, and it does not preclude helping others. A stockholder may invest to receive maximum corporate dividends and then donate a portion of them to the United Way or give them to grandchildren. A worker may take a second job to help pay college tuition for her or his children. An entrepreneur may make a fortune and donate much of it to a charitable foundation.

4.1
Self-interest

Competition

The market system depends on **competition** among economic units. The basis of this competition is freedom of choice exercised in pursuit of a monetary return. Very broadly defined, *competition* requires:

- Independently acting sellers and buyers operating in a particular product or resource market.
- Freedom of sellers and buyers to enter or leave markets, on the basis of their economic self-interest.

Competition diffuses economic power within the businesses and households that make up the economy. When there are independently acting sellers and buyers in a market, no one buyer or seller is able to dictate the price of the product.

Consider the supply side of the product market. When a product becomes scarce, its price rises. An unseasonable frost in Florida may seriously reduce the supply of citrus crops and sharply increase the price of oranges. Similarly, if a single producer can somehow restrict the total output of a product, it can raise the product's price. By controlling market supply, a firm can "rig the market" to its own advantage. But that is not possible in markets where suppliers compete. A firm that raises its price will lose part or all of its business to competitors.

The same reasoning applies to the demand side of the market. Because there are multiple buyers, single buyers cannot manipulate the market to their own advantage by refusing to pay the market price.

Competition also implies that producers can enter or leave an industry; there are no insurmountable barriers to an industry's expanding or contracting. This freedom of an industry to expand or contract provides the economy with the flexibility needed to remain efficient over time. Freedom of entry and exit enables the economy to adjust to changes in consumer tastes, technology, and resource availability.

The diffusion of economic power inherent in competition limits the potential abuse of that power. A producer that charges more than the competitive market price will lose sales to other producers. An employer who pays less than the competitive market wage rate will lose workers to other employers. A firm that fails to exploit new technology will lose profits to firms that do. Competition is the basic regulatory force in the market system.

Markets and Prices

Markets and prices are key characteristics of the market system. They give the system its ability to coordinate millions of daily economic decisions. We know from Chapters 2 and 3 that a market is a mechanism that brings buyers (demanders) and sellers (suppliers) into contact. A market system is necessary to convey the decisions made by buyers and sellers of products and resources. The decisions made on each side of the market determine a set of product and resource prices that guide resource owners, entrepreneurs, and consumers as they make and revise their free choices and pursue their self-interest.

Just as competition is the regulatory mechanism of the market system, the market system itself is the organizing mechanism. It serves as an elaborate communication network through which innumerable individual free choices are recorded, summarized, and balanced. Those who respond to market signals and obey market dictates are rewarded with greater profit and income; those who do not respond to these signals and choose to ignore market dictates are penalized. Through this mechanism society decides what the economy should produce, how production can be organized efficiently, and how the fruits of production are to be distributed among the various units that make up the economy.

QUICK REVIEW 4.1

- The market system rests on the private ownership of property and on freedom of enterprise and freedom of choice.
- The market system permits economic entities—businesses, resource suppliers, and consumers—to pursue and further their self-interest. It prevents any single economic entity from dictating the prices of products or resources.
- The coordinating mechanism of the market system is a system of markets and prices.

Reliance on Technology and Capital Goods

Another characteristic of the market system is the extensive use of capital goods. In the market system, competition, freedom of choice, self-interest, and personal reward provide the opportunity and motivation for technological advance. The monetary rewards for new products or production techniques accrue directly to the innovator. The market system therefore encourages extensive use and rapid development of complex capital goods: tools, machinery, large-scale factories, and facilities for storage, communication, transportation, and marketing.

Advanced technology and capital goods are important because the most direct methods of production are often the least efficient. The only way to avoid that inefficiency is to rely on **roundabout production.** It would be ridiculous for a farmer to go at production with bare hands. There are huge benefits—in the form of more efficient production and, therefore, more abundant output—to be derived from creating and using such tools of production (capital equipment) as plows, tractors, storage bins, and so on.

Specialization

The extent to which market economies rely on **specialization** is extraordinary. The majority of consumers produce virtually none of the goods and services they consume, and they consume little or nothing of what they produce. The worker who devotes 8 hours a day to installing windows in Fords may own a Honda. Many farmers sell their milk to the local dairy and then buy margarine at the local grocery store. Society learned long ago that self-sufficiency breeds inefficiency. The jack-of-all-trades may be a very colorful individual but is certainly not an efficient producer.

Division of Labor

Human specialization—called the **division of labor**—contributes to a society's output in several ways:

- *Specialization makes use of differences in ability.* Specialization enables individuals to take advantage of existing differences in their abilities and skills. If caveman A is strong and swift and good at tracking animals, and caveman B is weak and slow but patient, their distribution of talents can be most efficiently used if A hunts and B fishes.
- *Specialization fosters learning by doing.* Even if the abilities of A and B are identical, specialization may still be advantageous. By devoting all your time to a single task, you are more likely to develop the skills it requires and to devise improved techniques than you would by working at a number of different tasks. You learn to be a good hunter by going hunting every day.
- *Specialization saves time.* By devoting all your time to a single task, you avoid the loss of time incurred in shifting from one job to another.

For all these reasons, specialization increases the total output society derives from limited resources.

Geographic Specialization

Specialization also works on a regional and international basis. It is conceivable that oranges could be grown in Nebraska, but because of the unsuitability of the land, rainfall, and temperature, the costs would be very high. And it is conceivable that wheat could be grown in Florida. But for similar reasons such production would be costly. So Nebraskans produce products—wheat in particular—for which their resources are best suited, and Floridians do the same, producing oranges and other citrus fruits. By specializing, both economies produce more than is needed locally. Then, very sensibly, Nebraskans and Floridians swap some of their surpluses—wheat for oranges, oranges for wheat.

Similarly, on an international scale, the United States specializes in producing such items as commercial aircraft and computers, which it sells abroad in exchange for video recorders from Japan, bananas from Honduras, and woven baskets from Thailand. Both human specialization and geographic specialization are needed to achieve efficiency in the use of limited resources.

4.2
Specialization/
division of
labor

Use of Money

A rather obvious characteristic of the market system is the extensive use of money. Money performs several functions, but first and foremost it is a **medium of exchange.** It makes trade easier.

A convenient means of exchanging goods is required for specialization. Exchange can, and sometimes does, occur through **barter**—swapping goods for goods, say, wheat for oranges. But barter poses serious problems for the economy because it requires a *coincidence of wants* between the buyer and the seller. In our example, we assumed that Nebraskans had excess wheat to trade and wanted oranges. And we assumed that Floridians had excess oranges to trade and wanted wheat. So an exchange occurred. But if such a coincidence of wants is missing, trade is stymied.

Suppose that Nebraska has no interest in Florida's oranges but wants potatoes from Idaho. And suppose that Idaho wants Florida's oranges but not Nebraska's wheat. And, to complicate matters, suppose that Florida wants some of Nebraska's wheat but none of Idaho's potatoes. We summarize the situation in Figure 4.1.

In none of the cases shown in the figure is there a coincidence of wants. Trade by barter clearly would be difficult. Instead, people in each state use **money,** which is simply a convenient social invention to facilitate exchanges of goods and services. Historically, people have used cattle,

FIGURE 4.1

Money facilitates trade when wants do not coincide. The use of money as a medium of exchange permits trade to be accomplished despite a noncoincidence of wants. (1) Nebraska trades the wheat that Florida wants for money from Floridians; (2) Nebraska trades the money it receives from Florida for the potatoes it wants from Idaho; (3) Idaho trades the money it receives from Nebraska for the oranges it wants from Florida.

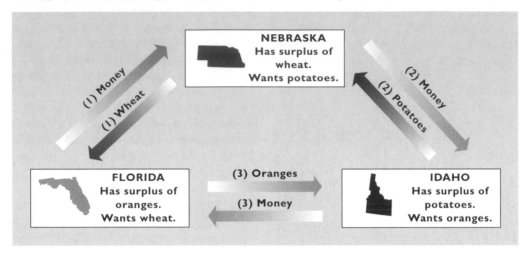

cigarettes, shells, stones, pieces of metal, and many other commodities, with varying degrees of success, as a medium of exchange. But to serve as money, an item needs to pass only one test: *It must be generally acceptable to sellers in exchange for their goods and services.* Money is socially defined; whatever society accepts as a medium of exchange *is* money.

Most economies use pieces of paper as money. The use of paper dollars (currency) as a medium of exchange is what enables Nebraska, Florida, and Idaho to overcome their trade stalemate, as demonstrated in Figure 4.1.

On a global basis the fact that different nations have different currencies complicates specialization and exchange. However, markets in which currencies are bought and sold make it possible for U.S. residents, Japanese, Germans, Britons, and Mexicans, through the swapping of dollars, yen, euros, pounds, and pesos, one for another, to exchange goods and services.

Active, but Limited, Government

The final characteristic of the market system, as evidenced in modern economies, is an active, but limited, government. Although a market system promotes a high degree of efficiency in the use of its resources, it has certain shortcomings. We will discover in Chapter 5 that government can increase the overall effectiveness of the economic system in several ways.

QUICK REVIEW 4.2

• The market systems of modern industrial economies are characterized by extensive use of technologically advanced capital goods. Such goods help these economies achieve greater efficiency in production.

• Specialization is extensive in market systems; it enhances efficiency and output by enabling individuals, regions, and nations to produce the goods and services for which their resources are best suited.

• The use of money in market systems facilitates the exchange of goods and services that specialization requires.

The Market System at Work

We have noted that a market system is characterized by competition, freedom of enterprise, and choice. Consumers are free to buy what they choose; entrepreneurs and firms are free to produce and sell what they choose; and resource suppliers are free to make their property and human resources available in whatever use or occupation they choose. We may wonder why such an economy does not collapse in chaos. If consumers want breakfast cereal but businesses choose to produce aerobic shoes and resource suppliers decide to manufacture computer software, production would seem to be dead-locked by the apparent inconsistency of these free choices.

In reality, the millions of decisions made by households and businesses are highly consistent with one another. Firms *do* produce the goods and services that consumers want, and households *do* provide the kinds of labor that businesses want.

To understand the operation of the market system, you must first recognize that every economy must respond to Four Fundamental Questions:

- What goods and services will be produced?
- How will the goods and services be produced?
- Who will get the goods and services?
- How will the system accommodate change?

The **Four Fundamental Questions** highlight the economic choices underlying the production possibilities curve discussed in Chapter 2. These questions are relevant because of scarce resources in a world of unlimited wants. Let's examine how the market system answers each of these questions and thus addresses the economizing problem.

What Will Be Produced?

With product and resource prices in place, established through competition in both the product and the resource markets, how will a market system decide on the specific types and quantities of goods to be produced? *Because businesses seek profits and avoid losses, the goods and services produced at a continuing profit* will *be produced and those produced at a continuing loss* will not. Profits and losses depend on the difference between the total revenue a firm receives from selling its product and the total cost of producing the product:

$$\text{Economic profit} = \text{total revenue} - \text{total cost}$$

Total revenue (TR) is found by multiplying the product price by the quantity of the product sold. Total cost (TC) is found by multiplying the price of each resource used by the amount employed and summing the results.

Economic Costs and Profits

Saying that the products that can be produced profitably *will* be produced and those that cannot *will not* is an accurate generalization only if the meaning of **economic costs** is clearly understood.

Let's think of businesses as simply organizational charts—that is, businesses "on paper," as distinct from the capital, raw materials, labor, and entrepreneurial ability that make them function. To become actual producing firms, these on-paper businesses must secure all four types of resources. *Economic costs are the payments that must be made to secure and retain the needed amounts of those resources.* The per-unit size of those costs—the resource prices—are determined by supply and demand in the resource market. As with land, labor, and capital, entrepreneurial ability is a scarce resource that carries a price tag. Consequently, costs must include not only wage and salary payments to labor, and interest and rental payments for capital and land, but also payments to the entrepreneur for organizing and combining the other resources to produce a commodity. The payment for (cost of) the entrepreneur's contributions is called **normal profit.**

A product is produced only if total revenue is large enough to pay wages, interest, rent, and a normal profit (a cost) to the entrepreneur. That way all the economic costs are covered, including the opportunity cost of the entrepreneur's time and talent. If the total revenue from the sale of a product exceeds all these economic costs, the remainder goes to the entrepreneur as an added reward. That return is called *pure profit* or **economic profit.** Economic profit is an above-normal profit, and it *is* what lures other producers to a particular industry.

Profits and Expanding Industries

An example will help explain how the market system determines what goods will be produced. With current technology, suppose the most favorable relationship between total revenue and total cost in producing product X occurs when a firm's output is 15 units. Assume, too, that the least-cost combination of resources in producing 15 units of X is 2 units of labor, 3 units of land, 1 unit of capital, and 1 unit of entrepreneurial ability, selling at prices of $2, $1, $3, and $3, respectively. Finally, suppose that the 15 units of X that these resources produce can be sold for $1 per unit, or $15 total. Will firms produce X? Yes, because each firm will be able to pay wages, rent, interest, and normal profit (a cost) of $13 [= (2 × $2) + (3 × $1) + (1 × $3) + (1 × $3)]. The difference between total revenue of $15 and total cost of $13 is an economic profit of $2.

This economic profit is evidence that industry X is prosperous. It will become an **expanding industry** as new firms, attracted by the above-normal profits, are formed or shift from less profitable industries.

But the entry of new firms will be self-limiting. As new firms enter industry X, the market supply of product X will increase relative to the market demand. This will lower the market price of X, as in Figure 3.6c, and economic profit will gradually diminish and finally disappear. The market supply and demand conditions prevailing when economic profit reaches zero will determine the total amount of X produced. At this point the industry will be at its "equilibrium size," at least until a further change in market demand or supply upsets that equilibrium.

Losses and Declining Industries

But what if the initial market situation for product X were less favorable? Suppose that demand conditions in the product market were such that a firm could sell the 15 units of X at a price of just $.75 per unit. Total revenue would then be $11.25 (= 15 × $.75). After paying wage, rental, and interest costs of $10, and figuring in the normal profit (a cost) of $3, the firm's total cost would again be $13. But because its total revenue is only $11.25, it would incur a loss of $1.75 (= $11.25 − $13).

Certainly, firms would not be attracted to this unprofitable **declining industry**. In fact, if these losses persisted, some of the firms in industry X would go out of business or migrate to more prosperous industries where normal or even economic profits prevailed. However, as that happened, the market supply of X would fall relative to the market demand. Product price would rise (as in Figure 3.6d), and the losses in industry X would eventually disappear. The industry would then stop shrinking. The supply and demand situation that prevailed when economic profit became zero would determine the total output of product X. Again, the industry would for the moment reach its equilibrium size.

Consumer Sovereignty and Dollar Votes

In the market system, consumers are sovereign (in command). **Consumer sovereignty** works through consumer demand, and consumer demand is crucial in determining the types and quantities of goods produced. Consumers spend the income they earn from the sale of their resources on the goods they are most willing and able to buy. Through these **"dollar votes"** consumers register their wants via the demand side of the product market. If the dollar votes for a certain product are great enough to provide a normal profit, businesses will produce that product. If there is an increase in consumer demand, so that enough dollar votes are cast to provide an economic profit, the industry will expand, as will the output of the product.

Conversely, a decrease in consumer demand—meaning fewer dollar votes cast for the product—will result in losses, and, in time, the industry will contract. As firms leave the industry, the output of the product will decline. Indeed, the industry may even cease to exist. Again, the consumers are sovereign; they collectively direct resources away from industries that are not meeting consumer wants.

The dollar votes of consumers determine not only which industries will continue to exist but also which

products will survive or fail. Example: In 1991, responding to doctors and nutritionists, McDonald's introduced its low-fat McLean burger. Good idea? Not really. Most consumers found the new product "too dry" and "not tasty," so sales were meager. In 1996 McDonald's quietly dropped the McLean burger from its menu at the same time that it introduced its higher-fat Arch Deluxe burger. In effect, consumers had collectively "voted out" the McLean burger.

Market Restraints on Freedom

In short, firms are not really free to produce whatever they wish. Consumers' buying decisions make the production of some products profitable and the production of other products unprofitable, thus restricting the choice of businesses in deciding what to produce. Businesses must match their production choices with consumer choices or else face losses and eventual bankruptcy.

The same holds true for resource suppliers. The demand for resources is a **derived demand**—derived, that is, from the demand for the goods and services that the resources help produce. There is a demand for autoworkers because there is a demand for automobiles. There is no demand for buggy-whip braiders because there is no demand for buggy whips. Resource suppliers are not free to allocate their resources to the production of goods that consumers do not value highly. Consumers register their preferences on the demand side of the product market; producers and resource suppliers, prompted by their own self-interest, respond appropriately.

How Will the Goods and Services Be Produced?

The market system steers resources to the industries whose products consumers want—simply because those industries survive, are profitable, and pay for resources. Within each industry, the firms that survive to do the producing also are the ones that are profitable. Because competition weeds out high-cost producers, continued profitability requires that firms produce their output at minimum cost. Achieving least-cost production necessitates, for example, that firms locate their production facilities optimally, considering such factors as resource prices, resource productivity, and transportation costs.

Least-cost production also means that firms must employ the most economically efficient technique of production in producing their output. The most efficient production technique depends on:

- The available technology, that is, the various combinations of resources that will produce the desired results.
- The prices of the needed resources.

A technique that requires just a few inputs of resources to produce a specific output may be highly *inefficient* economically *if* those resources are valued very highly in the market. *Economic efficiency means obtaining a particular output of product with the least input of scarce resources, when both output and resource inputs are measured in dollars and cents.*

The combination of resources that will produce, say, $15 worth of product X at the lowest possible cost is the most efficient.

Suppose there are three possible techniques for producing the desired $15 worth of product X. Suppose also that the quantity of each resource required by each production technique and the prices of the required resources are as shown in Table 4.1. By multiplying the required quantities of each resource by its price in each of the three techniques, we can determine the total cost of producing $15 worth of X by means of each technique.

Technique 2 is economically the most efficient, because it is the least costly. It enables society to obtain $15 worth of output by using a smaller amount of resources—$13 worth—than the $15 worth required by the two other techniques. Competition will dictate that producers use technique 2. Thus, the question of how goods will be produced is answered. They will be produced in a least-cost way.

A change in either technology *or* resource prices, however, may cause a firm to shift from the technology it is using. If the price of labor falls to $.50, technique 1 becomes more desirable than technique 2. Firms will find they can lower their costs by shifting to a technology that uses more of the resource whose price has fallen. Exercise: Would a new technique involving 1 unit of labor, 4 of land, 1 of capital, and 1 of entrepreneurial ability be preferable to the techniques listed in Table 4.1, assuming the resource prices shown there? **(Key Question 7)**

Who Will Get the Goods and Services?

The market system enters the picture in two ways when solving the problem of distributing total output. Generally, any product will be distributed to consumers on the basis of their ability and willingness to pay its

TABLE 4.1

Three Techniques for Producing $15 Worth of Product X

| | | Units of Resource | | | | | |
| | | Technique 1 | | Technique 2 | | Technique 3 | |
Resource	Price per Unit of Resource	Units	Cost	Units	Cost	Units	Cost
Labor	$2	4	$ 8	2	$ 4	1	$ 2
Land	1	1	1	3	3	4	4
Capital	3	1	3	1	3	2	6
Entrepreneurial ability	3	1	3	1	3	1	3
Total cost of $15 worth of X			$15		$13		$15

existing market price. If the price of some product, say, a pocket calculator, is $15, then buyers who are able and willing to pay that price will get a pocket calculator; those who are not, will not. This is the rationing function of equilibrium prices.

The ability to pay the equilibrium prices for pocket calculators and other products depends on the amount of income that consumers have, along with their preferences for various goods. If they have sufficient income and want to spend their money on a particular good, they can have it. And the amount of income they have depends on (1) the quantities of the property and human resources they supply and (2) the prices those resources command in the resource market. Resource prices (wages, interest, rent, profit) are key in determining the size of each household's income and therefore each household's ability to buy part of the economy's output.

How Will the System Accommodate Change?

Market systems are dynamic: Consumer preferences, technology, and supplies of resources all change. This means that the particular allocation of resources that is now the most efficient for a *specific* pattern of consumer tastes, range of technological alternatives, and amount of available resources will become obsolete and inefficient as consumer preferences change, new techniques of production are discovered, and resource supplies change over time. Can the market economy adjust to such changes and still use resources efficiently?

Guiding Function of Prices
Suppose consumer tastes change. For instance, assume that consumers decide they want more fruit juice and less milk than the economy currently provides. Those changes in consumer tastes will be communicated to producers through an increase in demand for fruit and a decline in demand for milk. Fruit prices will rise and milk prices will fall.

Now, assuming that firms in both industries were enjoying precisely normal profits before these changes in consumer demand set in, the higher fruit prices will mean economic profit for the fruit industry and the lower milk prices will mean losses for the milk industry. Self-interest will induce new competitors to enter the prosperous fruit industry and will in time force firms to leave the depressed milk industry.

The economic profit that initially follows the increase in demand for fruit will not only induce that industry to expand but will also give it the revenue needed to obtain the resources essential to its growth. Higher fruit prices will permit fruit producers to pay higher prices for resources, thereby increasing resource demand and drawing resources from less urgent alternative employment. The reverse occurs in the milk industry, where resource demand declines and fewer workers and other resources are employed. These adjustments in the economy are appropriate responses to the changes in consumer tastes. This is consumer sovereignty at work.

The market system is a gigantic communications system. Through changes in prices it communicates changes in such basic matters as consumer tastes and elicits appropriate responses from businesses and resource suppliers. By affecting product prices and profits, changes in consumer tastes direct the expansion of some industries and the contraction of others. Those adjustments are conveyed to the resource market as expanding industries demand more resources and contracting industries demand fewer; the resulting changes in resource prices guide resources from the contracting industries to the expanding industries.

This *directing* or **guiding function of prices** is a core element of the market system. Without such a system, some administrative agency such as a government planning board would have to direct businesses and resources into the appropriate industries. A similar analysis shows that the system can and does adjust to other fundamental changes—for example, to changes in technology and in the availability of various resources.

Role in Promoting Progress
Adjusting to changes is one thing; initiating desirable changes is another. How does the market system promote technological improvements and capital accumulation—two changes that lead to greater productivity and a higher level of economic well-being for society?

Technological Advance
The market system provides a strong incentive for technological advance and enables better products and processes to brush aside inferior ones. An entrepreneur or firm that introduces a popular new product will gain revenue and economic profit. Technological advance also includes new and improved methods that reduce production or distribution costs. By passing part of its cost reduction on to the consumer through a lower product price, the firm can increase sales and obtain economic profit at the expense of rival firms. Moreover, the market system is conducive to the *rapid spread* of technological advance throughout an industry. Rival firms must follow the lead of the most innovative

firm or else suffer immediate losses and eventual failure. In some cases, the result is **creative destruction:** The creation of new products and production methods completely destroys the market positions of firms that are wedded to existing products and older ways of doing business. Example: The advent of personal computers and word processing software demolished the market for electric typewriters.

Capital Accumulation   Most technological advances require additional capital goods. The market system provides the resources necessary to produce those goods by adjusting the product market and the resource market through increased dollar votes for capital goods. In other words, the market system acknowledges dollar voting for capital goods as well as for consumer goods.

But who will register votes for capital goods? Entrepreneurs and owners of businesses, as receivers of profit income, often use part of that income to purchase capital goods. Doing so yields even greater profit income in the future if the technological innovation is successful. Also, by paying interest or selling ownership shares, the entrepreneur and firm can attract some of the income of households to cast dollar votes for the production of more capital goods. **(Key Question 10)**

Competition and the "Invisible Hand"

In his 1776 book *The Wealth of Nations*, Adam Smith first noted that the operation of a market system creates a curious unity between private interests and social interests. Firms and resource suppliers, seeking to further their own self-interest and operating within the framework of a highly competitive market system, will simultaneously, as though guided by an **"invisible hand,"** promote the public or social interest. For example, we have seen that in a competitive environment, businesses use the least costly combination of resources to produce a specific output because it is in their self-interest to do so. To act otherwise would be to forgo profit or even to risk business failure. But, at the same time, to use scarce resources in the least costly (most efficient) way is clearly in the social interest as well.

In our more fruit juice–less milk illustration, it is self-interest, awakened and guided by the competitive market system, that induces responses appropriate to the change in society's wants. Businesses seeking to make higher profits and to avoid losses, and resource suppliers pursuing greater monetary rewards, negotiate changes in the

allocation of resources and end up with the output that society demands. Competition controls or guides self-interest in such a way that it automatically, and quite unintentionally, furthers the best interests of society. The invisible hand ensures that when firms maximize their profits, they also maximize society's output and income.

Of the many virtues of the market system three merit special emphasis:

- *Efficiency*   The basic economic argument for the market system is that it promotes the efficient use of resources, by guiding them into the production of the goods and services most wanted by society. It forces the use of the most efficient techniques in organizing resources for production, and it encourages the development and adoption of new and more efficient production techniques.

- *Incentives*   The market system encourages skill acquisition, hard work, and innovation. Greater work skills and effort mean greater production and higher incomes, which usually translate into a higher standard of living. Similarly, the assuming of risks by entrepreneurs can result in substantial profit incomes. Successful innovations generate economic rewards.

- *Freedom*   The major noneconomic argument for the market system is its emphasis on personal freedom. In contrast to central planning, the market system coordinates economic activity without coercion. The market system permits—indeed, it thrives on—freedom of enterprise and choice. Entrepreneurs and workers are free to further their own self-interest, subject to the rewards and penalties imposed by the market system itself.

QUICK REVIEW 4.3

- The output mix of the market system is determined by profits, which in turn depend heavily on consumer preferences. Economic profits cause efficient industries to expand; losses cause inefficient industries to contract.

- Competition forces industries to use the least costly (most efficient) production methods.

- In a market economy consumer income and product prices determine how output will be distributed.

- Competitive markets reallocate resources in response to changes in consumer tastes, technological advances, and changes in supplies of resources.

- The "invisible hand" of the market system channels the pursuit of self-interest to the good of society.

Economist Donald Boudreaux Marvels at the Way the Market System Systematically and Purposefully Arranges the World's Tens of Billions of Individual Resources.

In *The Future and Its Enemies,* Virginia Postrel notes the astonishing fact that if you thoroughly shuffle an ordinary deck of 52 playing cards, chances are practically 100 percent that the resulting arrangement of cards has never before existed. *Never.* Every time you shuffle a deck, you produce an arrangement of cards that exists for the first time in history.

The arithmetic works out that way. For a very small number of items, the number of possible arrangements is small. Three items, for example, can be arranged only six different ways. But the number of possible arrangements grows very large very quickly. The number of different ways to arrange five items is 120 ... for ten items it's 3,628,800 . . . for fifteen items it's 1,307,674,368,000.

The number of different ways to arrange 52 items is 8.066×10^{67}. This is a *big* number. No human can comprehend its enormousness. By way of comparison, the number of possible ways to arrange a mere 20 items is 2,432,902,008,176,640,000—a number larger than the total number of seconds that have elapsed since the beginning of time ten billion years ago—and this number is Lilliputian compared to 8.066×10^{67}.

What's the significance of these facts about numbers? Consider the number of different resources available in the world—my labor, your labor, your land, oil, tungsten, cedar, coffee beans, chickens, rivers, the Empire State Building, [Microsoft] Windows, the wharves at Houston, the classrooms at Oxford, the airport at Miami, and on and on and on. No one can possibly count all of the different productive resources available for our use. But we can be sure that this number is at least in the tens of billions.

When you reflect on how incomprehensibly large is the number of ways to arrange a deck containing a mere 52 cards, the mind boggles at the number of different ways to arrange all the world's resources.

If our world were random—if resources combined together haphazardly, as if a giant took them all into his hands and tossed them down like so many [cards]—it's a virtual certainty that the resulting combination of resources would be useless. Unless this chance arrangement were quickly rearranged according to some productive logic, nothing worthwhile would be produced. We would all starve to death. Because only a tiny fraction of possible arrangements serves human ends, any arrangement will be useless if it is chosen randomly or with inadequate knowledge of how each and every resource might be productively combined with each other.

And yet, we witness all around us an arrangement of resources that's productive and serves human goals. Today's arrangement of resources might not be perfect, but it is vastly superior to most of the trillions upon trillions of other possible arrangements.

How have we managed to get one of the minuscule number of arrangements that works? The answer is private property—a social institution that encourages mutual accommodation.

Private property eliminates the possibility that resource arrangements will be random, for each resource owner chooses a course of action only if it promises rewards to the owner that exceed the rewards promised by all other available courses.

[The result] is a breathtakingly complex and productive arrangement of countless resources. This arrangement emerged over time (and is still emerging) as the result of billions upon billions of individual, daily, small decisions made by people seeking to better employ their resources and labor in ways that other people find helpful.

Source: Abridged from Donald J. Boudreaux, "Mutual Accommodation," *Ideas on Liberty,* May 2000, pp. 4–5. Reprinted with permission.

SUMMARY

1. The market system—known also as the private-enterprise system or capitalism—is characterized by the private ownership of resources, including capital, and the freedom of individuals to engage in economic activities of their choice to advance their material well-being. Self-interest is the driving force of such an economy, and competition functions as a regulatory or control mechanism.

2. In the market system, markets and prices organize and make effective the many millions of individual decisions that determine what is produced, the methods of production, and the sharing of output.

3. Specialization, use of advanced technology, and the extensive use of capital goods are common features of market systems.

4. Functioning as a medium of exchange, money eliminates the problems of bartering and permits easy trade and greater specialization, both domestically and internationally.

5. Every economy faces Four Fundamental Questions: (a) What goods and services will be produced? (b) How will the goods and services be produced? (c) Who will get the goods and services? (d) How will the system used accommodate changes in consumer tastes, resource supplies, and technology?

6. The market system produces products whose production and sale yield total revenue sufficient to cover all costs, including a normal profit (a cost). It does not produce products that do not yield a normal profit, or more.

7. Economic profit indicates that an industry is prosperous and promotes its expansion. Losses signify that an industry is not prosperous and hasten its contraction.

8. Consumer sovereignty means that both businesses and resource suppliers are subject to the wants of consumers. Through their dollar votes, consumers decide on the composition of output.

9. Competition forces firms to use the lowest-cost and therefore the most economically efficient production techniques.

10. The prices that a household receives for the resources it supplies to the economy determine that household's income. This income determines the household's claim on the economy's output. Those who have income to spend get the products produced in the market system.

11. By communicating changes in consumer tastes to resource suppliers and entrepreneurs, the market system prompts appropriate adjustments in the allocation of the economy's resources. The market system also encourages technological advance and capital accumulation.

12. Competition, the primary mechanism of control in the market economy, promotes a unity of self-interest and social interests; as though directed by an invisible hand, competition harnesses the self-interest motives of businesses and resource suppliers to further the social interest.

TERMS AND CONCEPTS

private property	division of labor	normal profit	guiding function of prices
freedom of enterprise	medium of exchange	economic profit	creative destruction
freedom of choice	barter	expanding industry	"invisible hand"
self interest	money	declining industry	
competition	Four Fundamental Questions	consumer sovereignty	
roundabout production		dollar votes	
specialization	economic costs	derived demand	

STUDY QUESTIONS

1. Explain each of the following statements:
   a. The market system not only accepts self-interest as a fact of human existence; it relies on self-interest to achieve society's economic goals.
   b. The market system provides such a variety of desired goods and services precisely because no single individual or small group is deciding what the economy will produce.
   c. Entrepreneurs and businesses are at the helm of the economy, but their commanders are consumers.

2. Why is private property, and the protection of property rights, so critical to the success of the market system?

3. What are the advantages of "roundabout" production? What is meant by the term "division of labor"? What are the advantages of specialization in the use of human and material resources? Explain: "Exchange is the necessary consequence of specialization."

4. What problem does barter entail? Indicate the economic significance of money as a medium of exchange. What is meant by the statement "We want money only to part with it"?

5. Evaluate and explain the following statements:
   a. The market system is a profit-and-loss system.
   b. Competition is the indispensable disciplinarian of the market economy.
   c. Production methods that are inferior in the engineering sense may be the most efficient methods in the economic sense, once resource prices are considered.

6. In the 1990s thousands of "dot-com" companies emerged with great fanfare to take advantage of the Internet and new information technologies. A few, like Yahoo, eBay, and Amazon, generally thrived and prospered, but many others struggled and eventually failed. Explain these varied outcomes in terms of how the market system answers the question "What goods and services will be produced?"

7. *Key Question* Assume that a business firm finds that its profit will be at a maximum when it produces $40 worth of product A. Suppose also that each of the three techniques shown in the following table will produce the desired output:

| Resource | Price per Unit of Resource | Resource Units Required | | |
		Technique 1	Technique 2	Technique 3
Labor	$3	5	2	3
Land	4	2	4	2
Capital	2	2	4	5
Entrepreneurial ability	2	4	2	4

a. With the resource prices shown, which technique will the firm choose? Why? Will production entail profit or losses? Will the industry expand or contract? When will a new equilibrium output be achieved?

b. Assume now that a new technique, technique 4, is developed. It combines 2 units of labor, 2 of land, 6 of capital, and 3 of entrepreneurial ability. In view of the resource prices in the table, will the firm adopt the new technique? Explain your answer.

c. Suppose that an increase in the labor supply causes the price of labor to fall to $1.50 per unit, all other resource prices remaining unchanged. Which technique will the producer now choose? Explain.

d. "The market system causes the economy to conserve most in the use of resources that are particularly scarce in supply. Resources that are scarcest relative to the demand for them have the highest prices. As a result, producers use these resources as sparingly as is possible." Evaluate this statement. Does your answer to part *c*, above, bear out this contention? Explain.

8. With current technology, suppose the profit-maximizing or loss-minimizing relationship between total revenue and total cost in producing product Z occurs when a firm's output is 400 units. Also, assume that the least-cost combination of resources in producing 400 units of output of Z is 5 units of labor, 7 units of land, 2 units of capital, and 1 unit of entrepreneurial ability, selling at prices of $40, $60, $60, and $20, respectively. If the firm can sell these 400 units at $2 per unit, will the firm continue to produce Z? If this firm's situation is typical for the other firms in the industry, will this be an expanding industry or a declining industry?

9. Suppose the demand for bagels rises dramatically while the demand for breakfast cereal falls. Briefly explain how the competitive market economy will make the needed adjustments to reestablish an efficient allocation of society's scarce resources.

10. *Key Question* Some large hardware stores such as Home Depot boast of carrying as many as 20,000 different products in each store. What motivated the producers of those products—everything from screwdrivers to ladders to water heaters—to make them and offer them for sale? How did the producers decide on the best combinations of resources to use? Who made those resources available, and why? Who decides whether these particular hardware products should continue to get produced and offered for sale?

11. What is meant by the term "creative destruction"? How does the emergence of digital versatile disks (DVDs) relate to this idea?

12. In a single sentence, describe the meaning of the phrase "invisible hand."

13. *(Last Word)* What explains why millions of economic resources tend to get arranged logically and productively rather than haphazardly and unproductively?

14. *Web-Based Question: Diamonds—interested in buying one?* Go to the Internet auction site eBay at www.ebay.com and select the category Jewelry and Watches and then Loose Gemstones. How many loose diamonds are for sale at the moment? Note the wide array of sizes and prices of the diamonds. In what sense is there competition among the sellers in these markets? How does that competition influence prices? In what sense is there competition among buyers? How does that competition influence prices?

15. *Web-Based Question: Barter and the IRS* Bartering occurs when goods or services are exchanged without the exchange of money. For some, barter's popularity is that it enables them to avoid paying taxes to the government. How might such avoidance occur? Does the Internal Revenue Service (IRS), www.irs.ustreas.gov/, treat barter as taxable or nontaxable income? (Type "barter" in the site's search tool.) How is the value of a barter transaction determined? What are some IRS barter examples? What does the IRS require of the members of so-called barter exchanges?

5

The U.S. Economy: Private and Public Sectors

We now move from the general characteristics of the market system to specific information about the U.S. economy, including government's role. For convenience, we divide the economy into two sectors: the *private sector,* which includes *households* and *businesses,* and the *public sector,* or simply *government.*

Households as Income Receivers

The U.S. economy currently has about 109 million households. These households consist of one or more persons occupying a housing unit and are both the ultimate suppliers of all economic resources *and* the major spenders in the economy. We can categorize the income received by households by how it was earned and by how it was divided among households.

The Functional Distribution of Income

The **functional distribution of income** indicates how the nation's earned income is apportioned among wages, rents, interest, and profits, that is, according to the function performed by the income receiver. Wages are paid to labor; rents and interest are paid to owners of property resources; and profits are paid to the owners of corporations and unincorporated businesses.

Figure 5.1 shows the functional distribution of U.S. income earned in 2002. The largest source of income for households is the wages and salaries paid to workers. Notice that the bulk of total U.S. income goes to labor, not to capital. Proprietors' income—the income of doctors, lawyers, small-business owners, farmers, and owners of other unincorporated enterprises—also has a "wage" element. Some of this income is payment for one's own labor, and some of it is profit from one's own business.

The other three types of income are self-evident: Some households own corporate stock and receive dividend incomes on their holdings. Many households also own bonds and savings accounts that yield interest income. And some households receive rental income by providing buildings and natural resources (including land) to businesses and other individuals.

The Personal Distribution of Income

The **personal distribution of income** indicates how the nation's money income is divided among individual households. In Figure 5.2 households are divided into five numerically equal groups or quintiles; the heights of the bars show the percentage of total income received by each group. In 2001 the poorest 20 percent of all households received 3.5 percent of total personal income, and the richest 20 percent received 50.2 percent. Clearly there is considerable inequality in the personal distribution of U.S. income. **(Key Question 2)**

FIGURE 5.1

The functional distribution of U.S. income, 2002.   Nearly three-fourths of national income is received as wages and salaries. Income to property owners—corporate profit, interest, and rents—accounts for about one-fourth of total income.

Source: Bureau of Economic Analysis.

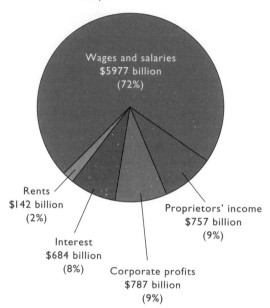

Wages and salaries
$5977 billion
(72%)

Rents
$142 billion
(2%)

Interest
$684 billion
(8%)

Corporate profits
$787 billion
(9%)

Proprietors' income
$757 billion
(9%)

Households as Spenders

How do households dispose of their income? Part of it flows to government as taxes, and the rest is divided between personal savings and personal consumption expenditures. In 2002, households disposed of their total personal income as shown in Figure 5.3.

Personal Taxes

U.S. households paid $1114 billion in personal taxes in 2002, or 13 percent of their $8709 billion of income. Personal taxes, of which the personal income tax is the major component, have risen in relative terms since the Second World War. In 1941, households paid just 3 percent of their total income in personal taxes.

Personal Saving

Economists define "saving" as that part of after-tax income that is not spent; hence, households have just two choices about what to do with their income after taxes—use it to consume, or save it. Saving is the portion of income that is not paid in taxes or used to purchase

consumer goods but instead flows into bank accounts, insurance policies, bonds and stocks, mutual funds, and other financial assets.

U.S. households saved about 3 percent of their income in 2002. Reasons for saving center on *security* and *speculation*. Households save to provide a nest egg for coping with unforeseen contingencies (sickness, accident, and unemployment), for retirement from the workforce, to finance the education of children, or simply for financial security. They may also channel part of their income to purchase stocks, speculating that their investments will increase in value.

The desire to save is not enough in itself, however. You must be able to save, and that depends on the size of your income. If your income is low, you may not be able to save any money at all. If your income is very, very low you may *dissave*—that is, spend more than your after-tax income. You do this by borrowing or by digging into savings you may have accumulated in years when your income was higher.

Both saving and consumption vary directly with income; as households garner more income, they save more

FIGURE 5.2

The personal distribution of income among U.S. households, 2001.   Personal income is unequally distributed in the United States, with the top 20 percent of households receiving about one-half of the total income. In an equal distribution, all five vertical bars would be as high as the horizontal line drawn at 20 percent; then each 20 percent of families would receive 20 percent of the nation's total income.

Source: Bureau of the Census.

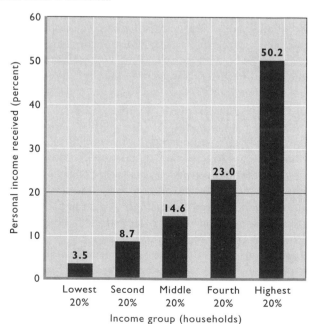

and consume more. In fact, the top 10 percent of income receivers account for most of the personal saving in the U.S. economy.

Personal Consumption Expenditures

As Figure 5.3 shows, more than four-fifths of the total income of households flows back into the business sector as personal consumption expenditures—money spent on consumer goods.

Figure 5.4 shows how consumers divide their expenditures among durable goods, nondurable goods, and services. Twelve percent of consumer expenditures are on **durable goods**—products that have expected lives of 3 years or more. Such goods include automobiles, furniture, and personal computers. Another 29 percent of consumer expenditures are on **nondurable goods**—products that have lives of less than 3 years. Included are such goods as food, clothing, and gasoline. About 59 percent of consumer expenditures are on **services**—the work done for consumers by lawyers, barbers, doctors, lodging personnel, and so on. This high percentage is the reason that the United States is often referred to as a *service-oriented economy.*

FIGURE 5.3

The disposition of household income, 2002.   Households apportion their income among taxes, saving, and consumption, with most going to consumption. (The way income is defined in this figure differs slightly from that used in Figure 5.1, accounting for the quantitative discrepancies between the "total income" amounts in the two figures.)
Source: Bureau of Economic Analysis.

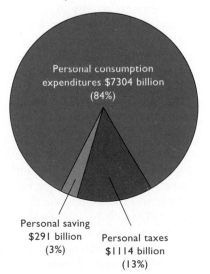

Personal consumption expenditures $7304 billion (84%)

Personal saving $291 billion (3%)

Personal taxes $1114 billion (13%)

FIGURE 5.4

The composition of consumer expenditures, 2002.   Consumers divide their spending among durable goods (goods that have expected lives of 3 years or more), nondurable goods, and services. About 59 percent of consumer spending is for services.
Source: Bureau of Economic Analysis.

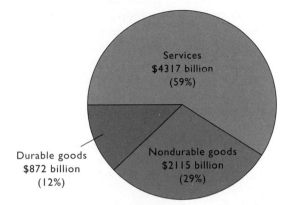

Services $4317 billion (59%)

Durable goods $872 billion (12%)

Nondurable goods $2115 billion (29%)

QUICK REVIEW 5.1

- The functional distribution of income indicates how income is apportioned among wages, rents, interest, and profits; the personal distribution of income indicates how income is divided among families.
- Wages and salaries are the major component of the functional distribution of income. The personal distribution of income reveals considerable inequality.
- More than 80 percent of household income is consumed; the rest is saved or paid in taxes.
- Consumer spending is directed to durable goods, nondurable goods, and services, with nearly 60 percent going to services.

The Business Population

Businesses constitute the second major part of the private sector. It will be useful to distinguish among a plant, a firm, and an industry:

- A **plant** is a physical establishment—a factory, farm, mine, store, or warehouse—that performs one or more functions in fabricating and distributing goods and services.
- A **firm** is a business organization that owns and operates plants. Some firms operate only one plant, but many own and operate several.

- An **industry** is a group of firms that produce the same, or similar, products.

The organizational structures of firms are often complex and varied. *Multiplant firms* may be organized horizontally, with several plants performing much the same function. Examples are the multiple bottling plants of Coca-Cola and the many individual Wal-Mart stores. Firms also may be *vertically integrated*, meaning they own plants that perform different functions in the various stages of the production process. For example, oil companies such as Shell own oil fields, refineries, and retail gasoline stations. Some firms are *conglomerates*, so named because they have plants that produce products in several industries. For example, Pfizer makes not only prescription medicines (Lipitor, Viagra) but also chewing gum (Trident, Dentyne), razors (Schick), cough drops (Halls), breath mints (Clorets, Certs), and antacids (Rolaids).

Legal Forms of Businesses

The business population is extremely diverse, ranging from giant corporations such as General Motors, with 2002 sales of $187 billion and hundreds of thousands of employees, to neighborhood specialty shops with one or two employees and sales of only $200 to $300 per day. There are three major legal forms of businesses:

- A **sole proprietorship** is a business owned and operated by one person. Usually, the proprietor (the owner) personally supervises its operation.
- The **partnership** form of business organization is a natural outgrowth of the sole proprietorship. In a partnership, two or more individuals (the partners) agree to own and operate a business together. Usually they pool their financial resources and business skills. Consequently, they share the risks and the profits or losses.
- A **corporation** is a legal creation that can acquire resources, own assets, produce and sell products, incur debts, extend credit, sue and be sued, and perform the functions of any other type of enterprise. A corporation is distinct and separate from the individual stockholders who own it. Hired managers run most corporations.

Figure 5.5a shows how the business population is distributed among the three major legal forms. About 72 percent of firms are sole proprietorships, whereas only 20 percent are corporations. But as Figure 5.5b indicates, corporations account for 87 percent of all sales (output).

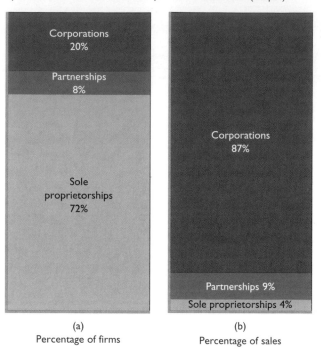

FIGURE 5.5

The business population and shares of domestic output. (a) Sole proprietorships dominate the business population numerically, but (b) corporations account for about 87 percent of total sales (output).

Corporations 20%

Partnerships 8%

Sole proprietorships 72%

Corporations 87%

Partnerships 9%

Sole proprietorships 4%

(a) Percentage of firms

(b) Percentage of sales

Advantages and Disadvantages

There are advantages and disadvantages to each form of business enterprise.

Sole Proprietorship Sole proprietorships are very numerous because they are so easy to set up and organize; there is virtually no complex paper work or legal expense. The proprietor is one's own boss and has substantial freedom of action. Because the proprietor's profit income depends on the enterprise's success, there is strong incentive to manage the business efficiently.

But there are also several disadvantages of sole proprietorships. With rare exceptions, the financial resources of a sole proprietorship are insufficient to permit the firm to grow into a large enterprise. Finances are usually limited to what the proprietor has in the bank and what he or she can borrow. Since proprietorships often fail, commercial banks are not eager to extend them credit.

Also, being totally in charge of an enterprise necessitates that the proprietor carry out all management functions. A proprietor must make decisions on buying, selling, and the hiring and training of personnel, as well as decisions on producing, advertising, and distributing the firm's product. In short, the potential benefits of specialization in business management are not available to the typical small-scale proprietorship.

Finally, and most important, the proprietor is subject to *unlimited liability*. Individuals in business for themselves risk not only the assets of the firm but their personal assets as well. If the assets of an unsuccessful sole proprietorship are insufficient to pay the firm's bills, creditors can file claims against the proprietor's personal property.

Partnership Like the sole proprietorship, a partnership is easy to organize. Although the partners usually sign a written agreement, there is not much paperwork or legal expense. Also, greater specialization in management is possible because there are two or more participants. And because there is more than one owner, the financial resources of a partnership are likely to be greater than the resources of a sole proprietorship. Consequently, commercial banks regard partnerships as somewhat better risks than sole proprietorships.

But partnerships have some of the shortcomings of the proprietorship as well as some of their own. Whenever several people participate in management, the divided authority may lead to inconsistent policies or to inaction when action is required. Worse, the partners may disagree on basic policy. And although the finances of partnerships are generally superior to those of sole proprietorships, partnerships are still severely limited. The combined financial resources of three or four partners may not be enough to ensure the growth of a successful enterprise.

The continuity of a partnership is precarious. Generally, when one partner dies or withdraws, the partnership must be dissolved and reorganized, with inevitable disruption of its operations. Finally, unlimited liability plagues a partnership, just as it does a proprietorship. Each partner is liable for all business debts incurred, not only as a result of his or her own performance but also as a result of the performance of any other partner. A wealthy partner risks his or her wealth on the prudence of less affluent partners.

Corporation The advantages of the corporate form of business enterprise have catapulted it into a dominant position in the United States. Although corporations are relatively small in number, many of them are large in size and in scale of operations. The corporation is by far the most effective form of business organization for raising financial capital (money). The corporation employs unique methods of finance—the selling of stocks and bonds—that enable it to pool the financial resources of large numbers of people. **Stocks** are shares of ownership of a corporation, whereas **bonds** are promises to repay a loan, usually at a set rate of interest. (See the Last Word.)

Financing via sales of stocks and bonds also provides advantages to those who purchase these *securities*. Such financing makes it possible for a household to own a part of the business and to share the expected monetary rewards without actively managing the firm. Moreover, an individual investor can spread risks by buying the securities of several corporations. And it is usually easy for holders of corporate securities to sell their holdings. Organized stock exchanges simplify the transfer of securities from sellers to buyers. This "ease of sale" increases the willingness of savers to make financial investments in corporate securities. Also, corporations have easier access to bank credit than do other types of business organizations. Corporations are better risks and are more likely to become profitable clients of banks.

Corporations have the distinct advantage of **limited liability.** The owners (stockholders) of a corporation risk only what they paid for their stock. Their personal assets are not at stake if the corporation defaults on its debts. Creditors can sue the corporation as a legal person but cannot sue the owners of the corporation as individuals.

Because of their ability to attract financial capital, successful corporations can easily expand the scope of their operations and realize the benefits of expansion. For example, they can take advantage of mass-production technologies and division of labor. A corporation can hire specialists in production, accounting, and marketing functions and thus improve efficiency.

As a legal entity, the corporation has a life independent of its owners and its officers. Legally, at least, corporations are immortal. The transfer of corporate ownership through inheritance or the sale of stock does not disrupt the continuity of the corporation. Corporations have permanence that is conducive to long-range planning and growth.

The corporation's advantages are of tremendous significance and typically override any associated disadvantages. Yet there are certain drawbacks to the corporate form. Some red tape and legal expense are involved in obtaining a corporate charter. And from the social point of view, the corporate form of enterprise lends itself to certain abuses. Because the corporation is a legal entity, unscrupulous business owners can sometimes avoid personal responsibility for questionable business activities by adopting the corporate form of enterprise.

A disadvantage to the owners of corporations is the **double taxation** of some corporate income. Corporate profit that is shared among stockholders as *dividends* is taxed twice—once as corporate profit and again as stockholders' personal income.

Hybrid Structures

A number of states have passed legislation authorizing "hybrid" business structures that extend some of the advantages of corporations to firms with one or relatively few owners. Two such structures are the *limited-liability company (LLC)* and the *S corporation.*

The LLC is like an ordinary partnership for tax purposes but resembles a corporation in matters of liability. Like a partnership, an LLC distributes all profit directly to its owners and investors. But like a corporation, an LLC shields the personal assets of owners from liability claims. LLCs have a limited life, typically 30 or 40 years.

The S corporation is a corporation with 75 or fewer shareholders. Because the profit from the corporation passes directly to the owners as if the firm were a sole proprietorship or a partnership, the owners avoid the double taxation on distributed profit. They also enjoy the benefit of limited liability.

The Principal-Agent Problem

Many U.S. corporations are extremely large. In 2002, 86 U.S. corporations had annual sales of more than $20 billion, and 187 firms had sales of more than $10 billion. Wal-Mart alone sold $247 billion of goods in 2002. Only 18 nations in the world had a total annual output that exceeded Wal-Mart's annual sales. (Global Perspective 5.1 lists the world's 10 largest corporations in terms of dollar revenue in 2002.)

Large size creates a potential problem. In sole proprietorships and partnerships, the owners of the real and financial assets of the firm enjoy direct control of those assets. But ownership of large corporations is spread over tens or hundreds of thousands of stockholders. The owners of a corporation usually do not manage it—they hire others to do so.

That practice can create a **principal-agent problem.** The *principals* are the stockholders who own the corporation and who hire executives as their *agents* to run the business on their behalf. But the interests of these managers (the agents) and the wishes of the owners (the principals) do not always coincide. The owners typically want maximum company profit and stock price. The agents, however, may want the power, prestige, and pay that usually accompany control over a large enterprise, independent of its profitability and stock price.

So a conflict of interest may develop. For example, executives may build expensive office buildings, enjoy excessive perks such as corporate jets, and pay too much

GLOBAL PERSPECTIVE 5.1

The World's 10 Largest Corporations

Five of the world's ten largest corporations, based on dollar revenue in 2002, were headquartered in the United States.

Wal-Mart (USA) $247 billion
General Motors (USA) $187 billion
Exxon Mobil (USA) $182 billion
Shell (Britain/Netherlands) $179 billion
BP (Britain) $179 billion
Ford Motor (USA) $164 billion
DaimlerChrysler (Germany) $141 billion
Toyota (Japan) $132 billion
General Electric (USA) $132 billion
Mitsubishi (Japan) $109 billion

Source: Fortune, www.fortune.com.

**5.1
Principal-agent problem**

to acquire other corporations. Consequently, the firm will have bloated costs. Profits and stock prices will not be maximized for the owners.

In the 1990s many corporations addressed the principal-agent problem by providing a substantial part of executive pay as shares of the firm's stock. The idea was to align the interest of the executives more closely with those of the broader corporate owners. By pursuing high profits and share prices, the executives would enhance their own wealth as well as that of all the stockholders.

This "solution" to the principal-agent problem had an unexpected side effect. It prompted a few executives to inflate their firm's share prices by hiding costs, overstating revenues, engaging in deceptive transactions, and, in general, exaggerating profits. These executives then sold large quantities of their inflated stock, making quick personal fortunes.

When the stock market bubble of the late 1990s burst, the business manipulations and fraudulent accounting were exposed. Several large American firms collapsed, among them Enron and WorldCom. Stockholders of those firms were left holding nearly worthless stock. In 2002 Congress strengthened the laws and penalties against corporate misconduct, but it is clear that the principal-agent problem is difficult to solve. **(Key Question 4)**

The Public Sector: Government's Role

The economic activities of the *public sector*—Federal, state, and local government—are extensive. We begin by discussing the economic functions of governments. What is government's role in the economy?

Providing the Legal Structure

Government provides the legal framework and the services needed for a market economy to operate effectively. The legal framework sets the legal status of business enterprises, ensures the rights of private ownership, and allows the making and enforcement of contracts. Government also establishes the legal "rules of the game" that control relationships among businesses, resource suppliers, and consumers. Discrete units of government referee economic relationships, seek out foul play, and impose penalties.

Government intervention is presumed to improve the allocation of resources. By supplying a medium of exchange, ensuring product quality, defining ownership rights, and enforcing contracts, the government increases the volume and safety of exchange. This widens the market and fosters greater specialization in the use of property and human resources. Such specialization promotes a more efficient allocation of resources.

Like the optimal amount of any "good," the optimal amount of regulation is that at which the marginal benefit and marginal cost are equal. Thus, there can be either too little regulation (MB exceeds MC) or too much regulation (MB is less than MC). The task is deciding on the right amount.

Maintaining Competition

Competition is the basic regulatory mechanism in the market system. It is the force that subjects producers and resource suppliers to the dictates of consumer sovereignty. With competition, buyers are the boss, the market is their agent, and businesses are their servants.

It is a different story where a single seller—a **monopoly**—controls an industry. By controlling supply, a monopolist can charge a higher-than-competitive price. Producer sovereignty then supplants consumer sovereignty. In the United States, government has attempted to control monopoly through *regulation* and through *antitrust*.

A few industries are natural monopolies—industries in which technology is such that only a single seller can achieve the lowest possible costs. In some cases government has allowed these monopolies to exist but has also created public commissions to regulate their prices and set their service standards. Examples of *regulated monopolies* are some firms that provide local electricity, telephone, and transportation services.

In nearly all markets, however, efficient production can best be attained with a high degree of competition. The Federal government has therefore enacted a series of antitrust (antimonopoly) laws, beginning with the Sherman Act of 1890, to prohibit certain monopoly abuses and, if necessary, break monopolists up into competing firms. Under these laws, for example, in 2000 Microsoft was found guilty of monopolizing the market for operating systems for personal computers. Rather than breaking up Microsoft, however, the government imposed a series of prohibitions and requirements that collectively limited Microsoft's ability to engage in anticompetitive actions.

Redistributing Income

The market system is impersonal and may distribute income more inequitably than society desires. It yields very large incomes to those whose labor, by virtue of inherent ability and acquired education and skills, command high wages. Similarly, those who, through hard work or inheritance, possess valuable capital and land, receive large property incomes.

But many other members of society have less productive ability, have received only modest amounts of education and training, and have accumulated or inherited no property resources. Moreover, some of the aged, the physically and mentally disabled, and the poorly educated earn small incomes or, like the unemployed, no income at all. Thus society chooses to redistribute a part of total income through a variety of government policies and programs. They are:

- **Transfer payments** *Transfer payments*, for example, in the form of welfare checks and food stamps, provide relief to the destitute, the dependent, the disabled, and older citizens; unemployment compensation payments provide aid to the unemployed.

- **Market intervention** Government also alters the distribution of income through *market intervention*, that is, by acting to modify the prices that are or would be established by market forces. Providing farmers with above-market prices for their output and requiring that firms pay minimum wages are illustrations of government interventions designed to raise the income of specific groups.

- **Taxation** Since the 1930s, government has used the personal income tax to take a larger proportion of the income of the rich than of the poor, thus narrowing the after-tax income difference between high-income and low-income earners.

The *extent* to which government should redistribute income is subject to lively debate. Redistribution involves both benefits and costs. The alleged benefits are greater "fairness," or "economic justice"; the alleged costs are reduced incentives to work, save, invest, and produce, and therefore a loss of total output and income.

Reallocating Resources

Market failure occurs when the competitive market system (1) produces the "wrong" amounts of certain goods and services or (2) fails to allocate any resources whatsoever to the production of certain goods and services whose output is economically justified. The first type of failure results from what economists call *spillovers*, and the second type involves *public goods*. Both kinds of market failure can be corrected by government action.

Spillovers or Externalities

When we say that competitive markets automatically bring about the efficient use of resources, we assume that all the benefits and costs for each product are fully reflected in the market demand and supply curves. That is not always the case. In some markets certain benefits or costs may escape the buyer or seller.

A spillover occurs when some of the costs or the benefits of a good are passed on to or "spill over to" someone other than the immediate buyer or seller. Spillovers

5.2 Externalities 🔍 are also called *externalities*, because they are benefits or costs that accrue to some third party that is external to the market transaction.

Spillover Costs Production or consumption costs inflicted on a third party without compensation are called **spillover costs.** Environmental pollution is an example. When a chemical manufacturer or a meatpacking plant dumps its wastes into a lake or river, swimmers, fishers, and boaters—and perhaps those who drink the water—suffer spillover costs. When a petroleum refinery pollutes the air with smoke or a paper mill creates obnoxious odors, the community experiences spillover costs for which it is not compensated.

What are the economic effects? Recall that costs determine the position of the firm's supply curve. When a firm avoids some costs by polluting, its supply curve lies farther to the right than it does when the firm bears the full costs of production. As a result, the price of the product is too low and the output of the product is too large to achieve allocative efficiency. A market failure occurs in the form of an overallocation of resources to the production of the good.

Correcting for Spillover Costs Government can do two things to correct the overallocation of resources. Both solutions are designed to internalize external costs, that is, to make the offending firm pay the costs rather than shift them to others:

- **Legislation** In cases of air and water pollution, the most direct action is legislation prohibiting or limiting the pollution. Such legislation forces potential polluters to pay for the proper disposal of industrial wastes—here, by installing smoke-abatement equipment or water-purification facilities. The idea is to force potential offenders, under the threat of legal action, to bear *all* the costs associated with production.

- **Specific taxes** A less direct action is based on the fact that taxes are a cost and therefore a determinant of a firm's supply curve. Government might levy a *specific tax*—that is, a tax confined to a particular product—on each unit of the polluting firm's output. The amount of this tax would roughly equal the estimated amount of the spillover cost arising from the production of each unit of output. Through this tax, government would pass back to the offending firm a cost equivalent to the spillover cost the firm is avoiding. This would shift the firm's supply curve to the left, reducing equilibrium output and eliminating the overallocation of resources.

Spillover Benefits Sometimes spillovers appear as benefits. The production or consumption of certain goods and services may confer spillover or external benefits on third parties or on the community at large without compensating payment. Immunization against measles and polio results in direct benefits to the immediate consumer of those vaccines. But it also results in widespread substantial spillover benefits to the entire community.

Education is another example of **spillover benefits.** Education benefits individual consumers: Better-educated people generally achieve higher incomes than less well educated people. But education also provides benefits to society, in the form of a more versatile and more productive labor force, on the one hand, and smaller outlays for crime prevention, law enforcement, and welfare programs, on the other.

Spillover benefits mean that the market demand curve, which reflects only private benefits, understates total benefits. The demand curve for the product lies farther to the left than it would if the market took all benefits into account. As a result, a smaller amount of the product will be produced, or, alternatively, there will be an *underallocation* of resources to the product—again a market failure.

Correcting for Spillover Benefits How might the underallocation of resources associated with spillover benefits be corrected? The answer is either to subsidize consumers (to increase demand), to subsidize producers (to increase supply), or, in the extreme, to have government produce the product:

- *Subsidize consumers* To correct the underallocation of resources to higher education, the U.S. government provides low-interest loans to students so that they can afford more education. Those loans increase the demand for higher education.
- *Subsidize suppliers* In some cases government finds it more convenient and administratively simpler to correct an underallocation by subsidizing suppliers. For example, in higher education, state governments provide substantial portions of the budgets of public colleges and universities. Such subsidies lower the costs of producing higher education and increase its supply. Publicly subsidized immunization programs, hospitals, and medical research are other examples.
- *Provide goods via government* A third policy option may be appropriate where spillover benefits are extremely large: Government may finance or, in the extreme, own and operate the industry that is involved.

Examples are the U.S. Postal Service and Federal aircraft control systems.

Public Goods and Services Certain goods called *private goods* are produced through the competitive market system. Examples are the wide variety of items sold in stores. Private goods have two characteristics—*rivalry* and *excludability*. "Rivalry" means that when one person buys and consumes a product, it is not available for purchase and consumption by another person. What Joan gets, Jane cannot have. *Excludability* means that buyers who are willing and able to pay the market price for the product obtain its benefits, but those unable or unwilling to pay that price do not. This characteristic enables profitable production by a private firm.

Certain other goods and services called **public goods** have the opposite characteristics—*nonrivalry* and *nonexcludability*. Everyone can simultaneously obtain the benefit from a public good such as a global positioning system, national defense, street lighting, and environmental protection. One person's benefit does not reduce the benefit available to others. More important, there is no effective way of excluding individuals from the benefit of the good once it comes into existence. The inability to exclude creates a **free-rider problem,** in which people can receive benefits from a public good without contributing to its costs. The free-rider problem makes the good unprofitable to provide by a private firm.

An example of a public good is the war on terrorism (which includes homeland defense and recent military actions abroad). This public good is thought to be economically justified by the majority of Americans because the benefits are perceived as exceeding the costs. Once the war efforts are undertaken, however, the benefits accrue to all Americans (nonrivalry). And, there is no practical way to exclude any American from receiving those benefits (nonexcluability).

No private firm will undertake the war on terrorism because the benefits cannot be profitably sold (due to the free-rider problem). So here we have a service that yields substantial benefits but to which the market system will not allocate sufficient resources. Like national defense in general, the pursuit of the war on terrorism is a public good. Society signals its desire for such goods by voting for particular political candidates who support their provision. Because of the free-rider problem, the public sector provides these goods and finances them through compulsory charges in the form of taxes.

Quasi-Public Goods Government provides many goods that fit the economist's definition of a public

---

Street Entertainers

© David Young-Wolff/
PhotoEdit

Street entertainers are often found in tourist areas of major cities. Some entertainers are highly creative and talented; others "need more practice." But, regardless of talent level, these entertainers illuminate the concepts of free riders and public goods.

Most street entertainers have a hard time earning a living from their activities (unless event organizers pay them) because they have no way of excluding nonpayers from the benefits of their entertainment. They essentially are providing public, not private, goods and must rely on voluntary payments.

The result is a significant free-rider problem. Only a few in the audience put money in the container or instrument case, and many who do so contribute only token amounts. The rest are free riders who obtain the benefits of the street entertainment and retain their money for purchases that *they* initiate.

Street entertainers are acutely aware of the free-rider problem, and some have found creative ways to lessen it. For example, some entertainers involve the audience directly in the act. This usually creates a greater sense of audience willingness (or obligation) to contribute money at the end of the performance.

"Pay for performance" is another creative approach to lessening the free-rider problem. A good example is the street entertainer painted up to look like a statue. When people drop coins into the container, the "statue" makes a slight movement. The greater the contributions, the greater the movement. But these human "statues" still face a free-rider problem: Nonpayers also get to enjoy the acts.

Finally, because talented street entertainers create a festive street environment, cities or retailers sometimes hire them to perform. The "free entertainment" attracts crowds of shoppers, who buy goods from nearby retailers. In these instances the cities or retailers use tax revenue or commercial funds to pay the entertainers, in the former case validating them as public goods.

---

good. However, it also provides other goods and services that could be produced and delivered in such a way that exclusion would be possible. Such goods, called **quasi-public goods,** include education, streets and highways, police and fire protection, libraries and museums, preventive medicine, and sewage disposal. They could all be priced and provided by private firms through the market system. But, as we noted earlier, because they all have substantial spillover benefits, they would be underproduced by the market system. Therefore, government often provides them to avoid the underallocation of resources that would otherwise occur.

The Reallocation Process How are resources reallocated from the production of private goods to the production of public and quasi-public goods? If the resources of the economy are fully employed, government must free up resources from the production of private goods and make them available for producing public and quasi-public goods. It does so by reducing private demand for them. And it does that by levying taxes on households and businesses, taking some of their income out of the circular flow. With lower incomes and hence less purchasing power, households and businesses must curtail their consumption and investment spending. As a result, the private demand for goods and services declines, as does the private demand for resources. So by diverting purchasing power from private spenders to government, taxes remove resources from private use.

Government then spends the tax proceeds to provide public and quasi-public goods and services. Taxation releases resources from the production of private consumer goods (food, clothing, television sets) and private investment goods (printing presses, boxcars, warehouses). Government shifts those resources to the production of public and quasi-public goods (post offices, submarines, parks), changing the composition of the economy's total output. **(Key Questions 9 and 10)**

Promoting Stability

An economy's level of output depends on its level of total spending relative to its production capacity. When the level of total spending matches the economy's production capacity, human and property resources are fully employed and prices in general are stable. But sometimes total spending is either inadequate or excessive and the result is either unemployment or inflation. Government promotes stability by addressing these two problems:

- *Unemployment* When private sector spending is too low, government may try to augment it so that total spending—private plus public—is sufficient to achieve full employment. It does this by increasing government spending or by lowering taxes to stimulate private spending. Also, the nation's central bank (Federal Reserve in the United States) often takes actions to lower interest rates, thereby stimulating private borrowing and spending.

- *Inflation* Inflation is a general increase in the level of prices. Prices of goods and services rise when spenders try to buy more than the economy's capacity to produce. When total spending is excessive and becomes inflationary, government may try to reduce total spending by cutting its own expenditures or by raising taxes to curtail private spending. The nation's central bank may also take actions to increase interest rates to reduce private borrowing and spending.

Government's Role: A Qualification

Government does not have an easy task in performing the aforementioned economic functions. In a democracy, government undertakes its economic role in the context of politics. To serve the public, politicians need to get elected. To stay elected, officials (presidents, senators, representatives, mayors, council members, school board members) need to satisfy their particular constituencies. At best the political realities complicate government's role in the economy; at worst, they produce undesirable economic outcomes.

In the political context, overregulation can occur in some cases; underregulation, in others. Income can be redistributed to such an extent that incentives to work, save, and invest suffer. Some public goods and quasi-public goods can be produced not because their benefits exceed their costs but because their benefits accrue to firms located in states served by powerful elected officials. Inefficiency can easily creep into government activities because of the lack of a profit incentive to hold down costs. Policies to correct spillover costs can be politically blocked by the very parties that are producing the spillovers. In short, the economic role of government, although critical to a well-functioning economy, is not always perfectly carried out.

QUICK REVIEW 5.3

- Government enhances the operation of the market system by providing an appropriate legal foundation and promoting competition.
- Transfer payments, direct market intervention, and taxation are among the ways in which government can lessen income inequality.
- Government can correct for the overallocation of resources associated with spillover costs through legislation or taxes; it can offset the underallocation of resources associated with spillover benefits by granting government subsidies.
- Government provides certain public goods for which there is nonrivalry in consumption and nonexcludability of benefits; government also provides many quasi-public goods because of their large spillover benefits.
- To try to stabilize the economy, the government can adjust its spending and tax revenues and the nation's central bank can take monetary actions that lower or increase interest rates.

The Circular Flow Revisited

In Figure 5.6 we integrate government into the circular flow model first shown in Figure 2.6. Here flows (1) through (4) are the same as the corresponding flows in that figure. Flows (1) and (2) show business expenditures for the resources provided by households. These expenditures are costs to businesses but represent wage, rent, interest, and profit income to households. Flows (3) and (4) show household expenditures for the goods and services produced by businesses.

Now consider what happens when we add government. Flows (5) through (8) illustrate that government makes purchases in both product and resource markets. Flows (5) and (6) represent government purchases of such products as paper, computers, and military hardware from private businesses. Flows (7) and (8) represent government purchases of resources. The Federal government employs and pays salaries to members of Congress, the armed forces, Justice Department lawyers, meat inspectors, and so on. State and local governments hire and pay teachers, bus drivers, police, and firefighters. The Federal government might also lease or purchase land to expand a military base, and a city might buy land on which to build a new elementary school.

Government then provides public goods and services to both households and businesses, as shown by flows (9) and (10). To finance those public goods and services, businesses and households are required to pay taxes, as shown by flows (11) and (12). These flows are labeled as *net* taxes to indicate that they also include "taxes in reverse" in the form of transfer payments to households and subsidies to businesses. Thus, flow (11) entails various subsidies to farmers, shipbuilders, and airlines as well as income, sales, and excise taxes paid by businesses to government. Most subsidies to business are "concealed" in the form of low-interest loans, loan guarantees, tax concessions, or public facilities provided at prices below their cost. Similarly, flow (12) includes both taxes (personal income taxes, payroll taxes) collected by government directly from households and transfer payments such as welfare payments and Social Security benefits paid by government.

Government Finance

How large is the U.S. public sector? What are the main expenditure categories of Federal, state, and local governments? How are these expenditures financed?

FIGURE 5.6

The circular flow and the public sector. Government buys products from the product market and employs resources from the resource market to provide public goods and services to households and businesses. Government finances its expenditures through the net tax revenues (taxes minus transfer payments) it receives from households and businesses.

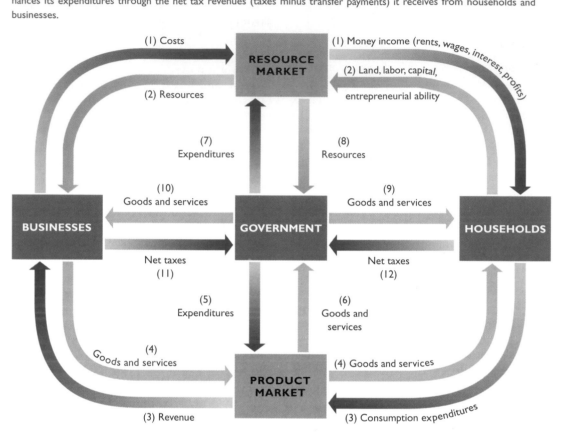

Government Purchases and Transfers

We can get an idea of the size of government's economic role by examining government purchases of goods and services and government transfer payments. There is a significant difference between these two kinds of outlays:

- **Government purchases** are *exhaustive;* the products purchased directly absorb (require the use of) resources and are part of the domestic output. For example, the purchase of a missile absorbs the labor of physicists and engineers along with steel, explosives, and a host of other inputs.

- **Transfer payments** are *nonexhaustive;* they do not directly absorb resources or create output. Social Security benefits, welfare payments, veterans' benefits, and unemployment compensation are examples of transfer payments. Their key characteristic is that recipients make no current contribution to domestic output in return for them.

Federal, state, and local governments spent $3126 billion in 2002. Of that total, government purchases were $1859 billion and government transfers were $1267 billion. Figure 5.7 shows these amounts as percentages of U.S. domestic output for 2002 and compares them to percentages for 1960. Government purchases have declined from about 22 to 18 percent of output since 1960. But transfer payments have more than doubled as a percentage of output—from 5 percent in 1960 to 12 percent in 2002. Relative to U.S. output, total government spending is thus higher today than it was 42 years ago. This means that the tax revenues required to finance government expenditures are also higher. Today, government spending and the tax revenues needed to finance it are about 30 percent of U.S. output.

In 2003 the so-called Tax Freedom Day in the United States was April 18. On that day the average worker had earned enough (from the start of the year) to pay his or her share of the taxes required to finance government

FIGURE 5.7

Government purchases, transfers, and total spending as percentages of U.S. output, 1960 and 2002. Government purchases have declined as a percentage of U.S. output since 1960. Transfer payments, however, have increased, so total government spending (purchases plus transfers) is now 30 percent of U.S. output.

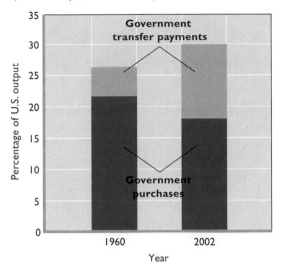

Year

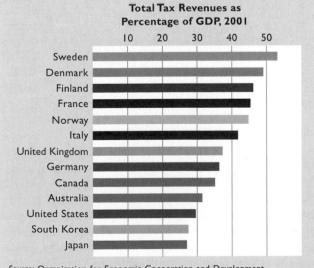

GLOBAL PERSPECTIVE 5.2

Total Tax Revenue as a Percentage of Total Output, Selected Nations

The percentage of tax revenues to total output is one measure of a country's tax burden. Among the world's industrialized nations, Japan, South Korea, the United States, and Australia have the lowest tax burdens.

Source: Organization for Economic Cooperation and Development, www.oecd.org.

spending for the year. Tax Freedom Day arrives even later in several other countries, as implied in Global Perspective 5.2.

Federal Finance

Now let's look separately at each of the Federal, state, and local units of government in the United States and compare their expenditures and taxes. Figure 5.8 tells the story for the Federal government.

Federal Expenditures

Four areas of Federal spending stand out: (1) pensions and income security, (2) national defense, (3) health, and (4) interest on the public debt. The *pensions and income security* category includes the many income-maintenance programs for the aged, persons with disabilities or handicaps, the unemployed, the retired, and families with no breadwinner. *National defense* accounts for about 17 percent of the Federal budget, underscoring the high cost of military preparedness. *Health* reflects the cost of government health programs for the retired and poor. *Interest on the public debt* is high because the public debt itself is large.

Federal Tax Revenues

The revenue side of Figure 5.8 shows that the personal income tax, payroll taxes, and the corporate income tax are the basic revenue sources, accounting respectively for 46, 38, and 8 cents of each dollar collected.

Personal Income Tax The **personal income tax** is the kingpin of the Federal tax system and merits special comment. This tax is levied on *taxable income*, that is, on the incomes of households and unincorporated businesses after certain exemptions ($3000 for each household member) and deductions (business expenses, charitable contributions, home mortgage interest payments, certain state and local taxes) are taken into account.

The Federal personal income tax is a *progressive tax*, meaning that people with higher incomes pay a larger percentage of their incomes as taxes than do people with lower incomes. The progressivity is achieved by applying higher tax rates to successive layers or brackets of income.

Columns 1 and 2 in Table 5.1 show the mechanics of the income tax for a married couple filing a joint return in 2003. Note that a 10 percent tax rate applies to all taxable income up to $14,000 and a 15 percent rate applies

FIGURE 5.8

Federal expenditures and tax revenues, 2002.   Federal expenditures are dominated by spending for pensions and income security, health, and national defense. A full 84 percent of Federal tax revenue is derived from just two sources: the personal income tax and payroll taxes. The $158 billion difference between expenditures and revenues reflects a budget deficit.

Source: U.S. Office of Management and Budget.

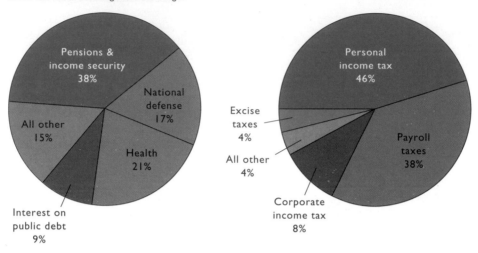

Total expenditures:
$2011 billion

Total tax revenues:
$1853 billion

to additional income up to $56,800. The rates on additional layers of income then go up to 25, 28, 33, and 35 percent.

The tax rates shown in column 2 in Table 5.1 are marginal tax rates. A **marginal tax rate** is the rate at which the tax is paid on each *additional* unit of taxable income. Thus, if a couple's taxable income is $60,000, they will pay the marginal rate of 10 percent on each dollar

TABLE 5.1

Federal Personal Income Tax Rates, 2003*

(1) Total Taxable Income	(2) Marginal Tax Rate, %	(3) Total Tax on Highest Income in Bracket	(4) Average Tax Rate on Highest Income in Bracket, % (3) ÷ (1)
$1–$14,000	10.0	$ 1,400.00	10.0
$14,001–$56,800	15.0	7,820.00	13.8
$56,801–$114,650	25.0	22,282.50	19.4
$114,651–$174,700	28.0	39,096.50	22.4
$174,701–$311,950	33.0	84,389.00	27.1
Over $311,950	35.0		

*For a married couple filing a joint return.

from $1 to $14,000, 15 percent on each dollar from $14,001 to $56,800, and 25 percent on each dollar from $56,801 to $60,000. You should confirm that their total income tax is $8,620.

The marginal tax rates in column 2 overstate the personal income tax bite because the rising rates in that column apply only to the income within each successive tax bracket. To get a better idea of the tax burden, we must consider average tax rates. The **average tax rate** is the total tax paid divided by total taxable income. The couple in our previous example is in the 25 percent tax bracket because they pay a top marginal tax rate of 25 percent on the highest dollar of their income. But their *average* tax rate is 14.4 percent (= $8,620/$60,000).

A tax whose average rate rises as income increases is a progressive tax. Such a tax claims both a larger absolute amount and a larger proportion of income as income rises. Thus we can say that the Federal personal income tax is progressive. **(Key Question 15)**

Payroll Taxes   Social Security contributions are **payroll taxes**—taxes based on wages and salaries—used to finance two compulsory Federal programs for retired workers: Social Security (an income-enhancement program) and Medicare (which pays for medical services). Employers and employees pay these taxes equally.

Improvements in, and extensions of, the Social Security programs, plus growth of the labor force, have resulted in significant increases in these payroll taxes in recent years. In 2003, employees and employers each paid 7.65 percent on the first $87,000 of an employee's annual earnings and 1.45 percent on all additional earnings.

Corporate Income Tax The Federal government also taxes corporate income. The **corporate income tax** is levied on a corporation's profit—the difference between its total revenue and its total expenses. For almost all corporations, the tax rate is 35 percent.

Excise Taxes Taxes on commodities or on purchases take the form of **sales and excise taxes.** The difference between the two is mainly one of coverage. Sales taxes fall on a wide range of products, whereas excises are levied individually on a small, select list of commodities. As Figure 5.8 suggests, the Federal government collects excise taxes (on the sale of such commodities as alcoholic beverages, tobacco, and gasoline) but does not levy a general sales tax; sales taxes are the primary revenue source of most state governments.

State and Local Finance

State and local governments have different mixes of revenues and expenditures than the Federal government has.

State Finances

The primary source of tax revenue for state governments is sales and excise taxes, which account for about 47 percent of all their tax revenue. State personal income taxes, which have much lower rates than the Federal income tax, are the second most important source of state tax revenue. They bring in about 36 percent of total state tax revenue. Corporate income taxes and license fees account for most of the remainder of state tax revenue.

Education expenditures account for about 36 percent of all state spending. State expenditures on public welfare are next in relative weight, at about 25 percent of the total. States also spend heavily on health and hospitals (8 percent), highway maintenance and construction (8 percent), and public safety (5 percent). That leaves about 18 percent of all state spending for a variety of other purposes.

These tax and expenditure percentages combine data from all the states, so they reveal little about the finances of individual states. States vary significantly in the taxes

levied. Thus, although personal income taxes are a major source of revenue for all state governments combined, seven states do not levy a personal income tax. Also, there are great variations in the sizes of tax revenues and disbursements among the states, both in the aggregate and as percentages of personal income.

Thirty-eight states augment their tax revenues with state-run lotteries to help close the gap between their tax receipts and expenditures. Individual states also receive large intergovernmental grants from the Federal government. In fact, about 22 percent of their total revenue is in that form. States also take in revenue from miscellaneous sources such as state-owned utilities and liquor stores.

Local Finances

The local levels of government include counties, municipalities, townships, and school districts as well as cities and towns. Local governments obtain about 72 percent of their tax revenue from **property taxes.** Sales and excise taxes contribute about 17 percent of all local government tax revenue.

About 44 percent of local government expenditures go to education. Welfare, health, and hospitals (12 percent); public safety (11 percent); housing, parks, and sewerage (8 percent); and streets and highways (5 percent) are also major spending categories.

The tax revenues of local government cover less than one-half of their expenditures. The remaining revenue comes from intergovernmental grants from the Federal and state governments. Also, local governments receive considerable amounts of proprietary income, for example, revenue from government-owned utilities providing water, electricity, natural gas, and transportation.

QUICK REVIEW 5.4

- Government purchases account for about 18 percent of U.S. output; the addition of transfers increases government spending to about 30 percent of domestic output.
- Income security and national defense are the main categories of Federal spending; personal income, payroll, and corporate income taxes are the primary sources of Federal revenue.
- States rely on sales and excise taxes for revenue; their spending is largely for education and public welfare.
- Education is the main expenditure for local governments, most of whose revenue comes from property taxes.

One Advantage of Corporations Is Their Ability to Raise Funds through the Sale of Stocks and Bonds.

Generally, corporations finance their activities in three ways. First, a very large portion of a corporation's activities is financed internally out of undistributed corporate profits. Second, as do individuals or unincorporated businesses, corporations may borrow from financial institutions. For example, a small corporation planning to build a new plant may obtain the needed funds from a commercial bank, a savings and loan association, or an insurance company. Third, unique to corporations, they can issue common stocks and bonds.

Stocks versus Bonds   A common stock represents a share in the ownership of a corporation. The purchaser of a stock certificate has the right to vote for corporate officers and to share in dividends. If you buy 1000 of the 100,000 shares issued by OutTell, Inc. (hereafter OT), then you own 1 percent of the company, are entitled to 1 percent of any dividends declared by the board of directors, and control 1 percent of the votes in the annual election of corporate officials.

In contrast, a bond does not bestow any corporate ownership on the purchaser. A bond purchaser is simply lending money to a corporation. A bond is an IOU, in acknowledgment of a loan, whereby the corporation promises to pay the holder a fixed amount set forth on the bond at some specified future date and other fixed amounts (interest payments) every year up to the bond's maturity date. For example, you might purchase a 10-year OT bond with a face value of $1000 and a 10 percent rate of interest. This means that, in exchange for your $1000, OT guarantees you a $100 interest payment for each of the next 10-years and then repays your $1000 principal at the end of that period.

Differences   There are clearly important differences between stocks and bonds. First, as noted above, the bondholder is only a lender, not an owner of the company. Second, bonds are considered to be less risky than stocks, for two reasons. On the one hand, bondholders have a "legal prior claim" on a corporation's earnings. Dividends cannot be paid to stockholders until all interest payments that are due to bondholders have been paid. On the other hand, holders of OT stock do not know how much their dividends will be or how much they might get for their stock if they decide to sell. If OutTell falls on hard times, stockholders may receive no dividends at all, and the value of their stock may plummet. Provided the corporation does not go bankrupt, the holder of an OT bond is guaranteed a $100 interest payment each year and the return of his or her $1000 at the end of 10 years.

Bond Risks   This is not to imply that the purchase of corporate bonds is without risk. The market value of your OT bond may vary over time in accordance with the financial health of the corporation. If OT encounters economic misfortunes that raise questions about its financial integrity, the market value of your bond may fall. Should you sell the bond prior to maturity, you may receive only $600 or $700 for it (rather than $1000) and thereby incur a capital loss.

Changes in the interest rate paid on bonds will also affect the market prices of bonds. An increase in the interest rate will cause the bond price to fall and a decrease in the interest rate will cause the bond price to rise. Assume you purchase a $1000 ten-year OT bond this year when the interest rate is 10 percent. That means that your bond will provide a $100 fixed interest payment each year. But suppose that next year the interest rate jumps to 15 percent. Now OT must guarantee a $150 fixed annual payment on its new $1000 ten-year bonds. Clearly, no sensible person will pay you $1000 for your bond, which pays only $100 of interest income per year, when a new bond can be purchased for $1000 and will pay the holder $150 per year. Hence, if you sell your original bond before it reaches maturity, you may suffer a capital loss.

Bondholders face another source of risk: inflation. If substantial inflation occurs over the 10-year period during which you hold an OT bond, the $1000 principal repaid to you at the end of that period will represent substantially less purchasing power than the $1000 you lent OT 10 years earlier. You will have lent "dear" dollars but will be repaid in "cheap" dollars.

SUMMARY

1. The functional distribution of income shows how society's total income is divided among wages, rents, interest, and profit; the personal distribution of income shows how total income is divided among individual households.

2. Households use all their income to pay personal taxes, for saving, and to buy consumer goods. Nearly 60 percent of their consumption expenditures are for services.

3. Sole proprietorships are firms owned and usually operated by single individuals. Partnerships are firms owned and usually operated by just a handful of individuals. Corporations are legal entities, distinct and separate from the individuals who own them. They often have thousands, or even millions, of owners—the stockholders.

4. Corporations finance their operations and purchases of new plant and equipment partly through the issuance of stocks and bonds. Stocks are ownership shares of a corporation, and bonds are promises to repay a loan, usually at a set rate of interest.

5. A principal-agent problem may occur in corporations when the agents (managers) hired to represent the interest of the principals (the stockholders) pursue their own objectives to the detriment of the objectives of the principals.

6. Government improves the operation of the market system by (a) providing an appropriate legal and social framework and (b) acting to maintain competition.

7. Government alters the distribution of income through the tax-transfer system and through market intervention.

8. Spillovers, or externalities, cause the equilibrium output of certain goods to vary from the socially efficient output. Spillover costs result in an overallocation of resources, which can be corrected by legislation or by specific taxes. Spillover benefits are accompanied by an underallocation of resources, which can be corrected by government subsidies to consumers or producers.

9. Only government is willing to provide public goods, which can be consumed by all simultaneously (nonrivalry) and entail benefits from which nonpaying consumers (free riders) cannot be excluded (nonexcludability). Because doing so is not profitable, private firms will not produce public goods. Quasi-public goods have some of the characteristics of public goods and some of the characteristics of private goods; government provides them because the private sector would underallocate resources to their production.

10. To try to stabilize the economy, the government adjusts its spending and taxes, and the nation's central bank (the Federal Reserve in the United States) uses monetary actions to alter interest rates.

11. Government purchases exhaust (use up or absorb) resources; transfer payments do not. Government purchases have declined from about 22 percent of domestic output in 1960 to 18 percent today. Transfer payments, however, have grown significantly. Total government spending now amounts to about 30 percent of domestic output.

12. The main categories of Federal spending are pensions and income security, national defense, health, and interest on the public debt; Federal revenues come primarily from personal income taxes, payroll taxes, and corporate income taxes.

13. States derive their revenue primarily from sales and excise taxes and personal income taxes; major state expenditures go to education, public welfare, health and hospitals, and highways. Local communities derive most of their revenue from property taxes; education is their most important expenditure.

14. State and local tax revenues are supplemented by sizable revenue grants from the Federal government.

TERMS AND CONCEPTS

functional distribution of income	industry	principal-agent problem	transfer payments
personal distribution of income	sole proprietorship	monopoly	personal income tax
durable goods	partnership	spillover costs	marginal tax rate
nondurable goods	corporation	spillover benefits	average tax rate
services	stocks	public goods	payroll taxes
plant	bonds	free-rider problem	corporate income tax
firm	limited liability	quasi-public goods	sales and excise taxes
	double taxation	government purchases	property taxes

STUDY QUESTIONS

1. Distinguish between the functional distribution and personal distribution of income. Which is being referred to in each of the following statements? "The combined share of wage income and proprietary income has remained remarkably stable at about 80 percent since the Second World War." "The relative income of the richest households is higher today than in 1970."

2. *Key Question* Assume that the five residents of Econoville receive incomes of $50, $75, $125, $250, and $500. Present the resulting distribution of income as a graph similar to Figure 5.2. Compare the incomes of the lowest fifth and the highest fifth of the income receivers.

3. Distinguish between a plant, a firm, and an industry. Contrast a vertically integrated firm, a horizontally integrated firm, and a conglomerate. Cite an example of a horizontally integrated firm from which you have recently made a purchase.

4. *Key Question* What are the three major legal forms of business organization? Which form is the most prevalent in terms of numbers? Why do you think that is so? Which form is dominant in terms of total sales? What major advantages of this form of business organization gave rise to its dominance?

5. What is the principal-agent problem as it relates to managers and stockholders? How did firms try to solve it in the 1990s? In what way did the "solution" backfire on some firms?

6. Identify and briefly describe the main economic functions of government. What function do you think is the most controversial? Explain why.

7. What divergences arise between equilibrium output and efficient output when (*a*) spillover costs and (*b*) spillover benefits are present? How might government correct these divergences? Cite an example (other than the text examples) of a spillover cost and a spillover benefit.

8. Explain why zoning laws, which allow certain land uses only in specific locations, might be justified in dealing with a problem of spillover costs. Explain why tax breaks to businesses that set up in areas of high unemployment might be justified in view of spillover benefits. Explain why excise taxes on beer might be justified in dealing with a problem of spillover costs.

9. *Key Question* What are the two characteristics of public goods? Explain the significance of each for public provision as opposed to private provision. What is the free-rider problem as it relates to public goods? Is U.S. border patrol a public good or a private good? Why? How about satellite TV? Explain.

10. *Key Question* Draw a production possibilities curve with public goods on the vertical axis and private goods on the horizontal axis. Assuming the economy is initially operating *on the curve*, indicate how the production of public goods

might be increased. How might the output of public goods be increased if the economy is initially operating at a point *inside the curve?*

11. Use the distinction between the characteristics of private and public goods to determine whether the following should be produced through the market system or provided by government: (*a*) French fries, (*b*) airport screening, (*c*) court systems, (*d*) mail delivery, and (*e*) medical care. State why you answered as you did in each case.

12. Use the circular flow diagram to show how each of the following government actions simultaneously affects the allocation of resources and the distribution of income:
    a. The construction of a new high school.
    b. A 2-percentage-point reduction of the corporate income tax.
    c. An expansion of preschool programs for disadvantaged children.
    d. The levying of an excise tax on polluters.

13. What do economists mean when they say government purchases are "exhaustive" expenditures whereas government transfer payments are "nonexhaustive" expenditures? Cite an example of a government purchase and a government transfer payment.

14. What is the most important source of revenue and the major type of expenditure at the Federal level? At the state level? At the local level?

15. *Key Question* Suppose in Fiscalville there is no tax on the first $10,000 of income, but a 20 percent tax on earnings between $10,000 and $20,000 and a 30 percent tax on income between $20,000 and $30,000. Any income above $30,000 is taxed at 40 percent. If your income is $50,000, how much will you pay in taxes? Determine your marginal and average tax rates. Is this a progressive tax? Explain.

16. *(Last Word)* Describe three ways to finance corporate activity. Make a case that stocks are more risky than bonds for the financial investor.

17. *Web-Based Question: Personal distribution of income—what is the trend?* Visit the U.S. Census Bureau website at www.census.gov/hhes/income/midclass/index.html and select Data Highlights. Since 1969, how has the share of aggregate household income received by the lowest and highest income quintiles (fifths) changed?

18. *Web-Based Question: State taxes and expenditures per capita—where does your state rank?* Go to the Census Bureau site, www.census.gov/govs/www/state.html, and find the table that ranks the states by tax revenue and expenditures per capita for the latest year. Where does your home state rank in each category? Where does the state in which you are attending college, if different, rank? Speculate as to why there is such a gap between the high-ranking and low-ranking states.

6 | The United States in the Global Economy

Backpackers in the wilderness like to think they are "leaving the world behind," but, like Atlas, they carry the world on their shoulders. Much of their equipment is imported—knives from Switzerland, rain gear from South Korea, cameras from Japan, aluminum pots from England, sleeping bags from China, and compasses from Finland. Moreover, they may have driven to the trailheads in Japanese-made Toyotas or German-made BMWs, sipping coffee from Brazil or snacking on bananas from Honduras.

International trade and the global economy affect all of us daily, whether we are hiking in the wilderness, driving our cars, listening to music, or working at our jobs. We cannot "leave the world behind." We are enmeshed in a global web of economic relationships—trading of goods and services, multinational corporations, cooperative ventures among the world's firms, and ties among the world's financial markets. That web is so complex that it is difficult to determine just what is—or isn't—an American product. A Finnish company owns Wilson sporting goods; a Swiss company owns Gerber baby food; and a South African corporation owns Miller Brewing. The Chrysler PT Cruiser is assembled in Mexico. Many "U.S." products are made with components from abroad, and, conversely, many "foreign" products contain numerous U.S.-produced parts.

International Linkages

Several economic flows link the U.S. economy and the economies of other nations. As identified in Figure 6.1, these flows are:

- *Goods and services flows* or simply *trade flows* The United States exports goods and services to other nations and imports goods and services from them.
- *Capital and labor flows* or simply *resource flows* U.S. firms establish production facilities—new capital—in foreign countries, and foreign firms establish production facilities in the United States. Labor also moves between nations. Each year many foreigners immigrate to the United States and some Americans move to other nations.
- *Information and technology flows* The United States transmits information to other nations about U.S. products, prices, interest rates, and investment opportunities and receives such information from abroad. Firms in other countries use technology created in the United States, and U.S. businesses incorporate technology developed abroad.

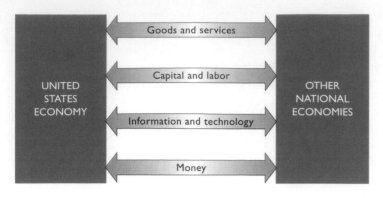

FIGURE 6.1

International linkages. The U.S. economy is intertwined with other national economies through goods and services flows (trade flows), capital and labor flows (resource flows), information and technology flows, and financial flows.

- *Financial flows* Money is transferred between the United States and other countries for several purposes, for example, paying for imports, buying foreign assets, paying interest on debt, and providing foreign aid.

The United States and World Trade

Our main goal in this chapter is to examine trade flows and the financial flows that pay for them. What is the extent and pattern of international trade, and how much has that trade grown? Who are the major participants?

Volume and Pattern

Table 6.1 suggests the importance of world trade for selected countries. Many countries, with restricted resources and limited domestic markets, cannot efficiently produce the variety of goods their citizens want. So they

must import goods from other nations. That, in turn, means that they must export, or sell abroad, some of their own products. For such countries, exports may run from 25 to 50 percent or more of their gross domestic product (GDP)—the market value of all goods and services produced in an economy. Other countries, the United States, for example, have rich and diversified resource bases and large internal markets. Although the total volume of trade is huge in the United States, it constitutes a smaller percentage of GDP than it does in a number of other nations.

Volume For the United States and for the world as a whole the volume of international trade has been increasing both absolutely and relative to their GDPs. A comparison of the boxed data in Figure 6.2 reveals substantial growth in the dollar amount of U.S. exports and imports over the past several decades. The graph shows the rapid growth of U.S. exports and imports of goods and services as percentages of GDP. In 2002, U.S. exports and imports were 11 and 16 percent of GDP, respectively.

Even so, the United States now accounts for a diminished percentage of total world trade. In 1950, it supplied about one-third of the world's total exports, compared with about one-eighth today. World trade has increased more rapidly for other nations than it has for the United States. *But in terms of absolute volumes of imports and exports, the United States is still the world's leading trading nation.*

Dependence The United States is almost entirely dependent on other countries for bananas, cocoa, coffee, spices, tea, raw silk, nickel, tin, natural rubber, and diamonds. Imported goods compete with U.S. goods in many of our domestic markets: Japanese cameras and cars, French and Italian wines, and Swiss and Austrian snow skis are a few examples. Even the "great American pastime" of baseball relies heavily on imported gloves and baseballs.

TABLE 6.1

Exports of Goods and Services as a Percentage of GDP, Selected Countries, 2002

Country	Exports as Percentage of GDP
Netherlands	62
Canada	41
Germany	36
New Zealand	33
Spain	29
Italy	28
France	27
United Kingdom	26
Japan	12
United States	11

Source: IMF, International Financial Statistics, 2002.

FIGURE 6.2

U.S. trade as percentage of GDP.   U.S. imports and exports have increased in volume and have greatly increased as a percentage of GDP since 1975.

Source: Bureau of Economic Analysis. Data are from the national income accounts and are adjusted for inflation (1996 dollars).

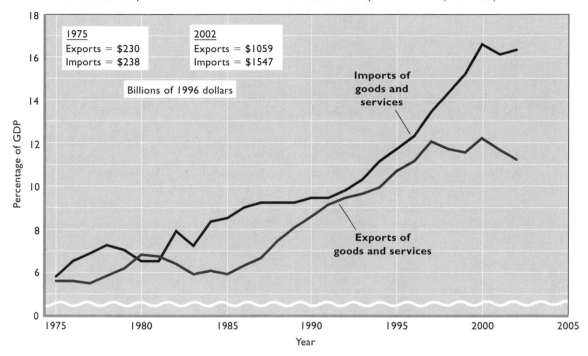

Of course, world trade is a two-way street. Many U.S. industries rely on foreign markets. Almost all segments of U.S. agriculture rely on sales abroad; for example, exports of rice, wheat, cotton, and tobacco vary from one-fourth to more than one-half of the total output of those crops.

The U.S. computer, chemical, semiconductor, aircraft, automobile, machine tool, and coal industries, among many others, sell significant portions of their output in international markets. Table 6.2 shows some of the major commodity exports and imports of the United States.

TABLE 6.2

**Principal U.S. Exports and Imports of Goods, 2002
(in Billions of Dollars)**

Exports	Amount	Imports	Amount
Chemicals	$49.8	Automobiles	$114.1
Semiconductors	42.3	Petroleum	103.6
Consumer durables	40.1	Computers	75.3
Computers	38.6	Household appliances	66.4
Generating equipment	27.6	Clothing	64.3
Aircraft	26.7	Chemicals	33.1
Telecommunications	22.2	Consumer electronics	32.8
Automobiles	20.5	Semiconductors	26.0
Grains	14.4	Telecommunications	23.2
Nonferrous metals	12.2	Iron and steel	17.7

Source: Consolidated from Department of Commerce data.

TABLE 6.3

U.S. Exports and Imports of Goods by Area, 2002*

Exports to	Value, Billions of Dollars	Percentage of Total	Imports from	Value, Billions of Dollars	Percentage of Total
Industrial countries	$381	56	Industrial countries	$ 594	51
Canada	$161	24	Canada	$213	18
Japan	50	7	Japan	121	10
Western Europe	154	23	Western Europe	246	21
Australia	13	2	Australia	6	1
Other	3	0	Other	8	1
Developing countries	302	44	Developing countries	573	49
Mexico	97	14	Mexico	136	12
China	35	5	China	135	12
Eastern Europe	6	1	Eastern Europe	15	1
OPEC countries	18	3	OPEC countries	53	5
Other	146	21	Other	234	20
Total	$683	100	Total	$1167	100

*Data are on an international transactions basis and exclude military shipments. The import percentages do not add to 100 percent because of rounding.

Source: Survey of Current Business, April 2003.

Trade Patterns   The following facts will give you an overview of U.S. international trade:

- The United States has a *trade deficit* in goods. In 2002, U.S. imports of goods exceeded U.S. exports of goods by $484 billion.
- The United States has a *trade surplus* in services (such as transportation services and financial services). In 2002, U.S. exports of services exceeded U.S. imports of services by $49 billion.
- The United States imports some of the same categories of goods that it exports, specifically, automobiles, computers, chemicals, semiconductors, and telecommunications equipment (see Table 6.2).
- As Table 6.3 shows, slightly more than half of U.S. export and import trade is with other industrially advanced countries. The remainder is with developing countries, including members of the Organization of Petroleum Exporting Countries (OPEC).
- Canada is the United States' most important trading partner quantitatively. In 2002, 24 percent of U.S. exported goods were sold to Canadians, who in turn provided 18 percent of the U.S. imports of goods (see Table 6.3).
- The United States has sizable trade deficits with China and Japan. In 2002, U.S. imported goods from China exceeded exported goods to China by $100 billion, and U.S. imported goods from Japan exceeded U.S. exported goods to Japan by $71 billion (see Table 6.3).

- The U.S. dependence on foreign oil is reflected in its trade with members of OPEC. In 2002, the United States imported $53 billion of goods (mainly oil) from OPEC members, while exporting $18 billion of goods to those countries (see Table 6.3).
- In terms of volume, the most significant U.S. export of *services* is airline transportation provided by U.S. carriers for foreign passengers.

Financial Linkages   International trade requires complex financial linkages among nations. How does a nation such as the United States obtain more goods from others than it provides to them? How does the United States finance its trade deficits, such as its 2002 goods and services deficit of $435 billion (= + $49 billion in services − $484 billion in goods) in 2002? The answer is by either borrowing from foreigners or selling real assets (for example, factories, real estate) to them. The United States is the world's largest borrower of foreign funds. Moreover, nations with which the United States has large trade deficits, such as Japan, often "recycle their excess dollars" by buying U.S. real assets.

Rapid Trade Growth

Several factors have propelled the rapid growth of international trade since the Second World War.

Transportation Technology

High transportation costs are a barrier to any type of trade, particularly among traders who are distant from one another. But improvements in transportation have shrunk the globe and have fostered world trade. Airplanes now transport low-weight, high-value items such as diamonds and semiconductors swiftly from one nation to another. We now routinely transport oil in massive tankers, significantly lowering the cost of transportation per barrel. Grain is loaded onto oceangoing ships at modern, efficient grain silos at Great Lakes and coastal ports. Natural gas flows through large-diameter pipelines from exporting to importing countries—for instance, from Russia to Germany and from Canada to the United States.

Communications Technology

Dramatic improvements in communications technology have also advanced world trade. Computers, the Internet, telephones, and fax (facsimile) machines now directly link traders around the world, enabling exporters to access overseas markets and to carry out trade deals. A distributor in New York can get a price quote on 1000 woven baskets in Thailand as quickly as a quotation on 1000 laptop computers in Texas. Money moves around the world in the blink of an eye. Exchange rates, stock prices, and interest rates flash onto computer screens nearly simultaneously in Los Angeles, London, and Lisbon.

General Decline in Tariffs

Tariffs are excise taxes (duties) on imported products. They have had their ups and downs over the years, but since 1940 they have generally fallen. A glance ahead to Figure 6.5 shows that U.S. tariffs as a percentage of imports (on which duties are levied) are now about 5 percent, down from 37 percent in 1940. Many nations still maintain barriers to free trade, but, on average, tariffs have fallen significantly, thus increasing international trade.

Participants in International Trade

All the nations of the world participate to some extent in international trade.

United States, Japan, and Western Europe

As Global Perspective 6.1 indicates, the top participants in world trade by total volume are the United States, Germany, and Japan. In 2001 those three nations had combined exports of $1.7 trillion. Along with Germany, other western European nations such as France, Britain, and Italy are major exporters and importers. The United

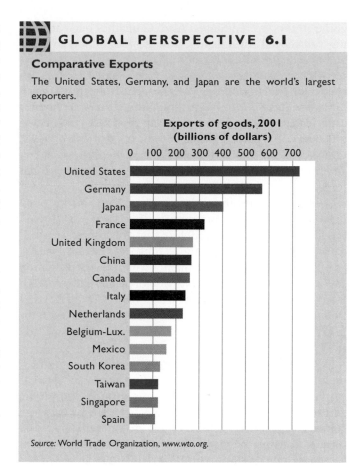

GLOBAL PERSPECTIVE 6.1

Comparative Exports

The United States, Germany, and Japan are the world's largest exporters.

Exports of goods, 2001
(billions of dollars)

Source: World Trade Organization, www.wto.org.

States, Japan, and the western European nations also form the heart of the world's financial system and provide headquarters for most of the world's large **multinational corporations**—firms that have sizable production and distribution activities in other countries. Examples of such firms are Unilever (Netherlands), Nestlé (Switzerland), Coca-Cola (United States), Bayer Chemicals (Germany), and Mitsubishi (Japan).

New Participants

Important new participants have arrived on the world trade scene. China, with its increased reliance on the market system and its reintegration of Hong Kong, is an emerging major trader. Since China initiated reforms in 1978, its annual growth of output has averaged 9 percent (compared with about 3 percent in the United States). At this remarkable rate, China's total output nearly doubles every 8 years! An upsurge of exports and imports has accompanied that economic growth. In 1990 Chinese exports were about $60 billion. In 2002 they topped $400 billion (including Hong Kong), with about one-third of China's exports going to the United States. Also, China has been attracting substantial foreign investment ($52 billion in 2002 and nearly $900 billion since 1990).

Other Asian economies are also active traders. In particular, Singapore, South Korea, and Taiwan are major exporters and importers. Although these three economies experienced economic difficulties in the 1990s, their combined exports exceed those of France, Britain, or Italy. Other economies of southeast Asia, particularly Malaysia and Indonesia, also have expanded their international trade.

Other changes in world trade patterns have resulted from the collapse of communism in eastern Europe and the former Soviet Union. Before that collapse, the eastern European nations of Poland, Hungary, Czechoslovakia, and East Germany traded mainly with the Soviet Union and such political allies as North Korea and Cuba. Today, East Germany is reunited with West Germany, and Poland, Hungary, and the Czech Republic have established new trade relationships with western Europe and the United States.

Russia itself has initiated far-reaching market reforms, including widespread privatization of industry, and has made major trade deals with firms around the globe. Although its transition to capitalism has been far from smooth, Russia may one day be a major trading nation. Other former Soviet republics—now independent nations—such as Estonia and Azerbaijan also have opened their economies to international trade and finance.

QUICK REVIEW 6.1

- There are four main categories of economic flows linking nations: goods and services flows, capital and labor flows, information and technology flows, and financial flows.

- World trade has increased globally and nationally. In terms of volume, the United States is the world's leading international trader. But with exports and imports of only about 11 to 16 percent of GDP, the United States is not as dependent on international trade as some other nations.

- Advances in transportation and communications technology and declines in tariffs have all helped expand world trade.

- The United States, Japan, and the western European nations dominate world trade. Recent new traders are the Asian economies of China (including Hong Kong), Singapore, South Korea, and Taiwan; the eastern European nations; and the former Soviet states.

Specialization and Comparative Advantage

Given the presence of an *open economy*—one that includes the international sector—the United States produces more of certain goods (exports) and fewer of other goods (imports) than it would otherwise. Thus U.S. labor and other resources are shifted toward export industries and away from import industries. For example, the United States uses more resources to make commercial aircraft and to grow wheat and less to make autos and clothing. So we ask: "Do shifts of resources like these make economic sense? Do they enhance U.S. total output and thus the U.S. standard of living?"

The answers are affirmative. *Specialization and international trade increase the productivity of a nation's resources and allow for greater total output than would otherwise be possible.* This idea is not new. Adam Smith had this to say in 1776:

> It is the maxim of every prudent master of a family, never to attempt to make at home what it will cost him more to make than to buy. The taylor does not attempt to make his own shoes, but buys them of the shoemaker. The shoemaker does not attempt to make his own clothes, but employs a taylor. The farmer attempts to make neither the one nor the other, but employs those different artificers. . . .
>
> What is prudence in the conduct of every private family, can scarce be folly in that of a great kingdom. If a foreign country can supply us with a commodity cheaper than we can make it, better buy it of them with some part of the produce of our own industry, employed in a way in which we have some advantage.[1]

Nations specialize and trade for the same reasons as individuals: Specialization and exchange result in greater overall output and income.

Basic Principle

In the early 1800s British economist David Ricardo expanded on Smith's idea by observing that it pays for a person or a country to specialize and trade even if some potential trading partner is more productive in *all* economic activities.

Consider the certified public accountant (CPA) who is also a skilled house painter. Suppose the CPA is a swifter painter than the professional painter she is thinking of hiring. Also suppose she can earn $50 per hour but would have to pay the painter $15 per hour. And say it would

---

[1]Adam Smith, *The Wealth of Nations* (New York: Modern Library, 1937), p. 424. (Originally published in 1776.)

take the accountant 30 hours to paint her house but the painter would take 40 hours.

Should the CPA take time from her accounting to paint her own house, or should she hire the painter? The CPA's opportunity cost of painting her house is $1500 (= 30 hours of sacrificed CPA time × $50 per CPA hour). The cost of hiring the painter is only $600 (= 40 hours of painting × $15 per hour of painting). Although the CPA is better at both accounting and painting, she *will get her house painted at lower cost by specializing in accounting and using some of her earnings from accounting to hire a house painter.*

Similarly, the house painter can reduce his cost of obtaining accounting services by specializing in painting and using some of his income to hire the CPA to prepare his income tax forms. Suppose it would take the painter 10 hours to prepare his tax return, while the CPA could handle the task in 2 hours. The house painter would sacrifice $150 of income (= 10 hours of painting time × $15 per hour) to do something he could hire the CPA to do for $100 (= 2 hours of CPA time × $50 per CPA hour). By using the CPA to prepare his tax return, the painter *lowers the cost of getting his tax return prepared.*

What is true for our CPA and house painter is also true for nations. Specializing enables nations to reduce the cost of obtaining the goods and services they desire.

Comparative Costs

Our simple example shows that the reason specialization is economically desirable is that it results in more efficient production. Now let's put specialization into the context of trading nations and use the familiar concept of the production possibilities table for our analysis. Suppose the production possibilities for one product in Mexico and for one product in the United States are as shown in Tables 6.4 and 6.5. In both tables we assume constant costs. Each country must give up a constant amount of one product to secure a certain increment of the other product. (This assumption simplifies our discussion without impairing the validity of our conclusions.)

Specialization and trade are mutually beneficial or "profitable" to the two nations if the comparative costs

TABLE 6.4

Mexico's Production Possibilities Table (in Tons)

Product	Production Alternatives				
	A	**B**	**C**	**D**	**E**
Avocados	0	20	24	40	60
Soybeans	15	10	9	5	0

TABLE 6.5

U.S. Production Possibilities Table (in Tons)

Product	Production Alternatives				
	R	**S**	**T**	**U**	**V**
Avocados	0	30	33	60	90
Soybeans	30	20	19	10	0

of producing the two products within the two nations differ. What are the comparative costs of avocados and soybeans in Mexico? By comparing production alternatives A and B in Table 6.4, we see that 5 tons of soybeans (= 15 − 10) must be sacrificed to produce 20 tons of avocados (= 20 − 0). Or, more simply, in Mexico it costs 1 ton of soybeans (S) to produce 4 tons of avocados (A); that is, 1S ≡ 4A. Because we assumed constant costs, this domestic *comparative-cost ratio* will not change as Mexico expands the output of either product. This is evident from production possibilities B and C, where we see that 4 more tons of avocados (= 24 − 20) cost 1 unit of soybeans (= 10 − 9).

Similarly, in Table 6.5, comparing U.S. production alternatives R and S reveals that in the United States it costs 10 tons of soybeans (= 30 − 20) to obtain 30 tons of avocados (= 30 − 0). That is, the domestic comparative-cost ratio for the two products in the United States is 1S ≡ 3A. Comparing production alternatives S and T reinforces this conclusion: an extra 3 tons of avocados (= 33 − 30) comes at the sacrifice of 1 ton of soybeans (= 20 − 19).

The comparative costs of the two products within the two nations are obviously different. Economists say that the United States has a domestic comparative advantage or, simply, a **comparative advantage** over Mexico in soybeans. The United States must forgo only 3 tons of avocados to get 1 ton of soybeans, but Mexico must forgo 4 tons of avocados to get 1 ton of soybeans. In terms of domestic opportunity costs, soybeans are relatively cheaper in the United States. *A nation has a comparative advantage in some product when it can produce that product at a lower domestic opportunity cost than can a potential trading partner.* Mexico, in contrast, has a comparative advantage in avocados. While 1 ton of avocados costs $\frac{1}{3}$ ton of soybeans in the United States, it costs only $\frac{1}{4}$ ton of soybeans in Mexico. Comparatively speaking, avocados are cheaper in Mexico. We summarize the situation in Table 6.6.

Because of these differences in domestic comparative costs, if both

6.1
Absolute and comparative advantage

TABLE 6.6

Comparative-Advantage Example: A Summary

Soybeans	Avocados
Mexico: Must give up 4 tons of avocados to get 1 ton of soybeans *United States*: Must give up 3 tons of avocados to get 1 ton of soybeans Comparative advantage: United States	*Mexico*: Must give up $\frac{1}{4}$ ton of soybeans to get 1 ton of avocados *United States*: Must give up $\frac{1}{3}$ ton of soybeans to get 1 ton of avocados Comparative advantage: Mexico

nations specialize, each according to its comparative advantage, each can achieve a larger total output with the same total input of resources. Together they will be using their scarce resources more efficiently.

Terms of Trade

The United States can shift production between soybeans and avocados at the rate of 1S for 3A. Thus, the United States would specialize in soybeans only if it could obtain *more than* 3 tons of avocados for 1 ton of soybeans by trading with Mexico. Similarly, Mexico can shift production at the rate of 4A for 1S. So it would be advantageous to Mexico to specialize in avocados if it could get 1 ton of soybeans for *less than* 4 tons of avocados.

Suppose that through negotiation the two nations agree on an exchange rate of 1 ton of soybeans for $3\frac{1}{2}$ tons of avocados. These **terms of trade** are mutually beneficial to both countries, since each can "do better" through such trade than through domestic production alone. The United States can get $3\frac{1}{2}$ tons of avocados by sending 1 ton of soybeans to Mexico, while it can get only 3 tons of avocados by shifting its own resources domestically from soybeans to avocados. Mexico can obtain 1 ton of soybeans

at a lower cost of $3\frac{1}{2}$ tons of avocados through trade with the United States, compared to the cost of 4 tons if Mexico produced the ton of soybeans itself.

Gains from Specialization and Trade

Let's pinpoint the gains in total output from specialization and trade. Suppose that, before specialization and trade, production alternative C in Table 6.4 and alternative T in 6.5 were the optimal product mixes for the two countries. That is, Mexico preferred 24 tons of avocados and 9 tons of soybeans (Table 6.4) and the United States preferred 33 tons of avocados and 19 tons of soybeans (Table 6.5) to all other available domestic alternatives. These outputs are shown in column 1 in Table 6.7.

Now assume that both nations specialize according to their comparative advantage, with Mexico producing 60 tons of avocados and no soybeans (alternative E) and the United States producing no avocados and 30 tons of soybeans (alternative R). These outputs are shown in column 2 in Table 6.7. Using our 1S $\equiv$ $3\frac{1}{2}$A terms of trade, assume that Mexico exchanges 35 tons of avocados for 10 tons of U.S. soybeans. Column 3 in Table 6.7 shows the quantities exchanged in this trade, with a minus sign indicating exports and a plus sign indicating imports. As shown in column 4, after the trade Mexico has 25 tons of avocados and 10 tons of soybeans, while the United States has 35 tons of avocados and 20 tons of soybeans. Compared with their optimum product mixes before specialization and trade (column 1), *both* nations now enjoy more avocados and more soybeans! Specifically, Mexico has gained 1 ton of avocados and 1 ton of soybeans. The United States has gained 2 tons of avocados and 1 ton of soybeans. These gains are shown in column 5.

Specialization based on comparative advantage improves global resource allocation. The same total inputs of world resources and technology result in a larger global output. If Mexico and the United States allocate all their resources to avocados

TABLE 6.7

Specialization According to Comparative Advantage and the Gains from Trade (in Tons)

Country	(1) Outputs before Specialization	(2) Outputs after Specialization	(3) Amounts Traded	(4) Outputs Available after Trade	(5) Gains from Specialization and Trade (4) − (1)
Mexico	24 avocados	60 avocados	−35 avocados	25 avocados	1 avocados
	9 soybeans	0 soybeans	+10 soybeans	10 soybeans	1 soybeans
United States	33 avocados	0 avocados	+35 avocados	35 avocados	2 avocados
	19 soybeans	30 soybeans	−10 soybeans	20 soybeans	1 soybeans

and soybeans, respectively, the same total inputs of resources can produce more output between them, indicating that resources are being allocated more efficiently.

We noted in Chapter 2 that through specialization and international trade a nation can overcome the production constraints imposed by its domestic production possibilities table and curve. Our discussion of Tables 6.4, 6.5, and 6.7 has shown just how this is done. The domestic production possibilities data (Tables 6.4 and 6.5) of the two countries have not changed, meaning that neither nation's production possibilities curve has shifted. But specialization and trade mean that citizens of both countries can enjoy increased consumption (column 5 of Table 6.7). Thus specialization and trade have the same effect as an increase in resources or in technological progress: They make more goods available to an economy. **(Key Question 4)**

The Foreign Exchange Market

Buyers and sellers, whether individuals, firms, or nations, use money to buy products or to pay for the use of resources. Within the domestic economy, prices are stated in terms of the domestic currency and buyers use that currency to purchase domestic products. In Mexico, for example, buyers have pesos, and that is what sellers want.

International markets are different. Sellers set their prices in terms of their domestic currencies, but buyers often possess entirely different currencies. How many dollars does it take to buy a truckload of Mexican avocados selling for 3000 pesos, a German automobile selling for 50,000 euros, or a Japanese motorcycle priced at 300,000 yen? Producers in Mexico, Germany, and Japan want payment in pesos, euros, and yen, respectively, so that they can pay their wages, rent, interest, dividends, and taxes. A **foreign exchange market,** *a market in which various national currencies are exchanged for one another,* serves this need. The equilibrium prices in these markets are called **exchange rates.** An exchange rate is the rate at which the currency of one nation can be exchanged for the currency of another nation. (See Global Perspective 6.2.) Two points about the foreign exchange market are particularly noteworthy:

- *A competitive market* Real-world foreign exchange markets conform closely to the markets discussed in Chapter 3. They are competitive markets characterized by large numbers of buyers and sellers dealing in standardized products such as the American dollar, the European euro, the British pound, and the Japanese yen.
- *Linkages to all domestic and foreign prices* The market price or exchange rate of a nation's currency is an unusual price; it links all domestic prices with all

GLOBAL PERSPECTIVE 6.2

Exchange Rates: Foreign Currency per U.S. Dollar

The amount of foreign currency that a dollar will buy varies greatly from nation to nation and fluctuates in response to supply and demand changes in the foreign exchange market. The amounts shown here are for March 2003.

$1 Will Buy

47.68	Indian rupees
.63	British pounds
1.48	Canadian dollars
10.91	Mexican pesos
1.36	Swiss francs
.93	European euros
119	Japanese yen
1237	South Korean won
8.54	Swedish kronors

foreign prices. Exchange rates enable consumers in one country to translate prices of foreign goods into units of their own currency: They need only multiply the foreign product price by the exchange rate. If the U.S. dollar–yen exchange rate is $.01 (1 cent) per yen, a Sony television set priced at ¥20,000 will cost $200 (= 20,000 × $.01) in the United States. If the exchange rate rises to $.02 (2 cents) per yen, the television will cost $400 (= 20,000 × $.02) in the United States. Similarly, all other Japanese products would double in price to U.S. buyers in response to the altered exchange rate. As you will see, a change in exchange rates has important implications for a nation's level of domestic production and employment.

Dollar-Yen Market

How does the foreign exchange market work? Let's look briefly at the market for dollars and yen. U.S. firms exporting goods to Japan want payment in dollars, not yen; but the Japanese importers of those U.S. goods possess yen, not dollars. So the Japanese importers supply their yen in exchange for dollars in the foreign exchange market. At the same time, there are U.S. importers of Japanese goods who need to pay the Japanese exporters in yen, not dollars. These importers go to the foreign exchange market as demanders of yen. We then have a market in which the "price" is in dollars and the "product" is yen.

CONSIDER THIS . . .

© Tony Freeman/PhotoEdit

A Ticket to Ride

Have you ever attended a county or state fair and spent time on the rides? If so, you are aware of the dual "currencies" often used there. One currency is the *dollar;* the other is the *ride ticket.* Rides are priced in number of ride tickets, but dollars are needed to buy tickets at the kiosks. Alternative rides require different numbers of tickets. For example, the roller-coaster may require 8 tickets; the twister, 6 tickets; and the merry-go-round, 2 tickets.

Exchange rates between dollars and other currencies are analogous to the exchange rate between dollars and ride tickets.* Such tickets are a "currency" used to buy rides, and dollars and tickets are exchanged.

Initially suppose that the dollar price of each ticket is $.25. If you were to exchange tickets for dollars on the midway, you would find that the ticket price of a dollar is 4; that is, 4 tickets will exchange for $1. The ticket-dollar exchange rate is 1 ticket = $.25, and the dollar-ticket exchange rate is $1 = 4 tickets.

Although the rides are priced in tickets, not dollars, the exchange rate permits quick conversion of ticket prices into dollars. For example, the 8-ticket price of the roller-coaster ride converts to $2 (= 8 tickets × $.25). *Exchange rates enable buyers to convert goods priced in another currency to prices in their own currency.*

Next suppose that in some year the fair increases the price of ride tickets from $.25 to $.50. The dollar has *depreciated* in value, because more dollars (one-half rather than one-fourth) are needed to buy each ticket. Ride tickets have *appreciated* in value, because fewer tickets (two rather than four) are needed to obtain a dollar. Specifically, the exchange rate has changed from 1 ticket = $.25 to 1 ticket = $.50 or, alternatively, from $1 = 4 tickets to $1 = 2 tickets.

If the fair charges the same number of tickets per ride as before, the dollar price of the roller-coaster ride increases from $2 (= 8 tickets × $.25) to $4 (= 8 tickets × $.50). *Other things equal, depreciation of the dollar relative to another currency increases the dollar price of goods and services that are priced in the other currency.*

*One difference, however, is that many exchange rates are free to fluctuate depending on currency supply and demand. The fair operators fix the dollar–ride ticket exchange rate. Another difference is that the fair operators offer an unlimited quantity of tickets at that price.

Figure 6.3 shows the supply of yen (by Japanese importers) and the demand for yen (by U.S. importers). The intersection of demand curve D_y and supply curve S_y establishes the equilibrium dollar price of yen. Here the equilibrium price of 1 yen—the dollar-yen exchange rate—is 1 cent per yen, or $.01 = ¥1. At this price, the market for yen clears; there is neither a shortage nor a surplus of yen. The

6.1
Exchange
rates

equilibrium $.01 price of 1 yen means that $1 will buy 100 yen or ¥100 worth of Japanese goods. Conversely, 100 yen will buy $1 worth of U.S. goods.

Changing Rates: Depreciation and Appreciation

What might cause the exchange rate to change? The determinants of the demand for and supply of yen are similar to the determinants of demand and supply for almost any product. In the United States, several things might increase the demand for—and therefore the dollar price of—yen. Incomes might rise in the United States, enabling residents to buy not only more domestic goods but also more Sony televisions, Nikon cameras, and Nissan automobiles from Japan. So people in the United States would need more yen, and the demand for yen would increase. Or a change in people's tastes might enhance their preferences for Japanese goods. When gas prices soared in the 1970s, many auto buyers in the United States shifted their demand from gas-guzzling domestic cars to gas-efficient Japanese compact cars. The result was an increased demand for yen.

The point is that an increase in the U.S. demand for Japanese goods will increase the demand for yen and raise the dollar price of yen. Suppose the dollar price of yen rises from $.01 = ¥1 to $.02 = ¥1. When the dollar price of yen increases, we say a **depreciation** of the dollar

FIGURE 6.3

The market for yen.   U.S. imports from Japan create a demand D_y for yen, while U.S. exports to Japan (Japan's imports) create a supply S_y of yen. The dollar price of 1 yen—the exchange rate—is determined at the intersection of the supply and demand curves. In this case the equilibrium price is $.01, meaning that 1 cent will buy 1 yen.

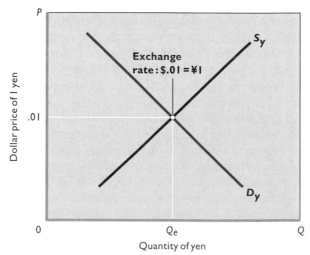

relative to the yen has occurred. It then takes more dollars (pennies in this case) to buy a single yen. Alternatively stated, the *international value of the dollar* has declined. A depreciated dollar buys fewer yen and therefore fewer Japanese goods; the yen and all Japanese goods have become more expensive to U.S. buyers. Result: Consumers in the United States shift their expenditures from Japanese goods to now less expensive American goods. The Ford Taurus becomes relatively more attractive than the Honda Accord to U.S. consumers. Conversely, because each yen buys more dollars—that is, because the international value of the yen has increased—U.S. goods become cheaper to people in Japan and U.S. exports to Japan rise.

If the opposite event occurred—if the Japanese demanded more U.S. goods—then they would supply more yen to pay for these goods. The increase in the supply of yen relative to the demand for yen would decrease the equilibrium price of yen in the foreign exchange market. For example, the dollar price of yen might decline from $.01 = ¥1 to $.005 = ¥1. A decrease in the dollar price of yen is called an **appreciation** of the dollar relative to the yen. It means that the international value of the dollar has increased. It then takes fewer dollars (or pennies) to buy a single yen; the dollar is worth more because it can purchase more yen and therefore more Japanese goods. Each Sony PlayStation becomes less expensive in terms of dollars, so people in the United States purchase more of them. In general, U.S. imports rise. Meanwhile, because it takes more yen to get a dollar, U.S. exports to Japan fall.

Figure 6.4 summarizes these currency relationships. **(Key Question 6)**

FIGURE 6.4

Currency appreciation and depreciation. Suppose the dollar price of a certain foreign currency rises (as illustrated by the upper left arrow). That means the international value of the dollar depreciates (upper right arrow). It also means that the foreign currency price of the dollar has declined (lower left arrow) and that the international value of the foreign currency has appreciated (lower right arrow).

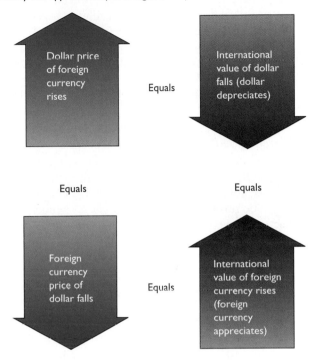

Government and Trade

If people and nations benefit from specialization and international exchange, why do governments sometimes try to restrict the free flow of imports or encourage exports? What kinds of world trade barriers can governments erect, and why would they do so?

Trade Impediments and Subsidies

There are four means by which governments commonly interfere with free trade:

- **Protective tariffs** are excise taxes or duties placed on imported goods. Protective tariffs are designed to shield domestic producers from foreign competition. They impede free trade by causing a rise in the prices of imported goods, thereby shifting demand toward domestic products. An excise tax on imported shoes, for example, would make domestically produced shoes more attractive to consumers.

- **Import quotas** are limits on the quantities or total value of specific items that may be imported. Once a quota is "filled," further imports of that product are choked off. Import quotas are more effective than tariffs in retarding international commerce. With a tariff, a product can go on being imported in large quantities; with an import quota, however, all imports are prohibited once the quota is filled.

- **Nontariff barriers** (and, implicitly, *nonquota* barriers) include onerous licensing requirements, unreasonable standards pertaining to product quality, or simply bureaucratic red tape in customs procedures. Some nations require that importers of foreign goods obtain licenses and then restrict the number of licenses issued. Although many nations carefully inspect imported agricultural products to prevent the introduction of potentially harmful insects, some countries use lengthy inspections to impede imports.

- **Export subsidies** consist of government payments to domestic producers of export goods. By reducing production costs, the subsidies enable producers to charge lower prices and thus to sell more exports in world markets. Two examples: Some European governments have heavily subsidized Airbus Industries, a European firm that produces commercial aircraft, to help Airbus compete against the American firm Boeing. The United States and other nations have subsidized domestic farmers to boost the domestic food supply. Such subsidies have lowered the market price of food and have artificially lowered export prices on agricultural produce.

Why Government Trade Interventions?

What accounts for the impulse to impede imports, boost exports, and create trade surpluses through government policy when free trade is beneficial to a nation? Why would a nation want to send more output abroad for consumption there than it gains as imported output in return? There are several reasons—some legitimate, most not.

Misunderstanding the Gains from Trade

It is a commonly accepted myth that the greatest benefit to be derived from international trade is greater domestic employment in the export sector. This suggests that exports are "good" because they increase domestic employment, whereas imports are "bad" because they deprive people of jobs at home. Actually, the true benefit created by international trade is the overall increase in output obtained through specialization and exchange. A nation can fully employ its resources, including labor, with or without international trade. International trade, however, enables society to use its resources in ways that increase its total output and therefore its overall well-being.

A nation does not need international trade to operate *on* its production possibilities curve. A closed (nontrading) national economy can have full employment without international trade. However, through world trade an economy can reach a point *beyond* its domestic production possibilities curve. The gain from trade is the extra output obtained from abroad—the imports obtained for less cost than the cost if they were produced at home.

Political Considerations

While a nation as a whole gains from trade, trade may harm particular domestic industries and particular groups of resource suppliers. In our earlier comparative-advantage example, specialization and trade adversely affected the U.S. avocado industry and the Mexican soybean industry. Those industries might seek to preserve their economic positions by persuading their respective governments to protect them from imports—perhaps through tariffs or import quotas.

Those who directly benefit from import protection are few in number but have much at stake. Thus, they have a strong incentive to pursue political activity to achieve their aims. However, the overall cost of tariffs and quotas typically greatly exceeds the benefits. It is not uncommon to find that it costs the public $200,000 or more a year to protect a domestic job that pays less than one-fourth that amount. Moreover, because these costs are buried in the price of goods and spread out over millions of citizens, the cost born by each individual citizen is quite small. In the political arena, the voice of the relatively few producers demanding *protectionism* is loud and constant, whereas the voice of those footing the bill is soft or nonexistent.

Indeed, the public may be won over by the apparent plausibility ("Cut imports and prevent domestic unemployment") and the patriotic ring ("Buy American!") of the protectionist arguments. The alleged benefits of tariffs are immediate and clear-cut to the public, but the adverse effects cited by economists are obscure and dispersed over the entire economy. When political deal making is added in—"You back tariffs for the apparel industry in my state, and I'll back tariffs on the auto industry in your state"—the outcome can be a network of protective tariffs, import quotas, and export subsidies.

Costs to Society

Tariffs and quotas benefit domestic producers of the protected products, but they harm domestic consumers, who must pay higher than world prices for the protected goods. They also hurt domestic firms that use the protected goods as inputs in their production processes. For example, a tariff on imported steel would boost the price of steel girders, thus hurting firms that construct large buildings. Also, tariffs and quotas reduce competition in the protected industries. With less competition from foreign producers, domestic firms may be slow to design and implement cost-saving production methods and introduce new or improved products.

Multilateral Trade Agreements and Free-Trade Zones

When one nation enacts barriers against imports, the nations whose exports suffer may retaliate with trade barriers of their own. In such a *trade war*, escalating tariffs choke world trade and reduce everyone's economic well-being. The **Smoot-Hawley Tariff Act** of 1930 is a classic example. Although that act was meant to reduce imports and stimulate U.S. production, the high tariffs it authorized prompted adversely affected nations to retaliate with tariffs equally high. International trade fell, lowering the output and income of all nations. Economic historians generally agree that the Smoot-Hawley Tariff Act was a

contributing cause of the Great Depression. Aware of that fact, nations have worked to lower tariffs worldwide. Their pursuit of free trade has been aided by powerful domestic interest groups: Exporters of goods and services, importers of foreign components used in "domestic" products, and domestic sellers of imported products all strongly support lower tariffs.

Figure 6.5 makes clear that while the United States has been a high-tariff nation over much of its history, U.S. tariffs have generally declined during the past half-century.

Reciprocal Trade Agreements Act

The **Reciprocal Trade Agreements Act** of 1934 started the downward trend of tariffs. Aimed at reducing tariffs, this act had two main features:

- *Negotiating authority* It authorized the president to negotiate with foreign nations agreements that would reduce existing U.S. tariffs by up to 50 percent. Those reductions were contingent on the actions other nations took to lower tariffs on U.S. exports.
- *Generalized reductions* The specific tariff reductions negotiated between the United States and any

FIGURE 6.5

U.S. tariff rates, 1860–2001. Historically, U.S. tariff rates have fluctuated. But beginning with the Reciprocal Trade Agreements Act of 1934, the trend has been downward.

Source: U.S. Department of Commerce data.

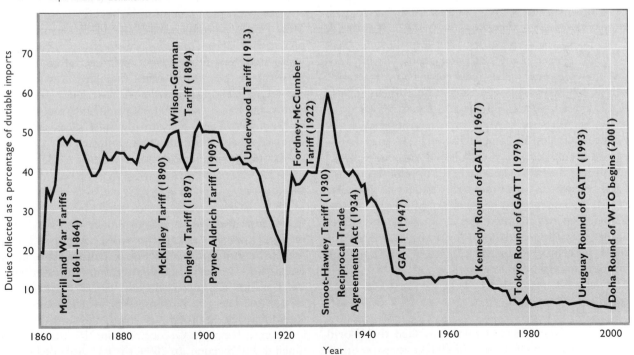

particular nation were generalized through **most-favored-nation clauses,** which often accompany such agreements. These clauses stipulate that any subsequently reduced U.S. tariffs, resulting from negotiation with any other nation, would apply equally to any nation that signed the original agreement. So if the United States negotiates a reduction in tariffs on wristwatches with, say, France, the lower U.S. tariffs on imported French watches also apply to the imports of the other nations having most-favored-nation status, say, Japan and Switzerland. This way, the reductions in U.S. tariffs automatically apply to many nations.

General Agreement on Tariffs and Trade

The Reciprocal Trade Agreements Act provided only bilateral (between two nations) negotiations. Its approach was broadened in 1947 when 23 nations, including the United States, signed the **General Agreement on Tariffs and Trade (GATT).** GATT was based on three principles: (1) equal, nondiscriminatory trade treatment for all member nations, (2) the reduction of tariffs by multilateral negotiation, and (3) the elimination of import quotas. Basically, GATT provided a forum for the negotiation of reduced trade barriers on a multilateral basis among nations.

Since the Second World War, member nations have completed eight "rounds" of GATT negotiations to reduce trade barriers. The eighth round of negotiations began in Uruguay in 1986. After 7 years of complex discussions, in 1993 the 128 member nations reached a new agreement. The *Uruguay Round* agreement took effect on January 1, 1995, and its provisions are to be phased in through 2005.

Under this agreement, tariffs on thousands of products have been eliminated or reduced, with overall tariffs eventually dropping by 33 percent. The agreement also liberalized government rules that in the past impeded the global market for such services as advertising, legal services, tourist services, and financial services. Quotas on imported textiles and apparel were phased out and replaced with tariffs. Other provisions reduced agricultural subsidies paid to farmers and protected intellectual property (patents, trademarks, copyrights) against piracy.

When fully implemented, the Uruguay Round agreement will boost the world's GDP by an estimated $6 trillion, or 8 percent. Consumers in the United States will save more than $30 billion annually.

World Trade Organization

The Uruguay Round agreement established the **World Trade Organization (WTO)** as GATT's successor. Some 145 nations belong to the WTO, with China being one of the latest entrants. The WTO oversees trade agreements reached by the member nations and rules on trade disputes among them. It also provides forums for further rounds of trade negotiations. The ninth and latest round of negotiations—the **Doha Round**—was launched in Doha, Qatar, in late 2001. (The trade rounds occur over several years in several venues but are named after the city or country of origination.) The negotiations are aimed at further reducing tariffs and quotas, as well as agricultural subsidies that distort trade. One of this chapter's web-based questions asks you to update the progress of the Doha Round.

GATT and the WTO have been positive forces in the trend toward liberalized world trade. The trade rules agreed upon by the member nations provide a strong and necessary bulwark against the protectionism called for by the special-interest groups in the various nations.

For that reason and others, the WTO is controversial. Critics are concerned that rules crafted to expand international trade and investment enable firms to circumvent national laws that protect workers and the environment. What good are minimum-wage laws, worker safety laws, collective bargaining rights, and environmental laws if firms can easily shift their production to nations that have weaker laws or consumers can buy goods produced in those countries?

Proponents of the WTO respond that labor and environmental protections should be pursued directly in nations that have low standards and via international organizations other than the WTO. These issues should not be linked to the process of trade liberalization, which confers widespread economic benefits across nations. Moreover, say proponents of the WTO, many environmental and labor concerns are greatly overblown. Most world trade is among advanced industrial countries, not between them and countries that have lower environmental and labor standards. Moreover, the free flow of goods and resources raises output and income in the developing nations. Historically, such increases in living standards have eventually resulted in stronger, not weaker, protections for the environment and for workers.

The European Union

Countries have also sought to reduce tariffs by creating regional *free-trade zones*—also called *trade blocs*. The most dramatic example is the **European Union (EU),** formerly called the European Economic Community. Initiated in 1958 as the Common Market, in 2003 the EU comprised 15 European nations—France, Germany, United Kingdom, Italy, Belgium, the Netherlands, Luxembourg, Denmark, Ireland, Greece, Spain, Portugal, Austria, Finland, and Sweden. In 2004, the EU expanded by 10 additional European countries—Poland, Hungary, Czech

Republic, Slovakia, Lithuania, Latvia, Estonia, Slovenia, Malta, and Cyprus.

The EU Trade Bloc   The EU has abolished tariffs and import quotas on nearly all products traded among the participating nations and established a common system of tariffs applicable to all goods received from nations outside the EU. It has also liberalized the movement of capital and labor within the EU and has created common policies in other economic matters of joint concern, such as agriculture, transportation, and business practices. The EU is now a strong **trade bloc:** a group of countries having common identity, economic interests, and trade rules.

EU integration has achieved for Europe what the U.S. constitutional prohibition on tariffs by individual states has achieved for the United States: increased regional specialization, greater productivity, greater output, and faster economic growth. The free flow of goods and services has created large markets for EU industries. The resulting economies of large-scale production have enabled these industries to achieve much lower costs than they could have achieved in their small, single-nation markets.

The effects of EU success on nonmember nations, such as the United States, have been mixed. A peaceful and increasingly prosperous EU makes its members better customers for U.S. exports. But U.S. firms and other nonmember firms have been faced with tariffs and other barriers that make it difficult for them to compete against firms within the EU trade bloc. For example, autos produced in Germany and sold in Spain or France face no tariffs, whereas U.S. and Japanese autos exported to EU countries do. This puts U.S. and Japanese firms at a serious disadvantage.

By giving preferences to countries within their free-trade zone, trade blocs such as the EU tend to reduce their members' trade with non-bloc members. Thus, the world loses some of the benefits of a completely open global trading system. Eliminating that disadvantage has been one of the motivations for liberalizing global trade through the World Trade Organization. Those liberalizations apply equally to all nations that belong to the WTO.

The Euro   One of the most significant accomplishments of the EU was the establishment of the so-called Euro Zone in the early 2000s. In 2003, 12 members of the EU used the **euro** as a common currency. Great Britain, Denmark, and Sweden have opted out of the common currency, at least for now. But gone are French francs, German marks, Italian liras, and other national currencies within the Euro Zone.

Economists expect the euro to raise the standard of living of the Euro Zone members over time. By ending the inconvenience and expense of exchanging currencies, the euro will enhance the free flow of goods, services, and resources among the Euro Zone members. It will also enable consumers and businesses to comparison shop for outputs and inputs, and this will increase competition, reduce prices, and lower costs.

North American Free Trade Agreement

In 1993 Canada, Mexico, and the United States formed a major trade bloc. The **North American Free Trade Agreement (NAFTA)** established a free-trade zone that has about the same combined output as the EU but encompasses a much larger geographic area. NAFTA has greatly reduced tariffs and other trade barriers between Canada, Mexico, and the United States and will eliminate them entirely by 2008.

Critics of NAFTA feared that it would cause a massive loss of U.S. jobs as firms moved to Mexico to take advantage of lower wages and weaker regulations on pollution and workplace safety. Also, there was concern that Japan and South Korea would build plants in Mexico and transport goods tariff-free to the United States, further hurting U.S. firms and workers.

In retrospect, critics were much too pessimistic. In the 7-year period (1993–2000) following passage of NAFTA, employment in the United States rose by more than 14 million workers and the unemployment rate fell from 6.9 to 4.2 percent. Increased trade between Canada, Mexico, and the United States has enhanced the standard of living in all three countries. **(Key Question 10)**

QUICK REVIEW 6.3

• Governments curtail imports and promote exports through protective tariffs, import quotas, nontariff barriers, and export subsidies.

• The General Agreement on Tariffs and Trade (GATT) established multinational reductions in tariffs and import quotas. The Uruguay Round of GATT (1993) reduced tariffs worldwide, liberalized international trade in services, strengthened protections for intellectual property, and reduced agricultural subsidies.

• The World Trade Organization (WTO)—GATT's successor—rules on trade disputes and provides forums for negotiations on further rounds of trade liberalization. The current round is called the Doha Round.

• The European Union (EU) and the North American Free Trade Agreement (NAFTA) have reduced internal trade barriers among their members by establishing large free-trade zones. Of the 25 EU members (as of 2004), 12 now have a common currency—the euro.

French Economist Frédéric Bastiat (1801–1850) Devastated the Proponents of Protectionism by Satirically Extending Their Reasoning to Its Logical and Absurd Conclusions.

Petition of the Manufacturers of Candles, Waxlights, Lamps, Candlesticks, Street Lamps, Snuffers, Extinguishers, and of the Producers of Oil Tallow, Rosin, Alcohol, and, Generally, of Everything Connected with Lighting.

TO MESSIEURS THE MEMBERS OF THE CHAMBER OF DEPUTIES.

Gentlemen—You are on the right road. You reject abstract theories, and have little consideration for cheapness and plenty. Your chief care is the interest of the producer. You desire to emancipate him from external competition, and reserve the national market for national industry.

We are about to offer you an admirable opportunity of applying your—what shall we call it? your theory? No; nothing is more deceptive than theory; your doctrine? your system? your principle? but you dislike doctrines, you abhor systems, and as for principles, you deny that there are any in social economy: we shall say, then, your practice, your practice without theory and without principle.

We are suffering from the intolerable competition of a foreign rival, placed, it would seem, in a condition so far superior to ours for the production of light, that he absolutely inundates our national market with it at a price fabulously reduced. The moment he shows himself, our trade leaves us—all consumers apply to him; and a branch of native industry, having countless ramifications, is all at once rendered completely stagnant. This rival . . . is no other than the Sun.

What we pray for is, that it may please you to pass a law ordering the shutting up of all windows, skylights, dormer windows, outside and inside shutters, curtains, blinds, bull's-eyes; in a word, of all openings, holes, chinks, clefts, and fissures, by or through which the light of the sun has been in use to enter houses, to the prejudice of the meritorious manufacturers with which we flatter ourselves we have accommodated our country,—a country which, in gratitude, ought not to abandon us now to a strife so unequal.

If you shut up as much as possible all access to natural light, and create a demand for artificial light, which of our French manufacturers will not be encouraged by it?

If more tallow is consumed, then there must be more oxen and sheep; and, consequently, we shall behold the multiplication of artificial meadows, meat, wool, hides, and, above all, manure, which is the basis and foundation of all agricultural wealth.

The same remark applies to navigation. Thousands of vessels will proceed to the whale fishery; and, in a short time, we shall possess a navy capable of maintaining the honor of France, and gratifying the patriotic aspirations of your petitioners, the undersigned candlemakers and others.

Only have the goodness to reflect, Gentlemen, and you will be convinced that there is, perhaps, no Frenchman, from the wealthy coalmaster to the humblest vender of lucifer matches, whose lot will not be ameliorated by the success of this our petition.

Source: Frédéric Bastiat, *Economic Sophisms* (Edinburgh: Oliver and Boyd, Tweeddale Court, 1873), pp. 49–53, abridged.

Global Competition

Globalization—the integration of industry, commerce, communication, travel, and culture among the world's nations—is one of the major trends of our time. (See Global Perspective 6.3 for a list of the top 12 globalized nations, according to one set of criteria.) There is a lively debate internationally as to whether globalization is a positive or negative force. Those who support globalization focus on the improvements to general standards of living that it brings. Those who oppose it express concerns about its impacts on the environment, unionized workers, and the poor. (We discuss this issue in detail in the Last Word to Chapter 37.)

One thing about globalization is certain and relevant to our present discussion: It has brought intense competition both within the United States and across the globe. In the United States, imports have gained major shares of many markets, including those for cars, steel, lumber, car tires, clothing, sporting goods, electronics, and toys. Nevertheless, hundreds of U.S. firms have prospered in the global marketplace. Such firms as Boeing,

GLOBAL PERSPECTIVE 6.3

The Top 12 Globalized Nations, 2002

Foreign Policy magazine publishes an annual list of the worlds' most globalized nations, based on 13 key indicators such as foreign trade, cross-border travel, Internet use, and international investment flows. Here is the magazine's list, in descending order, for 2002.

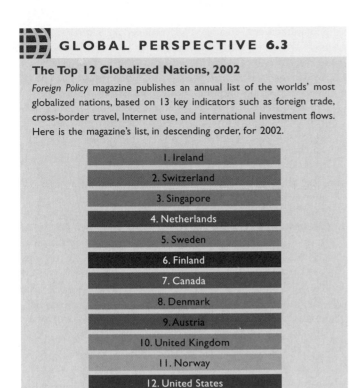

1. Ireland
2. Switzerland
3. Singapore
4. Netherlands
5. Sweden
6. Finland
7. Canada
8. Denmark
9. Austria
10. United Kingdom
11. Norway
12. United States

Source: A. T. Kearney, *Foreign Policy,* www.foreignpolicy.com.

McDonald's, Intel, Coca-Cola, Microsoft, Monsanto, Procter & Gamble, and Hewlett-Packard have contin-

ued to retain high market shares at home and have dramatically expanded their sales abroad. Of course, not all firms have been successful. Some have not been able to compete, because either their international competitors make higher-quality products, have lower production costs, or both.

Is the heightened competition that accompanies the global economy a good thing? Although some domestic producers *do* get hurt and their workers must find employment elsewhere, foreign competition clearly benefits consumers and society in general. Imports break down the monopoly power of existing firms, thereby lowering product prices and providing consumers with a greater variety of goods. Foreign competition also forces domestic producers to become more efficient and to improve product quality; that has already happened in several U.S. industries, including steel and autos. Most U.S. firms can and do compete quite successfully in the global marketplace.

What about the U.S. firms that cannot compete successfully in open markets? The harsh reality is that they should go out of business, much like an unsuccessful corner boutique. Persistent economic losses mean that scarce resources are not being used efficiently. Shifting those resources to alternative, profitable uses will increase total U.S. output. It will be far less expensive for the United States to provide training and, if necessary, relocation assistance to laid-off workers than to try to protect these jobs from foreign competition.

SUMMARY

1. Goods and services flows, capital and labor flows, information and technology flows, and financial flows link the United States and other countries.

2. International trade is growing in importance globally and for the United States. World trade is significant to the United States in two respects: (a) The absolute volumes of U.S. imports and exports exceed those of any other single nation. (b) The United States is completely dependent on trade for certain commodities and materials that cannot be obtained domestically.

3. Principal U.S. exports include chemicals, semiconductors, consumer durables, computers, and generating equipment; principal imports include automobiles, petroleum, computers, household appliances, and clothing. Quantitatively, Canada is the United States' most important trading partner.

4. Global trade has been greatly facilitated by (a) improvements in transportation technology, (b) improvements in communications technology, and (c) general declines in tar-

iffs. Although the United States, Japan, and the western European nations dominate the global economy, the total volume of trade has been increased by the contributions of several new trade participants. They include the Asian economies of Singapore, South Korea, Taiwan, and China (including Hong Kong), the eastern European countries (such as the Czech Republic, Hungary, and Poland), and the newly independent countries of the former Soviet Union (such as Estonia, Ukraine, and Azerbaijan).

5. Specialization based on comparative advantage enables nations to achieve higher standards of living through trade with other countries. A trading partner should specialize in products and services for which its domestic opportunity costs are lowest. The terms of trade must be such that both nations can obtain more of some product via trade than they could obtain by producing it at home.

6. The foreign exchange market sets exchange rates between currencies. Each nation's imports create a supply of its own currency and a demand for foreign currencies. The resulting

supply-demand equilibrium sets the exchange rate that links the currencies of all nations. Depreciation of a nation's currency reduces its imports and increases its exports; appreciation increases its imports and reduces its exports.

7. Governments influence trade flows through (a) protective tariffs, (b) quotas, (c) nontariff barriers, and (d) export subsidies. Such impediments to free trade result from misunderstandings about the advantages of free trade and from political considerations. By artificially increasing product prices, trade barriers cost U.S. consumers billions of dollars annually.

8. The Reciprocal Trade Agreements Act of 1934 marked the beginning of a trend toward lower U.S. tariffs. Most-favored-nation status allows a nation to export goods into the United States at the United States' lowest tariff level, then or at any later time.

9. In 1947 the General Agreement on Tariffs and Trade (GATT) was formed to encourage nondiscriminatory treatment for all member nations, to reduce tariffs, and to eliminate import quotas. The Uruguay Round of GATT negotiations (1993) reduced tariffs and quotas, liberalized trade in services, reduced agricultural subsidies, reduced pirating of intellectual property, and phased out quotas on textiles.

10. GATT's successor, the World Trade Organization (WTO), has 145 member nations. It implements WTO agreements, rules on trade disputes between members, and provides forums for continued discussions on trade liberalization. The latest round of trade negotiations—the Doha Round—was launched in late 2001 and is expected to continue for several years.

11. Free-trade zones (trade blocs) liberalize trade within regions but may at the same time impede trade with non-bloc members. Two examples of free-trade arrangements are the 25-member European Union (EU) and the North American Free Trade Agreement (NAFTA), comprising Canada, Mexico, and the United States. Twelve of the EU nations have abandoned their national currencies for a common currency called the euro.

12. The global economy has created intense foreign competition in many U.S. product markets, but most U.S. firms are able to compete well both at home and globally.

TERMS AND CONCEPTS

multinational corporations

comparative advantage

terms of trade

foreign exchange market

exchange rates

depreciation

appreciation

protective tariffs

import quotas

nontariff barriers

export subsidies

Smoot-Hawley Tariff Act

Reciprocal Trade Agreements Act

most-favored-nation clauses

General Agreement on Tariffs and Trade (GATT)

World Trade Organization (WTO)

Doha Round

European Union (EU)

trade bloc

euro

North American Free Trade Agreement (NAFTA)

STUDY QUESTIONS

1. Describe the four major economic flows that link the United States with other nations. Provide a specific example to illustrate each flow. Explain the relationships between the top and bottom flows in Figure 6.1.

2. How important is international trade to the U.S. economy? In terms of volume, does the United States trade more with the industrially advanced economies or with developing economies? What country is the United States' most important trading partner, quantitatively?

3. What factors account for the rapid growth of world trade since the Second World War? Who are the major players in international trade today? Besides Japan, what other Asian nations play significant roles in international trade?

4. *Key Question* The following are production possibilities tables for South Korea and the United States. Assume that before specialization and trade the optimal product mix for South Korea is alternative B and for the United States is alternative U.

	South Korea Production Possibilities					
Product	A	B	C	D	E	F
Radios (in thousands)	30	24	18	12	6	0
Chemicals (in tons)	0	6	12	18	24	30

	U.S. Production Possibilities					
Product	R	S	T	U	V	W
Radios (in thousands)	10	8	6	4	2	0
Chemicals (in tons)	0	4	8	12	16	20

a. Are comparative-cost conditions such that the two areas should specialize? If so, what product should each produce?

b. What is the total gain in radio and chemical output that would result from such specialization?

c. What are the limits of the terms of trade? Suppose actual terms of trade are 1 unit of radios for $1\frac{1}{2}$ units of chemicals and that 4 units of radios are exchanged for 6 units of chemicals. What are the gains from specialization and trade for each nation?

d. Can you conclude from this illustration that specialization according to comparative advantage results in more efficient use of world resources? Explain.

5. Suppose that the comparative-cost ratios of two products—baby formula and tuna fish—are as follows in the hypothetical nations of Canswicki and Tunata:

> Canswicki: 1 can baby formula ≡ 2 cans tuna fish
> Tunata: 1 can baby formula ≡ 4 cans tuna fish

In what product should each nation specialize? Explain why terms of trade of 1 can baby formula ≡ $2\frac{1}{2}$ cans tuna fish would be acceptable to both nations.

6. *Key Question* True or False? "U.S. exports create a demand for foreign currencies; foreign imports of U.S. goods create a supply of foreign currencies." Explain. Would a decline in U.S. consumer income or a weakening of U.S. preferences for foreign products cause the dollar to depreciate or to appreciate? Other things equal, what would be the effects of that depreciation or appreciation on U.S. exports and imports?

7. If the European euro were to decline in value (depreciate) in the foreign exchange market, would it be easier or harder for the French to sell their wine in the United States? Suppose you were planning a trip to Paris. How would depreciation of the euro change the dollar cost of your trip?

8. True or False? "An increase in the American dollar price of the South Korean won implies that the South Korean won has depreciated in value." Explain.

9. What measures do governments take to promote exports and restrict imports? Who benefits and who loses from protectionist policies? What is the net outcome for society?

10. *Key Question* Identify and state the significance of each of the following: (*a*) WTO; (*b*) EU; (*c*) euro; (*d*) NAFTA. What commonality do they share?

11. Explain: "Free-trade zones such as the EU and NAFTA lead a double life: They can promote free trade among members, but they pose serious trade obstacles for non-members." Do you think the net effects of trade blocs are good or bad for world trade? Why? How do the efforts of the WTO relate to these trade blocs?

12. Speculate as to why some U.S. firms strongly support trade liberalization while other U.S. firms favor protectionism. Speculate as to why some U.S. labor unions strongly support trade liberalization while other U.S. labor unions strongly oppose it.

13. What is the Doha Round and why is it so-named? How does it relate to the WTO? How does it relate to the Uruguay Round?

14. *(Last Word)* What point is Bastiat trying to make in his petition of the candlemakers?

15. *Web-Based Question: Trade balances with partner countries* The U.S. Census Bureau, at www.census.gov/foreign-trade/www/statistics.html, lists the top trading partners of the United States (imports and exports added together) as well as the top 10 countries with which the United States has a trade surplus and a trade deficit. Using the current year-to-date data, compare the top 10 deficit and surplus countries with the top 10 trading partners. Are deficit and surplus countries equally represented in the top 10 trading partners list, or does one group dominate the list? The top 10 trading partners represent what percent of U.S. imports and what percent of U.S. exports?

16. *Web-Based Question: Foreign exchange rates—the yen for dollars* The Federal Reserve System website, www.federalreserve.gov/releases/H10/hist/, provides historical foreign-exchange-rate data for a wide variety of currencies. Look at the data for the Japanese yen from 1995 to the present. Assume that you were in Tokyo every New Year's from January 1, 1995, to this year and bought a *bento* (box lunch) for 1000 yen each year. Convert this amount to dollars using the yen-dollar exchange rate for each January since 1995, and plot the dollar price of the *bento* over time. Has the dollar appreciated or depreciated against the yen? What was the least amount in dollars that your box lunch cost? The most?

17. *Web-Based Question: The Doha Round—what is the current status?* Determine and briefly summarize the current status of the Doha Round of trade negotiations by accessing the World Trade Organization site, www.wto.org. Is the round still in progress or has it been concluded with an agreement? If the former, when and where was the latest ministerial meeting? If the latter, what are the main features of the agreement?

Part II | Macroeconomic Measurement and Basic Concepts

7 | *Measuring Domestic Output and National Income*

"Disposable Income Flat." "Personal Consumption Surges." "Investment Spending Stagnates." "GDP Up 4 Percent."

These headlines, typical of those in *The Wall Street Journal,* give economists valuable information on the state of the economy. To beginning economics students, however, they may be gibberish. This chapter will help you learn the language of macroeconomics and national income accounting and will provide you with a basic understanding that you can build on in the next several chapters.

Assessing the Economy's Performance

National income accounting measures the economy's overall performance. It does for the economy as a whole what private accounting does for the individual firm or for the individual household.

A business firm measures its flows of income and expenditures regularly—usually every 3 months or once a year. With that information in hand, the firm can gauge its economic health. If things are going well and profits are good, the accounting data can be used to explain that success. Were costs down? Was output up? Have market prices risen? If things are going badly and profits are poor, the firm may be able to identify the reason by studying the record over several accounting periods. All this information helps the firm's managers plot their future strategy.

National income accounting operates in much the same way for the economy as a whole. The Bureau of Economic Analysis (BEA, an agency of the Commerce Department) compiles the National Income and Product Accounts (NIPA) for the U.S. economy. This accounting enables economists and policymakers to:
- Assess the health of the economy by comparing levels of production at regular intervals.
- Track the long-run course of the economy to see whether it has grown, been constant, or declined.
- Formulate policies that will safeguard and improve the economy's health.

Gross Domestic Product

The primary measure of the economy's performance is its annual total output of goods and services or, as it is called, its *aggregate output.* Aggregate output is labeled **gross domestic product (GDP):** *the total market value of all final goods and services produced in a given year.* GDP includes all goods and services produced by either citizen-supplied or foreign-supplied resources employed within the country. The U.S. GDP includes the market value of Fords produced by an American-owned factory in Michigan and the

TABLE 7.1

Comparing Heterogeneous Output by Using Money Prices

Year	Annual Output	Market Value
1	3 sofas and 2 computers	3 at $500 + 2 at $2000 = $5500
2	2 sofas and 3 computers	2 at $500 + 3 at $2000 = $7000

market value of Hondas produced by a Japanese-owned factory in Ohio.

A Monetary Measure

If the economy produces three sofas and two computers in year 1 and two sofas and three computers in year 2, in which year is output greater? We can't answer that question until we attach a price tag to each of the two products to indicate how society evaluates their relative worth.

That's what GDP does. It is a *monetary measure*. Without such a measure we would have no way of comparing the relative values of the vast number of goods and services produced in different years. In Table 7.1 the price of sofas is $500 and the price of computers is $2000. GDP would gauge the output of year 2 ($7000) as greater than the output of year 1 ($5500), because society places a higher monetary value on the output of year 2. Society is willing to pay $1500 more for the combination of goods produced in year 2 than for the combination of goods produced in year 1.

Avoiding Multiple Counting

To measure aggregate output accurately, all goods and services produced in a particular year must be counted once and only once. Because most products go through a series of production stages before they reach the market, some of their components are bought and sold many times. To avoid counting those components each time, GDP includes only the market value of *final goods* and ignores *intermediate goods* altogether.

Intermediate goods are goods and services that are purchased for resale or for further processing or manufacturing. **Final goods** are goods and services that are purchased for final use by the consumer, not for resale or for further processing or manufacturing.

Why is the value of final goods included in GDP but the value of intermediate goods excluded? Because the value of final goods already includes the value of all the intermediate goods that were used in producing them. Including the value of intermediate goods would amount to **multiple counting,** and that would distort the value of GDP.

To see why, suppose that there are five stages involved in manufacturing a wool suit and getting it to the consumer—the final user. Table 7.2 shows that firm A, a sheep ranch, sells $120 worth of wool to firm B, a wool processor. Firm A pays out the $120 in wages, rent, interest, and profit. Firm B processes the wool and sells it to firm C, a suit manufacturer, for $180. What does firm B do with the $180 it receives? It pays $120 to firm A for the wool and uses the remaining $60 to pay wages, rent, interest, and profit for the resources used in processing the wool. Firm C, the manufacturer, sells the suit to firm D, a wholesaler, which sells it to firm E, a retailer. Then at last a consumer, the final user, comes in and buys the suit for $350.

How much of these amounts should we include in GDP to account for the production of the suit? Just $350, the value of the final product. The $350 includes all the intermediate transactions leading up to the product's final sale. Including the sum of all the intermediate sales, $1140, in GDP would amount to multiple counting. The production and sale of the final suit generated just $350 of output, not $1140.

Alternatively, we could avoid multiple counting by measuring and cumulating only the *value added* at each stage. **Value added** is the market value of a firm's output *less* the value of the inputs the firm has bought from others. At each stage, the difference between what a firm pays for a product and what it receives from selling the product is paid out as wages, rent, interest, and profit. Column 3 of Table 7.2 shows that the value added by firm B is $60, the difference between the $180 value of its output and the $120 it paid for the input from firm A. We find the total value of the suit by adding together all the values added by the five firms. Similarly, by calculating and summing the values added to all the goods and services produced by all firms in the economy, we can find the market value of the economy's total output—its GDP.

GDP Excludes Nonproduction Transactions

Although many monetary transactions in the economy involve final goods and services, many others do not. Those nonproduction transactions must be excluded from GDP

TABLE 7.2

Value Added in a Five-Stage Production Process

(1) Stage of Production	(2) Sales Value of Materials or Product	(3) Value Added
	$ 0	
Firm A, sheep ranch	120	$120 (= $120 − $ 0)
Firm B, wool processor	180	60 (= 180 − 120)
Firm C, suit manufacturer	220	40 (= 220 − 180)
Firm D, clothing wholesaler	270	50 (= 270 − 220)
Firm E, retail clothier	**350**	80 (= 350 − 270)
Total sales values	$1140	
Value added (total income)		**$350**

because they have nothing to do with the generation of final goods. *Nonproduction transactions* are of two types: purely financial transactions and secondhand sales.

Financial Transactions   Purely financial transactions include the following:

- *Public transfer payments*   These are the social security payments, welfare payments, and veterans' payments that the government makes directly to households. Since the recipients contribute nothing to *current production* in return, to include such payments in GDP would be to overstate the year's output.
- *Private transfer payments*   Such payments include, for example, the money that parents give children or the cash gifts given at Christmas time. They produce no output. They simply transfer funds from one private individual to another and consequently do not enter into GDP.
- *Stock market transactions*   The buying and selling of stocks (and bonds) is just a matter of swapping bits of paper. Stock market transactions create nothing in the way of current production and are not included in GDP. Payments for the services of a security broker *are* included, however, because those services do contribute to current output.

Secondhand Sales   Secondhand sales contribute nothing to current production and for that reason are excluded from GDP. Suppose you sell your 1965 Ford Mustang to a friend; that transaction would be ignored in reckoning this year's GDP because it generates no current production. The same would be true if you sold a brand-new Mustang to a neighbor a week after you purchased it. **(Key Question 3)**

Two Ways of Looking at GDP: Spending and Income

Let's look again at how the market value of total output—or of any single unit of total output—is measured. Given the data listed in Table 7.2, how can we measure the market value of a suit?

One way is to see how much the final user paid for it. That will tell us the market value of the final product. Or we can add up the entire wage, rental, interest, and profit incomes that were created in producing the suit. The second approach is the value-added technique used in Table 7.2.

The final-product approach and the value-added approach are two ways of looking at the same thing. *What is spent on making a product is income to those who helped make it.* If $350 is spent on manufacturing a suit, then $350 is the total income derived from its production.

We can look at GDP in the same two ways. We can view GDP as the sum of all the money spent in buying it. That is the *output approach*, or **expenditures approach.** Or we can view GDP in terms of the income derived or created from producing it. That is the *earnings* or *allocations approach*, or the **income approach.**

As illustrated in Figure 7.1, we can determine GDP for a particular year either by adding up all that was spent to buy total output or by adding up all the money that was derived as income from its production. Buying (spending money) and selling (receiving income) are two aspects of the same transaction. On the expenditures side of GDP, all final goods produced by the economy are bought either by three domestic sectors (households, businesses, and government) or by foreign buyers. On the income side (once certain statistical adjustments are made), the total

FIGURE 7.1

The expenditures and income approaches to GDP. There are two general approaches to measuring gross domestic product. We can determine GDP as the value of output by summing all expenditures on that output. Alternatively, with some modifications, we can determine GDP by adding up all the components of income arising from the production of that output.

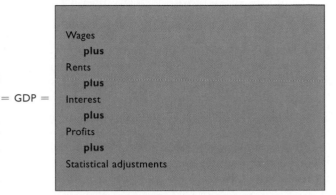

receipts acquired from the sale of that total output are allocated to the suppliers of resources as wage, rent, interest, and profit income.

The Expenditures Approach

To determine GDP using the expenditures approach, we add up all the spending on final goods and services that has taken place throughout the year. National income accountants use precise terms for the types of spending listed on the left side of Figure 7.1.

Personal Consumption Expenditures (C)

What we have called "consumption expenditures by households," the national income accountants call **personal consumption expenditures.** That term covers all expenditures by households on *durable consumer goods* (automobiles, refrigerators, video recorders), *nondurable consumer goods* (bread, milk, vitamins, pencils, toothpaste), and *consumer expenditures for services* (of lawyers, doctors, mechanics, barbers). The accountants use the symbol C to designate this component of GDP.

Gross Private Domestic Investment (I_g)

Under the heading **gross private domestic investment,** the accountants include the following items:
- All final purchases of machinery, equipment, and tools by business enterprises.
- All construction.
- Changes in inventories.

Notice that this list, except for the first item, includes more than we have meant by "investment" so far. The second item includes residential construction as well as the construction of new factories, warehouses, and stores. Why do the accountants regard residential construction as investment rather than consumption? Because apartment buildings and houses, like factories and stores, earn income when they are rented or leased. Owner-occupied houses are treated as investment goods because they *could be* rented to bring in an income return. So the national income accountants treat all residential construction as investment. Finally, increases in inventories (unsold goods) are considered to be investment because they represent, in effect, "unconsumed output." And, as we know from production possibilities analysis, that is precisely what investment is.

Positive and Negative Changes in Inventories

Let's look at changes in inventories more closely. Inventories can either increase or decrease over some period. Suppose they increased by $10 billion between December 31, 2001, and December 31, 2002. That means the economy produced $10 billion more output than was purchased in 2002. We need to count all output produced in 2002 as part of that year's GDP, even though some of it remained unsold at the end of the year. This is accomplished by including the $10 billion increase in inventories as investment in 2002. That way the expenditures in 2002 will correctly measure the output produced that year.

Alternatively, suppose that inventories decreased by $10 billion in 2002. This "drawing down of inventories" means that the economy sold $10 billion more of output in 2002 than it produced that year. It did this by selling goods produced in prior years—goods already counted as GDP in those years. Unless corrected, expenditures in 2002 will overstate GDP for 2002. So in 2002 we consider the $10 billion decline in inventories as "negative investment" and subtract it from total investment that year. Thus, expenditures in 2002 will correctly measure the output produced in 2002.

Noninvestment Transactions

So much for what investment is. You also need to know what it isn't. Investment does *not* include the transfer of paper assets (stocks, bonds) or the resale of tangible assets (houses, jewelry, boats). Such transactions merely transfer the ownership of existing assets. Investment has to do with the creation of *new* capital assets—assets that create jobs and income. The mere transfer (sale) of claims to existing capital goods does not create new capital.

Gross Investment versus Net Investment

As we have seen, the category gross private domestic investment includes (1) all final purchases of machinery, equipment, and tools; (2) all construction; and (3) changes in inventories. The words "private" and "domestic" mean that we are speaking of spending by private businesses, not by government (public) agencies, and that the investment is taking place inside the country, not abroad.

The word "gross" means that we are referring to all investment goods—both those that replace machinery, equipment, and buildings that were used up (worn out or made obsolete) in producing the current year's output and any net additions to the economy's stock of capital. Gross investment includes investment in replacement capital *and* in added capital.

In contrast, **net private domestic investment** includes *only* investment in the form of added capital. The amount of capital that is used up over the course of a year is called *depreciation*. So

Net investment = gross investment − depreciation

In typical years, gross investment exceeds depreciation. Thus net investment is positive and the nation's stock of capital rises, as illustrated in Figure 7.2. Such increases in capital shift the U.S. production possibilities curve outward and thus expand the nation's production capacity.

Gross investment need not always exceed depreciation, however. When gross investment and depreciation *are equal*, net investment is zero and there is no change in the size of the capital stock. When gross investment *is less than* depreciation, net investment is negative. The economy then is *disinvesting*—using up more capital than it is producing—and the nation's stock of capital shrinks. That happened in the Great Depression of the 1930s.

National income accountants use the symbol I for private domestic investment spending, along with the subscript g to signify gross investment. They use the subscript n to signify net investment. But it is gross investment, I_g, that they use in determining GDP.

Government Purchases (G)

The third category of expenditures in the national income accounts is **government purchases**, officially labeled "government consumption expenditures and gross investment." These expenditures have two components: (1) expenditures for goods and services that government consumes in providing public services and (2) expenditures for *social capital* such as schools and highways, which have long lifetimes. Government purchases (Federal, state, and local) include all government expenditures on final goods and all direct purchases of resources, including labor. It does *not* include government transfer payments, because, as we have seen, they merely transfer government receipts to certain households and generate no production of any sort. National income accountants use the symbol G to signify government purchases.

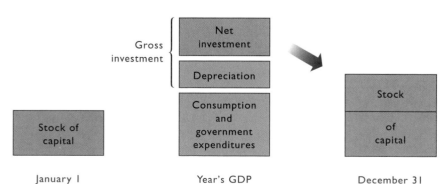

FIGURE 7.2

Gross investment, depreciation, net investment, and the stock of capital.   When gross investment exceeds depreciation, the economy is making a net addition to its stock of private capital; other things equal, the economy's production capacity expands.

CONSIDER THIS . . .

Stock Answers about Flows

© Lester Lefkowitz/CORBIS

An analogy of a reservoir is helpful in thinking about a nation's capital stock, investment, and depreciation. Picture a reservoir that has water flowing in from a river and flowing out from an outlet after it passes through turbines. The volume of water in the reservoir *at any particular point in time* is a "stock." In contrast, the inflow from the river and outflow from the outlet are "flows."

The volume or stock of water in the reservoir will rise if the weekly inflow exceeds the weekly outflow. It will fall if the inflow is less than the outflow. And it will remain constant if the two flows are equal.

Now let's apply this analogy to the stock of capital, gross investment, and depreciation. The stock of capital is the total capital in place at any point in time and is analogous to the level of water in the reservoir. Changes in this capital stock over some period, for example, 1 year, depend on *gross investment* and *depreciation*. Gross investment (analogous to the reservoir inflow) is an addition of capital goods and therefore adds to the stock of capital, while depreciation (analogous to the reservoir outflow) is the using up of capital and thus subtracts from the capital stock. The capital stock increases when gross investment exceeds depreciation, declines when gross investment is less than depreciation, and remains the same when gross investment and depreciation are equal.

Alternatively, the stock of capital increases when *net investment* (gross investment *minus* depreciation) is positive. When net investment is negative, the stock of capital declines, and when net investment is zero, the stock of capital remains constant.

Net Exports (X_n)

International trade transactions are a significant item in national income accounting. We know that GDP records all spending on goods and services produced in the United States, including spending on U.S. output by people abroad. So we must include the value of exports when we are using the expenditures approach to determine GDP.

At the same time, we know that Americans spend a great deal of money on imports—goods and services produced abroad. That spending shows up in other nations' GDP. We must subtract the value of imports from U.S. spending to avoid overstating total production in the United States.

Rather than add exports and then subtract imports, national income accountants use "exports less imports," or **net exports.** We designate exports as X, imports as M, and net exports as X_n:

$$\text{Net exports } (X_n) = \text{exports } (X) - \text{imports } (M)$$

Table 7.3 shows that in 2002 Americans spent $424 billion more on imports than foreigners spent on U.S. exports. That is, net exports in 2002 were a *minus* $424 billion.

Putting It All Together: GDP = C + I$_g$ + G + X$_n$

Taken together, these four categories of expenditures provide a measure of the market value of a given year's total output—its GDP. For the United States in 2002 (Table 7.3),

$$\begin{aligned} \text{GDP} &= \$7304 + 1593 + 1973 - 424 \\ &= \$10{,}446 \text{ billion} \end{aligned}$$

TABLE 7.3

Accounting Statement for the U.S. Economy, 2002 (in Billions)

Receipts: Expenditures Approach		Allocations: Income Approach	
Personal consumption expenditures (C)	$ 7304	Compensation of employees	$ 5977
Gross private domestic investment (I$_g$)	1593	Rents	142
Government purchases (G)	1973	Interest	684
Net exports (X$_n$)	−424	Proprietors' income	757
		Corporate income taxes	213
		Dividends	434
		Undistributed corporate profits	141
		National income	$ 8348
		Indirect business taxes	695
		Consumption of fixed capital	1393
		Net foreign factor income earned in the U.S.	10
Gross domestic product	$10,446	Gross domestic product	$10,446

Source: Bureau of Economic Analysis. Preliminary 2002 data.

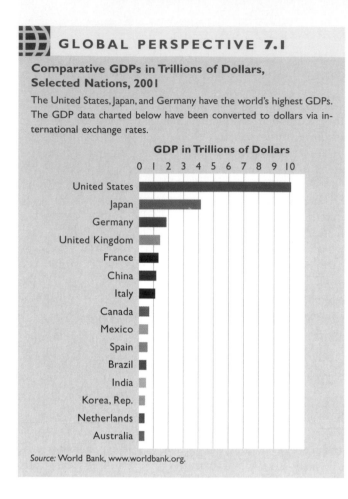

GLOBAL PERSPECTIVE 7.1

Comparative GDPs in Trillions of Dollars, Selected Nations, 2001

The United States, Japan, and Germany have the world's highest GDPs. The GDP data charted below have been converted to dollars via international exchange rates.

Source: World Bank, www.worldbank.org.

Global Perspective 7.1 lists the GDPs of several countries.

The Income Approach

Table 7.3 shows how 2002's expenditures of $10,446 billion were allocated as income to those responsible for producing the output. It would be simple if we could say that the entire amount flowed back to them in the form of wages, rent, interest, and profit. But we have to make a few adjustments to balance the expenditures and income sides of the account. We look first at the items that make up *national income*, shown on the right side of the table. Then we turn to the adjustments.

Compensation of Employees

By far the largest share of national income—$5977 billion—was paid as wages and salaries by business and government to their employees. That figure also includes wage and salary supplements, in particular, payments by employers into social insurance and into a variety of private pension, health, and welfare funds for workers.

Rents

Rents consist of the income received by the households and businesses that supply property resources. They include the monthly payments tenants make to landlords and the lease payments corporations pay for the use of office space. The figure used in the national accounts is *net rent*—gross rental income minus depreciation of the rental property.

Interest

Interest consists of the money paid by private businesses to the suppliers of money capital. It also includes such items as the interest households receive on savings deposits, certificates of deposit (CDs), and corporate bonds.

Proprietors' Income

What we have loosely termed "profits" is broken down by the national income accountants into two accounts: proprietors' income, which consists of the net income of sole proprietorships, partnerships, and other unincorporated businesses; and corporate profits. Proprietors' income flows to the proprietors.

Corporate Profits

Corporate profits are the earnings of owners of corporations. National income accountants subdivide corporate profits into three categories:
- *Corporate income taxes*   These taxes are levied on corporations' net earnings and flow to the government.
- *Dividends*   These are the part of corporate profits that are paid to the corporate stockholders and thus flow to households—the ultimate owners of all corporations.
- *Undistributed corporate profits*   These are monies saved by corporations to be invested later in new plants and equipment. They are also called *retained earnings*.

From National Income to GDP

The national income accountants add together employee compensation, rents, interest, proprietors' income, and corporate profits and get **national income**—*all the income that flows to American-supplied resources, whether here or abroad*. But notice that the figure for national income shown in Table 7.3—$8348 billion—is less than GDP as reckoned by the expenditures approach shown on the left side of the table. The account is balanced by adding three items to national income.

Indirect Business Taxes

Indirect business taxes include general sales taxes, excise taxes, business property taxes, license fees, and customs duties. Why do we add indirect business taxes to national income as a way of balancing expenditures and income?

Assume that a firm produces a product that sells for $1. The production and sale of that product create $1 of wage, rent, interest, and profit income. But now the government imposes a 5 percent sales tax on all products sold at retail. The retailer adds the tax to the price of the product and shifts it along to consumers, and this becomes part of consumption expenditures. But the $.05 is clearly not earned income because the government contributes nothing to the production of the product in return for it. Only $1 of what consumers pay goes out as wage, rent, interest, and profit income. So the national income accountants need to add the $.05 to the $1.00 of national income in calculating GDP and make the same adjustment for the entire economy.

Consumption of Fixed Capital

The useful lives of private capital equipment (such as bakery ovens or automobile assembly lines) extend far beyond the year in which they were produced. To avoid understating profit and income in the year of purchase and to avoid overstating profit and income in succeeding years, the cost of such capital must be allocated over its lifetime. The amount allocated is an estimate of how much of the capital is being used up each year. It is called *depreciation*. A bookkeeping entry, the depreciation allowance results in a more accurate statement of profit and income for the economy each year. Social capital, such as courthouses and bridges, also requires a depreciation allowance in the national income accounts.

The huge depreciation charge made against private and social capital each year is called **consumption of fixed capital** because it is the allowance for capital that has been "consumed" in producing the year's GDP. It is the portion of GDP that is set aside to pay for the ultimate replacement of those capital goods.

The money allocated to consumption of fixed capital (the depreciation allowance) is a cost of production and thus included in the gross value of output. But this money is not available for other purposes, and, unlike other costs of production, it does not add to anyone's income. So it is not included in national income. We must therefore add it to national income to achieve balance with the economy's expenditures, as in Table 7.3.

Net Foreign Factor Income

The last step in balancing the national account is to make a slight adjustment in "national" income versus "domestic" income. National income is *the total income of Americans, whether it was earned in the United States or abroad*. But GDP is a measure of domestic output—total output produced within the United States regardless of the nationality of those who provide the resources. So in moving from national income to GDP, we must consider the income Americans gain from supplying resources abroad and the income foreigners gain by supplying resources in the United States. In 2002, foreign-owned resources earned $10 billion more in the United States than American-owned resources earned abroad. That difference is called *net foreign factor income*. For that reason it is not included in U.S. national income. We must *add* it to national income in determining the value of U.S. domestic output (output produced within the U.S. borders).

Table 7.3 summarizes the expenditures approach and income approach to GDP. The left side shows what the U.S. economy produced in 2002 and what was spent to produce it. The right side shows how those expenditures, when appropriately adjusted, were allocated as income.

QUICK REVIEW 7.1

- Gross domestic product (GDP) is a measure of the total market value of all final goods and services produced by the economy in a given year.

- The expenditures approach to GDP sums the total spending on final goods and services: GDP = $C + I_g + G + X_n$

- The economy's stock of private capital expands when net investment is positive; stays constant when net investment is zero; and declines when net investment is negative.

- The income approach to GDP sums compensation to employees, rent, interest, proprietors' income, and corporate profits to obtain national income. To that amount is added indirect business taxes, consumption of fixed capital (depreciation), and net foreign factor income to measure GDP.

Other National Accounts

Several other national accounts provide additional useful information about the economy's performance. We can derive these accounts by making various adjustments to GDP.

Net Domestic Product

As a measure of total output, GDP does not make allowances for replacing the capital goods used up in each year's production. As a result, it does not tell us how much new output was available for consumption and for additions to the stock of capital. To determine that, we must subtract from GDP the capital that was consumed in producing the GDP and that had to be replaced. That is, we need to subtract consumption of fixed capital (depreciation) from GDP. The result is a measure of **net domestic product (NDP):**

$$NDP = GDP - \text{consumption of fixed capital (depreciation)}$$

For the United States in 2002:

	Billions
Gross domestic product	$10,446
Consumption of fixed capital	−1393
Net domestic product	$ 9053

NDP is simply GDP adjusted for depreciation. It measures the total annual output that the entire economy—households, businesses, government, and foreigners—can consume without impairing its capacity to produce in ensuing years.

National Income

Sometimes it is useful to know how much Americans earned for their contributions of land, labor, capital, and entrepreneurial talent. Recall that U.S. national income (NI) includes all income earned through the use of American-owned resources, whether they are located at home or abroad. To derive NI from NDP, we must make two adjustments:

- **Subtract net foreign factor income from NDP.** Net foreign factor income is factor (resource) income earned by foreigners in the United States in excess of factor income earned by Americans abroad. Since foreigners earn this income, it is not included in U.S. national income.
- **Subtract indirect business taxes from NDP.** Because government is not an economic resource, the indirect business taxes it collects do not qualify as payments to productive resources and thus are not included in national income.

For the United States in 2002:

	Billions
Net domestic product	$9053
Net foreign factor income earned	−10
Indirect business taxes	−695
National income	$8348

We know, too, that we can calculate national income through the income approach by simply adding up employee compensation, rent, interest, proprietors' income, and corporate profit.

Personal Income

Personal income (PI) includes all income received whether earned or unearned. It is likely to differ from national income (income earned) because some income earned—Social Security taxes (payroll taxes), corporate income taxes, and undistributed corporate profits—is not received by households. Conversely, some income received—such as Social Security payments, unemployment compensation payments, welfare payments, disability and education payments to veterans, and private pension payments—is not earned. These transfer payments must be added to obtain PI.

In moving from national income to personal income, we must subtract the income that is earned but not received and add the income that is received but not earned. For the United States in 2002:

	Billions
National income	$8348
Social Security contributions	−748
Corporate income taxes	−213
Undistributed corporate profits	−141
Transfer payments	+1683*
Personal income	$8929

*Includes a statistical discrepancy.

Disposable Income

Disposable income (DI) is personal income less personal taxes. Personal taxes include personal income taxes, personal property taxes, and inheritance taxes. Disposable income is the amount of income that households have left over after paying their personal taxes. They are free to divide that income between consumption (*C*) and saving (*S*):

$$DI = C + S$$

For the United States in 2002:

	Billions
Personal income	$8929
Personal taxes	−1113
Disposable income	$7816

Table 7.4 summarizes the relationships among GDP, NDP, NI, PI, and DI. **(Key Question 8)**

QUICK REVIEW 7.2

- Net domestic product (NDP) is the market value of GDP minus consumption of fixed capital (depreciation).
- National income (NI) is all income earned through the use of American-owned resources, whether located at home or abroad.
- Personal income (PI) is all income received by households, whether earned or not.
- Disposable income (DI) is all income received by households minus personal taxes.

The Circular Flow Revisited

Figure 7.3 is an elaborate flow diagram that shows the economy's four main sectors along with the flows of expenditures and allocations that determine GDP, NDP, NI, and PI. The blue arrows represent the spending flows—$C + I_g + G + X_n$—that together measure gross domestic product. To the right of the GDP rectangle are red arrows that show first the allocations of GDP and then the adjustments needed to derive NDP, NI, PI, and DI.

The diagram illustrates the adjustments necessary to determine each of the national income accounts. For example, net domestic product is smaller than GDP because

TABLE 7.4

The Relationships between GDP, NDP, NI, PI, and DI in the United States, 2002

	Billions
Gross domestic product (GDP)	$10,446
Consumption of fixed capital	−1393
Net domestic product (NDP)	$ 9053
Net foreign factor income earned in the U.S.	−10
Indirect business taxes	−695
National income (NI)	$ 8348
Social Security contributions	−748
Corporate income taxes	−213
Undistributed corporate profits	−141
Transfer payments	+1683
Personal income (PI)	$ 8929
Personal taxes	−1113
Disposable income (DI)	$ 7816

consumption of fixed capital flows away from GDP in determining NDP. National income is smaller than NDP because indirect business taxes and net foreign factor income earned in the United States flow away from NDP in determining NI. And so on.

Note the three domestic sectors of the economy: households, government, and businesses. The household sector has an inflow of disposable income and outflows of consumption spending and saving. The government sector has an inflow of revenue in the form of types of taxes and an outflow of government disbursements in the form of purchases and transfers. The business sector has inflows of three major sources of funds for business investment and an outflow of investment expenditures.

Finally, note the foreign sector (all other countries) in the flow diagram. Spending by foreigners on U.S. exports adds to U.S. GDP, but some of U.S. consumption, government, and investment expenditures buy imported products. The flow from foreign markets shows that we handle this complication by calculating net exports (U.S. exports minus U.S. imports). The net export flow may be a positive or negative amount, adding to or subtracting from U.S. GDP.

Figure 7.3 shows that flows of expenditures and income are part of a continuous, repetitive process. Cause and effect are intermingled: Expenditures create income, and from this income arise expenditures, which again flow to resource owners as income.

FIGURE 7.3

U.S. domestic output and the flows of expenditure and income. This figure is an elaborate circular flow diagram that fits the expenditures and allocations sides of GDP to one another. The expenditures flows are shown in blue; the allocations or income flows are shown in red. You should trace through the income and expenditures flows, relating them to the five basic national income accounting measures.

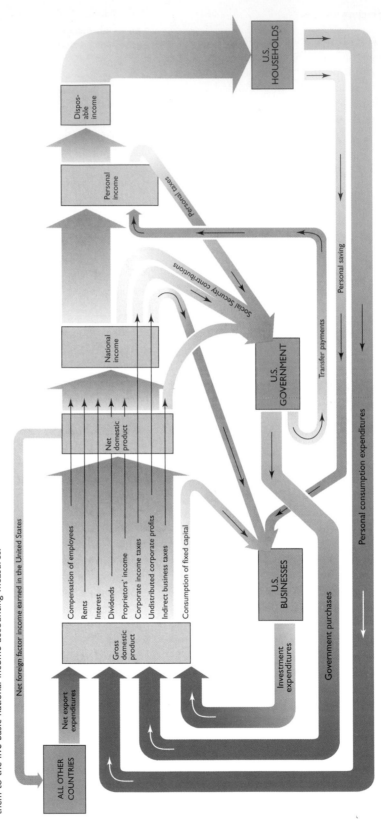

Nominal GDP versus Real GDP

Recall that GDP is a measure of the market or money value of all final goods and services produced by the economy in a given year. We use money or nominal values as a common denominator in order to sum that heterogeneous output into a meaningful total. But that creates a problem: How can we compare the market values of GDP from year to year if the value of money itself changes in response to inflation or deflation? After all, we determine the value of GDP by multiplying total output by market prices.

Whether there is a 5 percent increase in output with no change in prices or a 5 percent increase in prices with no change in output, the change in the value of GDP will be the same. And yet it is the *quantity* of goods that get produced and distributed to households that affects our standard of living, not the price of the goods. The hamburger that sold for $2 in 2000 yields the same satisfaction as an identical hamburger that sold for 50 cents in 1970.

The way around this problem is to *deflate* GDP when prices rise and to *inflate* GDP when prices fall. These adjustments give us a measure of GDP for various years as if the value of the dollar had always been the same as it was in some reference year. A GDP based on the prices that prevailed when the output was produced is called unadjusted GDP, or **nominal GDP.** A GDP that has been deflated or inflated to reflect changes in the price level is called adjusted GDP, or **real GDP.**

Adjustment Process in a One-Product Economy

There are two ways we can adjust nominal GDP to reflect price changes. For simplicity, let's assume that the economy produces only one good, pizza, in the amounts indicated in Table 7.5 for years 1, 2, and 3. Suppose that

we gather revenue data directly from the financial reports of the pizza businesses to measure nominal GDP in various years. After completing our effort, we will have determined nominal GDP for each year, as shown in column 4 of Table 7.5. We will have no way of knowing to what extent changes in price and/or changes in quantity of output have accounted for the increases or decreases in nominal GDP that we observe.

GDP Price Index How can we determine real GDP in our pizza economy? One way is to assemble data on the price changes that occurred over various years (column 2) and use them to establish an overall price index for the entire period. Then we can use the index in each year to adjust nominal GDP to real GDP for that year.

A **price index** is *a measure of the price of a specified collection of goods and services, called a "market basket," in a given year as compared to the price of an identical (or highly similar) collection of goods and services in a reference year.* That point of reference, or benchmark, is known as the base period or base year. More formally,

$$\text{Price index in given year} = \frac{\text{price of market basket in specific year}}{\text{price of same market basket in base year}} \times 100 \quad (1)$$

By convention, the price ratio between a given year and the base year is multiplied by 100 to facilitate computation. For example, a price ratio of 2/1 (= 2) is expressed as a price index of 200. A price ratio of 1/3 (= .33) is expressed as a price index of 33.

In our pizza-only example, of course, our market basket consists of only one product. Column 2 of Table 7.5 reveals that the price of pizza was $10 in year 1, $20 in year 2, $25 in year 3, and so on. Let's select year 1 as our base year. Now we can express the successive prices of the

TABLE 7.5
Calculating Real GDP

Year	(1) Units of Output	(2) Price of Pizza per Unit	(3) Price Index (Year 1 = 100)	(4) Unadjusted, or Nominal, GDP, (1) × (2)	(5) Adjusted, or Real, GDP
1	5	$10	100	$ 50	$50
2	7	20	200	140	70
3	8	25	250	200	80
4	10	30	—	—	—
5	11	28	—	—	—

contents of our market basket in, say, years 2 and 3 as compared to the price of the market basket in year 1:

$$\text{Price index, year 2} = \frac{\$20}{\$10} \times 100 = 200$$

$$\text{Price index, year 3} = \frac{\$25}{\$10} \times 100 = 250$$

For year 1 the index has to be 100, since that year and the base year are identical.

The index numbers tell us that the price of pizza rose from year 1 to year 2 by 100 percent {= [(200 − 100)/100] × 100} and from year 1 to year 3 by 150 percent {= [(250 − 100)/100] × 100}.

Dividing Nominal GDP by the Price Index
We can now use the index numbers shown in column 3 to deflate the nominal GDP figures in column 4. The simplest and most direct method of deflating is to express the index numbers as hundredths—in decimal form—and then to divide them into corresponding nominal GDP. That gives us real GDP:

$$\text{Real GDP} = \frac{\text{nominal GDP}}{\text{price index (in hundredths)}} \quad (2)$$

Column 5 shows the results. These figures for real GDP measure the market value of the output of pizza in years 1, 2, and 3 as if the price of pizza had been a constant $10 throughout the 3-year period. In short, real GDP reveals the market value of each year's output measured in terms of dollars that have the same purchasing power as dollars had in the base year.

> **7.1**
> **GDP price index**
>
> To test your understanding, extend Table 7.5 to years 4 and 5, using equations 1 and 2. Then run through the entire deflating procedure, using year 3 as the base period. This time you will have to inflate some of the nominal GDP data, using the same procedure as we used in the examples.

An Alternative Method

Another way to establish real GDP is to gather separate data on physical outputs (as in column 1) and their prices (as in column 2) of Table 7.5. We could then determine the market value of outputs in successive years *if the base-year price ($10) had prevailed*. In year 2, the 7 units of pizza would have a value of $70 (= 7 units × $10). As column 5 confirms, that $70 worth of output is year 2's real GDP. Similarly, we could determine the real GDP for year 3 by

---

TABLE 7.6

Steps for Deriving Real GDP from Nominal GDP

Method 1
1. Find nominal GDP for each year.
2. Compute a GDP price index.
3. Divide each year's nominal GDP by that year's price index (in hundredths) to determine real GDP.

Method 2
1. Break down nominal GDP into physical quantities of output and prices for each year.
2. Find real GDP for each year by determining the dollar amount that each year's physical output would have sold for if base-year prices had prevailed. (The GDP price index can then be found by dividing nominal GDP by real GDP.)

---

multiplying the 8 units of output that year by the $10 price in the base year.

Once we have determined real GDP through this method, we can identify the price index for a given year simply by dividing the nominal GDP by the real GDP for that year:

$$\frac{\text{Price index}}{\text{(in hundredths)}} = \frac{\text{nominal GDP}}{\text{real GDP}} \quad (3)$$

Example: In year 2 we get a price index of 200—or, in hundredths, 2.00—which equals the nominal GDP of $140 divided by the real GDP of $70. Note that equation 3 is simply a rearrangement of equation 2. Table 7.6 summarizes the two methods of determining real GDP in our single-good economy. **(Key Question 11)**

Real-World Considerations and Data

In the real world of many goods and services, of course, determining GDP and constructing a reliable price index are far more complex matters than in our pizza-only economy. The government accountants must assign a "weight" to each of several categories of goods and services based on the relative proportion of each category in total output. They update the weights annually as expenditure patterns change and roll the base year forward year by year using a moving average of expenditure patterns. The GDP price index used in the United States is called the *chain-type annual-weights price index*—which hints at its complexity. We spare you the details.

Table 7.7 shows some of the real-world relationships between nominal GDP, real GDP, and the GDP price index. Here the reference year is 1996, where the value of the index is set at 100. Because the price level has been

TABLE 7.7

Nominal GDP, Real GDP, and GDP Price Index, Selected Years

(1) Year	(2) Nominal GDP, Billions of $	(3) Real GDP, Billions of $	(4) GDP Price Index* (1996 = 100)
1975	1635.2	4084.4	——
1980	2795.6	——	57.05
1985	4213.0	5717.1	73.69
1990	5803.2	6707.9	——
1995	7400.5	——	98.10
1996	7813.2	7813.2	100.00
2002	10,446.2	9439.9	110.66

*Chain-type annual-weights price index.

Source: Bureau of Economic Analysis, www.bea.doc.gov.

rising over the long run, the pre-1996 values of real GDP (column 3) are higher than the nominal values of GDP for those years (column 2). This upward adjustment acknowledges that prices were lower in the years before 1996, and thus nominal GDP understated the real output of those years in 1996 prices and must be inflated to show the correct relationship to other years.

Conversely, the rising price level of the post-1996 years caused nominal GDP figures for those years to overstate real output. So the statisticians deflate those figures to determine what real GDP would have been in other years if 1996 prices had prevailed. Doing so reveals that real GDP has been less than nominal GDP since 1996.

By inflating the nominal pre-1996 GDP data and deflating the post-1996 data, government accountants determine annual real GDP, which can then be compared with the real GDP of any other year in the series of years. So the real GDP values in column 3 are directly comparable with one another.

Once we have determined nominal GDP and real GDP, we can fashion the price index. And once we have determined nominal GDP and the price index, we can calculate real GDP. Example: Nominal GDP in 2002 was $10,446.2 billion and real GDP was $9439.9 billion. So the price level in 2002 was 110.66 (= $10,446.2/$9439.9 × 100), or 10.7 percent higher than in 1996. If we knew the nominal GDP and the price level only, we could find the real GDP for 2002 by dividing the nominal GDP of $10,446.2 by the 2002 price index, expressed in hundredths (1.1066).

To test your understanding of the relationships between nominal GDP, real GDP, and the price level, determine the values of the price index for 1975 and 1990 in Table 7.7 and determine real GDP for 1980 and 1995. We have left those figures out on purpose. **(Key Question 12)**

Shortcomings of GDP

GDP is a reasonably accurate and highly useful measure of how well or how poorly the economy is performing. But it has several shortcomings as a measure of both total output and well-being (total utility).

Nonmarket Activities

Certain productive activities do not take place in any market—the services of homemakers, for example, and the labor of carpenters who repair their own homes. Such activities never show up in GDP, which measures only the *market value* of output. Consequently, GDP understates a nation's total output. There is one exception: The portion of farmers' output that farmers consume themselves *is* estimated and included in GDP.

Leisure

The average workweek in the United States has declined since the beginning of the 1900s—from about 53 hours to about 35 hours. Moreover, the greater frequency of paid vacations, holidays, and leave time has shortened the work year itself. This increase in leisure time has clearly had a positive effect on overall well-being. But our system of national income accounting understates well-being by ignoring leisure's value. Nor does the system accommodate the satisfaction—the "psychic income"—that many people derive from their work.

Improved Product Quality

Because GDP is a quantitative measure rather than a qualitative measure, it fails to take into account the value of improvements in product quality. There is a very real difference in quality between a $3000 personal computer with monitor purchased today and a computer that cost the same amount just a decade ago. Today's computer has far more speed and storage capacity, a clearer monitor, and enhanced multimedia capabilities.

Obviously quality improvement has a great effect on economic well-being, as does the quantity of goods produced. Although the BEA adjusts GDP for quality improvement for selected items, the vast majority of such improvement for the entire range of goods and services does not get reflected in GDP.

The Underground Economy

Embedded in our economy is a flourishing, productive underground sector. Some of the people who conduct business there are gamblers, smugglers, prostitutes, "fences" of stolen goods, drug growers, and drug dealers. They have good reason to conceal their incomes.

Most participants in the underground economy however, engage in perfectly legal activities but choose not to report their full incomes to the Internal Revenue Service (IRS). A bell captain at a hotel may report just a portion of the tips received from customers. Storekeepers may report only a portion of their sales receipts. Workers who want to hold on to their unemployment compensation benefits may take an "off-the-books" or "cash-only" job. A brick mason may agree to rebuild a neighbor's fireplace in exchange for the neighbor's repairing his boat engine. The value of none of these transactions shows up in GDP.

The value of underground transactions is estimated to be about 8 percent of the recorded GDP in the United States. That would mean that GDP in 2002 was understated by about $836 billion. Global Perspective 7.2 shows estimates of the relative sizes of underground economies in selected nations.

GDP and the Environment

The growth of GDP is inevitably accompanied by "gross domestic by-products," including dirty air and polluted water, toxic waste, congestion, and noise. The social costs of the negative by-products reduce our economic well-being. And since those costs are not deducted from total output, GDP overstates our national well-being. Ironically, when money is spent to clean up pollution and reduce congestion, those expenses are added to the GDP!

Composition and Distribution of Output

The composition of output is undoubtedly important for well-being. But GDP does not tell us whether the mix of

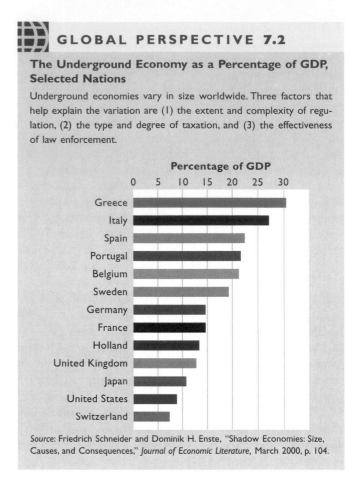

GLOBAL PERSPECTIVE 7.2

The Underground Economy as a Percentage of GDP, Selected Nations

Underground economies vary in size worldwide. Three factors that help explain the variation are (1) the extent and complexity of regulation, (2) the type and degree of taxation, and (3) the effectiveness of law enforcement.

Source: Friedrich Schneider and Dominik H. Enste, "Shadow Economies: Size, Causes, and Consequences," *Journal of Economic Literature*, March 2000, p. 104.

goods and services is enriching or potentially detrimental to society. GDP assigns equal weight to an assault rifle and a set of encyclopedias, as long as both sell for the same price. Moreover, GDP reveals nothing about the way output is distributed. Does 90 percent of the output go to 10 percent of the households, for example, or is the output more evenly distributed? The distribution of output may make a big difference for society's overall well-being.

Noneconomic Sources of Well-Being

Finally, the connection between GDP and well-being is problematic for another reason. Just as a household's income does not measure its total happiness, a nation's GDP does not measure its total well-being. There are many things that could make a society better off without necessarily raising GDP: a reduction of crime and violence, peaceful relations with other countries, people's greater civility toward one another, better understanding between parents and children, and a reduction of drug and alcohol abuse.

The Bureau of Economic Analysis (BEA), an Agency of the Department of Commerce, Compiles the NIPA Tables. Where Does It Get the Actual Data?

Discussions of national income accounting often leave the impression that a handful of economic sorcerers collect the data for the National Income and Product Accounts from some mysterious place. Let's see where the accountants get their data.

Consumption The BEA derives the data for the consumption component of the GDP accounts from four main sources:

- The Census Bureau's *Retail Trade Survey*, which gains sales information from a sample of 22,000 firms.
- The Census Bureau's *Survey of Manufacturers*, which gathers information on shipments of consumer goods from 50,000 establishments.
- The Census Bureau's *Service Survey*, which collects sales data from 30,000 service businesses.
- Industry trade sources. For example, data on auto sales and aircraft are collected directly from auto and aircraft manufacturers.

Investment The sources of the data for the investment component of GDP include:

- All the sources above used to determine consumption. Purchases of capital goods are separated from purchases of consumer goods. For example, estimates of investment in equipment and software are based on manufacturer's shipments reported in the *Survey of Manufacturers,* the *Service Survey,* and industry sources.
- Census construction surveys. The Census Bureau's *Housing Starts Survey* and *Housing Sales Survey* produce the data used to measure the amount of housing construction, and

the *Construction Progress Reporting Survey* is the source of data on nonresidential construction. The BEA determines changes in business inventories through the *Retail Trade Survey,* the *Wholesale Trade Survey* (of 7100 wholesale firms), and the *Survey of Manufacturing*.

Government Purchases The data for government purchases (officially "government consumption and investment expenditures") are obtained through the following sources:

- The U.S. Office of Personnel Management, which collects data on wages and benefits, broken out by the private and public sector. Wages and benefits of government employees are the single largest "purchase" by Federal, state, and local government.
- The previously mentioned Census Bureau's construction surveys, which break out private and public sector construction expenditures.
- The Census Bureau's *Survey of Government Finance,* which provides data on government consumption and investment expenditures.

Net Exports The BEA determines net exports through two main sources:

- The U.S. Customs Service, which collects data on exports and imports of goods.
- BEA surveys of potential domestic exporters and importers of services, which collect data on exports and imports of services.

So there you have it. Mystery solved!

Source: Based on Joseph A. Ritter, "Feeding the National Accounts," *Federal Reserve Bank of St. Louis Review,* March–April 2000, pp. 11–20. For those interested, this article also provides information on the sources of data for the income side of the national accounts.

SUMMARY

1. Gross domestic product (GDP), a basic measure of an economy's economic performance, is the market value of all final goods and services produced within the borders of a nation in a year.

2. Intermediate goods, nonproduction transactions, and secondhand sales are purposely excluded in calculating GDP.

3. GDP may be calculated by summing total expenditures on all final output or by summing the income derived from the production of that output.

4. By the expenditures approach, GDP is determined by adding consumer purchases of goods and services, gross investment spending by businesses, government purchases, and net exports: $GDP = C + I_g + G + X_n$.

5. Gross investment is divided into (a) replacement investment (required to maintain the nation's stock of capital at its existing level) and (b) net investment (the net increase in the stock of capital). In most years, net investment is positive and therefore the economy's stock of capital and production capacity increase.

6. By the income or allocations approach, GDP is calculated as the sum of compensation to employees, rents, interest, proprietors' income, corporate profits plus consumption of fixed capital, indirect business taxes, and net foreign factor income earned in the United States.

7. Other national accounts are derived from GDP. Net domestic product (NDP) is GDP less the consumption of fixed capital. National income (NI) is total income earned by a nation's resource suppliers; it is found by subtracting net foreign factor income earned in the United States and indirect business taxes from NDP. Personal income (PI) is the total income paid to households prior to any allowance for personal taxes. Disposable income (DI) is personal income after personal taxes have been paid. DI measures the amount of income available to households to consume or save.

8. Price indexes are computed by dividing the price of a specific collection or market basket of output in a particular period by the price of the same market basket in a base period and multiplying the result (the quotient) by 100. The GDP price index is used to adjust nominal GDP for inflation or deflation and thereby obtain real GDP.

9. Nominal (current-dollar) GDP measures each year's output valued in terms of the prices prevailing in that year. Real (constant-dollar) GDP measures each year's output in terms of the prices that prevailed in a selected base year. Because real GDP is adjusted for price-level changes, differences in real GDP are due only to differences in production activity.

10. GDP is a reasonably accurate and very useful indicator of a nation's economic performance, but it has its limitations. It fails to account for nonmarket and illegal transactions, changes in leisure and in product quality, the composition and distribution of output, and the environmental effects of production. The link between GDP and well-being is tenuous.

TERMS AND CONCEPTS

national income accounting	income approach	net exports (X_n)	disposable income (DI)
gross domestic product (GDP)	personal consumption expenditures (C)	national income	nominal GDP
intermediate goods	gross private domestic investment (I_g)	indirect business taxes	real GDP
final goods		consumption of fixed capital	price index
multiple counting	net private domestic investment	net domestic product (NDP)	
value added	government purchases (G)	personal income (PI)	
expenditures approach			

STUDY QUESTIONS

1. In what ways are national income statistics useful?
2. Explain why an economy's output, in essence, is also its income.
3. *Key Question* Why do national income accountants include only final goods in measuring GDP for a particular year? Why don't they include the value of the stocks and bonds bought and sold? Why don't they include the value of the used furniture bought and sold?
4. What is the difference between gross private domestic investment and net private domestic investment? If you were

to determine net domestic product (NDP) through the expenditures approach, which of these two measures of investment spending would be appropriate? Explain.

5. Why are changes in inventories included as part of investment spending? Suppose inventories declined by $1 billion during 2003. How would this affect the size of gross private domestic investment and gross domestic product in 2003? Explain.

6. Use the concepts of gross investment and net investment to distinguish between an economy that has a rising stock of capital and one that has a falling stock of capital. "In 1933 net private domestic investment was minus $6 billion. This means that in that particular year the economy produced no capital goods at all." Do you agree? Why or why not? Explain: "Though net investment can be positive, negative, or zero, it is quite impossible for gross investment to be less than zero."

7. Define net exports. Explain how U.S. exports and imports each affect domestic production. Suppose foreigners spend $7 billion on U.S. exports in a specific year and Americans spend $5 billion on imports from abroad in the same year. What is the amount of the United States' net exports? Explain how net exports might be a negative amount.

8. *Key Question* Below is a list of domestic output and national income figures for a certain year. All figures are in billions. The questions that follow ask you to determine the major national income measures by both the expenditures and the income approaches. The results you obtain with the different methods should be the same.

Personal consumption expenditures	$245
Net foreign factor income earned in the U.S.	4
Transfer payments	12
Rents	14
Consumption of fixed capital (depreciation)	27
Social Security contributions	20
Interest	13
Proprietors' income	33
Net exports	11
Dividends	16
Compensation of employees	223
Indirect business taxes	18
Undistributed corporate profits	21
Personal taxes	26
Corporate income taxes	19
Corporate profits	56
Government purchases	72
Net private domestic investment	33
Personal saving	20

a. Using the above data, determine GDP by both the expenditures and the income approaches. Then determine NDP.

b. Now determine NI in two ways: first, by making the required additions or subtractions from NDP; and second, by adding up the types of income that make up NI.

c. Adjust NI (from part *b*) as required to obtain PI.

d. Adjust PI (from part *c*) as required to obtain DI.

9. Using the following national income accounting data, compute (*a*) GDP, (*b*) NDP, and (*c*) NI. All figures are in billions.

Compensation of employees	$194.2
U.S. exports of goods and services	17.8
Consumption of fixed capital	11.8
Government purchases	59.4
Indirect business taxes	14.4
Net private domestic investment	52.1
Transfer payments	13.9
U.S. imports of goods and services	16.5
Personal taxes	40.5
Net foreign factor income earned in the U.S.	2.2
Personal consumption expenditures	219.1

10. Why do national income accountants compare the market value of the total outputs in various years rather than actual physical volumes of production? What problem is posed by any comparison over time of the market values of various total outputs? How is this problem resolved?

11. *Key Question* Suppose that in 1984 the total output in a single-good economy was 7000 buckets of chicken. Also suppose that in 1984 each bucket of chicken was priced at $10. Finally, assume that in 1996 the price per bucket of chicken was $16 and that 22,000 buckets were produced. Determine the GDP price index for 1984, using 1996 as the base year. By what percentage did the price level, as measured by this index, rise between 1984 and 1996? Use the two methods listed in Table 7.6 to determine real GDP for 1984 and 1996.

12. *Key Question* The following table shows nominal GDP and an appropriate price index for a group of selected years. Compute real GDP. Indicate in each calculation whether you are inflating or deflating the nominal GDP data.

Year	Nominal GDP, Billions	Price Index (1996 = 100)	Real GDP, Billions
1960	$ 527.4	22.19	$_____
1968	911.5	26.29	$_____
1978	2295.9	48.22	$_____
1988	4742.5	80.22	$_____
1998	8790.2	103.22	$_____

13. Which of the following are included in this year's GDP? Explain your answer in each case.

a. Interest on an AT&T corporate bond.

b. Social Security payments received by a retired factory worker.

c. The services of a painter in painting the family home.

d. The income of a dentist.

e. The money received by Smith when she sells her economics textbook to a book buyer.

f. The monthly allowance a college student receives from home.

g. Rent received on a two-bedroom apartment.

h. The money received by Josh when he resells his current-year-model Honda automobile to Kim.

i. The publication of a college textbook.

j. A 2-hour decrease in the length of the workweek.

k. The purchase of an AT&T corporate bond.

l. A $2 billion increase in business inventories.

m. The purchase of 100 shares of GM common stock.

n. The purchase of an insurance policy.

14. *(Last Word)* What government agency compiles the U.S. NIPA tables? In what U.S. department is it located? Of the several specific sources of information, name one source for each of the four components of GDP: consumption, investment, government purchases, and net exports.

15. *Web-Based Question: Update the key National Income and Product Account numbers* Go to the Bureau of Economic Analysis website, www.bea.gov, and access the BEA interactively by selecting National Income and Product Account Tables. Select Frequently Requested NIPA Tables, and find Table 1.1 on GDP. Update the data in the left column of the text's Table 7.3, using the latest available quarterly data. Search the full list of NIPA tables to find the latest reported data for national income (NI), personal income (PI), and disposable income (DI). Update the data in the text's Table 7.4 for these three items. By what percentages are GDP, NI, PI, and DI higher (or lower) than the numbers in the table?

16. *Web-Based Question: Nominal GDP and real GDP— both up?* Visit the Bureau of Economic Analysis website, www.bea.gov, and access the BEA interactively by selecting National Income and Product Account Tables. Select Frequently Requested NIPA Tables, and use Tables 1.1 and 1.2 to identify the GDP (nominal GDP) and real GDP for the past four quarters. Why was nominal GDP greater than real GDP in each of those quarters? What were the percentage changes in nominal GDP and real GDP for the most recent quarter? What accounts for the difference?

17. *Web-Based Question: GDPs in the Americas—how do nations compare?* Visit the World Bank website, www.worldbank.org, and type "GDP" in the search space. Find the latest data for total GDP (not PPP GDP) for the North and South America countries listed. Arrange the countries by highest to lowest GDPs, and express their GDPs as ratios of U.S. GDP. What general conclusion can you draw from your ratios?

8 | *Introduction to Economic Growth and Instability*

Between 1996 and 2000, real GDP in the United States expanded briskly and the price level rose only slowly. The economy experienced neither significant unemployment nor inflation. Some observers felt that the United States had entered a "new era" in which the business cycle was dead. But that wishful thinking came to an end in March 2001, when the economy entered its ninth recession since 1950. Since 1970, real GDP has declined in the United States in five periods: 1973–1975, 1980, 1981–1982, 1990–1991, and 2001.

Although the U.S. economy has experienced remarkable economic growth over time, high unemployment or inflation has sometimes been a problem. For example, between March 2001 and December 2001, unemployment rose by 2.2 million workers. The U.S. rate of inflation was 13.5 percent in 1980 and 5.4 percent in 1990. Further, other nations have suffered high unemployment rates or inflation rates in recent years. For example, the unemployment rate in Germany reached 8.7 percent in 2002. The inflation rate was 45 percent in Turkey in 2002.

In this chapter we provide an introductory look at the trend of real GDP growth in the United States and the macroeconomic instability that has occasionally accompanied it. Our specific topics are economic growth, the business cycle, unemployment, and inflation.

Economic Growth

Economists define and measure **economic growth** as either:
- An increase in real GDP occurring over some time period.
- An increase in real GDP per capita occurring over some time period.

With either definition, economic growth is calculated as a percentage rate of growth per quarter (3-month period) or per year. For the first definition, for example, if real GDP was $200 billion in the hypothetical country of Zorn last year and $210 billion this year, the rate of economic growth in Zorn would be 5 percent {= [($210 billion − $200 billion)/$200 billion] × 100}.

The second definition takes into consideration the size of the population. **Real GDP per capita** (or per capita output) is found by dividing real GDP by the size of the population. The resulting number is then compared in

131

percentage terms with that of the previous period. For example, if real GDP in Zorn was $200 billion last year and its population was 40 million, its real GDP per capita would be $5000. If real per capita GDP rose to $5100 this year, Zorn's rate of growth of real GDP per capita for the year would be 2 percent {= [($5100 − $5000)/$5000] × 100}.

For measuring expansion of military potential or political preeminence, the growth of real GDP is more useful. Unless specified otherwise, growth rates reported in the news and by international agencies use this definition of economic growth. For comparing living standards, however, the second definition is superior. While China's GDP in 2001 was $1131 billion compared with Denmark's $166 billion, Denmark's real GDP per capita was $31,090 compared with China's meager $890. And, in some cases, growth of real GDP can be misleading. Madagascar's real GDP grew at a rate of 2.4 percent per year from 1990 to 2001. But over the same period its annual population growth was 2.9 percent, resulting in a decline in real GDP per capita of .5 percent per year. **(Key Question 2)**

Growth as a Goal

Growth is a widely held economic goal. The expansion of total output relative to population results in rising real wages and incomes and thus higher standards of living. An economy that is experiencing economic growth is better able to meet people's wants and resolve socioeconomic problems. Rising real wages and income provide richer opportunities to individuals and families—a vacation trip, a personal computer, a higher education—without sacrificing other opportunities and pleasures. A growing economy can undertake new programs to alleviate poverty and protect the environment without impairing existing levels of consumption, investment, and public goods production.

In short, *growth lessens the burden of scarcity*. A growing economy, unlike a static economy, can consume more today while increasing its capacity to produce more in the future. By easing the burden of scarcity—by relaxing society's constraints on production—economic growth enables a nation to attain its economic goals more readily and to undertake new endeavors that require the use of goods and services to be accomplished.

Arithmetic of Growth

Why do economists pay so much attention to small changes in the rate of economic growth? Because those changes really matter! For the United States, with a current real GDP of about $10.5 trillion, the difference between a 3 percent and a 4 percent rate of growth is about $105 billion of output each year. For a poor country, a difference of one-half a percentage point in the rate of growth may mean the difference between starvation and mere hunger.

The mathematical approximation called the **rule of 70** provides a quantitative grasp of the effect of economic growth. It tells us that we can find the number of years it will take for some measure to double, given its annual percentage increase, by dividing that percentage increase into the number 70. So

$$\text{Approximate number of years required to double real GDP} = \frac{70}{\text{annual percentage rate of growth}}$$

Examples: A 3 percent annual rate of growth will double real GDP in about 23 (= 70 ÷ 3) years. Growth of 8 percent per year will double real GDP in about 9 (= 70 ÷ 8) years. The rule of 70 is applicable generally. For example, it works for estimating how long it will take the price level, or a savings account to double at various percentage rates of inflation or interest. When compounded over many years, an apparently small difference in the rate of growth thus becomes highly significant. Suppose Alta and Zorn have identical GDPs, but Alta grows at a 4 percent yearly rate, while Zorn grows at 2 percent. Alta's GDP would double in about 18 years, while Zorn's GDP would double in 35 years.

Main Sources of Growth

There are two fundamental ways society can increase its real output and income: (1) by increasing its inputs of resources, and (2) by increasing the productivity of those inputs. Other things equal, increases in land, labor, capital, and entrepreneurial resources yield additional output. But economic growth also occurs through increases in **productivity**—measured broadly as real output per unit of input. Productivity rises when the health, training, education, and motivation of workers are improved; when workers have more and better machinery and natural resources with which to work; when production is better organized and managed; and when labor is reallocated from less efficient industries to more efficient industries. About one-third of U.S. growth comes from more inputs. The remaining two-thirds results from improved productivity.

Growth in the United States

Table 8.1 gives an overview of economic growth in the United States over past periods. Column 2 reveals strong growth as measured by increases in real GDP. Note that between 1940 and 2002 real GDP increased about 10-fold. But the U.S. population also increased. Nevertheless, in column 4 we find that real GDP per capita rose more than fourfold over these years.

What has been the *rate* of U.S. growth? Real GDP grew at an annual rate of about 3.4 percent between 1950 and 2002. Real GDP per capita increased about 2.1 percent per year over that time. But we must qualify these raw numbers in several ways:

- ***Improved products and services***   Since the numbers in Table 8.1 do not fully account for the improvements in products and services, they understate the growth of economic well-being. Such purely quantitative data do not fully compare an era of iceboxes and LPs with an era of refrigerators and CDs.

- ***Added leisure***   The increases in real GDP and per capita GDP identified in Table 8.1 were accomplished despite large increases in leisure. The standard workweek, once 50 hours, is now about 35 hours. Again the raw growth numbers understate the gain in economic well-being.

- ***Other impacts***   These measures of growth do not account for any effects growth may have had on the environment and the quality of life. If growth debases the physical environment and creates a stressful work

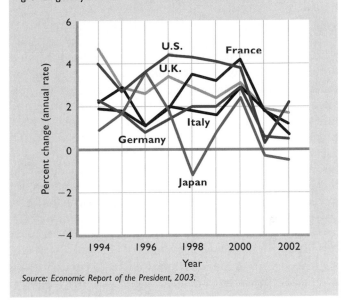

GLOBAL PERSPECTIVE 8.1

Average Annual Growth Rates, 1994–2002, Selected Nations

Between 1994 and 2002, economic growth in the United States exceeded that of several other major countries. But U.S. economic growth greatly slowed in 2001 and 2002.

Source: Economic Report of the President, 2003.

environment, the bare growth numbers will overstate the gains in well-being that result from growth. On the other hand, if growth leads to stronger environmental protections and greater human security, these numbers will understate the gains in well-being.

Relative Growth Rates

Viewed from the perspective of the last half-century, economic growth in the United States lagged behind that in Japan, Germany, Italy, Canada, and France. Japan's annual growth rate, in fact, averaged twice that of the United States. But economic growth since 1994 is quite another matter. As shown in Global Perspective 8.1, the U.S. growth rate surged ahead of the rates of growth in Japan and other major industrial nations in the late 1990s before greatly slowing in 2001 and 2002.

The Business Cycle

Long-run economic growth in the United States has been interrupted by periods of economic instability. At various times, growth has given way to recession and

TABLE 8.1

Real GDP and Per Capita Real GDP, Selected Years, 1929–2002

(1) Year	(2) Real GDP, Billions of 1996 $	(3) Population, Millions	(4) Real Per Capita GDP, 1996 $ (2) ÷ (3)
1929	$ 822	122	$ 6,738
1933	603	126	4,786
1940	981	132	7,432
1950	1687	152	11,099
1960	2377	181	13,133
1970	3578	205	17,454
1980	4901	228	21,496
1990	6708	250	26,832
1995	7544	267	28,255
2000	9191	282	32,592
2002	9440	289	32,664

Source: Data are from the Bureau of Economic Analysis, www.bea.doc.gov, and the U.S. Census Bureau, www.census.gov.

8.1
Business cycles 🔍

depression—that is, to declines in real GDP and significant increases in unemployment. At other times, rapid economic growth has been marred by rapid inflation. Both unemployment and inflation often are associated with *business cycles.*

Phases of the Business Cycle

The term **business cycle** refers to alternating rises and declines in the level of economic activity, sometimes extending over several years. Individual cycles (one "up" followed by one "down") vary substantially in duration and intensity. Yet all display certain phases, to which economists have assigned various labels. Figure 8.1 shows the four phases of a generalized business cycle:

- *Peak*   At a **peak,** such as the middle peak shown in Figure 8.1, business activity has reached a temporary maximum. Here the economy is near or at full employment and the level of real output is at or very close to the economy's capacity. The price level is likely to rise during this phase.

- *Recession*   A peak is followed by a **recession**—a period of decline in total output, income, employment, and trade. This downturn, which lasts 6 months or more, is marked by the widespread contraction of business activity in many sectors of the economy. But because many prices are downwardly inflexible, the price level is likely to fall only if the recession is severe and prolonged—that is, only if a depression occurs.

- *Trough*   In the **trough** of the recession or depression, output and employment "bottom out" at their lowest levels. The trough phase may be either short-lived or quite long.

- *Recovery*   In the expansion or **recovery** phase, output and employment rise toward full employment. As recovery intensifies, the price level may begin to rise before full employment and full-capacity production return.

Although business cycles all pass through the same phases, they vary greatly in duration and intensity. Many economists prefer to talk of business "fluctuations" rather than cycles because cycles imply regularity while fluctuations do not. The Great Depression of the 1930s resulted in a 40 percent decline in real GDP over a 3-year period in the United States and seriously impaired business activity for a decade. By comparison, more recent U.S. recessions, detailed in Table 8.2, were relatively mild in both intensity and duration.

Recessions, of course, occur in other countries, too. At one time or another during the past 10 years Argentina, Brazil, Canada, Colombia, Japan, Indonesia, Mexico, Germany, and South Korea experienced recessions.

Causation: A First Glance

Economists have suggested many theories to explain fluctuations in business activity. Some say that momentous innovations, such as the railroad, the automobile, synthetic fibers, and microchips, have great impact on investment and consumption spending and therefore on output, employment, and the price level. Such major innovations

---

FIGURE 8.1

The business cycle.   Economists distinguish four phases of the business cycle; the duration and strength of each phase may vary.

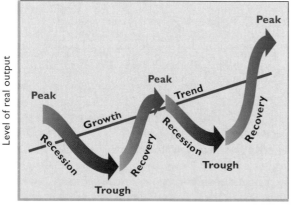

Time

TABLE 8.2

U.S. Recessions since 1950

Period	Duration, Months	Depth (Decline in Real Output)
1953–54	10	−3.7%
1957–58	8	−3.9
1960–61	10	−1.6
1969–70	11	−1.0
1973–75	16	−4.9
1980	6	−2.3
1981–82	16	−3.3
1990–91	8	−1.8
2001	8	−0.5

Source: Economic Report of the President, 1993, updated.

occur irregularly and thus contribute to the variability of economic activity.

Some economists see major changes in productivity as causes of business cycles. When productivity expands, the economy booms; when productivity falls, the economy recedes. Still others view the business cycle as a purely monetary phenomenon. When government creates too much money, they say, an inflationary boom occurs. Too little money triggers a decline in output and employment and, eventually, in the price level.

Most economists, however, believe that the immediate cause of cyclical changes in the levels of real output and employment is changes in the level of total spending. In a market economy, businesses produce goods or services only if they can sell them at a profit. If total spending sinks, many businesses find that it is no longer profitable to go on producing their current volume of goods and services. As a consequence, output, employment, and incomes all fall. When the level of spending rises, an increase in production becomes profitable, and output, employment, and incomes will rise accordingly. Once the economy nears full employment, however, further gains in real output become more difficult to achieve. Continued increases in spending may raise the price level as consumers bid for the limited amount of goods available.

We have seen that the long-run growth trend of the U.S. economy is one of expansion. Note that the stylized cycle in Figure 8.1 is drawn against a trend of economic growth.

Cyclical Impact: Durables and Nondurables

Although the business cycle is felt everywhere in the economy, it affects different segments in different ways and to different degrees.

Firms and industries producing *capital goods* (for example, housing, commercial buildings, heavy equipment, and farm implements) and *consumer durables* (for example, automobiles, personal computers, refrigerators) are affected most by the business cycle. Within limits, firms can postpone the purchase of capital goods. As the economy recedes, producers frequently delay the purchase of new equipment and the construction of new plants. The business outlook simply does not warrant increases in the stock of capital goods. In good times, capital goods are usually replaced before they depreciate completely. But when recession strikes, firms patch up their old equipment and make do. As a result, investment in capital goods declines sharply. Firms that have excess plant capacity may not even bother to replace all the capital that is depreciating. For

them, net investment may be negative. The pattern is much the same for consumer durables such as automobiles and major appliances. When recession occurs and households must trim their budgets, purchases of these goods are often deferred. Families repair their old cars and appliances rather than buy new ones, and the firms producing these products suffer. (Of course, producers of capital goods and consumer durables also benefit most from expansions.)

In contrast, *service* industries and industries that produce *nondurable consumer goods* are somewhat insulated from the most severe effects of recession. People find it difficult to cut back on needed medical and legal services, for example. And a recession actually helps some service firms, such as pawnbrokers and law firms that specialize in bankruptcies. Nor are the purchases of many nondurable goods such as food and clothing easy to postpone. The quantity and quality of purchases of nondurables will decline, but not so much as will purchases of capital goods and consumer durables. **(Key Question 4)**

QUICK REVIEW 8.1

- Economic growth can be measured as (a) an increase in real GDP over time or (b) an increase in real GDP per capita over time.
- Real GDP in the United States has grown at an average annual rate of about 3.4 percent since 1950; real GDP per capita has grown at roughly a 2.1 percent annual rate over that same period.
- The typical business cycle goes through four phases: peak, recession, trough, and recovery.
- During recession, industries that produce capital goods and consumer durables normally suffer greater output and employment declines than do service and nondurable consumer goods industries.

Unemployment

The twin problems that arise from the business cycle are unemployment and inflation. Let's look at unemployment first.

Measurement of Unemployment

To measure the unemployment rate, we must first determine who is eligible and available to work. Figure 8.2 provides a helpful starting point. It divides the total U.S. population into three groups. One group is made up of people less than 16 years of age and people who are

FIGURE 8.2

The labor force, employment, and unemployment, 2002. The labor force consists of persons 16 years of age or older who are not in institutions and who are (1) employed or (2) unemployed but seeking employment.

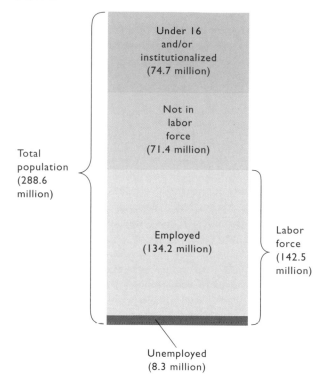

Total population (288.6 million)

Under 16 and/or institutionalized (74.7 million)

Not in labor force (71.4 million)

Employed (134.2 million)

Labor force (142.5 million)

Unemployed (8.3 million)

institutionalized, for example, in mental hospitals or correctional institutions. Such people are not considered potential members of the labor force.

A second group, labeled "Not in labor force," is composed of adults who are potential workers but are not employed and are not seeking work. For example, they are homemakers, full-time students, or retirees.

The third group is the **labor force,** which constituted about 50 percent of the total population in 2002. The labor force consists of people who are able and willing to work. Both those who are employed and those who are unemployed but actively seeking work are counted as being in the labor force. The **unemployment rate** is the percentage of the labor force unemployed:

$$\text{Unemployment rate} = \frac{\text{unemployed}}{\text{labor force}} \times 100$$

The statistics included in Figure 8.2 show that in 2002 the unemployment rate averaged

$$\frac{8,266,000}{142,535,000} \times 100 = 5.8\%$$

Unemployment rates for selected years between 1929 and 2002 appear on the back inside covers of this book.

The U.S. Bureau of Labor Statistics (BLS) conducts a nationwide random survey of some 60,000 households each month to determine who is employed and who is not employed. In a series of questions it asks which members of the household are working, unemployed and looking for work, not looking for work, and so on. From the answers it determines an unemployment rate for the entire nation. Despite the use of scientific sampling and interviewing techniques, the data collected in this survey are subject to criticism:

- *Part-time employment* The BLS lists all part-time workers as fully employed. In 2002 about 27 million people worked part-time as a result of personal choice. But another 4.2 million part-time workers either wanted to work full-time and could not find suitable full-time work or worked fewer hours because of a temporary slack in consumer demand. These last two groups were, in effect, partially employed and partially unemployed. By counting them as fully employed, say critics, the official BLS data understate the unemployment rate.

- *Discouraged workers* You must be actively seeking work in order to be counted as unemployed. An unemployed individual who is not actively seeking employment is classified as "not in the labor force." The problem is that many workers, after unsuccessfully seeking employment for a time, become discouraged and drop out of the labor force. The number of such **discouraged workers** is larger during recession than during prosperity; an estimated 369,000 people fell into this category in 2002, up from 262,000 in 2000. By not counting discouraged workers as unemployed, say critics, the official BLS data understate the unemployment rate. **(Key Question 6)**

Types of Unemployment

There are three *types* of unemployment: frictional, structural, and cyclical.

Frictional Unemployment

At any given time some workers are "between jobs." Some of them will be moving voluntarily from one job to another. Others will have been fired and will be seeking reemployment. Still others will have been laid off temporarily because of seasonal demand. In addition to those between jobs, many young workers will be searching for their first jobs.

As these unemployed people find jobs or are called back from temporary layoffs, other job seekers and laid-off workers will replace them in the "unemployment pool." So even though the workers who are unemployed for such reasons change from month to month, this type of unemployment persists.

Economists use the term **frictional unemployment**— consisting of *search unemployment* and *wait unemployment*— for workers who are either searching for jobs or waiting to take jobs in the near future. The word "frictional" implies that the labor market does not operate perfectly and instantaneously (without friction) in matching workers and jobs.

Frictional unemployment is inevitable and, at least in part, desirable. Many workers who are voluntarily between jobs are moving from low-paying, low-productivity jobs to higher-paying, higher-productivity positions. That means greater income for the workers, a better allocation of labor resources, and a larger real GDP for the economy.

Structural Unemployment

Frictional unemployment blurs into a category called **structural unemployment.** Here, economists use "structural" in the sense of "compositional." Changes over time in consumer demand and in technology alter the "structure" of the total demand for labor, both occupationally and geographically.

Occupationally, the demand for certain skills (for example, sewing clothes or working on farms) may decline or even vanish. The demand for other skills (for example, designing software or maintaining computer systems) will intensify. Unemployment results because the composition of the labor force does not respond immediately or completely to the new structure of job opportunities. Workers who find that their skills and experience have become obsolete or unneeded thus find that they have no marketable talents. They are structurally unemployed until they adapt or develop skills that employers want.

Geographically, the demand for labor also changes over time. An example: migration of industry and thus of employment opportunities from the Snow Belt to the Sun Belt over the past few decades. Another example is the movement of jobs from inner-city factories to suburban industrial parks. As job opportunities shift from one place to another, some workers become structurally unemployed.

The distinction between frictional and structural unemployment is hazy at best. The key difference is that *frictionally* unemployed workers have salable skills and either live in areas where jobs exist or are able to move to areas where they do. *Structurally* unemployed workers find it hard to obtain new jobs without retraining, gaining additional education, or relocating. Frictional unemployment is short-term; structural unemployment is more likely to be long-term and consequently more serious.

Cyclical Unemployment

Cyclical unemployment is caused by a decline in total spending and is likely to occur in the recession phase of the business cycle. As the demand for goods and services decreases, employment falls and unemployment rises. For this reason, **cyclical unemployment** is sometimes called *deficient-demand unemployment.* The 25 percent unemployment rate in the depth of the Great Depression in 1933 reflected mainly cyclical unemployment, as did significant parts of the 9.7 percent unemployment rate in 1982, the 7.5 percent rate in 1992, and the 5.8 percent rate in 2002.

Cyclical unemployment is a very serious problem when it occurs. We will say more about its high costs later, but first we need to define "full employment."

Definition of Full Employment

Because frictional and structural unemployment are largely unavoidable in a dynamic economy, *full employment* is something less than 100 percent employment of the labor force. Economists say that the economy is "fully employed" when it is experiencing only frictional and structural unemployment. That is, full employment occurs when there is no cyclical unemployment.

Economists describe the unemployment rate that is consistent with full employment as the **full-employment rate of unemployment,** or the **natural rate of unemployment (NRU).** At the NRU, the economy is said to be producing its **potential output.** This is the real GDP that occurs when the economy is "fully employed."

The NRU occurs when the number of *job seekers* equals the number of *job vacancies.* Even when labor markets are in balance, however, the NRU is some positive percentage because it takes time for frictionally unemployed job seekers to find open jobs they can fill. Also, it takes time for the structurally unemployed to achieve the skills and geographic relocation needed for reemployment.

"Natural" does not mean, however, that the economy will always operate at this rate and thus realize its potential output. When cyclical unemployment occurs, the economy has much more unemployment than that which would occur at the NRU. Moreover, the economy can operate for a while at an unemployment rate *below* the NRU. At times, the demand for labor may be so great that firms take a stronger initiative to hire and train the structurally unemployed. Also, some homemakers, teenagers, college students, and retirees who were casually looking for just the right part-time or full-time jobs may quickly find them. Thus the unemployment rate temporarily falls below the natural rate.

Also, the NRU can vary over time. In the 1980s, the NRU was about 6 percent. Today, it is 4 to 5 percent. Why the decline?

- The growing proportion of younger workers in the labor force has declined as the baby-boom generation has aged. The labor force now has a larger proportion of middle-aged workers, who traditionally have lower unemployment rates.

- The growth of temporary-help agencies and the improved information resulting from the Internet have lowered the NRU by enabling workers to find jobs more quickly.

- The work requirements under the new welfare laws have moved many people from the ranks of the unemployed to the ranks of the employed.

- The doubling of the U.S. prison population since 1985 has removed relatively high unemployment individuals from the labor force and thus lowered the overall unemployment rate.

A decade ago, a 4 to 5 percent rate of unemployment would have reflected excessive spending, an unbalanced labor market, and rising inflation; today, the same rate is consistent with a balanced labor market and a stable, low rate of inflation.

Economic Cost of Unemployment

Unemployment that is above the natural rate involves great economic and social costs.

GDP Gap and Okun's Law   The basic economic cost of unemployment is forgone output. *When the economy fails to create enough jobs for all who are able and willing to work, potential production of goods and services is irretrievably lost.* In terms of Chapter 2's analysis, unemployment above the natural rate means that society is operating at some point inside its production possibilities curve. Economists call this sacrifice of output a **GDP gap**—the difference between actual and potential GDP. That is:

$$\text{GDP gap} = \text{actual GDP} - \text{potential GDP}$$

The GDP gap can be either negative (actual GDP < potential GDP) or positive (actual GDP > potential GDP). In the case of unemployment above the natural rate, it is negative because actual GDP falls short of potential GDP.

Potential GDP is determined by assuming that the natural rate of unemployment prevails. The growth of potential GDP is simply projected forward on the basis of

the economy's "normal" growth rate of real GDP. Figure 8.3 shows the GDP gap for recent years in the United States. It also indicates the close correlation between the actual unemployment rate (Figure 8.3b) and the GDP gap (Figure 8.3a). The higher the unemployment rate, the larger is the GDP gap.

Macroeconomist Arthur Okun was the first to quantify the relationship between the unemployment rate and the GDP gap. On the basis of recent estimates, **Okun's law** indicates that *for every 1 percentage point by which the actual unemployment rate exceeds the natural rate, a negative GDP gap of about 2 percent occurs.* With this information, we can calculate the absolute loss of output associated with any above-natural unemployment rate. For example, in 1992 the unemployment rate was 7.4 percent, or 1.4 percentage points above the 6.0 percent natural rate of unemployment then existing. Multiplying this 1.4 percent by Okun's 2 indicates that 1992's GDP gap was 2.8 percent of potential GDP (in real terms). By applying this 2.8 percent loss to 1992's potential GDP of $6300 billion, we find that the economy sacrificed $176 billion of real output because the natural rate of unemployment was not achieved. **(Key Question 8)**

As you can see in Figure 8.3, sometimes the economy's actual output will exceed its potential or full-employment output. Figure 8.3 reveals that an economic expansion in 1999 and 2000, for example, caused actual GDP to exceed potential GDP in those years. There was a positive GDP gap in 1999 and 2000. Actual GDP for a time can exceed potential GDP, but positive GDP gaps create inflationary pressures and cannot be sustained indefinitely.

Unequal Burdens   An increase in the unemployment rate from 5 to, say, 7 or 8 percent might be more tolerable to society if every worker's hours of work and wage income were reduced proportionally. But this is not the case. Part of the burden of unemployment is that its cost is unequally distributed.

Table 8.3 examines unemployment rates for various labor market groups for 2 years. The 2001 recession pushed the 2002 unemployment rate to 5.8 percent. In 1999, the economy achieved full employment, with a 4.2 percent unemployment rate. By observing the large variance in unemployment rates for the different groups within each year and comparing the rates between the 2 years, we can generalize as follows:

- *Occupation*   Workers in lower-skilled occupations (for example, laborers) have higher unemployment rates than workers in higher-skilled occupations (for example, professionals). Lower-skilled workers have

FIGURE 8.3

Actual and potential GDP and the unemployment rate.   (a) The difference between actual and potential GDP is the GDP gap. A negative GDP gap measures the output the economy sacrifices when actual GDP falls short of potential GDP. A positive GDP gap indicates that actual GDP is above potential GDP. (b) A high unemployment rate means a large GDP gap (negative), and a low unemployment rate means a small or even positive GDP gap.

Source: Data are from the Federal Reserve Bank of St. Louis, www.research.stlouisfed.org/fred/, and Bureau of Economic Analysis, www.bea.gov.

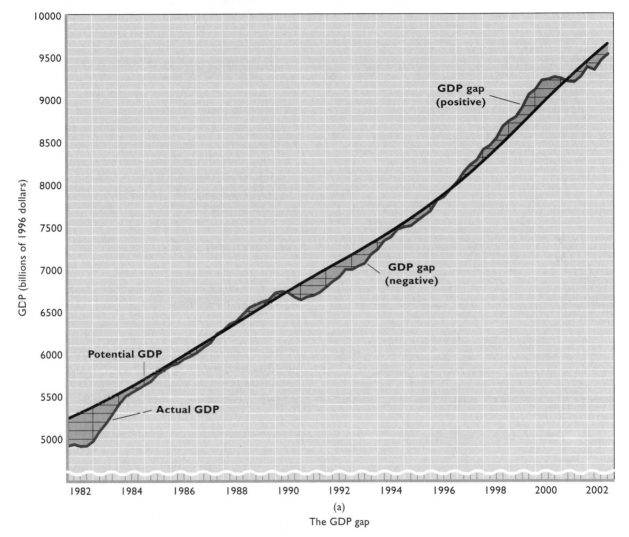

(a)
The GDP gap

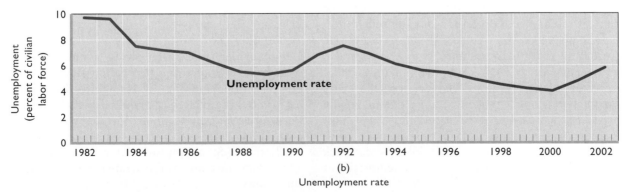

(b)
Unemployment rate

TABLE 8.3

Unemployment Rates by Demographic Group: Recession (2002) and Full Employment (1999)*

Demographic Group	Unemployment Rate	
	2002	1999
Overall	5.8%	4.2%
Occupation:		
Managerial and professional	3.1	1.9
Operators, fabricators, and laborers	8.9	6.3
Age:		
16–19	16.5	13.9
Black, 16–19	29.8	27.9
White, 16–19	14.5	12.0
Male, 20+	5.3	3.5
Female, 20+	5.1	3.8
Race and ethnicity:		
Black	10.2	8.0
Hispanic	7.5	6.4
White	5.1	3.7
Gender:		
Women	5.6	4.3
Men	5.9	4.2
Education:**		
Less than high school diploma	8.4	6.0
High school diploma only	5.3	3.5
College degree or more	2.9	1.8
Duration:		
15 or more weeks	2.0	1.1

*Civilian labor-force data. In 2002 the economy was suffering the lingering unemployment effects of the 2001 recession.

**People age 25 or over.

Source: *Economic Report of the President; Employment and Earnings;* Census Bureau, www.census.gov.

more and longer spells of structural unemployment than higher-skilled workers. They also are less likely to be self-employed than are higher-skilled workers. Moreover, lower-skilled workers usually bear the brunt of recessions. Businesses generally retain most of their higher-skilled workers, in whom they have invested the expense of training.

- **Age**   Teenagers have much higher unemployment rates than adults. Teenagers have lower skill levels, quit their jobs more frequently, are more frequently "fired," and have less geographic mobility than adults. Many unemployed teenagers are new in the labor market, searching for their first jobs. Male black teenagers, in particular, have very high unemployment rates.

- *Race and ethnicity*   The unemployment rate for blacks and Hispanics is higher than that for whites. The causes of the higher rates include lower rates of educational attainment, greater concentration in lower-skilled occupations, and discrimination in the labor market. In general, the unemployment rate for blacks is twice that of whites.

- *Gender*   The unemployment rates for men and women are very similar.

- *Education*   Less educated workers, on average, have higher unemployment rates than workers with more education. Less education is usually associated with lower-skilled, less permanent jobs, more time between jobs, and jobs that are more vulnerable to cyclical layoff.

- *Duration*   The number of persons unemployed for long periods—15 weeks or more—as a percentage of the labor force is much lower than the overall unemployment rate. But that percentage rises significantly during recessions.

Noneconomic Costs

Severe cyclical unemployment is more than an economic malady; it is a social catastrophe. Depression means idleness. And idleness means loss of skills, loss of self-respect, plummeting morale, family disintegration, and sociopolitical unrest. Widespread joblessness increases poverty, heightens racial and ethnic tensions, and reduces hope for material advancement.

History demonstrates that severe unemployment can lead to rapid and sometimes violent social and political change. Witness Hitler's ascent to power against a background of unemployment in Germany. Furthermore, relatively high unemployment among some racial and ethnic minorities has contributed to the unrest and violence that has periodically plagued some cities in the United States and abroad. At the individual level, research links increases in suicide, homicide, fatal heart attacks and strokes, and mental illness to high unemployment.

International Comparisons

Unemployment rates differ greatly among nations at any given time. One reason is that nations have different natural rates of unemployment. Another is that nations may be in different phases of their business cycles. Global Perspective 8.2 shows unemployment rates for five industrialized nations in recent years. Between 1992 and 2002, the U.S. unemployment rate was considerably lower than the rates in the United Kingdom, Germany, and France.

GLOBAL PERSPECTIVE 8.2

Unemployment Rates in Five Industrial Nations, 1992–2002

Compared with France, the United Kingdom, and Germany, the United States had a relatively low unemployment rate in recent years.

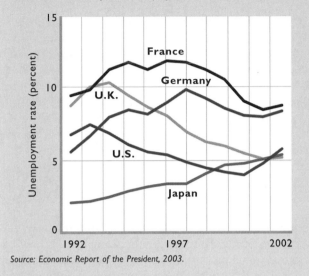

Source: *Economic Report of the President, 2003.*

QUICK REVIEW 8.2

• Unemployment is of three general types: frictional, structural, and cyclical.

• The natural unemployment rate (frictional plus structural) is presently 4 to 5 percent.

• Society loses real GDP when cyclical unemployment occurs; according to Okun's law, for each 1 percentage point of unemployment above the natural rate, the U.S. economy suffers a 2 percent decline in real GDP below its potential GDP.

• Lower-skilled workers, teenagers, blacks and Hispanics, and less educated workers bear a disproportionate burden of unemployment.

Inflation

We now turn to inflation, another aspect of macroeconomic instability. The problems inflation poses are subtler than those posed by unemployment.

Meaning of Inflation

Inflation is a rise in the *general level of prices*. When inflation occurs, each dollar of income will buy fewer goods and services than before. Inflation reduces the "purchasing power" of money. But inflation does not mean that *all* prices are rising. Even during periods of rapid inflation, some prices may be relatively constant while others are falling. For example, although the United States experienced high rates of inflation in the 1970s and early 1980s, the prices of video recorders, digital watches, and personal computers declined. As you will see, one troublesome aspect of inflation is that prices rise unevenly. Some shoot upward; others rise slowly; still others do not rise at all.

Measurement of Inflation

The main measure of inflation in the United States is the **Consumer Price Index (CPI),** compiled by the Bureau of Labor Statistics (BLS). The government uses this index to report inflation rates each month and each year. It also uses the CPI to adjust Social Security benefits and income tax brackets for inflation. The CPI reports the price of a "market basket" of some 300 consumer goods and services that presumably are purchased by a typical urban consumer. (The GDP price index of Chapter 7 is a much broader measure of inflation since it includes not only consumer goods and services but also capital goods, goods and services purchased by government, and goods and services that enter world trade.)

The composition of the market basket for the CPI is based on spending patterns of urban consumers in a specific period, presently 2000–2001. The BLS updates the composition of the market basket every 2 years so that it reflects the most recent patterns of consumer purchases and captures the inflation that consumers are currently experiencing. The BLS arbitrarily sets the CPI equal to 100 for 1982–1984. So the CPI for any particular year is found as follows:

$$CPI = \frac{\text{price of the most recent market basket in the particular year}}{\text{price of the same market basket in 1982–1984}} \times 100$$

The rate of inflation for a certain year (say, 2002) is found by comparing, in percentage terms, that year's index with the index in the previous year. For example, the CPI was 179.9 in 2002, up from 177.1 in 2001. So the rate of inflation for 2002 is calculated as follows:

$$\text{Rate of inflation} = \frac{179.9 - 177.1}{177.1} \times 100 = 1.6\%$$

Recall that the mathematical approximation called the *rule of 70* tells us that we can find the number of years

FIGURE 8.4

Annual inflation rates in the United States, 1960–2002. The major periods of inflation in the United States in the past 40 years were in the 1970s and 1980s.

Source: Bureau of Labor Statistics, stats.bls.gov.

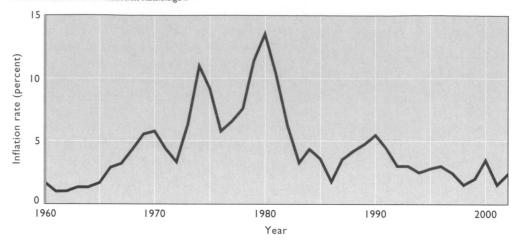

it will take for some measure to double, given its annual percentage increase, by dividing that percentage increase into the number 70. So a 3 percent annual rate of inflation will double the price level in about 23 (= 70 ÷ 3) years. Inflation of 8 percent per year will double the price level in about 9 (= 70 ÷ 8) years. **(Key Question 11)**

Facts of Inflation

Figure 8.4 shows the annual rates of inflation in the United States between 1960 and 2002. Observe that inflation reached double-digit rates in the 1970s and early 1980s but has since declined and has been relatively mild recently.

In recent years U.S. inflation has been neither unusually high nor low relative to inflation in several other industrial countries (see Global Perspective 8.3). Some nations (not shown) have had double-digit or even higher annual rates of inflation in recent years. In 2002, for example, the annual inflation rate in Romania was 23 percent; in Belarus, 43 percent; in Turkey, 45 percent; and in Myanmar, 57 percent.

Types of Inflation

Economists distinguish between two types of inflation: *demand-pull inflation* and *cost-push inflation*.

Demand-Pull Inflation Usually, changes in the price level are caused by an excess of total spending beyond the economy's capacity to produce. Where inflation is rapid and sustained, the cause invariably is an overissuance of money by the central bank (the Federal Reserve in the

United States). When resources are already fully employed, the business sector cannot respond to excess demand by expanding output. So the excess demand bids up the prices of the limited output, producing **demand-pull inflation.** The essence of this type of inflation is "too much spending chasing too few goods."

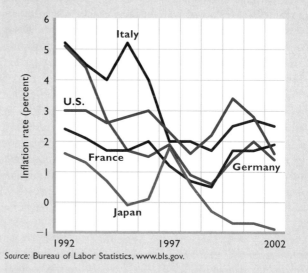

GLOBAL PERSPECTIVE 8.3

Inflation Rates in Five Industrial Nations, 1992–2002

Inflation rates in the United States in recent years were neither extraordinarily high nor extraordinarily low relative to rates in other industrial nations.

Source: Bureau of Labor Statistics, www.bls.gov.

Cost-Push Inflation   Inflation may also arise on the supply, or cost, side of the economy. During some periods in U.S. economic history, including the mid-1970s, the price level increased even though total spending was not excessive. These were periods when output and employment were both *declining* (evidence that total spending was not excessive) while the general price level was *rising*.

The theory of **cost-push inflation** explains rising prices in terms of factors that raise **per-unit production costs** at each level of spending. A per-unit production cost is the average cost of a particular level of output. This average cost is found by dividing the total cost of all resource inputs by the amount of output produced. That is,

$$\text{Per-unit production cost} = \frac{\text{total input cost}}{\text{units of output}}$$

Rising per-unit production costs squeeze profits and reduce the amount of output firms are willing to supply at the existing price level. As a result, the economy's supply of goods and services declines and the price level rises. In this scenario, costs are *pushing* the price level upward, whereas in demand-pull inflation demand is *pulling* it upward.

The major source of cost-push inflation has been so-called *supply shocks*. Specifically, abrupt increases in the costs of raw materials or energy inputs have on occasion driven up per-unit production costs and thus product prices. The rocketing prices of imported oil in 1973–1974 and again in 1979–1980 are good illustrations. As energy prices surged upward during these periods, the costs of producing and transporting virtually every product in the economy rose. Rapid cost-push inflation ensued.

Complexities

The real world is more complex than the distinction between demand-pull and cost-push inflation suggests. It is difficult to distinguish between demand-pull inflation and cost-push inflation unless the original source of inflation is known. For example, suppose a significant increase in total spending occurs in a fully employed economy, causing demand-pull inflation. But as the demand-pull stimulus works its way through various product and resource markets, individual firms find their wage costs, material costs, and fuel prices rising. From their perspective they must raise their prices because production costs (someone else's prices) have risen. Although this inflation is clearly demand-pull in origin, it may mistakenly appear to be cost-push inflation to business firms and to government. Without proper identification of the source of the inflation, government and the Federal Reserve may be slow to undertake policies to reduce excessive total spending.

Another complexity is that cost-push inflation and demand-pull inflation differ in their sustainability. Demand-pull inflation will continue as long as there is excess total spending. Cost-push inflation is automatically self-limiting; it will die out by itself. Increased per-unit costs will reduce supply, and this means lower real output and employment. Those decreases will constrain further per-unit cost increases. In other words, cost-push inflation generates a recession. And in a recession, households and businesses concentrate on keeping their resources employed, not on pushing up the prices of those resources.

QUICK REVIEW 8.3

- Inflation is a rising general level of prices and is measured as a percentage change in a price index such as the CPI.
- For the past several years, the U.S. inflation rate has been within the middle range of the rates of other advanced industrial nations and far below the rates experienced by some nations.
- Demand-pull inflation occurs when total spending exceeds the economy's ability to provide goods and services at the existing price level; total spending *pulls* the price level upward.
- Cost-push inflation occurs when factors such as rapid increases in the prices of imported raw materials drive up per-unit production costs at each level of output; higher costs *push* the price level upward.

Redistribution Effects of Inflation

Inflation hurts some people, leaves others unaffected, and actually helps still others. That is, inflation redistributes real income from some people to others. Who gets hurt? Who benefits? Before we can answer, we need some terminology.

Nominal and Real Income
There is a difference between money (or nominal) income and real income. **Nominal income** is the number of dollars received as wages, rent, interest, or profits. **Real income** is a measure of the amount of goods and services nominal income can buy; it is the purchasing power of nominal income, or income adjusted for inflation. That is,

$$\text{Real income} = \frac{\text{nominal income}}{\text{price index (in hundredths)}}$$

Inflation need not alter an economy's overall real income—its total purchasing power. It is evident from the above equation that real income will remain the same when nominal income rises at the same percentage rate as does the price index.

But when inflation occurs, not everyone's nominal income rises at the same pace as the price level. Therein lies the potential for redistribution of real income from some

to others. If the change in the price level differs from the change in a person's nominal income, his or her real income will be affected. The following rule tells us approximately by how much real income will change:

$$\begin{array}{ccc} \text{Percentage} & \text{percentage} & \text{percentage} \\ \text{change in} \cong & \text{change in} & - \text{ change in} \\ \text{real income} & \text{nominal income} & \text{price level} \end{array}$$

For example, suppose that the price level rises by 6 percent in some period. If Bob's nominal income rises by 6 percent, his real income will *remain unchanged*. But if his nominal income instead rises by 10 percent, his real income will *increase* by about 4 percent. And if Bob's nominal income rises by only 2 percent, his real income will *decline* by about 4 percent.[1]

Anticipations
The redistribution effects of inflation depend on whether or not it is expected. With fully expected or **anticipated inflation,** an income receiver may be able to avoid or lessen the adverse effects of inflation on real income. The generalizations that follow assume **unanticipated inflation**—inflation whose full extent was not expected.

Who Is Hurt by Inflation?

Unanticipated inflation hurts fixed-income recipients, savers, and creditors. It redistributes real income away from them and toward others.

Fixed-Income Receivers
People whose incomes are fixed see their real incomes fall when inflation occurs. The classic case is the elderly couple living on a private pension or annuity that provides a fixed amount of nominal income each month. They may have retired in, say, 1990 on what appeared to be an adequate pension. However, by 2000 they would have discovered that inflation had cut the purchasing power of that pension—their real income—by one-fourth.

---

[1] A more precise calculation uses our equation for real income. In our first illustration above, if nominal income rises by 10 percent from $100 to $110 and the price level (index) rises by 6 percent from 100 to 106, then real income has increased as follows:

$$\frac{\$110}{1.06} = \$103.77$$

The 4 percent increase in real income shown by the simple formula in the text is a reasonable approximation of the 3.77 percent yielded by our more precise formula.

Similarly, landlords who receive lease payments of fixed dollar amounts will be hurt by inflation as they receive dollars of declining value over time. Likewise, public sector workers whose incomes are dictated by fixed pay schedules may suffer from inflation. The fixed "steps" (the upward yearly increases) in their pay schedules may not keep up with inflation. Minimum-wage workers and families living on fixed welfare incomes will also be hurt by inflation.

Savers   Unanticipated inflation hurts savers. As prices rise, the real value, or purchasing power, of an accumulation of savings deteriorates. Paper assets such as savings accounts, insurance policies, and annuities that were once adequate to meet rainy-day contingencies or provide for a comfortable retirement decline in real value during inflation. The simplest case is the person who hoards money as a cash balance. A $1000 cash balance would have lost one-half its real value between 1981 and 2000. Of course, most forms of savings earn interest. But the value of savings will still decline if the rate of inflation exceeds the rate of interest.

Example: A household may save $1000 in a certificate of deposit (CD) in a commercial bank or savings and loan association at 6 percent annual interest. But if inflation is 13 percent (as it was in 1980), the real value or purchasing power of that $1000 will be cut to about $938 by the end of the year. Although the saver will receive $1060 (equal to $1000 plus $60 of interest), deflating that $1060 for 13 percent inflation means that its real value is only about $938 (= $1060 ÷ 1.13).

Creditors   Unanticipated inflation harms creditors (lenders). Suppose Chase Bank lends Bob $1000, to be repaid in 2 years. If in that time the price level doubles, the $1000 that Bob repays will have only half the purchasing power of the $1000 he borrowed. True, if we ignore interest charges, the same number of dollars will be repaid as was borrowed. But because of inflation, each of those dollars will buy only half as much as it did when the loan was negotiated. As prices go up, the value of the dollar goes down. So the borrower pays back less valuable dollars than those received from the lender. The owners of Chase Bank suffer a loss of real income.

Who Is Unaffected or Helped by Inflation?

Some people are unaffected by inflation and others are actually helped by it. For the second group, inflation redistributes real income toward them and away from others.

Flexible-Income Receivers   People who have flexible incomes may escape inflation's harm or even benefit from it. For example, individuals who derive their incomes solely from Social Security are largely unaffected by inflation because Social Security payments are *indexed* to the CPI. Benefits automatically increase when the CPI increases, preventing erosion of benefits from inflation. Some union workers also get automatic **cost-of-living adjustments (COLAs)** in their pay when the CPI rises, although such increases rarely equal the full percentage rise in inflation.

Some flexible-income receivers and all borrowers are helped by unanticipated inflation. The strong product demand and labor shortages implied by rapid demand-pull inflation may cause some nominal incomes to spurt ahead of the price level, thereby enhancing real incomes. For some, the 3 percent increase in nominal income that occurs when inflation is 2 percent may become a 7 percent increase when inflation is 5 percent. As an example, property owners faced with an inflation-induced real estate boom may be able to boost flexible rents more rapidly than the rate of inflation. Also, some business owners may benefit from inflation. If product prices rise faster than resource prices, business revenues will increase more rapidly than costs. In those cases, the growth rate of profit incomes will outpace the rate of inflation.

Debtors   Unanticipated inflation benefits debtors (borrowers). In our earlier example, Chase Bank's loss of real income from inflation is Bob's gain of real income. Debtor Bob borrows "dear" dollars but, because of inflation, pays back the principal and interest with "cheap" dollars whose purchasing power has been eroded by inflation. Real income is redistributed away from the owners of Chase Bank toward borrowers such as Bob.

As a historical example, the inflation of the 1970s and 1980s created a windfall of capital gains for people who purchased homes in earlier periods with low, fixed-interest-rate mortgages. Inflation greatly reduced the real burden of their mortgage indebtedness. They also benefited because the nominal value of housing in that period increased much more rapidly than the overall price level.

The Federal government, which had amassed $5.6 trillion of public debt through 2000, has also benefited from inflation. Historically, the Federal government regularly paid off its loans by taking out new ones. Inflation permitted the Treasury to pay off its loans with dollars of less purchasing power than the dollars originally borrowed. Nominal national income and therefore tax collections rise with inflation; the amount of public debt owed does not. Thus, inflation reduces the real burden of the public debt to the Federal government.

Anticipated Inflation

The redistribution effects of inflation are less severe or are eliminated altogether if people anticipate inflation and can adjust their nominal incomes to reflect the expected price-level rises. The prolonged inflation that began in the late 1960s prompted many labor unions in the 1970s to insist on labor contracts with cost-of-living adjustment clauses.

Similarly, if inflation is anticipated, the redistribution of income from lender to borrower may be altered. Suppose a lender (perhaps a commercial bank or a savings and loan institution) and a borrower (a household) both agree that 5 percent is a fair rate of interest on a 1-year loan provided the price level is stable. But assume that inflation has been occurring and is expected to be 6 percent over the next year. If the bank lends the household $100 at 5 percent interest, the bank will be paid back $105 at the end of the year. But if 6 percent inflation does occur during that year, the purchasing power of the $105 will have been reduced to about $99. The lender will, in effect, have paid the borrower $1 for the use of the lender's money for a year.

The lender can avoid this subsidy by charging an *inflation premium*—that is, by raising the interest rate by 6 percent, the amount of the anticipated inflation. By charging 11 percent, the lender will receive back $111 at the end of the year. Adjusted for the 6 percent inflation, that amount will have the purchasing power of today's $105. The result then will be a mutually agreeable transfer of purchasing power from borrower to lender of $5, or 5 percent, for the use of $100 for 1 year. Financial institutions have also developed variable-interest-rate mortgages to protect themselves from the adverse effects of inflation. (Incidentally, this example points out that, rather than being a *cause* of inflation, high nominal interest rates are a *consequence* of inflation.)

Our example reveals the difference between the real rate of interest and the nominal rate of interest. The **real interest rate** is the percentage increase in *purchasing power* that the borrower pays the lender. In our example the real interest rate is 5 percent. The **nominal interest rate** is the percentage increase in *money* that the borrower pays the lender, including

8.2
Real interest rates

that resulting from the built-in expectation of inflation, if any. In equation form:

$$\text{Nominal interest rate} = \text{real interest rate} + \text{inflation premium (the expected rate of inflation)}$$

As illustrated in Figure 8.5, the nominal interest rate in our example is 11 percent.

Addenda

We end our discussion of the redistribution effects of inflation by making three final points:

- *Deflation*   The effects of unanticipated **deflation**—declines in the price level—are the reverse of those of inflation. People with fixed nominal incomes will find their real incomes enhanced. Creditors will benefit at the expense of debtors. And savers will discover that the purchasing power of their savings has grown because of the falling prices.

- *Mixed effects*   A person who is an income earner, a holder of financial assets, and an owner of real assets simultaneously will probably find that the redistribution impact of inflation is cushioned. If the person owns fixed-value monetary assets (savings accounts, bonds, and insurance policies), inflation will lessen their real value. But that same inflation may increase the real value of any property assets (a house, land) that the person owns. In short, many individuals are

FIGURE 8.5

The inflation premium and nominal and real interest rates.
The inflation premium—the expected rate of inflation—gets built into the nominal interest rate. Here, the nominal interest rate of 11 percent comprises the real interest rate of 5 percent plus the inflation premium of 6 percent.

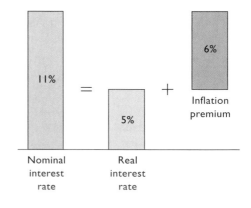

simultaneously hurt and benefited by inflation. All these effects must be considered before we can conclude that any particular person's net position is better or worse because of inflation.

- *Arbitrariness*   The redistribution effects of inflation occur regardless of society's goals and values. Inflation lacks a social conscience and takes from some and gives to others, whether they are rich, poor, young, old, healthy, or infirm.

QUICK REVIEW 8.4

- Inflation harms those who receive relatively fixed nominal incomes and either leaves unaffected or helps those who receive flexible nominal incomes.
- Unanticipated inflation hurts savers and creditors while benefiting debtors.
- The nominal interest rate equals the real interest rate plus the inflation premium (the expected rate of inflation).

Effects of Inflation on Output

Thus far, our discussion has focused on how inflation redistributes a given level of total real income. But inflation may also affect an economy's level of real output (and thus its level of real income). The direction and significance of this effect on output depends on the type of inflation and its severity.

Cost-Push Inflation and Real Output

Recall that abrupt and unexpected rises in key resource prices such as oil can sufficiently drive up overall production costs to cause cost-push inflation. As prices rise, the quantity of goods and services demanded falls. So firms respond by producing less output, and unemployment goes up.

Economic events of the 1970s provide an example of how inflation can reduce real output. In late 1973 the Organization of Petroleum Exporting Countries (OPEC), by exerting its market power, managed to quadruple the price of oil. The cost-push inflationary effects generated rapid price-level increases in the 1973–1975 period. At the same time, the U.S. unemployment rate rose from slightly less than 5 percent in 1973 to 8.5 percent in 1975. Similar outcomes occurred in 1979–1980 in response to a second OPEC oil supply shock.

In short, cost-push inflation reduces real output. It redistributes a decreased level of real income.

Demand-Pull Inflation and Real Output

Economists do not fully agree on the effects of mild inflation (less than 3 percent) on real output. One perspective is that even low levels of inflation reduce real output, because inflation diverts time and effort toward activities designed to hedge against inflation. Examples:

- Businesses must incur the cost of changing thousands of prices on their shelves and in their computers simply to reflect inflation.
- Households and businesses must spend considerable time and effort obtaining the information they need to distinguish between real and nominal values such as prices, wages, and interest rates.
- To limit the loss of purchasing power from inflation, people try to limit the amount of money they hold in their billfolds and checking accounts at any one time and instead put more money into interest-bearing accounts and stock and bond funds. But cash and checks are needed in even greater amounts to buy the higher-priced goods and services. So more frequent trips, phone calls, or Internet visits to financial institutions are required to transfer funds to checking accounts and billfolds, when needed.

Without inflation, these uses of resources, time, and effort would not be needed, and they could be diverted toward producing more valuable goods and services. Proponents of "zero inflation" bolster their case by pointing to cross-country studies that indicate that lower rates of inflation are associated with higher rates of economic growth. Even mild inflation, say these economists, is detrimental to economic growth.

In contrast, other economists point out that full employment and economic growth depend on strong levels of total spending. Such spending creates high profits, strong demand for labor, and a powerful incentive for firms to expand their plants and equipment. In this view, the mild inflation that is a by-product of strong spending is a small price to pay for full-employment and continued economic growth. Moreover, a little inflation may have positive effects because it makes it easier for firms to adjust real wages downward when the demands for their products fall. With mild inflation, firms can reduce real wages by holding nominal wages steady. With zero inflation firms would need to cut nominal wages to reduce real wages. Such cuts in nominal wages are highly visible and may cause considerable worker resistance and labor strife.

Finally, defenders of mild inflation say that it is much better for an economy to err on the side of strong spending, full employment, economic growth, and mild inflation than on the side of weak spending, unemployment, recession, and deflation.

Hyperinflation and Breakdown

All economists agree that the nation's policymakers must carefully monitor mild inflation so that it does not snowball into higher rates of inflation or even into **hyperinflation.** The latter is an extremely rapid inflation whose impact on real output and employment usually is devastating. When inflation begins to escalate, consumers, workers, and businesses assume that it will rise even further. So, rather than let their idle savings and current incomes depreciate, consumers "spend now" to beat the anticipated price rises. Businesses do the same by buying capital goods. Workers demand and receive higher nominal wages to recoup lost purchasing power and to maintain future purchasing power in the face of expected higher inflation. Actions based on these inflationary expectations then intensify the pressure on prices, and inflation feeds on itself.

Aside from its disruptive redistribution effects, hyperinflation may cause economic collapse. Severe inflation encourages speculative activity. Businesses, anticipating further price increases, may find it profitable to hoard both materials and finished products. But restricting the availability of materials and products intensifies the inflationary pressure. Also, rather than invest in capital equipment, businesses and individual savers may decide to purchase nonproductive wealth—jewels, gold and other precious metals, real estate, and so forth—as a hedge against inflation.

In the extreme, as prices shoot up sharply and unevenly, normal economic relationships are disrupted. Business owners do not know what to charge for their products. Consumers do not know what to pay. Resource suppliers want to be paid with actual output, rather than with rapidly depreciating money. Creditors avoid debtors to keep them from repaying their debts with cheap money. Money eventually becomes almost worthless and ceases to do its job as a medium of exchange. The economy may be thrown into a state of barter, and production and exchange drop dramatically. The net result is economic, social, and possibly political chaos. The hyperinflation has precipitated monetary collapse, depression, and sociopolitical disorder.

History reveals a number of examples that fit this scenario. Consider the effects of the Second World War on price levels in Hungary and Japan:

> The inflation in Hungary exceeded all known records of the past. In August 1946, 828 octillion (1 followed by 27 zeros) depreciated pengös equaled the value of 1 prewar pengö. The price of the American dollar reached a value of 3×10^{22} (3 followed by 22 zeros) pengös. Fishermen and farmers in 1947 Japan used scales to weigh currency and change, rather than bothering to count it. Prices rose some 116 times in Japan, 1938 to 1948.[2]

The German inflation of the 1920s also was catastrophic. The German Weimar Republic printed so much money to pay its bills that

> during 1922, the German price level went up 5,470 percent. In 1923, the situation worsened; the German price level rose 1,300,000,000,000 times. By October of 1923, the postage on the lightest letter sent from Germany to the United States was 200,000 marks. . . . Prices increased so rapidly that waiters changed the prices on the menu several times during the course of a lunch. Sometimes customers had to pay double the price listed on the menu when they ordered.[3]

There are also more recent examples of hyperinflation:[4]

- Between June 1986 and March 1991 the cumulative inflation in Nicaragua was 11,895,866,143 percent.
- From November 1993 to December 1994 the cumulative inflation rate in the Democratic Republic of Congo was 69,502 percent.
- From February 1993 to January 1994 the cumulative inflation rate in Serbia was 156,312,790 percent.

Such dramatic hyperinflations are almost invariably the consequence of highly imprudent expansions of the money supply by government. The rocketing money supply produces frenzied total spending and severe demand-pull inflation.

---

[2] Theodore Morgan, *Income and Employment,* 2d ed. (Englewood Cliffs, N.J.: Prentice-Hall, 1952), p. 361.

[3] Raburn M. Williams, *Inflation! Money, Jobs, and Politicians* (Arlington Heights, Ill.: AHM Publishing, 1980), p. 2.

[4] Stanley Fischer, Ratna Sahay, and Carlos Végh, "Modern Hyper- and High Inflations," *Journal of Economic Literature,* September 2002, p. 840.

How, If at All, Do Changes in Stock Prices Relate to Macroeconomic Instability?

Every day, the individual stocks (ownership shares) of thousands of corporations are bought and sold in the stock market. The owners of the individual stocks receive dividends—a portion of the firm's profit. Supply and demand in the stock market determine the price of each firm's stock, with individual stock prices generally rising and falling in concert with the collective expectations for each firm's profits. Greater profits normally result in higher dividends to the stock owners, and, in anticipation of higher dividends, people are willing to pay a higher price for the stock.

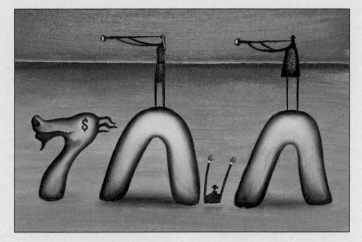

The media closely monitor and report stock market averages such as the Dow Jones Industrial Average (DJIA)—the weighted-average price of the stocks of 30 major U.S. industrial firms. It is common for these price averages to change over time or even to rise or fall sharply during a single day. On "Black Monday," October 19, 1987, the DJIA fell by 20 percent. A sharp drop in stock prices also occurred in October 1997, mainly in response to rapid declines in stock prices in Hong Kong and other southeast Asia stock markets. In contrast, the stock market averages rose spectacularly in 1998 and 1999, with the DJIA rising 16 and 25 percent in those two years. In 2002, the DJIA fell 17 percent.

The volatility of the stock market raises this question: Do changes in stock price averages and thus stock market wealth cause macroeconomic instability? There are linkages between the stock market and the economy that might lead us to answer "yes." Consider a sharp increase in stock prices. Feeling wealthier, stock owners respond by increasing their spending (the *wealth effect*). Firms react by increasing their purchases of new capital goods, because they can finance such purchases through issuing new shares of high-valued stock (the *investment effect*). Of course, sharp declines in stock prices would produce the opposite results.

Studies find that changes in stock prices do affect consumption and investment but that these consumption and investment impacts are relatively weak. For example, a 10 percent sustained increase in stock market values in 1 year is associated with a 4 percent increase in consumption spending over the next 3 years. The investment response is even weaker. So typical day-to-day and year-to-year changes in stock market values have little impact on the macroeconomy.

In contrast, *stock market bubbles* can be detrimental to an economy. Such bubbles are huge run-ups of overall stock prices, caused by excessive optimism and frenzied buying. The rising stock values are unsupported by realistic prospects of the future strength of the economy and the firms operating in it. Rather than slowly decompress, such bubbles may burst and cause harm to the economy. The free fall of stock values, if long-lasting, causes reverse wealth effects. The stock market crash may also create an overall pessimism about the economy that undermines consumption and investment spending even further.

A related question: Even though typical changes in stock prices do not cause recession or inflation, might they predict such maladies? That is, since stock market values are based on expected profits, wouldn't we expect rapid changes in stock price averages to forecast changes in future business conditions? Indeed, stock prices often do fall prior to recessions and rise prior to expansions. For this reason stock prices are among a group of 10 variables that constitute an index of leading indicators (Last Word, Chapter 12). Such an index may provide a useful clue to the future direction of the economy. But taken alone, stock market prices are not a reliable predictor of changes in GDP. Stock prices have fallen rapidly in some instances with no recession following. Black Monday itself did not produce a recession during the following 2 years. In other instances, recessions have occurred with no prior decline in stock market prices.

SUMMARY

1. Economic growth may be defined as either (a) an increase of real GDP over time or (b) an increase in real GDP per capita over time. Growth lessens the burden of scarcity and provides increases in real GDP that can be used to resolve socioeconomic problems. Since the Second World War, real GDP growth in the United States has been about 3.4 percent annually; real GDP per capita has grown at about a 2.1 percent annual rate.

2. The United States and other industrial economies have gone through periods of fluctuations in real GDP, employment, and the price level. Although they have certain phases in common—peak, recession, trough, recovery—business cycles vary greatly in duration and intensity.

3. Although economists explain the business cycle in terms of such causal factors as major innovations, political events, and money creation, they generally agree that the level of total spending is the immediate determinant of real output and employment.

4. The business cycle affects all sectors of the economy, though in varying ways and degrees. The cycle has greater effects on output and employment in the capital goods and durable consumer goods industries than in the services and nondurable goods industries.

5. Economists distinguish between frictional, structural, and cyclical unemployment. The full-employment or natural rate of unemployment, which is made up of frictional and structural unemployment, is currently between 4 and 5 percent. The presence of part-time and discouraged workers makes it difficult to measure unemployment accurately.

6. The economic cost of unemployment, as measured by the GDP gap, consists of the goods and services forgone by society when its resources are involuntarily idle. Okun's law suggests that every 1-percentage-point increase in unemployment above the natural rate causes an additional 2 percent negative GDP gap.

7. Inflation is a rise in the general price level and is measured in the United States by the Consumer Price Index (CPI). When inflation occurs, each dollar of income will buy fewer goods and services than before. That is, inflation reduces the purchasing power of money.

8. Unemployment rates and inflation rates vary widely globally. Unemployment rates differ because nations have different natural rates of unemployment and often are in different phases of their business cycles. Inflation and unemployment rates in the United States recently have been in the middle to low range compared with rates in other industrial nations.

9. Economists discern both demand-pull and cost-push (supply-side) inflation. Demand-pull inflation results from an excess of total spending relative to the economy's capacity to produce. The main source of cost-push inflation is abrupt and rapid increases in the prices of key resources. These supply shocks push up per-unit production costs and ultimately the prices of consumer goods.

10. Unanticipated inflation arbitrarily redistributes real income at the expense of fixed-income receivers, creditors, and savers. If inflation is anticipated, individuals and businesses may be able to take steps to lessen or eliminate adverse redistribution effects.

11. When inflation is anticipated, lenders add an inflation premium to the interest rate charged on loans. The nominal interest rate thus reflects the real interest rate plus the inflation premium (the expected rate of inflation).

12. Cost-push inflation reduces real output and employment. Proponents of zero inflation argue that even mild demand-pull inflation (1 to 3 percent) reduces the economy's real output. Other economists say that mild inflation may be a necessary by-product of the high and growing spending that produces high levels of output, full employment, and economic growth.

13. Hyperinflation, caused by highly imprudent expansions of the money supply, may undermine the monetary system and cause severe declines in real output.

TERMS AND CONCEPTS

economic growth
real GDP per capita
rule of 70
productivity
business cycle
peak
recession
trough
recovery
labor force

unemployment rate
discouraged workers
frictional unemployment
structural unemployment
cyclical unemployment
full-employment rate of unemployment
natural rate of unemployment (NRU)
potential output

GDP gap
Okun's law
inflation
Consumer Price Index (CPI)
demand-pull inflation
cost-push inflation
per-unit production costs
nominal income
real income

anticipated inflation
unanticipated inflation
cost-of-living adjustments (COLAs)
real interest rate
nominal interest rate
deflation
hyperinflation

STUDY QUESTIONS

1. Why is economic growth important? Why could the difference between a 2.5 percent and a 3 percent annual growth rate be of great significance over several decades?

2. *Key Question* Suppose an economy's real GDP is $30,000 in year 1 and $31,200 in year 2. What is the growth rate of its real GDP? Assume that population is 100 in year 1 and 102 in year 2. What is the growth rate of GDP per capita?

3. Briefly describe the growth record of the United States. Compare the rates of growth of real GDP and real GDP per capita, explaining any differences. Compare the average growth rates of Japan and the United States between 1992 and 2002. To what extent might growth rates understate or overstate economic well-being?

4. *Key Question* What are the four phases of the business cycle? How long do business cycles last? How do seasonal variations and long-run trends complicate measurement of the business cycle? Why does the business cycle affect output and employment in capital goods industries and consumer durable goods industries more severely than in industries producing consumer nondurables?

5. What factors make it difficult to determine the unemployment rate? Why is it difficult to distinguish between frictional, structural, and cyclical unemployment? Why is unemployment an economic problem? What are the consequences of a negative GDP gap? What are the noneconomic effects of unemployment?

6. *Key Question* Use the following data to calculate (*a*) the size of the labor force and (*b*) the official unemployment rate: total population, 500; population under 16 years of age or institutionalized, 120; not in labor force, 150; unemployed, 23; part-time workers looking for full-time jobs, 10.

7. Since the United States has an unemployment compensation program that provides income for those out of work, why should we worry about unemployment?

8. *Key Question* Assume that in a particular year the natural rate of unemployment is 5 percent and the actual rate of unemployment is 9 percent. Use Okun's law to determine the size of the GDP gap in percentage-point terms. If the potential GDP is $500 billion in that year, how much output is being forgone because of cyclical unemployment?

9. Explain how an increase in your nominal income and a decrease in your real income might occur simultaneously. Who loses from inflation? Who loses from unemployment? If you had to choose between (*a*) full employment with a 6 percent annual rate of inflation and (*b*) price stability with an 8 percent unemployment rate, which would you choose? Why?

10. What is the Consumer Price Index (CPI) and how is it determined each month? How does the Bureau of Labor Statistics calculate the rate of inflation from one year to the next? What effect does inflation have on the purchasing power of a dollar? How does it explain differences between nominal and real interest rates? How does deflation differ from inflation?

11. *Key Question* If the CPI was 110 last year and is 121 this year, what is this year's rate of inflation? What is the "rule of 70"? How long would it take for the price level to double if inflation persisted at (*a*) 2, (*b*) 5, and (*c*) 10 percent per year?

12. Distinguish between demand-pull inflation and cost-push inflation. Which of the two types is most likely to be associated with a negative GDP gap? Which with a positive GDP gap, in which actual GDP exceeds potential GDP?

13. Explain how hyperinflation might lead to a severe decline in total output.

14. Evaluate as accurately as you can how each of the following individuals would be affected by unanticipated inflation of 10 percent per year:
    a. A pensioned railroad worker.
    b. A department-store clerk.
    c. A unionized automobile assembly-line worker.
    d. A heavily indebted farmer.
    e. A retired business executive whose current income comes entirely from interest on government bonds.
    f. The owner of an independent small-town department store.

15. *(Last Word)* Suppose that stock prices were to fall by 10 percent in the stock market. All else equal, would the lower stock prices be likely to cause a decrease in real GDP? How might they predict a decline in real GDP?

16. *Web-Based Question: What is the current U.S. unemployment rate?* Visit the Bureau of Labor Statistics website, www.bls.gov/news.release/empsit.toc.htm, and select Employment Situation Summary. What month (and year) is summarized? What was the unemployment rate for that month? How does that rate compare with the rate in the previous month? What were the unemployment rates for adult men, adult women, teenagers, blacks, Hispanics, and whites? How did these rates compare with those a month earlier?

17. *Web-Based Question: What is the current U.S. inflation rate?* Visit the Bureau of Labor Statistics website, www.bls.gov/news.release/cpi.toc.htm, and select Consumer Price Index Summary. What month (and year) is summarized? What was the CPI-U for the month? What was the rate of inflation (change in the CPI-U) for the month? How does that rate of inflation compare with the rate for the previous month? Which two categories of goods or services had the greatest price increases for the month? Which two had the lowest price increases (or greatest price decreases) for the month?

9

*Basic Macroeconomic Relationships**

In Chapter 8 we described economic growth, the business cycle, recession, and inflation. Our eventual goal is to build economic models to explain those occurrences and assess the current status of the economy. This chapter begins that process by examining basic relationships between several economic aggregates. (Recall that to economists "aggregate" means "total" or "combined.") Specifically, this chapter looks at the relationships between:

- income and consumption (and income and saving).

- the interest rate and investment.

- changes in spending and changes in output.

What explains the trends in consumption (consumer spending) and saving reported in the news? How do changes in interest rates affect investment? How can initial changes in spending ultimately produce multiplied changes in GDP?

---

*Note to the Instructor: If you wish to bypass the aggregate expenditures model covered in full in Chapter 10, assigning the present chapter will provide a seamless transition to the AD-AS model of Chapter 11 and the chapters beyond. If you want to cover the aggregate expenditure model, this present chapter provides the necessary building blocks.

The Income-Consumption and Income-Saving Relationships

In examining the relationship between income and consumption, we are also exploring the relationship between income and saving. Recall that economists define *personal saving* as "not spending" or "that part of disposable (after-tax) income not consumed." Saving (*S*) equals disposable income (DI) *minus* consumption (*C*).

Many factors determine the nation's levels of consumption and saving, but the most significant is

disposable income. Consider some recent historical data for the United States. In Figure 9.1 each dot represents consumption and disposable income for 1 year since 1980. The line *C* fitted to these points shows that consumption is directly (positively) related to disposable income; moreover, households spend most of their income.

But we can say more. The **45° (degree) line** is a reference line. Because it bisects the 90° angle formed by the two axes of the graph, each point on it is equidistant from the two axes. At each point on the 45° line, consumption would equal disposable income, or *C* = DI. Therefore,

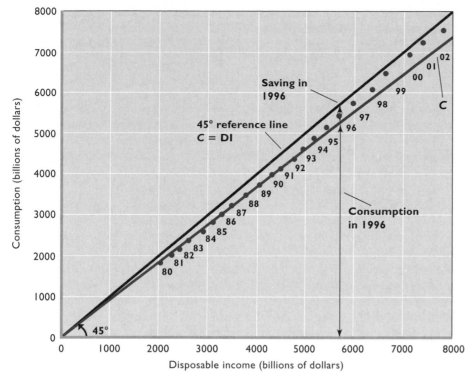

FIGURE 9.1

Consumption and disposable income, 1980–2002. Each dot in this figure shows consumption and disposable income in a specific year. The line *C*, which generalizes the relationship between consumption and disposable income, indicates a direct relationship and shows that households consume most of their incomes.

the vertical distance between the 45° line and any point on the horizontal axis measures either consumption *or* disposable income. If we let it measure disposable income, the vertical distance between it and the consumption line labeled *C* represents the amount of saving (*S*) in that year. Saving is the amount by which actual consumption in any year falls short of the 45° line—(*S* = DI − *C*). For example, in 1996 disposable income was $5678 billion and consumption was $5406 billion, so saving was $272 billion. Observe that the vertical distance between the 45° line and line *C* increases as we move rightward along the horizontal axis and decreases as we move leftward. Like consumption, saving varies directly with the level of disposable income: As DI rises, saving increases; as DI falls, saving decreases.

The Consumption Schedule

The dots in Figure 9.1 represent historical data—the actual amounts of DI, *C*, and *S* in the United States over a period of years. But, for analytical purposes, we need a schedule showing the various amounts that households would *plan* to consume at each of the various levels of disposable income that might prevail at some specific time. Columns 1 and 2 of Table 9.1, represented in **Figure 9.2a**

(Key Graph), show the hypothetical consumption schedule that we require. This **consumption schedule** (or "consumption function") reflects the direct consumption–disposable income relationship suggested by the data in Figure 9.1, and it is consistent with many household budget studies. In the aggregate, households increase their spending as their disposable income rises and spend a larger proportion of a small disposable income than of a large disposable income.

9.1 Income-consumption relationship

The Saving Schedule

It is relatively easy to derive a **saving schedule** (or "saving function"). Because saving equals disposable income less consumption (*S* = DI − *C*), we need only subtract consumption (Table 9.1, column 2) from disposable income (column 1) to find the amount saved (column 3) at each DI. Thus, columns 1 and 3 in Table 9.1 are the saving schedule, represented in Figure 9.2b. The graph shows that there is a direct relationship between saving and DI but that saving is a smaller proportion of a small DI than of a large DI. If households consume a smaller and smaller

TABLE 9.1

Consumption and Saving Schedules (in Billions) and Propensities to Consume and Save

(1) Level of Output and Income (GDP = DI)	(2) Consumption (C)	(3) Saving (S), (1) − (2)	(4) Average Propensity to Consume (APC), (2)/(1)	(5) Average Propensity to Save (APS), (3)/(1)	(6) Marginal Propensity to Consume (MPC), Δ(2)/Δ(1)*	(7) Marginal Propensity to Save (MPS), Δ(3)/Δ(1)*
(1) $370	$375	$−5	1.01	−.01	.75	.25
(2) 390	390	0	1.00	.00	.75	.25
(3) 410	405	5	.99	.01	.75	.25
(4) 430	420	10	.98	.02	.75	.25
(5) 450	435	15	.97	.03	.75	.25
(6) 470	450	20	.96	.04	.75	.25
(7) 490	465	25	.95	.05	.75	.25
(8) 510	480	30	.94	.06	.75	.25
(9) 530	495	35	.93	.07	.75	.25
(10) 550	510	40	.93	.07	.75	.25

*The Greek letter Δ, delta, means "the change in."

proportion of DI as DI increases, then they must be saving a larger and larger proportion.

Remembering that at each point on the 45° line consumption equals DI, we see that *dissaving* (consuming in excess of after-tax income) will occur at relatively low DIs. For example, at $370 billion (row 1, Table 9.1), consumption is $375 billion. Households can consume more than their incomes by liquidating (selling for cash) accumulated wealth or by borrowing. Graphically, dissaving is shown as the vertical distance of the consumption schedule above the 45° line or as the vertical distance of the saving schedule below the horizontal axis. We have marked the dissaving at the $370 billion level of income in Figure 9.2a and 9.2b. Both vertical distances measure the $5 billion of dissaving that occurs at $370 billion of income.

In our example, the **break-even income** is $390 billion (row 2). This is the income level at which households plan to consume their entire incomes (C = DI). Graphically, the consumption schedule cuts the 45° line, and the saving schedule cuts the horizontal axis (saving is zero) at the break-even income level.

At all higher incomes, households plan to save part of their incomes. Graphically, the vertical distance between the consumption schedule and the 45° line measures this saving (see Figure 9.2a), as does the vertical distance between the saving schedule and the horizontal axis (see Figure 9.2b). For example, at the $410 billion level of income (row 3), both these distances indicate $5 billion of saving.

Average and Marginal Propensities

Columns 4 to 7 in Table 9.1 show additional characteristics of the consumption and saving schedules.

APC and APS   The fraction, or percentage, of total income that is consumed is the **average propensity to consume (APC)**. The fraction of total income that is saved is the **average propensity to save (APS)**. That is,

$$APC = \frac{consumption}{income}$$

and

$$APS = \frac{saving}{income}$$

For example, at $470 billion of income (row 6) in Table 9.1, the APC is $\frac{450}{470} = \frac{45}{47}$, or about 96 percent, while the APS is $\frac{20}{470} = \frac{2}{47}$, or about 4 percent. Columns 4 and 5 in Table 9.1 show the APC and APS at each of the 10 levels of DI; note in the table that the APC falls and the APS rises as DI increases, as was implied in our previous comments.

Because disposable income is either consumed or saved, the fraction of any DI consumed plus the fraction saved (not consumed) must exhaust that income. Mathematically, APC + APS = 1 at any level of disposable income, as columns 4 and 5 in Table 9.1 illustrate.

KEY GRAPH

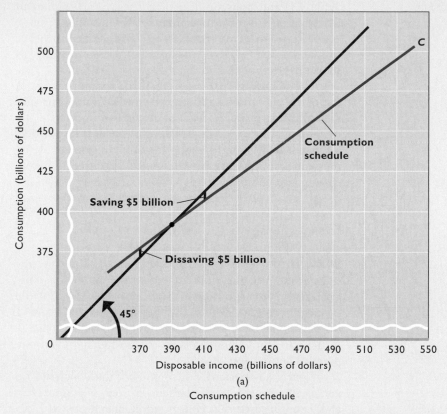

(a)
Consumption schedule

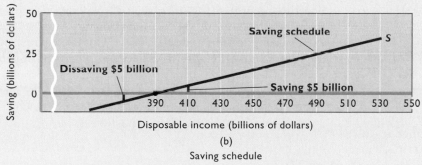

(b)
Saving schedule

FIGURE 9.2

(a) Consumption and (b) saving schedules.
The two parts of this figure show the income-consumption and income-saving relationships in Table 9.1 graphically. The saving schedule in (b) is found by subtracting the consumption schedule in (a) vertically from the 45° line. Consumption equals disposable income (and saving thus equals zero) at $390 billion for these hypothetical data.

QUICK QUIZ 9.2

1. The slope of the consumption schedule in this figure is .75. Thus the:
   a. slope of the saving schedule is 1.33.
   b. marginal propensity to consume is .75.
   c. average propensity to consume is .25.
   d. slope of the saving schedule is also .75.

2. In this figure, when consumption is a positive amount, saving:
   a. must be a negative amount.
   b. must also be a positive amount.
   c. can be either a positive or a negative amount.
   d. is zero.

3. In this figure:
   a. the marginal propensity to consume is constant at all levels of income.
   b. the marginal propensity to save rises as disposable income rises.
   c. consumption is inversely (negatively) related to disposable income.
   d. saving is inversely (negatively) related to disposable income.

4. When consumption equals disposable income:
   a. the marginal propensity to consume is zero.
   b. the average propensity to consume is zero.
   c. consumption and saving must be equal.
   d. saving must be zero.

Answers: 1. b; 2. c; 3. a; 4. d

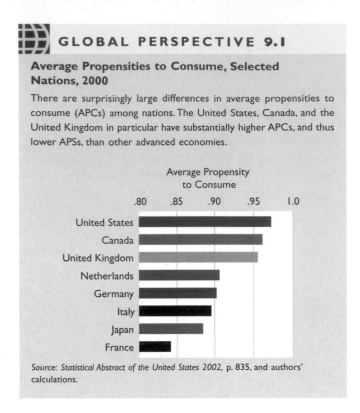

GLOBAL PERSPECTIVE 9.1

Average Propensities to Consume, Selected Nations, 2000

There are surprisingly large differences in average propensities to consume (APCs) among nations. The United States, Canada, and the United Kingdom in particular have substantially higher APCs, and thus lower APSs, than other advanced economies.

Source: *Statistical Abstract of the United States 2002*, p. 835, and authors' calculations.

Global Perspective 9.1 shows APCs for several countries.

MPC and MPS The fact that households consume a certain proportion of a particular total income, for example, $\frac{45}{47}$ of a $470 billion disposable income, does not guarantee they will consume the same proportion of any *change* in income they might receive. The proportion, or fraction, of any change in income consumed is called the **marginal propensity to consume (MPC),** "marginal" meaning "extra" or "a change in." Equivalently, the MPC is the ratio of a change in consumption to a change in the income that caused the consumption change:

$$\text{MPC} = \frac{\text{change in consumption}}{\text{change in income}}$$

Similarly, the fraction of any change in income saved is the **marginal propensity to save (MPS).** The MPS is the ratio of a change in saving to the change in income that brought it about:

$$\text{MPS} = \frac{\text{change in saving}}{\text{change in income}}$$

If disposable income is $470 billion (row 6 horizontally in Table 9.1) and household income rises by $20 billion to $490 billion (row 7), households will consume $\frac{15}{20}$, or $\frac{3}{4}$, and save $\frac{5}{20}$, or $\frac{1}{4}$, of that increase in income. In other words, the MPC is $\frac{3}{4}$ or .75, and the MPS is $\frac{1}{4}$ or .25, as shown in columns 6 and 7.

The sum of the MPC and the MPS for any change in disposable income must always be 1. Consuming or saving out of extra income is an either-or proposition; the fraction of any change in income not consumed is, by definition, saved. Therefore, the fraction consumed (MPC) plus the fraction saved (MPS) must exhaust the whole change in income:

$$\text{MPC} + \text{MPS} = 1$$

In our example, .75 plus .25 equals 1.

MPC and MPS as Slopes The MPC is the numerical value of the slope of the consumption schedule, and the MPS is the numerical value of the slope of the saving schedule. We know from the appendix to Chapter 1 that the slope of any line is the ratio of the vertical change to the horizontal change occasioned in moving from one point to another on that line.

Figure 9.3 measures the slopes of the consumption and saving lines, using enlarged portions of Figure 9.2a and 9.2b. Observe that consumption changes by $15 billion (the vertical change) for each $20 billion change in disposable income (the horizontal change). The slope of the consumption line is thus .75 (= $15/$20), which is the value of the MPC. Saving changes by $5 billion (shown as the vertical change) for every $20 billion change in disposable income (shown as the horizontal change). The slope of the saving line therefore is .25 (= $5/$20), which is the value of the MPS. **(Key Question 5)**

Nonincome Determinants of Consumption and Saving

The amount of disposable income is the basic determinant of the amounts households will consume and save. But certain determinants other than income might prompt households to consume more or less at each possible level of income and thereby change the locations of the consumption and saving schedules. Those other determinants are wealth, expectations, interest rates, indebtedness, and taxation.

Wealth The amount that households spend and save from current income depends partly on the value of the

FIGURE 9.3

The marginal propensity to consume and the marginal propensity to save.   The MPC is the slope (ΔC/ΔDI) of the consumption schedule, and the MPS is the slope (ΔS/ΔDI) of the saving schedule. The Greek letter delta (Δ) means "the change in."

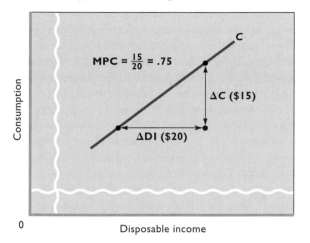

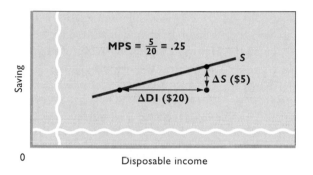

For example, expectations of rising prices tomorrow may trigger more spending and less saving today. Thus, the current consumption schedule shifts up and the current saving schedule shifts down. Or expectations of a recession and thus lower income in the future may lead households to reduce consumption and save more today. If so, the consumption schedule will shift down and the saving schedule will shift up.

Real Interest Rates   When real interest rates (those adjusted for inflation) fall, households tend to borrow more, consume more, and save less. A lower interest rate, for example, induces consumers to purchase automobiles and other goods bought on credit. A lower interest rate also diminishes the incentive to save because of the reduced interest "payment" to the saver. These effects on consumption and saving, however, are very modest. They mainly shift consumption toward some products (those bought on credit) and away from others. At best, lower interest rates shift the consumption schedule slightly upward and the saving schedule slightly downward. Higher interest rates do the opposite.

Household Debt   In drawing a particular consumption schedule, household debt as a percentage of DI is held constant. But when consumers as a group increase their household debt, they can increase current consumption at each level of DI. Increased borrowing shifts the consumption schedule upward. In contrast, when levels of household debt get abnormally high, households may be forced to reduce their consumption to pay off some of their loans. At that time, the consumption schedule shifts downward.

Taxation   When government is considered, changes in taxes shift the consumption and saving schedules. Taxes are paid partly at the expense of consumption and partly at the expense of saving. So an increase in taxes will shift both the consumption and the saving schedules downward. Conversely, a tax reduction will be partly consumed and partly saved by households. A tax decrease will shift both the consumption and the saving schedules upward.

Terminology, Shifts, and Stability

There are several additional important points regarding the consumption and saving schedules:

- *Terminology*   The movement from one point to another on a consumption schedule (for example, from

existing wealth they have already accumulated. By "wealth" we mean the value of both real assets (for example, houses, land) and financial assets (for example, cash, savings accounts, stocks, bonds, pensions) that households own. Households save to accumulate wealth. When events boost the value of existing wealth, households increase their spending and reduce their saving. This so-called **wealth effect** shifts the *consumption schedule upward and the saving schedule downward*. Examples: In the late 1990s, skyrocketing U.S. stock values expanded the value of household wealth. Predictably, households spent more and saved less. In contrast, a "reverse wealth effect" occurred in 2000 and 2001, when stock prices sharply fell.

Expectations   Household expectations about future prices and income may affect current spending and saving.

FIGURE 9.4

Shifts in the (a) consumption and (b) saving schedules. Normally, if households consume more at each level of DI, they are necessarily saving less. Graphically this means that an upward shift of the consumption schedule (C_0 to C_1) entails a downward shift of the saving schedule (S_0 to S_1). If households consume less at each level of DI, they are saving more. A downward shift of the consumption schedule (C_0 to C_2) is reflected in an upward shift of the saving schedule (S_0 to S_2). This pattern breaks down, however, when taxes change; then the consumption and saving schedules move in the *same* direction—opposite to the direction of the tax change.

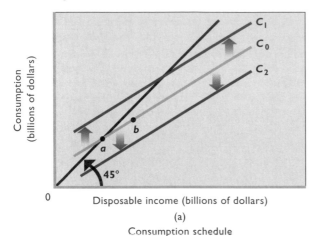

(a)
Consumption schedule

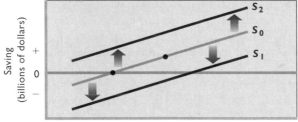

(b)
Saving schedule

a to *b* on C_0 in Figure 9.4a) is a *change in the amount consumed* and is solely caused by a change in disposable income (or GDP). On the other hand, an upward or downward shift of the entire schedule, for example, a shift from C_0 to C_1 or C_2 in Figure 9.4a, is caused by changes in any one or more of the five *nonincome* determinants of consumption just discussed.

A similar distinction in terminology applies to the saving schedule in Figure 9.4b.

- **Schedule shifts** Changes in wealth, expectations, interest rates, and household debt will shift the consumption schedule in one direction and the saving schedule in the opposite direction. If households decide to consume more at each possible level of disposable income, they want to save less, and vice versa. (Even when they spend more by borrowing, they are, in effect, reducing their current saving by the amount borrowed.) Graphically, if the consumption schedule shifts upward from C_0 to C_1 in Figure 9.4a, the saving schedule shifts downward, from S_0 to S_1 in Figure 9-4b. Similarly, a downward shift of the consumption schedule from C_0 to C_2 means an upward shift of the saving schedule from S_0 to S_2.

  In contrast, a change in taxes will result in the consumption and saving schedules moving in the same direction. A tax increase shifts both schedules downward, and a tax decrease shifts them upward.

- **Stability** Although changes in nonincome determinants can shift the consumption and saving schedules, usually these schedules are relatively stable. Their stability may be because consumption-saving decisions are strongly influenced by long-term considerations such as saving to meet emergencies or saving for retirement. It may also be because changes in the nonincome determinants frequently work in opposite directions and therefore may be self-canceling.

**9.1
Consumption
and saving
schedules**

QUICK REVIEW 9.1

- Both consumption spending and saving rise when disposable income increases; both fall when disposable income decreases.
- The average propensity to consume (APC) is the fraction of any specific level of disposable income that is spent on consumer goods; the average propensity to save (APS) is the fraction of any specific level of disposable income that is saved. The APC falls and the APS rises as disposable income increases.
- The marginal propensity to consume (MPC) is the fraction of a change in disposable income that is consumed and it is the slope of the consumption schedule; the marginal propensity to save (MPS) is the fraction of a change in disposable income that is saved and it is the slope of the saving schedule.
- Changes in consumer wealth, consumer expectations, interest rates, household debt, and taxes can shift the consumption and saving schedules.

The Interest-Rate–Investment Relationship

In our consideration of major macro relationships, we next turn to the relationship between the real interest rate and investment. Recall that investment consists of expenditures on new plants, capital equipment, machinery, inventories, and so on. The investment decision is a marginal-benefit–marginal-cost decision: The marginal benefit from investment is the expected rate of return businesses hope to realize. The marginal cost is the interest rate that must be paid for borrowed funds. We will see that businesses will invest in all projects for which the expected rate of return exceeds the interest rate. Expected returns (profits) and the interest rate therefore are the two basic determinants of investment spending.

Expected Rate of Return

Investment spending is guided by the profit motive; businesses buy capital goods only when they think such purchases will be profitable. Suppose the owner of a small cabinetmaking shop is considering whether to invest in a new sanding machine that costs $1000 and has a useful life of only 1 year. (Extending the life of the machine beyond 1 year complicates the economic decision but does not change the fundamental analysis.) The new machine will increase the firm's output and sales revenue. Suppose the net expected revenue from the machine (that is, after such operating costs as power, lumber, labor, and certain taxes have been subtracted) is $1100. Then, after operating costs have been accounted for, the remaining expected net revenue is sufficient to cover the $1000 cost of the machine and leave a profit of $100. Comparing this $100 profit to the $1000 cost of the machine, we find that the **expected rate of return,** r, on the machine is 10 percent (= $100/$1000). It is important to note that this is an *expected* rate of return, not a *guaranteed* rate of return. The investment may or may not pay off as anticipated. Investment involves risk.

The Real Interest Rate

One important cost associated with investing that our example has ignored is interest, which is the financial cost of borrowing the $1000 of *money* "capital" to purchase the $1000 of *real* capital (the sanding machine).

The interest cost of the investment is computed by multiplying the interest rate, i, by the $1000 borrowed to buy the machine. If the interest rate is, say, 7 percent, the total interest cost will be $70. This compares favorably with the net expected return of $100, which produced the 10 percent expected rate of return. If the investment works out as expected, it will add $30 to the firm's profit. We can generalize as follows: If the expected rate of return (10 percent) exceeds the interest rate (here, 7 percent), the investment should be undertaken. The firm expects the investment to be profitable. But if the interest rate (say, 12 percent) exceeds the expected rate of return (10 percent), the investment should not be undertaken. The firm expects the investment to be unprofitable. The firm should undertake all investment projects it thinks will be profitable. That means it should invest up to the point where $r = i$, because then it has undertaken all investment for which r exceeds i.

This guideline applies even if a firm finances the investment internally out of funds saved from past profit rather than borrowing the funds. The role of the interest rate in the investment decision does not change. When the firm uses money from savings to invest in the sander, it incurs an opportunity cost because it forgoes the interest income it could have earned by lending the funds to someone else.

That interest cost, converted to percentage terms, needs to be weighed against the expected rate of return.

The *real* rate of interest, rather than the *nominal* rate, is crucial in making investment decisions. Recall from Chapter 8 that the nominal interest rate is expressed in dollars of current value, while the real interest rate is stated in dollars of constant or inflation-adjusted value. Recall that the real interest rate is the nominal rate less the rate of inflation. In our sanding machine illustration our implicit assumption of a constant price level ensures that all our data, including the interest rate, are in real terms.

But what if inflation *is* occurring? Suppose a $1000 investment is expected to yield a real (inflation-adjusted) rate of return of 10 percent and the nominal interest rate is 15 percent. At first, we would say the investment would be unprofitable. But assume there is ongoing inflation of 10 percent per year. This means the investing firm will pay back dollars with approximately 10 percent less in purchasing power. While the nominal interest rate is 15 percent, the real rate is only 5 percent ($= 15$ percent $-$ 10 percent). By comparing this 5 percent real interest rate with the 10 percent expected real rate of return, we find that the investment is potentially profitable and should be undertaken. **(Key Question 7)**

Investment Demand Curve

We now move from a single firm's investment decision to total demand for investment goods by the entire business sector. Assume that every firm has estimated the expected rates of return from all investment projects and has recorded those data. We can cumulate (successively sum) these data by asking: How many dollars' worth of investment projects have an expected rate of return of, say, 16 percent or more? How many have 14 percent or more? How many have 12 percent or more? And so on.

Suppose no prospective investments yield an expected return of 16 percent or more. But suppose there are $5 billion of investment opportunities with expected rates of return between 14 and 16 percent; an additional $5 billion yielding between 12 and 14 percent; still an additional $5 billion yielding between 10 and 12 percent; and an additional $5 billion in each successive 2 percent range of yield down to and including the 0 to 2 percent range.

To cumulate these figures for each rate of return, *r*, we add the amounts of investment that will yield each particular rate of return *r* or higher. This provides the data in Table 9.2, shown graphically in **Figure 9.5 (Key Graph)**. In Table 9.2 the number opposite 12 percent, for example, means there are $10 billion of investment opportunities that will yield an expected rate of return of 12 percent or

TABLE 9.2

Rates of Expected Return and Investment

Expected Rate of Return (*r*)	Cumulative Amount of Investment Having This Rate of Return or Higher, Billions per Year
16%	$ 0
14	5
12	10
10	15
8	20
6	25
4	30
2	35
0	40

more. The $10 billion includes the $5 billion of investment expected to yield a return of 14 percent or more plus the $5 billion expected to yield between 12 and 14 percent.

We know from our example of the sanding machine that an investment project will be undertaken if its expected rate of return, *r*, exceeds the real interest rate, *i*. Let's first suppose *i* is 12 percent. Businesses will undertake all investments for which *r* exceeds 12 percent. That is, they will invest until the 12 percent rate of return equals the 12 percent interest rate. Figure 9.5 reveals that $10 billion of investment spending will be undertaken at a 12 percent interest rate; that means $10 billion of investment projects have an expected rate of return of 12 percent or more.

Put another way: At a financial "price" of 12 percent, $10 billion of investment goods will be demanded. If the interest rate is lower, say, 8 percent, the amount of investment for which *r* equals or exceeds *i* is $20 billion. Thus, firms will demand $20 billion of investment goods at an 8 percent real interest rate. At 6 percent, they will demand $25 billion of investment goods.

By applying the marginal-benefit–marginal-cost rule that investment projects should be undertaken up to the point where $r = i$, we see that we can add the real interest rate to the vertical axis in Figure 9.5. The curve in Figure 9.5 not only shows rates of return; it shows the quantity of investment demanded at each "price" *i* (interest rate) of investment. The vertical axis in Figure 9.5 shows the various possible real interest rates, and the horizontal axis shows the corresponding quantities of investment demanded. The inverse (downsloping) relationship between the interest rate (price) and dollar quantity of investment demanded conforms to

9.2 Interest-rate–investment relationship

KEY GRAPH

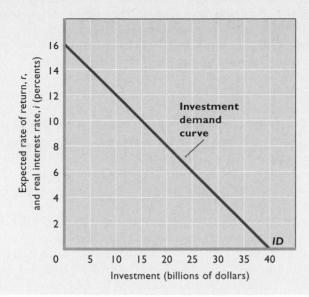

FIGURE 9.5

The investment demand curve. The investment demand curve is constructed by arraying all potential investment projects in descending order of their expected rates of return. The curve slopes downward, reflecting an inverse relationship between the real interest rate (the financial "price" of each dollar of investing) and the quantity of investment demanded.

QUICK QUIZ 9.5

1. The investment demand curve:
   a. reflects a direct (positive) relationship between the real interest rate and investment.
   b. reflects an inverse (negative) relationship between the real interest rate and investment.
   c. shifts to the right when the real interest rate rises.
   d. shifts to the left when the real interest rate rises.

2. In this figure:
   a. greater cumulative amounts of investment are associated with lower expected rates of return on investment.
   b. lesser cumulative amounts of investment are associated with lower expected rates of return on investment.
   c. higher interest rates are associated with higher expected rates of return on investment, and therefore greater amounts of investment.

   d. interest rates and investment move in the same direction.

3. In this figure, if the real interest rate falls from 6 to 4 percent:
   a. investment will increase from 0 to $30 billion.
   b. investment will decrease by $5 billion.
   c. the expected rate of return will rise by $5 billion.
   d. investment will increase from $25 billion to $30 billion.

4. In this figure, investment will be:
   a. zero if the real interest rate is zero.
   b. $40 billion if the real interest rate is 16 percent.
   c. $30 billion if the real interest rate is 4 percent.
   d. $20 billion if the real interest rate is 12 percent.

Answers: 1. b; 2. a; 3. d; 4. c

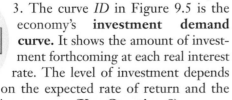

9.2
Investment demand curve

the law of demand discussed in Chapter 3. The curve *ID* in Figure 9.5 is the economy's **investment demand curve.** It shows the amount of investment forthcoming at each real interest rate. The level of investment depends on the expected rate of return and the real interest rate. **(Key Question 8)**

Shifts of the Investment Demand Curve

Figure 9.5 shows the relationship between the interest rate and the amount of investment demanded, other things equal.

When other things change, the investment demand curve shifts. In general, any factor that leads businesses collectively to expect greater rates of return on their investments increases investment demand. That factor shifts the investment demand curve to the right, as from ID_0 to ID_1 in Figure 9.6. Any factor that leads businesses collectively to expect lower rates of return on their investments shifts the curve to the left, as from ID_0 to ID_2. What are those non-interest-rate determinants of investment demand?

Acquisition, Maintenance, and Operating Costs

The initial costs of capital goods, and the estimated costs of operating and maintaining those goods, affect the expected

FIGURE 9.6

Shifts of the investment demand curve. Increases in investment demand are shown as rightward shifts of the investment demand curve; decreases in investment demand are shown as leftward shifts of the investment demand curve.

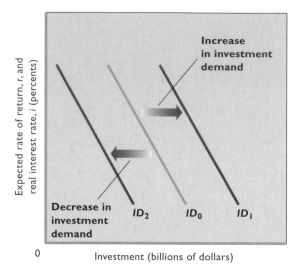

rate of return on investment. When these costs rise, the expected rate of return from prospective investment projects falls and the investment demand curve shifts to the left. Example: Higher electricity costs associated with operating tools and machinery shifts the investment demand curve to the left. Lower costs, in contrast, shift it to the right.

Business Taxes When government is considered, firms look to expected returns *after taxes* in making their investment decisions. An increase in business taxes lowers the expected profitability of investments and shifts the investment demand curve to the left; a reduction of business taxes shifts it to the right.

Technological Change Technological progress—the development of new products, improvements in existing products, and the creation of new machinery and production processes—stimulates investment. The development of a more efficient machine, for example, lowers production costs or improves product quality and increases the expected rate of return from investing in the machine. Profitable new products (for example, cholesterol medications, Internet services, high-resolution televisions, cellular phones, and so on) induce a flurry of investment as businesses tool up for expanded production. A rapid rate of technological progress shifts the investment demand curve to the right.

Stock of Capital Goods on Hand The stock of capital goods on hand, relative to output and sales,

influences investment decisions by firms. When the economy is overstocked with production facilities and when firms have excessive inventories of finished goods, the expected rate of return on new investment declines. Firms with excess production capacity have little incentive to invest in new capital. Therefore, less investment is forthcoming at each real interest rate; the investment demand curve shifts leftward.

When the economy is understocked with production facilities and when firms are selling their output as fast as they can produce it, the expected rate of return on new investment increases and the investment demand curve shifts rightward.

Expectations We noted that business investment is based on expected returns (expected additions to profit). Most capital goods are durable, with a life expectancy of 10 or 20 years. Thus, the expected rate of return on capital investment depends on the firm's expectations of future sales, future operating costs, and future profitability of the product that the capital helps produce. These expectations are based on forecasts of future business conditions as well as on such elusive and difficult-to-predict factors as changes in the domestic political climate, international relations, population growth, and consumer tastes. If executives become more optimistic about future sales, costs, and profits, the investment demand curve will shift to the right; a pessimistic outlook will shift the curve to the left.

Global Perspective 9.2 compares investment spending relative to GDP for several nations in a recent year. Domestic real interest rates and investment demand determine the levels of investment relative to GDP.

QUICK REVIEW 9.2

- A specific investment will be undertaken if the expected rate of return, *r*, equals or exceeds the real interest rate, *i*.
- The investment demand curve shows the total monetary amounts that will be invested by an economy at various possible real interest rates.
- The investment demand curve shifts when changes occur in (a) the costs of acquiring, operating, and maintaining capital goods, (b) business taxes, (c) technology, (d) the stock of capital goods on hand, and (e) business expectations.

Instability of Investment

In contrast to consumption, investment is unstable; it rises and falls quite often. Investment, in fact, is the most

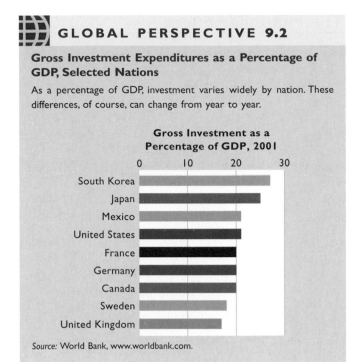

GLOBAL PERSPECTIVE 9.2

Gross Investment Expenditures as a Percentage of GDP, Selected Nations

As a percentage of GDP, investment varies widely by nation. These differences, of course, can change from year to year.

Gross Investment as a Percentage of GDP, 2001

Source: World Bank, www.worldbank.com.

volatile component of total spending. Figure 9.7 shows just how volatile investment in the United States has been. Note that its swings are much greater than those of GDP. Several factors explain the variability of investment.

Durability   Because of their durability, capital goods have an indefinite useful life. Within limits, purchases of capital goods are discretionary and therefore can be postponed. Firms can scrap or replace older equipment and buildings, or they can patch them up and use them for a few more years. Optimism about the future may prompt firms to replace their older facilities and such modernizing will call for a high level of investment. A less optimistic view, however, may lead to smaller amounts of investment as firms repair older facilities and keep them in use.

Irregularity of Innovation   We know that technological progress is a major determinant of investment. New products and processes stimulate investment. But history suggests that major innovations such as railroads, electricity, automobiles, fiber optics, and computers occur quite irregularly. When they do happen, they induce a

FIGURE 9.7

The volatility of investment.   Annual percentage changes in investment spending are often several times greater than the percentage changes in GDP. (Data are in real terms.)

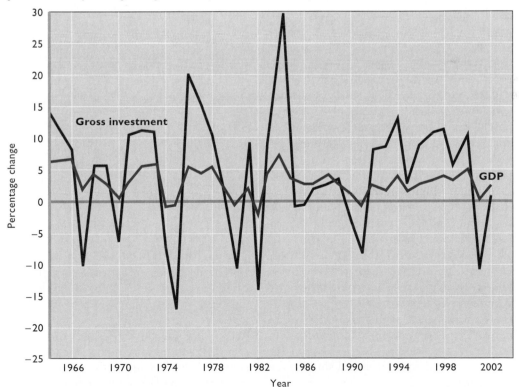

vast upsurge or "wave" of investment spending that in time recedes.

A contemporary example is the widespread acceptance of the personal computer and Internet, which has caused a wave of investment in those industries and in many related industries such as computer software and electronic commerce. Some time in the future, this surge of investment undoubtedly will level off.

Variability of Profits   The expectation of future profitability is influenced to some degree by the size of current profits. Current profits, however, are themselves highly variable. Thus, the variability of profits contributes to the volatile nature of the incentive to invest.

The instability of profits may cause investment fluctuations in a second way. Profits are a major source of funds for business investment. U.S. businesses sometimes prefer this internal source of financing to increases in external debt or stock issue.

In short, expanding profits give firms both greater incentives and greater means to invest; declining profits have the reverse effects. The fact that actual profits are variable thus adds doubly to the instability of investment.

Variability of Expectations   Firms tend to project current business conditions into the future. But their expectations can change quickly when some event suggests a significant possible change in future business conditions. Changes in exchange rates, changes in the outlook for international peace, court decisions in key labor or antitrust cases, legislative actions, changes in trade barriers, changes in governmental economic policies, and a host of similar considerations may cause substantial shifts in business expectations.

The stock market can influence business expectations because firms look to it as one of several indicators of society's overall confidence in future business conditions. Rising stock prices tend to signify public confidence in the business future, while falling stock prices may imply a lack of confidence. The stock market, however, is quite speculative. Some participants buy when stock prices begin to rise and sell as soon as prices begin to fall. This behavior can magnify what otherwise would be modest changes in stock prices. By creating swings in optimism and pessimism, the stock market may add to the instability of investment spending.

For all these reasons, changes in investment cause most of the fluctuations in output and employment. In terms of Figures 9.5 and 9.6, we would represent volatility of investment as occasional and substantial shifts in the investment demand curve.

The Multiplier Effect

Other things equal, there is a direct relationship between changes in spending and changes in real GDP. That is, more spending results in a higher GDP; less spending results in a lower GDP. But there is more to this relationship. A change in spending, say, investment, ultimately changes output and income by more than the initial change in investment spending. That surprising result is called the *multiplier effect:* a change in a component of total spending leads to a larger change in GDP. The **multiplier** determines how much larger that change will be; it is the ratio of a change in GDP to the initial change in spending (in this case, investment). Stated generally,

$$\text{Multiplier} = \frac{\text{change in real GDP}}{\text{initial change in spending}}$$

By rearranging this equation, we can also say that

Change in GDP = multiplier × initial change in spending

So if investment in an economy rises by $30 billion and GDP increases by $90 billion as a result, we then know from our first equation that the multiplier is 3 (= $90/30).

Note these three points about the multiplier:

- The "initial change in spending" is usually associated with investment spending because of investment's volatility. But changes in consumption (unrelated to changes in income), net exports, and government purchases also lead to the multiplier effect.
- The "initial change in spending" associated with investment spending results from a change in the real interest rate and/or a shift of the investment demand curve.
- Implicit in the preceding point is that the multiplier works in both directions. An increase in initial spending may create a multiple increase in GDP, and a decrease in spending may be multiplied into a larger decrease in GDP.

Rationale

The multiplier effect follows from two facts. First, the economy supports repetitive, continuous flows of expenditures and income through which dollars spent by Smith are received as income by Chin and then spent by Chin and received as income by Gonzales, and so on. (This chapter's Last Word presents this idea in a humorous way.) Second, any change in income will vary both consumption and saving in the same direction as, and by a fraction of, the change in income.

TABLE 9.3

The Multiplier: A Tabular Illustration (in Billions)

	(1) Change in Income	(2) Change in Consumption (MPC = .75)	(3) Change in Saving (MPS = .25)
Increase in investment of **$5.00**	$ 5.00	$ 3.75	$1.25
Second round	3.75	2.81	.94
Third round	2.81	2.11	.70
Fourth round	2.11	1.58	.53
Fifth round	1.58	1.19	.39
All other rounds	4.75	3.56	1.19
Total	**$20.00**	**$15.00**	**$5.00**

It follows that an initial change in spending will set off a spending chain throughout the economy. That chain of spending, although of diminishing importance at each successive step, will cumulate to a multiple change in GDP. Initial changes in spending produce magnified changes in output and income.

Table 9.3 illustrates the rationale underlying the multiplier effect. Suppose that a $5 billion increase in investment spending occurs. We assume that the MPC is .75 and the MPS is .25.

The initial $5 billion increase in investment generates an equal amount of wage, rent, interest, and profit income, because spending and receiving income are two sides of the same transaction. How much consumption will be induced by this $5 billion increase in the incomes of households? We find the answer by applying the marginal propensity to consume of .75 to this change in income. Thus, the $5 billion increase in income initially raises consumption by $3.75 (= .75 × $5) billion and saving by $1.25 (= .25 × $5) billion, as shown in columns 2 and 3 in Table 9.3.

Other households receive as income (second round) the $3.75 billion of consumption spending. Those households consume .75 of this $3.75 billion, or $2.81 billion, and save .25 of it, or $.94 billion. The $2.81 billion that is consumed flows to still other households as income to be spent or saved (third round). And the process continues, with the added consumption and income becoming less in each round. The process ends when there is no more additional income to spend.

Figure 9.8 shows several rounds of the multiplier process of Table 9.3 graphically. As shown by rounds 1 to 5, each round adds a smaller and smaller orange block to national income and GDP. The process, of course, continues beyond the five rounds shown (for convenience we have simply cumulated the subsequent declining blocks

into a single block labeled "All other"). The accumulation of the additional income in each round—the sum of the orange blocks—is the total change in income or GDP resulting from the initial $5 billion change in spending. Because the spending and respending effects of the increase in investment diminish with each successive round of spending, the cumulative increase in output and

FIGURE 9.8

The multiplier process (MPC = .75). An initial change in investment spending of $5 billion creates an equal $5 billion of new income in round 1. Households spend $3.75 (= .75 × $5) billion of this new income, creating $3.75 of added income in round 2. Of this $3.75 of new income, households spend $2.81 (= .75 × $3.75) billion, and income rises by that amount in round 3. Such income increments over the entire process get successively smaller but eventually produce a total change of income and GDP of $20 billion. The multiplier therefore is 4 (= $20 billion/$5 billion).

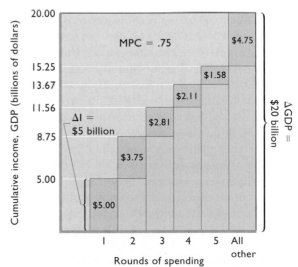

income eventually ends. In this case, the ending occurs when $20 billion of additional income accumulates. Thus, the multiplier is 4 (= $20 billion/$5 billion).

The Multiplier and the Marginal Propensities

You may have sensed from Table 9.3 that the fractions of an increase in income consumed (MPC) and saved (MPS) determine the cumulative respending effects of any initial change in spending and therefore determines the size of the multiplier. *The MPC and the multiplier are directly related and the MPS and the multiplier are inversely related.* The precise formulas are as shown in the next two equations:

$$\text{Multiplier} = \frac{1}{1 - \text{MPC}}$$

Recall, too, that MPC + MPS = 1. Therefore MPS = 1 − MPC, which means we can also write the multiplier formula as

$$\text{Multiplier} = \frac{1}{\text{MPS}}$$

This latter formula is a quick way to determine the multiplier. All you need to know is the MPS.

The smaller the fraction of any change in income saved, the greater the respending at each round and, therefore, the greater the multiplier. When the MPS is .25, as in our example, the multiplier is 4. If the MPS were .2, the multiplier would be 5. If the MPS were .33, the multiplier would be 3. Let's see why.

Suppose the MPS is .2 and businesses increase investment by $5 billion. In the first round of Table 9.3, consumption will rise by $4 billion (= MPC of .8 × $5 billion) rather than by $3.75 billion because saving will increase by $1 billion (= MPS of .2 × $5 billion) rather than $1.25 billion. The greater rise in consumption in round 1 will produce a greater increase in income in round 2. The same will be true for all successive rounds. If we worked through all rounds of the multiplier, we would find that the process ends when income has cumulatively increased by $25 billion, not the $20 billion shown in the table. When the MPS is .2 rather than .25, the multiplier is 5 (= $25 billion/$5 billion) as opposed to 4 (= $20 billion/$5 billion.)

If the MPS were .33 rather than .25, the successive increases in consumption and income would be less than those in Table 9.3. We would discover that the process ended with a $15 billion increase in income rather than the $20 billion shown. When the MPS is .33, the multiplier is 3 (= $15 billion/$5 billion). The mathematics works

FIGURE 9.9

The MPC and the multiplier. The larger the MPC (the smaller the MPS), the greater the size of the multiplier.

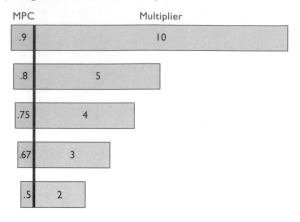

such that the multiplier is equal to the reciprocal of the MPS. The reciprocal of any number is the quotient you obtain by dividing 1 by that number.

A large MPC (small MPS) means the succeeding rounds of consumption spending shown in Figure 9.8 diminish slowly and thereby cumulate to a large change in income. Conversely, a small MPC (a large MPS) causes the increases in consumption to decline quickly, so the cumulative change in income is small. The relationship between the MPC (and thus the MPS) and the multiplier is summarized in Figure 9.9.

QUICK REVIEW 9.3

• The multiplier effect reveals that an initial change in spending can cause a larger change in domestic income and output. The multiplier is the factor by which the initial change is magnified: multiplier = change in real GDP/initial change in spending.

• The higher the marginal propensity to consume (the lower the marginal propensity to save), the larger the multiplier: multiplier = 1/(1 − MPC) or 1/MPS.

How Large Is the Actual Multiplier Effect?

The multiplier we have just described is based on simplifying assumptions. Consumption of domestic output rises by the increases in income minus the increases in saving. But in reality, consumption of domestic output increases in each round by a lesser amount than implied by the MPS alone. In addition to saving, households use some of the

Humorist Art Buchwald Examines the Multiplier.

WASHINGTON—The recession hit so fast that nobody knows exactly how it happened. One day we were the land of milk and honey and the next day we were the land of sour cream and food stamps.

This is one explanation.

Hofberger, the Chevy salesman in Tomcat, Va., a suburb of Washington, called up Littleton, of Littleton Menswear & Haberdashery, and said, "Good news, the new [Chevrolets] have just come in and I've put one aside for you and your wife."

Littleton said, "I can't, Hofberger, my wife and I are getting a divorce."

"I'm sorry," Littleton said, "but I can't afford a new car this year. After I settle with my wife, I'll be lucky to buy a bicycle."

Hofberger hung up. His phone rang a few minutes later.

"This is Bedcheck the painter," the voice on the other end said. "When do you want us to start painting your house?"

"I changed my mind," said Hofberger, "I'm not going to paint the house."

"But I ordered the paint," Bedcheck said. "Why did you change your mind?"

"Because Littleton is getting a divorce and he can't afford a new car."

That evening when Bedcheck came home his wife said, "The new color television set arrived from Gladstone's TV Shop."

"Take it back," Bedcheck told his wife.

"Why?" she demanded.

"Because Hofberger isn't going to have his house painted now that the Littletons are getting a divorce."

The next day Mrs. Bedcheck dragged the TV set in its carton back to Gladstone. "We don't want it."

Gladstone's face dropped. He immediately called his travel agent, Sandstorm. "You know that trip you had scheduled for me to the Virgin Islands?"

"Right, the tickets are all written up."

"Cancel it. I can't go. Bedcheck just sent back the color TV set because Hofberger didn't sell a car to Littleton because they're going to get a divorce and she wants all his money."

Sandstorm tore up the airline tickets and went over to see his banker, Gripsholm. "I can't pay back the loan this month because Gladstone isn't going to the Virgin Islands."

Gripsholm was furious. When Rudemaker came in to borrow money for a new kitchen he needed for his restaurant, Gripsholm turned him down cold. "How can I loan you money when Sandstorm hasn't repaid the money he borrowed?"

Rudemaker called up the contractor, Eagleton, and said he couldn't put in a new kitchen. Eagleton laid off eight men.

Meanwhile, General Motors announced it was giving a rebate on its new models. Hofberger called up Littleton immediately. "Good news," he said, "even if you are getting a divorce, you can afford a new car."

"I'm not getting a divorce," Littleton said. "It was all a misunderstanding and we've made up."

"That's great," Hofberger said. "Now you can buy the [Chevy]."

"No way," said Littleton. "My business has been so lousy I don't know why I keep the doors open."

"I didn't realize that," Hofberger said.

"Do you realize I haven't seen Bedcheck, Gladstone, Sandstorm, Gripsholm, Rudemaker or Eagleton for more than a month? How can I stay in business if they don't patronize my store?"

Source: Art Buchwald, "Squaring the Economic Circle," *Cleveland Plain Dealer,* Feb. 22, 1975. Reprinted by permission.

extra income in each round to purchase additional goods from abroad (imports) and pay additional taxes. Buying imports and paying taxes drains off some of the additional consumption spending (on domestic output) created by the increases in income. So the multiplier effect is reduced and the 1/MPS formula for the multiplier overstates the actual outcome. To correct that problem, we would need to change the multiplier equation to read "1 divided by the fraction of the change in income that is not spent on domestic output." Also, we will find in later chapters that an increase in spending may be partly dissipated as inflation rather than realized fully as an increase in real GDP. That, too, reduces the size of the multiplier effect. The Council of Economic Advisers, which advises the U.S. president on economic matters, has estimated that the actual multiplier effect for the United States is about 2. So keep in mind throughout later discussions that the actual multiplier is less than the multipliers in our simple examples. **(Key Question 9)**

SUMMARY

1. Other things equal, there is a direct (positive) relationship between income and consumption and income and saving. The consumption and saving schedules show the various amounts that households intend to consume and save at the various income and output levels, assuming a fixed price level.

2. The *average* propensities to consume and save show the fractions of any total income that are consumed and saved; APC + APS = 1. The *marginal* propensities to consume and save show the fractions of any change in total income that are consumed and saved; MPC + MPS = 1.

3. The locations of the consumption and saving schedules are determined by (a) the amount of wealth owned by households, (b) expectations of future prices and incomes, (c) real interest rates, (d) household debt, and (e) tax levels. The consumption and saving schedules are relatively stable.

4. The immediate determinants of investment are (a) the expected rate of return and (b) the real rate of interest. The economy's investment demand curve is found by cumulating investment projects, arraying them in descending order according to their expected rates of return, graphing the result, and applying the rule that investment should be undertaken up to the point at which the real interest rate, i, equals the expected rate of return, r. The investment demand curve reveals an inverse (negative) relationship between the interest rate and the level of aggregate investment.

5. Shifts of the investment demand curve can occur as the result of changes in (a) the acquisition, maintenance, and operating costs of capital goods, (b) business taxes, (c) technology, (d) the stocks of capital goods on hand, and (e) expectations.

6. Either changes in interest rates or shifts of the investment demand curve can change the level of investment.

7. The durability of capital goods, the irregular occurrence of major innovations, profit volatility, and the variability of expectations all contribute to the instability of investment spending.

8. Through the multiplier effect, an increase in investment spending (or consumption spending, government purchases, or net export spending) ripples through the economy, ultimately creating a magnified increase in real GDP. The multiplier is the ultimate change in GDP divided by the initiating change in investment or some other component of spending.

9. The multiplier is equal to the reciprocal of the marginal propensity to save: The greater is the marginal propensity to save, the smaller is the multiplier. Also, the greater is the marginal propensity to consume, the larger is the multiplier.

10. Economists estimate that the actual multiplier effect in the U.S. economy is about 2, which is less than the multiplier in the text examples.

TERMS AND CONCEPTS

45° (degree) line

consumption schedule

saving schedule

break-even income

average propensity to consume (APC)

average propensity to save (APS)

marginal propensity to consume (MPC)

marginal propensity to save (MPS)

wealth effect

expected rate of return

investment demand curve

multiplier

STUDY QUESTIONS

1. Very briefly summarize the relationships shown by (*a*) the consumption schedule, (*b*) the saving schedule, (*c*) the investment demand curve, and (*d*) the multiplier effect. Which of these relationships are direct (positive) relationships and which are inverse (negative) relationships? Why are consumption and saving in the United States greater today than they were a decade ago?

2. Precisely how do the APC and the MPC differ? Why must the sum of the MPC and the MPS equal 1? What are the

basic determinants of the consumption and saving schedules? Of your personal level of consumption?

3. Explain how each of the following will affect the consumption and saving schedules or the investment schedule, other things equal:
   a. A large increase in the value of real estate, including private houses.
   b. A decline in the real interest rate.
   c. A sharp, sustained decline in stock prices.

d. An increase in the rate of population growth.

e. The development of a cheaper method of manufacturing computer chips.

f. A sizable increase in the retirement age for collecting Social Security benefits.

g. The expectation that mild inflation will persist in the next decade.

h. An increase in the Federal personal income tax.

4. Explain why an upward shift of the consumption schedule typically involves an equal downshift of the saving schedule. What is the exception to this relationship?

5. *Key Question* Complete the following table:

Level of Output and Income (GDP = DI)	Consumption	Saving	APC	APS	MPC	MPS
$240	$ _____	$−4	—	—		
260	_____	0	—	—	—	—
280	_____	4	—	—	—	—
300	_____	8	—	—	—	—
320	_____	12	—	—	—	—
340	_____	16	—	—	—	—
360	_____	20	—	—	—	—
380	_____	24	—	—	—	—
400	_____	28	—	—		

a. Show the consumption and saving schedules graphically.

b. Find the break-even level of income. Explain how it is possible for households to dissave at very low income levels.

c. If the proportion of total income consumed (APC) decreases and the proportion saved (APS) increases as income rises, explain both verbally and graphically how the MPC and MPS can be constant at various levels of income.

6. What are the basic determinants of investment? Explain the relationship between the real interest rate and the level of investment. Why is investment spending unstable? How is it possible for investment spending to increase even in a period in which the real interest rate rises?

7. *Key Question* Suppose a handbill publisher can buy a new duplicating machine for $500 and the duplicator has a 1-year life. The machine is expected to contribute $550 to the year's net revenue. What is the expected rate of return? If the real interest rate at which funds can be borrowed to purchase the machine is 8 percent, will the publisher choose to invest in the machine? Explain.

8. *Key Question* Assume there are no investment projects in the economy that yield an expected rate of return of 25 percent or more. But suppose there are $10 billion of investment projects yielding expected returns of between 20 and 25 percent; another $10 billion yielding between 15 and

20 percent; another $10 billion between 10 and 15 percent; and so forth. Cumulate these data and present them graphically, putting the expected rate of return on the vertical axis and the amount of investment on the horizontal axis. What will be the equilibrium level of aggregate investment if the real interest rate is (*a*) 15 percent, (*b*) 10 percent, and (*c*) 5 percent? Explain why this curve is the investment demand curve.

9. *Key Question* What is the multiplier effect? What relationship does the MPC bear to the size of the multiplier? The MPS? What will the multiplier be when the MPS is 0, .4, .6, and 1? What will it be when the MPC is 1, .90, .67, .50, and 0? How much of a change in GDP will result if

firms increase their level of investment by $8 billion and the MPC is .80? If the MPC is .67?

10. Why is the actual multiplier for the U.S. economy less than the multiplier in this chapter's simple examples?

11. *Advanced Analysis* Linear equations for the consumption and saving schedules take the general form $C = a + bY$ and $S = -a + (1 - b)Y$, where C, S, and Y are consumption, saving, and national income, respectively. The constant a represents the vertical intercept, and b represents the slope of the consumption schedule.

a. Use the following data to substitute numerical values for a and b in the consumption and saving equations:

National Income (Y)	Consumption (C)
$ 0	$ 80
100	140
200	200
300	260
400	320

b. What is the economic meaning of b? Of $(1 - b)$?

c. Suppose that the amount of saving that occurs at each level of national income falls by $20 but that the values of b and $(1 - b)$ remain unchanged. Restate the saving and consumption equations for the new numerical values, and cite a factor that might have caused the change.

12. *Advanced Analysis* Suppose that the linear equation for consumption in a hypothetical economy is $C = 40 + .8Y$. Also suppose that income (Y) is $400. Determine (*a*) the marginal propensity to consume, (*b*) the marginal propensity to save, (*c*) the level of consumption, (*d*) the average propensity to consume, (*e*) the level of saving, and (*f*) the average propensity to save.

13. *(Last Word)* What is the central economic idea humorously illustrated in Art Buchwald's piece, "Squaring the Economic Circle"? How does the central idea relate to recessions, on the one hand, and vigorous expansions, on the other?

14. *Web-Based Question: The Beige Book and current consumer spending* Go to the Federal Reserve website, federalreserve.gov, and select About the Fed and then Federal Reserve Districts and Banks. Find your Federal Reserve District. Next, return to the Fed home page and select Monetary Policy and then Beige Book. What is the Beige Book? Locate the current Beige Book report and compare consumer spending for the entire U.S. economy with consumer spending in your Federal Reserve District. What are the economic strengths and weaknesses in both? Are retailers reporting that recent sales have met their expectations? What are their expectations for the future?

15. *Web-Based Question: Investment instability—changes in real private nonresidential fixed investment* The Bureau of Economic Analysis provides data for real private nonresidential fixed investment in table form at www.bea.gov. Access the BEA interactively and select National Income and Product Account Tables. Find Table 5.4, "Private Fixed Investment by Type." Has recent real private nonresidential fixed investment been volatile (as measured by percentage change from previous quarters)? Which is the largest component of this type of investment, (1) structures or (2) equipment and software? Which of these two components has been more volatile? How do recent quarterly percentage changes compare with the previous years' changes? Looking at the investment data, what investment forecast would you make for the forthcoming year?

Part III | Macroeconomic Models and Fiscal Policy

10 | The Aggregate Expenditures Model

Two of the most critical questions in macroeconomics are: (1) What determines the level of GDP, given a nation's production capacity? (2) What causes real GDP to rise in one period and to fall in another? To answer these questions we construct the aggregate expenditures model, which has its origins in 1936 in the writings of British economist John Maynard Keynes (pronounced "Caines"). The basic premise of the aggregate expenditures model—also known as the "Keynesian cross" model—is that the amount of goods and services produced and therefore the level of employment depend directly on the level of aggregate expenditures (total spending). Businesses will produce only a level of output that they think they can profitably sell. They will idle their workers and machinery when there are no markets for their goods and services. When aggregate expenditures fall, total output and employment decrease; when aggregate expenditures rise, total output and employment increase.

10.1
Aggregate
expenditures
model

Simplifications

Let's first look at aggregate expenditures and equilibrium GDP in a *private closed economy*—one without international trade or government. Then we will "open" the "closed" economy to exports and imports and also convert our "private" economy to a more realistic "mixed" economy that includes government purchases (or, more loosely, "government spending") and taxes.

Until we introduce taxes into the model, we will assume that real GDP equals disposable income (DI). If $500 billion of output is produced as GDP, households will receive exactly $500 billion of disposable income to

consume or to save. And, unless specified otherwise, we will assume the economy has excess production capacity and unemployed labor. Thus, an increase in aggregate expenditures will increase real output and employment but not raise the price level.

Consumption and Investment Schedules

In the private closed economy, the two components of aggregate expenditures are consumption, C, and gross investment, I_g. Because we examined the *consumption*

FIGURE 10.1

(a) The investment demand curve and (b) the investment schedule. (a) The level of investment spending (here, $20 billion) is determined by the real interest rate (here, 8 percent) together with the investment demand curve *ID*. (b) The investment schedule I_g relates the amount of investment ($20 billion) determined in (a) to the various levels of GDP.

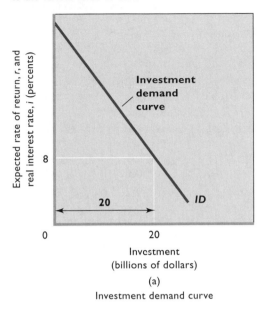

(a)
Investment demand curve

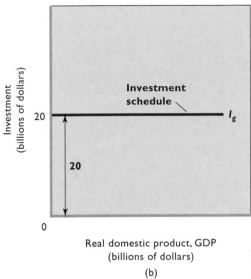

(b)
Investment schedule

schedule (Figure 9.2a) in the previous chapter, there is no need to repeat that analysis here. But to add the investment decisions of businesses to the consumption plans of households, we need to construct an investment schedule showing the amounts business firms collectively intend to invest—their **planned investment**—at each possible level of GDP. Such a schedule represents the investment plans of businesses in the same way the consumption schedule represents the consumption plans of households. In developing the investment schedule, we will assume that this planned investment is independent of the level of current disposable income or real output.

Suppose the investment demand curve is as shown in Figure 10.1a and the current real interest rate is 8 percent. This means that firms will spend $20 billion on investment goods. Our assumption tells us that this $20 billion of investment will occur at both low and high levels of GDP. The line I_g in Figure 10.1b shows this graphically; it is the economy's **investment schedule.** You should not confuse this investment schedule I_g with the investment demand curve *ID* in Figure 10.1a. The investment schedule shows the amount of investment forthcoming at each level of GDP. As indicated in Figure 10.1b, the interest rate and investment demand curve together determine this amount ($20 billion). Table 10.1 shows the investment

TABLE 10.1

The Investment Schedule (in Billions)

(1) Level of Real Output and Income	(2) Investment (I_g)
$370	$20
390	20
410	20
430	20
450	20
470	20
490	20
510	20
530	20
550	20

schedule in tabular form. Note that investment (I_g) in column 2 is $20 billion at all levels of real GDP.

Equilibrium GDP: $C + I_g = $ GDP

Now let's combine the consumption schedule of Chapter 9 and the investment schedule here to explain

TABLE 10.2

Determination of the Equilibrium Levels of Employment, Output, and Income: A Closed Private Economy

(1) Possible Levels of Employment, Millions	(2) Real Domestic Output (and Income) (GDP = DI),* Billions	(3) Consumption (C), Billions	(4) Saving (S), Billions	(5) Investment (I_g), Billions	(6) Aggregate Expenditures (C + I_g), Billions	(7) Unplanned Changes in Inventories, (+ or −)	(8) Tendency of Employment, Output, and Income
(1) 40	$370	$375	$−5	$20	$395	$−25	Increase
(2) 45	390	390	0	20	410	−20	Increase
(3) 50	410	405	5	20	425	−15	Increase
(4) 55	430	420	10	20	440	−10	Increase
(5) 60	450	435	15	20	455	−5	Increase
(6) **65**	**470**	**450**	**20**	**20**	**470**	**0**	**Equilibrium**
(7) 70	490	465	25	20	485	+5	Decrease
(8) 75	510	480	30	20	500	+10	Decrease
(9) 80	530	495	35	20	515	+15	Decrease
(10) 85	550	510	40	20	530	+20	Decrease

*If depreciation and net foreign factor income are zero, government is ignored and it is assumed that all saving occurs in the household sector of the economy. GDP as a measure of domestic output is equal to NI, PI, and DI. This means that households receive a DI equal to the value of total output.

the equilibrium levels of output, income, and employment in the private closed economy.

Tabular Analysis

Columns 2 through 5 in Table 10.2 repeat the consumption and saving schedules of Table 9.1 and the investment schedule of Table 10.1.

Real Domestic Output   Column 2 in Table 10.2 lists the various possible levels of total output—of real GDP—that the private sector might produce. Producers are willing to offer any of these 10 levels of output if they can expect to receive an identical level of income from the sale of that output. For example, firms will produce $370 billion of output, incurring $370 billion of costs (wages, rents, interest, and normal profit costs) only if they believe they can sell that output for $370 billion. Firms will offer $390 billion of output if they think they can sell that output for $390 billion. And so it is for all the other possible levels of output.

Aggregate Expenditures   In the private closed economy of Table 10.2, aggregate expenditures consist of consumption (column 3) plus investment (column 5). Their sum is shown in column 6, which with column 2 makes up the **aggregate expenditures schedule** for the private closed economy. This schedule shows the amount (C + I_g) that will be spent at each possible output or income level.

At this point we are working with *planned investment*— the data in column 5, Table 10.2. These data show the amounts firms plan or intend to invest, not the amounts they actually will invest if there are unplanned changes in inventories. More about that shortly.

Equilibrium GDP   Of the 10 possible levels of GDP in Table 10.2, which is the equilibrium level? Which total output is the economy capable of sustaining?

The equilibrium output is that output whose production creates total spending just sufficient to purchase that output. So the equilibrium level of GDP is the level at which the total quantity of goods produced (GDP) equals the total quantity of goods purchased (C + I_g). If you look at the domestic output levels in column 2 and the aggregate expenditures levels in column 6, you will see that this equality exists only at $470 billion of GDP (row 6). That is the only output at which the economy is willing to spend precisely the amount needed to move that output off the shelves. At $470 billion of GDP, the annual rates of production and spending are in balance. There is no overproduction, which would result in a piling up of unsold goods and consequently cutbacks in the production rate. Nor is there an excess of total spending, which would draw down inventories of goods and prompt increases in the rate of production. In short, there is no reason for businesses to alter this rate of production; $470 billion is the **equilibrium GDP.**

Disequilibrium   No level of GDP other than the equilibrium level of GDP can be sustained. At levels of

GDP *below* equilibrium, the economy wants to spend at higher levels than the levels of GDP the economy is producing. If, for example, firms produced $410 billion of GDP (row 3 in Table 10.2), they would find it would yield $405 billion in consumer spending. Supplemented by $20 billion of planned investment, aggregate expenditures ($C + I_g$) would be $425 billion, as shown in column 6. The economy would provide an annual rate of spending more than sufficient to purchase the $410 billion of annual production. Because buyers would be taking goods off the shelves faster than firms could produce them, an unintended decline in business inventories of $15 billion would occur (column 7) if this situation continued. But businesses can adjust to such an imbalance between aggregate expenditures and real output by stepping up production. Greater output will increase employment and total income. This process will continue until the equilibrium level of GDP is reached ($470 billion).

The reverse is true at all levels of GDP *above* the $470 billion equilibrium level. Businesses will find that these total outputs fail to generate the spending needed to clear the shelves of goods. Being unable to recover their costs, businesses will cut back on production. To illustrate: At the $510 billion output (row 8), business managers would find there is insufficient spending to permit the sale of all that output. Of the $510 billion of income that this output creates, $480 billion would be received back by businesses as consumption spending. Though supplemented by $20 billion of planned investment spending, total expenditures ($500 billion) would still be $10 billion below the $510 billion quantity produced. If this imbalance persisted, $10 billion of inventories would pile up (column 7). But businesses can adjust to this unintended accumulation of unsold goods by cutting back on the rate of production. The resulting decline in output would mean fewer jobs and a decline in total income.

Graphical Analysis

We can demonstrate the same analysis graphically. In **Figure 10.2 (Key Graph)** the 45° line developed in Chapter 9 now takes on increased significance. Recall that at any point on this line, the value of what is being measured on the horizontal axis (here, GDP) is equal to the value of what is being measured on the vertical axis (here, aggregate expenditures, or $C + I_g$). Having discovered in our tabular analysis that the equilibrium level of domestic output is determined where $C + I_g$ equals GDP, we can say that the 45° line in Figure 10.2 is a graphical statement of that equilibrium condition.

Now we must graph the aggregate expenditures schedule onto Figure 10.2. To do this, we duplicate the consumption schedule C in Figure 9.2a and add to it vertically the constant $20 billion amount of investment I_g from Figure 10.1b. This $20 billion is the amount we assumed firms plan to invest at all levels of GDP. Or, more directly, we can plot the $C + I_g$ data in column 6, Table 10.2.

Observe in Figure 10.2 that the aggregate expenditures line $C + I_g$ shows that total spending rises with income and output (GDP), but not as much as income rises. That is true because the marginal propensity to consume—the slope of line C—is less than 1. A part of any increase in income will be saved rather than spent. And because the aggregate expenditures line $C + I_g$ is parallel to the consumption line C, the slope of the aggregate expenditures line also equals the MPC for the economy and is less than 1. For our particular data, aggregate expenditures rise by $15 billion for every $20 billion increase in real output and income because $5 billion of each $20 billion increment is saved. Therefore, the slope of the aggregate expenditures line is .75 (= $\Delta$$15/$\Delta$$20).

The equilibrium level of GDP is determined by the intersection of the aggregate expenditures schedule and the 45° line. This intersection locates the only point at which aggregate expenditures (on the vertical axis) are equal to GDP (on the horizontal axis). Because Figure 10.2 is based on the data in Table 10.2, we once again find that equilibrium output is $470 billion. Observe that consumption at this output is $450 billion and investment is $20 billion.

It is evident from Figure 10.2 that no levels of GDP *above* the equilibrium level are sustainable because at those levels $C + I_g$ falls short of GDP. Graphically, the aggregate expenditures schedule lies below the 45° line in those situations. At the $510 billion GDP level, for example, $C + I_g$ is only $500 billion. This underspending causes inventories to rise, prompting firms to readjust production downward in the direction of the $470 billion output level.

Conversely, at levels of GDP *below* $470 billion, the economy wants to spend in excess of what businesses are producing. Then $C + I_g$ exceeds total output. Graphically, the aggregate expenditures schedule lies above the 45° line. At the $410 billion GDP level, for example, $C + I_g$ totals $425 billion. This excess spending causes unintended inventories to decline, prompting firms to raise production toward the $470 billion GDP. Unless there is some change in

10.1 Equilibrium GDP

KEY GRAPH

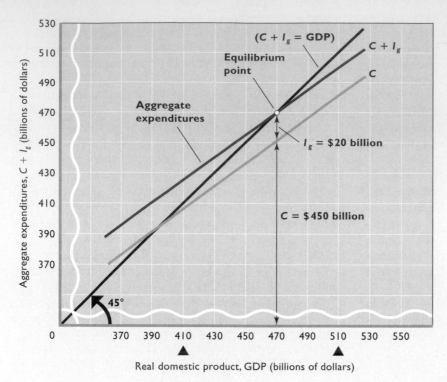

FIGURE 10.2

Equilibrium GDP. The aggregate expenditures schedule, $C + I_g$, is determined by adding the investment schedule I_g to the upsloping consumption schedule C. Since investment is assumed to be the same at each level of GDP, the vertical distances between C and $C + I_g$ do not change. Equilibrium GDP is determined where the aggregate expenditures schedule intersects the 45° line, in this case at $470 billion.

QUICK QUIZ 10.2

1. In this figure, the slope of the aggregate expenditures schedule $C + I_g$:
   a. increases as real GDP increases.
   b. falls as real GDP increases.
   c. is constant and equals the MPC.
   d. is constant and equals the MPS.

2. At all points on the 45° line:
   a. equilibrium GDP is possible.
   b. aggregate expenditures exceed real GDP.
   c. consumption exceeds investment.
   d. aggregate expenditures are less than real GDP.

3. The $490 billion level of real GDP is not at equilibrium because:
   a. investment exceeds consumption.
   b. consumption exceeds investment.
   c. planned $C + I_g$ exceeds real GDP.
   d. planned $C + I_g$ is less than real GDP.

4. The $430 billion level of real GDP is not at equilibrium because:
   a. investment exceeds consumption.
   b. consumption exceeds investment.
   c. planned $C + I_g$ exceeds real GDP.
   d. planned $C + I_g$ is less than real GDP.

Answers: 1. c; 2. a; 3. d; 4. c

the location of the aggregate expenditures line, the $470 billion level of GDP will be sustained indefinitely.

Other Features of Equilibrium GDP

We have seen that $C + I_g$ = GDP at equilibrium in the private closed economy. A closer look at Table 10.2 reveals two more characteristics of equilibrium GDP:
* Saving and planned investment are equal.
* There are no unplanned changes in inventories

Saving Equals Planned Investment

As shown by row 6 in Table 10.2, saving and planned investment are both $20 billion at the $470 billion equilibrium level of GDP.

Saving is a **leakage** or withdrawal of spending from the income-expenditures stream. Saving is what causes consumption to be less than total output or GDP. Because of saving, consumption by itself is insufficient to remove domestic output from the shelves, apparently setting the stage for a decline in total output.

However, firms do not intend to sell their entire output to consumers. Some of that output will be capital goods sold to other businesses. Investment—the purchases of capital goods—is therefore an **injection** of spending into the income-expenditures stream. As an adjunct to consumption, investment is thus a potential replacement for the leakage of saving.

If the leakage of saving at a certain level of GDP exceeds the injection of investment, then $C + I_g$ will be less than GDP and that level of GDP cannot be sustained. Any GDP for which saving exceeds investment is an above-equilibrium GDP. Consider GDP of $510 billion (row 8 in Table 10.2). Households will save $30 billion, but firms will plan to invest only $20 billion. This $10 billion excess of saving over planned investment will reduce total spending to $10 billion below the value of total output. Specifically, aggregate expenditures will be $500 billion while real GDP is $510 billion. This spending deficiency will reduce real GDP.

Conversely, if the injection of investment exceeds the leakage of saving, then $C + I_g$ will be greater than GDP and drive GDP upward. Any GDP for which investment exceeds saving is a below-equilibrium GDP. For example, at a GDP of $410 billion (row 3) households will save only $5 billion, but firms will invest $20 billion. So investment exceeds saving by $15 billion. The small leakage of saving at this relatively low GDP level is more than compensated for by the larger injection of investment spending. That causes $C + I_g$ to exceed GDP and drives GDP higher.

Only where $S = I_g$—where the leakage of saving of $20 billion is exactly offset by the injection of planned investment of $20 billion—will aggregate expenditures $(C + I_g)$ equal real output (GDP). That $C + I_g = $ GDP equality is what defines the equilibrium GDP. **(Key Question 2)**

No Unplanned Changes in Inventories

As part of their investment plans, firms may decide to increase or decrease their inventories. But, as confirmed in line 6 of Table 10.2, there are no **unplanned changes in inventories** at equilibrium GDP. This fact, along with $C + I_g = $ GDP, and $S = I$, is a characteristic of equilibrium GDP in the private closed economy.

Unplanned changes in inventories play a major role in achieving equilibrium GDP. Consider, as an example, the $490 billion *above-equilibrium* GDP shown in row 7 of Table 10.2. What happens if firms produce that output, thinking they can sell it? Households save $25 billion of their $490 billion DI, so consumption is only $465 billion. Planned investment (column 5) is $20 billion. So aggregate

expenditures $(C + I_g)$ are $485 billion and sales fall short of production by $5 billion. Firms retain that extra $5 billion of goods as an unplanned increase in inventories (column 7). It results from the failure of total spending to remove total output from the shelves.

Because changes in inventories are a part of investment, we note that *actual investment* is $25 billion. It consists of $20 billion of planned investment *plus* the $5 billion unplanned increase in inventories. Actual investment equals the saving of $25 billion, even though saving exceeds planned investment by $5 billion. Because firms cannot earn profits by accumulating unwanted inventories, the $5 billion unplanned increase in inventories will prompt them to cut back employment and production. GDP will fall to its equilibrium level of $470 billion, at which unplanned changes in inventories are zero.

Now look at the *below-equilibrium* $450 billion output (row 5, Table 10.2). Because households save only $15 billion of their $450 billion DI, consumption is $435 billion. Planned investment by firms is $20 billion, so aggregate expenditures are $455 billion. Sales exceed production by $5 billion. This is so only because a $5 billion unplanned decrease in business inventories has occurred. Firms must *disinvest* $5 billion in inventories (column 7). Note again that actual investment is $15 billion ($20 billion planned *minus* the $5 billion decline in inventory investment) and is equal to saving of $15 billion, even though planned investment exceeds saving by $5 billion. The unplanned decline in inventories, resulting from the excess of sales over production, will encourage firms to expand production. GDP will rise to $470 billion, at which unplanned changes in inventories are zero.

When economists say differences between investment and saving can occur and bring about changes in equilibrium GDP, they are referring to planned investment and saving. Equilibrium occurs only when planned investment and saving are equal. *But when unplanned changes in inventories are considered, investment and saving are always equal, regardless of the level of GDP.* That is true because actual investment consists of planned investment and unplanned investment (unplanned changes in inventories). Unplanned changes in inventories act as a balancing item that equates the actual amounts saved and invested in any period.

Changes in Equilibrium GDP and the Multiplier

In the private closed economy, the equilibrium GDP will change in response to changes in either the investment

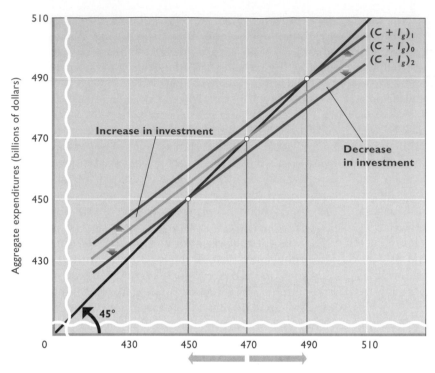

FIGURE 10.3

Changes in the equilibrium GDP caused by shifts in the aggregate expenditures schedule and the investment schedule. An upward shift of the aggregate expenditures schedule from $(C + I_g)_0$ to $(C + I_g)_1$ will increase the equilibrium GDP. Conversely, a downward shift from $(C + I_g)_0$ to $(C + I_g)_2$ will lower the equilibrium GDP.

schedule or the consumption schedule. Because changes in the investment schedule usually are the main source of instability, we will direct our attention toward them.

Figure 10.3 shows the effect of changes in investment spending on the equilibrium real GDP. Suppose that the expected rate of return on investment rises or that the real interest rate falls such that investment spending increases by $5 billion. That would be shown as an upward shift of the investment schedule in Figure 10.1b. In Figure 10.3, the $5 billion increase of investment spending will increase aggregate expenditures from $(C + I_g)_0$ to $(C + I_g)_1$ and raise equilibrium real GDP from $470 billion to $490 billion.

If the expected rate of return on investment decreases or if the real interest rate rises, investment spending will decline by, say, $5 billion. That would be shown as a downward shift of the investment schedule in Figure 10.1b and a downward shift of the aggregate expenditures schedule from $(C + I_g)_0$ to $(C + I_g)_2$ in Figure 10.3. Equilibrium GDP will fall from $470 billion to $450 billion.

In our examples, a $5 billion change in investment spending leads to a $20 billion change in output and income. So the *multiplier* is 4 (= $20/$5). The MPS is .25, meaning that for every $1 billion of new income, $.25

billion of new saving occurs. Therefore, $20 billion of new income is needed to generate $5 billion of new saving. Once that increase in income and saving occurs, the economy is back in equilibrium—$C + I_g$ = GDP; saving and investment are equal; and there are no unintended changes in inventories. You can see, then, that the multiplier process is an integral part of the aggregate expenditures model. (A brief review of Table 9.3 and Figure 9.8 will be helpful at this point.)

QUICK REVIEW 10.1

- In a private closed economy, equilibrium GDP occurs where aggregate expenditures equal real domestic output $(C + I_g = \text{GDP})$.

- At equilibrium GDP, saving equals planned investment $(S = I_g)$ and unplanned changes in inventories are zero.

- Actual investment consists of planned investment plus unplanned changes in inventories (+ or −) and is always equal to saving in a private closed economy.

- Through the multiplier effect, an initial change in investment spending can cause a magnified change in domestic output and income.

Adding International Trade

We next move from a closed economy to an open economy that incorporates exports (X) and imports (M). Our focus will be on **net exports** (exports minus imports), which may be either positive or negative.

Net Exports and Aggregate Expenditures

Like consumption and investment, exports create domestic production, income, and employment for a nation. Although U.S. goods and services produced for export are sent abroad, foreign spending on those goods and services increases production and creates jobs and incomes in the United States. We must therefore include exports as a component of each nation's aggregate expenditures.

Conversely, when an economy is open to international trade, it will spend part of its income on imports—goods and services produced abroad. To avoid overstating the value of domestic production, we must subtract from total spending the amount spent on imported goods because such spending generates production and income abroad. In measuring aggregate expenditures for domestic goods and services, we must subtract expenditures on imports.

In short, for a private closed economy, aggregate expenditures are $C + I_g$. But for an open economy, aggregate expenditures are $C + I_g + (X - M)$. Or, recalling that net exports (X_n) equal ($X - M$), we can say that aggregate expenditures for a private open economy are $C + I_g + X_n$.

The Net Export Schedule

A net export schedule lists the amount of net exports that will occur at each level of GDP. Table 10.3 shows two possible net export schedules for the hypothetical economy represented in Table 10.2. In net export schedule X_{n1} (columns 1 and 2), exports exceed imports by $5 billion at each level of GDP. Perhaps exports are $15 billion while imports are $10 billion. In schedule X_{n2} (columns 1 and 3), imports are $5 billion higher than exports. Perhaps imports are $20 billion while exports are $15 billion. To simplify our discussion, we assume in both schedules that net exports are independent of GDP.[1]

---

[1] In reality, although our exports depend on foreign incomes and are thus independent of U.S. GDP, our imports do vary directly with our own domestic national income. Just as our domestic consumption varies directly with our GDP, so do our purchases of foreign goods. As our GDP rises, U.S. households buy not only more Pontiacs and more Pepsi but also more Porsches and more Perrier. However, for now we will ignore the complications of the positive relationship between imports and U.S. GDP.

TABLE 10.3

Two Net Export Schedules (in Billions)

(1) Level of GDP	(2) Net Exports, X_{n1} ($X > M$)	(3) Net Exports, X_{n2} ($X < M$)
$370	$+5	$-5
390	+5	-5
410	+5	-5
430	+5	-5
450	+5	-5
470	+5	-5
490	+5	-5
510	+5	-5
530	+5	-5
550	+5	-5

Figure 10.4b represents the two net export schedules in Table 10.3. Schedule X_{n1} is above the horizontal axis and depicts positive net exports of $5 billion at all levels of GDP. Schedule X_{n2}, which is below the horizontal axis, shows negative net exports of $5 billion at all levels of GDP.

Net Exports and Equilibrium GDP

The aggregate expenditures schedule labeled $C + I_g$ in Figure 10.4a reflects the private closed economy. It shows the combined consumption and gross investment expenditures occurring at each level of GDP. With no foreign sector, the equilibrium GDP is $470 billion.

But in the private open economy net exports can be either positive or negative. Let's see how each of the net export schedules in Figure 10.4b affects equilibrium GDP.

Positive Net Exports   Suppose the net export schedule is X_{n1}. The $5 billion of additional net export expenditures by the rest of the world is accounted for by adding that $5 billion to the $C + I_g$ schedule in Figure 10.4a. Aggregate expenditures at each level of GDP are then $5 billion higher than $C + I_g$ alone. The aggregate expenditures schedule for the open economy thus becomes $C + I_g + X_{n1}$. In this case, international trade increases equilibrium GDP from $470 billion in the private closed economy to $490 billion in the private open economy.

Generalization: *Other things equal, positive net exports increase aggregate expenditures and GDP beyond what they would be in a closed economy.* Exports reduce the stock of available goods in an economy because some of an economy's output is sent abroad. But exports boost an economy's real GDP by increasing expenditures on domestically produced output. Adding net exports of $5 billion has increased GDP by $20 billion, in this case implying a multiplier of 4.

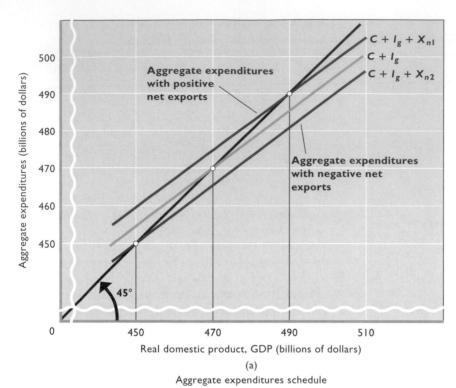

(a)
Aggregate expenditures schedule

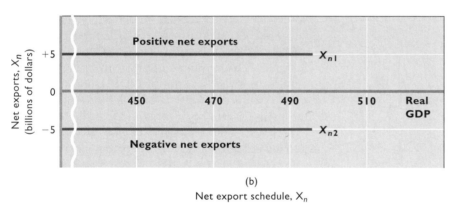

(b)
Net export schedule, X_n

FIGURE 10.4

Net exports and equilibrium GDP. Positive net exports such as shown by the net export schedule X_{n1} in (b) elevate the aggregate expenditures schedule in (a) from the closed-economy level of $C + I_g$ to the open-economy level of $C + I_g + X_{n1}$. Negative net exports such as depicted by the net export schedule X_{n2} in (b) lower the aggregate expenditures schedule in (a) from the closed-economy level of $C + I_g$ to the open-economy level of $C + I_g + X_{n2}$.

Negative Net Exports Conversely, suppose that net exports are a negative $5 billion as shown by X_{n2} in Figure 10.4b. This means that our hypothetical economy is importing $5 billion more of goods than it is exporting. The aggregate expenditures schedule shown as $C + I_g$ in Figure 10.4a therefore overstates the expenditures on domestic output at each level of GDP. We must reduce the sum of expenditures by the $5 billion net amount spent on imported goods. We do that by subtracting the $5 billion of net imports from $C + I_g$.

The relevant aggregate expenditures schedule in Figure 10.4a becomes $C + I_g + X_{n2}$ and equilibrium GDP falls from $470 billion to $450 billion. Again, a change in

net exports of $5 billion has produced a fourfold change in GDP, reminding us that the multiplier in this example is 4.

This gives us a corollary to our first generalization: *Other things equal, negative net exports reduce aggregate expenditures and GDP below what they would be in a closed economy.* Imports add to the stock of goods available in the economy, but they diminish real GDP by reducing expenditures on domestically produced products.

Our generalizations of the effects of net exports on GDP mean that a decline in X_n—a decrease in exports or an increase in imports—reduces aggregate expenditures and contracts a nation's GDP. Conversely, an increase in X_n—the result of either an increase in exports or a decrease

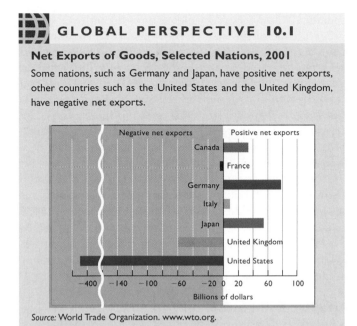

GLOBAL PERSPECTIVE 10.1

Net Exports of Goods, Selected Nations, 2001

Some nations, such as Germany and Japan, have positive net exports, other countries such as the United States and the United Kingdom, have negative net exports.

Negative net exports | Positive net exports

Canada
France
Germany
Italy
Japan
United Kingdom
United States

-400 -140 -100 -60 -20 0 20 60 100

Billions of dollars

Source: World Trade Organization. www.wto.org.

in imports—increases aggregate expenditures and expands GDP.

As is shown in Global Perspective 10-1, net exports vary greatly among the major industrial nations. **(Key Question 9)**

International Economic Linkages

Our analysis of net exports and real GDP suggests how circumstances or policies abroad can affect U.S. GDP.

Prosperity Abroad   A rising level of real output and income among U.S. foreign trading partners enables the United States to sell more goods abroad, thus raising U.S. net exports and increasing its real GDP (assuming initially there is excess capacity). There is good reason for Americans to be interested in the prosperity of our trading partners. Their good fortune enables them to buy more of our exports, increasing our income and enabling us in turn to buy more foreign imports. These lower-price imported goods are the ultimate benefit of international trade. Prosperity abroad transfers some of that prosperity to Americans.

Tariffs   Suppose foreign trading partners impose high tariffs on U.S. goods to reduce their imports from the United States and thus increase production in their economies. Their imports, however, are U.S. exports. So when they restrict their imports to stimulate *their*

economies, they are reducing U.S. exports and depressing *our* economy. We are likely to retaliate by imposing tariffs on their products. If so, their exports to us will decline and their net exports may fall. It is not clear, then, whether tariffs increase or decrease a nation's net exports. In the Great Depression of the 1930s various nations, including the United States, imposed trade barriers as a way of reducing domestic unemployment. But rounds of retaliation simply throttled world trade, worsened the Depression, and increased unemployment.

Exchange Rates   Depreciation of the dollar relative to other currencies (discussed in Chapter 6) enables people abroad to obtain more dollars with each unit of their own currencies. The price of U.S. goods in terms of those currencies will fall, stimulating purchases of U.S. exports. Also, U.S. customers will find they need more dollars to buy foreign goods and, consequently, will reduce their spending on imports. The increased exports and decreased imports will increase U.S. net exports and thus expand the nation's GDP.

Whether depreciation of the dollar will actually raise real GDP or produce inflation depends on the initial position of the economy relative to its full-employment output. If the economy is operating below its full-employment level, depreciation of the dollar and the resulting rise in net exports will increase aggregate expenditures and thus expand real GDP. But if the economy is already fully employed, the increase in net exports and aggregate expenditures will cause demand-pull inflation. Because resources are already fully employed, the increased spending cannot expand real output; but it can and does increase the prices of the existing output.

This last example has been cast only in terms of depreciation of the dollar. You should think through the impact that appreciation of the dollar would have on net exports and equilibrium GDP.

QUICK REVIEW 10.2

- Positive net exports increase aggregate expenditures relative to the closed economy and, other things equal, increase equilibrium GDP.

- Negative net exports decrease aggregate expenditures relative to the closed economy and, other things equal, reduce equilibrium GDP.

- In the open economy changes in (a) prosperity abroad, (b) tariffs, and (c) exchange rates can affect U.S. net exports and therefore U.S. aggregate expenditures and equilibrium GDP.

Adding the Public Sector

Our final step in constructing the full aggregate expenditures model is to move the analysis from a private (no-government) open economy to an economy with a public sector (sometimes called a "mixed economy"). This means adding government purchases and taxes to the model.

For simplicity, we will assume that government purchases do not cause any upward or downward shifts in the consumption and investment schedules. Also, government's net tax revenues—total tax revenues less "negative taxes" in the form of transfer payments—are derived entirely from personal taxes. Finally, a fixed amount of taxes is collected regardless of the level of GDP.

Government Purchases and Equilibrium GDP

Suppose the government decides to purchase $20 billion of goods and services regardless of the level of GDP and tax collections.

Tabular Example Table 10.4 shows the impact of this purchase on the equilibrium GDP. Columns 1 through 4 are carried over from Table 10.2 for the private closed economy, in which the equilibrium GDP was $470 billion. The only new items are exports and imports in column 5 and government purchases in column 6. (Observe in column 5 that net exports are zero.) As shown in column 7, the addition of government purchases to private spending $(C + I_g + X_n)$ yields a new, higher level of aggregate expenditures $(C + I_g + X_n + G)$. Comparing columns 1 and 7, we find that aggregate expenditures and real output are equal at a higher level of GDP. Without government purchases, equilibrium GDP was $470 billion (row 6); *with* government purchases, aggregate expenditures and real output are equal at $550 billion (row 10). *Increases in public spending, like increases in private spending, shift the aggregate expenditures schedule upward and produce a higher equilibrium GDP.*

Note, too, that government spending is subject to the multiplier. A $20 billion increase in government purchases has increased equilibrium GDP by $80 billion (from $470 billion to $550 billion). The multiplier in this example is 4.

This $20 billion increase in government spending is *not* financed by increased taxes. Shortly, we will demonstrate that increased taxes *reduce* equilibrium GDP.

Graphical Analysis In Figure 10.5, we vertically add $20 billion of government purchases, G, to the level of private spending, $C + I_g + X_n$. That added $20 billion raises the aggregate expenditures schedule (private plus public) to $C + I_g + X_n + G$, resulting in an $80 billion increase in equilibrium GDP, from $470 to $550 billion.

A decline in government purchases G will lower the aggregate expenditures schedule in Figure 10.5 and result in a multiplied decline in the equilibrium GDP. Verify in Table 10.4 that if government purchases were to decline from $20 billion to $10 billion, the equilibrium GDP would fall by $40 billion.

TABLE 10.4
The Impact of Government Purchases on Equilibrium GDP

(1) Real Domestic Output and Income (GDP = DI), Billions	(2) Consumption (C), Billions	(3) Savings (S), Billions	(4) Investment (I_g), Billions	(5) Net Exports (X_n), Billions		(6) Government Purchases (G), Billions	(7) Aggregate Expenditures $(C + I_g + X_n + G)$, Billions
				Exports (X)	Imports (M)		(2) + (4) + (5) + (6)
(1) $370	$375	$−5	$20	$10	$10	$20	$415
(2) 390	390	0	20	10	10	20	430
(3) 410	405	5	20	10	10	20	445
(4) 430	420	10	20	10	10	20	460
(5) 450	435	15	20	10	10	20	475
(6) 470	450	20	20	10	10	20	490
(7) 490	465	25	20	10	10	20	505
(8) 510	480	30	20	10	10	20	520
(9) 530	495	35	20	10	10	20	535
(10) *550*	*510*	*40*	*20*	*10*	*10*	*20*	*550*

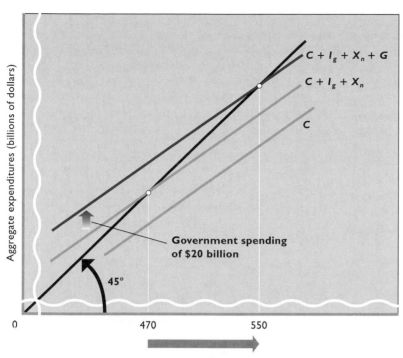

FIGURE 10.5

Government spending and equilibrium GDP. The addition of government expenditures of G to our analysis raises the aggregate expenditures ($C + I_g + X_n + G$) schedule and increases the equilibrium level of GDP, as would an increase in C, I_g, or X_n.

Taxation and Equilibrium GDP

The government not only spends but also collects taxes. Suppose it imposes a **lump-sum tax**, which is a *tax of a constant amount or, more precisely, a tax yielding the same amount of tax revenue at each level of GDP.* Suppose this tax is $20 billion, so that the government obtains $20 billion of tax revenue at each level of GDP regardless of the level of government purchases.

Tabular Example   In Table 10.5, which continues our example, we find taxes in column 2, and we see in column 3 that disposable (after-tax) income is lower than GDP (column 1) by the $20 billion amount of the tax. Because households use disposable income both to consume and to save, the tax lowers both consumption and saving. The MPC and MPS tell us how much consumption and saving will decline as a result of the $20 billion in taxes. Because the MPC is .75, the government tax collection of $20 billion will reduce consumption by $15 billion (= .75 × $20 billion). Since the MPS is .25, saving will drop by $5 billion (= .25 × $20 billion).

Columns 4 and 5 in Table 10.5 list the amounts of consumption and saving *at each level of GDP.* Note they are $15 billion and $5 billion smaller than those in Table 10.4. *Taxes reduce disposable income relative to GDP by the*

amount of the taxes. This decline in DI reduces both consumption and saving at each level of GDP. The MPC and the MPS determine the declines in C and S.

To find the effect of taxes on equilibrium GDP, we calculate aggregate expenditures again, as shown in column 9, Table 10.5. Aggregate spending is $15 billion less at each level of GDP than it was in Table 10.4. The reason is that after-tax consumption, designated by C_a, is $15 billion less at each level of GDP. A comparison of real output and aggregate expenditures in columns 1 and 9 shows that the aggregate amounts produced and purchased are equal only at $490 billion of GDP (row 7). The $20 billion lump-sum tax has reduced equilibrium GDP by $60 billion, from $550 billion (row 10, Table 10.3) to $490 billion (row 7, Table 10.4).

Graphical Analysis   In Figure 10.6 the $20 billion increase in taxes shows up as a $15 (not $20) billion decline in the aggregate expenditures ($C_a + I_g + X_n + G$) schedule. This decline in the schedule results solely from a decline in the consumption C component of aggregate expenditures. The equilibrium GDP falls from $550 billion to $490 billion because of this tax-caused drop in consumption. Assuming no change in government expenditures, *tax increases lower the aggregate expenditures schedule relative to the 45° line and reduce the equilibrium GDP.*

TABLE 10.5

Determination of the Equilibrium Levels of Employment, Output, and Income: Private and Public Sectors

(1) Real Domestic Output and Income (GDP = NI = PI), Billions	(2) Taxes (T), Billions	(3) Disposable Income (DI), Billions, (1) − (2)	(4) Consumption (C_a), Billions	(5) Saving (S_a), Billions, (3) − (4)	(6) Investment (I_g), Billions	(7) Net Exports (X_n), Billions — Exports (X)	(7) Net Exports (X_n), Billions — Imports (M)	(8) Government Purchases (G), Billions	(9) Aggregate Expenditures ($C_a + I_g + X_n + G$), Billions, (4) + (6) + (7) + (8)
(1) $370	$20	$350	$360	$−10	$20	$10	$10	$20	$400
(2) 390	20	370	375	−5	20	10	10	20	415
(3) 410	20	390	390	0	20	10	10	20	430
(4) 430	20	410	405	5	20	10	10	20	445
(5) 450	20	430	420	10	20	10	10	20	460
(6) 470	20	450	435	15	20	10	10	20	475
(7) **490**	**20**	**470**	**450**	**20**	**20**	**10**	**10**	**20**	**490**
(8) 510	20	490	465	25	20	10	10	20	505
(9) 530	20	510	480	30	20	10	10	20	520
(10) 550	20	530	495	35	20	10	10	20	535

In contrast to our previous case, a *decrease* in existing taxes will raise the aggregate expenditures schedule in Figure 10.6 as a result of an increase in consumption at all GDP levels. You should confirm that a tax reduction of $10 billion (from the present $20 billion to $10 billion) would increase the equilibrium GDP from $490 billion to $520 billion. **(Key Question 12)**

Differential Impacts   You may have noted that equal changes in *G* and *T* do not have equivalent impacts on GDP. The $60 billion increase in *G* in our illustration, subject to the multiplier of 4, produced an $80 billion increase in real GDP. But the $20 billion increase in taxes reduced GDP by only $60 billion. Given an MPC of .75, the tax increase of $20 billion reduced consumption by

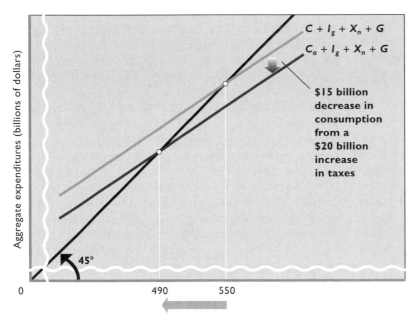

FIGURE 10.6

Taxes and equilibrium GDP.   If the MPC is .75, the $20 billion of taxes will lower the consumption schedule by $15 billion and cause a $60 billion decline in the equilibrium GDP. In the open economy with government, equilibrium GDP occurs where C_a (after-tax income) + I_g + X_n + G = GDP.

only $15 billion (not $20 billion) because saving also fell by $5 billion. Subjecting the $15 billion decline in consumption to the multiplier of 4, we find the tax increase of $20 billion reduced GDP by $60 billion (not $80 billion).

Table 10.5 and Figure 10.6 constitute the complete aggregate expenditures model for an open economy with government. When total spending equals total production, the economy's output is in equilibrium. In the open mixed economy, equilibrium GDP occurs where

$$C_a + I_g + X_n + G = \text{GDP}.$$

Injections, Leakages, and Unplanned Changes in Inventories

The related characteristics of equilibrium noted for the private closed economy also apply to the full model. Injections into the income-expenditures stream equal leakages from the income stream. For the private closed economy, $S = I_g$. For the expanded economy, imports and taxes are added leakages. Saving, importing, and paying taxes are all uses of income that subtract from potential consumption. Consumption will now be less than GDP—creating a potential spending gap—in the amount of after-tax saving (S_a), imports (M), and taxes (T). But exports (X) and government purchases (G), along with investment (I_g), are injections into the income-expenditures stream. At the equilibrium GDP, the sum of the leakages equals the sum of injections. In symbols:

$$S_a + M + T = I_g + X + G$$

You should use the data in Table 10.5 to confirm this equality between leakages and injections at the equilibrium GDP of $490 billion. Also, substantiate that a lack of such equality exists at all other possible levels of GDP.

Although not directly shown in Table 10.5, the equilibrium characteristic of "no unplanned changes in inventories" will also be fulfilled at the $490 billion GDP. Because aggregate expenditures equal GDP, all the goods and services produced will be purchased. There will be no unplanned increase in inventories, so firms will have no incentive to reduce their employment and production. Nor will they experience an unplanned decline in their inventories, which would prompt them to expand their employment and output in order to replenish their inventories.

10.2 Changes in GDP

Equilibrium versus Full-Employment GDP

Now let's use the complete aggregate expenditures model to evaluate the equilibrium GDP. The $490 billion equilibrium GDP in our complete analysis may or may not provide full employment. Indeed, we have assumed thus far that the economy is operating at less-than-full employment. The economy, we will see, need not always produce full employment and price-level stability.

Recessionary Gap

Suppose in **Figure 10.7 (Key Graph),** panel (a), that the full-employment level of GDP is $510 billion and the aggregate expenditures schedule is AE_1. (For simplicity, we will now dispense with the $C_a + I_g + X_n + G$ labeling.) This schedule intersects the 45° line to the left of the economy's full-employment output, so the economy's equilibrium GDP of $490 billion is $20 billion short of its full-employment output of $510 billion. According to column 1 in Table 10.2, total employment at the full-employment GDP is 75 million workers. But the economy depicted in Figure 10.7a is employing only 70 million workers; 5 million available workers are not employed. For that reason, the economy is sacrificing $20 billion of output.

A recessionary expenditure gap or, more simply, a **recessionary gap** is the amount by which aggregate expenditures *at the full-employment GDP* fall short of those required to achieve the full-employment GDP. Insufficient total spending contracts or depresses the economy. Table 10.5 shows that at the full-employment level of $510 billion (column 1), the corresponding level of aggregate expenditures is only $505 billion (column 9). The recessionary gap is thus $5 billion, the amount by which the aggregate expenditures curve would have to shift upward to realize equilibrium at the full-employment GDP. Graphically, the recessionary gap is the *vertical* distance (measured at the full-employment GDP) by which the actual aggregate expenditures schedule AE_1 lies below the hypothetical full-employment aggregate expenditures schedule AE_0. In Figure 10.7a, this recessionary gap is $5 billion. Because the multiplier is 4, there is a $20 billion differential (the recessionary gap of $5 billion times the multiplier of 4) between the equilibrium GDP and the full-employment GDP. This $20 billion difference is a negative *GDP gap*—an idea we first developed when discussing cyclical unemployment in Chapter 8.

KEY GRAPH

FIGURE 10.7

Recessionary and inflationary gaps. The equilibrium and full-employment GDPs may not coincide. (a) A recessionary gap is the amount by which aggregate expenditures at the full-employment GDP fall short of those needed to achieve the full-employment GDP. Here, the $5 billion recessionary gap causes a $20 billion negative GDP gap. (b) An inflationary gap is the amount by which aggregate expenditures at the full-employment GDP exceed those just sufficient to achieve the full-employment GDP. Here, the inflationary gap is $5 billion; this overspending produces demand-pull inflation.

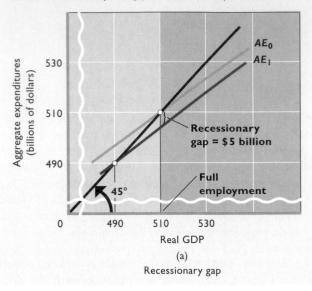

(a)
Recessionary gap

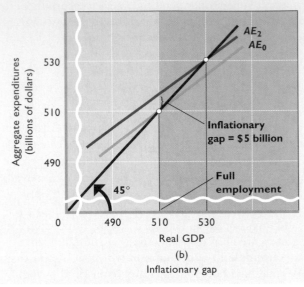

(b)
Inflationary gap

QUICK QUIZ 10.7

1. In the economy depicted:
   a. the MPS is .50.
   b. the MPC is .75.
   c. the full-employment level of real GDP is $530 billion.
   d. nominal GDP always equals real GDP.

2. The inflationary gap depicted will cause:
   a. demand-pull inflation.
   b. cost-push inflation.
   c. cyclical unemployment.
   d. frictional unemployment.

3. The recessionary gap depicted will cause:
   a. demand-pull inflation.
   b. cost-push inflation.
   c. cyclical unemployment.
   d. frictional unemployment.

4. In the economy depicted, the $5 billion inflationary gap:
   a. expands real GDP to $530 billion.
   b. leaves real GDP at $510 billion but causes inflation.
   c. could be remedied by equal $5 billion increases in taxes and government spending.
   d. implies that real GDP exceeds nominal GDP.

Answers: 1. b; 2. a; 3. c; 4. b

Application: The U.S. Recession of 2001

The U.S. economy grew briskly in the last half of the 1990s, with real GDP expanding at about 4 percent annually and the unemployment rate averaging roughly 4.5 percent. The economic boom and low rates of unemployment, however, did not spark inflation, as had been the case in prior business cycles. Exceptionally strong productivity growth in the late 1990s increased the economy's production capacity and enabled aggregate expenditures to expand without causing inflation. In terms of Figure 10.7b, it was as if the full-employment level of real GDP expanded from $510 billion to $530 billion at the same time the aggregate expenditures curve rose from AE_0 to AE_2. So the inflationary gap of $5 billion never materialized. Between 1995 and 1999, inflation averaged less than 2.5 percent annually.

But the booming economy of the second half of the 1990s produced notable excesses. A large number of ill-conceived Internet-related firms were born, attracting billions of investment dollars. Investment spending surged throughout the economy and eventually added too much production capacity. A stock market "bubble" developed as stock market investing became a national pastime. Consumers increased their household debt to expand their consumption. Some unscrupulous executives engaged in fraudulent business practices to further their own personal interests.

The boom ended in the early 2000s. Hundreds of Internet-related start-up firms folded. Many firms, particularly those in telecommunications and aircraft manufacturing, began to experience severe overcapacity. The stock market bubble burst, erasing billions of dollars of "paper" wealth. Firms significantly reduced their investment spending because of lower estimates of rates of return. In March 2001 aggregate expenditures declined sufficiently to push the economy into its ninth recession since 1950. The unemployment rate rose from 4.2 percent in February 2001 to 5.8 percent in December 2001. In terms of Figure 10.7a, a recessionary gap emerged. The terrorist attacks of September 11, 2001, damaged consumer confidence and prolonged the recession through 2001. In 2002 the economy resumed economic growth, but the unemployment rate remained a stubbornly high 6 percent at the end of 2002. Even so, the recession of 2001 was relatively mild by historical standards and in view of the unusual set of circumstances.

Inflationary Gap

An inflationary expenditure gap or, more simply, an **inflationary gap** is the amount by which an economy's aggregate expenditures *at the full-employment GDP* exceed those just necessary to achieve the full-employment GDP. In Figure 10.7b, there is a $5 billion inflationary gap at the $510 billion full-employment GDP. This is shown by the vertical distance between the actual aggregate expenditures schedule AE_2 and the hypothetical schedule AE_0, which would be just sufficient to achieve the $510 billion full-employment GDP. Thus, the inflationary gap is the amount by which the aggregate expenditures schedule would have to shift downward to realize equilibrium at the full-employment GDP.

The effect of this inflationary gap is that the excessive spending will pull up output prices. Since businesses cannot respond to the $5 billion in excessive spending by expanding their real output, demand-pull inflation will occur. Nominal GDP will rise because of a higher price

level, but real GDP will not. Excessive total spending causes inflation. **(Key Question 13)**

Application: U.S. Inflation in the Late 1980s

The United States has not had an episode of rising inflation since the late 1980s. During that period, however, a sizable U.S. inflationary gap developed. As the economy moved beyond its full-employment output between 1986 and 1990, the price level rose at an increasing rate. Specifically, the annual rate of inflation increased from 1.9 percent in 1986 to 3.6 percent in 1987 to 4.1 percent in 1988 to 4.8 percent in 1989. In terms of Figure 10.7b, the aggregate expenditures schedule moved upward from year to year and increased the inflationary gap. The gap closed as the expansion came to an end. In 1990–1991 a recessionary gap emerged. Inflation fell to 3 percent immediately after the recession of 1990–1991 and remained at or below 3 percent throughout the 1990s.

QUICK REVIEW 10.3

- Government purchases shift the aggregate expenditures schedule upward and raise the equilibrium GDP.
- Taxes reduce disposable income, lower consumption spending and saving, shift the aggregate expenditures schedule downward, and reduce the equilibrium GDP.
- A recessionary gap is the amount by which an economy's aggregate expenditures schedule must shift upward to achieve the full-employment GDP; an inflationary gap is the amount by which the economy's aggregate expenditures schedule must shift downward to eliminate demand-pull inflation and still achieve the full-employment GDP.

Limitations of the Model

This chapter's analysis demonstrates the power of the aggregate expenditures model to explain how the economy works, how recessions or depressions can occur, and how demand-pull inflation can arise. But this model has five well-known limitations:

- *It does not show price-level changes.* The model can account for demand-pull inflation, as in Figure 10.7b, but it does not indicate how much the price level will rise when aggregate expenditures are excessive relative to the economy's capacity. The aggregate expenditures model has no way of measuring the rate of inflation.

The Aggregate Expenditures Theory Emerged as a Critique of Classical Economics and as a Response to the Great Depression.

Until the Great Depression of the 1930s, many prominent economists, including David Ricardo (1772–1823) and John Stuart Mill (1806–1873), believed that the market system would ensure full employment of an economy's resources. These so-called *classical economists* acknowledged that now and then abnormal circumstances such as wars, political upheavals, droughts, speculative crises, and gold rushes would occur, deflecting the economy from full-employment status. But when such deviations occurred, the economy would automatically adjust and soon return to full-employment output. For example, a slump in output and employment would result in lower prices, wages, and interest rates, which in turn would increase consumer spending, employment, and investment spending. Any excess supply of goods and workers would soon be eliminated.

Classical macroeconomists denied that the level of spending in an economy could be too low to bring about the purchase of the entire full-employment output. They based their denial of inadequate spending in part on *Say's law,* attributed to the nineteenth-century French economist J. B. Say (1767–1832). This law is the disarmingly simple idea that the very act of producing goods generates income equal to the value of the goods produced. The production of any output automatically provides the income needed to buy that output. More succinctly stated, *supply creates its own demand.*

Say's law can best be understood in terms of a barter economy. A woodworker, for example, produces or supplies furniture as a means of buying or demanding the food and clothing produced by other workers. The woodworker's supply of furniture is the income that he will "spend" to satisfy his demand for other goods. The goods he buys (demands) will have a total value exactly equal to the goods he produces (supplies).

And so it is for other producers and for the entire economy. Demand must be the same as supply!

Assuming that the composition of output is in accord with consumer preferences, all markets would be cleared of their outputs. It would seem that all firms need to do to sell a full-employment output is to produce that level of output. Say's law guarantees there will be sufficient spending to purchase it all.

10.2
Say's law

The Great Depression of the 1930s called into question the theory that supply creates its own demand (Say's law). In the United States, real GDP declined by 40 percent and the unemployment rate rocketed to nearly 25 percent. Other nations experienced similar impacts. And cyclical unemployment lingered for a decade. An obvious inconsistency exists between a theory that says that unemployment is virtually impossible and the actual occurrence of a 10-year siege of substantial unemployment.

In 1936 British economist John Maynard Keynes (1883–1946) explained why cyclical unemployment could occur in a market economy. In his *General Theory of Employment, Interest, and Money,* Keynes attacked the foundations of classical theory and developed the ideas underlying the aggregate expenditures model. Keynes disputed Say's law, pointing out that not all income need be spent in the same period that it is produced. Investment spending, in particular, is volatile, said Keynes. A substantial decline in investment will lead to insufficient total spending. Unsold goods will accumulate in producers' warehouses, and producers will respond by reducing their output and discharging workers. A recession or depression will result, and widespread cyclical unemployment will occur. Moreover, said Keynes, recessions or depressions are not likely to correct themselves. In contrast to the more laissez-faire view of the classical economists, Keynes argued that government should play an active role in stabilizing the economy.

- *It ignores premature demand-pull inflation.* Mild demand-pull inflation can occur before an economy reaches its full-employment level of output. The aggregate expenditures model does not explain why that can happen.
- *It limits real GDP to the full-employment level of output.* For a time an actual economy can expand beyond its full-employment real GDP. The aggregate expenditures model does not allow for that possibility.
- *It does not deal with cost-push inflation.* We know from Chapter 8 that there are two general types of inflation: demand-pull inflation and cost-push inflation. The aggregate expenditures model does not address cost-push inflation.
- *It does not allow for "self-correction."* In reality, the economy contains some internal features that, given enough time, may correct a recessionary gap or an inflationary gap. The aggregate expenditures model does not contain those features.

In subsequent chapters we remedy these limitations while preserving the many valuable insights of the aggregate expenditures model.

SUMMARY

1. For a private closed economy the equilibrium level of GDP occurs when aggregate expenditures and real output are equal or, graphically, where the $C + I_g$ line intersects the 45° line. At any GDP greater than equilibrium GDP, real output will exceed aggregate spending, resulting in unintended investment in inventories and eventual declines in output and income (GDP). At any below-equilibrium GDP, aggregate expenditures will exceed real output, resulting in unintended disinvestment in inventories and eventual increases in GDP.

2. At equilibrium GDP, the amount households save (leakages) and the amount businesses plan to invest (injections) are equal. Any excess of saving over planned investment will cause a shortage of total spending, forcing GDP to fall. Any excess of planned investment over saving will cause an excess of total spending, inducing GDP to rise. The change in GDP will in both cases correct the discrepancy between saving and planned investment.

3. At equilibrium GDP, there are no unplanned changes in inventories. When aggregate expenditures diverge from real GDP, an unplanned change in inventories occurs. Unplanned increases in inventories are followed by a cutback in production and a decline of real GDP. Unplanned decreases in inventories result in an increase in production and a rise of GDP.

4. Actual investment consists of planned investment plus unplanned changes in inventories and is always equal to saving.

5. A shift in the investment schedule (caused by changes in expected rates of return or changes in interest rates) shifts the aggregate expenditures curve and causes a new equilibrium level of real GDP. Real GDP changes by more than the amount of the initial change in investment. This multiplier effect (Δ GDP/Δ I_g) accompanies both increases and decreases in aggregate expenditures and also applies to changes in net exports (X_n) and government purchases (G).

6. The net export schedule in the model of the open economy relates net exports (exports minus imports) to levels of real GDP. For simplicity, we assume that the level of net exports is the same at all levels of real GDP.

7. Positive net exports increase aggregate expenditures to a higher level than they would if the economy were "closed" to international trade. Negative net exports decrease aggregate expenditures relative to those in a closed economy, decreasing equilibrium real GDP by a multiple of their amount. Increases in exports or decreases in imports have an expansionary effect on real GDP, while decreases in exports or increases in imports have a contractionary effect.

8. Government purchases in the model of the mixed economy shift the aggregate expenditures schedule upward and raise GDP.

9. Taxation reduces disposable income, lowers consumption and saving, shifts the aggregate expenditures curve downward, and reduces equilibrium GDP.

10. In the complete aggregate expenditures model, equilibrium GDP occurs where $C_a + I_g + X_n + G$ = GDP. At the equilibrium GDP, *leakages* of after-tax saving (S_a), imports (M), and taxes (T) equal *injections* of investment (I_g), exports (X), and government purchases (G): $S_a + M + T = I_g + X_n + G$. Also, there are no unplanned changes in inventories.

11. The equilibrium GDP and the full-employment GDP may differ. A recessionary gap is the amount by which aggregate expenditures at the full-employment GDP fall short of those needed to achieve the full-employment GDP. This gap produces a negative GDP gap (actual GDP minus potential GDP). An inflationary gap is the amount by which aggregate expenditures at the full-employment GDP exceed those just sufficient to achieve the full-employment GDP. This gap causes demand-pull inflation.

12. The aggregate expenditures model provides many insights into the macroeconomy, but it does not (a) show price-level changes, (b) account for premature demand-pull inflation, (c) allow for real GDP to temporarily expand beyond the full-employment output, (d) account for cost-push inflation, or (e) allow for partial or full "self-correction" from a recessionary gap or inflationary gap.

TERMS AND CONCEPTS

planned investment

investment schedule

aggregate expenditures
schedule

equilibrium GDP

leakage

injection

unplanned changes in
inventories

net exports

lump-sum tax

recessionary gap

inflationary gap

STUDY QUESTIONS

1. What is an investment schedule and how does it differ from an investment demand curve?

2. *Key Question* Assuming the level of investment is $16 billion and independent of the level of total output, complete the following table and determine the equilibrium levels of output and employment in this private closed economy. What are the sizes of the MPC and MPS?

Possible Levels of Employment, Millions	Real Domestic Output (GDP = DI), Billions	Consumption, Billions	Saving, Billions
40	$240	$244	$ _____
45	260	260	_____
50	280	276	_____
55	300	292	_____
60	320	308	_____
65	340	324	_____
70	360	340	_____
75	380	356	_____
80	400	372	_____

3. Using the consumption and saving data in question 2 and assuming investment is $16 billion, what are saving and planned investment at the $380 billion level of domestic output? What are saving and actual investment at that level?

What are saving and planned investment at the $300 billion level of domestic output? What are the levels of saving and actual investment? Use the concept of unplanned investment to explain adjustments toward equilibrium from both the $380 billion and the $300 billion levels of domestic output.

4. Why is saving called a *leakage*? Why is planned investment called an *injection*? Why must saving equal planned investment at equilibrium GDP in the private closed economy? Are unplanned changes in inventories rising, falling, or constant at equilibrium GDP? Explain.

5. What effect will each of the changes listed in Study Question 3 of Chapter 9 have on the equilibrium level of GDP in the private closed economy? Explain your answers.

6. By how much will GDP change if firms increase their investment by $8 billion and the MPC is .80? If the MPC is .67?

7. Depict graphically the aggregate expenditures model for a private closed economy. Now show a decrease in the aggregate expenditures schedule and explain why the decline in real GDP in your diagram is greater than the initial decline in aggregate expenditures. What would be the ratio of a decline in real GDP to the initial drop in aggregate expenditures if the slope of your aggregate expenditures schedule was .8?

8. Suppose that a certain country has an MPC of .9 and a real GDP of $400 billion. If its investment spending decreases by $4 billion, what will be its new level of real GDP?

9. *Key Question* The data in columns 1 and 2 in the accompanying table are for a private closed economy:

(1) Real Domestic Output (GDP = DI), Billions	(2) Aggregate Expenditures, Private Closed Economy, Billions	(3) Exports, Billions	(4) Imports, Billions	(5) Net Exports, Billions	(6) Aggregate Expenditures, Private Open Economy, Billions
$200	$240	$20	$30	$ _____	$ _____
250	280	20	30	_____	_____
300	320	20	30	_____	_____
350	360	20	30	_____	_____
400	400	20	30	_____	_____
450	440	20	30	_____	_____
500	480	20	30	_____	_____
550	520	20	30	_____	_____

a. Use columns 1 and 2 to determine the equilibrium GDP for this hypothetical economy.

b. Now open up this economy to international trade by including the export and import figures of columns 3 and 4. Fill in columns 5 and 6 and determine the equilibrium GDP for the open economy. Explain why this equilibrium GDP differs from that of the closed economy.

c. Given the original $20 billion level of exports, what would be net exports and the equilibrium GDP if imports were $10 billion greater at each level of GDP?

d. What is the multiplier in this example?

10. Assume that, without taxes, the consumption schedule of an economy is as follows:

GDP, Billions	Consumption, Billions
$100	$120
200	200
300	280
400	360
500	440
600	520
700	600

a. Graph this consumption schedule and determine the MPC.

b. Assume now that a lump-sum tax is imposed such that the government collects $10 billion in taxes at all levels of GDP. Graph the resulting consumption schedule, and compare the MPC and the multiplier with those of the pretax consumption schedule.

11. Explain graphically the determination of equilibrium GDP for a private economy through the aggregate expenditures model. Now add government purchases (any amount you choose) to your graph, showing its impact on equilibrium GDP. Finally, add taxation (any amount of lump-sum tax that you choose) to your graph and show its effect on equilibrium GDP. Looking at your graph, determine whether equilibrium GDP has increased, decreased, or stayed the same given the sizes of the government purchases and taxes that you selected.

12. *Key Question* Refer to columns 1 and 6 in the table for question 9. Incorporate government into the table by assuming that it plans to tax and spend $20 billion at each possible level of GDP. Also assume that the tax is a personal tax and that government spending does not induce a shift in the private aggregate expenditures schedule. Compute and explain the change in equilibrium GDP caused by the addition of government.

13. *Key Question* Refer to the table in the next column in answering the questions that follow:

(1) Possible Levels of Employment, Billions	(2) Real Domestic Output, Billions	(3) Aggregate Expenditures $(C_a + I_g + X_n + G)$, Billions
90	$500	$520
100	550	560
110	600	600
120	650	640
130	700	680

a. If full employment in this economy is 130 million, will there be an inflationary gap or a recessionary gap? What will be the consequence of this gap? By how much would aggregate expenditures in column 3 have to change at each level of GDP to eliminate the inflationary gap or the recessionary gap? Explain. What is the multiplier in this example?

b. Will there be an inflationary gap or a recessionary gap if the full-employment level of output is $500 billion? Explain the consequences. By how much would aggregate expenditures in column 3 have to change at each level of GDP to eliminate the gap? What is the multiplier in this example?

c. Assuming that investment, net exports, and government expenditures do not change with changes in real GDP, what are the sizes of the MPC, the MPS, and the multiplier?

14. *Advanced Analysis* Assume that the consumption schedule for a private open economy is such that consumption $C = 50 + 0.8Y$. Assume further that planned investment I_g and net exports X_n are independent of the level of real GDP and constant at $I_g = 30$ and $X_n = 10$. Recall also that, in equilibrium, the real output produced (Y) is equal to aggregate expenditures: $Y = C + I_g + X_n$.

a. Calculate the equilibrium level of income or real GDP for this economy.

b. What happens to equilibrium Y if I_g changes to 10? What does this outcome reveal about the size of the multiplier?

15. Answer the following questions, which relate to the aggregate expenditures model:

a. If C_a is $100, I_g is $50, X_n is −$10, and G is $30, what is the economy's equilibrium GDP?

b. If real GDP in an economy is currently $200, C_a is $100, I_g is $50, X_n is −$10, and G is $30, will the economy's real GDP rise, fall, or stay the same?

c. Suppose that full-employment (and full-capacity) output in an economy is $200. If C_a is $150, I_g is $50, X_n is −$10, and G is $30, what will be the macroeconomic result?

16. *(Last Word)* What is Say's law? How does it relate to the view held by classical economists that the economy generally

will operate at a position on its production possibilities curve (Chapter 2). Use production possibilities analysis to demonstrate Keynes's view on this matter.

17. *Web-Based Question: The multiplier—calculating hypothetical changes in GDP* Go to the Bureau of Economic Analysis at www.bea.gov, and use the BEA interactivity feature to select National Income and Product Account Tables. Then find Table 1.1, which contains the most recent values for GDP = $C_a + I_g + G + (X - M)$. Assume that the MPC is .75 and that, for each of the following, the values of the initial variables are those you just discovered. Determine the new value of GDP if, other things equal, (*a*) investment increased by 5 percent, (*b*) imports increased by 5 percent while exports increased by 5 percent, (*c*) consumption

increased by 5 percent, and (*d*) government spending increased by 5 percent. Which of the changes, (*a*) through (*d*), caused the greatest change in GDP in absolute dollars?

18. *Web-Based Question: GDP gap and recessionary gap* The St. Louis Federal Reserve Bank at www.research.stlouisfed.org/fred2 provides data on both real GDP (chained 1996 dollars) and real potential GDP for the United States. Both sets of data are located as links under "Gross Domestic Product and Components." What was potential GDP for the third quarter of 2001? What was the actual level of real GDP for that quarter? What was the size difference between the two—the negative GDP gap? If the multiplier was 2 in that period, what was the size of the economy's recessionary gap?

11 | *Aggregate Demand and Aggregate Supply*

In early 2000, Alan Greenspan, chair of the Federal Reserve, made the following statement:

Through the so-called wealth effect, [recent stock market gains] have tended to foster increases in aggregate demand beyond the increases in supply. It is this imbalance . . . that contains the potential seeds of rising inflationary . . . pressures that could undermine the current expansion. Our goal [at the Federal Reserve] is to extend the expansion by containing its imbalances and avoiding the very recession that would complete the business cycle.[1]

Although the Federal Reserve held inflation in check, it did not accomplish its goal of extending the decade-long economic expansion. In March 2001 the U.S. economy experienced a recession and the expansionary phase of the business cycle ended.

We will say more about that later. Our immediate focus is the terminology in the Greenspan quotation, which is precisely the language of the **aggregate demand–aggregate supply model (AD-AS model).** The AD-AS model—the subject of this chapter—enables us to analyze changes in real GDP and the price level simultaneously. The AD-AS model therefore provides keen insights on inflation, recession, unemployment, and economic growth. In later chapters, we will see that it also explains the logic of macroeconomic stabilization policies, such as those implied by Greenspan.

---

[1] Alan Greenspan, speech to the New York Economics Club, Jan. 13, 2000.

Aggregate Demand

Aggregate demand is a schedule or curve that shows the amounts of real output that buyers collectively desire to purchase at each possible price level. The relationship between the price level and the amount of real GDP demanded is inverse or negative: When the price level rises, the quantity of real GDP demanded decreases; when the price level falls, the quantity of real GDP demanded increases.

Aggregate Demand Curve

The inverse relationship between the price level and real GDP is shown in Figure 11.1, where the aggregate

FIGURE 11.1

The aggregate demand curve. The downsloping aggregate demand curve AD indicates an inverse (or negative) relationship between the price level and the amount of real output purchased.

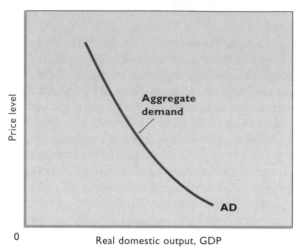

demand curve AD slopes downward, as does the demand curve for an individual product.

Why the downward slope? *The explanation is not the same as that for why the demand for a single product slopes downward.* That explanation centered on the income effect and the substitution effect. When the price of an *individual* product falls, the consumer's (constant) nominal income allows a larger purchase of the product (the income effect). And, as price falls, the consumer wants to buy more of the product because it becomes relatively less expensive than other goods (the substitution effect).

But these explanations do not work for aggregates. In Figure 11.1, when the economy moves down its aggregate demand curve, it moves to a lower general price level. But our circular flow model tells us that when consumers pay lower prices for goods and services, less nominal income flows to resource suppliers in the form of wages, rents, interest, and profits. As a result, a decline in the price level does not necessarily mean an increase in the nominal income of the economy as a whole. Thus, a decline in the price level need not produce an income effect, where more output is purchased because lower prices leave buyers with greater real income.

Similarly, in Figure 11.1 prices in general are falling as we move down the aggregate demand curve, so the rationale for the substitution effect (where more of a specific product is purchased because it becomes cheaper relative to all other products) is not applicable. There is no *overall* substitution effect among domestically produced goods when the price level falls.

If the conventional substitution and income effects do not explain the downward slope of the aggregate demand curve, what does? That explanation rests on three effects of a price-level change.

Real-Balances Effect

A change in the price level produces a **real-balances effect.** Here is how it works: A higher price level reduces the real value or purchasing power of the public's accumulated savings balances. In particular, the real value of assets with fixed money values, such as savings accounts or bonds, diminishes. Because of the erosion of the purchasing power of such assets, the public is poorer in real terms and will reduce its spending. A household might buy a new car or a projection TV if the purchasing power of its financial asset balances is, say, $50,000. But if inflation erodes the purchasing power of its asset balances to $30,000, the household may defer its purchase. So a higher price level means less consumption spending.

Interest-Rate Effect

The aggregate demand curve also slopes downward because of the **interest-rate effect.** When we draw an aggregate demand curve, *we assume that the supply of money in the economy is fixed.* But when the price level rises, consumers need more money for purchases and businesses need more money to meet their payrolls and to buy other resources. A $10 bill will do when the price of an item is $10, but a $10 bill plus a $1 bill is needed when the item costs $11. In short, a higher price level increases the demand for money. So, given a fixed supply of money, an increase in money demand will drive up the price paid for its use. That price is the interest rate.

Higher interest rates curtail investment spending and interest-sensitive consumption spending. Firms that expect a 6 percent rate of return on a potential purchase of capital will find that investment potentially profitable when the interest rate is, say, 5 percent. But the investment will be unprofitable and will not be made when the interest rate has risen to 7 percent. Similarly, consumers may decide not to purchase a new house or new automobile when the interest rate on loans goes up. So, by increasing the demand for money and consequently the interest rate, a higher price level reduces the amount of real output demanded.

Foreign Purchases Effect

The final reason why the aggregate demand curve slopes downward is the **foreign purchases effect.** When the U.S. price level rises relative to foreign price levels (and exchange rates do not respond quickly or completely), foreigners buy fewer U.S. goods and Americans buy more foreign goods. Therefore, U.S. exports fall and U.S. imports rise. In short, the rise in the price level reduces the quantity of U.S. goods demanded as net exports.

These three effects, of course, work in the opposite direction for a decline in the price level. Then the quantity demanded of consumption goods, investment goods, and net exports rises.

Determinants of Aggregate Demand

Other things equal, a change in the price level will change the amount of aggregate spending and therefore change the amount of real GDP demanded by the economy. Movements along a fixed aggregate demand curve represent these changes in real GDP. However, if one or more of those "other things" change, the entire aggregate demand curve will shift. We call these other things **determinants of aggregate demand** or, less formally, *aggregate demand shifters*. They are listed in Figure 11.2.

Changes in aggregate demand involve two components:

• A change in one of the determinants of demand that directly changes the amount of real GDP demanded.

• A multiplier effect that produces a greater ultimate change in aggregate demand than the initiating change in spending.

In Figure 11.2, the full rightward shift of the curve from AD₁ to AD₂ shows an increase in aggregate demand, separated into these two components. The horizontal distance between AD₁ and the broken curve to its right illustrates an initial increase in spending, say, $5 billion of added investment. If the economy's MPC is .75, for example, then the simple multiplier is 4. So the aggregate demand curve shifts rightward from AD₁ to AD₂—four times the distance between AD₁ and the broken line. The multiplier process magnifies the initial change in spending into successive rounds of new consumption spending. After the shift, $20 billion (= $5 × 4) of additional real goods and services are demanded at each price level.

Similarly, the leftward shift of the curve from AD₁ to AD₃ shows a decrease in aggregate demand, the lesser amount of real GDP demanded at each price level. It also involves the initial decline in spending (shown as the horizontal distance between AD₁ and the dashed line to its left), followed by multiplied declines in consumption spending and the ultimate leftward shift to AD₃.

Let's examine each of the determinants of aggregate demand listed in Figure 11.2.

FIGURE 11.2

Changes in aggregate demand. A change in one or more of the listed determinants of aggregate demand will shift the aggregate demand curve. The rightward shift from AD₁ to AD₂ represents an increase in aggregate demand; the leftward shift from AD₁ to AD₃ shows a decrease in aggregate demand. The vertical distances between AD₁ and the dashed lines represent the initial changes in spending. Through the multiplier effect, that spending produces the full shifts of the curves.

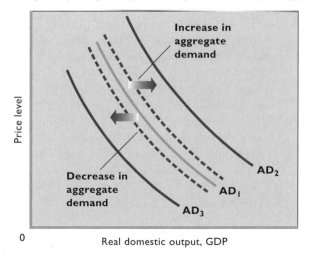

Determinants of Aggregate Demand: Factors that Shift the Aggregate Demand Curve

1. Change in consumer spending
   a. Consumer wealth
   b. Consumer expectations
   c. Household indebtedness
   d. Taxes
2. Change in investment spending
   a. Interest rates
   b. Expected returns
      • Expected future business conditions
      • Technology
      • Degree of excess capacity
      • Business taxes
3. Change in government spending
4. Change in net export spending
   a. National income abroad
   b. Exchange rates

Consumer Spending   Even when the U.S. price level is constant, domestic consumers may alter their purchases of U.S.-produced real output. If those consumers decide to buy more output at each price level, the aggregate demand curve will shift to the right, as from AD_1 to AD_2 in Figure 11.2. If they decide to buy less output, the aggregate demand curve will shift to the left, as from AD_1 to AD_3.

Several factors other than a change in the price level may change consumer spending and therefore shift the aggregate demand curve. As Figure 11.2 shows, those factors are real consumer wealth, consumer expectations, household indebtedness, and taxes. Because our discussion here parallels that of Chapter 9, we will be brief.

Consumer Wealth   Consumer wealth includes both financial assets such as stocks and bonds and physical assets such as houses and land. A sharp increase in the real value of consumer wealth (for example, because of a rise in stock market values) prompts people to save less and buy more products. The resulting increase in consumer spending—called the *wealth effect*—will shift the aggregate demand curve to the right. In contrast, a major decrease in the real value of consumer wealth at each price level will reduce consumption spending and thus shift the aggregate demand curve to the left.

Consumer Expectations   Changes in expectations about the future may alter consumer spending. When people expect their future real incomes to rise, they tend to spend more of their current incomes. Thus current consumption spending increases (current saving falls), and the aggregate demand curve shifts to the right. Similarly, a widely held expectation of surging inflation in the near future may increase aggregate demand today because consumers will want to buy products before their prices escalate. Conversely, expectations of lower future income or lower future prices may reduce current consumption and shift the aggregate demand curve to the left.

Household Indebtedness   Households finance some of their spending by borrowing. If household indebtedness from past spending rises beyond normal levels, consumers may be forced to cut current spending in order to pay the interest and principal on their debt. Consumption spending will then decline and the aggregate demand curve will shift to the left. Alternatively, when household indebtedness is unusually low, consumers have considerable leeway to borrow and spend today. Then the aggregate demand curve may shift to the right.

Taxes   A reduction in personal income tax rates raises take-home income and increases consumer purchases at each possible price level. Tax cuts shift the aggregate demand curve to the right. Tax increases reduce consumption spending and shift the curve to the left.

Investment Spending   Investment spending (the purchase of capital goods) is a second major determinant of aggregate demand. A decline in investment spending at each price level will shift the aggregate demand curve to the left. An increase in investment spending will shift it to the right. In Chapter 9 we saw that investment spending depends on the real interest rate and the expected return from the investment.

Real Interest Rates   Other things equal, an increase in interest rates will lower investment spending and reduce aggregate demand. We are not referring here to the "interest-rate effect" resulting from a change in the price level. Instead, we are identifying a change in the interest rate resulting from, say, a change in the nation's money supply. An increase in the money supply lowers the interest rate, thereby increasing investment and aggregate demand. A decrease in the money supply raises the interest rate, reducing investment and decreasing aggregate demand.

Expected Returns   Higher expected returns on investment projects will increase the demand for capital goods and shift the aggregate demand curve to the right. Alternatively, declines in expected returns will decrease investment and shift the curve to the left. Expected returns, in turn, are influenced by several factors:

- *Expectations about future business conditions*   If firms are optimistic about future business conditions, they are more likely to forecast high rates of return on current investment and therefore may invest more today. On the other hand, if they think the economy will deteriorate in the future, they will forecast low rates of return and perhaps will invest less today.
- *Technology*   New and improved technologies enhance expected returns on investment and thus increase aggregate demand. For example, recent advances in microbiology have motivated pharmaceutical companies to establish new labs and production facilities.
- *Degree of excess capacity*   A rise in excess capacity—unused capital—will reduce the expected return on new investment and hence decrease aggregate demand. Other things equal, firms operating factories at well below capacity have little incentive to build new factories. But when firms discover that their excess

capacity is dwindling or has completely disappeared, their expected returns on new investment in factories and capital equipment rise. Thus, they increase their investment spending, and the aggregate demand curve shifts to the right.

- *Business taxes* An increase in business taxes will reduce after-tax profits from capital investment and lower expected returns. So investment and aggregate demand will decline. A decrease in business taxes will have the opposite effects.

Government Spending Government purchases are the third determinant of aggregate demand. An increase in government purchases (for example, more military equipment) will shift the aggregate demand curve to the right, as long as tax collections and interest rates do not change as a result. In contrast, a reduction in government spending (for example, a cutback in orders for new computers) will shift the curve to the left.

Net Export Spending The final determinant of aggregate demand is net export spending. Other things equal, higher U.S. *exports* mean an increased foreign demand for U.S. goods. So a rise in net exports (higher exports relative to imports) shifts the aggregate demand curve to the right. In contrast, a decrease in U.S. net exports shifts the aggregate demand curve leftward. (These changes in net exports are *not* those prompted by a change in the U.S. price level—those associated with the foreign purchases effect. The changes here explain shifts of the curve, not movements along the curve.)

What might cause net exports to change, other than the price level? Two possibilities are changes in national income abroad and changes in exchange rates.

National Income Abroad Rising national income abroad encourages foreigners to buy more products, some of which are made in the United States. U.S. net exports thus rise, and the U.S. aggregate demand curve shifts to the right. Declines in national income abroad do the opposite: They reduce U.S. net exports and shift the U.S. aggregate demand curve to the left.

Exchange Rates Changes in exchange rates (Chapter 6) may affect U.S. net exports and therefore aggregate demand. Suppose the dollar depreciates in terms of the euro (meaning the euro appreciates in terms of the dollar). The new, relatively lower value of dollars and higher value of euros enables European consumers to obtain more dollars with each euro. From their perspective, U.S. goods are now less expensive; it takes fewer euros to obtain them. So

European consumers buy more U.S. goods, and U.S. exports rise. But American consumers can now obtain fewer euros for each dollar. Because they must pay more dollars to buy European goods, Americans reduce their imports. U.S. exports rise and U.S. imports fall. Conclusion: *Depreciation* of the dollar increases U.S. net exports, thereby shifting the U.S. aggregate demand curve to the right.

Think through the opposite scenario, in which the dollar *appreciates* and the euro depreciates.

QUICK REVIEW 11.1

- Aggregate demand reflects an inverse relationship between the price level and the amount of real output demanded.
- Changes in the price level create real-balances, interest-rate, and foreign purchases effects that explain the downward slope of the aggregate demand curve.
- Changes in one or more of the determinants of aggregate demand (Figure 11.2) alter the amounts of real GDP demanded at each price level; they shift the aggregate demand curve. The multiplier effect magnifies initial changes in spending into larger changes in aggregate demand.
- An increase in aggregate demand is shown as a rightward shift of the aggregate demand curve; a decrease, as a leftward shift of the curve.

Aggregate Supply

Aggregate supply is a schedule or curve showing the level of real domestic output that firms will produce at each price level. The production responses of firms to changes in the price level differ in the *long run*, which in macroeconomics is a period in which nominal wages (and other resource prices) match changes in the price level, and the *short run*, a period in which nominal wages (and other resource prices) do not respond to price-level changes. So the long and short runs vary by degree of wage adjustment, not by a set length of time such as 1 month, 1 year, or 3 years.

Aggregate Supply in the Long Run

In the long run, the aggregate supply curve is vertical at the economy's full-employment output (or its potential output), as represented by AS_{LR} in Figure 11.3. When changes in wages respond completely to changes in the price level, those price-level changes do not alter the amount of real GDP produced and offered for sale.

FIGURE 11.3

Aggregate supply in the long run. The long-run aggregate supply curve AS$_{LR}$ is vertical at the full-employment level of real GDP (Q_f) because in the long run wages and other input prices rise and fall to match changes in the price level. So price-level changes do not affect firms' profits and thus they create no incentive for firms to alter their output.

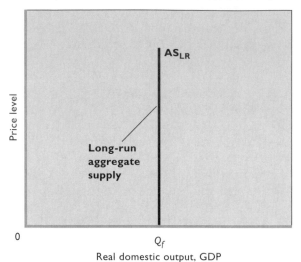

Consider a one-firm economy in which the firm's owners must receive a real profit of $20 in order to produce the full-employment output of 100 units. The real reward the owner receives, not the level of prices, is what really counts. Assume the owner's only input (aside from entrepreneurial talent) is 10 units of hired labor at $8 per worker, for a total wage cost of $80. Also, assume that the 100 units of output sell for $1 per unit, so total revenue is $100. The firm's nominal profit is $20 (= $100 − $80), and using the $1 price to designate the base-price index of 100, its real profit is also $20 (= $20/1.00). Well and good; the full-employment output is produced.

Next, suppose the price level doubles. Would the owner earn more than the $20 of real profit and therefore boost production beyond the 100-unit full-employment output? The answer is no, given the assumption that nominal wages and the price level rise by the same amount, as is true in the long run. Once the product price has doubled to $2, total revenue will be $200 (= 100 × $2). But the cost of 10 units of labor will double from $80 to $160 because the wage rate rises from $8 to $16. Nominal profit thus increases to $40 (= $200 − $160). What about real profit? By dividing the nominal profit of $40 by the new price index of 200 (expressed as a decimal), we obtain real profit of $20 (= $40/2.00). Because real profit does not change, the firm will not alter its production. Real GDP will remain at its full-employment level.

In the long run, wages and other input prices rise or fall to match changes in the price level. Changes in the price level therefore do not change real profit, and there is no change in real output. As shown in Figure 11.3, the **long-run aggregate supply curve** is vertical at the economy's potential output (or full-employment output).

Aggregate Supply in the Short Run

In reality, nominal wages adjust only slowly to changes in the price level and perfect adjustment may take several months or even a number of years. Reconsider our previous one-firm economy. If the $8 nominal wage for each of the 10 workers is unresponsive to the price-level change, the doubling of the price level will boost total revenue from $100 to $200 but leave total cost unchanged at $80. Nominal profit will rise from $20 (= $100 − $80) to $120 (= $200 − $80). Dividing that $120 profit by the new price index of 200 (= 2.0 in hundredths), we find that the real profit is now $60. The rise in the real reward from $20 to $60 prompts firms to produce more output. Conversely, price-level declines reduce real profits and cause firms collectively to reduce their output. So, in the short run, there is a direct or positive relationship between the price level and real output.

The **short-run aggregate supply curve** is upsloping, as shown in Figure 11.4. A rise in the price level increases real output; a fall in the price level reduces it. Per-unit production costs underlie the aggregate supply curve. Recall from Chapter 8 that

$$\text{Per-unit production cost} = \frac{\text{total input cost}}{\text{units of output}}$$

The per-unit production cost of any specific level of output establishes that output's price level because the price level must cover all the costs of production, including profit "costs."

As the economy expands in the short run, per-unit production costs generally rise because of reduced efficiency and rising input prices. But the extent of that rise depends on where the economy is operating relative to its capacity. The aggregate supply curve in Figure 11.4 is relatively flat at outputs below the full-employment output Q_f and relatively steep at outputs above it. Why the difference?

When the economy is operating below its full-employment output, it has large amounts of unused machinery and equipment and unemployed workers. Firms can put these idle human and property resources back to work with little upward pressure on per-unit production costs. Workers unemployed for 2 or 3 months will hardly expect a wage increase when recalled to their jobs. And as

FIGURE 11.4

The aggregate supply curve (short run). The upsloping aggregate supply curve AS indicates a direct (or positive) relationship between the price level and the amount of real output that firms will offer for sale. The AS curve is relatively flat below the full-employment output because unemployed resources and unused capacity allow firms to respond to price-level rises with large increases in real output. It is relatively steep beyond the full-employment output because resource shortages and capacity limitations make it difficult to expand real output as the price level rises.

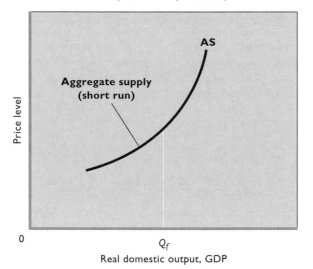

output expands, few if any shortages of inputs or production bottlenecks will arise to raise per-unit production costs.

When the economy is operating beyond its full-employment output, the vast majority of its available resources are already employed. Adding more workers to a relatively fixed number of highly used capital resources such as plant and equipment creates congestion in the workplace and reduces the efficiency (on average) of workers. Adding more capital, given the limited number of available workers, leaves equipment idle and reduces the efficiency of capital. Adding more land resources when capital and labor are highly constrained reduces the efficiency of land resources. Under these circumstances, total output rises less rapidly than total input cost. So per-unit production costs increase.

Moreover, individual firms may try to expand their own production by bidding resources away from other firms. But the resources and additional production that one firm gains will be largely lost by the other firms. The bidding will raise input prices, but real output will rise very little, if at all. That is a prescription for higher per-unit production costs.

Our focus in the remainder of this chapter, the rest of Part 3, and all of Part 4 is on short-run aggregate supply,

such as that shown in Figure 11.4. Unless stated otherwise, all references to "aggregate supply" are to aggregate supply in the short run. We will bring long-run aggregate supply prominently back into the analysis in Part 5, when we discuss long-run wage adjustments and economic growth.

Determinants of Aggregate Supply

An existing aggregate supply curve identifies the relationship between the price level and real output, other things equal. But when one or more of these other things change, the curve itself shifts. The rightward shift of the curve from AS_1 to AS_2 in Figure 11.5 represents an increase in aggregate supply, indicating that firms are willing to produce and sell more real output at each price level. The leftward shift of the curve from AS_1 to AS_3 represents a decrease in aggregate supply. At each price level, firms produce less output than before.

Figure 11.5 lists the other things that cause a shift of the aggregate supply curve. Called the **determinants of aggregate supply** or *aggregate supply shifters*, they collectively position the aggregate supply curve and shift the curve when they change. Changes in these determinants raise or lower per-unit production costs *at each price level (or each level of output)*. These changes in per-unit production cost affect profits, thereby leading firms to alter the amount of output they are willing to produce *at each price level*. For example, firms may collectively offer $7 trillion of real output at a price level of 1.0 (100 in index value), rather than $6.8 trillion. Or they may offer $6.5 trillion rather than $7 trillion. The point is that when one of the determinants listed in Figure 11.5 changes, the aggregate supply curve shifts to the right or left. Changes that reduce per-unit production costs shift the aggregate supply curve to the right, as from AS_1 to AS_2; changes that increase per-unit production costs shift it to the left, as from AS_1 to AS_3. *When per-unit production costs change for reasons other than changes in real output, the aggregate supply curve shifts.*

The aggregate supply determinants listed in Figure 11.5 require more discussion.

Input Prices   Input or resource prices—to be distinguished from the output prices that make up the price level—are a major ingredient of per-unit production costs and therefore a key determinant of aggregate supply. These resources can either be domestic or imported.

Domestic Resource Prices   Wages and salaries make up about 75 percent of all business costs. Other things equal, decreases in wages reduce per-unit production costs.

FIGURE 11.5

Changes in aggregate supply. A change in one or more of the listed determinants of aggregate supply will shift the aggregate supply curve. The rightward shift of the aggregate supply curve from AS$_1$ to AS$_2$ represents an increase in aggregate supply; the leftward shift of the curve from AS$_1$ to AS$_3$ shows a decrease in aggregate supply.

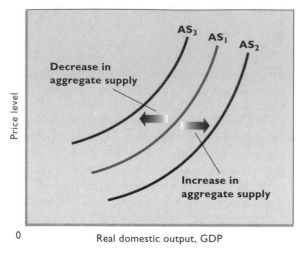

Determinants of Aggregate Supply: Factors That Shift the Aggregate Supply Curve

1. Change in input prices
   a. Domestic resource prices
   b. Prices of imported resources
   c. Market power
2. Change in productivity
3. Change in legal-institutional environment
   a. Business taxes and subsidies
   b. Government regulations

So the aggregate supply curve shifts to the right. Increases in wages shift the curve to the left. Examples:

- Labor supply increases because of substantial immigration. Wages and per-unit production costs fall, shifting the AS curve to the right.
- Labor supply decreases because of a rapid rise in pension income and early retirements. Wage rates and per-unit production costs rise, shifting the AS curve to the left.

Similarly, the aggregate supply curve shifts when the prices of land and capital inputs change. Examples:

- The price of machinery and equipment falls because of declines in the prices of steel and electronic components. Per-unit production costs decline, and the AS curve shifts to the right.
- Land resources expand through discoveries of mineral deposits, irrigation of land, or technical innovations that transform "nonresources" (say, vast desert lands) into valuable resources (productive lands). The price of land declines, per-unit production costs fall, and the AS curve shifts to the right.

Prices of Imported Resources Just as foreign demand for U.S. goods contributes to U.S. aggregate demand, resources imported from abroad (such as oil, tin, and copper) add to U.S. aggregate supply. Added supplies of resources—whether domestic or imported—typically reduce per-unit production costs. A decrease in the price of imported resources increases U.S. aggregate supply, while an increase in their price reduces U.S. aggregate supply.

Exchange-rate fluctuations are one factor that may alter the price of imported resources. Suppose that the dollar appreciates, enabling U.S. firms to obtain more foreign currency with each dollar. This means that domestic producers face a lower *dollar* price of imported resources. U.S. firms will respond by increasing their imports of foreign resources, thereby lowering their per-unit production costs at each level of output. Falling per-unit production costs will shift the U.S. aggregate supply curve to the right.

A depreciation of the dollar, in contrast, will have the opposite set of effects.

Market Power A change in the degree of market power—the ability to set prices above competitive levels—held by sellers of major inputs also can affect input prices and aggregate supply. An example is the fluctuating market power held by the Organization of Petroleum Exporting Countries (OPEC) over the past several decades. The 10-fold increase in the price of oil that OPEC achieved during the 1970s drove up per-unit production costs and jolted the U.S. aggregate supply curve leftward. Then a steep reduction in OPEC's market power during the mid-1980s resulted in a sharp decline in oil prices and a rightward shift of the U.S. aggregate supply curve. In 1999 OPEC temporarily reasserted its market power, raising oil prices and therefore per-unit production costs for some U.S. producers (for example, airlines and truckers).

Productivity The second major determinant of aggregate supply is **productivity,** which is a measure of the relationship between a nation's level of real output and the amount of resources used to produce that output.

Productivity is a measure of average real output, or of real output per unit of input:

$$\text{Productivity} = \frac{\text{total output}}{\text{total inputs}}$$

An increase in productivity enables the economy to obtain more real output from its limited resources. It does this by reducing the per-unit cost of output (per-unit production cost). Suppose, for example, that real output is 10 units, that 5 units of input are needed to produce that quantity, and that the price of each input unit is $2. Then

$$\text{Productivity} = \frac{\text{total output}}{\text{total inputs}} = \frac{10}{5} = 2$$

and

$$\text{Per-unit production cost} = \frac{\text{total input cost}}{\text{total output}}$$
$$= \frac{\$2 \times 5}{10} = \$1$$

Note that we obtain the total input cost by multiplying the unit input cost by the number of inputs used.

Now suppose productivity increases so that real output doubles to 20 units, while the price and quantity of the input remain constant at $2 and 5 units. Using the above equations, we see that productivity rises from 2 to 4 and that the per-unit production cost of the output falls from $1 to $.50. The doubled productivity has reduced the per-unit production cost by half.

By reducing the per-unit production cost, an increase in productivity shifts the aggregate supply curve to the right. The main source of productivity advance is improved production technology, often embodied within new plant and equipment that replaces old plant and equipment. Other sources of productivity increases are a better-educated and -trained workforce, improved forms of business enterprises, and the reallocation of labor resources from lower- to higher-productivity uses.

Legal-Institutional Environment

Changes in the legal-institutional setting in which businesses operate are the final determinant of aggregate supply. Such changes may alter the per-unit costs of output and, if so, shift the aggregate supply curve. Two changes of this type are (1) changes in taxes and subsidies and (2) changes in the extent of regulation.

Business Taxes and Subsidies

Higher business taxes, such as sales, excise, and payroll taxes, increase per-unit costs and reduce short-run aggregate supply in much the same way as a wage increase does. An increase in such taxes paid by businesses will increase per-unit production costs and shift aggregate supply to the left.

Similarly, a business subsidy—a payment or tax break by government to producers—lowers production costs and increases short-run aggregate supply. For example, the Federal government subsidizes firms that blend ethanol (derived from corn) with gasoline to increase the U.S. gasoline supply. This reduces the per-unit production cost of making blended gasoline. To the extent that this and other subsidies are successful, the aggregate supply curve shifts rightward.

Government Regulation

It is usually costly for businesses to comply with government regulations. More regulation therefore tends to increase per-unit production costs and shift the aggregate supply curve to the left. "Supply-side" proponents of deregulation of the economy have argued forcefully that, by increasing efficiency and reducing the paperwork associated with complex regulations, deregulation will reduce per-unit costs and shift the aggregate supply curve to the right. Other economists are less certain. Deregulation that results in accounting manipulations, monopolization, and business failures is likely to shift the AS curve to the left rather than to the right.

QUICK REVIEW 11.2

- The long-run aggregate supply curve is vertical because, given sufficient time, wages and other input prices rise and fall to match price-level changes; because price-level changes do not change real rewards, they do not change production decisions.

- The short run aggregate supply curve (or simply the "aggregate supply curve") is upward-sloping because wages and other input prices are slow to adjust to changes in price levels. The underlying upward slope of the aggregate supply curve reflects rising per-unit production costs as output expands.

- By altering per-unit production costs independent of changes in the level of output, changes in one or more of the determinants of aggregate supply (Figure 11.5) shift the aggregate supply curve.

- An increase in short-run aggregate supply is shown as a rightward shift of the aggregate supply curve; a decrease is shown as a leftward shift of the curve.

Equilibrium and Changes in Equilibrium

Of all the possible combinations of price levels and levels of real GDP, which combination will the economy gravitate toward, at least in the short run? **Figure 11.6**

KEY GRAPH

FIGURE 11.6

The equilibrium price level and equilibrium real GDP. The intersection of the aggregate demand curve and the aggregate supply curve determines the economy's equilibrium price level. At the equilibrium price level of 100 (in index-value terms) the $510 billion of real output demanded matches the $510 billion of real output supplied.

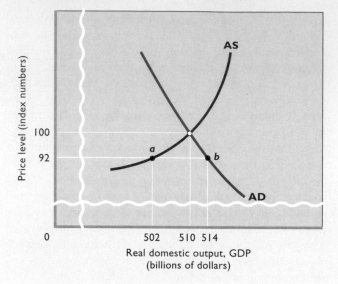

Real Output Demanded (Billions)	Price Level (Index Number)	Real Output Supplied (Billions)
$506	108	$513
508	104	512
510	**100**	**510**
512	96	507
514	92	502

QUICK QUIZ 11.6

1. The AD curve slopes downward because:
   a. per-unit production costs fall as real GDP increases.
   b. the income and substitution effects are at work.
   c. changes in the determinants of AD alter the amounts of real GDP demanded at each price level.
   d. decreases in the price level give rise to real-balances effects, interest-rate effects, and foreign purchases effects that increase the amounts of real GDP demanded.

2. The AS curve slopes upward because:
   a. per-unit production costs rise as real GDP expands toward and beyond its full-employment level.
   b. the income and substitution effects are at work.
   c. changes in the determinants of AS alter the amounts of real GDP supplied at each price level.
   d. increases in the price level give rise to real-balances effects, interest-rate effects, and foreign purchases effects that increase the amounts of real GDP supplied.

3. At price level 92:
   a. a GDP surplus of $12 billion occurs that drives the price level up to 100.
   b. a GDP shortage of $12 billion occurs that drives the price level up to 100.
   c. the aggregate amount of real GDP demanded is less than the aggregate amount of GDP supplied.
   d. the economy is operating beyond its capacity to produce.

4. Suppose real output demanded rises by $4 billion at each price level. The new equilibrium price level will be:
   a. 108.
   b. 104.
   c. 96.
   d. 92.

Answers: 1. d; 2. a; 3. b; 4. b

(Key Graph) and its accompanying table provide the answer. Equilibrium occurs at the price level that equalizes the amounts of real output demanded and supplied. The intersection of the aggregate demand curve AD and the aggregate supply curve AS establishes the economy's **equilibrium price level** and **equilibrium real output.** So aggregate demand and aggregate supply jointly establish the price level and level of real GDP.

In Figure 11.6 the equilibrium price level and level of real output are 100 and $510 billion, respectively. To illustrate why, suppose the price level is 92 rather than 100. We see from the table that the lower price level will encourage businesses to produce real output of $502 billion. This is shown by point *a* on the AS curve in the graph. But, as revealed by the table and point *b* on the aggregate demand curve, buyers will want to purchase $514 billion of real output at price level 92. Competition among buyers to purchase the lesser available real output of $502 billion will eliminate the $12 billion (= $514 billion − $502 billion) shortage and pull up the price level to 100.

As the table and graph show, the rise in the price level from 92 to 100 encourages producers to increase their real output from $502 billion to $510 billion and causes buyers to scale back their purchases from $514 billion to $510 billion. When equality occurs between the amounts of real output produced and purchased, as it does at price level 100, the economy has achieved equilibrium (here, at $510 billion of real GDP).

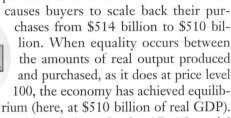

11.1
Aggregate demand–aggregate supply

Now let's apply the AD-AS model to various situations that can confront the economy. For simplicity we will use P and Q symbols, rather than actual numbers. Remember that these symbols represent price index values and amounts of real GDP.

Increases in AD: Demand-Pull Inflation

Suppose the economy is operating at its full-employment output and businesses and government decide to increase their spending—actions that shift the aggregate demand curve to the right. Our list of determinants of aggregate demand (Figure 11.2) provides several reasons why this shift might occur. Perhaps firms boost their investment spending because they anticipate higher future profits from investments in new capital. Those profits are predicated on having new equipment and facilities that incorporate a number of new technologies. And perhaps government increases spending to expand national defense.

As shown by the rise in the price level from P_1 to P_2 in Figure 11.7, the increase in aggregate demand beyond the full-employment level of output causes inflation. This is *demand-pull inflation*, because the price level is being pulled up by the increase in aggregate demand. Also, observe that the increase in demand expands real output from Q_f to Q_1. The distance between Q_1 and Q_f is a positive *GDP gap*. Actual GDP exceeds potential GDP.

The classic American example of demand-pull inflation occurred in the late 1960s. The escalation of the war in Vietnam resulted in a 40 percent increase in defense spending between 1965 and 1967 and another 15 percent increase in 1968. The rise in government spending, imposed on an already growing economy, shifted the economy's aggregate demand curve to the right, producing the worst inflation in two decades. Actual GDP exceeded potential GDP, and inflation jumped from 1.6 percent in 1965 to 5.7 percent by 1970. **(Key Question 4)**

FIGURE 11.7

An increase in aggregate demand that causes demand-pull inflation. The increase of aggregate demand from AD_1 to AD_2 causes demand-pull inflation, shown as the rise in the price level from P_1 to P_2. It also causes a positive GDP gap of Q_1 minus Q_f. The rise of the price level reduces the size of the multiplier effect. If the price level were constant, the increase in aggregate demand from AD_1 to AD_2 would increase output from Q_f to Q_2 and the multiplier would be at full strength. But because of the increase in the price level, real output increases only from Q_f to Q_1 and the multiplier effect is reduced.

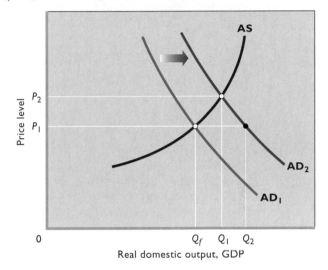

A careful examination of Figure 11.7 reveals an interesting point concerning the multiplier effect. The increase in aggregate demand from AD_1 to AD_2 increases real output only to Q_1, not to Q_2, because part of the increase in aggregate demand is absorbed as inflation as the price level rises from P_1 to P_2. Had the price level remained at P_1, the shift of aggregate demand from AD_1 to AD_2 would have increased real output to Q_2. The full-strength multiplier effect of Chapters 9 and 10 would have occurred. But in Figure 11.7 inflation reduced the increase in real output—and thus the multiplier effect—by about one-half. *For any initial increase in aggregate demand, the resulting increase in real output will be smaller the greater is the increase in the price level.* Price-level rises weaken the realized multiplier effect.

Decreases in AD: Recession and Cyclical Unemployment

Decreases in aggregate demand describe the opposite end of the business cycle: recession and cyclical unemployment (rather than above-full employment and demand-pull inflation). For example, in 2000 investment spending

FIGURE 11.8

A decrease in aggregate demand that causes a recession.   If the price level is downwardly inflexible at P_1, a decline of aggregate demand from AD_1 to AD_2 will move the economy leftward along the horizontal broken-line segment and reduce real GDP from Q_f to Q_1. Idle production capacity, cyclical unemployment, and a negative GDP gap (of Q_1 minus Q_f) will result.

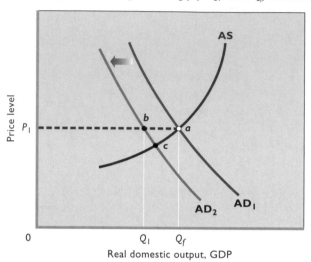

demand from AD_2 to AD_1 along this broken line, since none of the increase in output would be dissipated as inflation. We will say more about this in Chapter 12.

Real output takes the brunt of declines in aggregate demand in the U.S. economy because product prices tend to be "sticky" or inflexible in a downward direction. There are numerous reasons for this:

- **Wage contracts**   Wage rates often are inflexible downward, and it usually is not profitable for firms to cut their product prices if they cannot also cut their wage rates. Wages tend to be inflexible downward because large parts of the labor force work under contracts prohibiting wage cuts for the duration of the contract. (It is not uncommon for collective bargaining agreements in major industries to run for 3 years.) Similarly, the wages and salaries of nonunion workers are usually adjusted once a year, rather than quarterly or monthly.

- **Morale, effort, and productivity**   Wage inflexibility downward is reinforced by the reluctance of many employers to reduce wage rates. Current wages may be so-called **efficiency wages**—*wages that elicit maximum work effort and thus minimize labor cost per unit of output.* If worker productivity (output per hour of work) remains constant, lower wages *do* reduce labor costs per unit of output. But lower wages might impair worker morale and work effort, thereby reducing productivity. Considered alone, lower productivity raises labor costs per unit of output because less output is produced. If the higher labor costs resulting from reduced productivity exceed the cost savings from the lower wage, then wage cuts will increase rather than reduce labor costs per unit of output. In such situations, firms will resist lowering wages when they are faced with a decline in aggregate demand.

11.2
Efficiency wage

- **Minimum wage**   The minimum wage imposes a legal floor under the wages of the least skilled workers. Firms cannot reduce that wage rate when aggregate demand declines.

- **Menu costs**   Firms that think a recession will be relatively short lived may be reluctant to cut their prices. One reason is so-called **menu costs,** named after their most obvious example: the cost of printing new menus when a restaurant changes its prices. But changes in prices create other costs of changing prices. There are the costs of (1) estimating the magnitude and duration of the shift in demand to determine whether prices should be lowered, (2) repricing items held in inventory, (3) printing and mailing new catalogs, and (4) communicating new prices to customers,

substantially declined because of an overexpansion of capital during the second half of the 1990s. In Figure 11.8 we show the resulting decline in aggregate demand as a leftward shift from AD_1 to AD_2.

But now we add an important twist to the analysis. What goes up—the price level—does not always go down. *Deflation*—a decline in the price level—is a rarity in the American economy. Suppose, for example, that the economy represented by Figure 11.8 moves from *a* to *b*, rather than from *a* to *c*. The outcome is a decline of real output from Q_f to Q_1, with *no* change in the price level. In this case, it is as if the aggregate supply curve in Figure 11.8 is horizontal at P_1, to the left of Q_f, as indicated by the dashed line. This decline of real output from Q_f to Q_1 constitutes a *recession*, and since fewer workers are needed to produce the lower output, *cyclical unemployment* arises. The distance between Q_1 and Q_f is a negative GDP gap—the amount by which actual output falls short of potential output. Such a gap occurred during the U.S. recession of 2001, in which real GDP fell an average of $67 billion short of potential output for each of the last three quarters of 2001.

In this case, close inspection of Figure 11.8 reveals that, with the price level stuck at P_1, real GDP decreases by the full leftward shift of the AD curve. The multiplier of Chapter 9 and Chapter 10 is at full strength when changes in aggregate demand occur along what, in effect, is a horizontal segment of the AS curve. This full-strength multiplier would also exist for an increase in aggregate perhaps through advertising. When menu costs are present, firms may choose to avoid them by retaining current prices. That is, they will wait to see if the decline in aggregate demand is permanent.

- *Fear of price wars*   Some firms may be concerned that if they reduce their prices, rivals not only will match their price cuts but may retaliate by making even deeper cuts. An initial price cut may touch off an unwanted *price war*: successively deeper and deeper rounds of price cuts. In such a situation, all the firms end up with far less profit or higher losses than would be the case if they had simply maintained their prices. For this reason, each firm may resist making the initial price cut, choosing instead to reduce production and lay off workers.

But a major "caution" is needed: Although most economists agree that wages and prices tend to be inflexible downward, wages and prices are more flexible than in the past. The declining power of unions in the United States and intense foreign competition have undermined the ability of workers and firms to resist price and wage cuts when faced with falling aggregate demand. This increased flexibility may be one reason the recession of 2001 was relatively mild. The U.S. auto manufacturers, for example, maintained output in the face of falling demand by offering zero-interest loans on auto purchases. This, in effect, was a disguised price cut. But our description in Figure 11.8 remains valid. In the 2001 recession, the overall price level did not decline although output fell by .5 percent and unemployment rose by 1.8 million workers.

Decreases in AS: Cost-Push Inflation

Suppose that a major terrorist attack on oil facilities severely disrupts world oil supplies and drives up oil prices by, say, 300 percent. Higher energy prices would spread through the economy, driving up production and distribution costs on a wide variety of goods. The U.S. aggregate supply curve would spring to the left, say, from AS_1 to AS_2 in Figure 11.9. The resulting increase in the price level would be *cost-push inflation*.

The effects of a leftward shift in aggregate supply are doubly bad. When aggregate supply shifts from AS_1 to AS_2, the economy moves from *a* to *b*. The price level rises from P_1 to P_2 and real output declines from Q_f to Q_2. Along with the cost-push inflation, a recession (and negative GDP gap) occurs. That is exactly what happened in the United States in the mid-1970s when the price of oil rocketed upward. Then, oil expenditures were about 10 percent of U.S. GDP, compared to only 3 percent today. So the U.S. economy is now less vulnerable to cost-push inflation arising from such "aggregate supply shocks."

CONSIDER THIS . . .

© Index Stock Imagery, Inc

Ratchet Effect

A *ratchet analogy* is a good way to think about effects of changes in aggregate demand on the price level. A ratchet is a tool or mechanism such as a winch, car jack, or socket wrench that cranks a wheel forward but does not allow it to go backward. Properly set, each allows the operator to move an object (boat, car, or nut) in one direction while preventing it from moving in the opposite direction.

Product prices, wage rates, and per-unit production costs are highly flexible upward when aggregate demand increases along the aggregate supply curve. In the United States, the price level has increased in 52 of the 53 years since 1950.

But when aggregate demand decreases, product prices, wage rates, and per-unit production costs are inflexible downward. The U.S. price level has declined in only a single year (1955) since 1950, even though aggregate demand and real output have declined in a number of years.

In terms of our analogy, increases in aggregate demand ratchet the U.S. price level upward. Once in place, the higher price level remains until it is ratcheted up again. The higher price level tends to remain even with declines in aggregate demand.

Increases in AS: Full Employment with Price-Level Stability

Between 1996 and 2000, the United States experienced a combination of full employment, strong economic growth,

FIGURE 11.9

A decrease in aggregate supply that causes cost-push inflation. A leftward shift of aggregate supply from AS_1 to AS_2 raises the price level from P_1 to P_2 and produces cost-push inflation. Real output declines and a negative GDP gap (of Q_1 minus Q_f) occurs.

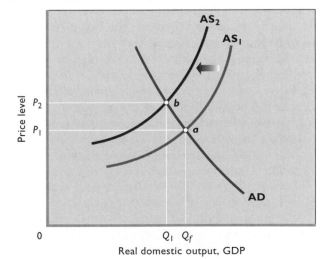

FIGURE 11.10

Growth, full employment, and relative price stability. Normally, an increase in aggregate demand from AD_1 to AD_2 would move the economy from a to b along AS_1. Real output would expand to its full-capacity level (Q_2), and inflation would result (P_1 to P_3). But in the late 1990s, significant increases in productivity shifted the aggregate supply curve, as from AS_1 to AS_2. The economy moved from a to c rather than from a to b. It experienced strong economic growth (Q_1 to Q_3), full employment, and only very mild inflation (P_1 to P_2) before receding in March 2001.

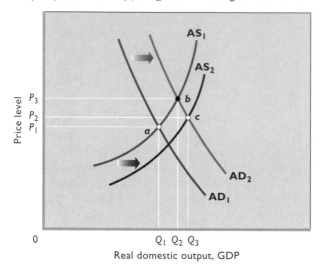

and very low inflation. Specifically, the unemployment rate fell to 4 percent and real GDP grew nearly 4 percent annually, *without igniting inflation*. At first thought, this "macroeconomic bliss" seems to be incompatible with the AD-AS model. The aggregate supply curve suggests that increases in aggregate demand that are sufficient for over-full employment will raise the price level (see Figure 11.7). Higher inflation, so it would seem, is the inevitable price paid for expanding output beyond the full-employment level.

But inflation remained very mild in the late 1990s. Figure 11.10 helps explain why. Let's first suppose that aggregate demand increased from AD_1 to AD_2 along aggregate supply curve AS_1. Taken alone, that increase in aggregate demand would move the economy from a to b. Real output would rise from full-employment output Q_1 to beyond-full-employment output Q_2. The economy would experience inflation, as shown by the increase in the price level from P_1 to P_3. Such inflation had occurred at the end of previous vigorous expansions of aggregate demand, including the expansion of the late 1980s.

Between 1990 and 2000, however, larger-than-usual increases in productivity occurred because of a burst of new technology relating to computers, the Internet, inventory management systems, electronic commerce, and

so on. We represent this higher-than-usual productivity growth as the rightward shift from AS_1 to AS_2 in Figure 11.10. The relevant aggregate demand and aggregate supply curves thus became AD_2 and AS_2, not AD_2 and AS_1. Instead of moving from a to b, the economy moved from a to c. Real output increased from Q_1 to Q_3, and the price level rose only modestly (from P_1 to P_2). The shift of the aggregate supply curve from AS_1 to AS_2 accommodated the rapid increase in aggregate demand and kept inflation mild. This remarkable combination of rapid productivity growth, rapid real GDP growth, full employment, and relative price-level stability led some observers to proclaim that the United States was experiencing a "new era" or a New Economy.

But in 2001 the New Economy came face-to-face with the old economic principles. Aggregate demand declined because of a substantial fall in investment spending, and in March 2001 the economy experienced a recession. The terrorist attacks of September 11, 2001, further dampened private spending and prolonged the recession throughout 2001. The unemployment rate rose from 4.2 percent in January 2001 to 6 percent in December 2002.

Throughout 2001 the Federal Reserve lowered interest rates to try to halt the recession and promote recovery. Those Fed actions, along with Federal tax cuts, increased military spending, and strong demand for new housing, helped spur recovery. The economy haltingly resumed its economic growth in 2002 and 2003.

We will examine stabilization policies, such as those carried out by the Federal government and the Federal Reserve, in chapters that follow. We will also discuss what remains of the New Economy thesis in more detail. **(Key Questions 5, 6, and 7)**

Are the High Unemployment Rates in Europe the Result of Structural Problems or of Deficient Aggregate Demand?

Several European economies have had high unemployment rates in the past several years. For example, in 2000 France had an unemployment rate of 9.3 percent; Italy, 10.4 percent; Germany, 7.8 percent; and Spain, 11.3 percent. These rates compared to a 4 percent unemployment rate in the United States in 2000. Even when the recession of 2001 pushed the unemployment rate in the United States to 5.8 percent, the European rates remained well above the U.S. rate. Specifically, in 2002 the percentage rates for France, Italy, Germany, and Spain were 8.7, 9, 8.2, and 11.4 percent, respectively.

Why are European unemployment rates so high? There are two views on this question.

High Natural Rates of Unemployment Many economists believe the high unemployment rates in Europe largely reflect high natural rates of unemployment. They envision a situation as in Figure 11.6, where aggregate demand and aggregate supply have produced the full-employment level of real output. But high levels of frictional and structural unemployment accompany such a level of output. In this view, the recent extensive unemployment in Europe has resulted from a high natural rate of unemployment, not from deficient aggregate demand. An increase in aggregate demand would push these economies beyond their full-employment levels of output, causing demand-pull inflation.

The sources of the high natural rates of unemployment are government policies and union contracts that have increased the costs of hiring workers and have reduced the cost of being unemployed. Examples: High minimum wages have discouraged employers from hiring low-skilled workers; generous welfare benefits have weakened incentives for people to take available jobs;

restrictions against firings have discouraged firms from employing workers; 30 to 40 days per year of paid vacations and holidays have boosted the cost of hiring workers; high worker absenteeism has reduced productivity; and high employer costs of health, pension, disability, and other benefits have discouraged hiring.

Deficient Aggregate Demand Not all economists agree that government and union policies have pushed up Europe's natural rate of unemployment. Instead, they point to insufficient aggregate demand as the problem. They see the European economies in terms of Figure 11.8, where the equilibrium real output Q_1 is less than it would be if aggregate demand were stronger. The argument is that the European governments have been so fearful of inflation that they have not undertaken appropriate fiscal and monetary policies (discussed in Chapters 12 and 15) to increase aggregate demand. In this view, increases in aggregate demand would not be inflationary, since these economies have considerable excess capacity. If they are operating in what in effect is a horizontal range of their aggregate supply curves, a rightward shift of their aggregate demand curves would expand output and employment without increasing inflation.

Conclusion: The debate over high unemployment in Europe reflects disagreement on where European aggregate demand curves lie relative to full-employment levels of output. If these curves are at the full-employment real GDP, as in Figure 11.6, then the high levels of unemployment are "natural." Public policies should focus on lowering minimum wages, reducing vacation time, reducing welfare benefits, easing restrictions on layoffs, and so on. But if the aggregate demand curves in the European nations lie to the left of their full-employment levels of output, as in Figure 11.8, then expansionary government policies such as reduced interest rates or tax cuts may be in order.

SUMMARY

1. The aggregate demand–aggregate supply model (AD-AS model) is a variable-price model that enables analysis of simultaneous changes of real GDP and the price level.

2. The aggregate demand curve shows the level of real output that the economy will purchase at each price level.

3. The aggregate demand curve is downsloping because of the real-balances effect, the interest-rate effect, and the foreign

purchases effect. The real-balances effect indicates that inflation reduces the real value or purchasing power of fixed-value financial assets held by households, causing cutbacks in consumer spending. The interest-rate effect means that, with a specific supply of money, a higher price level increases the demand for money, thereby raising the interest rate and reducing investment purchases. The foreign

207

purchases effect suggests that an increase in one country's price level relative to the price levels in other countries reduces the net export component of that nation's aggregate demand.

4. The determinants of aggregate demand consist of spending by domestic consumers, by businesses, by government, and by foreign buyers. Changes in the factors listed in Figure 11.2 alter the spending by these groups and shift the aggregate demand curve. The extent of the shift is determined by the size of the initial change in spending and the strength of the economy's multiplier.

5. The aggregate supply curve shows the levels of real output that businesses will produce at various possible price levels. The long-run aggregate supply curve assumes that nominal wages and other input prices fully match any change in the price level. The curve is vertical at the full-employment output.

6. The short-run aggregate supply curve (or simply "aggregate supply curve") assumes nominal wages and other input prices do not respond to price-level changes. The aggregate supply curve is generally upsloping because per-unit production costs, and hence the prices that firms must receive, rise as real output expands. The aggregate supply curve is relatively steep to the right of the full-employment output and relatively flat to the left of it.

7. Figure 11.5 lists the determinants of aggregate supply: input prices, productivity, and the legal-institutional environment. A change in any one of these factors will change per-unit production costs at each level of output and therefore will shift the aggregate supply curve.

8. The intersection of the aggregate demand and aggregate supply curves determines an economy's equilibrium price level and real GDP. At the intersection, the quantity of real GDP demanded equals the quantity of real GDP supplied.

9. Increases in aggregate demand to the right of the full-employment output cause inflation and positive GDP gaps (actual GDP exceeds potential GDP). An upsloping aggregate supply curve weakens the multiplier effect of an increase in aggregate demand because a portion of the increase in aggregate demand is dissipated in inflation.

10. Shifts of the aggregate demand curve to the left of the full employment output cause recession, negative GDP gaps, and cyclical unemployment. The price level may not fall during recessions because of downwardly inflexible prices and wages. This inflexibility results from wage contracts, efficiency wages, menu costs, minimum wages, and fear of price wars. When the price level is fixed, full multiplier effects occur along what, in essence, is a horizontal portion of the aggregate supply curve.

11. Leftward shifts of the aggregate supply curve reflect increases in per-unit production costs and cause cost-push inflation, with accompanying negative GDP gaps.

12. Rightward shifts of the aggregate supply curve, caused by large improvements in productivity, help explain the simultaneous achievement of full employment, economic growth, and price stability that occurred in the United States between 1996 and 2000. The recession of 2001, however, ended the expansionary phase of the business cycle.

TERMS AND CONCEPTS

aggregate demand–aggregate supply (AD-AS) model

aggregate demand

real-balances effect

interest-rate effect

foreign purchases effect

determinants of aggregate demand

aggregate supply

long-run aggregate supply curve

short-run aggregate supply curve

determinants of aggregate supply

productivity

equilibrium price level

equilibrium real output

efficiency wages

menu costs

STUDY QUESTIONS

1. Why is the aggregate demand curve downsloping? Specify how your explanation differs from the explanation for the downsloping demand curve for a single product. What role does the multiplier play in shifts of the aggregate demand curve?

2. Distinguish between "real-balances effect" and "wealth effect," as the terms are used in this chapter. How does each relate to the aggregate demand curve?

3. Why is the long-run aggregate supply curve vertical? Explain the shape of the short-run aggregate supply

curve. Why is the short-run curve relatively flat to the left of the full-employment output and relatively steep to the right?

4. *Key Question* Suppose that the aggregate demand and supply schedules for a hypothetical economy are as shown below:

Amount of Real GDP Demanded, Billions	Price Level (Price Index)	Amount of Real GDP Supplied, Billions
$100	300	$450
200	250	400
300	200	300
400	150	200
500	100	100

a. Use these sets of data to graph the aggregate demand and aggregate supply curves. What is the equilibrium price level and the equilibrium level of real output in this hypothetical economy? Is the equilibrium real output also necessarily the full-employment real output? Explain.

b. Why will a price level of 150 not be an equilibrium price level in this economy? Why not 250?

c. Suppose that buyers desire to purchase $200 billion of extra real output at each price level. Sketch in the new aggregate demand curve as AD_1. What factors might cause this change in aggregate demand? What is the new equilibrium price level and level of real output?

5. *Key Question* Suppose that a hypothetical economy has the following relationship between its real output and the input quantities necessary for producing that output:

Input Quantity	Real GDP
150.0	$400
112.5	300
75.0	200

a. What is productivity in this economy?

b. What is the per-unit cost of production if the price of each input unit is $2?

c. Assume that the input price increases from $2 to $3 with no accompanying change in productivity. What is the new per-unit cost of production? In what direction would the $1 increase in input price push the economy's aggregate supply curve? What effect would this shift of aggregate supply have on the price level and the level of real output?

d. Suppose that the increase in input price does not occur but, instead, that productivity increases by 100 percent. What would be the new per-unit cost of production? What effect would this change in per-unit production cost have on the economy's aggregate supply curve? What effect would this shift of aggregate supply have on the price level and the level of real output?

6. *Key Question* What effects would each of the following have on aggregate demand or aggregate supply? In each case use a diagram to show the expected effects on the equilibrium price level and the level of real output. Assume all other things remain constant.
   a. A widespread fear of depression on the part of consumers.
   b. A $2 increase in the excise tax on a pack of cigarettes.
   c. A reduction in interest rates at each price level.
   d. A major increase in Federal spending for health care.
   e. The expectation of rapid inflation.
   f. The complete disintegration of OPEC, causing oil prices to fall by one-half.
   g. A 10 percent reduction in personal income tax rates.
   h. A sizable increase in labor productivity (with no change in nominal wages).
   i. A 12 percent increase in nominal wages (with no change in productivity).
   j. Depreciation in the international value of the dollar.

7. *Key Question* Other things equal, what effect will each of the following have on the equilibrium price level and level of real output?
   a. An increase in aggregate demand in the steep portion of the aggregate supply curve.
   b. An increase in aggregate supply, with no change in aggregate demand (assume that prices and wages are flexible upward and downward).
   c. Equal increases in aggregate demand and aggregate supply.
   d. A reduction in aggregate demand in the flat portion of the aggregate supply curve.
   e. An increase in aggregate demand and a decrease in aggregate supply.

8. Explain how an upsloping aggregate supply curve weakens the realized multiplier effect.

9. Why does a reduction in aggregate demand reduce real output, rather than the price level? Why might a full-strength multiplier apply to a decrease in aggregate demand?

10. Explain: "Unemployment can be caused by a decrease of aggregate demand or a decrease of aggregate supply." In each case, specify the price-level outcomes.

11. Use shifts of the AD and AS curves to explain (*a*) the U.S. experience of strong economic growth, full employment, and price stability in the late 1990s and early 2000s and (*b*) how a strong negative wealth effect from, say, a precipitous drop in the stock market could cause a recession even though productivity is surging.

12. In early 2001 investment spending sharply declined in the United States. In the 2 months following the September 11, 2001, attacks on the United States, consumption also declined. Use AD-AS analysis to show the two impacts on real GDP.

13. *(Last Word)* State the alternative views on why unemployment in Europe has recently been so high. What are the policy implications of each view?

14. *Web-Based Question: Feeling wealthier; spending more?* Access the Bureau of Economic Analysis website, www.bea.gov/, interactively via the National Income and Product Account Tables. From Table 1.2 find the annual levels of real GDP and real consumption for 1996 and 1999. Did consumption increase more rapidly or less rapidly in percentage terms than real GDP? At http://dowjones.com in sequence select Dow Jones Industrial Average, Index Data, and Historical Values to find the level of the DJI on June 1, 1996, and June 1, 1999. What was the percentage change in the DJI over that period? How might that change help explain your findings about the growth of consumption versus real GDP between 1996 and 1999?

15. *Web-Based Question: The recession of 2001—which component of AD declined the most?* Use the interactive feature of the Bureau of Economic Analysis website, www.bea.gov/, to access the National Income and Product Account Tables. From Table 1.2 find the levels of real GDP, personal consumption expenditures (C), gross private investment (I_g), net exports (X_n), and government consumption expenditures and gross investment (G) in the first and third quarters of 2001. By what percentage did real GDP decline over this period? Which of the four broad components of aggregate demand decreased by the largest percentage amount?

The Relationship of the Aggregate Demand Curve to the Aggregate Expenditures Model*

The aggregate demand curve of this chapter and the aggregate expenditures model of Chapter 10 are intricately related.

Derivation of the Aggregate Demand Curve from the Aggregate Expenditures Model

We can directly connect the downward-sloping aggregate demand curve to the aggregate expenditures model by relating various possible price levels to corresponding equilibrium GDPs. In Figure 1 we have stacked the aggregate expenditures model (Figure 1a) and the aggregate demand curve (Figure 1b) vertically. This is possible because the horizontal axes of both models measure real GDP. Now let's derive the AD curve in three distinct steps. (Throughout this discussion, keep in mind that price level P_1 is lower than price level P_2, which is lower than price level P_3.)

- First suppose that the economy's price level is P_1 and its aggregate expenditures schedule is AE_1, the top schedule in Figure 1a. The equilibrium GDP is then Q_1 at point 1. So in Figure 1b we can plot the equilibrium real output Q_1 and the corresponding price level P_1. This gives us one point 1′ in Figure 1b.
- Now assume the price level rises from P_1 to P_2. Other things equal, this higher price level will (1) decrease the value of real balances (wealth), decreasing consumption expenditures; (2) increase the interest rate, reducing investment and interest-sensitive consumption expenditures; and (3) increase imports and decrease exports, reducing net export expenditures. The aggregate expenditures schedule will fall from AE_1 to, say, AE_2 in Figure 1a, giving us equilibrium Q_2 at point 2. In Figure 1b we plot this new price-level–real-output combination, P_2 and Q_2, as point 2′.

*This appendix presumes knowledge of the aggregate expenditures model discussed in Chapter 10 and should be skipped if Chapter 10 was not assigned.

FIGURE 1

Deriving the aggregate demand curve from the expenditures-output model. (a) Rising price levels from P_1 to P_2 to P_3 shift the aggregate expenditures curve downward from AE_1 to AE_2 to AE_3 and reduce real GDP from Q_1 to Q_2 to Q_3. (b) The aggregate demand curve AD is derived by plotting the successively lower real GDPs from the upper graph against the P_1, P_2, and P_3 price levels.

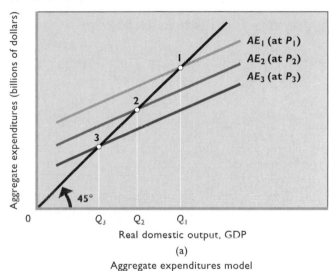

(a)
Aggregate expenditures model

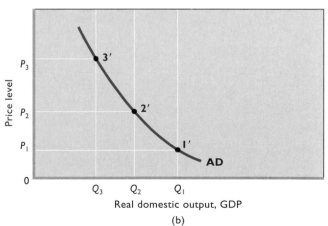

(b)
Aggregate demand–aggregate supply model

211

- Finally, suppose the price level rises from P_2 to P_3. The value of real balances falls, the interest rate rises, exports fall, and imports rise. Consequently, the consumption, investment, and net export schedules fall, shifting the aggregate expenditures schedule downward from AE_2 to AE_3, which gives us equilibrium Q_3 at point 3. In Figure 1b, this enables us to locate point 3′, where the price level is P_3 and real output is Q_3.

In summary, increases in the economy's price level will successively shift its aggregate expenditures schedule downward and will reduce real GDP. The resulting price-level–real-GDP combinations will yield various points such as 1′, 2′, and 3′ in Figure 1b. Together, such points locate the downward-sloping aggregate demand curve for the economy.

Aggregate Demand Shifts and the Aggregate Expenditures Model

The determinants of aggregate demand listed in Figure 11.2 are the components of the aggregate expenditures model discussed in Chapter 10. When there is a change in one of the determinants of aggregate demand, the aggregate expenditures schedule shifts upward or downward. We can easily link such shifts of the aggregate expenditures schedule to shifts of the aggregate demand curve.

Let's suppose that the price level is constant. In Figure 2 we begin with the aggregate expenditures schedule at AE_1 in the top diagram, yielding real output of Q_1. Assume now that investment increases in response to more optimistic business expectations, so the aggregate expenditures schedule rises from AE_1 to AE_2. (The notation "at P_1" reminds us that the price level is assumed constant.) The result will be a multiplied increase in real output from Q_1 to Q_2.

In Figure 2b the increase in investment spending is reflected in the horizontal distance between AD_1 and the broken curve to its right. The immediate effect of the increase in investment is an increase in aggregate demand by the exact amount of the new spending. But then the multiplier process magnifies the initial increase in investment into successive rounds of consumption spending and an ultimate multiplied increase in aggregate demand from AD_1 to AD_2. Equilibrium real output rises from Q_1 to Q_2, the same multiplied increase in real GDP as that in the top graph. The initial increase in investment in the top graph has shifted the AD curve in the lower graph by a horizontal distance equal to the change in investment

FIGURE 2

Shifts in the aggregate expenditures schedule and in the aggregate demand curve. (a) A change in some determinant of consumption, investment, or net exports (other than the price level) shifts the aggregate expenditures schedule upward from AE_1 to AE_2. The multiplier increases real output from Q_1 to Q_2. (b) The counterpart of this change is an initial rightward shift of the aggregate demand curve by the amount of initial new spending (from AD_1 to the broken curve). This leads to a multiplied rightward shift of the curve to AD_2, which is just sufficient to show the same increase or real output as that in the aggregate expenditures model.

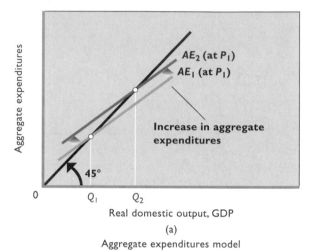

(a)
Aggregate expenditures model

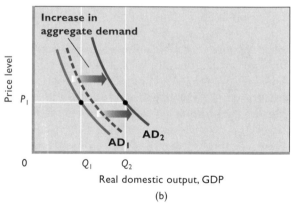

(b)
Aggregate demand–aggregate supply model

times the multiplier. This particular change in real GDP is still associated with the constant price level P_1. To generalize,

$$\text{Shift of AD curve} = \text{initial change in spending} \times \text{multiplier}$$

APPENDIX SUMMARY

1. A change in the price level alters the location of the aggregate expenditures schedule through the real-balances, interest-rate, and foreign purchases effects. The aggregate demand curve is derived from the aggregate expenditures model by allowing the price level to change and observing the effect on the aggregate expenditures schedule and thus on equilibrium GDP.

2. With the price level held constant, increases in consumption, investment, and net export expenditures shift the aggregate expenditures schedule upward and the aggregate demand curve to the right. Decreases in these spending components produce the opposite effects.

APPENDIX STUDY QUESTIONS

1. Explain carefully: "A change in the price level shifts the aggregate expenditures curve but not the aggregate demand curve."

2. Suppose that the price level is constant and that investment decreases sharply. How would you show this decrease in the aggregate expenditures model? What would be the outcome for real GDP? How would you show this fall in investment in the aggregate demand–aggregate supply model, assuming the economy is operating in what, in effect, is a horizontal range of the aggregate supply curve?

12 | *Fiscal Policy*

In the previous chapter we saw that a significant decline in aggregate demand can cause recession and cyclical unemployment, whereas an excessive increase in aggregate demand can cause demand-pull inflation. For those reasons, central governments sometimes use budgetary actions to try to "stimulate the economy" or "reign in inflation." Such countercyclical **fiscal policy** consists of deliberate changes in government spending and tax collections designed to achieve full employment, control inflation, and encourage economic growth.

12.1
Fiscal policy

What is the legal mandate for fiscal policy in the United States? What is the logic behind such policy? What is its current status? Why do some economists question its effectiveness?

Legislative Mandates

In the United States, the idea that government fiscal actions can exert a stabilizing influence on the economy emerged out of the Depression of the 1930s and the ascension of Keynesian economics. Since then, macroeconomic theory has played a major role both in the design of fiscal policy and in an improved understanding of its limitations.

Employment Act of 1946 In 1946, when the end of the Second World War raised anew the specter of unemployment, the Federal government passed the **Employment Act of 1946.** It commits the Federal government to use all practicable means, consistent with the market system, "to create economic conditions under

which there will be . . . employment opportunities, including self-employment, for those able, willing, and seeking to work, and to promote maximum employment, production, and purchasing power."

The Employment Act of 1946 is a landmark in American economic legislation. In effect, it commits the Federal government to take action through monetary and fiscal policy in order to maintain economic stability.

CEA and JEC The executive branch is responsible for fulfilling the purposes of the act; the president must submit an annual report to Congress that describes the current state of the economy and recommends policies to stabilize it. The act also established the **Council of Economic Advisers (CEA)** to assist and advise the president on economic matters and the *Joint Economic*

Committee (JEC) of Congress, which has since investigated a wide range of economic problems of national interest.

Fiscal Policy and the AD-AS Model

The fiscal policy that we have been describing is *discretionary* (or "active"). The changes in government spending and taxes are *at the option* of the Federal government. They do not occur automatically, independent of congressional action. The latter changes are *nondiscretionary* (or "passive" or "automatic"), and we will examine them later in this chapter.

Expansionary Fiscal Policy

When recession occurs, an **expansionary fiscal policy** may be in order. Consider Figure 12.1, where we suppose that a sharp decline in investment spending has shifted the economy's aggregate demand curve to the left from AD₁ to AD₂. (Disregard the arrows and dashed downsloping line for now.) The cause of the recession may be that profit expectations on investment projects have dimmed, curtailing investment spending and reducing aggregate demand.

Suppose the economy's potential or full-employment output is $510 billion in Figure 12.1. If the price level is inflexible downward at P_1, the broken horizontal line in effect becomes the relevant aggregate supply curve. The aggregate demand curve slides leftward along that broken line and reduces real GDP from $510 billion to $490 billion. A negative GDP gap of $20 (= $490 − $510)

billion arises. An increase in unemployment accompanies this negative GDP gap because fewer workers are needed to produce the reduced output. In short, the economy depicted is suffering both recession and cyclical unemployment.

What fiscal policy should the Federal government adopt to try to stimulate the economy? It has three main options: (1) Increase government spending, (2) reduce taxes, or (3) use some combination of the two. If the Federal budget is balanced at the outset, expansionary fiscal policy will create a government **budget deficit**—government spending in excess of tax revenues.

Increased Government Spending Other things equal, a sufficient increase in government spending will shift an economy's aggregate demand curve to the right, from AD₂ to AD₁ in Figure 12.1. To see why, suppose that the recession prompts the government to initiate $5 billion of new spending on highways, education, and health care. We represent this new $5 billion of government spending as the horizontal distance between AD₂ and the dashed line immediately to its right. At each price level, the amount of real output that is demanded is now $5 billion greater than that demanded before the expansion of government spending.

But the initial increase in aggregate demand is not the end of the story. Through the multiplier effect, the aggregate demand curve shifts to AD₁, a distance that exceeds that represented by the originating $5 billion increase in government purchases. This greater shift occurs because the multiplier process magnifies the initial change in spending into successive rounds of new consumption

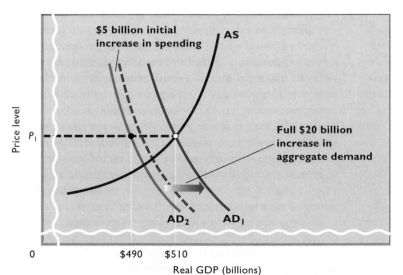

FIGURE 12.1

Expansionary fiscal policy. Expansionary fiscal policy uses increases in government spending or tax cuts to push the economy out of recession. In an economy with an MPC of .75, a $5 billion increase in government spending or a $6.67 billion decrease in personal taxes (producing a $5 billion initial increase in consumption) expands aggregate demand from AD₂ to the downsloping dashed curve. The multiplier then magnifies this initial increase in spending to AD₁. So real GDP rises along the horizontal broken aggregate supply segment by $20 billion.

spending. If the economy's MPC is .75, then the simple multiplier is 4. So the aggregate demand curve shifts rightward by four times the distance between AD_2 and the broken line. Because this *particular* increase in aggregate demand occurs along the horizontal broken-line segment of aggregate supply, real output rises by the full extent of the multiplier. Observe that real output rises to $510 billion, up $20 billion from its recessionary level of $490 billion. Concurrently, unemployment falls as firms increase their employment to the full-employment level that existed before the recession.

Tax Reductions Alternatively, the government could reduce taxes to shift the aggregate demand curve rightward, as from AD_2 to AD_1. Suppose the government cuts personal income taxes by $6.67 billion, which increases disposable income by the same amount. Consumption will rise by $5 billion (= MPC of .75 × $6.67 billion), and saving will go up by $1.67 billion (= MPS of .25 × $6.67 billion). In this case the horizontal distance between AD_2 and the dashed downsloping line in Figure 12.1 represents only the $5 billion initial increase in consumption spending. Again, we call it "initial" consumption spending because the multiplier process yields successive rounds of increased consumption spending. The aggregate demand curve eventually shifts rightward by four times the $5 billion initial increase in consumption produced by the tax cut. Real GDP rises by $20 billion, from $490 billion to $510 billion, implying a multiplier of 4. Employment increases accordingly.

You may have noted that a tax cut must be somewhat larger than the proposed increase in government spending if it is to achieve the same amount of rightward shift in the aggregate demand curve. This is because part of a tax reduction increases saving, rather than consumption. To increase initial consumption by a specific amount, the government must reduce taxes by more than that amount. With an MPC of .75, taxes must fall by $6.67 billion for $5 billion of new consumption to be forthcoming, because $1.67 billion is saved (not consumed). If the MPC had instead been, say, .6, an $8.33 billion reduction in tax collections would have been necessary to increase initial consumption by $5 billion. The smaller the MPC, the greater the tax cut needed to accomplish a specific initial increase in consumption and a specific shift in the aggregate demand curve.

Combined Government Spending Increases and Tax Reductions The government may combine spending increases and tax cuts to produce the desired initial increase in spending and the eventual increase in

aggregate demand and real GDP. In the economy depicted in Figure 12.1, the government might increase its spending by $1.25 billion while reducing taxes by $5 billion. As an exercise, you should explain why this combination will produce the targeted $5 billion initial increase in new spending.

If you were assigned Chapter 10, think through these three fiscal policy options in terms of the recessionary-gap analysis associated with the aggregate expenditures model (Figure 10.7). And recall from the appendix to Chapter 11 that rightward shifts of the aggregate demand curve relate directly to upward shifts of the aggregate expenditures schedule. **(Key Question 2)**

Contractionary Fiscal Policy

When demand-pull inflation occurs, a restrictive or **contractionary fiscal policy** may help control it. Take a look at Figure 12.2, where the full-employment level of real GDP is $510 billion. Suppose a sharp increase in investment and net export spending shifts the aggregate demand curve from AD_3 to AD_4. (Ignore the downsloping dashed line for now.) The outcomes are demand-pull inflation, as shown by the rise of the price level from P_1 to P_2, and a positive GDP gap of $12 billion (= $522 billion − $510 billion).

If the government looks to fiscal policy to control this inflation, its options are the opposite of those used to combat recession. It can (1) decrease government spending, (2) raise taxes, or (3) use some combination of those two policies. When the economy faces demand-pull inflation, fiscal policy should move toward a government **budget surplus**—tax revenues in excess of government spending.

Decreased Government Spending Reduced government spending shifts the aggregate demand curve leftward to control demand-pull inflation. In Figure 12.2, the horizontal distance between AD_4 and the dashed line to its left represents a $5 billion reduction in government spending. Once the multiplier process is complete, this spending cut will have shifted the aggregate demand curve leftward from AD_4 all the way to AD_3. If the price level were downwardly flexible, the price level would return to P_1, where it was before demand-pull inflation occurred. That is, deflation would occur.

Unfortunately, the actual economy is not as simple and tidy as Figure 12.2 suggests. Increases in aggregate demand tend to ratchet the price level upward, but declines in aggregate demand do not seem to push the price level

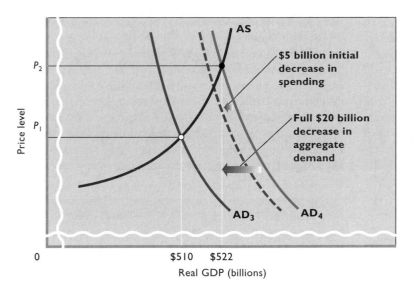

FIGURE 12.2

Contractionary fiscal policy. Contractionary fiscal policy uses decreases in government spending or increases in taxes to reduce demand-pull inflation. In an economy with an MPC of .75, a $5 billion decline in government spending or a $6.67 billion increase in taxes (producing a $5 billion initial decrease in consumption) shifts the aggregate demand curve from AD_4 to the dashed line. The multiplier effect then shifts the curve farther leftward to AD_3. The overall decrease in aggregate demand halts the demand-pull inflation.

downward. So stopping inflation is a matter of halting the rise of the price level, not trying to lower it to the previous level. Demand-pull inflation usually is experienced as a continual rightward shifting of the aggregate demand curve. Contractionary fiscal policy is designed to stop a further shift, not to restore a lower price level. Successful fiscal policy eliminates a continuing positive (and thus inflationary) GDP gap and prevents the price level from continuing its inflationary rise. Nevertheless, Figure 12.2 displays the basic principle: Reductions in government expenditures can be used as a fiscal policy action to tame demand-pull inflation.

Increased Taxes Just as government can use tax cuts to increase consumption spending, it can use tax *increases* to *reduce* consumption spending. If the economy in Figure 12.2 has an MPC of .75, the government must raise taxes by $6.67 billion to reduce consumption by $5 billion. The $6.67 billion tax reduces saving by $1.67 billion (= the MPS of .25 × $6.67 billion). This $1.67 billion reduction in saving, by definition, is not a reduction in spending. But the $6.67 billion tax increase also reduces consumption spending by $5 billion (= the MPC of .75 × $6.67 billion), as shown by the distance between AD_4 and the dashed line to its left in Figure 12.2. After the multiplier process is complete, aggregate demand will have shifted leftward by $20 billion at each price level (= multiplier of 4 × $5 billion) and the demand-pull inflation will have been controlled.

Combined Government Spending Decreases and Tax Increases The government may choose to combine spending decreases and tax increases in order to

reduce aggregate demand and check inflation. To check your understanding, determine why a $2 billion decline in government spending with a $4 billion increase in taxes would shift the aggregate demand curve from AD_4 to AD_3.

Also, if you were assigned Chapter 10, explain the three fiscal policy options for fighting inflation by referring to the inflationary-gap concept developed with the aggregate expenditures model (Figure 10.8). And recall from the appendix to Chapter 11 that leftward shifts of the aggregate demand curve are associated with downshifts of the aggregate expenditures schedule. **(Key Question 3)**

Financing of Deficits and Disposing of Surpluses

The expansionary effect of deficit spending on the economy depends on the method used to finance the deficit. Similarly, the anti-inflationary effect of a budget surplus depends on what is done with the surplus.

Borrowing versus New Money There are two ways the government can finance a deficit: borrowing from (selling interest-bearing bonds to) the public and, with the help of its monetary authorities, issuing new money to its creditors. The two methods have different effects on aggregate demand:

- *Borrowing from the public* If the government enters the money market and borrows, it will compete for funds with private business borrowers. This added demand for funds might drive up the interest rate and crowd out some private investment spending and interest-sensitive consumer spending. Any decline in private spending will weaken the expansionary effect of the deficit spending.

- *Money creation* If the central bank supports the deficit spending by creating new money, the crowding out of private spending can be avoided. In that case, federal spending can increase without adversely affecting investment or consumption. The creation of new money is more expansionary (but potentially more inflationary) than borrowing as a way of financing deficit spending.

Debt Retirement versus Idle Surplus Demand-pull inflation calls for fiscal action that will result in a budget surplus. But the anti-inflationary effect of the surplus depends on what the government does with it:

- *Debt reduction* Because the Federal government has a large public debt, it is logical to think that it should use the surplus to reduce the debt. Using the surplus to pay off debt, however, may reduce the anti-inflationary impact of the surplus. To retire its debt, the government buys back some of its bonds; by doing so, it transfers its surplus tax revenues back into the money market, causing interest rates to fall and thus private borrowing and spending to rise. The increase in private spending somewhat offsets the contractionary fiscal policy that created the budget surplus.

- *Impounding* The government can realize a greater anti-inflationary effect from its creation of a budget surplus by impounding the surplus funds—that is, by allowing them to stand idle. When a surplus is impounded, the government is extracting and withholding purchasing power from the economy. If surplus tax revenues are not put back into the economy, no portion of that surplus can be spent. Consequently, there is no chance that the surplus funds will create inflationary pressure to offset the anti-inflationary impact of the contractionary fiscal policy. Impounding a budget surplus is more anti-inflationary than using the surplus to retire public debt.

Policy Options: G or T?

Which is preferable as a means of eliminating recession and inflation? The use of government spending or the use of taxes? The answer depends largely on one's view as to whether the government is too large or too small.

Economists who believe there are many unmet social and infrastructure needs usually recommend that government spending be increased during recessions. In times of demand-pull inflation, they usually recommend tax

increases. Both actions either expand or preserve the size of government.

Economists who think that the government is too large and inefficient usually advocate tax cuts during recessions and cuts in government spending during times of demand-pull inflation. Both actions either restrain the growth of government or reduce its size.

The point is that discretionary fiscal policy designed to stabilize the economy can be associated with either an expanding government or a contracting government.

QUICK REVIEW 12.1

- The Employment Act of 1946 commits the Federal government to promoting "maximum employment, production, and purchasing power."
- Discretionary fiscal policy is the purposeful change of government expenditures and tax collections by government to promote full employment, price stability, and economic growth.
- The government uses expansionary fiscal policy to shift the aggregate demand curve rightward in order to expand real output. This policy entails increases in government spending, reductions in taxes, or some combination of the two.
- The government uses contractionary fiscal policy to shift the aggregate demand curve leftward in an effort to halt demand-pull inflation. This policy entails reductions in government spending, tax increases, or some combination of the two.
- The expansionary effect of fiscal policy is greater when the budget deficit is financed through money creation rather than through borrowing; the contractionary effect of the creation of a budget surplus is greater when the budget surplus is impounded rather than used for debt reduction.

Built-In Stability

To some degree, government tax revenues change automatically over the course of the business cycle and in ways that stabilize the economy. This automatic response, or built-in stability, constitutes nondiscretionary (or "passive" or "automatic") budgetary policy and results from the makeup of most tax systems. We did not include this built-in stability in our discussion of fiscal policy because we implicitly assumed that the same amount of tax revenue was being collected at each level of GDP. But the actual U.S. tax system is such that *net tax revenues* vary directly with GDP. (Net taxes are tax revenues less transfers and subsidies. From here on, we will use the simpler "taxes" to mean "net taxes.")

Virtually any tax will yield more tax revenue as GDP rises. In particular, personal income taxes have progressive rates and thus generate more-than-proportionate increases in tax revenues as GDP expands. Furthermore, as GDP rises and more goods and services are purchased, revenues from corporate income taxes and from sales taxes and excise taxes also increase. And, similarly, revenues from payroll taxes rise as economic expansion creates more jobs. Conversely, when GDP declines, tax receipts from all these sources also decline.

Transfer payments (or "negative taxes") behave in the opposite way from tax revenues. Unemployment compensation payments, welfare payments, and subsidies to farmers all decrease during economic expansion and increase during economic contraction.

Automatic or Built-In Stabilizers

A **built-in stabilizer** is anything that increases the government's budget deficit (or reduces its budget surplus) during a recession and increases its budget surplus (or reduces its budget deficit) during inflation without requiring explicit action by policymakers. As Figure 12.3 reveals, this is precisely what the U.S. tax system does. Government expenditures G are fixed and assumed to be independent of the level of GDP. Congress decides on a particular level of spending, but it does not determine the magnitude of tax revenues. Instead, it establishes tax rates, and the tax revenues then vary directly with the level of GDP that the economy achieves. Line T represents that direct relationship between tax revenues and GDP.

Economic Importance   The economic importance of the direct relationship between tax receipts and GDP becomes apparent when we consider that:
- Taxes reduce spending and aggregate demand.
- Reductions in spending are desirable when the economy is moving toward inflation, whereas increases in spending are desirable when the economy is slumping.

As shown in Figure 12.3, tax revenues automatically increase as GDP rises during prosperity, and since taxes reduce household and business spending, they restrain the economic expansion. That is, as the economy moves toward a higher GDP, tax revenues automatically rise and move the budget from deficit toward surplus. In Figure 12.3, observe that the high and perhaps inflationary income level GDP_3 automatically generates a contractionary budget surplus.

Conversely, as GDP falls during recession, tax revenues automatically decline, increasing spending and cushioning the economic contraction. With a falling GDP, tax receipts decline and move the government's budget from surplus toward deficit. In Figure 12.3, the low level of income GDP_1 will automatically yield an expansionary budget deficit.

Tax Progressivity   Figure 12.3 reveals that the size of the automatic budget deficits or surpluses—and therefore built-in stability—depends on the responsiveness of tax revenues to changes in GDP. If tax revenues change sharply as GDP changes, the slope of line T in the figure will be steep and the vertical distances between T and G (the deficits or surpluses) will be large. If tax revenues change very little when GDP changes, the slope will be gentle and built-in stability will be low.

The steepness of T in Figure 12.3 depends on the tax system itself. In a **progressive tax system,** the average tax rate (= tax revenue/GDP) rises with GDP. In a **proportional tax system,** the average tax rate remains constant as GDP rises. In a **regressive tax system,** the average tax rate falls as GDP rises. The progressive tax system has the steepest tax line T of the three. However, tax revenues will rise with GDP under both the progressive and the proportional tax systems, and they may rise, fall, or stay the same under a regressive tax system. The main point is this: *The more progressive the tax system, the greater the economy's built-in stability.*

FIGURE 12.3

Built-in stability. Tax revenues T vary directly with GDP, and government spending G is assumed to be independent of GDP. As GDP falls in a recession, deficits occur automatically and help alleviate the recession. As GDP rises during expansion, surpluses occur automatically and help offset possible inflation.

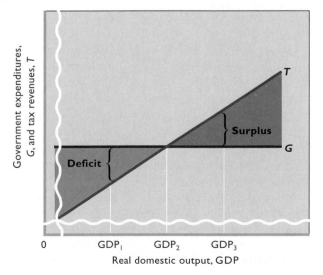

So changes in public policies or laws that alter the progressivity of the tax system affect the degree of built-in stability. For example, in 1993 the Clinton administration increased the highest marginal tax rate on personal income from 31 to 39.6 percent and boosted the corporate income tax 1 percentage point, to 35 percent. These increases in tax rates raised the overall progressivity of the tax system, bolstering the economy's built-in stability. As the economy expanded vigorously in the late 1990s, the Federal budget swung from deficit to surplus. That swing helped dampen private spending and forestall demand-pull inflation.

The built-in stability provided by the U.S. tax system has reduced the severity of business fluctuations, perhaps by as much as 8 to 10 percent of the change in GDP that otherwise would have occurred. But built-in stabilizers can only diminish, not eliminate, swings in real GDP. Discretionary fiscal policy (changes in tax rates and expenditures) or monetary policy (central bank–caused changes in interest rates) may be needed to correct recession or inflation of any appreciable magnitude.

Evaluating Fiscal Policy

How can we determine whether discretionary fiscal policy is expansionary, neutral, or contractionary in a particular period? We cannot simply examine changes in the actual budget deficits or surpluses, because those changes may reflect automatic changes in tax revenues that accompany changes in GDP, not changes in discretionary fiscal policy. Moreover, the strength of any deliberate change in government spending or taxes depends on how large it is relative to the size of the economy. So, in evaluating the status of fiscal policy, we must:

- Adjust deficits and surpluses to eliminate automatic changes in tax revenues.
- Compare the sizes of the adjusted budget deficits (or surpluses) to the levels of potential GDP.

Full-Employment Budget

Economists use the **full-employment budget** (also called the *standardized budget*) to adjust the actual Federal budget deficits and surpluses to eliminate the automatic changes in tax revenues. The full-employment budget measures what the Federal budget deficit or surplus would be with existing tax rates and government spending levels if the economy had achieved its full-employment level of GDP (its potential output) in each year. The idea is to compare *actual* government expenditures for each year with the tax revenues *that would have occurred* in that year if the

economy had achieved full-employment GDP. That procedure removes budget deficits or surpluses that arise simply because of changes in GDP and thus tell us nothing about changes in discretionary fiscal policy.

Consider Figure 12.4a, where line G represents government expenditures and line T represents tax revenues. In full-employment year 1, government expenditures of $500 billion equal tax revenues of $500 billion, as indicated by the intersection of lines G and T at point a. The full-employment budget deficit in year 1 is zero—government expenditures equal the tax revenues forthcoming at the full-employment output GDP_1. Obviously, the full-employment deficit *as a percentage of potential GDP* is also zero.

Now suppose that a recession occurs and GDP falls from GDP_1 to GDP_2, as shown in Figure 12.4a. Let's also assume that the government takes no discretionary action, so lines G and T remain as shown in the figure. Tax revenues automatically fall to $450 billion (point c) at GDP_2, while government spending remains unaltered at $500 billion (point b). A $50 billion budget deficit (represented by distance bc) arises. But this **cyclical deficit** is simply a by-product of the economy's slide into recession, not the result of discretionary fiscal actions by the government. We would be wrong to conclude from this deficit that the government is engaging in an expansionary fiscal policy.

That fact is highlighted when we consider the full-employment budget deficit for year 2 in Figure 12.4a. The $500 billion of government expenditures in year 2 are shown by b on line G. And, as shown by a on line T, $500 billion of tax revenues would have occurred if the economy had achieved its full-employment GDP. Because both b and a represent $500 billion, the full-employment budget deficit in year 2 is zero, as is this deficit as a percentage of potential GDP. Since the full-employment deficits are zero in both years, we know that government did not change its discretionary fiscal policy, even though a recession occurred and an actual deficit of $50 billion resulted.

Next, consider Figure 12.4b. Suppose that real output declined from full-employment GDP_3 to GDP_4. But also suppose that the Federal government responded to the recession by reducing tax rates in year 4, as represented by the downward shift of the tax line from T_1 to T_2. What has happened to the size of the full-employment deficit? Government expenditures in year 4 are $500 billion, as shown by e. We compare that amount with the $475 billion of tax revenues that would occur if the economy achieved its full-employment GDP. That is, we compare position e on line G with position h on line T_2.

FIGURE 12.4

Full-employment deficits. (a) In the left-hand graph the full-employment deficit is zero at the full-employment output GDP_1. But it is also zero at the recessionary output GDP_2, because the $500 billion of government expenditures at GDP_2 equals the $500 of tax revenues that would be forthcoming at the full-employment GDP_1. There has been no change in fiscal policy. (b) In the right-hand graph, discretionary fiscal policy, as reflected in the downward shift of the tax line from T_1 to T_2, has increased the full-employment budget deficit from zero in year 3 to $25 billion in year 4. This is found by comparing the $500 billion of government spending in year 4 with the $475 billion of taxes that would accrue at the full-employment GDP_3. Such a rise in the full-employment deficit (as a percentage of potential GDP) identifies an expansionary fiscal policy.

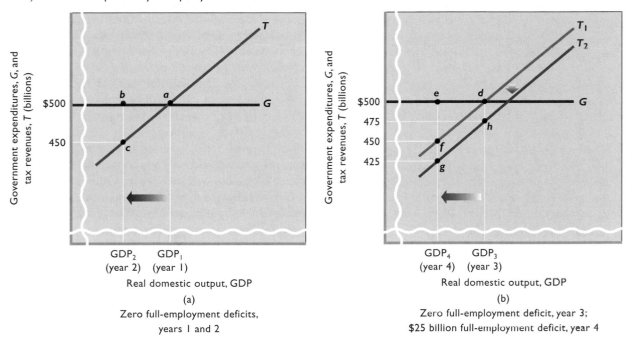

(a)
Zero full-employment deficits,
years 1 and 2

(b)
Zero full-employment deficit, year 3;
$25 billion full-employment deficit, year 4

The $25 billion of tax revenues by which e exceeds h is the full-employment budget deficit for year 4. (It is equal to the actual deficit of eg in year 4 *minus* the cyclical deficit of ef.) As a percentage of potential GDP, the full-employment budget deficit has increased from zero in year 3 (before the tax-rate cut) to some positive percent [= ($25 *billion*/$GDP_3$) $\times$ 100] in year 4. This increase in the relative size of the full-employment deficit between the two years reveals that fiscal policy is *expansionary*.

In contrast, if we observed a full-employment deficit (as a percentage of potential GDP) of zero in one year, followed by a full-employment budget surplus in the next, we could conclude that fiscal policy is contractionary. Because the full-employment budget adjusts for automatic changes in tax revenues, the increase in the full-employment budget surplus reveals that government either decreased its spending (G) or increased tax rates such that tax revenues (T) increased. These changes in G and T are precisely the discretionary actions that we have identified as elements of a *contractionary* fiscal policy.

Recent U.S. Fiscal Policy

Table 12.1 lists the actual Federal budget deficits and surpluses (column 2) and the full-employment deficits and surpluses (column 3), as percentages of actual and potential GDP, respectively, for recent years. Observe that the full-employment deficits are generally smaller than the actual deficits. This is because the actual deficits include cyclical deficits, whereas the full-employment deficits do not. The latter deficits provide the information needed to assess discretionary fiscal policy.

Column 3 shows that fiscal policy was expansionary in the early 1990s. Consider 1992, for example. From the table we see that the actual budget deficit was 4.7 percent of GDP and the full-employment budget deficit was 2.9 percent of potential GDP. The economy was recovering from the 1990–1991 recession, so tax revenues were relatively low. But even if the economy were at full employment in 1992, with the greater tax revenues that would imply, the Federal budget would have been in deficit by

TABLE 12.1

Federal Deficits (−) and Surpluses (+) as Percentages of GDP, 1990–2002

(1) Year	(2) Actual Deficit or Surplus	(3) Full-Employment Deficit or Surplus*
1990	−3.9%	−2.1%
1991	−4.5	−2.4
1992	−4.7	−2.9
1993	−3.9	−2.8
1994	−2.9	−2.1
1995	−2.2	−2.0
1996	−1.4	−1.3
1997	−0.3	−0.9
1998	+0.8	−0.4
1999	+1.4	+0.3
2000	+2.4	+1.1
2001	+1.3	+0.8
2002	−1.5	−1.5

*As a percentage of potential GDP.
Source: Congressional Budget Office, www.cbo.gov.

2.9 percent. And that percentage was greater than the deficits in the prior two years. So the full-employment budget deficit in 1992 clearly reflected expansionary fiscal policy.

But the large full-employment budget deficits were projected to continue even when the economy fully recovered from the 1990–1991 recession. The concern was that the large actual and full-employment deficits would cause high interest rates, low levels of investment, and slow economic growth. In 1993 the Clinton administration and Congress increased personal income and corporate income tax rates to prevent these potential outcomes. Observe from column 3 of Table 12.1 that the full-employment budget deficits shrunk each year and eventually gave way to surpluses in 1999, 2000, and 2001.

On the basis of projections that actual budget surpluses would accumulate to as much as $5 trillion between 2000 and 2010, the Bush administration and Congress passed a major tax reduction package in 2001. The tax cuts went into effect over a number of years. For example, the cuts reduced tax liabilities by an estimated $44 billion in 2001 and $52 billion in 2002. In terms of fiscal policy, the timing was good since the economy entered a recession in March 2001 and absorbed a second economic blow from the terrorist attacks on September 11, 2001. The government greatly increased its spending on war abroad and homeland security. Also, in March 2002 Congress passed a "recession-relief" bill that extended unemployment compensation benefits

and offered business tax relief. That legislation was specifically designed to interject $51 billion into the economy in 2002 and another $71 billion over the following 2 years.

As seen in Table 12.1, the full-employment budget moved from a *surplus* of 1.1 percent of potential GDP in 2000 to a *deficit* of 1.5 percent in 2002. Clearly, fiscal policy had turned expansionary. Nevertheless, the economy remained very sluggish in 2003. In June of that year, Congress again cut taxes, this time by an enormous $350 billion over several years. Specifically, the tax legislation accelerated the reduction of marginal tax rates already scheduled for future years and slashed tax rates on income from dividends and capital gains. It also increased tax breaks for families and small businesses. This tax package was expected to significantly increase the full-employment budget deficit as a percentage of potential GDP in 2003. The purpose of this expansionary fiscal policy was to prevent another recession, reduce unemployment, and increase economic growth. **(Key Question 7)**

Global Perspective 12.1 shows the extent of the full-employment budget deficits or surpluses of a number of countries in a recent year.

GLOBAL PERSPECTIVE 12.1

Full-Employment Budget Deficits or Surpluses as a Percentage of Potential GDP, Selected Nations

In 2002 some nations had full-employment budget surpluses, while others had full-employment budget deficits. These surpluses and deficits varied as a percentage of each nation's potential GDP. Generally, the surpluses represented contractionary fiscal policy and the deficits expansionary fiscal policy.

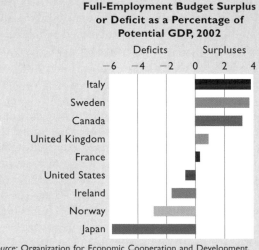

Full-Employment Budget Surplus or Deficit as a Percentage of Potential GDP, 2002

Source: Organization for Economic Cooperation and Development, www.oecd.org. Data are 2002 estimates.

Problems, Criticisms, and Complications

Economists recognize that governments may encounter a number of significant problems in enacting and applying fiscal policy.

Problems of Timing

Several problems of timing may arise in connection with fiscal policy:

- **Recognition lag**   The recognition lag is the time between the beginning of recession or inflation and the certain awareness that it is actually happening. This lag arises because of the difficulty in predicting the future course of economic activity. Although forecasting tools such as the index of leading indicators (see this chapter's Last Word) provide clues to the direction of the economy, the economy may be 4 or 6 months into a recession or inflation before that fact appears in relevant statistics and is acknowledged. Meanwhile, the economic downside or the inflation may become more serious than it would have if the situation had been identified and acted on sooner.

- **Administrative lag**   The wheels of democratic government turn slowly. There will typically be a significant lag between the time the need for fiscal action is recognized and the time action is taken. Following the terrorist attacks of September 11, 2001, the U.S. Congress was stalemated for 5 months before passing a compromise economic stimulus law in March 2002.

(In contrast, the Federal Reserve began lowering interest rates the week after the attacks.)

- **Operational lag**   A lag also occurs between the time fiscal action is taken and the time that action affects output, employment, or the price level. Although changes in tax rates can be put into effect relatively quickly, government spending on public works—new dams, interstate highways, and so on—requires long planning periods and even longer periods of construction. Such spending is of questionable use in offsetting short (for example, 6- to 12-month) periods of recession. Consequently, discretionary fiscal policy has increasingly relied on tax changes rather than on changes in spending as its main tool.

Political Considerations

Fiscal policy is conducted in a political arena. That reality not only may slow the enactment of fiscal policy but also may create the potential for political considerations swamping economic considerations in its formulation. It is a human trait to rationalize actions and policies that are in one's self-interest. Politicians are very human—they want to get reelected. A strong economy at election time will certainly help them. So they may favor large tax cuts under the guise of expansionary fiscal policy even though that policy is economically inappropriate. Similarly, they may rationalize increased government spending on popular items such as farm subsidies, health care, education, and homeland security.

At the extreme, elected officials and political parties might collectively "hijack" fiscal policy for political purposes, cause inappropriate changes in aggregate demand, and thereby cause (rather than avert) economic fluctuations. They may stimulate the economy using expansionary fiscal policy before elections and use contractionary fiscal policy to dampen excessive aggregate demand after the election. In short, elected officials may cause so-called **political business cycles.** Such scenarios are difficult to document and prove, but there is little doubt that political considerations weigh heavily in the formulation of fiscal policy. The question is how often, if ever, those political considerations run counter to "sound economics."

Future Policy Reversals

Fiscal policy may fail to achieve its intended objectives if households expect future reversals of policy. Consider a tax cut, for example. If taxpayers believe the tax reduction is temporary, they may save a large portion of their tax saving, reasoning that rates will return to their previous level in the future. At that time, they can draw on this extra saving to maintain their consumption then. So a tax reduction thought to be temporary may not increase present consumption spending and aggregate demand by as much as our simple model (Figure 12.1) suggests.

The opposite may be true for a tax increase. If tax-payers think it is temporary, they may reduce their saving to pay the tax while maintaining their present consumption. They may reason that they can restore their saving when the tax rate again falls. So the tax increase may not reduce current consumption and aggregate demand by as much as the policymakers desired.

To the extent that this so-called consumption smoothing occurs over time, fiscal policy will lose some of its strength. The lesson is that tax-rate changes that households view as permanent are more likely to alter consumption and aggregate demand than tax changes they view as temporary.

Offsetting State and Local Finance

The fiscal policies of state and local governments are frequently *pro-cyclical*, meaning that they worsen rather than correct recession or inflation. Unlike the Federal government, most state and local governments face constitutional or other legal requirements to balance their budgets. Like households and private businesses, state and local governments increase their expenditures during prosperity and cut them during recession. During the Great Depression of the 1930s, most of the increase in Federal spending was offset by decreases in state and local spending. During and immediately following the recession of 2001, many state and local governments had to increase tax rates, impose new taxes, and reduce spending to offset lower tax revenues resulting from the reduced personal income and spending of their citizens.

Crowding-Out Effect

Another potential flaw of fiscal policy is the so-called **crowding-out effect**: An expansionary fiscal policy (deficit spending) may increase the interest rate and reduce private spending, thereby weakening or canceling the stimulus of the expansionary policy. In this view, fiscal policy may be largely or totally ineffective!

Suppose the economy is in recession and government enacts a discretionary fiscal policy in the form of increased government spending. Also suppose that the monetary authorities hold the supply of money constant. To finance its budget deficit, the government borrows funds in the money market. The resulting increase in the

12.2 Crowding out

demand for money raises the price paid for borrowing money: the interest rate. Because investment spending varies inversely with the interest rate, some investment will be choked off or crowded out. (Some interest-sensitive consumption spending such as purchases of automobiles on credit may also be crowded out).

Graphical Presentation Figure 12.5 shows the crowding-out effect graphically. Figure 12.5a shows the relevant aggregate demand and supply conditions. Suppose the economy has slid into a recession, with the price level currently at P_1 and real GDP at $490 billion. Assuming that the full-employment GDP (or potential GDP) is $510 billion, the economy is experiencing a $20 billion negative GDP gap.

Suppose now that government undertakes an expansionary fiscal policy that shifts the aggregate demand curve rightward along the broken aggregate supply segment from AD_1 to AD_2. The economy thus achieves full-employment output without inflation at $510 billion of real GDP. For simplicity, we will continue to assume the MPC is .75 and the multiplier is 4 (although it is closer to 2 in the real world). So an increase in government spending of $5 billion or a decrease in taxes of $6.67 billion would create this $20 billion expansionary effect. With no offsetting or complicating factors, this "pure and simple" expansionary fiscal policy eliminates the negative GDP gap and restores full-employment real GDP.

Figure 12.5b shows the complication of crowding out. While fiscal policy is expansionary and designed to shift aggregate demand from AD_1 to AD_2, the borrowing needed to finance the deficit spending presumably increases the interest rate and crowds out some investment spending. For example, suppose the interest rate rises from 5 percent to 5.2 percent and investment declines by $2 billion. The initial increase in government spending of $5 billion therefore is reduced to a *net* spending increase of only $3 billion because $2 billion of investment has been crowded out. The aggregate demand curve thus shifts only to AD_2', not to AD_2. Equilibrium real GDP expands to $502 billion rather than to the desired $510 billion and does not fully close the $20 billion negative GDP gap. Lesson: The crowding-out effect may weaken expansionary fiscal policy. If it is strong enough, it could render fiscal policy completely ineffective.

Criticisms of the Crowding-Out Effect Nearly all economists agree that a full-employment deficit is

FIGURE 12.5

Fiscal policy: the effects of crowding out and the net export effect. In (a), fiscal policy is uncomplicated and works at full strength to eliminate the $20 billion negative GDP gap and produce the full-employment real GDP of $510 billion. In (b) we assume that the expansionary fiscal policy drives up the interest rate and crowds out some amount of private investment. Fiscal policy is weakened, as evidenced by the rise in GDP to $502 billion rather than $510 billion. In (c)—the same graph as (b)—we assume that fiscal policy increases the interest rate, thereby attracting foreign financial capital to the United States. The dollar appreciates and U.S. net exports fall, weakening the expansionary fiscal policy. GDP again rises only to $502 billion rather than to $510 billion.

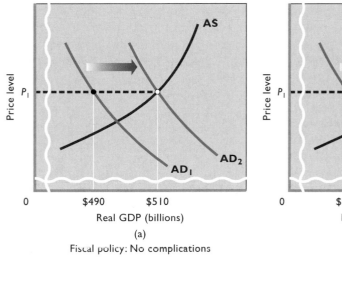

(a)
Fiscal policy: No complications

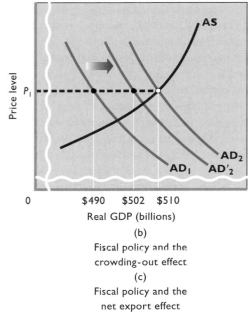

(b)
Fiscal policy and the
crowding-out effect
(c)
Fiscal policy and the
net export effect

inappropriate when the economy has achieved full employment. Such a deficit will surely crowd out private investment. But there is disagreement on whether crowding out exists under all circumstances. Many economists believe that little crowding out will occur when fiscal policy is used during a significant recession. Both increased government spending and increased consumption spending resulting from tax cuts will likely improve the profit expectations of businesses. The greater expected returns on private investment may encourage more of it. Thus, private investment need not fall, even though interest rates rise. (In terms of Figure 9.6, the investment demand curve *ID* may shift rightward sufficiently to offset a higher interest rate. So total investment need not decline.)

Critics also point out that policymakers (specifically the Federal Reserve) can counteract the crowding-out effect by increasing the supply of money just enough to offset the deficit-caused increase in the demand for money. Then the equilibrium interest rate would not change, and the crowding-out effect would be zero.

Fiscal Policy in the Open Economy

Additional complications arise from the fact that each national economy is a component of the world economy.

Shocks Originating from Abroad

Events and policies abroad that affect a nation's net exports also affect its own economy. National economies are vulnerable to unforeseen international aggregate demand shocks that can alter domestic GDP and make current domestic fiscal policy inappropriate.

Suppose the United States is in a recession and has enacted an expansionary fiscal policy to increase aggregate demand and GDP without igniting inflation (as from AD_1 to AD_2 in Figure 12.5a). Now suppose the economies of the major trading partners of the United States unexpectedly expand rapidly. Greater employment and rising incomes in those nations mean more purchases of U.S. goods. In the United States, net exports rise, and aggregate demand increases so rapidly that the nation experiences demand-pull inflation. If U.S. policymakers had known in advance that net exports might rise significantly, they would have enacted a less expansionary fiscal policy. Participation in the world economy inevitably brings with it the complications of mutual interdependence along with the gains derived from specialization and trade.

Net Export Effect

The **net export effect** may also work through international trade to reduce the effectiveness of fiscal policy. We concluded in our discussion of the crowding-out effect that an expansionary fiscal policy might boost interest rates, thereby reducing investment and weakening current fiscal policy. Now we ask what effect an interest-rate increase might have on a nation's net exports (exports minus imports).

Suppose the United States undertakes an expansionary fiscal policy that causes a higher U.S. interest rate. The higher interest rate will attract financial capital from abroad, where interest rates are unchanged. But foreign financial investors must acquire U.S. dollars in order to invest in U.S. securities. We know that an increase in the demand for a commodity (in this case, dollars) will cause its price to rise. So the price of dollars rises in terms of foreign currencies—that is, the dollar appreciates.

What will be the impact of that dollar appreciation on U.S. net exports? Because more units of foreign currencies are needed to buy goods from the United States, the rest of the world will see U.S. exports as being more expensive. Hence, U.S. exports will decline. Americans, who can now exchange their dollars for more units of foreign currencies, will buy more imports. Consequently, with U.S. exports falling and imports rising, net export expenditures in the United States will diminish. This is a contractionary change, so the expansionary fiscal policy of the United States will be partially negated.[1]

A return to our aggregate demand and supply analysis in Figure 12.5b, now labeled "c", will clarify this point. An expansionary fiscal policy aimed at increasing aggregate demand from AD_1 to AD_2 may hike the domestic interest rate and ultimately reduce net exports through the process just described. The decline in the net export component of aggregate demand will partially offset the expansionary fiscal policy. The aggregate demand curve might shift rightward from AD_1 to AD_2', *not* to AD_2, and equilibrium GDP would increase from $490 billion to $502 billion, *not* to $510 billion. Thus, the net export effect of fiscal policy joins the problems of timing, politics,

[1]The appreciation of the dollar will also reduce the dollar price of foreign resources imported into the United States. As a result, aggregate supply will increase and part of the contractionary net export effect described here may be offset.

TABLE 12.2
Fiscal Policy and the Net Export Effect

(1) Expansionary Fiscal Policy	(2) Contractionary Fiscal Policy
Problem: Recession, slow growth	Problem: Inflation
↓	↓
Expansionary fiscal policy	Contractionary fiscal policy
↓	↓
Higher domestic interest rate	Lower domestic interest rate
↓	↓
Increased foreign demand for dollars	Decreased foreign demand for dollars
↓	↓
Dollar appreciates	Dollar depreciates
↓	↓
Net exports decline (aggregate demand decreases, partially offsetting the expansionary fiscal policy)	Net exports increase (aggregate demand increases, partially offsetting the contractionary fiscal policy)

and crowding out in complicating the "management" of aggregate demand.

Table 12.2 summarizes the net export effect resulting from fiscal policy. Column 1 reviews the analysis just discussed (Figure 12.5c). But note that the net export effect works in both directions. By reducing the domestic interest rate, a contractionary fiscal policy increases net exports. With that in mind, follow through the analysis in column 2 in Table 12.2 and relate it to the aggregate demand–aggregate supply model. **(Key Question 10)**

QUICK REVIEW 12.3

- Time lags, political problems, expectations, and state and local finances complicate fiscal policy.
- The crowding-out effect indicates that an expansionary fiscal policy may increase the interest rate and reduce investment spending.
- Fiscal policy may be weakened by the net export effect, which works through changes in (a) the interest rate, (b) exchange rates, and (c) exports and imports.

One of Several Tools Policymakers Use to Forecast the Future Direction of Real GDP Is a Monthly Index of 10 Variables That in the Past Have Provided Advance Notice of Changes in GDP.

The Conference Board's *index of leading indicators* has historically reached a peak or a trough in advance of corresponding turns in the business cycle.* Thus changes in this composite index of 10 economic variables provide a clue to the future direction of the economy. Such advance warning helps policymakers formulate appropriate macroeconomic policy.

Here is how each of the 10 components of the index would change if it were predicting a decline in real GDP. The opposite changes would forecast a rise in real GDP.

1. Average workweek Decreases in the length of the average workweek of production workers in manufacturing foretell declines in future manufacturing output and possible declines in real GDP.

2. Initial claims for unemployment insurance Higher first-time claims for unemployment insurance are associated with falling employment and subsequently sagging real GDP.

3. New orders for consumer goods Decreases in the number of orders received by manufacturers for consumer goods portend reduced future production—a decline in real GDP.

4. Vendor performance Somewhat ironically, better on-time delivery by sellers of inputs indicates slackening business demand and potentially falling real GDP.

5. New orders for capital goods A drop in orders for capital equipment and other investment goods implies reduced future aggregate demand and thus lower real GDP.

6. Building permits for houses Decreases in the number of building permits issued for new homes imply future declines in investment and therefore the possibility that real GDP will fall.

7. Stock prices Declines in stock prices often are reflections of expected declines in corporate sales and profits. Also, lower stock prices diminish consumer wealth, leading to possible cutbacks in consumer spending. Lower stock prices also make it less attractive for firms to issue new shares of stock as a way

of raising funds for investment. Thus, declines in stock prices can bring forth declines in aggregate demand and real GDP.

8. Money supply Decreases in the nation's money supply are associated with falling real GDP.

9. Interest-rate spread Increases in short-term nominal interest rates typically reflect monetary policies designed to slow the economy. Such policies have much less effect on long-term interest rates, which usually are higher than short-term rates. So a smaller difference between short-term interest rates and long-term interest rates suggests restrictive monetary policies and potentially a future decline in GDP.

10. Consumer expectations Less favorable consumer attitudes about future economic conditions, measured by an index of consumer expectations, foreshadow lower consumption spending and potential future declines in GDP.

None of these factors alone consistently predicts the future course of the economy. It is not unusual in any month, for example, for one or two of the indicators to be decreasing while the other indicators are increasing. Rather, changes in the composite of the 10 components are what in the past have provided advance notice of a change in the direction of GDP. The rule of thumb is that three successive monthly declines or increases in the index indicate the economy will soon turn in that same direction.

Although the composite index has correctly signaled business fluctuations on numerous occasions, it has not been infallible. At times the index has provided false warnings of recessions that never happened. In other instances, recessions have so closely followed the downturn in the index that policymakers have not had sufficient time to make use of the "early" warning. Moreover, changing structural features of the economy have, on occasion, rendered the existing index obsolete and necessitated its revision.

Given these caveats, the index of leading indicators can best be thought of as a useful but not totally reliable signaling device that authorities must employ with considerable caution in formulating macroeconomic policy.

*The Conference Board is a private, nonprofit research and business membership group, with more than 2700 corporate and other members in 60 nations. See www.conferenceboard.org.

Current Thinking on Fiscal Policy

Where do these complications leave us as to the advisability and effectiveness of discretionary fiscal policy? In view of the complications and uncertain outcomes of fiscal policy, some economists argue that it is better not to engage in it at all. Those holding that view point to the superiority of monetary policy (changes in interest rates engineered by the Federal Reserve) as a stabilizing device or believe that most economic fluctuations tend to be mild and self-correcting. We will discuss monetary policy in Chapter 15 and the "self-correction" perspective in Chapter 19.

But most economists believe that fiscal policy remains an important, useful policy lever in the government's macroeconomic toolkit. The current popular view is that fiscal policy can help "push the economy" in a particular direction but cannot "fine-tune it" to a precise macroeconomic outcome. Mainstream economists generally agree that monetary policy is the best month-to-month stabilization tool for the U.S. economy. If monetary policy is doing its job, the government should maintain a relatively neutral fiscal policy, with a full-employment budget deficit or surplus of no more than 2 percent of potential GDP. It should hold major discretionary fiscal policy in reserve to help counter situations where recession threatens to be deep and long-lasting or where inflation threatens to escalate rapidly despite the efforts of the Federal Reserve to stabilize the economy.

Finally, there is general agreement that proposed fiscal policy should be evaluated for its potential positive and negative impacts on long-run productivity growth. The short-run policy tools used for conducting active fiscal policy often have long-run impacts. Countercyclical fiscal policy should be shaped to strengthen, or at least not impede, the growth of long-run aggregate supply (shown as a rightward shift of the long-run aggregate supply curve in Figure 11.3). For example, a tax cut might be structured to enhance work effort, strengthen investment, and encourage innovation. Or an increase in government spending might center on preplanned projects for "public capital" (highways, mass transit, ports, airports) that are complementary to private investment and thus conducive to long-term economic growth.

SUMMARY

1. Government responsibility for achieving and maintaining full employment is specified in the Employment Act of 1946. The Council of Economic Advisers (CEA) was established to advise the president on policies to fulfill the goals of the act.

2. Other things equal, increases in government spending expand, and decreases contract, aggregate demand and equilibrium GDP. Increases in taxes reduce, and decreases expand, aggregate demand and equilibrium GDP. Fiscal policy therefore calls for increases in government spending and decreases in taxes—a budget deficit—to correct for recession. Decreases in government spending and increases in taxes—a budget surplus—are appropriate fiscal policy for correcting demand-pull inflation.

3. Built-in stability arises from net tax revenues, which vary directly with the level of GDP. During recession, the Federal budget automatically moves toward a stabilizing deficit; during expansion, the budget automatically moves toward an anti-inflationary surplus. Built-in stability lessens, but does not fully correct, undesired changes in the real GDP.

4. The full-employment budget or standardized budget measures the Federal budget deficit or surplus that would occur if the economy operated at full employment throughout the year. Cyclical deficits or surpluses are those that result from changes in GDP.

5. Changes in the full-employment deficit or surplus provide meaningful information as to whether the government's fiscal policy is expansionary, neutral, or contractionary. Changes in the actual budget deficit or surplus do not, since such deficits or surpluses can include cyclical deficits or surpluses.

6. Certain problems complicate the enactment and implementation of fiscal policy. They include (a) timing problems associated with recognition, administrative, and operational lags; (b) the potential for misuse of fiscal policy for political rather than economic purposes; (c) the fact that state and local finances tend to be pro-cyclical; (d) potential ineffectiveness if households expect future policy reversals; (e) the possibility of fiscal policy crowding out private investment; and (f) complications relating to the effects of fiscal policy on exchange rates and net exports.

7. The current mainstream view by economists is that fiscal policy can help move the economy in a desired direction but cannot reliably be used to fine-tune the economy to a position of price stability and full employment. Nevertheless, fiscal policy is a valuable backup tool for aiding monetary policy in fighting significant recession or inflation.

TERMS AND CONCEPTS

fiscal policy	budget deficit	progressive tax system	cyclical deficit
Employment Act of 1946	contractionary fiscal policy	proportional tax system	political business cycle
Council of Economic Advisers (CEA)	budget surplus	regressive tax system	crowding-out effect
expansionary fiscal policy	built-in stabilizer	full-employment budget	net export effect

STUDY QUESTIONS

1. What is the central thrust of the Employment Act of 1946? What is the role of the Council of Economic Advisers (CEA) in response to this law? Class assignment: Determine the names and educational backgrounds of the present members of the CEA.

2. *Key Question* Assume that a hypothetical economy with an MPC of .8 is experiencing severe recession. By how much would government spending have to increase to shift the aggregate demand curve rightward by $25 billion? How large a tax cut would be needed to achieve the same increase in aggregate demand? Why the difference? Determine one possible combination of government spending increases and tax decreases that would accomplish the same goal.

3. *Key Question* What are government's fiscal policy options for ending severe demand-pull inflation? Use the aggregate demand–aggregate supply model to show the impact of these policies on the price level. Which of these fiscal options do you think might be favored by a person who wants to preserve the size of government? A person who thinks the public sector is too large?

4. (For students who were assigned Chapter 10) Use the aggregate expenditures model to show how government fiscal policy could eliminate either a recessionary gap or an inflationary gap (Figure 10.8). Explain how equal-size increases in G and T could eliminate a recessionary gap and how equal-size decreases in G and T could eliminate an inflationary gap.

5. Designate each of the following statements as true or false and justify your answer:
   a. Expansionary fiscal policy during a depression will have a greater positive effect on real GDP if the government borrows the money to finance the budget deficit than if the central bank creates new money to finance the deficit.
   b. Contractionary fiscal policy during severe demand-pull inflation will be more effective if the government impounds the budget surplus rather than using the surplus to pay off some of its debt.

6. Explain how built-in (or automatic) stabilizers work. What are the differences between proportional, progressive, and regressive tax systems as they relate to an economy's built-in stability?

7. *Key Question* Define the full-employment budget, explain its significance, and state why it may differ from the actual budget. Suppose the full-employment, noninflationary level of real output is GDP$_3$ (not GDP$_2$) in the economy depicted in Figure 12.3. If the economy is operating at GDP$_2$, instead of GDP$_3$, what is the status of its full-employment budget? Of its current fiscal policy? What change in fiscal policy would you recommend? How would you accomplish that in terms of the G and T lines in the figure?

8. As shown in Table 12.1, between 1990 and 1991 the actual budget deficit (as a percentage of GDP) grew more rapidly than the full-employment budget deficit. What could explain this fact?

9. Some politicians have suggested that the United States enact a constitutional amendment requiring that the Federal government balance its budget annually. Explain why such an amendment, if strictly enforced, would force the government to enact a *contractionary* fiscal policy whenever the economy experienced a severe recession.

10. *Key Question* Briefly state and evaluate the problem of time lags in enacting and applying fiscal policy. Explain the idea of a political business cycle. How might expectations of a near-term policy reversal weaken fiscal policy based on changes in tax rates? What is the crowding-out effect, and why is it relevant to fiscal policy? In what respect is the net export effect similar to the crowding-out effect?

11. In view of your answers to question 10, explain the following statement: "While fiscal policy clearly is useful in combating the extremes of severe recession and demand-pull inflation, it is impossible to use fiscal policy to fine-tune the economy to the full-employment, noninflationary level of real GDP and keep the economy there indefinitely."

12. Suppose that the government engages in deficit spending to push the economy away from recession and that this spending is directed toward new "public capital" such as roads, bridges, dams, harbors, office parks, and industrial sites. How might this spending increase the expected rate of return on some types of potential private investment projects? What are the implications for the crowding-out effect?

13. Use Figure 12.4b to explain why the deliberate increase of the full-employment budget deficit (resulting from the tax cut) will reduce the size of the actual budget deficit if the

fiscal policy succeeds in pushing the economy to its full-employment output of GDP_3. In requesting a tax cut in the early 1960s, President Kennedy said, "It is a paradoxical truth that tax rates are too high today and tax revenues are too low and the soundest way to raise tax revenues in the long run is to cut tax rates now." Relate this quotation to your previous answer in this question.

14. *Advanced Analysis* (For students who were assigned Chapter 10) Assume that, without taxes, the consumption schedule for an economy is as shown below:

GDP, Billions	Consumption, Billions
$100	$120
200	200
300	280
400	360
500	440
600	520
700	600

   a. Graph this consumption schedule, and determine the size of the MPC.

   b. Assume that a lump-sum (regressive) tax of $10 billion is imposed at all levels of GDP. Calculate the tax rate at each level of GDP. Graph the resulting consumption schedule, and compare the MPC and the multiplier with those of the pretax consumption schedule.

   c. Now suppose a proportional tax with a 10 percent tax rate is imposed instead of the regressive tax. Calculate

and graph the new consumption schedule, and note the MPC and the multiplier.

   d. Finally, impose a progressive tax such that the tax rate is 0 percent when GDP is $100, 5 percent at $200, 10 percent at $300, 15 percent at $400, and so forth. Determine and graph the new consumption schedule, noting the effect of this tax system on the MPC and the multiplier.

   e. Explain why proportional and progressive taxes contribute to greater economic stability, while a regressive tax does not. Demonstrate, using a graph similar to Figure 12.3.

15. *(Last Word)* What is the index of leading economic indicators, and how does it relate to discretionary fiscal policy?

16. *Web-Based Question: Leading economic indicators—how goes the economy?* The Conference Board, at www.conferenceboard.org/, tracks the leading economic indicators. Check the summary of the index of leading indicators and its individual components for the latest month. Is the index up or down? Which specific components are up, and which are down? What has been the trend of the composite index over the past 3 months?

17. *Web-Based Question: Text Table 12.1, column 3—what are the latest numbers?* Go to the Congressional Budget Office website, www.cbo.gov, and select Historical Budget Data. Find the historical data for the actual budget deficit or surplus (total). Update column 2 of text Table 12.1. Next, find the historical data for the standardized (full-employment) budget deficit or surplus as a percentage of potential GDP. Update column 3 of Table 12.1. Is fiscal policy more expansionary or less expansionary than it was in 2002?

Part IV | Money, Banking, and Monetary Policy

13 | Money and Banking

Money is a fascinating aspect of the economy:

Money bewitches people. They fret for it, and they sweat for it. They devise most ingenious ways to get it, and most ingenuous ways to get rid of it. Money is the only commodity that is good for nothing but to be gotten rid of. It will not feed you, clothe you, shelter you, or amuse you unless you spend it or invest it. It imparts value only in parting. People will do almost anything for money, and money will do almost anything for people. Money is a captivating, circulating, masquerading puzzle.[1]

In this chapter and the two chapters that follow we want to unmask the critical role of money and the monetary system in the economy. When the monetary system is working properly, it provides the lifeblood of the circular flows of income and expenditure. A well-operating monetary system helps the economy achieve both full employment and the efficient use of resources. A malfunctioning monetary system creates severe fluctuations in the economy's levels of output, employment, and prices and distorts the allocation of resources.

---

[1]Federal Reserve Bank of Philadelphia, "Creeping Inflation," *Business Review*, August 1957, p. 3.

The Functions of Money

Just what is money? There is an old saying that "money *is* what money *does*." In a general sense, anything that performs the functions of money *is* money. Here are those functions:

- *Medium of exchange* First and foremost, money is a **medium of exchange** that is usable for buying and selling goods and services. A bakery worker does not want to be paid 200 bagels per week. Nor does the bakery owner want to receive, say, halibut in exchange for bagels. Money, however, is readily acceptable as payment. As we saw in Chapter 4, money is a social invention with which resource suppliers and producers can be paid and that can be used to buy any of the full range of items available in the marketplace. As a medium of exchange, money allows society to escape the complications of barter. And because it provides a convenient way of exchanging goods, money enables society to gain the advantages of geographic and human specialization.

TABLE 13.1

Alternative Money Definitions for the United States: M1, M2, and M3

Definition	Absolute Amount, Billions	Percentage of Total		
		M1	M2	M3
Currency (coins and paper money)	$ 639	52%	11%	7%
plus Checkable deposits	597*	48	10	7
equals **M1**	**$1236**	100%		
plus Savings deposits, including money market deposit accounts (MMDAs)	2866		49	33
plus Small time deposits	818*		14	10
plus Money market mutual fund (MMMF) balances	979		16	11
equals **M2**	**$5899**		100%	
plus Large time deposits	2696*			32
equals **M3**	**$8595**			100%

*These figures include other quantitatively smaller components such as traveler's checks.

Source: *Federal Reserve Release*, May 8, 2003 (www.federalreserve.gov). Data are for March 2003.

- *Unit of account* Money is also a **unit of account.** Society uses monetary units—dollars, in the United States—as a yardstick for measuring the relative worth of a wide variety of goods, services, and resources. Just as we measure distance in miles or kilometers, we gauge the value of goods in dollars.

  With money as an acceptable unit of account, the price of each item need be stated only in terms of the monetary unit. We need not state the price of cows in terms of corn, crayons, and cranberries. Money aids rational decision making by enabling buyers and sellers to easily compare the prices of various goods, services, and resources. It also permits us to define debt obligations, determine taxes owed, and calculate the nation's GDP.

- *Store of value* Money also serves as a **store of value** that enables people to transfer purchasing power from the present to the future. People normally do not spend all their incomes on the day they receive them. In order to buy things later, they store some of their wealth as money. The money you place in a safe or a checking account will still be available to you a few weeks or months from now. Money is often the preferred store of value for short periods because it is the most liquid (spendable) of all assets. People can obtain their money nearly instantly and can immediately use it to buy goods or take advantage of financial investment opportunities. When inflation is nonexistent or mild, holding money is a relatively risk-free way to store your wealth for later use.

The Supply of Money

Societies have used many items as money, including whales' teeth, circular stones, elephant-tail bristles, gold coins, furs, and pieces of paper. Anything that is widely accepted as a medium of exchange can serve as money. In the United States, certain debts of government and of financial institutions are used as money, as you will see.

Money Definition M1

The narrowest definition of the U.S. money supply is called **M1.** It consists of:

- Currency (coins and paper money) in the hands of the public.
- All checkable deposits (all deposits in commercial banks and "thrift" or savings institutions on which checks of any size can be drawn).[2]

Coins and paper money are debts of government and government agencies. Checkable deposits are debts of commercial banks and savings institutions. Table 13.1 shows the amount of each sort of money in the M1 money supply.

---

[2]In the ensuing discussion, we do not discuss several of the quantitatively less significant components of the definitions of money in order to avoid a maze of details. For example, traveler's checks are included in the M1 money supply. The statistical appendix of any recent *Federal Reserve Bulletin* provides more comprehensive definitions.

Currency: Coins + Paper Money   From copper pennies to gold-colored dollars, coins are the "small change" of our money supply. They constitute only 2 to 3 percent of *M*1.

All coins in circulation in the United States are **token money.** This means that the *intrinsic value*, or the value of the metal contained in the coin itself, is less than the face value of the coin. This is to prevent people from melting down the coins for sale as a "commodity," in this case, the metal. If 50-cent pieces each contained 75 cents' worth of silver metal, it would be profitable to melt them and sell the metal. The 50-cent pieces would disappear from circulation.

Paper money constitutes about 50 percent of the U.S. economy's *M*1 money supply. All this paper currency is in the form of **Federal Reserve Notes,** issued by the Federal Reserve System (the U.S. central bank) with the authorization of Congress. Every bill carries the phrase "Federal Reserve Note" on its face.

Checkable Deposits   The safety and convenience of checks has made **checkable deposits** a large component of the *M*1 money supply. You would not think of stuffing $4896 in bills in an envelope and dropping it in a mailbox to pay a debt. But writing and mailing a check for a large sum is commonplace. The person cashing a check must endorse it (sign it on the reverse side); the writer of the check subsequently receives a record of the canceled check as a receipt attesting to the fulfillment of the obligation. Similarly, because the writing of a check requires endorsement, the theft or loss of your checkbook is not nearly as calamitous as losing an identical amount of currency. Finally, it is more convenient to write a check than to transport and count out a large sum of currency. For all these reasons, checkable deposits (checkbook money) are a large component of the stock of money in the United States. About 48 percent of *M*1 is in the form of checkable deposits, on which checks can be drawn.

It might seem strange that checking account balances are regarded as part of the money supply. But the reason is clear: Checks are nothing more than a way to transfer the ownership of deposits in banks and other financial institutions and are generally acceptable as a medium of exchange. Although checks are less generally accepted than currency for small purchases, for major purchases most sellers willingly accept checks as payment. Moreover, people can convert checkable deposits into paper money and coins on demand; checks drawn on those deposits are thus the equivalent of currency. To summarize:

$$\text{Money, } M1 = \text{currency} + \text{checkable deposits}$$

Institutions That Offer Checkable Deposits   In the United States, a variety of financial institutions allow customers to write checks in any amount on the funds they have deposited. **Commercial banks** are the primary depository institutions. They accept the deposits of households and businesses, keep the money safe until it is demanded via checks, and in the meantime use it to make available a wide variety of loans. Commercial bank loans provide short-term financial capital to businesses, and they finance consumer purchases of automobiles and other durable goods.

Savings and loan associations (S&Ls), mutual savings banks, and credit unions supplement the commercial banks and are known collectively as savings or **thrift institutions,** or simply "thrifts." *Savings and loan associations* and *mutual savings banks* accept the deposits of households and businesses and then use the funds to finance housing mortgages and to provide other loans. *Credit unions* accept deposits from and lend to "members," who usually are a group of people who work for the same company.

The checkable deposits of banks and thrifts are known variously as demand deposits, NOW (negotiable order of withdrawal) accounts, ATS (automatic transfer service) accounts, and share draft accounts. Their commonality is that depositors can write checks on them whenever, and in whatever amount, they choose.

A Qualification   We must qualify our discussion in an important way. Currency and checkable deposits owned by the government (the U.S. Treasury) and by Federal Reserve Banks, commercial banks, or other financial institutions are *excluded* from *M*1 and other measures of the money supply.

A paper dollar in the hands of, say, Emma Buck obviously constitutes just $1 of the money supply. But if we counted dollars held by banks as part of the money supply, the same $1 would count for $2 when it was deposited in a bank. It would count for a $1 checkable deposit owned by Buck and also for $1 of currency resting in the bank's till or vault. By excluding currency resting in banks in determining the total money supply, we avoid this problem of double counting.

Excluding government financial holdings from the money supply allows for better assessment of the amount of money available to firms and households for potential spending. That amount of money and potential spending is of keen interest to the Federal Reserve in conducting its monetary policy (a topic we cover in detail in Chapter 15).

Money Definition M2

A second and broader definition of money includes *M*1 plus several near-monies. **Near-monies** are certain highly liquid financial assets that do not function directly or fully as a medium of exchange but can be readily converted into currency or checkable deposits. There are three categories of near-monies included in the *M2* definition of money:

- *Savings deposits, including money market deposit accounts* A depositor can easily withdraw funds from a **savings account** at a bank or thrift or simply request that the funds be transferred from a savings account to a checkable account. A person can also withdraw funds from a **money market deposit account (MMDA),** which is an interest-bearing account through which banks and thrifts pool individual deposits to buy a variety of interest-bearing short-term securities. MMDAs, however, have a minimum-balance requirement and a limit on how often a person can withdraw funds.
- *Small (less than $100,000) time deposits* Funds from **time deposits** become available at their maturity. For example, a person can convert a 6-month time deposit ("certificate of deposit") to currency without penalty 6 months or more after it has been deposited. In return for this withdrawal limitation, the financial institution pays a higher interest rate on such deposits than it does on its MMDA. Also, a person can "cash in" a CD at any time but must pay a severe penalty.
- *Money market mutual funds* By making a telephone call, using the Internet, or writing a check for $500 or more, a depositor can redeem shares in a **money market mutual fund (MMMF)** offered by a mutual fund company. Such companies use the combined funds of individual shareholders to buy interest-bearing short-term credit instruments such as certificates of deposit and U.S. government securities. They in turn can offer interest on the money market accounts of their mutual fund customers (depositors).

All three categories of near-monies imply substantial liquidity. Thus, in equation form,

$$\text{Money, } M2 = \begin{array}{l} M1 + \text{savings deposits,} \\ \text{including MMDAs} + \text{small} \\ \text{(less than } \$100,000) \text{ time deposits} \\ + \text{MMMFs} \end{array}$$

In summary, *M2* includes the immediate medium-of-exchange items (currency and checkable deposits) that constitute *M1* plus certain near-monies that can be easily converted into currency and checkable deposits. In Table 13.1 we see that the addition of all these items yields an *M2* money supply of $5899 billion compared to the narrower *M1* money supply of $1236 billion.

Money Definition M3

A third definition of the money supply, *M3,* includes large ($100,000 or more) time deposits, usually owned by businesses as certificates of deposit. There is a market for these certificates, and they can be sold (liquidated) at any time, although perhaps at the risk of a loss. Businesses normally use large time deposits for saving, not as "money." But since businesses can convert these deposits into checkable deposits, they also are a near-money. Adding large time deposits to *M2* yields the still broader *M3* definition of the money supply:

$$\text{Money, } M3 = \begin{array}{l} M2 + \text{large (}\$100,000 \text{ or} \\ \text{more) time deposits} \end{array}$$

In Table 13.1 the *M3* money supply is $8595 billion.

Still other slightly less liquid assets, such as certain government securities (for example, Treasury bills and bonds), can be easily converted into *M1* money. Actually, there is an entire spectrum of assets that vary slightly in terms of their liquidity or "moneyness" that are not included in *M1*, *M2*, or *M3*.

Because the simple *M1* definition includes only items directly and immediately usable as a medium of exchange, it is usually cited in discussions of the money supply. However, for some purposes economists prefer the broader *M2* definition. For example, *M2* is used as 1 of the 10 trend variables in the index of leading indicators (Last Word, Chapter 12). *M3* and still broader definitions of money are so inclusive that many economists question their usefulness.

We will use the narrow *M1* definition of the money supply in our discussion and analysis, unless stated otherwise. The important principles we will develop relating to *M1* are also applicable to *M2* and *M3*, because *M1* is the base component of these broader measures. (**Key Question 4**)

QUICK REVIEW 13.1

- Money serves as a medium of exchange, a unit of account, and a store of value.
- The narrow *M1* definition of money includes currency held by the public plus checkable deposits in commercial banks and thrift institutions.
- Thrift institutions as well as commercial banks offer accounts on which checks can be written.
- The *M2* definition of money includes *M1* plus savings deposits, including money market deposit accounts, small (less than $100,000) time deposits, and money market mutual fund balances.
- Money supply *M3* consists of *M2* plus large (more than $100,000) time deposits.

CONSIDER THIS . . .

Are Credit Cards Money?

You may wonder why we have ignored credit cards such as Visa and MasterCard in our discussion of how the money supply is defined. After all, credit cards are a convenient way to buy things and account for about 25 percent of the

© Michael Newman/PhotoEdit

dollar value of all transactions in the United States. The answer is that a credit card is not money. Rather, it is a convenient means of obtaining a short-term loan from the financial institution that issued the card.

What happens when you purchase a sweatshirt with a credit card? The bank that issued the card will reimburse the store, charging it a transaction fee, and later you will reimburse the bank. Rather than reduce your cash or checking account with each purchase, you bunch your payments once a month. You may have to pay an annual fee for the services provided, and if you pay the bank in installments, you will pay a sizable interest charge on the loan. Credit cards are merely a means of deferring or postponing payment for a short period. Your checking account balance that you use to pay your credit card bill *is* money; the credit card is *not* money.*

However, credit cards allow individuals and businesses to "economize" in the use of money. Credit cards enable you to hold less currency in your billfold and fewer checkable deposits (prior to the due date for paying your credit card bill) in your bank account. Credit cards also help you coordinate the timing of your expenditures with your receipt of income.

*Nor is a debit card money. Like a check, it allows you to make payment directly from your checking account. The checking account balance *is* money; the check or debit card is *not.*

What "Backs" the Money Supply?

The money supply in the United States essentially is "backed" (guaranteed) by government's ability to keep the value of money relatively stable. Nothing more!

Money as Debt

The major components of the money supply—paper money and checkable deposits—are debts, or promises to pay. In the United States, paper money is the circulating debt of the Federal Reserve Banks. Checkable deposits are the debts of commercial banks and thrift institutions.

Paper currency and checkable deposits have no intrinsic value. A $5 bill is just an inscribed piece of paper. A checkable deposit is merely a bookkeeping entry. And coins, we know, have less intrinsic value than their face

value. Nor will government redeem the paper money you hold for anything tangible, such as gold. In effect, the government has chosen to "manage" the nation's money supply. Its monetary authorities attempt to provide the amount of money needed for the particular volume of business activity that will promote full employment, price-level stability, and economic growth.

Most economists agree that managing the money supply is more sensible than linking it to gold or to some other commodity whose supply might change arbitrarily and capriciously. A large increase in the nation's gold stock as the result of a new gold discovery might increase the money supply too rapidly and thereby trigger rapid inflation. Or a long-lasting decline in gold production might reduce the money supply to the point where recession and unemployment resulted.

In short, people cannot convert paper money into a fixed amount of gold or any other precious commodity. Money is exchangeable only for paper money. If you ask the government to redeem $5 of your paper money, it will swap one paper $5 bill for another bearing a different serial number. That is all you can get. Similarly, checkable deposits can be redeemed not for gold but only for paper money, which, as we have just seen, the government will not redeem for anything tangible.

Value of Money

So why are currency and checkable deposits money, whereas, say, Monopoly (the game) money is not? What gives a $20 bill or a $100 checking account entry its value? The answer to these questions has three parts.

Acceptability   Currency and checkable deposits are money because people accept them as money. By virtue of long-standing business practice, currency and checkable deposits perform the basic function of money: They are acceptable as a medium of exchange. We accept paper money in exchange because we are confident it will be exchangeable for real goods, services, and resources when we spend it.

Legal Tender   Our confidence in the acceptability of paper money is strengthened because government has designated currency as **legal tender.** Specifically, each bill contains the statement "This note is legal tender for all debts, public and private." That means paper money is a valid and legal means of payment of debt. (But private firms and government are not mandated to accept cash. It is not illegal for them to specify payment in noncash forms such as checks, cashier's checks, money orders, or credit cards.) The paper money in our economy is *fiat money;* it is money because the government has declared it so, not because it can be redeemed for precious metal.

The general acceptance of paper currency in exchange is more important than the government's decree that money is legal tender, however. The government has never decreed checks to be legal tender, and yet they serve as such in many of the economy's exchanges of goods, services, and resources. But it is true that government agencies—the Federal Deposit Insurance Corporation (FDIC) and the National Credit Union Administration (NCUA)—insure individual deposits of up to $100,000 at commercial banks and thrifts. That fact enhances our willingness to use checkable deposits as a medium of exchange.

Relative Scarcity

The value of money, like the economic value of anything else, depends on its supply and demand. Money derives its value from its scarcity relative to its utility (its want-satisfying power). The utility of money lies in its capacity to be exchanged for goods and services, now or in the future. The economy's demand for money thus depends on the total dollar volume of transactions in any period plus the amount of money individuals and businesses want to hold for future transactions. With a reasonably constant demand for money, the supply of money will determine the value or "purchasing power" of the monetary unit (dollar, yen, peso, or whatever).

Money and Prices

The purchasing power of money is the amount of goods and services a unit of money will buy. When money rapidly loses its purchasing power, it loses its role as money.

The Purchasing Power of the Dollar

The amount a dollar will buy varies inversely with the price level; that is, a reciprocal relationship exists between the general price level and the purchasing power of the dollar. When the consumer price index or "cost-of-living" index goes up, the value of the dollar goes down, and vice versa. Higher prices lower the value of the dollar, because more dollars are needed to buy a particular amount of goods, services, or resources. For example, if the price level doubles, the value of the dollar declines by one-half, or 50 percent.

Conversely, lower prices increase the purchasing power of the dollar, because fewer dollars are needed to obtain a specific quantity of goods and services. If the price level falls by, say, one-half, or 50 percent, the purchasing power of the dollar doubles.

In equation form, the relationship looks like this:

$$D = 1/P$$

To find the value of the dollar D, divide 1 by the price level P expressed as an index number (in hundredths). If the price level is 1, then the value of the dollar is 1. If the price level rises to, say, 1.20, D falls to .833; a 20 percent increase in the price level reduces the value of the dollar by 16.67 percent. Check your understanding of this reciprocal relationship by determining the value of D and its percentage rise when P falls by 20 percent to .80. **(Key Question 6)**

Inflation and Acceptability

In Chapter 8 we noted situations in which a nation's currency became worthless and unacceptable in exchange. They were circumstances in which the government issued so many pieces of paper currency that the value of each of these units of money was almost totally undermined. The infamous post-World War I inflation in Germany is an example. In December 1919 there were about 50 billion marks in circulation. Four years later there were 496,585,345,900 billion marks in circulation! The result? The German mark in 1923 was worth an infinitesimal fraction of its 1919 value.[3]

Runaway inflation may significantly depreciate the value of money between the time it is received and the time it is spent. Rapid declines in the value of a currency may cause it to cease being used as a medium of exchange. Businesses and households may refuse to accept paper money in exchange because they do not want to bear the loss in its value that will occur while it is in their possession. (All this despite the fact that the government says that paper currency is legal tender!) Without an acceptable domestic medium of exchange, the economy may simply revert to barter. Alternatively, more stable currencies such as the U.S. dollar may come into widespread use. At the extreme, a country may adopt a foreign currency as its own official currency as a way to counter hyperinflation. That is what Ecuador did in 2000 when it made the U.S. dollar its official currency.

Similarly, people will use money as a store of value only as long as there is no sizable deterioration in the value of that money because of inflation. And an economy can effectively employ money as a unit of account only when its purchasing power is relatively stable. A monetary yardstick that no longer measures a yard (in terms of

---

[3]Frank G. Graham, *Exchange, Prices and Production in Hyperinflation Germany, 1920-1923* (Princeton, N.J.: Princeton University Press, 1930), p. 13.

purchasing power) does not permit buyers and sellers to establish the terms of trade clearly. When the value of the dollar is declining rapidly, sellers will not know what to charge, and buyers will not know what to pay, for goods and services.

Stabilization of Money's Value

Stabilization of the value of money requires (1) appropriate *fiscal policy*, as explained in Chapter 12, and (2) intelligent management or regulation of the money supply *(monetary policy)*. In the United States a combination of legislation, government policy, and social practice inhibits imprudent expansion of the money supply that might jeopardize money's value in exchange.

What is true for paper money is also true for checkable deposits, which are debts of commercial banks and thrift institutions. Your checking account of $200 means that your bank or thrift is indebted to you for that number of dollars. You can collect this debt in one of two ways. You can go to the bank or thrift, write out a check for cash, and obtain paper money. This amounts to swapping bank or thrift debt for government-issued debt. Or, and this is more likely, you can "collect" the debt that the bank or thrift owes you by transferring your claim by check to someone else.

For example, if you buy a $200 leather coat from a store, you can pay for it by writing a check, which transfers your bank's indebtedness from you to the store. Your bank now owes the store the $200 it previously owed you. The store accepts this transfer of indebtedness (the check) as a medium of exchange because it can convert it into currency on demand or can transfer the debt to others in making purchases of its own. Thus, checks, as means of transferring the debts of banks and thrifts, are acceptable as money because we know banks and thrifts will honor these claims.

The ability of banks and thrifts to honor claims against them depends on their not creating too many of such claims. A decentralized system of private, profit-seeking banks might not contain sufficient safeguards against the creation of too many checkable deposits. For that reason, the U.S. banking and financial system exercises substantial centralization and government control to guard against the imprudent creation of those deposits.

A nation's monetary authorities make a particular quantity of money available, such as $M1$ in Table 13.1. In relation to the nation's real interest rate, this quantity of money establishes the economy's supply-of-money curve. Vertical line S_m in Figure 13.1c represents one such curve.

The Demand for Money

Why does the public want to hold some of its wealth as *money?* There are two main reasons: to make purchases with it and to hold it as an asset.

Transactions Demand, D_t

People hold money because, as a medium of exchange, it is convenient for purchasing goods and services. Households must have enough money on hand to buy groceries and pay mortgage and utility bills. Businesses need money to pay for labor, materials, power, and other inputs. The demand for money for such uses is called the **transactions demand** for money.

The main determinant of the amount of money demanded for transactions is the level of nominal GDP. The larger the total money value of all goods and services exchanged in the economy, the larger the amount of money needed to negotiate those transactions. The transactions demand for money varies directly with nominal GDP. We specify *nominal* GDP because households and firms will want more money for transactions if prices rise or if real output increases. In both instances there will be a need for a larger dollar volume to accomplish the desired transactions.

In **Figure 13.1a (Key Graph)** we graph the quantity of money demanded for transactions against the interest rate. For simplicity, we will assume that the amount demanded depends exclusively on the level of nominal GDP and is independent of the real interest rate. (In reality, higher interest rates are associated with slightly lower volumes of money demanded for transactions.) Our

KEY GRAPH

FIGURE 13.1

The demand for money and the money market. The total demand for money D_m is determined by horizontally adding the asset demand for money D_a to the transactions demand D_t. The transactions demand is vertical because it is assumed to depend on nominal GDP rather than on the interest rate. The asset demand varies inversely with the interest rate because of the opportunity cost involved in holding currency and checkable deposits that pay no interest or very low interest. Combining the money supply (stock) S_m with the total money demand D_m portrays the money market and determines the equilibrium interest rate i_e.

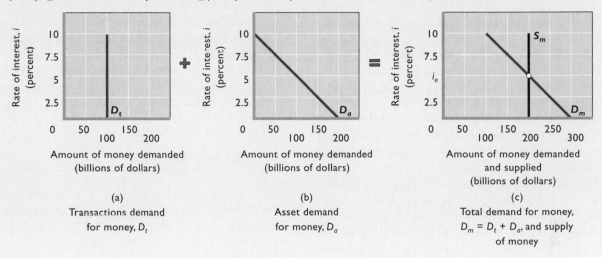

(a)
Transactions demand
for money, D_t

(b)
Asset demand
for money, D_a

(c)
Total demand for money,
$D_m = D_t + D_a$, and supply
of money

QUICK QUIZ 13.1

1. In this graph, at the interest rate i_e (5 percent):
   a. the amount of money demanded as an asset is $50 billion.
   b. the amount of money demanded for transactions is $200 billion.
   c. bond prices will decline.
   d. $100 billion is demanded for transactions, $100 billion is demanded as an asset, and the money supply is $200 billion.

2. In this graph, at an interest rate of 10 percent:
   a. no money will be demanded as an asset.
   b. total money demanded will be $200 billion.
   c. the Federal Reserve will supply $100 billion of money.
   d. there will be a $100 billion shortage of money.

3. Curve D_a slopes downward because:
   a. lower interest rates increase the opportunity cost of holding money.
   b. lower interest rates reduce the opportunity cost of holding money.

   c. the asset demand for money varies directly (positively) with the interest rate.
   d. the transactions-demand-for-money curve is perfectly vertical.

4. Suppose the supply of money declines to $100 billion. The equilibrium interest rate would:
   a. fall, the amount of money demanded for transactions would rise, and the amount of money demanded as an asset would decline.
   b. rise, and the amounts of money demanded both for transactions and as an asset would fall.
   c. fall, and the amounts of money demanded both for transactions and as an asset would increase.
   d. rise, the amount of money demanded for transactions would be unchanged, and the amount of money demanded as an asset would decline.

Answers: 1. d; 2. a; 3. b; 4. d

---

simplifying assumption allows us to graph the transactions demand, D_t, as a vertical line. The transactions demand curve is positioned at $100 billion, on the assumption that each dollar held for transactions purposes is spent on an average of three times per year and that nominal GDP is $300 billion. Thus the public needs $100 billion (= $300 billion/3) to purchase that GDP.

Asset Demand, D_a

The second reason for holding money derives from money's function as a store of value. People may hold their financial assets in many forms, including corporate stocks, private or government bonds, or money. Thus, there is an **asset demand** for money.

What determines the asset demand for money? First, we must recognize that each of the various ways of holding financial assets has advantages and disadvantages. To simplify, let's compare holding money as an asset with holding bonds. The advantages of holding money are its liquidity and lack of risk. Money is the most liquid of all assets; it is immediately usable in making purchases. Money is an attractive asset to be holding when the prices of goods, services, and other financial assets are expected to decline. But when the price of a bond falls, the bondholder who sells the bond before it matures will suffer a loss. There is no such risk in holding money.

The disadvantage of holding money as an asset is that, compared with holding bonds, it does not earn interest. Or, if it is in an interest-bearing checkable deposit account, it does not earn as much interest as do bonds or noncheckable deposits. Idle currency, of course, earns no interest at all.

Knowing this, the problem is deciding how much of your financial assets to hold as, say, bonds and how much as money. The answer depends primarily on the rate of interest. A household or a business incurs an opportunity cost when it holds money; in both cases, interest income is forgone or sacrificed. If a bond pays 6 percent interest, for example, it costs $6 per year of forgone income to hold $100 as cash or in a noninterest checkable account.

It is no surprise, then, that the asset demand for money varies inversely with the rate of interest. When the interest rate or opportunity cost of holding money as an asset is low, the public will choose to hold a large amount of money as assets. When the interest rate is high, it is costly to "be liquid" and the amount of assets held as money will be small. When it is expensive to hold money as an asset, people hold less of it; when money can be held cheaply, people hold more of it. This inverse relationship between the interest rate and the amount of money people want to hold as an asset is shown by D_a in Figure 13.1b.

13.1 Liquidity preference

Total Money Demand, D_m

As shown in Figure 13.1, we find the **total demand for money**, D_m, by horizontally adding the asset demand to the transactions demand. The resulting downward-sloping line in Figure 13.1c represents the total amount of money the public wants to hold, both for transactions and as an asset, at each possible interest rate.

Recall that the transactions demand for money depends on the nominal GDP. A change in the nominal GDP—working through the transactions demand for money—will shift the total money demand curve. Specifically, an increase in nominal GDP means that the public wants to hold a larger amount of money for transactions, and that extra demand will shift the total money demand curve to the right. In contrast, a decline in the nominal GDP will shift the total money demand curve to the left. As an example, suppose nominal GDP increases from $300 billion to $450 billion and the average dollar held for transactions is still spent three times per year. Then the transactions demand curve will shift from $100 billion (= $300 billion/3) to $150 billion (= $450 billion/3). The total money demand curve will then lie $50 billion farther to the right at each possible interest rate.

The Money Market

We can combine the demand for money with the supply of money to portray the **money market** and determine the equilibrium rate of interest. In Figure 13.1c the vertical line, S_m, represents the money supply. It is a vertical line because the monetary authorities and financial institutions have provided the economy with some particular stock of money, such as the $M1$ total shown in Table 13.1.

Just as in a product market or a resource market, the intersection of demand and supply determines equilibrium price. Here, the equilibrium "price" is the interest rate (i_e), which is the price paid for the use of money.

Adjustment to a Decline in the Money Supply

A decline in the supply of money will create a temporary shortage of money and increase the equilibrium interest rate. Consider Figure 13.2, which repeats Figure 13.1c and adds two alternative supply-of-money curves.

Suppose the monetary authorities reduce the supply of money from $200 billion, S_m, to $150 billion, S_{m1}. At the initial interest rate of 5 percent, the quantity of money demanded now exceeds the quantity supplied by $50 billion. People will attempt to make up for this shortage of money by selling some of the financial assets they own (we assume for simplicity that these assets are bonds). But one person's receipt of money through the sale of a bond is another person's loss of money through the purchase of that bond. *Overall, there is only $150 billion of money available*. The collective attempt to

FIGURE 13.2

Changes in the supply of money, bond prices, and interest rates.
When a decrease in the supply of money creates a temporary shortage of money in the money market, people and institutions try to gain more money by selling bonds. The supply of bonds therefore increases, and this reduces bond prices and raises interest rates. At higher interest rates, people reduce the amount of money they want to hold. Thus, the amounts of money supplied and demanded once again are equal at the higher interest rate. An increase in the supply of money creates a temporary surplus of money, resulting in an increase in the demand for bonds and higher bond prices. Interest rates fall and equilibrium is reestablished in the money market.

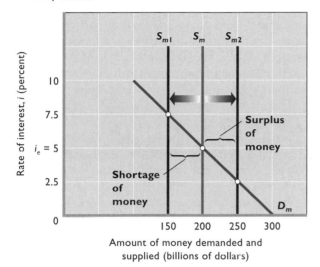

get more money by selling bonds will increase the supply of bonds relative to the demand for bonds in the bond market, but it will not increase the amount of money available as a whole. The outcome is that the price of bonds will fall and the interest rate will rise, here to $7\frac{1}{2}$ percent.

Generalization: *Lower bond prices are associated with higher interest rates.* To clarify, suppose a bond with no expiration date pays a fixed $50 annual interest and is selling for its face value of $1000. The interest yield on this bond is 5 percent:

$$\frac{\$50}{\$1000} = 5\%$$

Now suppose the price of this bond falls to $667 because of an increased supply of bonds. The $50 fixed annual interest payment will now yield $7\frac{1}{2}$ percent to whoever buys the bond:

$$\frac{\$50}{\$667} = 7\frac{1}{2}\%$$

Because all borrowers must compete by offering to pay lenders interest yields similar to those available on bonds, a higher general interest rate emerges. In Figure 13.2 the interest rate rises from 5 percent with the money supply at $200 billion to $7\frac{1}{2}$ percent when the money supply is $150 billion. This higher interest rate raises the opportunity cost of holding money and consequently reduces the amount of money firms and households want to hold. Here, the amount of money demanded declines from $200 billion at the 5 percent interest rate to $150 billion at the $7\frac{1}{2}$ percent interest rate. The money market has achieved a new equilibrium, now with $150 billion of money demanded and supplied at the new $7\frac{1}{2}$ percent interest rate.

Adjustment to an Increase in the Money Supply

An increase in the supply of money from $200 billion, S_m, to $250 billion, S_{m2}, in Figure 13.2 results in a surplus of $50 billion at the initial 5 percent interest rate. People will now try to get rid of money by purchasing more bonds. But one person's expenditure of money is another person's receipt of money. The collective attempt to buy more bonds will increase the demand for bonds, push bond prices upward, and lower interest rates.

Corollary: *Higher bond prices are associated with lower interest rates.* In our example, the $50 interest payment on a bond now priced at, say, $2000, will yield a bond buyer only $2\frac{1}{2}$ percent:

$$\frac{\$50}{\$2000} = 2\frac{1}{2}\%$$

The point is that interest rates in general will fall as people unsuccessfully attempt to reduce their money holdings below $250 billion by buying bonds. In this case, the interest rate will fall to a new equilibrium at $2\frac{1}{2}$ percent. Because the opportunity cost of holding money now is lower—that is, being liquid is less expensive—households and businesses will increase the amount of currency and checkable deposits they are willing to hold from $200 billion to $250 billion. Eventually, a new equilibrium in the money market will be achieved: The quantities of money demanded and supplied will each be $250 billion at an interest rate of $2\frac{1}{2}$ percent. **(Key Question 7)**

13.1
Equilibrium
interest rate

The Federal Reserve and the Banking System

In the United States, the "monetary authorities" we have been referring to are the members of the Board of Governors of the **Federal Reserve System** (the "Fed"). As shown in Figure 13.3, the Board directs the activities of the 12 Federal Reserve Banks, which in turn control the lending activity of the nation's banks and thrift institutions.

Historical Background

Early in the twentieth century, Congress decided that centralization and public control were essential for an efficient banking system. Decentralized, unregulated banking had fostered the inconvenience and confusion of numerous private bank notes being used as currency. It had also resulted in occasional episodes of monetary mismanagement such that the money supply was inappropriate to the needs of the economy. Sometimes "too much" money precipitated rapid inflation; other times "too little money" stunted the economy's growth by hindering the production and exchange of goods and services. There was no single entity charged with creating and implementing nationally consistent banking policies.

An unusually acute banking crisis in 1907 motivated Congress to appoint the National Monetary Commission to study the monetary and banking problems of the economy and to outline a course of action for Congress. The result was the Federal Reserve Act of 1913.

Let's examine the various parts of the Federal Reserve System and their relationship to one another.

Board of Governors

The central authority of the U.S. money and banking system is the **Board of Governors** of the Federal Reserve System. The U.S. president, with the confirmation of the Senate, appoints the seven Board members. Terms are 14 years and staggered so that one member is replaced every 2 years. In addition, new members are appointed when resignations occur. The president selects the chairperson and vice-chairperson of the Board from among the members. Those officers serve 4-year terms and can be reappointed to new 4-year terms by the president. The

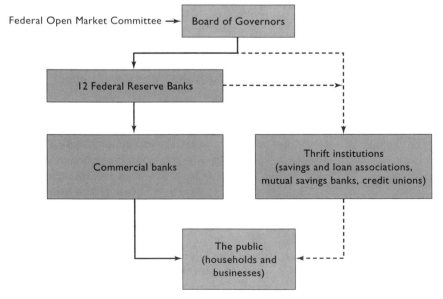

FIGURE 13.3

Framework of the Federal Reserve System and its relationship to the public. With the aid of the Federal Open Market Committee, the Board of Governors makes the basic policy decisions that provide monetary control of the U.S. money and banking systems. These decisions are implemented through the 12 Federal Reserve Banks.

FIGURE 13.4

The 12 Federal Reserve Districts. The Federal Reserve System divides the United States into 12 districts, each having one central bank and in some instances one or more branches of the central bank. Hawaii and Alaska are included in the twelfth district.

Source: Federal Reserve Bulletin.

long-term appointments provide the Board with continuity, experienced membership, and independence from political pressures that could result in inflation.

FOMC

The **Federal Open Market Committee (FOMC)** aids the Board of Governors in conducting monetary policy. The FOMC is made up of 12 individuals:

- The seven members of the Board of Governors.
- The president of the New York Federal Reserve Bank.
- Four of the remaining presidents of Federal Reserve Banks on a 1-year rotating basis.

The FOMC meets regularly to direct the purchase and sale of government securities (bills, notes, bonds) in the open market in order to maintain or change key interest rates. In Chapter 15 we will discover that these aptly named *open-market operations* are the most significant technique available to the Fed for controlling the nation's money supply.

The 12 Federal Reserve Banks

The 12 **Federal Reserve Banks,** which blend private and public control, collectively serve as the nation's "central bank." These banks also serve as bankers' banks.

Central Bank Most nations have a single central bank—for example, Britain's Bank of England or Japan's Bank of Japan. The United States' central bank consists of 12 banks whose policies are coordinated by the Fed's Board of Governors. The 12 Federal Reserve Banks accommodate the geographic size and economic diversity

of the United States and the nation's large number of commercial banks and thrifts.

Figure 13.4 locates the 12 Federal Reserve Banks and indicates the district that each serves. These banks implement the basic policy of the Board of Governors. The Federal Reserve Bank in New York City conducts most of the Fed's open-market operations.

Quasi-Public Banks The 12 Federal Reserve Banks are quasi-public banks, which blend private ownership and public control. Each Federal Reserve Bank is owned by the private commercial banks in its district. (Commercial banks are required to purchase shares of stock in the Federal Reserve Bank in their district.) But the Board of Governors, a government body, sets the basic policies that the Federal Reserve Banks pursue. The owners of these central banks thus control neither the central bank officials nor their policies.

Despite their private ownership, the Federal Reserve Banks are in practice public institutions. Unlike private firms, they are not motivated by profit. The policies they follow are designed by the Board of Governors to promote the well-being of the economy as a whole. Thus, the activities of the Federal Reserve Banks are frequently at odds with the profit motive.[4] Also, the Federal Reserve Banks do not compete with commercial banks. In general,

---

[4]Although it is not their goal, the Federal Reserve Banks have actually operated profitably, largely as a result of the Treasury debts they hold. Part of the profit is used to pay dividends to the commercial banks that hold stock in the Federal Reserve Banks; the remaining profit is usually turned over to the U.S. Treasury.

they do not deal with the public; rather, they interact with the government and commercial banks and thrifts.

Bankers' Banks The Federal Reserve Banks are "bankers' banks." They perform essentially the same functions for banks and thrifts as those institutions perform for the public. Just as banks and thrifts accept the deposits of and make loans to the public, so the central banks accept the deposits of and make loans to banks and thrifts. Normally, these loans average only about $150 million a day. But in emergency circumstances the Federal Reserve Banks become the "lender of last resort" to the banking system and can lend out as much as needed to ensure that banks and thrifts can meet their cash obligations. On the day after the September 11, 2001, terrorist attacks, the Fed lent $45 *billion* to U.S. banks and thrifts. The Fed wanted to make sure that the destruction and disruption in New York City and the Washington, D.C., area did not precipitate a nationwide banking crisis.

But the Federal Reserve Banks have a third function, which banks and thrifts do not perform: They issue currency when they are directed to do so by the Federal Reserve Board. Congress has authorized the Federal Reserve Banks to put into circulation Federal Reserve Notes, which constitute the economy's paper money supply.

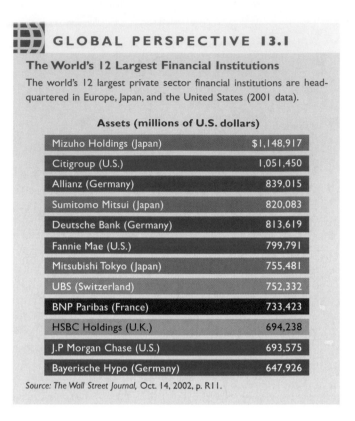

GLOBAL PERSPECTIVE 13.1

The World's 12 Largest Financial Institutions
The world's 12 largest private sector financial institutions are head-quartered in Europe, Japan, and the United States (2001 data).

Assets (millions of U.S. dollars)

Mizuho Holdings (Japan)	$1,148,917
Citigroup (U.S.)	1,051,450
Allianz (Germany)	839,015
Sumitomo Mitsui (Japan)	820,083
Deutsche Bank (Germany)	813,619
Fannie Mae (U.S.)	799,791
Mitsubishi Tokyo (Japan)	755,481
UBS (Switzerland)	752,332
BNP Paribas (France)	733,423
HSBC Holdings (U.K.)	694,238
J.P Morgan Chase (U.S.)	693,575
Bayerische Hypo (Germany)	647,926

Source: The Wall Street Journal, Oct. 14, 2002, p. R11.

Commercial Banks and Thrifts

There are about 7800 commercial banks. Roughly three-fourths are state banks. These are private banks chartered (authorized) by the individual states to operate within those states. One-fourth are private banks chartered by the Federal government to operate nationally; these are national banks. Some of the U.S. national banks are very large, ranking among the world's largest financial institutions (see Global Perspective 13.1).

The 11,800 thrift institutions—10,300 of which are credit unions—are regulated by agencies separate and apart from the Board of Governors and the Federal Reserve Banks. For example, the operations of savings and loan associations are regulated and monitored by the Treasury Department's Office of Thrift Supervision. But the thrifts *are* subject to monetary control by the Federal Reserve System. In particular, like the banks, thrifts are required to keep a certain percentage of their checkable deposits as "reserves." In Figure 13.3 we use dashed arrows to indicate that the thrift institutions are partially subject to the control of the Board of Governors and the central banks. Decisions concerning monetary policy affect the thrifts along with the commercial banks.

Fed Functions and the Money Supply

The Fed performs several functions, some of which we have already identified but they are worth repeating:

- *Issuing currency* The Federal Reserve Banks issue Federal Reserve Notes, the paper currency used in the U.S. monetary system. (The Federal Reserve Bank that issued a particular bill is identified in black in the upper left of the front of the newly designed bills. "A1," for example, identifies the Boston bank, "B2" the New York bank, and so on.)

- *Setting reserve requirements and holding reserves* The Fed sets reserve requirements, which are the fractions of checking account balances that banks must maintain as currency reserves. The central banks accept as deposits from the banks and thrifts any portion of their mandated reserves not held as vault cash.

- *Lending money to banks and thrifts* From time to time the Fed lends money to banks and thrifts and charges them an interest rate called the *discount rate*. In times of financial emergencies, the Fed serves as a lender of last resort to the U.S. banking industry.

- *Providing for check collection* The Fed provides the banking system with a means for collecting checks. If

Sue writes a check on her Miami bank or thrift to Joe, who deposits it in his Dallas bank or thrift, how does the Dallas bank collect the money represented by the check drawn against the Miami bank? Answer: The Fed handles it in 2 or 3 days by adjusting the reserves (deposits) of the two banks.

- *Acting as fiscal agent*   The Fed acts as the fiscal agent (provider of financial services) for the Federal government. The government collects huge sums through taxation, spends equally large amounts, and sells and redeems bonds. To carry out these activities, government uses the Fed's facilities.

- *Supervising banks*   The Fed supervises the operations of banks. It makes periodic examinations to assess bank profitability, to ascertain that banks perform in accordance with the many regulations to which they are subject, and to uncover questionable practices or fraud.[5]

- *Controlling the money supply*   Finally, and most important, the Fed has ultimate responsibility for regulating the supply of money, and this in turn enables it to influence interest rates. The major task of the Fed is to manage the money supply (and thus interest rates) according to the needs of the economy. This involves making an amount of money available that is consistent with high and rising levels of output and employment and a relatively constant price level. While all the other functions of the Fed are routine activities or have a service nature, managing the nation's money supply requires making basic, but unique, policy decisions. (We discuss those decisions in detail in Chapter 15.)

Federal Reserve Independence

Congress purposely established the Fed as an independent agency of government. The objective was to protect the Fed from political pressures so that it could effectively control the money supply and maintain price stability. Political pressures on Congress and the executive branch may at times result in inflationary fiscal policies, including tax cuts and special-interest spending. If Congress and the executive branch also controlled the nation's monetary policy, citizens and lobbying groups undoubtedly

would pressure elected officials to keep interest rates low even though at times high interest rates are necessary to reduce aggregate demand and thus control inflation. An independent monetary authority (the Fed) can take actions to increase interest rates when higher rates are needed to stem inflation. Studies show that countries that have independent central banks like the Fed have lower rates of inflation, on average, than countries that have little or no central bank independence.

Recent Developments in Money and Banking

The banking industry is undergoing a series of sweeping changes, spurred by competition from other financial institutions, the globalization of banking, and advances in information technology.

The Relative Decline of Banks and Thrifts

Banks and thrifts are just two of several types of firms that offer financial services. Table 13.2 lists the major categories of firms within the U.S. **financial services industry** and gives examples of firms in each category. Although banks and thrifts remain the only institutions that offer checkable deposits that have no restrictions on either the number or size of checks, their shares of total financial assets (value of things owned) are declining. In 1980 banks and thrifts together held nearly 60 percent of financial assets in the United States. By 2002 that percentage had declined to about 30 percent.

Where did the declining shares of the banks and thrifts go? Pension funds, insurance firms, and particularly securities firms and mutual fund companies expanded their shares of financial assets. (Mutual fund companies offer shares of a wide array of stock and bond funds, as well as the previously mentioned money market funds.) Clearly, between 1980 and 2002, U.S. households and businesses channeled relatively more saving away from banks and thrifts and toward other financial institutions. Those other institutions generally offered higher rates of return on funds than did banks and thrifts, largely because they could participate more fully in national and international stock and bond markets.

Consolidation among Banks and Thrifts

During the past two decades, many banks have purchased bankrupt thrifts or have merged with other banks.

---

[5]The Fed is not alone in this task of supervision. The individual states supervise all banks that they charter. The Comptroller of the Currency supervises all national banks, and the Office of Thrift Supervision supervises all thrifts. Also, the Federal Deposit Insurance Corporation supervises all banks and thrifts whose deposits it insures.

TABLE 13.2

Major U.S. Financial Institutions

Institution	Description	Examples
Commercial banks	State and national banks that provide checking and savings accounts, sell certificates of deposit, and make loans. The Federal Deposit Insurance Corporation (FDIC) insures checking and savings accounts up to $100,000.	J.P. Morgan Chase, Bank of America, Citibank, Wells Fargo
Thrifts	Savings and loan associations (S&Ls), mutual saving banks, and credit unions that offer checking and savings accounts and make loans. Historically, S&Ls made mortgage loans for houses while mutual savings banks and credit unions made small personal loans, such as automobile loans. Today, major thrifts offer the same range of banking services as commercial banks. The Federal Deposit Insurance Corporation and the National Credit Union Administration insure checking and savings deposits up to $100,000.	Washington Mutual, Golden State (owned by Citigroup), Golden West, Charter One
Insurance companies	Firms that offer policies (contracts) through which individuals pay premiums to insure against some loss, say, disability or death. In some life insurance policies and annuities, the funds are invested for the client in stocks and bonds and paid back after a specified number of years. Thus, insurance sometimes has a saving or financial-investment element.	Prudential, New York Life, Massachusetts Mutual
Mutual fund companies	Firms that pool deposits by customers to purchase stocks or bonds (or both). Customers thus own a part of a particular set of stocks or bonds, say stocks in companies expected to grow rapidly (a growth fund) or bonds issued by state governments (a municipal bond fund).	Fidelity, Putnam, Dreyfus, Kemper
Pension funds	For-profit or nonprofit institutions that collect savings from workers (or from employers on their behalf) throughout their working years and then buy stocks and bonds with the proceeds and make monthly retirement payments.	TIAA-CREF, Teamsters' Union
Securities firms	Firms that offer security advice and buy and sell stocks and bonds for clients. More generally known as *stock brokerage firms*.	Merrill Lynch, Solomon Smith Barney, Lehman Brothers, Charles Schwab

Major savings and loans have also merged. The purpose of such mergers is to create large regional or national banks or thrifts that can compete more effectively in the financial services industry. Consolidation of traditional banking is expected to continue; there are 5000 fewer banks today than there were in 1990. Today, the 10 largest U.S. banks hold roughly one-third of total bank deposits.

Convergence of Services Provided by Financial Institutions

In 1996 Congress greatly loosened the Depression-era prohibition against banks selling stocks, bonds, and mutual funds, and it ended the prohibition altogether in the Financial Services Modernization Act of 1999. Banks, thrifts, pension companies, insurance companies, and securities firms can now merge with one another and sell each other's products. Thus, the lines between the subsets of the financial industry are beginning to blur. Many banks have acquired stock brokerage firms and, in a few cases, insurance companies. For example, Citigroup now owns Salomon Smith Barney, a large securities firm. Many large banks (for example, Wells Fargo) and pension funds (for example, TIAA-CREF) now provide mutual funds, including money market funds that pay relatively high interest and on which checks of $500 or more can be written.

The lifting of restraints against banks and thrifts should work to their advantage because they can now provide their customers with "one-stop shopping" for financial services. In general, the reform will likely intensify competition and encourage financial innovation. The downside is that financial losses in securities subsidiaries—such as could occur during a major recession—could increase the number of bank failures. Such failures might undermine confidence in the entire banking system and complicate the Fed's task of maintaining an appropriate money supply.

Globalization of Financial Markets

Another significant banking development is the increasing integration of world financial markets. Major foreign financial institutions now have operations in the United States, and U.S. financial institutions do business abroad. For example, Visa, MasterCard, and American Express offer worldwide credit card services. Moreover, U.S. mutual fund companies now offer a variety of international stock and bond funds. Globally, financial capital increasingly flows in search of the highest risk-adjusted returns. As a result, U.S. banks increasingly compete with foreign banks for both deposits and loan customers.

Recent advances in computer and communications technology are likely to speed up the trend toward international financial integration. Yet studies indicate that the bulk of investment in the major nations is still financed through domestic saving within each nation.

Electronic Transactions

Finally, the rapid advance of Internet commerce and "banking" is potentially of great significance to financial institutions and central banks. Consumers have increasingly used the Internet for such **electronic transactions** as buying goods (using credit cards), buying and selling stock and mutual fund shares, transferring bank funds between accounts, and paying bills.

Some experts believe the next step will be the widespread use of electronic money, which is simply an entry in an electronic file stored in a computer. Electronic money will be deposited, or "loaded," into an account through Internet payments such as a paycheck, retirement benefit, or stock dividend. The owner of the account will withdraw, or "unload," the money from his or her account through Internet payments to others for a wide variety of goods and services.

In the future, account holders may be able to insert so-called stored-value cards into slots in their computers and load electronic money onto the card. These plastic "smart cards" contain computer chips that store information, including the amount of electronic money the

consumer has loaded. When purchases or payments are made, their amounts are automatically deducted from the balance in the card's memory. Consumers will be able to transfer traditional money to their smart cards through computers or cell phones or at automatic teller machines. Thus, it will be possible for nearly all payments to be made through the Internet or a smart card.

A few general-use smart cards that contain embedded programmable computer chips are available in the United States, including ones issued by Visa, MasterCard, and American Express ("Blue Cards"). More common are stored-value cards that facilitate specific purchases. Examples are prepaid phone cards, copy-machine cards, mass-transit cards, and single-store gift cards. Like the broader smart cards, these cards are "reloadable," meaning the amounts stored on them can be increased. A number of retailers—including Kinko's, Sears, Starbucks, Walgreens, and Wal-Mart—have recently made stored-value cards available to their customers.

Although smart-card use in the United States has increased, it remains far below that in Europe. Credit cards are more widely issued and more heavily used in the United States. They are as convenient as stored-value cards and provide interest-free loans between the time of purchase and the due date on the credit card statement. Because smart cards involve "instant payments," they do not offer this *interest-free float*. It is simply too early to predict whether stored-value cards will catch on in the United States and challenge credit cards, debit cards, currency, and checks as means of payment. In 2002 stored-value cards accounted for less than 2 percent of the dollar amount of purchases by American consumers.

A Large Amount of U.S. Currency Is Circulating Abroad.

Many Russians use American currency. So do Argentineans, Brazilians, Poles, Vietnamese, Chinese, and even Cubans. Like commercial aircraft, computer software, and movie videos, American currency has become a major U.S. "export." Russians hold about $40 billion of U.S. currency, and Argentineans hold $7 billion. The Polish government estimates that $6 billion of U.S. dollars is circulating in Poland. In all, perhaps as much as two-thirds of all U.S. currency is circulating abroad.

Dollars leave the United States when Americans buy imports, travel in other countries, or send dollars to relatives living abroad. The United States profits when the dollars stay in other countries. It costs the government about 4 cents to print a dollar. For someone abroad to obtain that new dollar, $1 worth of resources, goods, or services must be sold to Americans. These commodities are U.S. gains. The dollar goes abroad and, assuming it stays there, presents no claim on U.S. resources or goods or services. Americans in effect make 96 cents on the dollar (= $1 gain in resources, goods, or services — the 4-cent printing cost). It's like American Express selling traveler's checks that never get cashed.

Black markets and other illegal activity undoubtedly fuel some of the demand for U.S. cash abroad. The dollar is king in covert trading in diamonds, weapons, and pirated software. Billions of cash dollars are involved in the narcotics trade. But the illegal use of dollars is only a small part of the story. The massive volume of dollars in other nations reflects a global search for monetary stability. On the basis of past experience, foreign citizens are confident that the dollar's purchasing power will remain relatively steady.

Following the collapse of the Soviet Union in the early 1990s, high rates of inflation led many Russians to abandon rubles for U.S. dollars. While the dollar retained its purchasing power in Russia, the purchasing power of the ruble plummeted. As a result, many Russians still hold large parts of their savings in dollars today.

In Brazil, where inflation rates above 1000 percent annually were once common, people have long sought the stability of dollars. In the shopping districts of Beijing and Shanghai, Chinese consumers trade their domestic currency for dollars. In Bolivia half of all bank accounts are denominated in dollars. There is a thriving "dollar economy" in Vietnam, and even Cuba has partially legalized the use of U.S. dollars. The U.S. dollar is the official currency in Panama, Ecuador, and Liberia. Immediately after the war in Iraq in 2003, the purchasing power of the Iraqi dinar fell dramatically because looting of banks placed many more dinars into circulation. The United States and British forces began paying Iraqi workers in U.S. dollars, and dollars in effect became the transition currency in the country.

Is there any financial risk for those who hold dollars in foreign countries? While the dollar is likely to hold its purchasing power internally in those nations, holders of dollars do face *exchange-rate risk*. If the international value of the dollar depreciates, as it did in mid-2003, more dollars are needed to buy goods imported from countries other than the United States. Those goods, priced in say, euros, Swiss francs, or yen, become more expensive to holders of dollars. Offsetting that "downside risk," of course, is the "upside opportunity" of the dollar's appreciating.

There is little risk for the United States in satisfying the world's demand for dollars. If all the dollars came rushing back to the United States at once, the nation's money supply would surge, possibly causing demand-pull inflation. But there is not much chance of that happening. Overall, the global greenback is a positive economic force. It is a reliable medium of exchange, unit of account, and store of value that facilitates transactions that might not otherwise occur. Dollar holdings have helped buyers and sellers abroad overcome special monetary problems. The result has been increased output in those countries and thus greater output and income globally.

SUMMARY

1. Anything that is accepted as (a) a medium of exchange, (b) a unit of monetary account, and (c) a store of value can be used as money.

2. The Federal Reserve System recognizes three "official" definitions of the money supply. *M1* consists of currency and checkable deposits; *M2* consists of *M1* plus savings deposits, including money market deposit accounts, small (less than $100,000) time deposits, and money market mutual fund balances; and *M3* consists of *M2* plus large ($100,000 or more) time deposits.

3. Money represents the debts of government and institutions offering checkable deposits (commercial banks and

thrift institutions) and has value because of the goods, services, and resources it will command in the market. Maintaining the purchasing power of money depends largely on the government's effectiveness in managing the money supply.

4. The total demand for money consists of the transactions demand and the asset demand for money. The transactions demand varies directly with the nominal GDP; the asset demand varies inversely with the interest rate. The money market combines the total demand for money with the money supply to determine the equilibrium interest rate.

5. Other things equal, decreases in the supply of money raise interest rates, whereas increases in the supply of money decrease them. Interest rates and bond prices move in the opposite direction. At the equilibrium interest rate, bond prices tend to be stable and the amounts of money demanded and supplied are equal.

6. The U.S. banking system consists of (a) the Board of Governors of the Federal Reserve System, (b) the 12 Federal Reserve Banks, and (c) some 7800 commercial banks and 11,800 thrift institutions (mainly credit unions). The Board of Governors is the basic policymaking body for the entire banking system. The directives of the Board and the Federal Open Market Committee (FOMC) are made effective through the 12 Federal Reserve Banks, which are simultaneously (a) central banks, (b) quasi-public banks, and (c) bankers' banks.

7. The major functions of the Fed are to (a) issue Federal Reserve Notes, (b) set reserve requirements and hold reserves deposited by banks and thrifts, (c) lend money to banks and thrifts, (d) provide for the rapid collection of checks, (e) act as the fiscal agent for the Federal government, (f) supervise the operations of the banks, and (g) regulate the supply of money in the best interests of the economy.

8. The Fed is essentially an independent institution, controlled neither by the president of the United States nor by Congress. This independence shields the Fed from political pressure and allows it to raise and lower interest rates (via changes in the money supply) as needed to promote full employment, price stability, and economic growth.

9. Between 1980 and 2002, banks and thrifts lost considerable market share of the financial services industry to pension funds, insurance companies, mutual funds, and securities firms. Other recent banking developments of significance include the consolidation of the banking and thrift industry; the convergence of services offered by banks, thrifts, mutual funds, securities firms, and pension companies; the globalization of banking services; and the emergence of the Internet and electronic money, including smart cards.

TERMS AND CONCEPTS

medium of exchange	commercial banks	money market mutual fund (MMMF)	Federal Reserve System
unit of account	thrift institutions	legal tender	Board of Governors
store of value	near-monies	transactions demand	Federal Open Market Committee (FOMC)
$M1$, $M2$, $M3$	savings account	asset demand	Federal Reserve Banks
token money	money market deposit account (MMDA)	total demand for money	financial services industry
Federal Reserve Notes	time deposits	money market	electronic transactions
checkable deposits			

STUDY QUESTIONS

1. What are the three basic functions of money? Describe how rapid inflation can undermine money's ability to perform each of the three functions.

2. Which two of the following financial institutions offer checkable deposits included within the $M1$ money supply: mutual fund companies; insurance companies; commercial banks; securities firms; thrift institutions? Which of the following is not included in either $M1$ or $M2$: currency held by the public; checkable deposits; money market mutual

fund balances; small (less than $100,000) time deposits; currency held by banks; savings deposits.

3. Explain and evaluate the following statements:
    a. The invention of money is one of the great achievements of humankind, for without it the enrichment that comes from broadening trade would have been impossible.
    b. Money is whatever society says it is.
    c. In most economies of the world, the debts of government and commercial banks are used as money.

d. People often say they would like to have more money, but what they usually mean is that they would like to have more goods and services.

e. When the price of everything goes up, it is not because everything is worth more but because the currency is worth less.

f. Any central bank can create money; the trick is to create enough, but not too much, of it.

4. **Key Question** What are the components of the M1 money supply? What is the largest component? Which of the components of M1 is *legal tender?* Why is the face value of a coin greater than its intrinsic value? What near-monies are included in the M2 money supply? What distinguishes the M2 and M3 money supplies?

5. What "backs" the money supply in the United States? What determines the value (domestic purchasing power) of money? How does the value of money relate to the price level? Who in the United States is responsible for maintaining money's value?

6. **Key Question** Suppose the price level and value of the dollar in year 1 are 1 and $1, respectively. If the price level rises to 1.25 in year 2, what is the new value of the dollar? If, instead, the price level falls to .50, what is the value of the dollar? What generalization can you draw from your answers?

7. **Key Question** What is the basic determinant of (a) the transactions demand and (b) the asset demand for money? Explain how these two demands can be combined graphically to determine total money demand. How is the equilibrium interest rate in the money market determined? How might (a) the expanded use of credit cards, (b) a shortening of worker pay periods, and (c) an increase in nominal GDP each independently affect the transactions demand for money, the total demand for money, and the equilibrium interest rate?

8. Assume that the following data characterize a hypothetical economy: money supply = $200 billion; quantity of money demanded for transactions = $150 billion; quantity of money demanded as an asset = $10 billion at 12 percent interest, increasing by $10 billion for each 2-percentage-point fall in the interest rate.

    a. What is the equilibrium interest rate? Explain.

    b. At the equilibrium interest rate, what are the quantity of money supplied, the total quantity of money demanded, the amount of money demanded for transactions, and the amount of money demanded as an asset?

9. Suppose a bond with no expiration date has a face value of $10,000 and annually pays a fixed amount of interest of $800. Compute and enter in the spaces provided in the next column either the interest rate that the bond would yield to a bond buyer at each of the bond prices listed or the bond price at each of the interest yields shown. What generalization can be drawn from the completed table?

Bond Price	Interest Yield, %
$ 8,000	_____
_____	8.9
$10,000	_____
$11,000	_____
_____	6.2

10. Assume that the money market is initially in equilibrium and that the money supply is then increased. Explain the adjustments toward a new equilibrium interest rate. Will bond prices be higher or lower at the new equilibrium rate of interest? What effects would you expect the interest-rate change to have on the levels of output, employment, and prices? Answer the same questions for a *decrease* in the money supply.

11. How is the chairperson of the Federal Reserve System selected? Describe the relationship between the Board of Governors of the Federal Reserve System and the 12 Federal Reserve Banks. What is the composition and purpose of the Federal Open Market Committee (FOMC)?

12. What is meant when economists say that the Federal Reserve Banks are central banks, quasi-public banks, and bankers' banks? What are the seven basic functions of the Federal Reserve System?

13. Following are two hypothetical ways in which the Federal Reserve Board might be appointed. Would you favor either of these two methods over the present method? Why or why not?

    a. Upon taking office, the U.S. president appoints seven people to the Federal Reserve Board, including a chair. Each appointee must be confirmed by a majority vote of the Senate, and each serves the same 4-year term as the president.

    b. Congress selects seven members from its ranks (four from the House of Representatives and three from the Senate) to serve at its pleasure as the Board of Governors of the Federal Reserve System.

14. What are the major categories of firms that make up the U.S. financial services industry? Did the bank and thrift share of the financial services market rise, fall, or stay the same between 1980 and 2002? Are there more or fewer bank firms today than a decade ago? Why are the lines between the categories of financial firms becoming more blurred than in the past?

15. In what way are electronic money and smart cards potentially related? Do you think electronic money and smart cards will dominate transactions some time within the next 20 years? Why or why not?

16. **(Last Word)** Over the years, the Federal Reserve Banks have printed many billions of dollars more in currency than U.S. households, businesses, and financial institutions now hold. Where is this "missing" money? Why is it there?

17. ***Web-Based Question: Who are the members of the Federal Reserve Board?*** The Federal Reserve Board website, www.federalreserve.gov/BIOS/, provides a detailed biography of the seven members of the Board of Governors. What is the composition of the Board with regard to age, gender, education, previous employment, and ethnic background? Which Board members are near the ends of their terms?

18. ***Web-Based Question: Currency trivia*** Visit the website of the Federal Reserve Bank of Atlanta, www.frbatlanta.org/ publica/brochure/fundfac/money.htm, to answer the following questions: What are the denominations of Federal Reserve Notes now being printed? What was the largest-denomination Federal Reserve Note ever printed and circulated, and when was it last printed? What are some tips for spotting counterfeit currency? When was the last silver dollar minted? What have been the largest and smallest U.S. coin denominations since the Coinage Act of 1792?

14

How Banks and Thrifts Create Money

We have seen that the M1 money supply consists of currency (Federal Reserve Notes and coins) and checkable deposits. The U.S. Bureau of Engraving creates the Federal Reserve Notes and the U.S. Mint creates the coins. So who creates the checkable deposits that make up more than half the nation's M1 money supply? Surprisingly, it is loan officers! Although that may sound like something a congressional committee should investigate, the monetary authorities are well aware that banks and thrifts create checkable deposits. In fact, the Federal Reserve relies on these institutions to create this vital component of the nation's money supply.

This chapter explains how commercial banks and thrifts can create checkable deposits by issuing loans. Our examples will involve commercial banks, but remember that thrift institutions also provide checkable deposits. So the analysis applies to banks and thrifts alike.

The Balance Sheet of a Commercial Bank

We will analyze the workings of the U.S. monetary system by considering certain items on a commercial bank's balance sheet and the way various transactions alter those items.

The **balance sheet** of a commercial bank (or thrift) is a statement of assets and claims on assets that summarizes the financial position of the bank at a certain time. Every balance sheet must balance; this means that the value of *assets* must equal the amount of claims against those assets. The claims shown on a balance sheet are divided into two groups: the claims of nonowners against the firm's assets, called *liabilities*, and the claims of the

owners of the firm against the firm's assets, called *net worth*. A balance sheet is balanced because

$$\text{Assets} = \text{liabilities} + \text{net worth}$$

Prologue: The Goldsmiths

The United States, like most other countries today, has a **fractional reserve banking system** *in which only a fraction of the total money supply is held in reserve as currency.* Here is the history behind the idea.

When early traders began to use gold in making transactions, they soon realized that it was both unsafe and inconvenient to carry gold and to have it weighed and assayed (judged for purity) every time they negotiated a transaction. So by the sixteenth century they had begun to deposit their gold with goldsmiths, who would store it in vaults for a fee. On receiving a gold deposit, the goldsmith would issue a receipt to the depositor. Soon people were paying for goods with goldsmiths' receipts, which served as the first kind of paper money.

At this point the goldsmiths—embryonic bankers—used a 100 percent reserve system; they backed their circulating paper money receipts fully with the gold that they held "in reserve" in their vaults. But because of the public's acceptance of the goldsmiths' receipts as paper money, the goldsmiths soon realized that owners rarely redeemed the gold they had in storage. In fact, the goldsmiths observed that the amount of gold being deposited with them in any week or month was likely to exceed the amount that was being withdrawn.

Then some clever goldsmith hit on the idea that paper "receipts" could be issued in excess of the amount of gold held. Goldsmiths would put these receipts, which were redeemable in gold, into circulation by making interest-earning loans to merchants, producers, and consumers. Borrowers were willing to accept loans in the form of gold receipts because the receipts were accepted as a medium of exchange in the marketplace.

This was the beginning of the fractional reserve system of banking, in which reserves in bank vaults are a fraction of the total money supply. If, for example, the goldsmith issued $1 million in receipts for actual gold in storage and another $1 million in receipts as loans, then the total value of paper money in circulation would be $2 million—twice the value of the gold. Gold reserves would be a fraction (one-half) of outstanding paper money.

Fractional reserve banking has two significant characteristics:

- **Money creation and reserves** Banks can create money through lending. In fact, goldsmiths created money when they made loans by giving borrowers paper money that was not fully backed by gold reserves. The quantity of such money goldsmiths could create depended on the amount of reserves they deemed prudent to have available. The smaller the amount of reserves thought necessary, the larger the amount of paper money the goldsmiths could create. Today, gold is no longer used as bank reserves. Instead, the creation of checkable deposit money by banks (via their lending) is limited by the amount of *currency reserves* that the banks feel obligated, or are required by law, to keep.

- **Bank panics and regulation** Banks that operate on the basis of fractional reserves are vulnerable to "panics" or "runs." A goldsmith who issued paper money equal to twice the value of his gold reserves would be unable to convert all that paper money into gold in the event that all the holders of that money appeared at his door at the same time demanding their gold. In fact, many European and U.S. banks were once ruined by this unfortunate circumstance. However, a bank panic is highly unlikely if the banker's reserve and lending policies are prudent. Indeed, one reason why banking systems are highly regulated industries is to prevent runs on banks. This is also the reason why the United States has a system of deposit insurance.

A Single Commercial Bank

How can a commercial bank (or thrift) create money? If it can create money, can it destroy money too? What factors govern how a bank creates money?

Formation of a Commercial Bank

To answer these questions we must understand the items a bank carries on its balance sheet and how certain transactions affect the balance sheet. We begin with the organization of a local commercial bank.

Transaction 1: Creating a Bank Suppose some farsighted citizens of the town of Wahoo, Nebraska (yes, there is such a place), decide their town needs a new commercial bank to provide banking services for that growing community. Once they have secured a state or national charter for their bank, they turn to the task of selling, say, $250,000 worth of capital stock (equity shares) to buyers, both in and out of the community. Their efforts meet with success and the Bank of Wahoo comes into existence—at least on paper. What does its balance sheet look like at this stage?

The founders of the bank have sold $250,000 worth of shares of stock in the bank—some to themselves, some to other people. As a result, the bank now has $250,000 in cash on hand and $250,000 worth of capital stock outstanding. The cash is an asset to the bank. Cash held by a bank is sometimes called **vault cash** or till money. The shares of stock outstanding constitute an equal amount of claims that the owners have against the bank's assets. Those shares of stock constitute the net worth of the bank. The bank's balance sheet reads:

Creating a Bank			
Balance Sheet 1: Wahoo Bank			
Assets		Liabilities and net worth	
Cash	$250,000	Capital stock	$250,000

Each item listed in a balance sheet such as this is called an *account*.

Transaction 2: Acquiring Property and Equipment

The board of directors (who represent the bank's owners) must now get the new bank off the drawing board and make it a reality. First, property and equipment must be acquired. Suppose the directors, confident of the success of their venture, purchase a building for $220,000 and pay $20,000 for office equipment. This simple transaction changes the composition of the bank's assets. The bank now has $240,000 less in cash and $240,000 of new property assets. Using blue to denote accounts affected by each transaction, we find that the bank's balance sheet at the end of transaction 2 appears as follows:

Acquiring Property and Equipment Balance Sheet 2: Wahoo Bank			
Assets		Liabilities and net worth	
Cash	$ 10,000	Capital stock	$250,000
Property	240,000		

Note that the balance sheet still balances, as it must.

Transaction 3: Accepting Deposits

Commercial banks have two basic functions: to accept deposits of money and to make loans. Now that the bank is operating, suppose that the citizens and businesses of Wahoo decide to deposit $100,000 in the Wahoo bank. What happens to the bank's balance sheet?

The bank receives cash, which is an asset to the bank. Suppose this money is deposited in the bank as checkable deposits (checking account entries), rather than as savings accounts or time deposits. These newly created *checkable deposits* constitute claims that the depositors have against the assets of the Wahoo bank and thus are a new liability account. The bank's balance sheet now looks like this:

Accepting Deposits Balance Sheet 3: Wahoo Bank			
Assets		Liabilities and net worth	
Cash	$110,000	Checkable deposits	$100,000
Property	240,000		
		Capital stock	250,000

There has been no change in the economy's total supply of money as a result of transaction 3, but a change has occurred in the composition of the money supply. Bank money, or checkable deposits, has increased by $100,000,

and currency held by the public has decreased by $100,000. Currency held by a bank, you will recall, is not part of the economy's money supply.

A withdrawal of cash will reduce the bank's checkable-deposit liabilities and its holdings of cash by the amount of the withdrawal. This, too, changes the composition, but not the total supply, of money in the economy.

Transaction 4: Depositing Reserves in a Federal Reserve Bank

All commercial banks and thrift institutions that provide checkable deposits must by law keep **required reserves.** Required reserves are an amount of funds equal to a specified percentage of the bank's own deposit liabilities. A bank must keep these reserves on deposit with the Federal Reserve Bank in its district or as cash in the bank's vault. To simplify, we suppose the Bank of Wahoo keeps its required reserves entirely as deposits in the Federal Reserve Bank of its district. But remember that vault cash is counted as reserves and real-world banks keep a significant portion of their own reserves in their vaults.

The "specified percentage" of checkable-deposit liabilities that a commercial bank must keep as reserves is known as the **reserve ratio**—the ratio of the required reserves the commercial bank must keep to the bank's own outstanding checkable-deposit liabilities:

$$\text{Reserve ratio} = \frac{\text{commercial bank's required reserves}}{\text{commercial bank's checkable-deposit liabilities}}$$

If the reserve ratio is $\frac{1}{10}$, or 10 percent, the Wahoo bank, having accepted $100,000 in deposits from the public, would have to keep $10,000 as reserves. If the ratio is $\frac{1}{5}$, or 20 percent, $20,000 of reserves would be required. If $\frac{1}{2}$, or 50 percent, $50,000 would be required.

The Fed has the authority to establish and vary the reserve ratio within limits legislated by Congress. The limits now prevailing are shown in Table 14.1. The first $6 million of checkable deposits held by a commercial bank or thrift is exempt from reserve requirements. A 3 percent reserve is required on checkable deposits of between $6 million and $42.1 million. A 10 percent reserve is required on checkable deposits over $42.1 million, although the Fed can vary that percentage between 8 and 14 percent. Currently, no reserves are required against noncheckable nonpersonal (business) savings or time deposits, although up to 9 percent can be required. Also, after consultation with appropriate congressional committees, the Fed for 180 days may impose reserve requirements in excess of the requirements specified in Table 14.1.

TABLE 14.1

Reserve Requirements (Reserve Ratios) for Banks and Thrifts, 2003

Type of Deposit	Current Requirement	Statutory Limits
Checkable deposits:		
$0–$6 million	0%	3%
$6–$42.1 million	3	3
Over $42.1 million	10	8–14
Noncheckable nonpersonal savings and time deposits	0	0–9

Source: Federal Reserve, Regulation D, www.federalreserve.gov. Data are for 2003.

In order to simplify, we will suppose that the reserve ratio for checkable deposits in commercial banks is $\frac{1}{5}$, or 20 percent. Although 20 percent obviously is higher than the requirement really is, the figure is convenient for calculations. Because we are concerned only with checkable (spendable) deposits, we ignore reserves on noncheckable savings and time deposits. The main point is that reserve requirements are fractional, meaning that they are less than 100 percent. This point is critical in our analysis of the lending ability of the banking system.

By depositing $20,000 in the Federal Reserve Bank, the Wahoo bank will just be meeting the required 20 percent ratio between its reserves and its own deposit liabilities. We will use "reserves" to mean the funds commercial banks deposit in the Federal Reserve Banks, to distinguish those funds from the public's deposits in commercial banks.

But suppose the Wahoo bank anticipates that its holdings of the checkable deposits will grow in the future. Then, instead of sending just the minimum amount, $20,000, it sends an extra $90,000, for a total of $110,000. In so doing, the bank will avoid the inconvenience of sending additional reserves to the Federal Reserve Bank each time its own checkable-deposit liabilities increase. And, as you will see, it is these extra reserves that enable banks to lend money and earn interest income.

Actually, the bank would not deposit *all* its cash in the Federal Reserve Bank. However, because (1) banks as a rule hold vault cash only in the amount of $1\frac{1}{2}$ or 2 percent of their total assets and (2) vault cash can be counted as reserves, we can assume that all the bank's cash is deposited in the Federal Reserve Bank and therefore constitutes the commercial bank's actual reserves. Then we do not need to bother adding two assets—"cash" and "deposits in the Federal Reserve Bank"—to determine "reserves."

After the Wahoo bank deposits $110,000 of reserves at the Fed, its balance sheet becomes:

Depositing Reserves at the Fed Balance Sheet 4: Wahoo Bank			
Assets		Liabilities and net worth	
Cash	$　　0	Checkable	
Reserves	110,000	deposits	$100,000
Property	240,000	Capital stock	250,000

There are three things to note about this latest transaction.

Excess Reserves　A bank's **excess reserves** are found by subtracting its *required reserves* from its **actual reserves:**

$$\text{Excess reserves} = \text{actual reserves} - \text{required reserves}$$

In this case,

Actual reserves	$110,000
Required reserves	−20,000
Excess reserves	$ 90,000

The only reliable way of computing excess reserves is to multiply the bank's checkable-deposit liabilities by the reserve ratio to obtain required reserves ($100,000 × 20 percent = $20,000) and then to subtract the required reserves from the actual reserves listed on the asset side of the bank's balance sheet.

To test your understanding, compute the bank's excess reserves from balance sheet 4, assuming that the reserve ratio is (1) 10 percent, (2) $33\frac{1}{3}$ percent, and (3) 50 percent.

We will soon demonstrate that the ability of a commercial bank to make loans depends on the existence of excess reserves. Understanding this concept is crucial in seeing how the banking system creates money.

Control　You might think the basic purpose of reserves is to enhance the liquidity of a bank and protect commercial bank depositors from losses. Reserves would constitute a ready source of funds from which commercial banks could meet large, unexpected cash withdrawals by depositors.

But this reasoning breaks down under scrutiny. Although historically reserves have been seen as a source of liquidity and therefore as protection for depositors, a bank's required reserves are not great enough to meet sudden, massive cash withdrawals. If the banker's nightmare should materialize—everyone with checkable deposits appearing at once to demand those deposits in cash—the legal reserves held as vault cash or at the Federal Reserve Bank would be insufficient. The banker simply could not meet this "bank panic." Because reserves are fractional, checkable deposits may be much greater than a bank's required reserves.

So commercial bank deposits must be protected by other means. Periodic bank examinations are one way of promoting prudent commercial banking practices. Furthermore, insurance funds administered by the Federal Deposit Insurance Corporation (FDIC) and the National Credit Union Administration (NCUA) insure individual deposits in banks and thrifts up to $100,000.

If it is not the purpose of reserves to provide for commercial bank liquidity, then what is their function? *Control* is the answer. Required reserves help the Fed control the lending ability of commercial banks. The Fed can take certain actions that either increase or decrease commercial bank reserves and affect the ability of banks to grant credit. The objective is to prevent banks from overextending or underextending bank credit. To the degree that these policies successfully influence the volume of commercial bank credit, the Fed can help the economy avoid business fluctuations. Another function of reserves is to facilitate the collection or "clearing" of checks. **(Key Question 2)**

Asset and Liability Transaction 4 brings up another matter. Specifically, the reserves created in transaction 4 are an asset to the depositing commercial bank because they are a claim this bank has against the assets of another institution—the Federal Reserve Bank. The checkable deposit you get by depositing money in a commercial bank is an asset to you and a liability to the bank. In the same way, the reserves that a commercial bank establishes by depositing money in a bankers' bank are an asset to that bank and a liability to the Federal Reserve Bank.

Transaction 5: Clearing a Check Drawn against the Bank Assume that Clem Bradshaw, a Wahoo farmer, deposited a substantial portion of the $100,000 in checkable deposits that the Wahoo bank received in transaction 3. Now suppose that Clem buys $50,000 of farm machinery from the Ajax Farm Implement Company of Surprise, Nebraska. Bradshaw pays for this machinery by writing a $50,000 check, against his deposit in the Wahoo

bank, to the Ajax Company. (1) How is this check collected or cleared, and (2) what effect does the collection of the check have on the balance sheets of the banks involved in the transaction?

To answer these questions, we must consider the Wahoo bank (Bradshaw's bank), the Surprise bank (the Ajax Company's bank), and the Federal Reserve Bank of Kansas City. For simplicity, we deal only with changes that occur in the specific accounts affected by this transaction. We trace the transaction in three steps, keyed by letters to Figure 14.1.

(a) Bradshaw gives his $50,000 check, drawn against the Wahoo bank, to the Ajax Company. Ajax deposits the check in its account with the Surprise bank. The Surprise bank increases Ajax's checkable deposits by $50,000 when the check is deposited. Ajax is now paid in full. Bradshaw is pleased with his new machinery.

(b) Now the Surprise bank has Bradshaw's check. This check is simply a claim against the assets of the Wahoo bank. The Surprise bank will collect this claim by sending the check (along with checks drawn on other banks) to the Federal Reserve Bank of Kansas City. Here a clerk will clear, or collect, the check for the Surprise bank by increasing Surprise's reserve in the Federal Reserve Bank by $50,000 and decreasing the Wahoo bank's reserve by that same amount. The check is "collected" merely by making bookkeeping notations to the effect that Wahoo's claim against the Federal Reserve Bank is reduced by $50,000 and Surprise's claim is increased by $50,000. Note these changes on the balance sheets in Figure 14.1.

(c) Finally, the Federal Reserve Bank sends the cleared check back to the Wahoo bank, and for the first time the Wahoo bank discovers that one of its depositors has drawn a check for $50,000 against his checkable deposit. Accordingly, the Wahoo bank reduces Bradshaw's checkable deposit by $50,000 and notes that the collection of this check has caused a $50,000 decline in its reserves at the Federal Reserve Bank. Observe that the balance statements of all three banks balance. The Wahoo bank has reduced both its assets and its liabilities by $50,000. The Surprise bank has $50,000 more in assets (reserves) and in checkable deposits. Ownership of reserves at the Federal Reserve Bank has changed—with Wahoo owning $50,000 less, and Surprise owning $50,000 more—but total reserves stay the same.

Whenever a check is drawn against one bank and deposited in another bank, collection of that check will reduce both the

FIGURE 14.1

The collection of a check through a Federal Reserve Bank. The bank against which a check is drawn and cleared (Wahoo bank) loses both reserves and deposits; the bank in which the check is deposited (Surprise bank) acquires both reserves and deposits.

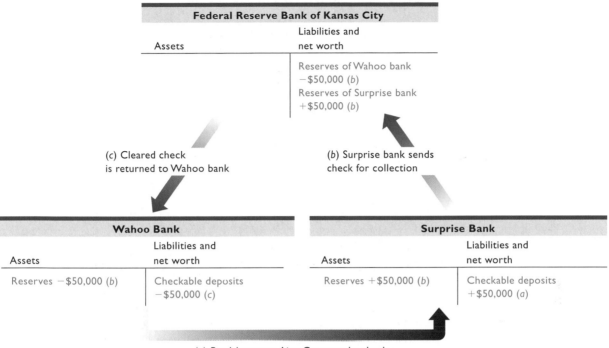

(a) Bradshaw pays Ajax Company by check

reserves and the checkable deposits of the bank on which the check is drawn. Conversely, if a bank receives a check drawn on another bank, the bank receiving the check will, in the process of collecting it, have its reserves and deposits increased by the amount of the check. In our example, the Wahoo bank loses $50,000 in both reserves and deposits to the Surprise bank. But there is no loss of reserves or deposits for the banking system as a whole. What one bank loses, another bank gains.

If we bring all the other assets and liabilities back into the picture, the Wahoo bank's balance sheet looks like this at the end of transaction 5:

Clearing a Check			
Balance Sheet 5: Wahoo Bank			
Assets		Liabilities and net worth	
Reserves	$ 60,000	Checkable	
Property	240,000	deposits	$ 50,000
		Capital stock	250,000

Verify that with a 20 percent reserve requirement, the bank's excess reserves now stand at $50,000.

Money-Creating Transactions of a Commercial Bank

The next three transactions are crucial because they explain (1) how a commercial bank can literally create money by making loans, (2) how money is destroyed when loans are repaid, and (3) how banks create money by purchasing government bonds from the public.

Transaction 6: Granting a Loan

In addition to accepting deposits, commercial banks grant loans to borrowers. What effect does lending by a commercial bank have on its balance sheet?

Suppose the Gristly Meat Packing Company of Wahoo decides it is time to expand its facilities. Suppose, too, that the company needs exactly $50,000—which just happens to be equal to the Wahoo bank's excess reserves—to finance this project.

Gristly goes to the Wahoo bank and requests a loan for this amount. The Wahoo bank knows the Gristly Company's fine reputation and financial soundness and is convinced of its ability to repay the loan. So the loan is granted. In return, the president of Gristly hands a promissory note—a fancy IOU—to the Wahoo bank. Gristly wants the convenience and safety of paying its obligations by check. So, instead of receiving a bushel basket full of currency from the bank, Gristly gets a $50,000 increase in its checkable-deposit account in the Wahoo bank.

The Wahoo bank has acquired an interest-earning asset (the promissory note, which it files under "Loans") and has created checkable deposits (a liability) to "pay" for this asset. Gristly has swapped an IOU for the right to draw an additional $50,000 worth of checks against its checkable deposit in the Wahoo bank. Both parties are pleased.

At the moment the loan is completed, the Wahoo bank's position is shown by balance sheet 6a:

When a Loan Is Negotiated		
Balance Sheet 6a: Wahoo Bank		
Assets	Liabilities and net worth	
Reserves	$ 60,000	Checkable
Loans	50,000	deposits	$100,000
Property	240,000	Capital stock	250,000

All this looks simple enough. But a close examination of the Wahoo bank's balance statement reveals a startling fact: *When a bank makes loans, it creates money*. The president of Gristly went to the bank with something that is *not* money—her IOU—and walked out with something that *is* money—a checkable deposit.

Contrast transaction 6a with transaction 3, in which checkable deposits were created but only as a result of currency having been taken out of circulation. There was a change in the *composition* of the money supply in that situation but no change in the *total supply* of money. But when banks lend, they create checkable deposits that *are* money.

By extending credit, the Wahoo bank has "monetized" an IOU. Gristly and the Wahoo bank have created and then swapped claims. The claim created by Gristly and given to the bank is not money; an individual's IOU is not acceptable as a medium of exchange. But the claim created by the bank and given to Gristly *is* money; checks drawn against a checkable deposit are acceptable as a medium of exchange.

Much of the money we use in our economy is created through the extension of credit by commercial banks. This checkable-deposit money may be thought of as "debts" of commercial banks and thrift institutions. Checkable deposits are bank debts in the sense that they are claims that banks and thrifts promise to pay "on demand."

But there are factors limiting the ability of a commercial bank to create checkable deposits ("bank money") by lending. The Wahoo bank can expect the newly created checkable deposit of $50,000 to be a very active account. Gristly would not borrow $50,000 at, say, 7, 10, or 12 percent interest for the sheer joy of knowing that funds were available if needed.

Assume that Gristly awards a $50,000 building contract to the Quickbuck Construction Company of Omaha. Quickbuck, true to its name, completes the expansion promptly and is paid with a check for $50,000 drawn by Gristly against its checkable deposit in the Wahoo bank. Quickbuck, with headquarters in Omaha, does not deposit this check in the Wahoo bank but instead deposits it in the Fourth National Bank of Omaha. Fourth National now has a $50,000 claim against the Wahoo bank. The check is collected in the manner described in transaction 5. As a result, the Wahoo bank loses both reserves and deposits equal to the amount of the check; Fourth National acquires $50,000 of reserves and deposits.

In summary, assuming a check is drawn by the borrower for the entire amount of the loan ($50,000) and is given to a firm that deposits it in some other bank, the Wahoo bank's balance sheet will read as follows *after the check has been cleared against it*:

After a Check Is Drawn on the Loan		
Balance Sheet 6b: Wahoo Bank		
Assets	Liabilities and net worth	
Reserves	$ 10,000	Checkable
Loans	50,000	deposits	$ 50,000
Property	240,000	Capital stock	250,000

After the check has been collected, the Wahoo bank just meets the required reserve ratio of 20 percent (= $10,000/$50,000). The bank has *no* excess reserves. This poses a question: Could the Wahoo bank have lent more than $50,000—an amount greater than its excess reserves—and still have met the 20 percent reserve requirement when a check for the full amount of the loan was cleared against it? The answer is no; the bank is "fully loaned up."

Here is why: Suppose the Wahoo bank had lent $55,000 to the Gristly company. Collection of the check against the Wahoo bank would have lowered its reserves to $5,000 (= $60,000 − $55,000), and checkable deposits would once again stand at $50,000 (= $105,000 − $55,000). The ratio of actual reserves to checkable deposits would then be $5,000/$50,000, or only 10 percent. The Wahoo bank could thus not have lent $55,000.

By experimenting with other amounts over $50,000, you will find that the maximum amount the Wahoo bank could lend at the outset of transaction 6 is $50,000. This amount is identical to the amount of excess reserves the bank had available when the loan was negotiated. *A single commercial bank in a multibank banking system can lend only an amount equal to its initial preloan excess reserves.* When it lends, the lending bank faces the possibility that checks for the entire amount of the loan will be drawn and cleared against it. If that happens, the lending bank will lose (to other banks) reserves equal to the amount it lends. So, to be safe, it limits its lending to the amount of its excess reserves.

Transaction 7: Repaying a Loan

If commercial banks create money in the form of checkable deposits when they make loans, is money destroyed when loans are repaid? Yes. Let's see what happens when Gristly repays the $50,000 it borrowed.

To simplify, we (1) suppose the loan is repaid not in installments but in one lump sum 2 years after it was made and (2) ignore interest charges on the loan. Gristly simply writes a check for $50,000 against its checkable deposit, which we assume was $50,000 before the Gristly loan was negotiated. As a result, the Wahoo bank's checkable-deposit liabilities decline by $50,000; Gristly has given up $50,000 worth of its claim against the bank's assets. In turn, the bank will surrender Gristly's IOU, which it has been holding these many months. The bank and the company have reswapped claims. But the claim given up by Gristly is money; the claim it is repurchasing—its IOU—is not. The supply of money has therefore been reduced by $50,000; that amount of checkable deposits has been destroyed, unaccompanied by an increase in the money supply elsewhere in the economy.

The Gristly Company's IOU has been "demonetized," as shown in balance sheet 7. The Wahoo bank's checkable deposits and loans have each returned to zero. The decline in checkable deposits lowers the bank's required reserves to zero and gives it new excess reserves (= its reserves of

$10,000); this provides the basis for making new loans. **(Key Questions 4 and 8)**

Repaying a Loan			
Balance Sheet 7: Wahoo Bank			
Assets		Liabilities and net worth	
Reserves	$ 10,000	Checkable	
Loans	0	deposits	$ 0
Property	240,000	Capital stock	250,000

In the unlikely event that Gristly repays the loan with cash, the money supply will still decline by $50,000. In this case, Gristly would repurchase its IOU by handing over $50,000 in cash to the bank. Loan balances decline in the bank's asset column by $50,000, and cash increases by $50,000. Remember, we exclude from the money supply currency held by banks, because to include such cash would be double-counting; it is apparent that this constitutes a $50,000 reduction in the supply of money.

Transaction 8: Buying Government Securities

When a commercial bank buys government bonds from the public, the effect is substantially the same as lending. New money is created.

Assume that the Wahoo bank's balance sheet initially stands as it did at the end of transaction 5. Now suppose that instead of making a $50,000 loan, the bank buys $50,000 of government securities from a securities dealer. The bank receives the interest-bearing bonds, which appear on its balance statement as the asset "Securities," and gives the dealer an increase in its checkable-deposit account. The Wahoo bank's balance sheet appears as follows:

Buying Government Securities			
Balance Sheet 8: Wahoo Bank			
Assets		Liabilities and net worth	
Reserves	$ 60,000	Checkable	
Securities	50,000	deposits	$100,000
Property	240,000	Capital stock	250,000

Checkable deposits, that is, the supply of money, have been increased by $50,000, as in transaction 6. *Bond purchases from the public by commercial banks increase the supply of money in the same way as lending to the public does.* The bank accepts government bonds (which are not money) and gives the securities dealer an increase in its checkable deposits (which *are* money).

Of course, when the securities dealer draws and clears a check for $50,000 against the Wahoo bank, the bank loses both reserves and deposits in that amount and then just meets the legal reserve requirement. Its balance sheet now reads precisely as in 6b except that "Securities" is substituted for "Loans" on the asset side.

Finally, the selling of government bonds to the public by a commercial bank—like the repayment of a loan—reduces the supply of money. The securities buyer pays by check, and both "Securities" and "Checkable deposits" (the latter being money) decline by the amount of the sale.

Profits, Liquidity, and the Federal Funds Market

The asset items on a commercial bank's balance sheet reflect the banker's pursuit of two conflicting goals:

- **Profit**   One goal is profit. Commercial banks, like any other businesses, seek profits, which is why the bank makes loans and buys securities—the two major earning assets of commercial banks.
- **Liquidity**   The other goal is safety. For a bank, safety lies in liquidity, specifically such liquid assets as cash and excess reserves. A bank must be on guard for depositors who want to transform their checkable deposits into cash. Similarly, it must guard against more checks clearing against it than are cleared in its favor, causing a net outflow of reserves. Bankers thus seek a balance between prudence and profit. The compromise is between assets that earn higher returns and highly liquid assets that earn no returns.

An interesting way in which banks can partly reconcile the goals of profit and liquidity is to lend temporary excess reserves held at the Federal Reserve Banks to other commercial banks. Normal day-to-day flows of funds to banks rarely leave all banks with their exact levels of legally required reserves. Also, funds held at the Federal Reserve Banks are highly liquid, but they do not draw interest. Banks therefore lend these excess reserves to other banks on an overnight basis as a way of earning additional interest without sacrificing long-term liquidity. Banks that borrow in this Federal funds market—the market for immediately available reserve balances at the Federal Reserve—do so because they are temporarily short of required reserves. The interest rate paid on these overnight loans is called the **Federal funds rate.**

In Figure 14.1, we would show an overnight loan of reserves from the Surprise bank to the Wahoo bank as a decrease in reserves at the Surprise bank and an increase in reserves at the Wahoo bank. Ownership of reserves at the Federal Reserve Bank of Kansas City would change, but total reserves would not be affected. Exercise: Determine what other changes would be required on the Wahoo and Surprise banks' balance sheets as a result of the overnight loan.

QUICK REVIEW 14.2

- Banks create money when they make loans; money vanishes when bank loans are repaid.
- New money is created when banks buy government bonds from the public; money disappears when banks sell government bonds to the public.
- Banks balance profitability and safety in determining their mix of earning assets and highly liquid assets.
- Banks borrow and lend temporary excess reserves on an overnight basis in the Federal funds market; the interest rate on these loans is the Federal funds rate.

The Banking System: Multiple-Deposit Expansion

Thus far we have seen that a single bank in a banking system can lend one dollar for each dollar of its excess reserves. The situation is different for all commercial banks as a group. We will find that the commercial banking system can lend—that is, can create money—by a multiple of its excess reserves. This multiple lending is accomplished even though each bank in the system can lend only "dollar for dollar" with its excess reserves.

How do these seemingly paradoxical results come about? To answer this question, we must keep our analysis uncluttered and rely on three simplifying assumptions:

- The reserve ratio for all commercial banks is 20 percent.
- Initially all banks are meeting this 20 percent reserve requirement exactly. No excess reserves exist; or, in the parlance of banking, they are "loaned up" (or "loaned out") fully in terms of the reserve requirement.
- If any bank can increase its loans as a result of acquiring excess reserves, an amount equal to those excess reserves will be lent to one borrower, who will write a check for the entire amount of the loan and give it to someone else, who will deposit the check in another bank. This third assumption means that the worst thing possible happens to every lending bank—a check for the entire amount of the loan is drawn and cleared against it in favor of another bank.

The Banking System's Lending Potential

Suppose a junkyard owner finds a $100 bill while dismantling a car that has been on the lot for years. He deposits the $100 in bank A, which adds the $100 to its reserves. We will record only changes in the balance sheets of the various commercial banks. The deposit changes bank A's balance sheet as shown by entries (a_1):

Multiple-Deposit Expansion Process			
Balance Sheet: Commercial Bank A			
Assets		Liabilities and net worth	
Reserves	$+100 (a_1)$	Checkable	
	$- 80 (a_3)$	deposits	$+100 (a_1)$
Loans	$+ 80 (a_2)$		$+ 80 (a_2)$
			$- 80 (a_3)$

Recall from transaction 3 that this $100 deposit of currency does not alter the money supply. While $100 of checkable-deposit money comes into being, it is offset by the $100 of currency no longer in the hands of the public (the junkyard owner). But bank A *has* acquired excess reserves of $80. Of the newly acquired $100 in currency, 20 percent, or $20, must be earmarked for the required reserves on the new $100 checkable deposit, and the remaining $80 goes to excess reserves. Remembering that a single commercial bank can lend only an amount equal to its excess reserves, we conclude that bank A can lend a maximum of $80. When a loan for this amount is made, bank A's loans increase by $80 and the borrower gets an $80 checkable deposit. We add these figures—entries (a_2)—to bank A's balance sheet.

But now we make our third assumption: The borrower draws a check ($80) for the entire amount of the loan, and gives it to someone who deposits it in bank B, a different bank. As we saw in transaction 6, bank A loses both reserves and deposits equal to the amount of the loan, as indicated in entries (a_3). The net result of these transactions is that bank A's reserves now stand at +$20 (= $100 − $80), loans at +$80, and checkable deposits at +$100 (= $100 + $80 − $80). When the dust has settled, bank A is just meeting the 20 percent reserve ratio.

Recalling transaction 5, we know that bank B acquires both the reserves and the deposits that bank A has lost. Bank B's balance sheet is changed as in entries (b_1):

Multiple-Deposit Expansion Process			
Balance Sheet: Commercial Bank B			
Assets		Liabilities and net worth	
Reserves	$+80 (b_1)$	Checkable	
	$-64 (b_3)$	deposits	$+80 (b_1)$
Loans	$+64 (b_2)$		$+64 (b_2)$
			$-64 (b_3)$

When the borrower's check is drawn and cleared, bank A loses $80 in reserves and deposits and bank B

gains $80 in reserves and deposits. But 20 percent, or $16, of bank B's new reserves must be kept as required reserves against the new $80 in checkable deposits. This means that bank B has $64 (= $80 − $16) in excess reserves. It can therefore lend $64 [entries (b_2)]. When the new borrower draws a check for the entire amount and deposits it in bank C, the reserves and deposits of bank B both fall by the $64 [entries (b_3)]. As a result of these transactions, bank B's reserves now stand at +$16 (= $80 − $64), loans at +$64, and checkable deposits at +$80 (= $80 + $64 − $64). After all this, bank B is just meeting the 20 percent reserve requirement.

We are off and running again. Bank C acquires the $64 in reserves and deposits lost by bank B. Its balance sheet changes as in entries (c_1):

Multiple-Deposit Expansion Process			
Balance Sheet: Commercial Bank C			
Assets		Liabilities and net worth	
Reserves	$+64.00 (c_1)$	Checkable	
	$-51.20 (c_3)$	deposits	$+64.00 (c_1)$
Loans	$+51.20 (c_2)$		$+51.20 (c_2)$
			$-51.20 (c_3)$

Exactly 20 percent, or $12.80, of these new reserves will be required reserves, the remaining $51.20 being excess reserves. Hence, bank C can safely lend a maximum of $51.20. Suppose it does [entries (c_2)]. And suppose the borrower draws a check for the entire amount and gives it to someone who deposits it in another bank [entries (c_3)].

Bank D—the bank receiving the $51.20 in reserves and deposits—now notes these changes on its balance sheet [entries (d_1)]:

Multiple-Deposit Expansion Process			
Balance Sheet: Commercial Bank D			
Assets		Liabilities and net worth	
Reserves	$+51.20 (d_1)$	Demand	
	$-40.96 (d_3)$	deposits	$+51.20 (d_1)$
Loans	$+40.96 (d_2)$		$+40.96 (d_2)$
			$-40.96 (d_3)$

It can now lend $40.96 [entries (d_2)]. The newest borrower draws a check for the full amount and deposits it in still another bank [entries (d_3)].

We could go ahead with this procedure by bringing banks E, F, G, H, . . . , N into the picture. But we suggest that you work through the computations for banks E, F, and G to be sure you understand the procedure.

TABLE 14.2

Expansion of the Money Supply by the Commercial Banking System

Bank	(1) Acquired Reserves and Deposits	(2) Required Reserves (Reserve Ratio = .2)	(3) Excess Reserves, (1) − (2)	(4) Amount Bank Can Lend; New Money Created = (3)
Bank A	$100.00 (a_1)	$20.00	**$80.00**	$ 80.00 (a_2)
Bank B	80.00 (a_3, b_1)	16.00	64.00	64.00 (b_2)
Bank C	64.00 (b_3, c_1)	12.80	51.20	51.20 (c_2)
Bank D	51.20 (c_3, d_1)	10.24	40.96	40.96 (d_2)
Bank E	40.96	8.19	32.77	32.77
Bank F	32.77	6.55	26.21	26.21
Bank G	26.21	5.24	20.97	20.97
Bank H	20.97	4.20	16.78	16.78
Bank I	16.78	3.36	13.42	13.42
Bank J	13.42	2.68	10.74	10.74
Bank K	10.74	2.15	8.59	8.59
Bank L	8.59	1.72	6.87	6.87
Bank M	6.87	1.37	5.50	5.50
Bank N	5.50	1.10	4.40	4.40
Other banks	21.99	4.40	17.59	17.59
Total amount of money created (sum of the amounts in column 4)				**$400.00**

The entire analysis is summarized in Table 14.2. Data for banks E through N are supplied so that you may check your computations. Our conclusion is startling: On the basis of only $80 in excess reserves (acquired by the banking system when someone deposited $100 of currency in bank A), the entire commercial banking system is able to lend $400, the sum of the amounts in column 4. The banking system can lend excess reserves by a multiple of 5 when the reserve ratio is 20 percent. Yet each single bank in the banking system is lending only an amount equal to its own excess reserves. How do we explain this? How can the banking system lend by a multiple of its excess reserves, when each individual bank can lend only dollar for dollar with its excess reserves?

The answer is that reserves lost by a single bank are not lost to the banking system as a whole. The reserves lost by bank A are acquired by bank B. Those lost by B are gained by C. C loses to D, D to E, E to F, and so forth. Although reserves can be, and are, lost by individual banks in the banking system, there is no loss of reserves for the banking system as a whole.

An individual bank can safely lend only an amount equal to its excess reserves, but the commercial banking system can lend by a multiple of its excess reserves. This contrast, incidentally, is an illustration of why it is imperative that we keep the fallacy of composition (Chapter 1)

firmly in mind. Commercial banks as a group can create money by lending in a manner much different from that of the individual banks in the group.

The Monetary Multiplier

The banking system magnifies any original excess reserves into a larger amount of newly created checkable-deposit money. The *checkable-deposit multiplier*, or **monetary multiplier**, is similar in concept to the spending-income multiplier in Chapter 10. That multiplier exists because the expenditures of one household become some other household's income; the multiplier magnifies a change in initial spending into a larger change in GDP. The spending-income multiplier is the reciprocal of the MPS (the leakage into saving that occurs at each round of spending).

Similarly, the monetary multiplier exists because the reserves and deposits lost by one bank become reserves of another bank. It magnifies excess reserves into a larger creation of checkable-deposit money. The monetary multiplier m is the reciprocal of the required reserve ratio R (the leakage into required reserves that occurs at each step in the lending process). In short,

$$\text{Monetary multiplier} = \frac{1}{\text{required reserve ratio}}$$

or, in symbols,

$$m = \frac{1}{R}$$

In this formula, m represents the maximum amount of new checkable-deposit money that can be created by a single dollar of excess reserves, given the value of R. By multiplying the excess reserves E by m, we can find the maximum amount of new checkable-deposit money, D, that can be created by the banking system. That is,

$$\text{Maximum checkable-deposit creation} = \text{excess reserves} \times \text{monetary multiplier}$$

or, more simply,

$$D = E \times m$$

In our example in Table 14.2, R is .20, so m is 5 (= 1/.20). Then

$$D = \$400 = \$80 \times 5$$

Higher reserve ratios mean lower monetary multipliers and therefore less creation of new checkable-deposit money via loans; smaller reserve ratios mean higher monetary multipliers and thus more creation of new checkable-deposit money via loans. With a high reserve ratio, say, 50 percent, the monetary multiplier would be 2 (= 1/.5), and in our example the banking system could create only $160 (= $80 of excess reserves × 2) of new checkable deposits. With a low reserve ratio, say, 5 percent, the monetary multiplier would be 20 (= 1/.05), and the banking system could create $1600 (= $80 of excess reserves × 20) of new checkable deposits. Again, note the similarities with the spending-income multiplier, in which higher MPSs mean lower multipliers and lower MPSs mean higher multipliers. Also, like the spending-income multiplier, the monetary multiplier works in both directions. The monetary multiplier applies to money destruction as well as to money creation.

But keep in mind that despite the similar rationales underlying the spending-income multiplier and the monetary multiplier, the former has to do with changes in income and output and the latter with changes in the supply of money.

Figure 14.2 depicts the final outcome of our example of a multiple-deposit expansion of the money supply. The initial deposit of $100 of currency into the bank (lower right-hand box) creates new reserves of an equal amount (upper box). With a 20 percent reserve ratio, however, only $20 of currency reserves is needed to "back up" this $100 checkable deposit. The excess reserves of $80 permit

FIGURE 14.2

The outcome of the money expansion process. A deposit of $100 of currency into a checking account creates an initial checkable deposit of $100. If the reserve ratio is 20 percent, only $20 of reserves is legally required to support the $100 checkable deposit. The $80 of excess reserves allows the banking system to create $400 of checkable deposits through making loans. The $100 of reserves supports a total of $500 of money ($100 + $400).

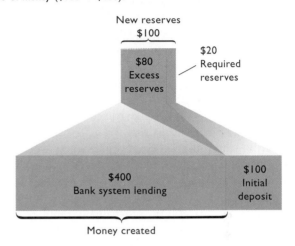

the creation of $400 of new checkable deposits via the making of loans, confirming a monetary multiplier of 5. The $100 of new reserves supports a total supply of money of $500, consisting of the $100 initial checkable deposit plus $400 of checkable deposits created through lending.

You might experiment with the following two brain-teasers to test your understanding of multiple credit expansion by the banking system:
- Rework the analysis in Table 14.2 (at least three or four steps of it) assuming the reserve ratio is 10 percent. What is the maximum amount of money the banking system can create upon acquiring $100 in new reserves and deposits? (The answer is not $800!)
- Suppose the banking system is loaned up and faces a 20 percent reserve ratio. Explain how it might have to reduce its outstanding loans by $400 when a $100 cash withdrawal from a checkable-deposit account forces one bank to draw down its reserves by $100. **(Key Question 13)**

Some Modifications

There are certain complications that might modify the preciseness of our analysis.

Other Leakages Aside from the leakage of required reserves at each step of the lending process, two other leakages of money from commercial banks might dampen the money-creating potential of the banking system:

- **Currency drains**   A borrower might request that part of his or her loan be paid in currency. Or the recipient of a check drawn by a borrower might ask the bank to redeem it partially or wholly in currency rather than add it to the recipient's account. If the person who borrowed the $80 from bank A in our illustration asked for $16 of it in cash and the remaining $64 as a checkable deposit, bank B would later receive only $64 in new reserves (of which only $51.20 would be excess) rather than $80 (of which $64 was excess). This decline in excess reserves would reduce the lending potential of the banking system accordingly. In fact, if the first borrower had taken the entire $80 in cash and if this currency remained in circulation, the multiple expansion process would have stopped then and there. But the convenience and safety of checkable deposits make this unlikely.

- **Excess reserves**   Our analysis of the commercial banking system's ability to expand the money supply by lending is based on the supposition that commercial banks are willing to meet precisely the legal reserve requirement. To the extent that bankers hold excess reserves, the overall credit expansion potential of the banking system will be reduced. For example, suppose bank A, upon receiving $100 in new cash, decided to add $25, rather than the legal minimum of $20, to its reserves. Then it would lend only $75, rather than $80, and the monetary multiplier would be diminished accordingly.[1] In fact, the amount of excess reserves that banks have held in recent years has been minimal. The explanation is simple: Excess reserves earn no interest income for a bank; loans and investments do. Hence, our assumption that a bank will lend an amount equal to its excess reserves is reasonable and generally accurate.

Need for Monetary Control

Our illustration of the banking system's ability to create money rests on the assumption that commercial banks are willing to create money by lending and that households

and businesses are willing to borrow. In reality, the willingness of banks to lend on the basis of excess reserves varies cyclically, and therein lies the rationale for government control of the money supply to promote economic stability.

When prosperity reigns, banks will expand credit to the maximum of their ability. Loans are interest-earning assets, and in good economic times there is little fear of borrowers defaulting. But, as you will find in Chapter 15, the money supply has an effect on aggregate demand. By lending and thereby creating money to the maximum of their ability during prosperity, commercial banks may contribute to excessive aggregate demand and therefore to inflation.

If recession appears on the economic horizon, bankers may hastily withdraw their invitations to borrow, seeking the safety of liquidity (excess reserves) even if this means sacrificing potential interest income. They may fear large-scale withdrawal of deposits by a panicky public and simultaneously doubt the ability of borrowers to repay. It is not surprising that during some years of the Great Depression of the 1930s banks had excess reserves but lending was at low ebb. The point is that during recession banks may decrease the money supply by cutting back on lending. This contraction of the money supply will restrain aggregate demand and intensify the recession. A rapid shrinkage of the money supply did indeed contribute to the Great Depression, as this chapter's Last Word indicates.

We thus conclude that profit-motivated bankers can be expected to vary the money supply in a way that reinforces cyclical fluctuations. For this reason the Federal Reserve System has at its disposal certain monetary tools to alter the money supply in a *countercyclical*, rather than *pro-cyclical*, fashion. We turn to an analysis of these tools in Chapter 15.

QUICK REVIEW 14.3

- A single bank in a multibank system can safely lend (create money) by an amount equal to its excess reserves; the banking system can lend (create money) by a multiple of its excess reserves.

- The monetary multiplier is the reciprocal of the required reserve ratio; it is the multiple by which the banking system can expand the money supply for each dollar of excess reserves.

- Currency drains and a desire by banks to hold excess reserves may reduce the size of the monetary multiplier.

---

[1]Specifically, in our $m = 1/R$ monetary multiplier, we now add to R, the required reserve ratio, the additional excess reserves that bankers choose to keep. For example, if banks want to hold additional excess reserves equal to 5 percent of any newly acquired checkable deposits, then the denominator becomes .25 (equal to the .20 reserve ratio plus the .05 addition to excess reserves). The monetary multiplier is reduced from 5 to $1/.25$, or 4.

A Series of Bank Panics in the Early 1930s Resulted in a Multiple Contraction of the Money Supply.

In the early months of the Great Depression, before there was deposit insurance, several financially weak banks went out of business. As word spread that customers of those banks had lost their deposits, a general concern arose that something similar could happen at other banks. Depositors became frightened that their banks did not, in fact, still have all the money they had deposited. And, of course, in a fractional reserve banking system, that is the reality. Acting on their fears, people en masse tried to withdraw currency—that is, to "cash out" their accounts—from their banks. They wanted to get their money before it was all gone. This "run on the banks" caused many previously financially sound banks to declare bankruptcy. More than 9000 banks failed within 3 years.

The massive conversion of checkable deposits to currency during 1930 to 1933 reduced the nation's money supply. This might seem strange, since a check written for "cash" reduces checkable-deposit money and increases currency in the hands of the public by the same amount. So how does the money supply decline? Our discussion of the money-creation process provides the answer, but now the story becomes one of money destruction.

Suppose that people collectively cash out $10 billion from their checking accounts. As an immediate result, checkable-deposit money declines by $10 billion, while currency held by the public increases by $10 billion. But here is the catch: Assuming a reserve ratio of 20 percent, the $10 billion of currency in the banks had been supporting $50 billion of deposit money, the $10 billion of deposits plus $40 billion created through loans. The $10 billion withdrawal of currency forces banks to reduce loans (and thus checkable-deposit money) by $40 billion to continue to meet their reserve requirement. In short, a $40 billion destruction of deposit money occurs. This is the scenario that occurred in the early years of the 1930s.

Accompanying this multiple contraction of checkable deposits was the banks' "scramble for liquidity" to try to meet further withdrawals of currency. To obtain more currency, they sold many of their holdings of government securities to the public. You know from this chapter that a bank's sale of government securities to the public, like a reduction in loans, reduces the money supply. People write checks for the securities, reducing their checkable deposits, and the bank uses the currency it obtains to meet the ongoing bank run. In short, the loss of reserves from the banking system, in conjunction with the scramble for security, reduced the amount of checkable-deposit money by far more than the increase in currency in the hands of the public. Thus, the money supply collapsed.

In 1933, President Franklin Roosevelt ended the bank panics by declaring a "national bank holiday," which closed all national banks for 1 week and resulted in the federally insured deposit program. Meanwhile, the nation's money supply had plummeted by 25 percent, the largest such drop in U.S. history. This decline in the money supply contributed to the nation's deepest and longest depression.

Today, a multiple contraction of the money supply of the 1930–1933 magnitude is unthinkable. FDIC insurance has kept individual bank failures from becoming general panics. Also, while the Fed stood idly by during the bank panics of 1930 to 1933, today it would take immediate and dramatic actions to maintain the banking system's reserves and the nation's money supply. Those actions are the subject of Chapter 15.

SUMMARY

1. The operation of a commercial bank can be understood through its balance sheet, where assets equal liabilities plus net worth.

2. Modern banking systems are fractional reserve systems: Only a fraction of checkable deposits is backed by currency.

3. Commercial banks keep required reserves on deposit in a Federal Reserve Bank or as vault cash. These required reserves are equal to a specified percentage of the commercial bank's checkable-deposit liabilities. Excess reserves are equal to actual reserves minus required reserves.

4. Banks lose both reserves and checkable deposits when checks are drawn against them.

5. Commercial banks create money—checkable deposits, or checkable-deposit money—when they make loans. The creation of checkable deposits by bank lending is the most important source of money in the U.S. economy. Money is destroyed when lenders repay bank loans.

6. The ability of a single commercial bank to create money by lending depends on the size of its excess reserves. Generally speaking, a commercial bank can lend only an amount equal to its excess reserves. Money creation is thus limited because, in all likelihood, checks drawn by borrowers will be deposited in other banks, causing a loss of reserves and deposits to the lending bank equal to the amount of money that it has lent.

7. Rather than making loans, banks may decide to use excess reserves to buy bonds from the public. In doing so, banks merely credit the checkable-deposit accounts of the bond sellers, thus creating checkable-deposit money. Money vanishes when banks sell bonds to the public, because bond buyers must draw down their checkable-deposit balances to pay for the bonds.

8. Banks earn interest by making loans and by purchasing bonds; they maintain liquidity by holding cash and excess reserves. Banks having temporary excess reserves often lend them overnight to banks that are short of required reserves. The interest rate paid on loans in this Federal funds market is called the Federal funds rate.

9. The commercial banking system as a whole can lend by a multiple of its excess reserves because the system as a whole cannot lose reserves. Individual banks, however, can lose reserves to other banks in the system.

10. The multiple by which the banking system can lend on the basis of each dollar of excess reserves is the reciprocal of the reserve ratio. This multiple credit expansion process is reversible.

11. The fact that profit-seeking banks would alter the money supply in a pro-cyclical direction underlies the need for the Federal Reserve System to control the money supply.

TERMS AND CONCEPTS

balance sheet	vault cash	excess reserves	Federal funds rate
fractional reserve banking system	required reserves	actual reserves	monetary multiplier
	reserve ratio		

STUDY QUESTIONS

1. Why must a balance sheet always balance? What are the major assets and claims on a commercial bank's balance sheet?

2. *Key Question* Why are commercial banks required to have reserves? Explain why reserves are an asset to commercial banks but a liability to the Federal Reserve Banks. What are excess reserves? How do you calculate the amount of excess reserves held by a bank? What is the significance of excess reserves?

3. "Whenever currency is deposited in a commercial bank, cash goes out of circulation and, as a result, the supply of money is reduced." Do you agree? Explain why or why not.

4. *Key Question* "When a commercial bank makes loans, it creates money; when loans are repaid, money is destroyed." Explain.

5. Explain why a single commercial bank can safely lend only an amount equal to its excess reserves but the commercial banking system as a whole can lend by a multiple of its excess reserves. What is the monetary multiplier, and how does it relate to the reserve ratio?

6. Assume that Jones deposits $500 in currency into her checkable-deposit account in First National Bank. A half-hour later Smith obtains a loan for $750 at this bank. By how much and in what direction has the money supply changed? Explain.

7. Suppose the National Bank of Commerce has excess reserves of $8000 and outstanding checkable deposits of $150,000. If the reserve ratio is 20 percent, what is the size of the bank's actual reserves?

8. *Key Question* Suppose that Continental Bank has the simplified balance sheet shown below and that the reserve ratio is 20 percent:
   a. What is the maximum amount of new loans that this bank can make? Show in column 1 how the bank's balance sheet will appear after the bank has lent this additional amount.
   b. By how much has the supply of money changed? Explain.
   c. How will the bank's balance sheet appear after checks drawn for the entire amount of the new loans have been cleared against the bank? Show the new balance sheet in column 2.

Assets		(1)	(2)	Liabilities and net worth		(1)	(2)
Reserves	$22,000	___	___	Checkable deposits	$100,000	___	___
Securities	38,000	___	___				
Loans	40,000	___	___				

d. Answer questions *a*, *b*, and *c* on the assumption that the reserve ratio is 15 percent.

9. The Third National Bank has reserves of $20,000 and checkable deposits of $100,000. The reserve ratio is 20 percent. Households deposit $5000 in currency into the bank that is added to reserves. What level of excess reserves does the bank now have?

10. Suppose again that the Third National Bank has reserves of $20,000 and checkable deposits of $100,000. The reserve ratio is 20 percent. The bank now sells $5000 in securities to the Federal Reserve Bank in its district, receiving a $5000 increase in reserves in return. What level of excess reserves does the bank now have? Why does your answer differ (yes, it does!) from the answer to question 9?

11. Suppose a bank discovers that its reserves will temporarily fall slightly short of those legally required. How might it remedy this situation through the Federal funds market? Now assume the bank finds that its reserves will be substantially and permanently deficient. What remedy is available to this bank? (Hint: Recall your answer to question 4.)

12. Suppose that Bob withdraws $100 of cash from his checking account at Security Bank and uses it to buy a camera from Joe, who deposits the $100 in his checking account in Serenity Bank. Assuming a reserve ratio of 10 percent and no initial excess reserves, determine the extent to which (*a*) Security Bank must reduce its loans and checkable deposits because of the cash withdrawal and (*b*) Serenity Bank can safely increase its loans and checkable deposits because of the cash deposit. Have the cash withdrawal and deposit changed the money supply?

13. *Key Question* Suppose the simplified consolidated balance sheet shown below is for the entire commercial banking system. All figures are in billions. The reserve ratio is 25 percent.

Assets			Liabilities and net worth		
		(1)			(1)
Reserves	$ 52	____	Checkable		
Securities	48	____	deposits	$200	____
Loans	100	____			

a. What amount of excess reserves does the commercial banking system have? What is the maximum amount the banking system might lend? Show in column 1 how the consolidated balance sheet would look after this amount has been lent. What is the monetary multiplier?

b. Answer the questions in part *a* assuming the reserve ratio is 20 percent. Explain the resulting difference in the lending ability of the commercial banking system.

14. What are banking leakages? How might they affect the money-creating potential of the banking system?

15. Explain why there is a need for the Federal Reserve System to control the money supply.

16. *(Last Word)* Explain how the bank panics of 1930 to 1933 produced a decline in the nation's money supply. Why are such panics highly unlikely today?

17. *Web-Based Question: How's your own bank doing?* Go to the FDIC's website, www.fdic.gov, and select Individual Banks. The FDIC's "Institution Directory" provides demographic data and financial profiles for each FDIC-insured institution. Use the directory to look up the financial statement of your personal bank or one in your community. How has it performed over the past year in the following categories: net worth, total assets, total liabilities, total deposits, net income, and number of branches?

18. *Web-Based Question: Assets and liabilities of all commercial banks in the United States* The Federal Reserve, at www.federalreserve.gov/releases/h8/Current/, provides an aggregate balance sheet for commercial banks in the United States. Check the current release, and look in the asset column for "Loans and leases." Rank the following components of loans and leases in terms of size: commercial and industrial, real estate, consumer, security, and other. Over the past 12 months, which component has increased by the largest percentage? By the largest absolute amount? Has the net worth (assets less liabilities) of all commercial banks in the United States increased, decreased, or remained constant during the past year?

19. *Web-Based Question: Reserve requirements—any changes to Table 14.1?* Go to the Fed's website, www.federalreserve.gov/, and select Subject Index. Under "R" choose Requirements, Regulation D. Check the latest amendment of reserve requirements to see if any part of Table 14.1 needs updating. If so, supply the new numbers in the table.

15 | *Monetary Policy*

Some newspaper commentators have stated that the chairperson of the Federal Reserve Board (currently Alan Greenspan) is the second most powerful person in the United States, after the U.S. president. That is undoubtedly an exaggeration because the chair has only a single vote on the 7-person Federal Reserve Board and 12-person Federal Open Market Committee. But there can be no doubt about the chair's influence, the overall importance of the Federal Reserve, and the **monetary policy** that it conducts. Such policy consists of deliberate changes in the money supply to influence interest rates and thus the total level of spending in the economy. The goal is to achieve and maintain price-level stability, full employment, and economic growth.

As indicated in Chapter 13, the 12 Federal Reserve Banks together constitute the U.S. "central bank" (nicknamed the "Fed"). In Global Perspective 15.1 we also list some of the other central banks in the world, along with their nicknames.

Consolidated Balance Sheet of the Federal Reserve Banks

The Fed's balance sheet helps us consider how the Fed conducts monetary policy. Table 15.1 consolidates the pertinent assets and liabilities of the 12 Federal Reserve Banks as of May 7, 2003. You will see that some of the Fed's assets and liabilities differ from those found on the balance sheet of a commercial bank.

Assets

The two main assets of the Federal Reserve Banks are securities and loans to commercial banks. (Again, we will simplify by referring only to *commercial banks*, even though the analysis also applies to *thrifts*—savings and loans, mutual savings banks, and credit unions.)

Securities The securities shown in Table 15.1 are government bonds that have been purchased by the

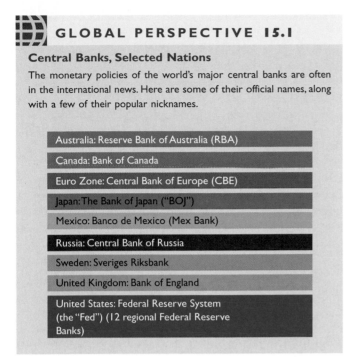

GLOBAL PERSPECTIVE 15.1

Central Banks, Selected Nations

The monetary policies of the world's major central banks are often in the international news. Here are some of their official names, along with a few of their popular nicknames.

- Australia: Reserve Bank of Australia (RBA)
- Canada: Bank of Canada
- Euro Zone: Central Bank of Europe (CBE)
- Japan: The Bank of Japan ("BOJ")
- Mexico: Banco de Mexico (Mex Bank)
- Russia: Central Bank of Russia
- Sweden: Sveriges Riksbank
- United Kingdom: Bank of England
- United States: Federal Reserve System (the "Fed") (12 regional Federal Reserve Banks)

Federal Reserve Banks. They consist largely of Treasury bills (short-term securities), Treasury notes (mid-term securities), and Treasury bonds (long-term securities) issued by the U.S. government to finance past budget deficits. These securities are part of the public debt—the money borrowed by the Federal government. The Federal Reserve Banks bought some of these securities directly from the Treasury but acquired most of them from commercial banks and the public. Although they are an important source of interest income to the Federal Reserve Banks, they are mainly bought and sold to influence the size of commercial bank reserves and,

therefore, the ability of those banks to create money by lending.

Loans to Commercial Banks   For reasons that will soon become clear, commercial banks occasionally borrow from Federal Reserve Banks. The IOUs that commercial banks give these "bankers' banks" in return for loans are listed on the Federal Reserve balance sheet as "Loans to commercial banks." They are assets to the Fed because they are claims against the commercial banks. To commercial banks, of course, these loans are liabilities in that they must be repaid. Through borrowing in this way, commercial banks can increase their reserves.

Liabilities

On the liability side of the Fed's consolidated balance sheet, we find three items: reserves, Treasury deposits, and Federal Reserve Notes.

Reserves of Commercial Banks   The Fed requires that the commercial banks hold reserves against their checkable deposits. When held in the Federal Reserve Banks, these reserves are listed as a liability on the Fed's balance sheet. They are assets on the books of the commercial banks, which still own them even though they are deposited at the Federal Reserve Banks.

Treasury Deposits   The U.S. Treasury keeps deposits in the Federal Reserve Banks and draws checks on them to pay its obligations. To the Treasury these deposits are assets; to the Federal Reserve Banks they are liabilities. The Treasury creates and replenishes these deposits by depositing tax receipts and money borrowed from the

TABLE 15.1

Consolidated Balance Sheet of the 12 Federal Reserve Banks, May 7, 2003 (in Millions)

Assets		Liabilities and Net Worth	
Securities	$647,580	Reserves of commercial banks	$ 21,417
Loans to commercial banks	59	Treasury deposits	6,050
All other assets	86,768	Federal Reserve Notes (outstanding)	657,217
		All other liabilities and net worth	49,723
Total	$734,407	Total	$734,407

Source: Federal Reserve Statistical Release, H.4.1, May 7, 2003, www.federalreserve.gov/.

public or from the commercial banks through the sale of bonds.

Federal Reserve Notes Outstanding

As we have seen, the supply of paper money in the United States consists of Federal Reserve Notes issued by the Federal Reserve Banks. When this money is circulating outside the Federal Reserve Banks, it constitutes claims against the assets of the Federal Reserve Banks. The Fed thus treats these notes as a liability.

Tools of Monetary Policy

With this look at the Federal Reserve Banks' consolidated balance sheet, we can now explore how the Fed can influence the money-creating abilities of the commercial banking system. The Fed has three tools of monetary control it can use to alter the reserves of commercial banks:

15.1
Tools of monetary policy

- Open-market operations
- The reserve ratio
- The discount rate

Open-Market Operations

Bond markets are "open" to all buyers and sellers of corporate and government bonds (securities). The Fed's **open-market operations** consist of the buying of government bonds from, or the selling of government bonds to, commercial banks and the general public. Open-market operations are the Fed's most important instrument for influencing the money supply.

Buying Securities

Suppose that the Fed decides to have the Federal Reserve Banks buy government bonds. They can purchase these bonds either from commercial banks or from the public. In both cases the reserves of the commercial banks will increase.

From Commercial Banks

When Federal Reserve Banks buy government bonds *from commercial banks,*

(*a*) The commercial banks give up part of their holdings of securities (the government bonds) to the Federal Reserve Banks.

(*b*) The Federal Reserve Banks, in paying for those securities, increase the reserves of the commercial banks by the amount of the purchase.

We show these outcomes as (*a*) and (*b*) on the following consolidated balance sheets of the commercial banks and the Federal Reserve Banks:

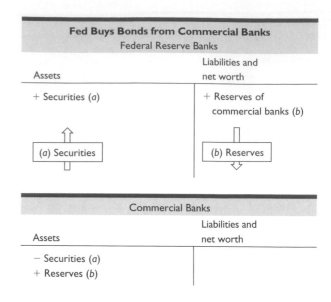

The upward arrow shows that securities have moved from the commercial banks to the Federal Reserve Banks. So we enter " − Securities" (minus securities) in the asset column of the balance sheet of the commercial banks. For the same reason, we enter " + Securities" in the asset column of the balance sheet of the Federal Reserve Banks.

The downward arrow indicates that the Federal Reserve Banks have provided reserves to the commercial banks. So we enter " + Reserves" in the asset column of the balance sheet for the commercial banks. In the liability column of the balance sheet of the Federal Reserve Banks, the plus sign indicates that although commercial bank reserves have increased, they are a liability to the Federal Reserve Banks because the reserves are owned by the commercial banks.

What is most important about this transaction is that when Federal Reserve Banks purchase securities from commercial banks, they increase the reserves in the banking system, which then increases the lending ability of the commercial banks.

From the Public

The effect on commercial bank reserves is much the same when Federal Reserve Banks purchase securities from the general public. Suppose the Gristly Meat Packing Company has government bonds that it sells in the open market to the Federal Reserve Banks. The transaction has several elements:

(*a*) Gristly gives up securities to the Federal Reserve Banks and gets in payment a check drawn by the Federal Reserve Banks on themselves.

(*b*) Gristly promptly deposits the check in its account with the Wahoo bank.

(*c*) The Wahoo bank sends this check against the Federal Reserve Banks to a Federal Reserve Bank for collection. As a result, the Wahoo bank enjoys an increase in its reserves.

The balance-sheet changes, labeled to correspond with the elements of the transaction, are as follows:

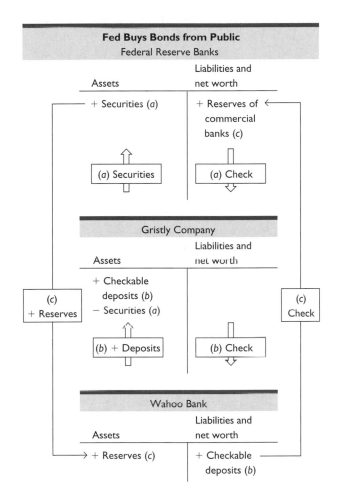

Fed Buys Bonds from Public

Two aspects of this transaction are particularly important. First, as with Federal Reserve purchases of securities directly from commercial banks, the purchases of securities from the public increases the lending ability of the commercial banking system. This is indicated by the " + Reserves," showing an increase in the assets of the Wahoo bank. Second, the supply of money is directly increased by the Federal Reserve Banks' purchase of government bonds (aside from any expansion of the money supply that may occur from the increase in commercial bank reserves). This direct increase in the money supply

has taken the form of an increased amount of checkable deposits in the economy as a result of Gristly's deposit; thus the " + Checkable deposits" in the Wahoo bank's balance sheet. Because these checkable deposits are an asset as viewed by Gristly, checkable deposits have increased (plus sign) on Gristly's balance sheet.

There is a slight difference between the Federal Reserve Banks' purchases of securities from the commercial banking system and their purchases of securities from the public. If we assume that all commercial banks are loaned up initially, Federal Reserve bond purchases *from commercial banks* increase the actual reserves and excess reserves of commercial banks by the entire amount of the bond purchases. As shown in the left panel in Figure 15.1, a $1000 bond purchase from a commercial bank increases both the actual and the excess reserves of the commercial bank by $1000.

In contrast, Federal Reserve Bank purchases of bonds from the public increase actual reserves but also increase checkable deposits when the sellers place the Fed's check into their personal checking accounts. Thus, a $1000 bond purchase from the public would increase checkable deposits by $1000 and hence the actual reserves of the loaned-up banking system by the same amount. But with a 20 percent reserve ratio applied to the $1000 checkable deposit, the excess reserves of the banking system would be only $800 since $200 of the $1000 would have to be held as reserves.

However, in both transactions the end result is the same: *When Federal Reserve Banks buy securities in the open market, commercial banks' reserves are increased.* When the banks lend out their excess reserves, the nation's money supply will rise. Observe in Figure 15.1 that a $1000 purchase of bonds by the Federal Reserve results in $5000 of additional money, regardless of whether the purchase was made from commercial banks or from the general public.

Selling Securities   As you may suspect, when the Federal Reserve Banks sell government bonds, commercial banks' reserves are reduced. Let's see why.

To Commercial Banks   When the Federal Reserve Banks sell securities in the open market to commercial banks,

(*a*) The Federal Reserve Banks give up securities that the commercial banks acquire.

(*b*) The commercial banks pay for those securities by drawing checks against their deposits—that is, against their reserves—in Federal Reserve Banks. The Fed collects those checks by reducing the commercial banks' reserves accordingly.

The balance-sheet changes—again identified by (*a*) and (*b*)—appear as shown below. The reduction in commercial bank reserves is indicated by the minus signs before the appropriate entries.

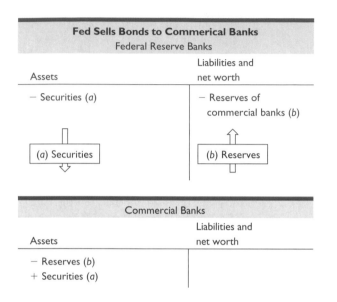

Fed Sells Bonds to Commerical Banks

Federal Reserve Banks

Assets	Liabilities and net worth
− Securities (*a*)	− Reserves of commercial banks (*b*)
(*a*) Securities	(*b*) Reserves

Commercial Banks

Assets	Liabilities and net worth
− Reserves (*b*) + Securities (*a*)	

To the Public When the Federal Reserve Banks sell securities to the public, the outcome is the same. Let's put the Gristly Company on the buying end of government bonds that the Federal Reserve Banks are selling:

(*a*) The Federal Reserve Banks sell government bonds to Gristly, which pays with a check drawn on the Wahoo bank.

(*b*) The Federal Reserve Banks clear this check against the Wahoo bank by reducing Wahoo's reserves.

(*c*) The Wahoo bank returns the canceled check to Gristly, reducing Gristly's checkable deposit accordingly.

We show these balance-sheet changes at the top of the next page.

Federal Reserve bond sales of $1000 to the commercial banking system reduce the system's actual and excess reserves by $1000. But a $1000 bond sale to the public reduces excess reserves by $800, because the public's checkable-deposit money is also reduced by $1000 by the sale. Since the commercial banking system's outstanding checkable deposits are reduced by $1000, banks need keep $200 less in reserves.

Whether the Fed sells bonds to the public or to commercial banks, the result is the same: *When Federal Reserve Banks sell securities in the open market, commercial bank reserves are reduced.* If all excess reserves are already lent out,

FIGURE 15.1

The Federal Reserve's purchase of bonds and the expansion of the money supply. Assuming all banks are loaned up initially, a Federal Reserve purchase of a $1000 bond from either a commercial bank or the public can increase the money supply by $5000 when the reserve ratio is 20 percent. In the left panel of the diagram, the purchase of a $1000 bond from a commercial bank creates $1000 of excess reserves that support a $5000 expansion of checkable deposits through loans. In the right panel, the purchase of a $1000 bond from the public creates a $1000 checkable deposit but only $800 of excess reserves, because $200 of reserves is required to "back up" the $1000 new checkable deposit. The commercial banks can therefore expand the money supply by only $4000 by making loans. This $4000 of checkable-deposit money plus the new checkable deposit of $1000 equals $5000 of new money.

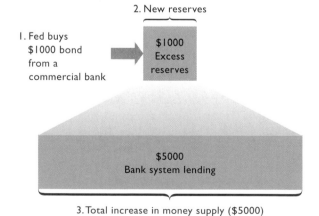

1. Fed buys $1000 bond from a commercial bank

2. New reserves

$1000 Excess reserves

$5000 Bank system lending

3. Total increase in money supply ($5000)

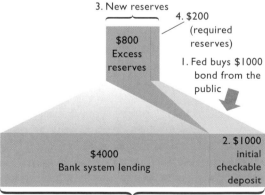

3. New reserves

$800 Excess reserves

4. $200 (required reserves)

1. Fed buys $1000 bond from the public

2. $1000 initial checkable deposit

$4000 Bank system lending

5. Total increase in money supply ($5000)

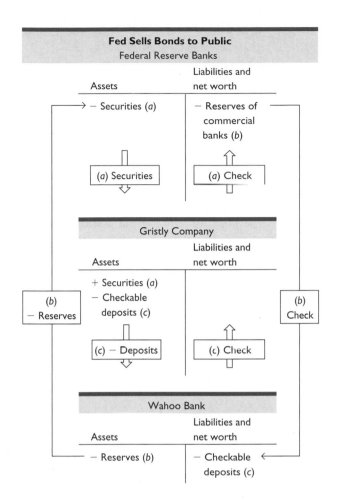

this decline in commercial bank reserves produces a decline in the nation's money supply. In our example, a $1000 sale of government securities results in a $5000 decline in the money supply whether the sale is made to commercial banks or to the general public. You can verify this by reexamining Figure 15.1 and tracing the effects of a *sale* of a $1000 bond by the Fed either to commercial banks or to the public.

What makes commercial banks and the public willing to sell government securities to, or buy them from, Federal Reserve Banks? The answer lies in the price of bonds and their interest rates. We know from Chapter 13 that bond prices and interest rates are inversely related. When the Fed buys government bonds, the demand for them increases. Government bond prices rise, and their interest rates decline. The higher bond prices and their lower interest rates prompt banks, securities firms, and individual holders of government bonds to sell them to the Federal Reserve Banks.

When the Fed sells government bonds, the additional supply of bonds in the bond market lowers bond prices and raises their interest rates, making government bonds attractive purchases for banks and the public.

The Reserve Ratio

The Fed can also manipulate the **reserve ratio** in order to influence the ability of commercial banks to lend. Suppose a commercial bank's balance sheet shows that reserves are $5000 and checkable deposits are $20,000. If the legal reserve ratio is 20 percent (row 2, Table 15.2), the bank's required reserves are $4000. Since actual reserves are $5000, the excess reserves of this bank are $1000. On the basis of $1000 of excess reserves, this one bank can lend $1000; however, the banking system as a whole can create a maximum of $5000 of new checkable-deposit money by lending (column 7).

Raising the Reserve Ratio   Now, what if the Fed raised the reserve ratio from 20 to 25 percent? (See row 3.) Required reserves would jump from $4000 to $5000, shrinking excess reserves from $1000 to zero. Raising the reserve ratio increases the amount of required reserves banks must keep. As a consequence, either banks lose excess reserves, diminishing their ability to create money by lending, or they find their reserves deficient and are forced

TABLE 15.2

The Effects of Changes in the Reserve Ratio on the Lending Ability of Commercial Banks

(1) Reserve Ratio, %	(2) Checkable Deposits	(3) Actual Reserves	(4) Required Reserves	(5) Excess Reserves, (3) − (4)	(6) Money-Creating Potential of Single Bank, = (5)	(7) Money-Creating Potential of Banking System
(1) 10	$20,000	$5000	$2000	$ 3000	$ 3000	$30,000
(2) 20	20,000	5000	4000	1000	1000	5,000
(3) 25	20,000	5000	5000	0	0	0
(4) 30	20,000	5000	6000	−1000	−1000	−3,333

to contract checkable deposits and therefore the money supply. In the example in Table 15.2, excess reserves are transformed into required reserves, and the money-creating potential of our single bank is reduced from $1000 to zero (column 6). Moreover, the banking system's money-creating capacity declines from $5000 to zero (column 7).

What if the Fed increases the reserve requirement to 30 percent? (See row 4.) The commercial bank, to protect itself against the prospect of failing to meet this requirement, would be forced to lower its checkable deposits and at the same time increase its reserves. To reduce its checkable deposits, the bank could let outstanding loans mature and be repaid without extending new credit. To increase reserves, the bank might sell some of its bonds, adding the proceeds to its reserves. Both actions would reduce the supply of money (to clarify this, see Chapter 14, transactions 6 and 8).

Lowering the Reserve Ratio   What would happen if the Fed lowered the reserve ratio from the original 20 percent to 10 percent? (See row 1.) In this case, required reserves would decline from $4000 to $2000, and excess reserves would jump from $1000 to $3000. The single bank's lending (money-creating) ability would increase from $1000 to $3000 (column 6), and the banking system's money-creating potential would expand from $5000 to $30,000 (column 7). *Lowering the reserve ratio transforms required reserves into excess reserves and enhances the ability of banks to create new money by lending.*

The examples in Table 15.2 show that a change in the reserve ratio affects the money-creating ability of the *banking system* in two ways:

- It changes the amount of excess reserves.
- It changes the size of the monetary multiplier.

For example, when the legal reserve ratio is raised from 10 to 20 percent, excess reserves are reduced from $3000 to $1000 and the checkable-deposit multiplier is reduced from 10 to 5. The money-creating potential of the banking system declines from $30,000 (= $3000 × 10) to $5000 (= $1000 × 5). *Raising the reserve ratio forces banks to reduce the amount of checkable deposits they create through lending.*

Although changing the reserve ratio is a powerful technique of monetary control, it is infrequently used. The last such change was in 1992, when the Fed lowered the reserve ratio from 12 percent to 10 percent.

The Discount Rate

One of the functions of a central bank is to be a "lender of last resort." Occasionally, commercial banks have unexpected and immediate needs for additional funds. In such cases, each Federal Reserve Bank will make short-term loans to commercial banks in its district.

When a commercial bank borrows, it gives the Federal Reserve Bank a promissory note (IOU) drawn against itself and secured by acceptable collateral—typically U.S. government securities. Just as commercial banks charge interest on their loans, so too Federal Reserve Banks charge interest on loans they grant to commercial banks. The interest rate they charge is called the **discount rate.**

As a claim against the commercial bank, the borrowing bank's promissory note is an asset to the lending Federal Reserve Bank and appears on its balance sheet as "Loans to commercial banks." To the commercial bank the IOU is a liability, appearing as "Loans from the Federal Reserve Banks" on the commercial bank's balance sheet. [See entries (*a*) on the balance sheets below.]

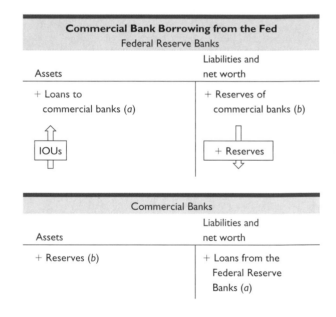

In providing the loan, the Federal Reserve Bank increases the reserves of the borrowing commercial bank. Since no required reserves need be kept against loans from Federal Reserve Banks, all new reserves acquired by borrowing from Federal Reserve Banks are excess reserves. [These changes are reflected in entries (*b*) on the balance sheets.]

In short, *borrowing from the Federal Reserve Banks by commercial banks increases the reserves of the commercial banks and enhances their ability to extend credit.*

The Fed has the power to set the discount rate at which commercial banks borrow from Federal Reserve Banks. From the commercial banks' point of view, the discount rate is a cost of acquiring reserves. A lowering of the discount rate encourages commercial banks to obtain additional reserves by borrowing from Federal Reserve Banks. When the commercial banks lend new reserves, the money supply increases.

An increase in the discount rate discourages commercial banks from obtaining additional reserves through borrowing from the Federal Reserve Banks. So the Fed may raise the discount rate when it wants to restrict the money supply. **(Key Question 2)**

Easy Money and Tight Money

Suppose the economy faces recession and unemployment. The Fed decides that an increase in the supply of money is needed to increase aggregate demand so as to employ idle resources. To increase the supply of money, the Fed must increase the excess reserves of commercial banks. How can it do that?

- *Buy securities* By purchasing securities in the open market, the Fed can increase commercial bank reserves. When the Fed's checks for the securities are cleared against it, the commercial banks discover that they have more reserves.
- *Lower the reserve ratio* By lowering the reserve ratio, the Fed changes required reserves into excess reserves and increases the size of the monetary multiplier.
- *Lower the discount rate* By lowering the discount rate, the Fed may entice commercial banks to borrow more reserves from the Fed.

These actions are called an **easy money policy** (or *expansionary monetary policy*). Its purpose is to make bank loans less expensive and more available and thereby increase aggregate demand, output, and employment.

Suppose, on the other hand, excessive spending is pushing the economy into an inflationary spiral. Then the Fed should try to reduce aggregate demand by limiting or contracting the supply of money. That means reducing the reserves of commercial banks. How is that done?

- *Sell securities* By selling government bonds in the open market, the Federal Reserve Banks can reduce commercial bank reserves.
- *Increase the reserve ratio* An increase in the reserve ratio will automatically strip commercial banks of their excess reserves and decrease the size of the monetary multiplier.
- *Raise the discount rate* A boost in the discount rate will discourage commercial banks from borrowing from Federal Reserve Banks in order to build up their reserves.

These actions are called a **tight money policy** (or *restrictive monetary policy*). The objective is to tighten the supply of money in order to reduce spending and control inflation.

Relative Importance

Of the three instruments of monetary control, *buying and selling securities in the open market is the most important*. This technique has the advantage of flexibility—government securities can be purchased or sold in large or small amounts—and the impact on bank reserves is prompt. And, compared with reserve-requirement changes, open-market operations work subtly and less directly. Furthermore, there is virtually no question about the ability of the Federal Reserve Banks to affect commercial bank reserves through the purchase and sale of bonds. A glance back at the consolidated balance sheet for the Federal Reserve Banks (Table 15.1) reveals very large holdings of government securities ($648 billion). The sale of those securities could theoretically reduce commercial bank reserves from $21 billion to zero.

Changing the reserve requirement is a less important instrument of monetary control, and the Fed has used this technique only sparingly. Normally, it can accomplish its monetary goals easier through open-market operations. The limited use of changes in the reserve ratio undoubtedly relates to the fact that reserves earn no interest. Consequently, raising or lowering reserve requirements has a substantial effect on bank profits.

The Fed often lowers or raises the discount rate, but this tool is much less important than open-market operations. On average, only 2 to 3 percent of commercial bank reserves are acquired from the Federal Reserve Banks. Indeed, open-market operations often lead the banks to borrow from Federal Reserve Banks. That is, if Fed sales of bonds to the public leave commercial banks temporarily short of reserves, commercial banks may seek loans from the Federal Reserve Banks. Commercial banks borrow from the Fed largely in response to open-market operations rather than in response to changes in the discount rate.

In recent years, the discount rate has become a passive element of monetary policy. The Fed actively uses open-market operations to change the money supply and thus the economy's short-term interest rates. Simultaneously, it adjusts the discount rate—the only rate it directly sets—to keep that rate in line with these other short-term rates.

KEY GRAPH

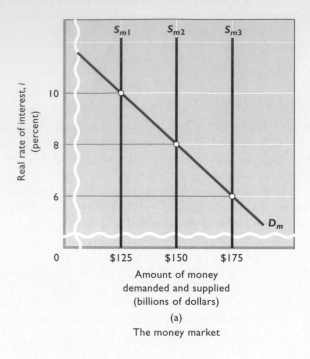

(a)
The money market

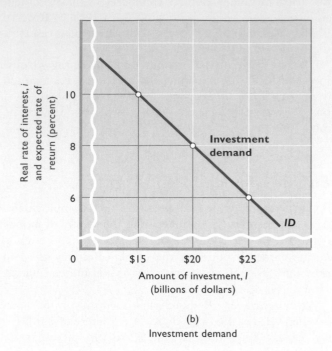

(b)
Investment demand

Monetary Policy, Real GDP, and the Price Level

 15.1
Monetary policy

So far we have explained only how the Fed can change the money supply. Now we need to link up the money supply, the interest rate, investment spending, and aggregate demand to see how monetary policy affects the economy. How does monetary policy work?

Cause-Effect Chain

The three diagrams in **Figure 15.2 (Key Graph)** will help you understand how monetary policy works toward achieving its goals.

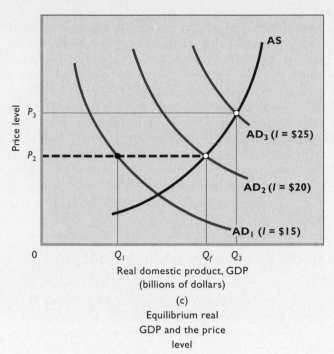

FIGURE 15.2

Monetary policy and equilibrium GDP. An easy money policy that shifts the money supply curve rightward from S_{m1} to S_{m2} lowers the interest rate from 10 to 8 percent. As a result, investment spending increases from $15 billion to $20 billion, shifting the aggregate demand curve rightward from AD_1 to AD_2, and real output rises from the recessionary level Q_1 to the full-employment level Q_f. A tight money policy that shifts the money supply curve leftward from S_{m3} to S_{m2} increases the interest rate from 6 to 8 percent. Investment spending thus falls from $25 billion to $20 billion, and the aggregate demand curve shifts leftward from AD_3 to AD_2, curtailing inflation.

3. The Federal Reserve could increase the money supply from S_{m1} to S_{m2} by:
   a. increasing the discount rate.
   b. reducing taxes.
   c. buying government securities in the open market.
   d. increasing the reserve requirement.

4. If the spending-income multiplier is 4 in the economy depicted, an increase in the money supply from $125 billion to $150 billion will:
   a. shift the aggregate demand curve rightward by $20 billion.
   b. increase real GDP by $25 billion.
   c. increase real GDP by $100 billion.
   d. shift the aggregate demand curve leftward by $5 billion.

Answers: 1. d; 2. c; 3. c; 4. a

Money Market Figure 15.2a represents the money market, in which the demand curve for money and the supply curve of money are brought together. Recall from Chapter 13 that the total demand for money is made up of the transactions and asset demands. The transactions demand is directly related to the nominal GDP. The asset demand is inversely related to the interest rate. The interest rate is the opportunity cost of holding money as an asset; the higher that cost, the smaller the amount of money the public wants to hold. The total demand for money D_m is thus inversely related to the interest rate, as is indicated in Figure 15.2a. Also, recall that an increase in nominal GDP will shift D_m to the right, and a decline in nominal GDP will shift D_m to the left.

This figure also shows three potential money supply curves, S_{m1}, S_{m2}, and S_{m3}. In each case the money supply is shown as a vertical line representing some fixed amount of money determined by the Fed. While monetary policy (specifically, the supply of money) helps determine the interest rate, the interest rate does not determine the location of the money supply curve.

The equilibrium interest rate is the rate at which the amount of money demanded and the amount supplied are equal. With money demand D_m in Figure 15.2a, if the supply of money is $125 billion ($S_{m1}$), the equilibrium interest rate is 10 percent. With a money supply of $150 billion ($S_{m2}$), the equilibrium interest rate is 8 percent; with a money supply of $175 billion ($S_{m3}$), it is 6 percent.

You know from Chapter 10 that the real, not the nominal, rate of interest is critical for investment decisions. So here we assume that Figure 15.2a portrays real interest rates.

Investment These 10, 8, and 6 percent real interest rates are carried rightward to the investment demand curve in Figure 15.2b. This curve shows the inverse relationship between the interest rate—the cost of borrowing to invest—and the amount of investment spending. At the 10 percent interest rate it will be profitable for the nation's businesses to invest $15 billion; at 8 percent, $20 billion; at 6 percent, $25 billion.

Changes in the interest rate mainly affect the investment component of total spending, although they also affect spending on durable consumer goods (such as autos) that are purchased on credit. The impact of changing interest rates on investment spending is great because of the large cost and long-term nature of capital purchases. Capital equipment, factory buildings, and warehouses are tremendously expensive. In absolute terms, interest charges on funds borrowed for these purchases are considerable.

Similarly, the interest cost on a house purchased on a long-term contract is very large: A $\frac{1}{2}$-percentage-point change in the interest rate could amount to thousands of dollars in the total cost of a home.

Also, changes in the interest rate may affect investment spending by changing the relative attractiveness of purchases of capital equipment versus purchases of bonds. In purchasing capital goods, the interest rate is the cost of borrowing the funds to make the investment. In purchasing bonds, the interest rate is the return on the financial investment. If the interest rate increases, the cost of buying capital goods increases while the return on bonds increases. Businesses are then more inclined to use business savings to buy securities than to buy equipment. Conversely, a drop in the interest rate makes purchases of capital goods relatively more attractive than bond ownership.

In brief, the impact of changing interest rates is mainly on investment (and, through that, on aggregate demand, output, employment, and the price level). Moreover, as Figure 15.2b shows, investment spending varies inversely with the interest rate.

Equilibrium GDP Figure 15.2c shows the impact of our three interest rates and corresponding levels of investment spending on aggregate demand. As noted, aggregate demand curve AD_1 is associated with the $15 billion level of investment, AD_2 with investment of $20 billion, and AD_3 with investment of $25 billion. That is, investment spending is one of the determinants of aggregate demand. Other things equal, the greater the investment spending, the farther to the right lies the aggregate demand curve.

Suppose the money supply in Figure 15.2a is $150 billion ($S_{m2}$), producing an equilibrium interest rate of 8 percent. In Figure 15.2b we see that this 8 percent interest rate will bring forth $20 billion of investment spending. This $20 billion of investment spending joins with consumption spending, net exports, and government spending to yield aggregate demand curve AD_2 in Figure 15.2c. The equilibrium levels of real output and prices are Q_f and P_2, as determined by the intersection of AD_2 and the aggregate supply curve AS.

To test your understanding of these relationships, explain why each of the other two levels of money supply in Figure 15.2a results in a different interest rate, level of investment, aggregate demand curve, and equilibrium real output.

Effects of an Easy Money Policy

Next, suppose that the money supply is $125 billion ($S_{m1}$) in Figure 15.2a. Because the resulting real output Q_1 in Figure 15.2c is far below the full-employment output, Q_f, the economy must be experiencing recession and substantial unemployment. The Fed therefore should institute an easy money policy.

To increase the money supply, the Federal Reserve Banks will take some combination of the following actions: (1) Buy government securities from banks and the public in the open market, (2) lower the legal reserve ratio, and (3) lower the discount rate. The intended outcome will be an increase in excess reserves in the commercial banking system. Because excess reserves are the basis on which commercial banks and thrifts can earn profit by lending and thus creating checkable-deposit money, the nation's money supply probably will rise. An increase in the money supply will lower the interest rate, increasing investment, aggregate demand, and equilibrium GDP.

For example, an increase in the money supply from $125 billion to $150 billion ($S_{m1}$ to S_{m2}) will reduce the interest rate from 10 to 8 percent, as indicated in Figure 15.2a, and will boost investment from $15 billion to $20 billion, as shown in Figure 15.2b. This $5 billion increase in investment will shift the aggregate demand curve rightward by more than the increase in investment because of the multiplier effect. If the economy's MPC is .75, the multiplier will be 4, meaning that the $5 billion increase in investment will shift the AD curve rightward by $20 billion (= 4 × $5) at each price level. Specifically, aggregate demand will shift from AD_1 to AD_2, as shown in Figure 15.2c. This rightward shift in the aggregate demand curve will eliminate the negative GDP gap by

TABLE 15.3

Monetary Policies for Recession and Inflation

(1) **Easy Money Policy**	(2) **Tight Money Policy**
Problem: unemployment and recession	*Problem:* inflation
↓	↓
Federal Reserve buys bonds, lowers reserve ratio, or lowers the discount rate	Federal Reserve sells bonds, increases reserve ratio, or increases the discount rate
↓	↓
Excess reserves increase	Excess reserves decrease
↓	↓
Money supply rises	Money supply falls
↓	↓
Interest rate falls	Interest rate rises
↓	↓
Investment spending increases	Investment spending decreases
↓	↓
Aggregate demand increases	Aggregate demand decreases
↓	↓
Real GDP rises by a multiple of the increase in investment	Inflation declines

increasing GDP from Q_1 to the full-employment GDP of Q_f.[1]

Column 1 in Table 15.3 summarizes the chain of events associated with an easy money policy.

Effects of a Tight Money Policy

Now let's assume that the money supply is $175 billion ($S_{m3}$) in Figure 15.2a. This results in an interest rate of 6 percent, investment spending of $25 billion, and aggregate demand AD$_3$. As you can see in Figure 15.2c, we

have depicted a positive GDP gap of $Q_3 - Q_f$ and demand-pull inflation. Aggregate demand AD$_3$ is excessive relative to the economy's full-employment level of real output Q_f. To rein in spending, the Fed will institute a tight money policy.

The Federal Reserve Board will direct Federal Reserve Banks to undertake some combination of the following actions: (1) Sell government securities to banks and the public in the open market, (2) increase the legal reserve ratio, and (3) increase the discount rate. Banks then will discover that their reserves are below those required. So they will need to reduce their checkable deposits by refraining from issuing new loans as old loans are paid back. This will shrink the money supply and increase the interest rate. The higher interest rate will discourage investment, lowering aggregate demand and restraining demand-pull inflation.

If the Fed reduces the money supply from $175 billion to $150 billion ($S_{m3}$ to S_{m2} in Figure 15.2a), the interest rate will rise from 6 to 8 percent and investment will decline from $25 billion to $20 billion (Figure 15.2b). This $5 billion decrease in investment, bolstered by the multiplier process, will shift the aggregate demand curve leftward from AD$_3$ to AD$_2$. For example, if the MPC is .75, the multiplier will be 4 and the aggregate demand curve will shift leftward by $20 billion (= 4 × $5 billion of investment) at each price level. This leftward shift of the aggregate demand curve will eliminate the excessive spending and thus the demand-pull inflation. In the real world, of course, the goal will be to stop inflation—that is, to halt further increases in the price level—rather than to actually drive down the price level.[2]

Column 2 in Table 15.3 summarizes the cause-effect chain of a tight money policy. **(Key Question 3)**

Monetary Policy in Action

We now turn from monetary policy in theory to monetary policy in action. Monetary policy has become the dominant component of U.S. national stabilization policy. It has two key advantages over fiscal policy:
- Speed and flexibility.
- Isolation from political pressure.

---

[1]To keep things simple, we assume that the increase in real GDP does not increase the demand for money. In reality, the transactions demand for money would rise, slightly dampening the decline in the interest rate shown in Figure 15.2a.

[2]Again, we assume for simplicity that the decrease in nominal GDP does not feed back to reduce the demand for money and thus the interest rate. In reality, this would occur, slightly dampening the increase in the interest rate shown in Figure 15.2a.

Compared with fiscal policy, monetary policy can be quickly altered. Recall that congressional deliberations may delay the application of fiscal policy for months. In contrast, the Fed can buy or sell securities from day to day and thus affect the money supply and interest rates almost immediately.

Also, because members of the Fed's Board of Governors are appointed and serve 14-year terms, they are relatively isolated from lobbying and need not worry about retaining their popularity with voters. Thus, the Board, more readily than Congress, can engage in politically unpopular policies (higher interest rates) that may be necessary for the long-term health of the economy. Moreover, monetary policy is a subtler and more politically conservative measure than fiscal policy. Changes in government spending directly affect the allocation of resources, and changes in taxes can have extensive political ramifications. Because monetary policy works more subtly, it is more politically palatable.

The Focus on the Federal Funds Rate

The Fed currently focuses monetary policy on altering the **Federal funds rate** as needed to stabilize the economy. Recall that this is the interest rate that banks charge one another on overnight loans of reserves held at the Federal Reserve Banks. When the Fed announces that it intends to raise the Federal funds rate, it signals that it will implement a "tighter" monetary policy. When it announces it intends to lower the Federal funds rate, it signals that it will implement an "easier" or "more

accommodating" monetary policy. Interest rates in general rise and fall with the Federal funds rate. For example, in Figure 15.3 observe that the **prime interest rate** generally parallels the Federal funds rate. The prime interest rate is the benchmark rate that banks use as a reference point for a wide range of interest rates on loans to businesses and individuals. By changing the Federal funds rate, the Fed therefore alters the economy's prime interest rate along with a wide array of other short-term rates.

The Fed actually sets neither the Federal funds rate nor the prime rate; each is an equilibrium "price." But the Fed is the monopoly supplier of bank reserves. When it reduces bank reserves through open-market operations, the Federal funds rate increases. When it increases bank reserves, the Federal funds rate declines. And because total bank reserves help determine total lending and the supply of money, changes in the supply of bank reserves also affect the overall money supply and thus the prime interest rate.

To increase the Federal funds interest rate, the Fed sells bonds in the open market. Such open-market operations reduce excess reserves in the banking system, lessening the supply of excess reserves available for overnight loans in the Federal funds market. The decreased supply of excess reserves in that market increases the Federal funds rate. In addition, reduced excess reserves decrease the amount of bank lending and hence the amount of checkable-deposit money. Declines in the supply of money produce lower interest rates in general, including the prime interest rate.

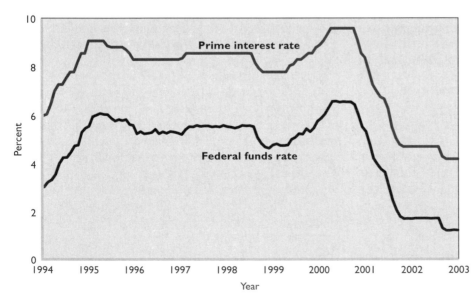

FIGURE 15.3

The prime interest rate and the Federal funds rate in the United States, 1994–2003. The prime interest rate rises and falls with changes in the Federal funds rate.

Source: Federal Reserve data, www.federalreserve.gov/.

In contrast, the Fed buys bonds from banks and the public when it wants to reduce the Federal funds rate. As a result, the supply of reserves in the Federal funds market increases and the Federal funds rate declines. The money supply rises because the increased supply of excess reserves leads to more lending and thus greater creation of checkable-deposit money. As a result, interest rates in general fall, including the prime interest rate. **(Key Question 6)**

Recent Monetary Policy

In the early 1990s, the Fed's easy money policy helped the economy recover from the 1990–1991 recession. The expansion of GDP that began in 1992 continued through the rest of the decade. By 2000 the U.S. unemployment rate had declined to 4 percent—the lowest rate in 30 years. To counter potential inflation during that strong expansion, in 1994 and 1995, and then again in early 1997, the Fed reduced reserves in the banking system to raise the interest rate. In 1998 the Fed temporarily reversed its course and moved to an easier monetary policy to make sure that the U.S. banking system had plenty of liquidity in the face of a severe financial crisis in southeast Asia. The economy continued to expand briskly, and in 1999 and 2000 the Fed, in a series of steps, boosted interest rates to make sure that inflation remained under control.

Significant inflation did not occur in the late 1990s. But in the last quarter of 2000 the economy abruptly slowed. The Fed responded by cutting interest rates by a full percentage point in two increments in January 2001. Despite these rate cuts, the economy entered a recession in March 2001. Between March 20, 2001, and August 21, 2001, the Fed cut the Federal funds rate from 5 to 3.5 percent in a series of steps. In the 3 months following the terrorist attacks of September 11, 2001, it lowered the Federal funds rate from 3.5 to 1.75 percent, and it left the rate there throughout 2002 as the economy began a slow recovery. Partly because of the Fed's actions, the prime interest rate sunk from 9.5 percent at the end of 2000 to 4.25 percent in December 2002.

Economists credit the Fed's adroit use of monetary policy as one of a number of factors that helped the U.S. economy achieve and maintain the rare combination of full employment, price stability, and strong economic growth that occurred between 1996 and 2000. The Fed also deserves high marks for helping to keep the recession of 2001 relatively mild, particularly in view of the adverse economic impacts of the terrorist attacks of September 11, 2001, and the steep stock market drop in 2001–2002.

Problems and Complications

Despite its recent successes in the United States, monetary policy has certain limitations and faces real-world complications.

Lags   Monetary policy is hindered by a recognition lag and an operational lag (but not an administrative lag). Because of monthly variations in economic activity and changes in the price level, it may take the Fed a while to recognize that the economy is receding or the rate of inflation is rising. And once the Fed acts, it may take 3 to 6 months for interest-rate changes to have their full impacts on investment, aggregate demand, real GDP, and the price level. These two lags complicate the timing of monetary policy.

Changes in Velocity   Total expenditures can be regarded as the money supply multiplied by the **velocity of money**—the number of times per year the average dollar is spent on goods and services. If the money supply is $150 billion and the velocity is 4, total spending will be $600 billion (= $150 × 4). But if velocity is 3, total expenditures will be only $450 (= $150 × 3).

Velocity may move counter to changes in the money supply in some circumstances, frustrating monetary policy. Velocity may increase at the same time the Fed reduces the money supply to control inflation. So aggregate demand and inflation may not be restrained by as much as the Fed wants. Conversely, velocity may decline at the same time the Fed takes measures to increase the money supply to combat recession. If so, aggregate demand and real GDP will not expand by the desired amounts.

Velocity might behave this way because of the asset demand for money. An easy money policy, for example, means an increase in the supply of money relative to its demand and therefore a reduction in the interest rate (Figure 15.2a). But the public will hold larger idle money balances when the interest rate (the opportunity cost of holding money as an asset) is lower. This means dollars will move from households to businesses and back again less rapidly. In short, the velocity of money will decline. A reverse sequence of events may cause a tight money policy to induce an increase in velocity. For monetary policy to work, the Fed may have to apply it quite vigorously in order to swamp these potentially offsetting changes in velocity.

Cyclical Asymmetry   Monetary policy may be highly effective in slowing expansions and controlling inflation but less reliable in pushing the economy from a severe

CONSIDER THIS . . .

© R. Ian Lloyd/Masterfile

Pushing on a String

In the late 1990s and early 2000s, the central bank of Japan used an easy money policy to reduce real interest rates to zero. Even with "interest-free" loans available, most consumers and businesses did not borrow and spend more. Japan's economy continued to sputter in and out of recession.

The Japanese circumstance illustrates the possible *asymmetry* of monetary policy, which economists have likened to "pulling versus pushing on a string." A string may be effective at pulling something back to a desirable spot, but it is ineffective at pushing it toward a desired location.

So it is with monetary policy, say some economists. Monetary policy can readily *pull* the aggregate demand curve to the left, reducing demand-pull inflation. There is no limit on how much a central bank can restrict a nation's money supply and hike interest rates. Eventually, a sufficiently tight money policy will reduce aggregate demand and inflation.

But during severe recession, participants in the economy may be highly pessimistic about the future. If so, an easy money policy may not be able to *push* the aggregate demand curve to the right, increasing real GDP. The central bank can produce excess reserves in the banking system by reducing the reserve ratio, lowering the discount rate, and purchasing government securities. But commercial banks may not be able to find willing borrowers for those excess reserves, no matter how low interest rates fall. Instead of borrowing and spending, consumers and businesses may be more intent on reducing debt and increasing saving in preparation for expected worse times ahead. If so, monetary policy will be ineffective. Using it under those circumstances will be much like pushing on a string.

recession. Economists say that monetary policy may suffer from **cyclical asymmetry.**

If pursued vigorously, a tight money policy could deplete commercial banking reserves to the point where banks would be forced to reduce the volume of loans. That would mean a contraction of the money supply, higher interest rates, and reduced aggregate demand. The Fed can turn down the monetary spigot and eventually achieve its goal.

But it cannot be certain of achieving its goal when it turns up the monetary spigot. An easy money policy suffers from a "You can lead a horse to water, but you cannot make it drink" problem. The Fed can create excess reserves, but it cannot guarantee that the banks will actually make the added loans and thus increase the supply of

money. If commercial banks seek liquidity and are unwilling to lend, the efforts of the Fed will be of little avail. Similarly, businesses can frustrate the intentions of the Fed by not borrowing excess reserves. And the public may use money paid to them through Fed sales of U.S. securities to pay off existing bank loans.

Furthermore, a severe recession may so undermine business confidence that the investment demand curve shifts to the left and frustrates an easy money policy. That is what happened in Japan in the 1990s and early 2000s. Although its central bank drove the real interest rate to zero percent, investment spending remained low and the Japanese economy stayed mired in recession. In fact, deflation—a fall in the price level—occurred. The Japanese experience reminds us that monetary policy is not an assured cure for the business cycle. (In March 2003 some members of the Fed's Open Market Committee expressed concern about potential deflation in the United States if the economy remained weak. As of August 2003, deflation had not occurred.)

"Artful Management" or "Inflation Targeting"?

Under the leadership of Alan Greenspan, the Fed and FOMC have artfully managed the money supply to avoid escalating inflation, on the one hand, and deep recession and deflation, on the other. The emphasis has been on achieving a multiple set of objectives: primarily to maintain price stability but also to smooth the business cycle, maintain high levels of employment, and promote strong economic growth. Greenspan and the FOMC have used their best judgment (and, some suggest, "Greenspan's personal intuition") to determine appropriate changes in monetary policy.

Some economists are concerned that this "artful management" may be unique to Greenspan and that someone less insightful may not be as successful. These economists say it would be beneficial to replace or combine the artful management of monetary policy with so-called **inflation targeting**—the annual statement of a target range of inflation, say, 1 to 2 percent, for the economy over some period, say, 2 years. The Fed would then undertake monetary policy to achieve that goal, explaining to the public how each monetary action fits within its overall strategy. If the Fed missed its target, it would need to explain what went wrong. So inflation targeting would increase the "transparency" (openness) of monetary policy and increase Fed accountability. Several countries, including Canada, New Zealand,

Sweden, and the United Kingdom, have adopted inflation targeting.

Proponents of inflation targeting say that, along with increasing transparency and accountability, it would focus the Fed on what should be its main mission: controlling inflation. They say that an explicit commitment to price-level stability will create more certainty for households and firms about future product and input prices and create greater output stability. In the advocates' view, setting and meeting an inflation target is the single best way for the Fed to achieve its important subsidiary goals of full employment and strong economic growth.

But many economists are unconvinced by the arguments for inflation targeting. They say that the overall success of the countries that have adopted the policy has come at a time in which inflationary pressures, in general, have been weak. The truer test will occur under more severe economic conditions. Critics of inflation targeting say that it assigns too narrow a role for the Fed. They do not want to limit the Fed's discretion to adjust the money supply and interest rates to smooth the business cycle, independent of meeting a specific inflation target. Those who oppose inflation targeting say the recent U.S. monetary policy owes its success to adherence to sound principles of monetary policy, not simply to Greenspan intuition. (In particular, they point out that the Fed's policy generally adheres to the so-called Taylor rule, the subject of Chapter 19's Last Word.) In view of the overall success of the Fed's monetary policies since 1990, ask critics, why saddle it with an explicit inflation target?

Monetary Policy and the International Economy

In Chapter 12 we noted that linkages among the economies of the world complicate domestic fiscal policy. Those linkages extend to monetary policy as well.

Net Export Effect   As we saw in Chapter 12, an expansionary U.S. fiscal policy (financed by government borrowing) may increase the domestic interest rate because the government competes with the private sector in obtaining loans. The higher interest rate causes the dollar to appreciate in the foreign exchange market. So imports rise and exports fall, and the resulting decline in net exports weakens the stimulus of the expansionary fiscal policy (review Figure 12.5c). This is the so-called *net export effect* of fiscal policy.

Will an easy money policy have a similar effect? The answer is no. As outlined in column 1, Table 15.4, an easy money policy does indeed produce a net export effect, but its direction strengthens the impact of that policy. An easy money policy in the United States reduces the domestic interest rate. The lower interest rate discourages the inflow of financial capital to the United States. The demand

QUICK REVIEW 15.2

• The Fed is engaging in an easy money policy when it increases the money supply to reduce interest rates and increase investment spending and real GDP; it is engaging in a tight money policy when it reduces the money supply to increase interest rates and reduce investment spending and inflation.

• The main strengths of monetary policy are (a) speed and flexibility and (b) political acceptability; its main weaknesses are (a) time lags, (b) the possibility that changes in velocity will offset it, and (c) potential ineffectiveness during severe recession.

• The Fed communicates changes in monetary policy by announcing the changes it targets for the Federal funds interest rate.

• The Fed's "artful management" of monetary policy has been highly successful in recent years, but some economists contend that this approach should be replaced or combined with explicit *inflation targeting*.

TABLE 15.4

Monetary Policy and the Net Export Effect

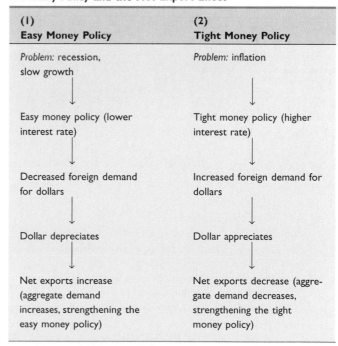

(1) Easy Money Policy	(2) Tight Money Policy
Problem: recession, slow growth	Problem: inflation
↓	↓
Easy money policy (lower interest rate)	Tight money policy (higher interest rate)
↓	↓
Decreased foreign demand for dollars	Increased foreign demand for dollars
↓	↓
Dollar depreciates	Dollar appreciates
↓	↓
Net exports increase (aggregate demand increases, strengthening the easy money policy)	Net exports decrease (aggregate demand decreases, strengthening the tight money policy)

KEY GRAPH

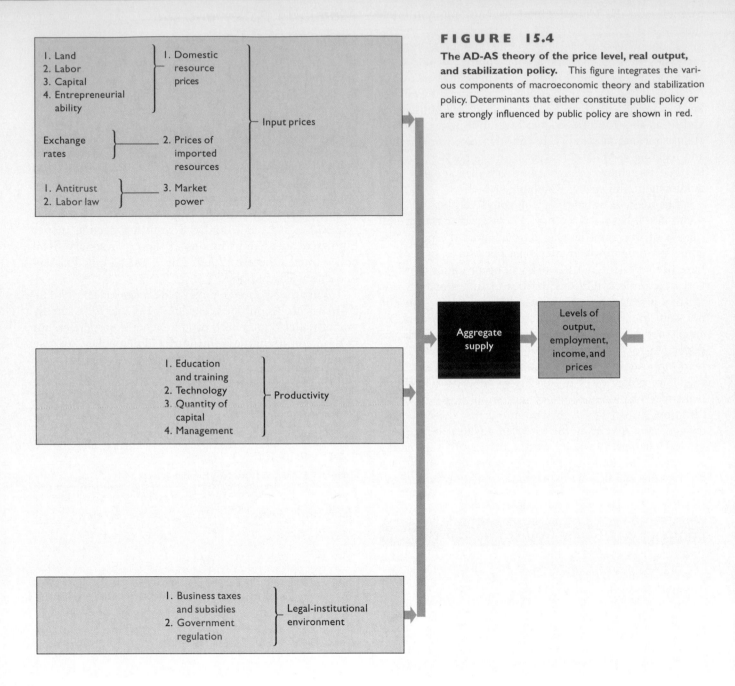

FIGURE 15.4

The AD-AS theory of the price level, real output, and stabilization policy. This figure integrates the various components of macroeconomic theory and stabilization policy. Determinants that either constitute public policy or are strongly influenced by public policy are shown in red.

QUICK QUIZ 15.4

1. All else equal, an increase in domestic resource availability will:
    a. increase input prices, reduce aggregate supply, and increase real output.
    b. raise labor productivity, reduce interest rates, and lower the international value of the dollar.
    c. increase net exports, increase investment, and reduce aggregate demand.
    d. reduce input prices, increase aggregate supply, and increase real output.

2. All else equal, an easy money policy during a recession will:
    a. lower the interest rate, increase investment, and reduce net exports.
    b. lower the interest rate, increase investment, and increase aggregate demand.
    c. increase the interest rate, increase investment, and reduce net exports.
    d. reduce productivity, aggregate supply, and real output.

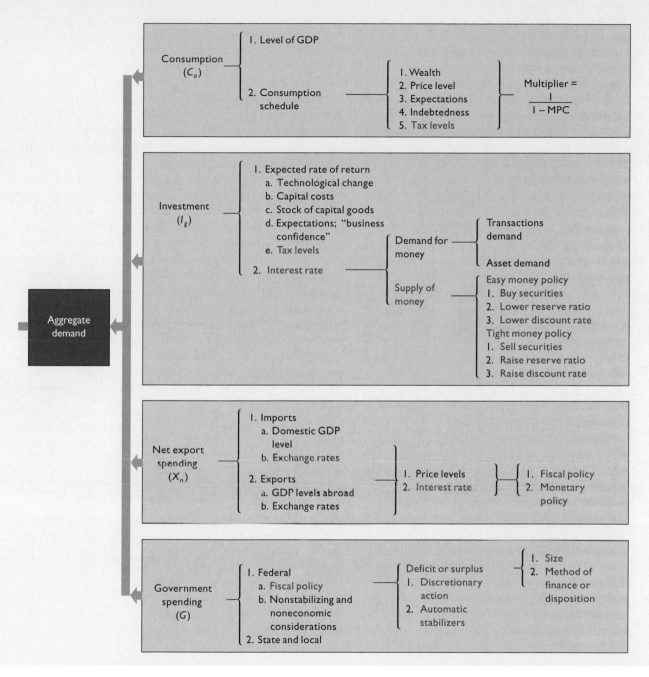

3. A personal income tax cut, combined with a reduction in corporate income and excise taxes, would:
   a. increase consumption, investment, aggregate demand, and aggregate supply.
   b. reduce productivity, raise input prices, and reduce aggregate supply.
   c. increase government spending, reduce net exports, and increase aggregate demand.
   d. increase the supply of money, reduce interest rates, increase investment, and expand real output.

4. An appreciation of the dollar would:
   a. reduce the price of imported resources, lower input prices, and increase aggregate supply.
   b. increase net exports and aggregate demand.
   c. increase aggregate supply and aggregate demand.
   d. reduce consumption, investment, net export spending, and government spending.

Answers: 1. d; 2. b; 3. a; 4. a

for dollars in foreign exchange markets falls, causing the dollar to depreciate in value. It takes more dollars to buy, say, a Japanese yen or a Swiss franc. All foreign goods become more expensive to U.S. residents, and U.S. goods become cheaper to foreigners. U.S. imports thus fall, and U.S. exports rise; so U.S. net exports increase. As a result, aggregate expenditures and equilibrium GDP expand in the United States.

Conclusion: In contrast to an expansionary fiscal policy (which decreases net exports), an expansionary monetary policy *increases* net exports and thus strengthens monetary policy. The depreciation of the dollar that results from the lower interest rate means that net exports rise along with domestic investment. Similarly, the net export effect strengthens a tight money policy. To see the full range of effects of a tight money policy, follow through the analysis in column 2, Table 15.4.

Macro Stability and the Trade Balance

Assume that, in addition to domestic macroeconomic stability, a widely held economic goal is that the United States should balance its exports and imports. That is, U.S. net exports should be zero. In simple terms, the United States wants to "pay its own way" in international trade by earning from its exports an amount of money sufficient to finance its imports.

Consider column 1 in Table 15.4 once again, but now suppose that the United States initially has a very large balance-of-international-trade deficit, which means its imports substantially exceed its exports and so it is not paying its way in world trade. By following through the cause-effect chain in column 1, we find that an easy money policy results in dollar depreciation and thus U.S. exports increase and U.S. imports decline. This increase in net exports eventually corrects the assumed initial balance-of-trade deficit.

Conclusion. *The easy money policy, which is appropriate for the alleviation of unemployment and sluggish growth, is compatible with the goal of correcting a balance-of-trade deficit.* Similarly, if the initial problem was a U.S. trade surplus, a tight money policy would tend to resolve it.

Now consider column 2 in Table 15.4, and assume again that the United States has a large balance-of-trade deficit. In using a tight money policy to restrain inflation, the Fed would cause net exports to decrease—U.S. exports would fall and imports would rise. That would mean a larger trade deficit.

Conclusion: *A tight money policy that is used to alleviate inflation conflicts with the goal of correcting a balance-of-trade deficit.* However, if the initial problem was a trade surplus, a tight money policy would help to resolve it.

Overall we find that an easy money policy alleviates a trade deficit and aggravates a trade surplus; a tight money policy alleviates a trade surplus and aggravates a trade deficit. The point is that certain combinations of circumstances create conflicts or tradeoffs between the use of monetary policy to achieve domestic stability and the realization of a balance in the nation's international trade. **(Key Question 8)**

The "Big Picture"

Figure 15.4 (Key Graph) on pages 284 and 285 brings together the analytical and policy aspects of macroeconomics discussed in this and the eight preceding chapters. This "big picture" shows how the many concepts and principles discussed relate to one another and how they constitute a coherent theory of the price level and real output in a market economy.

Study this diagram and you will see that the levels of output, employment, income, and prices all result from the interaction of aggregate supply and aggregate demand. The items shown in red relate to public policy.

The Popular Press Often Describes the Federal Reserve Board and Its Chair (Alan Greenspan, 1987–Present) in Colorful Terms.

The Federal Reserve Board leads a very dramatic life, or so it seems when one reads journalistic accounts of its activities. It loosens or tightens reins while riding herd on a rambunctious economy, goes to the rescue of an embattled dollar, tightens spigots on credit . . . you get the picture. For the Fed, life is a metaphor.

The Fed as Mechanic The Fed sometimes must roll up its sleeves and adjust the economic machinery. The Fed spends a lot of time tightening things, loosening things, or debating about whether to tighten or loosen.

Imagine a customer taking his car into Greenspan's Garage:

Normally calm, Skeezix Greenspan took one look at the car and started to sweat. This would be hard to fix—it was an economy car:

"What's the problem?" asked Greenspan.

"It's been running beautifully for over 6 years now," said the customer. "But recently it's been acting sluggish."

"These cars are tricky," said Greenspan. "We can always loosen a few screws, as long as you don't mind the side effects."

"What side effects?" asked the customer.

"Nothing at first," said Greenspan. "We won't even know if the repairs have worked for at least a year. After that, either everything will be fine, or your car will accelerate wildly and go totally out of control."

"Just as long as it doesn't stall," said the customer. "I hate that."

The Fed as Warrior The Fed must fight inflation. But can it wage a protracted war? There are only seven Fed governors, including Greenspan—not a big army:

Gen. Greenspan sat in the war room plotting strategy. You never knew where the enemy would strike next—producer prices, retail sales, factory payrolls, manufacturing inventories.

Suddenly, one of his staff officers burst into the room: "Straight from the Western European front, sir—the dollar is under attack by the major industrial nations."

Greenspan whirled around toward the big campaign map. "We've got to turn back this assault!" he said.

"Yes sir." The officer turned to go.

"Hold it!" Greenspan shouted. Suddenly, his mind reeled with conflicting data. A strong dollar was good for inflation, right? Yes, but it was bad for the trade deficit. Or was it the other way around? Attack? Retreat? Macroeconomic forces were closing in.

"Call out the Reserve!" he told the officer.

"Uh . . . we are the Reserve," the man answered.

The Fed as the Fall Guy Inflation isn't the only tough customer out there. The Fed must also withstand pressure from administration officials who are regularly described as "leaning heavily" on the Fed to ease up and relax. This always sounds vaguely threatening:

Alan Greenspan was walking down a deserted street late one night. Suddenly a couple of thugs wearing pin-stripes and wingtips cornered him in a dark alley.

"What do you want?" Greenspan asked.

"Just relax," said one.

"How can I relax?" asked Greenspan. "I'm in a dark alley talking to thugs."

"You know what we mean," said the other. "Ease up on the federal funds rate—or else."

"Or else what?" asked Greenspan.

"Don't make us spell it out. Let's just say that if anything unfortunate happens to the gross [domestic] product, I'm holding you personally responsible."

"Yeah," added the other. "A recession could get real painful."

The Fed as Cosmic Force The Fed may be a cosmic force. After all, it does satisfy the three major criteria—power, mystery, and a New York office. Some observers even believe the Fed can control the stock market, either by action, symbolic action, anticipated action, or non-action. But saner heads realize this is ridiculous—the market has always been controlled by sunspots.

I wish we could get rid of all these romantic ideas about the Federal Reserve. If you want to talk about the Fed, keep it simple. Just say the Fed is worried about the money. This is something we all can relate to.

Source: Paul Hellman, "Greenspan and the Feds: Captains Courageous," *The Wall Street Journal,* Jan. 31, 1991, p. 18. Reprinted with permission of *The Wall Street Journal,* © 1990 Dow Jones & Company, Inc. All rights reserved.

SUMMARY

1. The goal of monetary policy is to help the economy achieve price stability, full employment, and economic growth.

2. As they relate to monetary policy, the most important assets of the Federal Reserve Banks are securities and loans to commercial banks. The Federal Reserve Banks' most important liabilities are the reserves of member banks, Treasury deposits, and Federal Reserve Notes.

3. The three instruments of monetary policy are (a) open-market operations, (b) the reserve ratio, and (c) the discount rate.

4. Monetary policy operates through a complex cause-effect chain: (a) Policy decisions affect commercial bank reserves; (b) changes in reserves affect the money supply; (c) changes in the money supply alter the interest rate; (d) changes in the interest rate affect investment; (e) changes in investment affect aggregate demand; (f) changes in aggregate demand affect the equilibrium real GDP and the price level. Table 15-3 draws together all the basic ideas relevant to the use of monetary policy.

5. The advantages of monetary policy include its flexibility and political acceptability. Recently, the Fed has communicated its changes in monetary policy via announcements concerning its targets for the Federal funds rate. When it deems it necessary, the Fed uses open-market operations to change that rate, which is the interest rate banks charge one another on overnight loans of excess reserves. Interest rates in general, including the prime interest rate, rise and fall with the Federal funds rate. The prime interest rate is the benchmark rate that banks use as a reference rate for a wide range of interest rates on short-term loans to businesses and individuals.

6. In the recent past, the Fed has adroitly used monetary policy to hold inflation in check as the economy boomed, to limit the depth of the recession of 2001, and to promote economic recovery. Today, nearly all economists view monetary policy as a significant stabilization tool.

7. Monetary policy has some limitations and potential problems: (a) Recognition and operation lags complicate the timing of monetary policy. (b) Changes in the velocity of money may partially offset policy-instigated changes in the supply of money. (c) In a severe recession, the reluctance of firms to borrow and spend on capital goods may limit the effectiveness of an expansionary monetary policy.

8. Some economists recommend that the United States follow the lead of several other nations, including Canada and the United Kingdom, in replacing or combining the "artful management" of monetary policy with so-called *inflation targeting*.

9. The effect of an easy money policy on domestic GDP is strengthened by the increase in net exports that results from a lower domestic interest rate. Likewise, a tight money policy is strengthened by a decline in net exports. In some situations, there may be a tradeoff between the effect of monetary policy on the international value of a nation's currency (and thus on its trade balance) and the use of monetary policy to achieve domestic stability.

TERMS AND CONCEPTS

monetary policy	discount rate	Federal funds rate	cyclical asymmetry
open-market operations	easy money policy	prime interest rate	inflation targeting
reserve ratio	tight money policy	velocity of money	

STUDY QUESTIONS

1. Use commercial bank and Federal Reserve Bank balance sheets to demonstrate the impact of each of the following transactions on commercial bank reserves:

   a. Federal Reserve Banks purchase securities from private businesses and consumers.

   b. Commercial banks borrow from Federal Reserve Banks.

   c. The Fed reduces the reserve ratio.

2. *Key Question* In the table on page 289 you will find consolidated balance sheets for the commercial banking system and the 12 Federal Reserve Banks. Use columns 1 through 3 to indicate how the balance sheets would read after each of transactions *a* to *c* is completed. Do not cumulate your answers; that is, analyze each transaction separately, starting in each case from the figures provided. All accounts are in billions of dollars.

   a. A decline in the discount rate prompts commercial banks to borrow an additional $1 billion from the Federal Reserve Banks. Show the new balance-sheet figures in column 1 of each table.

		Consolidated Balance Sheet: All Commercial Banks		
		(1)	**(2)**	**(3)**
Assets:				
Reserves	$ 33	_____	_____	_____
Securities	60	_____	_____	_____
Loans	60	_____	_____	_____
Liabilities and net worth:				
Checkable deposits	$150	_____	_____	_____
Loans from the Federal Reserve Banks	3	_____	_____	_____

		Consolidated Balance Sheet: The 12 Federal Reserve Banks		
		(1)	**(2)**	**(3)**
Assets:				
Securities	$60	_____	_____	_____
Loans to commercial banks	3	_____	_____	_____
Liabilities and net worth:				
Reserves of commercial banks	$33	_____	_____	_____
Treasury deposits	3	_____	_____	_____
Federal Reserve Notes	27	_____	_____	_____

b. The Federal Reserve Banks sell $3 billion in securities to members of the public, who pay for the bonds with checks. Show the new balance-sheet figures in column 2 of each table.

c. The Federal Reserve Banks buy $2 billion of securities from commercial banks. Show the new balance-sheet figures in column 3 of each table.

d. Now review each of the above three transactions, asking yourself these three questions: (1) What change, if any, took place in the money supply as a direct and immediate result of each transaction? (2) What increase or decrease in the commercial banks' reserves took place in each transaction? (3) Assuming a reserve ratio of 20 percent, what change in the money-creating potential of the commercial banking system occurred as a result of each transaction?

3. *Key Question* Suppose that you are a member of the Board of Governors of the Federal Reserve System. The economy is experiencing a sharp and prolonged inflationary trend. What changes in (*a*) the reserve ratio, (*b*) the discount rate, and (*c*) open-market operations would you recommend? Explain in each case how the change you advocate would affect commercial bank reserves, the money supply, interest rates, and aggregate demand.

4. What is the basic objective of monetary policy? State the cause-effect chain through which monetary policy is made

effective. What are the major strengths of monetary policy?

5. What is "velocity" as it applies to money? Suppose the Fed decreases the money supply from $3 billion to $2 billion, but velocity rises from 3 to 5. By how much, if at all, will total spending decline? What do economists mean when they say that monetary policy can exhibit cyclical asymmetry?

6. *Key Question* Distinguish between the Federal funds rate and the prime interest rate. In what way is the Federal funds rate a measure of the tightness or looseness of monetary policy? In 2001 the Fed used open-market operations to significantly reduce the Federal funds rate. What was the logic of those actions? What was the effect on the prime interest rate?

7. What is inflation targeting, and how does it differ from the current Fed policy? What are the main benefits of inflation targeting, according to its supporters? Why do many economists feel it is not needed or even oppose it?

8. *Key Question* Suppose the Fed decides to engage in a tight money policy as a way to reduce demand-pull inflation. Use the aggregate demand–aggregate supply model to show what this policy is intended to accomplish in a closed economy. Now introduce the open economy and explain how changes in the international value of the dollar might affect the location of your aggregate demand curve.

9. *(Last Word)* How do each of the following metaphors apply to the Federal Reserve's role in the economy: Fed as a mechanic; Fed as a warrior; Fed as a fall guy?

10. *Web-Based Question: Current U.S. interest rates* Visit the Federal Reserve's website at www.federalreserve.gov, and select Research and Data, then Statistics: Releases and Historical Data, Selected Interest Rates (weekly), and Historical Data to find the most recent values for the following interest rates: the Federal funds rate, the discount rate, and the prime interest rate. Are these rates higher or lower than they were 3 years ago? Have they increased, decreased, or remained constant over the past year?

11. *Web-Based Question: The Federal Reserve annual report* Visit the Federal Reserve's website at www.federalreserve.gov, and select Testimony and Speeches and then Monetary Policy Report to the Congress to retrieve the current annual report (Sections 1 and 2). Summarize the policy actions of the Board of Governors during the most recent period. In the Fed's opinion, how did the U.S. economy perform?

Part V | Long-Run Perspectives and Macroeconomic Debates

16

Extending the Analysis of Aggregate Supply

Economist John Maynard Keynes once remarked, "In the long run we are all dead." If the long run is a century or more, nobody can argue with Keynes' statement. But if the long run is just a few years or even a few decades, it becomes tremendously important to households, businesses, and the economy. For that reason, macroeconomists have recently focused much attention on long-run macroeconomic adjustments and outcomes. As we will see in this and the next three chapters, that focus has produced significant insights relating to aggregate supply, economic growth, and government budgeting. We will also see that it has renewed debates over the causes of macro instability and the effectiveness of stabilization policy.

Our goals in this chapter are to extend the analysis of aggregate supply to the long run, examine the inflation-unemployment relationship, and evaluate the effect of taxes on aggregate supply. The latter is a key concern of so-called *supply-side economics.*

From Short Run to Long Run

Until now we have assumed the aggregate supply curve remains stable when the aggregate demand curve shifts. For example, an increase in aggregate demand along the upsloping short-run aggregate supply curve raises both the price level and real output. That analysis is accurate and realistic for the **short run,** which, you may recall from Chapter 11, is a period in which nominal wages (and other input prices) do not respond to price-level changes.

There are at least two reasons why nominal wages may be unresponsive to changes in the price level:
* Workers may not immediately be aware of the extent to which inflation (or deflation) has changed their real wages, and thus they may not adjust their labor supply decisions and wage demands accordingly.
* Many employees are hired under fixed-wage contracts. For unionized employees, for example, nominal wages are spelled out in their collective bargaining agreements for perhaps 2 or 3 years. Also, most managers and many professionals receive set salaries

established in annual contracts. For them, nominal wages remain constant for the life of the contracts, regardless of changes in the price level.

In such cases, price-level changes do not immediately give rise to changes in nominal wages. Instead, significant periods of time may pass before such adjustments occur.

Once contracts have expired and nominal wage adjustments have been made, the economy enters the **long run.** Recall that this is *the period in which nominal wages are fully responsive to previous changes in the price level.* As time passes, workers gain full information about price-level changes and how those changes affect their real wages. For example, suppose that Jessica received an hourly nominal wage of $10 when the price index was 100 (or, in decimals, 1.0) and that her real wage was also $10 (= $10 of nominal wage divided by 1.0). But when the price level rises to, say, 120, Jessica's $10 real wage declines to $8.33 (= $10/1.2). As a result, she and other workers will adjust their labor supply and wage demands such that their nominal wages eventually will rise to restore the purchasing power of an hour of work. In our example, Jessica's nominal wage will increase from $10 to $12, returning her real wage to $10 (= $12/1.2).

Short-Run Aggregate Supply

Our immediate objective is to demonstrate the *relationship* between short-run aggregate supply and long-run aggregate supply. We begin by briefly reviewing short-run aggregate supply.

Consider the short-run aggregate supply curve AS_1 in Figure 16.1a. This curve is based on three assumptions: (1) The initial price level is P_1, (2) firms and workers have established nominal wages on the expectation that this price level will persist, and (3) the price level is flexible both upward and downward. Observe from point a_1 that at price level P_1 the economy is operating at its full-employment output Q_f. This output is the real production forthcoming when the economy is operating at its natural rate of unemployment (or potential output.).

Now let's review the short-run effects of changes in the price level, say, from P_1 to P_2 in Figure 16.1a. The higher prices associated with price level P_2 increase firms' revenues, and because their nominal wages are unresponsive, their profits rise. Those higher profits lead firms to increase their output from Q_f to Q_2, and the economy moves from a_1 to a_2 on aggregate supply AS_1. At output Q_2 the economy is operating beyond its full-employment output.

FIGURE 16.1

Short-run and long-run aggregate supply. (a) In the short run, nominal wages are unresponsive to price-level changes and based on the expectation that price level P_1 will continue. An increase in the price level from P_1 to P_2 increases profits and output, moving the economy from a_1 to a_2; a decrease in the price level from P_1 to P_3 reduces profits and real output, moving the economy from a_1 to a_3. The short-run aggregate supply curve therefore slopes upward. (b) In the long run, a rise in the price level results in higher nominal wages and thus shifts the short-run aggregate supply curve to the left. Conversely, a decrease in the price level reduces nominal wages and shifts the short-run aggregate supply curve to the right. After such adjustments, the economy obtains equilibrium of points such as b_1 and c_1. Thus, the long-run aggregate supply curve is vertical at the full-employment output.

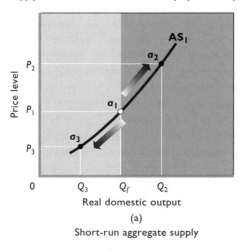

(a)
Short-run aggregate supply

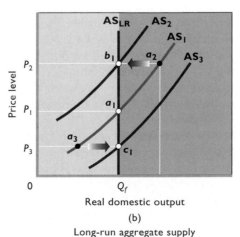

(b)
Long-run aggregate supply

The firms make this possible by extending the work hours of part-time and full-time workers, enticing new workers such as homemakers and retirees into the labor force, and hiring and training the structurally unemployed. Thus, the nation's unemployment rate declines below its natural rate.

How will the firms respond when the price level *falls*, say, from P_1 to P_3 in Figure 16.1a? Because the prices they receive for their products are lower while the nominal wages they pay workers are not, firms discover that their revenues and profits have diminished or disappeared. So they reduce their production and employment, and, as shown by the movement from a_1 to a_3, real output falls to Q_3. Increased unemployment and a higher unemployment rate accompany the decline in real output. At output Q_3 the unemployment rate is greater than the natural rate of unemployment associated with output Q_f.

Long-Run Aggregate Supply

The outcomes are different in the long run. To see why, we need to extend the analysis of aggregate supply to account for changes in nominal wages that occur *in response to changes in the price level*. That will enable us to derive the economy's long-run aggregate supply curve.

By definition, nominal wages in the long run are fully responsive to changes in the price level. We illustrate the implications for aggregate supply in Figure 16.1b. Again, suppose that the economy is initially at point a_1 (P_1 and Q_f). As we just demonstrated, an increase in the price level from P_1 to P_2 will move the economy from point a_1 to a_2 along the short-run aggregate supply curve AS_1. In the long run, however, workers discover that their real wages (their constant nominal wages divided by the price level) have declined because of this increase in the price level. They restore their previous level of real wages by gaining nominal wage increases. Because nominal wages are one of the determinants of aggregate supply (see Figure 11.5), the short-run supply curve then shifts leftward from AS_1 to AS_2, which now reflects the higher price level P_2 and the new expectation that P_2, not P_1, will continue. The leftward shift in the short-run aggregate supply curve to AS_2 moves the economy from a_2 to b_1. Real output falls back to its full-employment level Q_f, and the unemployment rate rises to its natural rate.

What is the long-run outcome of a *decrease* in the price level? *Assuming eventual downward wage flexibility*, a decline in the price level from P_1 to P_3 in Figure 16.1b works in the opposite way from a price-level increase. At first the economy moves from point a_1 to a_3 on AS_1. Profits are squeezed or eliminated because prices have fallen and nominal wages have not. But this movement along AS_1 is the

FIGURE 16.2

Equilibrium in the extended AD-AS model. The equilibrium price level P_1 and level of real output Q_f occur at the intersection of the aggregate demand curve AD_1, the long-run aggregate supply curve AS_{LR}, and the short-run aggregate supply curve AS_1.

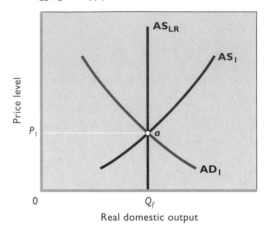

short-run supply response. With enough time the lower price level P_3 (which has increased real wages) results in a drop in nominal wages such that the original real wages are restored. Lower nominal wages shift the short-run aggregate supply curve rightward from AS_1 to AS_3, and real output returns to its full-employment level of Q_f at point c_1.

By tracing a line between the long-run equilibrium points b_1, a_1, and c_1, we obtain a long-run aggregate supply curve. Observe that it is vertical at the full-employment level of real GDP. After long-run adjustments in nominal wages, real output is Q_f regardless of the specific price level. **(Key Question 3)**

Equilibrium in the Extended AD-AS Model

Figure 16.2 shows the long-run equilibrium in the AD-AS model, now extended to include the distinction between short-run aggregate supply and long-run aggregate supply. (Hereafter, we will refer to this model as the *extended AD-AS model*, with "extended" referring to the inclusion of both the short-run and the long-run aggregate supply curves.) Equilibrium in the figure occurs at point *a*, where the economy's aggregate demand curve AD_1 intersects both its short-run aggregate supply curve AS_1 and the vertical long-run aggregate supply curve AS_{LR}. In long-run equilibrium, the economy's price level is P_1 and its real output is Q_f.

16.1 Extended AD-AS model

Applying the Extended AD-AS Model

Let's see how the extended AD-AS model helps us better understand the long-run aspects of demand-pull inflation, cost-push inflation, and recession.

Demand-Pull Inflation in the Extended AD-AS Model

Recall that demand-pull inflation occurs when an increase in aggregate demand pulls up the price level. Earlier, we depicted this inflation by shifting an aggregate demand curve rightward along a stable aggregate supply curve (see Figure 11.7).

In our more complex version of aggregate supply, however, an increase in the price level will eventually lead to an increase in nominal wages and thus a leftward shift of the short-run aggregate supply curve. This is shown in Figure 16.3, where we initially suppose the price level is P_1 at the intersection of aggregate demand curve AD_1, short-run supply curve AS_1, and long-run aggregate supply curve AS_{LR}. Observe that the economy is achieving its full-employment real output Q_f at point a.

Now consider the effects of an increase in aggregate demand as represented by the rightward shift from AD_1 to AD_2. This shift might result from any one of a number of factors, including an increase in investment spending and a rise in net exports. Whatever its cause, the increase in aggregate demand boosts the price level from P_1 to P_2 and expands real output from Q_f to Q_2 at point b. There, a positive GDP gap of $Q_2 - Q_f$ occurs.

So far, none of this is new to you. But now the distinction between short-run aggregate supply and long-run aggregate supply becomes important. Once workers have realized that their real wages have declined and their existing contracts have expired, nominal wages will rise.

FIGURE 16.3

Demand-pull inflation in the extended AD-AS model. An increase in aggregate demand from AD_1 to AD_2 drives up the price level and increases real output in the short run. But in the long run, nominal wages rise and the short-run aggregate supply curve shifts leftward, as from AS_1 to AS_2. Real output then returns to its prior level, and the price level rises even more. In this scenario, the economy moves from a to b and then eventually to c.

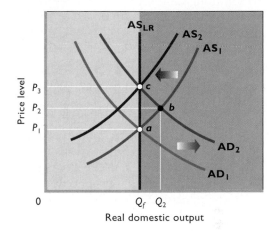

As they do, the short-run aggregate supply curve will ultimately shift leftward such that it intersects long-run aggregate supply at point c.[1] There, the economy has reestablished long-run equilibrium, with the price level and real output now P_3 and Q_f, respectively. Only at point c does the new aggregate demand curve AD_2 intersect both the short-run aggregate supply curve AS_2 and the long-run aggregate supply curve AS_{LR}.

In the short run, demand-pull inflation drives up the price level and increases real output; in the long run, only the price level rises. In the long run, the initial increase in aggregate demand has moved the economy along its vertical aggregate supply curve AS_{LR}. For a while, an economy can operate beyond its full-employment level of output. But the demand-pull inflation eventually causes adjustments of nominal wages that return the economy to its full-employment output Q_f.

---

[1] We say "ultimately" because the initial leftward shift in short-run aggregate supply will intersect the long-run aggregate supply curve AS_{LR} at price level P_2 (review Figure 16.1b). But the intersection of AD_2 and this new short-run aggregate supply curve (not shown) will produce a price level above P_2. (You may want to pencil this in to make sure that you understand this point.) Again nominal wages will rise, shifting the short-run aggregate supply curve farther leftward. The process will continue until the economy moves to point c, where the short-run aggregate supply curve is AS_2, the price level is P_3, and real output is Q_f.

Cost-Push Inflation in the Extended AD-AS Model

Cost-push inflation arises from factors that increase the cost of production at each price level, shifting the aggregate supply curve leftward and raising the equilibrium price level. Previously (Figure 11.9), we considered cost-push inflation using only the short-run aggregate supply curve. Now we want to analyze that type of inflation in its long-run context.

Analysis   Look at Figure 16.4, in which we again assume that the economy is initially operating at price level P_1 and output level Q_f (point a). Suppose that international oil producers agree to reduce the supply of oil to boost its price by, say, 100 percent. As a result, the per-unit production cost of producing and transporting goods and services rises substantially in the economy represented by Figure 16.4. This increase in per-unit production costs shifts the short-run aggregate supply curve to the left, as from AS_1 to AS_2, and the price level rises from P_1 to P_2 (as seen by comparing points a and b). In this case, the leftward shift of the aggregate supply curve is *not a response* to a price-level increase, as it was in our previous discussions of demand-pull inflation; it is the *initiating cause* of the price-level increase.

FIGURE 16.4

Cost-push inflation in the extended AD-AS model.   Cost-push inflation occurs when the short-run aggregate supply curve shifts leftward, as from AS_1 to AS_2. If government counters the decline in real output by increasing aggregate demand to the broken line, the price level rises even more. That is, the economy moves in steps from a to b to c. In contrast, if government allows a recession to occur, nominal wages eventually fall and the aggregate supply curve shifts back rightward to its original location. The economy moves from a to b and eventually back to a.

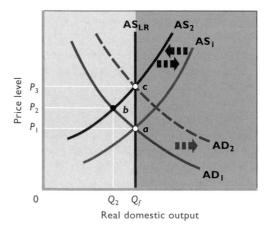

Policy Dilemma   Cost-push inflation creates a dilemma for policymakers. Without some expansionary stabilization policy, aggregate demand in Figure 16.4 remains in place at AD_1 and real output declines from Q_f to Q_2. Government can counter this recession, negative GDP gap, and attendant high unemployment by using fiscal policy and monetary policy to increase aggregate demand to AD_2. But there is a potential policy trap here: An increase in aggregate demand to AD_2 will further raise inflation by increasing the price level from P_2 to P_3 (a move from point b to c).

Suppose the government recognizes this policy trap and decides not to increase aggregate demand from AD_1 to AD_2 (you can now disregard the dashed AD_2 curve) and instead decides to allow a cost-push-created recession to run its course. How will that happen? Widespread layoffs, plant shutdowns, and business failures eventually occur. At some point the demand for oil, labor, and other inputs will decline so much that oil prices and nominal wages will decline. When that happens, the initial leftward shift of the short-run aggregate supply curve will reverse itself. That is, the declining per-unit production costs caused by the recession will shift the short-run aggregate supply curve rightward from AS_2 to AS_1. The price level will return to P_1, and the full-employment level of output will be restored at Q_f (point a on the long-run aggregate supply curve AS_{LR}).

This analysis yields two generalizations:

- If the government attempts to maintain full employment when there is cost-push inflation, an inflationary spiral may occur.
- If the government takes a hands-off approach to cost-push inflation, a recession will occur. Although the recession eventually may undo the initial rise in per-unit production costs, the economy in the meantime will experience high unemployment and a loss of real output.

Recession and the Extended AD-AS Model

By far the most controversial application of the extended AD-AS model is its application to recession (or depression) caused by decreases in aggregate demand. We will look at this controversy in detail in Chapter 19; here we simply identify the key point of contention.

Suppose in Figure 16.5 that aggregate demand initially is AD_1 and that the short-run and long-run aggregate supply curves are AS_1 and AS_{LR}, respectively. Therefore, as shown by point a, the price level is P_1 and

FIGURE 16.5

Recession in the extended AD-AS model. A recession occurs when aggregate demand shifts leftward, as from AD_1 to AD_2. If prices and wages are downwardly flexible, the price level falls from P_1 to P_2. That decline in the price level reduces nominal wages, and this eventually shifts the aggregate supply curve from AS_1 to AS_2. The price level declines to P_3, and real output increases back to Q_f. The economy moves from point a to b and then eventually to c.

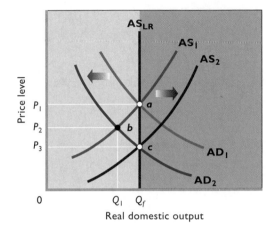

output is Q_f. Now suppose that investment spending declines dramatically, reducing aggregate demand to AD_2. Observe that real output declines from Q_f to Q_1, indicating that a recession has occurred. But if we make the controversial assumption that prices and wages are flexible downward, the price level falls from P_1 to P_2. The lower price level increases real wages for people who are still working, since each dollar of nominal wage has greater purchasing power. Eventually, nominal wages themselves fall to restore the previous real wage; when that happens, the short-run aggregate supply curve shifts rightward from AS_1 to AS_2. The negative GDP gap evaporates without the need for expansionary fiscal or monetary policy, since real output expands from Q_1 (point b) back to Q_f (point c). The economy is again located on its long-run aggregate supply curve AS_{LR}, but now at lower price level P_3.

There is much disagreement about this hypothetical scenario. The key point of dispute is how long it would take in the real world for the necessary downward price and wage adjustments to occur to regain the full-employment level of output. For now, suffice it to say that most economists believe that if such adjustments are forthcoming, they will occur only after the economy has experienced a relatively long-lasting recession with its accompanying high unemployment and large loss of output. **(Key Question 4)**

QUICK REVIEW 16.2

- In the short run, demand-pull inflation raises both the price level and real output; in the long run, nominal wages rise, the short-run aggregate supply curve shifts to the left, and only the price level increases.
- Cost-push inflation creates a policy dilemma for the government: If it engages in an expansionary policy to increase output, an inflationary spiral may occur; if it does nothing, a recession will occur.
- In the short run, a decline in aggregate demand reduces real output (creates a recession); in the long run, prices and nominal wages presumably fall, the short-run aggregate supply curve shifts to the right, and real output returns to its full-employment level.

The Inflation-Unemployment Relationship

Because both low inflation rates and low unemployment rates are major economic goals, economists are vitally interested in their relationship. Are low unemployment and low inflation compatible goals or conflicting goals? What explains situations in which high unemployment and high inflation coexist?

The extended AD-AS model supports three significant generalizations relating to these questions:
- Under normal circumstances, there is a short-run tradeoff between the rate of inflation and the rate of unemployment.
- Aggregate supply shocks can cause both higher rates of inflation and higher rates of unemployment.
- There is no significant tradeoff between inflation and unemployment over long periods of time.

Let's examine each of these generalizations.

The Phillips Curve

We can demonstrate the short-run tradeoff between the rate of inflation and the rate of unemployment through the **Phillips Curve**, named after A. W. Phillips, who developed the idea in Great Britain. This curve, generalized later in Figure 16.7, suggests an inverse relationship between the rate of inflation and the rate of unemployment. Lower unemployment rates (measured as leftward movements on the horizontal axis) are associated with higher rates

16.1
Phillips
Curve

of inflation (measured as upward movements on the vertical axis).

The underlying rationale of the Phillips Curve becomes apparent when we view the short-run aggregate supply curve in Figure 16.6 and perform a simple mental experiment. Suppose that in some period aggregate demand expands from AD_0 to AD_2, either because firms decided to buy more capital goods or the government decided to increase its expenditures. Whatever the cause, in the short run the price level rises from P_0 to P_2 and real output rises from Q_0 to Q_2. A decline in the unemployment rate accompanies the increase in real output.

Now let's compare what would have happened if the increase in aggregate demand had been larger, say, from AD_0 to AD_3. The new equilibrium tells us that the amount of inflation and the growth of real output would both have been greater (and that the unemployment rate would have been lower). Similarly, suppose aggregate demand during the year had increased only modestly, from AD_0 to AD_1. Compared with our shift from AD_0 to AD_2, the amount of inflation and the growth of real output would have been smaller (and the unemployment rate higher).

The generalization we draw from this mental experiment is this: Assuming a constant short-run aggregate supply curve, high rates of inflation are accompanied by low rates of unemployment, and low rates of inflation are accompanied by high rates of unemployment. Figure 16.7a

FIGURE 16.6

The effect of changes in aggregate demand on real output and the price level.   Comparing the effects of various possible increases in aggregate demand leads to the conclusion that the larger the increase in aggregate demand, the higher the rate of inflation and the greater the increase in real output. Because real output and the unemployment rate move in opposite directions, we can generalize that, given short-run aggregate supply, high rates of inflation should be accompanied by low rates of unemployment.

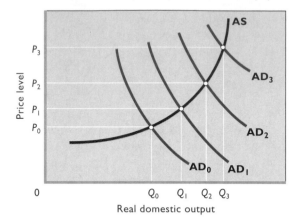

shows how the expected relationship should look, other things equal.

Figure 16.7b reveals that the facts for the 1960s nicely fit the theory. On the basis of that evidence and

FIGURE 16.7

The Phillips Curve: concept and empirical data.   (a) The Phillips Curve relates annual rates of inflation and annual rates of unemployment for a series of years. Because this is an inverse relationship, there presumably is a tradeoff between unemployment and inflation. (b) Data points for the 1960s seemed to confirm the Phillips Curve concept. (Note: Inflation rates are on a December-to-December basis.)

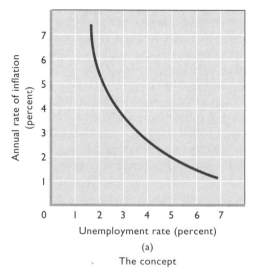

(a)

The concept

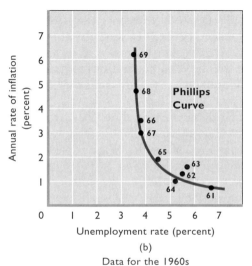

(b)

Data for the 1960s

evidence from other countries, most economists concluded there was a stable, predictable tradeoff between unemployment and inflation. Moreover, U.S. economic policy was built on that supposed tradeoff. According to this thinking, it was impossible to achieve "full employment without inflation": Manipulation of aggregate demand through fiscal and monetary measures would simply move the economy along the Phillips Curve. An expansionary fiscal and monetary policy that boosted aggregate demand and lowered the unemployment rate would simultaneously increase inflation. A restrictive fiscal and monetary policy could be used to reduce the rate of inflation but only at the cost of a higher unemployment rate and more forgone production. Society had to choose between the incompatible goals of price stability and full employment; it had to decide where to locate on its Phillips Curve.

For reasons we will soon see, modern economists reject the idea of a stable, predictable Phillips Curve. Nevertheless, they agree there is a short-run tradeoff between unemployment and inflation. Given aggregate supply, increases in aggregate demand increase real output and reduce the unemployment rate. As the unemployment rate falls and dips below the natural rate, the excessive spending produces demand-pull inflation. Conversely, when recession sets in and the unemployment rate increases, the weak aggregate demand that caused the recession also leads to lower inflation rates.

Periods of exceptionally low unemployment rates and inflation rates do occur, but only under special sets of economic circumstances. One such period was the late 1990s, when faster productivity growth increased aggregate supply and fully blunted the inflationary impact of rapidly rising aggregate demand (review Figure 11.10).

Aggregate Supply Shocks and the Phillips Curve

The unemployment-inflation experience of the 1970s and early 1980s demolished the idea of an always-stable Phillips Curve. In Figure 16.8 we show the Phillips Curve for the 1960s in blue and then add the data points for 1970 through 2002. Observe that in most of the years of the 1970s and early 1980s the economy experienced both higher inflation rates and higher unemployment rates than it did in the 1960s. In fact, inflation and unemployment rose simultaneously in some of those years. This condition is called **stagflation**—a media term that combines the words "stagnation" and "inflation." If there still was any such thing as a Phillips Curve, it had clearly shifted outward, perhaps as shown.

FIGURE 16.8

Inflation rates and unemployment rates, 1961–2002. A series of aggregate supply shocks in the 1970s resulted in higher rates of inflation and higher rates of unemployment. So data points for the 1970s and 1980s tended to be above and to the right of the Phillips Curve for the 1960s. In the 1990s the inflation-unemployment data points slowly moved back toward the original Phillips Curve. Points for the late 1990s and early 2000s are similar to those from the earlier era. (Note: Inflation rates are on a December-to-December basis.)

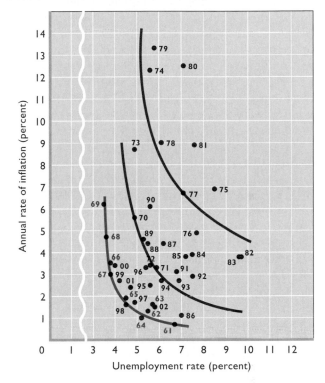

Adverse Aggregate Supply Shocks The Phillips data points for the 1970s and early 1980s support our second generalization: *Aggregate supply shocks can cause both higher rates of inflation and higher rates of unemployment.* A series of adverse **aggregate supply shocks**—sudden, large increases in resource costs that jolt an economy's short-run aggregate supply curve leftward—hit the economy in the 1970s and early 1980s. The most significant of these shocks was a quadrupling of oil prices by the Organization of Petroleum Exporting Countries (OPEC). Consequently, the cost of producing and distributing virtually every product and service rose rapidly. (Other factors working to increase U.S. costs during this period included major agricultural shortfalls, a greatly depreciated dollar, wage hikes previously held down by wage-price controls, and declining productivity.)

These shocks shifted the aggregate supply curve to the left and distorted the usual inflation-unemployment relationship. Remember that we derived the inverse relationship between the rate of inflation and the unemployment rate shown in Figure 16.7 by shifting the aggregate demand curve along a stable short-run aggregate supply curve (Figure 16.6). But the cost-push inflation model shown in Figure 16.4 tells us that a *leftward shift* of the short-run aggregate supply curve increases the price level and reduces real output (and increases the unemployment rate). This, say most economists, is what happened in two periods in the 1970s. The U.S. unemployment rate shot up from 4.9 percent in 1973 to 8.3 percent in 1975, contributing to a significant decline in real GDP. In the same period, the U.S. price level rose by 21 percent. The stagflation scenario recurred in 1978, when OPEC increased oil prices by more than 100 percent. The U.S. price level rose by 26 percent over the 1978–1980 period, while unemployment increased from 6.1 to 7.1 percent.

Stagflation's Demise Another look at Figure 16.8 reveals a generally inward movement of the inflation-unemployment points between 1982 and 1989. By 1989 the lingering effects of the early period had subsided. One precursor to this favorable trend was the deep recession of 1981–1982, largely caused by a tight money policy aimed at reducing double-digit inflation. The recession upped the unemployment rate to 9.5 percent in 1982. With so many workers unemployed, those who were working accepted smaller increases in their nominal wages—or, in some cases, wage reductions—in order to preserve their jobs. Firms, in turn, restrained their price increases to try to retain their relative shares of a greatly diminished market.

Other factors were at work. Foreign competition throughout this period held down wage and price hikes in several basic industries such as automobiles and steel. Deregulation of the airline and trucking industries also resulted in wage reductions or so-called wage givebacks. A significant decline in OPEC's monopoly power and a greatly reduced reliance on oil in the production process produced a stunning fall in the price of oil and its derivative products, such as gasoline.

All these factors combined to reduce per-unit production costs and to shift the short-run aggregate supply curve rightward (as from AS₂ to AS₁ in Figure 16.4). Employment and output expanded, and the unemployment rate fell from 9.6 percent in 1983 to 5.3 percent in 1989. Figure 16.8 reveals that the inflation-unemployment points for recent years are closer to the points associated with the Phillips Curve of the 1960s than to the points in the late 1970s and early 1980s. The points for 1997–2002, in fact, are very close to points on the 1960s curve. (The

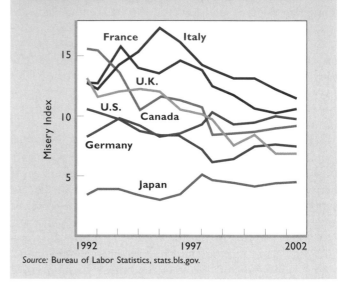

GLOBAL PERSPECTIVE 16.1

The Misery Index, Selected Nations, 1992–2002

The misery index adds together a nation's unemployment rate and its inflation rate to get a measure of national economic discomfort. For example, a nation with a 5 percent rate of unemployment and a 5 percent inflation rate would have a misery index number of 10, as would a nation with an 8 percent unemployment rate and a 2 percent inflation rate.

Source: Bureau of Labor Statistics, stats.bls.gov.

very low inflation and unemployment rates in this later period produced an exceptionally low value of the so-called *misery index*, as shown in Global Perspective 16.1.)

The Long-Run Phillips Curve

The overall set of data points in Figure 16.8 supports our third generalization relating to the inflation-unemployment relationship: There is no apparent *long-run* tradeoff between inflation and unemployment. Economists point out that when decades as opposed to a few years are considered, any rate of inflation is consistent with the natural rate of unemployment prevailing at that time. We know from Chapter 8 that the natural rate of unemployment is the unemployment rate that occurs when cyclical unemployment is zero; it is the full-employment rate of unemployment, or the rate of unemployment when the economy achieves it potential output.

How can there be a short-run inflation-unemployment tradeoff but not a long-run tradeoff? Figure 16.9 provides the answer.

Short-Run Phillips Curve

Consider Phillips Curve PC_1 in Figure 16.9. Suppose the economy initially is experiencing a 3 percent rate of inflation and a 5 percent natural rate of unemployment. Such short-term curves as PC_1, PC_2, and PC_3 (drawn as straight lines for simplicity) exist because the actual rate of inflation is not always the same as the expected rate.

Establishing an additional point on Phillips Curve PC_1 will clarify this. We begin at a_1, where we assume nominal wages are set on the assumption that the 3 percent rate of inflation will continue. But suppose that aggregate demand increases such that the rate of inflation rises to 6 percent. With a nominal wage rate set on the expectation that the 3 percent rate of inflation will continue, the higher product prices raise business profits. Firms respond to the higher profits by hiring more

FIGURE 16.9

The long-run vertical Phillips Curve. Increases in aggregate demand beyond those consistent with full-employment output may temporarily boost profits, output, and employment (as from a_1 to b_1). But nominal wages eventually will catch up so as to sustain real wages. When they do, profits will fall, negating the previous short-run stimulus to production and employment (the economy now moves from b_1 to a_2). Consequently, there is no tradeoff between the rates of inflation and unemployment in the long run; that is, the long-run Phillips Curve is roughly a vertical line at the economy's natural rate of unemployment.

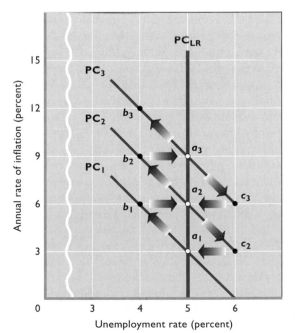

workers and increasing output. In the short run, the economy moves to b_1, which, in contrast to a_1, involves a lower rate of unemployment (4 percent) and a higher rate of inflation (6 percent). The move from a_1 to b_1 is consistent both with an upward-sloping aggregate supply curve and with the inflation-unemployment tradeoff implied by the Phillips Curve analysis. But this short-run Phillips Curve simply is a manifestation of the following principle: *When the actual rate of inflation is higher than expected, profits temporarily rise and the unemployment rate temporarily falls.*

Long-Run Vertical Phillips Curve

But point b_1 is not a stable equilibrium. Workers will recognize that their nominal wages have not increased as fast as inflation and will therefore obtain nominal wage increases to restore their lost purchasing power. But as nominal wages rise to restore the level of real wages that previously existed at a_1, business profits will fall to their prior level. The reduction in profits means that the original motivation to employ more workers and increase output has disappeared.

Unemployment then returns to its natural level at point a_2. Note, however, that the economy now faces a higher actual and expected rate of inflation—6 percent rather than 3 percent. The higher level of aggregate demand that originally moved the economy from a_1 to b_1 still exists, so the inflation it created persists.

In view of the higher 6 percent expected rate of inflation, the short-run Phillips Curve shifts upward from PC_1 to PC_2 in Figure 16.9. An "along-the-Phillips-Curve" kind of move from a_1 to b_1 on PC_1 is merely a short-run or transient occurrence. In the long run, after nominal wages catch up with price-level increases, unemployment returns to its natural rate at a_2, and there is a new short-run Phillips Curve PC_2 at the higher expected rate of inflation.

The scenario repeats if aggregate demand continues to increase. Prices rise momentarily ahead of nominal wages, profits expand, and employment and output increase (as implied by the move from a_2 to b_2). But, in time, nominal wages increase so as to restore real wages. Profits then fall to their original level, pushing employment back to the normal rate at a_3. The economy's "reward" for lowering the unemployment rate below the natural rate is a still higher (9 percent) rate of inflation.

Movements along the short-run Phillips curve (a_1 to b_1 on PC_1) cause the curve to shift to a less favorable position (PC_2, then PC_3, and so on). A stable Phillips Curve with the dependable series of unemployment-rate–inflation-rate tradeoffs simply does not exist in the long run. The economy is characterized by a **long-run vertical Phillips Curve.**

16.2
Long-run
vertical
Phillips
Curve

The vertical line through a_1, a_2, and a_3 shows the long-run relationship between unemployment and inflation. Any rate of inflation is consistent with the 5 percent natural rate of unemployment. So, in this view, society ought to choose a low rate of inflation rather than a high one.

Disinflation

The distinction between the short-run Phillips Curve and the long-run Phillips Curve also helps explain **disinflation**—reductions in the inflation rate from year to year. Suppose that in Figure 16.9 the economy is at a_3, where the inflation rate is 9 percent. And suppose that a decline in aggregate demand (such as that occurring in the 1981–1982 recession) reduces inflation below the 9 percent expected rate, say, to 6 percent. Business profits fall, because prices are rising less rapidly than wages. The nominal wage increases, remember, were set on the assumption that the 9 percent rate of inflation would continue. In response to the decline in profits, firms reduce their employment and consequently the unemployment rate rises. The economy temporarily slides downward from point a_3 to c_3 along the short-run Phillips Curve PC$_3$. *When the actual rate of inflation is lower than the expected rate, profits temporarily fall and the unemployment rate temporarily rises.*

Firms and workers eventually adjust their expectations to the new 6 percent rate of inflation, and thus newly negotiated wage increases decline. Profits are restored, employment rises, and the unemployment rate falls back to its natural rate of 5 percent at a_2. Because the expected rate of inflation is now 6 percent, the short-run Phillips Curve PC$_3$ shifts leftward to PC$_2$.

If aggregate demand declines more, the scenario will continue. Inflation declines from 6 percent to, say, 3 percent, moving the economy from a_2 to c_2 along PC$_2$. The lower-than-expected rate of inflation (lower prices) squeezes profits and reduces employment. But, in the long run, firms respond to the lower profits by reducing their nominal wage increases. Profits are restored and unemployment returns to its natural rate at a_1 as the short-run Phillips Curve moves from PC$_2$ to PC$_1$. Once again, the long-run Phillips Curve is vertical at the 5 percent natural rate of unemployment. **(Key Question 6)**

QUICK REVIEW 16.3

• As implied by the upward-sloping short-run aggregate supply curve, there may be a short-run tradeoff between the rate of inflation and the rate of unemployment. This tradeoff is reflected in the Phillips Curve, which shows that lower rates of inflation are associated with higher rates of unemployment.

• Aggregate supply shocks that produce severe cost-push inflation can cause stagflation—simultaneous increases in the inflation rate and the unemployment rate. Such stagflation occurred from 1973 to 1975 and recurred from 1978 to 1980, producing Phillips Curve data points above and to the right of the Phillips Curve for the 1960s.

• After all nominal wage adjustments to increases and decreases in the rate of inflation have occurred, the economy ends up back at its full-employment level of output and its natural rate of unemployment. The long-run Phillips Curve therefore is vertical at the natural rate of unemployment.

Taxation and Aggregate Supply

A final topic in our discussion of aggregate supply is taxation, a key aspect of **supply-side economics.** "Supply-side economists" or "supply-siders" stress that changes in aggregate supply are an active force in determining the levels of inflation, unemployment, and economic growth. Government policies can either impede or promote rightward shifts of the short-run and long-run aggregate supply curves shown in Figure 16.2. One such policy is taxation.

These economists say that the enlargement of the U.S. tax system has impaired incentives to work, save, and invest. In this view, high tax rates impede productivity growth and hence slow the expansion of long-run aggregate supply. By reducing the after-tax rewards of workers and producers, high tax rates reduce the financial attractiveness of work, saving, and investing.

Supply-siders focus their attention on *marginal tax rates*—the rates on extra dollars of income—because those rates affect the benefits from working, saving, or investing more. In 2003 the marginal tax rates varied from 10 to 35 percent in the United States (See Table 5.1 for details.)

Taxes and Incentives to Work

Supply-siders believe that how long and how hard people work depends on the amounts of additional after-tax earnings they derive from their efforts. They say that lower marginal tax rates on earned incomes induce more work, and therefore increase aggregate inputs of labor. Lower marginal tax rates increase the after-tax wage rate and make leisure more expensive and work more attractive. The higher opportunity cost of leisure encourages people to substitute work for leisure. This increase in productive effort is achieved in many ways: by increasing the number of hours worked per day or week, by encouraging workers to postpone retirement, by inducing more people to enter the labor force, by motivating people to work harder, and by avoiding long periods of unemployment.

Incentives to Save and Invest

High marginal tax rates also reduce the rewards for saving and investing. For example, suppose that Tony saves $10,000 at 8 percent interest, bringing him $800 of interest per year. If his marginal tax rate is 40 percent, his after-tax interest earnings will be $480, not $800, and his after-tax interest rate will fall to 4.8 percent. While Tony might be willing to save (forgo current consumption) for an 8 percent return on his saving, he might rather consume when the return is only 4.8 percent.

Saving, remember, is the prerequisite of investment. Thus supply-side economists recommend lower marginal tax rates on interest earned from saving. They also call for lower taxes on income from capital to ensure that there are ready investment outlets for the economy's enhanced pool of saving. A critical determinant of investment spending is the expected *after-tax* return on that spending.

To summarize: Lower marginal tax rates encourage saving and investing. Workers therefore find themselves equipped with more and technologically superior machinery and equipment. Labor productivity rises, and that expands long-run aggregate supply and economic growth, which in turn keeps unemployment rates and inflation low.

The Laffer Curve

In the supply-side view, reductions in marginal tax rates increase the nation's aggregate supply and can leave the nation's tax revenues unchanged or even enlarge them. Thus, supply-side tax cuts need not produce Federal budget deficits.

This idea is based on the **Laffer Curve,** named after Arthur Laffer, who developed it. As Figure 16.10 shows, the Laffer Curve depicts the relationship between tax rates and tax revenues. As tax rates increase from 0 to 100 percent, tax revenues increase from zero to some maximum level (at *m*) and then fall to zero. Tax revenues decline beyond some point because higher tax rates discourage economic activity, thereby shrinking the tax base (domestic

FIGURE 16.10

The Laffer Curve. The Laffer Curve suggests that up to point *m* higher tax rates will result in larger tax revenues. But higher tax rates will adversely affect incentives to work and produce, reducing the size of the tax base (output and income) to the extent that tax revenues will decline. It follows that if tax rates are above *m*, reductions in tax rates will produce increases in tax revenues.

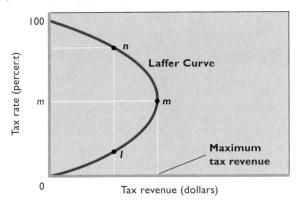

output and income). This is easiest to see at the extreme, where the tax rate is 100 percent. Tax revenues here are, in theory, reduced to zero because the 100 percent confiscatory tax rate has halted production. A 100 percent tax rate applied to a tax base of zero yields no revenue.

In the early 1980s Laffer suggested that the United States was at a point such as *n* on the curve in Figure 16.10. There, tax rates are so high that production is discouraged to the extent that tax revenues are below the maximum at *m*. If the economy is at *n*, then lower tax rates can either increase tax revenues or leave them unchanged. For example, lowering the tax rate from point *n* to point *l* would bolster the economy such that the government would bring in the same total amount of tax revenue as before.

Laffer's reasoning was that lower tax rates stimulate incentives to work, save and invest, innovate, and accept business risks, thus triggering an expansion of real output and income. That enlarged tax base sustains tax revenues even though tax rates are lowered. Indeed, between *n* and *m* lower tax rates result in increased tax revenue.

Also, when taxes are lowered, tax avoidance (which is legal) and tax evasion (which is not) decline. High marginal tax rates prompt taxpayers to avoid taxes through various tax shelters, such as buying municipal bonds, on which the interest earned is tax-free. High rates also encourage some taxpayers to conceal income from the Internal Revenue Service. Lower tax rates reduce the inclination to engage in either tax avoidance or tax evasion. **(Key Question 8)**

CONSIDER THIS . . .

Sherwood Forest

© Bettmann/CORBIS

The popularization of the idea that tax-rate reductions will increase tax revenues owed much to Arthur Laffer's ability to present his ideas simply. In explaining his thoughts to a *Wall Street Journal* editor over lunch, Laffer reportedly took out his pen and drew the curve on a napkin. The editor retained the napkin and later reproduced the curve in an editorial in the *Wall Street Journal*. The Laffer Curve was born. The idea it portrayed became the centerpiece of economic policy under the Reagan administration (1981–1989), which cut tax rates on personal income by 25 percent over a 3-year period.

Laffer illustrated his supply-side views with a story relating to Robin Hood, who, you may recall, stole from the rich to give to the poor. Laffer likened people traveling through Sherwood Forest to taxpayers, whereas Robin Hood and his band of merry men were government. As taxpayers passed through the forest, Robin Hood and his men intercepted them and forced them to hand over their money. Laffer asked audiences, "Do you think that travelers continued to go through Sherwood Forest?"

The answer he sought and got, of course, was "no." Taxpayers will avoid Sherwood Forest to the greatest extent possible. They will lower their taxable income by reducing work hours, retiring earlier, saving less, and engaging in tax avoidance and tax evasion activities. Robin Hood and his men may end up with less revenue than if they collected a relatively small "tax" from each traveler for passage through the forest.

Criticisms of the Laffer Curve

The Laffer Curve and its supply-side implications have been subject to severe criticism.

Taxes, Incentives, and Time A fundamental criticism relates to the degree to which economic incentives are sensitive to changes in tax rates. Skeptics say there is ample empirical evidence showing that the impact of a tax cut on incentives is small, of uncertain direction, and relatively slow to emerge. For example, with respect to work incentives, studies indicate that decreases in tax rates lead some people to work more but lead others to work less. Those who work more are enticed by the higher after-tax pay; they substitute work for leisure because the opportunity cost of leisure has increased. But other people work less because the higher after-tax pay enables them to "buy more leisure." With the tax cut, they can earn the same level of after-tax income as before with fewer work hours.

Inflation or Higher Real Interest Rates Most economists think that the demand-side effects of a tax cut exceed the supply-side effects. Thus, tax cuts undertaken when the economy is at or near full employment may produce increases in aggregate demand that overwhelm any increase in aggregate supply. The likely result is inflation or tight monetary policy to prevent it. If the latter, real interest rates will rise and investment will decline.

Position on the Curve Skeptics say that the Laffer Curve is merely a logical proposition and assert that there must be some level of tax rates between 0 and 100 percent at which tax revenues will be at their maximum. Economists of all persuasions can agree with this. But the issue of where a particular economy is located on its Laffer Curve is an empirical question. If we assume that we are at point *n* in Figure 16.10, then tax cuts will increase tax revenues. But if the economy is at any point below *m* on the curve, tax-rate reductions will reduce tax revenues.

Rebuttal and Evaluation

Supply-side advocates respond to the skeptics by contending that the Reagan tax cuts in the 1980s worked as Laffer predicted. Although the top marginal income tax rates on earned income were cut from 50 to 28 percent in that decade, real GDP and tax revenues were substantially higher at the end of the 1990s than at the beginning.

But the general view among economists is that the Reagan tax cuts, coming at a time of severe recession, helped boost aggregate demand and return real GDP to its full-employment output and normal growth path. As the economy expanded, so did tax revenues despite the lower tax rates. The rise in tax revenues caused by economic growth swamped the declines in revenues from lower tax rates. That is, the Laffer Curve shifted rightward, increasing net tax revenues. But the tax-rate cuts did not produce extraordinary rightward shifts of the long-run aggregate supply curve. Indeed, saving fell as a percentage of personal income during the period, productivity growth was sluggish, and real GDP growth was not extraordinarily strong.

Because government expenditures rose more rapidly than tax revenues in the 1980s, large budget deficits occurred. In 1993 the Clinton administration increased the top marginal tax rates from 31 to 39.6 percent to address these deficits. The economy boomed in the last half of the 1990s, and by the end of the decade tax revenues were so high relative to government expenditures that budget surpluses emerged. In 2001, the Bush administration reduced marginal tax rates over a series of years "to return excess

Significant Changes in Oil Prices Historically Have Had Major Impacts on the U.S. Economy. Have the Effects of Such Changes Weakened?

As indicated in this chapter, the United States has experienced several aggregate supply shocks caused by significant changes in oil prices. In the mid-1970s the price of oil rose from $4 to $12 per barrel, and then again in the late 1970s it increased to $24 per barrel and eventually to $35. These oil price increases caused significant aggregate supply shocks, rising unemployment, and rapid inflation.

In the late 1980s and through most of the 1990s oil prices fell, sinking to a low of $11 per barrel in late 1998. This decline created a "reverse" aggregate supply shock beneficial to the U.S. economy. But in response to those low oil prices, in late 1999 OPEC teamed with Mexico, Norway, and Russia to restrict oil output and thus boost prices. That action, along with a rapidly growing international demand for oil, sent oil prices upward once again. By March 2000 the price of a barrel of oil reached $34, before settling back to about $25 to $28 in 2001 and 2002. (You can find the current daily basket price of oil at OPEC's website, www.opec.org.)

Some economists feared that the rising price of oil would increase energy prices by so much that the U.S. aggregate supply curve would shift to the left, creating cost-push inflation. But inflation in the United States remained modest. Why did changes in oil prices seemingly lose their inflationary punch? There are several reasons.

First, other aggregate supply determinants swamped the potential inflationary impacts of the oil price increases of early 2000. The overall trend of lower costs resulting from the rapid productivity advance associated with the New Economy (discussed in the next chapter) more than compensated for the rise in oil prices. So aggregate supply did not decline as it had in earlier periods.

Second, oil prices are a less significant factor in the U.S. economy than they were in the 1970s. Prior to 1980, changes in oil prices greatly affected *core inflation* (the inflation rate after changes in the prices of food and energy have been subtracted).

Since 1980 changes in oil prices have had little effect on core inflation in the U.S.* The amount of oil and gas consumed in producing each dollar of U.S. GDP has significantly declined. In 2000 about 7000 BTUs of oil and gas were required to produce each dollar of real GDP, compared to 14,000 BTUs in 1970. Part of this decline resulted from new production techniques spawned by the higher oil and energy prices. But also important has been the changing relative composition of the GDP; away from larger, heavier items (such as earth-moving equipment) that are energy-intensive to make and transport and toward smaller, lighter items (such as microchips and software). Experts on energy economics estimate that the U.S. economy is about 33 percent less sensitive to oil price fluctuations than it was in the early 1980s and 50 percent less sensitive than in the mid-1970s.†

A final reason why changes in oil prices seem to have lost their inflationary punch is that the Federal Reserve has become more vigilant and adept at maintaining price stability through monetary policy. The Fed did not let the oil price increases of 1999–2000 become generalized as core inflation.

*Mark A. Hooker, "Are Oil Shocks Inflationary? Asymmetric and Nonlinear Specifications versus Changes in Regimes," *Journal of Money, Credit and Banking*, May 2002, pp. 540–561.
†Stephen P.A. Brown and Mine K. Yücel, "Oil Prices and the Economy," Federal Reserve Bank of Dallas *Southwest Economy*, July–August 2000, pp. 1–6.

---

revenues to taxpayers." In 2003 the top marginal tax rate fell to 35 percent.

Today, there is general agreement that the U.S. economy is operating at a point below *m*—rather than above *m*—on the Laffer Curve in Figure 16.10. Personal tax-rate increases raise tax revenue and personal tax-rate decreases reduce tax revenues. But economists recognize that, other things equal, cuts in tax rates reduce tax revenues in percentage terms by less than the tax-rate reductions. And tax-rate increases do not raise tax revenues by as much in percentage terms as the tax-rate increases. Changes in marginal tax rates *do* alter taxpayer behavior and thus affect taxable income. Although these effects are relatively modest, they need to be considered in designing tax policy.

SUMMARY

1. In macroeconomics, the short run is a period in which nominal wages do not change in response to changes in the price level. In contrast, the long run is a period in which nominal wages are fully responsive to changes in the price level.

2. The short-run aggregate supply curve is upward-sloping. Because nominal wages are unresponsive to price-level changes, increases in the price level (prices received by firms) increase profits and real output. Conversely, decreases in the price level reduce profits and real output. However, the long-run aggregate supply curve is vertical. With sufficient time for adjustment, nominal wages rise and fall with the price level, moving the economy along a vertical aggregate supply curve at the economy's full-employment output.

3. In the short run, demand-pull inflation raises the price level and real output. Once nominal wages rise to match the increase in the price level, the temporary increase in real output is reversed.

4. In the short run, cost-push inflation raises the price level and lowers real output. Unless the government expands aggregate demand, nominal wages eventually will decline under conditions of recession and the short-run aggregate supply curve will shift back to its initial location. Prices and real output will eventually return to their original levels.

5. If prices and wages are flexible downward, a decline in aggregate demand will lower output and the price level. The decline in the price level will eventually lower nominal wages and shift the short-run aggregate supply curve rightward. Full-employment output will thus be restored.

6. Assuming a stable, upward-sloping aggregate supply curve, rightward shifts of the aggregate demand curve of various sizes yield the generalization that high rates of inflation are associated with low rates of unemployment, and vice versa. This inverse relationship is known as the Phillips Curve, and empirical data for the 1960s seemed to be consistent with it.

7. In the 1970s and early 1980s the Phillips Curve apparently shifted rightward, reflecting stagflation—simultaneously rising inflation rates and unemployment rates. The higher unemployment rates and inflation rates resulted mainly from huge oil price increases that caused large leftward shifts in the short-run aggregate supply curve (so-called aggregate supply shocks). The Phillips Curve shifted inward toward its original position in the 1980s. By 1989 stagflation had subsided, and the data points for the late 1990s and early 2000s were similar to those of the 1960s.

8. Although there is a short-run tradeoff between inflation and unemployment, there is no long-run tradeoff. Workers will adapt their expectations to new inflation realities, and when they do, the unemployment rate will return to the natural rate. So the long-run Phillips Curve is vertical at the natural rate, meaning that higher rates of inflation do not permanently "buy" the economy less unemployment.

9. Supply-side economists focus attention on government policies such as high taxation that impede the expansion of aggregate supply. The Laffer Curve relates tax rates to levels of tax revenue and suggests that, under some circumstances, cuts in tax rates will expand the tax base (output and income) and increase tax revenues. Most economists, however, believe that the United States is currently operating in the range of the Laffer Curve where tax rates and tax revenues move in the same, not opposite, directions.

TERMS AND CONCEPTS

short run	stagflation	long-run vertical Phillips Curve	supply-side economics
long run	aggregate supply shocks	disinflation	Laffer Curve
Phillips Curve			

STUDY QUESTIONS

1. Distinguish between the short run and the long run as they relate to macroeconomics. Why is the distinction important?

2. Which of the following statements are true? Which are false? Explain why the false statements are untrue.

   a. Short-run aggregate supply curves reflect an inverse relationship between the price level and the level of real output.

   b. The long-run aggregate supply curve assumes that nominal wages are fixed.

   c. In the long run, an increase in the price level will result in an increase in nominal wages.

3. **Key Question** Suppose the full-employment level of real output (Q) for a hypothetical economy is $250 and the price level (P) initially is 100. Use the short-run aggregate

supply schedules below to answer the questions that follow:

AS (P_{100})		AS (P_{125})		AS (P_{75})	
P	Q	P	Q	P	Q
125	$280	125	$250	125	$310
100	250	100	220	100	280
75	220	75	190	75	250

a. What will be the level of real output in the short run if the price level unexpectedly rises from 100 to 125 because of an increase in aggregate demand? What if the price level unexpectedly falls from 100 to 75 because of a decrease in aggregate demand? Explain each situation, using figures from the table.

b. What will be the level of real output in the long run when the price level rises from 100 to 125? When it falls from 100 to 75? Explain each situation.

c. Show the circumstances described in parts *a* and *b* on graph paper, and derive the long-run aggregate supply curve.

4. *Key Question* Use graphical analysis to show how each of the following would affect the economy first in the short run and then in the long run. Assume that the United States is initially operating at its full-employment level of output, that prices and wages are eventually flexible both upward and downward, and that there is no counteracting fiscal or monetary policy.

a. Because of a war abroad, the oil supply to the United States is disrupted, sending oil prices rocketing upward.

b. Construction spending on new homes rises dramatically, greatly increasing total U.S. investment spending.

c. Economic recession occurs abroad, significantly reducing foreign purchases of U.S. exports.

5. Assume there is a particular short-run aggregate supply curve for an economy and the curve is relevant for several years. Use the AD-AS analysis to show graphically why higher rates of inflation over this period would be associated with lower rates of unemployment, and vice versa. What is this inverse relationship called?

6. *Key Question* Suppose the government misjudges the natural rate of unemployment to be much lower than it actually is, and thus undertakes expansionary fiscal and monetary policies to try to achieve the lower rate. Use the concept of the short-run Phillips Curve to explain why these policies might at first succeed. Use the concept of the long-run Phillips Curve to explain the long-run outcome of these policies.

7. What do the distinctions between short-run aggregate supply and long-run aggregate supply have in common with the distinction between the short-run Phillips Curve and the long-run Phillips Curve? Explain.

8. *Key Question* What is the Laffer Curve, and how does it relate to supply-side economics? Why is determining the economy's location on the curve so important in assessing tax policy?

9. Why might one person work more, earn more, and pay more income tax when his or her tax rate is cut, while another person will work less, earn less, and pay less income tax under the same circumstance?

10. *(Last Word)* Do oil prices play a smaller role or a larger role in the U.S. economy today than in the 1970s and 1980s? Explain why or why not.

11. *Web-Based Question: The Laffer Curve—does it shift?* Congress did not substantially change Federal income tax rates between 1993 and 2000. Visit the Bureau of Economic Analysis website, www.bea.gov/, and use the interactive feature for National Income and Product Accounts tables to find Table 3.2 on Federal government current receipts and expenditures. Find the annual revenues from the Federal income tax from 1993 to 2000. What happened to those revenues over those years? Given constant tax rates, what do the changes in tax revenues suggest about changes in the *location* of the Laffer Curve? If lower (or higher) tax rates do not explain the changes in tax revenues, what do you think does?

12. *Web-Based Question: Dynamic tax scoring—what is it, and who wants it?* Go to www.google.com and search for information on "dynamic tax scoring." What is it? How does it relate to supply-side economics? Which political groups support this approach, and why? What groups oppose it, and why?

17 | *Economic Growth*

The world's capitalist countries experienced impressive growth of real GDP and real GDP per capita during the last half of the twentieth century. In the United States, real GDP increased by 450 percent between 1950 and 2000, while population increased by only 80 percent. In 2000 the value of goods and services available to the average U.S. resident was three times greater than that of 50 years earlier. This expansion of real output—this **economic growth**—greatly increased material abundance and lifted the standard of living of most Americans.

In Chapter 8 we explained how economic growth is measured, briefly looked at economic growth in the United States, and compared growth rates among the major nations. In this chapter we want to explore economic growth in much greater depth. Then in Bonus Web Chapter 39W we extend the discussion of economic growth to the developing nations.

Ingredients of Growth

There are six main ingredients in economic growth. We can group them as supply, demand, and efficiency factors.

Supply Factors

Four of the ingredients of economic growth relate to the physical ability of the economy to expand. They are:
- Increases in the quantity and quality of natural resources.
- Increases in the quantity and quality of human resources.
- Increases in the supply (or stock) of capital goods.
- Improvements in technology.

These **supply factors**—changes in the physical and technical agents of production—enable an economy to expand its potential GDP.

Demand Factor

The fifth ingredient of economic growth is the **demand factor:**
- To achieve the higher production potential created by the supply factors, households, businesses, and government must *purchase* the economy's expanding output of goods and services.

When that occurs, there will be no unplanned increases in inventories and resources will remain fully employed. Economic growth requires increases in total spending to realize the output gains made available by increased production capacity.

Efficiency Factor

The sixth ingredient of economic growth is the **efficiency factor:**

- To reach its production potential, an economy must achieve economic efficiency as well as full employment. The economy must use its resources in the least costly way (productive efficiency) to produce the specific mix of goods and services that maximizes people's well-being (allocative efficiency). The ability to expand production, together with the full use of available resources, is not sufficient for achieving maximum possible growth. Also required is the efficient use of those resources.

The supply, demand, and efficiency factors in economic growth are related. Unemployment caused by insufficient total spending (the demand factor) may lower the rate of new capital accumulation (a supply factor) and delay expenditures on research (also a supply factor). Conversely, low spending on investment (a supply factor) may cause insufficient spending (the demand factor) and unemployment. Widespread inefficiency in the use of resources (the efficiency factor) may translate into higher costs of goods and services and thus lower profits, which in turn may slow innovation and reduce the accumulation of capital (supply factors). Economic growth is a dynamic process in which the supply, demand, and efficiency factors all interact.

Production Possibilities Analysis

To put the six factors underlying economic growth in proper perspective, let's first use the production possibilities analysis introduced in Chapter 2.

Growth and Production Possibilities

Recall that a curve like *AB* in Figure 17.1 is a production possibilities curve. It indicates the various *maximum* combinations of products an economy can produce with its fixed quantity and quality of natural, human, and capital resources and its stock of technological knowledge. An improvement in any of the supply factors will push the production possibilities curve outward, as from *AB* to *CD*.

But the demand factor reminds us that an increase in total spending is needed to move the economy from point *a* to a point on *CD*. And the efficiency factor reminds us that we need least-cost production and an optimal location on *CD* for the resources to make their maximum possible dollar

FIGURE 17.1

Economic growth and the production possibilities curve.
Economic growth is made possible by the four supply factors that shift the production possibilities curve outward, as from *AB* to *CD*. Economic growth is realized when the demand factor and the efficiency factor move the economy from point *a* to *b*.

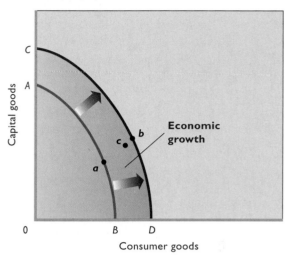

contribution to total output. You will recall from Chapter 2 that this "best allocation" is determined by expanding production of each good until its marginal benefit equals its marginal cost. Here, we assume that this optimal combination of capital and consumer goods occurs at point *b*.

Example: The net increase in the size of the labor force in the United States in recent years has been 1.5 to 2 million workers per year. That increment raises the economy's production capacity. But obtaining the extra output that these added workers could produce depends on their success in finding jobs. It also depends on whether or not the jobs are in firms and industries where the workers' talents are fully and optimally used. Society does not want new labor-force entrants to be unemployed. Nor does it want pediatricians working as plumbers or pediatricians producing services for which marginal costs exceed marginal benefits.

Normally, increases in total spending match increases in production capacity, and the economy moves from a point on the previous production possibilities curve to a point on the expanded curve. Moreover, the competitive market system tends to drive the economy toward productive and allocative efficiency. Occasionally, however, the curve may shift outward but leave the economy behind at some level of operation such as *c* in Figure 17.1. Because *c* is inside the new production possibilities curve *CD*, the economy has not realized its potential for economic growth. **(Key Question 1)**

Labor and Productivity

Although demand and efficiency factors are important, discussions of economic growth focus primarily on supply factors. Society can increase its real output and income in two fundamental ways: (1) by increasing its inputs of resources, and (2) by raising the productivity of those inputs. Figure 17.2 concentrates on the input of *labor* and provides a useful framework for discussing the role of supply factors in growth. A nation's real GDP in any year depends on the input of labor (measured in hours of work) multiplied by **labor productivity** (measured as real output per hour of work):

Real GDP = hours of work × labor productivity

So, thought of this way, a nation's economic growth from one year to the next depends on its *increase* in labor inputs (if any) and its *increase* in labor productivity (if any).

Illustration: Assume that the hypothetical economy of Ziam has 10 workers in year 1, each working 2000 hours per year (50 weeks at 40 hours per week). The total input of labor therefore is 20,000 hours. If productivity (average real output per hour of work) is $10, then real GDP in Ziam will be $200,000 (= 20,000 × $10). If work hours rise to 20,200 and labor productivity rises to $10.40, Ziam's real GDP will increase to $210,080 in year 2. Ziam's rate of economic growth will be about 5 percent [= ($210,080 − $200,000)/$200,000] for the year.

Hours of Work   What determines the number of hours worked each year? As shown in Figure 17.2, the

FIGURE 17.2

The supply determinants of real output.   Real GDP is usefully viewed as the product of the quantity of labor inputs (hours of work) multiplied by labor productivity.

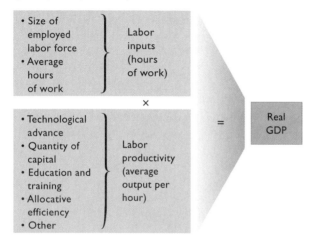

hours of labor input depend on the size of the employed labor force and the length of the average workweek. Labor-force size depends on the size of the working-age population and the **labor-force participation rate**—the percentage of the working-age population actually in the labor force. The length of the average workweek is governed by legal and institutional considerations and by collective bargaining.

Labor Productivity   Figure 17.2 tells us that labor productivity is determined by technological progress, the quantity of capital goods available to workers, the quality of the labor itself, and the efficiency with which inputs are allocated, combined, and managed. Productivity rises when the health, training, education, and motivation of workers improve, when workers have more and better machinery and natural resources with which to work, when production is better organized and managed, and when labor is reallocated from less efficient industries to more efficient industries.

Growth in the AD-AS Model

Let's now link the production possibilities analysis to long-run aggregate supply so that we can show the process of economic growth through the extended aggregate demand–aggregate supply model developed in Chapter 16.

Production Possibilities and Aggregate Supply

The supply factors that shift the economy's production possibilities curve outward also shift its long-run aggregate supply curve rightward. As shown in Figure 17.3, the outward shift of the production possibilities curve from *AB* to *CD* in graph (a) is equivalent to the rightward shift of the economy's long-run aggregate supply curve from AS_{LR1} to AS_{LR2} in graph (b). The long-run AS curves are vertical because an economy's potential output—its full-employment output—is determined by the supply and efficiency factors, not by its price level. Whatever the price level, the economy's potential output remains the same. Moreover, just as price-level changes do not shift an economy's production possibilities curve, they do not shift an economy's long-run aggregate supply curve.

Extended AD-AS Model   In Figure 17.4 we use the extended aggregate demand–aggregate supply model to depict the economic growth process. (The model is extended to include the distinction between short- and long-run aggregate supply. See Chapter 16.)

Suppose that an economy's aggregate demand curve, long-run aggregate supply curve, and short-run aggregate

FIGURE 17.3

Production possibilities and long-run aggregate supply. (a) Supply factors shift an economy's production possibilities curve outward, as from *AB* to *CD*. (b) The same factors (along with the efficiency factor) shift the economy's long-run aggregate supply curve to the right, as from AS_{LR1} to AS_{LR2}.

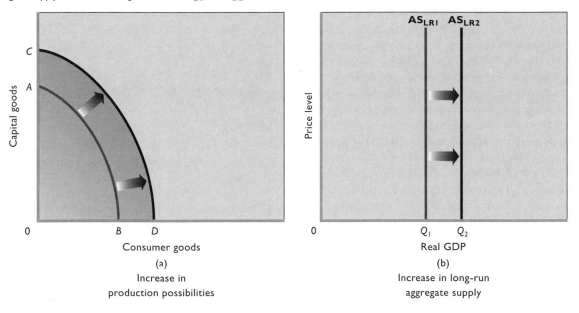

(a)
Increase in
production possibilities

(b)
Increase in long-run
aggregate supply

supply curve initially are AD_1, AS_{LR1}, and AS_1, as shown. The equilibrium price level and level of real output are P_1 and Q_1. At price level P_1, the short-run aggregate supply is AS_1; it slopes upward because, in the short run, changes in the price level cause firms to adjust their output. In the long run, however, price-level changes do not affect the

economy's real output, leaving the long-run aggregate supply curve vertical at the economy's potential level of output, here Q_1. This potential level of output depends on the supply and efficiency factors previously discussed.

Now let's assume that changes in the supply factors (quantity and quality of resources and technology) shift

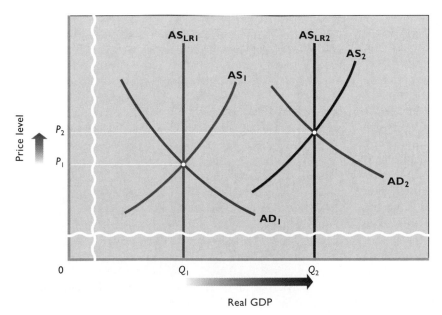

FIGURE 17.4

Economic growth in the extended AD-AS model. Long-run aggregate supply and short-run aggregate supply have increased over time, as from AS_{LR1} to AS_{LR2} and AS_1 to AS_2. Simultaneously, aggregate demand has shifted rightward, as from AD_1 to AD_2. The actual outcome of these combined shifts has been economic growth, shown as the increase in real output from Q_1 to Q_2, accompanied by mild inflation, shown as the rise in the price level from P_1 to P_2.

the long-run aggregate supply curve rightward from AS_{LR1} to AS_{LR2}. The economy's potential output has increased, as reflected by the expansion of available real output from Q_1 to Q_2.

If prices and wages are inflexible downward, the economy can realize its greater production potential only through an increase in aggregate demand. Under usual circumstances, such an increase is forthcoming because the production of additional output produces additional income to households and businesses. In Figure 17.4, suppose that this additional income results in increases in consumption and investment spending such that the aggregate demand curve shifts from AD_1 to AD_2. Also suppose that the economy continues to use its resources efficiently.

The increases of aggregate supply and aggregate demand in Figure 17.4 have increased real output from Q_1 to Q_2 and have boosted the price level from P_1 to P_2. At the higher price level P_2, the economy confronts a new short-run aggregate supply curve AS_2. The result of the dynamics described in Figure 17.4 is economic growth, accompanied in this case by mild inflation.

In brief, economic growth results from increases in aggregate supply and aggregate demand. Whether zero, mild, or rapid inflation accompanies economic growth depends on the extent to which aggregate demand increases relative to aggregate supply. **(Key Question 5)**

17.1 Growth theory

U.S. Economic Growth Rates

Figure 17.5 shows the average annual growth rates of real GDP and real per capita GDP in the United States for the past five decades. *Over the full 50 years, real GDP grew by about 3.5 percent annually, whereas real GDP per capita grew by about 2.3 percent annually.* Economic growth was particularly strong in the 1960s but declined during the 1970s and 1980s. Although the average annual growth rate for the 1990s only slightly exceeded that of the 1980s, real GDP surged between 1996 and 1999. Specifically, it grew by 3.6 percent in 1996, 4.4 percent in 1997, 4.3 percent in 1998, and 4.1 percent in 1999. These growth rates were not only higher than previous rates in the 1990s but higher than those in most other advanced industrial nations during that period.

Growth continued strong in 2000 in the United States, but it collapsed during the recessionary year 2001. Specifically, the rate was 3.8 percent in 2000 and 0.3 percent in 2001. In 2002 the U.S. growth rate was 2.3 percent.

QUICK REVIEW 17.1

• The ingredients of economic growth include (a) four supply factors (increases in the quantity and quality of natural resources, increases in the quantity and quality of human resources, increases in the stock of capital goods, and improvements in technology), (b) a demand factor (increased total spending), and (c) an efficiency factor (achieving economic efficiency).

• Economic growth is shown as an outward shift of a nation's production possibilities curve (accompanied by movement from some point on the old curve to a point on the new curve) and combined rightward shifts of the long-run aggregate supply curve, the short-run aggregate supply curve, and the aggregate demand curve.

• Real GDP grew by an average of 3.5 percent annually between 1950 and 2000; over that same period, real GDP per capita grew at an average annual rate of about 2.3 percent.

Accounting for Growth

The Council of Economic Advisers uses **growth accounting**—the bookkeeping of the supply-side elements that contribute to changes in real GDP—to assess

FIGURE 17.5

U.S. economic growth, annual averages for five decades. Growth of real GDP has averaged about 3.5 percent annually in the last half-century, and annual growth of real GDP per capita averaged about 2.3 percent. Growth rates in the 1970s and 1980s were less than those in the 1960s, but the rates rebounded in the last half of the 1990s.
Source: Bureau of Economic Analysis, www.bea.gov/.

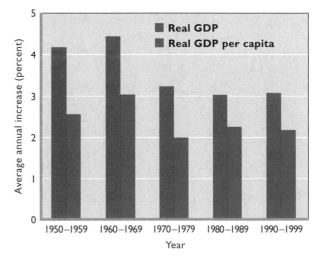

© Dennis O'Clair/Getty Images

Economic Growth Rates Matter!

When compounded over many decades, small absolute differences in rates of economic growth add up to substantial differences in real GDP and standards of living. Consider three hypothetical countries—Alpha, Bravo, and Charlie. Suppose that in 2003 these countries have identical levels of real GDP ($6 trillion), population (200 million), and real GDP per capita ($30,000). Also, assume that annual real GDP growth is 2 percent in Alpha, 3 percent in Bravo, and 4 percent in Charlie.

How will these alternative growth rates affect real GDP and real GDP per capita over a long period, say, the 70-year average life span of an American? By 2073 the 2, 3, and 4 percent growth rates would boost real GDP from $6 trillion to:

* $24 trillion in Alpha.
* $47 trillion in Bravo.
* $93 trillion in Charlie.

For illustration, let's assume that each country experienced an average annual population growth of 1 percent over the 70 years. Then, in 2073 real GDP per capita would be about:

* $60,000 in Alpha.
* $118,000 in Bravo.
* $233,000 in Charlie.

Economic growth rates matter!

the factors underlying economic growth. Ultimately, that accounting leads to two main categories:

* Increases in hours of work.
* Increases in labor productivity.

Labor Inputs versus Productivity

Table 17.1 provides the relevant data for four periods. The symbol "Q" in the table stands for "quarter" of the year. The end points for the first three periods are

business-cycle peaks, and the last period includes future projections by the Council of Economic Advisers. It is clear from the table that both increases in the quantity of labor and rises in labor productivity are important sources of economic growth. Between 1960 and 2002, the labor force increased from 70 million to 143 million workers. Over that period the length of the workweek remained relatively stable. Falling birthrates slowed the growth of the native population, but increased immigration partly offset that slowdown. Of particular significance was a surge of women's participation in the labor force (see this chapter's Last Word). Partly because of that increased participation, U.S. labor-force growth averaged 1.7 million workers per year during the past 25 years.

The growth of labor productivity has also been important to economic growth. In fact, productivity growth has usually been the more significant factor, with the exception of 1973–1990 when productivity growth greatly slowed. For example, between 1990 and 2002, productivity growth was responsible for 2 percentage points, or 68 percent, of the 3 percent average annual economic growth. Over the 2002–2008 period, productivity growth is projected to account for 56 percent of the growth of real GDP.

Technological Advance

The importance of productivity growth to economic growth calls for a fuller explanation of the factors that contribute to productivity growth. The largest contributor is technological advance, which is thought to account for about 40 percent of productivity growth. As economist Paul Romer stated, "Human history teaches us that economic growth springs from better recipes, not just from more cooking."

Technological advance includes not only innovative production techniques but new managerial methods and new forms of business organization that improve the process of production. Generally, technological advance is generated by the discovery of new knowledge, which allows resources to be combined in improved ways that

TABLE 17.1

Accounting for Growth of Real GDP, 1960–2008 (Average Annual Percentage Changes)*

Item	1960 Q2 to 1973 Q4	1973 Q4 to 1990 Q3	1990 Q3 to 2002 Q3	2002 Q3 to 2008 Q4
Increase in real GDP	4.2	2.9	2.9	3.2
Increase in quantity of labor	1.6	1.6	0.9	1.4
Increase in labor productivity	2.6	1.3	2.0	1.8

*Rates beyond 2002 are projected rates.

Source: Derived from *Economic Report of the President, 2003*, p. 66.

increase output. Once discovered and implemented, new knowledge soon becomes available to entrepreneurs and firms at relatively low cost. Technological advance therefore eventually spreads through the entire economy, boosting productivity and economic growth.

Technological advance and capital formation (investment) are closely related, since technological advance usually promotes investment in new machinery and equipment. In fact, technological advance is often *embodied* within new capital. For example, the purchase of new computers brings into industry speedier, more powerful computers that incorporate new technology.

Technological advance has been both rapid and profound. Gas and diesel engines, conveyor belts, and assembly lines are significant developments of the past. So, too, are fuel-efficient commercial aircraft, integrated microcircuits, personal computers, xerography, and containerized shipping. More recently, technological advance has exploded, particularly in the areas of information technology such as wireless communications and the Internet. Other fertile areas of recent innovation are medicine and biotechnology.

Quantity of Capital

A second major contributor to productivity growth is increased capital, which explains roughly 30 percent of productivity growth. More and better plant and equipment make workers more productive. And a nation acquires more capital by saving some of its income and using that saving to invest in plant and equipment.

Although some capital substitutes for labor, most capital is complementary to labor—it makes labor more productive. A key determinant of labor productivity is the amount of capital goods available *per worker*. If both the aggregate stock of capital goods and the size of the labor force increase over a given period, the individual worker is not necessarily better equipped and productivity will not necessarily rise. But the quantity of capital equipment available per U. S. worker has increased greatly over time. (In 2001 it was about $82,000 per worker.)

Public investment in the U.S. **infrastructure** (highways and bridges, public transit systems, wastewater treatment facilities, water systems, airports, educational facilities, and so on) has also grown over the years. This public capital (infrastructure) complements private capital. Investments in new highways promote private investment in new factories and retail stores along their routes. Industrial parks developed by local governments attract manufacturing and distribution firms.

Private investment in infrastructure also plays a large role in economic growth. One example is the tremendous growth of private capital relating to communications systems over the years.

Education and Training

Ben Franklin once said, "He that hath a trade hath an estate," meaning that education and training contribute to a worker's stock of **human capital**—the knowledge and skills that make a productive worker. Investment in human capital includes not only formal education but also on-the-job training. Like investment in physical capital, investment in human capital is an important means of increasing labor productivity and earnings. An estimated 15 percent of productivity growth owes to such investment in people's education and skills.

One measure of a nation's quality of labor is its level of educational attainment. Figure 17.6 shows large gains in education attainment over the past several decades. In 1960 only 41 percent of the U.S. population age 25 or older had at least a high school education; and only 8 percent had a college or postcollege education. By 2000, those numbers had increased to 84 and 26 percent, respectively. Clearly, education has become accessible to more people in the United States during the recent past.

But all is not upbeat with education in the United States. Many observers think that the quality of education in the United States has declined. Average scores on standardized college admission tests are lower than they were a few decades ago. U.S. students in science and mathematics do not do as well as students in many other nations (see Global Perspective 17.1). The United States has been producing fewer engineers and scientists, a problem that may trace back to inadequate training in math and science in

FIGURE 17.6

Changes in the educational attainment of the U.S. adult population. The percentage of the U.S. adult population, age 25 or more, completing high school and college has been rising over recent decades.
Source: U.S. Census Bureau, www.census.gov.

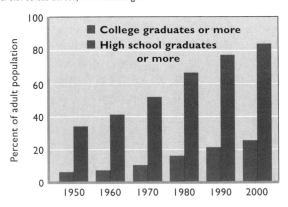

elementary and high schools. And it is argued that on-the-job training programs (apprenticeship programs) in several European nations are superior to those in the United States. For these reasons, much recent public policy discussion and legislation has been directed toward improving the quality of the U.S. education and training system.

 GLOBAL PERSPECTIVE 17.1

Average Test Scores of Eighth-Grade Students in Math and Science, Top 10 Countries and the United States

The test performance of U.S. eighth-grade students did not rank favorably with that of eighth-graders in several other nations in the Third International Math and Science Study (1999).

Mathematics

Rank		Score
1	Singapore	604
2	South Korea	587
3	Taiwan	585
4	Hong Kong (China)	582
5	Japan	579
6	Belgium	558
7	Netherlands	540
8	Slovak Republic	534
9	Hungary	532
10	Canada	531
19	United States	502

Science

Rank		Score
1	Taiwan	569
2	Singapore	568
3	Hungary	552
4	Japan	550
5	South Korea	549
6	Netherlands	545
7	Australia	540
8	Czech Republic	539
9	United Kingdom	538
10	Finland	535
18	United States	515

Economies of Scale and Resource Allocation

Economies of scale and improved resource allocation are a third and fourth source of productivity growth, and together explain about 15 percent of productivity growth.

Economies of Scale   Reductions in per-unit cost that result from increases in the size of markets and firms are called **economies of scale.** Markets have increased in size over time, allowing firms to achieve production advantages associated with greater size. As firms expand their size and output, they are able to use larger, more productive equipment and employ methods of manufacturing and delivery that increase productivity. They also are better able to recoup substantial investments in developing new products and production methods. Examples: A large manufacturer of autos can use elaborate assembly lines with computerization and robotics, while smaller producers must settle for less advanced technologies using more labor inputs. Large pharmaceutical firms greatly reduce the average amount of labor (researchers, production workers) needed to produce each pill as they increase the number of pills produced. Accordingly, economies of scale result in greater real GDP and thus contribute to economic growth.

Improved Resource Allocation   Improved resource allocation means that workers over time have moved from low-productivity employment to high-productivity employment. Historically, much labor has shifted from agriculture, where labor productivity is low, to manufacturing, where it is quite high. More recently, labor has shifted away from some manufacturing industries to even higher productivity industries such as computer software, business consulting, and pharmaceuticals. As a result of such shifts, the average productivity of U.S. workers has increased.

Also, discrimination in education and the labor market has historically deterred some women and minorities from entering high-productivity jobs. With the decline of such discrimination over time many members of those groups have shifted from low-productivity jobs to higher-productivity jobs. The result has been higher overall labor productivity and real GDP.

Finally, we know from discussions in Chapter 6 that tariffs, import quotas, and other barriers to international trade tend to relegate resources to relatively unproductive pursuits. The long-run movement toward liberalized international trade through international agreements has improved the allocation of resources, increased labor productivity, and expanded real output, both here and abroad. **(Key Question 6)**

Other Factors

Several difficult-to-measure factors influence a nation's rate of economic growth. The overall social-cultural-political environment of the United States, for example, has fostered economic growth. The market system that has prevailed in the United States since its founding has fostered many personal and corporate incentives that promote growth. The United States has also had a stable political system characterized by democratic principles, internal order, the right of property ownership, the legal status of enterprise, and the enforcement of contracts. Economic freedom and political freedom have been "growth-friendly."

Unlike some nations, there are virtually no social or moral taboos on production and material progress in the United States. The nation's social philosophy has embraced material advance as an attainable and desirable economic goal. The inventor, the innovator, and the businessperson are accorded high degrees of prestige and respect in American society.

Moreover, Americans have had positive attitudes toward work and risk taking, resulting in an ample supply of willing workers and innovative entrepreneurs. A flow of energetic immigrants has greatly augmented that supply.

QUICK REVIEW 17.2

• Improvements in labor productivity accounted for about two-thirds of increases in U.S. real GDP between 1990 and 2002; the use of more labor inputs accounted for the remainder.

• Improved technology, more capital, greater education and training, economies of scale, and better resource allocation have been the main contributors to U.S. productivity growth and thus to U.S. economic growth.

• Other factors that have been favorable to U.S. growth include reliance on the market system, a stable political system, a social philosophy that embraces material progress, an abundant supply of willing workers and entrepreneurs, and free-trade policies.

The Productivity Acceleration: A New Economy?

Figure 17.7 shows the growth of labor productivity (as measured by changes in the index of labor productivity) in the United States from 1973 to 2002, along with separate trend lines for 1973–1995 and 1995–2002. Labor productivity grew by an average of only 1.4 percent yearly

FIGURE 17.7

Growth of labor productivity in the United States, 1973–2002.   U.S. labor productivity increased at an average annual rate of only 1.4 percent from 1973 to 1995. But between 1995 and 2002 it accelerated to an annual rate of 2.8 percent.

Source: U.S. Bureau of Labor Statistics, www.bls.gov/.

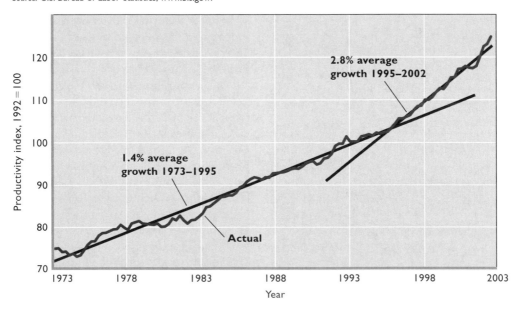

over the 1973–1995 period. But productivity growth averaged 2.8 percent between 1995 and 2002. Many economists believe that this higher productivity growth resulted from a significant new wave of technological advance, coupled with global competition. Some economists say that the United States has achieved a **New Economy**—one with a higher projected trend rate of productivity growth and therefore greater potential economic growth than in the 1973–1995 period.

This increase in productivity growth is important because real output, real income, and real wages are linked to labor productivity. To see why, suppose you are alone on an uninhabited island. The number of fish you can catch or coconuts you can pick per hour—your productivity—is your real wage (or real income) per hour. By *increasing* your productivity, you can improve your standard of living because greater output per hour means there are more fish and coconuts (goods) available to consume.

So it is for the economy as a whole: Over long periods, the economy's labor productivity determines its average real hourly wage. The economy's income per hour is equal to its output per hour. Productivity growth therefore is its main route for increasing its standard of living. It allows firms to pay higher wages without lowering their business profits. As we demonstrated in this chapter's Consider This box, even a seemingly small percentage change in productivity growth, if sustained over several years, can make a substantial difference as to how fast a nation's standard of living rises. We know from the *rule of 70* (Chapter 8) that if a nation's productivity grows by 2.5 percent annually rather than 1.5, its standard of living will double in 28 years rather than 47 years.

Reasons for the Productivity Acceleration

Why has productivity growth increased relative to earlier periods? What is "new" about the New Economy?

The Microchip and Information Technology

The core element of the productivity speedup is an explosion of entrepreneurship and innovation based on the microprocessor, or *microchip*, which bundles transistors on a piece of silicon. Advocates of the New Economy liken the invention of the microchip to that of electricity, the automobile, air travel, the telephone, and television in importance and scope.

The microchip has found its way into thousands of applications. It has helped create a wide array of new products and services and new ways of doing business. Its immediate result was the pocket calculator, the bar-code scanner, the personal computer, the laptop computer, and more powerful business computers. But the miniaturization of electronic circuits also advanced the development of many other products such as cell phones and pagers, computer-guided lasers, deciphered genetic codes, global positioning equipment, energy conservation systems, Doppler radar, and digital cameras.

Perhaps of greatest significance, the widespread availability of personal and laptop computers stimulated the desire to tie them together. That desire promoted rapid development of the Internet and all its many manifestations, such as business-to-household and business-to-business electronic commerce (e-commerce). The combination of the computer, fiber optic cable, wireless technology, and the Internet constitutes a spectacular advance in **information technology,** which has been used to connect all parts of the world.

New Firms and Increasing Returns

Hundreds of new **start-up firms** advanced various aspects of the new information technology. Many of these firms created more "hype" than goods and services and quickly fell by the wayside. But a number of firms flourished, eventually to take their places among the nation's largest firms. Examples of those firms include Intel (microchips); Apple, Dell, and Gateway (personal computers); Microsoft, Oracle, and Intuit (computer software); Cisco Systems (Internet switching systems); America Online (Internet service provision); Yahoo and Google (Internet search engines); and Amazon.com (electronic commerce). There are scores more! Most of these firms were either "not on the radar" or "a small blip on the radar" 25 years ago. Today each of them has large annual revenue and employs thousands of workers.

Successful new firms often experience **increasing returns,** which occur *when a firm's output increases by a larger percentage than the increase in its inputs (resources).* For example, suppose that Techco decides to double the size of its operations to meet the growing demand for its services. After doubling its plant and equipment and doubling its workforce, say, from 100 workers to 200 workers, it finds that its total output has tripled from 8000 units to 24,000 units. Techco has experienced increasing returns; its output has increased by 200 percent, while its inputs have increased by only 100 percent. That is, its labor productivity has gone up from $80 (= 8000 units/100 workers) to $120 (= 24,000 units/200 workers). Increasing returns boost labor productivity, which, other things equal, lowers per-unit costs of production. These reductions in costs resulting from larger firm size are called *economies of scale*.

There are a number of sources of increasing returns and economies of scale for emerging firms:

- *More specialized inputs* Firms can use more specialized and thus more productive capital and workers as they expand their operations. A growing new e-commerce business, for example, can purchase highly specialized inventory management systems and hire specialized personnel such as accountants, marketing managers, and system maintenance experts.

- *Spreading of development costs* Firms can spread high product development costs over greater output. For example, suppose that a new software product costs $100,000 to develop and only $2 per unit to manufacture and sell. If the firm sells 1000 units of the software, its per-unit cost will be $102 [= ($100,000 + $2000)/1000], but if it sells 500,000 units, that cost will drop to only $2.20 [= ($100,000 + $1 million)/500,000].

- *Simultaneous consumption* Many of the products and services of the New Economy can satisfy many customers at the same time. Unlike a gallon of gas that needs to be produced for each buyer, a software program needs to be produced only once. It then becomes available at very low expense to thousands or even millions of buyers. The same is true of entertainment delivered on CDs, movies distributed on DVDs, and information disseminated through the Internet.

- *Network effects* Software and Internet service becomes more beneficial to a buyer the greater the number of households and businesses that also buy them. When others have Internet service, you can send e-mail messages to them. And when they also have software that allows display of documents and photos, you can attach those items to your e-mail messages. These system advantages are called **network effects,** which are *increases in the value of the product to each user, including existing users, as the total number of users rises*. The domestic and global expansion of the Internet in particular has produced network effects, as have cell phones, pagers, palm computers, and other aspects of wireless communication. Network effects magnify the value of output well beyond the costs of inputs.

- *Learning by doing* Finally, firms that produce new products or pioneer new ways of doing business experience increasing returns through **learning by doing.** Tasks that initially may have taken firms hours

TABLE 17.2

Examples of Cost Reductions from Technology in the New Economy

- The cost of storing one megabit of information—enough for a 320-page book—fell from $5257 in 1975 to 17 cents in 1999.
- Prototyping each part of a car once took Ford weeks and cost $20,000 on average. Using an advanced 3-D object printer, it cut the time to just hours and the cost to less than $20.
- Studies show that telecommuting saves businesses about $20,000 annually for a worker earning $44,000—a saving in lost work time and employee retention costs, plus gains in worker productivity.
- Using scanners and computers, Weyerhaeuser increased the lumber yield and value from each log by 30 percent.
- Amoco has used 3-D seismic exploration technology to cut the cost of finding oil from nearly $10 per barrel in 1991 to under $1 per barrel today.
- Wal-Mart reduced the operating cost of its delivery trucks by 20 percent through installing computers, global positioning gear, and cell phones in 4300 vehicles.
- Banking transactions on the Internet cost 1 cent each, compared with $1.14 for face-to-face, pen-and-paper communication.

Source: Compiled and directly quoted from W. Michael Cox and Richard Alm, "The New Paradigm," Federal Reserve Bank of Dallas Annual Report, May 2000, various pages.

may take them only minutes once the methods are perfected.

Whatever the particular source of increasing returns, the result is higher productivity, which tends to reduce the per-unit cost of producing and delivering products. Table 17.2 lists a number of specific examples of cost reduction from technology in recent years.

Global Competition The recent economy is characterized not only by information technology and increasing returns but also by heightened global competition. The collapse of the socialist economies in the late 1980s and early 1990s, together with the success of market systems, has led to a reawakening of capitalism throughout the world. The new information technologies have "shrunk the globe" and made it imperative for all firms to lower their costs and prices and to innovate in order to remain competitive. Free-trade zones such as NAFTA and the European Union (EU), along with trade liberalization through the World Trade Organization (WTO), have also heightened competition internationally by removing trade protection from domestic firms. The larger geographic markets, in turn, have enabled the firms of the New Economy to expand beyond their national borders.

Macroeconomic Implications

Stronger productivity growth and heightened global competition have a number of important implications for the macroeconomy.

More Rapid Economic Growth

Of greatest importance, the productivity speedup allows the economy to achieve a higher rate of economic growth. A glance back at Figure 17.3 will help make this point. If the shifts of the curves reflect annual changes in the old economy, then the New Economy would be depicted by an outward shift of the production possibilities curve beyond *CD* in Figure 17.3a, and a shift of the long-run aggregate supply curve farther to the right than AS_{LR2} in Figure 17.3b. When coupled with economic efficiency and increased total spending, the economy's real GDP would rise by more than that shown. That is, the economy would achieve a higher rate of economic growth.

In this view, the New Economy has a higher "safe speed limit" than the old economy because production capacity rises more rapidly. The New Economy can grow by, say, 4 percent, rather than 2 or 3 percent, each year without igniting demand-pull inflation. Increases in aggregate demand that in the past would have caused inflation do not cause inflation because they are buffered by faster productivity growth. Even when nominal wage increases rise to match the productivity increases, as they usually do, per-unit production costs and therefore prices remain stable.

Global competition in the New Economy also contributes to price stability. Proponents of the New Economy say that increasing returns and global competition explain why inflation remained mild as real GDP rapidly increased between 1995 and 2000.

Low Natural Rate of Unemployment

A low natural rate of unemployment (NRU) such as that of 1995–2000 (4 to 5 percent) may also be consistent with the New Economy. The new information technology reduces frictional unemployment by enabling workers and employers to quickly find each other.

Growing Tax Revenues

Finally, the faster economic growth enabled by the productivity speedup produces larger increases in personal income and, given tax rates, larger increases in government tax revenues. The quick and unexpected elimination of the Federal budget deficit during the last half of the 1990s resulted largely from the higher rates of growth of real GDP. In 1995 the Federal government had a budget *deficit* of $160 billion; in 2000 it had a budget *surplus* of $167 billion.

A caution: Those who champion the idea of a New Economy emphasize that it does not mean that the business cycle is dead. Indeed, the economy slowed in the first two months of 2001 and receded over the following eight months of that year. The New Economy is simply one for which the *trend lin*es of productivity growth and economic growth are steeper than they were in the preceding two decades. Real output may periodically deviate below and above those trend lines.

Skepticism about Permanence

Although most macroeconomists have revised their forecasts for long-term productivity growth upward, at least slightly, others are still skeptical and urge a "wait-and-see" approach. Skeptics acknowledge that the economy has experienced a rapid advance of new technology, many new firms have experienced increasing returns, and global competition has increased. But they wonder if these factors are sufficiently profound to produce a 10- to 15-year period of substantially higher rates of productivity growth and real GDP growth.

The higher rates of productivity and real GDP growth between 1995 and 2002 *are* consistent with a long-lived New Economy. Unfortunately, they are also consistent with a rapid short-run economic expansion fueled by an extraordinarily brisk rise in consumption and investment spending. Such *economic booms* raise productivity by increasing real output faster than employment (labor inputs), but they are unsustainable over longer periods. Skeptics point out that productivity surged between 1975 and 1978 and between 1983 and 1986 but in each case soon reverted to its lower long-run trend.

For a time, economic expansions need not create inflation, as long as wage growth does not exceed the growth of productivity. But economic booms eventually create shortages, which produce inflationary pressures. Even industries that once had decreasing or constant costs can begin to experience rising costs when the pool of available workers dries up. The excessive demand that is causing the boom eventually raises all prices, including the price of labor. Rising inflation or the threat of rising inflation prompts the Federal Reserve to engineer increases in interest rates. For example, the Fed raised the Federal funds interest rate from 4.75 to 6 percent in a series of steps in 1999 and 2000.

By reducing investment spending, the higher interest rates dampen some of the inflationary pressure but may inadvertently slow the economy too much, causing recession. In any event, productivity and output growth stall. The higher trend line of productivity inferred from the short-run spurt of productivity proves to be an illusion. Only by looking backward over long periods can economists distinguish the start of a new long-run secular trend from a shorter-term boost in productivity related to the business cycle.

What Can We Conclude?

Given the different views on the New Economy, what should we conclude? Perhaps the safest conclusions are these:

- We should be pleased with the exceptional performance of the economy between 1995 and 2000, for its own sake, whether or not it represents a New Economy. These were remarkable times for the U.S. economy.

- The prospects for a more rapid long-run trend of productivity growth are good (see Global Perspective 17.2). Studies indicate that productivity advance related to information technology has spread to a wide range of industries, including services. Even in the

recession year 2001 and in 2002, when the economy was sluggish, productivity growth remained strong. Specifically, it averaged about 3 percent over these two years.

- Time will tell. It will be several more years before economists can declare the recent productivity acceleration a long-term reality. **(Key Question 9)**

QUICK REVIEW 17.3

- Over long time periods, labor productivity growth determines an economy's growth of real wages and its standard of living.

- Many economists believe that the United States has achieved a New Economy of faster productivity growth and higher rates of economic growth.

- The productivity acceleration is based on rapid technological change in the form of the microchip and information technology, increasing returns and lower per-unit costs, and heightened global competition that helps hold down prices.

- Faster productivity growth means the economy has a higher "economic speed limit": It can grow more rapidly than previously without producing inflation; the economy has a lower natural rate of unemployment; and it generates more rapid increases in tax revenues. Nonetheless, many economists caution that it is too early to determine whether the New Economy is a lasting long-run trend or a fortunate short-lived occurrence.

GLOBAL PERSPECTIVE 17.2

Growth Competitiveness Index

The World Economic Forum annually compiles a growth competitiveness index, which uses various factors (such as innovativeness, effective transfer of technology among sectors, efficiency of the financial system, rates of investment, and degree of integration with the rest of the world) to measure the ability of a country to achieve economic growth over time. Here is its latest top 10 list:

Country	Growth Competitiveness Ranking, 2002
United States	1
Finland	2
Taiwan	3
Singapore	4
Sweden	5
Switzerland	6
Australia	7
Canada	8
Norway	9
Denmark	10

Source: World Economic Forum, www.weforum.org/.

Is Growth Desirable and Sustainable?

Economists usually take for granted that economic growth is desirable and sustainable. But not everyone agrees.

The Antigrowth View

Critics of growth say industrialization and growth result in pollution, global warming, ozone depletion, and other environmental problems. These adverse spillover costs occur because inputs in the production process reenter the environment as some form of waste. The more rapid our growth and the higher our standard of living, the more waste the environment must absorb—or attempt to absorb. In an already wealthy society, further growth usually means satisfying increasingly trivial wants at the cost of mounting threats to the ecological system.

Critics of growth also argue that there is little compelling evidence that economic growth has solved

CHAPTER 17 | Economic Growth   **321**

sociological problems such as poverty, homelessness, and discrimination. Consider poverty: In the antigrowth view, American poverty is a problem of distribution, not production. The requisite for solving the problem is commitment and political courage to redistribute wealth and income, not further increases in output.

Antigrowth sentiment also says that while growth may permit us to "make a better living," it does not give us "the good life." We may be producing more and enjoying it less. Growth means frantic paces on jobs, worker burnout, and alienated employees who have little or no control over decisions affecting their lives. The changing technology at the core of growth poses new anxieties and new sources of insecurity for workers. Both high-level and low-level workers face the prospect of having their hard-earned skills and experience rendered obsolete by an onrushing technology. High-growth economies are high-stress economies, which may impair our physical and mental health.

Finally, critics of high rates of growth doubt that they are sustainable. The planet Earth has finite amounts of natural resources available, and they are being consumed at alarming rates. Higher rates of economic growth simply speed up the degradation and exhaustion of the earth's resources. In this view, slower economic growth that is sustainable is preferable to faster growth.

In Defense of Economic Growth

The primary defense of growth is that it is the path to the greater material abundance and higher living standards desired by the vast majority of people. Rising output and incomes allow people to buy

> more education, recreation, and travel, more medical care, closer communications, more skilled personal and professional services, and better-designed as well as more numerous products. It also means more art, music, and poetry, theater, and drama. It can even mean more time and resources devoted to spiritual growth and human development.[1]

Growth also enables society to improve the nation's infrastructure, enhance the care of the sick and elderly, provide greater access for the disabled, and provide more police and fire protection. Economic growth may be the only realistic way to reduce poverty, since there is little political support for greater redistribution of income. The

way to improve the economic position of the poor is to increase household incomes through higher productivity and economic growth. Also, a no-growth policy among industrial nations might severely limit growth in poor nations. Foreign investment and development assistance in those nations would fall, keeping the world's poor in poverty longer.

Economic growth has not made labor more unpleasant or hazardous, as critics suggest. New machinery is usually less taxing and less dangerous than the machinery it replaces. Air-conditioned workplaces are more pleasant than steamy workshops. Furthermore, why would an end to economic growth reduce materialism or alienation? The loudest protests against materialism are heard in those nations and groups that now enjoy the highest levels of material abundance! The high standard of living that growth provides has increased our leisure and given us more time for reflection and self-fulfillment.

Does growth threaten the environment? The connection between growth and environment is tenuous, say growth proponents. Increases in economic growth need not mean increases in pollution. Pollution is not so much a by-product of growth as it is a "problem of the commons." Much of the environment—streams, lakes, oceans, and the air—is treated as "common property," with no or insufficient restrictions on its use. The commons have become our dumping grounds; we have overused and debased them. Environmental pollution is a case of spillover or external costs, and correcting this problem involves regulatory legislation, specific taxes ("effluent charges"), or market-based incentives to remedy misuse of the environment.

Those who support growth admit there are serious environmental problems. But they say that limiting growth is the wrong solution. Growth has allowed economies to reduce pollution, be more sensitive to environmental considerations, set aside wilderness, create national parks and monuments, and clean up hazardous waste, while still enabling rising household incomes.

Is growth sustainable? Yes, say the proponents of growth. If we were depleting natural resources faster than their discovery, we would see the prices of those resources rise. That has not been the case for most natural resources; in fact, the prices of most of them have declined. And if one natural resource becomes too expensive, another resource will be substituted for it. Moreover, say economists, economic growth has to do with the expansion and application of human knowledge and information, not of extractable natural resources. In this view, economic growth is limited only by human imagination.

---

[1] Alice M. Rivlin, *Reviving the American Dream* (Washington, D.C.: Brookings Institution, 1992), p. 36.

A Large Increase in the Labor-Force Participation Rate of Women Has Shifted the U.S. Production Possibilities Curve Outward and Contributed to Economic Growth.

One of the major labor market trends of the past half-century in the United States has been the substantial rise in the number of women working in the paid workforce. Today 60 percent of women work full-time or part-time in paid jobs, compared to only 40 percent in 1965. This trend has greatly contributed to U.S. economic growth. There are many reasons for the surge of women to the workforce.

Women's Rising Wage Rates Over recent years, women have greatly increased their productivity in the workplace, mostly by becoming better educated and professionally trained. As a result, they can earn higher wages. Because those higher wages have increased the opportunity costs—the forgone wage earnings—of staying at home, women have substituted employment in the labor market for more "expensive" traditional home activities. This substitution has been particularly pronounced among married women.

Expanded Job Access Greater access to jobs is a second factor increasing the employment of women. Service industries—teaching, nursing, and clerical work, for instance—that traditionally have employed mainly women have expanded in the past several decades. Also, the population in general has shifted from farms and rural regions to urban areas, where jobs for women are more abundant and more geographically accessible. The decline in the average length of the workweek and the increased availability of part-time jobs have also made it easier for women to combine labor market employment with child-rearing and household activities. Also, antidiscrimination laws and enforcement efforts have reduced barriers that previously discouraged or prevented women from taking traditional male jobs such as managers, lawyers, professors, and physicians. More jobs are "open" to women today than a half-century ago.

SUMMARY

1. Economic growth—measured as either an increase in real output or an increase in real output per capita—increases material abundance and raises a nation's standard of living.

2. The supply factors in economic growth are (a) the quantity and quality of a nation's natural resources, (b) the quantity and quality of its human resources, (c) its stock of capital facilities, and (d) its technology. Two other factors—a sufficient level of aggregate demand and economic efficiency—are necessary for the economy to realize its growth potential.

3. The growth of production capacity is shown graphically as an outward shift of a nation's production possibilities curve or as a rightward shift of its long-run aggregate supply curve. Growth is realized when total spending rises sufficiently to match the growth of production capacity.

4. Between 1950 and 2000 the annual growth rate of real GDP for the United States averaged about 3.5 percent; the annual growth rate of real GDP per capita was about 2.3 percent.

5. U.S. real GDP has grown partly because of increased inputs of labor and primarily because of increases in the productivity of labor. The increases in productivity have resulted mainly from technological progress, increases in the quantity of capital per worker, improvements in the quality of labor, economies of scale, and an improved allocation of labor.

6. Over long time periods, the growth of labor productivity underlies an economy's growth of real wages and its standard of living.

7. Productivity rose by 2.8 percent annually between 1995 and 2002, compared to 1.4 percent annually between 1973 and 1995. Some economists think this productivity acceleration will be long-lasting and is reflective of a New Economy—one of faster productivity growth and greater noninflationary economic growth.

8. The New Economy is based on (a) rapid technological change in the form of the microchip and information technology, (b) increasing returns and lower per-unit costs, and (c) heightened global competition that holds down prices.

9. The main sources of increasing returns in the New Economy are (a) use of more specialized inputs as firms

Changing Preferences and Attitudes Women collectively have changed their preferences from household activities to employment in the labor market. Many find personal fulfillment in jobs, careers, and earnings, as evidenced by the huge influx of women into law, medicine, business, and other professions. More broadly, most industrial societies now widely accept and encourage labor-force participation by women, including those with very young children. Today about 65 percent of American mothers with preschool children participate in the labor force, compared to only 30 percent in 1970. More than half return to work before their youngest child has reached the age of 2.

Declining Birthrates There were 3.8 lifetime births per woman in 1957 at the peak of the baby boom. Today the number is less than 2. This marked decline in the size of the typical family, the result of changing lifestyles and the widespread availability of birth control, has freed up time for greater labor-force participation by women. Not only do women now have fewer children; their children are spaced closer together in age. Thus women who leave their jobs during their children's early years can return to the labor force sooner. Higher wage rates have also been at work. On average, women with relatively high wage earnings have fewer children than women with lower earnings. The opportunity cost of children—the income sacrificed by not being employed—rises as wage earnings rise. In the language of economics, the higher "price" associated with children has reduced the "quantity" of children demanded.

Rising Divorce Rates Marital instability, as evidenced by high divorce rates, may have motivated many women to enter and remain in the labor market. Because alimony and child-support payments are often erratic or nonexistent, the economic impact of divorce on nonworking women may be disastrous. Most nonworking women enter the labor force for the first time following divorce. And many married women—perhaps even women contemplating marriage—may have joined the labor force to protect themselves against the financial difficulties of potential divorce. Also, it is plausible that the greater economic independence of women has allowed them to abandon unfulfilling marriages.

Slower Growth of Male Wages The earnings of many low-wage and middle-wage male workers grew slowly or even fell in the United States over the past three decades. Many wives may have entered the labor force to ensure the rise of household living standards. The median income of couples with children grew 25 percent between 1969 and 1996. Without the mothers' incomes, that growth would have been only 2 percent. A related issue is that couples of all income levels may be concerned about their family incomes compared to those of other families. So the entry of some women into the labor force may have encouraged still other women to enter in order to maintain their families' *relative* standards of living.

Taken together, these factors have produced a rapid rise in the presence of women workers in the United States. This increase in the *quantity of resources* and their enhanced productivity have contributed greatly to U.S. economic growth.

---

grow, (b) the spreading of development costs, (c) simultaneous consumption by consumers, (d) network effects, and (e) learning by doing. Increasing returns mean higher productivity and lower per-unit production costs.

10. Those who champion the New Economy say that it has a lower natural rate of unemployment than did the old economy, can grow more rapidly without producing inflation, and generates higher tax revenues because of faster growth of personal income.

11. Skeptics of the New Economy urge a wait-and-see approach. They point out that surges in productivity and real GDP growth have previously occurred during vigorous economic expansions but do not necessarily represent long-lived trends.

12. Critics of rapid growth say that it adds to environmental degradation, increases human stress, and exhausts the earth's finite supply of natural resources. Defenders of rapid growth say that it is the primary path to the rising living standards nearly universally desired by people, that it need not debase the environment, and that there are no indications that we are running out of resources. Growth is based on the expansion and application of human knowledge, which is limited only by human imagination.

TERMS AND CONCEPTS

economic growth	labor productivity	human capital	start-up firms
supply factors	labor-force participation rate	economies of scale	increasing returns
demand factor	growth accounting	New Economy	network effects
efficiency factor	infrastructure	information technology	learning by doing

STUDY QUESTIONS

1. *Key Question* What are the four supply factors of economic growth? What is the demand factor? What is the efficiency factor? Illustrate these factors in terms of the production possibilities curve.

2. Suppose that Alpha and Omega have identically sized working-age populations but that annual hours of work are much greater in Alpha than in Omega. Provide two possible explanations.

3. Suppose that work hours in New Zombie are 200 in year 1 and productivity is $8. What is New Zombie's real GDP? If work hours increase to 210 in year 2 and productivity rises to $10, what is New Zombie's rate of economic growth?

4. What is the relationship between a nation's production possibilities curve and its long-run aggregate supply curve? How does each relate to the idea of a New Economy?

5. *Key Question* Between 1990 and 2002 the U.S. price level rose by about 38 percent while real output increased by about 41 percent. Use the aggregate demand–aggregate supply model to illustrate these outcomes graphically.

6. *Key Question* To what extent have increases in U.S. real GDP resulted from more labor inputs? From higher labor productivity? Rearrange the following contributors to the growth of real GDP in order of their quantitative importance: economics of scale, quantity of capital, improved resource allocation, education and training, technological advance.

7. True or false? If false, explain why.
   a. Technological advance, which to date has played a relatively small role in U.S. economic growth, is destined to play a more important role in the future.
   b. Many public capital goods are complementary to private capital goods.
   c. Immigration has slowed economic growth in the United States.

8. Explain why there is such a close relationship between changes in a nation's rate of productivity growth and changes in its average real hourly wage.

9. *Key Question* Relate each of the following to the New Economy:
   a. The rate of productivity growth
   b. Information technology
   c. Increasing returns
   d. Network effects
   e. Global competition

10. Provide three examples of products or services that can be simultaneously consumed by many people. Explain why labor productivity greatly rises as the firm sells more units of the product or service. Explain why the higher level of sales greatly reduces the per-unit cost of the product.

11. What is meant when economists say that the U.S. economy has "a higher safe speed limit" than it had previously? If the New Economy has a higher safe speed limit, what explains the series of interest-rate hikes engineered by the Federal Reserve in 1999 and 2000?

12. Productivity often rises during economic expansions and falls during economic recessions. Can you think of reasons why? Briefly explain. (Hint: Remember that the level of productivity involves both levels of output and levels of labor input.)

13. *(Last Word)* Which two of the six reasons listed in the Last Word do you think are the most important in explaining the rise in participation of women in the U.S. workplace? Explain your reasoning. How does the rising labor-force participation rate of women relate to economic growth?

14. *Web-Based Question: U.S. economic growth—what are the latest rates?* Go to the Bureau of Economic Analysis website, www.bea.gov, and use the data interactivity feature to find National Income and Product Account Table S.1. What are the quarterly growth rates (annualized) for the U.S. economy for the last six quarters? Is the average of those rates above or below the long-run U.S. annual growth rate of 3.5 percent? Expand the range of years, if necessary, to find the last time real GDP declined in two or more successive quarters. What were those quarters?

15. *Web-Based Question: What's up with productivity?* Visit the Bureau of Labor Statistics website, www.bls.gov. In sequence, select Productivity and Costs, Get Detailed Statistics, and Most Requested Statistics to find quarterly growth rates (annualized) for business output per hour for the last six quarters. Is the average of those rates higher or lower than the 1.4 percent average annual growth rate of productivity during the 1973–1995 period?

16. *Web-Based Question: Productivity and technology—examples of innovations in computers and communications* Recent innovations in computers and communications technologies are increasing productivity. Lucent Technologies (formerly Bell Labs), at www.lucent.com/minds/discoveries, provides a timeline of company innovations over the past 80 years. Cite five technological "home runs" (for example, the transistor in 1947) and five technological "singles" (for example, free space optical switching in 1990). Which single innovation do you think has increased productivity the most? List two innovations since 1990. How might they boost productivity?

18 | Deficits, Surpluses, and the Public Debt

By the year 2002, the United States had amassed $6.2 trillion of public debt. How large is $6.2 trillion? We can put it into perspective this way: "One million seconds have ticked by in the past 12 days. One billion seconds took more than 31 years to elapse. One trillion seconds ago, it was around 30,000 B.C.—the Ice Age—and much of America was buried by glaciers."[1] So a debt of $6.2 trillion is a large amount. This is a stunning number. Should we be concerned about it?

In this chapter we examine the public debt, budget deficits, and budget surpluses. What are the economic impacts of the public debt? Why did the Federal budget swing from a deficit to a surplus and back to a deficit in the past several years?

---

[1]Marcia Stepanek, "The National Debt: Red Ink Rising," *Seattle Post-Intelligencer* (Hearst Newspapers), Apr. 13, 1994, p. 1.

Deficits, Surpluses, and Debt: Definitions

A *budget deficit* is the amount by which government expenditures exceed government revenues in a given year. For example, in 2002 the Federal government spent $2011 billion while taking in revenues of $1853 billion, resulting in a $158 billion deficit. In contrast, a *budget surplus* is the amount by which government revenues exceed government expenditures in a given year. For example, in 2000 Federal revenues of $2025 billion exceeded Federal expenditures of $1789 billion, resulting in a $236 billion budget surplus.

The national or **public debt** is essentially the total accumulation of the deficits (minus the surpluses) the Federal government has incurred through time. It represents the total amount of money owed by the Federal government to the holders of **U.S. securities:** Treasury bills, Treasury notes, Treasury bonds, and U.S. saving bonds. In 2002 that amount was $6.2 trillion—$3.5 trillion held by the public and $2.7 trillion held by agencies of the Federal government.

Budget Philosophies

Is it good or bad to incur deficits or surpluses? Should the budget be balanced annually, if necessary by constitutional amendment? As we saw in Chapter 12, countercyclical fiscal policy should move the Federal budget toward a deficit during recession and toward a surplus during expansion.

This means that discretionary fiscal policy is unlikely to result in a balanced budget in any certain year. Is that a matter of concern?

Let's approach this question by examining the economic implications of several contrasting budget philosophies.

Annually Balanced Budget

Until the Great Depression of the 1930s, an **annually balanced budget** was viewed as the goal of public finance. On examination, however, it becomes clear that an annually balanced budget is not compatible with government fiscal activity viewed as a countercyclical, stabilizing force. Worse yet, an annually balanced budget may intensify the business cycle.

Illustration: Suppose the economy experiences the onset of unemployment and falling incomes. In such circumstances tax receipts automatically decline. To balance its budget, government must (1) increase tax rates, (2) reduce government expenditures, or (3) do both. But all three actions are *contractionary*; each further dampens, rather than expands, aggregate demand.

Similarly, an annually balanced budget may intensify inflation. As nominal incomes rise during the course of inflation, tax receipts automatically increase. To avoid the impending surplus, government must (1) cut tax rates, (2) increase government expenditures, or (3) do both. But each of these policies intensifies inflationary pressures.

An annually balanced budget is not economically neutral; the pursuit of such a policy may intensify the business cycle, not dampen it. Despite this problem, there is some support for a constitutional amendment requiring an annually balanced budget.

Some economists have advocated an annually balanced budget not because of a fear of deficits and a mounting public debt but because they feel that an annually balanced budget is needed to curtail the expansion of the public sector. They believe that government has a tendency to grow larger than it should because there is less popular opposition to such growth when it is financed by deficits rather than by taxes. And when budget surpluses do occur, the tendency is for government to spend down the surpluses on new government programs, rather than cut taxes. These economists, along with some politicians, want a constitutional amendment to force a balanced budget in order to slow government growth.

Cyclically Balanced Budget

Other economists contend that a **cyclically balanced budget** would enable the government to exert a counter-cyclical influence and at the same time balance its budget. They believe that the budget does not have to be balanced annually—there is nothing sacred about 12 months as an accounting period—but, rather, should be balanced over the course of the business cycle.

That rationale is simple, plausible, and appealing. To offset recession, the government should lower taxes and increase spending, purposely incurring a deficit. During the ensuing inflationary upswing, the government would raise taxes and slash spending. It would use the resulting surplus to retire the Federal debt incurred while financing the recession. Then government fiscal operations would exert a positive countercyclical force, and the government could still balance its budget over a period of years.

The problem with this budget philosophy is that the upswings and downswings of the business cycle are not always of equal magnitude and duration. A long severe slump followed by a modest, short period of prosperity would mean a large deficit during the slump, little or no surplus during prosperity, and a cyclical deficit in the budget.

Functional Finance

With **functional finance,** an annually or cyclically balanced budget is of secondary concern. The primary purpose of Federal finance is to provide for noninflationary full employment to balance the economy rather than the budget. If that objective causes either persistent deficits or persistent surpluses, so be it. In this philosophy, the problems of government deficits or surpluses are minor compared with prolonged recession or persistent inflation. The Federal budget is an instrument for achieving and maintaining macroeconomic stability. Government should not hesitate to incur deficits and surpluses to achieve macroeconomic stability and growth. **(Key Question 1)**

18.1
Functional
finance

The Public Debt: Facts and Figures

Over the years, budget deficits have greatly exceeded budget surpluses, leading to a large public debt. As column 2 in Table 18.1 shows, in nominal terms the public debt was considerably higher in 2002 than it was 60 years earlier. (Not shown: It is also considerably higher in real terms.)

TABLE 18.1

Quantitative Significance of the Public Debt: The Public Debt and Interest Payments in Relation to GDP, Selected Fiscal Years, 1940–2002*

(1) Year	(2) Public Debt, Billions†	(3) Gross Domestic Product, Billions†	(4) Interest Payments, Billions†	(5) Public Debt as Percentage of GDP, (2) ÷ (3)	(6) Interest Payments as Percentage of GDP, (4) ÷ (3)	(7) Per Capita Public Debt†
1940	$ 50.7	$ 101.3	$ 0.9	50%	0.9%	$ 384
1950	256.9	294.3	4.8	87	1.6	1,687
1960	290.5	527.4	6.9	55	1.3	1,608
1970	380.9	1,039.7	14.4	37	1.4	1,858
1980	909.1	2,795.6	52.5	33	1.9	3,992
1985	1817.5	4,213.0	129.5	43	3.1	7,622
1990	3206.6	5,803.2	184.3	55	3.2	12,828
1995	4921.0	7,400.5	232.1	66	3.1	18,705
2000	5629.0	9,824.6	223.0	57	2.3	20,441
2002	6198.0	10,446.2	171.0	59	1.6	21,476

*Fiscal years are 12-month periods ending September 30 of each year, rather than December 31 as in calendar years.

†In nominal terms.

Source: Compiled from Bureau of Economic Analysis, www.bea.gov/, and Congressional Budget Office, www.cbo.gov/, data.

Causes

The main sources of large budget deficits and thus the public debt have been wars, recessions, and lack of fiscal discipline by elected leaders.

Wars Some of the public debt has resulted from the deficit financing of wars. The public debt increased substantially during the First World War and grew more than fivefold during the Second World War.

Consider the Second World War and the options it posed. The task was to reallocate a substantial portion of the economy's resources from the production of civilian goods to the production of war goods. Government expenditures for armaments and military personnel soared. To finance those expenditures, three options were available: increase taxes, print the needed money, or borrow the funds. The government feared that financing by increasing taxes would require tax rates so high that they would impair the incentive to work. The national interest required attracting more people into the labor force and encouraging those already in it to work longer hours. Very high tax rates were felt to interfere with those goals. Printing and spending the needed money would be highly inflationary. Thus, much of the Second World War was financed by selling bonds to the public, thereby draining off spendable income and freeing resources from civilian production to make them available for defense industries.

Recessions Another cause of the public debt is recessions and the direct relationship between national income and tax revenues. In periods when the national income declines, tax collections automatically fall and budget deficits arise. Thus the public debt rose during the Great Depression of the 1930s and, more recently, during the recessions of 1974 to 1975, 1980 to 1982, 1990 to 1991, and 2001. Annual deficits, and thus the public debt, also rose between 1991 and 1993 because the Federal government incurred massive expenses in bailing out savings and loan associations that failed during the recession.

Lack of Fiscal Discipline Stated bluntly, a substantial part of the public debt reflects lack of fiscal discipline by elected leaders. Senators and representatives face tremendous pressures to secure government programs and provide government services for their constituents. They also know that tax-rate cuts are highly popular with the public. The combination for these two pressures—to increase Federal spending and to reduce Federal tax rates—has at times produced large Federal budget deficits even during periods of relative prosperity when budgets should be balanced or in surplus.

This lack of fiscal discipline accounted for much of the large growth in the public debt in the 1980s and early 1990s. Between 1982 and 1984 the Reagan administration and Congress enacted substantial cuts in both individual and corporate income tax rates. Even with the lower tax rates, tax revenue grew as the economy recovered from recession and returned to its long-term growth path. But government spending rose more rapidly, creating large deficits throughout the 1980s and into the early 1990s. The annual deficits between 1982 and 1990 added $1.3 trillion to the public debt. And the deficits remained even when the economy reached full employment. For example, the deficit in the full-employment year 1989 was $155 billion.

The taxation and expenditure policies of the 1980s resulted in the economy's entering the 1990–1991 recession with a large "built-in" budget deficit rather than a balanced budget or a budget surplus. The recession added large cyclical deficits to the mix and the public debt rose by another $1 trillion between 1990 and 1993. (We will examine budget deficits and surpluses in recent years later in this chapter.)

Quantitative Aspects

In 2002 the U.S. debt was $6.2 trillion, up from $0.9 trillion in 1980. But these large, seemingly incomprehensible numbers are misleading.

Debt and GDP   A simple statement of the absolute size of the debt ignores the fact that the wealth and productive ability of the U.S. economy is also vast. A wealthy, highly productive nation can incur and carry a large public debt more easily than a poor nation can. It is more meaningful to measure the public debt in relation to an economy's GDP, as shown in column 5 of Table 18.1. Instead of the many-fold increase in the public debt between 1950 and 2002 shown in column 2, observe that the relative size of the debt was considerably less in 2002 than in 1950. However, our data do show that the relative size of the debt doubled between 1980 and 1995. Between 1995 and 2000, that percentage again declined.

International Comparisons   As shown in Global Perspective 18.1, it is not uncommon for countries to have public debts. Many nations have larger public debts, as a percentage of GDP, than does the United States.

Interest Charges   Many economists conclude that the primary burden of the debt is the annual interest charge accruing on the bonds sold to finance the debt. We

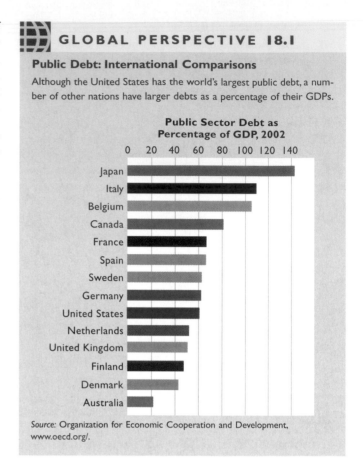

GLOBAL PERSPECTIVE 18.1

Public Debt: International Comparisons

Although the United States has the world's largest public debt, a number of other nations have larger debts as a percentage of their GDPs.

Source: Organization for Economic Cooperation and Development, www.oecd.org/.

show the size of the interest payments in column 4 of Table 18.1. Interest payments began to increase sharply in the 1970s, reflecting not only increases in the debt but also periods of very high interest rates. Interest on the debt is now the fourth-largest item in the Federal budget (see Figure 5.8, page 86).

Interest payments as a percentage of GDP, however, declined from 3.1 to 1.6 percent between 1995 and 2002, as shown in column 6 of Table 18.1. That percentage reflects the level of taxation (the average tax rate) required to pay the interest on the public debt. That is, in 2002 the Federal government had to collect taxes equal to 1.6 percent of GDP to service the public debt.

Ownership   Figure 18.1 shows that 57 percent of the public debt in 2002 was "held by the public" and that Federal government agencies and the Federal Reserve held the other 43 percent. In this case the "public" consists of individuals here and abroad, state and local governments, and U.S. financial institutions. People and institutions abroad held about 18 percent of the total debt. The

FIGURE 18.1

Ownership of the public debt, 2002. The total public debt can be divided into the proportion held by the public (57 percent) and the proportion held by Federal agencies and the Federal Reserve System (43 percent). Eighteen percent of the debt is foreign-owned.
Source: U.S. Treasury, www.fms.treas.gov/.

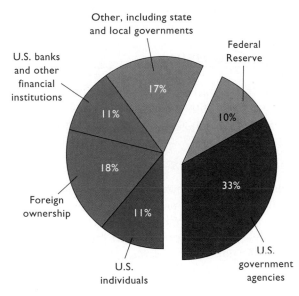

Debt held outside the Federal government and Federal Reserve (57%)

Debt held by the Federal government and Federal Reserve (43%)

Other, including state and local governments

Federal Reserve

U.S. banks and other financial institutions

17%

10%

11%

18%

33%

Foreign ownership

11%

U.S. individuals

U.S. government agencies

Total debt: $6.2 trillion

vast majority of the debt is thus internally held, not externally held. It is owed by Americans to Americans.

Social Security Considerations

Social Security is basically a "pay-as-you-go plan" in which the mandated benefits paid out each year are financed by the payroll tax revenues received each year. But current tax rates currently bring in more revenue than current payouts, in partial preparation for the opposite circumstance when the baby boomers retire in the next one or two decades. The Federal government saves the excess revenues by purchasing U.S. securities and holding them in the **Social Security trust fund.**

Some economists argue that these present Social Security surpluses should be excluded when calculating present Federal deficits or surpluses because they represent future government obligations on a dollar-for-dollar basis. In this view the Social Security surplus should not be considered as an offset to current government spending. For example, without the Social Security surplus, the

total budget deficit in 2002 would have been $160 billion more than the $158 billion reported.

QUICK REVIEW 18.1

• A budget deficit is an excess of government expenditures over tax revenues in a given year; a budget surplus is an excess of tax revenues over government expenditures in a given year; the public debt is essentially the total accumulation of budget deficits minus surpluses over time.

• The three major budget philosophies are (a) an annually balanced budget, (b) a budget balanced over the business cycle, and (c) functional finance.

• Wartime financing, recessions, and tax cuts (unaccompanied by expenditures cuts) are the main sources of the $6.2 trillion public debt in the United States.

• The U.S. public debt as a percentage of GDP was lower in 2002 than 7 years earlier and is in the middle range of such debt among major industrial nations.

False Concerns

You may wonder if the large public debt might bankrupt the United States or at least place a tremendous burden on your children and grandchildren. Fortunately, these are false concerns.

Bankruptcy

The large U.S. public debt does not threaten to bankrupt the Federal government, leaving it unable to meet its financial obligations. There are two main reasons:

• *Refinancing* The public debt is easily refinanced. As portions of the debt come due on maturing Treasury bills, notes, and bonds each month, the government does not cut expenditures or raise taxes to provide the funds required. Rather, it refinances the debt by selling new bonds and using the proceeds to pay off holders of the maturing bonds. The new bonds are in strong demand, because lenders can obtain a relatively good interest return with no risk of default by the Federal government.

• *Taxation* The Federal government has the constitutional authority to levy and collect taxes. A tax increase is a government option for gaining sufficient revenue to pay interest and principal on the public debt. Financially distressed private households and corporations cannot extract themselves from their financial difficulties by taxing the public. If their incomes or sales revenues fall short of their expenses, they can indeed go bankrupt. But the Federal government does have the option to impose new taxes or increase existing tax rates if necessary to finance its debt.

Burdening Future Generations

In 2002 public debt per capita was $21,476. Was each child born in 2002 handed a $21,476 bill from the Federal government? Not really. The public debt does not impose as much of a burden on future generations as generally thought.

The United States owes a substantial portion of the public debt to itself. U.S. citizens and institutions (banks, businesses, insurance companies, governmental agencies, and trust funds) own about 82 percent of the U.S. government securities. While that part of the public debt is a liability to Americans (as taxpayers), it is simultaneously an asset to Americans (as holders of Treasury bills, Treasury notes, Treasury bonds, and U.S. savings bonds).

To eliminate the American-owned part of the public debt would require a gigantic transfer payment from Americans to Americans. Taxpayers would pay higher taxes, and holders of the debt would receive an equal amount for their U.S. securities. Purchasing power in the United States would not change. Only the repayment of the 18 percent of the public debt owned by foreigners would negatively impact U.S. purchasing power.

We noted earlier that the public debt increased sharply during the Second World War. But the decision to finance military purchases through the sale of government bonds did not shift the economic burden of the war to future generations. The economic cost of the Second World War consisted of the civilian goods society had to forgo in shifting scarce resources to war goods production (recall production possibilities analysis). Regardless of whether society financed this reallocation through higher taxes or through borrowing, the real economic burden of the war would have been the same. That burden was borne almost entirely by those who lived during the war. They were the ones who did without a multitude of consumer goods to enable the United States to arm itself and its allies. The next generation inherited the debt from the war but also an equal amount of government bonds. It also inherited the enormous benefits from the victory—namely, preserved political and economic systems at home and the "export" of those systems to Germany, Italy, and Japan. Those outcomes enhanced postwar U.S. economic growth and helped raise the standards of living of future generations of Americans.

Substantive Issues

Although the above issues are of false concern, there are a number of substantive issues relating to the public debt. Economists, however, attach varying importance to them.

Income Distribution

The distribution of ownership of government securities is highly uneven. Some people own much more than the $21,476 per capita portion of government securities; other people own less or none at all. In general, the ownership of the public debt is concentrated among wealthier groups who own a large percentage of all stocks and bonds. Because the overall Federal tax system is only mildly progressive, payment of interest on the public debt probably increases income inequality. Income is transferred from people who, on average, have lower incomes to the higher-income bondholders. If greater income equality is one of society's goals, then this redistribution is undesirable.

Incentives

Table 18.1 indicates that the current public debt necessitates annual interest payments of $171 billion. With no increase in the size of the debt, that interest charge must be paid out of tax revenues. Higher taxes may dampen incentives to bear risk, to innovate, to invest, and to work. So, in this indirect way, a large public debt may impair economic growth.

Foreign-Owned Public Debt

The 18 percent of the U.S. debt held by citizens and institutions of foreign countries *is* an economic burden to Americans. Because we do not owe that portion of the debt "to ourselves," the payment of interest and principal on this **external public debt** enables foreigners to buy some of our output. In return for the benefits derived from the borrowed funds, the United States transfers goods and services to foreign lenders. Of course, Americans also own debt issued by foreign governments, so payment of principal and interest by those governments transfers some of their goods and services to Americans. **(Key Question 3)**

Crowding Out and the Stock of Capital

There is a potentially more serious problem. The financing (and continual refinancing) of the large public debt can transfer a real economic burden to future generations by passing on a smaller stock of capital goods. This possibility involves the *crowding-out effect:* the idea that a large public debt results in higher real interest rates, which reduce private investment spending. When crowding out is extensive, future generations will inherit an economy with a smaller production capacity and, other things equal, a lower standard of living.

Consider the investment demand curve ID_1 in Figure 18.2. (Ignore curve ID_2 for now.) If government borrowing increases the real interest rate from 6 to 10 percent, investment spending will fall from $25 billion to $15 billion, as shown by the economy's move from point *a* to point *b*. That is, the financing of the debt will crowd out $10 billion of private investment.

Qualifications But even with crowding out, there are two factors that could reduce the net economic burden shifted to future generations:

- *Public investment* Just as private goods may involve either consumption or investment, so it is with public goods. Part of the government spending enabled by the public debt is for public investment outlays (for example, highways, mass transit systems, and electric power facilities) and "human capital" (for example, investments in education, job training, and health). Like private expenditures on machinery and equipment, those **public investments** increase the economy's future production capacity. Because of the financing through debt, the stock of public capital passed on to future generations may be higher than otherwise. That greater stock of public capital may offset the diminished stock of private capital resulting from the crowding out effect, leaving overall production capacity unimpaired.
- *Public-private complementarities* Some public and private investments are complementary. Thus, the public investment financed through the debt could

FIGURE 18.2

The investment demand curve and the crowding-out effect. If the investment demand curve (ID_1) is fixed, the increase in the interest rate from 6 to 10 percent caused by financing a large public debt will move the economy from *a* to *b* and crowd out $10 billion of private investment and decrease the size of the capital stock inherited by future generations. However, if the government spending enabled by the debt improves the profit expectations of businesses, the private investment demand curve will shift rightward, as from ID_1 to ID_2. That shift may offset the crowding-out effect wholly or in part. In this case, it moves the economy from *a* to *c*.

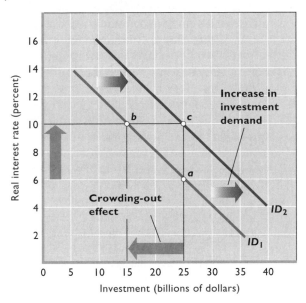

spur some private sector investment by increasing its expected rate of return. For example, a Federal building in a city may encourage private investment in the form of nearby office buildings, shops, and restaurants. Through its complementary effect, the spending on public capital may shift the private investment demand curve to the right, as from ID_1 to ID_2 in Figure 18.2. Even though the government borrowing boosts the interest rate from 6 to 10 percent, total private investment need not fall. In the case shown as the move from *a* to *c* in Figure 18.2, it remains at $25 billion. Of course, the increase in investment demand might be smaller than that shown. If it were smaller, the crowding-out effect would not be fully offset. But the point is that an increase in private investment demand may counter the decline in investment that would otherwise result from the higher interest rate. **(Key Question 7)**

18.1
Crowding
out

Deficits and Surpluses: 1992–2012

Whether the public debt will grow or shrink over the next several years largely depends on annual budget deficits. Figure 18.3 shows the actual budget deficits or surpluses from 1992 through 2002 and the projected deficits or surpluses from 2003 through 2012. The projected deficits and surpluses are those made by the Congressional Budget Office (CBO) as of May 2003. But at that time Congress was formulating a major tax cut to try to stimulate a sluggish U.S. economy. The revenue consequences of the tax package are *not* reflected in Figure 18.3. [Figure 18.3 is easy to update, and we strongly urge you to do so. Go to www.cbo.gov and select Current Budget Projections and then CBO Baseline Budget Projections. The relevant numbers are in the row "Surplus or Deficit (−)."]

From Deficits to Surpluses

Figure 18.3 shows that the absolute sizes of budget deficits were large between 1992 and 1996, adding more

than $800 billion to the public debt. The budget deficit of $221 billion in 1990 had jumped to $290 billion by 1992 because of the recession of 1990–1991 and a weak economic recovery, which slowed the inflow of tax revenues. The government's bailout of failing thrift institutions also contributed to the large deficits in 1992 and 1993.

Fiscal policy in the 1990s turned to reducing the huge deficits in order to promote a *reverse* crowding-out effect—that is, to lower interest rates and boost private investment spending. In 1993 the Clinton administration and Congress passed the Deficit Reduction Act, designed to increase tax revenues by $250 billion over the following 5 years and to reduce Federal spending by the same amount.

Specifically, this legislation (1) increased the top marginal tax rate on personal income from 31 to 39.6 percent, (2) raised the corporate income tax from 34 to 35 percent, and (3) added 4.3 cents per gallon to the Federal excise tax on gasoline. The largest spending "cut" resulted from holding all discretionary spending—spending not mandated by law—to 1993 nominal levels.

FIGURE 18.3

Federal budget deficits and surpluses, actual and projected, fiscal years 1992–2012 (in billions of nominal dollars). The annual budget deficits of 1992 through 1997 gave way to budget surpluses from 1998 through 2001. Deficits reappeared in 2002 and are projected to continue through 2007. Rising surpluses are projected from 2008 through 2012.

Source: Congressional Budget Office, www.cbo.gov/.

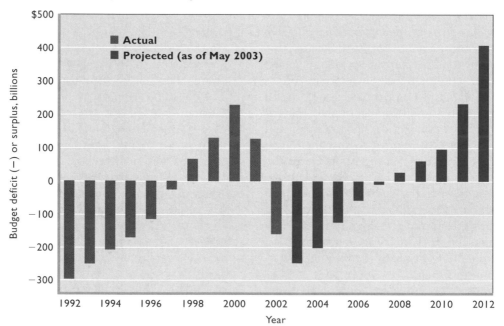

Normally, this spending would have increased at least as rapidly as inflation. In 1996 Congress reaffirmed its commitment to restraining spending by pledging in a "contract with America" to eliminate budget deficits by 2002.

Aided by stronger-than-expected economic growth, the congressional actions reduced the deficit to $22 billion in 1997. As evident in Figure 18.3, in 1998 the budget swung from deficit to a $69 billion surplus. Because of rapidly rising tax collections from the robust economy, budget surpluses were $126 billion in 1999, $236 billion in 2000, and $127 billion in 2001. We cannot overstress how remarkable this turnaround from deficits to surpluses was. Prior to 1998, the last Federal budget surplus was in 1969. And between 1969 and 1997, about $4.5 trillion was added to the public debt.

What to Do with the Surpluses?

In the early 2000s the public debate over the Federal budget turned 180 degrees from how to reduce large budget deficits to what to do with large budget surpluses. Without actions to reduce them, and barring recession, those surpluses were projected to accumulate to $5 trillion between 2000 and 2010. Even excluding the Social Security surpluses, the budget surpluses would accumulate to $3 trillion by 2010. Several options emerged for disposing of the surpluses.

Pay Down the Public Debt One option was for the Federal government to use its surpluses to pay down the public debt. The Federal government can do that by paying off its securities as they come due and not reissuing them. Also, because Treasury bills, notes, and bonds are bought and sold daily in financial markets, the Federal government can reduce the public debt by simply purchasing government securities and retiring them.

Those who advocated using budget surpluses to pay down the public debt said debt reduction would increase U.S. economic growth over the long run. The primary economic benefit from paying down the public debt would be the reverse crowding-out effect, as previously mentioned. Assuming no change in the nation's supply of money, less government borrowing in the money market would reduce the demand for money and therefore the real interest rate. That would boost private investment spending and thus increase the nation's stock of private capital. As we know, increases in capital per worker contribute to economic growth.

Some advocates of paying down the debt argued that the annual interest saving could be used to boost the size of the Social Security trust fund. That way, no major hikes of Social Security taxes or reductions of benefits would be necessary during the period when the large number of present workers retire. (This chapter's Last Word examines the serious fiscal imbalance in the Social Security program.)

Cut Taxes A second option for dealing with the budget surpluses was to cut tax rates. Proponents of this approach contended that the surplus revenues should be returned to taxpayers. The most direct way to return this money would be to reduce tax rates or eliminate certain taxes altogether. Some politicians suggested cutting income tax rates. Others suggested increasing tax deductions and tax credits to reduce the expense of elder care, college education, child care, and so on. Still others advocated repeal of the Federal estate tax and capital-gains tax (tax on the difference between the purchase price and sales price of assets such as stocks and bonds).

Increase Federal Expenditures A third option was to increase Federal expenditures. Supporters of this approach said there were a number of possible uses for the funds that would greatly benefit society and strengthen the economy over the long run. For example, one proposal was to spend part of the surpluses to add prescription drug coverage to Medicare. Another proposal was to undertake a massive effort to restore and upgrade a deteriorating infrastructure of such public capital as highways, bridges, air traffic control facilities, rail transit, school buildings, and textbooks. And, of course, there were many other proposals—about as many as the number of groups that would benefit from increased government spending.

Back to Deficits in 2002

A series of legislative actions and unforeseen events in the early 2000s combined to end—at least for some time—the budget surpluses. In 2002 the budget moved from surplus to a deficit of $158 billion, and as shown in Figure 18.3, deficits are now projected through 2007. What caused the recent swing to deficits?

The Bush Tax Cuts of 2001 Weighing the choices, the Bush administration and Congress decided to eliminate part of the projected surpluses through tax cuts. The

There Is a Severe Long-Run Shortfall in Social Security Funding because of Growing Payments to Retiring Baby Boomers.

The Social Security program (excluding Medicare) has grown from less than one-half of 1 percent of U.S. GDP in 1950 to 4.4 percent of GDP today. That percentage is projected to grow to 6.5 percent of GDP in 2035 and even higher thereafter.

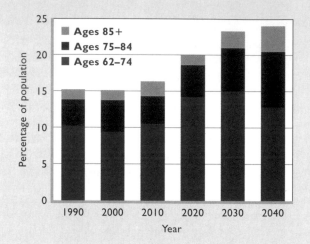

The Social Security program is largely a "pay-as-you-go" plan, meaning that most of the current revenues from the 12.4 percent Social Security tax (the rate when the 2.9 percent Medicare tax is excluded) are paid out to current Social Security retirees. In anticipation of the large benefits owed to the baby boomers when they retire, however, the Social Security Administration has been placing an excess of current revenues over current payouts into a trust fund consisting of U.S. Treasury securities. But the accumulation of money in the Social Security trust fund will be greatly inadequate for paying the retirement benefits promised to all future retirees.

In 2018 Social Security retirement revenues will fall below Social Security retirement benefits and the system will begin dipping into the trust fund to make up the difference. The trust fund will be exhausted in 2042, after which the promised retirement benefits will immediately exceed the Social Security tax revenues by an estimated 37 percent annually, rising to 56 percent annually in 2075. The Federal government faces a several-trillion-dollar shortfall of long-run revenues for funding Social Security.

As shown in the accompanying figure, the problem is one of demographics. The percentage of the American population age 62 or older will rise substantially over the next several decades, with the greatest increases for those age 75 and older. High fertility rates during the "baby boom" (1946–1964), declining birthrates thereafter, and rising life expectancies have combined to produce an aging population. In the future, more people will be receiving Social Security benefits for longer periods and each person's benefits will be paid for by fewer workers. The number of workers per Social Security beneficiary was 5:1 in 1960. Today it is 3:1, and by 2040 it will be only 2:1.

There is no easy way to restore long-run balance to Social Security funding. Either benefits must be reduced or revenues must be increased. The Social Security Administration concludes that bringing projected Social Security revenues and payments into balance over the next 75 years would require a 13 percent permanent reduction in Social Security benefits, a 15 percent permanent increase in tax revenues, or some combination of the two.*

Several suggestions have been offered to help make Social Security financially sound. One idea is to boost the trust fund by investing all or part of it in corporate stocks and bonds. The

Economic Growth and Tax Relief Reconciliation Act of 2001 (EGTRRA) phased in reductions of marginal tax rates through 2006. The top rate was scheduled to decline from 39.6 to 35 percent; the 36 percent rate, to 33 percent; the 31 percent rate, to 28 percent; and the 28 percent rate, to 25 percent. A new 10 percent bracket, split off from the 15 percent bracket, immediately went into effect. In 2001 the Federal government sent out the first half of the tax saving from those cuts as rebate checks to taxpayers totaling $36 billion. EGTRRA also set higher tax-free contribution limits for retirement, increased the child tax credit, and increased exemptions from the Federal estate tax in phases such that the tax will be eliminated in 2010.

The Bush tax cuts reduced the size of the surpluses but did not eliminate them. According to the Council of Economic Advisers (CEA), the EGTRRA tax cuts explain about 15 percent of the shift from a $127 billion surplus in 2001 to a $158 billion deficit in 2002.

The Economic Downturn The optimistic projections of rising budget surpluses were based on an assumption of continuing strong economic growth. But the recession of 2001 and the stock market crash of 2002 reduced tax revenues well below the earlier projections. We know from Chapter 12 that tax revenues automatically fall when personal income and corporate profits decline. Also, tax revenues from realized capital gains (asset-value increases) decline when the stock market crashes, as it did in 2001 and 2002. An estimated 70 percent of the swing from the $127 billion surplus in 2001

Federal government would own the stock investments, and an appointed panel would oversee the direction of those investments. The presumed higher returns on the investments relative to the lower returns on U.S. securities would stretch out the life of the trust fund. Nevertheless, a substantial increase in the payroll tax would still be needed to cover the shortfalls after the trust fund is exhausted.

Another option is to increase the payroll tax immediately—perhaps by as much as 1.5 percentage points—and allocate the new revenues to individual accounts. Government would own the accumulations in the accounts, but individuals could direct their investments to a restricted list of broad stock or bond funds. When they retire, recipients could convert these individual account balances to annuities—securities paying monthly payments for life. That annuity income would supplement reduced monthly benefits from the pay-as-you-go system when the trust fund is exhausted.

A different route is to place half the payroll tax into accounts that individuals, not the government, would own, maintain, and bequeath. Individuals could invest these funds in bank certificates of deposit or in approved stock and bond funds and

draw upon the accounts when they reach retirement age. A flat monthly benefit would supplement the accumulations in the private accounts. The personal security accounts would be phased in over time, so those individuals now receiving or about to receive Social Security benefits would continue to receive benefits.

These general ideas do not exhaust the possible reforms since the variations on each plan are nearly endless. Reaching consensus on Social Security reform will be difficult because every citizen has a direct economic stake in the outcome. Nevertheless, society will eventually need to confront the problem of trillions of dollars of unfunded Social Security liabilities.†

*Social Security Board of Trustees, "Status of the Social Security and Medicare Programs: A Summary of the 2002 Annual Reports," www.ssa.gov.
†Medicare (the health insurance that accompanies Social Security) is also severely underfunded. To bring projected Medicare revenues and expenditures into long-run balance would require an increase in the Medicare payroll tax from 2.9 to 4.92 percent, a 38 percent reduction of Medicare payments from their projected levels, or some combination of each. The total unfunded liabilities of Social Security and Medicare were $10 trillion in 2002.

to the $158 billion deficit in 2002 resulted from the bad economy.

September 11, 2001 According to the CEA, the final 15 percent of the change from budget surplus to budget deficit from 2001 to 2002 resulted from major spending increases related to the terrorist attacks of September 11, 2001. In the 12 months following the attacks, the Federal government spent or committed more than $100 billion of new spending, including $30 billion on the war on terrorism, $35 billion on homeland security, and $20 billion on helping New York City recover. Also, in 2002 Congress passed an "economic recovery" law that extended unemployment compensation benefits and offered tax relief for corporations. That law also added to the budget deficit.

The Tax Cuts of 2003

According to the May 2003 CBO projections presented in Figure 18.3, the Federal budget will return to surplus in 2007. But the U.S. economy remained sluggish in early 2003, and midway through that year the Bush administration and Congress enacted expansionary fiscal policy in the form of further tax cuts. Specifically, the legislation accelerated the phased tax-rate reductions scheduled in the 2001 tax law, expanded tax breaks for families, and reduced taxes on capital gains and dividends. Those changes will increase the size of the projected deficits shown in Figure 18.3 and extend them farther into the future. The point is that budget projections are subject to rapid change based on new tax policies, international events, and the health of the domestic economy.

QUICK REVIEW 18.3

- The borrowing and interest payments associated with the public debt may (a) increase income inequality, (b) require higher taxes, which dampen incentives, and (c) impede the growth of the nation's capital stock through crowding out of private investment.

- Only about 18 percent of the public debt is held by people and institutions abroad; Americans owe the rest to themselves.

- The large annual budget deficits of the 1980s and 1990s gave way to 4 years of budget surpluses between 1998 and 2001.

- The Federal budget returned to a deficit in 2002 because of the (a) recession of 2001, (b) stock market crash of 2001 and 2002, (c) phased tax-rate cuts enacted in 2001, and (d) increased government spending on the war on terrorism.

- In May 2003, the Congressional Budget Office projected budget deficits through 2007. In mid-2003, the Bush administration and Congress agreed on a new round of tax cuts, which advanced the phased tax-rate reductions scheduled under the 2001 tax law and reduced tax rates on capital gains and dividends. With those reductions, the projected budget deficits will be deeper and last longer than suggested by Figure 18.3.

SUMMARY

1. A budget deficit is the excess of government expenditures over receipts. A budget surplus is an excess of government revenues over expenditures. The public debt is the total accumulation of the government's deficits (minus surpluses) over time and consists of Treasury bills, Treasury notes, Treasury bonds, and U.S. savings bonds.

2. Among the various budget philosophies are the annually balanced budget, the cyclically balanced budget, and functional finance. The basic problem with an annually balanced budget is that it promotes swings in the business cycle rather than counters them. Similarly, it may be difficult to balance the budget over the course of the business cycle if upswings and downswings are not of roughly comparable magnitude. Functional finance is the view that the primary purpose of Federal finance is to stabilize the economy and that problems associated with consequent deficits or surpluses are of secondary importance.

3. Historically, the growth of the public debt has resulted from deficit financing of wars, revenue declines during recessions, and lack of fiscal discipline by elected leaders.

4. In 2002 the U.S. public debt was $6.2 trillion, or $21,476 per person. The public (here including banks and state and local governments) holds 57 percent of that debt, while the Federal Reserve and Federal agencies hold the other 43 percent. In the 1980s and early 1990s, the public debt increased sharply as a percentage of GDP. In more recent years, that percentage has substantially declined. Interest payments as a percentage of GDP were about 1.6 percent in 2002.

5. The concern that a large public debt may bankrupt the government is a false worry because (a) the debt needs only be refinanced rather than refunded and (b) the Federal government has the power to increase taxes to make interest payments on the debt.

6. The crowding-out effect aside, the public debt is not a vehicle for shifting economic burdens to future generations. In general, Americans inherit not only the public debt (a liability) but also the U.S. securities (an asset) that finance the debt.

7. More substantive problems associated with public debt include the following: (a) Payment of interest on the debt may increase income inequality. (b) Interest payments on the debt require higher taxes, which may impair incentives. (c) Paying interest or principal on the portion of the debt held by foreigners means a transfer of real output to abroad. (d) Government borrowing to refinance or pay interest on the debt may increase interest rates and crowd out private investment spending, leaving future generations with a smaller stock of capital than they would have otherwise.

8. The increase in investment in public capital that may result from debt financing may partly or wholly offset the crowding-out effect of the public debt on private investment. Also, the added public investment may stimulate private investment, if the two are complements.

9. The large Federal budget deficits of the 1980s and early 1990s prompted Congress in 1993 to increase tax rates and limit government spending. As a result of these policies, along with a very rapid and prolonged economic expansion, the deficits dwindled to $22 billion in 1997. Large budget surpluses occurred in 1999, 2000, and 2001. In 2001 the Congressional Budget Office projected that $5 trillion of annual budget surpluses would accumulate between 2000 and 2010.

10. The large actual and projected budget surpluses of the early 2000s set off a debate over what to do with them. The main options were (a) pay down the public debt, (b) reduce tax rates or eliminate some taxes, and (c) increase government spending.

11. In 2001 the Bush Administration and Congress chose to reduce marginal tax rates and phase out the Federal estate tax.

A recession occurred in 2001, the stock market crashed, and Federal spending relating to the war on terrorism rocketed. The Federal budget swung from a surplus of $127 billion in 2001 to a deficit of $158 billion in 2002. In 2003, budget deficits were projected to continue through 2007 before surpluses again reemerge.

12. In 2003 the Bush administration and Congress accelerated the tax reductions scheduled under the 2001 tax law and cut tax rates on capital gains and dividends. The purposes were to stimulate a sluggish economy and promote long-term economic growth.

TERMS AND CONCEPTS

public debt	annually balanced budget	functional finance	external public debt
U.S. securities	cyclically balanced budget	Social Security trust fund	public investments

STUDY QUESTIONS

1. *Key Question* Assess the leeway for using fiscal policy as a stabilization tool under (*a*) an annually balanced budget, (*b*) a cyclically balanced budget, and (*c*) functional finance.

2. What have been the three major sources of the public debt historically?

3. *Key Question* What are the two main ways the size of the public debt is measured? Distinguish between refinancing the debt and retiring the debt. How does an internally held public debt differ from an externally held public debt? Contrast the effects of retiring an internally held debt and retiring an externally held debt.

4. True or false? If the statement is false, explain why:
   a. An internally held public debt is like a debt of the left hand to the right hand.
   b. The Federal Reserve and Federal government agencies hold more than half the public debt.
   c. The U.S. public debt was smaller in percentage terms in 2000 than it was in 1990.
   d. In recent years, Social Security payments have exceeded Social Security tax revenues.

5. Why might economists be quite concerned if the annual interest payments on the debt sharply increased as a percentage of GDP?

6. Do you think that paying off the public debt would increase or decrease income inequality? Explain.

7. *Key Question* Trace the cause-and-effect chain through which financing and refinancing of the public debt might affect real interest rates, private investment, the stock of capital, and economic growth. How might investment in public capital and complementarities between public capital and private capital alter the outcome of the cause-effect chain?

8. Relate the Deficit Reduction Act of 1993 (Clinton tax increase) and the Economic Growth and Tax Relief Reconciliation Act of 2001 (Bush tax cut) to the Laffer Curve (Figure 16.10, page 303) and to their effects on U.S. budget deficits or surpluses.

9. What would happen to the stated sizes of Federal budget deficits or surpluses if the annual additions or subtractions from the Social Security trust fund were excluded?

10. Why did the budget deficits rise sharply in 1991 and 1992? What explains the large budget surpluses of the late 1990s and early 2000s? What caused the swing from the budget surpluses to a deficit in 2002?

11. *(Last Word)* What do economists mean when they refer to Social Security as a pay-as-you-go plan? What is the Social Security trust fund? What is the nature of the long-run fiscal imbalance in the Social Security system (Social Security payments and Medicare)? What are the broad options for fixing the long-run problem?

12. *Web-Based Question: The debt—to the penny* Go to the website of the Department of Treasury, Bureau of the Public Debt, at www.publicdebt.treas.gov/opd/opdpenny.htm and find the amount of the public debt, to the penny, as of the latest date. How does it compare to the debt of 10 years ago? What has been the trend over the past 12 months?

13. *Web-Based Question: Frequently asked questions about the public debt* Visit the U.S. Treasury's "Public Debt Frequently Asked Questions" (FAQ) site, www.publicdebt.treas.gov/opd/opdfaq.htm, and answer the following questions: Why does the public debt sometimes go down? Why does the public debt change only once a day? As of today, who owns the public debt?

Disputes over Macro Theory and Policy

As any academic discipline evolves, it naturally evokes a number of internal disagreements. Economics is no exception. In this chapter we examine a few alternative perspectives on macro theory and policy. After contrasting classical and Keynesian theories, we turn to recent disagreements on three interrelated questions: (1) What causes instability in the economy? (2) Is the economy self-correcting? (3) Should government adhere to *rules* or use *discretion* in setting economic policy?

Some History: Classical Economics and Keynes

Classical economics began with Adam Smith in 1776 and dominated economic thinking until the 1930s. It holds that full employment is the norm in a market economy and therefore a laissez-faire ("let it be") policy by government is best. Then, in the 1930s, John Maynard Keynes asserted that laissez-faire capitalism is subject to recurring recessions that bring widespread unemployment. In the Keynesian view, active government policy is required to stabilize the economy and to prevent valuable resources from standing idle.

Let's compare these two views through modern aggregate demand and aggregate supply analysis.

The Classical View

In the **classical view,** the aggregate supply curve is vertical and is the sole determinant of the level of real output.

The downsloping aggregate demand curve is stable and is the sole determinant of the price level.

Vertical Aggregate Supply Curve According to the classical perspective, the aggregate supply curve is a vertical line, as shown in Figure 19.1a. This line is located at the full-employment level of real GDP, Q_f. According to the classical economists, the economy will operate at its potential level of output because of (1) Say's law (Last Word, Chapter 10) and (2) responsive, flexible prices and wages.

We stress that classical economists believed that Q_f does not change in response to changes in the price level. Observe that as the price level falls from P_1 to P_2 in Figure 19.1a, real output remains anchored at Q_f.

But this stability of output is at odds with the upsloping supply curves for individual products that we discussed in Chapter 3. There we found that lower prices would make production less profitable and would cause producers to offer less output and employ fewer workers. The

FIGURE 19.1

Classical and Keynesian views of the macroeconomy. (a) In classical theory, aggregate supply determines the full-employment level of real output, while aggregate demand establishes the price level. Aggregate demand normally is stable, but if it should decline, say, from AD_1 to AD_2, the price level will quickly fall from P_1 to P_2 to eliminate the temporary excess supply of *ab* and to restore full employment at *c*. (b) The Keynesian view is that aggregate demand is unstable and that prices and wages are downwardly inflexible. An AD_1 to AD_2 decline in aggregate demand has no effect on the price level. Instead, the economy moves from point *x* to *y* and real output falls to Q_u, where it can remain for long periods.

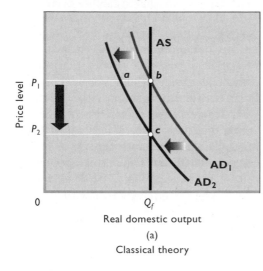

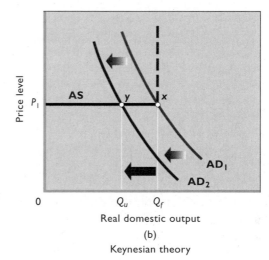

(a)
Classical theory

(b)
Keynesian theory

classical response to this view is that input costs in the economy would fall along with product prices and leave real profits and output unchanged. For example, if product prices on average fall from $10 to $5 and per-unit costs decline from $8 to $4, the real profit per unit of output will remain at $2. The new $1 of nominal profit (= $5 − $4) will equal $2 of real profit because prices have been halved. With flexible wages and other input prices, costs will move up and down with prices and leave real rewards and real output constant. A change in the price level will not cause the economy to stray from full employment.

Stable Aggregate Demand

Classical economists theorize that money underlies aggregate demand. The amount of real output that can be purchased depends on (1) the quantity of money households and businesses possess and (2) the purchasing power of that money as determined by the price level. The purchasing power of the dollar refers to the real quantity of goods and services a dollar will buy. Thus, as we move down the vertical axis of Figure 19.1a, the price level is falling. This means that the purchasing power of each dollar is rising. If the price level were to fall by one-half, a certain quantity of money would then purchase a real output twice as large. With a fixed money supply, the price level and real output are inversely related.

What about the location of the aggregate demand curve? According to the classical economists, aggregate demand will be stable as long as the nation's monetary authorities maintain a constant supply of money. With a fixed aggregate supply of output, increases in the supply of money will shift the aggregate demand curve rightward and spark demand-pull inflation. Reductions in the supply of money will shift the curve leftward and trigger deflation. The key to price-level stability, then, is to control the nation's money supply to prevent unwarranted shifts in aggregate demand.

Even if there are declines in the money supply and therefore in aggregate demand, the economy depicted in Figure 19.1a will not experience unemployment. Admittedly, the immediate effect of a decline in aggregate demand from AD_1 to AD_2 is an excess supply of output, since the aggregate output of goods and services exceeds aggregate spending by the amount *ab*. But, with the presumed downward flexibility of product and resource prices, that excess supply will reduce product prices along with workers' wages and the prices of other inputs. As a result, the price level will quickly decline from P_1 to P_2 until the amounts of output demanded and supplied are brought once again into equilibrium, this time at *c*. While the price level has fallen from P_1 to P_2, real output remains at the full-employment level.

The Keynesian View

The heart of the **Keynesian view** is that product prices and wages are downwardly inflexible over very long time periods. The result is graphically represented as a horizontal aggregate supply curve. Also, aggregate demand is subject to periodic changes caused by changes in the determinants of aggregate demand.

Horizontal Aggregate Supply Curve (to Full-Employment Output)

The downward inflexibility of prices and wages presumed by the Keynesians translates to the horizontal aggregate supply curve, shown in Figure 19.1b. Here, a decline in real output from Q_f to Q_u will have no impact on the price level. Nor will an increase in real output from Q_u to Q_f. The aggregate supply curve therefore extends from zero real output rightward to point x, where real output is at its full-employment level, Q_f. Once full employment is reached, the aggregate supply curve becomes vertical. The dashed line extending upward from the horizontal aggregate supply curve at x shows this.

Unstable Aggregate Demand

Keynesian economists view aggregate demand as unstable from one period to the next, even without changes in the money supply. In particular, the investment component of aggregate demand fluctuates, altering the location of the aggregate demand curve. Suppose aggregate demand in Figure 19.1b declines from AD_1 to AD_2. The sole impact is on output and employment. Real output falls from Q_f to Q_u, but the price level remains unchanged at P_1. Moreover, Keynesians believe that unless there is an offsetting increase in aggregate demand, real output may remain at Q_u, which is below the full-employment level Q_f. Active government policies to increase aggregate demand are essential to move the economy from point y to point x. Otherwise, the economy will suffer the wastes of recession and depression. **(Key Question 1)**

QUICK REVIEW 19.1

- In classical macroeconomics, the aggregate supply curve is vertical at the full-employment level of real output, and the aggregate demand curve is stable as long as the money supply is constant.
- In Keynesian macroeconomics, the aggregate supply curve is horizontal up to the full-employment level of output; then it becomes vertical. The aggregate demand curve is unstable largely because of the volatility of investment spending; such shifts cause either recession or demand-pull inflation.

What Causes Macro Instability?

As earlier chapters have indicated, capitalist economies experienced considerable instability during the twentieth century. The United States, for example, experienced the Great Depression, numerous recessions, and periods of inflation. Contemporary economists have different perspectives on why this instability occurs.

Mainstream View

For simplicity, we will use the term "mainstream view" to characterize the prevailing macroeconomic perspective of the majority of economists. According to that view, which retains a Keynesian flavor, instability in the economy arises from two sources: (1) significant changes in investment spending, which change aggregate demand, and, occasionally, (2) adverse aggregate supply shocks, which change aggregate supply. Although these factors are not new to you, let's quickly review them.

Changes in Investment Spending

Mainstream macroeconomics focuses on aggregate spending and its components. Recall that the basic equation underlying aggregate expenditures is

$$C_a + I_g + X_n + G = \text{GDP}$$

That is, the aggregate amount of after-tax consumption, gross investment, net exports, and government spending determines the total amount of goods and services produced and sold. In equilibrium, $C_a + I_g + X_n + G$ (aggregate expenditures) is equal to GDP (real output). A decrease in the price level increases equilibrium GDP and thus allows us to trace out a downsloping aggregate demand curve for the economy (see the appendix to Chapter 11). Any change in one of the spending components in the aggregate expenditures equation shifts the aggregate demand curve. This, in turn, changes equilibrium real output, the price level, or both.

Investment spending, in particular, is subject to wide "booms" and "busts." Significant increases in investment spending are multiplied into even greater increases in aggregate demand and thus can produce demand-pull inflation. In contrast, significant declines in investment spending are multiplied into even greater decreases in aggregate demand and thus can cause recessions.

Adverse Aggregate Supply Shocks

In the mainstream view, the second source of macroeconomic instability arises on the supply side. Occasionally, such external events as wars or an artificial supply restriction of a key resource can boost resource prices and significantly raise per-unit production costs. The result is a sizable decline in a nation's aggregate supply, which destabilizes the economy by simultaneously causing cost-push inflation and recession.

Monetarist View

Classical economics has reappeared in several modern forms. One is **monetarism,** which (1) focuses on the money supply, (2) holds that markets are highly competitive, and (3) says that a competitive market system gives the econ-omy a high degree of macroeconomic stability. Like classical economists, monetarists argue that the price and wage flexibility provided by competi-tive markets would cause fluctuations in aggregate demand to alter product and resource prices rather than output and employment. Thus the market system would provide substantial macroeconomic stability *were it not for government interference in the economy.*

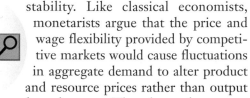

19.1
Monetarism

The problem, as monetarists see it, is that govern-ment has promoted downward wage inflexibility through the minimum-wage law, pro-union legislation, guaranteed prices for certain farm products, pro-business monopoly legislation, and so forth. The free-market system is capa-ble of providing macroeconomic stability, but, despite good intentions, government interference has undermined that capability. Moreover, monetarists say that govern-ment has contributed to the economy's business cycles through its clumsy and mistaken attempts to achieve greater stability through its monetary policies.

Equation of Exchange   The fundamental equation of monetarism is the **equation of exchange:**

$$MV = PQ$$

where M is the supply of money; V is the **velocity** of money, that is, *the average number of times per year a dollar is spent on final goods and services; P* is the price level or, more specifically, the average price at which each unit of physical output is sold; and Q is the physical volume of all goods and services produced.

19.2
Equation of
exchange

The left side of the equation of ex-change, *MV*, represents the total amount spent by purchasers of output, while the right side, *PQ*, represents the to-tal amount received by sellers of that output. The nation's money supply (M) multiplied by the number of times it is spent each year (V) must equal the nation's nominal GDP (= $P \times Q$). The dollar value of to-tal spending has to equal the dollar value of total output.

Stable Velocity   Monetarists say that velocity, V, in the equation of exchange is relatively stable. To them, "stable" is not synonymous with "constant," however. Monetarists are aware that velocity is higher today than it was several decades ago. Shorter pay periods, widespread use of credit cards, and faster means of making payments enable people to hold less money and to turn it over more rapidly than was possible in earlier times. These factors have enabled people to reduce their holdings of cash and checkbook money relative to the size of the nation's nominal GDP.

When monetarists say that velocity is stable, they mean that the factors altering velocity change gradually and pre-dictably and that changes in velocity from one year to the next can be readily anticipated. Moreover, they hold that velocity does not change in response to changes in the money supply itself. Instead, people have a stable desire to hold money relative to holding other financial assets, hold-ing real assets, and buying current output. The factors that determine the amount of money the public wants to hold depend mainly on the level of nominal GDP.

Example: Assume that when the level of nominal GDP is $400 billion, the public desires $100 billion of money to purchase that output. That means that V is 4 (= $400 billion of nominal GDP/$100 billion of money). If we further assume that the actual supply of money is $100 bil-lion, the economy is in equilibrium with respect to money; the actual amount of money supplied equals the amount the public wants to hold.

If velocity is stable, the equation of exchange suggests that there is a predictable relationship between the money supply and nominal GDP (= PQ). An increase in the money supply of, say, $10 billion would upset equilibrium in our example, since the public would find itself holding more money or liquidity than it wants. That is, the actual amount of money held ($110 billion) would exceed the amount of holdings desired ($100 billion). In that case, the reaction of the public (households and businesses) is to restore its desired balance of money relative to other items, such as stocks and bonds, factories and equipment, houses and automobiles, and clothing and toys. But the spending of money by individual households and busi-nesses would leave more cash in the checkable deposits or billfolds of other households and firms. And they too would try to "spend down" their excess cash balances. But, overall, the $110 billion supply of money cannot be spent down because a dollar spent is a dollar received.

Instead, the collective attempt to reduce cash balances increases aggregate demand, thereby boosting nominal

GDP. Because velocity in our example is 4—that is, the dollar is spent, on average, four times per year—nominal GDP rises from $400 billion to $440 billion. At that higher nominal GDP, the money supply of $110 billion equals the amount of money desired ($440 billion/4 = $110 billion), and equilibrium is reestablished.

The $10 billion increase in the money supply thus eventually increases nominal GDP by $40 billion. Spending on goods, services, and assets expands until nominal GDP has gone up enough to restore the original 4-to-1 equilibrium relationship between nominal GDP and the money supply.

Note that the relationship GDP/M defines V. A stable relationship between nominal GDP and M means a stable V. And a change in M causes a proportionate change in nominal GDP. Thus, changes in the money supply allegedly have a predictable effect on nominal GDP (= $P \times Q$). An increase in M increases P or Q, or some combination of both; a decrease in M reduces P or Q, or some combination of both. **(Key Question 4)**

Monetary Causes of Instability Monetarists say that inappropriate monetary policy is the single most important cause of macroeconomic instability. An increase in the money supply directly increases aggregate demand. Under conditions of full employment, that rise in aggregate demand raises the price level. For a time, higher prices cause firms to increase their real output, and the rate of unemployment falls below its natural rate. But once nominal wages rise to reflect the higher prices and thus to restore real wages, real output moves back to its full-employment level and the unemployment rate returns to its natural rate. The inappropriate increase in the money supply leads to inflation, together with instability of real output and employment.

Conversely, a decrease in the money supply reduces aggregate demand. Real output temporarily falls, and the unemployment rate rises above its natural rate. Eventually, nominal wages fall and real output returns to its full-employment level. The inappropriate decline in the money supply leads to deflation, together with instability of real GDP and employment.

The contrast between mainstream macroeconomics and monetarism on the causes of instability thus comes into sharp focus. Mainstream economists view the instability of investment as the main cause of the economy's instability. They see monetary policy as a stabilizing factor. Changes in the money supply raise or lower interest rates as needed, smooth out swings in investment, and thus reduce macroeconomic instability. In contrast, monetarists view changes in the money supply as the main cause of instability in the economy. For example, they say that the Great Depression occurred largely because the Fed allowed the money supply to fall by nearly 40 percent during that period. According to Milton Friedman, a prominent monetarist,

> And [the money supply] fell not because there were no willing borrowers—not because the horse would not drink. It fell because the Federal Reserve System forced or permitted a sharp reduction in the [money supply], because it failed to exercise the responsibilities assigned to it in the Federal Reserve Act to provide liquidity to the banking system. The Great Contraction is tragic testimony to the power of monetary policy—not, as Keynes and so many of his contemporaries believed, evidence of its impotence.[1]

Real-Business-Cycle View

A third modern view of the cause of macroeconomic instability is that business cycles are caused by real factors that affect aggregate supply rather than by monetary, or spending, factors that cause fluctuations in aggregate demand. In the **real-business-cycle theory,** business fluctuations result from significant changes in technology and resource availability. Those changes affect productivity and thus the long-run growth trend of aggregate supply.

An example focusing on recession will clarify this thinking. Suppose productivity (output per worker) declines sharply because of a large increase in oil prices, which makes it prohibitively expensive to operate certain types of machinery. That decline in productivity implies a reduction in the economy's ability to produce real output. The result would be a decrease in the economy's long-run aggregate supply curve, as represented by the leftward shift from AS_{LR1} to AS_{LR2} in Figure 19.2.

As real output falls from Q_1 to Q_2, the public needs less money to buy the reduced volume of goods and services. So the demand for money falls. Moreover, the slowdown in business activity means that businesses need to borrow less from banks, reducing the part of the money supply created by banks through their lending. Thus, the supply of money also falls. In this controversial scenario, changes in the supply of money respond to changes in the demand for money. The decline in the money supply then reduces aggregate demand, as from AD_1 to AD_2 in Figure 19.2. The outcome is a decline in real output from Q_1 to Q_2, with no change in the price level.

Conversely, a large increase in aggregate supply (not shown) caused by, say, major innovations in the

---

[1]Milton Friedman, *The Optimum Quantity of Money and Other Essays* (Chicago: Aldine, 1969), p. 97.

FIGURE 19.2

The real-business-cycle theory. In the real-business-cycle theory, a decline in resource availability shifts the nation's long-run aggregate supply curve to the left from AS_{LR1} to AS_{LR2}. The decline in real output from Q_1 to Q_2, in turn, reduces money demand (less is needed) and money supply (fewer loans are taken out) such that aggregate demand shifts leftward from AD_1 to AD_2. The result is a recession in which the price level remains constant.

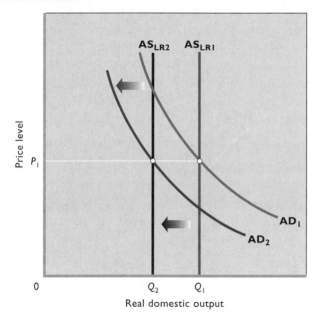

production process would shift the long-run aggregate supply curve rightward. Real output would increase, and money demand and money supply would both increase. Aggregate demand would shift rightward by an amount equal to the rightward shift of long-run aggregate supply. Real output would increase, without driving up the price level.

Conclusion: In the real-business-cycle theory, macro instability arises on the aggregate supply side of the economy, not on the aggregate demand side, as mainstream economists and monetarists usually claim.

Coordination Failures

A fourth and final modern view of macroeconomic instability relates to so-called **coordination failures.** Such failures occur when people fail to reach a mutually beneficial equilibrium because they lack a way to coordinate their actions.

Noneconomic Example Consider first a noneconomic example. Suppose you learn of an impending

informal party at a nearby beach, although it looks as though it might rain. If you expect others to be there, you will decide to go. If you expect that others will not go, you will decide to stay home. There are several possible equilibrium outcomes, depending on the mix of people's expectations. Let's consider just two. If each person assumes that all the others will be at the party, all will go. The party will occur and presumably everyone will have a good time. But if each person assumes that everyone else will stay home, all will stay home and there will be no party. When the party does not take place, even though all would be better off if it did take place, a coordination failure has occurred.

Macroeconomic Example Now let's apply this example to macroeconomic instability, specifically recession. Suppose that individual firms and households expect other firms and consumers to cut back their investment and consumption spending. As a result, each firm and household will anticipate a reduction of aggregate demand. Firms therefore will cut back their own investment spending, since they will anticipate that their future production capacity will be excessive. Households will also reduce their own spending (increase their saving), because they anticipate that they will experience reduced work hours, possible layoffs, and falling incomes in the future.

Aggregate demand will indeed decline and the economy will indeed experience a recession in response to what amounts to a self-fulfilling prophecy. Moreover, the economy will stay at a below-full-employment level of output because, once there, producers and households have no individual incentive to increase spending. If all producers and households would agree to increase their investment and consumption spending simultaneously, then aggregate demand would rise, and real output and real income would increase. Each producer and each consumer would be better off. However, this outcome does not occur because there is no mechanism for firms and households to agree on such a joint spending increase.

In this case, the economy is stuck in an *unemployment equilibrium* because of a coordination failure. With a different set of expectations, a coordination failure might leave the economy in an *inflation equilibrium*. In this view, there are a number of such potential equilibrium positions in the economy, some good and some bad, depending on people's mix of expectations. Macroeconomic instability, then, reflects the movement of the economy from one such equilibrium position to another as expectations change.

QUICK REVIEW 19.2

- Mainstream economists say that macroeconomic instability usually stems from swings in investment spending and, occasionally, from adverse aggregate supply shocks.

- Monetarists view the economy through the equation of exchange ($MV = PQ$). If velocity V is stable, changes in the money supply M lead directly to changes in nominal GDP ($P \times Q$). For monetarists, changes in M caused by inappropriate monetary policy are the single most important cause of macroeconomic instability.

- In the real-business-cycle theory, significant changes in "real" factors such as technology, resource availability, and productivity change the economy's long-run aggregate supply, causing macroeconomic instability.

- Macroeconomic instability can result from coordination failures—less-than-optimal equilibrium positions that occur because businesses and households lack a way to coordinate their actions.

Does the Economy "Self-Correct"?

Just as there are disputes over the causes of macroeconomic instability, there are disputes over whether or not the economy will correct itself when instability does occur. And economists also disagree on how long it will take for any such self-correction to take place.

New Classical View of Self-Correction

New classical economists tend to be either monetarists or adherents of **rational expectations theory:** *the idea that businesses, consumers, and workers expect changes in policies or circumstances to have certain effects on the economy and, in pursuing their own self-interest, take actions to make sure those changes affect them as little as possible.* The **new classical economics** holds that when the economy occasionally diverges from its full-employment output, internal mechanisms within the economy will automatically move it back to that output. Policymakers should stand back and let the automatic correction occur, rather than engaging in active fiscal and monetary policy. This perspective is that associated with the vertical long-run Phillips Curve, which we discussed in Chapter 16.

19.3
Rational
expectations
theory

Graphical Analysis Figure 19.3a relates the new classical analysis to the question of self-correction. Specifically, an increase in aggregate demand, say, from AD_1 to AD_2, moves the economy upward along its short-run aggregate supply curve AS_1 from *a* to *b*. The price level rises and real output increases. In the long run, however, nominal wages rise to restore real wages. Per-unit production costs then increase, and the short-run

FIGURE 19.3

New classical view of self-correction. (a) An unanticipated increase in aggregate demand from AD_1 to AD_2 first moves the economy from *a* to *b*. The economy then self-corrects to *c*. An anticipated increase in aggregate demand moves the economy directly from *a* to *c*. (b) An unanticipated decrease in aggregate demand from AD_1 to AD_3 moves the economy from *a* to *d*. The economy then self-corrects to *e*. An anticipated decrease in aggregate demand moves the economy directly from *a* to *e*. (Mainstream economists, however, say that if the price level remains at P_1, the economy will move from *a* to *f*, and even if the price level falls to P_4, the economy may remain at *d* because of downward wage inflexibility.)

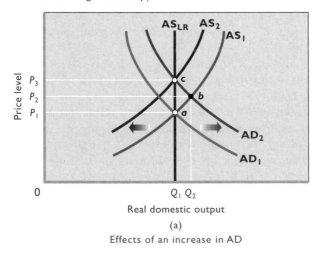

(a)
Effects of an increase in AD

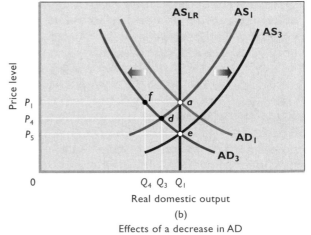

(b)
Effects of a decrease in AD

aggregate supply curve shifts leftward, eventually from AS_1 to AS_2. The economy moves from b to c, and real output returns to its full-employment level, Q_1. This level of output is dictated by the economy's vertical long-run aggregate supply curve, AS_{LR}.

Conversely, a decrease in aggregate demand from AD_1 to AD_3 in Figure 19.3b first moves the economy downward along its short-run aggregate supply curve AS_1 from point a to d. The price level declines, as does the level of real output. But in the long run, nominal wages decline such that real wages fall to their previous levels. When that happens, per-unit production costs decline and the short-run aggregate supply curve shifts to the right, eventually from AS_1 to AS_3. The economy moves to e, where it again achieves its full-employment level, Q_1. As in Figure 19.3a, the economy in Figure 19.3b has automatically self-corrected to its full-employment output and its natural rate of unemployment.

Speed of Adjustment

There is some disagreement among new classical economists on how long it will take for self-correction to occur. Monetarists usually hold the *adaptive* expectations view that people form their expectations on the basis of present realities and only gradually change their expectations as experience unfolds. This means that the shifts in the short-run aggregate supply curves shown in Figure 19.3 may not occur for 2 or 3 years or even longer. Other new classical economists, however, accept the rational expectations assumption that workers anticipate some future outcomes before they occur. When price-level changes are fully anticipated, adjustments of nominal wages are very quick or even instantaneous. Let's see why.

Although several new theories, including Keynesian ones, incorporate rational expectations, our interest here is in the new classical version of the rational expectations theory (hereafter, RET). RET is based on two assumptions:

- People behave rationally, gathering and intelligently processing information to form expectations about things that are economically important to them. They adjust those expectations quickly as new developments affecting future economic outcomes occur. Where there is adequate information, people's beliefs about future economic outcomes accurately reflect the likelihood that those outcomes will occur. For example, if it is clear that a certain policy will cause inflation, people will recognize that fact and adjust their economic behavior in anticipation of inflation.

- Like classical economists, RET economists assume that all product and resource markets are highly

competitive and that prices and wages are flexible both upward and downward. But the RET economists go further, assuming that new information is quickly (in some cases, instantaneously) taken into account in the demand and supply curves of such markets. The upshot is that equilibrium prices and quantities adjust rapidly to unforeseen events—say, technological change or aggregate supply shocks. They adjust instantaneously to events that have known outcomes—for example, changes in fiscal or monetary policy.

Unanticipated Price-Level Changes

The implication of RET is not only that the economy is self-correcting but that self-correction occurs quickly. In this thinking, unanticipated changes in the price level—so-called **price-level surprises**—do cause temporary changes in real output. Suppose, for example, that an unanticipated increase in foreign demand for U.S. goods increases U.S. aggregate demand from AD_1 to AD_2 in Figure 19.3a. The immediate result is an unexpected increase in the price level from P_1 to P_2.

But now an interesting question arises. If wages and prices are flexible, as assumed in RET, why doesn't the higher price level immediately cause nominal wages to rise, such that there is no increase in real output at all? Why does the economy temporarily move from point a to b along AS_1? In RET, firms increase output from Q_1 to Q_2 because of misperceptions about rising prices of their own products relative to the prices of other products (and to the prices of labor). They mistakenly think the higher prices of their own products have resulted from increased demand for those products relative to the demands for other products. Expecting higher profits, they increase their own production. But in fact *all* prices, including the price of labor (nominal wages), are rising because of the general increase in aggregate demand. Once firms see that *all* prices and wages are rising, they decrease their production to previous levels.

In terms of Figure 19.3a, the increase in nominal wages shifts the short-run aggregate supply curve leftward, ultimately from AS_1 to AS_2, and the economy moves from b to c. Thus, the increase in real output caused by the price-level surprise corrects itself.

The same analysis in reverse applies to an unanticipated price-level decrease. In the economy represented by Figure 19.3b, firms misperceive that the prices of their own products are falling due to decreases in the demand for those products relative to other products. They anticipate declines in profit and cut production. As a result of their collective actions, real output in the economy falls. But seeing that all prices and wages are dropping, firms increase their output to prior levels. The short-run aggregate supply curve in Figure 19.3b shifts rightward from AS_1 to AS_3, and the economy "self-corrects" by moving from d to e.

Fully Anticipated Price-Level Changes

In RET, fully *anticipated* price-level changes do not change real output, even for short periods. In Figure 19.3a, again consider the increase in aggregate demand from AD_1 to AD_2. Businesses immediately recognize that the higher prices being paid for their products are part of the inflation they had anticipated. They understand that the same forces that are causing the inflation result in higher nominal wages, leaving their profits unchanged. The economy therefore moves directly from a to c. The price level rises as expected, and output remains at its full-employment level Q_1.

Similarly, a fully *anticipated* price-level decrease will leave real output unchanged. Firms conclude that nominal wages are declining by the same percentage amount as the declining price level, leaving profits unchanged. The economy represented by Figure 19.3b therefore moves directly from a to e. Deflation occurs, but the economy continues to produce its full-employment output Q_1. The anticipated decline in aggregate demand causes no change in real output.

Mainstream View of Self-Correction

Almost all economists acknowledge that the new classical economists have made significant contributions to the theory of aggregate supply. In fact, mainstream economists have incorporated some aspects of RET into their own more detailed models. However, most economists strongly disagree with RET on the question of downward price and wage flexibility. While the stock market, foreign exchange market, and certain commodity markets experience day-to-day or minute-to-minute price changes, including price declines, that is not true of many product markets and most labor markets. There is ample evidence, say mainstream economists, that many prices and wages are inflexible downward for long periods. As a result, it may take years for the economy to move from recession back to full-employment output, unless it gets help from fiscal and monetary policy.

Graphical Analysis

To understand this mainstream view, again examine Figure 19.3b. Suppose aggregate demand declines from AD_1 to AD_3 because of a significant decline in investment spending. If the price level remains at P_1, the economy will not move from a to d to e, as suggested by RET. Instead, the economy will move from a to f, as if it were moving along a horizontal aggregate supply curve between those two points. Real output will decline from its full-employment level, Q_1, to the recessionary level, Q_4.

But let's assume that surpluses in product markets eventually cause the price level to fall to P_4. Will this lead to the decline in nominal wages needed to shift aggregate supply from AS_1 to AS_3, as suggested by the new classical economists? "Highly unlikely" say mainstream economists. Even more so than prices, nominal wages tend to be inflexible downward. If nominal wages do not decline in response to the decline in the price level, then the short-run aggregate supply curve will not shift rightward. The self-correction mechanism assumed by RET and new classical economists will break down. Instead, the economy will remain at d, experiencing less-than-full-employment output and a high rate of unemployment.

Downward Wage Inflexibility

In Chapter 11 we discussed several reasons why firms may not be able to, or may not want to, lower nominal wages. Firms may not be able to cut wages because of wage contracts and the legal minimum wage. And firms may not want to lower wages if they fear potential problems with morale, effort, and efficiency.

While contracts are thought to be the main cause of wage rigidity, so-called efficiency wages and insider-outsider relationships may also play a role. Let's explore both.

Efficiency Wage Theory

Recall from Chapter 11 that an **efficiency wage** is a wage that minimizes the firm's labor cost per unit of output. Normally, we would think that the market wage is the efficiency wage since it is the lowest wage at which a firm can obtain a particular type of labor. But where the cost of supervising workers is high or where worker turnover is great, firms may discover that paying a wage that is higher than the market wage will lower their wage cost per unit of output.

Example: Suppose a firm's workers, on average, produce 8 units of output at a $9 market wage but 10 units of output at a $10 above-market wage. The efficiency wage is $10, not the $9 market wage. At the $10 wage, the labor cost per unit of output is only $1 (= $10 wage/10 units of output), compared with $1.12 (= $9 wage/8 units of output) at the $9 wage.

How can a higher wage result in greater efficiency?

- *Greater work effort*   The above-market wage, in effect, raises the cost to workers of losing their jobs as a result of poor performance. Because workers have a strong incentive to retain their relatively high-paying jobs, they are more likely to provide greater work effort. Looked at differently, workers are more reluctant to shirk (neglect or avoid work) because the higher wage makes job loss more costly to them. Consequently, the above-market wage can be the efficient wage; it can enhance worker productivity so much that the higher wage more than pays for itself.

- *Lower supervision costs* With less incentive among workers to shirk, the firm needs fewer supervisory personnel to monitor work performance. This, too, can lower the firm's overall wage cost per unit of output.

- *Reduced job turnover* The above-market pay discourages workers from voluntarily leaving their jobs. The lower turnover rate reduces the firm's cost of hiring and training workers. It also gives the firm a more experienced, more productive workforce.

The key implication for macroeconomic instability is that efficiency wages add to the downward inflexibility of wages. Firms that pay efficiency wages will be reluctant to cut wages when aggregate demand declines, since such cuts may encourage shirking, require more supervisory personnel, and increase turnover. In other words, wage cuts that reduce productivity and raise per-unit labor costs are self-defeating.

19.4
Efficiency
wages

Insider-Outsider Relationships Other economists theorize that downward wage inflexibility may relate to relationships between "insiders" and "outsiders." Insiders are workers who retain employment even during recession. Outsiders are workers who have been laid off from a firm and unemployed workers who would like to work at that firm.

When recession produces layoffs and widespread unemployment, we might expect outsiders to offer to work for less than the current wage rate, in effect, bidding down wage rates. We might also expect firms to hire such workers in order to reduce their costs. But, according to the **insider-outsider theory,** outsiders may not be able to underbid existing wages because employers may view the nonwage cost of hiring them to be prohibitive. Employers might fear that insiders would view acceptance of such underbidding as undermining years of effort to increase wages or, worse, as "stealing" jobs. So insiders may refuse to cooperate with new workers who have undercut their pay. Where teamwork is critical for production, such lack of cooperation will reduce overall productivity and thereby lower the firms' profits.

Even if firms are willing to employ outsiders at less than the current wage, those workers might refuse to work for less than the existing wage. To do so might invite harassment from the insiders whose pay they have undercut. Thus, outsiders may remain unemployed, relying on past saving, unemployment compensation, and other social programs to make ends meet.

As in the efficiency wage theory, the insider-outsider theory implies that wages will be inflexible downward when aggregate demand declines. Self-correction may eventually occur but not nearly as rapidly as the new classical economists contend. **(Key Question 7)**

Rules or Discretion?

These different views on the causes of instability and on the speed of self-correction have led to vigorous debate on macro policy. Should the government adhere to policy rules that prohibit it from causing instability in an economy that is otherwise stable? Or should it use discretionary fiscal and monetary policy, when needed, to stabilize a sometimes-unstable economy?

In Support of Policy Rules

Monetarists and other new classical economists believe policy rules would reduce instability in the economy. They believe that such rules would prevent government from trying to "manage" aggregate demand. That would be a desirable trend, because in their view such management is misguided and thus is likely to *cause* more instability than it cures.

CONSIDER THIS . . .

© Photodisc/Getty Images

On the Road Again

Keynesian economist Abba Lerner (1903–1982) likened the economy to an automobile traveling down a road that had traffic barriers on each side. The problem was that the car had no steering wheel. It would hit one barrier, causing the car to veer to the opposite side of the road. There it would hit the other barrier, which in turn would send it careening to the opposite side. To avoid such careening in the form of business cycles, said Lerner, society must equip the economy with a steering wheel. Discretionary fiscal and monetary policy would enable government to steer the economy safely between the problems of recession and demand-pull inflation.

Economist Milton Friedman (b. 1912) modified Lerner's analogy, giving it a different meaning. He said that the economy does not need a skillful driver of the economic vehicle who is continuously turning the wheel to adjust to the unexpected irregularities of the route. Instead, the economy needs a way to prohibit the monetary passenger in the back seat from occasionally leaning over and giving the steering wheel a jerk that sends the car off the road. According to Friedman, the car will travel down the road just fine unless the Federal Reserve destabilizes it.

Lerner's analogy implies an internally unstable economy that needs steering through discretionary government stabilization policy. Friedman's modification of the analogy implies a generally stable economy that is destabilized by inappropriate monetary policy by the Federal Reserve. For Lerner, stability requires active use of fiscal and monetary policy. For Friedman, macroeconomic stability requires a monetary rule forcing the Federal Reserve to increase the money supply at a set, steady annual rate.

Monetary Rule
Since inappropriate monetary policy is the major source of macroeconomic instability, say monetarists, the enactment of a **monetary rule** would make sense. One such rule would be a requirement that the Fed expand the money supply each year at the same annual rate as the typical growth of the economy's production capacity. That fixed-rate expansion of the money supply would occur year after year regardless of the state of the economy. The Fed's sole monetary role would then be to use its tools (open-market operations, discount-rate changes, and changes in reserve requirements) to ensure

FIGURE 19.4

Rationale for a monetary rule. A monetary rule that required the Fed to increase the money supply at an annual rate linked to the long-run increase in potential GDP would shift aggregate demand rightward, as from AD_1 to AD_2, at the same pace as the shift in long-run aggregate supply, here AS_{LR1} to AS_{LR2}. Thus the economy would experience growth without inflation or deflation.

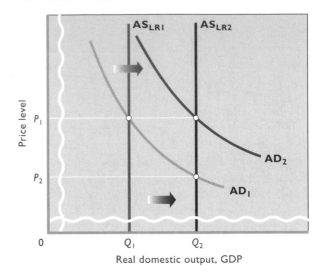

that the nation's money supply grew steadily by, say, 3 to 5 percent a year. According to Milton Friedman,

> Such a rule . . . would eliminate . . . the major cause of instability in the economy—the capricious and unpredictable impact of countercyclical monetary policy. As long as the money supply grows at a constant rate each year, be it 3, 4, or 5 percent, any decline into recession will be temporary. The liquidity provided by a constantly growing money supply will cause aggregate demand to expand. Similarly, if the supply of money does not rise at a more than average rate, any inflationary increase in spending will burn itself out for lack of fuel.[2]

Figure 19.4 illustrates the rationale for a monetary rule. Suppose the economy represented there is operating at its full-employment real output, Q_1. Also suppose the nation's long-run aggregate supply curve shifts rightward, as from AS_{LR1} to AS_{LR2}, each year, signifying the average annual potential increase in real output. As you saw in earlier chapters, such annual increases in "potential GDP" result from added resources, improved resources, and improved technology.

Monetarists argue that a monetary rule would tie increases in the money supply to the typical rightward shift

---

[2]As quoted in Lawrence S. Ritter and William L. Silber, *Money*, 5th ed. (New York: Basic Books, 1984), pp. 141–142.

of long-run aggregate supply. In view of the direct link between changes in the money supply and aggregate demand, this would ensure that the AD curve would shift rightward, as from AD_1 to AD_2, each year. As a result, real GDP would rise from Q_1 to Q_2 and the price level would remain constant at P_1. A monetary rule, then, would promote steady growth of real output along with price stability.

Generally, RET economists also support a monetary rule. They conclude that an easy or tight money policy would alter the rate of inflation but not real output. Suppose, for example, the Fed implements an easy money policy to reduce interest rates, expand investment spending, and boost real GDP. On the basis of past experience and economic knowledge, the public would anticipate that this policy is inflationary and would take protective actions. Workers would press for higher nominal wages; firms would raise their product prices; and lenders would lift their nominal interest rates on loans.

All these responses are designed to prevent inflation from having adverse effects on the real income of workers, businesses, and lenders. But collectively they would immediately raise wage and price levels. So the increase in aggregate demand brought about by the easy money policy would be completely dissipated in higher prices and wages. Real output and employment would not expand.

In this view, the combination of rational expectations and instantaneous market adjustments dooms discretionary monetary policy to ineffectiveness. If discretionary monetary policy produces only inflation (or deflation), say the RET economists, then it makes sense to limit the Fed's discretion and to require that Congress enact a monetary rule consistent with price stability at all times.

In recent decades, the call for a Friedman-type monetary rule has faded. Some economists who tend to favor monetary rules have advocated *inflation targeting*, which we discussed in Chapter 15. The Fed would be required to announce a targeted band of inflation rates, say, 1 to 2 percent, for some future period such as the following 2 years. It would then be expected to use its monetary policy tools to keep inflation rates within that range. If it did not hit the inflation target, it would have to explain why it failed.

Strictly interpreted, inflation targeting would focus the Fed's attention nearly exclusively on controlling inflation and deflation, rather than on counteracting business fluctuations. Proponents of inflation targeting generally believe the economy will have fewer, shorter, and less severe business cycles if the Fed adheres to the rule "Set a known inflation goal and achieve it."

We discuss another modern monetary rule—the so-called Taylor rule—in this chapter's Last Word.

Balanced Budget Monetarists and new classical economists question the effectiveness of fiscal policy. At the extreme, a few of them favor a constitutional amendment requiring that the Federal government balance its budget annually. Others simply suggest that government be "passive" in its fiscal policy, not intentionally creating budget deficits or surpluses. They believe that deficits and surpluses caused by recession or inflationary expansion will eventually correct themselves as the economy self-corrects to its full-employment output.

Monetarists are particularly strong in their opposition to expansionary fiscal policy. They believe that the deficit spending accompanying such a policy has a strong tendency to "crowd out" private investment. Suppose government runs a budget deficit by printing and selling U.S. securities—that is, by borrowing from the public. By engaging in such borrowing, the government is competing with private businesses for funds. The borrowing increases the demand for money, which then raises the interest rate and crowds out a substantial amount of private investment that would otherwise have been profitable. The net effect of a budget deficit on aggregate demand therefore is unpredictable and, at best, modest.

RET economists reject discretionary fiscal policy for the same reason they reject active monetary policy: They don't think it works. Business and labor will immediately adjust their behavior in anticipation of the price-level effects of a change in fiscal policy. The economy will move directly to the anticipated new price level. Like monetary policy, say the RET theorists, fiscal policy can move the economy along its vertical long-run aggregate supply curve. But because its effects on inflation are fully anticipated, fiscal policy cannot alter real GDP even in the short run. The best course of action for government is to balance its budget.

In Defense of Discretionary Stabilization Policy

Mainstream economists oppose both a strict monetary rule and a balanced-budget requirement. They believe that monetary policy and fiscal policy are important tools for achieving and maintaining full employment, price stability, and economic growth.

Discretionary Monetary Policy In supporting discretionary monetary policy, mainstream economists argue that the rationale for the Friedman monetary rule is flawed. While there is indeed a close relationship between the money supply and nominal GDP over long periods, in shorter periods this relationship breaks down. The reason is that the velocity of money has proved to be more variable and unpredictable than monetarists contend. Arguing that velocity is variable both cyclically and over time, mainstream economists contend that a constant annual rate of increase in the money supply might not eliminate fluctuations in aggregate demand. In terms of the equation of exchange, a steady rise of M does not guarantee a steady expansion of aggregate demand because V—the rate at which money is spent—can change.

Look again at Figure 19.4, in which we demonstrated the monetary rule: Expand the money supply annually by a fixed percentage, regardless of the state of the economy. During the period in question, optimistic business expectations might create a boom in investment spending and thus shift the aggregate demand curve to some location to the right of AD_2. (You may want to pencil in a new AD curve, labeling it AD_3.) The price level would then rise above P_1; that is, demand-pull inflation would occur. In this case, the monetary rule will not accomplish its goal of maintaining price stability. Mainstream economists say that the Fed can use a tight money policy to reduce the excessive investment spending and thereby hold the rightward shift of aggregate demand to AD_2, thus avoiding inflation.

Similarly, suppose instead that investment declines because of pessimistic business expectations. Aggregate demand will then increase by some amount less than the increase from AD_1 to AD_2 in Figure 19.4. Again, the monetary rule fails the stability test: The price level sinks below P_1 (deflation occurs). Or if the price level is inflexible downward at P_1, the economy will not achieve its full-employment output (unemployment rises). An easy money policy can help avoid each outcome.

Mainstream economists quip that the trouble with the monetary rule is that it tells the policymaker, "Don't do something, just stand there."

Discretionary Fiscal Policy   Mainstream economists support the use of fiscal policy to keep recessions from deepening or to keep mild inflation from becoming severe inflation. They recognize the possibility of crowding out but do not think it is a serious problem when business borrowing is depressed, as is usually the case in recession. Because politicians can abuse fiscal policy, most economists feel that it should be held in reserve for situations where monetary policy appears to be ineffective or working too slowly.

As indicated earlier, mainstream economists oppose requirements to balance the budget annually. Tax revenues fall sharply during recessions and rise briskly during periods of demand-pull inflation. Therefore, a law or a constitutional amendment mandating an annually balanced budget would require that the government increase tax rates and reduce government spending during recession and reduce tax rates and increase government spending during economic booms. The first set of actions would worsen recession, and the second set would fuel inflation.

Increased Macro Stability

Finally, mainstream economists point out that the U.S. economy has been much more stable in the last half-century than it had been in earlier periods. It is not a coincidence, they say, that use of discretionary fiscal and monetary policies characterized the latter period but not the former. These policies have helped tame the business cycle. Moreover, mainstream economists point out several specific policy successes in the past two decades:

- A tight money policy dropped inflation from 13.5 percent in 1980 to 3.2 percent in 1983.
- An expansionary fiscal policy reduced the unemployment rate from 9.7 percent in 1982 to 5.5 percent in 1988.
- An easy money policy helped the economy recover from the 1990–1991 recession.
- Judicious tightening of monetary policy in the mid-1990s, and then again in the late 1990s, helped the economy remain on a noninflationary, full-employment growth path.
- In late 2001 and 2002, expansionary fiscal and monetary policy helped the economy slowly recover from a series of economic blows, including the collapse of numerous Internet start-up firms, a severe decline in investment spending, the impacts of the terrorist attacks of September 11, 2001, and a precipitous decline in stock values. **(Key Question 13)**

Summary of Alternative Views

In Table 19.1 we summarize the central ideas and policy implications of three macroeconomic theories: mainstream macroeconomics, monetarism, and rational expectations theory. Note that we have broadly defined new classical economics to include both monetarism and the rational expectations theory, since both adhere to the view that the economy tends automatically to achieve equilibrium at its full-employment output. Also note that "mainstream macroeconomics" remains based on Keynesian ideas.

The Taylor Rule: Could a Robot Replace Alan Greenspan?

Macroeconomist John Taylor of Stanford University Calls for a New Monetary Rule That Would Institutionalize Appropriate Fed Policy Responses to Changes in Real Output and Inflation.

In our discussion of rules versus discretion, "rules" were associated with a *passive* monetary policy—one in which the monetary rule required that the Fed expand the money supply at a fixed annual rate regardless of the state of the economy. "Discretion," on the other hand, was associated with an *active* monetary policy in which the Fed changed interest rates in response to actual or anticipated changes in the economy.

Economist John Taylor has put a new twist on the rules-versus-discretion debate by suggesting a hybrid policy rule that dictates the precise active monetary actions the Fed should take when changes in the economy occur. This so-called *Taylor rule* combines traditional monetarism, with its emphasis on a monetary rule, and the more mainstream view that active monetary policy is a useful tool for taming inflation and limiting recession. Unlike the Friedman monetary rule, the Taylor rule holds, for example, that monetary policy should respond to changes in both real GDP and inflation, not simply inflation. The key adjustment instrument is the interest rate, not the money supply.

The Taylor rule has three parts:

- If real GDP rises 1 percent above potential GDP, the Fed should raise the Federal funds rate (the interbank interest rate of overnight loans), relative to the current inflation rate, by .5 percentage points.

- If inflation rises by 1 percentage point above its target of 2 percent, then the Fed should raise the Federal funds rate by .5 percentage points relative to the inflation rate.
- When real GDP is equal to potential GDP and inflation is equal to its target rate of 2 percent, the Federal funds rate should remain at about 4 percent, which would imply a real interest rate of 2 percent.*

Taylor has neither suggested nor implied that a robot, programmed with the Taylor rule, should replace Alan Greenspan, chairman of the Federal Reserve System. The Fed's discretion to override the rule (or "contingency plan for policy") would be retained, but the Fed would have to explain why its policies diverged from the rule. So the rule would remove the "mystery" associated with monetary policy and increase the Fed's accountability. Also, says Taylor, if used consistently, the rule would enable market participants to predict Fed behavior, and this would increase Fed credibility and reduce uncertainty.

Critics of the Taylor rule admit it is more in tune with countercyclical Fed policy than with Friedman's simple monetary rule. But they see no reason to limit the Fed's discretion in adjusting interest rates as it sees fit to achieve stabilization and growth. Monetary policy may be more art than science. The critics also point out that the Fed has done a good job of promoting price stability, full employment, and economic growth over the past two decades. In view of this success, they ask, "Why saddle the Fed with a highly mechanical monetary rule?"

*John Taylor, *Inflation, Unemployment, and Monetary Policy* (Cambridge, Mass.: MIT Press, 1998), pp. 44–47.

These different perspectives have obliged mainstream economists to rethink some of their fundamental principles and to revise many of their positions. Although considerable disagreement remains, mainstream macroeconomists agree with monetarists that "money matters" and that excessive growth of the money supply is the major cause of long-lasting, rapid inflation. They also agree with RET proponents and theorists of coordination failures that expectations matter. If government can create expectations of price stability, full employment, and economic growth, households and firms will tend to act in ways to make them happen. In short, thanks to ongoing challenges to conventional wisdom, macroeconomics continues to evolve.

TABLE 19.1

Summary of Alternative Macroeconomic Views

Issue	Mainstream Macroeconomics (Keynesian based)	New Classical Economics	
		Monetarism	Rational Expectations
View of the private economy	Potentially unstable	Stable in long run at natural rate of unemployment	Stable in long run at natural rate of unemployment
Cause of the observed instability of the private economy	Investment plans unequal to saving plans (changes in AD); AS shocks	Inappropriate monetary policy	Unanticipated AD and AS shocks in the short run
Appropriate macro policies	Active fiscal and monetary policy	Monetary rule	Monetary rule
How changes in the money supply affect the economy	By changing the interest rate, which changes investment and real GDP	By directly changing AD, which changes GDP	No effect on output because price-level changes are anticipated
View of the velocity of money	Unstable	Stable	No consensus
How fiscal policy affects the economy	Changes AD and GDP via the multiplier process	No effect unless money supply changes	No effect because price-level changes are anticipated
View of cost-push inflation	Possible (AS shock)	Impossible in the long run in the absence of excessive money supply growth	Impossible in the long run in the absence of excessive money supply growth

SUMMARY

1. In classical economics the aggregate supply curve is vertical and establishes the level of real output, while the aggregate demand curve tends to be stable and establishes the price level. So the economy is relatively stable.

2. In Keynesian economics the aggregate supply curve is horizontal at less-than-full-employment levels of real output, while the aggregate demand curve is inherently unstable. So the economy is relatively unstable.

3. The mainstream view is that macro instability is caused by the volatility of investment spending, which shifts the aggregate demand curve. If aggregate demand increases too rapidly, demand-pull inflation may occur; if aggregate demand decreases, recession may occur. Occasionally, adverse supply shocks also cause instability.

4. Monetarism focuses on the equation of exchange: $MV = PQ$. Because velocity is thought to be stable, changes in M create changes in nominal GDP ($= PQ$). Monetarists believe that the most significant cause of macroeconomic instability has been inappropriate monetary policy. Rapid increases in M cause inflation; insufficient growth of M causes recession. In this view, a major cause of the Great Depression was inappropriate monetary policy, which allowed the money supply to decline by nearly 40 percent.

5. Real-business-cycle theory views changes in resource availability and technology (real factors), which alter productivity, as the main causes of macroeconomic instability.

In this theory, shifts of the economy's long-run aggregate supply curve change real output. In turn, money demand and money supply change, shifting the aggregate demand curve in the same direction as the initial change in long-run aggregate supply. Real output thus can change without a change in the price level.

6. A coordination failure is said to occur when people lack a way to coordinate their actions in order to achieve a mutually beneficial equilibrium. Depending on people's expectations, the economy can come to rest at either a good equilibrium (noninflationary full-employment output) or a bad equilibrium (less-than-full-employment output or demand-pull inflation). A bad equilibrium is a result of a coordination failure.

7. The rational expectations theory (RET) rests on two assumptions: (1) With sufficient information, people's beliefs about future economic outcomes accurately reflect the likelihood that those outcomes will occur; and (2) markets are highly competitive, and prices and wages are flexible both upward and downward.

8. New classical economists (monetarists and rational expectations theorists) see the economy as automatically correcting itself when disturbed from its full-employment level of real output. In RET, unanticipated changes in aggregate demand change the price level, and in the short run this leads firms to change output. But once the firms realize that all prices

are changing (including nominal wages) as part of general inflation or deflation, they restore their output to the previous level. Anticipated changes in aggregate demand produce only changes in the price level, not changes in real output.

9. Mainstream economists reject the new classical view that all prices and wages are flexible downward. They contend that nominal wages, in particular, are inflexible downward because of several factors, including labor contracts, efficiency wages, and insider-outsider relationships. This means that declines in aggregate demand lower real output, not only wages and prices.

10. Monetarist and RET economists say the Fed should adhere to some form of policy rule, rather than rely exclusively on discretion. The Friedman rule would direct the Fed to increase the money supply at a fixed annual rate equal to

the long-run growth of potential GDP. An alternative approach—inflation targeting—would direct the Fed to establish a targeted range of inflation rates, say, 1 to 2 percent, and focus monetary policy on meeting that goal. They also support maintaining a "neutral" fiscal policy, as opposed to using discretionary fiscal policy to create budget deficits or budget surpluses. A few monetarists and RET economists favor a constitutional amendment requiring that the Federal government balance its budget annually.

11. Mainstream economists oppose strict monetary rules and a balanced-budget requirement, and defend discretionary monetary and fiscal policies. They say that both theory and evidence suggest that such policies are helpful in achieving full employment, price stability, and economic growth.

TERMS AND CONCEPTS

classical view

Keynesian view

monetarism

equation of exchange

velocity

real-business-cycle theory

coordination failures

rational expectations theory

new classical economics

price-level surprises

efficiency wage

insider-outsider theory

monetary rule

STUDY QUESTIONS

1. **Key Question** Use the aggregate demand aggregate supply model to compare the "old" classical and the Keynesian interpretations of (a) the aggregate supply curve and (b) the stability of the aggregate demand curve. Which of these interpretations seems more consistent with the realities of the Great Depression?

2. According to mainstream economists, what is the usual cause of macroeconomic instability? What role does the spending-income multiplier play in creating instability? How might adverse aggregate supply factors cause instability, according to mainstream economists?

3. State and explain the basic equation of monetarism. What is the major cause of macroeconomic instability, as viewed by monetarists?

4. **Key Question** Suppose that the money supply and the nominal GDP for a hypothetical economy are $96 billion and $336 billion, respectively. What is the velocity of money? How will households and businesses react if the central bank reduces the money supply by $20 billion? By how much will nominal GDP have to fall to restore equilibrium, according to the monetarist perspective?

5. Briefly describe the difference between a so-called real business cycle and a more traditional "spending" business cycle.

6. Craig and Kris were walking directly toward each other in a congested store aisle. Craig moved to his left to avoid Kris, and at the same time Kris moved to his right to avoid Craig. They bumped into each other. What concept does this example illustrate? How does this idea relate to macroeconomic instability?

7. **Key Question** Use an AD-AS graph to demonstrate and explain the price-level and real-output outcome of an anticipated decline in aggregate demand, as viewed by RET economists. (Assume that the economy initially is operating at its full-employment level of output.) Then demonstrate and explain on the same graph the outcome as viewed by mainstream economists.

8. What is an efficiency wage? How might payment of an above-market wage reduce shirking by employees and reduce worker turnover? How might efficiency wages contribute to downward wage inflexibility, at least for a time, when aggregate demand declines?

9. How might relationships between so-called insiders and outsiders contribute to downward wage inflexibility?

10. Use the equation of exchange to explain the rationale for a monetary rule. Why will such a rule run into trouble if V unexpectedly falls because of, say, a drop in investment spending by businesses?

11. Answer parts *a* and *b*, below, on the basis of the following information for a hypothetical economy in year 1: money supply = $400 billion; long-term annual growth of potential GDP = 3 percent; velocity = 4. Assume that the banking system initially has no excess reserves and that the reserve requirement is 10 percent. Also assume that velocity is constant and that the economy initially is operating at its full-employment real output.

   a. What is the level of nominal GDP in year 1?

   b. Suppose the Fed adheres to a monetary rule through open-market operations. What amount of U.S. securities will it have to sell to, or buy from, banks or the public between years 1 and 2 to meet its monetary rule?

12. Explain the difference between "active" discretionary fiscal policy advocated by mainstream economists and "passive" fiscal policy advocated by new classical economists. Explain: "The problem with a balanced-budget amendment is that it would, in a sense, require active fiscal policy—but in the wrong direction—as the economy slides into recession."

13. *Key Question* Place "MON," "RET," or "MAIN" beside the statements that most closely reflect monetarist, rational expectations, or mainstream views, respectively:

   a. Anticipated changes in aggregate demand affect only the price level; they have no effect on real output.

   b. Downward wage inflexibility means that declines in aggregate demand can cause long-lasting recession.

   c. Changes in the money supply *M* increase *PQ*; at first only *Q* rises because nominal wages are fixed, but once workers adapt their expectations to new realities, *P* rises and *Q* returns to its former level.

   d. Fiscal and monetary policies smooth out the business cycle.

   e. The Fed should increase the money supply at a fixed annual rate.

14. You have just been elected president of the United States, and the present chairperson of the Federal Reserve Board has resigned. You need to appoint a new person to this position, as well as a person to chair your Council of Economic Advisers. Using Table 19.1 and your knowledge of macroeconomics, identify the views on macro theory and policy you would want your appointees to hold. Remember, the economic health of the entire nation—and your chances for reelection—may depend on your selections.

15. *(Last Word)* Compare and contrast the Taylor rule for monetary policy with the older, simpler monetary rule advocated by Milton Friedman.

16. *Web-Based Question: The equation of exchange—what is the current velocity of money?* In the equation of exchange, $MV = PQ$, the velocity of money, *V*, is found by dividing nominal GDP ($= PQ$) by *M*, the money supply. Calculate the velocity of money for the past 4 years. How stable was *V* during that period? Is *V* increasing or decreasing? Get current-dollar GDP data from the "Gross Domestic Product" section at the Bureau of Economic Analysis website, www.bea.gov/. Find *M*1 money supply data (seasonally adjusted) at the Fed's website, www.federalreserve.gov/, by selecting, in sequence, Economic Research and Data, Statistics: Releases and Historical Data, and Money Stock—Historical Data.

Part VI | Microeconomics of Product Markets

20 | Elasticity of Demand and Supply

Modern market economies rely mainly on the activities of consumers, businesses, and resource suppliers to allocate resources efficiently. Those activities and their outcomes are the subject of *microeconomics*, to which we now turn. We start, in Part 6, by investigating the behaviors and decisions of consumers and businesses.

In this chapter we extend our previous discussion of demand and supply by introducing and applying three ideas: *price elasticity*—the buying and selling responses of consumers and producers to price changes; *cross elasticity*—the buying response of consumers of one product when the price of another product changes; and *income elasticity*—the buying response of consumers when their incomes change.

Price Elasticity of Demand

The law of demand tells us that consumers will buy more of a product when its price declines and less when its price increases. But how much more or less will they buy? The amount varies from product to product and over different price ranges for the same product. And such variations matter. For example, a firm contemplating a price hike will want to know how consumers will respond. If they remain highly loyal and continue to buy, the firm's revenue will rise. But if consumers defect en masse to other sellers or other products, its revenue will tumble.

The responsiveness (or sensitivity) of consumers to a price change is measured by a product's **price elasticity of demand.** For some products—for example, restaurant meals—consumers are highly responsive to price changes. Modest price changes cause very large changes in the quantity purchased. Economists say that the demand for such products is *relatively elastic* or simply *elastic.*

For other products—for example, salt—consumers pay much less attention to price changes. Substantial price changes cause only small changes in the amount purchased. The demand for such products is *relatively inelastic* or simply *inelastic.*

20.1 Price elasticity of demand

The Price-Elasticity Coefficient and Formula

Economists measure the degree of price elasticity or inelasticity of demand with the coefficient E_d, defined as

$$E_d = \frac{\text{percentage change in quantity demanded of product X}}{\text{percentage change in price of product X}}$$

356

The percentage changes in the equation are calculated by dividing the *change* in quantity demanded by the original quantity demanded and by dividing the *change* in price by the original price. So we can restate the formula as

$$E_d = \frac{\dfrac{\text{change in quantity demanded of X}}{\text{original quantity demanded of X}}}{\dfrac{\text{change in price of X}}{\text{original price of X}}}$$

Use of Percentages   Why use percentages rather than absolute amounts in measuring consumer responsiveness? There are two reasons.

First, if we use absolute changes, the choice of units will arbitrarily affect our impression of buyer responsiveness. To illustrate: If the price of a bag of popcorn at the local softball game is reduced from $3 to $2 and consumers increase their purchases from 60 to 100 bags, it will seem that consumers are quite sensitive to price changes and therefore that demand is elastic. After all, a price change of 1 unit has caused a change in the amount demanded of 40 units. But by changing the monetary unit from dollars to pennies (why not?), we find that a price change of 100 units (pennies) causes a quantity change of 40 units. This may falsely lead us to believe that demand is inelastic. We avoid this problem by using percentage changes. This particular price decline is 33 percent whether we measure it in dollars ($1/$3) or pennies (100¢/300¢).

Second, by using percentages, we can correctly compare consumer responsiveness to changes in the prices of different products. It makes little sense to compare the effects on quantity demanded of (1) a $1 increase in the price of a $10,000 used car with (2) a $1 increase in the price of a $1 soft drink. Here the price of the used car has increased by .01 percent while the price of the soft drink is up by 100 percent. We can more sensibly compare the consumer responsiveness to price increases by using some common percentage increase in price for both.

Elimination of Minus Sign   We know from the downsloping demand curve that price and quantity demanded are inversely related. Thus, the price-elasticity coefficient of demand E_d will always be a negative number. As an example, if price declines, then quantity demanded will increase. This means that the numerator in our formula will be positive and the denominator negative, yielding a negative E_d. For an increase in price, the numerator will be negative but the denominator positive, again yielding a negative E_d.

Economists usually ignore the minus sign and simply present the absolute value of the elasticity coefficient to avoid an ambiguity that might otherwise arise. It can be confusing to say that an E_d of -4 is greater than one of -2. This possible confusion is avoided when we say an E_d of 4 reveals greater elasticity than one of 2. So, in what follows, we ignore the minus sign in the coefficient of price elasticity of demand and show only the absolute value. Incidentally, the ambiguity does not arise with supply because price and quantity supplied are positively related.

Interpretations of E_d

We can interpret the coefficient of price elasticity of demand as follows.

Elastic Demand   Demand is **elastic** if a specific percentage change in price results in a larger percentage change in quantity demanded. Then E_d will be greater than 1. Example: Suppose that a 2 percent decline in the price of cut flowers results in a 4 percent increase in quantity demanded. Then demand for cut flowers is elastic and

$$E_d = \frac{.04}{.02} = 2$$

Inelastic Demand   If a specific percentage change in price produces a smaller percentage change in quantity demanded, demand is **inelastic.** Then E_d will be less than 1. Example: Suppose that a 2 percent decline in the price of coffee leads to only a 1 percent increase in quantity demanded. Then demand is inelastic and

$$E_d = \frac{.01}{.02} = .5$$

Unit Elasticity   The case separating elastic and inelastic demands occurs where a percentage change in price and the resulting percentage change in quantity demanded are the same. Example: Suppose that a 2 percent drop in the price of chocolate causes a 2 percent increase in quantity demanded. This special case is termed **unit elasticity** because E_d is exactly 1, or unity. In this example,

$$E_d = \frac{.02}{.02} = 1$$

Extreme Cases   When we say demand is "inelastic," we do not mean that consumers are completely unresponsive to a price change. In that extreme situation, where a price change results in no change whatsoever in the quantity demanded, economists say that demand is **perfectly inelastic.** The price-elasticity coefficient is zero because there is no response to a change in price. Approximate examples include an acute diabetic's demand

FIGURE 20.1

Perfectly inelastic and elastic demands. Demand curve D_1 in (a) represents perfectly inelastic demand ($E_d = 0$). A price increase will result in no change in quantity demanded. Demand curve D_2 in (b) represents perfectly elastic demand. A price increase will cause quantity demanded to decline from an infinite amount to zero ($E_d = \infty$).

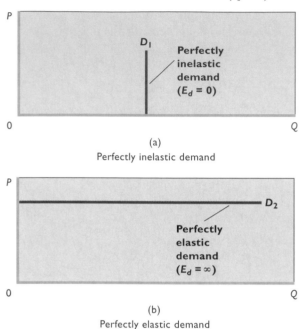

(a)
Perfectly inelastic demand

(b)
Perfectly elastic demand

© Photodisc/Getty Images

CONSIDER THIS . . .

A Bit of a Stretch

The following analogy might help you remember the distinction between "elastic" and "inelastic." Imagine two objects—one an Ace elastic bandage used to wrap injured joints and the other a relatively firm rubber tie-down used for securing items for transport. The Ace bandage stretches a great deal when pulled with a particular force; the rubber tie-down stretches some, but not a lot.

Similar differences occur for the quantity demanded of various products when their prices change. For some products, a price change causes a substantial "stretch" of quantity demanded. When this stretch in percentage terms exceeds the percentage change in price, demand is elastic. For other products, quantity demanded stretches very little in response to the price change. When this stretch in percentage terms is less than the percentage change in price, demand is inelastic.

In summary:

* Elastic demand displays considerable "quantity stretch" (as with the Ace bandage).
* Inelastic demand displays relatively little "quantity stretch" (as with the rubber tie-down).

And through extension:

* Perfectly elastic demand has infinite quantity stretch.
* Perfectly inelastic demand has zero quantity stretch.

for insulin or an addict's demand for heroin. A line parallel to the vertical axis, such as D_1 in Figure 20.1a, shows perfectly inelastic demand graphically.

Conversely, when we say demand is "elastic," we do not mean that consumers are completely responsive to a price change. In that extreme situation, where a small price reduction causes buyers to increase their purchases from zero to all they can obtain, the elasticity coefficient is infinite ($= \infty$) and economists say demand is **perfectly elastic.** A line parallel to the horizontal axis, such as D_2 in Figure 20.1b, shows perfectly elastic demand. You will see in Chapter 23 that such a demand applies to a firm—say, a raspberry grower—that is selling its product in a purely competitive market.

Refinement: Midpoint Formula

Unfortunately, there is an annoying problem that arises in computing the price-elasticity coefficient. To understand this problem and its solution, consider the hypothetical demand data for movie tickets in Table 20.1. To calculate E_d for, say, the $5–$4 price range, which price-quantity combination should we use as a point of reference? We

have two choices—the $5–4-unit combination and the $4–5-unit combination—and our choice will influence the outcome. (In this case, each "unit" represents 1000 tickets: 2 units are 2000, 3 units are 3000, and so on.)

For the $5–4-unit reference point, the price change is from $5 to $4, so the percentage decrease in price is 20 percent; the quantity change is from 4 to 5 units, so the percentage increase in quantity is 25 percent. Substituting in the formula, we get $E_d = 25/20$, or 1.25, indicating that demand is somewhat elastic.

But for the $4–5-unit reference point, the price change is from $4 to $5, making the percentage increase in price 25 percent; the quantity change is from 5 to 4 units, or a 20 percent decline in quantity. The elasticity coefficient is therefore 20/25, or .80, meaning that demand for tickets is slightly inelastic. Which is it? Is the hypothetical demand for movie tickets elastic or inelastic?

A solution to this problem is to use averages of the two ticket prices and two quantities as the reference point. For the same $5–$4 price range, the price reference is

TABLE 20.1

Price Elasticity of Demand for Movie Tickets as Measured by the Elasticity Coefficient and the Total-Revenue Test

(1) Total Quantity of Tickets Demanded per Week, Thousands	(2) Price per Ticket	(3) Elasticity Coefficient (E_d)	(4) Total Revenue, (1) × (2)	(5) Total-Revenue Test
1	$8		$ 8,000	
		5.00		Elastic
2	7		14,000	
		2.60		Elastic
3	6		18,000	
		1.57		Elastic
4	5		20,000	
		1.00		Unit elastic
5	4		20,000	
		0.64		Inelastic
6	3		18,000	
		0.38		Inelastic
7	2		14,000	
		0.20		Inelastic
8	1		8,000	

$4.50, and the quantity reference is 4.5 units. The percentage change in price is now $1/$4.50, or about 22 percent, and the percentage change in quantity is 1/4.50, or also about 22 percent, providing an E_d of 1. This solution estimates elasticity at the midpoint of the relevant price range. We now can state the *midpoint formula* for E_d as

$$E_d = \frac{\text{change in quantity}}{\text{sum of quantities}/2} \div \frac{\text{change in price}}{\text{sum of prices}/2}$$

Substituting data for the $5–$4 price range, we get

$$E_d = \frac{1}{9/2} \div \frac{1}{9/2} = 1$$

This indicates that at the $4.50–4.5-unit midpoint the price elasticity of demand is unity. Here a 1 percent price change will result in a 1 percent change in quantity demanded.

Assignment: Verify the elasticity coefficients for the $1–$2 and $7–$8 ticket price ranges in Table 20.1. The interpretation of E_d for the $1–$2 range is that a 1 percent change in price will change quantity demanded by .20 percent. For the $7–$8 range a 1 percent change in price will change quantity demanded by 5 percent.

Graphical Analysis

We used the hypothetical data for movie tickets in columns 1 and 2, Table 20.1, to plot the demand curve D in Figure 20.2a. The curve illustrates that elasticity typically varies over the different price ranges of the same demand schedule or curve. For all downsloping straight-line and most other demand curves, demand is more price-elastic to-

20.1 Elasticity and revenue

ward the upper left (the $5–$8 price range of D) than toward the lower right (the $4–$1 price range of D).

This is the consequence of the arithmetic properties of the elasticity measure. Specifically, in the upper left segment of the demand curve, the percentage change in quantity is large because the original reference quantity is small. Similarly, the percentage change in price is small in that segment because the original reference price is large. The relatively large percentage change in quantity divided by the relatively small change in price yields a large E_d—an elastic demand.

The reverse holds true for the lower right segment of the demand curve. Here the percentage change in quantity is small because the original reference quantity is large; similarly, the percentage change in price is large because the original reference price is small. The relatively small percentage change in quantity divided by the relatively large percentage change in price results in a small E_d—an inelastic demand.

The demand curve in Figure 20.2a also illustrates that the slope of a demand curve—its flatness or steepness—is not a sound basis for judging elasticity. The catch is that the slope of the curve is computed from *absolute* changes in price and quantity, while elasticity involves *relative* or *percentage* changes in price and quantity. The demand curve in Figure 20.2a is linear, which by definition means that the slope is constant throughout. But we have demonstrated that such a curve is elastic in its high-price ($8–$5) range and inelastic in its low-price ($4–$1) range. **(Key Question 2)**

FIGURE 20.2

The relation between price elasticity of demand for movie tickets and total revenue. Demand curve *D* in (a) is based on Table 20.1 and is marked to show that the hypothetical weekly demand for movie tickets is elastic at higher price ranges and inelastic at lower price ranges. The total-revenue curve TR in (b) is derived from demand curve *D*. When price falls and TR increases, demand is elastic; when price falls and TR is unchanged, demand is unit-elastic; and when price falls and TR declines, demand is inelastic.

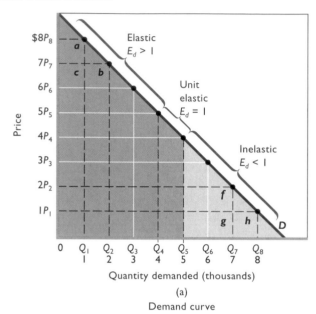

(a)
Demand curve

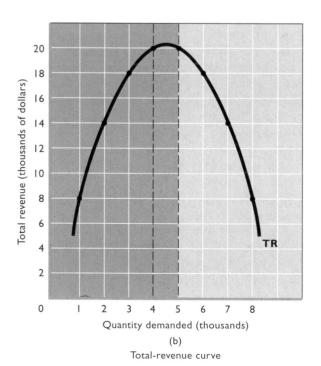

(b)
Total-revenue curve

The Total-Revenue Test

The importance of elasticity for firms relates to the effect of price changes on total revenue and thus on profits (total revenue minus total costs).

Total revenue (TR) is the total amount the seller receives from the sale of a product in a particular time period; it is calculated by multiplying the product price (*P*) by the quantity demanded and sold (*Q*). In equation form:

$$\text{TR} = P \times Q$$

Total revenue and the price elasticity of demand are related. Indeed, perhaps the easiest way to infer whether demand is elastic or inelastic is to employ the **total-revenue test,** which looks at what happens to total revenue when product price changes.

Elastic Demand If demand is elastic, a decrease in price will increase total revenue. Even though a lesser price is received per unit, enough additional units are sold to more than make up for the lower price. For an example, look at demand curve *D* in Figure 20.2a, specifically the elastic-demand region at the upper left. (Disregard Figure 20.2b for the moment.) At point *a* on the curve, price is $8 and quantity demanded is 1 unit, or 1000 tickets. So total revenue, or price times quantity, is $8000 (= $8 × 1000 tickets). Geometrically, total revenue is area $0P_8aQ_1$, found by multiplying one side of the rectangle ($0P_8$) by the other ($0Q_1$).

If the price of movie tickets declines to $7 (point *b*), the quantity demanded becomes 2 units, and total revenue is $14,000 (= $2 × 7000 tickets), or area $0P_7bQ_2$. As a result of the price decline from $8 to $7, total revenue has increased from $8000 to $14,000. This increase has occurred because the loss in revenue from the lower price per unit (area P_7P_8ac) is less than the gain in revenue from the larger quantity demanded (area Q_1cbQ_2) accompanying the lower price. Specifically, the $1 price reduction applies to the original 1000 tickets (Q_1), for a loss of $1000. But the lower price increases quantity demanded by 1000 tickets (Q_1 to Q_2), with a resulting gain in revenue of $7000. Thus, the movie theater achieves a net increase in total revenue of $6000 (= $7000 − $1000).

The analysis is reversible: If demand is elastic, a price increase will reduce total revenue. If we move along from b to a on the demand curve, the gain in total revenue caused by the higher ticket price (area P_7P_8ac) is less than the loss in revenue from the drop in sales (area Q_1cbQ_2). Combining these results tells us that demand is elastic if a price change causes total revenue to change in the opposite direction.

Inelastic Demand   If demand is inelastic, a price decrease will reduce total revenue. The modest increase in ticket sales will not offset the decline in revenue per unit, and the net result is that total revenue will decline. To see this, look at the lower right of demand curve D in Figure 20.2a, specifically the inelastic-demand region. At point f on the curve, price is $2 and quantity demanded is 7000 tickets. So total revenue is $14,000, or area $0P_2fQ_7$. If the price drops to $1 (point h), quantity demanded increases to 8000 tickets. Total revenue becomes $8000, which is clearly less than $14,000; area $0P_1hQ_8$ is smaller than area $0P_2fQ_7$. Total revenue has declined because the loss of revenue from the lower unit price (area P_1P_2fg) is larger than the gain in revenue from the accompanying increase in sales (area Q_7ghQ_8). The $1 decline in price applies to 7000 tickets, with a consequent revenue loss of $7000. The sales increase accompanying that lower price is 1000 tickets, which results in a revenue gain of $1000. The overall result is a net decrease in total revenue of $6000 (= $1000 − $7000).

Again, our analysis is reversible: If demand is inelastic, a price increase will increase total revenue. Together, these results tell us that demand is inelastic if a price change causes total revenue to change in the same direction.

Unit Elasticity   In the special case of unit elasticity, an increase or a decrease in price leaves total revenue unchanged. The loss in revenue from a lower unit price is exactly offset by the gain in revenue from the accompanying increase in sales. Conversely, the gain in revenue from a higher unit price is exactly offset by the revenue loss associated with the accompanying decline in the amount demanded.

In Figure 20.2a we find that at the $5 price, 4000 tickets will be sold, yielding total revenue of $20,000. At $4 a total of 5000 tickets will be sold, again resulting in $20,000 of total revenue. The $1 price reduction causes the loss of $4000 in revenue on the 4000 tickets that could have been sold for $5 each. This is exactly offset by a $4000 revenue gain that results from the sale of 1000 more tickets at the lower $4 price.

Price Elasticity and the Total-Revenue Curve

In Figure 20.2b we graphed the total revenue per week to the theater owner that corresponds to each price-quantity combination indicated along demand curve D in Figure 20.2a. The price–quantity-demanded combination represented by point a on the demand curve yields total revenue of $8000 (= $8 × 1000 tickets). In Figure 20.2b, we graphed this $8000 amount vertically at 1 unit (1000 tickets) demanded. Similarly, the price–quantity-demanded combination represented by point b in the upper panel yields total revenue of $14,000 (= $7 × 2000 tickets). This amount is graphed vertically at 2 units (2000 tickets) demanded in the lower panel. The ultimate result of such graphing is total-revenue curve TR, which first slopes upward, then reaches a maximum, and finally turns downward.

Comparison of curves D and TR sharply focuses the relationship between elasticity and total revenue. Lowering the ticket price in the elastic range of demand—for example, from $8 to $5—increases total revenue. Conversely, increasing the ticket price in that range reduces total revenue. In both cases, price and total revenue change in opposite directions, confirming that demand is elastic.

The $5–$4 price range of demand curve D reflects unit elasticity. When price either decreases from $5 to $4 or increases from $4 to $5, total revenue remains $20,000. In both cases, price has changed and total revenue has remained constant, confirming that demand is unit-elastic when we consider these particular price changes.

In the inelastic range of demand curve D, lowering the price—for example, from $4 to $1—decreases total revenue, as shown in Figure 20.2b. Raising the price boosts total revenue. In both cases, price and total revenue move in the same direction, confirming that demand is inelastic.

So here again is the total-revenue test: Note what happens to total revenue when the price of a product changes. If total revenue changes in the opposite direction from price, demand is elastic. If total revenue changes in the same direction as price, demand is inelastic. If total revenue does not change when price changes, demand is unit-elastic.

TABLE 20.2

Price Elasticity of Demand: A Summary

Absolute Value of Elasticity Coefficient	Demand Is:	Description	Impact on Total Revenue of a:	
			Price Increase	Price Decrease
Greater than 1 ($E_d > 1$)	Elastic or relatively elastic	Quantity demanded changes by a larger percentage than does price	Total revenue decreases	Total revenue increases
Equal to 1 ($E_d = 1$)	Unit or unitary elastic	Quantity demanded changes by the same percentage as does price	Total revenue is unchanged	Total revenue is unchanged
Less than 1 ($E_d < 1$)	Inelastic or relatively inelastic	Quantity demanded changes by a smaller percentage than does price	Total revenue increases	Total revenue decreases

Table 20.2 summarizes the characteristics of price elasticity of demand. You should review it carefully. **(Key Questions 4 and 5)**

Determinants of Price Elasticity of Demand

We cannot say just what will determine the price elasticity of demand in each individual situation. However, the following generalizations are often helpful.

Substitutability   Generally, *the larger the number of substitute goods that are available, the greater the price elasticity of demand.* We will find later that in a purely competitive market, where by definition there are many perfect substitutes for the product of any specific seller, the demand curve seen by that single seller is perfectly elastic. If one competitive seller of carrots or potatoes raises its price, buyers will turn to the readily available perfect substitutes provided by its many rivals. Similarly, we would expect the lowering of world trade barriers to increase the elasticity of demand for most products by making more substitutes available. With unimpeded foreign trade, Mercedes and BMWs become effective substitutes for domestic Cadillacs and Lincolns. At the other extreme, we saw earlier that the diabetic's demand for insulin is highly inelastic because there simply are no close substitutes.

The elasticity of demand for a product depends on how narrowly the product is defined. Demand for Reebok sneakers is more elastic than is the overall demand for shoes. Many other brands are readily substitutable for Reebok sneakers, but there are few, if any, good substitutes for shoes.

Proportion of Income   Other things equal, *the higher the price of a good relative to consumers' incomes, the greater the price elasticity of demand.* A 10 percent increase in the price of a good relative to consumers' incomes, the greater the price elasticity of demand. A 10 percent increase in the price of low-priced pencils or chewing gum amounts to a few more pennies relative to one's income, and quantity demanded will probably decline only slightly. Thus, price elasticity for such low-priced items tends to be low. But a 10 percent increase in the price of relatively high-priced automobiles or housing means additional expenditures of perhaps $2500 or $15,000, respectively. These price increases are significant fractions of the annual incomes and budgets of most families, and quantities demanded will likely diminish significantly. Price elasticity for such items tends to be high.

Luxuries versus Necessities   In general, *the more that a good is considered to be a "luxury" rather than a "necessity," the greater is the price elasticity of demand.* Bread and electricity are generally regarded as necessities; it is difficult to get along without them. A price increase will not significantly reduce the amount of bread consumed or the amount of lighting and power used in a household. (Note the very low price-elasticity coefficient of these goods in Table 20.3.) An extreme case: A person does not decline an operation for acute appendicitis because the physician's fee has just gone up.

On the other hand, travel vacations and jewelry are luxuries, which, by definition, can easily be forgone. If the prices of travel vacations and jewelry rise, a consumer need not buy them and will suffer no great hardship without them.

What about the demand for a common product like salt? It is highly inelastic on three counts: There are few good substitutes available; salt is a negligible item in the family budget; and it is a "necessity" rather than a luxury.

Time   Generally, *product demand is more elastic the longer the time period under consideration.* Consumers often need time to adjust to changes in prices. For example, when the

TABLE 20.3

Selected Price Elasticities of Demand

Product or Service	Coefficient of Price Elasticity of Demand (E_d)	Product or Service	Coefficient of Price Elasticity of Demand (E_d)
Newspapers	.10	Milk	.63
Electricity (household)	.13	Household appliances	.63
Bread	.15	Movies	.87
Major league baseball tickets	.23	Beer	.90
Telephone service	.26	Shoes	.91
Sugar	.30	Motor vehicles	1.14
Medical care	.31	Beef	1.27
Eggs	.32	China, glassware, tableware	1.54
Legal services	.37	Residential land	1.60
Automobile repair	.40	Restaurant meals	2.27
Clothing	.49	Lamb and mutton	2.65
Gasoline	.60	Fresh peas	2.83

Source: Compiled from numerous studies and sources reporting price elasticity of demand.

price of a product rises, it takes time to find and experiment with other products to see if they are acceptable. Consumers may not immediately reduce their purchases very much when the price of beef rises by 10 percent, but in time they may shift to chicken or fish.

Another consideration is product durability. Studies show that "short-run" demand for gasoline is more inelastic ($E_d = .2$) than is "long-run" demand ($E_d = .7$). In the short run, people are "stuck" with their present cars and trucks, but with rising gasoline prices they eventually replace them with smaller, more fuel-efficient vehicles.

Table 20.3 shows estimated price-elasticity coefficients for a number of products. Each reflects some combination of the elasticity determinants just discussed. As an exercise, you should select two or three of them and explain how they relate to the determinants. (**Key Question 6**)

QUICK REVIEW 20.2

- When the price of a good changes, total revenue will change in the opposite direction if demand for the good is price-elastic, in the same direction if demand is price-inelastic, and not at all if demand is unit-elastic.

- Price elasticity of demand is greater (a) the larger the number of substitutes available; (b) the higher the price of a product relative to one's budget; (c) the greater the extent to which the product is a luxury; and (d) the longer the time period involved.

Applications of Price Elasticity of Demand

The concept of price elasticity of demand has great practical significance, as the following examples suggest.

Large Crop Yields   The demand for most farm products is highly inelastic; E_d is perhaps .20 or .25. As a result, increases in the output of farm products arising from a good growing season or from increased productivity tend to depress both the prices of farm products and the total revenues (incomes) of farmers. For farmers as a group, the inelastic demand for their products means that large crop yields may be undesirable. For policymakers it means that achieving the goal of higher total farm income requires that farm output be restricted.

Excise Taxes   The government pays attention to elasticity of demand when it selects goods and services on which to levy excise taxes. If a $1 tax is levied on a product and 10,000 units are sold, tax revenue will be $10,000 (= $1 × 10,000 units sold). If the government raises the tax to $1.50 but the higher price that results reduces sales to 4000 because of elastic demand, tax revenue will decline to $6000 (= $1.50 × 4000 units sold). Because a higher tax on a product with elastic demand will bring in less tax revenue, legislatures tend to seek out products that have inelastic demand—such as liquor, gasoline, and cigarettes—when levying excises. In fact, the Federal government, in its effort to reduce the budget deficit, increased taxes on those very categories of goods in 1991.

But the government sometimes misjudges in such matters. For example, in 1991 Congress also imposed a 10 percent excise tax on yachts costing more than $100,000. Believing the demand for yachts was inelastic, Congress felt that the impact on sales would be small and therefore anticipated that the tax would raise $1.5 billion over 5 years. But demand turned out to be more elastic than the lawmakers thought. Many boat owners reponded by keeping their old boats longer, and some prospective first-time buyers abandoned plans to buy pleasure boats. Sales dropped by nearly 90 percent in Florida, where many prospective buyers avoided the tax by buying their boats in the Bahamas. Government revenue from the tax was further reduced by the 1990–1991 recession, which shifted the demand curve for most durable goods, yachts included, to the left. In 1991 the 10 percent tax raised only $30 million in revenue.

The tax, coupled with the recession, had a devastating effect on boat manufacturers. In the first year of the tax one-third of all U.S. yacht-building companies halted production, and more than 20,000 workers lost their jobs. In 1993 Congress repealed the tax.

Decriminalization of Illegal Drugs

In recent years proposals to legalize drugs have been widely debated. Proponents contend that drugs should be treated like alcohol; they should be made legal for adults and regulated for purity and potency. The current war on drugs, it is argued, has been unsuccessful, and the associated costs—including enlarged police forces, the construction of more prisons, an overburdened court system, and untold human costs—have increased markedly. Legalization would allegedly reduce drug trafficking significantly by taking the profit out of it. Crack cocaine and heroin, for example, are cheap to produce and could be sold at low prices in legal markets. Because the demand of addicts is highly inelastic, the amounts consumed at the lower prices would increase only modestly. Addicts' total expenditures for cocaine and heroin would decline, and so would the street crime that finances those expenditures.

Opponents of legalization say that the overall demand for cocaine and heroin is far more elastic than proponents think. In addition to the inelastic demand of addicts, there is another market segment whose demand is relatively elastic. This segment consists of the occasional users or "dabblers," who use hard drugs when their prices are low but who abstain or substitute, say, alcohol when their prices are high. Thus, the lower prices associated with the legalization of hard drugs would increase consumption by

dabblers. Also, removal of the legal prohibitions against using drugs might make drug use more socially acceptable, increasing the demand for cocaine and heroin.

Many economists predict that the legalization of cocaine and heroin would reduce street prices by up to 60 percent, depending on if and how much they were taxed. According to a recent study, price declines of that size would increase the number of occasional users of heroin by 54 percent and the number of occasional users of cocaine by 33 percent. The total quantity of heroin demanded would rise by an estimated 100 percent, and the quantity of cocaine demanded would rise by 50 percent.[1] Moreover, many existing and first-time dabblers might in time become addicts. The overall result, say the opponents of legalization, would be higher social costs, possibly including an increase in street crime.

Minimum Wage

In 2001 the Federal minimum wage prohibited employers from paying workers less than $5.15 per hour. Critics say that such a minimum wage, if it is above the equilibrium market wage, moves employers upward along their downsloping labor demand curves toward lower quantities of labor demanded and consequently causes unemployment, particularly among teenage workers. On the other hand, workers who remain employed at the minimum wage receive higher incomes than they otherwise would. The amount of income lost by the newly unemployed and the amount of income gained by those who keep their jobs depend on the elasticity of demand for teenage labor. Research suggests that the demand for teenage labor is relatively inelastic. If correct, this means that income gains associated with the minimum wage would exceed income losses. The "unemployment argument" made by critics of the minimum wage would be stronger if the demand for teenage workers were elastic.

Price Elasticity of Supply

The concept of price elasticity also applies to supply. If producers are relatively responsive to price changes, supply is elastic. If they are relatively insensitive to price changes, supply is inelastic.

20.2 Price elasticity of supply

We measure the degree of price elasticity or inelasticity of supply with the coefficient E_s, defined almost like E_d except that we

---

[1]Henry Saffer and Frank Chaloupka, "The Demand for Illegal Drugs," *Economic Inquiry*, July 1999, pp. 401–411.

substitute "percentage change in quantity supplied" for "percentage change in quantity demanded":

$$E_s = \frac{\text{percentage change in quantity supplied of product X}}{\text{percentage change in price of product X}}$$

For reasons explained earlier, the averages, or midpoints, of the before and after quantities supplied and the before and after prices are used as reference points for the percentage changes. Suppose an increase in the price of a good from $4 to $6 increases the quantity supplied from 10 units to 14 units. The percentage change in price would be 2/5, or 40 percent, and the percentage change in quantity would be 4/12, or 33 percent:

$$E_s = \frac{.33}{.40} = .83$$

In this case, supply is inelastic, since the price-elasticity coefficient is less than 1. If E_s is greater than 1, supply is elastic. If it is equal to 1, supply is unit-elastic. Also, E_s is never negative, since price and quantity supplied are directly related. Thus, there are no minus signs to drop, as was necessary with elasticity of demand.

The degree of **price elasticity of supply** depends on how easily—and therefore quickly—producers can shift resources between alternative uses. The easier and more rapidly producers can shift resources between alternative uses, the greater the price elasticity of supply. Take the case of Christmas trees. A firm's response to, say, an increase in the price of trees depends on its ability to shift resources from the production of other products (whose prices we assume remain constant) to the production of trees. And shifting resources takes time: The longer the time, the greater the resource "shiftability." So we can expect a greater response, and therefore greater elasticity of supply, the longer a firm has to adjust to a price change.

In analyzing the impact of time on elasticity, economists distinguish among the immediate market period, the short run, and the long run.

Price Elasticity of Supply: The Market Period

The **market period** is the period that occurs when the time immediately after a change in market price is too short for producers to respond with a change in quantity supplied. Suppose the owner of a small farm brings to market one truckload of tomatoes that is the entire season's output. The supply curve for the tomatoes is perfectly inelastic (vertical); the farmer will sell the truckload whether the price is high or low. Why? Because the farmer can offer only one truckload of tomatoes even if the price of tomatoes is much higher than anticipated. He or she might like to offer more tomatoes, but tomatoes cannot be produced overnight. Another full growing season is needed to respond to a higher-than-expected price by producing more than one truckload. Similarly, because the product is perishable, the farmer cannot withhold it from the market. If the price is lower than anticipated, he or she will still sell the entire truckload.

The farmer's costs of production, incidentally, will not enter into this decision to sell. Though the price of tomatoes may fall far short of production costs, the farmer will nevertheless sell out to avoid a total loss through spoilage. During the market period, our farmer's supply of tomatoes is fixed: Only one truckload is offered no matter how high or low the price.

Figure 20.3a shows the farmer's vertical supply curve during the market period. Supply is perfectly inelastic because the farmer does not have time to respond to a change in demand, say, from D_1 to D_2. The resulting price increase from P_0 to P_m simply determines which buyers get the fixed quantity supplied; it elicits no increase in output.

However, not all supply curves need be perfectly inelastic immediately after a price change. If the product is not perishable and the price rises, producers may choose to increase quantity supplied by drawing down their inventories of unsold, stored goods. This will cause the market supply curve to attain some positive slope. For our tomato farmer, the market period may be a full growing season; for producers of goods that can be inexpensively stored, there may be no market period at all.

Price Elasticity of Supply: The Short Run

The **short run** in microeconomics is a period of time too short to change plant capacity but long enough to use fixed plant more or less intensively. In the short run, our farmer's plant (land and farm machinery) is fixed. But he does have time in the short run to cultivate tomatoes more intensively by applying more labor and more fertilizer and pesticides to the crop. The result is a somewhat greater output in response to a presumed increase in demand; this greater output is reflected in a more elastic supply of tomatoes, as shown by S_s in Figure 20.3b. Note now that the increase in demand from D_1 to D_2 is met by an increase in quantity (from Q_0 to Q_s), so there is a smaller price adjustment (from P_0 to P_s) than would be the case in the market period. The equilibrium price is therefore lower in the short run than in the market period.

FIGURE 20.3

Time and the elasticity of supply. The greater the amount of time producers have to adjust to a change in demand, here from D_1 to D_2, the greater will be their output response. In the immediate market period (a) there is insufficient time to change output, and so supply is perfectly inelastic. In the short run (b) plant capacity is fixed, but changing the intensity of its use can alter output; supply is therefore more elastic. In the long run (c) all desired adjustments, including changes in plant capacity, can be made, and supply becomes still more elastic.

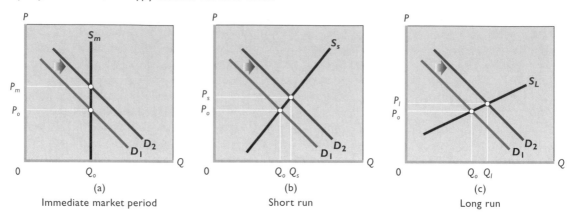

(a)
Immediate market period

(b)
Short run

(c)
Long run

Price Elasticity of Supply: The Long Run

The **long run** in microeconomics is a time period long enough for firms to adjust their plant sizes and for new firms to enter (or existing firms to leave) the industry. In the "tomato industry," for example, our farmer has time to acquire additional land and buy more machinery and equipment. Furthermore, other farmers may, over time, be attracted to tomato farming by the increased demand and higher price. Such adjustments create a larger supply response, as represented by the more elastic supply curve S_L in Figure 20.3c. The outcome is a smaller price rise (P_0 to P_l) and a larger output increase (Q_0 to Q_l) in response to the increase in demand from D_1 to D_2. **(Key Question 10)**

There is no total-revenue test for elasticity of supply. Supply shows a positive or direct relationship between price and amount supplied; the supply curve is upsloping. Regardless of the degree of elasticity or inelasticity, price and total revenue always move together.

Applications of Price Elasticity of Supply

The idea of price elasticity of supply has widespread applicability, as suggested by the following examples.

Antiques and Reproductions

The *Antiques Road Show* is a popular PBS television program in which people bring antiques to a central location for appraisal by experts. Some people are pleased to learn that their old

piece of furniture or funky folk art is worth a large amount, say, $30,000 or more.

The high price of an antique results from strong demand and limited, highly inelastic supply. Because a genuine antique can no longer be reproduced, its quantity supplied either does not rise or rises only slightly as its price goes up. The higher price might prompt the discovery of a few more of the remaining originals and thus add to the quantity available for sale, but this quantity response is usually quite small. So the supply of antiques and other collectibles tends to be inelastic. For one-of-a-kind antiques, the supply is perfectly inelastic.

Factors such as increased population, higher income, and greater enthusiasm for collecting antiques have increased the demand for antiques over time. Because the supply of antiques is limited and inelastic, those increases in demand have greatly boosted the prices of antiques.

Contrast the inelastic supply of original antiques with the elastic supply of modern "made-to-look-old" reproductions. Such faux antiques are quite popular and widely available at furniture stores and knickknack shops. When the demand for reproductions increases, the firms making them simply boost production. Because the supply of reproductions is highly elastic, increased demand raises their prices only slightly.

Volatile Gold Prices

The price of gold is quite volatile, sometimes shooting upward one period and plummeting downward the next. The main sources of these fluctuations are shifts in demand and highly inelastic supply. Gold production is a costly and time-consuming process of exploration, mining, and refining. Moreover, the physical availability of gold is highly limited. For both reasons, increases in gold prices do not elicit substantial increases in quantity supplied. Conversely, gold mining is costly to shut down and existing gold bars are expensive to store. Price decreases therefore do not produce large drops in the quantity of gold supplied. In short, the supply of gold is inelastic.

The demand for gold is partly derived from the demand for its uses, such as for jewelry, dental fillings, and coins. But people also demand gold as a speculative financial investment. They increase their demand for gold when they fear general inflation or domestic or international turmoil that might undermine the value of currency and more traditional investments. They reduce their demand when events settle down. Because of the inelastic supply of gold, even relatively small changes in demand produce relatively large changes in price. (Web-based question 17 at the end of the chapter provides you with a route for finding the current price of gold.)

Cross Elasticity and Income Elasticity of Demand

Price elasticities measure the responsiveness of the quantity of a product demanded or supplied when its price changes. The consumption of a good also is affected by a change in the price of a related product or by a change in income.

Cross Elasticity of Demand

The **cross elasticity of demand** measures how sensitive consumer purchases of one product (say, X) are to a change in the price of some other product (say, Y). We calculate the coefficient of cross elasticity of demand E_{xy} just as we do the coefficient of simple price elasticity, except that we relate the percentage change in the consumption of X to the percentage change in the price of Y:

$$E_{xy} = \frac{\text{percentage change in quantity demanded of product X}}{\text{percentage change in price of product Y}}$$

This cross-elasticity (or cross-price-elasticity) concept allows us to quantify and more fully understand substitute and complementary goods, introduced in Chapter 3.

Substitute Goods If cross elasticity of demand is positive, meaning that sales of X move in the same direction as a change in the price of Y, then X and Y are substitute goods. An example is Kodak film (X) and Fuji film (Y). An increase in the price of Kodak film causes consumers to buy more Fuji film, resulting in a positive cross elasticity. The larger the positive cross-elasticity coefficient, the greater is the substitutability between the two products.

Complementary Goods When cross elasticity is negative, we know that X and Y "go together"; an increase in the price of one decreases the demand for the other. So the two are complementary goods. For example, an increase in the price of cameras will decrease the amount of film purchased. The larger the negative cross-elasticity coefficient, the greater is the complementarity between the two goods.

Independent Goods A zero or near-zero cross elasticity suggests that the two products being considered are unrelated or independent goods. An example is walnuts and film: We would not expect a change in the price of walnuts to have any effect on purchases of film, and vice versa.

Applications The degree of substitutability of products, measured by the cross-elasticity coefficient, is important to businesses and government. For example, suppose that Coca-Cola is considering whether or not to lower the price of its Sprite brand. Not only will it want to know something about the price elasticity of demand for Sprite (will the price cut increase or decrease total revenue?), but it will also be interested in knowing if the increased sales of Sprite will come at the expense of its Coke brand. How sensitive are the sales of one of its products (Coke) to a change in the price of another of its products (Sprite)? By how much will the increased sales of Sprite "cannibalize" the sales of Coke? A low cross elasticity would indicate that Coke and Sprite are weak substitutes for each other and that a lower price for Sprite would have little effect on Coke sales.

Government also implicitly uses the idea of cross elasticity of demand in assessing whether a proposed merger between two large firms will substantially reduce competition and therefore violate the antitrust laws. For example, the cross elasticity between Coke and Pepsi is high, making them strong substitutes for each other. Consequently, the government would likely block a merger between them because the merger would lessen competition. In contrast, the cross elasticity between film and gasoline is low or zero. A merger between Kodak and Shell would have a minimal effect on competition. So government would let that merger happen.

TABLE 20.4

Cross and Income Elasticities of Demand

Value of Coefficient	Description	Type of Good(s)
Cross elasticity:		
Positive ($E_{wz} > 0$)	Quantity demanded of W changes in same direction as change in price of Z	Substitutes
Negative ($E_{xy} < 0$)	Quantity demanded of X changes in opposite direction from change in price of Y	Complements
Income elasticity:		
Positive ($E_i > 0$)	Quantity demanded of the product changes in same direction as change in income	Normal or superior
Negative ($E_i < 0$)	Quantity demanded of the product changes in opposite direction from change in income	Inferior

Income Elasticity of Demand

Income elasticity of demand measures the degree to which consumers respond to a change in their incomes by buying more or less of a particular good. The coefficient of income elasticity of demand E_i is determined with the formula

$$E_i = \frac{\text{percentage change in quantity demanded}}{\text{percentage change in income}}$$

Normal Goods   For most goods, the income-elasticity coefficient E_i is positive, meaning that more of them are demanded as incomes rises. Such goods are called normal or superior goods, which we first described in Chapter 3. But the value of E_i varies greatly among normal goods. For example, income elasticity of demand for automobiles is about +3, while income elasticity for most farm products is only about +.20.

Inferior Goods   A negative income-elasticity coefficient designates an inferior good. Retread tires, cabbage, long-distance bus tickets, used clothing, and muscatel wine are likely candidates. Consumers decrease their purchases of inferior goods as incomes rise.

Insights   Coefficients of income elasticity of demand provide insights into the economy. For example, income elasticity helps explain the expansion and contraction of industries in the United States. On average, total income in the economy has grown 2 to 3 percent annually. As income has expanded, industries producing products for which demand is quite income-elastic have expanded their outputs. Thus automobiles ($E_i = +3$), housing ($E_i = +1.5$), books ($E_i = +1.4$), and restaurant meals ($E_i = +1.4$) have all experienced strong growth of output. Meanwhile, industries producing products for which income elasticity is

low or negative have tended to grow less rapidly or to decline. For example, agriculture ($E_i = +.20$) has grown far more slowly than has the economy's total output. We do not eat twice as much when our income doubles.

As another example, when recessions occur and people's incomes decline, grocery stores fare relatively better than stores selling electronic equipment. People do not substantially cut back on their purchases of food when their incomes fall; income elasticity of demand for food is relatively low. But they do substantially cut back on their purchases of electronic equipment; income elasticity on such equipment is relatively high. **(Key Questions 12 and 13)**

In Table 20.4 we provide a convenient synopsis of the cross-elasticity and income-elasticity concepts.

QUICK REVIEW 20.3

- Price elasticity of supply measures the sensitivity of suppliers to changes in the price of a product. The price-elasticity-of-supply coefficient E_s is the ratio of the percentage change in quantity supplied to the percentage change in price. The elasticity of supply varies directly with the amount of time producers have to respond to the price change.

- The cross-elasticity-of-demand coefficient E_{xy} is computed as the percentage change in the quantity demanded of product X divided by the percentage change in the price of product Y. If the cross-elasticity coefficient is positive, the two products are substitutes; if negative, they are complements.

- The income-elasticity coefficient E_i is computed as the percentage change in quantity demanded divided by the percentage change in income. A positive coefficient indicates a normal or superior good. The coefficient is negative for an inferior good.

Firms and Nonprofit Institutions Often Recognize and Exploit Differences in Price Elasticity of Demand.

All buyers in a highly competitive market pay the same market price for the product, regardless of their individual demand elasticities. If the price rises, Jones may have an elastic demand and greatly reduce her purchases. Green may have a unit-elastic demand and reduce his purchases less than Jones. Lopez may have an inelastic demand and hardly curtail his purchases at all. But all three consumers will pay the single higher price regardless of their demand elasticities.

In later chapters we will find that not all sellers must passively accept a "one-for-all" price. Some firms have "market power" or "pricing power" that allows them to set their product prices in their best interests. For some goods and services, firms may find it advantageous to determine differences in price elasticity of demand and then charge different prices to different buyers.

It is extremely difficult to tailor prices for each customer on the basis of elasticity of demand, but it is relatively easy to observe differences in group elasticities. Consider airline tickets. Business travelers generally have inelastic demand for air travel. Because their time is highly valuable, they do not see slower modes of transportation as realistic substitutes. Also, their employers pay for their tickets as part of their business expenses. In contrast, leisure travelers tend to have elastic demand. They have the option to drive rather than fly or to simply not travel at all. They also pay for their tickets out of their own pockets and thus are more sensitive to price.

Airlines recognize this group difference in elasticity of demand and charge business travelers more than leisure travelers. To accomplish that, they have to dissuade business travelers from buying the less expensive round-trip tickets aimed at leisure travelers. So they place restrictions on the lower-priced tickets. For example, they make the tickets nonrefundable, require at least 2-week advance purchase, and require Saturday-night stays. These restrictions chase off most business travelers who engage in last-minute travel and want to be home for the weekend. As a result, a business traveler often pays hundreds of dollars more for a ticket than a leisure traveler on the same plane.

Discounts for children are another example of pricing based on group differences in price elasticity of demand. For many products, children have more elastic demands than adults because children have low budgets, often financed by their parents. Sellers recognize the elasticity difference and price accordingly. The barber spends as much time cutting a child's hair as an adult's but charges the child much less. A child takes up a full seat at the baseball game but pays a lower price than an adult. A child snowboarder occupies the same space on a chairlift as an adult snowboarder but qualifies for a discounted lift ticket.

Finally, consider pricing by colleges and universities. Prospective students from low-income families generally have more elastic demands for higher education than similar students from high-income families. This makes sense because tuition is a much larger proportion of household income for a low-income student or family than for his or her high-income counterpart. Desiring a diverse student body, colleges charge different *net* prices (= tuition *minus* financial aid) to the two groups on the basis of elasticity of demand. High-income students pay full tuition, unless they receive merit-based scholarships. Low-income students receive considerable financial aid in addition to merit-based scholarships and, in effect, pay a lower *net* price.

It is common for colleges to announce a large tuition increase and immediately cushion the news by emphasizing that they also are increasing financial aid. In effect, the college is increasing the tuition for students who have inelastic demand by the full amount and raising the *net* tuition of those with elastic demand by some lesser amount or not at all. Through this strategy, colleges boost revenue to cover rising costs while maintaining affordability for a wide range of students.

There are a number of other examples of dual or multiple pricing. All relate directly to price elasticity of demand. We will revisit this topic again in Chapter 24 when we discuss what economists call *price discrimination*—charging different prices to different customers for the same product.

SUMMARY

1. Price elasticity of demand measures consumer response to price changes. If consumers are relatively sensitive to price changes, demand is elastic. If they are relatively unresponsive to price changes, demand is inelastic.

2. The price-elasticity coefficient E_d measures the degree of elasticity or inelasticity of demand. The coefficient is found by the formula

$$E_d = \frac{\text{percentage change in quantity demanded of X}}{\text{percentage change in price of X}}$$

Economists use the averages of prices and quantities under consideration as reference points in determining percentage changes in price and quantity. If E_d is greater than 1, demand is elastic. If E_d is less than 1, demand is inelastic. Unit elasticity is the special case in which E_d equals 1.

3. Perfectly inelastic demand is graphed as a line parallel to the vertical axis; perfectly elastic demand is shown by a line above and parallel to the horizontal axis.

4. Elasticity varies at different price ranges on a demand curve, tending to be elastic in the upper left segment and inelastic in the lower right segment. Elasticity cannot be judged by the steepness or flatness of a demand curve.

5. If total revenue changes in the opposite direction from prices, demand is elastic. If price and total revenue change in the same direction, demand is inelastic. Where demand is of unit elasticity, a change in price leaves total revenue unchanged.

6. The number of available substitutes, the size of an item's price relative to one's budget, whether the product is a luxury or a necessity, and length of time to adjust are all determinants of elasticity of demand.

7. The elasticity concept also applies to supply. The coefficient of price elasticity of supply is found by the formula

$$E_s = \frac{\text{percentage change in quantity supplied of X}}{\text{percentage change in price of X}}$$

The averages of the prices and quantities under consideration are used as reference points for computing percentage changes. Elasticity of supply depends on the ease of shifting resources between alternative uses, which varies directly with the time producers have to adjust to a price change.

8. Cross elasticity of demand indicates how sensitive the purchase of one product is to changes in the price of another product. The coefficient of cross elasticity of demand is found by the formula

$$E_{xy} = \frac{\text{percentage change in quantity demanded of X}}{\text{percentage change in price of Y}}$$

Positive cross elasticity of demand identifies substitute goods; negative cross elasticity identifies complementary goods.

9. Income elasticity of demand indicates the responsiveness of consumer purchases to a change in income. The coefficient of income elasticity of demand is found by the formula

$$E_i = \frac{\text{percentage change in quantity demanded of X}}{\text{percentage change in income}}$$

The coefficient is positive for normal goods and negative for inferior goods.

TERMS AND CONCEPTS

price elasticity of demand	perfectly inelastic demand	price elasticity of supply	cross elasticity of demand
elastic demand	perfectly elastic demand	market period	income elasticity of demand
inelastic demand	total revenue (TR)	short run	
unit elasticity	total-revenue test	long run	

STUDY QUESTIONS

1. Explain why the choice between 1, 2, 3, 4, 5, 6, 7, and 8 "units," or 1000, 2000, 3000, 4000, 5000, 6000, 7000, and 8000 movie tickets, makes no difference in determining elasticity in Table 20.1.

2. *Key Question* Graph the accompanying demand data, and then use the midpoint formula for E_d to determine price elasticity of demand for each of the four possible $1 price changes. What can you conclude about the relationship between the slope of a curve and its elasticity? Explain in a nontechnical way why demand is elastic in the northwest segment of the demand curve and inelastic in the southeast segment.

Product Price	Quantity Demanded
$5	1
4	2
3	3
2	4
1	5

3. Draw two linear downsloping demand curves parallel to one another. Demonstrate that for any specific price change demand is more elastic on the curve closer to the origin.

4. *Key Question* Calculate total-revenue data from the demand schedule in question 2. Graph total revenue below your demand curve. Generalize about the relationship between price elasticity and total revenue.

5. *Key Question* How would the following changes in price affect total revenue? That is, would total revenue increase, decline, or remain unchanged?
   a. Price falls and demand is inelastic.
   b. Price rises and demand is elastic.
   c. Price rises and supply is elastic.
   d. Price rises and supply is inelastic.
   e. Price rises and demand is inelastic.
   f. Price falls and demand is elastic.
   g. Price falls and demand is of unit elasticity.

6. *Key Question* What are the major determinants of price elasticity of demand? Use those determinants and your own reasoning in judging whether demand for each of the following products is probably elastic or inelastic: (*a*) bottled water; (*b*) toothpaste; (*c*) Crest toothpaste; (*d*) ketchup; (*e*) diamond bracelets; (*f*) Microsoft Windows operating system.

7. What effect would a rule stating that university students must live in university dormitories have on the price elasticity of demand for dormitory space? What impact might this in turn have on room rates?

8. "If the demand for farm products is highly price-inelastic, an exceptionally large crop may reduce farm incomes." Evaluate and illustrate graphically.

9. You are chairperson of a state tax commission responsible for establishing a program to raise new revenue through excise taxes. Would elasticity of demand be important to you in determining the products on which the taxes should be levied? Explain.

10. *Key Question* In November 1998 Vincent van Gogh's self-portrait sold at auction for $71.5 million. Portray this sale in a demand and supply diagram, and comment on the elasticity of supply. Comedian George Carlin once mused, "If a painting can be forged well enough to fool some experts, why is the original so valuable?" Provide an answer.

11. Because of a legal settlement over state health care claims, in 1999 the U.S. tobacco companies had to raise the average price of a pack of cigarettes from $1.95 to $2.45. The projected decline in cigarette sales was 8 percent. What does this imply for the elasticity of demand for cigarettes? Explain.

12. *Key Question* Suppose the cross elasticity of demand for products A and B is +3.6 and for products C and D is −5.4. What can you conclude about how products A and B are related? Products C and D?

13. *Key Question* The income elasticities of demand for movies, dental services, and clothing have been estimated to be +3.4, +1, and +.5, respectively. Interpret these coefficients. What does it mean if an income elasticity coefficient is negative?

14. Research has found that an increase in the price of beer would reduce the amount of marijuana consumed. Is cross elasticity of demand between the two products positive or negative? Are these products substitutes or complements? What might be the logic behind this relationship?

15. In 2001 the organization representing apple growers in Washington State purchased and destroyed about half the 4 million boxes of apples remaining in cold storage from the 2000 crop. Use supply and demand analysis to show the effect on the equilibrium price and quantity of apples. What must this organization conclude about the elasticity of demand for apples? Explain.

16. *(Last Word)* What is the purpose of charging different groups of customers different prices? Supplement the three broad examples in the Last Word with two additional examples of your own. Hint: Think of price discounts based on group characteristic or time of purchase.

17. *Web-Based Question: The price of gold—today, yesterday, and throughout the year* Visit www.goldprices.com to find the very latest price of gold. Compare that price to the price at the beginning of the day. What was the highest price during the last 12 months? The lowest price? Assume the price fluctuations observed resulted exclusively from changes in demand. Would the observed price changes have been greater or less if the gold supply had been elastic rather than inelastic? Explain.

18. *Web-Based Question: Price, cross, and income elasticities—how do they relate to alcohol and cigarettes?* Go to the National Bureau of Economic Research (NBER) website, www.nber.org, and in the Google search space, type "alcohol." Use the titles and summaries of the papers to answer the following questions relating to elasticity: (*a*) Do the mentally ill have perfectly inelastic demands for cigarettes and alcohol? (*b*) Does alcohol consumption increase in bad times? (*c*) What is the effect of cigarette taxes (and smuggling) on the consumption of alcohol? What does that imply about the cross elasticity of demand between the two? (*d*) Is binge drinking among college students sensitive to the price of alcohol?

21

Consumer Behavior and Utility Maximization

If you were to compare the shopping carts of almost any two consumers, you would observe striking differences. Why does Paula have potatoes, peaches, and Pepsi in her cart while Sam has sugar, saltines, and 7-Up in his? Why didn't Paula also buy pasta and plums? Why didn't Sam have soup and spaghetti on his grocery list?

In this chapter, you will see how individual consumers allocate their incomes among the various goods and services available to them. Given a particular budget, how does a consumer decide what goods and services to buy? Why does the typical consumer buy more of a product when its price falls? As we answer these questions, you will also strengthen your understanding of the law of demand.

A Closer Look at the Law of Demand

The law of demand is based on common sense. A high price discourages consumers from buying; a low price encourages them to buy. In Chapter 3 we mentioned two explanations of the downward-sloping demand curve—income and substitution effects and the law of diminishing marginal utility—that backed up that everyday observation. We now want to say more about these explanations in the context of consumer behavior, the subject of this chapter. A third explanation, based on indifference curves, is more advanced and is summarized in the appendix to this chapter.

Income and Substitution Effects

Our first explanation of the downward slope of the demand curve involves the income and substitution effects.

The Income Effect The **income effect** is the impact that a change in the price of a product has on a consumer's real income and consequently on the quantity demanded of that good. Let's suppose our product is a coffee drink such as a latté or cappuccino. If the price of such drinks declines, the real income or purchasing power of anyone who buys them increases. That is, people are able to buy more with the same money income. The increase in real income will be reflected in increased purchases of many normal goods, including coffee drinks.

For example, with a constant money income of $20 every 2 weeks, you can buy 10 coffee drinks at $2 each. But if the price falls to $1 apiece and you buy 10 of them, you will have $10 per week left over to buy more coffee drinks and other goods. A decline in the price of coffee drinks increases the consumer's real income, enabling him or her to purchase more of them. This is the income effect.

The Substitution Effect   The **substitution effect** is the impact that a change in a product's price has on its relative expensiveness and consequently on the quantity demanded. When the price of a product falls, that product becomes cheaper relative to all other products. Consumers will substitute the cheaper product for other products that are now relatively more expensive. In our example, if the prices of other products remain unchanged and the price of coffee drinks falls, lattés and cappuccinos become more attractive to the buyer. Coffee drinks are a "relatively better buy" at $1 than at $2. The lower price will induce the consumer to substitute coffee drinks for some of the now relatively less attractive items in the budget—perhaps colas, bottled water, or iced tea. Because a lower price increases the relative attractiveness of a product, the consumer buys more of it. This is the substitution effect.

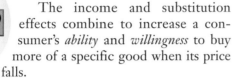

21.1
Income and substitution effects

The income and substitution effects combine to increase a consumer's *ability* and *willingness* to buy more of a specific good when its price falls.

Law of Diminishing Marginal Utility

A second explanation of the downward-sloping demand curve is that, although consumer wants in general may be insatiable, wants for particular commodities can be satisfied. In a specific span of time over which consumers' tastes remain unchanged, consumers can get as much of a particular good or service as they can afford. But the more of that product they obtain, the less they want still more of it.

Consider durable goods, for example. A consumer's desire for an automobile, when he or she has none, may be very strong. But the desire for a second car is less intense; and for a third or fourth, weaker and weaker. Unless they are collectors, even the wealthiest families rarely have more than a half-dozen cars, although their incomes would allow them to purchase a whole fleet of vehicles.

Terminology   Evidence indicates that consumers can fulfill specific wants with succeeding units of a commodity but that each added unit provides less utility than the last unit purchased. Recall that a product has utility if it can satisfy a want: **Utility** is want-satisfying power. The utility of a good or service is the satisfaction or pleasure one gets from consuming it. Three characteristics of this concept must be emphasized:

- "Utility" and "usefulness" are not synonymous. Paintings by Picasso may offer great utility to art connoisseurs but are useless functionally (other than for hiding a crack on a wall).

- Implied in the first characteristic is the fact that utility is subjective. The utility of a specific product may vary widely from person to person. A "jacked-up" truck may have great utility to someone who drives off-road but little utility to someone unable or unwilling to climb into the rig. Eyeglasses have tremendous utility to someone who has poor eyesight but no utility at all to a person with 20-20 vision.

- Because utility is subjective, it is difficult to quantify. But for purposes of illustration we assume that people can measure satisfaction with units called *utils* (units of utility). For example, a particular consumer may get 100 utils of satisfaction from a smoothie, 10 utils of satisfaction from a candy bar, and 1 util of satisfaction from a stick of gum. These imaginary units of satisfaction are convenient for quantifying consumer behavior.

Total Utility and Marginal Utility   We must distinguish carefully between total utility and marginal utility. **Total utility** is the total amount of satisfaction or pleasure a person derives from consuming some specific quantity—for example, 10 units—of a good or service. **Marginal utility** is the *extra* satisfaction a consumer realizes from an additional unit of that product—for example, from the eleventh unit. Alternatively, we can say that marginal utility is the change in total utility that results from the consumption of 1 more unit of a product.

Figure 21.1 (Key Graph) and the accompanying table reveal the relation between total utility and marginal utility. We have drawn the curves from the data in the table. Column 2 shows the total utility associated with each level of consumption of this particular product: tacos. Column 3 shows the marginal utility—the change in total utility—that results from the consumption of each successive taco. Starting at the origin in Figure 21.1a, we observe that each of the first 5 units increases total utility (TU), but by a diminishing amount. Total utility reaches a maximum with the addition of the sixth unit and then declines.

So in Figure 21.1b we find that marginal utility (MU) remains positive but diminishes through the first 5 units (because total utility increases at a declining rate). Marginal utility is zero for the sixth unit (because that unit doesn't change total utility). Marginal utility then becomes negative with the seventh unit and beyond (because total utility is falling).

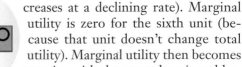

21.2
Diminishing marginal utility

KEY GRAPH

FIGURE 21.1

Total and marginal utility. Curves TU and MU are graphed from the data in the table. (a) As more of a product is consumed, total utility increases at a diminishing rate, reaches a maximum, and then declines. (b) Marginal utility, by definition, reflects the changes in total utility. Thus marginal utility diminishes with increased consumption, becomes zero when total utility is at a maximum, and is negative when total utility declines. As shown by the shaded rectangles in (a) and (b), marginal utility is the change in total utility associated with each additional taco. Or, alternatively, each new level of total utility is found by adding marginal utility to the preceding level of total utility.

(1) Tacos Consumed per Meal	(2) Total Utility, Utils	(3) Marginal Utility, Utils
0	0	
1	10	10
2	18	8
3	24	6
4	28	4
5	30	2
6	30	0
7	28	−2

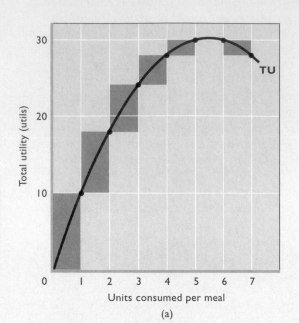

(a)
Total utility

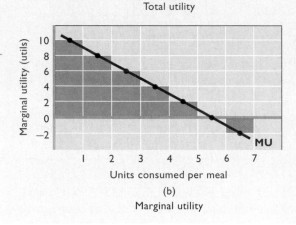

(b)
Marginal utility

QUICK QUIZ 21.1

1. Marginal utility:
   a. is the extra output a firm obtains when it adds another unit of labor.
   b. explains why product supply curves slope upward.
   c. typically rises as successive units of a good are consumed.
   d. is the extra satisfaction from the consumption of 1 more unit of some good or service.

2. Marginal utility in Figure 21.1b is positive, but declining, when total utility in Figure 21.1a is positive and:
   a. rising at an increasing rate.
   b. falling at an increasing rate.
   c. rising at a decreasing rate.
   d. falling at a decreasing rate.

3. When marginal utility is zero in graph (b), total utility in graph (a) is:
   a. also zero.
   b. neither rising nor falling.
   c. negative.
   d. rising, but at a declining rate.

4. Suppose the person represented by these graphs experienced a diminished taste for tacos. As a result the:
   a. TU curve would get steeper.
   b. MU curve would get flatter.
   c. TU and MU curves would shift downward.
   d. MU curve, but not the TU curve, would collapse to the horizontal axis.

Answers: 1. d; 2. c; 3. b; 4. c

374

CONSIDER THIS . . .

David Young-Wolff/PhotoEdit

Vending Machines and Marginal Utility

Newspaper dispensing devices and soft-drink vending machines are similar in their basic operations. Both enable consumers to buy a product by inserting coins. But there is an important difference in the two devices. The newspaper dispenser opens to the full stack of papers and seemingly "trusts" the customer to take only a single copy, whereas the vending machine displays no such "trust," requiring the consumer to buy one can at a time. Why the difference?

The idea of diminishing marginal utility is key to solving this puzzle. Most consumers take only single copies from the newspaper box because the marginal utility of a second newspaper is nearly zero. They could grab a few extra papers and try to sell them on the street, but the revenue obtained would be small relative to their time and effort. So, in selling their product, newspaper publishers rely on "zero marginal utility of the second unit," not on "consumer honesty." Also, newspapers have little "shelf life"; they are obsolete the next day. In contrast, soft-drink sellers do not allow buyers to make a single payment and then take as many cans as they want. If they did, consumers would clean out the machine because the marginal utility of successive cans of soda diminishes slowly and buyers could take extra sodas and consume them later. Soft-drink firms thus vend their products on a pay-per-can basis.

In summary, newspaper publishers and soft-drink firms use alternative vending techniques because of the highly different rates of decline in marginal utility for their products. The newspaper seller uses inexpensive dispensers that open to the full stack of papers. The soft-drink seller uses expensive vending machines that limit the consumer to a single can at a time. Each vending technique is optimal under the particular economic circumstance.

Marginal Utility, Demand, and Elasticity

How does the law of diminishing marginal utility explain why the demand curve for a given product slopes downward? The answer is that if successive units of a good yield smaller and smaller amounts of marginal, or extra, utility, then the consumer will buy additional units of a product only if its price falls. The consumer for whom Figure 21.1 is relevant may buy two tacos at a price of $1 each. But because he or she obtains less marginal utility from additional tacos, the consumer will choose not to buy more at that price. The consumer would rather spend additional dollars on products that provide more (or equal) utility, not less utility. Therefore, additional tacos with less utility are not worth buying unless the price declines. (When marginal utility becomes negative, Taco Bell would have to pay you to consume another taco!) Thus, diminishing marginal utility supports the idea that price must decrease in order for quantity demanded to increase. In other words, consumers behave in ways that make demand curves downward-sloping.

Moreover, the amount by which marginal utility declines as more units of a product are consumed helps us determine that product's price elasticity of demand. Other things equal, if marginal utility falls sharply as successive units of a product are consumed, demand is inelastic. A given decline in price will elicit only a relatively small increase in quantity demanded, since the MU of extra units drops off so rapidly. Conversely, modest declines in marginal utility as consumption increases imply an elastic demand. A particular decline in price will entice consumers to buy considerably more units of the product, since the MU of additional units declines so slowly.

Figure 21.1b and table column 3 tell us that each successive taco yields less extra utility, meaning fewer utils, than the preceding one as the consumer's want for tacos comes closer and closer to fulfillment.[1] The principle that marginal utility declines as the consumer acquires additional units of a given product is known as the **law of diminishing marginal utility. (Key Question 2)**

21.1
Total and marginal utility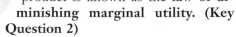

---

[1]Technical footnote: In Figure 21.1b we graphed marginal utility at half-units. For example, we graphed the marginal utility of 4 utils at $3\frac{1}{2}$ units because "4 utils" refers neither to the third nor the fourth unit per se but to the *addition* or *subtraction* of the fourth unit.

QUICK REVIEW 21.1

- The law of demand can be explained in terms of the income effect (a decline in price raises the consumer's purchasing power) and the substitution effect (a product whose price falls is substituted for other products).
- Utility is the benefit or satisfaction a person receives from consuming a good or a service.
- The law of diminishing marginal utility indicates that gains in satisfaction become smaller as successive units of a specific product are consumed.
- Diminishing marginal utility provides another rationale for the law of demand, as well as one for differing price elasticities.

Theory of Consumer Behavior

In addition to explaining the law of demand, the idea of diminishing marginal utility explains how consumers allocate their money incomes among the many goods and services available for purchase.

Consumer Choice and Budget Constraint

The typical consumer's situation has the following dimensions.

- **Rational behavior** The consumer is a rational person, who tries to use his or her money income to derive the greatest amount of satisfaction, or utility, from it. Consumers want to get "the most for their money" or, technically, to maximize their total utility. They engage in **rational behavior.**
- **Preferences** Each consumer has clear-cut preferences for certain of the goods and services that are available in the market. We assume buyers also have a good idea of how much marginal utility they will get from successive units of the various products they might purchase.
- **Budget constraint** At any point in time the consumer has a fixed, limited amount of money income. Since each consumer supplies a finite amount of human and property resources to society, he or she earns only limited income. Thus, every consumer faces what economists call a **budget constraint** (budget limitation), even those who earn millions of dollars a year. Of course, budget constraints are more severe for consumers with average incomes than for those with extraordinarily high incomes.
- **Prices** Goods are scarce relative to the demand for them, so every good carries a price tag. We assume that the price tags are not affected by the amounts of specific goods each person buys. After all, each person's purchase is a minuscule part of total demand. Moreover, since the consumer has a limited number of dollars, he or she can buy only a limited amount of goods. The consumer cannot buy everything wanted. This point drives home the reality of scarcity to each consumer.

So the consumer must compromise; he or she must choose the most satisfying mix of goods and services. Different individuals will choose different mixes.

Utility-Maximizing Rule

Of all the different combinations of goods and services a consumer can obtain within his or her budget, which spe-

cific combination will yield the maximum utility or satisfaction? To maximize satisfaction, *the consumer should allocate his or her money income so that the last dollar spent on each product yields the same amount of extra (marginal) utility.* We call this the **utility-maximizing rule.** When the consumer has "balanced his or her margins" using this rule, there is no incentive to alter the expenditure pattern. The consumer is in equilibrium and would be worse off—total utility would decline—if there were any alteration in the bundle of goods purchased, providing there is no change in taste, income, products, or prices.

Numerical Example

An illustration will help explain the utility-maximizing rule. For simplicity our example is limited to two products, but the analysis applies as well if there are more. Suppose consumer Holly is trying to decide which combination of two products she should purchase with her fixed daily income of $10. These products might be asparagus and breadsticks, apricots and bananas, or apples and broccoli. Let's just call them A and B.

Holly's preferences for products A and B and their prices are the basic data determining the combination that will maximize her satisfaction. Table 21.1 summarizes those data, with column 2a showing the amount of marginal utility she will derive from each successive unit of A and with column 3a showing the same thing for product B.

T A B L E 21.1

The Utility-Maximizing Combination of Products A and B
Obtainable with an Income of $10*

(1) Unit of Product	(2) Product A: Price = $1		(3) Product B: Price = $2	
	(a) Marginal Utility, Utils	(b) Marginal Utility per Dollar (MU/Price)	(a) Marginal Utility, Utils	(b) Marginal Utility per Dollar (MU/Price)
First	10	10	24	12
Second	8	*8*	20	10
Third	7	7	18	9
Fourth	6	6	16	*8*
Fifth	5	5	12	6
Sixth	4	4	6	3
Seventh	3	3	4	2

*It is assumed in this table that the amount of marginal utility received from additional units of each of the two products is independent of the quantity of the other product. For example, the marginal-utility schedule for product A is independent of the amount of B obtained by the consumer.

Both columns reflect the law of diminishing marginal utility, which is assumed to begin with the second unit of each product purchased.

Marginal Utility per Dollar

Before applying the utility-maximizing rule to these data, we must put the marginal-utility information in columns 2a and 3a on a per-dollar-spent basis. A consumer's choices are influenced not only by the extra utility that successive units of product A will yield but also by how many dollars (and therefore how many units of alternative product B) she must give up to obtain those added units of A.

The rational consumer must compare the extra utility from each product with its added cost (that is, its price). Suppose you prefer a pizza whose marginal utility is, say, 36 utils to a movie whose marginal utility is 24 utils. But if the pizza's price is $12 and the movie costs only $6, you would choose the movie rather than the pizza! Why? Because the marginal utility per dollar spent would be 4 utils for the movie (= 24 utils/$6) compared to only 3 utils for the pizza (= 36 utils/$12). You could see two movies for $12 and, assuming that the marginal utility of the second movie is, say, 16 utils, your total utility would be 40 utils. Clearly, 40 units of satisfaction from two movies are superior to 36 utils from the same $12 expenditure on one pizza.

To make the amounts of extra utility derived from differently priced goods comparable, marginal utilities must be put on a per-dollar-spent basis. We do this in columns 2b and 3b by dividing the marginal-utility data of columns 2a and 3a by the prices of A and B—$1 and $2, respectively.

Decision-Making Process

In Table 21.1 we have Holly's preferences on a unit basis and a per-dollar basis as well as the price tags of A and B. With $10 to spend, in what order should Holly allocate her dollars on units of A and B to achieve the highest degree of utility within the $10 limit imposed by her income? And what specific combination of A and B will she have obtained at the time she uses up her $10?

Concentrating on columns 2b and 3b in Table 21.1, we find that Holly should first spend $2 on the first unit of B, because its marginal utility per dollar of 12 utils is higher than A's 10 utils. But now Holly finds herself indifferent about whether she should buy a second unit of B or the first unit of A because the marginal utility per dollar of both is 10 utils. So she buys both of them. Holly now has 1 unit of A and 2 units of B. Also, the last dollar she spent on each good yielded the same marginal utility per dollar (10 utils). But this combination of A and B does not represent the maximum amount of utility that Holly can obtain. It cost her only $5 [= (1 × $1) + (2 × $2)], so she has $5 remaining, which she can spend to achieve a still higher level of total utility.

Examining columns 2b and 3b again, we find that Holly should spend the next $2 on a third unit of B because marginal utility per dollar for the third unit of B is 9 compared with 8 for the second unit of A. But now, with 1 unit of A and 3 units of B, we find she is again indifferent between a second unit of A and a fourth unit of B because both provide 8 utils per dollar. So Holly purchases 1 more unit of each. Now the last dollar spent on each product provides the same marginal utility per dollar (8 utils), and Holly's money income of $10 is exhausted.

The utility-maximizing combination of goods attainable by Holly is 2 units of A and 4 of B. By summing marginal-utility information from columns 2a and 3a, we find that Holly is obtaining 18 (= 10 + 8) utils of satisfaction from the 2 units of A and 78 (= 24 + 20 + 18 + 16) utils of satisfaction from the 4 units of B. Her $10, optimally spent, yields 96 (= 18 + 78) utils of satisfaction.

Table 21.2, which summarizes our step-by-step process for maximizing Holly's utility, merits careful study.

TABLE 21.2

Sequence of Purchases to Achieve Consumer Equilibrium, Given the Data in Table 21.1

Choice Number	Potential Choices	Marginal Utility per Dollar	Purchase Decision	Income Remaining
1	First unit of A	10	First unit of B for $2	$8 = $10 − $2
	First unit of B	12		
2	First unit of A	10	First unit of A for $1	$5 = $8 − $3
	Second unit of B	10	and second unit of B for $2	
3	Second unit of A	8	Third unit of B for $2	$3 = $5 − $2
	Third unit of B	9		
4	Second unit of A	8	Second unit of A for $1	$0 = $3 − $3
	Fourth unit of B	8	and fourth unit of B for $2	

Note that we have implicitly assumed that Holly spends her entire income. She neither borrows nor saves. However, saving can be regarded as a "commodity" that yields utility and can be incorporated into our analysis. In fact, we treat it that way in question 4 at the end of this chapter. **(Key Question 4)**

Inferior Options   Holly can obtain other combinations of A and B with $10, but none will yield as great a total utility as do 2 units of A and 4 of B. As an example, she can obtain 4 units of A and 3 of B for $10. However, this combination yields only 93 utils, clearly inferior to the 96 utils provided by 2 of A and 4 of B. Furthermore, there are other combinations of A and B (such as 4 of A and 5 of B or 1 of A and 2 of B) in which the marginal utility of the last dollar spent is the same for both A and B. But all such combinations either are unobtainable with Holly's limited money income (as 4 of A and 5 of B) or do not exhaust her money income (as 1 of A and 2 of B) and therefore fail to yield the maximum utility attainable.

Problem: Suppose Holly's money income is $14 rather than $10. What now is the utility-maximizing combination of A and B? Are A and B normal or inferior goods?

Algebraic Restatement

Our allocation rule says that a consumer will maximize her satisfaction when she allocates her money income so that the last dollar spent on product A, the last on product B, and so forth, yield equal amounts of additional, or marginal, utility. The marginal utility per dollar spent on A is indicated by the MU of product A divided by the price of A (column 2b in Table 21.1), and the marginal utility per dollar spent on B by the MU of product B divided by the price of B (column 3b in Table 21.1). Our utility-maximizing rule merely requires that these ratios be equal. Algebraically,

$$\frac{\text{MU of product A}}{\text{Price of A}} = \frac{\text{MU of product B}}{\text{Price of B}}$$

And, of course, the consumer must exhaust her available income. Table 21.1 shows us that the combination of 2 units of A and 4 of B fulfills these conditions in that

$$\frac{8 \text{ utils}}{\$1} = \frac{16 \text{ utils}}{\$2}$$

and the consumer's $10 income is spent.

If the equation is not fulfilled, then some reallocation of the consumer's expenditures between A and B (from the low to the high marginal-utility-per-dollar product) will increase the consumer's total utility. For example, if

the consumer spent $10 on 4 of A and 3 of B, we would find that

$$\frac{\text{MU of A: 6 utils}}{\text{Price of A: \$1}} < \frac{\text{MU of B: 18 utils}}{\text{Price of B: \$2}}$$

Here the last dollar spent on A provides only 6 utils of satisfaction, and the last dollar spent on B provides 9 (= 18/$2). So the consumer can increase total satisfaction by purchasing more of B and less of A. As dollars are reallocated from A to B, the marginal utility per dollar of A will increase while the marginal utility per dollar of B will decrease. At some new combination of A and B the two will be equal and consumer equilibrium will be achieved. Here that combination is 2 of A and 4 of B.

Utility Maximization and the Demand Curve

Once you understand the utility-maximizing rule, you can easily see why product price and quantity demanded are inversely related. Recall that the basic determinants of an individual's demand for a specific product are (1) preferences or tastes, (2) money income, and (3) the prices of other goods. The utility data in Table 21.1 reflect our consumer's preferences. We continue to suppose that her money income is $10. And, concentrating on the construction of a simple demand curve for product B, we assume that the price of A, representing "other goods," is still $1.

Deriving the Demand Schedule and Curve

We can derive a single consumer's demand schedule for product B by considering alternative prices at which B might be sold and then determining the quantity the consumer will purchase. We have already determined one such price-quantity combination in the utility-maximizing example: Given tastes, income, and prices of other goods, our rational consumer will purchase 4 units of B at $2.

Now let's assume the price of B falls to $1. The marginal-utility-per-dollar data of column 3b in Table 21.1 will double, because the price of B has been halved; the new data for column 3b are in fact identical to those in column 3a. But the purchase of 2 units of A and 4 of B is no longer an equilibrium combination. By applying the same reasoning we used in the initial utility-maximizing example, we now find that Holly's utility-maximizing combination is 4 units of A and 6 units of B. As summarized

FIGURE 21.2

Deriving an individual demand curve. At a price of $2 for product B, the consumer represented by the data in the table maximizes utility by purchasing 4 units of product B. The decline in the price of product B to $1 upsets the consumer's initial utility-maximizing equilibrium. The consumer restores equilibrium by purchasing 6 rather than 4 units of product B. Thus, a simple price-quantity schedule emerges, which locates two points on a downward-sloping demand curve.

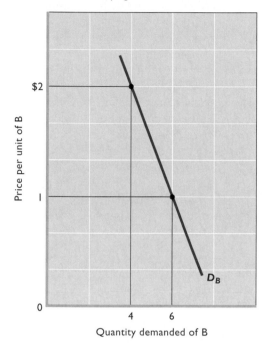

Price per Unit of B	Quantity Demanded
$2	4
1	6

in the table in Figure 21.2, Holly will purchase 6 units of B when the price of B is $1. Using the data in this table, we can sketch the downward-sloping demand curve D_B shown in Figure 21.2. This exercise, then, clearly links the utility-maximizing behavior of a consumer and that person's demand curve for a particular product.

Income and Substitution Effects Revisited

At the beginning of this chapter we mentioned that the law of demand can be understood in terms of the substitution and income effects. Our analysis does not let us sort out these two effects quantitatively. However, we can see

through utility maximization how each is involved in the increased purchase of product B when the price of B falls.

To see the substitution effect, recall that before the price of B declined, Holly was in equilibrium when purchasing 2 units of A and 4 units of B in that $MU_A(8)/P_A(\$1) = MU_B(16)/P_B(\$2)$. But after B's price falls from $2 to $1, we have $MU_A(8)/P_A(\$1) < MU_B(16)/P_B(\$1)$; more simply stated, the last dollar spent on B now yields more utility (16 utils) than does the last dollar spent on A (8 utils). This indicates that a switching of purchases from A to B is needed to restore equilibrium; that is, a *substitution* of now cheaper B for A will occur when the price of B drops.

What about the *income effect?* The assumed decline in the price of B from $2 to $1 increases Holly's real income. Before the price decline, Holly was in equilibrium when buying 2 of A and 4 of B. But at the lower $1 price for B, Holly would have to spend only $6 rather than $10 on the same combination of goods. She has $4 left over to spend on more of A, more of B, or more of both. In short, the price decline of B has caused Holly's *real* income to increase, so she can now obtain larger amounts of A and B with the same $10 of *money* income. The portion of the increase in her purchases of B due to this increase in real income is the income effect. **(Key Question 5)**

Applications and Extensions

Many real-world phenomena can be explained by applying the theory of consumer behavior.

DVDs and DVD Players

Every now and then a new product captures consumers' imagination. One such product is the digital versatile disk

(DVD) and the DVD player. DVDs and DVD players made their debut in 1997 in the United States and about 320,000 DVD players were sold that year. In 2002 annual U.S. sales of DVD players reached 17 million and the cumulative number of players in the United States was 48 million. Nearly $12 billion was spent buying and renting DVD movies in 2002.

This swift ascendancy of the DVD and DVD player has resulted from both price and quality considerations. Although the price of DVDs has declined only slightly, the price of DVD players has nose-dived. Costing $1000 or more when first introduced, most players currently sell for under $200. DVDs and DVD players are *complementary goods*. The lower price for DVD players has expanded their sales and greatly increased the demand for DVD movies.

Moreover, DVDs provide higher-quality audio and video than videocassettes (VCs) and are much easier to store. For playing movies, DVDs and VCs are *substitute goods*. The improved audio and video experience of DVDs—the greater consumer satisfaction—has produced a substitution away from VCs and toward DVDs.

In terms of our analysis, many consumers have concluded that DVDs have higher ratios of marginal utility to price (= MU/*P*) than the ratios for VCs. Those consumers have increased their total utility by purchasing DVDs rather than VCs.

The Diamond-Water Paradox

Early economists such as Adam Smith were puzzled by the fact that some "essential" goods had much lower prices than some "unimportant" goods. Why would water, essential to life, be priced below diamonds, which have much less usefulness? The paradox is resolved when we acknowledge that water is in great supply relative to demand and thus has a very low price per gallon. Diamonds, in contrast, are rare and are costly to mine, cut, and polish. Because their supply is small relative to demand, their price is very high per carat.

Moreover, the marginal utility of the last unit of water consumed is very low. The reason follows from our utility-maximizing rule. Consumers (and producers) respond to the very low price of water by using a great deal of it—for generating electricity, irrigating crops, heating buildings, watering lawns, quenching thirst, and so on. Consumption is expanded until marginal utility, which declines as more water is consumed, equals its low price. On the other hand, relatively few diamonds are purchased because of their prohibitively high price,

meaning that their marginal utility remains high. In equilibrium:

$$\frac{\text{MU of water (low)}}{\text{Price of water (low)}} = \frac{\text{MU of diamonds (high)}}{\text{Price of diamonds (high)}}$$

Although the marginal utility of the last unit of water consumed is low and the marginal utility of the last diamond purchased is high, the total utility of water is very high and the total utility of diamonds quite low. The total utility derived from the consumption of water is large because of the enormous amounts of water consumed. Total utility is the sum of the marginal utilities of all the gallons of water consumed, including the trillions of gallons that have far higher marginal utilities than the last unit consumed. In contrast, the total utility derived from diamonds is low since their high price means that relatively few of them are bought. Thus the water-diamond "paradox" is solved: Water has much more total utility (roughly, usefulness) than diamonds even though the price of diamonds greatly exceeds the price of water. These relative prices relate to marginal utility, not total utility.

21.3
Diamond-water paradox

The Value of Time

The theory of consumer behavior has been generalized to account for the economic value of *time*. Both consumption and production take time. Time is a valuable economic commodity; by using an hour in productive work a person can earn $6, $10, $50, or more, depending on her or his education and skills. By using that hour for leisure or in consumption activities, the individual incurs the opportunity cost of forgone income; she or he sacrifices the $6, $10, or $50 that could have been earned by working.

Imagine a self-employed consumer who is considering buying a round of golf, on the one hand, and a concert, on the other. The market price of the golf game is $30 and that of the concert is $40. But the golf game takes more time than the concert. Suppose this consumer spends 4 hours on the golf course but only 2 hours at the concert. If her time is worth $10 per hour, as evidenced by the $10 wage she can obtain by working, then the "full price" of the golf game is $70 (the $30 market price plus $40 worth of time). Similarly, the full price of the concert is $60 (the $40 market price plus $20 worth of time). We find that, contrary to what market prices alone indicate, the full price of the concert is really less than the full price of the golf game.

If we now assume that the marginal utilities derived from successive golf games and concerts are identical, traditional theory would indicate that our consumer should consume more golf games than concerts because the market price of the former ($30) is lower than that of the latter ($40). But when time is taken into account, the situation is reversed and golf games ($70) are more expensive than concerts ($60). So it is rational for this person to consume more concerts than golf games.

By accounting for time, we can explain certain observable phenomena that traditional theory does not explain. It may be rational for the unskilled worker or retiree whose time has little market value to ride a bus from Chicago to Pittsburgh. But the corporate executive, whose time is very valuable, will find it cheaper to fly, even though bus fare is only a fraction of plane fare. It is sensible for the retiree, living on a modest company pension and a Social Security check, to spend many hours shopping for bargains at the mall or taking long trips in a motor home. It is equally intelligent for the highly paid physician, working 55 hours per week, to buy a new personal computer over the Internet and take short vacations at expensive resorts.

People in other nations often feel affluent Americans are "wasteful" of food and other material goods but "overly economical" in their use of time. Americans who visit developing countries find that time is used casually or "squandered," while material goods are very highly prized and carefully used. These differences are not a paradox or a case of radically different temperaments. The differences are primarily a rational reflection of the fact that the high productivity of labor in an industrially advanced society gives time a high market value, whereas the opposite is true in a low-income, developing country.

Medical Care Purchases

The method of payment for certain goods and services affects their prices at the time we buy them and significantly changes the amount purchased. Let's go back to Table 21.1. Suppose the $1 price for A is its "true" unit value or opportunity cost. But now, for some reason, its price is only, say, $.20. A rational consumer clearly would buy more units at $.20 than at the $1 price.

That is what happens with medical care. People in the United States who have health insurance pay a fixed premium once a month that covers, say, 80 percent of all incurred health care costs. This means that when they actually need health care, its price to them will be only 20 percent of the actual market price. How would you act

in such a situation? When you are ill, you would likely purchase a great deal more medical care than you would if you were confronted with the full price. As a result, financing health care through insurance is an important factor in explaining today's high expenditures on health care and the historical growth of such spending as a percentage of domestic output.

Similar reasoning applies to purchases of buffet meals. If you buy a meal at an all-you-can-eat buffet, you will tend to eat more than if you purchased it item by item. Why not eat that second dessert? Its marginal utility is positive and its "price" is zero!

Cash and Noncash Gifts

Marginal-utility analysis also helps us understand why people generally prefer cash gifts to noncash gifts costing the same amount. The reason is simply that the noncash gifts may not match the recipient's preferences and thus may not add as much as cash to total utility. Thought of differently, consumers know their own preferences better than the gift giver does, and the $100 cash gift provides more choices.

Look back at Table 21.1. Suppose Holly has zero earned income but is given the choice of a $2 cash gift or a noncash gift of 2 units of A. Because 2 units of A can be bought with $2, these two gifts are of equal monetary value. But by spending the $2 cash gift on the first unit of B, Holly could obtain 24 utils. The noncash gift of the first 2 units of A would yield only 18 (= 10 + 8) units of utility. Conclusion: The noncash gift yields less utility to the beneficiary than does the cash gift.

Since giving noncash gifts is common, a considerable value of those gifts is potentially lost because they do not match their recipients' tastes. For example, Uncle Fred may have paid $15 for the Frank Sinatra CD he gave you for Christmas, but you would pay only $7.50 for it. Thus, a $7.50, or 50 percent, value loss is involved. Multiplied by billions spent on gifts each year, the potential loss of value is large.

But some of that loss is avoided by the creative ways individuals handle the problem. For example, newlyweds set up gift registries for their weddings to help match up their wants to the noncash gifts received. Also, people obtain cash refunds or exchanges for gifts, so they can buy goods that provide more utility. And people have even been known to "recycle gifts" by giving them to someone else at a later time. All three actions support the proposition that individuals take actions to maximize their total utility.

Although Economic Analysis Is Not Particularly Relevant in Explaining Some Crimes of Passion and Violence (for Example, Murder and Rape), It Does Provide Interesting Insights on Such Property Crimes as Robbery, Burglary, and Auto Theft.

Through extension, the theory of rational consumer behavior provides some useful insights on criminal behavior. Both the lawful consumer and the criminal try to maximize their total utility (or net benefit). For example, you can remove a textbook from the campus bookstore by either purchasing it or stealing it. If you *buy* the book, your action is legal; you have fully compensated the bookstore for the product. (The bookstore would rather have your money than the book.) If you *steal* the book, you have broken the law. Theft is outlawed because it imposes uncompensated costs on others. In this case, your action reduces the bookstore's revenue and profit and also may impose costs on other buyers who now must pay higher prices for their textbooks.

Why might someone engage in criminal activity such as stealing? Just like the consumer who compares the marginal utility of a good with its price, the potential criminal compares the marginal benefit from his or her action with the "price" or cost. If the marginal benefit (to the criminal) exceeds the price or marginal cost (also to the criminal), the individual undertakes the criminal activity.

Most people, however, do not engage in theft, burglary, or fraud. Why not? The answer is that they perceive the personal price of engaging in these illegal activities to be too high relative to the marginal benefit. That price or marginal cost to the potential criminal has several facets. First, there are the "guilt costs," which for many people are substantial. Such individuals would not steal from others even if there were no penalties for doing so. Their moral sense of right and wrong would entail too great a guilt cost relative to the benefit from the stolen good. Other types of costs include the direct costs of the criminal activity (supplies and tools) and the forgone income from legitimate activities (the opportunity cost to the criminal).

Unfortunately, guilt costs, direct costs, and forgone income are not sufficient to deter some people from stealing. So society imposes other costs, mainly fines and imprisonment, on lawbreakers. The potential of being fined increases the marginal cost to the criminal. The potential of being imprisoned boosts marginal cost still further. Most people highly value their personal freedom and lose considerable legitimate earnings while incarcerated.

Given these types of costs, the potential criminal estimates the marginal cost and benefit of committing the crime. As a simple example, suppose that the direct cost and opportunity cost of stealing an $80 textbook both are zero. The probability of getting caught is 10 percent and, if apprehended, there will be a $500 fine. The potential criminal will estimate the marginal cost of stealing the book as $50 (= $500 fine × .10 chance of apprehension). Someone who has a guilt cost of zero will choose to steal the book because the marginal benefit of $80 will exceed the marginal cost of $50. In contrast, someone having a guilt cost of, say, $40, will not steal the book. The marginal benefit of $80 will not be as great as the marginal cost of $90 (= $50 of penalty cost + $40 of guilt cost).

This perspective on illegal behavior has some interesting implications. For example, other things equal, crime will rise (more of it will be "bought") when its price falls. This explains, for instance, why some people who do not steal from stores under normal circumstances participate in looting stores during riots, when the marginal cost of being apprehended has substantially declined.

Another implication is that society can reduce unlawful behavior by increasing the "price of crime." It can nourish and increase guilt costs through family, educational, and religious efforts. It can increase the direct costs of crime by using more sophisticated security systems (locks, alarms, video surveillance) so that criminals will have to buy and use more sophisticated tools. It can undertake education and training initiatives to enhance the legitimate earnings of people who might otherwise engage in illegal activity. It can increase policing to raise the probability of being apprehended for crime. And it can impose greater penalties for those who are caught and convicted.

SUMMARY

1. The income and substitution effects and the law of diminishing marginal utility help explain why consumers buy more of a product when its price drops and less of the product when its price increases.

2. The income effect implies that a decline in the price of a product increases the consumer's real income and enables the consumer to buy more of that product with a fixed money income. The substitution effect implies that a lower price makes a product relatively more attractive and therefore increases the consumer's willingness to substitute it for other products.

3. The law of diminishing marginal utility states that beyond a certain quantity, additional units of a specific good will yield declining amounts of extra satisfaction to a consumer.

4. We assume that the typical consumer is rational and acts on the basis of well-defined preferences. Because income is limited and goods have prices, the consumer cannot purchase all the goods and services he or she might want. The consumer therefore selects the attainable combination of goods that maximizes his or her utility or satisfaction.

5. A consumer's utility is maximized when income is allocated so that the last dollar spent on each product purchased yields the same amount of extra satisfaction. Algebraically, the utility-maximizing rule is fulfilled when

$$\frac{\text{MU of product A}}{\text{Price of A}} = \frac{\text{MU of product B}}{\text{Price of B}}$$

and the consumer's total income is spent.

6. The utility-maximizing rule and the demand curve are logically consistent. Because marginal utility declines, a lower price is needed to induce the consumer to buy more of a particular product.

TERMS AND CONCEPTS

income effect

substitution effect

utility

total utility

marginal utility

law of diminishing marginal utility

rational behavior

budget constraint

utility-maximizing rule

STUDY QUESTIONS

1. Explain the law of demand through the income and substitution effects, using a price increase as a point of departure. Explain the law of demand in terms of diminishing marginal utility.

2. *Key Question* Complete the following table and answer the questions below:

Units Consumed	Total Utility	Marginal Utility
0	0	
1	10	10
2	—	8
3	25	—
4	30	—
5	—	3
6	34	—

  a. At which rate is total utility increasing: a constant rate, a decreasing rate, or an increasing rate? How do you know?

  b. "A rational consumer will purchase only 1 unit of the product represented by these data, since that amount maximizes marginal utility." Do you agree? Explain why or why not.

  c. "It is possible that a rational consumer will not purchase any units of the product represented by these data." Do you agree? Explain why or why not.

3. Mrs. Wilson buys loaves of bread and quarts of milk each week at prices of $1 and 80 cents, respectively. At present she is buying these products in amounts such that the marginal utilities from the last units purchased of the two products are 80 and 70 utils, respectively. Is she buying the utility-maximizing combination of bread and milk? If not, how should she reallocate her expenditures between the two goods?

4. *Key Question* Columns 1 through 4 in the table on the next page show the marginal utility, measured in utils, that Ricardo would get by purchasing various amounts of products A, B, C, and D. Column 5 shows the marginal utility Ricardo gets from saving. Assume that the prices of A, B, C, and D are $18, $6, $4, and $24, respectively, and that Ricardo has an income of $106.

Column 1		Column 2		Column 3		Column 4		Column 5	
Units of A	MU	Units of B	MU	Units of C	MU	Units of D	MU	Number of Dollars Saved	MU
1	72	1	24	1	15	1	36	1	5
2	54	2	15	2	12	2	30	2	4
3	45	3	12	3	8	3	24	3	3
4	36	4	9	4	7	4	18	4	2
5	27	5	7	5	5	5	13	5	1
6	18	6	5	6	4	6	7	6	$\frac{1}{2}$
7	15	7	2	7	$3\frac{1}{2}$	7	4	7	$\frac{1}{4}$
8	12	8	1	8	3	8	2	8	$\frac{1}{8}$

a. What quantities of A, B, C, and D will Ricardo purchase in maximizing his utility?

b. How many dollars will Ricardo choose to save?

c. Check your answers by substituting them into the algebraic statement of the utility-maximizing rule.

5. **Key Question** You are choosing between two goods, X and Y, and your marginal utility from each is as shown below. If your income is $9 and the prices of X and Y are $2 and $1, respectively, what quantities of each will you purchase to maximize utility? What total utility will you realize? Assume that, other things remaining unchanged, the price of X falls to $1. What quantities of X and Y will you now purchase? Using the two prices and quantities for X, derive a demand schedule (price–quantity-demanded table) for X.

Units of X	MU_x	Units of Y	MU_y
1	10	1	8
2	8	2	7
3	6	3	6
4	4	4	5
5	3	5	4
6	2	6	3

6. How can time be incorporated into the theory of consumer behavior? Explain the following comment: "Want to make millions of dollars? Devise a product that saves Americans lots of time."

7. Explain:

a. Before economic growth, there were too few goods; after growth, there is too little time.

b. It is irrational for an individual to take the time to be completely rational in economic decision making.

c. Telling Santa what you want for Christmas makes sense in terms of utility maximization.

8. In the last decade or so there has been a dramatic expansion of small retail convenience stores (such as Kwik Shops, 7-Elevens, Gas 'N Shops), although their prices are generally much higher than prices in large supermarkets. What explains the success of the convenience stores?

9. Many apartment-complex owners are installing water meters for each apartment and billing the occupants according to the amount of water they use. This is in contrast to the former procedure of having a central meter for the entire complex and dividing up the water expense as part of the rent. Where individual meters have been installed, water usage has declined 10 to 40 percent. Explain that drop, referring to price and marginal utility.

10. **Advanced Analysis** A mathematically "fair bet" is one in which a gambler bets, say, $100, for a 10 percent chance to win $1000 dollars ($100 = .10 × $1000). Assuming diminishing marginal utility of dollars, explain why this is *not* a fair bet in terms of utility. Why is it even a less fair bet when the "house" takes a cut of each dollar bet? So is gambling irrational?

11. **Advanced Analysis** Let $MU_A = z = 10 - x$ and $MU_B = z = 21 - 2y$, where z is marginal utility per dollar measured in utils, x is the amount spent on product A, and y is the amount spent on product B. Assume that the consumer has $10 to spend on A and B—that is, $x + y = 10$. How is the $10 best allocated between A and B? How much utility will the marginal dollar yield?

12. **(Last Word)** In what way is criminal behavior similar to consumer behavior? Why do most people obtain goods via legal behavior as opposed to illegal behavior? What are society's main options for reducing illegal behavior?

13. **Web-Based Question: The ESPN Sportszone—to fee or not to fee** The ESPN Sportszone, at espn.go.com/, is a major sports information site. Most of the content is free, but ESPN has a premium membership (see its "Insider") available for a monthly or an annual fee. Similar, but fee-free, sports content can be found at the websites of CNN/Sports Illustrated,

www.cnnsi.com/, and CBS Sports Line, cbs.sportsline.com/. Since ESPN has put a price tag on some of its sports content, it implies that the utility of a premium membership cannot be found at a no-fee site and is therefore worth the price. Is this the case? Use the utility maximization rule to justify your subscribing or not subscribing to the premium membership.

14. *Web-Based Question: Here is $500—go spend it at Wal-Mart* Assume that you and several classmates each receive a $500 credit voucher (good for today only) from Wal-Mart Online. Go to www.wal-mart.com/ and select $500 worth of merchandise. Use Add to Cart to keep a running total, and use Review Cart to print your final selection. Compare your list with your classmates' lists. What explains the differences? Would you have purchased your items if you had received $500 in cash to be spent whenever and wherever you pleased?

Indifference Curve Analysis

A more advanced explanation of consumer behavior and equilibrium is based on (1) budget lines and (2) so-called indifference curves.

The Budget Line: What Is Attainable

A **budget line** (or, more technically, the *budget constraint*) is a schedule or curve that shows various combinations of two products a consumer can purchase with a specific money income. If the price of product A is $1.50 and the price of product B is $1, a consumer could purchase all the combinations of A and B shown in Table 1 with $12 of money income. At one extreme, the consumer might spend all of his or her income on 8 units of A and have nothing left to spend on B. Or, by giving up 2 units of A and thereby "freeing" $3, the consumer could have 6 units of A and 3 of B. And so on to the other extreme, at which the consumer could buy 12 units of B at $1 each, spending his or her entire money income on B with nothing left to spend on A.

Figure 1 shows the same budget line graphically. Note that the graph is not restricted to whole units of A and B as is the table. Every point on the graph represents a possible combination of A and B, including fractional quantities. The slope of the graphed budget line measures the ratio of the price of B to the price of A; more precisely, the absolute value of the slope is $P_B/P_A = \$1.00/\$1.50 = \frac{2}{3}$. This is the mathematical way of saying that the consumer must forgo 2 units of A (measured on the vertical axis) to

TABLE 1

The Budget Line: Whole-Unit Combinations of A and B Attainable with an Income of $12

Units of A (Price = $1.50)	Units of B (Price = $1)	Total Expenditure
8	0	$12 (= $12 + $0)
6	3	$12 (= $9 + $3)
4	6	$12 (= $6 + $6)
2	9	$12 (= $3 + $9)
0	12	$12 (= $0 + $12)

FIGURE 1

A consumer's budget line. The budget line shows all the combinations of any two products that can be purchased, given the prices of the products and the consumer's money income.

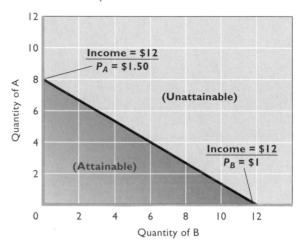

buy 3 units of B (measured on the horizontal axis). In moving down the budget or price line, 2 units of A (at $1.50 each) must be given up to obtain 3 more units of B (at $1 each). This yields a slope of $\frac{2}{3}$.

The budget line has two other significant characteristics:

- **Income changes** The location of the budget line varies with money income. An increase in money income shifts the budget line to the right; a decrease in money income shifts it to the left. To verify this, recalculate Table 1, assuming that money income is (a) $24 and (b) $6, and plot the new budget lines in Figure 1.
- **Price changes** A change in product prices also shifts the budget line. A decline in the prices of both products—the equivalent of an increase in real income—shifts the curve to the right. (You can verify this by recalculating Table 1 and replotting Figure 1 assuming that $P_A = \$.75$ and $P_B = \$.50$.) Conversely, an increase in the prices of A and B shifts the curve to the left. (Assume $P_A = \$3$ and $P_B = \$2$, and rework Table 1 and Figure 1 to substantiate this statement.)

Note what happens if P_B changes while P_A and money income remain constant. In particular, if P_B drops, say, from $1 to $.50, the lower end of the budget line fans outward to the right. Conversely, if P_B increases, say, from $1 to $1.50, the lower end of the line fans inward to the left. In both instances the line remains "anchored" at 8 units on the vertical axis because P_A has not changed.

Indifference Curves: What Is Preferred

Budget lines reflect "objective" market data, specifically income and prices. They reveal combinations of products A and B that can be purchased, given current money income and prices.

Indifference curves, on the other hand, reflect "subjective" information about consumer preferences for A and B. An **indifference curve** shows all the combinations of two products A and B that will yield the same total satisfaction or total utility to a consumer. Table 2 and Figure 2 present a hypothetical indifference curve for products A and B. The consumer's subjective preferences are such that he or she will realize the same total utility from each combination of A and B shown in the table or on the curve. So the consumer will be indifferent (will not care) as to which combination is actually obtained.

Indifference curves have several important characteristics.

21.4 Indifference curves

Indifference Curves Are Downsloping An indifference curve slopes downward because more of one product means less of the other if total utility is to remain unchanged. Suppose the consumer moves from one combination of A and B to another, say, from *j* to *k* in Figure 2. In so doing, the consumer obtains more of product B, increasing his or her total utility. But because total utility is the same everywhere on the curve, the consumer must give up some of the other product, A, to reduce to-

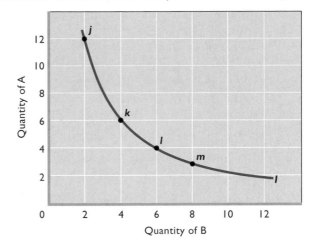

FIGURE 2

A consumer's indifference curve. Every point on indifference curve *I* represents some combination of products A and B, and all those combinations are equally satisfactory to the consumer. That is, each combination of A and B on the curve yields the same total utility.

tal utility by a precisely offsetting amount. Thus "more of B" necessitates "less of A," and the quantities of A and B are inversely related. A curve that reflects inversely related variables is downward-sloping.

Indifference Curves Are Convex to the Origin

Recall from the appendix to Chapter 1 that the slope of a curve at a particular point is measured by drawing a straight line that is tangent to that point and then measuring the "rise over run" of the straight line. If you drew such straight lines for several points on the curve in Figure 2, you would find that their slopes decline (in absolute terms) as you move down the curve. An indifference curve is therefore convex (bowed inward) to the origin of the graph. Its slope diminishes or becomes flatter as we move down the curve from *j* to *k* to *l*, and so on. Technically, the slope of an indifference curve at each point measures the **marginal rate of substitution (MRS)** of the combination of two goods represented by that point. The slope or MRS shows the rate at which the consumer who possesses the combination will substitute one good for the other (say, B for A) to remain equally satisfied. The diminishing slope of the indifference curve means that the willingness to substitute B for A diminishes as more of B is obtained.

The rationale for this convexity—that is, for a diminishing MRS—is that a consumer's subjective willingness to substitute B for A (or A for B) will depend on the

TABLE 2

An Indifference Schedule (Whole Units)

Combination	Units of A	Units of B
j	12	2
k	6	4
l	4	6
m	3	8

amounts of B and A he or she has to begin with. Consider Table 2 and Figure 2 again, beginning at point *j*. Here, in relative terms, the consumer has a substantial amount of A and very little of B. Within this combination, a unit of B is very valuable (that is, its marginal utility is high), while a unit of A is less valuable (its marginal utility is low). The consumer will then be willing to give up a substantial amount of A to get, say, 2 more units of B. In this case, the consumer is willing to forgo 6 units of A to get 2 more units of B; the MRS is $\frac{6}{2}$, or 3, for the *jk* segment of the curve.

But at point *k* the consumer has less A and more B. Here A is somewhat more valuable, and B less valuable, "at the margin." In a move from point *k* to point *l*, the consumer is willing to give up only 2 units of A to get 2 more units of B, so the MRS is only $\frac{2}{2}$, or 1. Having still less of A and more of B at point *l*, the consumer is willing to give up only 1 unit of A in return for 2 more units of B and the MRS falls to $\frac{1}{2}$ between *l* and *m*.[1]

In general, as the amount of B *increases*, the marginal utility of additional units of B *decreases*. Similarly, as the quantity of A *decreases*, its marginal utility *increases*. In Figure 2 we see that in moving down the curve, the consumer will be willing to give up smaller and smaller amounts of A to offset acquiring each additional unit of B. The result is a curve with a diminishing slope, a curve that is convex to the origin. The MRS declines as one moves southeast along the indifference curve.

The Indifference Map

The single indifference curve of Figure 2 reflects some constant (but unspecified) level of total utility or satisfaction. It is possible and useful to sketch a whole series of indifference curves or an **indifference map,** as shown in Figure 3. Each curve reflects a different level of total utility. Specifically, each curve to the right of our original curve (labeled I_3 in Figure 3) reflects combinations of A and B that yield more utility than I_3. Each curve to the left of I_3 reflects less total utility than I_3. As we move out from the origin, each successive indifference curve represents a higher level of utility. To demonstrate this fact, draw a line in a northeasterly direction from the origin; note that its points of intersection with successive curves entail larger amounts of both A and B and therefore higher levels of total utility.

---

[1]MRS declines continuously between *j* and *k*, *k* and *l*, and *l* and *m*. Our numerical values for MRS relate to the curve segments between points and are not the actual values of the MRS at each point. For example, the MRS *at* point *l* is $\frac{2}{3}$.

FIGURE 3

An indifference map. An indifference map is a set of indifference curves. Curves farther from the origin indicate higher levels of total utility. Thus any combination of products A and B represented by a point on I_4 has greater total utility than any combination of A and B represented by a point on I_3, I_2, or I_1.

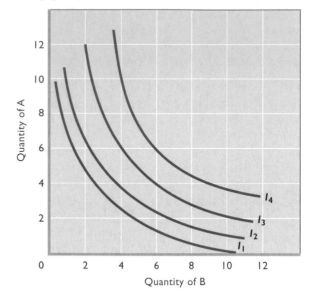

Equilibrium at Tangency

Since the axes in Figures 1 and 3 are identical, we can superimpose a budget line on the consumer's indifference map, as shown in Figure 4. By definition, the budget line indicates all the combinations of A and B that the consumer can attain with his or her money income, given the prices of A and B. Of these attainable combinations, the consumer will prefer the combination that yields the greatest satisfaction or utility. Specifically, the utility-maximizing combination will be the combination lying on the highest attainable indifference curve. It is called the consumer's **equilibrium position.**

In Figure 4 the consumer's equilibrium position is at point *X*, where the budget line is *tangent* to I_3. Why not point *Y*? Because *Y* is on a lower indifference curve, I_2. By moving "down" the budget line—by shifting dollars from purchases of A to purchases of B—the consumer can attain an indifference curve farther from the origin and thereby increase the total utility derived from the same income. Why not point *Z*? For the same reason: Point *Z* is on a lower indifference curve, I_1. By moving "up" the budget line—by reallocating dollars from B to A—the consumer can get on higher indifference curve I_3 and increase total utility.

FIGURE 4

The consumer's equilibrium position. The consumer's equilibrium position is represented by point X, where the black budget line is tangent to indifference curve I_3. The consumer buys 4 units of A at $1.50 per unit and 6 of B at $1 per unit with a $12 money income. Points Z and Y represent attainable combinations of A and B but yield less total utility, as is evidenced by the fact that they are on lower indifference curves. Point W would entail more utility than X, but it requires a greater income than the $12 represented by the budget line.

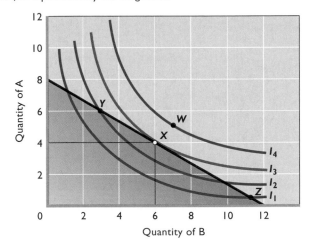

CONSIDER THIS . . .

Indifference Maps and Topographical Maps

The familiar topographical map may help you understand the idea of indifference curves and indifference maps. Each line on a topographical map represents a particular elevation above sea level, say, 4000 feet. Similarly, an indifference curve represents a particular level of total utility. When you move from one point on a specific elevation line to another, the elevation remains the same. So it is with an indifference curve. A move from one position to another on the curve leaves total utility unchanged. Neither elevation lines nor indifference curves can intersect. If they did, the meaning of each line or curve would be violated. An elevation line is "an equal-elevation line"; an indifference curve is "an equal-total-utility curve."

Like the topographical map, an indifference map contains not just one line but a series of lines. That is, the topographical map may have elevation lines representing successively higher elevations of 1000, 2000, 3000, 4000, and 5000 feet. Similarly, the indifference curves on the indifference map represent successively higher levels of total utility. The climber whose goal is to maximize elevation wants to get to the highest possible elevation line; the consumer desiring to maximize total utility wants to get to the highest possible indifference curve.

Finally, both topographical maps and indifference maps show only a few of the many such lines that could be drawn. The topographical map, for example, leaves out the elevation lines for 1001 feet, 1002, 1003, and so on. The indifference map leaves out all the indifference curves that could be drawn between those illustrated.

How about point W on indifference curve I_4? While it is true that W would yield a greater total utility than X, point W is beyond (outside) the budget line and hence is *not* attainable by the consumer. Point X represents the optimal *attainable* combination of products A and B. Note that, according to the definition of tangency, the slope of the highest attainable indifference curve equals the slope of the budget line. Because the slope of the indifference curve reflects the MRS (marginal rate of substitution) and the slope of the budget line is P_B/P_A, the consumer's optimal or equilibrium position is the point where

$$\text{MRS} = \frac{P_B}{P_A}$$

(You may benefit by trying **Appendix Key Question 3** at this time.)

The Measurement of Utility

There is an important difference between the marginal-utility theory of consumer demand and the indifference curve theory. The marginal-utility theory assumes that utility is *numerically* measurable, that is, that the consumer can say how much extra utility he or she derives from each extra unit of A or B. The consumer needs that informa-tion to realize the utility-maximizing (equilibrium) position, as indicated by

$$\frac{\text{Marginal utility of A}}{\text{Price of A}} = \frac{\text{Marginal utility of B}}{\text{Price of B}}$$

The indifference curve approach imposes a less stringent requirement on the consumer. He or she need only specify whether a particular combination of A and B will yield more than, less than, or the same amount of utility as some other combination of A and B will yield. The consumer need only say, for example, that 6 of A and 7 of B will yield more (or less) satisfaction than will 4 of A and 9 of B. Indifference curve theory does not require that the consumer specify *how much* more (or less) satisfaction will be realized.

When we compare the equilibrium situations in the two theories, we find that in the indifference curve analysis the MRS equals P_B/P_A at equilibrium; however, in the marginal-utility approach the ratio of marginal utilities equals P_B/P_A. We therefore deduce that at equilibrium the MRS is equivalent in the marginal-utility approach to the ratio of the marginal utilities of the last purchased units of the two products.[2]

The Derivation of the Demand Curve

We noted earlier that with a fixed price for A, an increase in the price of B will cause the bottom of the budget line to fan inward to the left. We can use that fact to derive a demand curve for product B. In Figure 5a we reproduce the part of Figure 4 that shows our initial consumer equilibrium at point X. The budget line determining this equilibrium position assumes that money income is $12 and that $P_A = \$1.50$ and $P_B = \$1$. Let's see what happens to the equilibrium position when we increase P_B to $1.50 and hold both money income and the price of A constant.

The result is shown in Figure 5a. The budget line fans to the left, yielding a new equilibrium point X' where it is tangent to lower indifference curve I_2. At X' the consumer buys 3 units of B and 5 of A, compared with 4 of A and 6 of B at X. Our interest is in B, and we now have sufficient information to locate two points on the demand curve for product B. We know that at equilibrium point X the price of B is $1 and 6 units are purchased; at equilibrium point X' the price of B is $1.50 and 3 units are purchased.

These data are shown graphically in Figure 5b as points on the consumer's demand curve for B. Note that the horizontal axes of Figure 5a and 5b are identical; both measure the quantity demanded of B. We can therefore drop vertical reference lines from Figure 5a down to the horizontal axis of Figure 5b. On the vertical axis of Figure 5b we locate the two chosen prices of B. Knowing that these prices yield the relevant quantities demanded, we locate two points on the demand curve for B. By simple manipulation of the price of B in an indifference curve–budget line context, we have obtained a downward-sloping demand curve for B. We have thus again derived the law of demand assuming "other things equal," since only the price of B was changed (the price of A and the consumer's money income and tastes remained constant). But, in this

[2]Technical footnote: If we begin with the utility-maximizing rule, $MU_A/P_A = MU_B/P_B$, and then multiply through by P_B and divide through by MU_A, we obtain $P_B/P_A = MU_B/MU_A$. In indifference curve analysis we know that at the equilibrium position MRS = P_B/P_A. Hence, at equilibrium, MRS also equals MU_B/MU_A.

FIGURE 5

Deriving the demand curve. (a) When the price of product B is increased from $1 to $1.50, the equilibrium position moves from X to X', decreasing the quantity of product B demanded from 6 to 3 units. (b) The demand curve for product B is determined by plotting the $1–6-unit and the $1.50–3-unit price-quantity combinations for product B.

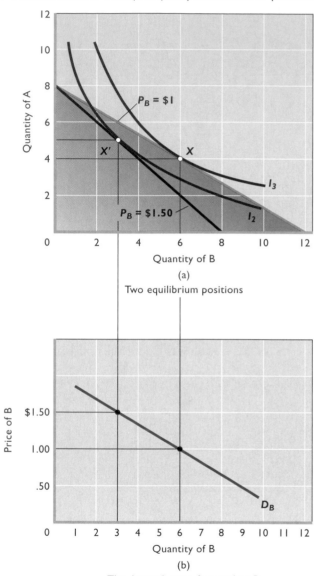

case, we have derived the demand curve without resorting to the questionable assumption that consumers can measure utility in units called "utils." In this indifference curve approach, consumers simply compare combinations of products A and B and determine which combination they prefer, given their incomes and the prices of the two products.

APPENDIX SUMMARY

1. The indifference curve approach to consumer behavior is based on the consumer's budget line and indifference curves.

2. The budget line shows all combinations of two products that the consumer can purchase, given product prices and his or her money income.

3. A change in either product prices or money income moves the budget line.

4. An indifference curve shows all combinations of two products that will yield the same total utility to a consumer. Indifference curves are downward-sloping and convex to the origin.

5. An indifference map consists of a number of indifference curves; the farther from the origin, the higher the total utility associated with a curve.

6. The consumer is in equilibrium (utility is maximized) at the point on the budget line that lies on the highest attainable indifference curve. At that point the budget line and indifference curve are tangent.

7. Changing the price of one product shifts the budget line and determines a new equilibrium point. A downsloping demand curve can be determined by plotting the price-quantity combinations associated with two or more equilibrium points.

APPENDIX TERMS AND CONCEPTS

budget line

indifference curve

marginal rate of substitution (MRS)

indifference map

equilibrium position

APPENDIX STUDY QUESTIONS

1. What information is embodied in a budget line? What shifts occur in the budget line when money income (*a*) increases and (*b*) decreases? What shifts occur in the budget line when the price of the product shown on the vertical axis (*a*) increases and (*b*) decreases?

2. What information is contained in an indifference curve? Why are such curves (*a*) downward-sloping and (*b*) convex to the origin? Why does total utility increase as the consumer moves to indifference curves farther from the origin? Why can't indifference curves intersect?

3. *Appendix Key Question* Using Figure 4, explain why the point of tangency of the budget line with an indifference curve is the consumer's equilibrium position. Explain why any point where the budget line intersects an indifference curve is not equilibrium. Explain: "The consumer is in equilibrium where MRS = P_B/P_A."

4. Assume that the data in the accompanying table give an indifference curve for Mr. Chen. Graph this curve, putting A on the vertical axis and B on the horizontal axis. Assuming

that the prices of A and B are $1.50 and $1, respectively, and that Mr. Chen has $24 to spend, add his budget line to your graph. What combination of A and B will Mr. Chen purchase? Does your answer meet the MRS = P_B/P_A rule for equilibrium?

Units of A	Units of B
16	6
12	8
8	12
4	24

5. Explain graphically how indifference analysis can be used to derive a demand curve.

6. *Advanced Analysis* Demonstrate mathematically that the equilibrium condition MRS = P_B/P_A is the equivalent of the utility-maximizing rule $MU_A/P_A = MU_B/P_B$.

22 | The Costs of Production

Our attention now turns from the behavior of consumers to the behavior of producers. In market economies, a wide variety of businesses produce an even wider variety of goods and services. Each of those businesses requires economic resources in order to produce its products. In obtaining and using resources, a firm makes monetary payments to resource owners (for example, workers) and incurs opportunity costs when using resources it already owns (for example, entrepreneurial talent). Those payments and opportunity costs together make up the firm's *costs of production,* which we discuss in this chapter.

Then, in the next several chapters, we bring product demand, product prices, and revenue back into the analysis and explain how firms compare revenues and costs in determining how much to produce. Our ultimate purpose is to show how those comparisons relate to economic efficiency.

Economic Costs

Costs exist because resources are scarce, productive, and have alternative uses. When society uses a combination of resources to produce a particular product, it forgoes all alternative opportunities to use those resources for other purposes. The measure of the **economic cost,** or **opportunity cost,** of any resource used to produce a good is the value or worth the resource would have in its best alternative use.

We stressed this view of costs in our analysis of production possibilities in Chapter 2, where we found that the opportunity cost of producing more pizzas is the industrial robots that must be forgone. Similarly, the opportunity cost of the steel used in constructing office buildings is the value it would have in manufacturing automobiles or refrigerators. The paper used for printing economics textbooks is not available for printing encyclopedias or romance novels. And if an assembly-line worker is capable of assembling either personal computers or washing machines, then the cost to society of employing that worker in a computer plant is the contribution he or she would otherwise have made in producing washing machines.

Explicit and Implicit Costs

Now let's consider costs from the firm's viewpoint. Keeping opportunity costs in mind, we can say that *economic costs are the payments a firm must make, or the* incomes it must provide, to attract the resources it needs away from alternative production opportunities. Those payments to resource suppliers are explicit (revealed and expressed) or implicit (present but not obvious). So in producing products firms incur *explicit costs* and *implicit costs.*

- A firm's **explicit costs** are the monetary payments (or cash expenditures) it makes to those who supply labor services, materials, fuel, transportation services, and the like. Such money payments are for the use of resources owned by others.
- A firm's **implicit costs** are the opportunity costs of using its self-owned, self-employed resources. To the firm, implicit costs are the money payments that self-employed resources could have earned in their best alternative use.

Example: Suppose you are earning $22,000 a year as a sales representative for a T-shirt manufacturer. At some point you decide to open a retail store of your own to sell T-shirts. You invest $20,000 of savings that have been earning you $1000 per year. And you decide that your new firm will occupy a small store that you own and have been renting out for $5000 per year. You hire one clerk to help you in the store, paying her $18,000 annually.

A year after you open the store, you total up your accounts and find the following:

Total sales revenue		$120,000
Cost of T-shirts	$40,000	
Clerk's salary	18,000	
Utilities	5,000	
Total (explicit) costs		63,000
Accounting profit		57,000

Looks good. But unfortunately your accounting profit of $57,000 ignores your implicit costs and thus overstates the economic success of your venture. By providing your own financial capital, building, and labor, you incur implicit costs (forgone incomes) of $1000 of interest, $5000 of rent, and $22,000 of wages. If your entrepreneurial talent is worth, say, $5000 annually in other business endeavors of similar scope, you have also ignored that implicit cost. So:

Accounting profit		$57,000
Forgone interest	$ 1,000	
Forgone rent	5,000	
Forgone wages	22,000	
Forgone entrepreneurial income	5,000	
Total implicit costs		33,000
Economic profit		24,000

Normal Profit as a Cost

The $5000 implicit cost of your entrepreneurial talent in the above example is a **normal profit.** As is true of the forgone rent and forgone wages, the payment you could otherwise receive for performing entrepreneurial functions is indeed an implicit cost. If you did not realize at least this minimum, or normal, payment for your effort, you could withdraw from this line of business and shift to a more attractive endeavor. So a normal profit is a cost of doing business.

The economist includes as costs of production all the costs— explicit and implicit, including a normal profit—required to attract and retain resources in a specific line of production. For economists, a firm's economic costs are the opportunity costs of the resources used, whether those resources are owned by others or by the firm. In our example, economic costs are $96,000 (= $63,000 of explicit costs + $33,000 of implicit costs).

Economic Profit (or Pure Profit)

Obviously, then, economists use the term "profit" differently from the way accountants use it. To the accountant, profit is the firm's total revenue less its explicit costs (or accounting costs). To the economist, **economic profit** is total revenue less economic costs (explicit and implicit costs, the latter including a normal profit to the entrepreneur). So when an economist says a certain firm is earning only enough revenue to cover its costs, this means it is meeting all explicit and implicit costs and the entrepreneur is receiving a payment just large enough to retain his or her talents in the present line of production.

If a firm's total revenue exceeds all its economic costs (explicit + implicit), any residual goes to the entrepreneur. That residual is called an *economic*, or *pure*, *profit*. In short:

$$\frac{\text{Economic}}{\text{profit}} = \frac{\text{total}}{\text{revenue}} - \frac{\text{economic}}{\text{cost}}$$

In our example, economic profit is $24,000, found by subtracting the $96,000 of economic cost from the $120,000 of revenue. An *economic* profit is not a cost, because it is a return in excess of the normal profit that is required to retain the entrepreneur in this particular line of production. Even if the economic profit is zero, the entrepreneur is still covering all explicit and implicit costs, including a normal profit. In our example, as long as accounting profit is $33,000 or more (so economic profit is zero or more), you will be earning a $5000 normal profit and will therefore continue to operate your T-shirt store.

FIGURE 22.1

Economic profit versus accounting profit.   Economic profit is equal to total revenue less economic costs. Economic costs are the sum of explicit and implicit costs and include a normal profit to the entrepreneur. Accounting profit is equal to total revenue less accounting (explicit) costs.

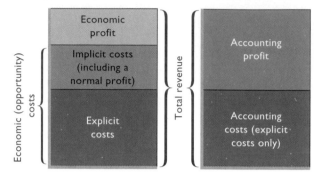

Figure 22.1 shows the relationship among the various cost and profit concepts that we have just discussed. To test yourself, you might want to enter cost data from our example in the appropriate blocks. **(Key Question 2)**

Short Run and Long Run

When the demand for a firm's product changes, the firm's profitability may depend on how quickly it can adjust the amounts of the various resources it employs. It can easily and quickly adjust the quantities employed of many resources such as hourly labor, raw materials, fuel, and power. It needs much more time, however, to adjust its *plant capacity*—the size of the factory building, the amount of machinery and equipment, and other capital resources. In some heavy industries such as aircraft manufacturing, a firm may need several years to alter plant capacity. Because of these differences in adjustment time, economists find it useful to distinguish between two conceptual periods: the short run and the long run. We will discover that costs differ in these two time periods.

Short Run: Fixed Plant   The **short run** is a period too brief for a firm to alter its plant capacity, yet long enough to permit a change in the degree to which the fixed plant is used. The firm's plant capacity is fixed in the short run. However, the firm can vary its output by applying larger or smaller amounts of labor, materials, and other resources to that plant. It can use its existing plant capacity more or less intensively in the short run.

Long Run: Variable Plant   From the viewpoint of an existing firm, the **long run** is a period long enough for it

to adjust the quantities of all the resources that it employs, including plant capacity. From the industry's viewpoint, the long run also includes enough time for existing firms to dissolve and leave the industry or for new firms to be created and enter the industry. While the short run is a "fixed-plant" period, the long run is a "variable-plant" period.

Illustrations   If Boeing hires 100 extra workers for one of its commercial airline plants or adds an entire shift of workers, we are speaking of the short run. If it adds a new production facility and installs more equipment, we are referring to the long run. The first situation is a *short-run adjustment*; the second is a *long-run adjustment*.

The short run and the long run are conceptual periods rather than calendar time periods. In light-manufacturing industries, changes in plant capacity may be accomplished almost overnight. A small T-shirt manufacturer can increase its plant capacity in a matter of days by ordering and installing two or three new cutting tables and several extra sewing machines. But for heavy industry the long run is a different matter. Shell Oil may require several years to construct a new gasoline refinery.

QUICK REVIEW 22.1

- Explicit costs are money payments a firm makes to outside suppliers of resources; implicit costs are the opportunity costs associated with a firm's use of resources it owns.
- Normal profit is the implicit cost of entrepreneurship. Economic profit is total revenue less all explicit and implicit costs, including normal profit.
- In the short run, a firm's plant capacity is fixed; in the long run, a firm can vary its plant size and firms can enter or leave the industry.

Short-Run Production Relationships

A firm's costs of producing a specific output depend on the prices of the needed resources and the quantities of resources (inputs) needed to produce that output. Resource supply and demand determine resource prices. The technological aspects of production, specifically the relationships between inputs and output, determine the quantities of resources needed. Our focus will be on the *labor*-output relationship, given a fixed plant capacity. But before examining that relationship, we need to define three terms:

- **Total product (TP)** is the total quantity, or total output, of a particular good produced.

- **Marginal product (MP)** is the extra output or added product associated with adding a unit of a variable resource, in this case labor, to the production process. Thus,

$$\text{Marginal product} = \frac{\text{change in total product}}{\text{change in labor input}}$$

- **Average product (AP),** also called labor productivity, is output per unit of labor input:

$$\text{Average product} = \frac{\text{total product}}{\text{units of labor}}$$

In the short run, a firm can for a time increase its output by adding units of labor to its fixed plant. But by how much will output rise when it adds the labor? Why do we say "for a time"?

Law of Diminishing Returns

The answers are provided in general terms by the **law of diminishing returns.** This law assumes that technology is fixed and thus the techniques of production do not change. It states that *as successive units of a variable resource (say, labor) are added to a fixed resource (say, capital or land), beyond some point the extra, or marginal, product that can be attributed to each additional unit of the variable resource will decline.* For example, if additional workers are hired to work with a constant amount of capital equipment, output will eventually rise by smaller and smaller amounts as more workers are hired.

22.1
Law of
diminishing
returns

Rationale   Suppose a farmer has a fixed resource of 80 acres planted in corn. If the farmer does not cultivate the cornfields (clear the weeds) at all, the yield will be 40 bushels per acre. If he cultivates the land once, output may rise to 50 bushels per acre. A second cultivation may increase output to 57 bushels per acre, a third to 61, and a fourth to 63. Succeeding cultivations will add less and less to the land's yield. If this were not so, the world's needs for corn could be fulfilled by extremely intense cultivation of this single 80-acre plot of land. Indeed, if diminishing returns did not occur, the world could be fed out of a flowerpot. Why not? Just keep adding more seed fertilizer, and harvesters!

The law of diminishing returns also holds true in nonagricultural industries. Assume a wood shop is manufacturing furniture frames. It has a specific amount of equipment such as lathes, planers, saws, and sanders. If this shop hired just one or two workers, total output and productivity (output per worker) would be very low. The

workers would have to perform many different jobs, and the advantages of specialization would not be realized. Time would be lost in switching from one job to another, and machines would stand idle much of the time. In short, the plant would be understaffed, and production would be inefficient because there would be too much capital relative to the amount of labor.

The shop could eliminate those difficulties by hiring more workers. Then the equipment would be more fully used, and workers could specialize on doing a single job. Time would no longer be lost switching from job to job. As more workers were added, production would become more efficient and the marginal product of each succeeding worker would rise.

TABLE 22.1

Total, Marginal, and Average Product: The Law of Diminishing Returns

(1) Units of the Variable Resource (Labor)	(2) Total Product (TP)	(3) Marginal Product (MP), Change in (2)/ Change in (1)		(4) Average Product (AP), (2)/(1)
0	0	10 ⎫	Increasing marginal returns	—
1	10	15 ⎬		10.00
2	25	20 ⎭		12.50
3	45	15 ⎫	Diminishing marginal returns	15.00
4	60	10 ⎬		15.00
5	70	5 ⎭		14.00
6	75	0 ⎫	Negative marginal returns	12.50
7	75	−5 ⎬		10.71
8	70			8.75

But the rise could not go on indefinitely. If still more workers were added, beyond a certain point, overcrowding would set in. Since workers would then have to wait in line to use the machinery, they would be underused. Total output would increase at a diminishing rate, because, given the fixed size of the plant, each worker would have less capital equipment to work with as more and more labor was hired. The marginal product of additional workers would decline, because there would be more labor in proportion to the fixed amount of capital. Eventually, adding still more workers would cause so much congestion that marginal product would become negative and total product would decline. At the extreme, the addition of more and more labor would exhaust all the standing room, and total product would fall to zero.

Note that the law of diminishing returns assumes that all units of labor are of equal quality. Each successive worker is presumed to have the same innate ability, motor coordination, education, training, and work experience. Marginal product ultimately diminishes, not because successive workers are less skilled or less energetic but because more workers are being used relative to the amount of plant and equipment available.

Tabular Example   Table 22.1 is a numerical illustration of the law of diminishing returns. Column 2 shows the total product, or total output, resulting from combining each level of a variable input (labor) in column 1 with a fixed amount of capital.

Column 3 shows the marginal product (MP), the change in total product associated with each additional unit of labor. Note that with no labor input, total product is zero; a plant with no workers will produce no output. The first 3 units of labor reflect increasing marginal

returns, with marginal products of 10, 15, and 20 units, respectively. But beginning with the fourth unit of labor, marginal product diminishes continuously, becoming zero with the seventh unit of labor and negative with the eighth.

Average product, or output per labor unit, is shown in column 4. It is calculated by dividing total product (column 2) by the number of labor units needed to produce it (column 1). At 5 units of labor, for example, AP is 14 (= 70/5).

Graphical Portrayal   Figure 22.2 (Key Graph) shows the diminishing-returns data in Table 22.1 graphically and further clarifies the relationships between total, marginal, and average products. (Marginal product in Figure 22.2b is plotted halfway between the units of labor, since it applies to the addition of each labor unit.)

Note first in Figure 22.2a that total product, TP, goes through three phases: It rises initially at an increasing rate; then it increases, but at a diminishing rate; finally, after reaching a maximum, it declines.

Geometrically, marginal product—shown by the MP curve in Figure 22.2b—is the slope of the total-product curve. Marginal product measures the change in total product associated with each succeeding unit of labor. Thus, the three phases of total product are also reflected in marginal product. Where total product is increasing at an increasing rate, marginal product is rising. Here, extra units of labor are adding larger and larger amounts to total product. Similarly, where total product is increasing but at a decreasing rate, marginal product is positive but falling. Each additional unit of labor adds less to total product than did the previous unit. When total product is at a maximum, marginal product is zero. When total product declines, marginal product becomes negative.

KEY GRAPH

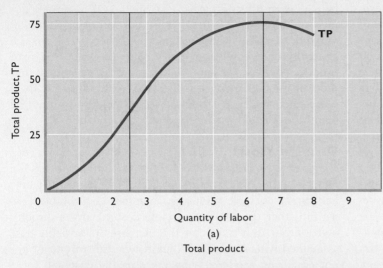

(a)
Total product

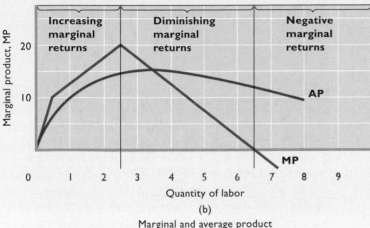

(b)
Marginal and average product

FIGURE 22.2

The law of diminishing returns. (a) As a variable resource (labor) is added to fixed amounts of other resources (land or capital), the total product that results will eventually increase by diminishing amounts, reach a maximum, and then decline. (b) Marginal product is the change in total product associated with each new unit of labor. Average product is simply output per labor unit. Note that marginal product intersects average product at the maximum average product.

QUICK QUIZ 22.2

1. Which of the following is an assumption underlying these figures?
   a. Firms first hire "better" workers and then hire "poorer" workers.
   b. Capital and labor are both variable, but labor increases more rapidly than capital.
   c. Consumers will buy all the output (total product) produced.
   d. Workers are of equal quality.

2. Marginal product is:
   a. the change in total product divided by the change in the quantity of labor.
   b. total product divided by the quantity of labor.
   c. always positive.
   d. unrelated to total product.

3. Marginal product in graph (b) is zero when:
   a. average product in graph (b) stops rising.
   b. the slope of the marginal-product curve in graph (b) is zero.
   c. total product in graph (a) begins to rise at a diminishing rate.
   d. the slope of the total-product curve in graph (a) is zero.

4. Average product in graph (b):
   a. rises when it is less than marginal product.
   b. is the change in total product divided by the change in the quantity of labor.
   c. can never exceed marginal product.
   d. falls whenever total product in graph (a) rises at a diminishing rate.

Answers: 1. d; 2. a; 3. d; 4. a

Average product, AP (Figure 22.2b), displays the same tendencies as marginal product. It increases, reaches a maximum, and then decreases as more and more units of labor are added to the fixed plant. But note the relationship between marginal product and average product: Where marginal product exceeds average product, average product rises. And where marginal product is less than average product, average product declines. It follows that marginal product intersects average product where average product is at a maximum.

This relationship is a mathematical necessity. If you add a larger number to a total than the current average of that total, the average must rise. And if you add a smaller number to a total than the current average of that total, the average must fall. You raise your average examination grade only when your score on an additional (marginal) examination is greater than the average of all your past scores. You lower your average when your grade on an additional exam is below your current average. In our production example, when the amount an extra worker adds to total product exceeds the average product of all workers currently employed, average product will rise. Conversely, when an extra worker adds to total product an amount that is less than the current average product, then average product will decrease.

The law of diminishing returns is embodied in the shapes of all three curves. But, as our definition of the law of diminishing returns indicates, economists are most concerned with its effects on marginal product. The regions of increasing, diminishing, and negative marginal product (returns) are shown in Figure 22.2b. **(Key Question 4)**

22.2
Production
relationships

Short-Run Production Costs

Production information such as that provided in Table 22.1 and Figure 22.2a and 22.2b must be coupled with resource prices to determine the total and per-unit costs of producing various levels of output. We know that in the short run some resources, those associated with the firm's plant, are fixed. Other resources, however, are variable. So short-run costs are either fixed or variable.

Fixed, Variable, and Total Costs

Let's see what distinguishes fixed costs, variable costs, and total costs from one another.

Fixed Costs Fixed costs are *those costs that in total do not vary with changes in output.* Fixed costs are associated with the very existence of a firm's plant and therefore must be paid even if its output is zero. Such costs as rental payments, interest on a firm's debts, a portion of depreciation on equipment and buildings, and insurance premiums are generally fixed costs; they do not increase even if a firm produces more. In column 2 of Table 22.2 we assume that the firm's total fixed cost is $100. By definition, this fixed cost is incurred at all levels of output, including zero. The firm cannot avoid paying fixed costs in the short run.

Variable Costs Variable costs are *those costs that change with the level of output.* They include payments for materials, fuel, power, transportation services, most labor, and similar variable resources. In column 3 of Table 22.2 we find that the total of variable costs changes directly with output. But note that the increases in variable cost associated with succeeding 1-unit increases in output are not equal. As production begins, variable cost will for a time increase by a decreasing amount; this is true through the fourth unit of output in Table 22.2. Beyond the fourth unit, however, variable cost rises by increasing amounts for succeeding units of output.

The reason lies in the shape of the marginal-product curve. At first, as in Figure 22.2b, marginal product is increasing, so smaller and smaller increases in the amounts of variable resources are needed to produce successive units of output. Hence the variable cost of successive units of output decreases. But when, as diminishing returns are encountered, marginal product begins to decline, larger and larger additional amounts of variable resources are needed to produce successive units of output. Total variable cost therefore increases by increasing amounts.

Total Cost Total Cost is *the sum of fixed cost and variable cost at each level of output.* It is shown in column 4 of Table 22.2. At zero units of output, total cost is equal to the firm's fixed cost. Then for each unit of the 10 units of production, total cost increases by the same amount as variable cost.

Figure 22.3 shows graphically the fixed-, variable-, and total-cost data given in Table 22.2. Observe that total variable cost, TVC, is measured vertically from the horizontal axis at each level of output. The amount of fixed cost, shown as TFC, is added vertically to the total-variable-cost curve to obtain the points on the total-cost curve TC.

The distinction between fixed and variable costs is significant to the business manager. Variable costs can be controlled or altered in the short run by changing production levels. Fixed costs are beyond the business manager's current control; they are incurred in the short run and must be paid regardless of output level.

TABLE 22.2

Total-, Average-, and Marginal-Cost Schedules for an Individual Firm in the Short Run

				Average-Cost Data			Marginal Cost
	Total-Cost Data			(5) Average Fixed Cost (AFC) $AFC = \dfrac{TFC}{Q}$	(6) Average Variable Cost (AVC) $AVC = \dfrac{TVC}{Q}$	(7) Average Total Cost (ATC) $ATC = \dfrac{TC}{Q}$	(8) Marginal Cost (MC) $MC = \dfrac{\text{change in TC}}{\text{change in Q}}$
(1) Total Product (Q)	(2) Total Fixed Cost (TFC)	(3) Total Variable Cost (TVC)	(4) Total Cost (TC) TC = TFC + TVC				
0	$100	$ 0	$ 100				
1	100	90	190	$100.00	$90.00	$190.00	$ 90
2	100	170	270	50.00	85.00	135.00	80
3	100	240	340	33.33	80.00	113.33	70
4	100	300	400	25.00	75.00	100.00	60
5	100	370	470	20.00	74.00	94.00	70
6	100	450	550	16.67	75.00	91.67	80
7	100	540	640	14.29	77.14	91.43	90
8	100	650	750	12.50	81.25	93.75	110
9	100	780	880	11.11	86.67	97.78	130
10	100	930	1030	10.00	93.00	103.00	150

Per-Unit, or Average, Costs

Producers are certainly interested in their total costs, but they are equally concerned with per-unit, or average, costs. In particular, average-cost data are more meaning-

FIGURE 22.3

Total cost is the sum of fixed cost and variable cost. Total variable cost (TVC) changes with output. Total fixed cost (TFC) is independent of the level of output. The total cost (TC) at any output is the vertical sum of the fixed cost and variable cost at that output.

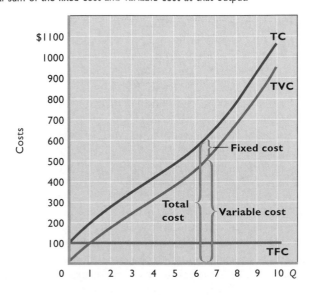

ful for making comparisons with product price, which is always stated on a per-unit basis. Average fixed cost, average variable cost, and average total cost are shown in columns 5 to 7, Table 22.2.

AFC Average fixed cost (AFC) for any output level is found by dividing total fixed cost (TFC) by that output (Q). That is,

$$AFC = \frac{TFC}{Q}$$

Because the total fixed cost is, by definition, the same regardless of output, AFC must decline as output increases. As output rises, the total fixed cost is spread over a larger and larger output. When output is just 1 unit in Table 22.2, TFC and AFC are the same at $100. But at 2 units of output, the total fixed cost of $100 becomes $50 of AFC or fixed cost per unit; then it becomes $33.33 per unit as $100 is spread over 3 units, and $25 per unit when spread over 4 units. This process is sometimes referred to as "spreading the overhead." Figure 22.4 shows that AFC graphs as a continuously declining curve as total output is increased.

AVC Average variable cost (AVC) for any output level is calculated by dividing total variable cost (TVC) by that output (Q):

$$AVC = \frac{TVC}{Q}$$

FIGURE 22.4

The average-cost curves. AFC falls as a given amount of fixed costs is apportioned over a larger and larger output. AVC initially falls because of increasing marginal returns but then rises because of diminishing marginal returns. Average total cost (ATC) is the vertical sum of average variable cost (AVC) and average fixed cost (AFC).

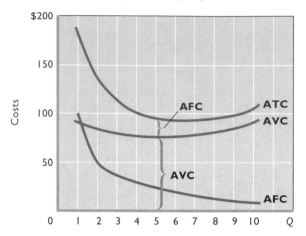

As added variable resources increase output, AVC declines initially, reaches a minimum, and then increases again. A graph of AVC is a U-shaped or saucer-shaped curve, as shown in Figure 22.4.

Because total variable cost reflects the law of diminishing returns, so must AVC, which is derived from total variable cost. Because marginal returns increase initially, it takes fewer and fewer additional variable resources to produce each of the first 4 units of output. As a result, variable cost per unit declines. AVC hits a minimum with the fifth unit of output, and beyond that point AVC rises as diminishing returns require more and more variable resources to produce each additional unit of output.

In simpler terms, at very low levels of output production is relatively inefficient and costly. Because the firm's fixed plant is understaffed, average variable cost is relatively high. As output expands, however, greater specialization and better use of the firm's capital equipment yield more efficiency, and variable cost per unit of output declines. As still more variable resources are added, a point is reached where diminishing returns are incurred. The firm's capital equipment is now staffed more intensively, and therefore each added input unit does not increase output by as much as preceding inputs. This means that AVC eventually increases.

You can verify the U or saucer shape of the AVC curve by returning to Table 22.1. Assume the price of labor is $10 per unit. By dividing average product (output per labor unit) into $10 (price per labor unit), we determine the labor

cost per unit of output. Because we have assumed labor to be the only variable input, the labor cost per unit of output is the variable cost per unit of output, or AVC. When average product is initially low, AVC is high. As workers are added, average product rises and AVC falls. When average product is at its maximum, AVC is at its minimum. Then, as still more workers are added and average product declines, AVC rises. The "hump" of the average-product curve is reflected in the saucer or U shape of the AVC curve. As you will soon see, the two are mirror images of each other.

ATC   **Average total cost (ATC)** for any output level is found by dividing total cost (TC) by that output (Q) or by adding AFC and AVC at that output:

$$\text{ATC} = \frac{\text{TC}}{Q} = \frac{\text{TFC}}{Q} + \frac{\text{TVC}}{Q} = \text{AFC} + \text{AVC}$$

Graphically, ATC can be found by adding vertically the AFC and AVC curves, as in Figure 22.4. Thus the vertical distance between the ATC and AVC curves measures AFC at any level of output.

Marginal Cost

One final and very crucial cost concept remains: **Marginal cost (MC)** is *the extra, or additional, cost of producing 1 more unit of output.* MC can be determined for each added unit of output by noting the change in total cost which that unit's production entails:

$$\text{MC} = \frac{\text{change in TC}}{\text{change in } Q}$$

Calculations   In column 4, Table 22.2, production of the first unit of output increases total cost from $100 to $190. Therefore, the additional, or marginal, cost of that first unit is $90 (column 8). The marginal cost of the second unit is $80 (= $270 − $190); the MC of the third is $70 (= $340 − $270); and so forth. The MC for each of the 10 units of output is shown in column 8.

MC can also be calculated from the total-variable-cost column, because the only difference between total cost and total variable cost is the constant amount of fixed costs ($100). Thus, the change in total cost and the change in total variable cost associated with each additional unit of output are always the same.

Marginal Decisions   Marginal costs are costs the firm can control directly and immediately. Specifically, MC designates all the cost incurred in producing the last unit of output. Thus, it also designates the cost that can be "saved" by not producing that last unit. Average-cost

KEY GRAPH

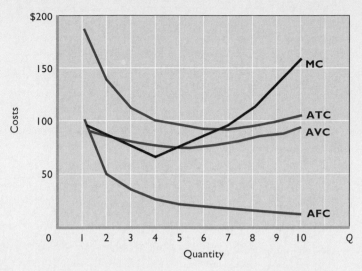

FIGURE 22.5

The relationship of the marginal-cost curve to the average-total-cost and average-variable-cost curves. The marginal-cost (MC) curve cuts through the average-total-cost (ATC) curve and the average-variable-cost (AVC) curve at their minimum points. When MC is below average total cost, ATC falls; when MC is above average total cost, ATC rises. Similarly, when MC is below average variable cost, AVC falls; when MC is above average variable cost, AVC rises.

QUICK QUIZ 22.5

1. The marginal-cost curve first declines and then increases because of:
   a. increasing, then diminishing, marginal utility.
   b. the decline in the gap between ATC and AVC as output expands.
   c. increasing, then diminishing, marginal returns.
   d. constant marginal revenue.

2. The vertical distance between ATC and AVC measures:
   a. marginal cost.
   b. total fixed cost.
   c. average fixed cost.
   d. economic profit per unit.

3. ATC is:
   a. AVC − AFC.
   b. MC + AVC.
   c. AFC + AVC.
   d. (AFC + AVC) × Q.

4. When the marginal-cost curve lies:
   a. above the ATC curve, ATC rises.
   b. above the AVC curve, ATC rises.
   c. below the AVC curve, total fixed cost increases.
   d. below the ATC curve, total fixed cost falls.

Answers: 1. c; 2. c; 3. c; 4. a

---

figures do not provide this information. For example, suppose the firm is undecided whether to produce 3 or 4 units of output. At 4 units Table 22.2 indicates that ATC is $100. But the firm does not increase its total costs by $100 by producing the fourth unit, nor does it save $100 by not producing that unit. Rather, the change in costs involved here is only $60, as the MC column in Table 22.2 reveals.

A firm's decisions as to what output level to produce are typically marginal decisions, that is, decisions to produce a few more or a few less units. Marginal cost is the change in costs when 1 more or 1 less unit of output is produced. When coupled with marginal revenue (which, as you will see in Chapter 23, indicates the change in revenue from 1 more or 1 less unit of output), marginal cost allows a firm to determine if it is profitable to expand or contract its production. The analysis in the next three chapters focuses on those marginal calculations.

Graphical Portrayal Marginal cost is shown graphically in **Figure 22.5 (Key Graph).** Marginal cost at first declines sharply, reaches a minimum, and then rises rather abruptly. This reflects the fact that variable costs, and therefore total cost, increase first by decreasing amounts and then by increasing amounts (see columns 3 and 4, Table 22.2).

22.1
Production
and costs

MC and Marginal Product The marginal-cost curve's shape is a consequence of the law of diminishing returns. Looking back at Table 22.1, we can see the relationship between marginal product and marginal cost. If all units of a variable resource (here labor) are hired at the same price, the marginal cost of each extra unit of output will fall as long as the marginal product of each additional

401

worker is rising. This is true because marginal cost is the (constant) cost of an extra worker divided by his or her marginal product. Therefore, in Table 22.1, suppose that each worker can be hired for $10. Because the first worker's marginal product is 10 units of output, and hiring this worker increases the firm's costs by $10, the marginal cost of each of these 10 extra units of output is $1 (= $10/10 units). The second worker also increases costs by $10, but the marginal product is 15, so the marginal cost of each of these 15 extra units of output is $.67 (= $10/15 units). Similarly, the MC of each of the 20 extra units of output contributed by the third worker is $.50 (= $10/20 units). To generalize, as long as marginal product is rising, marginal cost will fall.

But with the fourth worker diminishing returns set in and marginal cost begins to rise. For the fourth worker, marginal cost is $.67 (= $10/15 units); for the fifth worker, MC is $1 ($10/10 units); for the sixth, MC is $2 (= $10/5 units); and so on. If the price (cost) of the variable resource remains constant, increasing marginal returns will be reflected in a declining marginal cost, and diminishing marginal returns in a rising marginal cost. The MC curve is a mirror reflection of the marginal-product curve. As you can see in Figure 22.6, when marginal product is rising, marginal cost is necessarily falling. When marginal product is at its maximum, marginal cost is at its minimum. And when marginal product is falling, marginal cost is rising.

Relation of MC to AVC and ATC

Figure 22.5 shows that the marginal-cost curve MC intersects both the AVC and the ATC curves at their minimum points. As noted earlier, this marginal-average relationship is a mathematical necessity, which a simple illustration will reveal. Suppose a baseball pitcher has allowed his opponents an average of 3 runs per game in the first three games he has pitched. Now, whether his average falls or rises as a result of pitching a fourth (marginal) game will depend on whether the additional runs he allows in that extra game are fewer or more than his current 3-run average. If in the fourth game he allows fewer than 3 runs, for example, 1, his total runs will rise from 9 to 10 and his average will fall from 3 to $2\frac{1}{2}$ (= 10/4). Conversely, if in the fourth game he allows more than 3 runs, say, 7, his total will increase from 9 to 16 and his average will rise from 3 to 4 (= 16/4).

So it is with costs. When the amount (the marginal cost) added to total cost is less than the current average total cost, ATC will fall. Conversely, when the marginal cost exceeds ATC, ATC will rise. This means in Figure 22.5 that as long as MC lies below ATC, ATC will fall, and

FIGURE 22.6

The relationship between productivity curves and cost curves. The marginal-cost (MC) curve and the average-variable-cost (AVC) curve in (b) are mirror images of the marginal-product (MP) and average-product (AP) curves in (a). Assuming that labor is the only variable input and that its price (the wage rate) is constant, then when MP is rising, MC is falling, and when MP is falling, MC is rising. Under the same assumptions, when AP is rising, AVC is falling, and when AP is falling, AVC is rising.

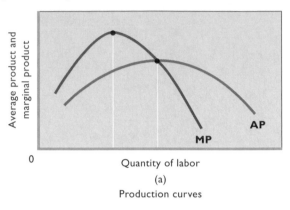

(a)
Production curves

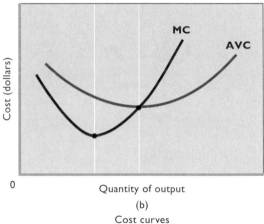

(b)
Cost curves

whenever MC lies above ATC, ATC will rise. Therefore, at the point of intersection where MC equals ATC, ATC has just ceased to fall but has not yet begun to rise. This, by definition, is the minimum point on the ATC curve. The marginal-cost curve intersects the average-total-cost curve at the ATC curve's minimum point.

Marginal cost can be defined as the addition either to total cost or to total variable cost resulting from 1 more unit of output; thus this same rationale explains why the MC curve also crosses the AVC curve at the AVC curve's minimum point. No such relationship exists between the MC curve and the average-fixed-cost curve, because the two are not related; marginal cost includes only those costs that change with output, and fixed costs by definition are those that are independent of output. **(Key Question 7)**

Shifts of the Cost Curves

Changes in either resource prices or technology will cause costs to change and therefore the cost curves to shift. If fixed costs double from $100 to $200, the AFC curve in Figure 22.5 would be shifted upward. At each level of output, fixed costs are higher. The ATC curve would also move upward, because AFC is a component of ATC. But the positions of the AVC and MC curves would be unaltered, because their locations are based on the prices of variable rather than fixed resources. However, if the price (wage) of labor or some other variable input rose, AVC, ATC, and MC would rise and those cost curves would all shift upward. The AFC curve would remain in place because fixed costs have not changed. And, of course, reductions in the prices of fixed or variable resources would reduce costs and produce shifts of the cost curves exactly opposite to those just described.

The discovery of a more efficient technology would increase the productivity of all inputs. The cost figures in Table 22.2 would all be lower. To illustrate, if labor is the only variable input, if wages are $10 per hour, and if average product is 10 units, then AVC would be $1. But if a technological improvement increases the average product of labor to 20 units, then AVC will decline to $.50. More generally, an upward shift in the productivity curves shown in Figure 22.6a means a downward shift in the cost curves portrayed in Figure 22.6b.

QUICK REVIEW 22.2

- The law of diminishing returns indicates that, beyond some point, output will increase by diminishing amounts as more units of a variable resource (labor) are added to a fixed resource (capital).
- In the short run, the total cost of any level of output is the sum of fixed and variable costs (TC = TFC + TVC).
- Average fixed, average variable, and average total costs are fixed, variable, and total costs per unit of output; marginal cost is the extra cost of producing 1 more unit of output.
- Average fixed cost declines continuously as output increases; average-variable-cost and average-total-cost curves are U-shaped, reflecting increasing and then diminishing returns; the marginal-cost curve falls but then rises, intersecting both the average-variable-cost curve and the average-total-cost curve at their minimum points.

Long-Run Production Costs

In the long run an industry and the individual firms it comprises can undertake all desired resource adjustments. That is, they can change the amount of all inputs used. The firm can alter its plant capacity; it can build a larger plant or revert to a smaller plant than that assumed in Table 22.2. The industry also can change its plant size; the long run allows sufficient time for new firms to enter or for existing firms to leave an industry. We will discuss the impact of the entry and exit of firms to and from an industry in the next chapter; here we are concerned only with changes in plant capacity made by a single firm. Let's couch our analysis in terms of average total cost (ATC), making no distinction between fixed and variable costs because all resources, and therefore all costs, are variable in the long run.

Firm Size and Costs

Suppose a single-plant manufacturer begins on a small scale and, as the result of successful operations, expands to successively larger plant sizes with larger output capacities. What happens to average total cost as this occurs? For a time, successively larger plants will lower average total cost. However, eventually the building of a still larger plant may cause ATC to rise.

Figure 22.7 illustrates this situation for five possible plant sizes. ATC-1 is the short-run average-total-cost curve for the smallest of the five plants, and ATC-5 the curve for the largest. Constructing larger plants will lower the minimum average total costs through plant size 3. But then larger plants will mean higher minimum average total costs.

The Long-Run Cost Curve

The vertical lines perpendicular to the output axis in Figure 22.7 indicate the outputs at which the firm should change plant size to realize the lowest attainable average total costs of production. These are the outputs at which the per-unit costs for a larger plant drop below those for the current, smaller plant. For all outputs up to 20 units, the lowest average total costs are attainable with plant size 1. However, if the firm's volume of sales expands beyond 20 units but less than 30, it can achieve lower per-unit costs by constructing a larger plant, size 2. Although total cost will be higher at the expanded levels of production, the cost per unit of output will be less. For any output between 30 and 50 units, plant size 3 will yield the lowest average total costs. From 50 to 60 units of output, the firm must build the size-4 plant to achieve the lowest unit costs.

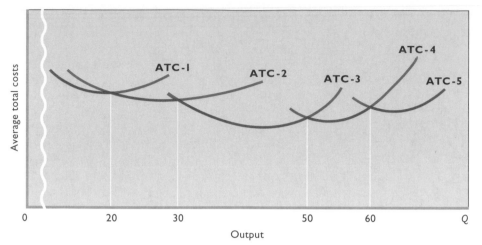

FIGURE 22.7

The long-run average-total-cost curve: five possible plant sizes. The long-run average-total-cost curve is made up of segments of the short-run cost curves (ATC-1, ATC-2, etc.) of the various-size plants from which the firm might choose. Each point on the bumpy planning curve shows the lowest unit cost attainable for any output when the firm has had time to make all desired changes in its plant size.

Lowest average total costs for any output over 60 units require construction of the still larger plant, size 5.

Tracing these adjustments, we find that the long-run ATC curve for the enterprise is made up of segments of the short-run ATC curves for the various plant sizes that can be constructed. The long-run ATC curve shows the lowest average total cost at which *any output level* can be produced after the firm has had time to make all appropriate adjustments in its plant size. In Figure 22.7 the red, bumpy curve is the firm's long-run ATC curve or, as it is often called, the firm's *planning curve.*

In most lines of production the choice of plant size is much wider than in our illustration. In many industries the number of possible plant sizes is virtually unlimited, and in time quite small changes in the volume of output will lead to changes in plant size. Graphically, this implies an unlimited number of short-run ATC curves, one for each output level, as suggested by **Figure 22.8 (Key Graph).** Then, rather than being made up of segments of short-run ATC curves as in Figure 22.7, the long-run ATC curve is made up of all the points of tangency of the unlimited number of short-run ATC curves from which the long-run ATC curve is derived. Therefore, the planning curve is smooth rather than bumpy. Each point on it tells us the minimum ATC of producing the corresponding level of output.

Economies and Diseconomies of Scale

We have assumed that for a time larger and larger plant sizes will lead to lower unit costs but that beyond some point successively larger plants will mean higher average total costs. That is, we have assumed the long-run ATC curve is U-shaped. But why should this be? Note, first,

that the law of diminishing returns does not apply in the long run. That's because diminishing returns presume one resource is fixed in supply while the long run means all resources are variable. Also, our discussion assumes resource prices are constant. We can explain the U-shaped long-run average-total-cost curve in terms of economies and diseconomies of large-scale production.

Economies of Scale Economies of scale, or economies of mass production, explain the downsloping part of the long-run ATC curve, as indicated in Figure 22.9, graphs (a), (b), and (c). As plant size increases, a number of factors will for a time lead to lower average costs of production.

Labor Specialization Increased specialization in the use of labor becomes more achievable as a plant increases in size. Hiring more workers means jobs can be divided and subdivided. Each worker may now have just one task to perform instead of five or six. Workers can work full-time on the tasks for which they have special skills. In a small plant, skilled machinists may spend half their time performing unskilled tasks, leading to higher production costs.

Further, by working at fewer tasks, workers become proficient at those tasks. The jack-of-all-trades doing five or six jobs is not likely to be efficient in any of them. Concentrating on one task, the same worker may become highly efficient.

Finally, greater labor specialization eliminates the loss of time that accompanies each shift of a worker from one task to another.

Managerial Specialization Large-scale production also means better use of, and greater specialization in,

KEY GRAPH

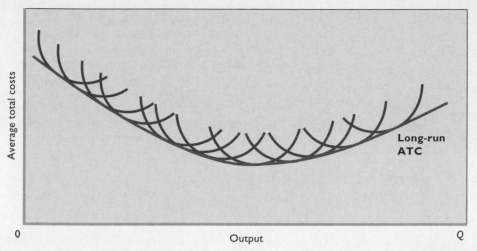

FIGURE 22.8

The long-run average-total-cost curve: unlimited number of plant sizes. If the number of possible plant sizes is very large, the long-run average-total-cost curve approximates a smooth curve. Economies of scale, followed by diseconomies of scale, cause the curve to be U-shaped.

QUICK QUIZ 22.8

1. The unlabeled blue curves in this figure illustrate the:
   a. long-run average-total-cost curves of various firms constituting the industry.
   b. short-run average-total-cost curves of various firms constituting the industry.
   c. short-run average-total-cost curves of various plant sizes available to a particular firm.
   d. short-run marginal-cost curves of various plant sizes available to a particular firm.

2. The unlabeled blue curves in this figure derive their shapes from:
   a. decreasing, then increasing, short-run returns.
   b. increasing, then decreasing, short-run returns.
   c. economies, then diseconomies, of scale.
   d. diseconomies, then economies, of scale.

3. The long-run ATC curve in this figure derives its shape from:
   a. decreasing, then increasing, short-run returns.
   b. increasing, then decreasing, short-run returns.
   c. economies, then diseconomies, of scale.
   d. diseconomies, then economies, of scale.

4. The long-run ATC curve is often called the firm's:
   a. planning curve.
   b. capital-expansion path.
   c. total-product curve.
   d. production possibilities curve.

Answers: 1. c; 2. b; 3. c; 4. a

---

management. A supervisor who can handle 20 workers is underused in a small plant that employs only 10 people. The production staff could be doubled with no increase in supervisory costs.

Small firms cannot use management specialists to best advantage. In a small plant a sales specialist may have to divide his or her time between several executive functions, for example, marketing, personnel, and finance. A larger scale of operations means that the marketing expert can supervise marketing full-time, while specialists perform other managerial functions. Greater efficiency and lower unit costs are the net result.

Efficient Capital Small firms often cannot afford the most efficient equipment. In many lines of production such machinery is available only in very large and extremely expensive units. Furthermore, effective use of the

equipment demands a high volume of production, and that again requires large-scale producers.

In the automobile industry the most efficient fabrication method employs robotics and elaborate assembly-line equipment. Effective use of this equipment demands an annual output of perhaps 200,000 to 400,000 automobiles. Only very large scale producers can afford to purchase and use this equipment efficiently. The small-scale producer is faced with a dilemma. To fabricate automobiles using other equipment is inefficient and therefore more costly per unit. The alternative of purchasing the efficient equipment and underusing it at low levels of output is also inefficient and costly.

Other Factors Many products entail design and development costs, as well as other "start-up" costs, which

405

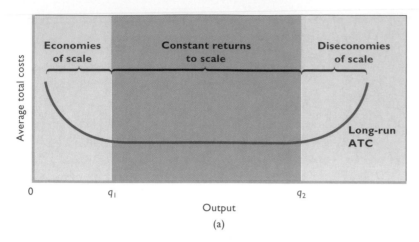

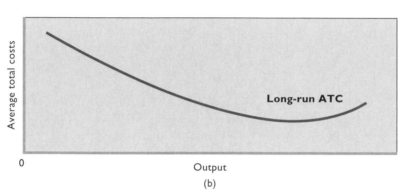

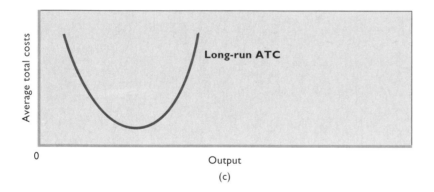

FIGURE 22.9

Various possible long-run average-total-cost curves. In (a), economies of scale are rather rapidly obtained as plant size rises, and diseconomies of scale are not encountered until a considerably large scale of output has been achieved. Thus, long-run average total cost is constant over a wide range of output. In (b), economies of scale are extensive, and diseconomies of scale occur only at very large outputs. Average total cost therefore declines over a broad range of output. In (c), economies of scale are exhausted quickly, followed immediately by diseconomies of scale. Minimum ATC thus occurs at a relatively low output.

must be incurred irrespective of projected sales. These costs decline per unit as output is increased. Similarly, advertising costs decline per auto, per computer, per stereo system, and per box of detergent as more units are produced and sold. Also, the firm's production and marketing expertise usually rises as it produces and sells more output. This *learning by doing* is a further source of economies of scale.

All these factors contribute to lower average total costs for the firm that is able to expand its scale of operations. Where economies of scale are possible, an increase in all resources of, say, 10 percent will cause a more-than-proportionate increase in output of, say, 20 percent. The result will be a decline in ATC.

In many U.S. manufacturing industries economies of scale have been of great significance. Firms that have expanded their scale of operations to obtain economies of mass production have survived and flourished. Those unable to expand have become relatively high-cost producers, doomed to a struggle to survive.

Diseconomies of Scale

In time the expansion of a firm may lead to diseconomies and therefore higher average total costs.

The main factor causing **diseconomies of scale** is the difficulty of efficiently controlling and coordinating a firm's operations as it becomes a large-scale producer. In a small plant a single key executive may make all the basic decisions for the plant's operation. Because of the firm's small size, the executive is close to the production line, understands the firm's operations, and can digest information and make efficient decisions.

This neat picture changes as a firm grows. There are now many management levels between the executive suite and the assembly line; top management is far removed from the actual production operations of the plant. One person cannot assemble, digest, and understand all the information essential to decision making on a large scale. Authority must be delegated to many vice-presidents, second vice-presidents, and so forth. This expansion of the management hierarchy leads to problems of communication and cooperation, bureaucratic red tape, and the possibility that decisions will not be coordinated. Similarly, decision making may be slowed down to the point that decisions fail to reflect changes in consumer tastes or technology quickly enough. The result is impaired efficiency and rising average total costs.

Also, in massive production facilities workers may feel alienated from their employers and care little about working efficiently. Opportunities to shirk, by avoiding work in favor of on-the-job leisure, may be greater in large plants than in small ones. Countering worker alienation and shirking may require additional worker supervision, which increases costs.

Where diseconomies of scale are operative, an increase in all inputs of, say, 10 percent will cause a less-than-proportionate increase in output of, say, 5 percent. As a consequence, ATC will increase. The rising portion of the long-run cost curves in Figure 22.9 illustrates diseconomies of scale.

Constant Returns to Scale

In some industries there may exist a rather wide range of output between the output at which economies of scale end and the output at which diseconomies of scale begin. That is, there may be a range of **constant returns to scale** over which long-run average cost does not change. The q_1q_2 output range of Figure 22.9a is an example. Here a given percentage increase in all inputs of, say, 10 percent will cause a proportionate 10 percent increase in output. Thus, in this range ATC is constant.

Minimum Efficient Scale and Industry Structure

Economies and diseconomies of scale are an important determinant of an industry's structure. Here we introduce the concept of **minimum efficient scale (MES),** which is the lowest level of output at which a firm can minimize long-run average costs. In Figure 22.9a that level occurs at q_1 units of output. Because of the extended range of constant returns to scale, firms producing substantially greater outputs could also realize the minimum attainable average costs. Specifically, firms within the q_1 to q_2 range would be equally efficient. So we would not be surprised to find an industry with such cost conditions to be populated by firms of quite different sizes. The apparel, food processing, furniture, wood products, snowboard, and small-appliance industries are examples. With an extended range of constant returns to scale, relatively large and relatively small firms can coexist in an industry and be equally successful. Another example appears to be banking.

Compare this with Figure 22.9b, where economies of scale prevail over a wide range of outputs and diseconomies of scale appear only at very high levels of output. This pattern of declining long-run average total cost may occur over an extended range of outputs, as in the automobile, aluminum, steel, and other heavy industries. The same pattern holds in several of the new industries related to information technology, for example, computer microchips, operating system software, and Internet service provision.

Given consumer demand, efficient production will be achieved with a few large-scale producers. Small firms cannot realize the minimum efficient scale and will not be able to compete. In the extreme, economies of scale might extend beyond the market's size, resulting in what is termed **natural monopoly,** a relatively rare market situation in which average total cost is minimized when only one firm produces the particular good or service.

Where economies of scale are few and diseconomies come into play quickly, the minimum efficient size occurs at a low level of output, as shown in Figure 22.9c. In such industries a particular level of consumer demand will support a large number of relatively small producers. Many retail trades and some types of farming fall into this category. So do certain kinds of light manufacturing, such as the baking, clothing, and shoe industries. Fairly small firms are more efficient than larger-scale producers in such industries.

Our point here is that the shape of the long-run average-total-cost curve is determined by technology and the economies and diseconomies of scale that result. The shape of the long-run ATC curve, in turn, can be significant in determining whether an industry is populated by a relatively large number of small firms or is dominated by a few large producers, or lies somewhere in between.

But we must be cautious in our assessment because industry structure does not depend on cost conditions alone. Government policies, the geographic size of markets, managerial strategy and skill, and other factors must be considered in explaining the structure of a particular industry. **(Key Question 10).**

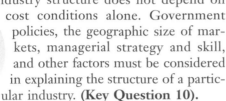

22.3
Minimum efficient scale and natural monopoly

QUICK REVIEW 22.3

- Most firms have U-shaped long-run average-total-cost curves, reflecting economies and then diseconomies of scale.
- Economies of scale are the consequence of greater specialization of labor and management, more efficient capital equipment, and the spreading of start-up costs among more units of output.
- Diseconomies of scale are caused by the problems of coordination and communication that arise in large firms.
- Minimum efficient scale is the lowest level of output at which a firm's long-run average total cost is at a minimum.

Applications and Illustrations

The business world offers many examples relating to short-run costs, economies of scale, and minimum efficient scale (MES). Here are just a few.

Rising Cost of Insurance and Security

Following the terrorist attacks of September 11, 2001, and the threat of additional attacks, insurance premiums rose for many American businesses. In the short run, insurance premiums are fixed costs because they are independent of the level of production. The terrorist attacks also increased security costs, some of which are fixed (for example, video cameras) and others of which are variable (security workers). Together, higher insurance premiums and added security costs shifted short-run ATC curves upward for many firms.

Successful Start-Up Firms

The U.S. economy has greatly benefited over the past several decades by explosive growth of scores of highly successful start-up firms. These firms typically reduce their costs by moving from higher to lower points on their short-run cost curves and by downward and to-the-right shifts of their short-run cost curves via economies of scale. That has certainly been the case for such former start-up firms as CNN (television news), Intel (microchips), Starbucks (coffee), Microsoft (software), Dell (personal computers), Yahoo (Internet search engine), Cisco Systems (Internet switching), and America Online (Internet access).

A major source of cost savings for rapidly growing firms is the ability to spread huge product development and advertising costs over a larger number of units of output. These firms also achieve economies of scale from learning by doing and through increased specialization of labor, management, and equipment. Many successful start-up firms experience declining average total costs over the years or even decades it takes them to reach MES.

The Verson Stamping Machine

In 1996 Verson (a U.S. firm located in Chicago) introduced a 49-foot-tall metal-stamping machine that is the size of a house and weighs as much as 12 locomotives. This $30 million machine, which cuts and sculpts raw sheets of steel into automobile hoods and fenders, enables automakers to make new parts in just 5 minutes compared with 8 hours for older stamping presses. A single machine is designed to make 5 million auto parts per year. So, to achieve the cost saving from the machine, an auto manufacturer must have sufficient auto production to use all these parts. By allowing the use of this cost-saving piece of equipment, large firm size achieves economies of scale.

The Daily Newspaper

The daily newspaper is undoubtedly one of the economy's great bargains. Think of all the resources that combine to produce it: reporters, delivery people, photographers, editors, management, printing presses, pulp mills, pulp mill workers, ink makers, loggers, logging truck drivers, and so on. Yet for 50 cents you can buy a high-quality newspaper in major cities.

The main reason for such low prices is the low average total costs that result from the spreading of fixed costs and the achieving of economies of scale. If only 100 or 200 people bought the paper each day, the average cost of each paper would be exceedingly high because the overhead costs would be spread over so few buyers. But when publishers sell thousands or hundreds of thousands of newspapers each day, they spread the overhead costs very

Sunk Costs Should Be Disregarded in Decision Making.

There is an old saying: Don't cry over spilt milk. The message is that once you have spilled a glass of milk, there is nothing you can do to recover it, so you should forget about it and "move on from there." This saying has great relevance to what economists call sunk costs. Such costs are like sunken ships on the ocean floor: Once these costs are incurred, they cannot be recovered.

Let's gain an understanding of this idea by applying it first to consumers and then to businesses. Suppose you buy an expensive ticket to an upcoming football game, but the morning of the game you wake up with a bad case of the flu. Feeling miserable, you step outside to find that the wind chill is about −10 degrees. You absolutely do not want to go to the game, but you remind yourself that you paid a steep price for the ticket. You call several people to try to sell the ticket, but you soon discover that no one is interested in it, even at a discounted price. You conclude that everyone who wants a ticket has one.

Should you go to the game? Economic analysis says that you should not take actions for which marginal cost exceeds marginal benefit. And, in this situation, the price you paid for the ticket is irrelevant to the decision. Both marginal or additional cost and marginal or additional benefit are forward-looking. If the marginal cost of going to the game is greater than the marginal benefit, the best decision is to go back to bed. This decision should be the same whether you paid $2, $20, or $200 for the game ticket, because the price that you pay for something does not affect its marginal benefit. Once the ticket has been purchased and cannot be resold, its cost is irrelevant to the decision to attend the game. Since "you absolutely do not want to go," clearly the marginal cost exceeds the marginal benefit of the game.

Here is a second consumer example: Suppose a family is on vacation and stops at a roadside stand to buy some apples. The kids get back into the car and bite into their apples, immediately pronouncing them "totally mushy" and unworthy of another bite. Both parents agree that the apples are "terrible," but the father continues to eat his, because, as he says, "We paid a premium price for them." One of the older children replies, "Dad, that is irrelevant." Although not stated very diplomatically, the child is exactly right. In making a new decision, you should ignore all costs that are not affected by the decision. The prior bad decision (in retrospect) to buy the apples should not dictate a second decision for which marginal benefit is less than marginal cost.

Now let's apply the idea of sunk costs to firms. Some of a firm's costs are not only fixed (recurring, but unrelated to the level of output) but sunk (unrecoverable). For example, a nonrefundable annual lease payment for the use of a store cannot be recouped once it has been paid. A firm's decision about whether to move from the store to a more profitable location does not depend on the amount of time remaining on the lease. If moving means greater profit, it makes sense to move whether there are 300 days, 30 days, or 3 days left on the lease.

Or, as another example, suppose a firm spends $1 million on R&D to bring out a new product, only to discover that the product sells very poorly. Should the firm continue to produce the product at a loss even when there is no realistic hope for future success? Obviously, it should not. In making this decision, the firm realizes that the amount it has spent in developing the product is irrelevant; it should stop production of the product and cut its losses. In fact, many firms have dropped products after spending millions of dollars on their development. Examples are the quick decision by Coca-Cola to drop its New Coke and the eventual decision by McDonald's to drop its McLean Burger.

In short, if a cost has been incurred and cannot be partly or fully recouped by some other choice, a rational consumer or firm should ignore it. Sunk costs are irrelevant. Or, as the saying goes, don't cry over spilt milk.

widely. The large volume of sales also enables them to use specialized labor and large, highly efficient printing presses. Given sufficient scale and volume, the average total cost of a paper sinks to a few dimes. Moreover, the greater the number of readers, the greater is the amount of money that advertisers are willing to pay for advertising space. That added revenue helps keep the price of the newspaper low.

Aircraft and Concrete Plants

Why are there only three plants in the United States (all operated by Boeing) that produce large commercial aircraft and thousands of plants (owned by hundreds of firms) that produce ready-mixed concrete? The simple answer is that MES is radically different in the two industries. Why is that? First, economies of scale are extensive in assembling large commercial aircraft and very modest in mixing

concrete. Manufacturing airplanes is a complex process that requires huge facilities, thousands of workers, and very expensive, specialized machinery. Economies of scale extend to huge plant sizes. But mixing Portland cement, sand, gravel, and water efficiently to produce concrete requires only a handful of workers and relatively inexpensive equipment. Economies of scale are exhausted at relatively small size.

The differing MESs also derive from the vastly different sizes of the geographic markets. The market for commercial airplanes is global, and aircraft manufacturers can deliver new airplanes anywhere in the world by flying them there. In contrast, the geographic market for a concrete plant is roughly the 50-mile radius that enables the concrete to be delivered before it "sets up." So thousands of small concrete plants locate close to their customers in hundreds of different small and large cities in the United States.

SUMMARY

1. Economic costs include all payments that must be received by resource owners to ensure a continued supply of needed resources to a particular line of production. Economic costs include explicit costs, which flow to resources owned and supplied by others, and implicit costs, which are payments for the use of self-owned and self-employed resources. One implicit cost is a normal profit to the entrepreneur. Economic profit occurs when total revenue exceeds total cost (= explicit costs + implicit costs, including a normal profit).

2. In the short run a firm's plant capacity is fixed. The firm can use its plant more or less intensively by adding or subtracting units of variable resources, but it does not have sufficient time in the short run to alter plant size.

3. The law of diminishing returns describes what happens to output as a fixed plant is used more intensively. As successive units of a variable resource, such as labor are added to a fixed plant, beyond some point the marginal product associated with each additional unit of a resource declines.

4. Because some resources are variable and others are fixed, costs can be classified as variable or fixed in the short run. Fixed costs are independent of the level of output; variable costs vary with output. The total cost of any output is the sum of fixed and variable costs at that output.

5. Average fixed, average variable, and average total costs are fixed, variable, and total costs per unit of output. Average fixed cost declines continuously as output increases because a fixed sum is being spread over a larger and larger number of units of production. A graph of average variable cost is

U-shaped, reflecting the law of diminishing returns. Average total cost is the sum of average fixed and average variable costs; its graph is also U-shaped.

6. Marginal cost is the extra, or additional, cost of producing 1 more unit of output. It is the amount by which total cost and total variable cost change when 1 more or 1 less unit of output is produced. Graphically, the marginal-cost curve intersects the ATC and AVC curves at their minimum points.

7. Lower resource prices shift cost curves downward, as does technological progress. Higher input prices shift cost curves upward.

8. The long run is a period of time sufficiently long for a firm to vary the amounts of all resources used, including plant size. In the long run all costs are variable. The long-run ATC, or planning, curve is composed of segments of the short-run ATC curves, and it represents the various plant sizes a firm can construct in the long run.

9. The long-run ATC curve is generally U-shaped. Economies of scale are first encountered as a small firm expands. Greater specialization in the use of labor and management, the ability to use the most efficient equipment, and the spreading of start-up costs among more units of output all contribute to economies of scale. As the firm continues to grow, it will encounter diseconomies of scale stemming from the managerial complexities that accompany large-scale production. The output ranges over which economies and diseconomies of scale occur in an industry are often an important determinant of the structure of that industry.

TERMS AND CONCEPTS

economic (opportunity) cost

explicit costs

implicit costs

normal profit

economic profit

short run

long run

total product (TP)

marginal product (MP)

average product (AP)

law of diminishing returns

fixed costs

variable costs

total cost

average fixed cost (AFC)

average variable cost (AVC)

average total cost (ATC)

marginal cost (MC)

economies of scale

diseconomies of scale

constant returns to scale

minimum efficient scale (MES)

natural monopoly

STUDY QUESTIONS

1. Distinguish between explicit and implicit costs, giving examples of each. What are some explicit and implicit costs of attending college? Why does the economist classify normal profit as a cost? Is economic profit a cost of production?

2. *Key Question* Gomez runs a small pottery firm. He hires one helper at $12,000 per year, pays annual rent of $5000 for his shop, and spends $20,000 per year on materials. He has $40,000 of his own funds invested in equipment (pottery wheels, kilns, and so forth) that could earn him $4000 per year if alternatively invested. He has been offered $15,000 per year to work as a potter for a competitor. He estimates his entrepreneurial talents are worth $3000 per year. Total annual revenue from pottery sales is $72,000. Calculate the accounting profit and the economic profit for Gomez's pottery firm.

3. Which of the following are short-run and which are long-run adjustments?
   a. Wendy's builds a new restaurant.
   b. Acme Steel Corporation hires 200 more production workers.
   c. A farmer increases the amount of fertilizer used on his corn crop.
   d. An Alcoa aluminum plant adds a third shift of workers.

4. *Key Question* Complete the following table by calculating marginal product and average product from the data given:

Inputs of Labor	Total Product	Marginal Product	Average Product
0	0		
1	15	_____	_____
2	34	_____	_____
3	51	_____	_____
4	65	_____	_____
5	74	_____	_____
6	80	_____	_____
7	83	_____	_____
8	82	_____	_____

Plot the total, marginal, and average products and explain in detail the relationship between each pair of curves. Explain why marginal product first rises, then declines, and ultimately becomes negative. What bearing does the law of diminishing returns have on short-run costs? Be specific. "When marginal product is rising, marginal cost is falling. And when marginal product is diminishing, marginal cost is rising." Illustrate and explain graphically.

5. Why can the distinction between fixed costs and variable costs be made in the short run? Classify the following as fixed or variable costs: advertising expenditures, fuel, interest on company-issued bonds, shipping charges, payments for raw materials, real estate taxes, executive salaries, insurance premiums, wage payments, depreciation and obsolescence charges, sales taxes, and rental payments on leased office machinery. "There are no fixed costs in the long run; all costs are variable." Explain.

6. List several fixed and variable costs associated with owning and operating an automobile. Suppose you are considering whether to drive your car or fly 1000 miles to Florida for spring break. Which costs—fixed, variable, or both—would you take into account in making your decision? Would any implicit costs be relevant? Explain.

7. *Key Question* A firm has fixed costs of $60 and variable costs as indicated in the table on the following page. Complete the table and check your calculations by referring to question 4 at the end of Chapter 23.
   a. Graph total fixed cost, total variable cost, and total cost. Explain how the law of diminishing returns influences the shapes of the variable-cost and total-cost curves.
   b. Graph AFC, AVC, ATC, and MC. Explain the derivation and shape of each of these four curves and their relationships to one another. Specifically, explain in nontechnical terms why the MC curve intersects both the AVC and the ATC curves at their minimum points.
   c. Explain how the location of each curve graphed in question 7b would be altered if (1) total fixed cost had been $100 rather than $60 and (2) total variable cost had been $10 less at each level of output.

Total Product	Total Fixed Cost	Total Variable Cost	Total Cost	Average Fixed Cost	Average Variable Cost	Average Total Cost	Marginal Cost
0	$_____	$ 0	$_____	$_____	$_____	$_____	$_____
1	_____	45	_____	_____	_____	_____	_____
2	_____	85	_____	_____	_____	_____	_____
3	_____	120	_____	_____	_____	_____	_____
4	_____	150	_____	_____	_____	_____	_____
5	_____	185	_____	_____	_____	_____	_____
6	_____	225	_____	_____	_____	_____	_____
7	_____	270	_____	_____	_____	_____	_____
8	_____	325	_____	_____	_____	_____	_____
9	_____	390	_____	_____	_____	_____	_____
10	_____	465	_____	_____	_____	_____	_____

8. Indicate how each of the following would shift the (1) marginal-cost curve, (2) average-variable-cost curve, (3) average-fixed-cost curve, and (4) average-total-cost curve of a manufacturing firm. In each case specify the direction of the shift.
   a. A reduction in business property taxes.
   b. An increase in the nominal wages of production workers.
   c. A decrease in the price of electricity.
   d. An increase in insurance rates on plant and equipment.
   e. An increase in transportation costs.

9. Suppose a firm has only three possible plant-size options, represented by the ATC curves shown in the accompanying figure. What plant size will the firm choose in producing (a) 50, (b) 130, (c) 160, and (d) 250 units of output? Draw the firm's long-run average-cost curve on the diagram and describe this curve.

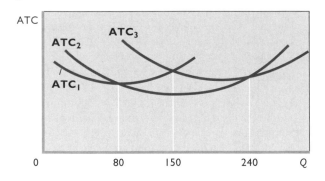

10. *Key Question* Use the concepts of economies and diseconomies of scale to explain the shape of a firm's long-run ATC curve. What is the concept of minimum efficient scale? What bearing can the shape of the long-run ATC curve have on the structure of an industry?

11. *(Last Word)* What is a sunk cost? Provide an example of a sunk cost other than one from this book. Why are such costs irrelevant in making decisions about future actions?

12. *Web-Based Question: The 10 largest U.S. firms—what are their sources of economies of scale?* Find the Forbes 500s list of the largest U.S. firms at www.forbes.com/lists/. From the top 10 list, select three firms from three different industries and discuss the likely sources of the economies of scale that underlie their large size.

13. *Web-Based Question: Corporate annual reports—identify fixed and variable costs* Use the Yahoo search engine at www.yahoo.com to locate the home page of a company of your choice. Find and review the company's income statement in its annual report, and classify the nonrevenue items as either fixed or variable costs. Are all costs clearly identifiable as either fixed or variable? What item would be considered accounting profit? Would economic profit be higher or lower than this accounting profit?

23

Pure Competition

In Chapter 21 we examined the relationship between product demand and total revenue, and in Chapter 22 we discussed costs of production. Now we want to put revenues and costs together to see how a business decides what price to charge and how much output to produce. But a firm's decisions concerning price and production depend greatly on the character of the industry in which it is operating. There is no "average" or "typical" industry. At one extreme is a single producer that dominates the market; at the other extreme are industries in which thousands of firms each produce a tiny fraction of market supply. Between these extremes are many other industries.

Since we cannot examine each industry individually, we will focus on several basic *models* of market structure. Together, these models will help you understand how price and output are determined in the many product markets in the economy. They will also help you evaluate the efficiency or inefficiency of those markets.

Four Market Models

Economists group industries into four distinct market structures: pure competition, pure monopoly, monopolistic competition, and oligopoly. These four market models differ in several respects: the number of firms in the industry, whether those firms produce a standardized product or try to differentiate their products from those of other firms, and how easy or how difficult it is for firms to enter the industry.

Very briefly the four models are as follows:

- **Pure competition** involves a very large number of firms producing a standardized product (that is, a product identical to that of other producers, such as

corn or cucumbers). New firms can enter or exit the industry very easily.
- **Pure monopoly** is a market structure in which one firm is the sole seller of a product or service (for example, a local electric utility). Since the entry of additional firms is blocked, one firm constitutes the entire industry. Because the monopolist produces a unique product, it makes no effort to differentiate its product.
- **Monopolistic competition** is characterized by a relatively large number of sellers producing differentiated products (clothing, furniture, books). There is widespread *nonprice competition*, a selling strategy in which one firm tries to distinguish its product or service from all competing products on the basis of attributes like

TABLE 23.1

Characteristics of the Four Basic Market Models

	Market Model			
Characteristic	Pure Competition	Monopolistic Competition	Oligopoly	Pure Monopoly
Number of firms	A very large number	Many	Few	One
Type of product	Standardized	Differentiated	Standardized or differentiated	Unique; no close substitutes
Control over price	None	Some, but within rather narrow limits	Limited by mutual interdependence; considerable with collusion	Considerable
Conditions of entry	Very easy, no obstacles	Relatively easy	Significant obstacles	Blocked
Nonprice competition	None	Considerable emphasis on advertising, brand names, trademarks	Typically a great deal, particularly with product differentiation	Mostly public relations advertising
Examples	Agriculture	Retail trade, dresses, shoes	Steel, automobiles, farm implements, many household appliances	Local utilities

design and workmanship (an approach called *product differentiation*). Either entry to or exit from monopolistically competitive industries is quite easy.

- **Oligopoly** involves only a few sellers of a standardized or differentiated product; so each firm is affected by the decisions of its rivals and must take those decisions into account in determining its own price and output.

Table 23.1 summarizes the characteristics of the four models for easy comparison. In discussing these four market models, we will occasionally distinguish the characteristics of *pure competition* from those of the three other basic market structures, which together we will designate as **imperfect competition**.

Pure Competition: Characteristics and Occurrence

Let's take a fuller look at pure competition, the focus of the remainder of this chapter:

- *Very large numbers*   A basic feature of a purely competitive market is the presence of a large number of independently acting sellers, often offering their products in large national or international markets. Examples: markets for farm commodities, the stock market, and the foreign exchange market.
- *Standardized product*   Purely competitive firms produce a standardized (identical or homogeneous) product. As long as the price is the same, consumers will

be indifferent about which seller to buy the product from. Buyers view the products of firms B, C, D, and E as perfect substitutes for the product of firm A. Because purely competitive firms sell standardized products, they make no attempt to differentiate their products and do not engage in other forms of nonprice competition.

- *"Price takers"*   In a purely competitive market individual firms exert no significant control over product price. Each firm produces such a small fraction of total output that increasing or decreasing its output will not perceptibly influence total supply or, therefore, product price. In short, the competitive firm is a **price taker:** It cannot change market price; it can only adjust to it. That means that the individual competitive producer is at the mercy of the market. Asking a price higher than the market price would be futile. Consumers will not buy from firm A at $2.05 when its 9999 competitors are selling an identical product, and therefore a perfect substitute, at $2 per unit. Conversely, because firm A can sell as much as it chooses at $2 per unit, there is no reason for it to charge a lower price, say, $1.95, for to do so would shrink its profit.
- *Free entry and exit*   New firms can freely enter and existing firms can freely leave purely competitive industries. No significant legal, technological, financial, or other obstacles prohibit new firms from selling their output in any competitive market.

Relevance of Pure Competition

Although pure competition is relatively rare in the real world, this market model is highly relevant. A few industries more closely approximate pure competition than any other market structure. In particular, we can learn much about markets for agricultural goods, fish products, foreign exchange, basic metals, and stock shares by studying the pure-competition model. Also, pure competition is a meaningful starting point for any discussion of price and output determination. Moreover, the operation of a purely competitive economy provides a standard, or norm, for evaluating the efficiency of the real-world economy.

Demand as Seen by a Purely Competitive Seller

To develop a tabular and graphical model of pure competition, we first examine demand from a competitive seller's viewpoint and see how it affects revenue. This seller might be a wheat farmer, a strawberry grower, a sheep rancher, a catfish raiser, or the like. Because each purely competitive firm offers only a negligible fraction of total market supply, it must accept the price predetermined by the market; it is a price taker, not a price maker.

Perfectly Elastic Demand

The demand curve of the competitive firm, as represented by columns 1 and 2 in Table 23.2, is perfectly elastic. As

shown in the table, the market price is $131. The firm represented cannot obtain a higher price by restricting its output, nor does it need to lower its price to increase its sales volume.

We are *not* saying that *market* demand is perfectly elastic in a competitive market. Rather, market demand graphs as a downsloping curve, as a glance ahead at Figure 23.7b will reveal. In fact, the total-demand curves for most agricultural products are quite inelastic, even though agriculture is the most competitive industry in the U.S. economy. An entire industry (all firms producing a particular product) can affect price by changing industry output. For example, all firms, acting independently but simultaneously, can increase price by reducing output. But the individual firm cannot do that. So the demand schedule faced by the *individual firm* in a purely competitive industry is perfectly elastic at the market price, as demonstrated in Figure 23.1.

Average, Total, and Marginal Revenue

The firm's demand schedule is also its average revenue schedule. What appears as price per unit to the purchaser is also revenue per unit, or average revenue, to the seller. To say that all buyers must pay $131 per unit is to say that the revenue per unit, or **average revenue,** received by the seller is $131. Price and average revenue are the same thing seen from different viewpoints.

The **total revenue** for each sales level is found by multiplying price by the corresponding quantity the firm can sell. (Column 1 multiplied by column 2 in Table 23.2 yields

TABLE 23.2

The Demand and Revenue Schedules for a Purely Competitive Firm

Firm's Demand Schedule		Firm's Revenue Data	
(1) Product Price (P) (Average Revenue)	(2) Quantity Demanded (Q)	(3) Total Revenue (TR), (1) × (2)	(4) Marginal Revenue (MR)
$131	0	$ 0	
131	1	131	$131
131	2	262	131
131	3	393	131
131	4	524	131
131	5	655	131
131	6	786	131
131	7	917	131
131	8	1048	131
131	9	1179	131
131	10	1310	131

FIGURE 23.1

Demand, marginal revenue, and total revenue of a purely competitive firm.   Because a purely competitive firm can sell additional units of output at the market price, its marginal-revenue curve (MR) coincides with its perfectly elastic demand curve (D). The firm's total-revenue curve (TR) is a straight upward-sloping line.

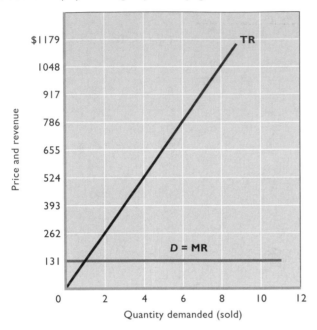

column 3.) In this case, total revenue increases by a constant amount, $131, for each additional unit of sales. Each unit sold adds exactly its constant price to total revenue.

When a firm is pondering a change in its output, it will consider how its total revenue will change as a result. What will be the additional revenue from selling another unit of output? **Marginal revenue** is the change in total revenue, that is, the extra revenue, that results from selling 1 more unit of output. In column 3, Table 23.2, total revenue is zero when zero units are sold. The first unit of output sold increases total revenue from zero to $131; so marginal revenue for that unit is $131. The second unit sold increases total revenue from $131 to $262, and marginal revenue is again $131. Note in column 4 that, as is price, marginal revenue is a constant $131. In pure competition, marginal revenue and price are equal. **(Key Question 3)**

Graphical Portrayal

Figure 23.1 shows the purely competitive firm's demand curve and total-revenue and marginal-revenue curves. The demand curve (D) is horizontal, indicating perfect price

elasticity. The marginal-revenue curve (MR) coincides with the demand curve because the product price (and hence MR) is constant. Total revenue (TR) is a straight line that slopes upward to the right. Its slope is constant because each extra unit of sales increases TR by $131.

Profit Maximization in the Short Run

Because the purely competitive firm is a price taker, it can maximize its economic profit (or minimize its loss) only by adjusting its *output*. And, in the short run, the firm has a fixed plant. Thus it can adjust its output only through changes in the amount of variable resources (materials, labor) it uses. It adjusts its variable resources to achieve the output level that maximizes its profit.

There are two ways to determine the level of output at which a competitive firm will realize maximum profit or minimum loss. One method is to compare total revenue and total cost; the other is to compare marginal revenue and marginal cost. Both approaches apply to all firms, whether they are pure competitors, pure monopolists, monopolistic competitors, or oligopolists.[1]

Total-Revenue–Total-Cost Approach: Profit-Maximization Case

Confronted with the market price of its product, the competitive producer will ask: (1) Should we produce this product? (2) If so, in what amount? (3) What economic profit (or loss) will we realize?

---

[1]To make sure you understand these two approaches, we will apply both of them to output determination under pure competition. But since we want to emphasize the marginal approach, we will limit our graphical application of the total-revenue approach to a situation where the firm maximizes profits. We will then use the marginal approach to examine three cases: profit maximization, loss minimization, and shutdown.

TABLE 23.3

The Profit-Maximizing Output for a Purely Competitive Firm: Total-Revenue–Total-Cost
Approach (Price = $131)

(1) Total Product (Output) (Q)	(2) Total Fixed Cost (TFC)	(3) Total Variable Cost (TVC)	(4) Total Cost (TC)	(5) Total Revenue (TR)	(6) Profit (+) or Loss (−)
0	$100	$ 0	$ 100	$ 0	$ −100
1	100	90	190	131	− 59
2	100	170	270	262	− 8
3	100	240	340	393	+ 53
4	100	300	400	524	+124
5	100	370	470	655	+185
6	100	450	550	786	+236
7	100	540	640	917	+277
8	100	650	750	1048	+298
9	100	780	**880**	**1179**	**+299**
10	100	930	1030	1310	+280

Price: $131

Let's demonstrate how a pure competitor answers these questions, given certain cost data and a specific market price. Our cost data are already familiar to you because they are the fixed-cost, variable-cost, and total-cost data in Table 22.2, repeated in columns 1 to 4 in Table 23.3. (Recall that these data reflect explicit and implicit costs, including a normal profit.) Assuming that the market price is $131, the total revenue for each output level is found by multiplying output (total product) by price. Total-revenue data are in column 5. Then in column 6 we find the profit or loss at each output level by subtracting total cost, TC (column 4), from total revenue, TR (column 5).

Should the firm produce? Definitely. It can realize a profit by doing so. How much should it produce? Nine units. Column 6 tells us that this is the output at which total economic profit is at a maximum. What economic profit (or loss) will it realize? A $299 economic profit—the difference between total revenue ($1179) and total cost ($880).

Figure 23.2a compares total revenue and total cost graphically for this profit-maximizing case. Observe again that the total-revenue curve for a purely competitive firm is a straight line (Table 23.2). Total cost increases with output in that more production requires more resources. But the rate of increase in total cost varies with the relative efficiency of the firm. Specifically, the cost data reflect Chapter 22's law of diminishing marginal returns. From zero to 4 units of output, total cost increases at a decreasing rate as the firm uses its

fixed resources more efficiently. With additional output, total cost begins to rise by ever-increasing amounts because of the diminishing returns accompanying more intensive use of the plant.

Total revenue and total cost are equal where the two curves in Figure 23.2a intersect (at roughly 2 units of output). Total revenue covers all costs (including a normal profit, which is included in the cost curve), but there is no economic profit. For this reason economists call this output a **break-even point:** an output at which a firm makes a *normal profit* but not an economic profit. If we extended the data beyond 10 units of output, another break-even point would occur where total cost catches up with total revenue, somewhere between 13 and 14 units of output in Figure 23.2a. Any output within the two break-even points identified in the figure will produce an economic profit. The firm achieves maximum profit, however, where the vertical distance between the total-revenue and total-cost curves is greatest. For our particular data, this is at 9 units of output, where maximum profit is $299.

The profit-maximizing output is easier to see in Figure 23.2b, where total profit is graphed for each level of output. Where the total-revenue and total-cost curves intersect in Figure 23.2a, economic profit is zero, as shown by the total-profit line in Figure 23.2b. Where the vertical distance between TR and TC is greatest in the upper graph, economic profit is at its peak ($299), as shown in the lower graph. This firm will choose to produce 9 units, since that output maximizes its profit.

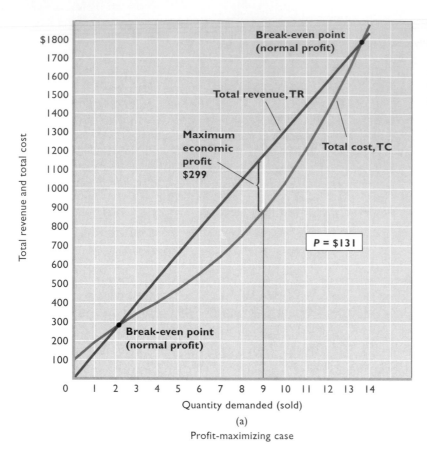

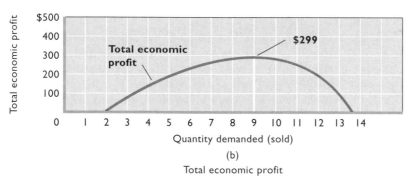

FIGURE 23.2

Total-revenue–total-cost approach to profit maximization for a purely competitive firm. (a) The firm's profit is maximized at that output (9 units) where total revenue, TR, exceeds total cost, TC, by the maximum amount. (b) The vertical distance between TR and TC in (a) is plotted as a total-economic-profit curve. Maximum economic profit is $299 at 9 units of output.

Marginal-Revenue–Marginal-Cost Approach

In the second approach, the firm compares the amounts that each *additional* unit of output would add to total revenue and to total cost. In other words, the firm compares the *marginal revenue* (MR) and the *marginal cost* (MC) of each successive unit of output. Assuming that producing is preferable to shutting down, the firm should produce any unit of output whose marginal revenue exceeds its marginal cost because the firm would gain more in revenue from selling that unit than it would add to its costs by producing it. Conversely, if the marginal cost of a unit of output exceeds its marginal revenue, the firm should not produce that unit. Producing it would add more to costs than to revenue, and profit would decline or loss would increase.

MR = MC Rule In the initial stages of production, where output is relatively low, marginal revenue will usually (but not always) exceed marginal cost. So it is profitable to produce through this range of output. But at later stages of production, where output is relatively high, rising marginal costs will exceed marginal revenue. Obviously, a profit-maximizing firm will want to avoid output levels in that range. Separating these two production ranges is a unique point at which marginal revenue equals marginal cost. This point is the key to the output-determining rule: *In the short run, the firm will maximize profit or minimize loss by producing the output at which marginal revenue equals marginal cost (as long as producing is preferable to shutting down).* This profit-maximizing guide is known as the **MR = MC rule.** (For most sets of MR and MC data, MR and MC will be precisely equal at a fractional level of output. In such instances the firm should produce the last complete unit of output for which MR exceeds MC.)

Three Characteristics of the MR = MC Rule

Keep in mind these three features of the MR = MC rule:
* As noted, the rule applies only if producing is preferable to shutting down. We will show shortly that if marginal revenue does not equal or exceed average variable cost, the firm will shut down rather than produce the MR = MC output.
* The rule is an accurate guide to profit maximization for all firms whether they are purely competitive, monopolistic, monopolistically competitive, or oligopolistic.
* The rule can be restated as *P* = MC when applied to a purely competitive firm. Because the demand schedule faced by a competitive seller is perfectly elastic at the going market price, product price and marginal revenue are equal. So under pure competition (and only under pure competition) we may substitute *P* for MR in the rule: *When producing is preferable to shutting down, the competitive firm that wants to maximize its profit or minimize its loss should produce at that point where price equals marginal cost* (P = MC).

Now let's apply the MR = MC rule or, because we are considering pure competition, the *P* = MC rule, first using the same price as used in our total-revenue–total-cost approach to profit maximization. Then, by considering other prices, we will demonstrate two additional cases: loss minimization and shutdown. *It is crucial that you understand the MR = MC analysis that follows since it reappears in Chapters 24 and 25.*

Profit-Maximizing Case

The first five columns in Table 23.4 reproduce the AFC, AVC, ATC, and MC data derived for our product in Table 22.2. It is the marginal-cost data of column 5 that we will compare with price (equals marginal revenue) for each unit of output. Suppose first that the market price, and therefore marginal revenue, is $131, as shown in column 6.

What is the profit-maximizing output? Every unit of output up to and including the ninth unit represents greater marginal revenue than marginal cost of output. Each of the first 9 units therefore adds to the firm's profit and should be produced. The tenth unit, however, should not be produced. It would add more to cost ($150) than to revenue ($131).

TABLE 23.4

The Profit-Maximizing Output for a Purely Competitive Firm: Marginal-Revenue–Marginal-Cost Approach (Price = $131)

(1) Total Product (Output)	(2) Average Fixed Cost (AFC)	(3) Average Variable Cost (AVC)	(4) Average Total Cost (ATC)	(5) Marginal Cost (MC)	(6) Price = Marginal Revenue (MR)	(7) Total Economic Profit (+) or Loss (−)
0						$ −100
1	$100.00	$90.00	$190.00	$ 90	$131	− 59
2	50.00	85.00	135.00	80	131	− 8
3	33.33	80.00	113.33	70	131	+ 53
4	25.00	75.00	100.00	60	131	+124
5	20.00	74.00	94.00	70	131	+185
6	16.67	75.00	91.67	80	131	+236
7	14.29	77.14	91.43	90	131	+277
8	12.50	81.25	93.75	110	131	+298
9	11.11	86.67	97.78	130	131	+299
10	10.00	93.00	103.00	150	131	+280

KEY GRAPH

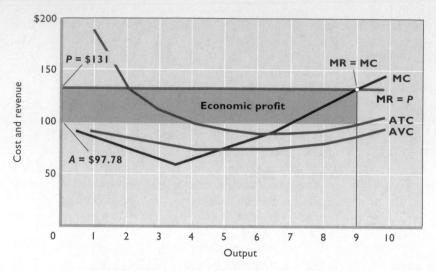

FIGURE 23.3

The short-run profit-maximizing position of a purely competitive firm. The MR = MC output enables the purely competitive firm to maximize profits or to minimize losses. In this case MR (= P in pure competition) and MC are equal at an output Q of 9 units. There P exceeds the average total cost A = $97.78, so the firm realizes an economic profit of P − A per unit. The total economic profit is represented by the blue rectangle and is 9 × (P − A).

Profit Calculations The economic profit realized by producing 9 units can be calculated from the average-total-cost data. Multiplying price ($131) by output (9), we find that total revenue is $1179. Multiplying average total cost ($97.78) by output (9) gives us total cost of $880.[2] The difference of $299 (= $1179 − $880) is the economic profit. Clearly, this firm will prefer to operate rather than shut down.

Perhaps an easier way to calculate the economic profit is to determine the profit per unit by subtracting the average total cost ($97.78) from the product price ($131) and multiplying the difference (a per-unit profit of $33.22) by output (9). Take some time now to verify the numbers in column 7 in Table 23.4. You will find that any output other than that which adheres to the MR = MC rule will mean either profits below $299 or losses.

Graphical Portrayal Figure 23.3 (Key Graph) shows price (= MR) and marginal cost graphically. Price equals marginal cost at the profit-maximizing output of 9 units. There the per-unit economic profit is P − A, where P is the market price and A is the average total cost for an

---

[2]Most of the unit-cost data are rounded figures. Therefore, economic profits calculated from them will typically vary by a few cents from the profits determined in the total-revenue–total-cost approach. Here we simply ignore the few-cents differentials to make our answers consistent with the results of the total-revenue–total-cost approach.

23.1
Short-run profit maximization

output of 9 units. The total economic profit is 9 × (P − A), shown by the blue rectangular area.

Note that the firm wants to maximize its total profit, not its per-unit profit. Per-unit profit is greatest at 7 units of output, where price exceeds average total cost by $39.57 (= $131 − $91.43). But by producing only 7 units, the firm would be forgoing the production of 2 additional units of output that would clearly contribute to total profit. The firm is happy to accept lower per-unit profits for additional units of output because they nonetheless add to total profit.

Loss-Minimizing Case Now let's assume that the market price is $81 rather than $131. Should the firm still produce? If so, how much? And what will be the resulting profit or loss? The answers, respectively, are "Yes," "Six units," and "A loss of $64."

The first five columns in Table 23.5 are the same as those in Table 23.4. Column 6 shows the new price (equal to MR), $81. Comparing columns 5 and 6, we find that the first unit of output adds $90 to total cost but only $81 to total revenue. One might conclude: "Don't produce—close down!" But that would be hasty. Remember that in the very early stages of production, marginal product is low, making marginal cost unusually high. The price–marginal-cost relationship improves with increased production. For units 2 through 6, price exceeds marginal cost. Each of these 5 units adds more to revenue than to

cost, and as shown in column 7, they decrease the total loss. Together they more than compensate for the "loss" taken on the first unit. Beyond 6 units, however, MC exceeds MR (= P). The firm should therefore produce 6 units. In general, the profit-seeking producer should always compare marginal revenue (or price under pure competition) with the rising portion of the marginal-cost schedule or curve.

Loss Determination Will production be profitable? No, because at 6 units of output the average total cost of $91.67 exceeds the price of $81 by $10.67 per unit. If we multiply that by the 6 units of output, we find the firm's total loss is $64. Alternatively, comparing the total revenue of $486 (= 6 × $81) with the total cost of $550 (= 6 × $91.67), we see again that the firm's loss is $64.

Then why produce? Because this loss is less than the firm's $100 of fixed costs, which is the $100 loss the firm would incur in the short run by closing down. The firm receives enough revenue per unit ($81) to cover its average variable costs of $75 and also provide $6 per unit, or a total of $36, to apply against fixed costs. Therefore, the firm's loss is only $64 (= $100 − $36), not $100.

Graphical Portrayal This loss-minimizing case is shown graphically in Figure 23.4. Wherever price P exceeds average variable cost AVC but is less than ATC, the firm can pay part, but not all, of its fixed costs by producing. The loss is minimized by producing the output at which MC = MR (here, 6 units). At that output, each unit contributes P − V to covering fixed cost, where V is the

TABLE 23.5
The Loss-Minimizing Outputs for a Purely Competitive Firm: Marginal-Revenue–Marginal-Cost Approach (Prices = $81 and $71)

(1) Total Product (Output)	(2) Average Fixed Cost (AFC)	(3) Average Variable Cost (AVC)	(4) Average Total Cost (ATC)	(5) Marginal Cost (MC)	(6) $81 Price = Marginal Revenue (MR)	(7) Profit (+) or Loss (−), $81 Price	(8) $71 Price = Marginal Revenue (MR)	(9) Profit (+) or Loss (−), $71 Price
0						$ −100		$−100
1	$100.00	$90.00	$190.00	$ 90	$81	−109	$71	−119
2	50.00	85.00	135.00	80	81	−108	71	−128
3	33.33	80.00	113.33	70	81	− 97	71	−127
4	25.00	75.00	100.00	60	81	− 76	71	−116
5	20.00	74.00	94.00	70	81	− 65	71	−115
6	16.67	75.00	91.67	80	81	− 64	71	−124
7	14.29	77.14	91.43	90	81	− 73	71	−143
8	12.50	81.25	93.75	110	81	−102	71	−182
9	11.11	86.67	97.78	130	81	−151	71	−241
10	10.00	93.00	103.00	150	81	−220	71	−320

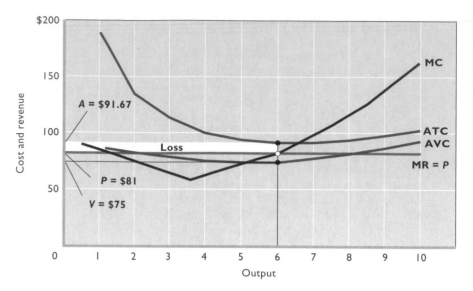

FIGURE 23.4

The short-run loss-minimizing position of a purely competitive firm. If price P exceeds the minimum AVC (here $74 at Q = 5) but is less than ATC, the MR = MC output (here 6 units) will permit the firm to minimize its losses. In this instance the loss is A − P per unit, where A is the average total cost at 6 units of output. The total loss is shown by the white area and is equal to 6 × (A − P).

AVC at 6 units of output. The per-unit loss is $A − P = \$10.67$, and the total loss is $6 \times (A − P)$, or \$64, as shown by the white area.

Shutdown Case

Suppose now that the market yields a price of only $71. Should the firm produce? No, because at every output the firm's average variable cost is greater than the price (compare columns 3 and 8 in Table 23.5). The smallest loss it can incur by producing is greater than the $100 fixed cost it will lose by shutting down (as shown by column 9). The best action is to shut down.

You can see this shutdown situation in Figure 23.5. Price comes closest to covering average variable costs at the MR (= P) = MC output of 5 units. But even here, price or revenue per unit would fall short of average variable cost by $3 (= $74 − $71). By producing at the MR (= P) = MC output, the firm would lose its $100 worth of fixed cost plus $15 ($3 of variable cost on each of the 5 units), for a total loss of $115. This compares unfavorably with the $100 fixed-cost loss the firm would incur by shutting down and producing no output. So it will make sense for the firm to shut down rather than produce at a $71 price—or at any price less than the minimum average variable cost of $74.

The shutdown case reminds us of the qualifier to our MR (= P) = MC rule. A competitive firm will maximize

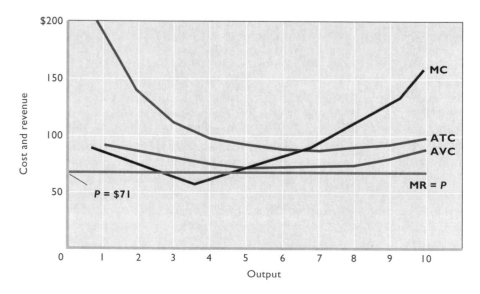

FIGURE 23.5

The short-run shutdown position of a purely competitive firm. If price P falls below the minimum AVC (here $74 at Q = 5), the competitive firm will minimize its losses in the short run by shutting down. There is no level of output at which the firm can produce and realize a loss smaller than its total fixed cost.

CONSIDER THIS . . .

© Douglas Kirkland/CORBIS

The Still There Motel

Have you ever driven by a poorly maintained business facility and wondered why the owner does not either fix up the property or go out of business? The somewhat surprising reason is that it may be unprofitable to improve the facility yet profitable to continue to operate the business as it deteriorates. Seeing why will aid your understanding of the "stay open or shut down" decision facing firms experiencing declining demand.

Consider the story of the Still There Motel on Old Highway North, Anytown, USA. The owner built the motel on the basis of traffic patterns and competition existing several decades ago. But as interstate highways were built, the motel found itself located on a relatively vacant stretch of road. Also, it faced severe competition from "chain" motels located much closer to the interstate highway.

As demand and revenue fell, Still There moved from profitability to loss. But at first its room rates and annual revenue were sufficient to cover its total variable costs and contribute some to the payment of fixed costs (or $P > \text{AVC}$; $P < \text{ATC}$). By staying open, Still There lost less than it would have if it shut down. But since its total revenue did not cover its total costs (or $P < \text{ATC}$), the owner realized that something must be done in the long run. The owner decided to lower costs by reducing annual maintenance. In effect, the owner decided to allow the motel to deteriorate as a way of regaining temporary profitability.

This renewed profitability of Still There cannot last because in time the deterioration of the motel structure will produce even lower room rates, and therefore even less total revenue. The owner of Still There knows that sooner or later total revenue will again fall below total cost (or P will again fall below ATC), even with an annual maintenance expense of zero. When that occurs, the owner will close down the business, tear down the structure, and sell the vacant property. But, in the meantime, the motel is still there—open, deteriorating, and profitable.

profit or minimize loss in the short run by producing that output at which MR ($= P$) = MC, *provided that market price exceeds minimum average variable cost.*

Marginal Cost and Short-Run Supply

In the preceding section we simply selected three different prices and asked what quantity the profit-seeking competitive firm, faced with certain costs, would choose to of-

TABLE 23.6

The Supply Schedule of a Competitive Firm Confronted with the Cost Data in Table 23.4

Price	Quantity Supplied	Maximum Profit (+) or Minimum Loss (−)
$151	10	$ +480
131	9	+299
111	8	+138
91	7	− 3
81	6	− 64
71	0	−100
61	0	−100

fer in the market at each price. This set of product prices and corresponding quantities supplied constitutes part of the supply schedule for the competitive firm.

Table 23.6 summarizes the supply schedule data for those three prices ($131, $81, and $71) and four others. This table confirms the direct relationship between product price and quantity supplied that we identified in Chapter 3. Note first that the firm will not produce at price $61 or $71, because both are less than the $74 minimum AVC. Then note that quantity supplied increases as price increases. Observe finally that economic profit is higher at higher prices.

Generalized Depiction

Figure 23.6 (Key Graph) generalizes the MR = MC rule and the relationship between short-run production costs and the firm's supply behavior. The ATC, AVC, and MC curves are shown, along with several marginal-revenue lines drawn at possible market prices. Let's observe quantity supplied at each of these prices:

- Price P_1 is below the firm's minimum average variable cost, so at this price the firm won't operate at all. Quantity supplied will be zero, as it will be at all other prices below P_2.
- Price P_2 is just equal to the minimum average variable cost. The firm will supply Q_2 units of output (where MR_2 = MC) and just cover its total variable cost. Its loss will equal its total fixed cost. (Actually, the firm would be indifferent as to shutting down or supplying Q_2 units of output, but we assume it produces.)
- At price P_3 the firm will supply Q_3 units of output to minimize its short-run losses. At any other price between P_2 and P_4 the firm will minimize its losses by producing and supplying the quantity at which MR ($= P$) = MC.

KEY GRAPH

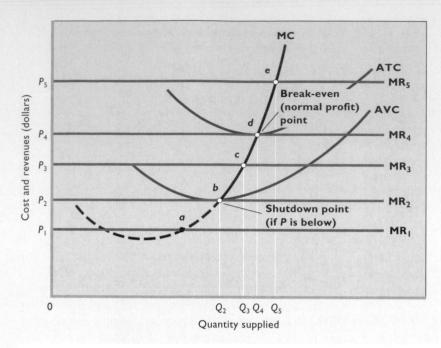

FIGURE 23.6

The $P = MC$ rule and the competitive firm's short-run supply curve. Application of the $P = MC$ rule, as modified by the shutdown case, reveals that the (solid) segment of the firm's MC curve that lies above AVC is the firm's short-run supply curve. More specifically, at price P_1, $P = MC$ at point a, but the firm will produce no output because P_1 is less than minimum AVC. At price P_2 the firm will operate at point b, where it produces Q_2 units and incurs a loss equal to its total fixed cost. At P_3 it operates at point c, where output is Q_3 and the loss is less than total fixed cost. With the price of P_4, the firm operates at point d; in this case the firm earns a normal profit because at output Q_4 price equals ATC. At price P_5 the firm operates at point e and maximizes its economic profit by producing Q_5 units.

QUICK QUIZ 23.6

1. Which of the following might increase product price from P_3 to P_5?
    a. An improvement in production technology.
    b. A decline in the price of a substitute good.
    c. An increase in the price of a complementary good.
    d. Rising incomes if the product is a normal good.

2. An increase in price from P_3 to P_5 would:
    a. shift this firm's MC curve to the right.
    b. mean that MR_5 exceeds MC at Q_3 units, inducing the firm to expand output to Q_5.
    c. decrease this firm's average variable costs.
    d. enable this firm to obtain a normal, but not an economic, profit.

3. At P_4:
    a. this firm has no economic profit.
    b. this firm will earn only a normal profit and thus will shut down.
    c. MR_4 will be less than MC at the profit-maximizing output.
    d. the profit-maximizing output will be Q_5.

4. Suppose P_4 is $10, P_5 is $15, Q_4 is 8 units, and Q_5 is 10 units. This firm's:
    a. supply curve is elastic over the Q_4–Q_5 range of output.
    b. supply curve is inelastic over the Q_4–Q_5 range of output.
    c. total revenue will decline if price rises from P_4 to P_5.
    d. marginal-cost curve will shift downward if price falls from P_5 to P_4.

Answers: 1. d; 2. b; 3. a; 4. b

- The firm will just break even at price P_4. There it will supply Q_4 units of output (where $MR_4 = MC$), earning a normal profit but not an economic profit. Total revenue will just cover total cost, including a normal profit, because the revenue per unit ($MR_4 = P_4$) and the total cost per unit (ATC) are the same.

- At price P_5 the firm will realize an economic profit by producing and supplying Q_5 units of output. In fact, at any price above P_4 the firm will obtain economic profit by producing to the point where MR ($= P$) $= MC$.

Note that each of the MR ($= P$) $= MC$ intersection points labeled b, c, d and e in Figure 23.6 indicates a possible product price (on the vertical axis) and the corresponding quantity that the firm would supply at that price (on the horizontal axis). Thus, points such as these are on the upsloping supply curve of the competitive firm. Note too that quantity supplied would be zero at any price below the minimum average variable cost (AVC). We can conclude that the portion of the firm's marginal-cost curve lying above its average-variable-cost curve is its short-run supply curve. In Figure 23.6, the solid segment of the marginal-cost curve MC is this firm's **short-run supply curve.** It tells us the amount of output the firm will supply at each price in a series of prices.

Diminishing Returns, Production Costs, and Product Supply

We have now identified the links between the law of diminishing returns (Chapter 22), production costs, and product supply in the short run. Because of the law of diminishing returns, marginal costs eventually rise as more units of output are produced. And because marginal costs rise with output, a purely competitive firm must get successively higher prices to motivate it to produce additional units of output.

Viewed alternatively, higher product prices and marginal revenue encourage a purely competitive firm to expand output. As its output increases, the firm's marginal costs rise as a result of the law of diminishing returns. At some now greater output, the higher MC equals the new product price and MR. Profit once again is maximized, but at a greater total amount. Quantity supplied has increased in direct response to an increase in product price and the desire to maximize profit.

Changes in Supply

In Chapter 22 we saw that changes in such factors as the prices of variable inputs or in technology will alter costs and shift the marginal-cost or short-run supply curve to a new location. All else equal, for example, a wage increase would increase marginal cost and shift the supply curve in Figure 23.6 upward as viewed from the horizontal axis (leftward as viewed from the vertical axis). That is, supply would decrease. Similarly, technological progress that increases the productivity of labor would reduce marginal cost and shift the marginal-cost or supply curve downward as viewed from the horizontal axis (rightward as viewed from the vertical axis). This represents an increase in supply.

Firm and Industry: Equilibrium Price

In the preceding section we developed the competitive firm's short-run supply curve by applying the MR (= P) = MC rule. We now determine which of the various possible prices will actually be the market equilibrium price.

TABLE 23.7

Firm and Market Supply and Market Demand

(1) Quantity Supplied, Single Firm	(2) Total Quantity Supplied, 1000 Firms	(3) Product Price	(4) Total Quantity Demanded
10	10,000	$151	4,000
9	9,000	131	6,000
8	*8,000*	*111*	*8,000*
7	7,000	91	9,000
6	6,000	81	11,000
0	0	71	13,000
0	0	61	16,000

From Chapter 3 we know that in a purely competitive market, equilibrium price is determined by total, or market, supply and total demand. To derive total supply, the supply schedules or curves of the individual competitive sellers must be summed. Columns 1 and 3 in Table 23.7 repeat the supply schedule for the individual competitive firm, as derived in Table 23.6. We now assume that there are 1000 competitive firms in this industry, all having the same total and unit costs as the single firm we discussed. This lets us calculate the market supply schedule (columns 2 and 3) by multiplying the quantity-supplied figures of the single firm (column 1) by 1000.

Market Price and Profits   To determine the equilibrium price and output, these total-supply data must be compared with total-demand data. Let's assume that total demand is as shown in columns 3 and 4 in Table 23.7. By comparing the total quantity supplied and the total quantity demanded at the seven possible prices, we determine that the equilibrium price is $111 and the equilibrium quantity is 8000 units for the industry—8 units for each of the 1000 identical firms.

Will these conditions of market supply and demand make this a profitable or unprofitable industry? Multiplying produce price ($111) by output (8 units), we find that the total revenue of each firm is $888. The total cost is $750, found by looking at column 4 in Table 23.3. The $138 difference is the economic profit of each firm. For the industry, total economic profit is $138,000. This, then, is a profitable industry.

Another way of calculating economic profit is to determine per-unit profit by subtracting average total cost

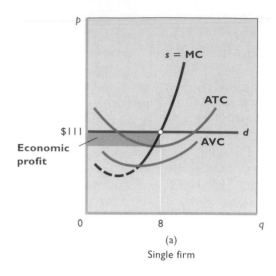

(a)
Single firm

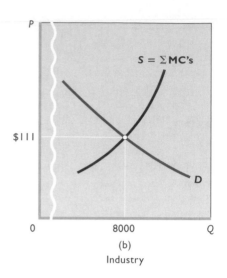

(b)
Industry

FIGURE 23.7

Short-run competitive equilibrium for (a) a firm and (b) the industry. The horizontal sum of the 1000 firms' individual supply curves (*s*) determines the industry supply curve (*S*). Given industry demand (*D*), the short-run equilibrium price and output for the industry are $111 and 8000 units. Taking the equilibrium price as given, the individual firm establishes its profit-maximizing output at 8 units and, in this case, realizes the economic profit represented by the blue area.

($93.75) from product price ($111) and multiplying the difference (per-unit profit of $17.25) by the firm's equilibrium level of output (8). Again we obtain an economic profit of $138 per firm and $138,000 for the industry.

Graphical Portrayal   Figure 23.7 shows this analysis graphically. The individual supply curves of each of the 1000 identical firms—one of which is shown as *s* = MC in Figure 23.7a—are summed horizontally to get the total-supply curve *S* = ΣMC of Figure 23.7b. With total-demand curve *D*, it yields the equilibrium price $111 and equilibrium quantity (for the industry) 8000 units. This equilibrium price is given and unalterable to the individual firm; that is, each firm's demand curve is perfectly elastic at the equilibrium price, as indicated by *d* in Figure 23.7a. Because the individual firm is a price taker, the marginal-revenue curve coincides with the firm's demand curve *d*. This $111 price exceeds the average total cost at the firm's equilibrium MR = MC output of 8 units, so the firm earns an economic profit represented by the blue area in Figure 23.7a.

Assuming no changes in costs or market demand, these diagrams reveal a genuine equilibrium in the short run. There are no shortages or surpluses in the market to cause price or total quantity to change. Nor can any firm in the industry increase its profit by altering its output. Note, too, that higher unit and marginal costs, on the one hand, or weaker market demand, on the other, could change the situation so that Figure 23.7a resembles Figure 23.4 or Figure 23.5. In Figure 23.7a and 23.7b, sketch how higher costs or decreased demand could produce short-run losses.

Firm versus Industry   Figure 23.7 underscores a point made earlier: Product price is a given fact to the *individual* competitive firm, but the supply plans of all competitive producers *as a group* are a basic determinant of product price. If we recall the fallacy of composition, we find there is no inconsistency here. Although one firm, supplying a negligible fraction of total supply, cannot affect price, the sum of the supply curves of all the firms in the industry constitutes the industry supply curve, and that curve does have an important bearing on price. **(Key Question 4)**

QUICK REVIEW 23.2

• Profit is maximized, or loss minimized, at the output at which marginal revenue (or price in pure competition) equals marginal cost, provided that price exceeds average variable cost.

• If the market price is below the minimum average variable cost, the firm will minimize its losses by shutting down.

• The segment of the firm's marginal-cost curve that lies above the average-variable-cost curve is its short-run supply curve.

• Table 23.8 summarizes the MR = MC approach to determining the competitive firm's profit-maximizing output. It also shows the equivalent analysis in terms of total revenue and total cost.

• Under competition, equilibrium price is a given to the individual firm and simultaneously is the result of the production (supply) decisions of all firms as a group.

TABLE 23.8

Output Determination in Pure Competition in the Short Run

Question	Answer
Should this firm produce?	Yes, if price is equal to, or greater than, minimum average variable cost. This means that the firm is profitable or that its losses are less than its fixed cost.
What quantity should this firm produce?	Produce where MR (= P) = MC; there, profit is maximized (TR exceeds TC by a maximum amount) or loss is minimized.
Will production result in economic profit?	Yes, if price exceeds average total cost (TR will exceed TC). No, if average total cost exceeds price (TC will exceed TR).

Profit Maximization in the Long Run

In the short run the industry is composed of a specific number of firms, each with a fixed, unalterable plant. Firms may shut down in the sense that they can produce zero units of output in the short run, but they do not have sufficient time to liquidate their assets and go out of business. By contrast, in the long run firms already in an industry have sufficient time either to expand or to contract their plant capacities. More important, the number of firms in the industry may either increase or decrease as new firms enter or existing firms leave. We now examine how these long-run adjustments modify our conclusions concerning short-run output and price determination.

Assumptions

We make three simplifying assumptions, none of which affects our conclusions:

- *Entry and exit only* The only long-run adjustment is the entry or exit of firms. Moreover, we ignore all short-run adjustments in order to concentrate on the effects of the long-run adjustments.
- *Identical costs* All firms in the industry have identical cost curves. This assumption lets us discuss an "average," or "representative," firm, knowing that all other firms in the industry are similarly affected by any long-run adjustments that occur.
- *Constant-cost industry* The industry is a constant-cost industry. This means that the entry and exit of firms does not affect resource prices or, consequently, the locations of the average-total-cost curves of individual firms.

Goal of Our Analysis

The basic conclusion we seek to explain is this: After all long-run adjustments are completed, product price will be exactly equal to, and production will occur at, each firm's minimum average total cost.

This conclusion follows from two basic facts: (1) Firms seek profits and shun losses, and (2) under pure competition, firms are free to enter and leave an industry. If market price initially exceeds average total costs, the resulting economic profits will attract new firms to the industry. But this industry expansion will increase supply until price is brought back down to equality with minimum average total cost. Conversely, if price is initially less than average total cost, resulting losses will cause firms to leave the industry. As they leave, total supply will decline, bringing the price back up to equality with minimum average total cost.

Long-Run Equilibrium

Consider the average firm in a purely competitive industry that is initially in long-run equilibrium. This firm is represented in Figure 23.8a, where MR = MC and price and minimum average total cost are equal at $50. Economic profit here is zero; the industry is in equilibrium or "at rest" because there is no tendency for firms to enter or to leave. The existing firms are earning normal profits, which, recall, are included in their cost curves. The $50 market price is determined in Figure 23.8b by market or industry demand D_1 and supply S_1. (S_1 is a short-run supply curve; we will develop the long-run industry supply curve in our discussion.)

As shown on the quantity axes of the two graphs, equilibrium output in the industry is 100,000 while equilibrium output for the single firm is 100. If all firms in the industry are identical, there must be 1000 firms (= 100,000/100).

Entry Eliminates Economic Profits Let's upset the long-run equilibrium in Figure 23.8 and see what happens. Suppose a change in consumer tastes increases

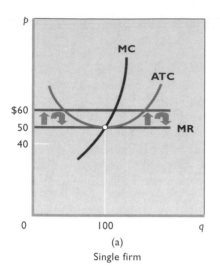

(a)

Single firm

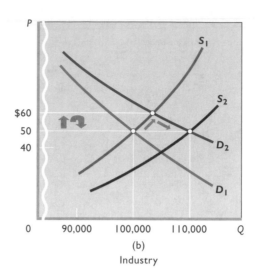

(b)

Industry

FIGURE 23.8

Temporary profits and the reestablishment of long-run equilibrium in (a) a representative firm and (b) the industry. A favorable shift in demand (D_1 to D_2) will upset the original industry equilibrium and produce economic profits. But those profits will cause new firms to enter the industry, increasing supply (S_1 to S_2) and lowering product price until economic profits are once again zero.

product demand from D_1 to D_2. Price will rise to $60, as determined at the intersection of D_2 and S_1, and the firm's marginal-revenue curve will shift upward to $60. This $60 price exceeds the firm's average total cost of $50 at output 100, creating an economic profit of $10 per unit. This economic profit will lure new firms into the industry. Some entrants will be newly created firms; others will shift from less prosperous industries.

As firms enter, the market supply of the product increases, pushing the product price below $60. Economic profits persist, and entry continues until short-run supply increases to S_2. Market price falls to $50, as does marginal revenue for the firm. Price and minimum average total cost are again equal at $50. The economic profits caused by the

boost in demand have been eliminated, and, as a result, the previous incentive for more firms to enter the industry has disappeared. Long-run equilibrium has been restored.

Observe in Figure 23.8a and 23.8b that total quantity supplied is now 110,000 units and each firm is producing 100 units. Now 1100 firms rather than the original 1000 populate the industry. Economic profits have attracted 100 more firms.

Exit Eliminates Losses Now let's consider a shift in the opposite direction. We begin in Figure 23.9b with curves S_1 and D_1 setting the same initial long-run equilibrium situation as in our previous analysis, including the $50 price.

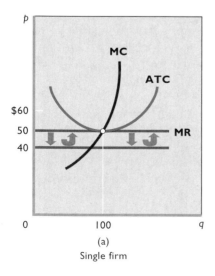

(a)

Single firm

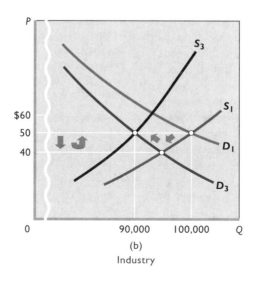

(b)

Industry

FIGURE 23.9

Temporary losses and the reestablishment of long-run equilibrium in (a) a representative firm and (b) the industry. An unfavorable shift in demand (D_1 to D_3) will upset the original industry equilibrium and produce losses. But those losses will cause firms to leave the industry, decreasing supply (S_1 to S_3) and increasing product price until all losses have disappeared.

Suppose consumer demand declines from D_1 to D_3. This forces the market price and marginal revenue down to $40, making production unprofitable at the minimum ATC of $50. In time the resulting losses will induce firms to leave the industry. Their owners will seek a normal profit elsewhere rather than accept the below-normal profits (loss) now confronting them. And as capital equipment wears out, some firms will simply go out of business. As this exodus of firms proceeds, however, industry supply decreases, pushing the price up from $40 toward $50. Losses continue and more firms leave the industry until the supply curve shifts to S_3. Once this happens, price is again $50, just equal to the minimum average total cost. Losses have been eliminated and long-run equilibrium is restored.

In Figure 23.9a and 23.9b, total quantity supplied is now 90,000 units and each firm is producing 100 units. Only 900 firms, not the original 1000, populate the industry. Losses have forced 100 firms out.

You may have noted that we have sidestepped the question of which firms will leave the industry when losses occur by assuming that all firms have identical cost curves. In the "real world," of course, entrepreneurial talents differ. Even if resource prices and technology are the same for all firms, inferior entrepreneurs tend to incur higher costs and therefore are the first to leave an industry when demand declines. Similarly, firms with less productive labor forces will be higher-cost producers and likely candidates to quit an industry when demand decreases.

We have now reached an intermediate goal: Our analysis verifies that competition, reflected in the entry and exit of firms, eliminates economic profits or losses by adjusting price to equal minimum long-run average total cost. In addition, this competition forces firms to select output levels at which average total cost is minimized.

Long-Run Supply for a Constant-Cost Industry

Although our analysis has dealt with the long run, we have noted that the market supply curves in Figures 23.8b and 23.9b are short-run curves. What then is the character of the **long-run supply curve** of a competitive industry? The analysis points us toward an answer. The crucial factor here is the effect, if any, that changes in the number of firms in the industry will have on costs of the individual firms in the industry.

Constant-Cost Industry   In our analysis of long-run competitive equilibrium we assumed that the industry un-

der discussion was a **constant-cost industry.** This means that industry expansion or contraction will not affect resource prices and therefore production costs. Graphically, it means that the entry or exit of firms does not shift the long-run ATC curves of individual firms. This is the case when the industry's demand for resources is small in relation to the total demand for those resources. Then the industry can expand or contract without significantly affecting resource prices and costs.

Perfectly Elastic Long-Run Supply   What does the long-run supply curve of a constant-cost industry look like? The answer is contained in our previous analysis. There we saw that the entry and exit of firms changes industry output but always brings the product price back to its original level, where it is just equal to the constant minimum ATC. Specifically, we discovered that the industry would supply 90,000, 100,000, or 110,000 units of output, all at a price of $50 per unit. In other words, the long-run supply curve of a constant-cost industry is perfectly elastic.

This is demonstrated graphically in Figure 23.10, which uses data from Figures 23.8 and 23.9. Suppose industry demand is originally D_1, industry output is Q_1 (100,000 units), and product price is P_1 ($50). This situation, from Figure 23.8, is one of long-run equilibrium. We saw that when demand increases to D_2, upsetting this equilibrium, the resulting economic profits attract new

FIGURE 23.10

The long-run supply curve for a constant-cost industry is horizontal. Because the entry or exodus of firms does not affect resource prices or, therefore, unit costs, an increase in demand (D_1 to D_2) causes an expansion in industry output (Q_1 to Q_2) but no alteration in price ($50). Similarly, a decrease in demand (D_1 to D_3) causes a contraction of output (Q_1 to Q_3) but no change in price. This means that the long-run industry supply curve (S) is horizontal through points Z_1, Z_2 and Z_3.

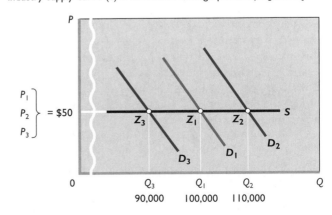

firms. Because this is a constant-cost industry, entry continues and industry output expands until the price is driven back down to the level of the unchanged minimum ATC. This is at price P_2 ($50) and output Q_2 (110,000).

From Figure 23.9, we saw that a decline in market demand from D_1 to D_3 causes an exit of firms and ultimately restores equilibrium at price P_3 ($50) and output Q_3 (90,000 units). The points Z_1, Z_2, and Z_3 in Figure 23.10 represent these three price-quantity combinations. A line or curve connecting all such points shows the various price-quantity combinations that firms would produce if they had enough time to make all desired adjustments to changes in demand. This line or curve is the industry's long-run supply curve. In a constant-cost industry this curve (straight line) is horizontal, as in Figure 23.10, thus representing perfectly elastic supply.

Long-Run Supply for an Increasing-Cost Industry

Constant-cost industries are a special case. Most industries are **increasing-cost industries,** in which firms' ATC curves shift upward as the industry expands and downward as the industry contracts. Usually, the entry of new firms will increase resource prices, particularly in industries using specialized resources whose supplies are not readily increased in response to an increase in resource demand. Higher resource prices result in higher long-run average total costs for all firms in the industry. These higher costs cause upward shifts in each firm's long-run ATC curve.

Thus, when an increase in product demand results in economic profits and attracts new firms to an increasing-cost industry, a two-way squeeze works to eliminate those profits. As before, the entry of new firms increases market supply and lowers the market price. But now the entire ATC curve shifts upward. The overall result is a higher-than-original equilibrium price. The industry produces a larger output at a higher product price because the industry expansion has increased resource prices and the minimum average total cost. We know that, in the long run, the product price must cover ATC.

Since greater output will be supplied at a higher price, the long-run industry supply curve is upsloping. Instead of supplying 90,000, 100,000, or 110,000 units at the same price of $50, an increasing-cost industry might supply 90,000 units at $45, 100,000 units at $50, and 110,000 units at $55. A higher price is required to induce more production, because costs per unit of output increase as production rises.

FIGURE 23.11

The long-run supply curve for an increasing-cost industry is up-sloping. In an increasing-cost industry the entry of new firms in response to an increase in demand (D_3 to D_1 to D_2) will bid up resource prices and thereby increase unit costs. As a result, an increased industry output (Q_3 to Q_1 to Q_2) will be forthcoming only at higher prices ($55 > $50 > $45). The long-run industry supply curve (S) therefore slopes upward through points Y_3, Y_1, and, Y_2.

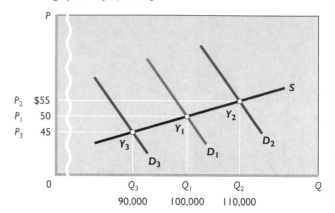

We show this in Figure 23.11. Original market demand is D_1 and industry price and output are P_1 ($50) and Q_1 (100,000 units), respectively, at equilibrium point Y_1. An increase in demand to D_2 upsets this equilibrium and leads to economic profits. New firms enter the industry, increasing both market supply and production costs of individual firms. A new price is established at point Y_2, where P_2 is $55 and Q_2 is 110,000 units.

Conversely, a decline in demand from D_1 to D_3 makes production unprofitable and causes firms to leave the industry. The resulting decline in resource prices reduces the minimum average total cost of production for firms that stay. A new equilibrium price is established at some level below the original price, say, at point Y_3, where P_3 is $45 and Q_3 is 90,000 units. Connecting these three equilibrium positions, we derive the upsloping long-run supply curve S in Figure 23.11.

Long-Run Supply for a Decreasing-Cost Industry

In **decreasing-cost industries,** firms experience lower costs as the industry expands. The personal computer industry is an example. As demand for personal computers increased, new manufacturers of computers entered the industry and greatly increased the resource demand for the components used to build them (for example, memory chips, hard drives, monitors, and operating software).

KEY GRAPH

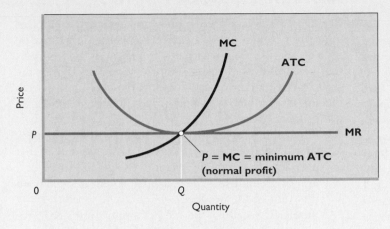

FIGURE 23.12

The long-run equilibrium position of a competitive firm:
P = MC = minimum ATC. The equality of price and minimum average total cost indicates that the firm is using the most
efficient known technology and is charging the lowest price P and
producing the greatest output Q consistent with its costs. The
equality of price and marginal cost indicates that resources are
being allocated in accordance with consumer preferences.

QUICK QUIZ 23.12

1. We know this firm is a price taker because:
   a. its MC curve slopes upward.
   b. its ATC curve is U-shaped.
   c. its MR curve is horizontal.
   d. MC and ATC are equal at the profit-maximizing output.

2. This firm's MC curve is rising because:
   a. it is a price taker,
   b. of the law of diminishing marginal utility.
   c. wage rates rise as output expands.
   d. of the law of diminishing marginal returns.

3. At this firm's profit-maximizing output:
   a. total revenue equals total cost.

   b. it is earning an economic profit.
   c. allocative, but not necessarily productive, efficiency is achieved.
   d. productive, but not necessarily allocative, efficiency is achieved.

4. The equality of P, MC, and minimum ATC:
   a. occurs only in constant-cost Industries.
   b. encourages entry of new firms.
   c. means that the "right goods" are being produced in the "right ways."
   d. results in a zero accounting profit.

Answers: 1. c; 2. d; 3. a; 4. c

The expanded production of the components enabled the producers of those items to achieve substantial economies of scale. The decreased production costs of the components reduced their prices, which greatly lowered the computer manufacturers' average costs of production. The supply of personal computers increased by more than demand, and the price of personal computers declined.

We urge you to rework the analysis underlying Figure 23.11 to show that the long-run supply curve of a decreasing-cost industry is *downsloping*. **(Key Question 6)**

Pure Competition and Efficiency

Our final goal in this chapter is to relate pure competition to efficiency. Whether a purely competitive indus-

try is a constant-cost industry or an increasing-cost industry, the final long-run equilibrium positions of all firms have the same basic characteristics relating to economic efficiency. As shown in **Figure 23.12 (Key Graph)**, price (and marginal revenue) will settle where it is equal to minimum average total cost: P (and MR) = minimum ATC. Moreover, since the marginal-cost curve intersects the average-total-cost curve at its minimum point, marginal cost and average total cost are equal: MC = minimum ATC. Thus in long-run equilibrium there is a multiple equality: P (and MR) = MC = minimum ATC.

This triple equality tells us that although a competitive firm may realize economic profit or loss in the short run, it will earn only a normal profit by producing in accordance with the MR (= P) = MC rule in the long run. Also, this triple equality suggests certain conclusions of great social significance concerning the efficiency of a purely competitive economy.

Economists agree that, subject to qualifications discussed in later chapters, an idealized purely competitive economy leads to an efficient use of society's scarce resources. A competitive market economy uses the limited amounts of resources available to society in a way that maximizes the satisfaction of consumers. As we demonstrated in Chapter 2, efficient use of limited resources requires both productive efficiency and allocative efficiency.

Productive efficiency requires that goods be produced in the least costly way. **Allocative efficiency** requires that resources be apportioned among firms and industries so as to yield the mix of products and services that is most wanted by society (consumers). Allocative efficiency has been realized when it is impossible to alter the combination of goods produced and achieve a net gain for society. Let's look at how productive and allocative efficiency would be achieved under purely competitive conditions.

23.1
Allocative
efficiency

Productive Efficiency: P = Minimum ATC

In the long run, pure competition forces firms to produce at the minimum average total cost of production and to charge a price that is just consistent with that cost. That is a highly favorable situation from the consumer's point of view. It means that unless firms use the best-available (least-cost) production methods and combinations of inputs, they will not survive. Stated differently, it means that the minimum amount of resources will be used to produce any particular output. Let's suppose that output is cucumbers.

In the final equilibrium position shown in Figure 23.9a, each firm in the cucumber industry is producing 100 units (say, pickup truckloads) of output by using $5000 (equal to average total cost of $50 × 100 units) worth of resources. If one firm produced that same output at a total cost of, say, $7000, its resources would be used inefficiently. Society would be faced with a net loss of $2000 worth of alternative products. But this cannot happen in pure competition; this firm would incur a loss of $2000, requiring it either to reduce its costs or go out of business.

Note, too, that consumers benefit from productive efficiency by paying the lowest product price possible under the prevailing technology and cost conditions.

Allocative Efficiency: P = MC

Productive efficiency alone does not ensure the efficient allocation of resources. Least-cost production must be used to provide society with the "right goods"—the goods that consumers want most. Before we can show that the competitive market system does just that, we must discuss the social meaning of product prices. There are two critical elements here:

• The money price of any product is society's measure of the relative worth of an additional unit of that product—for example, cucumbers. So the price of a unit of cucumbers is the marginal benefit derived from that unit of the product.

• Similarly, recalling the idea of opportunity cost, we see that the marginal cost of an additional unit of a product measures the value, or relative worth, of the other goods sacrificed to obtain it. In producing cucumbers, resources are drawn away from producing other goods. The marginal cost of producing a unit of cucumbers measures society's sacrifice of zucchinis or other goods.

To understand why $P = MC$ defines allocative efficiency, let's first look at situations where that is not the case.

Underallocation: P > MC   In pure competition, a firm will realize the maximum possible profit only by producing where price equals marginal cost (Figure 23.12). Producing fewer cucumbers such that MR (and thus P) exceeds MC yields less than maximum profit. It also entails, from society's viewpoint, an underallocation of resources to this product. The fact that price still exceeds marginal cost indicates that society values additional units of cucumbers more highly than the alternative products the appropriate resources could otherwise produce.

To illustrate, if the price or marginal benefit of a unit of cucumbers is $100 and its marginal cost is $60, producing an additional unit will cause a net increase in total well-being of $40. Society will gain cucumbers valued at $100, while the alternative products sacrificed by allocating more resources to cucumbers would be valued at only $60. Whenever society can gain something valued at $100 by giving up something valued at $60, the initial allocation of resources must have been inefficient.

Overallocation: P < MC   For similar reasons, the production of cucumbers should not go beyond the output at which price equals marginal cost. To produce where MC exceeds MR (and thus P) would yield less than the maximum profit for the producer and, from the viewpoint of society, would entail an overallocation of resources to cucumbers. Producing cucumbers at a level where marginal cost exceeds price (or marginal benefit) means that society is producing cucumbers by sacrificing alternative goods that society values more highly.

For example, if the price of a unit of cucumbers is $75 and its marginal cost is $100, then the production of 1 less unit of cucumbers would result in a net increase in society's total well-being of $25. Society would lose cucumbers valued at $75, but reallocating the freed resources to their best alternative uses would increase the output of some other good valued at $100. Whenever society is able to give up something of lesser value in return for something of greater value, the original allocation of resources must have been inefficient.

Efficient Allocation   Our conclusion must be that in pure competition, when profit-motivated firms produce each good or service to the point where price (marginal benefit) and marginal cost are equal, society's resources are being allocated efficiently. Each item is being produced to the point at which the value of the last unit is equal to the value of the alternative goods sacrificed by its production. Altering the production of cucumbers would reduce consumer satisfaction. Producing cucumbers beyond the $P = MC$ point would sacrifice alternative goods whose value to society exceeds that of the extra cucumbers. Producing cucumbers short of the $P = MC$ point would sacrifice cucumbers that society values more than the alternative goods its resources could produce.[3] **(Key Question 7)**

Dynamic Adjustments   A further attribute of purely competitive markets is their ability to restore efficiency when disrupted by changes in the economy. A change in consumer tastes, resource supplies, or technology will automatically set in motion the appropriate realignments of resources. For example, suppose that cucumbers and pickles become dramatically more popular. First, the price of cucumbers will increase and so, at current output, the price of cucumbers will exceed their marginal cost. At this

point efficiency will be lost, but the higher price will create economic profits in the cucumber industry and stimulate its expansion. The profitability of cucumbers will permit the industry to bid resources away from now less pressing uses, say, watermelons. Expansion of the industry will end only when the price of cucumbers and their marginal cost are equal—that is, when allocative efficiency has been restored.

Similarly, a change in the supply of a particular resource—for example, the field laborers who pick cucumbers—or in a production technique will upset an existing price–marginal-cost equality by either raising or lowering marginal cost. The resulting inequality will cause business managers, in either pursuing profit or avoiding loss, to reallocate resources until price once again equals marginal cost. In so doing, they will correct any inefficiency in the allocation of resources that the original change may have temporarily imposed on the economy.

"Invisible Hand" Revisited   Finally, the highly efficient allocation of resources that a purely competitive economy promotes comes about because businesses and resource suppliers seek to further their self-interest. The "invisible hand" (Chapter 4) is at work in a competitive market system. The competitive system not only maximizes profits for individual producers but, at the same time, creates a pattern of resource allocation that maximizes consumer satisfaction. The invisible hand thus organizes the private interests of producers in a way that is fully in accord with society's interest in using scarce resources efficiently.

---

[3]If you were assigned Internet Chapter 3W, you may recall that the efficient $P = MC$ output has two other characteristics: (1) Maximum willingness to pay for the last unit equals minimum acceptable price, and (2) combined consumer surplus and producer surplus is at a maximum.

QUICK REVIEW 23.3

- In the long run, the entry of firms into an industry will compete away any economic profits, and the exit of firms will eliminate losses, so price and minimum average total cost are equal.
- The long-run supply curves of constant-, increasing-, and decreasing-cost industries are horizontal, upsloping, and downsloping, respectively.
- In purely competitive markets both productive efficiency (price equals minimum average total cost) and allocative efficiency (price equals marginal cost) are achieved in the long run.

Pure Competition Provides Consumers with the Largest Utility Surplus That Is Consistent with Keeping the Product in Production.

In almost all markets, consumers collectively obtain more utility (total satisfaction) from their purchases than the amount of their expenditures (product price × quantity). This surplus of utility arises because some consumers are willing to pay more than the equilibrium price but need not do so.

Consider the open-air market for oranges depicted in the accompanying figure and drawing. The market demand curve D tells us that some consumers of oranges are willing to pay more than the $8 equilibrium price per bag. For example, assume Bob is willing to pay $18; Barb, $16; Bill, $14; Bart, $12; and Brent, $10. Betty, in contrast, is unwilling to pay one penny more than the $8 equilibrium price.

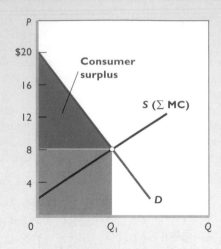

There are many other consumers besides Bob, Barb, Bill, Bart, and Brent in this market who are willing to pay prices above $8. Only Betty pays exactly the price she is willing to pay; the others receive some amount of utility beyond their expenditures. The difference between that utility value (measured by the vertical height of the points on the demand curve) and the $8 price is called *consumer surplus*. When we add together each buyer's utility surplus, we obtain the consumer surplus for all the consumers in the market. To get the Q_1 bags of oranges, consumers collectively are willing to pay the sum of

23.2 Consumer surplus 🔍

the amounts represented by the blue triangle and brown rectangle. However, they have to pay only the amount represented by the brown rectangle. The blue triangle thus represents consumer surplus.

A glance at the figure shows that the amount of consumer surplus—the size of the blue triangle—would be less if the sellers could charge some price above $8. As just one example, at a price of $16, only a very small triangle of consumer surplus would exist. But purely competitive firms cannot charge $16, because they are price takers. Any firm that charged a price above $8 would immediately lose all its business to the other firms.

Moreover, we know that in pure competition the equilibrium price equals the marginal cost of the Q_1 bags of oranges. And, since we are assuming that entry and exit have resulted in this price being equal to the lowest average total cost, each seller is earning only a normal profit. By definition, this profit is just sufficient to continue production of oranges.

The principle that emerges is this: By establishing the lowest price (here $8) consistent with continued production, pure competition yields the largest sustainable amount of consumer surplus.

SUMMARY

1. Economists group industries into four models based on their market structures: (a) pure competition, (b) pure monopoly, (c) monopolistic competition, and (d) oligopoly.

2. A purely competitive industry consists of a large number of independent firms producing a standardized product. Pure competition assumes that firms and resources are mobile among different industries.

3. In a competitive industry, no single firm can influence market price. This means that the firm's demand curve is perfectly elastic and price equals marginal revenue.

4. We can analyze short-run profit maximization by a competitive firm by comparing total revenue and total cost or by applying marginal analysis. A firm maximizes its short-run profit by producing the output at which total revenue exceeds total cost by the greatest amount.

5. Provided price exceeds minimum average variable cost, a competitive firm maximizes profit or minimizes loss in the short run by producing the output at which price or marginal revenue equals marginal cost. If price is less than average variable cost, the firm minimizes its loss by shutting down. If price is greater than average variable cost but is less than average total cost, the firm minimizes its loss by producing the $P = MC$ output. If price also exceeds average total cost, the firm maximizes its economic profit at the $P = MC$ output.

6. Applying the MR $(= P) = MC$ rule at various possible market prices leads to the conclusion that the segment of the firm's short-run marginal-cost curve that lies above the firm's average-variable-cost curve is its short-run supply curve.

7. In the long run, the market price of a product will equal the minimum average total cost of production. At a higher price, economic profits would cause firms to enter the industry until those profits had been competed away. At a lower price, losses would force the exit of firms from the industry until the product price rose to equal average total cost.

8. The long-run supply curve is horizontal for a constant-cost industry, upsloping for an increasing-cost industry, and downsloping for a decreasing-cost industry.

9. The long-run equality of price and minimum average total cost means that competitive firms will use the most efficient known technology and charge the lowest price consistent with their production costs.

10. The long-run equality of price and marginal cost implies that resources will be allocated in accordance with consumer tastes. The competitive price system will reallocate resources in response to a change in consumer tastes, in technology, or in resource supplies and will thereby maintain allocative efficiency over time.

TERMS AND CONCEPTS

pure competition	price taker	MR = MC rule	decreasing-cost industry
pure monopoly	average revenue	short-run supply curve	productive efficiency
monopolistic competition	total revenue	long-run supply curve	allocative efficiency
oligopoly	marginal revenue	constant-cost industry	
imperfect competition	break-even point	increasing-cost industry	

STUDY QUESTIONS

1. Briefly state the basic characteristics of pure competition, pure monopoly, monopolistic competition, and oligopoly. Under which of these market classifications does each of the following most accurately fit? (*a*) a supermarket in your hometown; (b) the steel industry; (c) a Kansas wheat farm; (d) the commercial bank in which you or your family has an account; (e) the automobile industry. In each case justify your classification.

2. Strictly speaking, pure competition has never existed and probably never will. Then why study it?

3. *Key Question* Use the following demand schedule to determine total revenue and marginal revenue for each possible level of sales:

Product Price	Quantity Demanded	Total Revenue	Marginal Revenue
$2	0	$_____	$_____
2	1	_____	_____
2	2	_____	_____
2	3	_____	_____
2	4	_____	_____
2	5	_____	

a. What can you conclude about the structure of the industry in which this firm is operating? Explain.

b.   Graph the demand, total-revenue, and marginal-revenue curves for this firm.

c.   Why do the demand and marginal-revenue curves coincide?

d.   "Marginal revenue is the change in total revenue associated with additional units of output." Explain verbally and graphically, using the data in the table.

4. **Key Question** Assume the following cost data are for a purely competitive producer:

Total Product	Average Fixed Cost	Average Variable Cost	Average Total Cost	Marginal Cost
0				$45
1	$60.00	$45.00	$105.00	40
2	30.00	42.50	72.50	35
3	20.00	40.00	60.00	30
4	15.00	37.50	52.50	35
5	12.00	37.00	49.00	40
6	10.00	37.50	47.50	45
7	8.57	38.57	47.14	55
8	7.50	40.63	48.13	65
9	6.67	43.33	50.00	75
10	6.00	46.50	52.50	

a.   At a product price of $56, will this firm produce in the short run? Why or why not? If it is preferable to produce, what will be the profit-maximizing or loss-minimizing output? Explain. What economic profit or loss will the firm realize per unit of output?

b.   Answer the relevant questions of 4a assuming product price is $41.

c.   Answer the relevant questions of 4a assuming product price is $32.

d.   In the table below, complete the short-run supply schedule for the firm (columns 1 and 2) and indicate the profit or loss incurred at each output (column 3).

(1) Price	(2) Quantity Supplied, Single Firm	(3) Profit (+) or Loss (−)	(4) Quantity Supplied, 1500 Firms
$26	_____	$_____	_____
32	_____	_____	_____
38	_____	_____	_____
41	_____	_____	_____
46	_____	_____	_____
56	_____	_____	_____
66	_____	_____	_____

e.   Explain: "That segment of a competitive firm's marginal-cost curve that lies above its average-variable-cost curve constitutes the short-run supply curve for the firm." Illustrate graphically.

f.   Now assume that there are 1500 identical firms in this competitive industry; that is, there are 1500 firms, each of which has the cost data shown in the table. Complete the industry supply schedule (column 4).

g.   Suppose the market demand data for the product are as follows:

Price	Total Quantity Demanded
$26	17,000
32	15,000
38	13,500
41	12,000
46	10,500
56	9,500
66	8,000

What will be the equilibrium price? What will be the equilibrium output for the industry? For each firm? What will profit or loss be per unit? Per firm? Will this industry expand or contract in the long run?

5. Why is the equality of marginal revenue and marginal cost essential for profit maximization in all market structures? Explain why price can be substituted for marginal revenue in the MR = MC rule when an industry is purely competitive.

6. **Key Question** Using diagrams for both the industry and a representative firm, illustrate competitive long-run equilibrium. Assuming constant costs, employ these diagrams to show how (a) an increase and (b) a decrease in market demand will upset that long-run equilibrium. Trace graphically and describe verbally the adjustment processes by which long-run equilibrium is restored. Now rework your analysis for increasing- and decreasing-cost industries and compare the three long-run supply curves.

7. **Key Question** In long-run equilibrium, P = minimum ATC = MC. Of what significance for economic efficiency is the equality of P and minimum ATC? The equality of P and MC? Distinguish between productive efficiency and allocative efficiency in your answer.

8. **(Last Word)** Suppose that improved technology causes the supply curve for oranges to shift rightward in the market discussed in this Last Word (see the figure there). Assuming no change in the location of the demand curve, what will happen to consumer surplus? Explain why.

9. **Web-Based Question: You are a pure competitor—what was your revenue yesterday?** Suppose that you operate a

purely competitive firm that buys and sells foreign currencies. Also suppose that yesterday your business activity consisted of buying 100,000 Swiss francs at the market exchange rate and selling them for a 3 percent commission.
Go to the Federal Reserve website at federalreserve.gov and
select, in order, Economic Research and Data, Statistics,
and Foreign Exchange Rates. What was your total revenue
in dollars yesterday (be sure to include your commission)?
Why would your profit for the day be considerably less
than this total revenue?

10. *Web-Based Question: Entry and exit of firms—where
   have they occurred?* Go to the Census Bureau website
   at www.census.gov and select Economic Census, then
   Manufacturing, and then Comparative Statistics. Identify
   three manufacturing industries that experienced large percentage increases in the number of firms between 1992 and
   1997. Identify three manufacturing industries that experienced large percentage decreases. What single factor is the
   most likely cause of the entry and exit differences between
   your two groups? Explain.

24

Pure Monopoly

We turn now from pure competition to pure monopoly, which is at the opposite end of the spectrum of industry structures listed in Table 23.1. You deal with monopolies—sole sellers of products and services—more often than you might think. When you see the logo for Microsoft's Windows on your computer, you are dealing with a monopoly (or, at least, a near-monopoly). When you purchase certain prescription drugs, you are buying monopolized products. When you make a local telephone call, turn on your lights, or subscribe to cable TV, you may be patronizing a monopoly, depending on your location.

What precisely do we mean by pure monopoly, and what conditions enable it to arise and survive? How does a pure monopolist determine its profit-maximizing price and output quantity? Does a pure monopolist achieve the efficiency associated with pure competition? If not, what should the government do about it? A simplified model of pure monopoly will help us answer these questions.

An Introduction to Pure Monopoly

Pure monopoly exists when a single firm is the sole producer of a product for which there are no close substitutes. Here are the main characteristics of pure monopoly:

- *Single seller*   A pure, or absolute, monopoly is an industry in which a single firm is the sole producer of a specific good or the sole supplier of a service; the firm and the industry are synonymous.
- *No close substitutes*   A pure monopoly's product is unique in that there are no close substitutes. The

consumer who chooses not to buy the monopolized product must do without it.

- *Price maker*   The pure monopolist controls the total quantity supplied and thus has considerable control over price; it is a *price maker*. (Unlike the pure competitor that has no such control and therefore is a *price taker*.) The pure monopolist confronts the usual downward-sloping product demand curve. It can change its product price by changing the quantity of the product it supplies. The monopolist will use this power whenever it is advantageous to do so.

- ***Blocked entry***   A pure monopolist has no immediate competitors because certain barriers keep potential competitors from entering the industry. Those barriers may be economic, technological, legal, or of some other type. But entry is totally blocked in pure monopoly.
- ***Nonprice competition***   The product produced by a pure monopolist may be either standardized (as with natural gas and electricity) or differentiated (as with Windows or Frisbees). Monopolists that have standardized products engage mainly in public relations advertising, whereas those with differentiated products sometimes advertise their products' attributes.

24.1
Monopoly

Examples of Monopoly

Examples of *pure* monopoly are relatively rare, but there are many examples of less pure forms. In most cities, government-owned or government-regulated public utilities—natural gas and electric companies, the water company, the cable TV company, and the local telephone company—are all monopolies or virtually so.

There are also many "near-monopolies" in which a single firm has the bulk of sales in a specific market. Intel, for example, provides 80 percent of the central microprocessors used in personal computers. First Data Corporation, via its Western Union subsidiary, accounts for 80 percent of the market for money order transfers. Brannock Device Company has an 80 percent market share of the shoe sizing devices found in shoe stores. Wham-O, through its Frisbee brand, sells 90 percent of plastic throwing disks. The De Beers diamond syndicate effectively controls 65 percent of the world's supply of rough-cut diamonds (see this chapter's Last Word).

Professional sports teams are, in a sense, monopolies because they are the sole suppliers of specific services in large geographic areas. With a few exceptions, a single major-league team in each sport serves each large American city. If you want to see a live major-league baseball game in St. Louis or Seattle, you must patronize the Cardinals or the Mariners, respectively. Other geographic monopolies exist. For example, a small town may be served by only one airline or railroad. In a small, isolated community, the local bank, movie, or bookstore may approximate a monopoly.

Of course, there is almost always some competition. Satellite television is a substitute for cable, and amateur softball is a substitute for professional baseball. The Linux operating system can substitute for Windows, and so on.

But such substitutes are typically either more costly or in some way less appealing.

Dual Objectives of the Study of Monopoly

We want to examine pure monopoly not only for its own sake but also because such a study will help you understand the more common market structures of monopolistic competition and oligopoly, to be discussed in Chapter 25. These two market structures combine, in differing degrees, characteristics of pure competition and pure monopoly.

Barriers to Entry

The factors that prohibit firms from entering an industry are called **barriers to entry.** In pure monopoly, strong barriers to entry effectively block all potential competition. Somewhat weaker barriers may permit oligopoly, a market structure dominated by a few firms. Still weaker barriers may permit the entry of a fairly large number of competing firms giving rise to monopolistic competition. And the absence of any effective entry barriers permits the entry of a very large number of firms, which provide the basis of pure competition. So barriers to entry are pertinent not only to the extreme case of pure monopoly but also to other market structures in which there is some degree of monopoly-like conditions and behavior.

Economies of Scale

Modern technology in some industries is such that economies of scale—declining average total cost with added firm size—are extensive. So a firm's long-run average-cost schedule will decline over a wide range of output. Given market demand, only a few large firms or, in the extreme, only a single large firm can achieve low average total costs.

Figure 24.1 indicates economies of scale over a wide range of outputs. If total consumer demand is within that output range, then only a single producer can satisfy demand at least cost. Note, for example, that a monopolist can produce 200 units at a per-unit cost of $10 and a total cost of $2000. If there are two firms in the industry and each produces 100 units, the unit cost is $15 and total cost rises to $3000 (= 200 units × $15). A still more competitive situation with four firms each producing 50 units would boost unit and total cost to $20 and $4000, respectively. Conclusion: When long-run ATC is

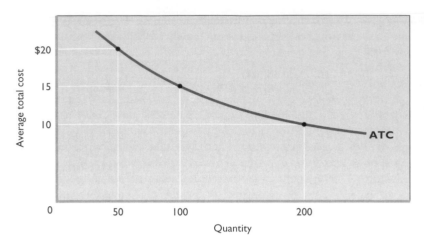

FIGURE 24.1

Economies of scale: the natural monopoly case. A declining long-run average-total-cost curve over a wide range of output quantities indicates extensive economies of scale. A single monopoly firm can produce, say, 200 units of output at lower cost ($10 each) than could two or more firms that had a combined output of 200 units.

declining, only a single producer, a monopolist, can produce any particular output at minimum total cost.

If a pure monopoly exists in such an industry, economies of scale will serve as an entry barrier and will protect the monopolist from competition. New firms that try to enter the industry as small-scale producers cannot realize the cost economies of the monopolist and therefore cannot obtain the normal profits necessary for survival or growth. A new firm might try to start out big, that is, to enter the industry as a large-scale producer so as to achieve the necessary economies of scale. But the massive plant facilities required would necessitate huge amounts of financing, which a new and untried enterprise would find difficult to secure. In most cases the financial obstacles and risks to "starting big" are prohibitive. This explains why efforts to enter such industries as automobiles, computer operating software, commercial aircraft, and basic steel are so rare.

In the extreme circumstance, in which the market demand curve cuts the long-run ATC curve where average total costs are still declining, the single firm is called a *natural monopoly*. It might seem that a natural monopolist's lower unit cost would enable it to charge a lower price than if the industry were more competitive. But that won't necessarily happen. A pure monopolist may, instead, set its price far above ATC and obtain substantial economic profit. In that event, the lowest-unit-cost advantage of a natural monopolist would accrue to the monopolist as profit and not as lower prices to consumers. That is why the government regulates some natural monopolies, specifying the price they may charge. We will say more about that later.

24.2
Minimum efficient scale

Legal Barriers to Entry: Patents and Licenses

Government also creates legal barriers to entry by awarding patents and licenses.

Patents   A *patent* is the exclusive right of an inventor to use, or to allow another to use, her or his invention. Patents and patent laws aim to protect the inventor from rivals who would use the invention without having shared in the effort and expense of developing it. At the same time, patents provide the inventor with a monopoly position for the life of the patent. The world's nations have agreed on a uniform patent length of 20 years from the time of application. Patents have figured prominently in the growth of modern-day giants such as IBM, Merck, Kodak, Xerox, Polaroid, General Electric, and DuPont.

Research and development (R&D) is what leads to most patentable inventions and products. Firms that gain monopoly power through their own research or by purchasing the patents of others can use patents to strengthen their market position. The profit from one patent can finance the research required to develop new patentable products. In the pharmaceutical industry, patents on prescription drugs have produced large monopoly profits that have helped finance the discovery of new patentable medicines. So monopoly power achieved through patents may well be self-sustaining, even though patents eventually expire and generic drugs then compete with the original brand.

Licenses   Government may also limit entry into an industry or occupation through *licensing*. At the national level, the Federal Communications Commission licenses only so many radio and television stations in each geographic area. In many large cities one of a limited number of municipal licenses is required to drive a taxicab. The consequent restriction of the supply of cabs creates economic profit for cab owners and drivers. New cabs cannot enter the industry to drive down prices and profits. In a few instances the government might "license" itself to provide some product and thereby create a public monopoly. For example, in some states only state-owned retail outlets can sell liquor. Similarly, many states have "licensed" themselves to run lotteries.

Ownership or Control of Essential Resources

A monopolist can use private property as an obstacle to potential rivals. For example, a firm that owns or controls a resource essential to the production process can prohibit the entry of rival firms. At one time the International Nickel Company of Canada (now called Inco) controlled 90 percent of the world's known nickel reserves. A local firm may own all the nearby deposits of sand and gravel. And it is very difficult for new sports leagues to be created because existing professional sports leagues have contracts with the best players and have long-term leases on the major stadiums and arenas.

Pricing and Other Strategic Barriers to Entry

Even if a firm is not protected from entry by, say, extensive economies of scale or ownership of essential resources, entry may effectively be blocked by the way the monopolist responds to attempts by rivals to enter the industry. Confronted with a new entrant, the monopolist may "create an entry barrier" by slashing its price, stepping up its advertising, or taking other strategic actions to make it difficult for the entrant to succeed.

Examples of entry deterrence: In 1999 the U.S. Justice Department accused Dentsply, the dominant American maker of false teeth (70 percent market share) of unlawfully precluding independent distributors of false teeth from carrying competing brands. The lack of access to the distributors allegedly deterred potential foreign competitors from entering the U.S. market. As another example, in 2001 a U.S. court of appeals upheld a lower court's finding that Microsoft used a series of illegal actions to maintain its monopoly in Intel-compatible PC operating systems (95 percent market share). One such action was charging higher prices for its Windows operating system

to computer manufacturers that featured Netscape's Navigator rather than Microsoft's Internet Explorer.

Monopoly Demand

Now that we have explained the sources of monopoly, we want to build a model of pure monopoly so that we can analyze its price and output decisions. Let's start by making three assumptions:

- Patents, economies of scale, or resource ownership secure our monopolist's status.
- No unit of government regulates the firm.
- The firm is a single-price monopolist; it charges the same price for all units of output.

The crucial difference between a pure monopolist and a purely competitive seller lies on the demand side of the market. The purely competitive seller faces a perfectly elastic demand at the price determined by market supply and demand. It is a price taker that can sell as much or as little as it wants at the going market price. Each additional unit sold will add the amount of the constant product price to the firm's total revenue. That means that marginal revenue for the competitive seller is constant and equal to product price. (Refer to Table 23.2 and Figure 23.1 for price, marginal-revenue, and total-revenue relationships for the purely competitive firm.)

The demand curve for the monopolist (and for any imperfectly competitive seller) is very different from that of the pure competitor. Because the pure monopolist *is* the industry, its demand curve is *the market demand curve*. And because market demand is not perfectly elastic, the monopolist's demand curve is downsloping. Columns 1 and 2 in Table 24.1 illustrate this concept. Note that quantity demanded increases as price decreases.

In Chapter 23 we drew separate demand curves for the purely competitive industry and for a single firm in such an industry. But only a single demand curve is needed in pure monopoly. The firm and the industry are one and the same. We have graphed part of the demand data in Table 24.1 as demand curve D in Figure 24.2. This is the monopolist's demand curve *and* the market demand curve. The downward-sloping demand curve has three implications that are essential to understanding the monopoly model.

Marginal Revenue Is Less Than Price

The monopolist's downward-sloping demand curve means that it can increase sales only by charging a lower price. Consequently, marginal revenue is less than price (average

TABLE 24.1

Revenue and Cost Data of a Pure Monopolist

	Revenue Data			Cost Data			
(1) Quantity of Output	(2) Price (Average Revenue)	(3) Total Revenue, (1) × (2)	(4) Marginal Revenue	(5) Average Total Cost	(6) Total Cost, (1) × (5)	(7) Marginal Cost	(8) Profit [+] or Loss [−]
0	$172	$ 0			$ 100		$−100
			$162			$ 90	
1	162	162		$190.00	190		− 28
			142			80	
2	152	304		135.00	270		+ 34
			122			70	
3	142	426		113.33	340		+ 86
			102			60	
4	132	528		100.00	400		+128
			82			70	
5	122	610		94.00	470		+140
			62			80	
6	112	672		91.67	550		+122
			42			90	
7	102	714		91.43	640		+ 74
			22			110	
8	92	736		93.75	750		− 14
			2			130	
9	82	738		97.78	880		−142
			−18			150	
10	72	720		103.00	1030		−310

revenue) for every level of output except the first. Why so? The reason is that the lower price applies not only to the extra output sold but also to all prior units of output. The monopolist could have sold these prior units at a higher price if it had not produced and sold the extra output. Each additional unit of output sold increases total

FIGURE 24.2

Price and marginal revenue in pure monopoly. A pure monopolist, or any other imperfect competitor with a downsloping demand curve such as D, must set a lower price in order to sell more output. Here, by charging $132 rather than $142, the monopolist sells an extra unit (the fourth unit) and gains $132 from that sale. But from this gain must be subtracted $30, which reflects the $10 less the monopolist charged for each of the first 3 units. Thus, the marginal revenue of the fourth unit is $102 (= $132 − $30), considerably less than its $132 price.

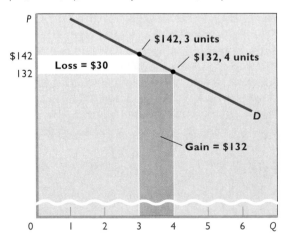

revenue by an amount equal to its own price less the sum of the price cuts that apply to all prior units of output.

Figure 24.2 confirms this point. There, we have highlighted two price-quantity combinations from the monopolist's demand curve. The monopolist can sell 1 more unit at $132 than it can at $142 and that way obtain $132 of extra revenue. But to sell that fourth unit for $132, the monopolist must also sell the first 3 units at $132 rather than $142. The $10 reduction in revenue on 3 units results in a $30 revenue loss. The net difference in total revenue from selling a fourth unit is $102: the $132 gain from the fourth unit minus the $30 forgone on the first 3 units. This net gain (marginal revenue) of $102 from the fourth unit is clearly less than the $132 price of the fourth unit.

Column 4 in Table 24.1 shows that marginal revenue is always less than the corresponding product price in column 2, except for the first unit of output. Because marginal revenue is the change in total revenue associated with each additional unit of output, the declining amounts of marginal revenue in column 4 mean that total revenue increases at a diminishing rate (as shown in column 3).

We show the relationship between the monopolist's marginal-revenue curve and total-revenue curve in Figure 24.3. For this figure, we extended the demand and revenue data of columns 1 through 4 in Table 24.1, assuming that successive $10 price cuts each elicit 1 additional unit of sales. That is, the monopolist can sell 11 units at $62, 12 units at $52, and so on.

Note that the monopolist's MR curve lies below the demand curve, indicating that marginal revenue is less

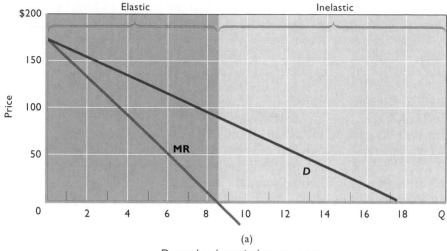

(a)
Demand and marginal-revenue curves

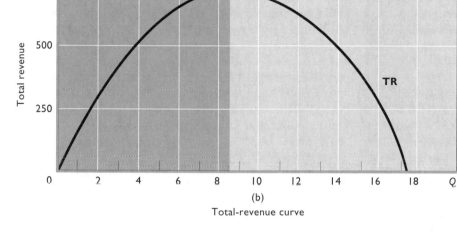

(b)
Total-revenue curve

FIGURE 24.3

Demand, marginal revenue, and total revenue for an imperfectly competitive firm. (a) Because it must lower price on all units sold in order to increase its sales, an imperfectly competitive firm's marginal-revenue curve (MR) lies below its downsloping demand curve (D). The elastic and inelastic regions of demand are highlighted. (b) Total revenue (TR) increases at a decreasing rate, reaches a maximum, and then declines. Note that in the elastic region, TR is increasing and hence MR is positive. When TR reaches its maximum, MR is zero. In the inelastic region of demand, TR is declining, so MR is negative.

than price at every output quantity but the very first unit. Observe also the special relationship between total revenue and marginal revenue. Because marginal revenue is the change in total revenue, marginal revenue is positive while total revenue is increasing. When total revenue reaches its maximum, marginal revenue is zero. When total revenue is diminishing, marginal revenue is negative.

The Monopolist Is a Price Maker

All imperfect competitors, whether pure monopoly, oligopoly, or monopolistic competition, face downward-sloping demand curves. So firms in those industries can to one degree or another influence total supply through their own output decisions. In changing market supply, they can also influence product price. Firms with downward-sloping demand curves are *price makers.*

This is most evident in pure monopoly, where one firm controls total output. The monopolist faces a downsloping demand curve in which each output is associated with some unique price. Thus, in deciding on what volume of output to produce, the monopolist is also indirectly determining the price it will charge. Through control of output, it can "make the price." From columns 1 and 2 in Table 24.1 we find that the monopolist can charge a price of $72 if it produces and offers for sale 10 units, a price of $82 if it produces and offers for sale 9 units, and so forth.

The Monopolist Sets Prices in the Elastic Region of Demand

The total-revenue test for price elasticity of demand is the basis for our third implication. Recall from Chapter 20 that the total-revenue test reveals that when demand is elastic, a decline in price will increase total revenue. Similarly, when demand is inelastic, a decline in price will reduce total revenue. Beginning at the top of demand curve *D* in Figure 24.3a, observe that as the price declines from $172 to approximately $82, total revenue increases (and marginal revenue therefore is positive). This means that demand is elastic in this price range. Conversely, for price declines below $82, total revenue decreases (marginal revenue is negative), indicating that demand is inelastic there.

The implication is that a monopolist will never choose a price-quantity combination where price reductions cause total revenue to decrease (marginal revenue to be negative). The profit-maximizing monopolist will always want to avoid the inelastic segment of its demand curve in favor of some price-quantity combination in the elastic region. Here's why: To get into the inelastic region, the monopolist must lower price and increase output. In the inelastic region a lower price means less total revenue. And increased output always means increased total cost. Less total revenue and higher total cost yield lower profit. **(Key Question 4)**

QUICK REVIEW 24.1

- A pure monopolist is the sole supplier of a product or service for which there are no close substitutes.
- A monopoly survives because of entry barriers such as economies of scale, patents and licenses, the ownership of essential resources, and strategic actions to exclude rivals.
- The monopolist's demand curve is downsloping, and its marginal-revenue curve lies below its demand curve.
- The downsloping demand curve means that the monopolist is a price maker.
- The monopolist will operate in the elastic region of demand since in the inelastic region it can increase total revenue and reduce total cost by reducing output.

Output and Price Determination

At what specific price-quantity combination will a profit-maximizing monopolist choose to operate? To answer this question, we must add production costs to our analysis.

Cost Data

On the cost side, we will assume that although the firm is a monopolist in the product market, it hires resources competitively and employs the same technology as Chapter 23's competitive firm does. This lets us use the cost data we developed in Chapter 22 and applied in Chapter 23, so we can compare the price-output decisions of a pure monopoly with those of a pure competitor. Columns 5 through 7 in Table 24.1 restate the pertinent cost data from Table 22.2.

MR = MC Rule

A monopolist seeking to maximize total profit will employ the same rationale as a profit-seeking firm in a competitive industry. If producing is preferable to shutting down, it will produce up to the output at which marginal revenue equals marginal cost (MR = MC).

A comparison of columns 4 and 7 in Table 24.1 indicates that the profit-maximizing output is 5 units, because the fifth unit is the last unit of output whose marginal revenue exceeds its marginal cost. What price will the monopolist charge? The demand schedule shown as columns 1 and 2 in Table 24.1 indicates there is only one price at which 5 units can be sold: $122.

This analysis is shown in **Figure 24.4 (Key Graph)**, where we have graphed the demand, marginal-revenue, average-total-cost, and marginal-cost data of Table 24.1. The profit-maximizing output occurs at 5 units of output (Q_m), where the marginal-revenue (MR) and marginal-cost (MC) curves intersect. There, MR = MC.

To find the price the monopolist will charge, we extend a vertical line from Q_m up to the demand curve *D*. The unique price P_m at which Q_m units can be sold is $122. In this case, it is the profit-maximizing price. The monopolist sets the quantity at Q_m to charge its profit-maximizing price of $122.

In columns 2 and 5 in Table 24.1 we see that at 5 units of output, the product price ($122) exceeds the average total cost ($94). The monopolist thus earns an economic profit of $28 per unit, and the total economic profit is then $140 (= 5 units × $28). In Figure 24.4, per-unit profit is $P_m - A$, where *A* is the average total cost of producing Q_m units. We find total economic profit by multiplying this per-unit profit by the profit-maximizing output Q_m.

Another way we can determine the profit-maximizing output is by comparing total revenue and total cost at each possible level of production and choosing the output with the greatest positive difference. Use columns 3 and 6 in Table 24.1 to verify our conclusion that 5 units is the profit-maximizing output. An accurate graphing of total revenue and total cost

24.1
Monopoly

KEY GRAPH

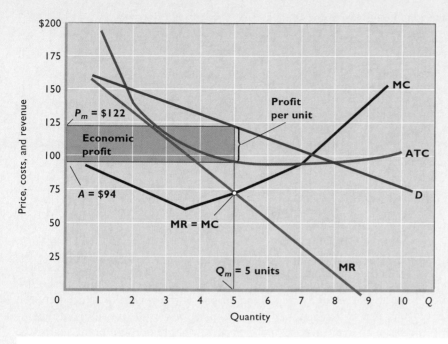

FIGURE 24.4

The profit-maximizing position of a pure monopolist. The pure monopolist maximizes profit by producing the MR = MC output, here $Q_m = 5$ units. Then, as seen from the demand curve, it will charge price $P_m = \$122$. Average total cost will be $A = \$94$, meaning that per-unit profit is $P_m - A$ and total profit is $5 \times (P_m - A)$. Total economic profit is thus represented by the blue rectangle.

QUICK QUIZ 24.4

1. The MR curve lies below the demand curve in this figure because the:
  - a. demand curve is linear (a straight line).
  - b. demand curve is highly inelastic throughout its full length.
  - c. demand curve is highly elastic throughout its full length.
  - d. gain in revenue from an extra unit of output is less than the price charged for that unit of output.

2. The area labeled "Economic profit" can be found by multiplying the difference between P and ATC by quantity. It also can be found by:
  - a. dividing profit per unit by quantity.
  - b. subtracting total cost from total revenue.
  - c. multiplying the coefficient of demand elasticity by quantity.
  - d. multiplying the difference between P and MC by quantity.

3. This pure monopolist:
  - a. charges the highest price that it could achieve.
  - b. earns only a normal profit in the long run.
  - c. restricts output to create an insurmountable entry barrier.
  - d. restricts output to increase its price and total economic profit.

4. At this monopolist's profit-maximizing output:
  - a. price equals marginal revenue.
  - b. price equals marginal cost.
  - c. price exceeds marginal cost.
  - d. profit per unit is maximized.

Answers: 1. d; 2. b; 3. d; 4. c

---

against output would also show the greatest difference (the maximum profit) at 5 units of output. Table 24.2 is a step-by-step summary of the process for determining the profit-maximizing output, profit-maximizing price, and economic profit in pure monopoly. **(Key Question 5)**

No Monopoly Supply Curve

Recall that MR equals P in pure competition and that the supply curve of a purely competitive firm is determined by applying the MR $(= P) =$ MC profit-maximizing rule.

At any specific market-determined price the purely competitive seller will maximize profit by supplying the quantity at which MC is equal to that price. When the market price increases or decreases, the competitive firm produces more or less output. Each market price is thus associated with a specific output, and all such price-output pairs define the supply curve. This supply curve turns out to be the portion of the firm's MC curve that lies above the average-variable-cost curve (see Figure 23.6).

At first glance we would suspect that the pure monopolist's marginal-cost curve would also be its supply curve.

445

TABLE 24.2

Steps for Graphically Determining the Profit-Maximizing Output, Profit-Maximizing Price, and Economic Profit (if Any) in Pure Monopoly

Step 1. Determine the profit-maximizing output by finding where MR = MC.
Step 2. Determine the profit-maximizing price by extending a vertical line upward from the output determined in step 1 to the pure monopolist's demand curve.

Step 3. Determine the pure monopolist's economic profit using one of two methods:
  Method 1. Find profit per unit by substracting the average total cost of the profit-maximizing output from the profit-maximizing price. Then multiply the difference by the profit-maximizing output to determine economic profit (if any).
  Method 2. Find total cost by multiplying the average total cost of the profit-maximizing output by that output. Find total revenue by multiplying the profit-maximizing output by the profit-maximizing price. Then subtract total cost from total revenue to determine economic profit (if any).

But that is *not* the case. *The pure monopolist has no supply curve.* There is no unique relationship between price and quantity supplied for a monopolist. Like the competitive firm, the monopolist equates marginal revenue and marginal cost to determine output, but for the monopolist marginal revenue is less than price. Because the monopolist does not equate marginal cost to price, it is possible for different demand conditions to bring about different prices for the same output. To convince yourself of this, refer to Figure 24.4 and pencil in a new, steeper marginal-revenue curve that intersects the marginal-cost curve at the same point as does the present marginal-revenue curve. Then draw in a new demand curve that roughly corresponds with your new marginal-revenue curve. With the new curves, the same MR = MC output of 5 units now corresponds with a higher profit-maximizing price. Conclusion: There is no single, unique price associated with each output level Q_m, and so there is no supply curve for the pure monopolist.

Misconceptions Concerning Monopoly Pricing

Our analysis exposes two fallacies concerning monopoly behavior.

Not Highest Price   Because a monopolist can manipulate output and price, people often believe it "will charge the highest price possible." That is incorrect. There are many prices above P_m in Figure 24.4, but the monopolist shuns them because they yield a smaller-than-maximum total profit. The monopolist seeks maximum total profit, not maximum price. Some high prices that could be charged would reduce sales and total revenue too severely to offset any decrease in total cost.

Total, Not Unit, Profit   The monopolist seeks maximum *total* profit, not maximum *unit* profit. In Figure 24.4 a careful comparison of the vertical distance between average total cost and price at various possible outputs indicates that per-unit profit is greater at a point slightly to the left of the profit-maximizing output Q_m. This is seen in Table 24.1, where unit profit at 4 units of output is $32 (= $132 − $100) compared with $28 (= $122 − $94) at the profit-maximizing output of 5 units. Here the monopolist accepts a lower-than-maximum per-unit profit because additional sales more than compensate for the lower unit profit. A profit-seeking monopolist would rather sell 5 units at a profit of $28 per unit (for a total profit of $140) than 4 units at a profit of $32 per unit (for a total profit of only $128).

Possibility of Losses by Monopolist

The likelihood of economic profit is greater for a pure monopolist than for a pure competitor. In the long run the pure competitor is destined to have only a normal profit, whereas barriers to entry mean that any economic profit realized by the monopolist can persist. In pure monopoly there are no new entrants to increase supply, drive down price, and eliminate economic profit.

But pure monopoly does not guarantee profit. The monopolist is not immune from changes in tastes that reduce the demand for its product. Nor is it immune from upward-shifting cost curves caused by escalating resource prices. If the demand and cost situation faced by the monopolist is far less favorable than that in Figure 24.4, the monopolist will incur losses in the short run. Despite its dominance in the market (as, say, a seller of home sewing machines), the monopoly enterprise in Figure 24.5 suffers

FIGURE 24.5

The loss-minimizing position of a pure monopolist. If demand D is weak and costs are high, the pure monopolist may be unable to make a profit. Because P_m exceeds V, the average variable cost at the MR = MC output Q_m, the monopolist will minimize losses in the short run by producing at that output. The loss per unit is $A - P_m$, and the total loss is indicated by the blue rectangle.

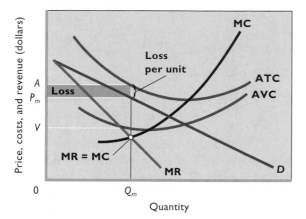

Quantity

a loss, as shown, because of weak demand and relatively high costs. Yet it continues to operate for the time being because its total loss is less than its fixed cost. More precisely, at output Q_m the monopolist's price P_m exceeds its average variable cost V. Its loss per unit is $A - P_m$, and the total loss is shown by the blue rectangle.

Like the pure competitor, the monopolist will not persist in operating at a loss. Faced with continuing losses, in the long run the firm's owners will move their resources to alternative industries that offer better profit opportunities. Thus we can expect the monopolist to realize a normal profit or better in the long run.

Economic Effects of Monopoly

Let's now evaluate pure monopoly from the standpoint of society as a whole. Our reference for this evaluation will be the outcome of long-run efficiency in a purely competitive market, identified by the triple equality $P =$ MC = minimum ATC.

Price, Output, and Efficiency

Figure 24.6 graphically contrasts the price, output, and efficiency outcomes of pure monopoly and a purely competitive *industry*. Starting with Figure 24.6a, we are reminded that the purely competitive industry's market supply curve S is the horizontal sum of the marginal-cost curves of all the firms in the industry. Let's suppose there

FIGURE 24.6

Inefficiency of pure monopoly relative to a purely competitive industry. (a) In a purely competitive industry, entry and exit of firms ensures that price (P_c) equals marginal cost (MC) and that the minimum average-total-cost output (Q_c) is produced. Both productive efficiency (P = minimum ATC) and allocative efficiency (P = MC) are obtained. (b) In pure monopoly, the MR curve lies below the demand curve. The monopolist maximizes profit at output Q_m, where MR = MC, and charges price P_m. Thus, output is lower (Q_m rather than Q_c) and price is higher (P_m rather than P_c) than they would be in a purely competitive industry. Monopoly is inefficient, since output is less than that required for achieving minimum ATC (here at Q_c) and because the monopolist's price exceeds MC.

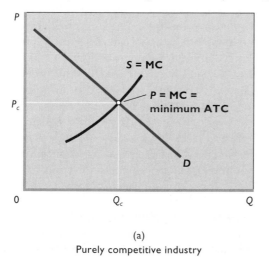

(a)
Purely competitive industry

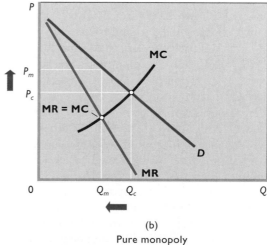

(b)
Pure monopoly

are 1000 such firms. Comparing their combined supply curves S with market demand D, we get the purely competitive price and output of P_c and Q_c.

Recall that this price-output combination results in both productive efficiency and allocative efficiency. *Productive efficiency* is achieved because free entry and exit forces firms to operate where average total cost is at a minimum. The sum of the minimum-ATC outputs of the 1000 pure competitors is the industry output, here, Q_c. Product price is at the lowest level consistent with minimum average total cost. The *allocative efficiency* of pure competition results because production occurs up to that output at which price (the measure of a product's value or marginal benefit to society) equals marginal cost (the worth of the alternative products forgone by society in producing any given commodity). In short: $P = MC = $ minimum ATC.

Now let's suppose that this industry becomes a pure monopoly (Figure 24.6b) as a result of one firm buying out all its competitors. We also assume that no changes in costs or market demand result from this dramatic change in the industry structure. What were formerly 1000 competing firms are now a single pure monopolist consisting of 1000 noncompeting branches.

The competitive market supply curve S has become the marginal-cost curve (MC) of the monopolist, the summation of the MC curves of its many branch plants. (Since the monopolist does not have a supply curve, as such, we have removed the S label.) The important change, however, is on the demand side. From the viewpoint of each of the 1000 individual competitive firms, demand was perfectly elastic, and marginal revenue was therefore equal to price. Each firm equated MR (= price) and MC in maximizing profits. But market demand and individual demand are the same to the pure monopolist. The firm *is* the industry, and thus the monopolist sees the downsloping demand curve D shown in Figure 24.6b.

This means that marginal revenue is less than price, that graphically the MR curve lies below demand curve D. In using the MR = MC rule, the monopolist selects output Q_m and price P_m. A comparison of both graphs in Figure 24.6 reveals that the monopolist finds it profitable to sell a smaller output at a higher price than do the competitive producers. Monopoly yields neither productive nor allocative efficiency. The monopolist's output is less than Q_c, the output at which average total cost is lowest. And price is higher than the competitive price P_c, which in long-run equilibrium pure competition equals minimum average total cost. Thus the monopoly price *exceeds* minimum average total cost. Also, at the monopolist's Q_m output, product price is considerably higher than marginal cost, meaning that society values additional units of this monopolized product more highly than it values the alternative products the resources could otherwise produce. So the monopolist's profit-maximizing output results in an underallocation of resources. The monopolist finds it profitable to restrict output and therefore employ fewer resources than is justified from society's standpoint. So the monopolist does not achieve allocative efficiency.

In monopoly, then, P exceeds MC and P exceeds minimum ATC.

Income Transfer

In general, monopoly transfers income from consumers to the stockholders who own the monopoly. By virtue of their market power, monopolists charge a higher price than would a purely competitive firm with the same costs. So monopolists in effect levy a "private tax" on consumers and obtain substantial economic profits. These monopolistic profits are not equally distributed, because higher-income groups largely own corporate stock. The owners of monopolistic enterprises thus tend to benefit at the expense of the consumers, who "overpay" for the product. Because, on average, these owners have more income than the buyers, monopoly increases income inequality.

Exception: If the buyers of a monopoly product are wealthier than the owners of the monopoly, the income transfer from consumers to owners may reduce income inequality. But, in general, this is not the case, and we thus conclude that monopoly contributes to income inequality.

Cost Complications

Our evaluation of pure monopoly has led us to conclude that, given identical costs, a purely monopolistic industry will charge a higher price, produce a smaller output, and allocate economic resources less efficiently than a purely competitive industry. These inferior results are rooted in the entry barriers characterizing monopoly.

Now we must recognize that costs may not be the same for purely competitive and monopolistic producers. The unit cost incurred by a monopolist may be either larger or smaller than that incurred by a purely competitive firm. There are four reasons why costs may differ: (1) economies of scale, (2) a factor called "X-inefficiency," (3) the need for monopoly-preserving expenditures, and (4) the "very long run" perspective, which allows for technological advance.

Economies of Scale Once Again   Where there are extensive economies of scale, market demand may not be sufficient to support a large number of competing firms, each producing at minimum efficient scale. In such cases,

an industry of one or two firms would have a lower average total cost than would the same industry made up of numerous competitive firms. At the extreme, only a single firm—a natural monopoly—might be able to achieve the lowest long-run average total cost.

Some firms relating to new information technologies—for example, computer software, Internet service, and wireless communications—have displayed extensive economies of scale. As these firms have grown, their long-run average total costs have declined because of greater use of specialized inputs, the spreading of product development costs, and learning by doing. Also, *simultaneous consumption* and *network effects* have reduced costs.

A product's ability to satisfy a large number of consumers at the same time is called **simultaneous consumption** (or *nonrivalous consumption*). Dell Computers needs to produce a personal computer for each customer, but Microsoft needs to produce its Windows program only once. Then, at very low marginal cost, Microsoft delivers its program by disk or Internet to millions of consumers. The same is true for Internet service providers, music producers, and wireless communication firms. Because marginal costs are so low, the average total cost of output declines as more customers are added.

Network effects are increases in the value of a product to each user, including existing users, as the total number of users rises. Good examples are computer software, cell phones, pagers, palm computers, and other products related to the Internet. When other people have Internet service and devices to access it, a person can conveniently send e-mail messages to them. And when they have similar software, documents, spreadsheets, and photos can be attached to the e-mail messages. The greater the number of persons connected to the system, the more the benefits of the product to each person are magnified.

Such network effects may drive a market toward monopoly because consumers tend to choose standard products that everyone else is using. The focused demand for these products permits their producers to grow rapidly and thus achieve economies of scale. Smaller firms, which have the higher-cost "right" products or the "wrong" products get acquired or go out of business.

Economists generally agree that some new information firms have not yet exhausted their economies of scale. But most economists question whether such firms are truly natural monopolies. Most firms eventually achieve their minimum efficient scale at less than the full size of the market.

Even if natural monopoly develops, it's unlikely that the monopolist will pass cost reductions along to consumers as price reductions. So, with perhaps a handful of exceptions, economies of scale do not change the general conclusion that monopolies yield less efficiency than do more competitive industries.

X-Inefficiency   In constructing all the average-total-cost curves used in this book, we have assumed that the firm uses the most efficient existing technology. In other words, it uses the technology that permits it to achieve the lowest average total cost of whatever level of output it chooses to produce. **X-inefficiency** occurs when a firm's actual cost of producing any output is greater than the lowest possible cost of producing it. In Figure 24.7 X-inefficiency is represented by operation at points X and X' above the lowest-cost ATC curve. At these points, per-unit costs are ATC_x (as opposed to ATC_1) for output Q_1 and $ATC_{x'}$ (as opposed to ATC_2) for output Q_2. Any point above the average-total-cost curve

24.3
X-inefficiency

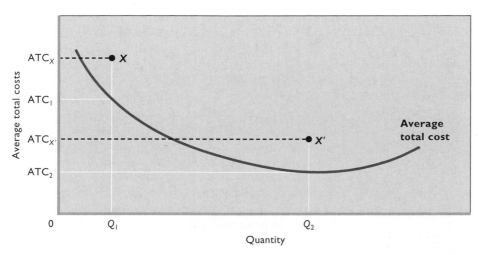

FIGURE 24.7

X-inefficiency. The average-total-cost curve (ATC) is assumed to reflect the minimum cost of producing each particular level of output. Any point above this "lowest-cost" ATC curve, such as X or X', implies X-inefficiency: operation at greater than lowest cost for a particular level of output.

in Figure 24.7 is possible but reflects inefficiency or "bad management" by the firm.

Why is X-inefficiency allowed to occur if it reduces profits? The answer is that managers may have goals, such as corporate growth, an easier work life, avoidance of business risk, or giving jobs to incompetent relatives, that conflict with cost minimization. Or X-inefficiency may arise because a firm's workers are poorly motivated or ineffectively supervised. Or a firm may simply become lethargic and inert, relying on rules of thumb in decision making as opposed to relevant calculations of costs and revenues.

For our purposes the relevant question is whether monopolistic firms tend more toward X-inefficiency than competitive producers do. Presumably they do. Firms in competitive industries are continually under pressure from rivals, forcing them to be internally efficient to survive. But monopolists are sheltered from such competitive forces by entry barriers, and that lack of pressure may lead to X-inefficiency.

There is no indisputable evidence regarding X-inefficiency, but what evidence we have suggests that it increases as competition decreases. A reasonable estimate is that X-inefficiency may be 10 percent or more of costs for monopolists but only 5 percent for an "average" oligopolistic industry in which the four largest firms produce 60 percent of total output.[1] In the words of one authority: "The evidence is fragmentary, but it points in the same direction. X-inefficiency exists, and it is more apt to be reduced when competitive pressures are strong than when firms enjoy insulated market positions."[2]

Rent-Seeking Expenditures
Rent-seeking behavior is any activity designed to transfer income or wealth to a particular firm or resource supplier at someone else's, or even society's, expense. We have seen that a monopolist can obtain an economic profit even in the long run. Therefore, it is no surprise that a firm may go to great expense to acquire or maintain a monopoly granted by government through legislation or an exclusive license. Such rent-seeking expenditures add nothing to the firm's output, but they clearly increase its costs. They imply that monopoly involves higher costs and less efficiency than suggested in Figure 24.6b.

Technological Advance
In the very long run, firms can reduce their costs through the discovery and implementation of new technology. If monopolists are more likely than competitive producers to develop more efficient production techniques over time, then the inefficiency of monopoly might be overstated. Since research and development (R&D) is the topic of Chapter 26, we will provide only a brief assessment here.

The general view of economists is that a pure monopolist will not be technologically progressive. Although its economic profit provides ample means to finance research and development, it has little incentive to implement new techniques (or products). The absence of competitors means that there is no external pressure for technological advance in a monopolized market. Because of its sheltered market position, the pure monopolist can afford to be inefficient and lethargic; there simply is no penalty for being so.

One caveat: Research and technological advance may be one of the monopolist's barriers to entry. Thus, the monopolist may continue to seek technological advance to avoid falling prey to new rivals. In this case technological advance is essential to the maintenance of monopoly. But then it is potential competition, not the monopoly market structure, that is driving the technological advance. By assumption, no such competition exists in the pure monopoly model; entry is completely blocked.

Assessment and Policy Options

For reasons we have discussed, monopoly is a legitimate concern to an economy. Monopolists can charge higher-than-competitive prices that result in an underallocation of resources to the monopolized product. They can stifle innovation, engage in rent-seeking behavior, and foster X-inefficiency. Even when their costs are low because of economies of scale, there is no guarantee that the price they charge will reflect those low costs. The cost savings may simply accrue to the monopoly as greater economic profit.

Fortunately, however, monopoly is not widespread in the economy. Barriers to entry are seldom completely successful. Although research and technological advance may strengthen the market position of a monopoly, technology may also undermine monopoly power. Over time, the creation of new technologies may work to destroy monopoly positions. For example, the development of courier delivery, fax machines, and e-mail has eroded the monopoly power of the U.S. Postal Service. Cable television monopolies are now challenged by satellite TV and by new technologies that permit the transmission of audio and visual signals over the Internet.

[1]William G. Shepherd, *The Economics of Industrial Organization*, 4th ed. (Englewood Cliffs, N.J.: Prentice-Hall, 1997), p. 107.

[2]F. M. Scherer and David Ross, *Industrial Market Structure and Economic Performance*, 3d ed. (Chicago: Rand McNally College Publishing, 1990), p. 672.

GLOBAL PERSPECTIVE 24.1

Competition from Foreign Multinational Corporations

Competition from foreign multinational corporations diminishes the market power of firms in the United States. Here are just a few of the hundreds of foreign multinational corporations that compete strongly with U.S. firms in certain American markets.

Company (Country)	Main Products
Bayer (Germany)	chemicals
BP Amoco (United Kingdom)	gasoline
Michelin (France)	tires
NEC (Japan)	computers
Nestlé (Switzerland)	food products
Nokia (Finland)	wireless phones
Royal Dutch/Shell (Netherlands)	gasoline
Royal Philips (Netherlands)	electronics
Sony (Japan)	electronics
Toyota (Japan)	automobiles
Unilever (Netherlands)	food products

Source: Compiled from the Fortune 500 listing of the world's largest firms, www.fortune.com.

Similarly, patents eventually expire, and before they do, the development of new and distinct substitutable products often circumvents existing patent advantages. New sources of monopolized resources sometimes are found and competition from foreign firms may emerge. (See Global Perspective 24.1.) Finally, if a monopoly is sufficiently fearful of future competition from new products, it may keep its prices relatively low so as to discourage rivals from developing such products. If so, consumers may pay nearly competitive prices even though competition is currently lacking.

So what should government do about monopoly when it arises in the real world? Economists agree that government needs to look carefully at monopoly on a case-by-case basis. Three general policy options are available:

- If the monopoly is achieved and sustained through anticompetitive actions, creates substantial economic inefficiency, and appears to be long-lasting, the government can file charges against the monopoly under the antitrust laws. If found guilty of monopoly abuse, the firm can either be expressly prohibited from engaging in certain business activities or be broken into

two or more competing firms. An example of the breakup approach was the dissolution of Standard Oil into several competing firms in 1911. In contrast, in 2001 an appeals court overruled a lower-court decision to divide Microsoft into two firms. Instead, Microsoft was prohibited from engaging in a number of specific anticompetitive business activities. (We discuss the antitrust laws and the Microsoft case in Chapter 32.)

- If the monopoly is a natural monopoly, society can allow it to continue to expand. If no competition emerges from new products, government may then decide to regulate its prices and operations. (We discuss this option later in this chapter and in Chapter 32.)

- If the monopoly appears to be unsustainable over a long period of time, say, because of emerging new technology, society can simply choose to ignore it. (In Chapter 26 we discuss the potential for real-world monopoly to collapse in the very long run.)

QUICK REVIEW 24.2

- The monopolist maximizes profit (or minimizes loss) at the output where MR 5 MC and charges the price that corresponds to that output on its demand curve.
- The monopolist has no supply curve, since any of several prices can be associated with a specific quantity of output supplied.
- Assuming identical costs, a monopolist will be less efficient than a purely competitive industry because the monopolist produces less output and charges a higher price.
- The inefficiencies of monopoly may be offset or lessened by economies of scale and, less likely, by technological progress, but they may be intensified by the presence of X-inefficiency and rent-seeking expenditures.

Price Discrimination

We have assumed in this chapter that the monopolist charges a single price to all buyers. But under certain conditions the monopolist can increase its profit by charging different prices to different buyers. In so doing, the monopolist is engaging in **price discrimination**, the practice of selling a specific product at more than one price when the price differences are not justified by cost differences.

24.4 Price discrimination

Conditions

The opportunity to engage in price discrimination is not readily available to all sellers. Price discrimination is possible when the following conditions are realized:

- *Monopoly power* The seller must be a monopolist or, at least, must possess some degree of monopoly power, that is, some ability to control output and price.

- *Market segregation* At relatively low cost to itself, the seller must be able to segregate buyers into distinct classes, each of which has a different willingness or ability to pay for the product. This separation of buyers is usually based on different elasticities of demand, as the examples below will make clear.

- *No resale* The original purchaser cannot resell the product or service. If buyers in the low-price segment of the market could easily resell in the high-price segment, the monopolist's price-discrimination strategy would create competition in the high-price segment. This competition would reduce the price in the high-price segment and undermine the monopolist's price-discrimination policy. This condition suggests that service industries such as the transportation industry or legal and medical services, where resale is impossible, are candidates for price discrimination.

Examples of Price Discrimination

Price discrimination is widely practiced in the U.S. economy. For example, we noted in Chapter 20's Last Word that airlines charge high fares to business travelers, whose demand for travel is inelastic, and offer lower "Saturday night stayover rates" and "14-day advance purchase fares" to attract vacationers and others whose demands are more elastic.

Electric utilities frequently segment their markets by end uses, such as lighting and heating. The absence of reasonable lighting substitutes means that the demand for electricity for illumination is inelastic and that the price per kilowatt-hour for such use is high. But the availability of natural gas and petroleum for heating makes the demand for electricity for this purpose less inelastic and the price lower.

Movie theaters and golf courses vary their charges on the basis of time (for example, higher evening and weekend rates) and age (for example, lower rates for children, senior discounts). Railroads vary the rate charged per ton-mile of freight according to the market value of the product being shipped. The shipper of 10 tons of television sets or refrigerators is charged more than the shipper of 10 tons of gravel or coal.

CONSIDER THIS ...

© Richard Gross/CORBIS

Price Discrimination at the Ballpark

Take me out to the ball game . . .
Buy me some peanuts and Cracker Jack . . .

Professional baseball teams earn substantial revenues through ticket sales. To maximize profit, they offer significantly lower ticket prices for children (whose demand is elastic) than those for adults (whose demand is inelastic). This discount may be as much as 50 percent.

If this type of price discrimination increases revenue and profit, why don't teams also price discriminate at the concession stands? Why don't they offer half-price hot dogs, soft drinks, peanuts, and Cracker Jack to children?

The answer involves the three requirements for successful price discrimination. All three requirements are met for game tickets: (1) The team has monopoly power; (2) it can segregate ticket buyers by age group, each group having a different elasticity of demand; and (3) children cannot resell their discounted tickets to adults.

It's a different situation at the concession stands. Specifically, the third condition is *not* met. If the team had dual prices, it could not prevent the exchange or "resale" of the concession goods from children to adults. Many adults would send children to buy food and soft drinks for them: "Here's some money, Billy. Go buy *six* hot dogs." In this case, price discrimination would reduce, not increase, team profit. Thus, children and adults are charged the same high prices at the concession stands. (These prices are high relative to those for the same goods at the local convenience store because the stadium sellers have a captured audience and thus considerable monopoly power.)

The issuance of discount coupons, redeemable at purchase, is a form of price discrimination. It permits firms to give price discounts to their most price-sensitive customers who have elastic demand. Less price-sensitive consumers who have less elastic demand are not as likely to undertake the clipping and redeeming of coupons. The firm thus makes a larger profit than if it had used a single-price, no-coupon strategy.

Finally, price discrimination often occurs in international trade. A Russian aluminum producer, for example, might sell aluminum for less in the United States than in Russia. In the United States, this seller faces an elastic demand because several substitute suppliers are available. But in Russia, where the manufacturer dominates the market and trade barriers impede imports, consumers have fewer choices and thus demand is less elastic.

Price Discrimination Outcomes

As you will see shortly, a monopolist can increase its profit by practicing price discrimination. At the same time, *perfect price discrimination* results in more output than would be purchased at a single monopoly price. Such price discrimination occurs when the monopolist charges each customer the price that he or she would be willing to pay rather than go without the product.

More Profit   Let's again consider our monopolist's downsloping demand curve in Figure 24.4, this time to see why price discrimination can yield additional profit. In that figure we saw that the profit-maximizing single price is $P_m = \$122$. However, the segment of the demand curve above the economic profit area (in blue) reveals that some buyers are willing to pay more than $122 rather than forgo the product.

If the monopolist can identify those buyers, segregate them, and charge the maximum price each would be willing to pay, total revenue and economic profit would increase. Observe from columns 1 and 2 in Table 24.1 that buyers of the first 4 units of output would be willing to pay $162, $152, $142, and $132, respectively, for those units. If the seller could practice perfect price discrimination by charging the maximum price for each unit, total revenue would increase from $610 (= $122 × 5) to $710 (= $122 + $132 + $142 + $152 + $162) and profit would increase from $140 (= $610 − $470) to $240 (= $710 − $470).

More Production   Other things equal, the monopolist practicing perfect price discrimination will produce a larger output than the monopolist that does not. When the nondiscriminating monopolist lowers its price to sell additional output, the lower price not only applies to the additional output but also to all the prior units of output. So the single-price monopolist's marginal revenue falls more rapidly than price and, graphically, its marginal-revenue curve lies below its demand curve. The decline of marginal revenue is a disincentive to increase production.

But when a discriminating monopolist lowers price, the reduced price applies only to the additional unit sold and not to the prior units. Thus, marginal revenue equals price for each unit of output, and the firm's marginal revenue curve and demand curve coincide. The disincentive to increase production is removed.

We can show the outcome through Table 24.1. Because marginal revenue and price are equal, the discriminating monopolist finds it profitable to produce 7 units, not 5 units, of output. The additional revenue from the sixth and seventh units is $214 (= $112 + $102).

Thus total revenue for 7 units is $924 (= $710 + $214). Since total cost for 7 units is $640, profit is $284.

Ironically, although perfect price discrimination results in higher monopoly profit than that achieved by a nondiscriminating monopolist, it also results in greater output and thus greater allocative efficiency. In our example, the output level of 7 units matches the output that would have occurred in pure competition. That is, allocative efficiency ($P = MC$) is achieved.

Graphical Portrayal   Figure 24.8 shows the effects of price discrimination graphically. Figure 24.8a merely restates Figure 24.4 in a generalized form to show the position of a nondiscriminating monopolist as a benchmark. The nondiscriminating monopolist produces output Q_1 (where MR = MC) and charges price P_1. Total revenue is area 0*bce* and economic profit is area *abcd*.

The monopolist in Figure 24.8b engages in perfect price discrimination, charging each buyer the highest price he or she is willing to pay. Starting at the very first unit, each additional unit is sold for the price indicated by the corresponding point on the demand curve. This monopolist's demand and marginal-revenue curves coincide, because the monopolist does not cut price on preceding units to sell more output. Thus, the most profitable output is Q_2 (where MR = MC), which is greater than Q_1. Total revenue is area 0*fgk* and total cost is area 0*hjk*. The economic profit of *hfgj* for the discriminating monopolist is clearly larger than the profit of *abcd* for the single-price monopolist.

The impact of price discrimination on consumers is mixed. Those buying each unit out to Q_1 will pay more than the nondiscriminatory price of P_1. But those additional consumers brought into the market by discrimination will pay less than P_1. Specifically, they will pay the various prices shown on segment *cg* of the $D = MR$ curve.

Overall, then, (1) perfect price discrimination results in greater profit and greater output than is the case in single-price monopoly; (2) some consumers pay more than the single price, but other consumers pay less; and (3) perfect price discrimination and pure competition are equally efficient. **(Key Question 6)**

Regulated Monopoly

Natural monopolies traditionally have been subject to *rate regulation* (price regulation), although the recent trend has been to deregulate the parts of the industries where competition seems possible. For example, long-distance telephone, natural gas at the wellhead, wireless communications, cable television, and long-distance electricity

FIGURE 24.8

Single-price versus perfectly discriminating monopoly pricing. (a) The single-price monopolist produces output Q_1 at which MR = MC, charges price P_1 for all units, incurs an average total cost of A_1, and realizes an economic profit represented by area *abcd*. (b) The perfectly discriminating monopolist has MR = D and, as a result, produces output Q_2 (where MR = MC). It then charges the maximum price for each unit of output, incurs average total cost A_2, and realizes an economic profit represented by area *hfgj*.

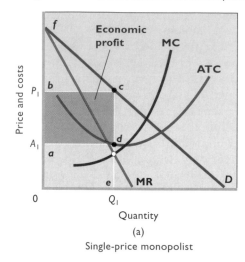

(a)

Single-price monopolist

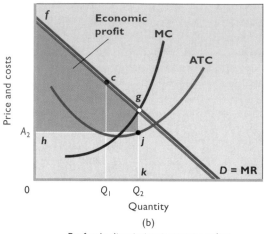

(b)

Perfectly discriminating monopolist

transmission have been, to one degree or another, deregulated over the past several decades. And regulators in some states are beginning to allow new entrants to compete with existing local telephone and electricity providers. Nevertheless, state and local regulatory commissions still regulate the prices that most local natural gas distributors, regional telephone companies, and local electricity suppliers can charge.

Let's consider the regulation of a local natural monopoly, for example, a natural gas provider. Figure 24.9 shows the demand and the long-run cost curves facing our firm. Because of extensive economies of scale, the demand curve cuts the natural monopolist's long-run average-total-cost curve at a point where that curve is still falling. It would be inefficient to have several firms in this industry because each would produce a much smaller output, operating well to the left on the long-run average-total-cost curve. In short, each firm's lowest average total cost would be substantially higher than that of a single firm. So efficient, low-cost production requires a single seller.

We know by application of the MR = MC rule that Q_m and P_m are the profit-maximizing output and price that an unregulated monopolist would choose. Because price exceeds average total cost at output Q_m, the monopolist enjoys a substantial economic profit. Furthermore, price exceeds marginal cost, indicating an underallocation of resources to this product or service. Can government regulation bring about better results from society's point of view?

Socially Optimal Price: P = MC

If the objective of a regulatory commission is to achieve allocative efficiency, it should attempt to establish a legal (ceiling) price for the monopolist that is equal to marginal cost. Remembering that each point on the market demand curve designates a price-quantity combination, and noting that the marginal-cost curve cuts the demand curve

FIGURE 24.9

Regulated monopoly. The socially optimal price P_r, found where D and MC intersect, will result in an efficient allocation of resources but may entail losses to the monopoly. The fair-return price P_f will allow the monopolist to break even but will not fully correct the underallocation of resources.

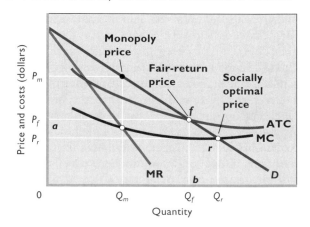

only at point r, we see that P_r is the only price on the demand curve equal to marginal cost. The maximum or ceiling price effectively causes the monopolist's demand curve to become horizontal (indicating perfectly elastic demand) from zero out to point r, where the regulated price ceases to be effective. Also, out to point r we have MR $= P_r$.

Confronted with the legal price P_r, the monopolist will maximize profit or minimize loss by producing Q_r units of output, because at this output MR $(= P_r) =$ MC. By making it illegal to charge more than P_r per unit, the regulatory agency has removed the monopolist's incentive to restrict output to Q_m to obtain a higher price and greater profit.

In short, the regulatory commission can simulate the allocative forces of pure competition by imposing the legal price P_r and letting the monopolist choose its profit-maximizing or loss-minimizing output. Production takes place where $P_r =$ MC, and this equality indicates an efficient allocation of resources to this product or service. The price that achieves allocative efficiency is called the **socially optimal price.**

Fair-Return Price: P = ATC

But the socially optimal price P_r that equals marginal cost may be so low that average total costs are not covered, as is the case in Figure 24.9. The result is a loss for the firm. The reason lies in the basic character of our firm. Because it is required to meet the heaviest "peak" demands (both daily and seasonally) for natural gas, it has substantial excess production capacity when demand is relatively "normal." Its high level of investment in production facilities and economies of scale mean that its average total cost is likely to be greater than its marginal cost over a very wide range of outputs. In particular, as in Figure 24.9, average total cost is likely to be greater than the price P_r at the intersection of the demand curve and marginal-cost curve. Therefore, forcing the socially optimal price P_r on the regulated monopolist would result in short-run losses and long-run bankruptcy for the utility.

What to do? One option is to provide a public subsidy to cover the loss that marginal-cost pricing would entail. Another possibility is to condone price discrimination and hope that the additional revenue gained will permit the firm to cover costs.

In practice, regulatory commissions have pursued a third option: They modify the objective of allocative efficiency and $P =$ MC pricing. Most regulatory agencies in the United States establish a **fair-return price.** They do so because the courts have ruled that a socially optimal price leading to losses and bankruptcy deprives the monopoly's owners of their private property without due process of law. The Supreme Court has held that regulatory agencies must permit a "fair return" to utility owners.

Remembering that total cost includes a normal or "fair" profit, we see in Figure 24.9 that a fair-return price should be on the average-total-cost curve. Because the demand curve cuts average total cost only at point f, clearly P_f is the only price on the demand curve that permits a fair return. The corresponding output at regulated price P_f will be Q_f. Total revenue of $0afb$ will equal the utility's total cost of the same amount, and the firm will realize a normal profit.

Dilemma of Regulation

Comparing results of the socially optimal price ($P =$ MC) and the fair-return price ($P =$ ATC) suggests a policy dilemma, sometimes termed the *dilemma of regulation*. When its price is set to achieve the most efficient allocation of resources ($P =$ MC), the regulated monopoly is likely to suffer losses. Survival of the firm would presumably depend on permanent public subsidies out of tax revenues. On the other hand, although a fair-return price ($P =$ ATC) allows the monopolist to cover costs, it only partially resolves the underallocation of resources that the unregulated monopoly price would foster. That is, the fair-return price would increase output only from Q_m to Q_f in Figure 24.9, while the socially optimal output is Q_r. Despite this dilemma, regulation can improve on the results of monopoly from the social point of view. Price regulation (even at the fair-return price) can simultaneously reduce price, increase output, and reduce the economic profits of monopolies. **(Key Question 12)**

QUICK REVIEW 24.3

- Price discrimination occurs when a firm sells a product at different prices that are not based on cost differences.
- The conditions necessary for price discrimination are (a) monopoly power, (b) the ability to segregate buyers on the basis of demand elasticities, and (c) the inability of buyers to resell the product.
- Compared with single pricing by a monopolist, perfect price discrimination results in greater profit and greater output. Many consumers pay higher prices, but other buyers pay prices below the single price.
- Monopoly price can be reduced and output increased through government regulation.
- The socially optimal price ($P =$ MC) achieves allocative efficiency but may result in losses; the fair-return price ($P =$ ATC) yields a normal profit but fails to achieve allocative efficiency.

De Beers Was One of the World's Strongest and Most Enduring Monopolies. But in Mid-2000 It Announced That It Could No Longer Control the Supply of Diamonds and Thus Would Abandon Its 66-Year Policy of Monopolizing the Diamond Trade.

De Beers, a Swiss-based company controlled by a South African corporation, produces about 50 percent of the world's rough-cut diamonds and purchases for resale a sizable number of the rough-cut diamonds produced by other mines worldwide. As a result, De Beers markets about 65 percent of the world's diamonds to a select group of diamond cutters and dealers. But that percentage has declined from 80 percent in the mid-1980s. Therein lies the company's problem.

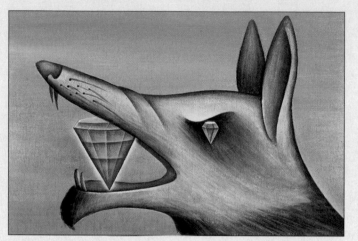

Classic Monopoly Behavior   De Beers' past monopoly behavior and results are a classic example of the unregulated monopoly model illustrated in Figure 24.4. No matter how many diamonds it mined or purchased, it sold only the quantity of diamonds that would yield an "appropriate" (monopoly) price. That price was well above production costs, and De Beers and its partners earned monopoly profits.

When demand fell, De Beers reduced its sales to maintain price. The excess of production over sales was then reflected in growing diamond stockpiles held by De Beers. It also attempted to bolster demand through advertising ("Diamonds are forever"). When demand was strong, it increased sales by reducing its diamond inventories.

De Beers used several methods to control the production of many mines it did not own. First, it convinced a number of independent producers that "single-channel" or monopoly marketing through De Beers would maximize their profit. Second, mines that circumvented De Beers often found their market suddenly flooded with similar diamonds from De Beers' vast stockpiles. The resulting price decline and loss of profit often would encourage a "rogue" mine into the De Beers fold. Finally, De Beers simply purchased and stockpiled diamonds produced by independent mines so that their added supplies would not "undercut" the market.

An End of an Era?   Several factors have come together to unravel the monopoly. New diamond discoveries resulted in a growing leakage of diamonds into world markets outside De Beers' control. For example, significant prospecting and trading in Angola occurred. Recent diamond discoveries in Canada's Northwest Territories pose another threat. Although De Beers is a participant in that region, a large uncontrolled supply of diamonds is expected to emerge. Similarly, although Russia's diamond monopoly Alrosa is part of the De Beers monopoly, it is allowed to sell one-half of its large diamond stock directly to diamond cutters.

If that was not enough, Australian diamond producer Argyle opted to withdraw from the De Beers monopoly. Its annual production of mostly low-grade industrial diamonds accounts for about 6 percent of the global $8 billion diamond market. Moreover, the international media began to focus heavily on the role that diamonds play in financing the bloody civil wars in Africa. Fearing a consumer boycott of diamonds, De Beers pledged not to buy these "conflict" diamonds or do business with any firms that did. These diamonds, however, continue to find their way into the marketplace, eluding De Beers' control.

In mid-2000 De Beers abandoned its attempt to control the supply of diamonds. It announced that it planned to transform itself from a diamond cartel to a modern firm selling "premium" diamonds and other luxury goods under the De Beers label. It therefore would gradually reduce its $4 billion stockpile of diamonds and turn its efforts to increasing the overall demand for diamonds through advertising. De Beers proclaimed that it was changing its strategy to being "the diamond supplier of choice."

With its high market share and ability to control its own production levels, De Beers will still wield considerable influence over the price of rough-cut diamonds. But it turns out that the De Beers monopoly was not forever.

SUMMARY

1. A pure monopolist is the sole producer of a commodity for which there are no close substitutes.

2. The existence of pure monopoly and other imperfectly competitive market structures is explained by barriers to entry in the form of (a) economies of scale, (b) patent ownership and research, (c) ownership or control of essential resources, and (d) pricing and other strategic behavior.

3. The pure monopolist's market situation differs from that of a competitive firm in that the monopolist's demand curve is downsloping, causing the marginal-revenue curve to lie below the demand curve. Like the competitive seller, the pure monopolist will maximize profit by equating marginal revenue and marginal cost. Barriers to entry may permit a monopolist to acquire economic profit even in the long run. However, (a) the monopolist does not charge "the highest price possible"; (b) the price that yields maximum total profit to the monopolist rarely coincides with the price that yields maximum unit profit; (c) high costs and a weak demand may prevent the monopolist from realizing any profit at all; and (d) the monopolist avoids the inelastic region of its demand curve.

4. With the same costs, the pure monopolist will find it profitable to restrict output and charge a higher price than would sellers in a purely competitive industry. This restriction of output causes resources to be misallocated, as is evidenced by the fact that price exceeds marginal cost in monopolized markets.

5. In general, monopoly transfers income from consumers to the owners of the monopoly. Because, on average, con-

sumers of monopolized products have less income than the corporate owners, monopoly increases income inequality.

6. The costs monopolists and competitive producers face may not be the same. On the one hand, economies of scale may make lower unit costs available to monopolists but not to competitors. Also, pure monopoly may be more likely than pure competition to reduce costs via technological advance because of the monopolist's ability to realize economic profit, which can be used to finance research. On the other hand, X-inefficiency—the failure to produce with the least costly combination of inputs—is more common among monopolists than among competitive firms. Also, monopolists may make costly expenditures to maintain monopoly privileges that are conferred by government. Finally, the blocked entry of rival firms weakens the monopolist's incentive to be technologically progressive.

7. A monopolist can increase its profit by practicing price discrimination, provided (a) it can segregate buyers on the basis of elasticities of demand and (b) its product or service cannot be readily transferred between the segregated markets. Other things equal, the perfectly discriminating monopolist will produce a larger output than the nondiscriminating monopolist.

8. Price regulation can be invoked to eliminate wholly or partially the tendency of monopolists to underallocate resources and to earn economic profits. The socially optimal price is determined where the demand and marginal-cost curves intersect; the fair-return price is determined where the demand and average-total-cost curves intersect.

TERMS AND CONCEPTS

pure monopoly	network effects	rent-seeking behavior	socially optimal price
barriers to entry	X-inefficiency	price discrimination	fair-return price
simultaneous consumption			

STUDY QUESTIONS

1. "No firm is completely sheltered from rivals; all firms compete for consumer dollars. If that is so, then pure monopoly does not exist." Do you agree? Explain. How might you use Chapter 20's concept of cross elasticity of demand to judge whether monopoly exists?

2. Discuss the major barriers to entry into an industry. Explain how each barrier can foster either monopoly or oligopoly. Which barriers, if any, do you feel give rise to monopoly that is socially justifiable?

3. How does the demand curve faced by a purely monopolistic seller differ from that confronting a purely competitive firm? Why does it differ? Of what significance is the difference? Why is the pure monopolist's demand curve not perfectly inelastic?

4. *Key Question* Use the demand schedule that follows to calculate total revenue and marginal revenue at each quantity. Plot the demand, total-revenue, and marginal-revenue curves and explain the relationships between them. Explain

why the marginal revenue of the fourth unit of output is $3.50, even though its price is $5. Use Chapter 20's total-revenue test for price elasticity to designate the elastic and inelastic segments of your graphed demand curve. What generalization can you make as to the relationship between marginal revenue and elasticity of demand? Suppose the marginal cost of successive units of output was zero. What output would the profit-seeking firm produce? Finally, use your analysis to explain why a monopolist would never produce in the inelastic region of demand.

Price (P)	Quantity Demanded (Q)	Price (P)	Quantity Demanded (Q)
$7.00	0	$4.50	5
6.50	1	4.00	6
6.00	2	3.50	7
5.50	3	3.00	8
5.00	4	2.50	9

5. **Key Question** Suppose a pure monopolist is faced with the demand schedule shown below and the same cost data as the competitive producer discussed in question 4 at the end of Chapter 23. Calculate the missing total-revenue and marginal-revenue amounts, and determine the profit-maximizing price and profit-earning output for this monopolist. What is the monopolist's profit? Verify your answer graphically and by comparing total revenue and total cost.

Price	Quantity Demanded	Total Revenue	Marginal Revenue
$115	0	$_____	
100	1	_____	$_____
83	2	_____	_____
71	3	_____	_____
63	4	_____	_____
55	5	_____	_____
48	6	_____	_____
42	7	_____	_____
37	8	_____	_____
33	9	_____	_____
29	10	_____	_____

6. **Key Question** If the firm described in question 5 could engage in perfect price discrimination, what would be the level of output? Of profits? Draw a diagram showing the relevant demand, marginal-revenue, average-total-cost, and marginal-cost curves and the equilibrium price and output for a nondiscriminating monopolist. Use the same diagram to show the equilibrium position of a monopolist that is able to practice perfect price discrimination. Compare

equilibrium outputs, total revenues, economic profits, and consumer prices in the two cases. Comment on the economic desirability of price discrimination.

7. Assume that a pure monopolist and a purely competitive firm have the same unit costs. Contrast the two with respect to (a) price, (b) output, (c) profits, (d) allocation of resources, and (e) impact on the distribution of income. Since both monopolists and competitive firms follow the MC = MR rule in maximizing profits, how do you account for the different results? Why might the costs of a purely competitive firm and a monopolist be different? What are the implications of such a cost difference?

8. Critically evaluate and explain each statement:
   a. Because they can control product price, monopolists are always assured of profitable production by simply charging the highest price consumers will pay.
   b. The pure monopolist seeks the output that will yield the greatest per-unit profit.
   c. An excess of price over marginal cost is the market's way of signaling the need for more production of a good.
   d. The more profitable a firm, the greater its monopoly power.
   e. The monopolist has a pricing policy; the competitive producer does not.
   f. With respect to resource allocation, the interests of the seller and of society coincide in a purely competitive market but conflict in a monopolized market.
   g. In a sense the monopolist makes a profit for not producing; the monopolist produces profit more than it does goods.

9. Assume a monopolistic publisher has agreed to pay an author 15 percent of the total revenue from the sales of a text. Will the author and the publisher want to charge the same price for the text? Explain.

10. U.S. pharmaceutical companies charge different prices for prescription drugs to buyers in different nations, depending on elasticity of demand and government-imposed price ceilings. Explain why these companies oppose laws allowing reimportation of drugs to the United States.

11. Explain verbally and graphically how price (rate) regulation may improve the performance of monopolies. In your answer distinguish between (a) socially optimal (marginal-cost) pricing and (b) fair-return (average-total-cost) pricing. What is the "dilemma of regulation"?

12. **Key Question** It has been proposed that natural monopolists should be allowed to determine their profit-maximizing outputs and prices and then government should tax their profits away and distribute them to consumers in proportion to their purchases from the monopoly. Is this proposal as socially desirable as requiring monopolists to equate price with marginal cost or average total cost?

13. **(Last Word)** How was De Beers able to control the world price of diamonds over the past several decades even though

it produced only 50 percent of the diamonds? What factors ended its monopoly? What is its new strategy for earning economic profit, rather than just normal profit?

14. ***Web-Based Question: Is Microsoft a monopoly—what did the courts conclude?*** In 2002 a U.S. court of appeals imposed remedies relating to a lower court's findings that Microsoft had a monopoly in personal computer (PC) operating systems and had maintained its monopoly through illegal actions. At the U.S. Justice Department's website, www.usdoj.gov, use the alphabetical listing to find Antitrust Division and then Antitrust Case Filings. Locate *U.S. v. Microsoft* and select District Court filings and then Court's Findings of Fact (11/5/99). On what basis did the court conclude that Microsoft was a monopoly (see "Market Share")? What was Microsoft's market share of Intel-compatible PC operating systems? Of all operating systems, including those of Apple computers? What evidence did the court cite in claiming that Microsoft charged above-competitive prices (see "Microsoft's Pricing Behavior")?

15. ***Web-Based Question: Getting to know your state regulatory commission*** Go to www.yahoo.com or some other standard search engine and type "public utility commissions" in the search line. Find the utilities commission for the state where you reside (or another state if you cannot find the website for your state commission). What industries does the state commission regulate? How many specific firms are registered or regulated? List the names of 10 such specific firms. Why are these and the other firms regulated?

25

Monopolistic Competition and Oligopoly

Most markets in the U.S. economy fall between the two poles of pure competition and pure monopoly. Real-world industries usually have fewer than the hundreds of producers required for pure competition and more than the single producer that defines pure monopoly. Most firms have distinguishable rather than standardized products and have some discretion over the prices they charge. Competition often occurs on the basis of price, quality, location, service, and advertising. Entry to most real-world industries ranges from easy to very difficult but is rarely completely blocked.

This chapter examines two models that more closely approximate these widespread markets. You will discover that *monopolistic competition* mixes a small amount of monopoly power with a large amount of competition. *Oligopoly,* in contrast, blends a large amount of monopoly power, a small amount of competition through entry, and considerable rivalry among industry firms.

Monopolistic Competition

Let's begin by examining **monopolistic competition,** which is characterized by (1) a relatively large number of sellers, (2) differentiated products (often promoted by heavy advertising), and (3) easy entry to, and exit from, the industry. The first and third characteristics provide the "competitive" aspect of monopolistic competition; the second characteristic provides the "monopolistic" aspect. In general, however, monopolistically competitive industries are much more competitive than they are monopolistic.

25.1
Monopolistic
competition

Relatively Large Number of Sellers

Monopolistic competition is characterized by a fairly large number of firms, say, 25, 35, 60, or 70, not by the hundreds or thousands of firms in pure competition. Consequently, monopolistic competition involves:

- **Small market shares**   Each firm has a comparatively small percentage of the total market and consequently has limited control over market price.
- **No collusion**   The presence of a relatively large number of firms ensures that collusion by a group of firms to restrict output and set prices is unlikely.
- **Independent action**   With numerous firms in an industry, there is no feeling of interdependence among

them; each firm can determine its own pricing policy without considering the possible reactions of rival firms. A single firm may realize a modest increase in sales by cutting its price, but the effect of that action on competitors' sales will be nearly imperceptible and will probably trigger no response.

Differentiated Products

In contrast to pure competition, in which there is a standardized product, monopolistic competition is distinguished by **product differentiation.** Monopolistically competitive firms turn out variations of a particular product. They produce products with slightly different physical characteristics, offer varying degrees of customer service, provide varying amounts of locational convenience, or proclaim special qualities, real or imagined, for their products.

Let's examine these aspects of product differentiation in more detail.

Product Attributes   Product differentiation may entail physical or qualitative differences in the products themselves. Real differences in functional features, materials, design, and workmanship are vital aspects of product differentiation. Personal computers, for example, differ in terms of storage capacity, speed, graphic displays, and included software. There are dozens of competing principles of economics textbooks that differ in content, organization, presentation and readability, pedagogical aids, and graphics and design. Most cities have a variety of retail stores selling men's and women's clothes that differ greatly in styling, materials, and quality of work. Similarly, one furniture manufacturer may feature its solid oak furniture, while a competitor stresses its solid maple furniture.

Service   Service and the conditions surrounding the sale of a product are forms of product differentiation too. One grocery store may stress the helpfulness of its clerks who bag your groceries and carry them to your car. A warehouse competitor may leave bagging and carrying to its customers but feature lower prices. Customers may prefer 1-day over 3-day dry cleaning of equal quality. The prestige appeal of a store, the courteousness and helpfulness of clerks, the firm's reputation for servicing or exchanging its products, and the credit it makes available are all service aspects of product differentiation.

Location   Products may also be differentiated through the location and accessibility of the stores that sell them. Small convenience stores manage to compete with large supermarkets, even though these minimarts have a more limited range of products and charge higher prices. They compete mainly on the basis of location—being close to customers and situated on busy streets. A motel's proximity to an interstate highway gives it a locational advantage that may enable it to charge a higher room rate than nearby motels in less convenient locations.

Brand Names and Packaging   Product differentiation may also be created through the use of brand names and trademarks, packaging, and celebrity connections. Most aspirin tablets are very much alike, but many headache sufferers believe that one brand—for example, Bayer, Anacin, or Bufferin—is superior and worth a higher price than a generic substitute. A celebrity's name associated with jeans, perfume, or athletic equipment may enhance the appeal of those products for some buyers. Many customers prefer one style of ballpoint pen to another. Packaging that touts "natural spring" bottled water may attract additional customers.

Some Control over Price   Despite the relatively large number of firms, monopolistic competitors do have some control over their product prices because of product differentiation. If consumers prefer the products of specific sellers, then within limits they will pay more to satisfy their preferences. Sellers and buyers are not linked randomly, as in a purely competitive market. But the monopolistic competitor's control over price is quite limited, since there are numerous potential substitutes for its product.

Easy Entry and Exit

Entry into monopolistically competitive industries is relatively easy compared to oligopoly or pure monopoly. Because monopolistic competitors are typically small firms, both absolutely and relatively, economies of scale are few and capital requirements are low. On the other hand, compared with pure competition, financial barriers may result from the need to develop and advertise a product that differs from rivals' products. Some firms may hold patents on their products or copyrights on their brand names, making it difficult and costly for other firms to imitate them.

Exit from monopolistically competitive industries is relatively easy. Nothing prevents an unprofitable monopolistic competitor from holding a going-out-of-business sale and shutting down.

Advertising

The expense and effort involved in product differentiation would be wasted if consumers were not made aware

TABLE 25.1

Percentage of Output Produced by Firms in Selected Low-Concentration U.S. Manufacturing Industries

(1) Industry	(2) Percentage of Industry Output* Produced by the Four Largest Firms	(3) Herfindahl Index	(1) Industry	(2) Percentage of Industry Output* Produced by the Four Largest Firms	(3) Herfindahl Index
Curtains and draperies	27	295	Wooden kitchen cabinets	18	133
Wood furniture	26	238	Asphalt paving	17	125
Lighting fixtures	25	266	Sawmills	17	112
Paperboard boxes	25	246	Women's dresses	14	111
Manufactured ice	24	302	Jewelry	13	81
Textile machinery	24	269	Quick printing	10	27
Plastic pipe	24	260	Signs	8	35
Textile bags	19	180	Ready-mix concrete	7	29
Leather goods	19	167	Wood pallets	6	16
Bolts, nuts, and rivets	19	153	Sheet metal work	4	16

*As measured by value of shipments. Data are for 1997. See www.census.gov/epcd/www/concentration.html.

Source: Bureau of Census, Census of Manufacturers, 1997.

of product differences. Thus, monopolistic competitors advertise their products, often heavily. The goal of product differentiation and advertising—so-called **nonprice competition**—is to make price less of a factor in consumer purchases and make product differences a greater factor. If successful, the firm's demand curve will shift to the right and will become less elastic.

Monopolistically Competitive Industries

Table 25.1 lists several manufacturing industries that approximate monopolistic competition. (The data in column 2 are self-explanatory. We will explain the data in column 3 later in this chapter.) In addition, many retail establishments in metropolitan areas are monopolistically competitive, including grocery stores, gasoline stations, barbershops, dry cleaners, clothing stores, and restaurants. Also, many providers of professional services such as medical care, legal assistance, real estate sales, and basic bookkeeping are monopolistic competitors.

Price and Output in Monopolistic Competition

We now analyze the price and output decisions of a monopolistically competitive firm. Initially, we assume that each firm in the industry is producing a specific

differentiated product and engaging in a particular amount of advertising. Later we'll see how changes in the product and in the amount of advertising modify our conclusions.

The Firm's Demand Curve

Our explanation is based on **Figure 25.1 (Key Graph).** The basic feature of that diagram is the elasticity of demand, as shown by the individual firm's demand curve. The demand curve faced by a monopolistically competitive seller is highly, but not perfectly, elastic. It is precisely this feature that distinguishes monopolistic competition from pure monopoly and pure competition. The monopolistic competitor's demand is more elastic than the demand faced by a pure monopolist because the monopolistically competitive seller has many competitors producing closely substitutible goods. The pure monopolist has no rivals at all. Yet, for two reasons, the monopolistic competitor's demand is not perfectly elastic like that of the pure competitor. First, the monopolistic competitor has fewer rivals; second, its products are differentiated, so they are not perfect substitutes.

The price elasticity of demand faced by the monopolistically competitive firm depends on the number of rivals and the degree of product differentiation. The larger the number of rivals and the weaker the product differentiation, the greater the price elasticity of each seller's

KEY GRAPH

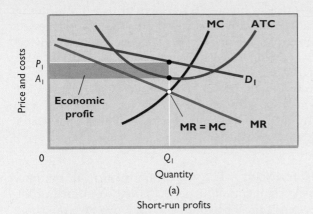

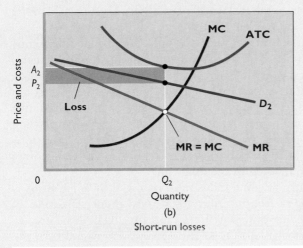

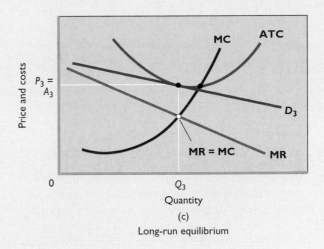

FIGURE 25.1

A monopolistically competitive firm: short run and long run. The monopolistic competitor maximizes profit or minimizes loss by producing the output at which MR = MC. The economic profit shown in (a) will induce new firms to enter, eventually eliminating economic profit. The loss shown in (b) will cause an exit of firms until normal profit is restored. After such entry and exit, the price will settle in (c) to where it just equals average total cost at the MR = MC output. At this price P_3 and output Q_3, the monopolistic competitor earns only a normal profit, and the industry is in long-run equilibrium.

QUICK QUIZ 25.1

1. Price exceeds MC in:
   a. graph (a) only.
   b. graph (b) only.
   c. graphs (a) and (b) only.
   d. graphs (a), (b), and (c).

2. Price exceeds ATC in:
   a. graph (a) only.
   b. graph (b) only.
   c. graphs (a) and (b) only.
   d. graphs (a), (b), and (c).

3. The firm represented by Figure 25.1c is:
   a. making a normal profit.
   b. incurring a loss.

c. producing at the same level of output as a purely competitive firm.
   d. producing a standardized product.

4. Which of the following pairs are both "competition-like elements" in monopolistic competition?
   a. Price exceeds MR; standardized product.
   b. Entry is relatively easy; only a normal profit in the long run.
   c. Price equals MC at the profit-maximizing output; economic profits are likely in the long run.
   d. The firms' demand curve is downsloping; differentiated products.

demand, that is, the closer monopolistic competition will be to pure competition.

The Short Run: Profit or Loss

The monopolistically competitive firm maximizes its profit or minimizes its loss in the short run just as do the other firms we have discussed: by producing the output at which marginal revenue equals marginal cost (MR = MC). In Figure 25.1a the firm produces output Q_1, where MR = MC. As shown by demand curve D_1, it then can charge price P_1. It realizes an economic profit, shown by the blue area [= $(P_1 - A_1) \times Q_1$].

But with less favorable demand or costs, the firm may incur a loss in the short run. We show this possibility in Figure 25.1b, where the firm's best strategy is to minimize its loss. It does so by producing output Q_2 (where MR = MC) and, as determined by demand curve D_2, by charging price P_2. Because price P_2 is less than average total cost A_2, the firm incurs a per-unit loss of $A_2 - P_2$ and a total loss represented as the blue area [= $(A_2 - P_2) \times Q_2$].

The Long Run: Only a Normal Profit

In the long run, firms will enter a profitable monopolistically competitive industry and leave an unprofitable one. So a monopolistic competitor will earn only a normal profit in the long run or, in other words, will only break even. (Remember that the cost curves include both explicit and implicit costs, including a normal profit.)

Profits: Firms Enter   In the case of short-run profit (Figure 25.1a), economic profits attract new rivals, because entry to the industry is relatively easy. As new firms enter, the demand curve faced by the typical firm shifts to the left (falls). Why? Because each firm has a smaller share of total demand and now faces a larger number of close-substitute products. This decline in the firm's demand reduces its economic profit. When entry of new firms has reduced demand to the extent that the demand curve is tangent to the average-total-cost curve at the profit-maximizing output, the firm is just making a normal profit. This situation is shown in Figure 25.1c, where demand is D_3 and the firm's long-run equilibrium output is Q_3. As Figure 25.1c indicates, any greater or lesser output will entail an average total cost that exceeds product price P_3, meaning a loss for the firm. At the tangency point between the demand curve and ATC, total revenue equals total costs. With the economic profit gone, there is no further incentive for additional firms to enter.

Losses: Firms Leave   When the industry suffers short-run losses, as in Figure 25.1b, some firms will exit in the long run. Faced with fewer substitute products and blessed with an expanded share of total demand, the surviving firms will see their demand curves shift to the right (rise), as to D_3. Their losses will disappear and give way to normal profits (Figure 25.1c). (For simplicity we have assumed constant costs; shifts in the cost curves as firms enter or leave would complicate our discussion slightly but would not alter our conclusions.)

Complications   The representative firm in the monopolistic competition model earns only a normal profit in the long run. That outcome may not always occur, however, in the real world of small firms as opposed to the theoretical model.

- Some firms may achieve sufficient product differentiation such that other firms cannot duplicate them, even over time. One hotel in a major city may have the best location relative to business and tourist activities. Or a firm may have developed a well-known brand name that gives it a slight but very long-lasting advantage over imitators. Such firms may have sufficient monopoly power to realize modest economic profits even in the long run.

- Entry to some industries populated by small firms is not as free in reality as it is in theory. Because of product differentiation, there are likely to be greater financial barriers to entry than there would be if the product were standardized. This suggests some monopoly power, with small economic profits continuing even in the long run.

25.1
Monopolistic
competition

With all things considered, however, the normal profit outcome—the long-run equilibrium shown in Figure 25.1c—is a reasonable portrayal of reality.

Monopolistic Competition and Efficiency

We know from Chapter 23 that economic efficiency requires the triple equality P = MC = minimum ATC. The equality of price and minimum average total cost yields *productive efficiency*. The good is being produced in the least costly way, and the price is just sufficient to cover average total cost, including a normal profit. The equality of price and marginal cost yields *allocative efficiency*. The right amount of output is being produced, and thus the

FIGURE 25.2

The inefficiency of monopolistic competition. In long-run equilibrium a monopolistic competitor achieves neither productive nor allocative efficiency. Productive efficiency is not realized because production occurs where the average total cost A_3 exceeds the minimum average total cost A_4. Allocative efficiency is not realized because the product price P_3 exceeds the marginal cost M_3. The result is an underallocation of resources and excess productive capacity of $Q_4 - Q_3$.

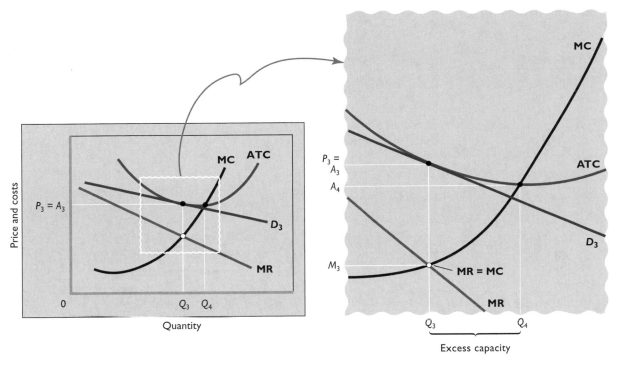

right amount of society's scarce resources is being devoted to this specific use.

How efficient is monopolistic competition, as measured against this triple equality?

Neither Productive nor Allocative Efficiency

In monopolistic competition, neither productive nor allocative efficiency occurs in long-run equilibrium. We show this in Figure 25.2, which includes an enlargement of part of Figure 25.1c. First note that the profit-maximizing price P_3 slightly exceeds the lowest average total cost, A_4. Therefore, in producing the profit-maximizing output Q_3, the firm's average total cost is slightly higher than optimal from society's perspective—productive efficiency is not achieved. Also note that the profit-maximizing price P_3 exceeds marginal cost (here M_3), meaning that monopolistic competition causes an underallocation of resources. Society values each unit of output between Q_3

and Q_4 more highly than the goods it would have to forgo to produce those units. Thus, to a modest extent, monopolistic competition also fails the allocative-efficiency test. Consumers pay a higher-than-competitive price and obtain a less-than-optimal output. Indeed, monopolistic competitors must charge a higher-than-competitive price in the long run in order to achieve a normal profit.

Excess Capacity

In monopolistic competition, the gap between the minimum-ATC output and the profit-maximizing output identifies **excess capacity:** plant and equipment that are underused because firms are producing less than the minimum-ATC output. We show this gap as the distance between Q_4 and Q_3 in Figure 25.2. If each monopolistic competitor could profitably produce at the minimum-ATC output, fewer firms could produce the same total output, and the product could be sold at a lower price.

Monopolistically competitive industries thus are over-crowded with firms, each operating below its optimal capacity. This situation is typified by many kinds of retail establishments. For example, in most cities there is an abundance of small motels and restaurants that operate well below half capacity. **(Key Question 2)**

Product Variety

The situation portrayed in Figures 25.1c and 25.2 is not very satisfying to monopolistic competitors, since it foretells only a normal profit. But the profit-realizing firm of Figure 25.1a need not stand by and watch new competitors eliminate its profit by imitating its product, matching its customer service, and copying its advertising. Each firm has a product that is distinguishable in some way from those of the other producers. So the firm can attempt to stay ahead of competitors and sustain its profit through further product differentiation and better advertising. By developing or improving its product, it may be able to postpone, at least for a while, the outcome of Figure 25.1c.

Although product differentiation and advertising will add to the firm's costs, they can also increase the demand for its product. If demand increases by more than enough to compensate for the added costs, the firm will have improved its profit position. As Figure 25.2 suggests, the firm has little or no prospect of increasing profit by price cutting. So why not engage in nonprice competition?

Benefits of Product Variety

The product variety and product improvement that accompany the drive to maintain economic profit in monopolistic competition are a benefit for society—one that may offset the cost of the inefficiency associated with monopolistic competition. Consumers have a wide diversity of tastes: Some like regular fries, others like curly fries; some like contemporary furniture, others like traditional furniture. If a product is differentiated, then at any time the consumer will be offered a wide range of types, styles, brands, and quality gradations of that product. Compared with pure competition, this provides an advantage to the consumer. The range of choice is widened, and producers more fully meet the wide variation in consumer tastes.

The product improvement promoted by monopolistic competition further differentiates products and expands choices. And a successful product improvement by one firm obligates rivals to imitate or improve on that firm's temporary market advantage or else lose business. So society benefits from better products.

In fact, product differentiation creates a tradeoff between consumer choice and productive efficiency. The stronger the product differentiation, the greater is the excess capacity and, hence, the greater is the productive inefficiency. But the greater the product differentiation, the more likely the firms will satisfy the great diversity of consumer tastes. The greater is the excess-capacity problem, the wider the range of consumer choice.

Further Complexity

Finally, the ability to engage in nonprice competition makes the market situation of a monopolistic competitor more complex than Figure 25.1 indicates. That figure assumes a given (unchanging) product and a given level of advertising expenditures. But we know that, in practice, product attributes and advertising are not fixed. The monopolistically competitive firm juggles three factors—price, product, and advertising—in seeking maximum profit. It must determine what variety of product, selling at what price, and supplemented by what level of advertising will result in the greatest profit. This complex situation is not easily expressed in a simple, meaningful economic model. At best, we can say that each possible combination of price, product, and advertising poses a different demand and cost (production cost plus advertising cost) situation for the firm and that one combination yields the maximum profit. In practice, this optimal combination cannot be readily forecast but must be found by trial and error.

QUICK REVIEW 25.1

- Monopolistic competition involves a relatively large number of firms operating in a noncollusive way and producing differentiated products with easy industry entry and exit.

- In the short run, a monopolistic competitor will maximize profit or minimize loss by producing that output at which marginal revenue equals marginal cost.

- In the long run, easy entry and exit of firms cause monopolistic competitors to earn only a normal profit.

- A monopolistic competitor's long-run equilibrium output is such that price exceeds the minimum average total cost (implying that consumers do not get the product at the lowest price attainable) and price exceeds marginal cost (indicating that resources are underallocated to the product).

Oligopoly

In terms of competitiveness, the spectrum of market structures reaches from pure competition, to monopolistic competition, to oligopoly, to pure monopoly (review Table 23.1). We now direct our attention to **oligopoly,** a market dominated by a few large producers of a homogeneous or differentiated product. Because of their "fewness," oligopolists have considerable control over their prices, but each must consider the possible reaction of rivals to its own pricing, output, and advertising decisions.

A Few Large Producers

The phrase "a few large producers" is necessarily vague because the market model of oligopoly covers much ground, ranging between pure monopoly, on the one hand, and monopolistic competition, on the other. Oligopoly encompasses the U.S. aluminum industry, in which three huge firms dominate an entire national market, and the situation in which four or five much smaller auto-parts stores enjoy roughly equal shares of the market in a medium-size town. Generally, however, when you hear a term such as "Big Three," "Big Four," or "Big Six," you can be sure it refers to an oligopolistic industry.

Homogeneous or Differentiated Products

An oligopoly may be either a **homogeneous oligopoly** or a **differentiated oligopoly,** depending on whether the firms in the oligopoly produce standardized or differentiated products. Many industrial products (steel, zinc, copper, aluminum, lead, cement, industrial alcohol) are virtually standardized products that are produced in oligopolies. Alternatively, many consumer goods industries (automobiles, tires, household appliances, electronics equipment, breakfast cereals, cigarettes, and many sporting goods) are differentiated oligopolies. These differentiated oligopolies typically engage in considerable nonprice competition supported by heavy advertising.

Control over Price, but Mutual Interdependence

Because firms are few in oligopolistic industries, each firm is a "price maker"; like the monopolist, it can set its price and output levels to maximize its profit. But unlike the monopolist, which has no rivals, the oligopolist must consider how its rivals will react to any change in its price, output, product characteristics, or advertising. Oligopoly is thus characterized by *strategic behavior* and *mutual interdependence.* By **strategic behavior,** we simply mean self-interested behavior that takes into account the reactions of others. Firms develop and implement price, quality, location, service, and advertising strategies to "grow their business" and expand their profits. But because rivals are few, there is **mutual interdependence:** a situation in which each firm's profit depends not entirely on its own price and sales strategies but also on those of the other firms. So oligopolistic firms base their decisions on how they think rivals will react. Example: In deciding whether to increase the price of its baseball gloves, Rawlings will try to predict the response of the other major producers, such as Wilson. Second example: In deciding on its advertising strategy, Burger King will take into consideration how McDonald's might react.

Entry Barriers

The same barriers to entry that create pure monopoly also contribute to the creation of oligopoly. Economies of scale are important entry barriers in a number of oligopolistic industries, such as the aircraft, rubber, and copper industries. In those industries, three or four firms might each have sufficient sales to achieve economies of scale, but new firms would have such a small market share that they could not do so. They would then be high-cost producers, and as such they could not survive. A closely related barrier is the large expenditure for capital—the cost of obtaining necessary plant and equipment—required for entering certain industries. The jet engine, automobile, commercial aircraft, and petroleum-refining industries, for example, are all characterized by very high capital requirements.

The ownership and control of raw materials help explain why oligopoly exists in many mining industries, including gold, silver, and copper. In the electronics, chemicals, photographic equipment, office equipment, and pharmaceutical industries, patents have served as entry barriers. Moreover, oligopolists can preclude the entry of new competitors through preemptive and retaliatory pricing and advertising strategies.

Mergers

Some oligopolies have emerged mainly through the growth of the dominant firms in a given industry (examples: breakfast cereals, chewing gum, candy bars). But for other industries the route to oligopoly has been through mergers (examples: steel, in its early history, and, more recently, airlines, banking, and entertainment). The merging, or combining, of two or more competing firms may substantially increase their market share, and this in turn may allow the new firm to achieve greater economies of scale.

Another motive underlying the "urge to merge" is the desire for monopoly power. The larger firm that results from a merger has greater control over market supply and thus the price of its product. Also, since it is a larger buyer of inputs, it will probably be able to demand and obtain lower prices (costs) on its production inputs.

Measures of Industry Concentration

Several means are used to measure the degree to which oligopolistic industries are concentrated in the "hands" of their largest firms. The most-often-used measures are *concentration ratios* and the *Herfindahl index*.

Concentration Ratio
A **concentration ratio** reveals the percentage of total output produced and sold by an industry's largest firms. Previously, we listed the four-firm concentration ratio—the percentage of total industry sales accounted for by the four largest firms—for a number of monopolistically competitive industries (see Table 25.1). Column 2 of Table 25.2 shows the four-firm concentration ratios for 20 oligopolistic industries. For example, the four largest U.S. producers of breakfast cereals make 83 percent of all breakfast cereals produced in the United States.

When the largest four firms in an industry control 40 percent or more of the market (as in Table 25.2), that industry is considered oligopolistic. Using this benchmark, about one-half of all U.S. manufacturing industries are oligopolies.

Although concentration ratios provide useful insights into the competitiveness or monopoly power of various industries, they have three shortcomings.

Localized Markets
Concentration ratios pertain to the nation as a whole, whereas the markets for some products are highly localized because of high transportation costs. For example, the four-firm concentration ratio for ready-mix concrete is only 7 percent, suggesting a highly competitive industry. But the sheer bulk of this product limits the relevant market to a specific town or metropolitan area,

TABLE 25.2

Percentage of Output Produced by Firms in Selected High-Concentration U.S. Manufacturing Industries

(1) Industry	(2) Percentage of Industry Output* Produced by the Four Largest Firms	(3) Herfindahl Index	(1) Industry	(2) Percentage of Industry Output* Produced by the Four Largest Firms	(3) Herfindahl Index
Cigarettes	99	ND†	Photo equipment and supplies	81	ND
Cane sugar refining	99	ND†	Turbines and generators	78	2390
Primary copper	95	2392	Flat glass	77	1829
Glass containers	91	2960	Fiber-optic cable	71	2364
Beer	90	ND†	Men's slacks	69	2254
Small-arms ammunition	90	ND†	Tires	69	1518
Electric light bulbs	89	2849	Motorcycles and bicycles	68	2037
Aircraft	85	ND	Gypsum products	68	1557
Breakfast cereals	83	2446	Soap and detergents	66	1619
Motor vehicles	82	2506	Lawn and garden equipment	64	1707
Household refrigerators and freezers	82	2025			

*As measured by value of shipments. Data are for 1997. See www.census.gov/epcd/www/concentration.html.

†ND = not disclosed.

Source: Bureau of Census, Census of Manufacturers, 1997.

and in such localized markets we often find oligopolistic concrete producers.

Interindustry Competition Since definitions of industries are somewhat arbitrary, we must be aware of **interindustry competition**—that is, competition between two products associated with different industries. The high concentration ratio for the copper industry shown in Table 25.2 understates the competition in that industry, because aluminum competes with copper in many applications (for example, in the market for electric transmission lines).

World Trade The data in Table 25.2 are only for products produced in the United States and may overstate concentration because they do not account for the **import competition** of foreign suppliers. The motorcycle and bicycle industry is a good example. Although Table 25.2 shows that four U.S. firms produce 68 percent of the domestic output of those goods, it ignores the fact that a very large portion of the motorcycles and bicycles bought in the United States are imports. Many of the world's largest corporations are foreign, and many of them do business in the United States.

Herfindahl Index The concentration-ratio shortcomings listed above actually apply to many measures of concentration, but one of those shortcomings can be eliminated: Suppose that in industry X one firm produces all the market output. In a second industry, Y, there are four firms, each of which has 25 percent of the market. The concentration ratio is 100 percent for both these industries. But industry X is a pure monopoly, while industry Y is an oligopoly that may be facing significant economic rivalry. Most economists would agree that monopoly power (or market power) is substantially greater in industry X than in industry Y, a fact disguised by their identical 100 percent concentration ratios.

The **Herfindahl index** addresses this problem. This index is the sum of the squared percentage market shares of all firms in the industry. In equation form:

$$\text{Herfindahl index} = (\%S_1)^2 + (\%S_2)^2 + (\%S_3)^2 + \cdots + (\%S_n)^2$$

where $\%S_1$ is the percentage market share of firm 1, $\%S_2$ is the percentage market share of firm 2, and so on for each firm in the industry. By squaring the percentage market shares of all firms in the industry, the Herfindahl index gives much greater weight to larger, and thus more

powerful, firms than to smaller ones. In the case of the single-firm industry X, the index would be at its maximum of 100^2 or 10,000, indicating an industry with complete monopoly power. For our supposed four-firm industry Y, the index would be $25^2 + 25^2 + 25^2 + 25^2$, or 2500, indicating much less market power. (For a purely competitive industry, the index would approach zero, since each firm's market share—$\%S$ in the equation—is extremely small.)

To generalize, the larger the Herfindahl index, the greater the market power within an industry. Note in Table 25.2 that the four-firm concentration ratios for the men's slacks industry and the tire industry are both 69 percent. But the Herfindahl index of 2254 for the men's slacks industry suggests greater market power than the 1518 index for the tire industry. Also, contrast the much larger Herfindahl indexes in Table 25.2 with those for the low-concentration industries in Table 25.1. (**Key Question 7**)

Oligopoly Behavior: A Game-Theory Overview

Oligopoly pricing behavior has the characteristics of certain games of strategy, such as poker, chess, and bridge. The best way to play such a game depends on the way one's opponent plays. Players (and oligopolists) must pattern their actions according to the actions and expected reactions of rivals. The study of how people behave in strategic situations is called *game theory*. And we will use a simple **game-theory model** to analyze the pricing behavior of oligopolists. We assume a duopoly, or two-firm oligopoly, producing athletic shoes. Each of the two firms—let's call them RareAir and Uptown—has a choice of two pricing strategies: price high or price low. The profit each firm earns will depend on the strategy it chooses and the strategy its rival chooses.

25.2 Game theory

There are four possible combinations of strategies for the two firms, and a lettered cell in Figure 25.3 represents each combination. For example, cell C represents a low-price strategy for Uptown along with a high-price strategy for RareAir. Figure 25.3 is called a *payoff matrix*, because each cell shows the payoff (profit) to each firm that would result from each combination of strategies. Cell C shows that if Uptown adopts a low-price strategy and RareAir a high-price strategy, then Uptown will earn $15 million (lavender portion) and RareAir will earn $6 million (rose portion).

FIGURE 25.3

Profit payoff (in millions) for a two-firm oligopoly. Each firm has two possible pricing strategies. RareAir's strategies are shown in the top margin, and Uptown's in the left margin. Each lettered cell of this four-cell payoff matrix represents one combination of a RareAir strategy and an Uptown strategy and shows the profit that combination would earn for each firm.

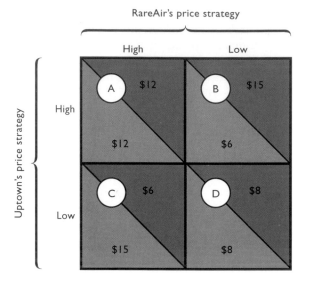

Figure 25.3 are acting independently and following high-price strategies. Each realizes a $12 million profit (cell A).

Note that either RareAir or Uptown could increase its profit by switching to a low-price strategy (cell B or C). The low-price firm would increase its profit to $15 million, and the high-price firm's profit would fall to $6 million. The high-price firm would be better off if it, too, adopted a low-price policy. Doing so would increase its profit from $6 million to $8 million (cell D). The effect of all this independent strategy shifting would be the reduction of both firms' profits from $12 million (cell A) to $8 million (cell D).

In real situations, too, independent action by oligopolists may lead to mutually "competitive" low-price

Mutual Interdependence Revisited

The data in Figure 25.3 are hypothetical, but their relationships are typical of real situations. Recall that oligopolistic firms can increase their profits, and influence their rivals' profits, by changing their pricing strategies. Each firm's profit depends on its own pricing strategy and that of its rivals. This mutual interdependence of oligopolists is the most obvious point demonstrated by Figure 25.3. If Uptown adopts a high-price strategy, its profit will be $12 million provided that RareAir also employs a high-price strategy (cell A). But if RareAir uses a low-price strategy against Uptown's high-price strategy (cell B), RareAir will increase its market share and boost its profit from $12 to $15 million. RareAir's higher profit will come at the expense of Uptown, whose profit will fall from $12 to $6 million. Uptown's high-price strategy is a good strategy only if RareAir also employs a high-price strategy.

Collusive Tendencies

Figure 25.3 also suggests that oligopolists often can benefit from collusion—that is, cooperation with rivals. To see the benefits of collusion, first suppose that both firms in

CONSIDER THIS . . .

Creative Strategic Behavior

The following story, offered with tongue in cheek, illustrates a localized market that exhibits some characteristics of oligopoly, including strategic behavior.

© Richard Cummins/CORBIS

Tracy Martinez's Native American Arts and Crafts store is located in the center of a small tourist town that borders on a national park. In its early days, Tracy had a minimonopoly. Business was brisk, and prices and profits were high.

To Tracy's annoyance, two "copycat" shops opened adjacent to her store, one on either side of her shop. Worse yet, the competitors named their shops to take advantage of Tracy's advertising. One was "Native Arts and Crafts," the other, "Indian Arts and Crafts." These new sellers drew business away from Tracy's store, forcing her to lower her prices. The three side-by-side stores in the small, isolated town constituted a localized oligopoly for Native American arts and crafts.

Tracy began to think strategically about ways to boost profit. She decided to distinguish her shop from those on either side by offering a greater mix of high-quality, expensive products and a lesser mix of inexpensive souvenir items. The tactic worked for a while, but the other stores eventually imitated her product mix.

Then, one of the competitors next door escalated the rivalry by hanging up a large sign proclaiming "We Sell for Less!" Shortly thereafter, the other shop put up a large sign stating "We Won't Be Undersold!"

Not to be outdone, Tracy painted a colorful sign of her own and hung it above her door. It read "Main Entrance."

strategies: Independent oligopolists compete with respect to price, and this leads to lower prices and lower profits. This outcome is clearly beneficial to consumers but not to the oligopolists, whose profits decrease.

How could oligopolists avoid the low-profit outcome of cell D? The answer is that they could collude, rather than establish prices competitively or independently. In our example, the two firms could agree to establish and maintain a high-price policy. So each firm will increase its profit from $8 million (cell D) to $12 million (cell A).

Incentive to Cheat

The payoff matrix also explains why an oligopolist might be strongly tempted to cheat on a collusive agreement. Suppose Uptown and RareAir agree to maintain high-price policies, with each earning $12 million in profit (cell A). Both are tempted to cheat on this collusive pricing agreement, because either firm can increase its profit to $15 million by lowering its price. If Uptown secretly cheats on the agreement by charging low prices, the payoff moves from cell A to cell C. Uptown's profit rises to $15 million, and RareAir's falls to $6 million. If RareAir cheats, the payoff moves from cell A to cell B, and RareAir gets the $15 million. **(Key Question 8)**

25.2
Game
theory

QUICK REVIEW 25.2

- An oligopoly is made up of relatively few firms producing either homogeneous or differentiated products; these firms are mutually interdependent.

- Barriers to entry such as scale economies, control of patents or strategic resources, or the ability to engage in retaliatory pricing characterize oligopolies. Oligopolies may result from internal growth of firms, mergers, or both.

- The four-firm concentration ratio shows the percentage of an industry's sales accounted for by its four largest firms; the Herfindahl index measures the degree of market power in an industry by summing the squares of the percentage market shares held by the individual firms in the industry.

- Game theory reveals that (a) oligopolies are mutually interdependent in their pricing policies; (b) collusion enhances oligopoly profits; and (c) there is a temptation for oligopolists to cheat on a collusive agreement.

Three Oligopoly Models

To gain further insight into oligopolistic pricing and output behavior, we will examine three distinct pricing models: (1) the kinked-demand curve, (2) collusive pricing, and (3) price leadership.

Why not a single model, as in our discussions of the other market structures? There are two reasons:

- *Diversity of oligopolies* Oligopoly encompasses a greater range and diversity of market situations than do other market structures. It includes the *tight* oligopoly, in which two or three firms dominate an entire market, and the *loose* oligopoly, in which six or seven firms share, say, 70 or 80 percent of a market while a "competitive fringe" of firms shares the remainder. It includes both differentiated and standardized products. It includes cases in which firms act in collusion and those in which they act independently. It embodies situations in which barriers to entry are very strong and situations in which they are not quite so strong. In short, the diversity of oligopoly does not allow us to explain all oligopolistic behaviors with a single market model.

- *Complications of interdependence* The mutual interdependence of oligopolistic firms complicates matters significantly. Because firms cannot predict the reactions of their rivals with certainty, they cannot estimate their own demand and marginal-revenue data. Without such data, firms cannot determine their profit-maximizing price and output, even in theory, as we will see.

Despite these analytical difficulties, two interrelated characteristics of oligopolistic pricing have been observed. First, if the macroeconomy is generally stable, oligopolistic prices are typically inflexible (or "rigid" or "sticky"). Prices change less frequently under oligopoly than under pure competition, monopolistic competition, and, in some instances, pure monopoly. Second, when oligopolistic prices do change, firms are likely to change their prices together, suggesting that there is a tendency to act in concert, or collusively, in setting and changing prices (as we mentioned in the preceding section). The diversity of oligopolies and the presence of mutual interdependence are reflected in the models that follow.

Kinked-Demand Theory: Noncollusive Oligopoly

Imagine an oligopolistic industry made up of three hypothetical firms (Arch, King, and Dave's), each having about one-third of the total market for a differentiated product. Assume that the firms are "independent," meaning that they do not engage in collusive price practices. Assume, too, that the going price for Arch's product is P_0 and its current sales are Q_0, as shown in **Figure 25.4a (Key Graph)**.

Now the question is, "What does the firm's demand curve look like?" Mutual interdependence and the uncertainty about rivals' reactions make this question hard to answer. The location and shape of an oligopolist's demand curve depend on how the firm's rivals will react to a price change introduced by Arch. There are two plausible assumptions about the reactions of Arch's rivals:

- *Match price changes*   One possibility is that King and Dave's will exactly match any price change initiated by Arch. In this case, Arch's demand and marginal-revenue curves will look like the straight lines labeled D_1 and MR_1 in Figure 25.4a. Why are they so steep? Reason: If Arch cuts its price, its sales will increase only modestly because its two rivals will also cut their prices to prevent Arch from gaining an advantage over them. The small increase in sales that Arch (and its two rivals) will realize is at the expense of other industries; Arch will gain no sales from King and Dave's. If Arch raises its price, its sales will fall only modestly, because King and Dave's will match its price increase. The industry will lose sales to other industries, but Arch will lose no customers to King and Dave's.

- *Ignore price changes*   The other possibility is that King and Dave's will ignore any price change by Arch. In this case, the demand and marginal-revenue curves faced by Arch will resemble the straight lines D_2 and MR_2 in Figure 25.4a. Demand in this case is considerably more elastic than it was under the previous assumption. The reasons are clear: If Arch lowers its price and its rivals do not, Arch will gain sales significantly at the expense of its two rivals because it will be underselling them. Conversely, if Arch raises its price and its rivals do not, Arch will lose many customers to King and Dave's, which will be underselling it. Because of product differentiation, however, Arch's sales will not fall to zero when it raises its price; some of Arch's customers will pay the higher price because they have a strong preference for Arch's product.

A Combined Strategy

Now, which is the most logical assumption for Arch to make about how its rivals will react to any price change it might initiate? The answer is, "It depends on the direction of price." Common sense

and observation of oligopolistic industries suggest that a firm's rivals will match price declines below P_0 as they act to prevent the price cutter from taking their customers. But they will ignore price increases above P_0, because the rivals of the price-increasing firm stand to gain the business lost by the price booster. In other words, the dark-blue left-hand segment of the "rivals ignore" demand curve D_2 seems relevant for price increases, and the dark-blue right-hand segment of the "rivals match" demand curve D_1 seems relevant for price cuts. It is logical, then, or at least a reasonable assumption, that the noncollusive oligopolist faces the **kinked-demand curve** $D_2 e D_1$, as shown in Figure 25.4b. Demand is highly elastic above the going price P_0 but much less elastic or even inelastic below that price.

Note also that if it is correct to suppose that rivals will follow a price cut but ignore an increase, the marginal-revenue curve of the oligopolist will also have an odd shape. It, too, will be made up of two segments: the dark gray left-hand part of marginal-revenue curve MR_2 in Figure 25.4a and the dark gray right-hand part of marginal-revenue curve MR_1. Because of the sharp difference in elasticity of demand above and below the going price, there is a gap, or what we can simply treat as a vertical segment, in the marginal-revenue curve. We show this gap as the dashed segment in the combined marginal-revenue curve $MR_2 fg MR_1$ in Figure 25.4b.

Price Inflexibility

This analysis helps explain why prices are generally stable in noncollusive oligopolistic industries. There are both demand and cost reasons.

On the demand side, the kinked-demand curve gives each oligopolist reason to believe that any change in price will be for the worse. If it raises its price, many of its customers will desert it. If it lowers its price, its sales at best will increase very modestly, since rivals will match the lower price. Even if a price cut increases the oligopolist's total revenue somewhat, its costs may increase by a greater amount. And if its demand is inelastic to the right of Q_0, as it may well be, then the firm's profit will surely fall. A price decrease in the inelastic region lowers the firm's total revenue, and the production of a larger output increases its total costs.

On the cost side, the broken marginal-revenue curve suggests that even if an oligopolist's costs change substantially, the firm may have no reason to change its price. In particular, all positions of the marginal-cost curve between MC_1 and MC_2 in Figure 25.4b will result in the firm's deciding on exactly the same price and output. For all those positions, MR equals MC at output Q_0; at that output, it will charge price P_0.

KEY GRAPH

FIGURE 25.4

The kinked-demand curve. (a) The slope of a noncollusive oligopolist's demand and marginal-revenue curves depends on whether its rivals match (straight lines D_1 and MR_1) or ignore (straight lines D_2 and MR_2) any price changes that it may initiate from the current price P_0. (b) In all likelihood an oligopolist's rivals will ignore a price increase but follow a price cut. This causes the oligopolist's demand curve to be kinked (D_2eD_1) and the marginal-revenue curve to have a vertical break, or gap (fg). Because any shift in marginal costs between MC_1 and MC_2 will cut the vertical (dashed) segment of the marginal-revenue curve, no change in either price P_0 or output Q_0 will result from such a shift.

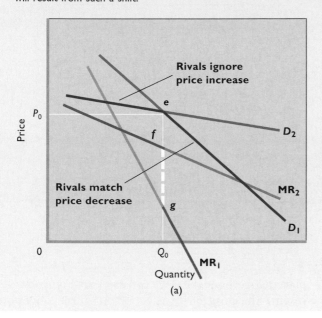

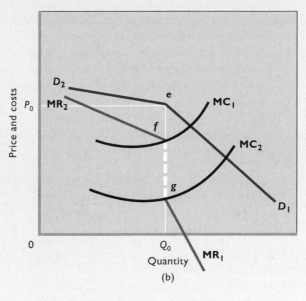

QUICK QUIZ 25.4

1. Suppose Q_0 in this figure represents annual sales of 5 million units for this firm. The other two firms in this three-firm industry sell 3 million and 2 million units, respectively. The Herfindahl Index for this industry is:
   a. 100 percent.
   b. 400.
   c. 10.
   d. 3800.

2. The D_2e segment of the demand curve D_2eD_1 in graph (b) implies that:
   a. this firm's total revenue will fall if it increases its price above P_0.
   b. other firms will match a price increase above P_0.
   c. the firm's relevant marginal-revenue curve will be MR_1 for price increases above P_0.

   d. the product in this industry is necessarily standardized.

3. By matching a price cut, this firm's rivals can:
   a. increase their market shares.
   b. increase their marginal revenues.
   c. maintain their market shares.
   d. lower their total costs.

4. A shift of the marginal-cost curve from MC_2 to MC_1 in graph (b) would:
   a. increase the "going price" above P_0.
   b. leave price at P_0, but reduce this firm's total profit.
   c. leave price at P_0, but reduce this firm's total revenue.
   d. make this firm's demand curve more elastic.

Answers: 1. d; 2. a; 3. c; 4. b

473

Criticisms of the Model   The kinked-demand analysis has two shortcomings. First, it does not explain how the going price gets to be at P_0 in Figure 25.4 in the first place. It only helps explain why oligopolists tend to stick with an existing price. The kinked-demand curve explains price inflexibility but not price itself.

Second, when the macroeconomy is unstable, oligopoly prices are not as rigid as the kinked-demand theory implies. During inflationary periods, many oligopolists have raised their prices often and substantially. And during downturns (recessions), some oligopolists have cut prices. In some instances these price reductions have set off a **price war:** *successive and continuous rounds of price cuts by rivals as they attempt to maintain their market shares.* **(Key Question 9)**

Cartels and Other Collusion

Our game-theory model demonstrated that oligopolists might benefit from collusion. We can say that collusion occurs whenever firms in an industry reach an agreement to fix prices, divide up the market, or otherwise restrict competition among themselves. The disadvantages and uncertainties of noncollusive, kinked-demand oligopolies are obvious. There is always the danger of a price war breaking out, especially during a general business recession. Then each firm finds that, because of unsold goods and excess capacity, it can reduce per-unit costs by increasing market share. Then, too, a new firm may surmount entry barriers and initiate aggressive price cutting to gain a foothold in the market. In addition, the kinked-demand curve's tendency toward rigid prices may adversely affect profits if general inflationary pressures increase costs. However, by controlling price through collusion, oligopolists may be able to reduce uncertainty, increase profits, and perhaps even prohibit the entry of new rivals.

Price and Output   Assume once again that there are three hypothetical oligopolistic firms (Gypsum, Sheetrock, and GSR) producing, in this instance, gypsum drywall panels for finishing interior walls. All three firms produce a homogeneous product and have identical cost curves. Each firm's demand curve is indeterminate unless we know how its rivals will react to any price change. Therefore, we suppose each firm assumes that its two rivals will match either a price cut or a price increase. In other words, each firm has a demand curve like the straight line D_1 in Figure 25.4a. And since they have identical cost data, and the same demand and thus

FIGURE 25.5

Collusion and the tendency toward joint-profit maximization.   If oligopolistic firms face identical or highly similar demand and cost conditions, they may collude to limit their joint output and to set a single, common price. Thus each firm acts as if it were a pure monopolist, setting output at Q_0 and charging price P_0. This price and output combination maximizes each oligopolist's profit (blue area) and thus their combined or joint profit.

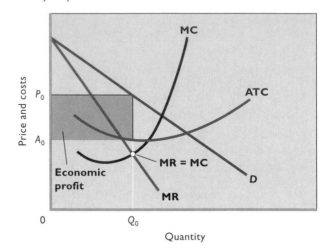

marginal-revenue data, we can say that Figure 25.5 represents the position of each of our three oligopolistic firms.

What price and output combination should, say, Gypsum select? If Gypsum were a pure monopolist, the answer would be clear: Establish output at Q_0, where marginal revenue equals marginal cost, charge the corresponding price P_0, and enjoy the maximum profit attainable. However, Gypsum does have two rivals selling identical products, and if Gypsum's assumption that its rivals will match its price of P_0 proves to be incorrect, the consequences could be disastrous for Gypsum. Specifically, if Sheetrock and GSR actually charge prices below P_0, then Gypsum's demand curve D will shift sharply to the left as its potential customers turn to its rivals, which are now selling the same product at a lower price. Of course, Gypsum can retaliate by cutting its price too, but this will move all three firms down their demand curves, lowering their profits. It may even drive them to a point where average total cost exceeds price and losses are incurred.

So the question becomes, "Will Sheetrock and GSR want to charge a price below P_0?" Under our assumptions, and recognizing that Gypsum has little choice except to match any price they may set below P_0, the answer is no. Faced with the same demand and cost circumstances,

Sheetrock and GSR will find it in their interest to produce Q_0 and charge P_0. This is a curious situation; each firm finds it most profitable to charge the same price, P_0, but only if its rivals actually do so! How can the three firms ensure the price P_0 and quantity Q_0 solution in which each is keenly interested? How can they avoid the less profitable outcomes associated with either higher or lower prices?

The answer is evident: They can collude. They can get together, talk it over, and agree to charge the same price, P_0. In addition to reducing the possibility of price wars, this will give each firm the maximum profit. (But it will also subject them to antitrust prosecution if they are caught!) For society, the result will be the same as would occur if the industry were a pure monopoly composed of three identical plants.

Overt Collusion: The OPEC Cartel

Collusion may assume a variety of forms. The most comprehensive form of collusion is the **cartel,** *a group of producers that typically creates a formal written agreement specifying how much each member will produce and charge.* Output must be controlled—the market must be divided up—in order to maintain the agreed-upon price. The collusion is overt, or open to view.

Undoubtedly the most significant international cartel is the Organization of Petroleum Exporting Countries (OPEC), comprising 11 oil-producing nations (see Global Perspective 25.1). OPEC produces 40 percent of the world's oil and supplies 60 percent of all oil traded internationally. In the late 1990s it reacted vigorously to very low oil prices by greatly restricting supply. Some non-OPEC producers supported the cutback in production, and within a 15-month period the price of oil shot up from $11 a barrel to $34 a barrel. Gasoline prices in the United States rose by as much as $1 a gallon in some markets. Fearing a global political and economic backlash from the major industrial nations, OPEC upped the production quotas for its members in mid-2000. The increases in oil supply that resulted reduced the price of oil to about $25, where it remained through 2002. It is clear that the OPEC cartel has sufficient market power to hold the price of oil substantially above its marginal cost of production.

Covert Collusion: Relatively Recent Examples

Cartels are illegal in the United States, and hence any collusion that exists is covert or secret. Yet there are numerous examples, as shown by evidence from antitrust (antimonopoly) cases. In 1993 the Borden, Pet, and Dean

---

GLOBAL PERSPECTIVE 25.1

The 11 OPEC Nations, Daily Oil Production, June 1, 2003

The OPEC nations produce about 40 percent of the world's oil and 60 percent of the oil sold in world markets.

OPEC Country	Barrels of Oil
Saudi Arabia	8,256,000
Iran	3,729,000
Venezuela	2,923,000
UAE	2,217,000
Nigeria	2,092,000
Kuwait	2,038,000
Libya	1,360,000
Indonesia	1,317,000
Algeria	811,000
Qatar	658,000
Iraq	(U.S./U.N. determined)

Source: OPEC, www.opec.org/.

---

food companies, among others, either pleaded guilty or were convicted of rigging bids on the prices of milk products sold to schools and military bases. By phone or at luncheons, company executives agreed in advance on which firm would submit the low bid for each school district or military base. In 1996 American agribusiness Archer Daniels Midland and three Japanese and South Korean firms were found to have conspired to fix the worldwide price and sales volume of a livestock feed additive. Executives for the firms secretly met in Hong Kong, Paris, Mexico City, Vancouver, and Zurich to discuss their plans.

In many other instances collusion is much subtler. **Tacit understandings** (historically called "gentlemen's agreements") are frequently made at cocktail parties, on golf courses, through phone calls, or at trade association meetings. In such agreements, competing firms reach a verbal understanding on product price, leaving market shares to be decided by nonprice competition. Although these agreements, too, violate antitrust laws—and can result in severe personal and corporate penalties—the elusive character of tacit understandings makes them more difficult to detect.

Obstacles to Collusion Normally, cartels and similar collusive arrangements are difficult to establish and maintain. Here are several barriers to collusion:

Demand and Cost Differences When oligopolists face different costs and demand curves, it is difficult for them to agree on a price. This is particularly the case in industries where products are differentiated and change frequently. Even with highly standardized products, firms usually have somewhat different market shares and operate with differing degrees of productive efficiency. Thus it is unlikely that even homogeneous oligopolists would have the same demand and cost curves.

In either case, differences in costs and demand mean that the profit-maximizing price will differ among firms; no single price will be readily acceptable to all, as we assumed was true in Figure 25.5. So price collusion depends on compromises and concessions that are not always easy to obtain and hence act as an obstacle to collusion.

Number of Firms Other things equal, the larger the number of firms, the more difficult it is to create a cartel or some other form of price collusion. Agreement on price by three or four producers that control an entire market may be relatively easy to accomplish. But such agreement is more difficult to achieve where there are, say, 10 firms, each with roughly 10 percent of the market, or where the Big Three have 70 percent of the market while a competitive fringe of 8 or 10 smaller firms battles for the remainder.

Cheating As the game-theory model makes clear, there is a temptation for collusive oligopolists to engage in secret price cutting to increase sales and profit. The difficulty with such cheating is that buyers who are paying a high price for a product may become aware of the lower-priced sales and demand similar treatment. Or buyers receiving a price concession from one producer may use the concession as a wedge to get even larger price concessions from a rival producer. Buyers' attempts to play producers against one another may precipitate price wars among the producers. Although secret price concessions are potentially profitable, they threaten collusive oligopolies over time. Collusion is more likely to succeed when cheating is easy to detect and punish. Then the conspirators are less likely to cheat on the price agreement.

Recession Long-lasting recession usually serves as an enemy of collusion because slumping markets increase average total cost. In technical terms, as the oligopolists' demand and marginal-revenue curves shift to the left in Figure 25.5 in response to a recession, each firm moves leftward and upward to a higher operating point on its average-total-cost curve. Firms find they have substantial excess production capacity, sales are down, unit costs are up, and profits are being squeezed. Under such conditions, businesses may feel they can avoid serious profit reductions (or even losses) by cutting price and thus gaining sales at the expense of rivals.

Potential Entry The greater prices and profits that result from collusion may attract new entrants, including foreign firms. Since that would increase market supply and reduce prices and profits, successful collusion requires that colluding oligopolists block the entry of new producers.

Legal Obstacles: Antitrust Law U.S. antitrust laws prohibit cartels and price-fixing collusion. So less obvious means of price control have evolved in this country.

Price Leadership Model

Price leadership entails a type of implicit understanding by which oligopolists can coordinate prices without engaging in outright collusion based on formal agreements and secret meetings. Rather, a practice evolves whereby the "dominant firm"—usually the largest or most efficient in the industry—initiates price changes and all other firms more or less automatically follow the leader. Many industries, including farm machinery, cement, copper, newsprint, glass containers, steel, beer, fertilizer, cigarettes, and tin, are practicing, or have in the recent past practiced, price leadership.

Leadership Tactics An examination of price leadership in a variety of industries suggests that the price leader is likely to observe the following tactics.

Infrequent Price Changes Because price changes always carry the risk that rivals will not follow the lead, price adjustments are made only infrequently. The price leader does not respond to minuscule day-to-day changes in costs and demand. Price is changed only when cost and demand conditions have been altered significantly and on an industrywide basis as the result of, for example, industrywide wage increases, an increase in excise taxes, or an increase in the price of some basic input such as energy.

In the automobile industry, price adjustments traditionally have been made when new models are introduced each fall.

Communications The price leader often communicates impending price adjustments to the industry through speeches by major executives, trade publication interviews, or press releases. By publicizing "the need to raise prices," the price leader seeks agreement among its competitors regarding the actual increase.

Limit Pricing The price leader does not always choose the price that maximizes short-run profits for the industry because the industry may want to discourage new firms from entering. If the cost advantages (economies of scale) of existing firms are a major barrier to entry, new entrants could surmount that barrier if the price leader and the other firms set product price high enough. New firms that are relatively inefficient because of their small size might survive and grow if the industry sets price very high. So, in order to discourage new competitors and to maintain the current oligopolistic structure of the industry, the price leader may keep price below the short-run profit-maximizing level. The strategy of establishing a price that blocks the entry of new firms is called *limit pricing*.

Breakdowns in Price Leadership: Price Wars
Price leadership in oligopoly occasionally breaks down, at least temporarily, and sometimes results in a price war. An example of disruption of price leadership occurred in the breakfast cereal industry, in which Kellogg traditionally had been the price leader. General Mills countered Kellogg's leadership in 1995 by reducing the prices of its cereals by 11 percent. In 1996 Post responded with a 20 percent price cut, which Kellogg then followed. Not to be outdone, Post reduced its prices by another 11 percent.

As another example, in late 2002 Burger King set off a price war by offering its bacon cheeseburger for 99¢. McDonald's countered by placing a price tag of $1 on its Big "N" Tasty burger, which competes directly against Burger King's popular Whopper. Burger King then offered a "limited-time special" of 99¢ for Whoppers.

Most price wars eventually run their course. When all firms recognize that low prices are severely reducing their profits, they again yield price leadership to one of the industry's leading firms. That firm then begins to raise prices, and the other firms willingly follow suit.

Oligopoly and Advertising

We have noted that oligopolists would rather not compete on the basis of price and may become involved in price collusion. Nonetheless, each firm's share of the total market is typically determined through product development and advertising, for two reasons:

• Product development and advertising campaigns are less easily duplicated than price cuts. Price cuts can be quickly and easily matched by a firm's rivals to cancel any potential gain in sales derived from that strategy. Product improvements and successful advertising, however, can produce more permanent gains in market share because they cannot be duplicated as quickly and completely as price reductions.

• Oligopolists have sufficient financial resources to engage in product development and advertising. For most oligopolists, the economic profits earned in the past can help finance current advertising and product development.

Product development (or, more broadly, "research and development") is the subject of the next chapter, so we will confine our present discussion to advertising. In 2002, firms spent an estimated $248 billion on advertising in the United States and $448 billion worldwide. *Advertising is prevalent in both monopolistic competition and oligopoly.* Table 25.3 lists the 10 leading U.S. advertisers in 2002.

Advertising may affect prices, competition, and efficiency both positively and negatively, depending on the

TABLE 25.3

The Largest U.S. Advertisers, 2002

Company	Advertising Spending Millions of $
General Motors	$3652
AOL Time Warner	2923
Procter & Gamble	2673
Pfizer	2566
Ford Motor	2252
DaimlerChrysler	2032
Walt Disney	1803
Johnson & Johnson	1799
Sears	1661
Unilever	1640

Source: Advertising Age, www.adage.com/.

circumstances. While our focus here is on advertising by oligopolists, the analysis is equally applicable to advertising by monopolistic competitors.

Positive Effects of Advertising

In order to make rational (efficient) decisions, consumers need information about product characteristics and prices. Advertising may be a low-cost means of providing that information. Suppose you are in the market for a high-quality camera and there is advertising of such a product in newspapers or magazines. To make a rational choice, you may have to spend several days visiting stores to determine the prices and features of various brands. This search entails both direct costs (gasoline, parking fees) and indirect costs (the value of your time). Advertising reduces your search time and minimizes these costs.

By providing information about the various competing goods that are available, advertising diminishes monopoly power. In fact, advertising is frequently associated with the introduction of new products designed to compete with existing brands. Could Toyota and Honda have so strongly challenged U.S. auto producers without advertising? Could Federal Express have sliced market share away from UPS and the U.S. Postal Service without advertising?

Viewed this way, advertising is an efficiency-enhancing activity. It is a relatively inexpensive means of providing useful information to consumers and thus lowering their search costs. By enhancing competition, advertising results in greater economic efficiency. By facilitating the introduction of new products, advertising speeds up technological progress. By increasing output, advertising

can reduce long-run average total cost by enabling firms to obtain economies of scale.

Potential Negative Effects of Advertising

Not all the effects of advertising are positive, of course. Much advertising is designed simply to manipulate or persuade consumers—that is, to alter their preferences in favor of the advertiser's product. A television commercial that indicates that a popular personality drinks a particular brand of soft drink—and therefore that you should too—conveys little or no information to consumers about price or quality. In addition, advertising is sometimes based on misleading and extravagant claims that confuse consumers rather than enlighten them. Indeed, in some cases advertising may well persuade consumers to pay high prices for much-acclaimed but inferior products, forgoing better but unadvertised products selling at lower prices. Example: *Consumer Reports* has found that heavily advertised premium motor oils and fancy additives provide no better engine performance and longevity than do cheaper brands.

Firms often establish substantial brand-name loyalty and thus achieve monopoly power via their advertising (see Global Perspective 25.2). As a consequence, they are

GLOBAL PERSPECTIVE 25.2

The World's Top 10 Brand Names

Here are the world's top 10 brands, based on four criteria: the brand's market share within its category, the brand's world appeal across age groups and nationalities, the loyalty of customers to the brand, and the ability of the brand to "stretch" to products beyond the original product.

World's Top 10 Brands

- Coca-Cola
- Microsoft
- IBM
- General Electric
- Intel
- Nokia
- Disney
- McDonald's
- Marlboro
- Mercedes

Source: Interbrand, www.brandchannel.com/. Data are for 2002.

able to increase their sales, expand their market shares, and enjoy greater profits. Larger profit permits still more advertising and further enlargement of the firm's market share and profit. In time, consumers may lose the advantages of competitive markets and face the disadvantages of monopolized markets. Moreover, new entrants to the industry need to incur large advertising costs in order to establish their products in the marketplace; thus, advertising costs may be a barrier to entry. **(Key Question 11)**

Advertising can also be self-canceling. The advertising campaign of one fast-food hamburger chain may be offset by equally costly campaigns waged by rivals, so each firm's demand actually remains unchanged. Few, if any, extra burgers will be purchased, and each firm's market share will stay the same. But because of the advertising, the cost and hence the price of hamburgers will be higher.

When advertising either leads to increased monopoly power or is self-canceling, economic inefficiency results.

Oligopoly and Efficiency

Is oligopoly, then, an efficient market structure from society's standpoint? How do the price and output decisions of the oligopolist measure up to the triple equality $P = MC = $ minimum ATC that occurs in pure competition?

Productive and Allocative Efficiency

Many economists believe that the outcome of some oligopolistic markets is approximately as shown in Figure 25.5. This view is bolstered by evidence that many oligopolists sustain sizable economic profits year after year. In that case, the oligopolist's production occurs where price exceeds marginal cost and average total cost. Moreover, production is below the output at which average total cost is minimized. In this view, neither productive efficiency ($P = $ minimum ATC) nor allocative efficiency ($P = MC$) is likely to occur under oligopoly.

A few observers assert that oligopoly is actually less desirable than pure monopoly, because government usu-ally regulates pure monopoly in the United States to guard against abuses of monopoly power. Informal collusion among oligopolists may yield price and output results similar to those under pure monopoly yet give the outward appearance of competition involving independent firms.

Qualifications

We should note, however, three qualifications to this view:

- *Increased foreign competition*   In recent decades foreign competition has increased rivalry in a number of oligopolistic industries—steel, automobiles, photographic film, electric shavers, outboard motors, and copy machines, for example. This has helped to break down such cozy arrangements as price leadership and to stimulate much more competitive pricing.

- *Limit pricing*   Recall that some oligopolists may purposely keep prices below the short-run profit-maximizing level in order to bolster entry barriers. In essence, consumers and society may get some of the benefits of competition—prices closer to marginal cost and minimum average total cost—even without the competition that free entry would provide.

- *Technological advance*   Over time, oligopolistic industries may foster more rapid product development and greater improvement of production techniques than would be possible if they were purely competitive. Oligopolists have large economic profits from which they can fund expensive research and development (R&D). Moreover, the existence of barriers to entry may give the oligopolist some assurance that it will reap the rewards of successful R&D. Thus, the short-run economic inefficiencies of oligopolists may be partly or wholly offset by the oligopolists' contributions to better products, lower prices, and lower costs over time. We will have more to say about these more dynamic aspects of rivalry in Chapter 26.

The Beer Industry Was Once Populated by Hundreds of Firms and an Even Larger Number of Brands. But It Now Is an Oligopoly Dominated by a Handful of Producers.

The brewing industry has undergone profound changes since the Second World War that have increased the degree of concentration in the industry. In 1947 more than 400 independent brewing companies existed in the United States. By 1967 there were 124, and by 1980 only 33. While the five largest brewers sold only 19 percent of the nation's beer in 1947, the Big Four brewers (Anheuser-Busch, SABMiller, Coors, and Pabst) currently sell 84 percent of the nation's beer. The Big Two—Anheuser-Busch (at 49 percent) and Miller (at 20 percent)—produce 69 percent. The industry is clearly an oligopoly.

Changes on the demand side of the market have contributed to the "shakeout" of small brewers from the industry. First, consumer tastes have generally shifted from the stronger-flavored beers of the small brewers to the light products of the larger brewers. Second, there has been a shift from the consumption of beer in taverns to consumption of it in the home. The beer consumed in taverns was mainly "draft" or "tap" beer from kegs, supplied by local and regional brewers who could deliver the kegs in a timely fashion at relatively low transportation cost. But the large increase in the demand for beer consumed at home opened the door for large brewers that sold their beer in bottles and aluminum cans. The large brewers could ship their beer by truck or rail over long distances and compete directly with the local brewers.

Developments on the supply side of the market have been even more profound. Technological advances speeded up the bottling and canning lines. Today, large brewers can fill and close

2000 cans per line per minute. Large plants are also able to reduce labor costs through the automating of brewing and warehousing. Furthermore, plant construction costs per barrel are about one-third less for a 4.5-million-barrel plant than for a 1.5-million-barrel plant. As a consequence of these and other factors, the minimum efficient scale in brewing is a plant size of about 4.5 million barrels, with multiple plants. Because the construction cost of a modern brewery of that size averages about $300 million, economies of scale may now constitute a significant barrier to entry.

"Blindfold" taste tests confirm that most mass-produced American beers taste alike. So brewers greatly emphasize advertising. And here Anheuser-Busch, SABMiller, and Coors, which sell national brands, enjoy major cost advantages over producers such as Pabst that have many regional brands (for example, Lonestar, Rainer, Schaefer, and Schmidts). The reason is because national television advertising is less costly *per viewer* than local spot TV advertising.

Although mergers have occurred in the brewing industry, they have not been a fundamental cause of the rising concentration. Rather, they largely have been the result of failing smaller breweries (such as Heileman) selling out. Dominant firms have expanded by heavily advertising their main brands and by creating new brands such as Lite, Bud Light, Genuine Draft, Keystone, and Icehouse rather than acquiring other brewers. This has sustained significant product differentiation, despite the declining number of major brewers.

The rise of the Miller Brewing Company from the seventh- to the second-largest producer in the 1970s was due in large measure to advertising and product differentiation. When the Philip Morris Company acquired Miller in 1970, the new management made two big changes. First, it

SUMMARY

1. The distinguishing features of monopolistic competition are (a) there are enough firms in the industry to ensure that each firm has only limited control over price, mutual interdependence is absent, and collusion is nearly impossible; (b) products are characterized by real or perceived differences so that economic rivalry entails both price and nonprice competition; and (c) entry to the industry is relatively easy. Many aspects of retailing, and some manufacturing industries in which economies of scale are few, approximate monopolistic competition.

2. Monopolistically competitive firms may earn economic profits or incur losses in the short run. The easy entry and exit of firms result in only normal profits in the long run.

3. The long-run equilibrium position of the monopolistically competitive producer is less efficient than that of the pure competitor. Under monopolistic competition, price exceeds marginal cost, suggesting an underallocation of resources to the product, and price exceeds minimum average total cost, indicating that consumers do not get the product at the lowest price that cost conditions might allow.

4. Nonprice competition provides a way that monopolistically competitive firms can offset the long-run tendency for economic profit to fall to zero. Through product differentiation, product development, and advertising, a firm may strive to increase the demand for its product

"repositioned" Miller High Life beer into that segment of the market where potential sales were the greatest. Sold previously as the "champagne of beers," High Life had appealed heavily to upper-income consumers and to occasional women beer drinkers. Miller's new television ads featured young blue-collar workers, who were inclined to be greater beer consumers. Second, Miller then developed its low-calorie Lite beer, which was extensively promoted with Philip Morris advertising dollars. Lite proved to be the most popular new product in the history of the beer industry. Miller later introduced its Genuine Draft beer, which found its place within the top 10 brands.

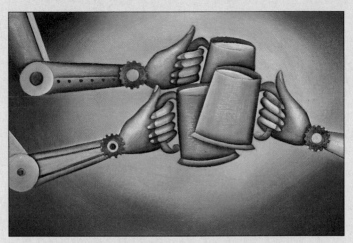

But the story of the last two decades has been not Miller but, rather, Anheuser-Busch (A-B), which has greatly expanded its market share. A-B now makes the nation's top two brands: Bud Light and Budweiser account for nearly half the beer sold in the United States. Part of A-B's success owes to the demise of regional competitors. But part also is the result of A-B's strategic prowess. It has constructed state-of-the-art breweries, created effective advertising campaigns, and forged strong relationships with regional distributors. Meanwhile, Miller's market share has declined slightly in recent years. In 2002 Philip Morris sold Miller to South African Breweries (SAB). SABMiller, as the firm is now called, plans to redesign Miller's labeling to enhance its appeal and to expand its presence overseas.

Imported beers such as Beck, Corona, and Guinness constitute about 9 percent of the market, with individual brands seeming to wax and wane in popularity. Some local or regional microbreweries such as Samuel Adams and Pyramid, which brew "craft" or specialty beers and charge super-premium prices, have slightly whittled into the sales of the major brewers. A-B and Miller have taken notice, responding with specialty brands of their own (for example, Red Wolf, Red Dog, Killarney's, and Ice House) and bought stakes in microbrewers Redhook Ale and Celis. But despite their local success, microbreweries account for only about 3 percent of the beer consumed in the United States and pose less of a threat to the majors than does "trendy" imported beer.

Sources: Based on Kenneth G. Elzinga, "Beer," in Walter Adams and James Brock (eds.), *The Structure of American Industry,* 10th ed. (Upper Saddle River, N.J.: Prentice-Hall, 2001), pp. 85–113; and Douglas F. Greer, "Beer: Causes of Structural Change," in Larry Duetsch (ed.), *Industry Studies,* 2d ed. (New York: M. E. Sharpe, 1998), pp. 28–64. Updated data and information are mainly from *Beer Marketer's Insights,* www.beerinsights.com, and the Association of Brewers, www.beertown.com.

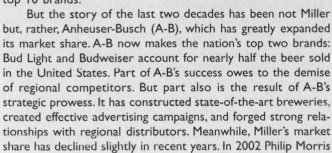

more than enough to cover the added cost of such non-price competition. Consumers benefit from the wide diversity of product choice that monopolistic competition provides.

5. In practice, the monopolistic competitor seeks the specific combination of price, product, and advertising that will maximize profit.

6. Oligopolistic industries are characterized by the presence of few firms, each having a significant fraction of the market. Firms thus situated engage in strategic behavior and are mutually interdependent: The behavior of any one firm directly affects, and is affected by, the actions of rivals. Products may be either virtually uniform or significantly differentiated. Various barriers to entry, including economies of scale, underlie and maintain oligopoly.

7. High concentration ratios are an indication of oligopoly (monopoly) power. By giving more weight to larger firms, the Herfindahl index is designed to measure market dominance in an industry.

8. Game theory (a) shows the interdependence of oligopolists' pricing policies, (b) reveals the tendency of oligopolists to collude, and (c) explains the temptation of oligopolists to cheat on collusive arrangements.

9. Noncollusive oligopolists may face a kinked-demand curve. This curve and the accompanying marginal-revenue curve help explain the price rigidity that often characterizes oligopolies; they do not, however, explain how the actual prices of products were first established.

10. The uncertainties inherent in oligopoly promote collusion. Collusive oligopolists such as cartels maximize joint

profits—that is, they behave like pure monopolists. Demand and cost differences, a "large" number of firms, cheating through secret price concessions, recessions, and the antitrust laws are all obstacles to collusive oligopoly.

11. Price leadership is an informal means of collusion whereby one firm, usually the largest or most efficient, initiates price changes and the other firms in the industry follow the leader.

12. Market shares in oligopolistic industries are usually determined on the basis of product development and advertising. Oligopolists emphasize nonprice competition because (a) advertising and product variations are less easy for rivals to match and (b) oligopolists frequently have ample resources to finance nonprice competition.

13. Advertising may affect prices, competition, and efficiency either positively or negatively. Positive: It can provide consumers with low-cost information about competing products, help introduce new competing products into concentrated industries, and generally reduce monopoly power and its attendant inefficiencies. Negative: It can promote monopoly power via persuasion and the creation of entry barriers. Moreover, it can be self-canceling when engaged in by rivals; then it boosts costs and creates inefficiency while accomplishing little else.

14. Neither productive nor allocative efficiency is realized in oligopolistic markets, but oligopoly may be superior to pure competition in promoting research and development and technological progress.

15. Table 23.1, page 414, provides a concise review of the characteristics of monopolistic competition and oligopoly as they compare to those of pure competition and pure monopoly.

TERMS AND CONCEPTS

monopolistic competition	homogeneous oligopoly	interindustry competition	kinked-demand curve
product differentiation	differentiated oligopoly	import competition	price war
nonprice competition	strategic behavior	Herfindahl index	cartel
excess capacity	mutual interdependence	game-theory model	tacit understandings
oligopoly	concentration ratio	collusion	price leadership

STUDY QUESTIONS

1. How does monopolistic competition differ from pure competition in its basic characteristics? From pure monopoly? Explain fully what product differentiation may involve. Explain how the entry of firms into its industry affects the demand curve facing a monopolistic competitor and how that, in turn, affects its economic profit.

2. *Key Question* Compare the elasticity of the monopolistic competitor's demand with that of a pure competitor and a pure monopolist. Assuming identical long-run costs, compare graphically the prices and outputs that would result in the long run under pure competition and under monopolistic competition. Contrast the two market structures in terms of productive and allocative efficiency. Explain: "Monopolistically competitive industries are characterized by too many firms, each of which produces too little."

3. "Monopolistic competition is monopolistic up to the point at which consumers become willing to buy close-substitute products and competitive beyond that point." Explain.

4. "Competition in quality and service may be just as effective as price competition in giving buyers more for their money."

Do you agree? Why? Explain why monopolistically competitive firms frequently prefer nonprice competition to price competition.

5. Critically evaluate and explain:
   a. In monopolistically competitive industries economic profits are competed away in the long run; hence, there is no valid reason to criticize the performance and efficiency of such industries.
   b. In the long run, monopolistic competition leads to a monopolistic price but not to monopolistic profits.

6. Why do oligopolies exist? List five or six oligopolists whose products you own or regularly purchase. What distinguishes oligopoly from monopolistic competition?

7. *Key Question* Answer the following questions, which relate to measures of concentration:
   a. What is the meaning of a four-firm concentration ratio of 60 percent? 90 percent? What are the shortcomings of concentration ratios as measures of monopoly power?
   b. Suppose that the five firms in industry A have annual sales of 30, 30, 20, 10, and 10 percent of total industry sales.

For the five firms in industry B the figures are 60, 25, 5, 5, and 5 percent. Calculate the Herfindahl index for each industry and compare their likely competitiveness.

8. *Key Question* Explain the general meaning of the following profit payoff matrix for oligopolists C and D. All profit figures are in thousands.

C's possible prices

		$40	$35
D's possible prices	$40	$57 / $60	$59 / $55
	$35	$50 / $69	$55 / $58

a. Use the payoff matrix to explain the mutual interdependence that characterizes oligopolistic industries.

b. Assuming no collusion between C and D, what is the likely pricing outcome?

c. In view of your answer to 8*b*, explain why price collusion is mutually profitable. Why might there be a temptation to cheat on the collusive agreement?

9. *Key Question* What assumptions about a rival's response to price changes underlie the kinked-demand curve for oligopolists? Why is there a gap in the oligopolist's marginal-revenue curve? How does the kinked-demand curve explain price rigidity in oligopoly? What are the shortcomings of the kinked-demand model?

10. Why might price collusion occur in oligopolistic industries? Assess the economic desirability of collusive pricing. What are the main obstacles to collusion? Speculate as to why price leadership is legal in the United States, whereas price fixing is not.

11. *Key Question* Why is there so much advertising in monopolistic competition and oligopoly? How does such advertising help consumers and promote efficiency? Why might it be excessive at times?

12. *Advanced Analysis* Construct a game-theory matrix involving two firms and their decisions on high versus low advertising budgets and the effects of each on profits. Show a circumstance in which both firms select high advertising budgets even though both would be more profitable with low advertising budgets. Why won't they unilaterally cut their advertising budgets?

13. *(Last Word)* What firm dominates the beer industry? What demand and supply factors have contributed to "fewness" in this industry?

14. *Web-Based Question: Bookselling on the Internet—how do sellers differentiate identical books?* Upstart company Amazon introduced bookselling on the Web through its site at www.amazon.com. Amazon's success enticed a long-time bookseller, Barnes & Noble, to go online with a major website, www.barnesandnoble.com. Search both sites for Viktor Frankl's *Man's Search for Meaning* (paperback). Find the price, including shipping to your address. Is one company cheaper? Identify the nonprice competition that might lead you to order from one company rather than the other.

15. *Web-Based Question: Market shares—top 10 lists* *Advertising Age*, at adage.com, compiles statistics on the market shares of many familiar products. Go to "Data Center" to find 100 leading national advertisers. Then scroll down to the "Market share charts" and select the top 10 lists for five separate products. In general, do the very top sellers in the top 10 lists advertise more or less than the sellers toward the bottoms of the lists? Are there exceptions? Do you think the top 10 lists would get turned upside down if the pattern of advertising were turned upside down? Why or why not?

26 | Technology, R&D, and Efficiency

- **"Just do it!"** In 1968 two entrepreneurs from Oregon developed a lightweight sport shoe and formed a new company called Nike, incorporating a "swoosh" logo (designed by a graduate student for $35). Today, Nike sells more than $10 billion worth of goods annually.

- "Intel inside." In 1967 neither Intel nor its product existed. Today it is the world's largest producer of microprocessors for personal computers, with about $27 billion of annual sales.

- "Always low prices. Always." Expanding from a single store in 1962 to more than 2800 stores today, Wal-Mart's annual revenue ($245 billion) exceeds that of General Motors or IBM.

Nike, Intel, and Wal-Mart owe much of their success to **technological advance,** broadly defined *as new and better goods and services or new and better ways of producing or distributing them.* Nike and Intel pioneered innovative new products, and Wal-Mart developed creative ways to manage inventories and distribute goods.

Multiply these examples—perhaps on a smaller scale—by thousands in the economy! The pursuit of technological advance is a major competitive activity among firms. In this chapter, we examine some of the microeconomics of that activity.

Invention, Innovation, and Diffusion

For economists, technological advance occurs over a theoretical time period called the *very long run,* which can be as short as a few months or as long as many years. Recall that in our four market models (pure competition, monopolistic competition, oligopoly, and pure monopoly), the short run is a period in which technology and plant and equipment are fixed. In the long run, technology is

constant but firms can change their plant sizes and are free to enter or exit industries. In contrast, the **very long run** is a period in which technology can change and in which firms can develop and offer entirely new products.

In Chapter 2 we saw that technological advance shifts an economy's production possibilities curve outward, enabling the economy to obtain more goods and services. Technological advance is a three-step process of invention, innovation, and diffusion.

Invention

The basis of technological advance is **invention:** *the discovery of a product or process through the use of imagination, ingenious thinking, and experimentation and the first proof that it will work.* Invention is a process, and the result of the process is also called an invention. The prototypes (basic working model) of the telephone, the automobile, and the microchip are inventions. Invention usually is based on scientific knowledge and is the product of individuals, either working on their own or as members of corporate R&D staffs. Later on you will see how governments encourage invention by providing the inventor with a **patent,** an exclusive right to sell any new and useful process, machine, or product for a set period of time. In 2002 the five firms that secured the most U.S. patents were IBM (3288), Canon (1893), Micron (1833), NEC (1821), and Hitachi (1602). Such patents have a worldwide duration of 20 years from the time of application for the patent.

Innovation

Innovation draws directly on invention. While invention is the "discovery and first proof of workability," **innovation** is *the first successful commercial introduction of a new product, the first use of a new method, or the creation of a new form of business enterprise.* Innovation is of two types: **product innovation,** which refers to new and improved products or services; and **process innovation,** which refers to new and improved methods of production or distribution.

Unlike inventions, innovations cannot be patented. Nevertheless, innovation is a major factor in competition, since it sometimes enables a firm to "leapfrog" competitors by rendering their products or processes obsolete. For example, personal computers coupled with software for word processing pushed some major typewriter manufacturers into obscurity. More recently, innovations in hardware retailing (large warehouse stores such as Home Depot) have threatened the existence of smaller, more traditional hardware stores.

But innovation need not weaken or destroy existing firms. Aware that new products and processes may threaten their survival, existing firms have a powerful incentive to engage continuously in R&D of their own. Innovative products and processes often enable such firms to maintain or increase their profit. The aluminum cans introduced by Reynolds, disposable contact lenses by Johnson & Johnson, and scientific calculators by Hewlett-Packard are good examples. Thus, innovation can either diminish or strengthen market power.

Diffusion

Diffusion is the spread of an innovation through imitation or copying. To take advantage of new profit opportunities or to slow the erosion of profit, both new and existing firms emulate the successful innovations of others. Years ago, Alamo greatly increased its auto rentals by offering customers unlimited mileage, and Hertz, Avis, Budget, and others eventually followed. DaimlerChrysler profitably introduced a luxury version of its Jeep Grand Cherokee; other manufacturers, including Acura, Mercedes, and Lexus, countered with luxury sport-utility vehicles of their own. In 1996 Palm introduced its Palm Pilot, a palm-size personal computer. Microsoft, Handspring, OmniSky, and other firms soon brought out similar products. In each of these cases, innovation led eventually to widespread imitation—that is, to diffusion.

R&D Expenditures

As related to *businesses,* the term "research and development" is used loosely to include direct efforts toward invention, innovation, and diffusion. However, *government* also engages in R&D, particularly R&D having to do with national defense. In 2002 *total* U.S. R&D expenditures (business *plus* government) were $292 billion. Relative to GDP that amount was 2.79 percent, which is a reasonable measure of the emphasis the U.S. economy puts on technological advance. As shown in Global Perspective 26.1, this is a high percentage of GDP compared to several other nations.

American businesses spent $211 billion on R&D in 2002. Figure 26.1 shows how these R&D expenditures were allocated. Observe that U.S. firms collectively channeled 72 percent of their R&D expenditures to "development" (innovation and imitation, the route to diffusion). They spent another 22 percent on applied research, or on pursuing invention. For reasons we will mention later, only 6 percent of business R&D expenditures went for basic research, the search for general scientific principles. Of course, industries, and firms within industries, vary greatly in the amount of emphasis they place on these three processes.

Modern View of Technological Advance

For decades most economists regarded technological advance as being external to the economy—a random outside force to which the economy adjusted. From time to time fortuitous advances in scientific and technological knowledge occurred, paving the way for major new products (automobiles, airplanes) and new production processes (assembly lines). Firms and industries, each at its own

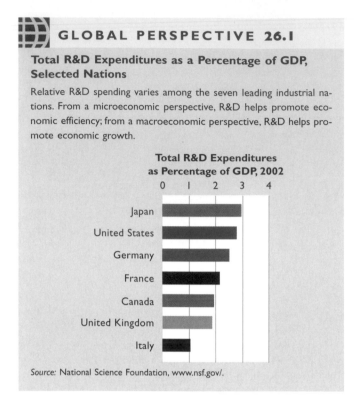

GLOBAL PERSPECTIVE 26.1

Total R&D Expenditures as a Percentage of GDP, Selected Nations

Relative R&D spending varies among the seven leading industrial nations. From a microeconomic perspective, R&D helps promote economic efficiency; from a macroeconomic perspective, R&D helps promote economic growth.

Total R&D Expenditures
as Percentage of GDP, 2002

Japan
United States
Germany
France
Canada
United Kingdom
Italy

Source: National Science Foundation, www.nsf.gov/.

pace, then incorporated the new technology into their products or processes to enhance or maintain their profit. Then, after making the appropriate adjustments, they settled back into new long-run equilibrium positions. Although technological advance has been vitally important to the economy, economists believed it was rooted in

FIGURE 26.1

The composition of business R&D outlays in the United States, 2002. Firms channel the bulk of their R&D spending to innovation and imitation, because both have direct commercial value; less to applied research, that is, invention; and a relatively small amount to basic scientific research.

Source: National Science Foundation, www.nsf.gov/; authors' estimates for 2002.

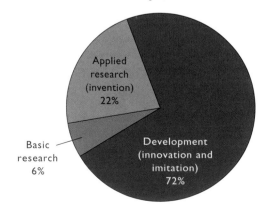

Applied research (invention) 22%

Basic research 6%

Development (innovation and imitation) 72%

the independent advance of science, which is largely external to the market system.

Most contemporary economists have a different view. They see capitalism itself as the driving force of technological advance. In their view, invention, innovation, and diffusion occur in response to incentives within the economy, meaning that technological advance is *internal* to capitalism. Specifically, technological advance arises from intense rivalry among individuals and firms that motivates them to seek and exploit new profit opportunities or to expand existing opportunities. That rivalry occurs both among existing firms and between existing firms and new firms. Moreover, many advances in "pure" scientific knowledge are motivated, at least in part, by the prospect of commercial applicability and eventual profit. In the modern view, entrepreneurs and other innovators are at the heart of technological advance.

Role of Entrepreneurs and Other Innovators

It will be helpful to distinguish between "entrepreneurs" and "other innovators":

- **Entrepreneurs**   Recall that the entrepreneur is an initiator, innovator, and risk bearer—the catalyst who combines land, labor, and capital resources in new and unique ways to produce new goods and services. In the past a single individual, for example, Andrew Carnegie in steel, Henry Ford in automobiles, or Levi Strauss in blue jeans, carried out the entrepreneurial role. Such advances as air conditioning, the ballpoint pen, cellophane, the jet engine, insulin, xerography, and the helicopter all have an individualistic heritage. But in today's more technologically complex economy, entrepreneurship is just as likely to be carried out by entrepreneurial teams. Such teams may include only two or three people working "as their own bosses" on some new product idea or it may consist of larger groups of entrepreneurs who have pooled their financial resources.

- **Other innovators**   This designation includes other key people involved in the pursuit of innovation who do not bear personal financial risk. Among them are key executives, scientists, and other salaried employees engaged in commercial R&D activities. (They are sometimes referred to as *intrapreneurs*, since they provide the spirit of entrepreneurship within existing firms.)

Forming Start-Ups

Entrepreneurs often form small new companies called **start-ups** that focus on creating and introducing a new product or employing a new production or distribution technique. Two people, working out of their garages, formed such a start-up in the mid-1970s. Since neither of their employers—Hewlett-Packard and Atari, the developer of Pong (the first video game)—was interested in their prototype personal computer, they founded their own company: Apple Computers. Other examples of successful start-ups are Amgen, a biotechnology firm specializing in new medical treatments; Starbucks, a seller of gourmet coffee; and Amazon, an Internet retailer.

Innovating within Existing Firms

Innovators are also at work within existing corporations, large and small. Such innovators are salaried workers, although many firms have pay systems that provide them with substantial bonuses or shares of the profit. Examples of firms known for their skillful internal innovators are 3M Corporation, the U.S. developer of Scotch tape, Post-it Note Pads, and Thinsulate insulation; and Canon, the Japanese developer of the "laser engine" for personal copiers and printers. R&D work in major corporations has produced significant technological improvements in such products as television sets, telephones, home appliances, automobiles, automobile tires, and sporting equipment.

Some large firms, aware that excessive bureaucracy can stifle creative thinking and technological advance, have separated part of their R&D and manufacturing divisions to form new, more flexible, innovative firms. Three significant examples of such "spin-off firms" are Lucent Technologies, a telephone equipment and R&D firm created by AT&T; Imation, a high-technology firm spun off by the 3M Corporation; and Palm, a maker of hand-held computers, spun off by 3Com.

Anticipating the Future

Some 50 years ago a writer for *Popular Mechanics* magazine boldly predicted, "Computers in the future may weigh no more than 1.5 tons." Today's notebook computers weigh less than 3 pounds.

It is difficult to anticipate the future, but that is what innovators try to do. Those with strong anticipatory ability and determination have a knack for introducing new and improved products or services at just the right time.

The rewards for success are both monetary and nonmonetary. Product innovation and development are creative endeavors, with such intangible rewards as personal satisfaction. Also, many people simply enjoy participating in the competitive "contest." Of course, the "winners" can reap huge monetary rewards in the form of economic profits, stock appreciation, or large bonuses. Extreme examples are Bill Gates and Paul Allen, who founded Microsoft in 1975, and had a net worth in 2002 of $43 billion and $21 billion, respectively, mainly in the form of Microsoft stock.

Past successes often give entrepreneurs and innovative firms access to resources for further innovations that anticipate consumer wants. Although they may not succeed a second time, the market tends to entrust the production of goods and services to businesses that have consistently succeeded in filling consumer wants. And the market does not care whether these "winning" entrepreneurs and innovative firms are American, Brazilian, Japanese, German, or Swiss. Entrepreneurship and innovation are global in scope.

Exploiting University and Government Scientific Research

In Figure 26.1 we saw that only 6 percent of business R&D spending in the United States goes to basic scientific research. The reason the percentage is so small is that scientific principles, as such, cannot be patented, nor do they usually have immediate commercial uses. Yet new scientific knowledge is highly important to technological advance. For that reason, entrepreneurs study the scientific output of university and government laboratories to identify discoveries with commercial applicability.

Government and university labs have been the scene of many technological breakthroughs, including hybrid seed corn, nuclear energy, satellite communications, the computer "mouse," genetic engineering, and the Internet. Entire high-tech industries such as computers and biotechnology have their roots in major research universities and government laboratories. And nations with strong scientific communities tend to have the most technologically progressive firms and industries.

Also, firms increasingly help fund university research that relates to their products. Business funding of R&D at universities has grown rapidly, rising to more than $2.3 billion in 2002. Today, the separation between university scientists and innovators is narrowing; scientists and universities increasingly realize that their work may have commercial value and are teaming up with innovators to share in the potential profit.

A few firms, of course, find it profitable to conduct basic scientific research on their own. New scientific knowledge can give them a head start in creating an invention or a new product. This is particularly true in the pharmaceutical industry, where it is not uncommon for firms to parlay new scientific knowledge generated in their corporate labs into new, patentable drugs.

A Firm's Optimal Amount of R&D

How does a firm decide on its optimal amount of research and development? That amount depends on the firm's perception of the marginal benefit and marginal cost of R&D activity. The decision rule here flows from basic economics: to earn the greatest profit, expand a particular activity until its marginal benefit (MB) equals its marginal cost (MC). A firm that sees the marginal benefit of a particular R&D activity, say, innovation, as exceeding the marginal cost should expand that activity. In contrast, an activity whose marginal benefit promises to be less than its marginal cost should be cut back. But the R&D spending decision is complex, since it involves a present sacrifice for a future expected gain. While the cost of R&D is immediate, the expected benefits occur at some future time and are highly uncertain. So estimating those benefits is often more art than science. Nevertheless, the MB = MC way of thinking remains relevant for analyzing R&D decisions.

Interest-Rate Cost of Funds

Firms have several ways of obtaining the funds they need to finance R&D activities:

- *Bank loans*   Some firms are able to obtain a loan from a bank or other financial institution. Then the cost of using the funds is the interest paid to the lender. The marginal cost is the cost per extra dollar borrowed, which is simply the market interest rate for borrowed funds.

- *Bonds*   Established, profitable firms may be able to borrow funds for R&D by issuing bonds and selling them in the bond market. In this case, the cost is the interest paid to the lenders—the bondholders. Again

the marginal cost of using the funds is the interest rate. (We discussed bonds in Chapter 5's Last Word.)

- *Retained earnings*   A large, well-established firm may be able to draw on its own corporate savings to finance R&D. Typically, such a firm retains part of its profit rather than paying it all out as dividends to corporate owners. Some of the undistributed corporate profit, called *retained earnings*, can be used to finance R&D activity. The marginal cost is the rate at which those funds could have earned interest as deposits in a financial institution.

- *Venture capital*   A smaller start-up firm might be able to attract venture capital to finance its R&D projects. Venture capital is financial capital, or simply money, not real capital. **Venture capital** consists of that part of household saving used to finance high-risk business ventures in exchange for shares of the profit if the ventures succeed. The marginal cost of venture capital is the share of expected profit that the firm will have to pay to those who provided the money. This can be stated as a percentage of the venture capital, so it is essentially an interest rate.

- *Personal savings*   Finally, individual entrepreneurs might draw on their own savings to finance the R&D for a new venture. The marginal cost of the financing is again the forgone interest rate.

Thus, whatever the source of the R&D funds, we can state the marginal cost of these funds as an interest rate i. For simplicity, let's assume that this interest rate is the same no matter how much financing is required. Further, we assume that a certain firm called MedTech must pay an interest rate of 8 percent, the least expensive funding available to it. Then a graph of the marginal cost of each funding amount for this firm is a horizontal line at the 8 percent interest rate, as shown in Figure 26.2. Such a graph is called an **interest-rate cost-of-funds curve.** This one tells us that MedTech can borrow $10, $10,000, $10,000,000, or more at the 8 percent interest rate. The table accompanying the graph contains the data used to construct the graph and tells us much the same thing.

With these data in hand, MedTech wants to determine how much R&D to finance in the coming year.

Expected Rate of Return

A firm's marginal benefit from R&D is its expected profit (or return) from the last (marginal) dollar spent on R&D. That is, the R&D is expected to result in a new product or production method that will increase revenue, reduce production costs, or both (in ways we will soon explain). This return is expected, not certain—there is risk in R&D

FIGURE 26.2

The interest-rate cost-of-funds schedule and curve. As it relates to R&D, a firm's interest-rate cost-of-funds schedule (the table) and curve (the graph) show the interest rate the firm must pay to obtain any particular amount of funds to finance R&D. Curve *i* indicates the firm can finance as little or as much R&D as it wants at a constant 8 percent rate of interest.

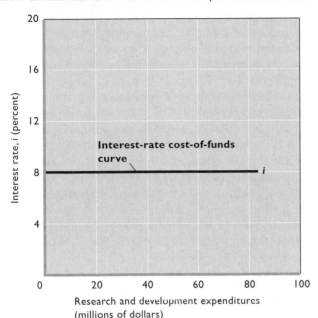

Research and development expenditures
(millions of dollars)

R&D, millions	Interest-rate cost of funds, %
$10	8
20	8
30	8
40	8
50	8
60	8
70	8
80	8

FIGURE 26.3

The expected-rate-of-return schedule and curve. As they relate to R&D, a firm's expected-rate-of-return schedule (the table) and curve (the graph) show the firm's expected gain in profit, as a percentage of R&D spending, for each level of R&D spending. Curve *r* slopes downward because the firm assesses its potential R&D projects in descending order of expected rates of return.

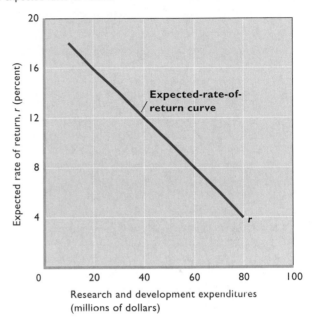

Research and development expenditures
(millions of dollars)

R&D, millions	Expected rate of return, %
$10	18
20	16
30	14
40	12
50	10
60	8
70	6
80	4

decisions. Let's suppose that after considering such risks, MedTech anticipates that an R&D expenditure of $1 million will result in a new product that will yield a one-time added profit of $1.2 million a year later. The expected rate of return *r* on the $1 million R&D expenditure (after the $1 million has been repaid) is 20 percent (= $200,000/$1,000,000). This is the marginal benefit of the first $1 million of R&D. (Stretching the return over several years complicates the computation of *r*; but it does not alter the basic analysis.)

MedTech can use this same method to estimate the expected rates of return for R&D expenditures of $2

million, $3 million, $4 million, and so on. Suppose those marginal rates of return are the ones indicated in the table in Figure 26.3, where they are also graphed as the **expected-rate-of-return curve.** This curve shows the expected rate of return, which is the marginal benefit of each dollar of expenditure on R&D. The curve slopes downward because of diminishing returns to R&D expenditures. A firm will direct its initial R&D expenditures to the highest expected-rate-of-return activities and then use additional funding for activities with successively lower expected rates of return. That is, as the firm increases R&D spending, it uses it to

FIGURE 26.4

A firm's optimal level of R&D expenditures. The firm's optimal level of R&D expenditures ($60 million) occurs where its expected rate of return equals the interest-rate cost of funds, as shown in both the table and the graph. At $60 million of R&D spending, the firm has taken advantage of all R&D opportunities for which the expected rate of return, r, exceeds or equals the 8 percent interest cost of borrowing, i.

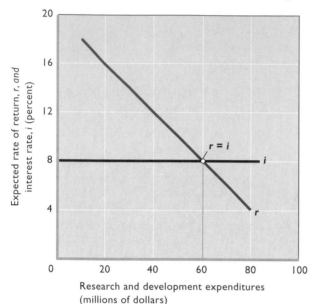

Research and development expenditures (millions of dollars)

Expected rate of return, %	R&D, millions	Interest-rate cost of funds, %
18	$10	8
16	20	8
14	30	8
12	40	8
10	50	8
8	*60*	*8*
6	70	8
4	80	8

finance R&D activities with lower and lower expected rates of return.

Optimal R&D Expenditures

Figure 26.4 combines the interest-rate cost-of-funds curve (Figure 26.2) and the expected-rate-of-return curve (Figure 26.3). The curves intersect at MedTech's **optimal amount of R&D,** which is $60 million. This amount can also be determined from the table as the amount of funding for which the expected rate of return and the interest cost of borrowing are equal (here, 8 percent).

Both the curve and the table in Figure 26.4 tell us that at $60 million of R&D expenditures, the marginal benefit and marginal cost of the last dollar spent on R&D are equal. MedTech should undertake all R&D expenditures up to $60 million, since those outlays yield a higher marginal benefit or expected rate of return, r, than the 8 percent marginal cost or interest-rate cost of borrowing, i. But it should not undertake R&D expenditures beyond $60 million; for these outlays, r (marginal benefit) is less than i (marginal cost). Only at $60 million do we have $r = i$, telling us that MedTech will spend $60 million on R&D.

Our analysis reinforces three important points:

- *Optimal versus affordable R&D*   From earlier discussions we know there can be too much, as well as too little, of a "good thing." So it is with R&D and technological advance. Figure 26.4 shows that R&D expenditures make sense to a firm only as long as the expected return from the outlay equals or exceeds the cost of obtaining the funds needed to finance it. Many R&D expenditures may be affordable but not worthwhile because their marginal benefit is likely to be less than their marginal cost.

- *Expected, not guaranteed, returns*   The outcomes from R&D are expected, not guaranteed. With 20-20 hindsight, a firm can always look back and decide whether a particular expenditure for R&D was worthwhile. But that assessment is irrelevant to the original decision. At the time of the decision, the expenditure was thought to be worthwhile on the basis of existing information and expectations. Some R&D decisions may be more like an informed gamble than the typical business decision. Invention and innovation, in particular, carry with them a great deal of risk. For every successful outcome, there are scores of costly disappointments.

- *Adjustments*   Firms adjust their R&D expenditures when expected rates of return on various projects change (when curves such as r in Figure 26.4 shift). The U.S. war on terrorism, for example, increased the expected rate of return on R&D for improved security devices used at airports, train stations, harbors, and other public places. It also increased the expected return on new methods of detecting and responding to potential bioterrorism. The revised realities prompted many firms to increase their R&D expenditures for these purposes. **(Key Questions 4 and 5)**

Increased Profit via Innovation

In discussing how a firm determines its optimal amount of R&D spending, we sidestepped the question of how technological change can increase a firm's profit. Although the answer may seem obvious—by increasing revenue or reducing production costs—there are insights to be gained by exploring these two potential outcomes in some detail.

Increased Revenue via Product Innovation

Firms here and abroad have profitably introduced hundreds of new products in the past two or three decades. Examples include roller blades, microwave popcorn, cordless drills, digital cameras, camcorders, and projection TVs. Other new products are snowboards, cellular phones, telephone pagers, and automobile air bags. All these items reflect technological advance in the form of product innovation.

How do such new products gain consumer acceptance? As you know from Chapter 21, to maximize their satisfaction, consumers purchase products that have the highest marginal utility per dollar. They determine which products to buy in view of their limited money incomes by comparing the ratios of MU/price for the various goods. They first select the unit of the good with the highest MU/price ratio, then the one with the next highest, and so on, until their incomes are used up.

The first five columns of Table 26.1 repeat some of the information in Table 21.1. Before the introduction of new product C, the consumer maximized total utility from $10 of income by buying 2 units of A at $1 per unit and 4 units of B at $2 per unit. The total $10 budget was thus expended, with $2 spent on A and $8 on B. As shown in columns 2b and 3b, the marginal utility per dollar spent on the last unit of each product was 8 (= 8/$1 = 16/$2). The total utility, derived from columns 2a and 3a, was 96 utils (= 10 + 8 from the first 2 units of A plus 24 + 20 + 18 + 16 from the first 4 units of B). (If you are uncertain about this outcome, please review the discussion of Table 21.1.)

Now suppose an innovative firm offers new product C (columns 4a and 4b in Table 26.1), priced at $4 per unit. Note that the first unit of C has a higher marginal utility per dollar (13) than any unit of A and B and that the second unit of C and the first unit of B have equal MU/price ratios of 12. To maximize satisfaction, the consumer now buys 2 units of C at $4 per unit, 1 unit of B at $2 per unit, and zero units of A. Our consumer has spent the entire $10 of income ($8 on C and $2 on B), and the MU/price ratios of the last units of B and C are equal at 12. But as determined via columns 3a and 4a, the consumer's total utility is now 124 utils (= 24 from the first unit of B plus 52 + 48 from the first 2 units of C).

Total utility has increased by 28 utils (= 124 utils − 96 utils), and that is why product C was purchased. *Consumers will buy a new product only if it increases the total utility they obtain from their limited incomes.*

From the innovating firm's perspective, these "dollar votes" represent new product demand that yields increased revenue. When per-unit revenue exceeds per-unit cost, the product innovation creates per-unit profit. Total profit rises by the per-unit profit multiplied by the number of units sold. As a percentage of the original R&D expenditure, the rise in total profit is the return on that R&D expenditure. It was the basis for the expected-rate-of-return curve *r* in Figure 26.4.

Other related points:

- *Importance of price* Consumer acceptance of a new product depends on both its marginal utility and its price. (Confirm that the consumer represented in Table 26.1 would buy zero units of new product C if its price were $8 rather than $4.) To be successful, a new product must not only deliver utility to consumers but do so at an acceptable price.

TABLE 26.1
Utility Maximization with the Introduction of a New Product (Income = $10)*

(1) Unit of Product	(2) Product A: Price = $1		(3) Product B: Price = $2		(4) New Product C: Price = $4	
	(a) Marginal Utility, Utils	(b) Marginal Utility per Dollar (MU/Price)	(a) Marginal Utility, Utils	(b) Marginal Utility per Dollar (MU/Price)	(a) Marginal Utility, Utils	(b) Marginal Utility per Dollar (MU/Price)
First	10	10	24	*12*	52	13
Second	8	*8*	20	10	48	*12*
Third	7	7	18	9	44	11
Fourth	6	6	16	*8*	36	9
Fifth	5	5	12	6	32	8

*It is assumed in this table that the amount of marginal utility received from additional units of each of the three products is independent of the quantity purchased of the other products. For example, the marginal-utility schedule for product C is independent of the amount of A and B purchased by the consumer.

- *Unsuccessful new products*   For every successful new product, there are hundreds that do not succeed; the expected return that motivates product innovation is not always realized. Examples of colossal product flops are Ford's Edsel automobile, 3-D movies, quadraphonic stereo, New Coke by Coca-Cola, Kodak disc cameras, and XFL football. Less dramatic failures include the hundreds of "dot-com" firms that have recently gone out of business. In each case, millions of dollars of R&D and promotion expense ultimately resulted in loss, not profit.

- *Product improvements*   Most product innovation consists of incremental improvements to existing products rather than radical inventions. Examples: more fuel-efficient automobile engines, new varieties of pizza, lighter-weight shafts for golf clubs, more flavorful bubble-gum, "rock shocks" for mountain bikes, and clothing made of wrinkle-free fabrics. (**Key Question 6**)

Reduced Cost via Process Innovation

The introduction of better methods of producing products—process innovation—is also a path toward enhanced profit and a positive return on R&D expenditures. Suppose a firm introduces a new and better production process, say, assembling its product by teams rather than by a standard assembly line. Alternatively, suppose this firm replaces old equipment with more productive equipment embodying technological advance. In either case, the innovation yields an upward shift in the firm's total-product curve from TP_1 to TP_2 in Figure 26.5a. Now more units of output can be produced at each level of resource usage. Note from the figure, for example, that this firm can now produce 2500 units of output, rather than 2000 units, when using 1000 units of labor. So its average product has increased from 2 (= 2000 units of output/1000 units of labor) to 2.5 (= 2500 units of output/1000 units of labor).

The result is a downward shift in the firm's average-total-cost curve, from ATC_1 to ATC_2 in Figure 26.5b. To understand why, let's assume this firm pays $1000 for the use of its capital and $9 for each unit of labor. Since it uses 1000 units of labor, its labor cost is $9000 (= $9 × 1000); its capital cost is $1000; and thus its total cost is $10,000. When its output increases from 2000 to 2500 units as a result of the process innovation, its total cost remains $10,000. So its average total cost declines from $5 (= $10,000/2000) to $4 (= $10,000/2500). Alternatively, the firm could

FIGURE 26.5

Process innovation, total product, and average total cost.   (a) Process innovation shifts a firm's total-product curve upward from TP_1 to TP_2, meaning that with a given amount of capital the firm can produce more output at each level of labor input. As shown, with 1000 units of labor it can produce 2500 rather than 2000 units of output. (b) The upward shift in the total-product curve results in a downward shift in the firm's average-total-cost curve, from ATC_1 to ATC_2. This means the firm can produce any particular unit of output at a lower average total cost than it could previously. For example, the original 2000 units can be produced at less than $4 per unit, versus $5 per unit originally. Or 2500 units can now be produced at $4 per unit.

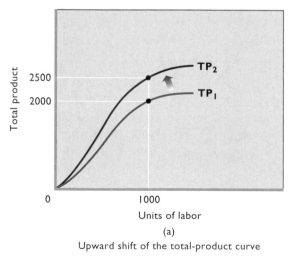

(a)
Upward shift of the total-product curve

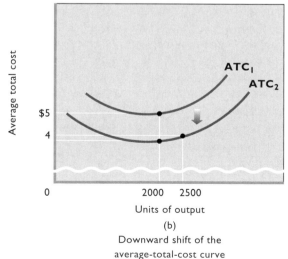

(b)
Downward shift of the
average-total-cost curve

produce the original 2000 units of output with fewer units of labor at an even lower average total cost.

This reduction in average total cost enhances the firm's profit. As a percentage of the R&D expenditure that fostered it, this extra profit is the expected return r, the basis for the rate-of-return-curve in Figure 26.3. In this case, the expected rate of return arose from the prospect of lower production costs through process innovation.

Example: Computer-based inventory control systems, such as those pioneered by Wal-Mart, enabled innovators to reduce the number of people keeping track of inventories and placing reorders of sold goods. They also enabled firms to keep goods arriving "just in time," reducing the cost of storing inventories. The consequence? Significant increases in sales per worker, declines in average total cost, and increased profit. **(Key Question 8)**

Imitation and R&D Incentives

Our analysis of product and process innovation explains how technological advance enhances a firm's profit. But it also hints at a potential **imitation problem:** A firm's rivals may be able to imitate its new product or process, greatly reducing the originator's profit from its R&D effort. As just one example, in the 1980s U.S. auto firms took apart Japanese Honda Accords, piece by piece, to discover the secrets of their high quality. This reverse engineering—which ironically was perfected earlier by the Japanese—helped the U.S. firms incorporate innovative features into their own cars. This type of imitation is perfectly legitimate and fully anticipated; it is often the main path to widespread diffusion of an innovation.

In fact, a dominant firm that is making large profits from its existing products may let smaller firms in the industry incur the high costs of product innovation while it closely monitors their successes and failures. The dominant firm then moves quickly to imitate any successful new product; its goal is to become the second firm to embrace the innovation. In using this so-called **fast-second strategy,** the dominant firm counts on its own product-improvement abilities, marketing prowess, or economies of scale to prevail.

Examples abound: Royal Crown introduced the first diet cola, but Diet Coke and Diet Pepsi dominate diet-cola sales today. Meister-Brau introduced the first low-calorie beer, but Miller popularized the product with its Miller Lite. Gillette moved quickly with its own stainless-steel razor blade only after a smaller firm, Wilkinson, introduced this product innovation.

Benefits of Being First

Imitation and the fast-second strategy raise an important question: What incentive is there for any firm to bear the expenses and risks of innovation if competitors can imitate its new or improved product? Why not let others bear the costs and risks of product development and then just imitate the successful innovations? Although we have seen that this may be a plausible strategy in some situations, there are several protections for, and potential advantages to, taking the lead.

Patents   Some technological breakthroughs, specifically inventions, can be patented. Once patented, they cannot be legally imitated for two decades. The purpose of patents is, in fact, to reduce imitation and its negative effect on the incentive for engaging in R&D. Example: Polaroid's patent of its instant camera enabled it to earn high economic profits for many years. When Kodak "cloned" the camera, Polaroid won a patent-infringement lawsuit against its rival. Kodak not only had to stop producing its version of the camera but had to buy back the Kodak instant cameras it had sold and pay millions of dollars in damages to Polaroid.

There are hundreds of other examples of long-run profits based on U.S. patents; they involve products from prescription drugs to pop-top cans to weed trimmers. As shown in Global Perspective 26.2, foreign citizens and firms hold U.S. patents along with American citizens and firms.

Copyrights and Trademarks   *Copyrights* protect publishers of books, computer software, movies, videos, and musical compositions from having their works copied. *Trademarks* give the original innovators of products the exclusive right to use a particular product name ("M&Ms," "Barbie Doll," "Wheaties"). By reducing the problem of direct copying, these legal protections increase the incentive for product innovation. They have been strengthened worldwide through recent international trade agreements.

Brand-Name Recognition   Along with trademark protection, brand-name recognition may give the original innovator a major marketing advantage for years or even decades. Consumers often identify a new product with the firm that first introduced and popularized it in the mass market. Examples: Levi's blue jeans, Kleenex soft tissues, Johnson and Johnson's Band-Aids, Sony's Walkman, and Kellogg's Corn Flakes.

Trade Secrets and Learning by Doing   Some innovations involve trade secrets, without which competitors cannot imitate the product or process. Example: Coca-Cola has successfully kept its formula for Coke a secret from potential rivals. Many other firms have perfected special production techniques known only to them. In a related advantage, a firm's head start with a new product often allows it to achieve substantial cost reductions through learning by doing. The innovator's lower cost may enable it to continue to profit even after imitators have entered the market.

Time Lags   Time lags between innovation and diffusion often enable innovating firms to realize a substantial economic profit. It takes time for an imitator to gain knowledge of the properties of a new innovation. And once it has that knowledge, the imitator must design a substitute product, gear up a factory for its production, and conduct a marketing campaign. Various entry barriers, such as large financial requirements, economies of scale, and price-cutting, may extend the time lag between innovation and imitation. In practice, it may take years or even decades before rival firms can successfully imitate a profitable new product and cut into the market share of the innovator. In the meantime, the innovator continues to profit.

Profitable Buyouts   A final advantage of being first arises from the possibility of a buyout (outright purchase)

CONSIDER THIS . . .

Trade Secrets

© David Katzenstein/CORBIS

Trade secrets have long played an important role in maintaining returns from research and development (R&D). Long before Coca-Cola's secret formula or Colonel Sander's secret herbs and spices, the Roman citizen Erasmo (c. 130 A. D.) had a secret ingredient for violin strings.* As the demand for his new product grew, he falsely identified his strings as *catgut*, when they were actually made of sheep intestines. Why the deception? At the time, it was considered to be extremely bad luck to kill a cat. By identifying his strings as catgut, he hoped that nobody would imitate his product and reduce his monopoly profit. Moreover, his product name would help him preserve his valuable trade secret.

*We discovered this anecdote in Dennis W. Carleton and Jeffrey Perloff, *Modern Industrial Organization*, 2d ed. (New York: HarperCollins, 1994), p. 139. Their source, in turn, was L. Boyd, *San Francisco Chronicle*, October 27, 1984, p. 35.

of the innovating firm by a larger firm. Here, the innovative entrepreneurs take their rewards immediately, as cash or as shares in the purchasing firm, rather than waiting for perhaps uncertain long-run profits from their own production and marketing efforts.

Examples: Once the popularity of cellular communications became evident, AT&T bought out McCaw Communications, an early leader in this new technology. When Minnetonka's Softsoap became a huge success, it sold its product to Colgate-Palmolive. More recently, Swiss conglomerate Nestlé bought out Chef America, the highly successful maker of Hot Pockets frozen meat-and-cheese sandwiches. Such buyouts are legal under current antitrust laws as long as they do not substantially lessen competition in the affected industry. For this to be the case, there must be other strong competitors in the market. That was not true, for example, when Microsoft tried to buy out Intuit (maker of Quicken, the best-selling financial software). That buyout was disallowed because Intuit and Microsoft were the two main suppliers of financial software for personal computers.

In short, despite the imitation problem, there are significant protections and advantages that enable most innovating firms to profit from their R&D efforts, as implied by the continuing high levels of R&D spending by firms year after year. As shown in Figure 26.6, business

GLOBAL PERSPECTIVE 26.2

Distribution of U.S. Patents, by Foreign Nation

Foreign citizens, corporations, and governments hold 43 percent of U.S. patents. The top 10 foreign countries in terms of U.S. patent holdings are listed below, with the number of U.S. patents (through 2001) in parentheses.

Top 10 Foreign Countries

Japan (464,244)
Germany (185,653)
France (72,669)
U. K. (71,773)
Canada (52,413)
Taiwan (36,993)
Switzerland (32,443)
Italy (30,953)
Sweden (24,857)
Netherlands (23,468)

Source: U.S. Patent and Trademark Office, www.uspto.gov.

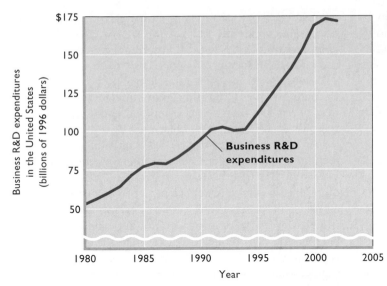

FIGURE 26.6

The growth of business R&D expenditures in the United States, 1980–2002. Inflation-adjusted R&D expenditures by firms are substantial and growing, suggesting that R&D continues to be profitable for firms, even in the face of possible imitation.

Source: National Science Foundation, www.nsf.gov/.

R&D spending in the United States not only remains substantial but has grown over the past quarter-century. The high levels of spending simply would not continue if imitation consistently and severely depressed rates of return on R&D expenditures.

QUICK REVIEW 26.2

• A firm's optimal R&D expenditure is the amount at which the expected rate of return (marginal benefit) from the R&D expenditure just equals the interest-rate cost of borrowing (marginal cost) required to finance it.

• Product innovation can entice consumers to substitute a new product for existing products to increase their total utility, thereby increasing the innovating firm's revenue and profit.

• Process innovation can lower a firm's production costs and increase its profit by increasing total product and decreasing average total cost.

• A firm faces reduced profitability from R&D if competitors can successfully imitate its new product or process. Nevertheless, there are significant potential protections and benefits to being first, including patents, copyrights, and trademarks; brand-name recognition; trade secrets; cost reductions from learning by doing; and major time lags between innovation and imitation.

Role of Market Structure

In view of our discussion of market structures in the last three chapters, it is logical to ask whether there is some particular market structure or firm size that is best suited to technological progress. Is a highly competitive industry consisting of thousands of relatively small firms preferable to an industry comprising only two or three large firms? Or is some intermediate structure best?

Market Structure and Technological Advance

As a first step toward answering these questions, we survey the strengths and shortcomings of our four market models as related to technological advance.

Pure Competition Does a pure competitor have a strong incentive and strong ability to undertake R&D? On the positive side, strong competition provides a reason for such firms to innovate; competitive firms tend to be less complacent than monopolists. If a pure competitor does not seize the initiative, one or more rivals may introduce a new product or cost-reducing production technique that could drive it from the market. As a matter of short-term profit and long-term survival, the pure competitor is under continual pressure to improve products and lower costs through innovation. Also, where there are many competing firms, there is less chance that an idea for improving a product or process will be overlooked by a single firm.

On the negative side, the expected rate of return on R&D may be low or even negative for a pure competitor. Because of easy entry, its profit rewards from innovation may quickly be competed away by existing or entering firms that also produce the new product or adopt the new technology. Also, the small size of competitive firms and the fact that they earn only a normal profit in the long run lead to serious questions as to whether they can finance substantial R&D programs. Observers have noted that the high rate of technological advance in the purely competitive agricultural industry, for example, has come not from the R&D of individual farmers but from government-sponsored research and from the development of fertilizers, hybrid seed, and farm implements by oligopolistic firms.

Monopolistic Competition   Like pure competitors, monopolistic competitors cannot afford to be complacent. But unlike pure competitors, which sell standardized products, monopolistic competitors have a strong profit incentive to engage in product innovation. This incentive to differentiate products from those of competitors stems from the fact that sufficiently novel products may create monopoly power and thus economic profit. There are many examples of innovative firms (McDonald's, Blockbuster Video, Krispy Crème Donuts) that started out as monopolistic competitors in localized markets but soon gained considerable national market power, with the attendant economic profit.

For the typical firm, however, the shortcomings of monopolistic competition in relation to technological advance are the same as those of pure competition. Most monopolistic competitors remain small, which limits their ability to secure inexpensive financing for R&D. In addition, monopolistic competitors find it difficult to extract large profits from technological advances. Any economic profits from innovation are usually temporary, because entry to monopolistically competitive industries is relatively easy. In the long run, new entrants with similar goods reduce the demand for the innovator's product, leaving the innovator with only a normal profit. Monopolistic competitors therefore usually have relatively low expected rates of return on R&D expenditures.

Oligopoly   Many of the characteristics of oligopoly are conducive to technological advance. First, the large size of oligopolists enables them to finance the often large R&D costs associated with major product or process innovation. In particular, the typical oligopolist realizes ongoing economic profits, a part of which is retained. This undistributed profit serves as a major source of readily available, relatively low-cost funding for R&D. Moreover, the existence of barriers to entry gives the oligopolist some assurance that it can maintain any economic profit it gains from innovation. Then, too, the large sales volume of the oligopolist enables it to spread the cost of specialized R&D equipment and teams of specialized researchers over a great many units of output. Finally, the broad scope

of R&D activity within oligopolistic firms helps them offset the inevitable R&D "misses" with more-than-compensating R&D "hits." Thus, oligopolists clearly have the means and incentive to innovate.

But there is also a negative side to R&D in oligopoly. In many instances, the oligopolist's incentive to innovate may be far less than we have implied above, because oligopoly tends to breed complacency. An oligopolist may reason that it makes little sense to introduce costly new technology and produce new products when it currently is earning a sizable economic profit without them. The oligopolist wants to maximize its profit by exploiting fully all its capital assets. Why rush to develop a new product (say, batteries for electric automobiles) when that product's success will render obsolete much of the firm's current equipment designed to produce its existing product (say, gasoline engines)? It is not difficult to cite oligopolistic industries in which the largest firms' interest in R&D has been quite modest. Examples: the steel, cigarette, and aluminum industries.

Pure Monopoly   In general, the pure monopolist has little incentive to engage in R&D; it maintains its high profit through entry barriers that, in theory, are complete. The only incentive for the pure monopolist to engage in R&D is defensive: to reduce the risk of being blindsided by some new product or production process that destroys its monopoly. If such a product is out there to be discovered, the monopolist may have an incentive to find it. By so doing, it can either exploit the new product or process for continued monopoly profit or suppress the product until the monopolist has extracted the maximum profit from its current capital assets. But, in general, economists agree that pure monopoly is the market structure least conducive to innovation.

Inverted-U Theory

Analysis like this has led some experts on technological progress to postulate a so-called **inverted-U theory** of the relationship between market structure and technological advance. This theory is illustrated in Figure 26.7, which relates R&D spending as a percentage of a firm's sales (vertical axis) to the industry's four-firm concentration ratio (horizontal axis). The "inverted-U" shape of the curve suggests that R&D effort is at best weak in both very low concentration industries (pure competition) and very high concentration industries (pure monopoly). Starting from the lowest concentrations, R&D spending as a percentage of sales rises with concentration until a concentration ratio of 50 percent or so is reached, meaning

FIGURE 26.7

The inverted-U theory of R&D expenditures. The inverted-U theory suggests that R&D expenditures as a percentage of sales rise with industry concentration until the four-firm concentration ratio reaches about 50 percent. Further increases in industry concentration are associated with lower relative R&D expenditures.

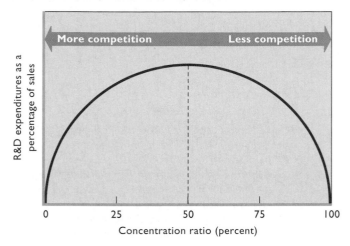

that the four largest firms account for about one-half the total industry output. Beyond that, relative R&D spending decreases as concentration rises.

The logic of the inverted-U theory follows from our discussion. Firms in industries with very low concentration ratios are mainly competitive firms. They are small, and this makes it difficult for them to finance R&D. Moreover, entry to these industries is easy, making it difficult to sustain economic profit from innovations that are not supported by patents. As a result, firms in these industries spend little on R&D relative to their sales. At the other end (far right) of the curve, where concentration is exceptionally high, monopoly profit is already high and innovation will not add much more profit. Furthermore, innovation typically requires costly retooling of very large factories, which will cut into whatever additional profit is realized. As a result, the expected rate of return from R&D is quite low, as are expenditures for R&D relative to sales. Finally, the lack of rivals makes the monopolist quite complacent about R&D.

The optimal industry structure for R&D is one in which expected returns on R&D spending are high and funds to finance it are readily available and inexpensive. From our discussion, those factors seem to occur in industries where a few firms are absolutely and relatively large but where the concentration ratio is not so high as to prohibit vigorous competition by smaller rivals. Rivalry among the larger oligopolistic firms and competition between the larger and the smaller firms then provide a strong incentive for R&D. The inverted-U theory, as represented by Figure 26.7, also points toward this "loose" oligopoly as the optimal structure for R&D spending.

Market Structure and Technological Advance: The Evidence

Dozens of industry studies have tried to pin down the relationship between market structure and technological advance. Because those studies dealt with different industries and time periods, and used different methodologies, they are not easy to compare and summarize. Nevertheless, they provide general support for the inverted-U theory.[1] Other things equal, the optimal market structure for technological advance seems to be an industry in which there is a mix of large oligopolistic firms (a 40 to 60 percent concentration ratio), with several highly innovative smaller firms.

But our "other-things-equal" qualification is quite important here. Whether or not a particular industry is highly technical may well be a more important determinant of R&D than its structure. While some concentrated industries (electronics, aircraft, and petroleum) devote large quantities of resources to R&D and are very innovative, others (cigarettes, aluminum, gypsum products) are not. The level of R&D spending within an industry seems to depend as much on its technical character and "technological opportunities" as on its market structure. There simply may be more opportunities to innovate in the computer and pharmaceutical industries, for example, than in the brick-making and coal-mining industries.

Conclusion: The inverted-U curve shown in Figure 26.7 is a useful depiction of the general relationship between R&D spending and market structure, other things equal.

Technological Advance and Efficiency

Technological advance contributes significantly to economic efficiency. New and better processes and products enable society to produce more output, as well as a higher-valued mix of output.

Productive Efficiency

Technological advance as embodied in process innovation improves *productive efficiency* by increasing the productivity

---

[1]Douglas F. Greer, *Industrial Organization and Public Policy*, 3d ed. (New York: Macmillan, 1992), pp. 680–687.

Technological Advance Is Clearly Evident in the Development of the Modern Personal Computer and the Emergence of the Internet. Here Is a Brief History of Those Events.

1945 Grace Murray Hopper finds a dead moth between relay contacts in the experimental Mark II computer at Harvard University. Whenever the computer subsequently malfunctions, workers set out to "debug" the device.

1946 ENIAC is revealed. A precursor to the modern-day computer, it relies on 18,000 vacuum tubes and fills 3000 cubic feet of space.

1947 AT&T scientists invent the "transfer resistance device," later known as the transistor. It replaces the less reliable vacuum tubes in computers.

1961 Bob Noyce (who later founded Intel Corporation) and Jack Kilby invent the first integrated circuit, which miniaturizes electronic circuitry onto a single silicon chip.

1964 IBM introduces the System/360 computer. Configured as a system, it takes up nearly the same space as two tennis courts.

1965 Digital Equipment Corporation unveils its PDP-8, the first relatively small-size computer (a "minicomputer").

1969 A networking system called ARPANET is born; it is the beginning of the Internet.

1971 Intel introduces its 4004 processor (a "microprocessor"). The $200 chip is the size of a thumbnail and has as much computing capability as the earlier ENIAC.

1975 Xerox markets Alto, the first personal computer (a "microcomputer"). Bill Gates and Paul Allen found Microsoft. MITS Corporation's Altair 8800 arrives on the scene. It contains Intel's 8080 microprocessor that Intel developed a year earlier to control traffic lights.

1977 Apple II, Commodore's PET, and Tandy Radio Shack TRS-80 go on sale, setting the stage for the personal computer revolution.

1981 IBM enters the market with its personal computer powered by the Intel 8800 chip and operated by the Microsoft Disc Operating System (MS-DOS). Osborne Computer markets the Osborne 1, the first self-contained microcomputer, but within 2 years the firm declares bankruptcy. Logitech commercializes the "X-Y Position Indicator for a Display System," invented earlier by Douglas Engelbart in a government-funded research lab. Someone dubs it a "computer mouse" because it appears to have a tail.

1982 Compaq Computer "clones" the IBM machines; others do the same. Eventually Compaq becomes one of the leading sellers of personal computers.

1984 Apple introduces its Macintosh computer, with its "user-friendly" icons, attached mouse, and preloaded software. College student Michael Dell founds Dell Computers, which builds personal computers and sells them through mail order. IBM, Sears Roebuck, and CBS team up to launch Prodigy Services, the first online computer business.

1985 Microsoft releases its Windows graphical interface operating system that improves upon MS-DOS. Ted Waitt

---

of inputs (as indicated in Figure 26.5a) and by reducing average total costs (as in Figure 26.5b). In other words, it enables society to produce the same amount of a particular good or service while using fewer scarce resources, thereby freeing the unused resources to produce other goods and services. Or if society desires more of the now less expensive good, process innovation enables it to have that greater quantity without sacrificing other goods. Viewed either way, process innovation enhances productive efficiency: It reduces society's per-unit cost of whatever mix of goods and services it chooses. It thus is an important means of shifting an economy's production possibilities curve rightward.

Allocative Efficiency

Technological advance as embodied in *product* (or service) innovation enhances allocative efficiency by giving society

a more preferred mix of goods and services. Recall from our earlier discussion that consumers buy a new product rather than an old product only when buying the new one increases the total utility obtained from their limited incomes. Obviously, then, the new product—and the new mix of products it implies—creates a higher level of total utility for society.

In terms of markets, the demand for the new product rises and the demand for the old product declines. The high economic profit engendered by the new product attracts resources away from less valued uses and to the production of the new product. In theory, such shifting of resources continues until the price of the new product equals its marginal cost.

There is a caveat here, however. Innovation (either product or process) can create monopoly power through patents or through the many advantages of being first.

starts a mail-order personal computer business (Gateway 2000) out of his South Dakota barn.

1990 Microsoft introduces Windows 3.0, which, like Macintosh, features windows, icons, and pull-down menus. Apple sues Microsoft for copyright infringement.

1991 The World Wide Web (an Internet system) is invented.

1993 Intel introduces its first of several Pentium chips, which greatly speed up computing. The courts reject Apple's claim that Microsoft violated its copyrights on its Macintosh operating system.

1994 Marc Andreessen starts up Netscape Communications and markets Netscape Navigator, which quickly becomes the leading software browser for the emerging Internet. David Filo and Jerry Yang develop Yahoo, a system for locating material stored on the Internet.

1995 Microsoft releases the Windows 95 operating system, which becomes the dominant operating system of personal computers (90 percent market share). Microsoft is now well established as the world's leading software producer. Sun Microsystems introduces Java, an Internet programming language.

1996 Playing catch-up with Netscape, Microsoft develops Microsoft Internet Explorer and gives it away free.

1999 Netscape's market share plunges and it merges with America Online. More than 100 million personal computers are manufactured worldwide this year alone.

2000 Sixty percent of American households have access to the Internet either at home or at work, and the Internet spreads worldwide. Internet commerce in the United States reaches $300 billion, and an estimated 1.2 million U.S. jobs are Internet-related.

2002 A Federal court of appeals finds that Microsoft has a monopoly in operating system software for Intel-compatible personal computers and has maintained its monopoly through illegal actions aimed at thwarting threats from rivals. The court imposes a set of specific restrictions on Microsoft's anticompetitive business practices.

Source: Based partly on Diedtra Henderson, "Moore's Law Still Reigns," *Seattle Times*, Nov. 24, 1996, augmented and updated.

When new monopoly power results from an innovation, society may lose part of the improved efficiency it otherwise would have gained from that innovation. The reason is that the profit-maximizing monopolist restricts output to keep its product price above marginal cost. For example, Microsoft's innovative Windows product has resulted in dominance in the market for Intel-compatible operating systems for personal computers. Microsoft's substantial monopoly power permits it to charge prices that are well above marginal cost and minimum average total cost.

Creative Destruction

Although innovation can create monopoly power, it also can reduce or eliminate it. By creating competition where it previously was weak, innovation can push prices down toward marginal cost. For example, Intel's microprocessor enabled personal computers, and their ease of production eventually diminished IBM's monopoly power in the sale of computer hardware. More recently, Linux's new computer operating system has provided some promising competition for Microsoft Windows.

At the extreme, innovation may cause **creative destruction,** where the creation of new products and new production methods simultaneously destroys the monopoly market positions of firms committed to existing products and old ways of doing business. As stated many years ago by Joseph Schumpeter, who championed this view:

In capitalist reality . . . it is . . . competition from the new commodity, the new technology, the new source of supply, the new type of business organization—competition which commands a decisive cost or quality advantage and which strikes not at the margins of profits of the existing firms but at their foundation and their very lives. This

499

kind of competition is . . . so . . . important that it becomes a matter of comparative indifference whether competition in the ordinary sense functions more or less promptly; the powerful lever that in the [very] long run expands output and brings down prices is in any case made of other stuff.[2]

There are many examples of creative destruction: In the 1800s wagons, ships, and barges were the only means of transporting freight until the railroads broke up their monopoly; the dominant market position of the railroads was, in turn, undermined by trucks and, later, by airplanes. Movies brought new competition to live theater, at one time the "only show in town," but movies were later challenged by television. Vinyl long-playing records supplanted acetate 78-rpm phonograph records; cassettes then challenged LP records; and compact discs undermined cassettes. Now Internet music-recording technology such as MP3 threaten sales of traditional CDs. Aluminum cans and plastic bottles have displaced glass bottles in many uses. E-mail has challenged the postal service. Mass discounters such as Wal-Mart and Costco have gained market share at the expense of Sears and Montgomery Ward.

26.1
Creative
destruction

According to Schumpeter, an innovator will automatically displace any monopolist that no longer delivers superior performance. But many contemporary economists think this notion reflects more wishful thinking than fact. In this view, the idea that creative destruction is automatic

. . . neglects the ability of powerful established firms to erect private storm shelters—or lobby government to build public storm shelters for them—in order to shield themselves from the Schumpeterian gales of creative destruction. It ignores the difference between the legal freedom of entry and the economic reality deterring the entry of potential newcomers into concentrated industries.[3]

That is, some dominant firms may be able to use strategies such as selective price cutting, buyouts, and massive advertising to block entry and competition from even the most innovative new firms and existing rivals. Moreover, rent-seeking dominant firms have been known to persuade government to give them tax breaks, subsidies, and tariff protection that strengthen their market power.

In short, while innovation in general enhances economic efficiency, in some cases it may lead to entrenched monopoly power. Further innovation may eventually destroy that monopoly power, but the process of creative destruction is neither automatic nor inevitable. On the other hand, rapid technological change, innovation, and efficiency clearly are not necessarily inconsistent with possession of monopoly power.

---

[2]Joseph A. Schumpeter, *Capitalism, Socialism, and Democracy*, 3d ed. (New York: Harper & Row, 1950), pp. 84–85.

[3]Walter Adams and James Brock, *The Structure of American Industry*, 10th ed. (Upper Saddle River, N.J.: Prentice-Hall, 2001), pp. 363–364.

SUMMARY

1. Technological advance is evidenced by new and improved goods and services and new and improved production or distribution processes. In economists' models, technological advance occurs only in the *very long run*.

2. Invention is the discovery of a product or process through the use of imagination, ingenuity, and experimentation. Innovation is the first successful commercial introduction of a new product, the first use of a new method, or the creation of a new form of business enterprise. Diffusion is the spread of an earlier innovation among competing firms. Firms channel a majority of their R&D expenditures to innovation and imitation, rather than to basic scientific research and invention.

3. Historically, most economists viewed technological advance as a random, external force to which the economy adjusted. Many contemporary economists see technological advance as occurring in response to profit incentives within the economy and thus as an integral part of capitalism.

4. Entrepreneurs and other innovators try to anticipate the future. They play a central role in technological advance by initiating changes in products and processes. Entrepreneurs often form start-up firms that focus on creating and introducing new products. Sometimes, innovators work in the R&D labs of major corporations. Entrepreneurs and innovative firms often rely heavily on the basic research done by university and government scientists.

5. A firm's optimal amount of R&D spending occurs where its expected return (marginal benefit) from the R&D equals its interest-rate cost of funds (marginal cost) to finance the R&D. Entrepreneurs and firms use several sources to finance R&D, including (a) bank loans, (b) bonds, (c) venture capital (funds lent in return for a share of the profits if the

business succeeds), (d) undistributed corporate profits (retained earnings), and (e) personal savings.

6. Product innovation, the introduction of new products, succeeds when it provides consumers with higher marginal utility per dollar spent than do existing products. The new product enables consumers to obtain greater total utility from a given income. From the firm's perspective, product innovation increases net revenue sufficiently to yield a positive rate of return on the R&D spending that produced the innovation.

7. Process innovation can lower a firm's production costs by improving its internal production techniques. Such improvement increases the firm's total product, thereby lowering its average total cost and increasing its profit. The added profit provides a positive rate of return on the R&D spending that produced the process innovation.

8. Imitation poses a potential problem for innovators, since it threatens their returns on R&D expenditures. Some dominant firms use a fast-second strategy, letting smaller firms initiate new products and then quickly imitating the successes. Nevertheless, there are significant protections and potential benefits for firms that take the lead with R&D and innovation, including (a) patent protection, (b) copy-rights and trademarks, (c) lasting brand-name recognition, (d) benefits from trade secrets and learning by doing, (e) high economic profits during the time lag between a product's introduction and its imitation, and (f) the possibility of lucrative buyout offers from larger firms.

9. Each of the four basic market structures has potential strengths and weaknesses regarding the likelihood of R&D and innovation. The inverted-U theory holds that a firm's R&D spending as a percentage of its sales rises with its industry four-firm concentration ratio, reaches a peak at a 50 percent concentration ratio, and then declines as concentration increases further. Empirical evidence is not clear-cut but lends general support to this theory. For any specific industry, however, the technological opportunities that are available may count more than market structure in determining R&D spending and innovation.

10. In general, technological advance enhances both productive and allocative efficiency. But in some situations patents and the advantages of being first with an innovation can increase monopoly power. While in some cases creative destruction eventually destroys monopoly, most economists doubt that this process is either automatic or inevitable.

TERMS AND CONCEPTS

technological advance	product innovation	interest-rate cost-of-funds curve	imitation problem
very long run	process innovation	expected-rate-of-return curve	fast-second strategy
invention	diffusion		inverted-U theory of R&D
patent	start-ups	optimal amount of R&D	creative destruction
innovation	venture capital		

STUDY QUESTIONS

1. What is meant by technological advance, as broadly defined? How does technological advance enter into the definition of the very long run? Which of the following are examples of technological advance, and which are not: an improved production process; entry of a firm into a profitable purely competitive industry; the imitation of a new production process by another firm; an increase in a firm's advertising expenditures?

2. Listed below are several possible actions by firms. Write "INV" beside those that reflect invention, "INN" beside those that reflect innovation, and "DIF" beside those that reflect diffusion.
    a. An auto manufacturer adds "heated seats" as a standard feature in its luxury cars to keep pace with a rival firm whose luxury cars already have this feature.

    b. A television production company pioneers the first music video channel.
    c. A firm develops and patents a working model of a self-erasing whiteboard for classrooms.
    d. A lightbulb firm is the first to produce and market lighting fixtures with halogen lamps.
    e. A rival toy maker introduces a new Jenny doll to compete with Mattel's Barbie doll.

3. Contrast the older and the modern views of technological advance as they relate to the economy. What is the role of entrepreneurs and other innovators in technological advance? How does research by universities and government affect innovators and technological advance? Why do you think some university researchers are becoming more like entrepreneurs and less like "pure scientists"?

4. *Key Question* Suppose a firm expects that a $20 million expenditure on R&D will result in a new product that will increase its revenue by a total of $30 million 1 year from now. The firm estimates that the production cost of the new product will be $29 million.

   a. What is the expected rate of return on this R&D expenditure?

   b. Suppose the firm can get a bank loan at 6 percent interest to finance its $20 million R&D project. Will the firm undertake the project? Explain why or why not.

   c. Now suppose the interest-rate cost of borrowing, in effect, falls to 4 percent because the firm decides to use its own retained earnings to finance the R&D. Will this lower interest rate change the firm's R&D decision? Explain.

5. *Key Question* Answer the following lettered questions on the basis of the information in this table:

Amount of R&D, Millions	Expected Rate of Return on R&D, %
$10	16
20	14
30	12
40	10
50	8
60	6

   a. If the interest-rate cost of funds is 8 percent, what will be the optimal amount of R&D spending for this firm?

   b. Explain why $20 million of R&D spending will not be optimal.

   c. Why won't $60 million be optimal either?

6. *Key Question* Refer to Table 26.1 and suppose the price of new product C is $2 instead of $4. How does this affect the optimal combination of products A, B, and C for the person represented by the data? Explain: "The success of a new product depends not only on its marginal utility but also on its price."

7. Learning how to use software takes time. So once customers have learned to use a particular software package, it is easier to sell them software upgrades than to convince them to switch to new software. What implications does this have for expected rates of return on R&D spending for software firms developing upgrades versus firms developing imitative products?

8. *Key Question* Answer the following questions on the basis of this information for a single firm: total cost of capital = $1000; price paid for labor = $12 per labor unit; price paid for raw materials = $4 per raw-material unit.

   a. Suppose the firm can produce 5000 units of output by combining its fixed capital with 100 units of labor and 450 units of raw materials. What are the total cost and

average total cost of producing the 5000 units of output?

   b. Now assume the firm improves its production process so that it can produce 6000 units of output by combining its fixed capital with 100 units of labor and 450 units of raw materials. What are the total cost and average cost of producing the 6000 units of output?

   c. Refer to your answers to 8a and 8b and explain how process innovation can improve economic efficiency.

9. Why might a firm making a large economic profit from its existing product employ a fast-second strategy in relationship to new or improved products? What risks does it run in pursuing this strategy? What incentive does a firm have to engage in R&D when rivals can imitate its new product?

10. Do you think the overall level of R&D would increase or decrease over the next 20 to 30 years if the lengths of new patents were extended from 20 years to, say, "forever"? What if the duration were reduced from 20 years to, say, 3 years?

11. Make a case that neither pure competition nor pure monopoly is conducive to a great deal of R&D spending and innovation. Why might oligopoly be more favorable to R&D spending and innovation than either pure competition or pure monopoly? What is the inverse-U theory, and how does it relate to your answers to these questions?

12. Evaluate: "Society does not need laws outlawing monopolization and monopoly. Inevitably, monopoly causes its own self-destruction, since its high profit is the lure for other firms or entrepreneurs to develop substitute products."

13. *(Last Word)* Identify a specific example of each of the following in this chapter's Last Word: (a) entrepreneurship, (b) invention, (c) innovation, and (d) diffusion.

14. *Web-Based Question: The National Science Foundation R&D statistics—what's happening?* Go to the Division of Science Resource Statistics website, www.nsf.gov/sbe/srs/stats.htm, and find Publications by Type and then select Detailed Statistical Tables. In the report titled "National Patterns of Research and Development Resources," use the table on comparative measures to determine whether the following R&D numbers have increased, remained constant, or decreased over the last 5 years listed: (a) Total U.S. R&D expenditures in constant dollars, (b) Federal support for R&D in constant dollars, (c) R&D as a percentage of U.S. GDP, and (d) Federal support of R&D as a percentage of GDP. What are the technological implications of these figures for the United States?

15. *Web-Based Question: NASA—are there commercial spin-offs?* Visit the website of NASA's Technology Transfer Office, at www.sti.nasa.gov/tto, to identify significant commercial benefits from secondary use of NASA technology. Search the database to find and describe five such spin-offs. How does the NASA Commercial Technology Network (nctn.hq.nasa.gov/) move technology from the lab to the marketplace?

Part VII | Microeconomics of Resource Markets

27 | *The Demand for Resources*

We now turn from the pricing and production of *goods and services* to the pricing and employment of *resources*. Although firms come in various sizes and operate under highly different market conditions, they each have a demand for productive resources. They obtain those resources from households—the direct or indirect owners of land, labor, capital, and entrepreneurial resources. So, referring to the circular flow model (Figure 2.6, page 34), we shift our attention from the bottom loop of the diagram (where businesses supply products that households demand) to the top loop (where businesses demand resources that households supply).

This chapter looks at the *demand* for economic resources. Although the discussion is couched in terms of labor, the principles developed also apply to land, capital, and entrepreneurial ability. In Chapter 28 we will combine resource (labor) demand with labor *supply* to analyze wage rates. Then in Chapter 29 we will use resource demand and resource supply to examine the prices of, and returns to, other productive resources.

Significance of Resource Pricing

There are several good reasons to study resource pricing:

- *Money-income determination*   Resource prices are a major factor in determining the income of households. The expenditures that firms make in acquiring economic resources flow as wage, rent, interest, and profit incomes to the households that supply those resources.

- *Resource allocation*   Just as product prices allocate finished goods and services to consumers, resource prices allocate resources among industries and firms. In a dynamic economy, where technology and product demand often change, the efficient allocation of resources over time calls for the continuing shift of resources from one use to another. Resource pricing is a major factor in producing those shifts.

- *Cost minimization*   To the firm, resource prices are costs. And to obtain the greatest profit, the firm must produce the profit-maximizing output with the most efficient (least costly) combination of resources. Resource prices play the main role in determining the quantities of land, labor, capital, and entrepreneurial ability that will be combined in producing each good or service (see Table 4.1).

- *Policy issues*   There are many policy issues surrounding the resource market. Examples: To what extent should government redistribute income through taxes and transfers? Should government do anything to discourage "excess" pay to corporate executives? Is it efficient to provide subsidies to farmers? Should it encourage or restrict labor unions? The facts and debates relating to these policy questions are grounded on resource pricing.

Marginal Productivity Theory of Resource Demand

To make things simple, let's first assume that a firm hires a certain resource in a purely competitive resource market and sells its output in a purely competitive product market. The simplicity of this situation is twofold: In a competitive product market the firm is a "price taker" and can dispose of as little or as much output as it chooses at the market price. The firm is selling such a negligible fraction of total output that its output decisions exert no influence on product price. Similarly, in the competitive resource market, the firm is a "wage taker." It hires such a negligible fraction of the total supply of the resource that its hiring decisions do not influence the resource price.

Resource Demand as a Derived Demand

The demand for resources is a **derived demand:** It is derived from the products that they help produce. Resources usually do not directly satisfy customer wants but do so indirectly through their use in producing goods and services. No one wants to consume an acre of land, a John Deere tractor, or the labor services of a farmer, but households do want to consume the food and fiber products that these resources help produce. Similarly, the demand for airplanes generates a demand for assemblers, and the demands for such services as income-tax preparation, haircuts, and child care create derived demands for accountants, barbers, and child care workers. Global Perspective 27.1 demonstrates that the global demand for labor is derived.

Marginal Revenue Product

The derived nature of resource demand means that the strength of the demand for any resource will depend on:
- The productivity of the resource in helping to create a good or service.

 GLOBAL PERSPECTIVE 27.1

Labor Demand and Allocation: Developing Countries, Industrially Advanced Countries, and the United States

The idea of derived demand implies that the composition of a country's product market demand will determine the allocation of its labor force among agricultural products, industrial goods, and services. Because lower-income nations must spend large portions of their incomes for food and fiber, the bulk of their labor is allocated to agriculture. The industrially advanced economies, with higher incomes, allocate most of their labor to industrial products and services.

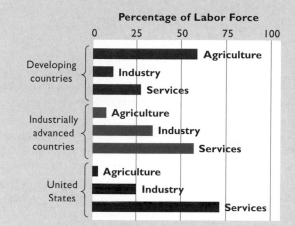

Source: International Labour Organization data, www.ilo.org/, based on latest available data.

- The market value or price of the good or service it helps produce.

A resource that is highly productive in turning out a highly valued commodity will be in great demand. On the other hand, a relatively unproductive resource that is capable of producing only a minimally valued commodity will be in little demand. And there will be no demand at all for a resource that is phenomenally efficient in producing something that no one wants to buy.

Productivity Table 27.1 shows the roles of productivity and product price in determining resource demand. Here we assume that a firm adds one variable resource, labor, to its fixed plant. Columns 1 and 2 give the number of units of the resource applied to production and the resulting total product (output). Column 3 provides the **marginal product (MP),** or additional output, resulting from using each additional unit of labor. Columns 1 through 3 remind us that the law of diminishing returns applies here, causing the marginal product of labor to fall

TABLE 27.1

The Demand for Labor: Pure Competition in the Sale of the Product

(1) Units of Resource	(2) Total Product (Output)	(3) Marginal Product (MP)	(4) Product Price	(5) Total Revenue, (2) × (4)	(6) Marginal Revenue Product (MRP)
0	0		$2	$ 0	
		7			$14
1	7		2	14	
		6			12
2	13		2	26	
		5			10
3	18		2	36	
		4			8
4	22		2	44	
		3			6
5	25		2	50	
		2			4
6	27		2	54	
		1			2
7	28		2	56	

beyond some point. For simplicity, we assume that those diminishing marginal returns—those declines in marginal product—begin with the first worker hired.

Product Price   But the derived demand for a resource depends also on the price of the commodity it produces. Column 4 in Table 27.1 adds this price information. Product price is constant, in this case at $2, because we are assuming a competitive product market. The firm is a price taker and will sell units of output only at this market price.

Multiplying column 2 by column 4 gives us the total-revenue data of column 5. These are the amounts of revenue the firm realizes from the various levels of resource usage. From these total-revenue data we can compute **marginal revenue product (MRP)**—*the change in total revenue resulting from the use of each additional unit of a resource* (labor, in this case). In equation form,

$$\frac{\text{Marginal}}{\text{revenue}} = \frac{\text{change in total revenue}}{\text{unit change in resource quantity}}$$
product

The MRPs are listed in column 6 in Table 27.1.

Rule for Employing Resources: MRP = MRC

The MRP schedule, shown as columns 1 and 6, is the firm's demand schedule for labor. To explain why, we must first discuss the rule that guides a profit-seeking firm in hiring any resource: *To maximize profit, a firm should hire additional units of a specific resource as long as each successive unit adds more to the firm's total revenue than it adds to total cost.*

Economists use special terms to designate what each additional unit of labor or other variable resource adds to

total cost and what it adds to total revenue. We have seen that MRP measures how much each successive unit of a resource adds to total revenue. The amount that each additional unit of a resource adds to the firm's total (resource) cost is called its **marginal resource cost (MRC)**.

In equation form,

$$\frac{\text{Marginal}}{\text{resource}} = \frac{\text{change in total (resource) cost}}{\text{unit change in resource quantity}}$$
cost

So we can restate our rule for hiring resources as follows: It will be profitable for a firm to hire additional units of a resource up to the point at which that resource's MRP is equal to its MRC. If the number of workers a firm is currently hiring is such that the MRP of the last worker exceeds his or her MRC, the firm can profit by hiring more workers. But if the number being hired is such that the MRC of the last worker exceeds his or her MRP, the firm is hiring workers who are not "paying their way" and it can increase its profit by discharging some workers. You may have recognized that this **MRP = MRC rule** is similar to the MR = MC profit-maximizing rule employed throughout our discussion of price and output determination. The rationale of the two rules is the same, but the point of reference is now *inputs* of a resource, not *outputs* of a product.

MRP as Resource Demand Schedule

In a purely competitive labor market, market supply and market demand establish the wage rate. Because each firm hires such a small fraction of market supply, it cannot influence the market wage rate; it is a wage taker, not a wage maker. This means that for each additional unit of labor hired, total resource cost increases by exactly the amount of the constant market wage rate. The MRC of labor exactly equals the market wage rate. Thus, resource "price" (the market wage rate) and resource "cost" (marginal resource cost) are equal for a firm that hires a resource in a competitive labor market. Then the MRP = MRC rule tells us that, in pure competition, the firm will hire workers up to the point at which the market *wage rate* (its MRC) is equal to its MRP.

In terms of the data in columns 1 and 6 in Table 27.1, if the market wage rate is, say, $13.95, the firm will hire only one worker. This is so because the first worker adds $14 to total revenue and slightly less—$13.95—to total cost. In other words, because MRP exceeds MRC for the first worker, it is profitable to hire that worker. For each successive worker, however, MRC (= $13.95) exceeds MRP (= $12 or less), indicating that it will not be profitable to hire any of those workers. If the wage rate is $11.95, by the same reasoning we discover that it will pay the firm to hire both the first and second workers. Similarly, if the wage rate is $9.95, three will be hired. If it is $7.95, four. If it is $5.95, five. And so forth. *The MRP schedule therefore constitutes the firm's demand for labor, because each point on this schedule (or curve) indicates the number of workers the firm would hire at each possible wage rate.* In Figure 27.1, we show the D = MRP curve based on the data in Table 27.1.[1]

Resource Demand under Imperfect Product Market Competition

Our analysis of labor demand becomes more complex when the firm is selling its product in an imperfectly competitive market, one in which the firm is a price maker. Pure monopoly, oligopoly, and monopolistic competition in the product market all mean that the firm's product demand curve is downsloping; the firm must set a lower price to increase its sales.

The productivity data in Table 27.1 are retained in columns 1 to 3 in Table 27.2. But here we show in column 4 that product price must be lowered to sell the marginal product of each successive worker. The MRP of the purely competitive seller of Table 27.1 falls for a single reason: Marginal product diminishes. But the MRP of the imperfectly competitive seller of Table 27.2 falls for two

---

[1]Note that we plot the points in Figure 27.1 halfway between succeeding numbers of resource units, because MRP is associated with the addition of 1 more unit. Thus, in Figure 27.1, for example, we plot the MRP of the second unit ($12) not at 1 or 2 but at $1\frac{1}{2}$. This "smoothing" enables us to sketch a continuously downsloping curve rather than one that moves downward in discrete steps as each new unit of labor is hired.

FIGURE 27.1

The purely competitive seller's demand for a resource. The MRP curve is the resource demand curve; each of its points relates a particular resource price (= MRP when profit is maximized) with a corresponding quantity of the resource demanded. Under pure competition, product price is constant; therefore, the downward slope of the D = MRP curve is due solely to the decline in the resource's marginal product (law of diminishing marginal returns).

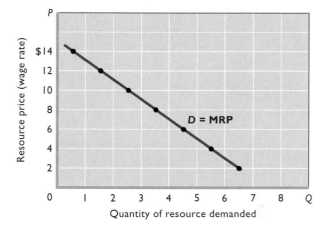

reasons: Marginal product diminishes *and* product price falls as output increases.

We emphasize that the lower price accompanying each increase in output (total product) applies not only to the marginal product of each successive worker but also *to all prior output units that otherwise could have been sold at a higher price.* Observe that the marginal product of the second worker is 6 units of output. These 6 units can be sold for $2.40 each, or, as a group, for $14.40. But this is not the MRP of the second worker. To sell these 6 units, the firm must take a 20-cent price cut on the 7 units produced by the first worker—units that otherwise could have been sold for $2.60 each. Thus, the MRP of the second worker is only $13 [= $14.40 − (7 × 20 cents)], as shown.

Similarly, the third worker adds 5 units to total product, and these units are worth $2.20 each, or $11 total. But to sell these 5 units, the firm must take a 20-cent price cut on the 13 units produced by the first two workers. So the third worker's MRP is only $8.40 [= $11 − (13 × 20 cents)]. The other figures in column 6 are derived similarly.

In Figure 27.2 we graph the MRP data from Table 27.2 and label it "D = MRP (imperfect competition)." The broken-line resource demand curve, in contrast, is that of the purely competitive seller represented in Figure 27.1. A comparison of the two curves demonstrates that, other things equal, the resource demand curve of an imperfectly competitive seller is less elastic than that of a

TABLE 27.2

The Demand for Labor: Imperfect Competition in the Sale of the Product

(1) Units of Resource	(2) Total Product (Output)	(3) Marginal Product (MP)	(4) Product Price	(5) Total Revenue, (2) × (4)	(6) Marginal Revenue Product (MRP)
0	0		$2.80	$ 0	
		7			$18.20
1	7		2.60	18.20	
		6			13.00
2	13		2.40	31.20	
		5			8.40
3	18		2.20	39.60	
		4			4.40
4	22		2.00	44.00	
		3			2.25
5	25		1.85	46.25	
		2			1.00
6	27		1.75	47.25	
		1			−1.05
7	28		1.65	46.20	

purely competitive seller. Consider the effects of an identical percentage decline in the wage rate (resource price) from $11 to $6 in Figure 27.2. Comparison of the two curves reveals that the imperfectly competitive seller (solid curve) does not expand the quantity of labor by as large a percentage as does the purely competitive seller (broken curve).

It is not surprising that the imperfectly competitive producer is less responsive to resource price cuts than the purely competitive producer. The imperfect competitor's relative reluctance to employ more resources, and produce more output, when resource prices fall reflects the imperfect competitor's tendency to restrict output in the product market. Other things equal, the imperfectly competitive seller produces less of a product than a purely competitive seller. In producing that smaller output, it demands fewer resources. **(Key Question 2)**

Market Demand for a Resource

We have now explained the individual firm's demand curve for a resource. Recall that the total, or market, demand curve for a *product* is found by summing horizontally the demand curves of all individual buyers in the market. The market demand curve for a particular *resource* is derived in essentially the same way—by summing the individual demand or MRP curves for all firms hiring that resource.

FIGURE 27.2

The imperfectly competitive seller's demand curve for a resource. An imperfectly competitive seller's resource demand curve *D* (solid) slopes downward because both marginal product and product price fall as resource employment and output rise. This downward slope is greater than that for a purely competitive seller (dashed resource demand curve) because the pure competitor can sell the added output at a constant price.

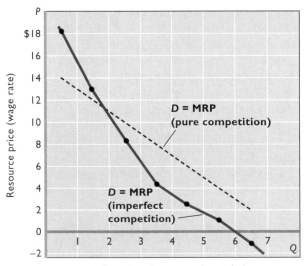

Quantity of resource demanded

QUICK REVIEW 27.1

- To maximize profit, a firm will use a resource in an amount at which the resource's marginal revenue product equals its marginal resource cost (MRP = MRC).

- Application of the MRP = MRC rule to a firm's MRP curve demonstrates that the MRP curve is the firm's resource demand curve. In a purely competitive resource market, resource price (the wage rate) equals MRC.

- The resource demand curve of a purely competitive seller is downsloping solely because the marginal product of the resource diminishes; the resource demand curve of an imperfectly competitive seller is downsloping because marginal product diminishes and product price falls as output is increased.

© Adriane Jaeckle/
Getty Images

She's The One

In what economist Robert Frank calls "winner-take-all-markets," a few highly talented performers have huge earnings relative to the average performers in the market. Because consumers and firms seek out "top" performers, small differences in talent or popularity get magnified into huge differences in pay.

In these markets, consumer spending gets channeled toward a few performers. The media then "hypes" these individuals, which further increases the public's awareness of their talents. Many more consumers then buy the stars' products. Although it is not easy to stay on top, several superstars emerge.

The high earnings of superstars results from the high revenues they generate from their work. Consider Shania Twain. If she sold only a few thousand CDs and attracted only a few hundred fans to each concert, the revenue she would produce—her marginal revenue product—would be quite modest. So, too, would be her earnings.

But consumers have anointed Shania as queen of country/pop. For the moment, "she's the one" and thus the demand for her CDs and concerts is extraordinarily high. She sells *millions* of CDs (nearly 50 million thus far), not thousands, and draws *thousands* to her concerts, not hundreds. Her extraordinarily high net earnings derive from her extraordinarily high MRP.

So it is for the other superstars in the "winner-take-all markets." Influenced by the media, but coerced by no one, consumers direct their spending toward a select few. The resulting strong demand for these stars' services reflects their high MRP. And because top talent (by definition) is very limited, superstars receive amazingly high earnings.

Determinants of Resource Demand

What will alter the demand for a resource—that is, shift the resource demand curve? The fact that resource demand is derived from *product demand* and depends on *resource productivity* suggests two "resource demand shifters." Also, our analysis of how changes in the prices of other products can shift a product's demand curve (Chapter 3) suggests another factor: changes in the prices of other *resources*.

Changes in Product Demand

Other things equal, *an increase in the demand for a product will increase the demand for a resource used in its production, whereas a decrease in product demand will decrease the resource demand.*

Let's see how this works. The first thing to recall is that a change in the demand for a product will change its price. In Table 27.1, let's assume that an increase in product demand boosts product price from $2 to $3. You should calculate the new resource demand schedule (columns 1 and 6) that would result, and plot it in Figure 27.1 to verify that the new resource demand curve lies to the right of the old demand curve. Similarly, a decline in the product demand (and price) will shift the resource demand curve to the left. This effect—resource demand changing along with product demand—demonstrates that resource demand is derived from product demand.

Example: Assuming no offsetting change in supply, an increase in the demand for new houses will drive up house prices. Those higher prices will increase the MRP of construction workers, and therefore the demand for construction workers will rise. The resource demand curve such as in Figure 27.1 or Figure 27.2 will shift to the right.

Changes in Productivity

Other things equal, *an increase in the productivity of a resource will increase the demand for the resource and a decrease in productivity will reduce the resource demand.* If we doubled the MP data of column 3 in Table 27.1, the MRP data of column 6 would also double, indicating a rightward shift of the resource demand curve.

The productivity of any resource may be altered in several ways:

- **Quantities of other resources** The marginal productivity of any resource will vary with the quantities of the other resources used with it. The greater the amount of capital and land resources used with, say, labor, the greater will be labor's marginal productivity and, thus, labor demand.

- **Technological advance** Technological improvements that increase the quality of other resources, such as capital, have the same effect. The better the *quality* of capital, the greater the productivity of labor used with it. Dockworkers employed with a specific amount of real capital in the form of unloading cranes are more productive than dockworkers with the same amount of real capital embodied in older conveyor-belt systems.

- **Quality of the variable resource** Improvements in the quality of the variable resource, such as labor, will increase its marginal productivity and therefore its demand. In effect, there will be a new demand curve for a different, more skilled, kind of labor.

All these considerations help explain why the average level of (real) wages is higher in industrially advanced nations (for example, the United States, Germany, Japan, and France) than in developing nations (for example, India, Ethiopia, Angola, and Cambodia). Workers in industrially advanced nations are generally healthier, better educated, and better trained than are workers in developing countries. Also, in most industries they work with a larger and more efficient stock of capital goods and more abundant natural resources. This creates a strong demand for labor. On the supply side of the market, labor is *relatively* scarce compared with that in most developing nations. A strong demand and a relatively scarce supply of labor result in high wage rates in the industrially advanced nations.

Changes in the Prices of Other Resources

Changes in the prices of other resources may change the demand for a specific resource. For example, a change in the price of capital may change the demand for labor. The direction of the change in labor demand will depend on whether labor and capital are substitutes or complements in production.

Substitute Resources   Suppose the technology in a certain production process is such that labor and capital are substitutable. A firm can produce some specific amount of output using a relatively small amount of labor and a relatively large amount of capital, or vice versa. Now assume that the price of machinery (capital) falls. The effect on the demand for labor will be the net result of two opposed effects: the substitution effect and the output effect.

- *Substitution effect*   The decline in the price of machinery prompts the firm to substitute machinery for labor. This allows the firm to produce its output at lower cost. So at the fixed wage rate, smaller quantities of labor are now employed. This **substitution effect** decreases the demand for labor. More generally, the substitution effect indicates that a firm will purchase more of an input whose relative price has declined and, conversely, use less of an input whose relative price has increased.

- *Output effect*   Because the price of machinery has fallen, the costs of producing various outputs must also decline. With lower costs, the firm finds it profitable to produce and sell a greater output. The greater output increases the demand for all resources, including labor. So this **output effect** increases the demand for labor. More generally, the output effect means that the firm will purchase more of one particular input when the price of the other input falls and less of that particular input when the price of the other input rises.

- *Net effect*   The substitution and output effects are both present when the price of an input changes, but they work in opposite directions. For a decline in the price of capital, the substitution effect decreases the demand for labor and the output effect increases it. The net change in labor demand depends on the relative sizes of the two effects: *If the substitution effect outweighs the output effect, a decrease in the price of capital decreases the demand for labor. If the output effect exceeds the substitution effect, a decrease in the price of capital increases the demand for labor.*

Complementary Resources   Recall from Chapter 3 that certain products, such as computers and software, are complementary goods; they "go together" and are jointly demanded. Resources may also be complementary; an increase in the quantity of one of them used in the production process requires an increase in the amount used of the other as well, and vice versa. Suppose a small design firm does computer-assisted design (CAD) with relatively expensive personal computers as its basic piece of capital equipment. Each computer requires a single design engineer to operate it; the machine is not automated—it will not run itself—and a second engineer would have nothing to do.

Now assume that a technological advance in the production of these computers substantially reduces their price. There can be no substitution effect, because labor and capital must be used in *fixed proportions*, one person for one machine. Capital cannot be substituted for labor. But there *is* an output effect. Other things equal, the reduction in the price of capital goods means lower production costs. It will therefore be profitable to produce a larger output. In doing so, the firm will use both more capital and more labor. *When labor and capital are complementary, a decline in the price of capital increases the demand for labor through the output effect.*

We have cast our analysis of substitute resources and complementary resources mainly in terms of a decline in the price of capital. Table 27.3 summarizes the effects of an *increase* in the price of capital on the demand for labor. Please study it carefully.

Now that we have discussed the full list of the determinants of labor demand, let's again review their effects. Stated in terms of the labor resource, the demand for labor will increase (the labor demand curve will shift rightward) when:

- The demand for (and therefore the price of) the product produced by that labor *increases*.
- The productivity (MP) of labor *increases*.
- The price of a substitute input *decreases*, provided the output effect exceeds the substitution effect.

TABLE 27.3

The Effect of an Increase in the Price of Capital on the Demand for Labor, D_L

(1) Relationship of Inputs	(2) Increase in the Price of Capital		
	(a) Substitution Effect	(b) Output Effect	(c) Combined Effect
Substitutes in production	Labor substituted for capital	Production costs up, output down, and less of both capital and labor used	D_L increases if the substitution effect exceeds the output effect; D_L decreases if the output effect exceeds the substitution effect
Complements in production	No substitution of labor for capital	Production costs up, output down, and less of both capital and labor used	D_L decreases

- The price of a substitute input *increases*, provided the substitution effect exceeds the output effect.
- The price of a complementary input *decreases*.

Be sure that you can "reverse" these effects to explain a *decrease* in labor demand.

Table 27.4 provides several illustrations of the determinants of labor demand, listed by the categories of determinants we have discussed. You will benefit by giving them a close look.

Occupational Employment Trends

Changes in labor demand have considerable significance since they affect wage rates and employment in specific occupations. Increases in labor demand for certain occupational groups result in increases in their employment, and decreases in labor demand result in decreases in their employment. For illustration, let's look at occupations that are growing and declining in demand. (Wage rates are the subject of the next chapter.)

The Fastest-Growing Occupations
Table 27.5 lists the 10 fastest-growing U.S. occupations for 2000 to 2010, as measured by percentage changes and projected by the Bureau of Labor Statistics. It is no coincidence that the service occupations dominate the list. In general, the demand for service workers is rapidly outpacing the demand for manufacturing, construction, and mining workers.

TABLE 27.4

Determinants of Labor Demand: Factors That Shift the Labor Demand Curve

Determinant	Examples
Change in product demand	Gambling increases in popularity, increasing the demand for workers at casinos.
	Consumers decrease their demand for leather coats, decreasing the demand for tanners.
	The Federal government increases spending on homeland security, increasing the demand for military personnel.
Change in productivity	An increase in the skill levels of physicians increases the demand for their services.
	Computer-assisted graphic design increases the productivity of, and demand for, graphic artists.
Change in the price of another resource	An increase in the price of electricity increases the cost of producing aluminum and reduces the demand for aluminum workers.
	The price of security equipment used by businesses to protect against illegal entry falls, decreasing the demand for night guards.
	The price of cell phone equipment decreases, reducing the cost of cell phone service; this in turn increases the demand for cell phone assemblers.
	Health-insurance premiums rise, and firms substitute part-time workers who are not covered by insurance for full-time workers who are.

TABLE 27.5

The 10 Fastest-Growing U.S. Occupations in Percentage Terms, 2000–2010

Occupation	Employment, Thousands of Jobs		Percentage Increase
	2000	2010	
Computer software engineers, applications	380	760	100%
Computer support specialists	506	996	97
Computer software engineers, systems	317	601	90
Computer systems administrators	229	416	82
Data communications analysts	119	211	77
Desktop publishers	38	63	66
Database administrators	106	176	66
Personal and home care aides	414	672	62
Computer system analysts	431	689	60
Medical assistants	329	516	57

Source: Bureau of Labor Statistics, "Employment Projections," www.bls.gov.

Of the 10 fastest-growing occupations in percentage terms, the top 7 are directly related to computers. The increase in the demand for computer software engineers, computer support specialists, systems and database administrators, data communication analysts, and desktop publishing specialists relates to the rapid rise in the demand for computers, computer services, and the Internet. It also relates to the rising productivity of these particular workers, given the vastly improved quality of the computer and communications equipment they work with. Moreover, price declines on such equipment have had stronger output effects than substitution effects, increasing the demand for these kinds of labor.

Two of the other fastest-growing occupations relate to health care: personal and home care aides and medical assistants. The growing demands for these types of labor are derived from the growing demand for health services, caused by several factors. The aging of the U.S. population has brought with it more medical problems, the rising standard of income has led to greater expenditures on health care, and the growing presence of private and public insurance has allowed people to buy more health care than most could afford individually.

The Most Rapidly Declining Occupations

Table 27.6 lists the 10 U.S. occupations with the greatest projected job loss in percentage terms between 2000 and 2010. These occupations are more diverse than the fastest-growing occupations, although 4 of the 10 relate to railroads and agriculture. Some of the declines in occupations (for example, shoe machine operators, radio mechanics, and rail track layers) reflect falling domestic

product demand. Several others (for example, loan interviewers, meter readers, telephone operators, and motion picture projectionists) reflect technological advances that have reduced the price of capital relative to labor. Employers have found it economical to replace workers with automated or computerized equipment that appraises creditworthiness, reads meters, handles long-distance calls, projects movies, and so on. In these particular cases, the drop in the price of capital has had a modest output effect relative to its substitution effect, so the demands for these types of labor have declined.

TABLE 27.6

The 10 Most Rapidly Declining U.S. Occupations in Percentage Terms, 2000–2010

Occupation	Employment, Thousands of Jobs		Percentage Decrease
	2000	2010	
Railroad brake, signal, and switch operators	22	9	−59%
Shoe machine operators	9	4	−56
Telephone operators	54	35	−35
Radio mechanics	7	5	−29
Loan interviewers	139	101	−27
Motion picture projectionists	11	8	−27
Meter readers	49	36	−27
Rail track layers	12	9	−25
Farmers and ranchers	1294	965	−25
Shoe and leather workers	19	15	−21

Source: Bureau of Labor Statistics, "Employment Projections," www.bls.gov.

Elasticity of Resource Demand

The employment changes we have just discussed have resulted from shifts in the locations of resource demand curves. Such changes in demand must be distinguished from changes in the quantity of a resource demanded caused by a change in the price of the specific resource under consideration. Such a change is caused not by a shift of the demand curve but, rather, by a movement from one point to another on a fixed resource demand curve. Example: In Figure 27.1 we note that an increase in the wage rate from $5 to $7 will reduce the quantity of labor demanded from 5 to 4 units. This is a change in the *quantity of labor demanded* as distinct from a *change in demand*.

The sensitivity of producers to changes in resource prices is measured by the **elasticity of resource demand.** In coefficient form,

$$E_{rd} = \frac{\text{percentage change in resource quantity}}{\text{percentage change in resource price}}$$

27.1
Elasticity of resource demand

When E_{rd} is greater than 1, resource demand is elastic; when E_{rd} is less than 1, resource demand is inelastic; and when E_{rd} equals 1, resource demand is unit-elastic. What determines the elasticity of resource demand? Several factors are at work.

Ease of Resource Substitutability
The degree to which resources are substitutable is a fundamental determinant of elasticity. *The larger the number of satisfactory substitute resources available, the greater the elasticity of demand for a particular resource.* If a furniture manufacturer finds that five or six different types of wood are equally satisfactory in making coffee tables, a rise in the price of any one type of wood may cause a sharp drop in the amount demanded as the producer substitutes one of the other woods. At the other extreme, there may be no reasonable substitutes; bauxite is absolutely essential in the production of aluminum ingots. Thus, the demand for bauxite by aluminum producers is inelastic.

Time can play a role in the input substitution process. For example, a firm's truck drivers may obtain a substantial wage increase with little or no immediate decline in employment. But over time, as the firm's trucks wear out and are replaced, that wage increase may motivate the company to purchase larger trucks and in that way deliver the same total output with fewer drivers.

Elasticity of Product Demand
The elasticity of demand for any resource depends on the elasticity of

demand for the product it helps produce. *The greater the elasticity of product demand, the greater the elasticity of resource demand.* The derived nature of resource demand leads us to expect this relationship. A small rise in the price of a product with great elasticity of demand will sharply reduce output, bringing about a relatively large decline in the amounts of various resources demanded. This means that the demand for the resource is elastic.

Remember that the resource demand curve in Figure 27.1 is more elastic than the resource demand curve shown in Figure 27.2. The difference arises because in Figure 27.1 we assume a perfectly elastic product demand curve, while Figure 27.2 is based on a downsloping or less than perfectly elastic product demand curve.

Ratio of Resource Cost to Total Cost
The larger the proportion of total production costs accounted for by a resource, the greater the elasticity of demand for that resource. In the extreme, if labor cost is the only production cost, then a 20 percent increase in wage rates will shift all the firm's cost curves upward by 20 percent. If product demand is elastic, this substantial increase in costs will cause a relatively large decline in sales and a sharp decline in the amount of labor demanded. So labor demand is highly elastic. But if labor cost is only 50 percent of production cost, then a 20 percent increase in wage rates will increase costs by only 10 percent. With the same elasticity of product demand, this will cause a relatively small decline in sales and therefore in the amount of labor demanded. In this case the demand for labor is much less elastic. **(Key Question 5)**

QUICK REVIEW 27.2

- A resource demand curve will shift because of changes in product demand, changes in the productivity of the resource, and changes in the prices of other inputs.
- If resources A and B are substitutable, a decline in the price of A will decrease the demand for B provided the substitution effect exceeds the output effect. But if the output effect exceeds the substitution effect, the demand for B will increase.
- If resources C and D are complements, a decline in the price of C will increase the demand for D.
- Elasticity of resource demand measures the extent to which producers change the quantity of a resource they hire when its price changes.
- The elasticity of resource demand will be less the more rapid the decline in marginal product, the smaller the number of substitutes, the smaller the elasticity of product demand, and the smaller the proportion of total cost accounted for by the resource.

Optimal Combination of Resources

So far, our main focus has been on one variable input, labor. But in the long run firms can vary the amounts of all the resources they use. That's why we need to consider what combination of resources a firm will choose when *all* its inputs are variable. While our analysis is based on two resources, it can be extended to any number of inputs.

We will consider two interrelated questions:
- What combination of resources will minimize costs at a specific level of output?
- What combination of resources will maximize profit?

The Least-Cost Rule

A firm is producing a specific output with the **least-cost combination of resources** *when the last dollar spent on each resource yields the same marginal product.* That is, the cost of any output is minimized when the ratios of marginal product to price of the last units of resources used are the same for each resource. In competitive resource markets, recall, marginal resource cost is the market resource price; the firm can hire as many or as few units of the resource as it wants at that price. Then, with just two resources, labor and capital, a competitive firm minimizes its total cost of a specific output when

$$\frac{\text{Marginal product of labor (MP}_L)}{\text{Price of labor (}P_L)} = \frac{\text{Marginal product of capital (MP}_C)}{\text{Price of capital (}P_C)} \quad (1)$$

Throughout, we will refer to the marginal products of labor and capital as MP_L and MP_C, respectively, and symbolize the price of labor by P_L and the price of capital by P_C.

A concrete example will show why fulfilling the condition in equation 1 leads to least-cost production. Assume that the price of both capital and labor is $1 per unit but that Siam Soups currently employs them in such amounts that the marginal product of labor is 10 and the marginal product of capital is 5. Our equation immediately tells us that this is not the least costly combination of resources:

$$\frac{MP_L = 10}{P_L = \$1} > \frac{MP_C = 5}{P_C = \$1}$$

Suppose Siam spends $1 less on capital and shifts that dollar to labor. It loses 5 units of output produced by the last dollar's worth of capital, but it gains 10 units of output from the extra dollar's worth of labor. Net output increases by 5 (= 10 − 5) units for the same total cost. More such shifting of dollars from capital to labor will

push the firm *down* along its MP curve for labor and *up* along its MP curve for capital, increasing output and moving the firm toward a position of equilibrium where equation 1 is fulfilled. At that equilibrium position, the MP per dollar for the last unit of both labor and capital might be, for example, 7. And Siam will be producing a greater output for the same (original) cost.

Whenever the same total-resource cost can result in a greater total output, the cost per unit—and therefore the total cost of any specific level of output—can be reduced. Being able to produce a *larger* output with a *specific* total cost is the same as being able to produce a *specific* output with a *smaller* total cost. If Siam buys $1 less of capital, its output will fall by 5 units. If it spends only $.50 of that dollar on labor, the firm will increase its output by a compensating 5 units (= $\frac{1}{2}$ of the MP per dollar). Then the firm will realize the same total output at a $.50 lower total cost.

The cost of producing any specific output can be reduced as long as equation 1 does not hold. But when dollars have been shifted between capital and labor to the point where equation 1 holds, no additional changes in the use of capital and labor will reduce costs further. Siam is now producing that output using the least-cost combination of capital and labor.

All the long-run cost curves developed in Chapter 22 and used thereafter assume that the least-cost combination of inputs has been realized at each level of output. Any firm that combines resources in violation of the least-cost rule would have a higher-than-necessary average total cost at each level of output. That is, it would incur *X-inefficiency*, as discussed in Figure 24.7.

The producer's least-cost rule is analogous to the consumer's utility-maximizing rule described in Chapter 21. In achieving the utility-maximizing combination of goods, the consumer considers both his or her preferences as reflected in diminishing-marginal-utility data and the prices of the various products. Similarly, in achieving the cost-minimizing combination of resources, the producer considers both the marginal-product data and the price (costs) of the various resources.

The Profit-Maximizing Rule

Minimizing cost is not sufficient for maximizing profit. A firm can produce any level of output in the least costly way by applying equation 1. But there is only one unique level of output that maximizes profit. Our earlier analysis of product markets showed that this profit-maximizing output occurs where marginal revenue equals marginal cost (MR = MC). Near the beginning of this chapter we determined that we could write this profit-maximizing condition as MRP = MRC as it relates to resource inputs.

In a purely competitive resource market the marginal resource cost (MRC) is equal to the resource price P. Thus, for any competitive resource market, we have as our profit-maximizing equation

$$\text{MRP (resource)} = P \text{ (resource)}$$

This condition must hold for every variable resource, and in the long run all resources are variable. In competitive markets, a firm will therefore achieve its **profit-maximizing combination of resources** when each resource is employed to the point at which its marginal revenue product equals its resource price. For two resources, labor and capital, we need both

$$P_L = \text{MRP}_L \quad \text{and} \quad P_C = \text{MRP}_C$$

We can combine these conditions by dividing both sides of each equation by their respective prices and equating the results to get

$$\frac{\text{MRP}_L}{P_L} = \frac{\text{MRP}_C}{P_C} = 1 \qquad (2)$$

Note in equation 2 that it is not sufficient that the MRPs of the two resources be *proportionate* to their prices; the MRPs must be *equal* to their prices and the ratios therefore equal to 1. For example, if $\text{MRP}_L = \$15$, $P_L = \$5$, $\text{MRP}_C = \$9$, and $P_C = \$3$, Siam is underemploying both capital and labor even though the ratios of MRP to resource price are identical for both resources. The firm can expand its profit by hiring additional amounts of both capital and labor until it moves down their downsloping MRP curves to the points at which $\text{MRP}_L = \$5$ and $\text{MRP}_C = \$3$. The ratios will then be 5/5 and 3/3 and equal to 1.

The profit-maximizing position in equation 2 includes the cost-minimizing condition of equation 1. That is, if a firm is maximizing profit according to equation 2, then it must be using the least-cost combination of inputs to do so. However, the converse is not true: A firm operating at least cost according to equation 1 may not be operating at the output that maximizes its profit.

Numerical Illustration

A numerical illustration will help you understand the least-cost and profit-maximizing rules. In columns 2, 3, 2′, and 3′ in Table 27.7 we show the total products and marginal products for various amounts of labor and capital that are assumed to be the only inputs Siam needs in producing its soup. Both inputs are subject to diminishing returns.

We also assume that labor and capital are supplied in competitive resource markets at $8 and $12, respectively, and that Siam soup sells competitively at $2 per unit. For both labor and capital we can determine the total revenue associated with each input level by multiplying total product by the $2 product price. These data are shown in columns 4 and 4′. They enable us to calculate the marginal revenue product of each successive input of labor and capital as shown in columns 5 and 5′, respectively.

Producing at Least Cost What is the least-cost combination of labor and capital for Siam to use in

TABLE 27.7

Data for Finding the Least-Cost and Profit-Maximizing Combination of Labor and Capital, Siam Soups*

	Labor (Price = $8)					Capital (Price = $12)			
(1) Quantity	(2) Total Product (Output)	(3) Marginal Product	(4) Total Revenue	(5) Marginal Revenue Product	(1′) Quantity	(2′) Total Product (Output)	(3′) Marginal Product	(4′) Total Revenue	(5′) Marginal Revenue Product
0	0		$ 0		0	0		$ 0	
		12		$24			13		$26
1	12		24		1	13		26	
		10		20			9		18
2	22		44		2	22		44	
		6		12			6		12
3	28		56		3	28		56	
		5		10			4		8
4	33		66		4	32		64	
		4		8			3		6
5	37		74		5	35		70	
		3		6			2		4
6	40		80		6	37		74	
		2		4			1		2
7	42		84		7	38		76	

*To simplify, it is assumed in this table that the productivity of each resource is independent of the quantity of the other. For example, the total and marginal products of labor are assumed not to vary with the quantity of capital employed.

producing, say, 50 units of output? The answer, which we can obtain by trial and error, is 3 units of labor and 2 units of capital. Columns 2 and 2′ indicate that this combination of labor and capital does, indeed, result in the required 50 (= 28 + 22) units of output. Now, note from columns 3 and 3′ that hiring 3 units of labor gives us $MP_L/P_L = \frac{6}{8} = \frac{3}{4}$ and hiring 2 units of capital gives us $MP_C/P_C = \frac{9}{12} = \frac{3}{4}$. So equation (1) is fulfilled. How can we verify that costs are actually minimized? First, we see that the total cost of employing 3 units of labor and 2 of capital is $48 [= (3 × $8) + (2 × $12)].

Other combinations of labor and capital will also yield 50 units of output, but at a higher cost than $48. For example, 5 units of labor and 1 unit of capital will produce 50 (= 37 + 13) units, but total cost is higher, at $52 [= (5 × $8) + (1 × $12)]. This comes as no surprise, because 5 units of labor and 1 unit of capital violate the least-cost rule—$MP_L/P_L = \frac{4}{8}$, $MP_C/P_C = \frac{13}{12}$. Only the combination (3 units of labor and 2 units of capital) that minimizes total cost will satisfy equation 1. All other combinations capable of producing 50 units of output violate the cost-minimizing rule, and therefore cost more than $48.

Maximizing Profit

Will 50 units of output maximize Siam's profit? No, because the profit-maximizing terms of equation 2 are not satisfied when the firm employs 3 units of labor and 2 of capital. To maximize profit, each input should be employed until its price equals its marginal revenue product. But for 3 units of labor, labor's MRP in column 5 is $12 while its price is only $8. This means the firm could increase its profit by hiring more labor. Similarly, for 2 units of capital, we see in column 5′ that capital's MRP is $18 and its price is only $12. This indicates that more capital should also be employed. By producing only 50 units of output (even though they are produced at least cost), labor and capital are being used in less-than-profit-maximizing amounts. The firm needs to expand its employment of labor and capital, thereby increasing its output.

Table 27.7 shows that the MRPs of labor and capital are equal to their prices, so equation 2 is fulfilled, when Siam is employing 5 units of labor and 3 units of capital. So this is the profit-maximizing combination of inputs.[2] The firm's total cost will be $76, made up of $40 (= 5 × $8) of labor and $36 (= 3 × $12) of capital. Total revenue

will be $130, found either by multiplying the total output of 65 (= 37 + 28) by the $2 product price or by summing the total revenues attributable to labor ($74) and to capital ($56). The difference between total revenue and total cost in this instance is $54 (= $130 − $76). Experiment with other combinations of labor and capital to demonstrate that they yield an economic profit of less than $54.

Note that the profit-maximizing combination of 5 units of labor and 3 units of capital is also a least-cost combination for this particular level of output. Using these resource amounts satisfies the least-cost requirement of equation 1 in that $MP_L/P_L = \frac{4}{8} = \frac{1}{2}$ and $MP_C/P_C = \frac{6}{12} = \frac{1}{2}$. **(Key Questions 6 and 7)**

Marginal Productivity Theory of Income Distribution

Our discussion of resource pricing is the cornerstone of the controversial view that fairness and economic justice are one of the outcomes of a competitive capitalist economy. Table 27.7 tells us, in effect, that workers receive income payments (wages) equal to the marginal contributions they make to their employers' outputs and revenues. In other words, workers are paid according to the value of the labor services that they contribute to production. Similarly, owners of the other resources receive income based on the value of the resources they supply in the production process.

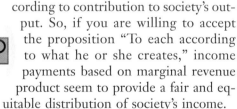

27.2
Marginal productivity theory of distribution

In this **marginal productivity theory of income distribution,** income gets distributed according to contribution to society's output. So, if you are willing to accept the proposition "To each according to what he or she creates," income payments based on marginal revenue product seem to provide a fair and equitable distribution of society's income.

This sounds fair enough, but there are serious criticisms of this theory of income distribution:

- *Inequality* Critics argue that the distribution of income resulting from payment according to marginal productivity may be highly unequal because productive resources are very unequally distributed in the first place. Aside from their differences in mental and physical attributes, individuals encounter substantially different opportunities to enhance their productivity through education and training and the use of more and better equipment. Some people may not be able to participate in production at all because of mental or physical disabilities, and they would obtain no income under a system of distribution based solely on

---

[2]Because we are dealing with discrete (nonfractional) units of the two outputs here, the use of 4 units of labor and 2 units of capital is equally profitable. The fifth unit of labor's MRP and its price (cost) are equal at $8, so that the fifth labor unit neither adds to nor subtracts from the firm's profit; similarly, the third unit of capital has no effect on profit.

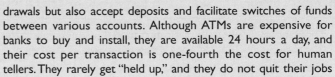

Banks Are Using More Automatic Teller Machines (ATMs) and Employing Fewer Human Tellers.

As you have learned from this chapter, a firm achieves its least-cost combination of inputs when the last dollar it spends on each input makes the same contribution to total output. This raises an interesting real-world question: What happens when technological advance makes available a new, highly productive capital good for which MP/P is greater than it is for other inputs, say, a particular type of labor? The answer is that the least-cost mix of resources abruptly changes, and the firm responds accordingly. If the new capital is a substitute for labor (rather than a complement), the firm replaces the particular type of labor with the new capital.

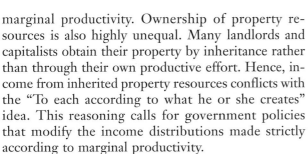

That is exactly what is happening in the banking industry, in which ATMs are replacing human bank tellers.

ATMs made their debut about 30 years ago when Diebold, a U.S. firm, introduced the product. Today, Diebold and NCR (also a U.S. firm) dominate global sales, with the Japanese firm Fujitsu being a distant third. The number of ATMs and their usage has exploded, and currently there are 325,000 ATMs in the United States. In 1975, about 10 *million* ATM transactions occurred in the United States. In contrast, in 2002 there were 14 *billion* U.S. ATM transactions. There are now an estimated 1.14 million ATMs worldwide.

ATMs are highly productive: A single machine can handle hundreds of transactions daily, thousands weekly, and millions over the course of several years. ATMs can not only handle cash with-

drawals but also accept deposits and facilitate switches of funds between various accounts. Although ATMs are expensive for banks to buy and install, they are available 24 hours a day, and their cost per transaction is one-fourth the cost for human tellers. They rarely get "held up," and they do not quit their jobs (turnover among human tellers is nearly 50 percent per year). Moreover, ATMs are highly convenient; unlike human tellers, they are located not only at banks but also at busy street corners, workplaces, universities, and shopping malls. The same bank card that enables you to withdraw cash from your local ATM also enables you to withdraw pounds from an ATM in London, yen from an ATM in Tokyo, and even rubles from an ATM in Moscow. (All this, of course, assumes that you have money in your checking account.)

In the terminology of this chapter, the more productive, lower-priced ATMs have reduced the demand for a substitute in production—human tellers. Between 1990 and 2000, an estimated 80,000 human teller positions were eliminated, and more positions will disappear in the coming years. Where will the people holding these jobs go? Most will eventually move to other occupations. Although the lives of individual tellers are disrupted, society clearly wins. Society obtains more convenient banking services as well as the other goods that these "freed-up" labor resources help produce.

Source: Based partly on Ben Craig, "Where Have All the Tellers Gone?" Federal Reserve Bank of Cleveland, *Economic Commentary*, Apr. 15, 1997; and statistics provided by the American Bankers Association.

---

marginal productivity. Ownership of property resources is also highly unequal. Many landlords and capitalists obtain their property by inheritance rather than through their own productive effort. Hence, income from inherited property resources conflicts with the "To each according to what he or she creates" idea. This reasoning calls for government policies that modify the income distributions made strictly according to marginal productivity.

- *Market imperfections* The marginal productivity theory rests on the assumptions of competitive markets. Yet labor markets, for example, are riddled with imperfections, as you will see in Chapter 28. Some

employers exert pricing power in hiring workers. And some workers, through labor unions, professional associations, and occupational licensing laws, wield monopoly power in selling their services. Even the process of collective bargaining over wages suggests a power struggle over the division of income. In this struggle, market forces—and income shares based on marginal productivity—may get pushed into the background. In addition, discrimination in the labor market can distort earnings patterns. In short, because of real-world market imperfections, wage rates and other resource prices frequently are not based solely on contributions to output.

517

SUMMARY

1. Resource prices help determine money incomes, and they simultaneously ration resources to various industries and firms.

2. The demand for any resource is derived from the product it helps produce. That means the demand for a resource will depend on its productivity and on the market value (price) of the good it is producing.

3. Marginal revenue product is the extra revenue a firm obtains when it employs 1 more unit of a resource. The marginal revenue product curve for any resource is the demand curve for that resource, because the firm equates resource price and MRP in determining its profit-maximizing level of resource employment. Thus each point on the MRP curve indicates how many resource units the firm will hire at a specific resource price.

4. The firm's demand curve for a resource slopes downward, because the marginal product of additional units declines in accordance with the law of diminishing returns. When a firm is selling in an imperfectly competitive market, the resource demand curve falls for a second reason: Product price must be reduced for the firm to sell a larger output. The market demand curve for a resource is derived by summing horizontally the demand curves of all the firms hiring that resource.

5. The demand curve for a resource will shift as the result of (a) a change in the demand for, and therefore the price of, the product the resource is producing; (b) changes in the productivity of the resource; and (c) changes in the prices of other resources.

6. If resources A and B are substitutable for each other, a decline in the price of A will decrease the demand for B provided the substitution effect is greater than the output effect. But if the output effect *exceeds* the substitution effect, a decline in the price of A will increase the demand for B.

7. If resources C and D are complementary or jointly demanded, there is only an output effect; a change in the price of C will change the demand for D in the opposite direction.

8. The majority of the 10 fastest-growing occupations in the United States relate to computers or health care (see Table 27.5); the 10 most rapidly declining occupations, however, are more mixed (see Table 27.6).

9. The elasticity of demand for a resource measures the responsiveness of producers to a change in the resource's price. The coefficient of the elasticity of resource demand is

$$E_{rd} = \frac{\text{percentage change in resource quantity}}{\text{percentage change in resource price}}$$

When E_{rd} is greater than 1, resource demand is elastic; when E_{rd} is less than 1, resource demand is inelastic; and when E_{rd} equals 1, resource demand is unit-elastic.

10. The elasticity of demand for a resource will be greater (a) the larger the number of good substitute resources available, (b) the greater the elasticity of demand for the product, and (c) the larger the proportion of total production costs attributable to the resource.

11. Any specific level of output will be produced with the least costly combination of variable resources when the marginal product per dollar's worth of each input is the same—that is, when

$$\frac{\text{MP of labor}}{\text{Price of labor}} = \frac{\text{MP of capital}}{\text{Price of capital}}$$

12. A firm is employing the profit-maximizing combination of resources when each resource is used to the point where its marginal revenue product equals its price. In terms of labor and capital, that occurs when the MRP of labor equals the price of labor and the MRP of capital equals the price of capital—that is, when

$$\frac{\text{MRP of labor}}{\text{Price of labor}} = \frac{\text{MRP of capital}}{\text{Price of capital}} = 1$$

13. The marginal productivity theory of income distribution holds that all resources are paid according to their marginal contribution to output. Critics say that such an income distribution is too unequal and that real-world market imperfections result in pay above and below marginal contributions to output.

TERMS AND CONCEPTS

derived demand

marginal product (MP)

marginal revenue product (MRP)

marginal resource cost (MRC)

MRP = MRC rule

substitution effect

output effect

elasticity of resource demand

least-cost combination of resources

profit-maximizing combination of resources

marginal productivity theory of income distribution

STUDY QUESTIONS

1. What is the significance of resource pricing? Explain how the factors determining resource demand differ from those determining product demand. Explain the meaning and significance of the fact that the demand for a resource is a derived demand. Why do resource demand curves slope downward?

2. ***Key Question*** At the bottom of the page, complete the labor demand table for a firm that is hiring labor competitively and selling its product in a competitive market.
   a. How many workers will the firm hire if the market wage rate is $27.95? $19.95? Explain why the firm will not hire a larger or smaller number of units of labor at each of these wage rates.
   b. Show in schedule form and graphically the labor demand curve of this firm.
   c. Now again determine the firm's demand curve for labor, assuming that it is selling in an imperfectly competitive market and that, although it can sell 17 units at $2.20 per unit, it must lower product price by 5 cents in order to sell the marginal product of each successive labor unit. Compare this demand curve with that derived in question 2b. Which curve is more elastic? Explain.

3. Suppose that marginal product tripled while product price fell by one-half in Table 27.1. What would be the new MRP values in Table 27.1? What would be the net impact on the location of the resource demand curve in Figure 27.1?

4. In 2002 Boeing reduced employment by 33,000 workers. What does this decision reveal about how it viewed its marginal revenue product (MRP) and marginal resource cost (MRC)? Why didn't Boeing reduce employment by more than 33,000 workers? By less than 33,000 workers?

5. ***Key Question*** What factors determine the elasticity of resource demand? What effect will each of the following have on the elasticity or the location of the demand for resource C, which is being used to produce commodity X? Where there is any uncertainty as to the outcome, specify the causes of that uncertainty.

   a. An increase in the demand for product X.
   b. An increase in the price of substitute resource D.
   c. An increase in the number of resources substitutable for C in producing X.
   d. A technological improvement in the capital equipment with which resource C is combined.
   e. A fall in the price of complementary resource E.
   f. A decline in the elasticity of demand for product X due to a decline in the competitiveness of the product market.

6. ***Key Question*** Suppose the productivity of capital and labor are as shown in the accompanying table. The output of these resources sells in a purely competitive market for $1 per unit. Both capital and labor are hired under purely competitive conditions at $3 and $1, respectively.

Units of Capital	MP of Capital	Units of Labor	MP of Labor
0		0	
1	24	1	11
2	21	2	9
3	18	3	8
4	15	4	7
5	9	5	6
6	6	6	4
7	3	7	1
8	1	8	$\frac{1}{2}$

   a. What is the least-cost combination of labor and capital the firm should employ in producing 80 units of output? Explain.
   b. What is the profit-maximizing combination of labor and capital the firm should use? Explain. What is the resulting level of output? What is the economic profit? Is this the least costly way of producing the profit-maximizing output?

Units of Labor	Total Product	Marginal Product	Product Price	Total Revenue	Marginal Revenue Product
0	0		$2	$_____	
1	17	_____	2	_____	$_____
2	31	_____	2	_____	
3	43	_____	2	_____	
4	53	_____	2	_____	
5	60	_____	2	_____	
6	65	_____	2	_____	

7. **Key Question** In each of the following four cases, MRP_L and MRP_C refer to the marginal revenue products of labor and capital, respectively, and P_L and P_C refer to their prices. Indicate in each case whether the conditions are consistent with maximum profits for the firm. If not, state which resource(s) should be used in larger amounts and which resource(s) should be used in smaller amounts.

   a. $MRP_L = \$8$; $P_L = \$4$; $MRP_C = \$8$; $P_C = \$4$
   b. $MRP_L = \$10$; $P_L = \$12$; $MRP_C = \$14$; $P_C = \$9$
   c. $MRP_L = \$6$; $P_L = \$6$; $MRP_C = \$12$; $P_C = \$12$
   d. $MRP_L = \$22$; $P_L = \$26$; $MRP_C = \$16$; $P_C = \$19$

8. Florida citrus growers say that the recent crackdown on illegal immigration is increasing the market wage rates necessary to get their oranges picked. Some are turning to $100,000 to $300,000 mechanical harvesters known as "trunk, shake, and catch" pickers, which vigorously shake oranges from the trees. If widely adopted, what will be the effect on the demand for human orange pickers? What does that imply about the relative strengths of the substitution and output effects?

9. **(Last Word)** Explain the economics of the substitution of ATMs for human tellers. Some banks are beginning to assess transaction fees when customers use human tellers rather than ATMs. What are these banks trying to accomplish?

10. **Web-Based Question: Selected occupations—what are their employment outlooks?** Use the A to Z index in the Bureau of Labor Statistics *Occupational Outlook*, at www.bls.gov/oco/, to determine the general and specific employment outlooks for (a) textile machinery operators, (b) financial managers, (c) computer operators, and (d) dental hygienists. Why do these job outlooks differ?

11. **Web-Based Question: The overall demand for labor—in which countries has it increased the most?** In countries where real wages are steady or rising, increases in total employment reflect increases in labor demand. Go to the Bureau of Labor Statistics website, www.bls.gov/fls/, and select Comparative Civilian Labor Force Statistics. Find the percentage increases in civilian employment for the United States, Japan, Germany, France, Great Britain, Italy, and Canada for the most recent 10-year period. Which three countries have had the fastest growth of labor demand, as measured by the percentage change in employment? Which three the slowest?

28 | *Wage Determination*

Nearly 135 million of us go to work each day in the United States. We work at an amazing variety of jobs for thousands of different firms and receive considerable differences in pay. What determines our hourly wage or annual salary? Why is the salary for, say, a topflight major league baseball player $15 million or more a year, whereas the pay for a first-rate schoolteacher is $50,000? Why are starting salaries for college graduates who major in engineering and accounting so much higher than those for graduates majoring in journalism and sociology?

Having explored the major factors that underlie labor demand, we now bring *labor supply* into our analysis to help answer these questions. Generally speaking, labor supply and labor demand interact to determine the level of hourly wage rates or annual salaries in each occupation. Collectively, those wages and salaries make up 72 percent of the national income.

Labor, Wages, and Earnings

Economists use the term "labor" broadly to apply to (1) blue- and white-collar workers of all varieties; (2) professional people such as lawyers, physicians, dentists, and teachers; and (3) owners of small businesses, including barbers, plumbers, and a host of retailers who provide labor as they carry on their own businesses.

Wages are the price that employers pay for labor. Wages not only take the form of direct money payments such as hourly pay, annual salaries, bonuses, commissions, and royalties but also fringe benefits such as paid vacations, health insurance, and pensions. Unless stated otherwise, we will use the term "wages" to mean all such payments and benefits converted to an hourly basis. That will remind

us that the **wage rate** is the price paid per unit of labor services, in this case an hour of work. It will also let us distinguish between the wage rate and labor earnings, the latter determined by multiplying the number of hours worked by the hourly wage rate.

We must also distinguish between nominal wages and real wages. A **nominal wage** is the amount of money received per hour, day, or year. A **real wage** is the quantity of goods and services a worker can obtain with nominal wages; real wages reveal the "purchasing power" of nominal wages.

Your real wage depends on your nominal wage and the prices of the goods and services you purchase. Suppose you receive an 8 percent increase in your nominal wage during a certain year but in that same year the price level increases by 5 percent. Then your real wage has increased by 3 percent (= 8 percent − 5 percent). Unless otherwise indicated, we will assume that the overall level of prices remains constant. In other words, we will discuss only *real* wages.

General Level of Wages

Wages differ among nations, regions, occupations, and individuals. Wage rates are much higher in the United States than in China or India. They are slightly higher in the north and east of the United States than in the south. Plumbers are paid less than NFL punters. And physician Adam may earn twice as much as physician Bennett for the same number of hours of work. Wage rates also differ by gender, race, and ethnic background.

The general, or average, level of wages, like the general level of prices, includes a wide range of different wage rates. It includes the wages of bakers, barbers, brick masons, and brain surgeons. By averaging such wages, we can more easily compare wages among regions and among nations.

As Global Perspective 28.1 suggests, the general level of real wages in the United States is relatively high—although not the highest in the world.

The simplest explanation for the high real wages in the United States and other industrially advanced economies (referred to hereafter as advanced economies) is that the demand for labor in those nations is relatively large compared to the supply of labor.

Role of Productivity

We know from the previous chapter that the demand for labor, or for any other resource, depends on its productivity. In general, the greater the productivity of labor, the greater is the demand for it. And if the total supply of labor is fixed, then the stronger the demand for labor, the higher is the average level of real wages. The demand for labor in the United States and the other major advanced economies is large because labor in those countries is highly productive. There are several reasons for that high productivity:

- *Plentiful capital* Workers in the advanced economies have access to large amounts of physical capital equipment (machinery and buildings). In the United States there is $82,000 of physical capital available, on average, for each worker.

- *Access to abundant natural resources* In advanced economies, natural resources tend to be abundant in

GLOBAL PERSPECTIVE 28.1

Hourly Wages of Production Workers, Selected Nations

Wage differences are pronounced worldwide. The data shown here indicate that hourly compensation in the United States is not as high as in some European nations. It is important to note, however, that the prices of goods and services vary greatly among nations and the process of converting foreign wages into dollars may not accurately reflect such variations.

Hourly Pay in U.S. Dollars, 2001

Germany, Denmark, Switzerland, United States, Japan, Sweden, United Kingdom, France, Canada, Italy, Australia, Korea, Taiwan, Mexico

Source: U.S. Bureau of Labor Statistics, www.bls.gov/, 2003.

relation to the size of the labor force. Some of those resources are available domestically and others are imported from abroad. The United States, for example, is richly endowed with arable land, mineral resources, and sources of energy for industry.

- *Advanced technology* The level of technological progress is generally high in advanced economies. Not only do workers in these economies have more capital equipment to work with, but that equipment is technologically superior to the equipment available to the vast majority of workers worldwide. Moreover, work methods in the advanced economies are steadily being improved through scientific study and research.

- *Labor quality* The health, vigor, education, and training of workers in advanced economies are generally superior to those in developing nations. This means that, even with the same quantity and quality of natural and capital resources, workers in advanced

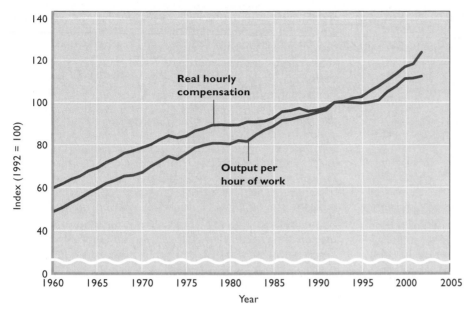

FIGURE 28.1

Output per hour and real hourly compensation in the United States. Over long periods of years there is a close relationship between output per hour of work and real hourly compensation.

Source: Bureau of Labor Statistics, stat.bls.gov.

economies tend to be more efficient than many of their foreign counterparts.

- *Other factors* Less obvious factors also may underlie the high productivity in some of the advanced economies. In the United States, for example, such factors include (a) the efficiency and flexibility of management; (b) a business, social, and political environment that emphasizes production and productivity; (c) the vast size of the domestic market, which enables firms to engage in mass production; and (d) the increased specialization of production enabled by free-trade agreements with other nations.

Real Wages and Productivity

Figure 28.1 shows the close long-run relationship in the United States between output per hour of work and real hourly compensation (= wages and salaries + employers' contributions to social insurance and private benefit plans). Because real income and real output are two ways of viewing the same thing, real income (compensation) per worker can increase only at about the same rate as output per worker. When workers produce more real output per hour, more real income is available to distribute to them for each hour worked.

In the real world, however, suppliers of land, capital, and entrepreneurial talent also share in the income from production. Real wages therefore do not always rise in lockstep with gains in productivity over short spans of time. But over long periods, productivity and real wages tend to rise together.

Secular Growth of Real Wages

Basic supply and demand analysis helps explain the long-term trend of real-wage growth in the United States. The nation's labor force has grown significantly over the decades. But, as a result of the productivity-increasing factors we have mentioned, labor demand has increased more rapidly than labor supply. Figure 28.2 shows several such increases in labor supply and labor demand. The result has been a long-run, or secular, increase in wage rates and employment.

FIGURE 28.2

The long-run trend of real wages in the United States. The productivity of U.S. labor has increased substantially over the long run, causing the demand for labor *D* to shift rightward (that is, to increase) more rapidly than increases in the supply of labor *S*. The result has been increases in real wages.

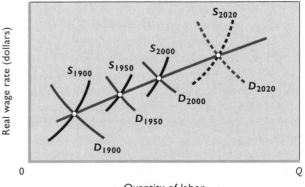

A Purely Competitive Labor Market

We now turn from the average level of wages to specific wage rates. What determines the wage rate paid for some specific type of labor? Demand and supply analysis again is revealing. Let's begin by examining labor demand and labor supply in a **purely competitive labor market.** In this type of market:

- Many firms compete with one another in hiring a specific type of labor.
- Each of numerous qualified workers with identical skills supplies that type of labor.
- Individual firms and individual workers are "wage takers," since neither can exert any control over the market wage rate.

Market Demand for Labor

Suppose 200 firms demand a particular type of labor, say, carpenters. These firms need not be in the same industry; industries are defined according to the products they produce and not the resources they employ. Thus, firms producing wood-framed furniture, wood windows and doors, houses and apartment buildings, and wood cabinets will demand carpenters. To find the total, or market, labor demand curve for a particular labor service, we sum horizontally the labor demand curves (the marginal revenue product curves) of the individual firms, as indicated in **Figure 28.3 (Key Graph).** The horizontal summing of the 200 labor demand curves like *d* in Figure 28.3b yields the market labor demand curve *D* in Figure 28.3a.

Market Supply of Labor

On the supply side of a purely competitive labor market, we assume that there is no union and that workers individually compete for available jobs. The supply curve for each type of labor slopes upward, indicating that employers as a group must pay higher wage rates to obtain more workers. This is so because they must bid workers away from other industries, occupations, and localities. Within limits, workers have alternative job opportunities. For example, they may work in other industries in the same locality, or they may work in their present occupations in different cities or states, or they may work in other occupations.

Firms that want to hire these workers (here, carpenters) must pay higher wage rates to attract them away from the alternative job opportunities available to

them. They must also pay higher wages to induce people who are not currently in the labor force—who are perhaps doing household activities or enjoying leisure—to seek employment. In short, assuming that wages are constant in other labor markets, higher wages in a particular labor market entice more workers to offer their labor services in that market—a fact confirmed by the upward-sloping market supply-of-labor curve *S* in Figure 28.3a.

Labor Market Equilibrium

The intersection of the market labor demand curve and the market supply curve determines the equilibrium wage rate and level of employment in purely competitive labor markets. In Figure 28.3a the equilibrium wage rate is W_c ($10), and the number of workers hired is Q_c (1000). To the individual firm the market wage rate W_c is given. Each of the many firms employs such a small fraction of the total available supply of this type of labor that none of them can influence the wage rate. The supply of this labor is perfectly elastic to the individual firm, as shown by horizontal line *s* in Figure 28.3b.

Each individual firm will find it profitable to hire this type of labor up to the point at which marginal revenue product is equal to marginal resource cost. This is merely an application of the MRP = MRC rule we developed in Chapter 27.

As Table 28.1 indicates, when the price of a resource is given to the individual competitive firm, the marginal cost of that resource (MRC) is constant and is equal to the resource price. Here, MRC is constant and is equal to the wage rate. Each additional worker hired adds precisely his or her own wage rate ($10 in this case) to the firm's total resource cost. So the firm in a purely competitive labor market maximizes its profit by hiring workers to the point at which its wage rate equals MRP. In Figure 28.3b this firm will hire q_c (five) workers, paying each of them the market wage rate W_c ($10). So, too, will the other 199 firms (not shown) that are hiring workers in this labor market.

To determine a firm's total revenue from employing a particular number of labor units, we sum the MRPs of those units. For example, if a firm employs 3 labor units with marginal revenue products of $14, $13, and $12, respectively, then the firm's total revenue is $39 (= $14 + $13 + $12). In Figure 28.3b, where we are not restricted to whole units of labor, total revenue is represented by area 0*abc* under the MRP curve to the left of q_c. And what area represents the firm's total cost, including a normal profit? Answer: For q_c units, the same area—0*abc*.

KEY GRAPH

FIGURE 28.3

Labor supply and labor demand in (a) a purely competitive labor market and (b) a single competitive firm. In a purely competitive labor market (a) the equilibrium wage rate W_c and the number of workers Q_c are determined by labor supply S and labor demand D. Because this market wage rate is given to the individual firm (b) hiring in this market, its labor supply curve $s = MRC$ is perfectly elastic. Its labor demand curve is its MRP curve (here labeled *mrp*). The firm maximizes its profit by hiring workers up to where MRP = MRC. Area $0abc$ represents both the firm's total revenue and its total cost. The red area is its total wage cost; the blue area is its nonlabor costs, including a normal profit—that is, the firm's payments to the suppliers of land, capital, and entrepreneurship.

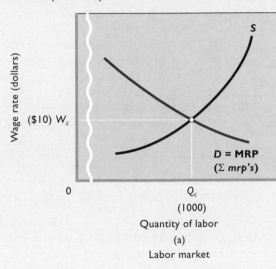

(a)

Labor market

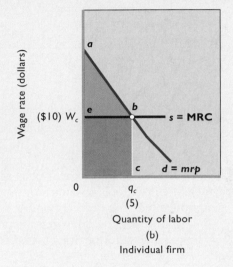

(b)

Individual firm

TABLE 28.1

The Supply of Labor: Pure Competition in the Hire of Labor

(1) Units of Labor	(2) Wage Rate	(3) Total Labor Cost (Wage Bill)	(4) Marginal Resource (Labor) Cost
0	$10	$ 0	
1	10	10	$10
2	10	20	10
3	10	30	10
4	10	40	10
5	10	50	10
6	10	60	10

The red rectangle represents the firm's total wage cost $(0q_c \times 0W_c)$. The blue triangle (total revenue minus total wage cost) represents the firm's nonlabor costs—its explicit and implicit payments to land, capital, and entrepreneurship. Thus, in this case, total cost (wages plus other income payments) equals total revenue. This firm and others like it are earning only a normal profit. Figure 28.3b represents a long-run equilibrium for a firm that is selling its product in a purely competitive product market and "buying" its labor in a purely competitive labor market. **(Key Questions 3 and 4)**

28.1
Competitive
labor market

Monopsony Model

In the purely competitive labor market described in the preceding section, each employer hires too small an amount of labor to influence the wage rate. Each firm can hire as little or as much labor as it needs, but only at the market wage rate, as reflected in its horizontal labor supply curve. The situation is quite different in **monopsony**, a market in which a single employer of labor has substantial buying (hiring) power. Labor market monopsony has the following characteristics:

- There is only a single buyer of a particular type of labor.
- This type of labor is relatively immobile, either geographically or because workers would have to acquire new skills.
- The firm is a "wage maker," because the wage rate it must pay varies directly with the number of workers it employs.

As is true of monopoly power, there are various degrees of monopsony power. In *pure* monopsony such power is at its maximum, because there is only a single employer in the labor market. The best real-world examples are probably the labor markets in some towns that depend almost entirely on one major firm. For example, a silver-mining company may be almost the only source of employment in a remote Idaho or Colorado town. A New England textile mill, a Wisconsin paper mill, or a farm-belt food processor may provide most of the employment in its locale. Maytag (the maker of home appliances) is the dominant employer in Newton, Iowa.

28.1
Monopsony

In other cases three or four firms may each hire a large portion of the supply of labor in a certain market and therefore have some monopsony power. Moreover, if they tacitly or openly act in concert in hiring labor, they greatly enhance their monopsony power.

Upward-Sloping Labor Supply to Firm

When a firm hires most of the available supply of a particular type of labor, its decision to employ more or fewer workers affects the wage rate it pays to those workers. Specifically, if a firm is large in relation to the size of the labor market, it will have to pay a higher wage rate to obtain more labor. Suppose there is only one employer of a particular type of labor in a certain geographic area. In that extreme case, the labor supply curve for that firm and the total supply curve for the labor market are identical. This supply curve is upward-sloping, indicating that the firm must pay a higher wage rate to attract more workers. The supply curve, S in Figure 28.4, is also the average-cost-of-labor curve for the firm; each point on it indicates the wage rate (cost) per worker that must be paid to attract the corresponding number of workers.

MRC Higher than the Wage Rate

When a monopsonist pays a higher wage to attract an additional worker, it must pay that higher wage to all the workers it is currently employing at a lower wage. If not, labor morale will deteriorate, and the employer will be plagued with labor unrest because of wage-rate differences existing for the same job. Paying a uniform wage to all workers means that the cost of an extra worker—the marginal resource (labor) cost (MRC)—is the sum of that worker's wage rate and the amount necessary to bring the wage rate of all current workers up to the new wage level.

FIGURE 28.4

The wage rate and level of employment in a monopsonistic labor market. In a monopsonistic labor market the employer's marginal resource (labor) cost curve (MRC) lies above the labor supply curve S. Equating MRC with MRP at point b, the monopsonist hires Q_m workers (compared with Q_c under competition). As indicated by point c on S, it pays only wage rate W_m (compared with the competitive wage W_c).

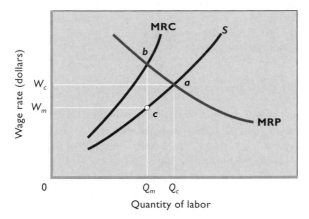

Table 28.2 illustrates this point. One worker can be hired at a wage rate of $6. But hiring a second worker forces the firm to pay a higher wage rate of $7. The marginal resource (labor) cost of the second worker is $8—the $7 paid to the second worker plus a $1 raise for the first worker. From another viewpoint, total labor cost is now $14 (= 2 × $7), up from $6. So the MRC of the second worker is $8 (= $14 − $6), not just the $7 wage rate paid to that worker. Similarly, the marginal labor cost of the third worker is $10—the $8 that must be paid to attract this worker from alternative employment plus $1 raises, from $7 to $8, for the first two workers.

The important point is that to the monopsonist, marginal resource (labor) cost exceeds the wage rate.

TABLE 28.2

The Supply of Labor: Monopsony in the Hire of Labor

(1) Units of Labor	(2) Wage Rate	(3) Total Labor Cost (Wage Bill)	(4) Marginal Resource (Labor) Cost
0	$ 5	$ 0	
			$ 6
1	6	6	
			8
2	7	14	
			10
3	8	24	
			12
4	9	36	
			14
5	10	50	
			16
6	11	66	

Graphically, the MRC curve lies above the average-cost-of-labor curve, or labor supply curve S, as is clearly shown in Figure 28.4.

Equilibrium Wage and Employment

How many units of labor will the monopsonist hire, and what wage rate will it pay? To maximize profit, the monopsonist will employ the quantity of labor Q_m in Figure 28.4, because at that quantity MRC and MRP are equal (point b).[1] The monopsonist next determines how much it must pay to attract these Q_m workers. From the supply curve S, specifically point c, it sees that it must pay wage rate W_m. Clearly, it need not pay a wage equal to MRP; it can attract exactly the number of workers it wants (Q_m) with wage rate W_m. And that is what it will pay.

Contrast these results with those that would prevail in a competitive labor market. With competition in the hiring of labor, the level of employment would be greater (at Q_c) and the wage rate would be higher (at W_c). Other things equal, the monopsonist maximizes its profit by hiring a smaller number of workers and thereby paying a less-than-competitive wage rate. Society gets a smaller output, and workers get a wage rate that is less by bc than their marginal revenue product. Just as a monopolistic seller finds it profitable to restrict product output to realize an above-competitive price for its goods, the monopsonistic employer of resources finds it profitable to restrict employment in order to depress wage rates and therefore costs, that is, to realize wage rates below those that would occur under competitive conditions.

28.2 Monopsony

---

[1] The fact that MRC exceeds resource price when resources are hired or purchased under imperfectly competitive (monopsonistic) conditions calls for adjustments in Chapter 27's least-cost and profit-maximizing rules for hiring resources. (See equations 1 and 2 in the "Optimal Combination of Resources" section of Chapter 27.) Specifically, we must substitute MRC for resource price in the denominators of our two equations. That is, with imperfect competition in the hiring of both labor and capital, equation 1 becomes

$$\frac{MP_L}{MRC_L} = \frac{MP_C}{MRC_C} \qquad (1')$$

and equation 2 is restated as

$$\frac{MRP_L}{MRC_L} = \frac{MRP_C}{MRC_C} = 1 \qquad (2')$$

In fact, equations 1 and 2 can be regarded as special cases of 1′ and 2′ in which firms happen to be hiring under purely competitive conditions and resource price is therefore equal to, and can be substituted for, marginal resource cost.

Examples of Monopsony Power

Monopsonistic labor markets are not common in the U.S. economy; typically, many potential employers compete for most workers, particularly for workers who are occupationally and geographically mobile. Also, where monopsony labor market outcomes might have otherwise occurred, unions have sprung up to counteract that power by forcing firms to negotiate wages. Nevertheless, economists have found evidence of monopsony power in such diverse labor markets as the markets for nurses, professional athletes, public school teachers, newspaper employees, and some building-trade workers.

In the case of nurses, the major employers in most locales are a relatively small number of hospitals. Further, the highly specialized skills of nurses are not readily transferable to other occupations. It has been found, in accordance with the monopsony model, that, other things equal, the smaller the number of hospitals in a town or city (that is, the greater the degree of monopsony), the lower the beginning salaries of nurses.

Professional sports leagues also provide a good example of monopsony, particularly as it relates to the pay of first-year players. The National Football League, the National Basketball Association, and Major League Baseball assign first-year players to teams through "player drafts." That device prohibits other teams from competing for the player's services, at least for several years, until the player becomes a "free agent." In this way the league exercises monopsony power, which results in lower salaries than would occur under competitive conditions. **(Key Question 6).**

QUICK REVIEW 28.1

- Real wages have increased historically in the United States because labor demand has increased relative to labor supply.

- Over the long term, real wages per worker have increased at approximately the same rate as worker productivity.

- The competitive employer is a wage taker and employs workers at the point where the wage rate (= MRC) equals MRP.

- The labor supply curve to a monopsonist is upward-sloping, causing MRC to exceed the wage rate for each worker. Other things equal, the monopsonist, hiring where MRC = MRP, will employ fewer workers and pay a lower wage rate than would a purely competitive employer.

Three Union Models

We have assumed so far that workers compete with one another in selling their labor services. In some labor markets, however, workers sell their labor services collectively through unions. When a union is formed in an otherwise competitive labor market, it bargains with a relatively large number of employers. It has many goals, the most important of which is to raise wage rates. It can pursue that objective in several ways.

Demand-Enhancement Model

From the union's viewpoint, the most desirable technique for raising wage rates is to increase the demand for labor. As Figure 28.5 shows, an increase in labor demand will create both higher wage rates and more jobs. How great those increases will be depends on the elasticity of labor supply. The less elastic the labor supply, the greater will be the wage increase; the more elastic the labor supply, the greater will be the employment increase.

To increase labor demand, the union might alter one or more of the determinants of demand. For example, a union can attempt to increase the demand for the product or service it is producing, enhance the productivity of labor, or alter the prices of other inputs.

Increase Product Demand   Unions can increase the demand for the products they help produce—and thus raise the demand for their own labor services—through advertising or political lobbying.

FIGURE 28.5

Unions and demand enhancement.   When unions can increase the demand for labor (say, from D_1 to D_2), they can realize higher wage rates (W_c to W_u) and more jobs (Q_c to Q_u).

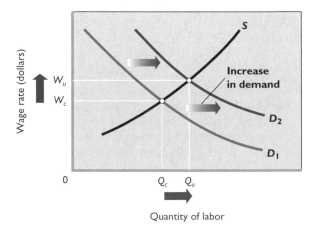

Occasionally, unions advertise union-produced goods or services. The long-running campaign urging consumers to "look for the union label" is an example. Less often, unions join with their employers to finance advertising campaigns designed to bolster product demand. The Communications Workers of America (CWA) once helped finance a large "Call or Buy Union" campaign to convince telephone users to choose the long-distance services and equipment of AT&T and Western Union, which together provided thousands of CWA jobs.

On the political front construction unions have lobbied for new highway, mass-transit, and stadium projects. Teachers' unions and associations have pushed for increased public spending on education. Unions in the aerospace industry have lobbied to increase spending on the military and on space exploration. And the steelworkers' union has at times supported employers in seeking protective tariffs designed to exclude competing foreign steel. The steelworkers recognize that an increase in the price of imported steel through tariffs or international agreements will increase the demand for highly substitutable domestically made steel, boosting the derived demand for U.S. steelworkers.

Increase Productivity Many decisions affecting labor productivity—for example, decisions concerning the quantity and quality of real capital used by workers—are made unilaterally by management. There is a growing tendency, however, to set up joint labor-management committees designed to increase labor productivity.

Alter the Price of Other Inputs Unions sometimes have tried to strengthen the demand for their labor by working to increase the price of substitute resources. For example, although union members are generally paid significantly more than the minimum wage, unions have strongly supported increases in the minimum wage. The purpose may be to raise the price of low-wage, nonunion labor, which in some cases is substitutable for union labor. A higher minimum wage for nonunion workers will discourage employers from substituting such workers for union workers and will thereby bolster the demand for union members.

Similarly, unions have sometimes sought to increase the demand for their labor by supporting public actions that will reduce the price of a complementary resource. For example, unions in industries that use large amounts of imported resources might urge reductions in tariffs on those imports. Where labor and the other resource are complementary, a price decrease for the other resource will increase the demand for labor through Chapter 27's output effect.

Unions recognize that their ability to influence the demand for labor is very limited. So it is not surprising that their efforts to raise wage rates have concentrated on the supply side of the labor market.

Exclusive or Craft Union Model

One way in which unions can boost wage rates is to reduce the supply of labor, and over the years organized labor has favored policies to do just that. For example, labor unions have supported legislation that has (1) restricted immigration, (2) reduced child labor, (3) encouraged compulsory retirement, and (4) enforced a shorter workweek.

Moreover, certain types of workers have adopted techniques designed to restrict the number of workers who can join their union. This is especially true of *craft unions*, whose members possess a particular skill, such as carpenters or brick masons or plumbers. Craft unions have frequently forced employers to agree to hire only union members, thereby gaining virtually complete control of the labor supply. Then, by following restrictive membership policies—for example, long apprenticeships, very high initiation fees, and limits on the number of new members admitted—they have artificially restricted labor supply. As indicated in Figure 28.6, such practices result in higher wage rates and constitute what is called **exclusive unionism.** By excluding workers from unions and therefore from the labor supply, craft unions succeed in elevating wage rates.

FIGURE 28.6

Exclusive or craft unionism. By reducing the supply of labor (say, from S_1 to S_2) through the use of restrictive membership policies, exclusive unions achieve higher wage rates (W_c to W_u). However, restriction of the labor supply also reduces the number of workers employed (Q_c to Q_u).

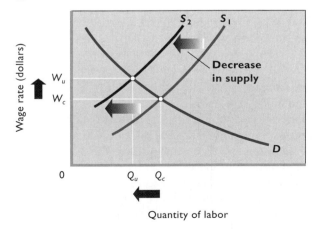

This craft union model is also applicable to many professional organizations, such as the American Medical Association, the National Education Association, the American Bar Association, and hundreds of others. Such groups seek to limit competition for their services from less qualified labor suppliers. One way to accomplish that is through **occupational licensing.** Here a group of workers in a given occupation pressure Federal, state, or municipal government to pass a law that says that some occupational group (for example, barbers, physicians, lawyers, plumbers, cosmetologists, egg graders, pest controllers) can practice their trade only if they meet certain requirements. Those requirements might include level of education, amount of work experience, the passing of an examination, and personal characteristics ("the practitioner must be of good moral character"). Members of the licensed occupation typically dominate the licensing board that administers such laws. The result is self-regulation, which often leads to policies that serve only to restrict entry to the occupation and reduce labor supply.

The purpose of licensing is supposedly to protect consumers from incompetent practitioners—surely a worthy goal. But such licensing, if abused, results in above-competitive wages and earnings for those in the licensed occupation (Figure 28.6). Moreover, licensing requirements often include a residency requirement, which inhibits the interstate movement of qualified workers. Some 600 occupations are now licensed in the United States.

Inclusive or Industrial Union Model

Instead of trying to limit their membership, however, most unions seek to organize all available workers. This is especially true of the *industrial unions*, such as those of the automobile workers and steelworkers. Such unions seek as members all available unskilled, semiskilled, and skilled workers in an industry. A union can afford to be exclusive when its members are skilled craftspersons for whom there are few substitutes. But for a union composed of unskilled and semiskilled workers, a policy of limited membership would make available to the employers numerous nonunion workers who are highly substitutable for the union workers.

An industrial union that includes virtually all available workers in its membership can put firms under great pressure to agree to its wage demands. Because of its legal right to strike, such a union can threaten to deprive firms of their entire labor supply. And an actual strike can do just that.

We illustrate such **inclusive unionism** in Figure 28.7. Initially, the competitive equilibrium wage rate is W_c and

FIGURE 28.7

Inclusive or industrial unionism. By organizing virtually all available workers in order to control the supply of labor, inclusive industrial unions may impose a wage rate, such as W_u, which is above the competitive wage rate W_c. In effect, this changes the labor supply curve from S to aeS. At wage rate W_u, employers will cut employment from Q_c to Q_u.

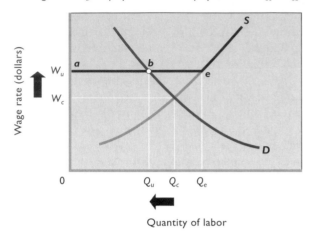

Quantity of labor

the level of employment is Q_c. Now suppose an industrial union is formed that demands a higher, above-equilibrium wage rate of, say, W_u. That wage rate W_u would create a perfectly elastic labor supply over the range ae in Figure 28.7. If firms wanted to hire any workers in this range, they would have to pay the union-imposed wage rate. If they decide against meeting this wage demand, the union will supply no labor at all, and the firms will be faced with a strike. If firms decide it is better to pay the higher wage rate than to suffer a strike, they will cut back on employment from Q_c to Q_u.

By agreeing to the union's W_u wage demand, individual employers become wage takers. Because labor supply is perfectly elastic over range ae, the marginal resource (labor) cost is equal to the wage rate W_u over this range. The Q_u level of employment is the result of employers' equating this MRC (now equal to the wage rate) with MRP, according to our profit-maximizing rule.

Note from point e on labor supply curve S that Q_e workers desire employment at wage W_u. But as indicated by point b on labor demand curve D, only Q_u workers are employed. The result is a surplus of labor of $Q_e - Q_u$ (also shown by distance eb). In a purely competitive labor market without the union, the effect of a surplus of unemployed workers would be lower wages. Specifically, the wage rate would fall to the equilibrium level W_c, where the quantity of labor supplied equals the quantity of labor demanded (each Q_c). But this drop in wages does not happen, because workers are acting collectively through their union. Individual workers cannot offer to work for less than W_u; nor can employers pay less than that.

Wage Increases and Unemployment

Have U.S. unions been successful in raising the wages of their members? Evidence suggests that union members on average achieve a 15 percent wage advantage over nonunion workers.

As Figures 28.6 and 28.7 suggest, the effect of wage-raising actions achieved by both exclusive and inclusive unionism is reduced employment. A union's success in achieving above-equilibrium wage rates thus tends to be accompanied by a decline in the number of workers employed. That result acts as a restraining influence on union wage demands. A union cannot expect to maintain solidarity within its ranks if it seeks a wage rate so high that joblessness will result for, say, 20 or 30 percent of its members.

The unemployment effect created by union-induced wage increases may be reduced in two ways:

- *Growth* The normal growth of the economy increases the demand for most kinds of labor over time. This continual rightward shift of the labor demand curves in Figures 28.6 and 28.7 might offset, or more than offset, the unemployment effect associated with the indicated wage increases. In that event, the increases in unemployment prompted by the unions would tend to *slow* the growth of job opportunities but would not reduce total employment by firms.

- *Elasticity* The size of the unemployment effect resulting from a union-induced wage increase depends on the elasticity of demand for labor. The more inelastic that demand, the smaller is the amount of unemployment that accompanies a given wage-rate increase. And if unions have sufficient bargaining strength, they may be able to win provisions in their collective bargaining agreements that reduce the elasticity of demand for union labor by reducing the substitutability of other inputs for that labor. For example, a union may force employers to accept rules slowing the introduction of new machinery and equipment. Or the union may bargain successfully for severance pay or layoff pay, which increases the cost to the firm of substituting capital for labor when wage rates are increased. Similarly, the union may gain a contract provision prohibiting the firm from subcontracting production to nonunion (lower-wage) firms or from relocating work to low-wage workers overseas, thereby restricting the substitution of cheaper labor for union workers.

Bilateral Monopoly Model

Suppose a strong industrial union is formed in a labor market that is monopsonistic rather than competitive, creating a combination of the monopsony model and the inclusive unionism model. The result is called **bilateral monopoly** because in its pure form there is a single seller and a single buyer. The union is a monopolistic "seller" of labor that controls labor supply and can influence wage rates, but it faces a monopsonistic "buyer" of labor that can also affect wages by altering its employment. This is not an uncommon case, particularly in less pure forms in which a single union confronts two, three, or four large employers. Examples: steel, automobiles, construction equipment, professional sports, and commercial aircraft.

Indeterminate Outcome of Bilateral Monopoly

We show this situation in Figure 28.8, where we superimpose Figure 28.7 onto Figure 28.4. The monopsonistic employer will seek the below-competitive-equilibrium wage rate W_m, and the union presumably will press for some above-competitive-equilibrium wage rate such as W_u. Which will be the outcome? We cannot say with certainty. The outcome is "logically indeterminate" because the bilateral monopoly model does not explain what will happen at the collective bargaining table. We can expect the wage outcome to lie somewhere between W_m and W_u.

FIGURE 28.8

Bilateral monopoly in the labor market. A monopsonist seeks to hire Q_m workers (where MRC = MRP) and pay wage rate W_m corresponding to quantity Q_m on labor supply curve S. The inclusive union it faces seeks the above-equilibrium wage rate W_u. The actual outcome cannot be predicted by economic theory.

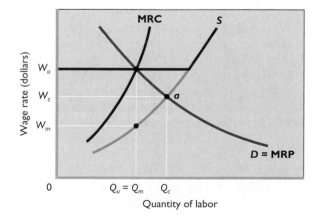

Beyond that, about all we can say is that the party with the greater bargaining power and the more effective bargaining strategy will probably get a wage closer to the one it seeks.

Desirability of Bilateral Monopoly

The wage and employment outcomes in this situation might be more socially desirable than the term "bilateral monopoly" implies. The monopoly on one side of the market might in effect cancel out the monopoly on the other side, yielding competitive or near-competitive results. If either the union or management prevailed in this market—that is, if the actual wage rate were determined at either W_u or W_m—employment would be restricted to Q_m (where MRP = MRC), which is below the competitive level.

But now suppose the monopoly power of the union roughly offsets the monopsony power of management, and the union and management agree on wage rate W_c, which is the competitive wage. Once management accepts this wage rate, its incentive to restrict employment disappears; no longer can it depress wage rates by restricting employment. Instead, management hires at the most profitable resource quantity, where the bargained wage rate W_c (which is now the firm's MRC) is equal to the MRP. It hires Q_c workers. Thus, with monopoly on both sides of the labor market, the resulting wage rate and level of employment may be closer to competitive levels than would be the case if monopoly existed on only one side of the market. **(Key Question 7)**

QUICK REVIEW 28.2

- In the demand-enhancement union model, a union increases the wage rate by increasing labor demand through actions that increase product demand, raise labor productivity, or alter the prices of related inputs.

- In the exclusive (craft) union model, a union increases wage rates by artificially restricting labor supply, through, say, long apprenticeships or occupational licensing.

- In the inclusive (industrial) union model, a union raises the wage rate by gaining control over a firm's labor supply and threatening to withhold labor via a strike unless a negotiated wage is obtained.

- Bilateral monopoly occurs in a labor market where a monopsonist bargains with an inclusive, or industrial, union. Wage and employment outcomes are determined by collective bargaining in this situation.

The Minimum-Wage Controversy

Since the passage of the Fair Labor Standards Act in 1938, the United States has had a Federal **minimum wage.** That wage has ranged between 35 and 50 percent of the average wage paid to manufacturing workers and was $5.15 per hour in 2003. The purpose of the minimum wage is to provide a "wage floor" that will help less skilled workers earn enough income to escape poverty.

Case against the Minimum Wage

Critics, reasoning in terms of Figure 28.7, contend that an above-equilibrium minimum wage (say, W_u) will simply push employers back up their labor demand curves, causing them to hire fewer workers. The higher labor costs may even force some firms out of business. Then some of the poor, low-wage workers whom the minimum wage was designed to help will find themselves out of work. Critics point out that a worker who is *unemployed* at a minimum wage of $5.15 per hour is clearly worse off than he or she would be if *employed* at a market wage rate of, say, $4.85 per hour.

A second criticism of the minimum wage is that it is "poorly targeted" to reduce household poverty. Critics point out that much of the benefit of the minimum wage accrues to workers, including many teenagers, who do not live in poverty households.

Case for the Minimum Wage

Advocates of the minimum wage say that critics analyze its impact in an unrealistic context. Figure 28.7, advocates claim, assumes a competitive, static market. But in a more real, low-pay labor market where there is some monopsony power (Figure 28.8), the minimum wage can increase wage rates without causing unemployment. Indeed, a higher minimum wage may even produce more jobs by eliminating the motive that monopsonistic firms have for restricting employment. For example, a minimum-wage floor of W_c in Figure 28.8 would change the firm's labor supply curve to W_caS and prompt the firm to increase its employment from Q_m workers to Q_c workers.

Moreover, a minimum wage may increase labor productivity, shifting the labor demand curve to the right and offsetting any reduced employment that the minimum wage might cause. For example, the higher wage rate might prompt firms to find more productive tasks for low-paid workers, thereby raising their productivity. Alternatively, the minimum wage may reduce *labor turnover* (the rate at which workers voluntarily quit). With fewer low-productive trainees, the *average* productivity of the firm's workers would rise. In either case, the higher labor productivity would justify paying the higher minimum wage. So the alleged negative employment effects of the minimum wage might not occur.

Evidence and Conclusions

Which view is correct? Unfortunately, there is no clear answer. All economists agree there is some minimum wage so high that it would severely reduce employment. Consider $20 an hour, as an absurd example. But no current consensus exists on the employment effects of the present level of the minimum wage. Evidence in the 1980s suggested that minimum-wage hikes reduced employment of minimum-wage workers, particularly teenagers (16- to 19-year-olds). The consensus then was that a 10 percent increase in the minimum wage would reduce teenage employment by about 1 to 3 percent. But the minimum-wage hikes in 1991, 1996, and 1997 seemed to produce smaller, and perhaps zero, employment declines among teenagers.[2]

The overall effect of the minimum wage is thus uncertain. On the one hand, the employment and unemployment effects of the minimum wage do not appear to be as great as many critics fear. On the other hand, because a large part of its effect is dissipated on nonpoverty families, the minimum wage is not as strong an antipoverty tool as many supporters contend.

It is clear, however, that the minimum wage has strong political support. Perhaps this stems from two realities: (1) More workers are helped by the minimum wage than are hurt, and (2) the minimum wage gives society some assurance that employers are not "taking undo advantage" of vulnerable, low-skilled workers.

Wage Differentials

Hourly wage rates and annual salaries differ greatly among occupations. In Table 28.3 we list average annual salaries for a number of occupations to illustrate such occupational **wage differentials.** For example, observe that surgeons on average earn seven times as much as retail salespersons. Not shown, there are also large wage differentials within some of the occupations listed. For example, some highly experienced surgeons earn several

[2]Alan Krueger, "Teaching the Minimum Wage in Econ 101 in Light of the New Economics of the Minimum Wage," *Journal of Economic Education*, Summer 2001.

TABLE 28.3

Average Annual Wages in Selected Occupations, 2001

Occupation	Average Annual Wages
Surgeons	$137,050
Aircraft pilots	99,400
Petroleum engineers	81,800
Law professors	79,130
Financial managers	75,430
Chemical engineers	72,780
Dental hygienists	56,770
Registered nurses	48,240
Electricians	43,160
Police officers	41,950
Travel agents	27,230
Barbers	21,190
Retail salespersons	20,920
Recreation workers	20,270
Teacher aides	19,430
Fast food cooks	14,530

Source: Bureau of Labor Statistics, www.bls.gov/, 2003.

times as much income as surgeons just starting their careers. And, although average wages for retail salespersons are relatively low, some top salespersons selling on commission make several times the average wages listed for their occupation.

What explains wage differentials such as these? Once again, the forces of demand and supply are revealing. As we demonstrate in Figure 28.9, wage differentials can arise on either the supply or the demand side of labor markets. Figure 28.9a and 28.9b represent labor markets for two occupational groups that have identical *labor supply curves*. Labor market (a) has a relatively high equilibrium wage (W_a) because labor demand is very strong. In labor market (b) the equilibrium wage is relatively low (W_b) because labor demand is weak. Clearly, the wage differential between occupations (a) and (b) results solely from differences in the magnitude of labor demand.

Contrast that situation with Figure 28.9c and 28.9d, where the *labor demand curves* are identical. In labor market (c) the equilibrium wage is relatively high (W_c) because labor supply is highly restricted. In labor market (d) labor supply is highly abundant, so the equilibrium wage (W_d) is relatively low. The wage differential between (c) and (d) results solely from the differences in the magnitude of labor supply.

Although Figure 28.9 provides a good starting point for understanding wage differentials, we need to know *why* demand and supply conditions differ in various labor markets. There are several reasons.

Marginal Revenue Productivity

The strength of labor demand—how far rightward the labor demand curve is located—differs greatly among occupations due to differences in how much various occupational groups contribute to their employer's revenue. This revenue contribution, in turn, depends on the workers' productivity and the strength of the demand for the products they are helping to produce. Where labor is highly productive and product demand is strong, labor demand also is strong and, other things equal, pay is high. Top professional athletes, for example, are highly productive at producing sports entertainment, for which millions of people are willing to pay billions of dollars over the course of a season. So the **marginal revenue productivity** of these top players is exceptionally high, as are their salaries (as represented in Figure 28.9a). In contrast, in most occupations workers generate much more modest

revenue for their employers, so their pay is lower (as in Figure 28.9b).

Noncompeting Groups

On the supply side of the labor market, workers are not homogeneous; they differ in their mental and physical capacities and in their education and training. At any given time the labor force is made up of many **noncompeting groups** of workers, each representing several occupations for which the members of a particular group qualify. In some groups qualified workers are relatively few, whereas in others they are highly abundant. And workers in one group do not qualify for the occupations of other groups.

Ability   Only a few workers have the ability or physical attributes to be brain surgeons, concert violinists, top fashion models, research chemists, or professional athletes. Because the supply of these particular types of labor is very small in relation to labor demand, their wages are

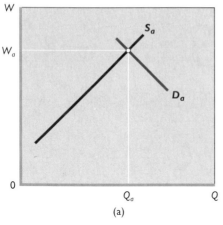

(a)

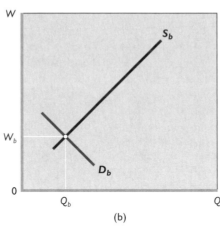

(b)

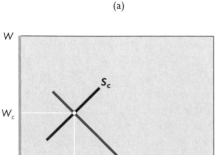

(c)

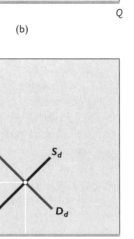
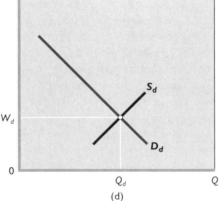

(d)

FIGURE 28.9

Labor demand, labor supply, and wage differentials. The wage differential between labor markets (a) and (b) results solely from differences in labor demand. In labor markets (c) and (d), differences in labor supply are the sole cause of the wage differential.

high (as in Figure 28.9c). The members of these and similar groups do not compete with one another or with other skilled or semiskilled workers. The violinist does not compete with the surgeon, nor does the surgeon compete with the violinist or the fashion model.

The concept of noncompeting groups can be applied to various subgroups and even to specific individuals in a particular group. Some especially skilled violinists can command higher salaries than colleagues who play the same instrument. A handful of top corporate executives earn 10 to 20 times as much as the average chief executive officer. In each of these cases, the supply of top talent is highly limited, since less talented colleagues are only imperfect substitutes.

Education and Training

Another source of wage differentials has to do with differing amounts of investment in human capital. An **investment in human capital** is *an expenditure on education or training that improves the skills and therefore the productivity of workers.* Like expenditures on machinery and equipment, expenditures on education or training that increase a worker's productivity can be regarded as investments. In both cases, current costs are incurred with the intention that they will lead to a greater *future* flow of earnings.

28.2 Human capital

Figure 28.10 indicates that workers who have made greater investments in education achieve higher incomes during their careers. The reason is twofold: (1) There are fewer such workers, so their supply is limited relative to less educated workers, and (2) more educated workers tend to be more productive and thus in greater demand. Figure 28.10 also indicates that the earnings of better-educated workers rise more rapidly than those of poorly educated workers. The primary reason is that employers provide more on-the-job training to the better-educated workers, boosting their marginal revenue productivity and therefore their earnings.

Although education yields higher incomes, it carries substantial costs. A college education involves not only direct costs (tuition, fees, books) but indirect or opportunity costs (forgone earnings) as well. Does the higher pay received by better-educated workers compensate for these costs? The answer is yes. Rates of return are estimated to be 10 to 13 percent for investments in secondary education and 8 to 12 percent for investments in college education. One generally accepted estimate is that each year of schooling raises a worker's wage by about 8 percent. Also, the pay gap between college graduates and high school graduates increased sharply between 1980 and

FIGURE 28.10

Education levels and individual annual earnings. Annual income by age is higher for workers with more education than less. Investment in education yields a return in the form of earnings differences enjoyed over one's work life.

Source: U.S. Bureau of the Census. Data are for males in 2001.

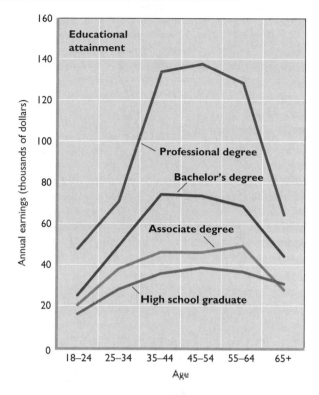

2000. Specifically, it rose from 37 to 66 percent for women and from 34 to 60 percent for men.

Compensating Differences

If the workers in a particular noncompeting group are equally capable of performing several different jobs, you might expect the wage rates to be identical for all these jobs. Not so. A group of high school graduates may be equally capable of becoming salesclerks or general construction workers. But these jobs pay different wages. In virtually all locales, construction laborers receive much higher wages than salesclerks. These wage differentials are called **compensating differences,** because they must be paid to compensate for nonmonetary differences in various jobs.

The construction job involves dirty hands, a sore back, the hazard of accidents, and irregular employment, both seasonally and cyclically. The retail sales job means clean clothing, pleasant air-conditioned surroundings, and

CONSIDER THIS . . .

© Réunion des Musées Nationaux/Art Resource, NY. © 2004 Estate of Pablo Picasso/Artists Rights Society (ARS), New York.

My Entire Life

Human capital is the accumulation of outcomes of prior investments in education, training, and other factors that increase productivity and earnings. It is the stock of knowledge, know-how, and skills that enables individuals to be productive and thus earn income. A valuable stock of human capital, together with a strong demand for one's services, can add up to a large capacity to earn income. For some people, high earnings have little to do with actual hours of work and much to do with their tremendous skill, which reflects their accumulated stock of human capital.

The point is demonstrated in the following story: It is said that a tourist once spotted the famous Spanish artist Pablo Picasso (1881–1973) in a Paris café. The tourist asked Picasso if he would do a sketch of his wife for pay. Picasso sketched the wife in a matter of minutes and said, "That will be 10,000 francs [roughly $2000]." Hearing the high price, the tourist became irritated, saying, "But that took you only a few minutes."

"No," replied Picasso, "it took me my entire life! "

little fear of injury or layoff. Other things equal, it is easy to see why workers would rather pick up a credit card than a shovel. So labor supply is more limited to construction firms (as in Figure 28.9c) than to retail shops (as in Figure 28.9d). Construction firms must pay higher wages than retailers to compensate for the unattractive nonmonetary aspects of construction jobs.

Compensating differences play an important role in allocating society's scarce labor resources. If very few workers want to be garbage collectors, then society must pay high wages to garbage collectors to get the garbage collected. If many more people want to be salesclerks, then society need not pay them as much as it pays garbage collectors to get those services performed.

Market Imperfections

Differences in marginal revenue productivity, amounts of human capital, and nonmonetary aspects of jobs explain most of the wage differentials in the economy. But some persistent differentials result from various market imperfections that impede workers from moving from lower-paying jobs to higher-paying jobs.

Lack of Job Information   Workers may simply be unaware of job opportunities and wage rates in other geographic areas and in other jobs for which they qualify. Consequently, the flow of qualified labor from lower-paying to higher-paying jobs—and thus the adjustments in labor supply—may not be sufficient to equalize wages within occupations.

Geographic Immobility   Workers take root geographically. Many are reluctant to move to new places, to leave friends, relatives, and associates, to force their children to change schools, to sell their houses, or to incur the costs and inconveniences of adjusting to a new job and a new community. As Adam Smith noted over two centuries ago, "A [person] is of all sorts of luggage the most difficult to be transported." The reluctance or inability of workers to move enables geographic wage differentials within the same occupation to persist.

Unions and Government Restraints   Wage differentials may be reinforced by artificial restrictions on mobility imposed by unions and government. We have noted that craft unions find it to their advantage to restrict membership. After all, if carpenters and bricklayers become too plentiful, the wages they can command will decline. Thus the low-paid nonunion carpenter of Brush, Colorado, may be willing to move to Chicago in the pursuit of higher wages. But her chances for succeeding are slim. She may be unable to get a union card, and no card means no job. Similarly, an optometrist or lawyer qualified to practice in one state may not meet licensing requirements of other states, so his or her ability to move is limited. Other artificial barriers involve pension plans, health insurance benefits, and seniority rights that might be jeopardized by moving from one job to another.

Discrimination   Despite legislation to the contrary, discrimination sometimes results in lower wages being paid to women and minority workers than to white males doing virtually identical work. Also, women and minorities may be crowded into certain low-paying occupations, driving down wages there and raising them elsewhere. If discrimination keeps qualified women and minorities from taking higher-paying jobs, then differences in pay will persist. (We discuss discrimination in Chapter 35.)

All four considerations—differences in marginal revenue productivity, noncompeting groups, nonmonetary differences, and market imperfections—come into play in explaining actual wage differentials. For example, the differential between the wages of a physician and those of a construction worker can be explained on the basis of marginal revenue productivity and noncompeting groups. Physicians generate considerable revenue because of their high productivity and the strong willingness of consumers (via insurance) to pay for health care. Physicians also fall into a noncompeting group where, because of stringent training requirements, only relatively few persons qualify. So the supply of labor is small in relation to demand.

In construction work, where training requirements are much less significant, the supply of labor is great relative to demand. So wages are much lower for construction workers than for physicians. However, if not for the unpleasantness of the construction worker's job and the fact that his or her craft union observes restrictive membership policies, the differential would be even greater than it is.

Pay for Performance

The models of wage determination we have described in this chapter assume that worker pay is always a standard amount for each hour's work, for example, $15 per hour. But pay schemes are often more complex than that both in composition and in purpose. For instance, many workers receive annual salaries rather than hourly pay. And workers receive differing proportions of fringe benefits (health insurance, life insurance, paid vacations, paid sick-leave days, pension contributions, and so on) as part of their pay. Finally, some pay plans are designed to elicit a desired level of performance from workers. This last aspect of pay plans requires further elaboration.

The Principal-Agent Problem Revisited

In Chapter 5 we identified the *principal-agent problem* as it relates to possible differences in the interests of corporate stockholders (principals) and the executives (agents) they hire. This problem extends to all workers. Firms hire workers because they are needed to help produce the goods and services the firms sell for a profit. Workers are the firms' agents; they are hired to advance the interest (profit) of the firms. The principals are the firms; they hire agents to advance their goals. Firms and workers have one interest in common: They both want the firm to survive and thrive. That will ensure profit for the firm and continued employment and wages for the workers.

28.3 Principal-agent problem

But the interests of the firm and of workers are not identical. A principal-agent problem arises when those interests diverge. Workers may seek to increase their utility by shirking on the job, that is, by providing less than the agreed-upon effort or by taking unauthorized breaks. They may improve their well-being by increasing their leisure during paid work hours, without forfeiting income. The night security guard in a warehouse may leave work early or spend time reading a novel rather than making the assigned rounds. A salaried manager may spend time away from the office visiting with friends rather than attending to company business.

Firms (principals) have a profit incentive to reduce or eliminate shirking. One option is to monitor workers, but monitoring is difficult and costly. Hiring another worker to supervise or monitor the security guard might double the cost of maintaining a secure warehouse. Another way of resolving a principal-agent problem is through some sort of **incentive pay plan** that ties worker compensation more closely to worker output or performance. Such incentive pay schemes include piece rates; commissions and royalties; bonuses, stock options, and profit sharing; and efficiency wages.

Piece Rates Piece rates consist of compensation paid according to the number of units of output a worker produces. If a principal pays fruit pickers by the bushel or typists by the page, it need not be concerned with shirking or with monitoring costs.

Commissions or Royalties Unlike piece rates, commissions and royalties tie compensation to the value of sales. Employees who sell products or services—including real estate agents, insurance agents, stockbrokers, and retail salespersons—commonly receive *commissions* that are computed as a percentage of the monetary value of their sales. Recording artists and authors are paid *royalties*, computed as a certain percentage of sales revenues from their works. Such types of compensation link the financial interests of the salespeople, artists, and authors to the profit interest of the firms.

Bonuses, Stock Options, and Profit Sharing *Bonuses* are payments in addition to one's annual salary that are based on some factor such as the performance of the individual worker, or of a group of workers, or of the firm itself. A professional baseball player may receive a bonus based on a high batting average, the number of home runs hit, or the number of runs batted in. A business manager may receive a bonus based on the profitability of her or his unit. *Stock options* allow workers to buy shares of their employer's stock at a fixed, lower price when the stock price rises. Such options are part of the compensation packages of top corporate officials, as well as many workers in relatively new high-technology firms. *Profit-sharing plans* allocate a percentage of a firm's profit to its employees. Such plans have in recent years resulted in large annual payments to many U.S. autoworkers.

Efficiency Wages   The rationale behind *efficiency wages* is that employers will enjoy greater effort from their workers by paying them above-equilibrium wage rates. Glance back at Figure 28.3, which shows a competitive labor market in which the equilibrium wage rate is $10. What if an employer decides to pay an above-equilibrium wage of $12 per hour? Rather than putting the firm at a cost disadvantage compared with rival firms paying only $10, the higher wage might improve worker effort and productivity so that unit labor costs actually fall. For example, if each worker produces 10 units of output per hour at the $12 wage rate compared with only 6 units at the $10 wage rate, unit labor costs for the high-wage firm will be only $1.20 (= $12/10) compared to $1.67 (= $10/6) for firms paying the equilibrium wage.

An above-equilibrium wage may enhance worker efficiency in several ways. It enables the firm to attract higher-quality workers. It lifts worker morale. And it lowers turnover, resulting in a more experienced workforce, greater worker productivity, and lower recruitment and training costs. Because the opportunity cost of losing a higher-wage job is greater, workers are more likely to put forth their best efforts with less supervision and monitoring. In fact, efficiency wage payments have proved effective for many employers.

28.4
Efficiency
wages

Addenda: Negative Side Effects of Pay for Performance

Although pay for performance may help overcome the principal-agent problem and enhance worker productivity, such plans may have negative side effects and require careful design. Here are a few examples:

- The rapid production pace that piece rates encourage may result in poor product quality and may compro-

mise the safety of workers. Such outcomes can be costly to the firm over the long run.

- Commissions may cause some salespeople to engage in questionable or even fraudulent sales practices, such as making exaggerated claims about products or recommending unneeded repairs. Such practices may lead to private lawsuits or government legal action.

- Bonuses based on personal performance may disrupt the close cooperation needed for maximum team production. A professional basketball player who receives a bonus for points scored may be reluctant to pass the ball to teammates.

- Since profit sharing is usually tied to the performance of the entire firm, less energetic workers can "free ride" by obtaining their profit share on the basis of hard work by others.

- Stock options may prompt some unscrupulous executives to manipulate cost and revenue streams of their firms to create a false appearance of rapidly rising profit. When the firm's stock value rises, the executives exercise their stock options at inflated share prices and reap a personal fortune. In the early 2000s, some firms collapsed when the wrongdoings of their executives were exposed.

- There may be a downside to the reduced turnover resulting from above-market wages: Firms that pay efficiency wages have fewer opportunities to hire new workers and suffer the loss of new blood that sometimes energizes the workplace.

QUICK REVIEW 28.3

- Proponents of the minimum wage argue that it is needed to assist the working poor and to counter monopsony where it might exist; critics say that it is poorly targeted to reduce poverty and reduces employment.

- Wage differentials are attributable in general to the forces of supply and demand, influenced by differences in workers' marginal revenue productivity, education, and skills and by nonmonetary differences in jobs. But several labor market imperfections also play a role.

- As it applies to labor, the principal-agent problem is one of workers' pursuing their own interests to the detriment of the employer's profit objective.

- Pay-for-performance plans (piece rates, commissions, royalties, bonuses, stock options, profit sharing, and efficiency wages) are designed to improve worker productivity by overcoming the principal-agent problem.

Are Chief Executive Officers (CEOs) Overpaid?

The Multimillion-dollar Pay of Major Corporate CEOs Has Drawn Considerable Criticism.

Top executives of U.S. corporations typically receive total annual pay (salary, bonuses, and stock options) in the millions of dollars. As shown in Table 1, each of the top five paid U.S. executives earned more than $60 million in 2002.

CEO pay in the United States is not only exceptionally high relative to the average pay of U.S. managers and workers but also high compared to the CEO pay in other industrial countries. For example, in 2001 the CEO pay at firms with about $500 million in annual sales averaged $1,933,000 in the United States, $787,000 in Canada, $669,000 in the United Kingdom, $600,000 in Italy, $519,000 in France, $508,000 in Japan, and $455,000 in Germany.*

Is high CEO pay simply the outcome of labor supply and labor demand, as is the pay for star athletes and entertainers? Does it reflect marginal revenue productivity—that is, the contributions by CEOs to their company's output and revenue?

Observers who answer affirmatively point out that decisions made by the CEOs of large corporations affect the productivity of every employee in the organization. Good decisions enhance productivity throughout the organization and increase revenue; bad decisions reduce productivity and revenue. Only executives who have consistently made good business decisions

attain the top positions in large corporations. Because the supply of these people is highly limited and their marginal revenue productivity is enormous, they command huge salaries and performance bonuses.

Also, some economists note that CEO pay in the United States may be like the prizes professional golfers and tennis players receive for winning tournaments. These high prizes are designed to promote the productivity of all those who aspire to achieve them. In corporations the top prizes go to the winners of the "contests" among managers to attain, at least eventually, the CEO positions. Thus high CEO pay does not derive solely from the CEO's direct productivity. Instead, it may exist because the high pay creates incentives that raise the productivity of scores of other corporate executives who seek to achieve the top position. In this view, high CEO pay remains grounded on high productivity.

Critics of existing CEO pay acknowledge that CEOs deserve substantially higher salaries than ordinary workers or typical managers, but they question pay packages that run into the millions of dollars. They reject the "tournament pay" idea on the grounds that corporations require cooperative team effort by managers and executives, not the type of high-stakes competition promoted by "winner-take-most" pay. They believe that corporations, although owned by their shareholders, are controlled by corporate boards and professional executives. Because many board members are present or past CEOs of other corporations, they often exaggerate CEO importance and, consequently, overpay their own CEOs. These overpayments are at the expense of the firm's stockholders.

In summary, defenders of CEO pay say that high pay is justified by the direct or indirect marginal-revenue contribution of CEOs. Like it or not, CEO pay is market-determined pay. In contrast, critics say that multimillion-dollar CEO pay bears little relationship to marginal revenue productivity and is unfair to ordinary stockholders. It is clear from our discussion that this issue remains unsettled.

TABLE 1

The Five Highest-Paid U.S. CEOs, 2002

Name	Company	Total Pay, Millions
1. Alfred Lerner	MBNA	$195
2. Jeffrey Barbakow	Tenet Healthcare	117
3. Millard Drexler	GAP	91
4. Dennis Kozlowski	Tyco International	71
5. Irwin Jacobs	Qualcomm	63

Source: Business Week, Apr. 21, 2003. This list is updated each year in the mid-April issue of *Business Week.*

*Worldwide Total Remuneration, (New York: Towers Perrin, December, 2001, p. 20).

SUMMARY

1. The term "labor" encompasses all people who work for pay. The wage rate is the price paid per unit of time for labor. Labor earnings comprise total pay and are found by multiplying the number of hours worked by the hourly wage rate. The nominal wage rate is the amount of money received per unit of time; the real wage rate is the purchasing power of the nominal wage.

2. The long-run growth of real hourly compensation—the average real wage—roughly matches that of productivity, with both increasing over the long run.

3. Global comparisons suggest that real wages in the United States are relatively high, but not the highest, internationally. High real wages in the advanced industrial countries stem largely from high labor productivity.

4. Specific wage rates depend on the structure of the particular labor market. In a competitive labor market the equilibrium wage rate and level of employment are determined at the intersection of the labor supply curve and labor demand curve. For the individual firm, the market wage rate establishes a horizontal labor supply curve, meaning that the wage rate equals the firm's constant marginal resource cost. The firm hires workers to the point where its MRP equals its MRC.

5. Under monopsony the marginal resource cost curve lies above the resource supply curve because the monopsonist must bid up the wage rate to hire extra workers and must pay that higher wage rate to all workers. The monopsonist hires fewer workers than are hired under competitive conditions, pays less-than-competitive wage rates (has lower labor costs), and thus obtains greater profit.

6. A union may raise competitive wage rates by (a) increasing the derived demand for labor, (b) restricting the supply of labor through exclusive unionism, or (c) directly enforcing an above-equilibrium wage rate through inclusive unionism.

7. In many industries the labor market takes the form of bilateral monopoly, in which a strong union "sells" labor to a monopsonistic employer. The wage-rate outcome of this labor market model depends on union and employer bargaining power.

8. On average, unionized workers realize wage rates 15 percent higher than comparable nonunion workers.

9. Economists disagree about the desirability of the minimum wage as an antipoverty mechanism. While it causes unemployment for some low-income workers, it raises the incomes of those who retain their jobs.

10. Wage differentials are largely explainable in terms of (a) marginal revenue productivity of various groups of workers; (b) noncompeting groups arising from differences in the capacities and education of different groups of workers; (c) compensating wage differences, that is, wage differences that must be paid to offset nonmonetary differences in jobs; and (d) market imperfections in the form of lack of job information, geographic immobility, union and government restraints, and discrimination.

11. The principal-agent problem arises when workers provide less-than-expected effort. Firms may combat this by monitoring workers or by creating incentive pay schemes that link worker compensation to performance.

TERMS AND CONCEPTS

wage rate	monopsony	minimum wage	investment in human capital
nominal wage	exclusive unionism	wage differentials	compensating differences
real wage	occupational licensing	marginal revenue productivity	incentive pay plan
purely competitive labor market	inclusive unionism	noncompeting groups	
	bilateral monopoly		

STUDY QUESTIONS

1. Explain why the general level of wages is high in the United States and other industrially advanced countries. What is the single most important factor underlying the long-run increase in average real-wage rates in the United States?

2. Why is a firm in a purely competitive labor market a *wage taker?* What would happen if it decided to pay less than the going market wage rate?

3. *Key Question* Describe wage determination in a labor market in which workers are unorganized and many firms actively compete for the services of labor. Show this situation graphically, using W_1 to indicate the equilibrium wage rate and Q_1 to show the number of workers hired by the firms as a group. Show the labor supply curve of the individual firm, and compare it with that of the total market.

Why the differences? In the diagram representing the firm, identify total revenue, total wage cost, and revenue available for the payment of nonlabor resources.

4. *Key Question* Complete the following labor supply table for a firm hiring labor competitively:

Units of Labor	Wage Rate	Total Labor Cost (Wage Bill)	Marginal Resource (Labor) Cost
0	$14	$ _____	
1	14	_____	$ _____
2	14	_____	_____
3	14	_____	_____
4	14	_____	_____
5	14	_____	_____
6	14	_____	_____

   a. Show graphically the labor supply and marginal resource (labor) cost curves for this firm. Explain the relationship of these curves to one another.

   b. Plot the labor demand data of question 2 in Chapter 27 on the graph used in part *a* above. What are the equilibrium wage rate and level of employment? Explain.

5. Suppose the formerly competing firms in question 3 form an employers' association that hires labor as a monopsonist would. Describe verbally the effect on wage rates and employment. Adjust the graph you drew for question 3, showing the monopsonistic wage rate and employment level as W_2 and Q_2, respectively. Using this monopsony model, explain why hospital administrators sometimes complain about a "shortage" of nurses. How might such a shortage be corrected?

6. *Key Question* Assume a firm is a monopsonist that can hire its first worker for $6 but must increase the wage rate by $3 to attract each successive worker. Draw the firm's labor supply and marginal resource cost curves and explain their relationships to one another. On the same graph, plot the labor demand data of question 2 in Chapter 27. What are the equilibrium wage rate and level of employment? Why do these differ from your answer to question 4?

7. *Key Question* Assume a monopsonistic employer is paying a wage rate of W_m and hiring Q_m workers, as indicated in Figure 28.8. Now suppose an industrial union is formed that forces the employer to accept a wage rate of W_c. Explain verbally and graphically why in this instance the higher wage rate will be accompanied by an increase in the number of workers hired.

8. Have you ever worked for the minimum wage? If so, for how long? Would you favor increasing the minimum wage by a dollar? By two dollars? By five dollars? Explain your reasoning.

9. "Many of the lowest-paid people in society—for example, short-order cooks—also have relatively poor working conditions. Hence, the notion of compensating wage differentials is disproved." Do you agree? Explain.

10. What is meant by investment in human capital? Use this concept to explain (*a*) wage differentials, and (*b*) the long-run rise of real wage rates in the United States.

11. What is the principal-agent problem? Have you ever worked in a setting where this problem has arisen? If so, do you think increased monitoring would have eliminated the problem? Why don't firms simply hire more supervisors to eliminate shirking?

12. *(Last Word)* Do you think exceptionally high pay to CEOs is economically justified? Why or why not?

13. *Web-Based Question: Real wages and productivity—are workers' paychecks keeping up?* Over the long run, real wages grow at about the same pace as labor productivity. Go to the Bureau of Labor Statistics website, www.bls.gov/lpc/, and select Get Detailed Statistics and then Most Requested Statistics for current information on percentage changes in output per hour of all persons in the business sector (labor productivity) and percentage changes in real compensation per hour. Has real compensation per hour kept up with output per hour over the latest 3 years shown?

14. *Web-Based Question: Men's and women's earnings in professional golf—why the differences?* Go to espn.go.com and select Golf and then Money Leaders. What are the annual earnings to date of the top 10 men golfers on the PGA tour? What are the earnings of the top 10 women golfers on the LPGA tour? Why the general differences in earnings between the men and the women golfers?

29 | *Rent, Interest, and Profit*

How do land prices (and land rents) get established, and why do they differ? For example, why do 20 acres of land in the middle of the Nevada desert sell for $5000 while 20 acres along the Las Vegas strip command $100 million or more?

What determines interest rates and causes them to change? For instance, why were interest rates on 3-month bank certificates of deposit 6.7 percent in July 2000 but only 1.3 percent in January 2003?

What are the sources of profit and losses and why do they vary? For example, why did Wal-Mart earn profits of $6.7 billion in 2001 whereas rival K-Mart experienced losses of $95 million?

In Chapter 28 we focused on resource payments in the forms of wages and salaries, which account for about 72 percent of national income. This chapter examines the other 28 percent of national income, specifically rent, interest, and profit. We begin by looking at rent.

Economic Rent

To most people, "rent" means the money paid for the use of an apartment or a dormitory room. To the business executive, "rent" is a payment made for the use of a factory building, machine, or warehouse facility. Such definitions of rent can be confusing and ambiguous, however. Dormitory room rent, for example, may include other payments as well: interest on money the university borrowed to finance the dormitory, wages for custodial services, utility payments, and so on.

Economists use "rent" in a much narrower sense. **Economic rent** is *the price paid for the use of land and other natural resources that are completely fixed in total supply.* As

you will see, this fixed overall supply distinguishes rental payments from wage, interest, and profit payments.

Let's examine this idea and some of its implications through supply and demand analysis. We first assume that all land is of the same grade or quality, meaning that each arable (tillable) acre of land is as productive as every other acre. We assume, too, that all land has a single use, for example, producing wheat. And we suppose that land is rented or leased in a competitive market in which many producers are demanding land and many landowners are offering land in the market.

In Figure 29.1, curve S represents the supply of arable land available in the economy as a whole, and curve D_2 represents the demand of producers for use of that land.

FIGURE 29.1

The determination of land rent. Because the supply S of land (and other natural resources) is perfectly inelastic, demand is the sole active determinant of land rent. An increase in demand from D_2 to D_1 or a decrease in demand from D_2 to D_3 will cause a considerable change in rent: from R_2 to R_1 in the first instance and from R_2 to R_3 in the second. But the amount of land supplied will remain at L_0. If demand is very weak (D_4) relative to supply, land will be a "free good," commanding no rent.

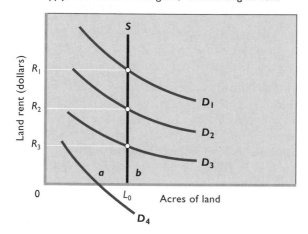

As with all economic resources, this demand is derived from the demand for the product being produced. The demand curve for land is downward-sloping because of diminishing returns and because, for producers as a group, product price must be reduced in order to sell additional units of output.

Perfectly Inelastic Supply

The unique feature of our analysis is on the supply side. For all practical purposes the supply of land is perfectly inelastic (in both the short run and the long run), as reflected in supply curve S. Land has no production cost; it is a "free and nonreproducible gift of nature." The economy has only so much land, and that's that. Of course, within limits any parcel of land can be made more usable by clearing, drainage, and irrigation. But these are capital improvements and not changes in the amount of land itself. Moreover, increases in the usability of land affect only a small fraction of the total amount of land and do not change the basic fact that land and other natural resources are fixed in supply.

Changes in Demand

Because the supply of land is fixed, demand is the only active determinant of land rent; supply is passive. And what determines the demand for land? The factors we discussed in Chapter 27: the price of the product produced on the land, the productivity of land (which depends in part on the quantity and quality of the resources with which land is combined), and the prices of the other resources that are combined with land.

If the demand for land in Figure 29.1 increased from D_2 to D_1, land rent would rise from R_2 to R_1. On the other hand, if the demand for land declined from D_2 to D_3, land rent would fall from R_2 to R_3. But, in either case, the amount of land supplied would remain the same at quantity L_0. Changes in economic rent have no effect on the amount of land available because the supply of land cannot be augmented. If the demand for land were only D_4, land rent would be zero. Land would be a *free good*—a good for which demand is so weak relative to supply that there is an excess supply of it even if the market price is zero. In Figure 29.1, we show this excess supply as distance $b - a$ at rent of zero. This essentially was the situation in the free-land era of U.S. history.

The ideas underlying Figure 29.1 help answer one of our chapter-opening questions. Land prices and rents are so high along the Las Vegas strip because the demand for that land is tremendous. It is capable of producing exceptionally high revenue from gambling, lodging, and entertainment. In contrast, the demand for isolated land in the middle of the desert is highly limited because very little revenue can be generated from its use. (It is an entirely different matter, of course, if gold can be mined from the land, as is true of some isolated lands in Nevada!)

Land Rent: A Surplus Payment

The perfectly inelastic supply of land must be contrasted with the relatively elastic supply of capital, such as apartment buildings, machinery, and warehouses. In the long run, capital is *not* fixed in total supply. A higher price gives entrepreneurs the incentive to construct and offer larger quantities of property resources. Conversely, a decline in price induces suppliers to allow existing facilities to depreciate and not be replaced. The supply curves of these nonland resources are upward-sloping, meaning that the prices paid to such resources provide an **incentive function.** A high price provides an incentive to offer more of the resource, whereas a low price prompts resource suppliers to offer less.

Not so with land. Rent serves no incentive function because the total supply of land is fixed. Whether rent is $10,000, $500, $1, or $0 per acre, the same amount of land is available to society for use in production. This is why economists consider rent a *surplus payment* not necessary to ensure that land is available to the economy as a whole.

Application: A Single Tax on Land

If land is a gift of nature, costs nothing to produce, and would be available even without rental payments, why should rent be paid to those who by historical accident, by inheritance, or by misdeed happen to be landowners? Socialists have long argued that all land rents are unearned incomes. They urge that land should be nationalized (owned by the state) so that any payments for its use can be used by the government to further the well-being of the entire population rather than being used by a landowning minority.

Henry George's Proposal
In the United States, criticism of rental payments has taken the form of a **single-tax movement,** which gained significant support in the late nineteenth century. Spearheaded by Henry George's provocative book *Progress and Poverty* (1879), supporters of this reform movement held that economic rent could be heavily taxed, or even taxed away, without diminishing the available supply of land or, therefore, the productive potential of the economy as a whole.

George observed that as population grew and the geographic frontier closed, landowners enjoyed larger and larger rents from their landholdings. That increase in rents was the result of a growing demand for a resource whose supply was perfectly inelastic. Some landlords were receiving fabulously high incomes, not through any productive effort but solely through their owning advantageously located land. George insisted that these increases in land rent belonged to the economy; he held that land rents should be heavily taxed and the revenue spent for public uses. In seeking popular support for his ideas on land taxation, George proposed that taxes on rental income be the *only* tax levied by government.

George's case for taxing land was based not only on equity or fairness but also on efficiency. That is, a tax on land is efficient because, unlike virtually every other tax, it does not alter the use of the resource being taxed. A tax on wages reduces after-tax wages and may weaken the incentive to work; an individual who decides to work for a $10 before-tax wage may decide to retire when an income tax reduces the wage to an after-tax $8. Similarly, a property tax on buildings lowers returns to investors in such property and might cause some to look for other investments. But no such reallocations of resources occur when

land is taxed. The most profitable use of land before it is taxed remains the most profitable use after it is taxed. Of course, a landlord could withdraw land from production when a tax is imposed, but that would mean no rental income at all. And some rental income, no matter how small, is better than none.

Criticisms
There are very few remaining advocates of a single tax on land. Critics of the idea have pointed out that:

- Current levels of government spending are such that a land tax alone would not bring in enough revenue; it is unrealistic to consider it as a single tax.
- Most income payments consist of a mixture of such elements as interest, rent, wages, and profits. Land is typically improved in some way, and economic rent cannot be readily disentangled from payments for such improvements. So in practice it would be difficult to determine how much of any specific income payment actually amounted to economic rent.
- So-called *unearned income* accrues to many people other than landowners, especially when the economy is growing. For example, consider the capital-gains income received by someone who, some 20 or 25 years ago, chanced to purchase (or inherit) stock in a firm that has experienced rapid profit growth. Is such income more "earned" than the rental income of the landowner?
- Historically, a piece of land is likely to have changed ownership many times. Former owners may have been the beneficiaries of past increases in the value of the land (and in land rent). It would hardly be fair to impose a heavy tax on current owners who paid the competitive market price for the land.

Productivity Differences and Rent Differences

So far we have assumed that all units of land are of the same grade. That is plainly not so. Different pieces of land vary greatly in productivity, depending on soil fertility and on such climatic factors as rainfall and temperature. Such factors explain, for example, why Kansas soil is excellently suited to wheat production, why the sagebrush plains of Wyoming are much less well suited, and why the desert of Arizona is nearly incapable of wheat production. Such productivity differences are reflected in resource demand and prices. Competitive bidding by producers will establish a high rent for highly productive Kansas land; less productive Wyoming land will command a much lower rent; and Arizona desert land may command no rent at all.

Location itself may be just as important in explaining differences in land rent. Other things equal, renters will pay more for a unit of land that is strategically located with respect to materials, transportation, labor, and customers than they will for a unit of land whose location is remote from these things. Examples: the enormously high land prices in major ski resorts and the high price of land that contains oil beneath it.

Figure 29.1, viewed from a slightly different perspective, reveals the rent differentials from quality differences in land. Assume, again, that only wheat can be produced on four grades of land, each of which is available in the fixed amount L_0. When combined with identical amounts of labor, capital, and entrepreneurial talent, the productivity or, more specifically, the marginal revenue product of each of the four grades of land is reflected in demand curves D_1, D_2, D_3, and D_4. Grade 1 land is the most productive, as shown by D_1, while grade 4 is the least productive, as shown by D_4. The resulting economic rents for grades 1, 2, and 3 land will be R_1, R_2, and R_3, respectively; the rent differential will mirror the differences in productivity of the three grades of land. Grade 4 land is so poor in quality that, given its supply S, farmers won't pay anything to use it. It will be a free good because it is not sufficiently scarce in relation to the demand for it to command a price or a rent.

Alternative Uses of Land

We have assumed that land has only one use. Actually, we know that land normally has alternative uses. An acre of Kansas farmland may be useful for raising not only wheat but corn, oats, barley, and cattle; or it may be useful for building a house or a highway or as a factory site. In other words, any particular use of land involves an opportunity cost—the forgone production from the next best use of the resource. Where there are alternative uses, individual firms must pay rent to cover those opportunity costs in order to secure the use of land for their particular purposes. To the individual firm, rent is a cost of production, just as are wages and interest.

Recall that, as viewed by society, economic rent is not a cost. Society would have the same amount of land with or without the payment of economic rent. From society's perspective, economic rent is a surplus payment above that needed to gain the use of a resource. But individual firms do need to pay rent to attract land resources away from alternative uses. For firms, rental payments *are* a cost. **(Key Question 2)**

Interest

Interest is the price paid for the use of money. It is the price that borrowers need to pay lenders for transferring purchasing power from the present to the future. It can be thought of as the amount of money that must be paid for the use of $1 for 1 year.

- ***Interest is stated as a percentage.*** Interest is paid in kind; that is, money (interest) is paid for the loan of money. For that reason, interest is typically stated as a percentage of the amount of money borrowed rather than as a dollar amount. It is less clumsy to say that interest is "12 percent annually" than to say that interest is "$120 per year per $1000." Also, stating interest as a percentage makes it easier to compare the interest paid on loans of different amounts. By expressing interest as a percentage, we can immediately compare an interest payment of, say, $432 per year per $2880 with one of $1800 per year per $12,000. Both interest payments are 15 percent per year, which is not obvious from the actual dollar figures. This interest of 15 percent per year is referred to as a 15 percent interest rate.
- ***Money is not a resource.*** Money is *not* an economic resource. In the form of coins, paper currency, or checking accounts, money is not productive; it cannot produce goods and services. However, businesses "buy" the use of money because it can be used to acquire capital goods such as factories, machinery, warehouses, and so on. Such facilities clearly do contribute to production. Thus, in "hiring" the use of money capital, business executives are indirectly buying the use of real capital goods.

Loanable Funds Theory of Interest

In macroeconomics the interest rate is often viewed through the lens of the economy's total supply of and demand for money. But because our present focus is on microeconomics, it will be useful to consider a more micro-based theory of interest here. Specifically, the **loanable funds theory of interest** explains the interest rate not in terms of the total supply of and demand for *money* but, rather, in terms of the supply of and demand for *funds available for lending (and borrowing)*. As Figure 29.2 shows, the equilibrium interest rate (here, 8 percent) is the rate at which the quantities of loanable funds supplied and demanded are equal.

29.1
Loanable
funds

Let's first consider the loanable funds theory in simplified form. Specifically, assume households or consumers are the sole suppliers of loanable funds and businesses are the sole demanders. Also assume that lending occurs directly between households and businesses; there are no intermediate financial institutions.

Supply of Loanable Funds
The supply of loanable funds is represented by curve *S* in Figure 29.2. Its upward slope indicates that households will make available a larger quantity of funds at high interest rates than at low interest rates. Most people prefer to use their incomes to purchase pleasurable goods and services *today*, rather than

FIGURE 29.2

The market for loanable funds. The upsloping supply curve *S* for loanable funds reflects the idea that at higher interest rates, households will defer more of their present consumption (save more), making more funds available for lending. The downsloping demand curve *D* for loanable funds indicates that businesses will borrow more at lower interest rates than at higher interest rates. At the equilibrium interest rate (here, 8 percent), the quantities of loanable funds lent and borrowed are equal (here, F_0 each).

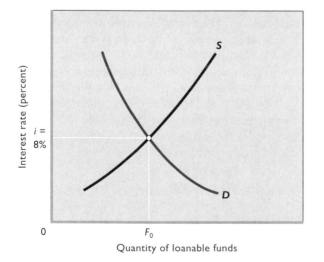

delay purchases to sometime in the *future*. For people to delay consumption and increase their saving, they must be "bribed" or compensated by an interest payment. The larger the amount of that payment, the greater the deferral of household consumption and thus the greater the amount of money made available for loans.

There is disagreement among economists as to how much the quantity of loanable funds made available by suppliers changes in response to changes in the interest rate. Most economists view saving as being relatively insensitive to changes in the interest rate because people also save for reasons other than to secure interest. For example, they may save out of habit, or to have funds available for a "rainy day," or to accumulate funds for an expensive purchase. The supply curve of loanable funds may therefore be more inelastic than *S* in Figure 29.2 implies.

Demand for Loanable Funds
Businesses borrow loanable funds primarily to add to their stocks of capital goods, such as new plants or warehouses, machinery, and equipment. Assume that a firm wants to buy a machine that will increase output and sales such that the firm's total revenue will rise by $110 for the year. Also assume that the machine costs $100 and has a useful life of just 1 year. Comparing the $10 earned with the $100 cost of the machine, we find that the expected rate of return on this investment is 10 percent (= $10/$100) for the 1 year.

To determine whether the investment would be profitable and whether it should be made, the firm must compare the interest rate—the price of loanable funds—with the 10 percent expected rate of return. If funds can be borrowed at some rate less than the rate of return, say, at 8 percent, as in Figure 29.2, then the investment is profitable and should be made. But if funds can be borrowed only at an interest rate above the 10 percent rate of return, say, at 14 percent, the investment is unprofitable and should not be made.

Why is the demand for loanable funds down-sloping, as in Figure 29.2? At higher interest rates fewer investment projects will be profitable and hence a smaller quantity of loanable funds will be demanded. At lower interest rates, more investment projects will be profitable and therefore more loanable funds will be demanded. Indeed, as we have just seen, it is profitable to purchase the $100 machine if funds can be borrowed at 8 percent but not if the firm must borrow at 14 percent.

29.1
Interest
rates

That Is Interest

© Matthew Borkoski/
Index Stock Imagery, Inc.

Viewed from the supply side of the market for loanable funds, interest rates are the payments needed to entice individuals to sacrifice their present consumption, that is, to let someone else use their money for a period of time. The following story told by economist Irving Fisher (1867–1947) helps illustrate this "time-value of money."

In the process of a massage, a masseur informed Fisher that he was a socialist who believed that "interest is the basis of capitalism and is robbery." Following the massage, Fisher asked, "How much do I owe you?"

The masseur replied, "Thirty dollars."

"Very well," said Fisher, "I will give you a note payable a hundred years hence. I suppose you have no objections to taking this note without any interest. At the end of that time, you, or perhaps your grandchildren, can redeem it."

"But I cannot afford to wait that long," said the masseur.

"I thought you said that interest was robbery. If interest is robbery, you ought to be willing to wait indefinitely for the money. If you are willing to wait ten years, how much would you require?"

"Well, I would have to get more than thirty dollars."

His point now made, Fisher replied, "That is interest."*

*Irving Fisher, as quoted in Irving Norton Fisher, *My Father Irving Fisher* (New York: Comet, 1956), p. 77.

Extending the Model

We now make this simple model more realistic in several ways.

Financial Institutions

Households rarely lend their savings directly to businesses that are borrowing funds for investment. Instead, they place their savings in banks (and other financial institutions). The banks pay interest to savers in order to attract loanable funds and in turn lend those funds to businesses. Businesses borrow the funds from the banks, paying them interest for the use of the money. Financial institutions profit by charging borrowers higher interest rates than the interest rates they pay savers. Both interest rates, however, are based on the supply of and demand for loanable funds.

Changes in Supply

Anything that causes households to be thriftier will prompt them to save more at each interest rate, shifting the supply curve rightward. For example, if interest earned on savings were to be suddenly exempted from taxation, we would expect the supply of loanable funds to increase and the equilibrium interest rate to decrease.

Conversely, a decline in thriftiness would shift the supply-of-loanable-funds curve leftward and increase the equilibrium interest rate. Illustration: If the government expanded social insurance to cover the costs of hospitalization, prescription drugs, and retirement living more fully, the incentive of households to save might diminish.

Changes in Demand

On the demand side, anything that increases the rate of return on potential investments will increase the demand for loanable funds. Let's return to our earlier example, where a firm would receive additional revenue of $110 by purchasing a $100 machine and, therefore, would realize a 10 percent return on investment. What factors might increase or decrease the rate of return? Suppose a technological advance raised the productivity of the machine such that the firm's total revenue increased by $120 rather than $110. The rate of return would then be 20 percent, not 10 percent. Before the technological advance, the firm would have demanded zero loanable funds at, say, an interest rate of 14 percent. But now it will demand $100 of loanable funds at that interest rate, meaning that the demand curve for loanable funds has been shifted to the right.

Similarly, an increase in consumer demand for the firm's product will increase the price of its product. So even though the productivity of the machine is unchanged, its potential revenue will rise from $110 to perhaps $120, increasing the firm's rate of return from 10 to 20 percent. Again the firm will be willing to borrow more than previously at our presumed 8 or 14 percent interest rate, implying that the demand curve for loanable funds has shifted rightward. This shift in demand increases the equilibrium interest rate.

Conversely, a decline in productivity or in the price of the firm's product would shift the demand curve for loanable funds leftward, reducing the equilibrium interest rate.

Other Participants

We must recognize that there are more participants on both the demand and the supply sides of the loanable funds market. For example, while households are suppliers of loanable funds, many are also demanders of such funds. Households borrow to finance expensive purchases such as housing, automobiles, furniture, and household appliances. Governments also are on the demand side of the loanable funds market when they borrow to finance budgetary deficits. And businesses that have revenues in excess of their current expenditures may offer some of those revenues in the market for loanable funds. Thus, like households, businesses operate on both the supply and the demand sides of the market.

Finally, in addition to gathering and making available the savings of households, banks and other financial institutions also increase funds through the lending process and decrease funds when loans are paid back and not lent back out. The Federal Reserve (the nation's central bank) controls the amount of this bank activity and thus influences interest rates.

This fact helps answer one of our chapter-opening questions: Why did the interest rate on 3-month certificates of deposit in the United States fall from 6.7 percent in 2000 to only 1.3 percent in early 2003? There are two reasons: (1) The demand for loanable funds sharply declined because businesses reduced their desire to purchase more capital goods, and (2) the Federal Reserve, fighting recession and sluggish recovery, took monetary actions that greatly increased the supply of loanable funds. **(Key Question 6)**

Range of Interest Rates

Although economists often speak in terms of a single interest rate, there are actually a number of interest rates. Table 29.1 lists several interest rates often referred to in the media. These rates range from 1 to 14 percent. Why the differences?

- **Risk** Loans to different borrowers for different purposes carry varying degrees of risk. The greater the chance that the borrower will not repay the loan, the higher the interest rate the lender will charge to compensate for that risk.

- **Maturity** The time length of a loan or its *maturity* (when it needs to be paid back) also affects the interest rate. Other things equal, longer-term loans command higher interest rates than shorter-term loans. The long-term lender suffers the inconvenience and possible financial sacrifice of forgoing alternative uses of his or her money for a greater period.

- **Loan size** If there are two loans of equal maturity and risk, the interest rate on the smaller of the two loans usually will be higher. The costs of issuing a large loan and a small loan are about the same in dollars, but the cost is greater *as a percentage* of the smaller loan.

- **Taxability** Interest on certain state and municipal bonds is exempt from Federal income taxation. Because lenders are interested in their after-tax rate of interest, borrowing by states and local governments can attract lenders even though the borrowers pay low interest rates. Consider a high-income lender

TABLE 29.1

Selected Interest Rates, May 2003

Type of Interest Rate	Annual Percentage
20-year Treasury bond rate (interest rate on Federal government security used to finance the public debt)	4.91%
90-day Treasury Bill rate (interest rate on Federal government security used to finance the public debt)	1.13
Prime interest rate (interest rate used as a reference point for a wide range of bank loans)	4.25
30-year mortgage rate (fixed-interest rate on loans for houses)	5.10
4-year automobile loan rate (interest rate for new autos by automobile finance companies)	5.40
Tax-exempt state and municipal bond rate (interest rate paid on a low-risk bond issued by a state or local government)	4.74
Federal funds rate (interest rate on overnight loans between banks)	1.26
Consumer credit card rate (interest rate charged for credit card purchases)	13.72

Sources: Federal Reserve, www.federalreserve.gov, and Bankrate.com, www.bankrate.com.

who pays a 35 percent Federal income tax (2003) on marginal income. He or she may prefer a 5 percent interest rate on a tax-exempt municipal bond to a 6 percent taxable interest rate on a corporate bond.

- **Market imperfections** Market imperfections also explain some interest-rate differentials. The small-town bank that monopolizes local lending may charge high interest rates on consumer loans because households find it inconvenient and costly to "shop around" at banks in distant cities. The large corporation, on the other hand, can survey a number of rival lenders to float a new bond issue and secure the lowest obtainable rate.

Pure Rate of Interest

Economists and financial specialists talk of "the" interest rate to simplify the cluster of rates (Table 29.1). When they do so, they usually have in mind the **pure rate of interest.** The pure rate is best approximated by the interest paid on long-term, virtually riskless securities such as long-term bonds of the U.S. government (20-year Treasury bonds). This interest payment can be thought of as being made solely for the use of money over an extended time period, because risk and administrative costs are negligible and the interest rate on these bonds is not distorted by market imperfections. In spring 2003 the pure rate of interest in the United States was 4.9 percent.

Role of the Interest Rate

The interest rate is a critical price that affects the *level* and *composition* of investment goods production, as well as the *amount* of R&D spending.

Interest and Total Output
A lower equilibrium interest rate encourages businesses to borrow more for investment. As a result, total spending in the economy rises, and if the economy has unused resources, so does total output. Conversely, a higher equilibrium interest rate discourages business from borrowing for investment, thereby reducing investment and total spending. Such a decrease in spending may be desirable if an economy is experiencing inflation.

The Federal Reserve often manipulates the interest rate to try to expand investment and output, on the one hand, or to reduce investment and inflation, on the other. It affects the interest rate by changing the supply of money. Increases in the money supply increase the supply of loanable funds, causing the equilibrium interest rate to fall. This boosts investment spending and expands the economy. In contrast, decreases in the money supply decrease the supply of loanable funds, boosting the equilibrium interest rate. As a result, investment is constrained and so is the economy.

Interest and the Allocation of Capital
Prices are rationing devices. The price of money—the interest rate—is certainly no exception. The interest rate rations the available supply of loanable funds to investment projects that have expected rates of return at or above the interest rate cost of the borrowed funds.

If, say, the computer industry expects to earn a return of 12 percent on the money it invests in physical capital and it can secure the required funds at an interest rate of 8 percent, it can borrow and expand its physical capital. If the expected rate of return on additional capital in the steel industry is only 6 percent, that industry will find it unprofitable to expand its capital at 8 percent interest. The interest rate allocates money, and ultimately physical capital, to the industries in which it will be most productive

and therefore most profitable. Such an allocation of capital goods benefits society.

But the interest rate does not perfectly ration capital to its most productive uses. Large oligopolistic borrowers may be better able than competitive borrowers to pass interest costs on to consumers because they can change prices by controlling output. Also, the size, prestige, and monopsony power of large corporations may help them obtain funds on more favorable terms than can smaller firms, even when the smaller firms have similar rates of profitability.

Interest and R&D Spending
Recall from Chapter 26 that, like the investment decision, the decision on how much to spend on R&D depends on the cost of borrowing funds in relationship to the expected rate of return. Other things equal, the lower the interest rate and thus the lower the cost of borrowing funds for R&D, the greater the amount of R&D spending that is profitable. The higher the interest rate, the less is the amount of R&D spending.

Also, the interest rate allocates R&D funds to firms and industries for which the expected rate of return on R&D is the greatest. Ace Microcircuits may have an expected rate of return of 16 percent on an R&D project, while Glow Paints has only a 2 percent expected rate of return on its R&D project. With the interest rate at 8 percent, loanable funds will flow to Ace, not to Glow. Society will benefit by having R&D spending allocated to projects that have high enough expected rates of return to justify using scarce resources for R&D rather than for other purposes.

Nominal and Real Interest Rates
This discussion of the role of interest in investment decisions and in R&D decisions assumes that there is no inflation. If inflation exists, we must distinguish between nominal and real interest rates, just like we needed to distinguish between nominal and real wages in Chapter 28. The **nominal interest rate** is the rate of interest expressed in dollars of current value. The **real interest rate** is the rate of interest expressed in purchasing power—dollars of inflation-adjusted value. (For a comparison of nominal interest rates on bank loans in selected countries, see Global Perspective 29.1.)

Example: Suppose the nominal interest rate and the rate of inflation are both 10 percent. If you borrow $100, you must pay back $110 a year from now. However, because of 10 percent inflation, each of these 110 dollars will be worth 10 percent less. Thus, the real value or purchasing power of your $110 at the end of the year is only $100. In inflation-adjusted dollars you are borrowing $100 and at year's end you are paying back $100. While the nominal interest rate is 10 percent, the real interest rate is zero. We determine the real interest rate by subtracting the 10 percent inflation rate from the 10 percent nominal interest rate.

It is the real interest rate, not the nominal rate, that affects investment and R&D decisions. **(Key Question 8)**

Application: Usury Laws

A number of states have passed **usury laws,** which specify a maximum interest rate at which loans can be made. Such rates are a special case of *price ceilings,* discussed in Chapter 3. The purpose of usury laws is to hold down the interest cost of borrowing, particularly for low-income borrowers. ("Usury" simply means exorbitant interest.)

Figure 29.2 helps us assess the impact of such legislation. The equilibrium interest rate there is 8 percent, but suppose a usury law specifies that lenders cannot charge more than 6 percent. The effects are as follows:

* *Nonmarket rationing* At 6 percent, the quantity of loanable funds demanded exceeds the quantity supplied: There is a shortage of loanable funds. Because

the market interest rate no longer can ration the available loanable funds to borrowers, lenders (banks) have to do the rationing. We can expect them to make loans only to the most creditworthy borrowers (mainly wealthy, high-income people), thus defeating the goal of the usury law. Low-income, riskier borrowers are excluded from the market and may be forced to turn to loan sharks who charge illegally high interest rates.

* *Gainers and losers* Creditworthy borrowers gain from usury laws, because they pay below-market interest rates. Lenders (ultimately bank shareholders) are losers, because they receive 6 percent rather than 8 percent on each dollar lent.

* *Inefficiency* We have just seen how the equilibrium interest rate allocates money to the investments and the R&D projects whose expected rates of return are greatest. Under usury laws, funds are much less likely to be allocated by banks to the most productive projects. Suppose Mendez has a project so promising she would pay 10 percent for funds to finance it. Chen has a less promising investment, and he would be willing to pay only 7 percent for financing. If the market were rationing funds, Mendez's highly productive project would be funded and Chen's would not. That allocation of funds would be in the interest of both Mendez and society. But with a 6 percent usury rate, Chen may get to the bank before Mendez and receive the loanable funds at 6 percent. So Mendez may not get funded. Legally controlled interest rates may thus inefficiently ration funds to less productive investments or R&D projects.

Economic Profit

Recall from previous chapters that economists define profit narrowly. To accountants, "profit" is what remains of a firm's total revenue after it has paid individuals and other firms for the materials, capital, and labor they have supplied to the firm. To the economist, this definition overstates profit. The reason is that the accountant's view of profit considers only **explicit costs:** payments made by the firm to outsiders. It ignores **implicit costs:** the monetary income the firm sacrifices when it uses resources that it owns, rather than supplying those resources to the market. The economist considers implicit costs to be opportunity costs, and hence to be real costs that must be accounted for in determining profit. **Economic,** or **pure, profit** is what remains after all costs—both explicit and implicit costs, the latter including a normal profit—have been subtracted from a firm's total revenue. Economic profit may be either positive or negative (a loss).

Role of the Entrepreneur

The economist views profit as the return to a particular type of human resource: entrepreneurial ability. We know from earlier chapters that the entrepreneur (1) combines resources to produce a good or service, (2) makes basic, nonroutine policy decisions for the firm, (3) introduces innovations in the form of new products or new production processes, and (4) bears the economic risks associated with all those functions.

Part of the entrepreneur's return is a **normal profit.** This is the minimum payment necessary to retain the entrepreneur in his or her current line of production. We saw in Chapter 22 that normal profit is a cost—the cost of using entrepreneurial ability for a particular purpose. We saw also that a firm's total revenue may exceed its total cost; the excess revenue above all costs is its economic profit. This *residual profit* also goes to the entrepreneur. The entrepreneur is the *residual claimant:* the resource that receives what is left after all costs are paid.

Why should there be residual profit? There are three possible reasons, two relating to the risks involved in business and one based on monopoly power.

Sources of Economic Profit

Let's first construct an artificial economic environment in which economic profit would be zero. Then, by noting how the real world differs from such an environment, we will see where economic profit arises.

We begin with a purely competitive, static economy. A **static economy** is one in which the basic forces such as resource supplies, technological knowledge, and consumer tastes are constant and unchanging. As a result, all cost and supply data, on the one hand, and all demand and revenue data, on the other, are constant.

Given the nature of these data, the economic future is perfectly certain and foreseeable; there is no uncertainty. The outcome of any price or production policy can be accurately predicted. Furthermore, no product or production process is ever improved. Under pure competition any economic profit or loss that might have existed in an industry will disappear with the entry or exit of firms in the long run. All costs, explicit and implicit, are just covered in the long run, so there is no economic profit in this static economy.

The idea of zero economic profit in a static competitive economy suggests that profit is linked to the dynamic nature of real-world capitalism and its accompanying uncertainty. Moreover, it indicates that economic profit may arise from a source other than the directing, innovating, and risk-bearing functions of the entrepreneur. That source is the presence of some amount of monopoly power.

Risk and Profit In a real, dynamic economy the future is not certain and predictable; there is uncertainty. This means that the entrepreneur must assume risks. Some or all of economic profit may be a reward for assuming risks.

In linking economic profit with uncertainty and risk bearing, we must distinguish between risks that are insurable and risks that are not. Some types of risk such as fire, floods, theft, and accidents to employees are measurable; that is, their frequency of occurrence can be estimated accurately. Firms can avoid losses due to **insurable risks** by paying an annual fee (an insurance premium) to an insurance company. The entrepreneur need not bear such risks.

However, the entrepreneur must bear the uninsurable risks of business, and those risks are a potential source of economic profit. **Uninsurable risks** are mainly the uncontrollable and unpredictable changes in the demand and supply conditions facing the firm (and hence its revenues and costs). Uninsurable risks stem from three general sources:

- *Changes in the general economic environment* A downturn in business (a recession), for example, can lead to greatly reduced demand, sales, and revenues, and thus to business losses. An otherwise-prosperous firm may experience such losses through no fault of its own.

- *Changes in the structure of the economy* Consumer tastes, technology, resource availability, and prices change constantly in the real world, bringing changes in production costs and revenues. For example, an airline earning economic profit one year may find its profit plunging the next year as the result of a significant increase in the price of jet fuel.

- **Changes in government policy** A newly instituted regulation, the removal of a tariff, or a change in national defense policy may significantly alter the cost and revenue data of the affected industry and firms.

Regardless of how such revenue and cost changes come about, they are risks that the firm and entrepreneur must take in order to stay in business. *Some or all of the economic profit in a real, dynamic economy may be compensation for taking risks.*

Innovations and Profit

Such uninsurable risks are beyond the control of the individual firm or industry and thus external to it. But one dynamic feature of capitalism—innovation—occurs at the initiative of the entrepreneur. Business firms deliberately introduce new methods of production to affect their costs favorably and new and improved products to affect their revenues favorably. The entrepreneur purposely undertakes to upset existing cost and revenue data in a way that promises to be profitable.

But again, uncertainty enters the picture. Despite exhaustive market surveys, new products or modifications of existing products may be economic failures. Similarly, of the many new novels, textbooks, movies, and compact discs that appear every year, only a handful garners large profits. Nor is it known with certainty whether new production machinery will actually yield projected cost economies. Thus, innovations undertaken by entrepreneurs entail uncertainty and the possibility of losses, not just the potential for increased profit. *Some of the economic profit in an innovative economy may be compensation for dealing with the uncertainty of innovation.*

Monopoly and Profit

So far, we have linked economic profit with the uncertainties surrounding (1) the dynamic environment to which enterprises are exposed and (2) the dynamic business processes they initiate themselves. *The existence of monopoly power is a final source of economic profit.* Because a monopolist can restrict output and deter entry, it may persistently enjoy above-competitive prices and economic profit if demand is strong relative to cost.

Economic uncertainty and monopoly are closely intertwined as sources of economic profit. A firm with some monopoly power can reduce business risk, or at least manipulate it enough to reduce its adverse effects, and thus

increase and prolong economic profit. Furthermore, a firm can use innovation as a source of monopoly power and a means of sustaining itself and its economic profit.

An important distinction between profit stemming from uncertainty and profit resulting from monopoly has to do with the social desirability of these two sources of profit. Bearing business risk and undertaking innovation in an uncertain economic environment are socially desirable functions. Obtaining monopoly profit is not socially desirable, because it is typically founded on reduced output, above-competitive prices, and economic inefficiency. **(Key Question 10)**

Functions of Profit

Economic profit is the main energizer of the capitalistic economy. It influences both the level of economic output and the allocation of resources among alternative uses.

Profit and Total Output

The expectation of economic profit motivates firms to innovate. Innovation stimulates new investment, thereby increasing total output and employment. Thus, the pursuit of profit enhances economic growth by promoting innovation.

Profit and Resource Allocation

Profit also helps allocate resources among alternative lines of production, distribution, and sales. Entrepreneurs seek profit and shun losses. The occurrence of continuing profits in a firm or industry is a signal that society wants that particular firm or industry to expand. It attracts resources from firms and industries that are not profitable. But the rewards of profits are more than an inducement for a firm to expand; they also attract the financing needed for expansion. In contrast, continuing losses penalize firms or industries that fail to adjust their productive efforts to match consumer wants. Such losses signal society's desire for the afflicted entities to contract.

So, in terms of our chapter-opening question, Wal-Mart experienced large profit because it was locating its stores close to customers and delivering the mix of products many consumers wanted at exceptionally low prices. This profit signaled that society wanted more of its scarce resources allocated to Wal-Mart stores. Kmart, in contrast, was not delivering products equivalent in value to the costs of the resources used to provide them—so the firm suffered losses. The losses signaled that society would benefit from a reallocation of all or a part of those resources to some other use. Indeed, Kmart announced in early 2003 that it was closing 326 stores in 44 states and Puerto Rico.

A Variety of Lending Practices May Cause the Effective Interest Rate to Be Quite Different from What It Appears to Be.

Borrowing and lending—receiving and granting credit—are a way of life. Individuals receive credit when they negotiate a mortgage loan and when they use their credit cards. Individuals make loans when they open a savings account in a commercial bank or buy a government bond.

It is sometimes difficult to determine exactly how much interest we pay and receive when we borrow and lend. Let's suppose that you borrow $10,000 that you agree to repay plus $1000 of interest at the end of 1 year. In this instance, the interest rate is 10 percent per year. To determine the interest rate i, we compare the interest paid with the amount borrowed:

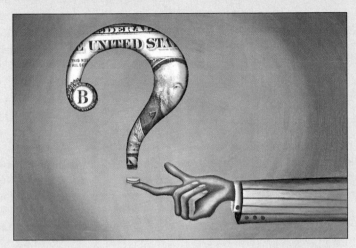

$$i = \frac{\$1000}{\$10,000} = 10\%$$

But in some cases a lender—say, a bank—will discount the interest payment at the time the loan is made. Thus, instead of giving the borrower $10,000, the bank discounts the $1000 interest payment in advance, giving the borrower only $9000. This increases the interest rate:

$$i = \frac{\$1000}{\$9000} = 11\%$$

While the absolute amount of interest paid is the same, in the second case the borrower has only $9000 available for the year.

An even more subtle point is that, to simplify their calculations, many financial institutions assume a 360-day year (twelve 30-day months). This means the borrower has the use of the lender's funds for 5 days less than the normal year. This use of a "short year" also increases the actual interest rate paid by the borrower.

The interest rate paid may change dramatically if a loan is repaid in installments. Suppose a bank lends you $10,000 and charges interest in the amount of $1000 to be paid at the end of the year. But the loan contract requires that you repay the $10,000 loan in 12 equal monthly installments. In effect, then, the average amount of the loan outstanding during the year is only $5000. Therefore:

$$i = \frac{\$1000}{\$5000} = 20\%$$

Here interest is paid on the total amount of the loan ($10,000) rather than on the outstanding balance (which averages $5000 for the year), making for a much higher interest rate.

Another factor that influences the effective interest rate is whether or not interest is compounded. Suppose you deposit $10,000 in a savings account that pays a 10 percent interest rate compounded semiannually. In other words, interest is paid on your "loan" to the bank twice a year. At the end of the first 6 months, $500 of interest (10 percent of $10,000 for half a year) is added to your account. At the end of the year, interest is calculated on $10,500 so that the second interest payment is $525 (10 percent of $10,500 for half a year). Thus:

$$i = \frac{\$1025}{\$10,000} = 10.25\%$$

This means that a bank advertising a 10 percent interest rate compounded semiannually is actually paying more interest to its customers than is a competitor paying a simple (noncompounded) interest rate of 10.2 percent.

Two pieces of legislation have attempted to clarify interest charges and payments. The Truth in Lending Act of 1968 requires that lenders state the costs and terms of consumer credit in concise and uniform language, in particular, as an annual percentage rate (APR). More recently, the Truth in Savings Act of 1991 requires that all advertisements of deposit accounts by banks and other financial institutions disclose all fees connected with such accounts and the interest rate and annual percentage return on each account. Nevertheless, some check-cashing firms that lend money to people in return for postdated personal checks have been found to receive interest equivalent to 261 to 913 percent a year. These interest rates prompted calls for state legislators to protect consumers from "predatory lenders." More recently, many banks have established fee-based "bounce (overdraft) protection" for checking accounts. The bank agrees to pay each overdraft for a flat $20 to $35 fee. These fees are essentially interest on a loan for the amount of the overdraft. When the overdraft amount is small, the annual interest on the loan can easily exceed 1000 percent. "Let the borrower (or depositor) beware" remains a fitting motto in the world of credit.

QUICK REVIEW 29.3

- Pure or economic profit is what remains after all explicit and implicit costs (including a normal profit) are subtracted from a firm's total revenue.

- Economic profit has three sources: the bearing of uninsurable risk, the uncertainty of innovation, and monopoly power.

- Profit and profit expectations affect the levels of investment, total spending, and domestic output; profit and loss also allocate resources among alternative uses.

Income Shares

Our discussion in this and in the preceding chapter would not be complete without a brief reexamination of how U.S. national income is distributed among wages, rent, interest, and profit.

It will be worth your while to look back at Figure 5.1, page 74. Although the income categories shown in that chart do not neatly fit the economic definitions of wages, rent, interest, and profits, they do provide insights about income shares in the United States. Note the dominant role of the labor resource and thus labor income in the U.S. economy. Even with labor income defined narrowly as "wages and salaries," labor receives about 70 percent of national income in a typical year. But some economists contend that the income of proprietors is largely composed of implicit wages and salaries and therefore should be added to the "wages and salaries" category to determine labor income. When we use this broad definition, labor's share rises to about 80 percent of national income, a percentage that has been remarkably stable in the United States since 1900. That leaves about 20 percent for capitalists in the form of rent, interest, and profit. Ironically, capitalist income is a relatively small share of the U.S. economy, which we call a capitalist system.

SUMMARY

1. Economic rent is the price paid for the use of land and other natural resources whose total supplies are fixed.

2. Rent is a surplus payment that is socially unnecessary because land would be available to the economy even without rental payments. The idea of land rent as a surplus payment gave rise to the single-tax movement of the late 1800s.

3. Differences in land rent result from differences in the fertility and climatic features of the land and differences in location.

4. Although land rent is a surplus payment rather than a cost to the economy as a whole, to individual firms and industries, rental payments are correctly regarded as costs. These payments must be made to gain the use of land, which has alternative uses.

5. Interest is the price paid for the use of money. In the loanable funds theory, the equilibrium interest rate is determined by the demand for and supply of loanable funds. Other things equal, an increase in the supply of loanable funds reduces the equilibrium interest rate, whereas a decrease in supply increases it; increases in the demand for loanable funds raise the equilibrium interest rate, whereas decreases in demand reduce it.

6. Interest rates vary in size because loans differ as to risk, maturity, amount, and taxability. Market imperfections cause additional variations. The pure rate of interest is the interest rate on long-term, virtually riskless, 20-year U.S. Treasury bonds.

7. The equilibrium interest rate influences the level of investment and helps ration financial and physical capital to specific firms and industries. Similarly, this rate influences the size and composition of R&D spending. The real interest rate, not the nominal rate, is critical to investment and R&D decisions.

8. Although designed to make funds available to low-income borrowers, usury laws tend to allocate credit to high-income persons, subsidize high-income borrowers at the expense of lenders, and lessen the efficiency with which loanable funds are allocated.

9. Economic, or pure, profit is the difference between a firm's total revenue and the sum of its explicit and implicit costs, the latter including a normal profit. Profit accrues to entrepreneurs for assuming the uninsurable risks associated with organizing and directing economic resources and for innovating. Profit also results from monopoly power.

10. Profit expectations influence innovating and investment activities and therefore the economy's levels of employment and economic growth. The basic function of profits and losses, however, is to allocate resources in accord with consumers' preferences.

11. The largest share of national income—about 70 percent—goes to labor, a share narrowly defined as "wages and salaries." When labor's share is more broadly defined to include "proprietors' income," it rises to about 80 percent of national income, leaving about 20 percent as capital's share.

TERMS AND CONCEPTS

economic rent	pure rate of interest	explicit costs	static economy
incentive function	nominal interest rate	implicit costs	insurable risks
single-tax movement	real interest rate	economic or pure profit	uninsurable risks
loanable funds theory of interest	usury laws	normal profit	

STUDY QUESTIONS

1. How does the economist's use of the term "rent" differ from everyday usage? Explain: "Though rent need not be paid by society to make land available, rental payments are very useful in guiding land into the most productive uses."

2. *Key Question* Explain why economic rent is a surplus payment when viewed by the economy as a whole but a cost of production from the standpoint of individual firms and industries. Explain: "Land rent performs no 'incentive function' for the overall economy."

3. In the 1980s land prices in Japan surged upward in a "speculative bubble." Land prices then fell for 11 straight years between 1990 and 2001. What can we safely assume happened to *land rent* in Japan over those 11 years? Use graphical analysis to illustrate your answer.

4. How does Henry George's proposal for a single tax on land relate to the elasticity of supply of land? Why are there so few remaining advocates of George's proposal?

5. If money is not an economic resource, why is interest paid and received for its use? What considerations account for the fact that interest rates differ greatly on various types of loans? Use those considerations to explain the relative sizes of the interest rates on the following:
   a. A 10-year $1000 government bond.
   b. A $20 pawnshop loan.
   c. A 30-year mortgage loan on a $145,000 house.
   d. A 24-month $12,000 commercial bank loan to finance the purchase of an automobile.
   e. A 60 day $100 loan from a personal finance company.

6. *Key Question* Why is the supply of loanable funds upsloping? Why is the demand for loanable funds downsloping? Explain the equilibrium interest rate. List some factors that might cause it to change.

7. What are the major economic functions of the interest rate? How might the fact that many businesses finance their investment activities internally affect the efficiency with which the interest rate performs its functions?

8. *Key Question* Distinguish between nominal and real interest rates. Which is more relevant in making investment and R&D decisions? If the nominal interest rate is 12 percent and the inflation rate is 8 percent, what is the real rate of interest?

9. Historically, usury laws that put below-equilibrium ceilings on interest rates have been used by some states to make credit available to poor people who could not otherwise afford to borrow. Critics contend that poor people are those most likely to be hurt by such laws. Which view is correct?

10. *Key Question* How do the concepts of accounting profit and economic profit differ? Why is economic profit smaller than accounting profit? What are the three basic sources of economic profit? Classify each of the following according to those sources:
    a. A firm's profit from developing and patenting a new medication that greatly reduces cholesterol and thus diminishes the likelihood of heart disease and stroke.
    b. A restaurant's profit that results from the completion of a new highway past its door.
    c. The profit received by a firm due to an unanticipated change in consumer tastes.

11. Why is the distinction between insurable and uninsurable risks significant for the theory of profit? Carefully evaluate: "All economic profit can be traced to either uncertainty or the desire to avoid it." What are the major functions of economic profit?

12. Explain the absence of economic profit in a purely competitive, static economy. Realizing that the major function of profit is to allocate resources according to consumer preferences, describe the allocation of resources in such an economy.

13. What is the rent, interest, and profit share of national income in a typical year if proprietors' income is included within the labor (wage) share?

14. *(Last Word)* Assume that you borrow $5000 and pay back the $5000 plus $250 in interest at the end of the year. Assuming no inflation, what is the real interest rate? What would the interest rate be if the $250 of interest had been discounted at the time the loan was made? What would the interest rate be if you were required to repay the loan in 12 equal monthly installments?

15. *Web-Based Question: What are the current nominal and real interest rates?* Go to www.federalreserve.gov (Research and Data; Statistics: Releases and Historical Data; Selected Interest Rates) and www.bankrate.com to update the interest

rates in Table 29.1 to their latest recorded values. In what direction, if any, have the interest rates changed? Find the current annual rate of inflation at www.bls.gov/cpi (Latest Numbers; CPI-U, U.S. City Average, All Items, 12-months ending with the last month). Subtract this annual rate of inflation from your updated interest rates in the table to determine the real interest rates in each category.

16. *Web-Based Question: Corporate profits—which industries are making the most?* The Bureau of Economic Analysis provides profit data for various industries in the United States. Go to www.bea.gov/ and find "National Income and Product Account Table 6.16C on Corporate Profits by Industry Group." Based on current figures, which of the following categories of industry classifications has the greatest profits: (*a*) financial or nonfinancial; (*b*) manufacturing, transportation, wholesale trade, or retail trade; (*c*) durable goods or nondurable goods? During the past year, which sectors had the largest and smallest percentage increases in profit? Which sectors, if any, experienced losses? What are the implications of the profit changes for expansion or contraction of the particular industries?

Part VIII | Microeconomics of Government

Government and Market Failure

The economic activities of government affect your well-being every day. If you drive to work or classes, you are using publicly provided highways and streets. If you attend a public college or university, taxpayers subsidize your education. When you receive a check from your part-time or summer job, you see deductions for income taxes and Social Security taxes. Government antipollution laws affect the air you breathe. Laws requiring seat belts, motorcycle helmets, and the sprinkler system in college dormitories are all government mandates.

This chapter examines government and *market failure*—a circumstance in which private markets do not bring about the allocation of resources that best satisfies society's wants. Where private markets fail, an economic role for government may arise. We want to examine that role as it relates to three kinds of market failure: public goods, externalities, and information asymmetries. Our discussion of externalities in turn facilitates a discussion of pollution and pollution policies.

In Chapter 31 we continue our discussion of the microeconomics of government by first analyzing potential government inefficiencies—called *government failure*—and then considering the economics of taxation.

Public Goods

Recall from Chapter 5 that a private good is characterized by *rivalry* and *excludability*. "Rivalry" means that when one person buys and consumes a product, it is not available for purchase and consumption by another person. "Excludability" means that sellers can keep people who do not pay for the product from obtaining its benefits. Because of these characteristics, the demand for a private good gets expressed in the market, and profit-seeking suppliers satisfy that demand. In contrast, a public good has the opposite characteristics: *nonrivalry* and *nonexcludability*. Once a producer has provided a public good, everyone can obtain the benefit. One person's consumption of the good does not preclude consumption of the same good by others. And, once a producer has provided a public good, it cannot bar nonpayers from receiving the benefit. Because of free riders, the demand for a public good does not get expressed in the market and therefore the good does not get produced. Only government will provide it. Two simple examples will help clarify these ideas.

The market demand for a private good is the horizontal summation of the demand curves representing all individual buyers (review Table 3.2 and Figure 3.2). Suppose there are just two people in society who enjoy hot dogs, which cost $.80 each to produce. If Adams wants to buy three hot dogs at $1 each and Benson wants to buy two hot dogs at that same price, the market demand curve will reflect that five hot dogs are demanded at a $1 price. A seller charging $1 for each hot dog can gain $5 of revenue and earn $1 of profit [$5 of total revenue minus $4 (= $.80 × 5) of cost].

The situation is different with public goods. Suppose an enterprising sculptor creates a piece of art costing $600 and places it in the town square. Also suppose that Adams gets $300 of enjoyment from the art and Benson gets $400. Sensing this enjoyment and hoping to make a profit, the sculptor approaches Adams for a donation equal to his satisfaction. Adams falsely says that, unfortunately, he doesn't much like the piece. The sculptor then tries Benson, hoping to get $400 or so. Same deal: Benson professes not to like the piece either. Adams and Benson have become free riders. Although feeling a bit guilty, both reason that it makes no sense to pay for something when you can receive the benefits without paying for them. The artist is a quick learner; he vows never to try anything like that again.

Conclusion: Because of nonrivalry and nonexcludability, private firms cannot profitably produce a public good. If society wants the good, it will have to direct government to provide it. Government can finance the provision of the good through taxation.

Demand for Public Goods

If consumers need not reveal their true demand for a public good in the marketplace, then how can the optimal amount of that good be determined? The answer is that the government has to try to estimate the demand for a public good through surveys or public votes. Suppose Adams and Benson are the only two people in the society, and their marginal willingness to pay for a public good, this time national defense, is as shown in columns 1 and 2 and columns 1 and 3 in Table 30.1. Economists might have discovered these schedules through a survey asking hypothetical questions about how much each citizen was willing to pay for various types and amounts of public goods rather than go without them.

Notice that the schedules in Table 30.1 are price-quantity schedules, implying that they are demand schedules. Rather than depicting demand in the usual way—the quantity of a product someone is willing to buy at each

TABLE 30.1

Demand for a Public Good, Two Individuals

(1) Quantity of Public Good	(2) Adams' Willingness to Pay (Price)		(3) Benson's Willingness to Pay (Price)		(4) Collective Willingness to Pay (Price)
1	$4	+	$5	=	$9
2	3	+	4	=	7
3	2	+	3	=	5
4	1	+	2	=	3
5	0	+	1	=	1

possible price—these schedules show the price someone is willing to pay for the extra unit of each possible quantity. That is, Adams is willing to pay $4 for the first unit of the public good, $3 for the second, $2 for the third, and so on.

Suppose the government produces 1 unit of this public good. Because of nonrivalry, Adams' consumption of the good does not preclude Benson from also consuming it, and vice versa. So both consume the good, and neither volunteers to pay for it. But from Table 30.1 we can find the amount these two people would be willing to pay, together, rather than do without this 1 unit of the good. Columns 1 and 2 show that Adams would be willing to pay $4 for the first unit of the public good; columns 1 and 3 show that Benson would be willing to pay $5 for it. So the two people are jointly willing to pay $9 (= $4 + $5) for this first unit.

For the second unit of the public good, the collective price they are willing to pay is $7 (= $3 from Adams + $4 from Benson); for the third unit they will pay $5 (= $2 + $3); and so on. By finding the collective willingness to pay for each additional unit (column 4), we can construct a collective demand schedule (a willingness-to-pay schedule) for the public good. Here we are not adding the quantities demanded at each possible price, as we do when we determine the market demand for a private good. Instead, we are adding *the prices that people are willing to pay for the last unit of the public good at each possible quantity demanded.*

Figure 30.1 shows the same adding procedure graphically, using the data from Table 30.1. Note that we sum Adams' and Benson's willingness-to-pay curves *vertically* to derive the collective willingness-to-pay curve (demand curve). For example, the height of the collective demand curve D_c at 2 units of output is $7, the sum of the amounts that Adams and Benson are each willing to pay for the second unit (= $3 + $4). Likewise, the height of the collective demand curve at 4 units of the public good is $3 (= $1 + $2).

FIGURE 30.1

The optimal amount of a public good.   The collective demand curve for a public good, as shown by D_c in (c), is found by summing vertically the individual willingness-to-pay curves D_1 in (a) and D_2 in (b) of Adams and Benson, the only two people in the economy. The supply curve of the public good represented in (c) slopes upward and to the right, reflecting rising marginal costs. The optimal amount of the public good is 3 units, determined by the intersection of D_c and S. At that output, marginal benefit (reflected in the collective demand curve D_c) equals marginal cost (reflected in the supply curve S).

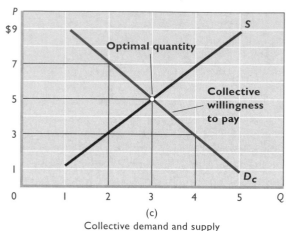

(c)
Collective demand and supply

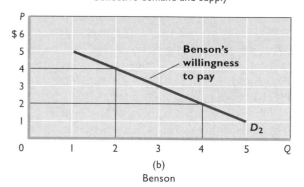

(b)
Benson

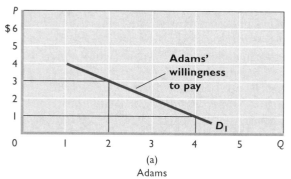

(a)
Adams

What does it mean in Figure 30.1a that, for example, Adams is willing to pay $3 for the second unit of the public good? It means that Adams expects to receive $3 of

extra benefit or utility from that unit. And we know from the law of diminishing marginal utility that successive units of any good yield less and less added benefit. This is also true for public goods, explaining the downward slope of the willingness-to-pay curves of Adams, Benson, and society. These curves, in essence, are marginal-benefit curves. **(Key Question 1)**

Supply of Public Goods

The supply curve for any good, private or public, is its marginal-cost curve. Marginal cost rises as more of a good is produced. The reason is the law of diminishing returns, which applies whether a society is making missiles (a public good) or mufflers (a private good). In the short run, government has fixed resources (public capital) with which to "produce" public goods such as national defense. As it adds more units of a variable resource (labor) to these fixed resources, total product eventually rises at a diminishing rate. That means that marginal product falls and marginal cost rises, explaining why curve S in Figure 30.1c slopes upward.

Optimal Quantity of a Public Good

We can now determine the optimal quantity of the public good. The collective demand curve D_c in Figure 30.1c measures society's marginal benefit of each unit of this particular good. The supply curve S in that figure measures society's marginal cost of each unit. The optimal quantity of this public good occurs where marginal benefit equals marginal cost, or where the two curves intersect. In Figure 30.1c that point is 3 units of the public good, where the collective willingness to pay for the last (third) unit—the marginal benefit—just matches that unit's marginal cost ($5 = $5). As we saw in Chapter 2, equating marginal benefit and marginal cost efficiently allocates society's scarce resources. **(Key Question 2)**

Cost-Benefit Analysis

The above example suggests a practical means, called **cost-benefit analysis,** for deciding whether to provide a particular public good and how much of it to provide. Like our example, cost-benefit analysis (or marginal-benefit–marginal-cost analysis) involves a comparison of marginal costs and marginal benefits.

Concept   Suppose the Federal government is contemplating a highway construction plan. Because the economy's resources are limited, any decision to use more resources in the public sector will mean fewer resources for the private sector. There will be both a cost and a benefit. The cost is the loss of satisfaction resulting from the accompanying decline in the production of private goods; the benefit is the extra satisfaction resulting from the output of more public goods. Should the needed resources be shifted from the private to the public sector? The answer is yes if the benefit from the extra public goods exceeds the cost that results from having fewer private goods. The answer is no if the cost of the forgone private goods is greater than the benefit associated with the extra public goods.

Cost-benefit analysis, however, can indicate more than whether a public program is worth doing. It can also help the government decide on the extent to which a project should be pursued. Real economic questions cannot usually be answered simply by "yes" or "no" but, rather, by questions such as "how much" or "how little."

Illustration Although a few private toll roads exist, highways clearly have public goods characteristics because the benefits are widely diffused and highway use is difficult to price. Should the Federal government expand the Federal highway system? If so, what is the proper size or scope for the overall project?

Table 30.2 lists a series of increasingly ambitious and increasingly costly highway projects: widening existing two-lane highways; building new two-lane highways; building new four-lane highways; building new six-lane highways. The extent to which government should undertake highway construction depends on the costs and benefits. The costs are largely the costs of constructing and maintaining the highways; the benefits are an improved flow of people and goods throughout the nation.

The table shows that total annual benefit (column 4) exceeds total annual cost (column 2) for plans A, B, and C, indicating that some highway construction is econom-

ically justifiable. We see this directly in column 6, where total costs (column 2) are subtracted from total annual benefits (column 4). Net benefits are positive for plans A, B, and C. Plan D is not economically justifiable because net benefits are negative.

But the question of optimal size or scope for this project remains. Comparing the additional, or marginal, cost and the additional, or marginal, benefit relating to each plan determines the answer. The guideline is well known to you from previous discussions: Increase an activity, project, or output as long as the marginal benefit (column 5) exceeds the marginal cost (column 3). Stop the activity at, or as close as possible to, the point at which the marginal benefit equals the marginal cost. Do not undertake a project for which marginal cost exceeds marginal benefit.

In this case plan C (building new four-lane highways) is the best plan. Plans A and B are too modest; the marginal benefits exceed the marginal costs. Plan D's marginal cost ($10 billion) exceeds the marginal benefit ($3 billion) and therefore cannot be justified; it overallocates resources to the project. Plan C is closest to the theoretical optimum because its marginal benefit ($10 billion) still exceeds marginal cost ($8 billion) but approaches the MB = MC (or MC = MB) ideal.

This **marginal-cost–marginal-benefit rule** actually tells us which plan provides the maximum excess of total benefits over total costs or, in other words, the plan that provides society with the maximum net benefit. You can confirm directly in column 6 that the maximum net benefit (of $5 billion) is associated with plan C.

Cost-benefit analysis shatters the myth that "economy in government" and "reduced government spending" are synonymous. "Economy" is concerned with using scarce resources efficiently. If the marginal cost of a proposed government program exceeds its marginal benefit, then the proposed public program should not be undertaken. But if the marginal benefit exceeds

TABLE 30.2

Cost-Benefit Analysis for a National Highway Construction Project (in Billions)

(1) Plan	(2) Total Cost of Project	(3) Marginal Cost	(4) Total Benefit	(5) Marginal Benefit	(6) Net Benefit (4) − (2)
No new construction	$ 0		$ 0		$ 0
		$ 4		$ 5	
A: Widen existing highways	4		5		1
		6		8	
B: New 2-lane highways	10		13		3
		8		10	
C: New 4-lane highways	*18*		*23*		*5*
		10		3	
D: New 6-lane highways	28		26		−2

the marginal cost, then it would be uneconomical or "wasteful" not to spend on that government program. Economy in government does not mean minimization of public spending. It means allocating resources between the private and public sectors to achieve maximum net benefit. **(Key Question 3)**

QUICK REVIEW 30.1

- Public goods are characterized by nonrivalry and nonexcludability.
- The demand (marginal-benefit) curve for a public good is found by vertically adding the prices all the members of society are willing to pay for the last unit of output at various output levels.
- The socially optimal amount of a public good is the amount at which the marginal cost and marginal benefit of the good are equal.
- Cost-benefit analysis is the method of evaluating alternative projects or sizes of projects by comparing the marginal cost and marginal benefit and applying the MC = MB rule.

Externalities

In performing its allocation function, government not only produces public goods but also corrects for a market failure called **externalities,** or spillovers. Recall from Chapter 5 that a spillover is a cost or a benefit accruing to an individual or group—a third party—that is *external* to a market transaction. An example of a spillover cost or a negative externality is the cost of breathing polluted air; an example of a spillover benefit or a positive externality is the benefit of having everyone else inoculated against

some disease. When there are spillover costs, an overproduction of the related product occurs and there is an overallocation of resources to this product. Conversely, underproduction and underallocation of resources result when spillover benefits are present. We can demonstrate both graphically.

Spillover Costs

Figure 30.2a illustrates how spillover costs affect the allocation of resources. When producers shift some of their costs onto the community as spillover costs, producers' marginal costs are lower than otherwise. So their supply curves do not include or "capture" all the costs legitimately associated with the production of their goods. A polluting producer's supply curve such as S in Figure 30.2a therefore understates the total cost of production. The firm's supply curve lies to the right of (or below) the full-cost supply curve S_t, which would include the spillover cost. Through polluting and thus transferring cost to society, the firm enjoys lower production costs and has the supply curve S.

30.1
Externalities

The outcome is shown in Figure 30.2a, where equilibrium output Q_e is larger than the optimal output Q_o. This means that resources are overallocated to the production of this commodity; too many units of it are produced.

Spillover Benefits

Figure 30.2b shows the impact of spillover benefits on resource allocation. When spillover benefits occur, the market demand curve D lies to the left of (or below) the full-benefits demand curve. That is, D does not include the

---

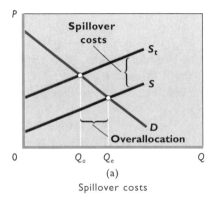

(a)
Spillover costs

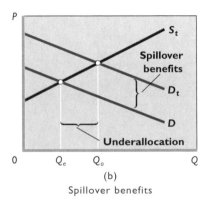

(b)
Spillover benefits

FIGURE 30.2

Spillover costs and spillover benefits.
(a) With spillover costs borne by society, the producers' supply curve S is to the right of (below) the full-cost curve S_t. Consequently, the equilibrium output Q_e is greater than the optimal output Q_o. (b) When spillover benefits accrue to society, the market demand curve D is to the left of (below) the full-benefit demand curve D_t. As a result, the equilibrium output Q_e is less than the optimal output Q_o.

spillover benefits of the product, whereas D_t does. Consider inoculations against a communicable disease. Watson and Weinberg benefit when they get vaccinated, but so do their associates Alvarez and Anderson who are less likely to contract the disease from them. The market demand curve reflects only the direct, private benefits to Watson and Weinberg. It does not reflect the spillover benefits—the positive externalities—to Alvarez and Anderson, which are included in D_t.

The outcome is that the equilibrium output Q_e is less than the optimal output Q_o. The market fails to produce enough vaccinations, and resources are underallocated to this product.

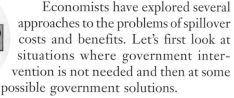

30.1 Externalities

Economists have explored several approaches to the problems of spillover costs and benefits. Let's first look at situations where government intervention is not needed and then at some possible government solutions.

Individual Bargaining: Coase Theorem

In the **Coase theorem,** conceived decades ago by economist Ronald Coase at the University of Chicago, government is not needed to remedy spillover costs or benefits where (1) property ownership is clearly defined, (2) the number of people involved is small, and (3) bargaining costs are negligible. Under these circumstances the government should confine its role to encouraging bargaining between affected individuals or groups. Property rights place a price tag on an externality, creating opportunity costs for all parties. Because the economic self-interests of the parties are at stake, bargaining will enable them to find a mutually acceptable solution to the externality problem.

30.2 Coase theorem

Example of the Coase Theorem

Suppose the owner of a large parcel of forestland is considering a plan to clear-cut (totally level) thousands of acres of mature fir trees. The complication is that the forest surrounds a lake with a popular resort on its shore. The resort is on land owned by the resort. The unspoiled beauty of the general area attracts vacationers from all over the nation to the resort, and the resort owner is against the clear-cutting. Should state or local government intervene to allow or prevent the tree cutting?

According to the Coase theorem, the forest owner and the resort owner can resolve this situation without

government intervention. As long as one of the parties to the dispute has property rights to what is at issue, an incentive will exist for both parties to negotiate a solution acceptable to each. In our example, the owner of the timberland holds the property rights to the land to be logged and thus has the right to clear-cut it. The owner of the resort therefore has an economic incentive to negotiate with the forest owner to reduce the logging impact. Excessive logging of the forest surrounding the resort will reduce tourism and revenues to the resort owner.

But what is the economic incentive to the forest owner to negotiate with the resort owner? The answer draws directly on the idea of opportunity cost. One cost incurred in logging the forest is the forgone payment that the forest owner could obtain from the resort owner for agreeing not to clear-cut the fir trees. The resort owner might be willing to make a lump-sum or annual payment to the owner of the forest to avoid or minimize the spillover cost. Or perhaps the resort owner might be willing to buy the forested land to prevent the logging. As viewed by the forest owner, a payment for not clear-cutting or a purchase price above the prior market value of the land is an opportunity cost of logging the land.

It is likely that both parties would regard a negotiated agreement as better than clear-cutting the firs.

Limitations   Unfortunately, many externalities involve large numbers of affected parties, high bargaining costs, and community property such as air and water. In such situations private bargaining cannot be used as a remedy. As an example, the global-warming problem affects millions of people in many nations. The vast number of affected parties could not individually negotiate an agreement to remedy this problem. Instead, they must rely on their governments to represent the millions of affected parties and find an acceptable solution.

Liability Rules and Lawsuits

Although private negotiation may not be a realistic solution to many externality problems, clearly established property rights may help in another way. The government has erected a framework of laws that define private property and protect it from damage done by other parties. Those laws, and the damage recovery system to which they give rise, permit parties suffering spillover costs to sue for compensation.

Suppose the Ajax Degreaser Company regularly dumps leaky barrels containing solvents into a nearby canyon owned by Bar Q Ranch. Bar Q eventually discovers this dump site and, after tracing the drums to Ajax, immediately contacts its lawyer. Soon after, Bar Q sues Ajax. Not only will Ajax have to pay for the cleanup; it may also have to pay Bar Q additional damages for ruining its property.

Clearly defined property rights and government liability laws thus help remedy some externality problems. They do so directly by forcing the perpetrator of the harmful externality to pay damages to those injured. They do so indirectly by discouraging firms and individuals from generating spillover costs for fear of being sued. It is not surprising, then, that many spillovers do not involve private property but rather property held in common by society. It is the public bodies of water, the public lands, and the public air, where ownership is less clear, that often bear the brunt of spillovers.

Caveat: Like private negotiations, private lawsuits to resolve externalities have their own limitations. Large legal fees and major time delays in the court system are commonplace. Also, the uncertainty associated with the court outcome reduces the effectiveness of this approach. Will the court accept your claim that your emphysema has resulted from the smoke emitted by the factory next door, or will it conclude that your ailment is unrelated to the plant's pollution? Can you prove that a specific firm in the area is the source of the contamination of your well? What happens to Bar Q's suit if Ajax Degreaser goes out of business during the litigation?

Government Intervention

Government intervention may be needed to achieve economic efficiency when externalities affect large numbers of people or when community interests are at stake. Government can use direct controls and taxes to counter spillover costs; it may provide subsidies or public goods to deal with spillover benefits.

Direct Controls The direct way to reduce spillover costs from a certain activity is to pass legislation limiting that activity. Such direct controls force the offending firms to incur the actual costs of the offending activity. To date, this approach has dominated public policy in the United States. Historically, direct controls in the form of uniform emission standards—limits on allowable pollution—have dominated American air pollution policy. For example, the Clean Air Act of 1990 (1) forced factories and businesses to install "maximum achievable control technology" to reduce emissions of 189 toxic chemicals by 90 percent between 1990 and 2000; (2) required a 30 to 60 percent reduction in tailpipe emissions from automobiles by 2000; (3) mandated a 50 percent reduction in the use of chlorofluorocarbons (CFCs), which deplete the ozone layer (CFCs are used widely as a coolant in refrigeration, a blowing agent for foam, and a solvent in the electronics industry); and (4) forced coal-burning utilities to cut their emissions of sulfur dioxide by about 50 percent to reduce the acid-rain destruction of lakes and forests. Clean-water legislation limits the amount of heavy metals, detergents, and other pollutants firms can discharge into rivers and bays. Toxic-waste laws dictate special procedures and dump sites for disposing of contaminated soil and solvents. Violating these laws means fines and, in some cases, imprisonment.

Direct controls raise the marginal cost of production because the firms must operate and maintain pollution-control equipment. The supply curve S in Figure 30.3b,

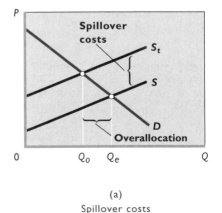

(a)
Spillover costs

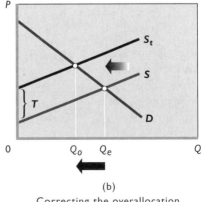

(b)
Correcting the overallocation
of resources via direct controls
or via a tax

FIGURE 30.3

Correcting for spillover costs (negative externalities). (a) Spillover costs result in an overallocation of resources. (b) Government can correct this overallocation in two ways: (1) use of direct controls, which would shift the supply curve from S to S_t and reduce output from Q_e to Q_o, or (2) imposition of a specific tax T, which would also shift the supply curve from S to S_t, eliminating the overallocation of resources.

which does not reflect the spillover costs, shifts leftward (upward) to the full-cost supply curve, S_t. Product price increases, equilibrium output falls from Q_e to Q_o, and the initial overallocation of resources shown in Figure 30.3a is corrected.

Specific Taxes
A second policy approach to spillover costs is for government to levy taxes or charges specifically on the related good. For example, the government has placed a manufacturing excise tax on CFCs, which deplete the stratospheric ozone layer protecting the earth from excessive solar ultraviolet radiation. Facing such an excise tax, manufacturers must decide whether to pay the tax or expend additional funds to purchase or develop substitute products. In either case, the tax raises the marginal cost of producing CFCs, shifting the private supply curve for this product leftward (or upward).

In Figure 30.3b, a tax equal to T per unit increases the firm's marginal cost, shifting the supply curve from S to S_t. The equilibrium price rises, and the equilibrium output declines from Q_e to the economically efficient level Q_o. The tax thus eliminates the initial overallocation of resources.

Subsidies and Government Provision
Where spillover benefits are large and diffuse, as in our earlier example of inoculations, government has three options for correcting the underallocation of resources:

- *Subsidies to buyers* Figure 30.4a again shows the supply-demand situation for spillover benefits. Government could correct the underallocation of resources, for example, to inoculations, by subsidizing consumers of the product. It could give each new mother in the United States a discount coupon to be used to obtain a series of inoculations for her child. The coupon would reduce the "price" to the mother by, say, 50 percent. As shown in Figure 30.4b, this program would shift the demand curve for inoculations from too low D to the appropriate D_t. The number of inoculations would rise from Q_e to the economically optimal Q_o, eliminating the underallocation of resources shown in Figure 30.4a.

- *Subsidies to producers* A subsidy to producers is a specific tax in reverse. Taxes impose an extra cost on producers, while subsidies reduce producers' costs. As shown in Figure 30.4c, a subsidy of U per inoculation to physicians and medical clinics would reduce their marginal costs and shift their supply curve rightward from S_t to S_t'. The output of inoculations would increase from Q_e to the optimal level Q_o, correcting the underallocation of resources shown in Figure 30.4a.

- *Government provision* Finally, where spillover benefits are extremely large, the government may decide to provide the product as a public good. The U.S. government largely eradicated the crippling disease

---

FIGURE 30.4

Correcting for spillover benefits (positive externalities).   (a) Spillover benefits result in an underallocation of resources. (b) This underallocation can be corrected by a subsidy to consumers, which shifts market demand from D to D_t and increases output from Q_e to Q_o. (c) Alternatively, the underallocation can be eliminated by providing producers with a subsidy of U, which shifts their supply curve from S_t to S_t', increasing output from Q_e to Q_o.

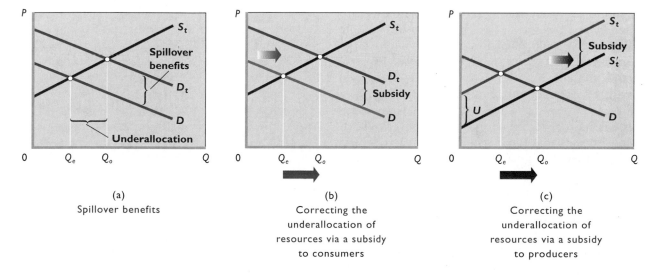

(a)
Spillover benefits

(b)
Correcting the underallocation of resources via a subsidy to consumers

(c)
Correcting the underallocation of resources via a subsidy to producers

polio by administering free vaccines to all children. India ended smallpox by paying people in rural areas to come to public clinics to have their children vaccinated. **(Key Question 4)**

A Market-Based Approach to Spillover Costs

One novel approach to spillover costs involves only limited government action. The idea is to create a market for externality rights. But before describing that approach, we first need to understand the idea called the **tragedy of the commons.**

The Tragedy of the Commons
The air, rivers, lakes, oceans, and public lands, such as parks and streets, are all objects for pollution because the rights to use those resources are held "in common" by society. No private individual or institution has a monetary incentive to maintain the purity or quality of such resources.

We maintain the property we own—for example, we paint and repair our homes periodically—in part because we will recoup the value of these improvements at the time of sale. But as long as "rights" to air, water, and certain land resources are commonly held and are freely available, there is no incentive to maintain them or use them carefully. As a result, these natural resources are overused and thereby degraded or polluted.

For example, a common pasture in which anyone can graze cattle will quickly be overgrazed because each rancher has an incentive to graze as many cattle as possible. Similarly, commonly owned resources such as rivers, lakes, oceans, and the air get used beyond their capacity to absorb pollution. Manufacturers will choose the least-cost combination of inputs and bear only unavoidable costs. If they can dump waste chemicals into rivers and lakes rather than pay for proper disposal, some businesses will be inclined to do so. Firms will discharge smoke into the air if they can, rather than purchase expensive abatement facilities. Even Federal, state, and local governments sometimes discharge inadequately treated waste into rivers, lakes, or oceans to avoid the expense of constructing expensive treatment facilities. Many individuals avoid the costs of proper refuse pickup and disposal by burning their garbage or dumping it in the woods.

The problem is mainly one of incentives. There is no incentive to incur internal costs associated with reducing or eliminating pollution when those costs can be transferred externally to society. The fallacy of composition also comes into play. Each person and firm reasons their individual contribution to pollution is so small that it is of little or no overall consequence. But their actions, multiplied by hundreds, thousands, or millions, overwhelm the absorptive capacity of the common resources. Society ends up with a degradation or pollution problem.

A Market for Externality Rights
This outcome gives rise to a market-based approach to spillover costs. The idea is that the government can create a **market for externality rights.** We confine our discussion to pollution, although the same approach might be used with other externalities.

Operation of the Market
In this market approach, an appropriate pollution-control agency determines the amount of pollutants that firms can discharge into the water or air of a specific region annually while maintaining the water or air quality at some acceptable level. Suppose the agency ascertains that 500 tons of pollutants can be discharged into Metropolitan Lake and "recycled" by nature each year. Then 500 pollution rights, each entitling the owner to dump 1 ton of pollutants into the lake in 1 year, are made available for sale to producers each year. The supply of these pollution rights is fixed and therefore perfectly inelastic, as shown in Figure 30.5.

FIGURE 30.5

A market for pollution rights. The supply of pollution rights S is set by the government, which determines that a specific body of water can safely recycle 500 tons of waste. In 2004, the demand for pollution rights is D_{2004} and the 1-ton price is $100. The quantity of pollution is 500 tons, not the 750 tons it would have been without the pollution rights. Over time, the demand for pollution rights increases to D_{2012} and the 1-ton price rises to $200. But the amount of pollution stays at 500 tons, rather than rising to 1000 tons.

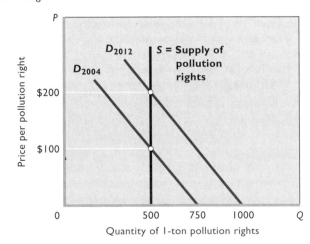

The demand for pollution rights, represented by D_{2004} in the figure, takes the same downsloping form as the demand for any other input. At higher prices there is less pollution, as polluters either stop polluting or pollute less by acquiring pollution-abatement equipment. An equilibrium market price for pollution rights, here $100, will be determined at which the environment-preserving quantity of pollution rights is rationed to polluters. Figure 30.5 shows that if the use of the lake as a dump site for pollutants were instead free, 750 tons of pollutants would be discharged into the lake; it would be "overconsumed," or polluted, in the amount of 250 tons.

Over time, as human and business populations expand, demand will increase, as from D_{2004} to D_{2012}. Without a market for pollution rights, pollution in 2012 would be 1000 tons, 500 tons beyond what can be assimilated by nature. With the market for pollution rights, the price would rise from $100 to $200, and the amount of pollutants would remain at 500 tons—the amount that the lake can recycle.

Advantages   This scheme has several advantages over direct controls. Most important, it reduces society's costs by allowing pollution rights to be bought and sold. Suppose it costs Acme Pulp Mill $20 a year to reduce a specific noxious discharge by 1 ton while it costs Zemo Chemicals $8000 a year to accomplish the same 1-ton reduction. Also assume that Zemo wants to expand production, but doing so will increase its pollution discharge by 1 ton.

Without a market for pollution rights, Zemo would have to use $8000 of society's scarce resources to keep the 1-ton pollution discharge from occurring. But with a market for pollution rights, Zemo has a better option: It buys 1 ton of pollution rights for the $100 price shown in Figure 30.5. Acme is willing to sell Zemo 1 ton of pollution rights for $100 because that amount is more than Acme's $20 cost of reducing its pollution by 1 ton. Zemo increases its discharge by 1 ton; Acme reduces its discharge by 1 ton. Zemo benefits (by $8000 − $100), Acme benefits (by $100 − $20), and society benefits (by $8000 − $20). Rather than using $8000 of its scarce resources to hold the discharge at the specified level, society uses only $20 of those resources.

Market-based plans have other advantages. Potential polluters have a monetary incentive not to pollute, because they must pay for the right to discharge effluent. Conservation groups can fight pollution by buying up and withholding pollution rights, thereby reducing pollution below governmentally determined standards. As the demand for pollution rights increases over time, the growing revenue from the sale of a fixed quantity of pollution rights could be devoted to environmental improvement. At the same time, the rising price of pollution rights should stimulate the search for improved pollution-control techniques.

Real-World Examples   Administrative and political problems have kept the government from replacing direct controls—such as uniform emission limits—with a full-scale market for pollution rights. But the Environmental Protection Agency (EPA) established a system of pollution rights, or "tradeable emission allowances," in the 1980s as part of a plan to reduce the sulfur dioxide emitted by coal-burning public utilities. Those emissions are the major source of acid rain. The market for such rights was greatly expanded by legislation in the 1990s.

The Clean Air Act of 1990 established a limited market for pollution rights, similar to that shown in Figure 30.5, by allowing utilities to trade emission credits provided by government. Utilities can obtain credits by reducing sulfur-dioxide emissions by more than the specified amount. They can then sell their emission credits to other utilities that find it less costly to buy the credits than to install additional pollution-control equipment.

This market for sulfur-dioxide-emission credits complements other air pollution policies that also permit the exchange of pollution rights. The EPA now allows firms to exchange pollution rights internally and externally. Polluters are allowed to transfer air pollution internally between individual sources within their plants. That is, as long as it meets the overall pollution standard assigned to it, a firm may increase one source of pollution by offsetting it with reduced pollution from another part of its operations.

The EPA also permits external trading of pollution rights. It has set targets for reducing air pollution in regions where the minimum standards are not being met. Previously, new pollution sources could not enter these regions unless existing polluters went out of business. But under the system of external trading rights, the EPA allows firms that reduce their pollution below set standards to sell their pollution rights to other firms. A new firm that wants to locate in the Los Angeles area, for example, might be able to buy rights to emit 20 tons of nitrous oxide annually from an existing firm that has reduced its emissions below its allowable limit. The price of emission rights depends on their supply and demand.

Finally, in 2003 the EPA extended the market-based approach to the Clean Water Act. Industry, agriculture, and municipalities within a defined watershed can meet their EPA-approved maximum daily discharge limits

TABLE 30.3

Methods for Dealing with Externalities

Problem	Resource Allocation Outcome	Ways to Correct
Spillover costs (negative externalities)	Overallocation of resources	1. Individual bargaining 2. Liability rules and lawsuits 3. Tax on producers 4. Direct controls 5. Market for externality rights
Spillover benefits (positive externalities)	Underallocation of resources	1. Individual bargaining 2. Subsidy to consumers 3. Subsidy to producers 4. Government provision

through trading "water quality credits." Entities that find it extremely expensive to reduce water pollution can buy credits from entities that can reduce pollution relatively inexpensively. Therefore, society incurs less total cost in improving water quality.

Table 30.3 reviews the major methods for correcting externalities.

Society's Optimal Amount of Externality Reduction

Negative externalities such as pollution reduce the utility of those affected, rather than increase it. These spillovers are not economic goods but economic "bads." If something is bad, shouldn't society eliminate it? Why should society allow firms or municipalities to discharge *any* impure waste into public waterways or to emit *any* pollution into the air?

Reducing a negative externality has a "price." Society must decide how much of a reduction it wants to "buy." Eliminating pollution might not be desirable, even if it were technologically feasible. Because of the law of diminishing returns, cleaning up the second 10 percent of pollutants from an industrial smokestack normally is more costly than cleaning up the first 10 percent. Eliminating the third 10 percent is more costly than cleaning up the second 10 percent, and so on. Therefore, cleaning up the last 10 percent of pollutants is the most costly reduction of all.

The marginal cost (MC) to the firm and hence to society—the opportunity cost of the extra resources used—rises as pollution is reduced more and more. At some point MC may rise so high that it exceeds society's marginal benefit (MB) of further pollution abatement

(reduction). Additional actions to reduce pollution will therefore lower society's well-being; total cost will rise more than total benefit.

MC, MB, and Equilibrium Quantity Figure 30.6 shows both the rising marginal-cost curve, MC, for pollution reduction and the downsloping marginal-benefit curve, MB, for this outcome. MB slopes downward because of the law of diminishing marginal utility: The

FIGURE 30.6

Society's optimal amount of pollution abatement. The optimal amount of externality reduction—in this case, pollution abatement—occurs at Q_1, where society's marginal cost MC and marginal benefit MB of reducing the spillover are equal.

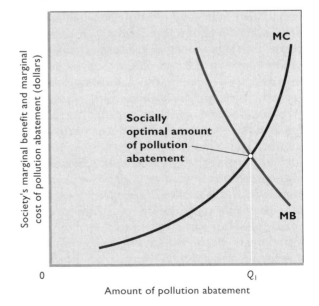

more pollution reduction society accomplishes, the lower the utility (and benefit) of the next unit of pollution reduction.

The **optimal reduction of an externality** occurs when society's marginal cost and marginal benefit of reducing that externality are equal (MC = MB). In Figure 30.6 this optimal amount of pollution abatement is Q_1 units. When MB exceeds MC, additional abatement moves society toward economic efficiency; the added benefit of cleaner air or water exceeds the benefit of any alternative use of the required resources. When MC exceeds MB, additional abatement reduces economic efficiency; there would be greater benefits from using resources in some other way than to further reduce pollution.

In reality, it is difficult to measure the marginal costs and benefits of pollution control. Nevertheless, Figure 30.6 demonstrates that some pollution may be economically efficient. This is so not because pollution is desirable but because beyond some level of control, further abatement may reduce society's net well-being.

Shifts in Locations of Curves
The locations of the marginal-cost and marginal-benefit curves in Figure 30.6 are not forever fixed. They can, and probably do, shift over time. For example, suppose that the technology of pollution-control equipment were to improve noticeably. We would expect the cost of pollution abatement to fall, society's MC curve to shift rightward, and the optimal level of abatement to rise. Or suppose that society were to decide that it wanted cleaner air and water because of new information about the adverse health effects of pollution. The MB curve in Figure 30.6 would shift rightward, and the optimal level of pollution control would increase beyond Q_1. Test your understanding of these statements by drawing the new MC and MB curves in Figure 30.6. **(Key Question 7)**

QUICK REVIEW 30.2

- Policies for coping with the overallocation of resources caused by spillover costs are (a) private bargaining, (b) liability rules and lawsuits, (c) direct controls, (d) specific taxes, and (e) markets for externality rights.
- Policies for correcting the underallocation of resources associated with spillover benefits are (a) private bargaining, (b) subsidies to producers, (c) subsidies to consumers, and (d) government provision.
- The optimal amount of negative-externality reduction occurs where society's marginal cost and marginal benefit of reducing the externality are equal.

Recycling

Production and consumption of goods and services result in millions of tons of solid waste (garbage) annually in the United States. The major means of disposing of solid waste are garbage dumps and incinerators, but these methods often produce spillover costs to nearby communities. Therefore, increasing attention has been given to *recycling*: the reuse of old materials to make new products. According to the EPA, 96 percent of lead-acid batteries, 58 percent of steel cans, 47 percent of aluminum cans, 45 percent of corrugated boxes, 35 percent of plastic soft-drink bottles, 26 percent of glass bottles, and 26 percent of tires are now being recycled. Should government encourage more recycling? If so, how and to what extent?

Market for Recyclable Inputs Figure 30.7a, which shows the demand and supply curves for some recyclable product, such as glass, suggests the incentives for recycling.

The demand for recyclable glass derives from manufacturers that use recycled glass as a resource in producing new glass. This demand curve slopes downward, telling us that manufacturers will increase their purchases of recyclable glass as its price falls.

The location of the demand curve in Figure 30.7a depends partly on the demand for the products for which the recycled glass is used. The greater the demand for those products, the greater is the demand for the recyclable input. The location of the curve also depends on the technology and thus the cost of using original raw materials rather than recycled glass in the production process. The more costly it is to use original materials relative to recycled glass, the farther to the right will be the demand curve for recyclable glass.

The supply curve for recyclable glass slopes upward, because higher prices increase the incentive for households to recycle. The location of the supply curve depends on such factors as the attitudes of households toward recycling and the cost to them of alternative disposal.

The equilibrium price P_1 and quantity Q_1 in Figure 30.7a are determined at the intersection of the supply and demand curves. At price P_1 the market clears; there is neither a shortage nor a surplus of recyclable glass.

Policy Suppose the government wants to encourage recycling as an alternative to land dumps or incineration. It could do that in one of two ways.

Demand Incentives The government could increase recycling by increasing the demand for recycled inputs.

FIGURE 30.7

The economics of recycling. (a) The equilibrium price and amount of materials recycled are determined by supply S_1 and demand D_1. (b) Policies that increase the incentives for producers to buy recyclable inputs shift the demand curve rightward, say, to D_2, and raise both the equilibrium price and the amount of recycling. (c) Policies that encourage households to recycle shift the supply curve rightward, say, to S_2, and expand the equilibrium amount of recycling. These policies, however, also reduce the equilibrium price of the recycled inputs.

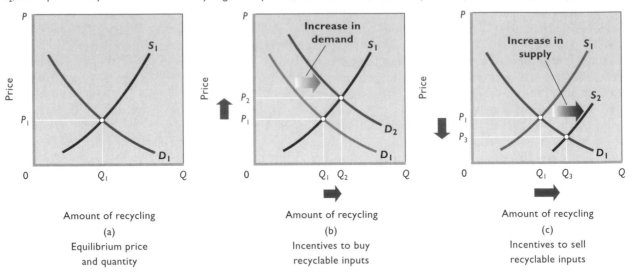

If the demand curve in Figure 30.7b shifts from D_1 rightward to D_2, the equilibrium price and quantity of recycled glass will increase to P_2 and Q_2; more recycling will occur. A policy that might increase demand would be to place taxes on the inputs that are substitutable for recycled glass in the production process. Such taxes would encourage firms to use more of the untaxed recycled glass and less of the taxed inputs. Or the government could shift its purchases toward goods produced with recycled inputs and require that its contractors do the same. Example: In 1993 the Federal government announced a new policy requiring 20 percent or more recycled content in every piece of writing and copying paper purchased by Federal agencies.

Also, environmental awareness by the public can contribute to rightward shifts of the demand curve for recycled resources. Many large firms that produce waste-intensive goods have concluded that it is in their interest to support recycling, for fear of a consumer backlash against their products. Examples: Procter & Gamble (disposable diapers) and McDonald's (packaging of fast foods) have undertaken multimillion-dollar campaigns to use recycled plastic and paper.

Supply Incentives As shown in Figure 30.7c, government can also increase recycling by shifting the supply curve rightward, as from S_1 to S_2. The equilibrium price

would fall from P_1 to P_3, but the equilibrium quantity—of, in this case, recyclable glass—would rise from Q_1 to Q_3. That is, more recycling would occur. Many local governments have implemented specific policies to do so. For example, they encourage recycling by providing curbside pickup of recyclable goods such as glass, aluminum cans, and newspapers at a lower monthly fee than that for the pickup of other garbage.

In a few cases, supply incentives for recyclables have been so effective that the price of a recycled item has fallen to zero. You can envision this outcome by shifting the supply curve in Figure 30.7c farther rightward. Some cities now are paying users of recyclable inputs such as mixed paper to truck them away from the recycling center; this means that these items have a negative price. If the cost of paying firms to take away recyclable products is lower than the cost of alternative methods, even such paid-for recycling will promote economic efficiency. However, if it is more costly to recycle trash than to bury or incinerate it, even when externalities are considered, such recycling will reduce efficiency rather than increase it. Again we are reminded that there can be either too little or too much of a good thing.

The government's task is to find the optimal amount of recycling compared with the alternative disposal of garbage. It can do this by estimating and comparing the marginal benefit and marginal cost of recycling. And, incidentally, consumers as a group can reduce the accumulation of garbage by buying products that have minimal packaging.

Global Warming

The United States has made significant progress in cleaning its air. According to the EPA, between 1990 and 2000 clean-air laws and antipollution efforts by businesses and local governments reduced concentrations of lead by 60 percent, carbon monoxide and sulfur dioxide by 36 percent each, particulate matter by 18 percent, nitrogen dioxide by 10 percent, and smog by 4 percent.

But significant air pollution problems remain, including the controversial problem of *global warming*. The earth's surface has warmed over the last century by about 1 degree Fahrenheit, with an acceleration of warming during the past two decades. Some of this surface warming may simply reflect natural fluctuations of warming and cooling, but the balance of scientific evidence suggests that human activity is a contributing factor. According to the EPA (2003), carbon dioxide and other gas emissions from factories, power plants, automobiles, and other human sources are cumulating in the earth's atmosphere and creating a greenhouse effect.

Because of the greenhouse effect, average temperatures are predicted to rise by 1 to 4.5 degrees Fahrenheit over the next 50 years and 2.2 to 10 degrees by 3000. Although there will be significant regional variation, scientists say many parts of the world will experience noticeable climatic changes. Rainfall will increase, rainfall patterns will change, and ocean levels will gradually rise by as much as 2 feet. Snow accumulations may decline in some regions and rise in others. More violent storms such as tornadoes and hurricanes may occur in some regions. (Global Perspective 30.1 lists *per capita* carbon-dioxide emissions for selected nations.)

The world's nations have responded to the global-warming threat collectively and individually. In the Kyoto Protocol of 1997, representatives of the industrially advanced nations agreed to cut their greenhouse-gas emissions to 6 to 8 percent below their 1990 levels by 2012. Since 1997 all major nations except the United States have ratified the Kyoto agreement, although few are actually likely to meet the 2012 goals. In 2001 the United States opted out of the Kyoto agreement, concluding that the limitations on greenhouse gas would severely damage the U.S. economy. A year later the United States announced a "Global Climate Change" initiative designed to use clean-energy investments to reduce greenhouse gases per dollar of GDP by 18 percent by 2012.

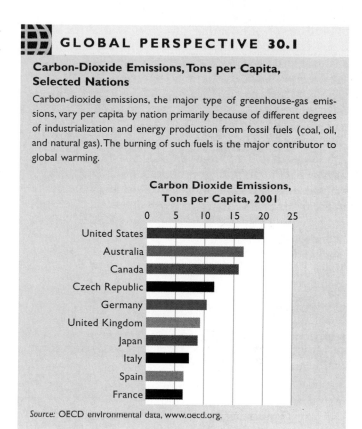

GLOBAL PERSPECTIVE 30.1

Carbon-Dioxide Emissions, Tons per Capita, Selected Nations

Carbon-dioxide emissions, the major type of greenhouse-gas emissions, vary per capita by nation primarily because of different degrees of industrialization and energy production from fossil fuels (coal, oil, and natural gas). The burning of such fuels is the major contributor to global warming.

Carbon Dioxide Emissions, Tons per Capita, 2001

United States	~20
Australia	~17
Canada	~15
Czech Republic	~12
Germany	~10
United Kingdom	~10
Japan	~9
Italy	~7
Spain	~7
France	~6

Source: OECD environmental data, www.oecd.org.

Economists stress that global-warming policies that reduce greenhouse-gas emissions and thus slow or eliminate global warming create costs as well as benefits. Therefore it is imperative to consider the marginal costs and marginal benefits carefully in making policy decisions. Greenhouse-gas limits should not be so stringent that they end up costing society more than the value of the benefits they produce. But limits should not be so lenient that society forgoes substantial potential benefits that it would have otherwise achieved.

Economists also stress that the market mechanism, through its system of prices and profits and losses, will make appropriate adjustments based on new climatic realities. Air-conditioner sales may rise; snow shovel sales may fall. Some agricultural lands probably will be deserted; others farther north will be cultivated. The maple syrup industry in New England may shift to Canada. Nevertheless, the *transition costs*—the costs associated with making economic adjustments—of global warming will undoubtedly be very high if no actions are taken to reduce greenhouse gases. The reduction or elimination of these transition costs is part of the benefit of slowing or eliminating the greenhouse effect. Such benefits must be fully considered in the cost-benefit analysis.

QUICK REVIEW 30.3

- Society's pollution problem has largely resulted from increasing population, rising per capita consumption, certain changes in technology, and the so-called tragedy of the commons.
- The government can encourage recycling through demand and supply incentives; its task is to determine the optimal amount of recycling.
- The world's industrial nations are struggling to reduce emissions of greenhouse gases, which most scientists think are contributing to global warming.

Information Failures

Thus far we have added new details and insights concerning two types of market failure: public goods and externalities. There is another, subtler, market failure. This one results when either buyers or sellers have incomplete or inaccurate information and their cost of obtaining better information is prohibitive. Technically stated, this market failure occurs because of **asymmetric information**—unequal knowledge possessed by the parties to a market transaction. Buyers and sellers do not have identical information about price, quality, or some other aspect of the good or service.

Sufficient market information normally is available to ensure that goods and services are produced and purchased efficiently. But in some cases inadequate information makes it difficult to distinguish trustworthy from untrustworthy sellers or trustworthy from untrustworthy buyers. In these markets, society's scarce resources may not be used efficiently, thus implying that the government should intervene by increasing the information available to the market participants. Under rare circumstances the government may itself supply a good for which information problems have prohibited efficient production.

30.3
Information
failures

Inadequate Information Involving Sellers

Inadequate information about sellers and their products can cause market failure in the form of underallocation

© Michael Newman/PhotoEdit

"Lemons"

Why does a new car lose substantial market value when it is purchased, even though the same car can sit on the dealer's lot for weeks, or even months, and still retain its market value? One plausible explanation for this paradox is based on the ideas of *asymmetric information* and *adverse selection.**

Used-car owners (potential sellers) have much better information about the mechanical condition of their cars than do potential buyers. Because of this asymmetric information, an *adverse selection problem* occurs. Owners of defective used cars—so-called lemons—have an incentive to sell their cars to unsuspecting buyers, whereas owners of perfectly operating used cars have an incentive to retain their used cars. Although a mix of both good and bad used cars is offered for sale, the mix is tilted toward the poorer-quality used cars. So the average quality of the used cars is lower than that of the same makes and models that are not for sale.

The typical consumer finds it difficult to identify the higher-quality used cars from the average- (lower-) quality used cars simply by looking at them or taking them for a test drive. Anticipating repair costs, the customer is willing to pay only a price that reflects the lower quality.†

So we have a solution to the paradox: When purchased, the market values of new cars drop quickly to the value of the average-quality used cars of the same year, make, and model in the market. This is true even though many individual used cars may be in perfect operating condition. Adverse selection, asymmetric information, and the resulting risk of "buying someone else's problem" drop the value of used cars relative to new cars still on the lot.

*This explanation is based on the work of economist George Akerlof.

†Transferable warrantees reduce, but do not eliminate, the potential repair costs of used cars. Consumers lose time in arranging repairs and forgo the use of their cars when the repairs are being done.

of resources. Examining the markets for gasoline and for the services of surgeons will show us how this comes about.

Example: Gasoline Market Assume an absurd situation: Suppose there is no system of weights and measures established by law, no government inspection of gasoline pumps, and no law against false advertising. Each gas station can use whatever measure it chooses; it can define a gallon of gas as it pleases. A station can advertise that its gas is 87 octane when in fact it is only 75. It can rig its pumps to indicate that it is providing more gas than the amount being delivered.

Obviously, the consumer's cost of obtaining reliable information under such chaotic conditions is exceptionally high, if not prohibitive. Customers or their representatives would have to buy samples of gas from various gas stations, have them tested for octane level, and test the accuracy of calibrations at the pump. And these activities would have to be repeated regularly, since a station owner could alter the product quality and the accuracy of the pump at will.

Because of the high costs of obtaining information about the seller, many customers would opt out of this chaotic market. One tankful of a 50 percent solution of gasoline and water would be enough to discourage most motorists from further driving. More realistically, the conditions in this market would encourage consumers to vote for political candidates who promise to provide a government solution. The oil companies and honest gasoline stations would not object to government intervention. They would realize that accurate information, by enabling this market to work, would expand their total sales and profit.

The government has in fact intervened in the market for gasoline and other markets with similar potential information difficulties. It has established a system of weights and measures, employed inspectors to check the accuracy of gasoline pumps, and passed laws against fraudulent claims and misleading advertising. There can be no doubt that these government activities have produced net benefits for society.

Example: Licensing of Surgeons

Suppose now that anyone could hang out a shingle and claim to be a surgeon, much as anyone can become a house painter. The market would eventually sort out the true surgeons from those who are "learning by doing" or are fly-by-night operators who move into and out of an area. As people died from unsuccessful surgery, lawsuits for malpractice eventually would eliminate the medical impostors. People needing surgery for themselves or their loved ones could obtain information from newspaper reports or from people who have undergone similar operations.

But this process of obtaining information for those needing surgery would take considerable time and would impose unacceptably high human and economic costs. There is a fundamental difference between getting an amateurish paint job on one's house and being on the receiving end of heart surgery by a bogus physician. The marginal cost of obtaining information about sellers in the surgery market would be excessively high. The risk of proceeding without good information would result in much less surgery than desirable—an underallocation of resources to surgery.

The government has remedied this market failure through a system of qualifying tests and licensing. The licensing provides consumers with inexpensive information about a service they only infrequently buy. The government has taken a similar role in several other areas of the economy. For example, it approves new medicines, regulates the securities industry, and requires warnings on containers of potentially hazardous substances. It also requires warning labels on cigarette packages and disseminates information about communicable diseases. And it issues warnings about unsafe toys and inspects restaurants for health-related violations.

Inadequate Information Involving Buyers

Just as inadequate information involving sellers can keep markets from achieving economic efficiency, so can inadequate information relating to buyers. The buyers may be consumers who buy products or firms that buy resources.

Moral Hazard Problem

Private markets may underallocate resources to a particular good or service for which there is a severe **moral hazard problem.** The moral hazard problem is the tendency of one party to a contract or agreement to alter her or his behavior, after the contract is signed, in ways that could be costly to the other party.

Suppose a firm offers an insurance policy that pays a set amount of money per month to people who suffer divorces. The attractiveness of such insurance is that it would pool the economic risk of divorce among thousands of people and, in particular, would protect spouses and children from the economic hardship that divorce often brings. Unfortunately, the moral hazard problem reduces the likelihood that insurance companies can profitably provide this type of insurance.

After taking out such insurance, some people would alter their behavior in ways that impose heavy costs on the insurer. For example, married couples would have less of an incentive to get along and to iron out marital difficulties. At the extreme, some people might be motivated to obtain a divorce, collect the insurance, and then continue to live together. Such insurance could even promote more divorces, the very outcome it is intended to protect against. The moral hazard problem would force the insurer to charge such high premiums for this insurance that few policies would be bought. If the insurer could identify in advance those people most prone to alter their behavior, the firm could exclude them from buying it. But the firm's marginal cost of getting such information is too high compared with the marginal benefit. Thus, this market would fail.

Although divorce insurance is not available in the marketplace, society recognizes the benefits of insuring against the hardships of divorce. It has corrected for this underallocation of "hardship insurance" through child-support laws that dictate payments to the spouse who retains the children, when the economic circumstances warrant them. Alimony laws also play a role.

Since, unlike private firms, the government does not have to earn a profit when supplying services, it provides "divorce insurance" of sorts through the Temporary Assistance to Needy Families (TANF) program. If a divorce leaves a spouse with children destitute, the family is eligible for TANF payments for a period of time. Government intervention does not eliminate the moral hazard problem, but it does offset the problem's adverse effects.

The moral hazard problem is also illustrated in the following statements:

- Drivers may be less cautious because they have car insurance.
- Medical malpractice insurance may increase the amount of malpractice.
- Guaranteed contracts for professional athletes may reduce the quality of their performance.
- Unemployment compensation insurance may lead some workers to shirk.
- Government insurance on bank deposits may encourage banks to make risky loans.

Adverse Selection Problem Another information problem resulting from inadequate information involving buyers is the **adverse selection problem**. This problem arises when information known by the first party to a contract or agreement is not known by the second and, as a result, the second party incurs major costs. Unlike the moral hazard problem, which arises after a person signs a contract, the adverse selection problem arises at the time a person signs a contract.

In insurance, the adverse selection problem is that people who are most likely to need insurance payouts are those who buy insurance. For example, those in poorest health will seek to buy the most generous health insurance

policies. Or, at the extreme, a person planning to hire an arsonist to "torch" his failing business has an incentive to buy fire insurance.

Our hypothetical divorce insurance sheds further light on the adverse selection problem. If the insurance firm sets the premiums on the basis of the average divorce rate, many married couples who are about to obtain a divorce will buy insurance. An insurance premium based on average probabilities will make a great buy for those about to get divorced. Meanwhile, those in highly stable marriages will not buy it.

The adverse selection problem thus tends to eliminate the pooling of low and high risks, which is the basis of profitable insurance. Insurance rates then must be so high that few people would want to (or be able to) buy such insurance.

Where private firms underprovide insurance because of information problems, the government often establishes some type of social insurance. It can require that everyone in a particular group take the insurance and thereby can overcome the adverse selection problem. Example: Although the Social Security system in the United States is partly insurance and partly an income transfer program, in its broadest sense it is insurance against poverty during old age. The Social Security program requires nearly universal participation: People who are most likely to need the minimum benefits that Social Security provides are automatically participants in the program. So, too, are those not likely to need the benefits. There is, then, no adverse selection problem.

Workplace Safety The labor market also provides an example of how inadequate information about buyers (employers) can produce market failures.

For several reasons employers have an economic incentive to provide safe workplaces. A safe workplace reduces the amount of disruption of the production process created by job accidents and lowers the costs of recruiting, screening, training, and retaining new workers. It also reduces a firm's worker compensation insurance premiums (legally required insurance against job injuries).

But a safe workplace is expensive: Safe equipment, protective gear, and a slower work pace all entail costs. The firm will decide how much safety to provide by comparing the marginal cost and marginal benefit of providing a safer workplace. Will this amount of job safety achieve economic efficiency, as well as maximize the firm's profit?

The answer is yes if the labor and product markets are competitive and if workers are fully aware of the job risks at various places of employment. With full information, workers will avoid employers having unsafe workplaces. The supply of labor to these establishments will be greatly restricted, forcing them to boost their wages to attract a workforce. The higher wages will then give these employers an incentive to provide increased workplace safety; safer workplaces will reduce wage expenses. Only firms that find it very costly to provide safer workplaces will choose to pay high compensating wage differentials rather than reduce workplace hazards.

But a serious problem arises when workers do not know that particular occupations or workplaces are unsafe. Because information involving the buyer—that is, about the employer and the workplace—is inadequate, the firm may not need to pay a wage premium to attract its workforce. Its incentive to remove safety hazards therefore will be diminished, and its profit-maximizing level of workplace safety will be less than economically desirable. In brief, the labor market will fail because of asymmetric information—in this case, sellers (workers) having less information than buyers (employers).

The government has several options for remedying this information problem:

- It can directly provide information to workers about the injury experience of various employers, much as it publishes the on-time performance of airlines.

- It can require that firms provide information to workers about known workplace hazards.

- It can establish standards of workplace safety and enforce them through inspections and penalties.

Although the Federal government has mainly employed the standards and enforcement approach to improve workplace safety, some critics contend that an information strategy might be less costly and more effective. **(Key Question 13)**

Qualification

People have found many ingenious ways to overcome information difficulties without government intervention. For example, many firms offer product warranties to overcome the lack of information about themselves and their products. Franchising also helps overcome this problem. When you visit a Wendy's or a Marriott, you know what you are going to get, as opposed to stopping at Bob's Hamburger Shop or the Bates Motel.

Also, some private firms and organizations specialize in providing information to buyers and sellers. *Consumer Reports* and the *Mobil Travel Guide* provide product information; labor unions collect and disseminate information about job safety; and credit bureaus provide information to insurance companies. Brokers, bonding agencies, and intermediaries also provide information to clients.

Economists agree, however, that the private sector cannot remedy all information problems. In some situations, government intervention is desirable to promote an efficient allocation of society's scarce resources.

QUICK REVIEW 30.4

- Asymmetric information is a source of potential market failure, causing society's scarce resources to be allocated inefficiently.

- Inadequate information about sellers and their products may lead to an underallocation of resources to those products.

- The moral hazard problem is the tendency of one party to a contract or agreement to alter its behavior in ways that are costly to the other party; for example, a person who buys insurance may willingly incur added risk.

- The adverse selection problem arises when one party to a contract or agreement has less information than the other party and incurs a cost because of that asymmetrical information. For example, an insurance company offering "no-medical-exam-required" life insurance policies may attract customers who have life-threatening diseases.

Economists Ian Ayres and Steven Levitt Find That an Auto Antitheft Device Called *Lojack* Produces Large Spillover Benefits.

Private expenditures to reduce crime are estimated to be $300 billion annually and are growing at a faster rate than is spending on public crime prevention. Unfortunately, some forms of private crime prevention simply redistribute crime rather than reduce it. For example, car alarm systems that have red blinking warning lights may simply divert professional auto thieves to vehicles that do not have such lights and alarms. The owner of a car with such an alarm system benefits through reduced likelihood of theft but imposes a cost on other car owners who do not have such alarms. Their cars are more likely to be targeted for theft by thieves because other cars have visible security systems.

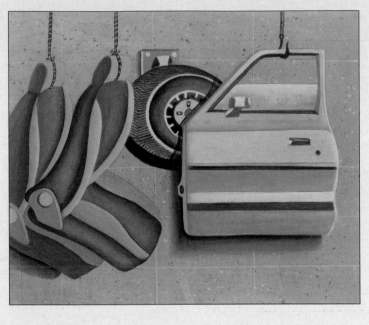

Some private crime prevention measures, however, actually reduce crime, rather than simply redistribute it. One such measure is installation of a Lojack (or some similar) car retrieval system. Lojack is a tiny radio transmitter that is hidden in one of many possible places within the car. When an owner reports a stolen car, the police can remotely activate the transmitter. Police then can determine the car's precise location and track its subsequent movements.

The owner of the car benefits because the 95 percent retrieval rate on cars with the Lojack system is higher than the 60 percent retrieval rate for cars without the system. But, according to a study by Ayres and Levitt, the benefit to the car owner is only 10 percent of the total benefit. Ninety percent of the total benefit is external; it is a spillover benefit to other car owners in the community.

There are two sources of this positive externality. First, the presence of the Lojack device sometimes enables police to intercept the car while the thief is still driving it. For example, in California the arrest rate for cars with Lojack was three times greater than that for cars without it. The arrest puts the car thief out of commission for a time and thus reduces subsequent car thefts in the community. Second, and far more important, the device enables police to trace cars to "chop shops," where crooks disassemble cars for resale of the parts. When police raid the chop shop, they put the entire theft ring out of business. In Los Angeles alone, Lojack has eliminated 45 chop shops in just a few years. The purging of the chop shop and theft ring reduces auto theft in the community. So auto owners who do not have Lojack devices in their cars benefit from car owners who do. Ayres and Levitt estimate the *marginal social benefit* of Lojack—the marginal benefit to the Lojack car owner *plus* the spillover benefit to other car owners—is 15 times greater than the marginal cost of the device.

We saw in Figure 30.4a that the existence of positive externalities causes an insufficient quantity of a product and thus an underallocation of scarce resources to its production. The two general ways to correct the outcome are to subsidize the consumer, as shown in Figure 30.4b, or to subsidize the producer, as shown in Figure 30.4c. Currently, there is only one form of government intervention in place: state-mandated insurance discounts for people who install auto retrieval systems such as Lojack. Those discounts on insurance premiums, in effect, subsidize the consumer by lowering the "price" of the system to consumers. The lower price raises the number of systems installed. But, on the basis of their research, Ayres and Levitt contend that the current levels of insurance discounts are far too small to correct the underallocation that results from the positive externalities created by Lojack.

Source: Based on Ian Ayres and Steven D. Levitt, "Measuring Positive Externalities from Unobservable Victim Precaution: An Empirical Analysis of Lojack," *Quarterly Journal of Economics,* February 1998, pp. 43–77. The authors point out that Lojack did not fund their work in any way, nor do they have any financial stake in Lojack.

SUMMARY

1. Graphically, the collective demand curve for a particular public good can be found by summing vertically the individual demand curves for that good. The demand curve resulting from this process indicates the collective willingness to pay for the last unit of any given amount of the public good.

2. The optimal quantity of a public good occurs where the combined willingness to pay for the last unit—the marginal benefit of the good—equals the good's marginal cost.

3. Cost-benefit analysis can provide guidance as to the economic desirability and most efficient scope of public goods output.

4. Spillovers or externalities cause the equilibrium output of certain goods to vary from the optimal output. Spillover costs (negative externalities) result in an overallocation of resources that can be corrected by legislation or specific taxes. Spillover benefits (positive externalities) are accompanied by an underallocation of resources that can be corrected by subsidies to consumers, subsidies to producers, or government provision.

5. According to the Coase theorem, private bargaining is capable of solving potential externality problems where (a) the property rights are clearly defined, (b) the number of people involved is small, and (c) bargaining costs are negligible.

6. Clearly established property rights and liability rules permit some spillover costs to be prevented or remedied through private lawsuits. Lawsuits, however, can be costly, time-consuming, and uncertain as to their results.

7. Direct controls and specific taxes can improve resource allocation in situations where negative externalities affect many people and community resources. Both direct controls (for example, smokestack emission standards) and specific taxes (for example, taxes on firms producing toxic chemicals) increase production costs and hence product

price. As product price rises, the externality is reduced, since less of the output is bought and sold.

8. Markets for pollution rights, where firms can buy and sell the right to discharge a fixed amount of pollution, put a price on pollution and encourage firms to reduce or eliminate it.

9. The socially optimal amount of externality abatement occurs where society's marginal cost and marginal benefit of reducing the externality are equal. This optimal amount of pollution abatement is likely to be less than a 100 percent reduction. Changes in technology or changes in society's attitudes toward pollution can affect the optimal amount of pollution abatement.

10. Extensive recycling is a relatively recent response to the growing garbage disposal problem. The equilibrium price and quantity of recyclable inputs depend on their demand and supply. The government can encourage recycling through either demand or supply incentives.

11. A growing body of scientific evidence suggests that accumulation of carbon dioxide and other greenhouse gases in the earth's atmosphere may be contributing to a global-warming problem. In the Kyoto Protocol of 1997 the world's industrial nations agreed to reduce their emissions of greenhouse gases to 6 to 8 percent below 1990 levels by 2012. The United States refused to ratify the Kyoto agreement, instead opting for a less aggressive policy of using clean-energy investments to reduce greenhouse emissions by 18 percent per dollar of GDP by 2012.

12. Asymmetric information between sellers and buyers can cause markets to fail. The moral hazard problem occurs when people alter their behavior after they sign a contract or reach an agreement, imposing costs on the other party. The adverse selection problem occurs when one party to a contract or agreement takes advantage of the other party's inadequate information, resulting in an unanticipated loss to the latter party.

TERMS AND CONCEPTS

cost-benefit analysis

marginal-cost–marginal-benefit rule

externalities

Coase theorem

tragedy of the commons

market for externality rights

optimal reduction of an externality

asymmetric information

moral hazard problem

adverse selection problem

STUDY QUESTIONS

1. **Key Question** On the basis of the three individual demand schedules on the next page, and assuming these three people are the only ones in the society, determine (a) the market demand schedule on the assumption that the good is a private good and (b) the collective demand schedule on the assumption that the good is a public good. Explain the differences, if any, in your schedules.

Individual 1		Individual 2		Individual 3	
P	**Q_d**	**P**	**Q_d**	**P**	**Q_d**
$8	0	$8	1	$8	0
7	0	7	2	7	0
6	0	6	3	6	1
5	1	5	4	5	2
4	2	4	5	4	3
3	3	3	6	3	4
2	4	2	7	2	5
1	5	1	8	1	6

2. **Key Question** Use your demand schedule for a public good, determined in question 1, and the following supply schedule to ascertain the optimal quantity of this public good. Why is this the optimal quantity?

P	**Q_s**
$19	10
16	8
13	6
10	4
7	2
4	1

3. **Key Question** The following table shows the total costs and total benefits in billions for four different antipollution programs of increasing scope. Which program should be undertaken? Why?

Program	**Total Cost**	**Total Benefit**
A	$ 3	$ 7
B	7	12
C	12	16
D	18	19

4. **Key Question** Why are spillover costs and spillover benefits also called negative and positive externalities? Show graphically how a tax can correct for a spillover cost and how a subsidy to producers can correct for a spillover benefit. How does a subsidy to consumers differ from a subsidy to producers in correcting for a spillover benefit?

5. An apple grower's orchard provides nectar to a neighbor's bees, while the beekeeper's bees help the apple grower by pollinating the apple blossoms. Use Figure 30.2b to explain why this situation might lead to an underallocation of

resources to apple growing and to beekeeping. How might this underallocation get resolved via the means suggested by the Coase theorem?

6. Explain: "Without a market for pollution rights, dumping pollutants into the air or water is costless; in the presence of the right to buy and sell pollution rights, dumping pollutants creates an opportunity cost for the polluter." What is the significance of this opportunity cost to the search for better technology to reduce pollution?

7. **Key Question** Explain the following statement, using the MB curve in Figure 30.6 to illustrate: "The optimal amount of pollution abatement for some substances, say, water from storm drains, is very low; the optimal amount of abatement for other substances, say, cyanide poison, is close to 100 percent."

8. Explain the tragedy of the commons, as it relates to pollution?

9. What is the global-warming problem? How is it being addressed? Using an example other than one in the text, explain how global warming might hurt one industry, particular region, or country but help another.

10. Explain how marketable emission credits add to overall economic efficiency, compared to across-the-board limitations on maximum discharges of air pollutants by firms?

11. Explain why there may be insufficient recycling of products when the externalities associated with landfills and garbage incinerators are not considered. What demand and supply incentives might the government provide to promote more recycling? Explain how there could be too much recycling in some situations.

12. Why is it in the interest of new homebuyers and builders of new homes to have government building codes and building inspectors?

13. **Key Question** Place an "M" beside the items in the following list that describe a moral hazard problem and an "A" beside those that describe an adverse selection problem:
    a. A person with a terminal illness buys several life insurance policies through the mail.
    b. A person drives carelessly because he or she has automobile insurance.
    c. A person who intends to "torch" his warehouse takes out a large fire insurance policy.
    d. A professional athlete who has a guaranteed contract fails to stay in shape during the off-season.
    e. A woman who anticipates having a large family takes a job with a firm that offers exceptional child care benefits.

14. **(Last Word)** Explain how a global-positioning antitheft device installed by one car owner can produce a positive spillover to thousands of others in a city.

15. **Web-Based Question: Global warming—the EPA's view** Go to www.epa.gov and use the search feature to find the

EPA's Global Warming site. What are the major greenhouse gases? How much greenhouse gas does the United States emit per person? What is the trend of emissions on a per-person basis? What is the trend of emissions per dollar of GDP in the United States? Use your own analysis to explain how total emissions can rise even though emissions per dollar of GDP substantially decline. Which of the two is most relevant for global warming?

16. ***Web-Based Question: Workplace safety—OSHA's role*** Visit www.osha.gov and first select Workers (under Audiences). How does a worker file a complaint or report a hazard? Where is the nearest OSHA office to you? Go back to the OSHA home page and select News Releases. In a sentence or two each, summarize the latest three news releases that relate to OSHA enforcement of workers' safety and health standards.

31 Public Choice Theory and the Economics of Taxation

In Chapter 30 we saw that private markets can occasionally produce *market failures,* which impede economic efficiency and justify government intervention in the economy. But the government's response to market failures is not without its own problems and pitfalls. Perhaps that is why government policies and decisions are the focus of hundreds of radio talk shows, television debates, and newspaper articles each day.

31.1
Public
choice
theory

In this chapter, we explore a number of *government failures* that impede economic efficiency in the public sector. Our spotlight is first on selected aspects of **public choice theory**—the economic analysis of government decision making, politics, and elections—and then on the economics of taxation.

Revealing Preferences through Majority Voting

Which public goods should government produce and in what amounts? To what extent should government intervene to correct externalities? How should the tax burden of financing government be apportioned?

Decisions like these are made collectively in the United States through a democratic process that relies heavily on majority voting. Candidates for office offer alternative policy packages, and citizens elect people who they think will make the best decisions on their collective behalf. Voters "retire" officials who do not adequately represent their collective wishes and elect persons they

think do. Also, citizens periodically have opportunities at the state and local levels to vote directly on public expenditures or new legislation.

Although the democratic process does a reasonably good job of revealing society's preferences, it is imperfect. Public choice theory demonstrates that majority voting can produce inefficiencies and inconsistencies.

Inefficient Voting Outcomes

Society's well-being is enhanced when government provides a public good whose total benefit exceeds its total cost. Unfortunately, majority voting does not always produce that outcome.

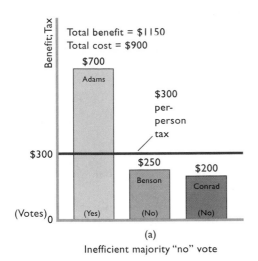

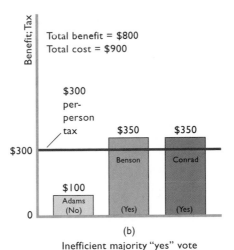

FIGURE 31.1

Inefficient voting outcomes.
Majority voting can produce inefficient decisions. (a) Majority voting leads to rejection of a public good that would entail a greater total benefit than total cost. (b) Majority voting results in acceptance of a public good that has a higher total cost than total benefit.

Illustration: Inefficient "No" Vote Assume that the government can provide a public good, say, national defense, at a total expense of $900. Also assume that there are only three individuals—Adams, Benson, and Conrad—in the society and that they will share the $900 tax expense equally, each being taxed $300 if the proposed public good is provided. And assume, as Figure 31.1a illustrates, that Adams would receive $700 worth of benefits from having this public good; Benson, $250; and Conrad, $200.

What will be the result if a majority vote determines whether or not this public good is provided? Although people do not always vote strictly according to their own economic interest, it is likely Benson and Conrad will vote "no" because they will incur tax costs of $300 each while gaining benefits of only $250 and $200, respectively. Adams will vote "yes." So the majority vote will defeat the proposal even though the total benefit of $1150 (= $700 for Adams + $250 for Benson + $200 for Conrad) exceeds the total cost of $900. Resources should be devoted to this good, but they will not be. There will be too little of this public good produced.

Illustration: Inefficient "Yes" Vote Now consider a situation in which the majority favors a public good even though its total cost exceeds its total benefit. Figure 31.1b shows the details. Again, Adams, Benson, and Conrad will equally share the $900 cost of the public good; they will each be taxed $300. But since Adams' benefit now is only $100 from the public good, she will vote against it. Meanwhile, Benson and Conrad will benefit by $350 each. They will vote for the public good because that benefit ($350) exceeds their tax payments ($300).

The majority vote will provide a public good costing $900 that produces total benefits of only $800 (= $100 for Adams + $350 for Benson + $350 for Conrad). Society's resources will be inefficiently allocated to this public good. There will be too much of it produced.

Implications So an inefficient outcome may occur as either an overproduction or an underproduction of a specific public good, and therefore as an overallocation or underallocation of resources for that particular use. In Chapter 30 we saw that government can improve economic efficiency by providing public goods that the market system will not make available. Now we have extended that analysis to reveal that government might fail to provide some public goods whose production is economically justifiable while providing other goods that are not economically warranted.

In our examples, each person has only a single vote, no matter how much he or she might gain or lose from a public good. In the first example (inefficient "no" vote), Adams would be willing to purchase a vote from either Benson or Conrad if buying votes were legal. That way Adams could be assured of obtaining the national defense he so highly values. But since buying votes is illegal, many people with strong preferences for certain public goods may have to go without them.

When individual consumers have a strong preference for a specific *private good*, they usually can find that good in the marketplace even though it may be unpopular with the majority of consumers. A consumer can buy beef tongue, liver, and squid in some supermarkets, although it is doubtful that these products would be available if majority voting stocked the shelves. But a person cannot easily "buy" a *public good* such as national defense once the majority has decided against it.

On the other hand, a consumer in the marketplace can decide not to buy a particular product, even a popular one. But although you may not want national defense, you must "buy" it through your tax payments when it is favored by the majority.

Conclusion: *Because majority voting fails to incorporate the strength of the preferences of the individual voter, it may produce economically inefficient outcomes.*

Interest Groups and Logrolling

There are avenues for resolving the inefficiencies associated with majority voting. Two examples follow.

Interest Groups

Those who have a strong preference for a public good may band together into interest groups and use advertisements, mailings, and direct persuasion to convince others of the merits of that public good. Adams might try to persuade Benson and Conrad that it is in their best interest to vote for national defense—that national defense is much more valuable to them than their $250 and $200 valuations. Such appeals are common in democratic politics. Sometimes they are successful; sometimes they are not.

Political Logrolling

Logrolling—the trading of votes to secure favorable outcomes—can also turn an inefficient outcome into an efficient one. In our first example (Figure 31.1a), perhaps Benson has a strong preference for a different public good, for example, a new road, which Adams and Conrad do not think is worth the tax expense. That would provide an opportunity for Adams and Benson to trade votes to ensure provision of both national defense and the new road. That is, Adams and Benson would each vote "yes" on both measures. Adams would get the national defense and Benson would get the road. Without the logrolling, both public goods would have been rejected. Moreover, the logrolling will add to society's well-being if, as was true for national defense, the road creates a greater overall benefit than cost.

But logrolling need not increase economic efficiency. Even if national defense and the road each cost more than the total benefit each produces, both might still be provided because of the vote trading. Adams and Benson might still engage in logrolling if each expects to secure a sufficient net gain from her or his favored public good, even though the gains would come at the clear expense of Conrad.

Logrolling is very common in state legislatures and Congress. It can either increase or diminish economic efficiency, depending on the circumstances.

Paradox of Voting

31.2 Paradox of voting 🔍

Another difficulty with majority voting is the **paradox of voting,** *a situation in which society may not be able to rank its preferences consistently through paired-choice majority voting.*

Preferences   Consider Table 31.1, in which we again assume a community of three voters: Adams, Benson, and Conrad. Suppose the community has three alternative public goods from which to choose: national defense, a road, and a weather warning system. We expect that each member of the community prefers the three alternatives in a certain order. For example, one person might prefer national defense to a road and a road to a weather warning system. We can attempt to determine the preferences of the community through paired-choice majority voting. Specifically, a vote can be held between any two of the public goods, and the winner of that vote can then be matched against the third public good in another vote.

The three goods and the assumed individual preferences of the three voters are listed in the top part of Table 31.1. The data indicate that Adams prefers national defense to the road and the road to the weather warning system. This implies also that Adams prefers national defense to the weather warning system. Benson values the road more than the weather warning system and the

TABLE 31.1

Paradox of Voting

Public Good	Preferences		
	Adams	**Benson**	**Conrad**
National defense	1st choice	3d choice	2d choice
Road	2d choice	1st choice	3d choice
Weather warning system	3d choice	2d choice	1st choice

Election	Voting Outcomes: Winner
1. National defense vs. road	National defense (preferred by Adams and Conrad)
2. Road vs. weather warning system	Road (preferred by Adams and Benson)
3. National defense vs. weather warning system	Weather warning system (preferred by Benson and Conrad)

warning system more than national defense. Conrad's order of preference is weather warning system, national defense, and road.

Voting Outcomes The lower part of Table 31.1 shows the outcomes of three hypothetical elections decided through majority vote. In the first, national defense wins against the road, because a majority of voters (Adams and Conrad) prefer national defense to the road. In the second election, to see whether this community wants a road or a weather warning system, a majority of voters (Adams and Benson) prefer the road.

We have determined that the majority of people in this community prefer national defense to a road and prefer a road to a weather warning system. It seems logical to conclude that the community prefers national defense to a weather warning system. But it does not!

To demonstrate this conclusion, we hold a direct election between national defense and the weather warning system. Row 3 shows that a majority of voters (Benson and Conrad) prefer the weather warning system to national defense. As listed in Table 31.1, then, the three paired-choice majority votes imply that this community is irrational: It seems to prefer national defense to a road and a road to a weather warning system, but would rather have a weather warning system than national defense.

The problem is not irrational community preferences but rather a flawed procedure for determining those preferences. We see that the outcome from paired-choice majority voting may depend on the order in which the votes are taken up. Under some circumstances majority voting fails to make consistent choices that reflect the community's underlying preferences. As a consequence, government may find it difficult to provide the "correct" public goods by acting in accordance with majority voting. Important note: This critique is not meant to suggest that there is some better procedure. Majority voting is much more likely to reflect community preferences than decisions by, say, a dictator or a group of self-appointed leaders. **(Key Question 2)**

Median-Voter Model

One final aspect of majority voting reveals insights into real-world phenomena. The **median-voter model** suggests that, under majority rule and consistent voting preferences, the median voter will in a sense determine the outcomes of elections. The median voter is the person holding the middle position on an issue: Half the other voters have stronger preferences for a public good, amount of taxation, or degree of government regulation, and half

have weaker or negative preferences. The extreme voters on each side of an issue prefer the median choice rather than the other extreme position, so the median voter's choice predominates.

Example Suppose a society composed of Adams, Benson, and Conrad has reached agreement that as a society it needs a weather warning system. Each person independently is to submit a total dollar amount he or she thinks should be spent on the warning system, assuming each will be taxed one-third of that amount. An election will determine the size of the system. Because each person can be expected to vote for his or her own proposal, no majority will occur if all the proposals are placed on the ballot at the same time. Thus, the group decides on a paired-choice vote: They will first vote between two of the proposals and then match the winner of that vote against the remaining proposal.

The three proposals are as follows: Adams desires a $400 system; Benson wants an $800 system; Conrad opts for a $300 system. Which proposal will win? The median-voter model suggests it will be the $400 proposal submitted by the median voter, Adams. Half the other voters favor a more costly system; half favor a less costly system. To understand why the $400 system will be the outcome, let's conduct the two elections.

First, suppose that the $400 proposal is matched against the $800 proposal. Adams naturally votes for her $400 proposal, and Benson votes for his own $800 proposal. Conrad, who proposed the $300 expenditure for the warning system, votes for the $400 proposal because it is closer to his own. So Adams' $400 proposal is selected by a 2-to-1 majority vote.

Next, we match the $400 proposal against the $300 proposal. Again the $400 proposal wins. It gets a vote from Adams and one from Benson, who proposed the $800 expenditure and for that reason prefers a $400 expenditure to a $300 one. Adams, the median voter in this case, is in a sense the person who has decided the level of expenditure on a weather warning system for this society.

Real-World Applicability Although our illustration is a simple one, it explains a great deal. We do note a tendency for public choices to match most closely the median view. Political candidates, for example, take one set of positions to win the nomination of their political parties; in so doing, they tend to appeal to the median voter within the party to get the nomination. They then shift their views more closely to the political center when they square off against opponents from the opposite political party. In effect, they redirect their appeal toward the median voter within the total population. They also try to label their opponents as being too liberal, or too conservative, and out of touch with "mainstream America." And they conduct polls and adjust their positions on issues accordingly.

Implications   The median-voter model has two important implications:

- Many people will be dissatisfied by the extent of government involvement in the economy. The size of government will largely be determined by the median preference, leaving many people desiring a much larger, or a much smaller, public sector. In the marketplace you can buy zero zucchinis, 2 zucchinis, or 200 zucchinis, depending on how much you enjoy them. In the public sector you get the number of Stealth bombers and interstate highways the median voter prefers.

- Some people may "vote with their feet" by moving into political jurisdictions where the median voter's preferences are closer to their own. They may move from the city to a suburb where the level of government services, and therefore taxes, is lower. Or they may move into an area known for its excellent, but expensive, school system.

For these reasons, and because our personal preferences for government activity are not static, the median preference shifts over time. Moreover, information about people's preferences is imperfect, leaving much room for politicians to misjudge the true median position. When they do, they may have a difficult time getting reelected. **(Key Question 3)**

Government Failure

As implied in our discussion of voting problems, government does not always perform its economic functions effectively and efficiently. In fact, public choice theory suggests that inherent shortcomings within the public sector can produce inefficient outcomes. Such shortcomings may result in **government failure**—inefficiency due to certain characteristics of the public sector. Let's consider some of these characteristics and outcomes.

Special Interests and Rent Seeking

Casual reflection suggests there may be a significant gap between "sound economics" and "good politics." Sound economics calls for the public sector to pursue various programs as long as marginal benefits exceed marginal costs. Good politics, however, suggests that politicians support programs and policies that will maximize their chance of getting elected and staying in office. The result may be that the government will promote the goals of groups of voters that have special interests to the detriment of the larger public. In the process, economic inefficiency may result.

Special-Interest Effect   Efficient public decision making is often impaired by the **special-interest effect.** This is any outcome of the political process whereby a small number of people obtain a government program or policy that gives them large gains at the expense of a much greater number of persons who individually suffer small losses.

The small group of potential beneficiaries is well informed and highly vocal on the issue in question, and they press politicians for approval. The large numbers facing very small individual losses, however, are generally uninformed on the issue. Politicians feel they will lose the campaign contributions and votes of the small special-interest group that backs the issue if they legislate against it but will not lose the support of the large group of uninformed voters, who are likely to evaluate the politicians on other issues of greater importance to them.

The special-interest effect is also evident in so-called *pork-barrel politics*, a means of securing a government project that yields benefits mainly to a single political district and its political representative. In this case, the special-interest group comprises local constituents, while the larger group consists of relatively uninformed taxpayers scattered across a much larger geographic area. Politicians clearly have a strong incentive to secure public goods ("pork") for their local constituents. Such goods win political favor because they are highly valued by constituents and the much larger group of relatively uninformed taxpayers bears the cost. Moreover, logrolling typically enters the picture. "Vote for my special local project and I will vote for yours" become part of the overall strategy for securing "pork" and remaining elected.

Finally, a politician's inclination to support the smaller group of special beneficiaries is enhanced because special-interest groups are often quite willing to help finance the campaigns of "right-minded" politicians and politicians who "bring home the pork." The result is that politicians may support special-interest programs and projects that cannot be justified on economic grounds.

Rent-Seeking Behavior   The appeal to government for special benefits at taxpayers' or someone else's expense is called **rent seeking.** To economists, "rent" is a payment beyond what is necessary to keep a resource supplied in its current use. Corporations, trade associations, labor unions, and professional organizations employ vast resources to secure favorable government policies that result in rent— higher profit or income than would occur under competitive market conditions. The government is able to dispense such rent directly or indirectly through laws, rules, hiring, and purchases. Elected officials are willing to provide such rent because they want to be responsive to key constituents, who in turn help them remain in office.

Here are some examples of "rent-providing" legislation or policies: tariffs on foreign products that limit competition and raise prices to consumers; tax breaks that benefit specific corporations; government construction projects that create union jobs but cost more than the benefits they yield; occupational licensing that goes beyond what is needed to protect consumers; and large subsidies to farmers by taxpayers. None of these is justified by economic efficiency.

Clear Benefits, Hidden Costs

Some critics say that vote-seeking politicians will not weigh objectively all the costs and benefits of various programs, as economic rationality demands in deciding which to support and which to reject. Because political officeholders must seek voter support every few years, they favor programs that have immediate and clear-cut benefits and vague or deferred costs. Conversely, politicians will reject programs with immediate and easily identifiable costs but with less measurable but very high long-term benefits.

Such biases may lead politicians to reject economically justifiable programs and to accept programs that are economically irrational. Example: A proposal to construct or expand mass-transit systems in large metropolitan areas may be economically rational on the basis of cost-benefit analysis. But if (1) the program is to be financed by immediate increases in highly visible income or sales taxes and (2) benefits will occur only years from now when the project is completed, then the vote-seeking politician may oppose the program.

Assume, on the other hand, that a program of Federal aid to municipal police forces is not justifiable on the basis of cost-benefit analysis. But if the cost is paid for from budget surpluses, the program's modest benefits may seem so large that it will gain approval.

Limited and Bundled Choice

Public choice theorists point out that the political process forces citizens and their elected representatives to be less selective in choosing public goods and services than they are in choosing private goods and services.

In the marketplace, the citizen as a consumer can exactly satisfy personal preferences by buying certain goods and not buying others. However, in the public sector the citizen as a voter is confronted with, say, only two or three candidates for an office, each representing a different "bundle" of programs (public goods and services). None of these bundles of public goods is likely to fit exactly the preferences of any particular voter. Yet the voter must choose one of them. The candidate who comes closest to voter Smith's preference may endorse national health insurance, increases in Social Security benefits, subsidies to tobacco farmers, and tariffs on imported goods. Smith is likely to vote for that candidate even though Smith strongly opposes tobacco subsidies.

In other words, the voter must take the bad with the good. In the public sector, people are forced to "buy" goods and services they do not want. It is as if, in going to a sporting-goods store, you were forced to buy an unwanted pool cue to get a wanted pair of running shoes. This is a situation where resources are not being used efficiently to satisfy consumer wants. In this sense, the provision of public goods and services is inherently inefficient.

Congress is confronted with a similar limited-choice, bundled-goods problem. Appropriations legislation combines hundreds, even thousands, of spending items into a single bill. Many of these spending items may be completely unrelated to the main purpose of the legislation. Yet congressional representatives must vote the entire package—yea or nay. Unlike consumers in the marketplace, they cannot be selective. **(Key Question 4)**

Bureaucracy and Inefficiency

Some economists contend that public agencies are generally less efficient than private businesses. The reason is not that lazy and incompetent workers somehow end up in the public sector while ambitious and capable people gravitate to the private sector. Rather, it is that the market system creates incentives and pressures for internal efficiency that are absent from the public sector. Private enterprises have a clear goal—profit. Whether a private firm is in a competitive or monopolistic market, efficient management means lower costs and higher profit. The higher profit not only benefits the firm's owners but enhances the promotion prospects of managers. Moreover, part of the managers' pay may be tied to profit via profit-sharing plans, bonuses, and stock options. There is no similar gain to government agencies and their managers—no counterpart to profit—to create a strong incentive to achieve efficiency.

The market system imposes a very obvious test of performance on private firms: the test of profit and loss. An efficient firm is profitable and therefore successful; it survives, prospers, and grows. An inefficient firm is unprofitable and unsuccessful; it declines and in time goes bankrupt and ceases to exist. But there is no similar, clear-cut test with which to assess the efficiency or inefficiency of public agencies. How can anyone determine whether a public hydroelectricity provider, a state university, a local fire department, the Department of Agriculture, or the Bureau of Indian Affairs is operating efficiently?

Cynics even argue that a public agency that inefficiently uses its resources is likely to survive and grow! In the private sector, inefficiency and monetary loss lead to the abandonment of certain activities or products or even firms. But the government, they say, does not like to abandon activities in which it has failed. Some suggest that the typical response of the government to a program's failure is to increase its budget and staff. This means that public sector inefficiency just continues on a larger scale.

Furthermore, economists assert that government employees, together with the special-interest groups they serve, often gain sufficient political clout to block attempts to pare down or eliminate their agencies. Politicians who attempt to reduce the size of huge Federal bureaucracies such as those relating to agriculture, education, health and welfare, and national defense incur sizable political risk because bureaucrats and special-interest groups will team up to defeat them.

Finally, critics point out that there is a tendency for government bureaucrats to justify their continued employment by looking for and eventually finding new problems to solve. It is not surprising that social "problems," as defined by government, tend to persist or even expand.

The Last Word at the end of this chapter highlights several recent media-reported examples of the special-interest effect, the problem of limited and bundled choices, and problems of government bureaucracy. You might want to read through these examples now, relating each to the section just completed.

Imperfect Institutions

It is possible to argue that such criticisms of public sector inefficiency are exaggerated and cynical. Perhaps they are. Nevertheless, they do tend to shatter the concept of a benevolent government that responds with precision and efficiency to the wants of its citizens. The market system of the private sector is far from perfectly efficient, and government's economic function is mainly to correct that system's shortcomings. But the public sector too is subject to deficiencies in fulfilling its economic function. "The relevant comparison is not between perfect markets and imperfect governments, nor between faulty markets and all-knowing, rational, benevolent governments, but between inevitably imperfect institutions."[1]

Because the market system and public agencies are both imperfect, it is sometimes difficult to determine whether a particular activity can be performed with greater success in the private sector or in the public sector. It is easy to reach agreement on opposite extremes: National defense must lie with the public sector, while computer production can best be accomplished by the private sector. But what about health insurance? Parks and recreation areas? Fire protection? Garbage collection? Housing? Education? It is hard to assess every good or service and to say absolutely that it should be assigned to either the public sector or the private sector. Evidence: All the goods and services just mentioned are provided in part by *both* private enterprises and public agencies.

QUICK REVIEW 31.1

- Majority voting can produce voting outcomes that are inefficient; projects having greater total benefits than total costs may be defeated, and projects having greater total costs than total benefits may be approved.

- The paradox of voting occurs when voting by majority rule does not provide a consistent ranking of society's preferences for public goods and services.

- The median-voter model suggests that under majority rule and consistent voting preferences, the voter who has the middle preference will determine the outcome of an election.

- Government failure allegedly occurs as a result of rent seeking, pressure by special-interest groups, shortsighted political behavior, limited and bundled choices, and bureaucratic inefficiency.

Apportioning the Tax Burden

We now turn from the difficulties of making collective decisions about public goods to the difficulties of deciding how those goods should be financed.

---

[1] Otto Eckstein, *Public Finance*, 3d ed. (Englewood Cliffs, N.J.: Prentice-Hall, 1973), p. 17.

It is difficult to measure precisely how the benefits of public goods are apportioned among individuals and institutions. We cannot accurately determine how much citizen Mildred Moore benefits from military installations, a network of highways, a public school system, the national weather bureau, and local police and fire protection.

The situation is different when it comes to paying for those benefits. Studies reveal with reasonable clarity how the overall tax burden is apportioned. (By "tax burden" we mean the total cost of taxes imposed on society.) This apportionment question affects each of us. The overall level of taxes is important, but the average citizen is much more concerned with his or her part of the overall tax burden.

Benefits Received versus Ability to Pay

There are two basic philosophies on how the economy's tax burden should be apportioned.

Benefits-Received Principle

The **benefits-received principle** of taxation asserts that households and businesses should purchase the goods and services of government in the same way they buy other commodities. Those who benefit most from government-supplied goods or services should pay the taxes necessary to finance them. A few public goods are now financed on this basis. For example, money collected as gasoline taxes is typically used to finance highway construction and repairs. Thus people who benefit from good roads pay the cost of those roads. Difficulties immediately arise, however, when we consider widespread application of the benefits-received principle:

- How will the government determine the benefits that individual households and businesses receive from national defense, education, the court system, and police and fire protection? Recall that public goods are characterized by nonrivalry and nonexcludability. So benefits from public goods are especially widespread and diffuse. Even in the seemingly straightforward case of highway financing it is difficult to measure benefits. Owners of cars benefit in different degrees from good roads. But others also benefit. For example, businesses benefit because good roads bring them customers.

- The benefits-received principle cannot logically be applied to income redistribution programs. It would be absurd and self-defeating to ask poor families to pay the taxes needed to finance their welfare payments. It would be ridiculous to think of taxing only unemployed workers to finance the unemployment compensation payments they receive.

Ability-to-Pay Principle

The **ability-to-pay principle** of taxation asserts that the tax burden should be apportioned according to taxpayers' income and wealth. In the United States this means that individuals and businesses with larger incomes should pay more taxes in both absolute and relative terms than those with smaller incomes.

What is the rationale of ability-to-pay taxation? Proponents argue that each additional dollar of income received by a household yields a smaller amount of satisfaction or marginal utility when it is spent. Because consumers act rationally, the first dollars of income received in any time period will be spent on high-urgency goods that yield the greatest marginal utility. Successive dollars of income will go for less urgently needed goods and finally for trivial goods and services. This means that a dollar taken through taxes from a poor person who has few dollars represents a greater utility sacrifice than a dollar taken through taxes from a rich person who has many dollars. To balance the sacrifices that taxes impose on income receivers, taxes should be apportioned according to the amount of income a taxpayer receives.

This argument is appealing, but application problems arise here too. Although we might agree that the household earning $100,000 per year has a greater ability to pay taxes than a household receiving $10,000, we don't know exactly how much more ability to pay the first family has. Should the wealthier family pay the *same* percentage of its larger income, and hence a larger absolute amount, as taxes? Or should it be made to pay a *larger* fraction of its income as taxes? And how much larger should that fraction be?

There is no scientific way of measuring someone's ability to pay taxes—and that's the main problem. In practice, the solution hinges on guesswork, the tax views of the political party in power, expediency, and how urgently the government needs revenue.

Progressive, Proportional, and Regressive Taxes

Any discussion of taxation leads ultimately to the question of tax rates. Recall from Chapter 5 that an *average tax rate* is the total tax paid divided by some base against which the tax is compared.

Definitions

Taxes are classified as progressive, proportional, or regressive, depending on the relationship between average tax rates and taxpayer incomes. We focus on incomes because all taxes, whether on income or on a product or a building or a parcel of land, are ultimately paid out of someone's income.

- A tax is **progressive** if its average rate increases as income increases. Such a tax claims not only a larger absolute (dollar) amount but also a larger percentage of income as income increases.
- A tax is **regressive** if its average rate declines as income increases. Such a tax takes a smaller proportion of income as income increases. A regressive tax may or may not take a larger absolute amount of income as income increases. (You may want to derive an example to substantiate this conclusion.)
- A tax is **proportional** if its average rate *remains the same* regardless of the size of income.

We can illustrate these ideas with the personal income tax. Suppose tax rates are such that a household pays 10 percent of its income in taxes regardless of the size of its income. This is a *proportional* income tax. Now suppose the rate structure is such that a household with an annual taxable income of less than $10,000 pays 5 percent in income taxes; a household with an income of $10,000 to $20,000 pays 10 percent; one with a $20,000 to $30,000 income pays 15 percent; and so forth. This is a *progressive* income tax. Finally, suppose the rate declines as taxable income rises: You pay 15 percent if you earn less than $10,000; 10 percent if you earn $10,000 to $20,000; 5 percent if you earn $20,000 to $30,000; and so forth. This is a *regressive* income tax.

In general, progressive taxes are those that fall relatively more heavily on people with high incomes; regressive taxes are those that fall relatively more heavily on the poor. **(Key Question 7)**

Applications   Let's examine the progressivity, or regressivity, of several taxes.

Personal Income Tax   We noted in Chapter 5 that the Federal personal income tax is progressive, with marginal tax rates (those assessed on additional income) ranging from 10 to 35 percent in 2003. Rules that allow individuals to deduct from income interest on home mortgages and property taxes and that exempt interest on state and local bonds from taxation tend to make the tax less progressive than these marginal rates suggest. Nevertheless, average tax rates rise with income.

Sales Taxes   At first thought, a general sales tax with, for example, a 5 percent rate would seem to be proportional. But in fact it is regressive with respect to income. A larger portion of a low-income person's income is exposed to the tax than is the case for a high-income person; the rich pay no tax on the part of income that is saved, whereas the poor are unable to save. Example:

"Low-income" Smith has an income of $15,000 and spends it all. "High-income" Jones has an income of $300,000 but spends only $200,000 and saves the rest. Assuming a 5 percent sales tax applies to all expenditures of each individual, we find that Smith pays $750 (5 percent of $15,000) in sales taxes and Jones pays $10,000 (5 percent of $200,000). But Smith pays $750/$15,000, or 5 percent of income, as sales taxes, while Jones pays $10,000/$300,000, or 3.3 percent of income. The general sales tax therefore is regressive.

Corporate Income Tax   The Federal corporate income tax is essentially a proportional tax with a flat 35 percent tax rate. But this assumes that corporation owners (shareholders) bear the tax. Some tax experts argue that at least part of the tax is passed through to consumers in the form of higher product prices. To the extent that this occurs, the tax is like a sales tax and is thus regressive.

Payroll Taxes   Payroll (Social Security and Medicare) taxes are regressive because the Social Security tax applies to only a fixed amount of income. For example, in 2003 the Social Security tax rate was 6.2 percent, but only of the first $87,000 of a person's wage income. The Medicare tax was 1.45 percent of all wage income. Someone earning exactly $87,000 would pay $6655.50, or 7.65 percent (6.2 percent + 1.45 percent) of his or her income. Someone with twice that wage income, or $174,000, would pay $7917 (= $6655.50 on the first $87,000 + $1261.50 on the second $87,000), which is only 4.55 percent of his or her wage income. So the average payroll tax falls as income rises, confirming that the payroll tax is regressive.

Moreover, government does not collect payroll taxes on nonwage income (such as interest, dividends, or rents). This makes them even more regressive. If our individual with the $174,000 of wage income also received $174,000 of nonwage income, then the $7917 of payroll tax would be only 2.23 percent of his or her total income.

Property Taxes   Most economists conclude that property taxes on buildings are regressive for the same reasons as are sales taxes. First, property owners add the tax to the rents that tenants are charged. Second, property taxes, as a percentage of income, are higher for low-income families than for high-income families because the poor must spend a larger proportion of their incomes for housing. This alleged regressivity of property taxes may be increased by differences in property-tax rates from locality to locality. In general, property-tax rates are higher in poorer areas, to make up for lower property values.

Tax Incidence and Efficiency Loss

Determining whether a particular tax is progressive, proportional, or regressive is complicated, because those on whom taxes are levied do not always pay the taxes. We therefore need to try to locate the final resting place of a tax, or the **tax incidence.** The tools of elasticity of supply and demand will help. Let's focus on a hypothetical excise tax levied on wine producers. Do the producers really pay this tax, or do they shift it to wine consumers?

Elasticity and Tax Incidence

In Figure 31.2, S and D represent the pretax market for a certain domestic wine; the no-tax equilibrium price and quantity are $8 per bottle and 15 million bottles. Suppose that government levies an excise tax of $2 per bottle at the winery. Who will actually pay this tax?

Division of Burden   Since the government imposes the tax on the sellers (suppliers), we can view the tax as an

addition to the marginal cost of the product. Now sellers must get $2 more for each bottle to receive the same per-unit profit they were getting before the tax. While sellers are willing to offer, for example, 5 million bottles of untaxed wine at $4 per bottle, they must now receive $6 per bottle (= $4 + $2 tax) to offer the same 5 million bottles. The tax shifts the supply curve upward (leftward) as shown in Figure 31.2, where S_t is the "after-tax" supply curve.

The after-tax equilibrium price is $9 per bottle, whereas the before-tax equilibrium price was $8. So, in this case, consumers pay half the $2 tax as a higher price; producers pay the other half in the form of a lower after-tax per-unit revenue. That is, after remitting the $2 tax per unit to government, producers receive $7, or $1 less than the $8 before-tax price. So, in this case, consumers and producers share the burden of the tax equally: Producers shift half the tax to consumers in the form of a higher price and bear the other half themselves.

Note also that the equilibrium quantity declines because of the tax levy and the higher price that it imposes on consumers. In Figure 31.2 that decline in quantity is from 15 million bottles to 12.5 million bottles per month.

Elasticities   If the elasticities of demand and supply were different from those shown in Figure 31.2, the incidence of tax would also be different. Two generalizations are relevant.

With a specific supply, the more inelastic the demand for the product, the larger is the portion of the tax shifted to consumers. To verify this, sketch graphically the extreme cases in which demand is perfectly elastic and perfectly inelastic. In the first case, the incidence of the tax is entirely on sellers; in the second, the tax is shifted entirely to consumers.

Figure 31.3 contrasts the more usual cases where demand is either relatively elastic or relatively inelastic in the relevant price range. With elastic demand (Figure 31.3a), a small portion of the tax ($P_e - P_1$) is shifted to consumers and most of the tax ($P_1 - P_a$) is borne by the producers. With inelastic demand (Figure 31.3b), most of the tax ($P_i - P_1$) is shifted to consumers and only a small amount ($P_1 - P_b$) is paid by producers. In both graphs the per-unit tax is represented by the vertical distance between S_t and S.

Note also that the decline in equilibrium quantity ($Q_1 - Q_2$) is smaller when demand is more inelastic. This is the basis of our previous applications of the elasticity concept: Revenue-seeking legislatures place heavy excise

FIGURE 31.2

The incidence of an excise tax.   An excise tax of a specified amount, here $2 per unit, shifts the supply curve upward by the amount of the tax per unit: the vertical distance between S and S_t. This results in a higher price (here $9) to consumers and a lower after-tax price (here $7) to producers. Thus consumers and producers share the burden of the tax in some proportion (here equally at $1 per unit).

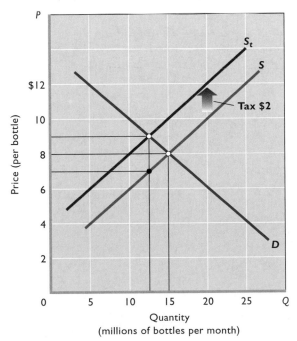

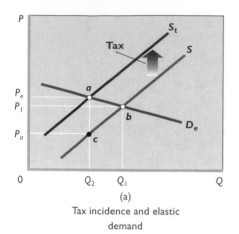

(a)
Tax incidence and elastic
demand

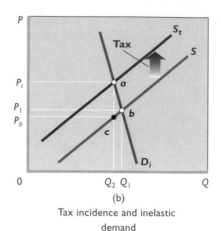

(b)
Tax incidence and inelastic
demand

FIGURE 31.3

Demand elasticity and the incidence of an excise tax. (a) If demand is elastic in the relevant price range, price rises modestly (P_1 to P_e) when an excise tax is levied. Hence, the producer bears most of the tax burden. (b) If demand is inelastic, the price to the buyer increases substantially (P_1 to P_i) and most of the tax is shifted to consumers.

taxes on liquor, cigarettes, automobile tires, telephone service, and other products whose demand is thought to be inelastic. Since demand for these products is relatively inelastic, the tax does not reduce sales by much, so the tax revenue stays high.

The second generalization is that, *with a specific demand, the more inelastic the supply, the larger is the portion of the tax borne by producers.* When supply is elastic (Figure 31.4a), the producers shift most of the tax ($P_e - P_1$) to consumers and bear only a small portion ($P_1 - P_a$) themselves. But where supply is inelastic (Figure 31.4b), the reverse is true: The major portion of the tax ($P_1 - P_b$) falls on sellers, and a relatively small amount ($P_i - P_1$) is shifted to buyers. The equilibrium quantity also declines less with an inelastic supply than it does with an elastic supply.

Gold is an example of a product with an inelastic supply and therefore one where the burden of an excise tax (such as an extraction tax) would mainly fall on producers.

On the other hand, because the supply of baseballs is relatively elastic, producers would pass on to consumers much of an excise tax on baseballs.

Efficiency Loss of a Tax

We just observed that producers and consumers typically each bear part of an excise tax levied on producers. Let's now look more closely at the overall economic effect of the excise tax. Consider Figure 31.5, which is identical to Figure 31.2 but contains the additional detail we need for our discussion.

Tax Revenues   In our example, a $2 excise tax on wine increases its market price from $8 to $9 per bottle and reduces the equilibrium quantity from 15 million bottles to 12.5 million. Government tax revenue is $25 million (= $2 × 12.5 million bottles), an amount shown as the

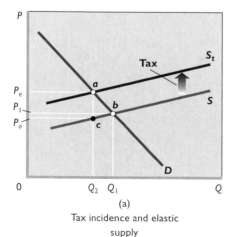

(a)
Tax incidence and elastic
supply

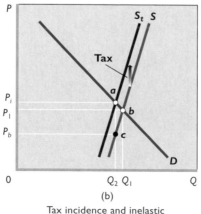

(b)
Tax incidence and inelastic
supply

FIGURE 31.4

Supply elasticity and the incidence of an excise tax. (a) With elastic supply, an excise tax results in a large price increase (P_1 to P_e) and the tax is therefore paid mainly by consumers. (b) If supply is inelastic, the price rise is small (P_1 to P_i) and sellers bear most of the tax.

FIGURE 31.5

Efficiency loss of a tax. The levy of a $2 tax per bottle of wine increases the price per bottle from $8 to $9 and reduces the equilibrium quantity from 15 million to 12.5 million. Tax revenue to the government is $25 million (area *efac*). The efficiency loss of the tax arises from the 2.5 million decline in output; the amount of that loss is shown as triangle *abc*.

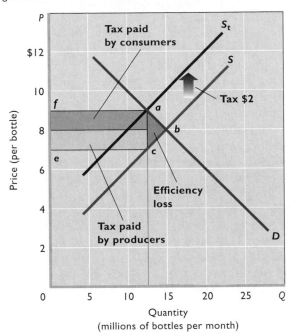

For all but the very last one of these 2.5 million bottles, the marginal benefit (shown by a point on *ab*) exceeds the marginal cost (shown by a point on *cb*). Not producing all 2.5 million bottles of wine reduces well-being by an amount represented by the triangle *abc*. The area of this triangle identifies the **efficiency loss of the tax** (also called the *deadweight loss of the tax*). This loss is society's sacrifice of net benefit, because the tax reduces production and consumption of the product below their levels of economic efficiency, where marginal benefit and marginal cost are equal.

Role of Elasticities   Most taxes create some degree of efficiency loss, but just how much depends on the supply and demand elasticities. Glancing back at Figure 31.3, we see that the efficiency loss area *abc* is greater in Figure 31.3a, where demand is relatively elastic, than in Figure 31.3b, where demand is relatively inelastic. Similarly, area *abc* is greater in Figure 31.4a than in Figure 31.4b, indicating a larger efficiency loss where supply is more elastic. *Other things equal, the greater the elasticities of supply and demand, the greater the efficiency loss of a particular tax.*

Two taxes yielding equal revenues do not necessarily impose equal costs on society. The government must keep this fact in mind in designing a tax system to finance beneficial public goods and services. In general, it should minimize the efficiency loss of the tax system in raising any specific dollar amount of tax revenue.

Qualifications   We must acknowledge, however, that there may be other tax goals as important as, or even more important than, minimizing efficiency losses from taxes. Here are two examples:

- **Redistributive goals**   Government may wish to impose progressive taxes as a way to redistribute income. The 10 percent excise tax the Federal government placed on selected luxuries in 1990 was an example. Because the demand for luxuries is elastic, substantial efficiency losses from this tax were to be expected. However, Congress apparently concluded that the benefits from the redistribution effects of the tax would exceed the efficiency losses.

  Ironically, in 1993 Congress repealed the luxury taxes on personal airplanes and yachts, mainly because the taxes had reduced quantity demanded so much that widespread layoffs of workers were occurring in those industries. But the 10 percent tax on luxury automobiles remained in place until it expired in 2003.

- **Reducing negative externalities**   The government may have intended the $2 tax on wine in Figure 31.5 to reduce the consumption of wine by 2.5 million

rectangle *efac* in Figure 31.5. The elasticities of supply and demand in this case are such that consumers and producers each pay half this total amount, or $12.5 million apiece (= $1 × 12.5 million bottles). The government uses this $25 million of tax revenue to provide public goods and services. So this transfer of dollars from consumers and producers to government involves no loss of well-being to society.

Efficiency Loss   The $2 tax on wine does more than require consumers and producers to pay $25 million of taxes; it also reduces the equilibrium amount of wine produced and consumed by 2.5 million bottles. The fact that consumers and producers demanded and supplied 2.5 million more bottles of wine before the tax means that those 2.5 million bottles provided benefits in excess of their production costs. This is clear from the following analysis.

Segment *ab* of demand curve *D* in Figure 31.5 indicates the willingness to pay—the marginal benefit— associated with each of the 2.5 million bottles consumed before (but not after) the tax. Segment *cb* of supply curve *S* reflects the marginal cost of each of the bottles of wine.

bottles. It may have concluded that such consumption of alcoholic beverages produces certain negative externalities. Therefore, it might have purposely levied this tax to shift the market supply curve such that the price of wine increased and the amount of resources allocated to wine declined (as in Figure 31.3b). **(Key Question 9)**

Probable Incidence of U.S. Taxes

Let's look now at the probable incidence of each of the major sources of tax revenue in the United States.

Personal Income Tax   The incidence of the personal income tax generally is on the individual, because there is little chance for shifting it. But there might be exceptions. Individuals and groups who can control the price of their labor services may be able to shift a part of the tax. Doctors, dentists, lawyers, and other professional people who can readily increase their fees may do so because of the tax. Unions might regard personal income taxes as part of the cost of living and, as a result, strengthen their bargaining resolve for higher wages when personal income tax rates rise. If they are successful, they may shift part of the tax from workers to employers, who, by increasing prices, shift the wage increase to the public. Generally, however, the individual on whom the tax is initially levied bears the burden of the personal income tax. The same ordinarily holds true for payroll and inheritance taxes.

Corporate Income Tax   The incidence of the corporate income tax is much less certain. The traditional view is that a firm currently charging the profit-maximizing price and producing the profit-maximizing output will have no reason to change price or output when a tax on corporate income (profit) is imposed. The price and output combination yielding the greatest profit before the tax will still yield the greatest profit after a fixed percentage of the firm's profit is taken away via an income tax. In this view, the company's stockholders (owners) must bear the burden of the tax through lower dividends or a smaller amount of retained earnings.

However, economists recognize that where a small number of firms control a market, producers may be able to shift part of their corporate income tax to consumers through higher prices and to resource suppliers through lower prices and wages. That is, some firms may be able to use their monopoly power as sellers and monopsony power as buyers to reduce the actual amount of the tax paid by their corporate stockholders.

There simply is no consensus among experts on the overall incidence of the corporate income tax. Stockholders, customers, and resource suppliers may share the tax burden in some unknown proportions.

Sales and Excise Taxes   A *sales tax* is a general excise tax levied on a full range of consumer goods and services, whereas a *specific excise tax* is one levied only on a particular product. Sales taxes are usually transparent to the buyer, whereas excise taxes are often "hidden" in the price of the product. Sellers often shift both taxes partly or largely to consumers through higher product prices. There may be some difference in the extent to which sales taxes and excise taxes are shifted, however. Because a sales tax covers a much wider range of products than an excise tax, there is little chance for consumers to resist the price boosts that sales taxes entail. They cannot reallocate their expenditures to untaxed, lower-priced products. Therefore, sales taxes tend to be shifted from producers in their entirety to consumers.

Excise taxes, however, fall on a select list of goods. Therefore, the possibility of consumers turning to substitute goods and services is greater. An excise tax on theater tickets that does not apply to other types of entertainment might be difficult to pass on to consumers via price increases. Why? The answer is provided in Figure 31.3a, where demand is elastic. A price boost to cover the excise tax on theater tickets might cause consumers to substitute alternative types of entertainment. The higher price would reduce sales so much that a seller would be better off to bear all, or a large portion of, the excise tax.

With other products, modest price increases to cover taxes may have smaller effects on sales. The excise taxes on gasoline, cigarettes, and alcoholic beverages provide examples. Here there are few good substitute products to which consumers can turn as prices rise. For these goods, the seller is better able to shift nearly all the excise tax to consumers. Example: Prices of cigarettes have gone up nearly in lockstep with the recent, substantial increases in excise taxes on cigarettes.

As indicated in Global Perspective 31.1, the United States depends less on sales and excise taxes for tax revenue than do several other nations.

Property Taxes   Many property taxes are borne by the property owner, because there is no other party to whom they can be shifted. This is typically true for taxes on land, personal property, and owner-occupied residences. Even when land is sold, the property tax is not likely to be shifted. The buyer will understand that future taxes will have to be paid on it, and this expected taxation would be

TABLE 31.2
The Probable Incidence of Taxes

Type of Tax	Probable Incidence
Personal income tax	The household or individual on which it is levied.
Corporate income tax	Some economists conclude the firm on which it is levied bears the tax; others conclude the tax is shifted, wholly or in part, to consumers and resource suppliers.
Sales tax	Consumers who buy the taxed products.
Specific excise taxes	Consumers, producers, or both, depending on elasticities of demand and supply.
Property taxes	Owners in the case of land and owner-occupied residences; tenants in the case of rented property; consumers in the case of business property.

reflected in the price the buyer is willing to offer for the land.

Taxes on rented and business property are a different story. Taxes on rented property can be, and usually are, shifted wholly or in part from the owner to the tenant by the process of boosting the rent. Business property taxes are treated as a business cost and are taken into account in establishing product price; hence such taxes are ordinarily shifted to the firm's customers.

Table 31.2 summarizes this discussion of the shifting and incidence of taxes.

The U.S. Tax Structure

Is the overall U.S. tax structure—Federal, state, and local taxes combined—progressive, proportional, or regressive? This question is difficult to answer, because estimates of the distribution of the total tax burden depend on the assumptions we make regarding tax incidence. The extent to which the various taxes are shifted and who bears the ultimate burden are subject to dispute. We have already noted, for example, that there is no consensus among experts as to who actually pays the corporate income tax.

But the majority view of experts can be summarized as follows:

- **The Federal tax system is progressive.** In 1999, the 20 percent of families with the lowest income paid an average Federal tax rate (on Federal income, payroll, and excise taxes) of only 4.6 percent. The 20 percent with the highest income paid a 29.1 percent average rate; the top 10 percent paid 30.6 percent; and the top 1 percent paid 34.4 percent.[2]

    In 2000 the top 5 percent of all taxpayers paid 56 percent of the total Federal income tax collected (here, excluding payroll and excise taxes). The bottom 50 percent paid only 4 percent. (Because wealthy Americans earn a disproportionately high amount of the total income, they pay a disproportionately high amount of the total tax. This would be true even for a proportional tax system.)

GLOBAL PERSPECTIVE 31.1

Taxes on Goods and Services as a Percentage of Total Tax Revenues, Selected Nations

A number of industrial nations rely more heavily on goods and services taxes—sales taxes, value-added taxes, and specific excise taxes—than does the United States. (A value-added tax applies only to the difference between the value of a firm's sales and the value of its purchases from other firms.)

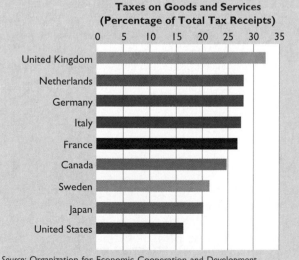

Taxes on Goods and Services (Percentage of Total Tax Receipts)

Source: Organization for Economic Cooperation and Development, www.oecd.org/. Data are for 1999.

---

[2]Henry J. Aaron, William Gale, and James Sly, *Setting National Priorities: The 2000 Election and Beyond* (Washington, D.C.: Brookings Institution, 1999), p. 224. Congressional Budget Office data.

The Media Continually Report Government Actions That Illustrate the Special-Interest Effect, Limited and Bundled Choices, or Bureaucratic Inefficiency.

Examples:

- Several years ago, it took 23 Federal employees to approve the purchase of laptop computers bought for $3500 each. Those computers were priced at $1500 each at the local retail computer store. *(Newsweek)*
- As part of a radiation cleanup project in Pennsylvania in the late 1990s, the EPA spent an average of $651,700 to custom-build 10 new houses for homeowners. This was in addition to the cleanup costs. The old houses were worth an average of $147,000 each. (Gannet News Services)
- Government departments and their contractors must buy all security locks for government buildings from a single firm, which is in a state formerly represented by a powerful senator. (Senator McCain's Congressional "Pork" website, mccain.senate.gov)
- Emergency legislation in 1999 to finance U.S. bombing in Yugoslavia and help rebuild homes destroyed by Hurricane Mitch contained several unrelated "riders," including the approval of an open-pit gold mine in eastern Washington State. The gold-mine provision overturned the decisions of two Federal agencies. *(Washington Post)*
- Appropriations bills for 2000 contained language that (a) prevented the Coast Guard from decommissioning 11 harbor tugs that provide ice-breaking services for the mid-Atlantic and New England ports; (b) prohibited the establishment of a national wildlife refuge in the Kankakee watershed in Indiana and Illinois; (c) designated funding for the 2000 census as "emergency spending," which removed it from congressional spending limitations. (Senator McCain's Congressional "Pork" website, mccain.senate.gov)
- In 2001, Congress appropriated $350,000 for the Chicago Wilderness Program, $273,000 for the Blue Springs (Missouri) Youth Outreach Unit for educational training in combating the Goth culture, and $400,000 for the Montana Sheep Institute. (Citizens Against Waste, as reported in the *Lincoln Journal Star*)
- In 2001, Congress appropriated $1 million of Federal funds to establish a museum at the Atomic Testing History Institute in Las Vegas, $300,000 for aquatic-weed removal in the Lavaca and Navidad Rivers in Texas, and $350,000 for a study of beach erosion on Waikiki Beach in Hawaii. *(Washington Post)* Alaska got $400,000 for a parking lot in Talkeetna (population 300) and $176,000 for the Alaska Reindeer Herders Association. (Citizens Against Waste, as reported in *Newsweek*)
- The 2001 Senate "economic stimulus" bill contained a $220 million subsidy for bison meat producers and eggplant, cauliflower, and pumpkin growers that experienced low prices during the 2000 and 2001 crop years. *(Los Angles Times)*
- The 2003 Appropriations bill directed the U.S. Agency for International Development to provide $2.5 million for the Orangutan Foundation located in Indonesia and $1.5 million to the Dian Fossey Gorilla Fund. Senator McCain asked: "Why stop at giving special preference to these two primates? What about the other members of the animal kingdom?" McCain also noted that the disaster emergency relief section of the bill contained a provision to qualify catfish farmers for livestock compensation payments. McCain asked, "When did a catfish become analogous to a cow?" (Senator McCain's Congressional "Pork" website, mccain.senate.gov)

- *The state and local tax structures are largely regressive.* As a percentage of income, property taxes and sales taxes fall as income rises. Also, state income taxes are generally less progressive than the Federal income tax.
- *The overall U.S. tax system is slightly progressive.* This means that the tax system alone only slightly redistributes income from the wealthy to the poor. Caution:

While the U.S. tax system does not substantially alter the distribution of income, the system of transfer payments does considerably reduce income inequality. Transfer payments to the poorest fifth of U.S. households almost quadruple their collective incomes. The tax-transfer system redistributes income by much more than does the tax system alone.

SUMMARY

1. Public choice theory examines the economics of government decision making, politics, and elections.

2. Majority voting creates a possibility of (a) an underallocation or an overallocation of resources to a particular public good and (b) inconsistent voting outcomes. The median-voter model predicts that, under majority rule, the person holding the middle position on an issue will determine the outcome of an election involving that issue.

3. Public choice theorists cite reasons why government might be inefficient in providing public goods and services. (a) There are strong reasons for politicians to support special-interest legislation. (b) Politicians may be biased in favor of programs with immediate and clear-cut benefits and difficult-to-identify costs and against programs with immediate and easily identified costs and vague or deferred benefits. (c) Citizens as voters and congressional representatives face limited and bundled choices as to public goods and services, whereas consumers in the private sector can be highly selective in their choices. (d) Government bureaucracies have less incentive to operate efficiently than do private businesses.

4. The benefits-received principle of taxation states that those who receive the benefits of goods and services provided by government should pay the taxes required to finance them. The ability-to-pay principle states that those who have greater income should be taxed more, absolutely and relatively, than those who have less income.

5. The Federal personal income tax is progressive. The corporate income tax is roughly proportional. General sales, excise, payroll, and property taxes are regressive.

6. Excise taxes affect supply and therefore equilibrium price and quantity. The more inelastic the demand for a product, the greater is the portion of an excise tax that is shifted to consumers. The greater the inelasticity of supply, the larger is the portion of the tax that is borne by the seller.

7. Taxation involves the loss of some output whose marginal benefit exceeds its marginal cost. The more elastic the supply and demand curves, the greater is the efficiency loss resulting from a particular tax.

8. Sales taxes normally are shifted to consumers; personal income taxes are not shifted. Specific excise taxes may or may not be shifted to consumers, depending on the elasticities of demand and supply. There is disagreement as to whether corporate income taxes are shifted. Property taxes on owner-occupied property are borne by the owner; those on rental property are borne by tenants.

9. The Federal tax structure is progressive; the state and local tax structure is regressive; and the overall tax structure is slightly progressive.

TERMS AND CONCEPTS

public choice theory	government failure	ability-to-pay principle	tax incidence
logrolling	special-interest effect	progressive tax	efficiency loss of a tax
paradox of voting	rent seeking	regressive tax	
median-voter model	benefits-received principle	proportional tax	

STUDY QUESTIONS

1. Explain how affirmative and negative majority votes can sometimes lead to inefficient allocations of resources to public goods. Is this problem likely to be greater under a benefits-received or under an ability-to-pay tax system? Use the information in Figures 31.1a and 31.1b to show how society might be better off if Adams were allowed to buy votes.

2. *Key Question* Explain the paradox of voting through reference to the accompanying table, which shows the ranking of three public goods by voters Jay, Dave, and Conan:

	Rankings		
Public good	Jay	Dave	Conan
Courthouse	2d choice	1st choice	3d choice
School	3d choice	2d choice	1st choice
Park	1st choice	3d choice	2d choice

3. *Key Question* Suppose there are only five people in a society and each favors one of the five highway construction

options in Table 30.2 (include no highway construction as one of the options). Explain which of these highway options will be selected using a majority paired-choice vote. Will this option be the optimal size of the project from an economic perspective?

4. *Key Question* How does the problem of limited and bundled choice in the public sector relate to economic efficiency? Why are public bureaucracies alleged to be less efficient than private enterprises?

5. Explain: "Politicians would make more rational economic decisions if they weren't running for reelection every few years."

6. Distinguish between the benefits-received and the ability-to-pay principles of taxation. Which philosophy is more evident in our present tax structure? Justify your answer. To which principle of taxation do you subscribe? Why?

7. *Key Question* Suppose a tax is such that an individual with an income of $10,000 pays $2000 of tax, a person with an income of $20,000 pays $3000 of tax, a person with an income of $30,000 pays $4000 of tax, and so forth. What is each person's average tax rate? Is this tax regressive, proportional, or progressive?

8. What is meant by a progressive tax? A regressive tax? A proportional tax? Comment on the progressivity or regressivity of each of the following taxes, indicating in each case where you think the tax incidence lies: (*a*) the Federal personal income tax; (*b*) a 4 percent state general sales tax; (*c*) a Federal excise tax on automobile tires; (*d*) a municipal property tax on real estate; (*e*) the Federal corporate income tax.

9. *Key Question* What is the incidence of an excise tax when demand is highly inelastic? Elastic? What effect does the elasticity of supply have on the incidence of an excise tax? What is the efficiency loss of a tax, and how does it relate to elasticity of demand and supply?

10. *Advanced Analysis* Suppose the equation for the demand curve for some product X is $P = 8 - .6Q$ and the supply curve is $P = 2 + .4Q$. What are the equilibrium price and quantity? Now suppose an excise tax is imposed on X such

that the new supply equation is $P = 4 + .4Q$. How much tax revenue will this excise tax yield the government? Graph the curves, and label the area of the graph that represents the tax collection "TC" and the area that represents the efficiency loss of the tax "EL." Briefly explain why area EL is the efficiency loss of the tax but TC is not.

11. *(Last Word)* How do the concepts of pork-barrel politics and logrolling relate to the items listed in the Last Word?

12. *Web-Based Question: Bureaucracy and inefficiency—the post office versus UPS* Some economists contend that public agencies generally are less efficient than private businesses. United Parcel Service (UPS) competes directly with the U.S. Postal Service for express mail and packages. Assume you need to send an express letter and a 3-pound package from your address to either New York City or Los Angeles. On the basis of their interactive rate and options calculators at www.ups.com and www.usps.com, which service is more competitive as to price and delivery? Does a lower rate with greater delivery options mean greater efficiency? Why or why not?

13. *Web-Based Question: Calculating taxes and determining average rates* The Internal Revenue Service provides current tax-rate tables online at www.irs.gov. Enter "Tax Tables" in the search line for forms and publications and find "1040 Instructions (Tax Tables)" for the latest tax year. Find the tax payment you would owe if you were a single taxpayer with a taxable income of (1) $23,360, (2) $46,200, and (3) $85,010 in the taxable year. Compare the average tax rates (taxable income/tax payment) for the three levels of income. Next, suppose that you live in a state with a 7 percent sales tax and that you spent 90 percent of your taxable income in the year. How much total sales tax would you pay at each income level? Add the total sales tax to the income tax for each income level and compute new average tax rates based on the combined income tax and sales tax as a percentage of taxable income. Compare the new percentages with the previous ones. What can you conclude from the comparison?

Part IX | Microeconomic Issues and Policies

32

Antitrust Policy and Regulation

We now can apply the economics of product markets (Part 6), resource markets (Part 7), and government (Part 8) to selected microeconomic issues and policies.

In this chapter we look at three sets of government policies toward business: antitrust policy, industrial regulation, and social regulation. **Antitrust policy** consists of the laws and government actions designed to prevent monopoly and promote competition. **Industrial regulation** consists of government regulation of firms' prices (or "rates") within selected industries. **Social regulation** is government regulation of the conditions under which goods are produced, the physical characteristics of goods, and the impact of the production and consumption of goods on society.

Then, in the remaining four chapters of Part 9, we discuss issues and policies relating to agriculture, income inequality, labor markets (unions, discrimination, and immigration), and health care.

The Antitrust Laws

The underlying purpose of antitrust policy (antimonopoly policy) is to prevent monopolization, promote competition, and achieve allocative efficiency. Although all economists would agree that these are meritorious goals, there is sharp conflict of opinion about the appropriateness and effectiveness of U.S. antitrust policy. As we will see, antitrust policy over the years has been neither clear-cut nor consistent.

Historical Background

Just after the U.S. Civil War (1861–1865), local markets widened into national markets because of improved trans-

portation facilities, mechanized production methods, and sophisticated corporate structures. In the 1870s and 1880s, dominant firms formed in several industries, including petroleum, meatpacking, railroads, sugar, lead, coal, whiskey, and tobacco. Some of these oligopolists, near-monopolists, or monopolists were known as *trusts*—business combinations that assign control to a single decision group ("trustees"). Because these trusts "monopolized" industries, the word "trust" became synonymous with "monopoly" in common usage. The public, government, and historians began to define a business monopoly as a large-scale dominant seller, even though that seller was not always "a sole seller" as specified in the model of pure monopoly.

These dominant firms often used questionable tactics in consolidating their industries and then charged high prices to customers and extracted price concessions from resource suppliers. Farmers and owners of small businesses were particularly vulnerable to the power of large corporate monopolies and were among the first to oppose them. Consumers, labor unions, and economists were not far behind in their opposition.

The main economic case against monopoly is familiar to you from Chapter 24. Monopolists tend to produce less output and charge higher prices than would be the case if their industries were competitive. With pure competition, production occurs where $P = MC$. This equality represents an efficient allocation of resources because P measures the marginal benefit to society of an extra unit of output while marginal cost MC reflects the cost of an extra unit. When $P = MC$, society cannot gain by producing 1 more or 1 less unit of the product. In contrast, a monopolist maximizes profit by equating marginal revenue (not price) with marginal cost. At this $MR = MC$ point, price exceeds marginal cost, meaning that society would obtain more benefit than it would incur cost by producing extra units. There is an underallocation of resources to the monopolized product, and so the economic well-being of society is less than it would be with greater competition.

Government concluded in the late 1800s and early 1900s that market forces in monopolized industries did not provide sufficient control to protect consumers, achieve fair competition, and achieve allocative efficiency. So it instituted two alternative means of control as substitutes for, or supplements to, market forces:

- *Regulatory agencies* In the few markets where the nature of the product or technology creates a *natural monopoly*, the government established public regulatory agencies to control economic behavior.
- *Antitrust laws* In most other markets, social control took the form of antitrust (antimonopoly) legislation designed to inhibit or prevent the growth of monopoly.

Four particular pieces of Federal legislation, as refined and extended by various amendments, constitute the basic law relating to monopoly structure and conduct.

Sherman Act of 1890

The public resentment of trusts that emerged in the 1870s and 1880s culminated in the **Sherman Act** of 1890. This cornerstone of antitrust legislation is surprisingly brief and, at first glance, directly to the point. The core of the act resides in two provisions:

- *Section 1* Every contract, combination in the form of a trust or otherwise, or conspiracy, in restraint of trade or commerce among the several states, or with foreign nations is hereby declared to be illegal.

- *Section 2* Every person who shall monopolize, or attempt to monopolize, or combine or conspire with any person or persons, to monopolize any part of the trade or commerce among the several states, or with foreign nations, shall be deemed guilty of a felony (as later amended from "misdemeanor").

The Sherman Act thus outlawed *restraints of trade* (for example, collusive price fixing and dividing up markets) as well as *monopolization*. Today, the U.S. Department of Justice, the Federal Trade Commission, injured private parties, or state attorney generals can file antitrust suits against alleged violators of the act. The courts can issue injunctions to prohibit anticompetitive practices or, if necessary, break up monopolists into competing firms. Courts can also fine and imprison violators. Further, parties injured by illegal combinations and conspiracies can sue the perpetrators for *treble damages*—awards of three times the amount of the monetary injury done to them.

The Sherman Act seemed to provide a sound foundation for positive government action against business monopolies. However, early court interpretations limited the scope of the act and created ambiguities of law. It became clear that a more explicit statement of the government's antitrust sentiments was needed. The business community itself sought a clearer statement of what was legal and what was illegal.

Clayton Act of 1914

The **Clayton Act** of 1914 contained the desired elaboration of the Sherman Act. Four sections of the act, in particular, were designed to strengthen and make explicit the intent of the Sherman Act:

- Section 2 outlaws *price discrimination* when such discrimination is not justified on the basis of cost differences and when it reduces competition.

- Section 3 prohibits **tying contracts,** in which a producer requires that a buyer purchase another (or others) of its products as a condition for obtaining a desired product.

- Section 7 prohibits the acquisition of stocks of competing corporations when the outcome would be less competition.

- Section 8 prohibits the formation of **interlocking directorates**—situations where a director of one firm is also a board member of a competing firm—in large corporations where the effect would be reduced competition.

The Clayton Act simply sharpened and clarified the general provisions of the Sherman Act. It also sought to outlaw the techniques that firms might use to develop monopoly power and, in that sense, was a preventive measure. Section 2 of the Sherman Act, by contrast, was aimed more at breaking up existing monopolies.

Federal Trade Commission Act of 1914

The **Federal Trade Commission Act** created the five-member Federal Trade Commission (FTC), which has joint Federal responsibility with the U.S. Justice Department for enforcing the antitrust laws. The act gave the FTC the power to investigate unfair competitive practices on its own initiative or at the request of injured firms. It can hold public hearings on such complaints and, if necessary, issue **cease-and-desist orders** in cases where it discovers "unfair methods of competition in commerce."

The **Wheeler-Lea Act** of 1938 gave the FTC the additional responsibility of policing "deceptive acts or practices in commerce." In so doing, the FTC tries to protect the public against false or misleading advertising and the misrepresentation of products. So the Federal Trade Commission Act, as modified by the Wheeler-Lea Act, (1) established the FTC as an independent antitrust agency and (2) made unfair and deceptive sales practices illegal.

Celler-Kefauver Act of 1950

The **Celler-Kefauver Act** amended the Clayton Act, Section 7, which prohibits a firm from merging with a competing firm (and thereby lessening competition) by acquiring its stock. Firms could evade Section 7, however, by instead acquiring the physical assets (plant and equipment) of competing firms. The Celler-Kefauver Act closed that loophole by prohibiting one firm from obtaining the physical assets of another firm when the effect would be reduced competition. Section 7 of the Clayton Act now prohibits anticompetitive mergers no matter how they are undertaken. **(Key Question 2)**

Antitrust Policy: Issues and Impacts

The effectiveness of any law depends on how the courts interpret it and on the vigor of government enforcement. The courts have been inconsistent in interpreting the antitrust laws. At times, they have applied them vigorously, adhering closely to their spirit and objectives. At other times, their interpretations have rendered certain laws nearly powerless. The Federal government itself has varied considerably in its willingness to apply the antitrust laws. Administrations holding a laissez-faire philosophy about monopoly have sometimes ignored them or have reduced the budgets of the enforcement agencies.

Issues of Interpretation

Differences in judicial interpretations have led to vastly different applications of the antitrust laws. Two questions, in particular, have arisen: (1) Should the focus of antitrust policy be on monopoly behavior or on monopoly structure? (2) How broadly should markets be defined in antitrust cases?

Monopoly Behavior versus Monopoly Structure

A comparison of three landmark Supreme Court decisions reveals two distinct interpretations of Section 2 of the Sherman Act as it relates to monopoly behavior and structure.

In the 1911 **Standard Oil case,** the Supreme Court found Standard Oil guilty of monopolizing the petroleum industry through a series of abusive and anticompetitive actions. The Court's remedy was to divide Standard Oil into several competing firms. But the Standard Oil case left open an important question: Is every monopoly in violation of Section 2 of the Sherman Act or just those created or maintained by anticompetitive actions?

In the 1920 **U.S. Steel case,** the courts established a **rule of reason,** saying that not every monopoly is illegal. Only monopolies that "unreasonably" restrain trade violate Section 2 of the Sherman Act and are subject to antitrust action. Size alone was not an offense. Although U.S. Steel clearly possessed monopoly power, it was innocent of "monopolizing" because it had not resorted to illegal acts against competitors in obtaining that power nor had it unreasonably used its monopoly power. Unlike Standard Oil, which was a so-called bad trust, U.S. Steel was a "good trust" and therefore not in violation of the law.

In the **Alcoa case** of 1945 the courts touched off a 20-year turnabout. The Supreme Court sent the case to the U.S. court of appeals in New York because four of the Supreme Court justices had been involved with litigation of the case before their appointments. Led by Judge Hand the court of appeals held that, even though a firm's behavior might be legal, the mere possession of monopoly power (Alcoa held 90 percent of the aluminum ingot market) violated the antitrust laws. So Alcoa was found guilty of violating the Sherman Act.

These two cases point to a controversy in antitrust policy. Should a firm be judged by its behavior (as in the U.S. Steel case) or by its structure, or market share (as in the Alcoa case)?

"Structuralists" say that a firm with a very high market share will behave like a monopolist. Since the economic performance of such firms will be undesirable, they are legitimate targets for antitrust action. Changes in the structure of the industry, say, by splitting the monopolist into several smaller firms, will improve behavior and performance.

"Behavioralists" assert that the relationship between structure, behavior, and performance is tenuous and unclear. They feel a monopolized or highly concentrated industry may be technologically progressive and have a good record of providing products of increasing quality at reasonable prices. If a firm has served society well and has engaged in no anticompetitive practices, it should not be accused of antitrust violation just because it has an extraordinarily large market share. That share may be the product of superior technology, superior products, and economies of scale. "Why use antitrust laws to penalize efficient, technologically progressive, well-managed firms?" they ask.

Over the past 20 years, the courts have returned to the rule of reason, and most contemporary economists and antitrust enforcers reject strict structuralism. For instance, in 1982 the government dropped its 13-year-long monopolization case against IBM on the grounds that IBM had not unreasonably restrained trade. More recently, the government has made no attempt to break up Intel's monopoly in the sale of microcircuits for personal computers. And in prosecuting the Microsoft case (the subject of this chapter's Last Word), the Federal government made it clear that the behavior used by Microsoft to maintain and extend its monopoly, not the presence of its large market share, violated the Sherman Act. That is, the goverment in effect declared Microsoft "a bad monopoly."

The Relevant Market   Courts often decide whether or not market power exists by considering the share of the market held by the dominant firm. If the market is defined broadly to include a wide range of somewhat similar products, the firm's market share will appear small. If the market is defined narrowly to exclude such products, the market share will seem large. The Supreme Court's task is to determine how broadly to define relevant markets, and it has not always been consistent.

In the Alcoa case, the Court used a narrow definition of the relevant market: the aluminum ingot market. But in the **DuPont cellophane case** of 1956 the Court defined the market very broadly. The government contended that DuPont, along with a licensee, controlled 100 percent of the cellophane market. But the Court accepted DuPont's contention that the relevant market included all "flexible packaging materials"—waxed paper, aluminum foil, and so forth, in addition to cellophane. Despite DuPont's monopoly in the "cellophane market," it controlled only 20 percent of the market for "flexible

wrapping materials." The Court ruled that this did not constitute a monopoly.

Issues of Enforcement

Some U.S. presidential administrations have enforced the antitrust laws more strictly than others. The degree of Federal antitrust enforcement makes a difference in the overall degree of antitrust action in the economy. It is true that individual firms can sue other firms under the antitrust laws, but major antitrust suits often last years and are highly expensive. Injured parties therefore often look to the Federal government to initiate and litigate such cases. Once the Federal government gains a conviction, the injured parties no longer need to prove guilt and can simply sue the violator to obtain treble damages. In many cases, lack of Federal antitrust action therefore means diminished legal action by firms.

Why might one administration enforce the antitrust laws more or less strictly than another? The main reason is differences in political philosophies about the market economy and the wisdom of intervention by government. There are two contrasting general perspectives on antitrust policy.

The *active antitrust perspective* is that competition is insufficient in some circumstances to achieve allocative efficiency and ensure fairness to consumers and competing firms. Firms occasionally use illegal tactics against competitors to dominate markets. In other instances, competitors collude to fix prices or merge to enhance their monopoly power. Active, strict enforcement of the antitrust laws is needed to stop illegal business practices, prevent anticompetitive mergers, and remedy monopoly. This type of government intervention maintains the viability and vibrancy of the market system and thus allows society to reap its full benefits. In this view, the antitrust authorities need to act much like the officials in a football game. They must observe the players, spot infractions, and enforce the rules.

In contrast, the *laissez-faire perspective* holds that antitrust intervention is largely unnecessary, particularly as it relates to monopoly. Economists holding this position view competition as a long-run dynamic process in which firms battle against each other for dominance of markets. In some markets, a firm successfully monopolizes the market, usually because of its superior innovativeness or business skill. But in exploiting its monopoly power to raise prices, these firms inadvertently create profit incentives and profit opportunities for other entrepreneurs and firms to develop alternative technologies and new products to better serve consumers. A process of *creative destruction* (review

Chapter 26) occurs, in which today's monopolies are eroded and eventually destroyed by tomorrow's technologies and products. The government therefore should not try to break up monopoly. It should stand aside and allow the long-run competitive process to work.

32.1 Creative destruction

The extent to which a particular administration adheres to—or leans toward—one of these contrasting antitrust perspectives usually gets reflected in the appointments to the agencies overseeing antitrust policy. Those appointees help determine the degree of strictness in enforcement of the laws.

Effectiveness of Antitrust Laws

Have the antitrust laws been effective? Although this question is difficult to answer, we can at least observe how the laws have been applied to monopoly, mergers, price fixing, price discrimination, and tying contracts.

Monopoly   On the basis of the rule of reason, the government has generally been lenient in applying antitrust laws to monopolies that have developed naturally. Generally, a firm will be sued by the Federal government only if it has a very high market share and there is evidence of abusive conduct in achieving, maintaining, or extending its market dominance.

Since the 1980s there have been two particularly noteworthy monopoly cases in which the issue of remedy arose.

The first was the AT&T (American Telephone and Telegraph) case in which the government charged AT&T with violating the Sherman Act by engaging in anticompetitive practices designed to maintain its domestic telephone monopoly. As part of an out-of-court settlement between the government and AT&T, in 1982 AT&T agreed to divest itself of its 22 regional telephone-operating companies.

A second significant monopoly case was the **Microsoft case.** In 2000 Microsoft was found guilty of violating the Sherman Act by taking several unlawful actions designed to maintain its monopoly of operating systems for personal computers. A lower court ordered that Microsoft be split into two competing firms. A court of appeals upheld the lower-court finding of abusive monopoly but rescinded the breakup of Microsoft. Instead of the structural remedy, the eventual outcome was a behavioral remedy in which Microsoft was prohibited from engaging in a set of specific anticompetitive business practices.

Mergers   The treatment of mergers, or combinations of existing firms, varies with the type of merger and its effect on competition.

Merger Types   There are three basic types of mergers, as represented in Figure 32.1. This figure shows two stages of production (the input stage and the output, or final-product, stage) for two distinct final-goods industries (autos and blue jeans). Each rectangle (A, B, C, . . . X, Y, Z) represents a particular firm.

FIGURE 32.1

Types of mergers.   Horizontal mergers (T + U) bring together firms selling the same product in the same geographic market; vertical mergers (F + Z) connect firms having a buyer-seller relationship; and conglomerate mergers (C + D) join firms in different industries or firms operating in different geographic areas.

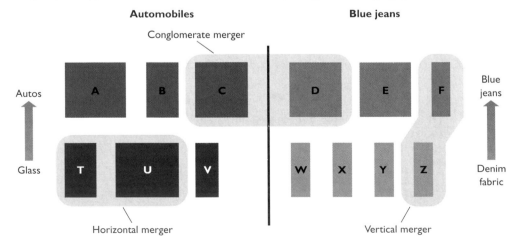

A **horizontal merger** is *a merger between two competitors that sell similar products in the same geographic market.* In Figure 32.1 this type of merger is shown as a combination of glass producers T and U. Actual examples of such mergers include Chase Manhattan's merger with Chemical Bank, Boeing's merger with McDonnell Douglas, and Exxon's merger with Mobil.

A **vertical merger** is *a merger between firms at different stages of the production process.* In Figure 32.1, the merger between firm Z, a producer of denim fabric, and firm F, a producer of blue jeans, is a vertical merger. Vertical mergers are mergers between firms that have buyer-seller relationships. Actual examples of such mergers are PepsiCo's mergers with Pizza Hut, Taco Bell, and Kentucky Fried Chicken. PepsiCo supplies soft drinks to each of these fast-food outlets. (In 1997, PepsiCo spun off these entities into a separate company now called Yum! Brands.)

A **conglomerate merger** is officially defined as *any merger that is not horizontal or vertical; in general, it is the combination of firms in different industries or firms operating in different geographic areas.* Conglomerate mergers can extend the line of products sold, extend the territory in which products are sold, or combine totally unrelated companies. In Figure 32.1, the merger between firm C, an auto manufacturer, and firm D, a blue jeans producer, is a conglomerate merger. Real-world examples of conglomerate mergers include the merger between Walt Disney Company (movies) and the American Broadcasting Company (radio and television) and the merger between America Online (Internet service provider) and Time Warner (communications).

Merger Guidelines: The Herfindahl Index

The Federal government has established very loose merger guidelines based on the Herfindahl index. Recall from Chapter 25 that this measure of concentration is the sum of the squared percentage market shares of the firms within an industry. An industry of only four firms, each with a 25 percent market share, has a Herfindahl index of $2500 (= 25^2 + 25^2 + 25^2 + 25^2)$. In pure competition, where each firm's market share is minuscule, the index approaches $0 (= 0^2 + 0^2 + \ldots + 0^2)$. In pure monopoly, the index for that single firm is $10{,}000 (= 100^2)$.

The U.S. government uses Section 7 of the Clayton Act to block horizontal mergers that will substantially lessen competition. It is likely to challenge a horizontal merger if the postmerger Herfindahl index would be high (above 1800) and if the merger has substantially increased the index (added 100 or more points). However, other factors, such as economies of scale, the degree of foreign competition, and the ease of entry of new firms, are also

considered. Furthermore, horizontal mergers are usually allowed if one of the merging firms is suffering major and continuing losses. (This is one reason Boeing was allowed to acquire McDonnell Douglas in 1996: MD was losing money in producing its commercial airplanes.)

In recent years, the Federal government has blocked several proposed horizontal mergers. For example, it blocked the mergers between Staples and Office Depot, two major office-supply retailers, and between WorldCom and Sprint, two competing telecommunications firms.

Most *vertical mergers* escape antitrust prosecution because they do not substantially lessen competition in either of the two markets. (In Figure 32.1 neither the Herfindahl index in the industry producing denim fabric nor the index in the blue jeans industry changes when firms Z and F merge vertically.) However, a vertical merger between large firms in highly concentrated industries may be challenged. For example, in 1999 the threat of FTC action spurred Barnes & Noble to abandon its merger with Ingram Book group, the nation's largest book wholesaler. The merger would have enabled Barnes & Noble to set the wholesale price of books charged to its direct retail competitors such as Borders and Amazon.com.

Conglomerate mergers are generally permitted. If an auto manufacturer acquires a blue jeans producer, no antitrust action is likely, since neither firm has increased its own market share as a result. That means the Herfindahl index remains unchanged in each industry. **(Key Question 5)**

Price Fixing

Price fixing is treated strictly. Evidence of price fixing, even by small firms, will bring antitrust action, as will other collusive activities such as scheming to rig bids on government contracts or dividing up sales in a market. In antitrust law, these activities are known as **per se violations;** they are "in and of themselves" illegal, and therefore are *not* subject to the rule of reason. To gain a conviction, the government or other party making the charge need show only that there was a conspiracy to fix prices, rig bids, or divide up markets, not that the conspiracy succeeded or caused serious damage to other parties.

Price-fixing investigations and court actions are common. We list several recent price-fixing cases in the Consider This box on the next page.

Price Discrimination

Price discrimination is a common business practice that rarely reduces competition and therefore is rarely challenged by government. The exception occurs when a firm engages in price discrimination as part of a strategy to block entry or drive out competitors.

© Lawson Wood/CORBIS

Of Catfish and Sneakers (and Other Things in Common)

There are many recent examples of price fixing. Here are just a few:

* Archer Daniels Midland (ADM) and other agribusinesses admitted fixing the prices of an additive to livestock feed, citric acid, and a sweetener made from corn.
* ConAgra and Hormel agreed to pay more than $21 million to settle their roles in a nationwide price-fixing case involving catfish.
* Reebok agreed to pay nearly $10 million in damages to settle a lawsuit in which it was accused of fixing the minimum price retailers could charge for footwear.
* The U.S. Justice Department fined UCAR International $110 million for scheming with competitors to fix prices and divide the world market for graphite electrodes used in steel mills.
* The auction houses Sotheby's and Christy's were found guilty of conspiring over a 6-year period to set the same commission rates for sellers at auctions.
* The music industry agreed to pay $143 million to settle a price-fixing case involving "minimum advertised prices" on compact discs.

Tying Contracts The Federal government strictly enforces the prohibition of tying contracts, particularly when practiced by dominant firms. For example, it stopped movie distributors from forcing theaters to buy the projection rights to a full package of films as a condition of showing a blockbuster movie. Also, it prevented Kodak—the dominant maker of photographic film—from requiring that consumers process their film only through Kodak.

What then can we conclude about the overall effectiveness of antitrust laws? Antitrust policy has not been very effective in restricting the rise of or in breaking up monopolies or oligopolies resulting from legally undertaken internal expansions of firms. But most economists do not deem that to be a flaw. The antitrust laws have been used more effectively against predatory or abusive monopoly, but that effectiveness has been diminished by the slow legal process and consequently long time between the filing of charges and the implementation of remedies. In contrast, antitrust policy *has* been effective in

blocking blatantly anticompetitive mergers and in identifying and prosecuting price fixing and tying contracts.

Most economists conclude that, overall, U.S. antitrust policy has been moderately effective in achieving its goal of promoting competition and efficiency. Much of the success of antitrust policy arises from its deterrent effect on price fixing and anticompetitive mergers. Some economists, however, think that enforcement of antitrust laws has been too weak. Others believe that parts of U.S. antitrust policy are anachronistic in an era of rapidly changing technology that continuously undermines existing monopoly power.

Industrial Regulation

Antitrust policy assumes that society will benefit if monopoly is prevented from evolving or if it is dissolved where it already exists. We now return to a special situation in which there is an economic reason for an industry to be organized monopolistically.

Natural Monopoly

A **natural monopoly** exists when economies of scale are so extensive that a single firm can supply the entire market at a lower unit cost than could a number of competing firms. Clear-cut circumstances of natural monopoly are relatively rare, but such conditions exist for many *public utilities*, such as local electricity, water, natural gas, and telephone providers. As we discussed in Chapter 24, large-scale operations in some cases are necessary to obtain low unit costs and a low product price. Where there is natural monopoly, competition is uneconomical. If the market were divided among many producers, economies of scale would not be achieved and unit costs and prices would be higher than necessary.

There are two possible alternatives for promoting better economic outcomes where natural monopoly exists. One is public ownership, and the other is public regulation.

Public ownership or some approximation of it has been established in a few instances. Examples: the Postal Service, the Tennessee Valley Authority, and Amtrak at the national level and mass transit, water supply systems, and garbage collection at the local level.

But *public regulation*, or what economists call *industrial regulation*, has been the preferred option in the United States. In this type of regulation, government commissions regulate the prices (usually called "rates") charged by natural monopolists. Table 32.1 lists the two major Federal regulatory commissions and their jurisdictions. It also notes that all 50 states have commissions that regulate the intrastate activities and "utility rates" of remaining natural monopolies.

The economic objective of industrial regulation is embodied in the **public interest theory of regulation.** In that theory, industrial regulation is necessary to keep a natural monopoly from charging monopoly prices and thus harming consumers and society. The goal of such regulation is to garner for society at least part of the cost reductions associated with natural monopoly while avoid-ing the restrictions of output and high prices associated with unregulated monopoly. If competition is inappropriate or impractical, society should allow or even encourage a monopoly but regulate its prices. Regulation should then be structured so that ratepayers benefit from the economies of scale—the lower per-unit costs—that natural monopolists are able to achieve.

In practice, regulators seek to establish rates that will cover production costs and yield a "fair" return to the enterprise. The goal is to set price equal to average total cost so that the regulated firm receives a normal profit, as described in the "Regulated Monopoly" section of Chapter 24. In particular, you should carefully review Figure 24.9.

Problems with Industrial Regulation

There is considerable disagreement on the effectiveness of industrial regulation. Let's examine two criticisms.

Costs and Inefficiency
An unregulated firm has a strong incentive to reduce its costs at each level of output because that will increase its profit. The regulatory commission, however, confines the regulated firm to a normal profit or a "fair return" on the value of its assets. If a regulated firm lowers its operating costs, the rising profit eventually will lead the regulatory commission to require that the firm lower its rates in order to return its profits to normal. The regulated firm therefore has little or no incentive to reduce its operating costs.

Worse yet, higher costs do not result in lower profit. Because the regulatory commission must allow the public utility a fair return, the regulated monopolist can simply pass through higher production costs to consumers by charging higher rates. A regulated firm may reason that it might as well have high salaries for its workers, opulent working conditions for management, and the like, since the "return" is the same in percentage terms whether costs are minimized or not. So, although a natural monopoly reduces cost through economies of scale, industrial regulation fosters considerable X-inefficiency (Figure 24.7). Due to the absence of competition, the potential cost savings from natural monopoly may never actually materialize.

Perpetuating Monopoly
A second general problem with industrial regulation is that it sometimes perpetuates monopoly long after the conditions of natural monopoly have ended.

Technological change often creates the potential for competition in at least some or all portions of the regulated industry. Examples: Trucks began competing with

TABLE 32.1
The Main Regulatory Commissions Providing Industrial Regulation

Commission (Year Established)	Jurisdiction
Federal Energy Regulatory Commission (1930)*	Electricity, gas, gas pipelines, oil pipelines, water-power sites
Federal Communications Commission (1934)	Telephones, television, cable television, radio, telegraph, CB radios, ham operators, etc.
State public utility commissions (50 states)	Electricity, gas, telephones

*Originally called the Federal Power Commission; renamed in 1977.

railroads; transmission of voice and data by microwave and satellites began competing with transmission over telephone wires; satellite television began competing with cable television; and cell phones began competing with regular phones.

But spurred by the firms they regulate, commissions often protect the regulated firms from new competition by either blocking entry or extending regulation to competitors. Industrial regulation therefore may perpetuate a monopoly that is no longer a natural monopoly and would otherwise erode. Ordinary monopoly, protected by government, may supplant natural monopoly. If so, the regulated prices may exceed those that would occur with competition. The beneficiaries of outdated regulation are the regulated firms and their employees. The losers are consumers and the potential entrants.

Example: Regulation of the railroads by the Interstate Commerce Commission (ICC) was justified in the late 1800s and early 1900s. But by the 1930s, with the emergence of a network of highways, the trucking industry had seriously undermined the monopoly power of the railroads. That is, for the transport of many goods over many routes, railroad service was no longer a natural monopoly. At that time it would have been desirable to dismantle the ICC and let railroads and truckers, along with barges and airlines, compete with one another. Instead, in the 1930s the ICC extended regulation of rates to interstate truckers. The ICC remained in place until its elimination in 1996.

Second example: Until recently, unregulated long-distance telephone companies such as AT&T and MCI have been prohibited from offering local telephone services in competition with regulated local and regional telephone companies. But the very fact that these and other firms wanted to compete with regulated monopolies calls into question whether those local providers are in fact natural monopolies or, rather, are government-protected monopolies. **(Key Question 10)**

Legal Cartel Theory

The regulation of potentially competitive industries has produced the **legal cartel theory of regulation.** In place of having socially minded officials forcing regulation on natural monopolies to protect consumers, holders of this view see practical politicians "supplying" regulation to local, regional, and national firms that fear the impact of competition on their profits or even on their long-term survival. These firms desire regulation because it yields a legal monopoly that can virtually guarantee a profit. Specifically, the regulatory commission performs such

functions as blocking entry (for example, in local telephone service). Or, where there are several firms, the commission divides up the market much like an illegal cartel (for example, prior to airline deregulation, the Civil Aeronautics Board assigned routes to specific airlines). The commission may also restrict potential competition by enlarging the "cartel" (for example, the ICC's addition of trucking to its regulatory domain).

While private cartels are illegal and unstable and often break down, the special attraction of a government-sponsored cartel under the guise of regulation is that it endures. The legal cartel theory of regulation suggests that regulation results from the rent-seeking activities of private firms and the desire of politicians to be responsive (Chapter 31).

Proponents of the legal cartel theory of regulation note that the Interstate Commerce Commission was welcomed by the railroads and that the trucking and airline industries both supported the extension of ICC regulation to their industries, arguing that unregulated competition was severe and destructive.

Occupational licensing is a labor market application of the legal cartel theory. Certain occupational groups—barbers, dentists, hairstylists, interior designers, dietitians, lawyers—demand stringent licensing on the grounds that it protects the public from charlatans and quacks. But skeptics say the real reason may be to limit entry into the occupational group so that practitioners can receive monopoly incomes. It is not surprising to these skeptics that a recent study found that, other things equal, dental fees were about 15 percent higher and dentists' income 10 percent higher in states with the most restrictive licensing laws compared to states with the least restricitive laws. The quality of dentistry apparently was not affected.[1]

Deregulation

Beginning in the 1970s, evidence of inefficiency in regulated industries and the contention that the government was regulating potentially competitive industries contributed to a wave of deregulation. Since then, Congress and many state legislatures have passed legislation that has deregulated in varying degrees the airline, trucking, banking, railroad, natural gas, television, and electricity industries. Deregulation has also occurred in the telecommunications industry, where antitrust authorities dismantled the

---

[1]Morris Kleiner and Robert Kudrle, "Does Regulation Affect Economic Outcomes? The Case of Dentistry," *Journal of Law and Economics,* October 2000, pp. 547–582.

regulated monopoly known as the Bell System (AT&T). Deregulation in the 1970s and 1980s was one of the most extensive experiments in economic policy to take place during the last 50 years.

While there are still some critics of deregulation, most economists believe that deregulation has clearly benefited consumers and the economy. Studies reveal that deregulation of formerly regulated industries is contributing more than $50 billion annually to society's well-being through lower prices, lower costs, and increased output.[2] Most of those gains are accruing in three industries: airlines, railroads, and trucking. Airfares (adjusted for inflation) have declined by about one-third, and airline safety has continued to improve. Trucking and railroad freight rates (again, adjusted for inflation) have dropped by about one-half.

Significant efficiency gains also have occurred in long-distance telecommunications, and there have been slight efficiency gains in cable television, stock brokerage services, and the natural gas industry. Moreover, deregulation has unleashed a wave of technological advances that have resulted in such new and improved products and services as fax machines, cellular phones, fiber-optic cable, microwave systems in communications, and the Internet.

The most recent and perhaps controversial industry to be deregulated is electricity. Deregulation is relatively advanced at the wholesale level, where firms can buy and sell electricity at market prices. They are also free to build generating facilities and sell electricity to local electricity providers at unregulated prices. In addition, several states have deregulated retail prices and encouraged households and businesses to choose among available electricity suppliers. This competition has generally lowered electricity rates for consumers and enhanced allocative efficiency.

But deregulation suffered a severe setback in California, where wholesale electricity prices, but not retail rates, were deregulated. Wholesale electricity prices surged in 2001 when California experienced electricity shortages. Because they could not pass on wholesale price increases to consumers, California electric utilities suffered large financial losses. California has recently filed lawsuits against several energy-trading companies that allegedly manipulated electricity supplies to boost the wholesale price of electricity during the California energy crisis. One multibillion-dollar energy trader—Enron—

collapsed in 2002 when Federal investigators uncovered a pattern of questionable and fraudulent business and accounting practices.

The California deregulation debacle and the Enron collapse have muddied the overall assessment of electricity deregulation in the United States. It is simply far too soon to declare deregulation either a success or a failure.

QUICK REVIEW 32.2

- Natural monopoly occurs where economies of scale are so extensive that only a single firm can produce the product at minimum average total cost.

- The public interest theory of regulation says that government must regulate natural monopolies to prevent abuses arising from monopoly power. Regulated firms, however, have less incentive than competitive firms to reduce costs. That is, regulated firms tend to be X-inefficient.

- The legal cartel theory of regulation suggests that some firms seek government regulation to reduce price competition and ensure stable profits.

- Deregulation initiated by government in the past three decades has yielded large annual efficiency gains for society.

Social Regulation

The industrial regulation discussed in the preceding section has focused on the regulation of prices (or rates) in natural monopolies. But in the early 1960s a new type of regulation began to emerge. This *social regulation* is concerned with the conditions under which goods and services are produced, the impact of production on society, and the physical qualities of the goods themselves.

The Federal government carries out most of the social regulation, although states also play a role. In Table 32.2 we list the main Federal regulatory commissions engaged in social regulation.

Distinguishing Features

Social regulation differs from industrial regulation in several ways.

First, social regulation applies to far more firms than does industrial regulation. Social regulation is often applied "across the board" to all industries and directly affects more producers than does industrial regulation. For instance, while the industrial regulation of the Federal Energy Regulatory Commission (FERC) applies to a relatively small number of firms, Occupational Safety and

---

[2]Clifford Winston, "Economic Deregulation: Days of Reckoning for Microeconomists," *Journal of Economic Literature*, September 1993, p. 1284; and Robert Crandall and Jerry Ellig, "Economic Deregulation and Consumer Choice," Center for Market Processes, Fairfax, Virginia.

TABLE 32.2

The Main Federal Regulatory Commissions Providing Social Regulation

Commission (Year Established)	Jurisdiction
Food and Drug Administration (1906)	Safety and effectiveness of food, drugs, and cosmetics
Equal Employment Opportunity Commission (1964)	Hiring, promotion, and discharge of workers
Occupational Safety and Health Administration (1971)	Industrial health and safety
Environmental Protection Agency (1972)	Air, water, and noise pollution
Consumer Product Safety Commission (1972)	Safety of consumer products

Health Administration (OSHA) rules and regulations apply to firms in all industries.

Second, social regulation intrudes into the day-to-day production process to a greater extent than industrial regulation. While industrial regulation focuses on rates, costs, and profits, social regulation often dictates the design of products, the conditions of employment, and the nature of the production process. As examples, the Consumer Product Safety Commission (CPSC) regulates the design of potentially unsafe products, and the Environmental Protection Agency (EPA) regulates the amount of pollution allowed during production.

Finally, social regulation has expanded rapidly during the same period in which industrial regulation has waned. Between 1970 and 1980, the U.S. government created 20 new social regulatory agencies. More recently, Congress has established new social regulations to be enforced by existing regulatory agencies. For example, the Equal Employment Opportunity Commission, which is responsible for enforcing laws against workplace discrimination on the basis of race, gender, age, or religion, has been given the added duty of enforcing the Americans with Disabilities Act of 1990. Under this social regulation, firms must provide reasonable accommodations for qualified workers and job applicants with disabilities. Also, sellers must provide reasonable access for customers with disabilities.

The names of the regulatory agencies in Table 32.2 suggest the reasons for their creation and growth: As much of our society had achieved a fairly affluent standard of living by the 1960s, attention shifted to improvement in the nonmaterial quality of life. That focus called for safer products, less pollution, improved working conditions, and greater equality of economic opportunity.

The Optimal Level of Social Regulation

While economists agree on the need for social regulation, they disagree on whether or not the current level of such regulation is optimal. Recall that an activity should be expanded as long as its marginal benefit (MB) exceeds its marginal cost (MC). If the MB of social regulation exceeds its MC, then there is too little social regulation. But if MC exceeds MB, there is too much (review Figure 30.6). Unfortunately, the marginal costs and benefits of social regulation are not always easy to measure and therefore may be illusive. So ideology about the proper size and role of government often drives the debate over social regulation as much as, or perhaps more than, economic cost-benefit analysis.

In Support of Social Regulation   Defenders of social regulation say that it has achieved notable successes and, overall, has greatly enhanced society's well-being. They point out that the problems that social regulation confronts are serious and substantial. According to the National Safety Council, about 5000 workers die annually in job-related accidents and 3.8 million workers suffer injuries that force them to miss a day or more of work. Air pollution continues to cloud major U.S. cities, imposing large costs in terms of reduced property values and increased health care expense. Numerous children and adults die each year because of poorly designed or manufactured products (for example, car tires) or tainted food (for example, *E. coli* in beef). Discrimination against some ethnic and racial minorities, persons with disabilities, and older workers reduces their earnings and imposes heavy costs on society.

Proponents of social regulation acknowledge that social regulation is costly. But they correctly point out that a high "price" for something does not necessarily mean that it should not be purchased. They say that the appropriate economic test should be not whether the costs of social regulation are high or low but, rather, whether the benefits of social regulation exceed the costs. After decades of neglect, they further assert, society cannot expect to cleanse the environment, enhance the safety of the workplace, and promote economic opportunity for all without incurring substantial costs. So statements about the huge costs of social regulation are irrelevant, say defenders, since the benefits are even greater. The public often underestimates those benefits, since they are more difficult to measure than costs and often become apparent only after some time has passed (for example, the benefits of reducing global warming).

Proponents of social regulation point to its many specific benefits. Here are just a few examples: It is estimated that highway fatalities would be 40 percent greater annually in the absence of auto safety features mandated through regulation. Compliance with child safety-seat and seat belt laws has significantly reduced the auto fatality rate for small children. The national air quality standards set by law have been reached in nearly all parts of the nation for sulfur dioxide, nitrogen dioxide, and lead. Moreover, recent studies clearly link cleaner air, other things equal, with increases in the values of homes. Affirmative action regulations have increased the labor demand for racial and ethnic minorities and females. The use of childproof lids has resulted in a 90 percent decline in child deaths caused by accidental swallowing of poisonous substances.

Some defenders of social regulation say there are many remaining areas in which greater regulation would generate net benefits to society. For instance, some call for greater regulation of the meat, poultry, and seafood industries to improve food safety. Others favor greater regulation of health care organizations and insurance companies to ensure "patients' rights" for consumers of health care services. Still others say that more regulation is needed to ensure that violent movies, CDs, and video games are not marketed to children.

Advocates of social regulation say that the benefits of such regulation are well worth the considerable costs. The costs are simply the price we must pay to create a hospitable, sustainable, and just society. **(Key Question 12)**

Criticisms of Social Regulation Critics of social regulation contend that, in many instances, it has been expanded to the point where the marginal costs exceed the marginal benefits. In this view, society would achieve net benefits by cutting back on mettlesome social regulation. Critics say that many social regulation laws are poorly written, making regulatory objectives and standards difficult to understand. As a result, regulators pursue goals well beyond the original intent of the legislation. Businesses complain that regulators often press for additional increments of improvement, unmindful of costs.

Also, decisions must often be made and rules formed on the basis of inadequate information. Examples: Consumer Product Safety Commission (CPSC) officials may make decisions about certain cancer-causing ingredients in products on the basis of limited laboratory experiments with animals. Or government agencies may establish costly pollution standards to attack the global-warming problem without knowing for certain whether pollution is the main cause of the problem. These efforts, say critics, lead to excessive regulation of business.

Moreover, critics argue that social regulations produce many unintended and costly side effects. For instance, the Federal gas mileage standard for automobiles has been blamed for an estimated 2000 to 3900 traffic deaths a year because auto manufacturers have reduced the weight of vehicles to meet the higher miles-per-gallon standards. Other things equal, drivers of lighter cars have a higher fatality rate than drivers of heavier vehicles.

Finally, opponents of social regulation say that the regulatory agencies may attract overzealous workers who are hostile toward the market system and "believe" too fervently in regulation. For example, the EPA staff allegedly sees all pollution as bad and all polluters as "bad guys." They have been accused of avoiding the challenge of trying to identify the optimal amount of pollution based on a careful analysis of marginal costs and marginal benefits.

Two Reminders

The debate over the proper amount of social regulation will surely continue. We leave both proponents and opponents of social regulation with pertinent economic "reminders."

There Is No Free Lunch On the one hand, fervent supporters of social regulation need to remember that "there is no free lunch." Social regulation can produce higher prices, stifle innovation, and reduce competition.

Social regulation raises product prices in two ways. It does so directly because compliance costs normally get passed on to consumers, and it does so indirectly by reducing labor productivity. Resources invested in making workplaces accessible to disabled workers, for example, are not available for investment in new machinery designed to increase output per worker. Where the wage rate is fixed, a drop in labor productivity increases the marginal and average total costs of production. In effect, the supply curve for the product shifts leftward, causing the price of the product to rise.

Social regulation may have a negative impact on the rate of innovation. Technological advance may be stifled by, say, the fear that a new plant will not meet EPA guidelines or that a new medicine will require years of testing before being approved by the Food and Drug Administration (FDA).

Social regulation may weaken competition, since it usually places a relatively greater burden on small firms than on large ones. The costs of complying with social regulation are, in effect, fixed costs. Because smaller firms produce less output over which to distribute those costs,

The Recent Microsoft Antitrust Case Is the Most Significant Monopoly Case since the Breakup of AT&T in the Early 1980s.

The Charges In May 1998 the U.S. Justice Department (under President Clinton), 19 individual states, and the District of Columbia (hereafter, "the government") filed antitrust charges against Microsoft under the Sherman Antitrust Act. The government charged that Microsoft had violated Section 2 of the act through a series of unlawful actions designed to maintain its "Windows" monopoly. It also charged that some of that conduct violated Section 1 of the Sherman Act.

Microsoft denied the charges, arguing it had achieved its success through product innovation and lawful business practices. Microsoft contended it should not be penalized for its superior foresight, business acumen, and technological prowess. It also pointed out that its monopoly was highly transitory because of rapid technological advance.

The District Court Findings In June 2000 the district court ruled that the relevant market was software used to operate Intel-compatible personal computers (PCs). Microsoft's 95 percent share of that market clearly gave it monopoly power. The court pointed out, however, that being a monopoly is not illegal. The violation of the Sherman Act occurred because Microsoft used anticompetitive means to maintain its monopoly power.

According to the court, Microsoft feared that the success of Netscape's Navigator, which allowed people to browse the Internet, might allow Netscape to expand its software to include a competitive PC operating system—software that would threaten the Windows monopoly. It also feared that Sun's Internet applications of its Java programming language might eventually threaten Microsoft's Windows monopoly.

To counter these and similar threats, Microsoft illegally signed contracts with PC makers that required them to feature Internet Explorer on the PC desktop and penalized companies that promoted software products that competed with Microsoft products. Moreover, it gave friendly companies coding that linked Windows to software applications and withheld such coding from companies featuring Netscape. Finally, under license from Sun, Microsoft developed Windows-related Java software that made Sun's own software incompatible with Windows.

The District Court Remedy The district court ordered Microsoft to split into two competing companies, one initially selling the Windows operating system and the other initially selling Microsoft applications (such as Word, Hotmail, MSN, PowerPoint, and Internet Explorer). Both companies would be free to develop new products that compete with each other, and both could derive those products from the intellectual property embodied in the common products existing at the time of divestiture.

The Appeals Court Ruling In late 2000 Microsoft appealed the district court decision to a U.S. court of appeals. In 2001 the

their compliance costs per unit of output put them at a competitive disadvantage with their larger rivals. Social regulation is more likely to force smaller firms out of business, thus contributing to the increased concentration of industry.

Less Government Is Not Always Better than More

On the other hand, fervent opponents of social regulation need to remember that less government is not always better than more government. While the market system is a powerful engine of producing goods and services and generating income, it has its flaws. Through social regulation government can clearly increase economic efficiency and thus society's well-being. Ironically, by "taking the rough edges off of capitalism," social regulation may be a strong pro-capitalist force. Properly conceived and executed, social regulation helps maintain political support for the market system. Such support could quickly wane should there be a steady drumbeat of reports of unsafe workplaces, unsafe products, discriminatory hiring,

choking pollution, ill-served medical patients, and the like. Social regulation helps the market system deliver not only goods and services but also a "good society."

QUICK REVIEW 32.3

- Social regulation is concerned with the conditions under which goods and services are produced, the effects of production on society, and the physical characteristics of the goods themselves.

- Defenders of social regulation point to the benefits arising from policies that keep dangerous products from the marketplace, reduce workplace injuries and deaths, contribute to clean air and water, and reduce employment discrimination.

- Critics of social regulation say uneconomical policy goals, inadequate information, unintended side effects, and overzealous personnel create excessive regulation, for which regulatory costs exceed regulatory benefits.

higher court affirmed that Microsoft illegally maintained its monopoly, but tossed out the district court's decision to break up Microsoft. It agreed with Microsoft that the company was denied due process during the penalty phase of the trial and concluded that the district court judge had displayed an appearance of bias by holding extensive interviews with the press. The appeals court sent the remedial phase of the case to a new district court judge to determine appropriate remedies. The appeals court also raised issues relating to the wisdom of a structural remedy.

The Final Settlement At the urging of the new district court judge, the Federal government (now under President Bush) and Microsoft negotiated a proposed settlement. With minor modification, the settlement became the final court order in 2002. The breakup was rescinded and replaced with a behavioral remedy. It (1) prevents Microsoft from retaliating against any firm that is developing, selling, or using software that competes with Microsoft Windows or Internet Explorer or is shipping a personal computer that includes both Windows and a non-Microsoft operating system; (2) requires Microsoft to establish uniform royalty and licensing terms for computer manufacturers wanting to include Windows on their PCs; (3) requires that manufacturers be allowed to remove Microsoft icons and replace them with other icons on the Windows desktop; and (4) calls for Microsoft to provide technical information to other companies so that they can develop programs that work as well with Windows as Microsoft's own products.

Source: United States v. Microsoft (District Court Conclusions of Law), April 2000; *United States v. Microsoft* (Court of Appeals), June 2001; *U.S. v. Microsoft* (Final Judgment), November 2002; and Reuters and Associated Press News Services.

SUMMARY

1. The cornerstones of antitrust policy are the Sherman Act of 1890 and the Clayton Act of 1914. The Sherman Act specifies that "every contract, combination . . . or conspiracy in the restraint of interstate trade . . . is . . . illegal" and that any person who monopolizes or attempts to monopolize interstate trade is guilty of a felony.

2. The Clayton Act was designed to bolster and make more explicit the provisions of the Sherman Act. It declares that price discrimination, tying contracts, intercorporate stock acquisitions, and interlocking directorates are illegal when their effect is to reduce competition.

3. The Federal Trade Commission Act of 1914 created the Federal Trade Commission to investigate antitrust violations and to prevent the use of "unfair methods of competition." Empowered to issue cease-and-desist orders, the commission also serves as a watchdog agency over false and deceptive representation of products.

4. The Celler-Kefauver Act of 1950 prohibits one firm from acquiring the assets of another firm when the result will curtail competition.

5. Issues in applying antitrust laws include (a) determining whether an industry should be judged by its structure or by its behavior; (b) defining the scope and size of the dominant firm's market; and (c) deciding how strictly to enforce the antitrust laws.

6. Antitrust officials are more likely to challenge price fixing, tying contracts, and horizontal mergers than they are to break up existing monopolies. Nevertheless, antitrust suits by the Federal government led to the breakup of the AT&T monopoly in the early 1980s.

7. The objective of industrial regulation is to protect the public from the market power of natural monopolies by regulating prices and quality of service.

8. Critics of industrial regulation contend that it can lead to inefficiency and rising costs and that in many instances it constitutes a legal cartel for the regulated firms. Legislation passed in the late 1970s and the 1980s has brought about varying degrees of deregulation in the airline, trucking, banking, railroad, and television broadcasting industries.

9. Studies indicate that deregulation of airlines, railroads, trucking, and telecommunications is producing sizable annual gains to society through lower prices, lower costs, and increased output. Less certain is the effect of the more recent deregulation of the electricity industry.

10. Social regulation is concerned with product safety, working conditions, and the effects of production on society. Whereas industrial regulation is on the wane, social regulation continues to expand. The optimal amount of social regulation occurs where MB = MC.

11. Those who support social regulation point to its numerous specific successes and assert that it has greatly enhanced society's well-being. Critics of social regulation contend that businesses are excessively regulated to the point where marginal costs exceed marginal benefits. They also say that social regulation often produces unintended and costly side effects.

TERMS AND CONCEPTS

antitrust policy

industrial regulation

social regulation

Sherman Act

Clayton Act

tying contracts

interlocking directorates

Federal Trade Commission Act

cease-and-desist order

Wheeler-Lea Act

Celler-Kefauver Act

Standard Oil case

U.S. Steel case

rule of reason

Alcoa case

DuPont cellophane case

Microsoft case

horizontal merger

vertical merger

conglomerate merger

per se violations

natural monopoly

public interest theory of regulation

legal cartel theory of regulation

STUDY QUESTIONS

1. Both antitrust policy and industrial regulation deal with monopoly. What distinguishes the two approaches? How does government decide to use one form of remedy rather than the other?

2. *Key Question* Describe the major provisions of the Sherman and Clayton acts. What government entities are responsible for enforcing those laws? Are firms permitted to initiate antitrust suits on their own against other firms?

3. Contrast the outcomes of the Standard Oil and U.S. Steel cases. What was the main antitrust issue in the DuPont cellophane case? In what major way do the Microsoft and Standard Oil cases differ?

4. Why might one administration interpret and enforce the antitrust laws more strictly than another? How might a change of administrations affect a major monopoly case in progress?

5. *Key Question* How would you expect antitrust authorities to react to:
   a. A proposed merger of Ford and General Motors.
   b. Evidence of secret meetings by contractors to rig bids for highway construction projects.
   c. A proposed merger of a large shoe manufacturer and a chain of retail shoe stores.
   d. A proposed merger of a small life-insurance company and a regional candy manufacturer.
   e. An automobile rental firm that charges higher rates for last-minute rentals than for rentals reserved weeks in advance.

6. Suppose a proposed merger of firms would simultaneously lessen competition and reduce unit costs through economies of scale. Do you think such a merger should be allowed?

7. In the 1980s, PepsiCo Inc., which then had 28 percent of the soft-drink market, proposed to acquire the Seven-Up Company. Shortly thereafter the Coca-Cola Company, with 39 percent of the market, indicated it wanted to acquire the Dr. Pepper Company. Seven-Up and Dr. Pepper each controlled about 7 percent of the market. In your judgment, was the government's decision to block these mergers appropriate?

8. Why might a firm charged with violating the Clayton Act, Section 7, try arguing that the products sold by the merged firms are in separate markets? Why might a firm charged with violating Section 2 of the Sherman Act try convincing the court that none of its behavior in achieving and maintaining its monopoly was illegal?

9. "The social desirability of any particular firm should be judged not on the basis of its market share but on the basis of its conduct and performance." Make a counterargument, referring to the monopoly model in your statement.

10. *Key Question* What types of industries, if any, should be subjected to industrial regulation? What specific problems does industrial regulation entail?

11. In view of the problems involved in regulating natural monopolies, compare socially optimal (marginal-cost) pricing

and fair-return pricing by referring again to Figure 24.9. Assuming that a government subsidy might be to cover any loss resulting from marginal-cost pricing, which pricing policy would you favor? Why? What problems might such a subsidy entail?

12. *Key Question* How does social regulation differ from industrial regulation? What types of benefits and costs are associated with social regulation?

13. Use economic analysis to explain why the optimal amount of product safety may be less than the amount that would totally eliminate risks of accidents and deaths. Use automobiles as an example.

14. *(Last Word)* Under what law and on what basis did the Federal district court find Microsoft guilty of violating the antitrust laws? What was the initial district court's remedy? How did Microsoft fare with its appeal to the court of appeals? Was the final remedy in the case a structural remedy or a behavioral remedy?

15. *Web-Based Question: The FTC and the Antitrust Division—recent antitrust actions* Go to the FTC website, www.ftc.gov/ftc/antitrust.htm, to find recent press releases. Briefly summarize two recent legal actions taken by the FTC. Next, go to the website of the U.S. Department of Justice's Antitrust Division, www.usdoj.gov/atr/index.html, and select What's New and All Press Releases. Briefly summarize two recent legal actions taken by the Antitrust Division.

16. *Web-Based Question: The Consumer Product Safety Commission—what is it and what does it do?* What are the major functions of the Consumer Product Safety Commission (www.cpsc.gov)? What products are the subjects of the latest CPSC press release? Identify two product categories of interest to you from Recalls by Product. List three specific product recalls for each of your two product categories. What products are covered by other government agencies and not by the CPSC?

33 | *Agriculture: Economics and Policy*

If you eat, you are part of agriculture!

In the United States, agriculture is economically important for a number of reasons:

- It is one of the nation's largest industries and provides a real-world example of the pure-competition model (Chapter 23).

- It shows the effects of government policies that interfere with supply and demand.

- It provides excellent illustrations of Chapter 31's special-interest effect and rent-seeking behavior.

- It demonstrates the increasing globalization of markets.

This chapter examines the problems in agriculture that have resulted in government intervention, the types and outcomes of government intervention, and recent major changes in farm policy.

Economics of Agriculture

Partly because of large government subsidies, agriculture remains a generally profitable industry in the United States. U.S. consumers allocate 14 percent of their spending to food, and farmers receive about $250 billion of revenue annually. But, over the years, American farmers have faced severely fluctuating prices and periodically low incomes. Agriculture has always been a risky and difficult business. There are actually two separate farm problems. The **short-run farm problem** is the year-to-year fluctuations of farm prices and incomes, and the **long-run farm problem** is the decline of agriculture as an industry and the need to reallocate agricultural resources to other uses.

Short-Run Problem: Price and Income Instability

The short-run farm problem is the result of (1) an inelastic demand for agricultural products, combined with (2) fluctuations in farm output and (3) shifts of the demand curve for farm products.

Inelastic Demand for Agricultural Products   In industrially advanced economies, the price elasticity of demand for agricultural products is low. For farm products in the aggregate, the elasticity coefficient is between .20 and .25. These figures suggest that the prices of agricultural products would have to fall by 40 to 50 percent for

consumers to increase their purchases by a mere 10 percent. Consumers apparently put a low value on additional farm output compared with the value they put on additional units of alternative goods.

Why is this so? Recall that the basic determinant of elasticity of demand is substitutability. When the price of one product falls, the consumer tends to substitute that product for other products whose prices have not fallen. But in relatively wealthy societies this "substitution effect" is very modest for food. Although people may eat more, they do not switch from three meals a day to, say, five or six meals a day in response to a decline in the relative prices of farm products. Real biological factors constrain an individual's capacity to substitute food for other products.

The inelasticity of agricultural demand is also related to diminishing marginal utility. In a high-income economy, the population is generally well fed and well clothed; it is relatively saturated with the food and fiber of agriculture. Consequently, additional farm products are subject to rapidly diminishing marginal utility. So it takes very large price cuts to induce small increases in food and fiber consumption.

Fluctuations in Output Farm output tends to fluctuate from year to year, mainly because farmers have limited control over their output. Floods, droughts, unexpected frost, insect damage, and similar disasters can mean poor crops, while an excellent growing season means bumper crops. Such natural phenomena are beyond the control of farmers, yet those phenomena exert an important influence on output.

In addition to natural phenomena, the highly competitive nature of agriculture makes it difficult for farmers to form huge combinations to control production. If the thousands of widely scattered and independent producers happened to plant an unusually large or an abnormally small portion of their land one year, an extra-large or a very small farm output would result even if the growing season were normal.

Curve D in Figure 33.1 suggests the inelastic demand for agricultural products. Combining that inelastic demand with the instability of farm production, we can see why farm prices and incomes are unstable. Even if the market demand for agricultural products remains fixed at D, its price inelasticity will magnify small changes in output into relatively large changes in farm prices and income. For example, suppose that a "normal" crop of Q_n results in a "normal" price of P_n and a "normal" farm income represented by the brown rectangle. A bumper crop or a poor crop will cause large deviations from

FIGURE 33.1

The effect of output changes on farm prices and income.
Because of the inelasticity of demand for farm products, a relatively small change in output (from Q_n to Q_p or Q_b) will cause a relatively large change in farm prices (from P_n to P_p or P_b). Farm income will change from the brown area to $0P_ppQ_p$ or $0P_bbQ_b$.

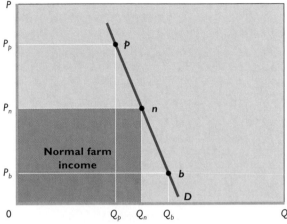

these normal prices and incomes because of the inelasticity of demand.

If a good growing season occurs, the resulting large crop of Q_b will reduce farm income to that of area $0P_bbQ_b$. When demand is inelastic, an increase in the quantity sold will be accompanied by a more-than-proportionate decline in price. The net result is that total revenue, that is, total farm income, will decline disproportionately.

Similarly, a small crop caused by, say, drought will boost total farm income to that represented by area $0P_ppQ_p$. A decline in output will cause a more-than-proportionate increase in price and in income when demand is inelastic. Ironically, for farmers as a group, a poor crop may be a blessing, and a bumper crop a hardship.

Conclusion: With a stable market demand for farm products, the inelasticity of that demand will turn relatively small changes in output into relatively larger changes in farm prices and income.

Fluctuations in Demand The third factor in the short-run instability of farm income results from shifts in the demand curve for agricultural products. Suppose that somehow agricultural output is stabilized at the "normal" level of Q_n in Figure 33.2. Now, because of the inelasticity of the demand for farm products, short-run changes in the demand for those products will cause markedly different prices and incomes to be associated with this fixed level of output.

FIGURE 33.2

The effect of demand shifts on farm prices and income.
Because of the highly inelastic demand for agricultural products, a small shift in demand (from D_1 to D_2) will cause drastically different levels of farm prices (P_1 to P_2) and farm income (area $0P_1aQ_n$ to area $0P_2bQ_n$) to be associated with a fixed level of production Q_n.

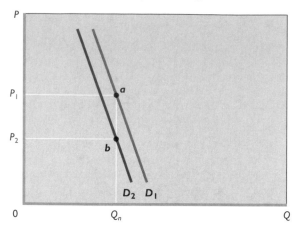

A slight drop in demand from D_1 to D_2 will reduce farm income from area $0P_1aQ_n$ to $0P_2bQ_n$. So a relatively small decline in demand gives farmers significantly less income for the same amount of farm output. Conversely, a slight increase in demand—as from D_2 to D_1—provides a sizable increase in farm income for the same volume of output. Again, large price and income changes occur because demand is inelastic.

It is tempting to argue that the sharp declines in farm prices that accompany a decrease in demand will cause many farmers to close down in the short run, reducing total output and alleviating the price and income declines. But farm production is relatively insensitive to price changes in the short run because farmers' fixed costs are high compared with their variable costs.

Interest, rent, tax, and mortgage payments on land, buildings, and equipment are the major costs faced by the farmer. These are all fixed charges. Furthermore, the labor supply of farmers and their families can also be regarded as a fixed cost. As long as they stay on their farms, farmers cannot reduce their costs by firing themselves. Their variable costs are the costs of the small amounts of extra help they may employ, as well as expenditures for seed, fertilizer, and fuel. As a result of their high proportion of fixed costs, farmers are usually better off working their land even when they are losing money, since they would lose much more by shutting down their operations for the year. Only in the long run will it make sense for them to exit the industry.

But why is agricultural demand unstable? The major source of demand volatility in U.S. agriculture springs from its dependence on world markets. As we show in Figure 33.3, that dependency has increased since 1950.

FIGURE 33.3

U.S. farm exports as a percentage of farm output, 1950–2001. Exports of farm output have increased as a percentage of total farm output in the United States. This percentage, however, has been quite variable, contributing greatly to the instability of the demand for U.S. farm output.
Source: U.S. Department of Agriculture and Federal Reserve Bank of St. Louis.

FIGURE 33.4

Inflation-adjusted U.S. agricultural prices, selected commodities, 1950–1998. Inflation-adjusted U.S. prices (in 1998 dollars) for cattle, hogs, corn, and wheat during the second half of the twentieth century reflected both volatility and general decline. *Source:* Federal Reserve Bank of Minneapolis.

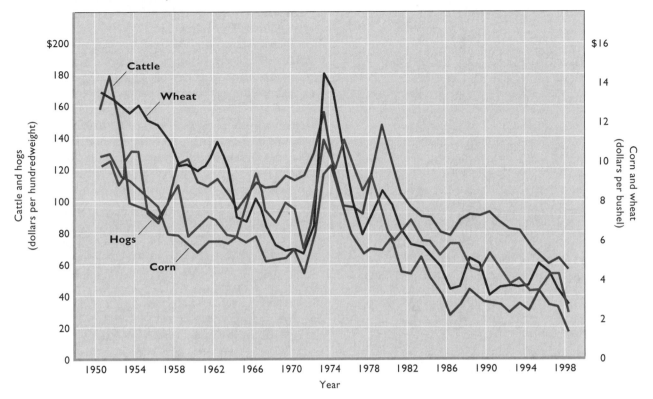

The figure also reveals that, as a percentage of total U.S. farm output, farm exports are quite unstable.

The incomes of U.S. farmers are sensitive to changes in weather and crop production in other countries: Better crops abroad mean less foreign demand for U.S. farm products. Similarly, cyclical fluctuations in incomes in Europe or Southeast Asia, for example, may shift the demand for U.S. farm products. Changes in foreign economic policies may also change demand. For instance, if the nations of western Europe decide to provide their farmers with greater protection from foreign competition, U.S. farmers will have less access to those markets and demand for U.S. farm exports will fall.

International politics also add to demand instability. Changing political relations between the United States and China and the United States and Russia have boosted exports to those countries in some periods and reduced them in others. Changes in the international value of the dollar may also be critical. Depreciation of the dollar increases the demand for U.S. farm products (which become cheaper to foreigners), whereas appreci-ation of the dollar diminishes foreign demand for U.S. farm products.

To summarize: The increasing importance of exports has amplified the short-run instability of the demand for U.S. farm products. Farm exports are affected not only by weather, income fluctuations, and economic policies abroad but also by international politics and changes in the international value of the dollar. **(Key Question 1)**

Figure 33.4 shows inflation-adjusted U.S. prices for cattle, hogs, corn, and wheat from 1950 to 1998. The short-run problem of price volatility is clearly evident. So too is the long-run problem of generally declining farm prices.

Long-Run Problem: A Declining Industry

Two other characteristics of agricultural markets explain why agriculture has been a declining industry:

- Over time, the *supply* of farm products has increased rapidly because of technological progress.

- The *demand* for farm products has increased slowly, because it is inelastic with respect to income.

Let's examine each of these supply and demand forces.

Technology and Supply Increases

A rapid rate of technological advance has significantly increased the supply of agricultural products. This technological progress has many roots: the mechanization of farms, improved techniques of land management, soil conservation, irrigation, development of hybrid crops, availability of improved fertilizers and insecticides, polymer-coated seeds, and improvements in the breeding and care of livestock. The amount of capital used per farmworker increased 15 times between 1930 and 1980, permitting a fivefold increase in the amount of land cultivated per farmer. The simplest measure of these advances is the increasing number of people a single farmer's output will support. In 1820 each farmworker produced enough food and fiber to support 4 people; by 1948, about 13. By 2002 each farmer produced enough to support 106 people. Unquestionably, the physical volume of farm output per unit of farm labor in agriculture has risen spectacularly. Over the last 50 years, this physical productivity in agriculture has advanced twice as fast as that in the nonfarm economy.

Most of the technological advances in agriculture have *not* been initiated by farmers but, rather, are the result of government-sponsored programs of research and education and the initiative of farm machinery producers. Land-grant colleges, experiment stations, county agents of the Agricultural Extension Service, educational pamphlets issued by the United States Department of Agriculture (USDA), and the research departments of farm machinery, pesticide, and fertilizer producers have been the primary sources of technological advance in U.S. agriculture.

Lagging Demand

Increases in demand for agricultural products, however, have failed to keep pace with technologically created increases in the supply of the products. The reason lies in the two major determinants of agricultural demand: income and population.

Income-Inelastic Demand

In developing countries, consumers must devote most of their meager incomes to agricultural products—food and clothing—to sustain themselves. But as income expands beyond subsistence and the problem of hunger diminishes, consumers increase their outlays on food at ever-declining rates. Once consumers' stomachs are filled, they turn to the amenities of life that manufacturing and services, not agriculture, provide. Economic growth in the United States has boosted average per capita income far beyond the level of subsistence. As a result, increases in the incomes of U.S. consumers now produce less-than-proportionate increases in spending on farm products.

The demand for farm products in the United States is *income-inelastic*; it is quite insensitive to increases in income. Estimates indicate that a 10 percent increase in real per capita after-tax income produces about a 2 percent increase in consumption of farm products. That means a coefficient of income elasticity of .2 ($= .02/.10$). So as the incomes of Americans rise, the demand for farm products increases far less rapidly than the demand for products in general.

Population Growth

Once a certain income level has been reached, each consumer's intake of food and fiber becomes relatively fixed. Thus subsequent increases in demand depend directly on growth in the number of consumers. In most advanced nations, including the United States, the demand for farm products increases at a rate roughly equal to the rate of population growth. Because U.S. population growth has not been rapid, the increase in U.S. demand for farm products has not kept pace with the rapid growth of farm output.

Graphical Portrayal

The combination of an inelastic and slowly increasing demand for agricultural products with a rapidly increasing supply puts strong downward pressure on farm prices and income. Figure 33.5 shows a large increase in agricultural supply accompanied by a very modest increase in demand. Because of the inelasticity of demand, those modest shifts result in a sharp decline in farm prices, accompanied by a relatively small increase in output. So farm income declines. On the graph, we see that farm income before the increases in demand and supply (measured by rectangle $0P_1aQ_1$) exceeds farm income after those increases ($0P_2bQ_2$). Because of an inelastic demand for farm products, an increase in supply of such products relative to demand creates persistent downward pressure on farm income.

Consequences

The actual consequences over time have been those predicted by the pure-competition model. The supply and demand conditions just outlined have increased the *minimum efficient scale (MES)* in agriculture and reduced crop prices. Farms that are too small to realize productivity gains and take advantage of

FIGURE 33.5

A graphical depiction of the long-run U.S. farm problem. In the long run, increases in the demand for U.S. farm products (from D_1 to D_2) have not kept pace with the increases in supply (from S_1 to S_2) that technological advances have permitted. Because agricultural demand is inelastic, these shifts have tended to depress farm prices (from P_1 to P_2) and reduce farm income (from $0P_1aQ_1$ to $0P_2bQ_2$) while increasing output only modestly (from Q_1 to Q_2).

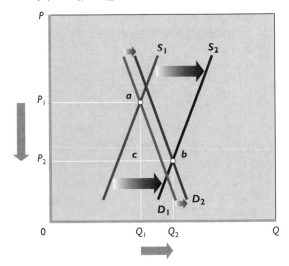

economies of scale have discovered that their average total costs exceed the (declining) prices for their crops. So they can no longer operate profitably. In the long run, financial losses in agriculture have triggered a massive exit of workers to other sectors of the economy, as shown by Table 33.1. They have also caused a major consolidation of smaller farms into larger ones. A person farming,

TABLE 33.1

U.S. Farm Employment and Number of Farms, 1950–2000

	Farm Employment*		
Year	In Millions of People	As Percentage of Total Employment	Number of Farms, Thousands
1950	9.9	17	5388
1960	7.1	11	3962
1970	4.5	6	2954
1980	3.7	4	2440
1990	2.9	2	2146
2000	3.0	2	2172

*Includes self-employed farmers, unpaid farmworkers, and hired farmworkers.
Sources: U.S. Department of Agriculture, Economic Research Service, www.usda.gov/nass, and U.S. Department of Commerce, Census Bureau, www.census.gov/.

say, 240 acres of corn three decades ago is today likely to be farming two or three times that number of acres. Large corporate firms called **agribusinesses** have emerged in some areas of farming such as potatoes, beef, fruits, vegetables, and poultry. Today, there are about 2 million farms compared to 4 million in 1960 and farm labor constitutes about 2 percent of the U.S. labor force compared to 11 percent in 1960. (Global Perspective 33.1 compares the most recent labor-force percentages for several nations.)

The income of farm households traditionally was well below that of nonfarm households. But that imbalance has ended. In 2001 the average income of farm households was $64,117 compared to $58,208 for all U.S. households. Outmigration and consolidation has boosted income *per farm household* (of which there are fewer than before). More important, members of farm households have increasingly taken jobs in nearby towns and cities. On average, only 10 percent of the income of farm households derives from farming activities. **(Key Question 3)**

GLOBAL PERSPECTIVE 33.1

Percentage of Labor Force in Agriculture, Selected Nations

High-income nations devote a much smaller percentage of their labor forces to agriculture than do low-income nations. Because their workforces are so heavily committed to producing the food and fiber needed for their populations, low-income nations have relatively less labor available to produce housing, schools, autos, and the other goods and services that contribute to a high standard of living.

Source: International Labour Office, www.ilo.org/. Latest data.

Economics of Farm Policy

The U.S. government has subsidized agriculture since the 1930s with a "farm program" that includes (1) support for farm prices, income, and output; (2) soil and water conservation; (3) agricultural research; (4) farm credit; (5) crop insurance; and (6) subsidized sale of farm products in world markets.

We will focus on the main element of farm policy: the programs designed to prop up prices and income. This topic is particularly timely because in recent years (specifically, 1996 and 2002) Congress has passed new farm laws that have replaced traditional forms of farm subsidies with new forms. To understand these new policies, we need to understand the policies they replaced and the purposes and outcomes of farm subsidies. Between 1999 and 2002, American farmers received an average of $20 billion of subsidies each year. (As indicated in Global Perspective 33.2, farm subsidies are common in many nations.)

Rationale for Farm Subsidies

A variety of arguments have been made to justify farm subsidies over the decades:

- Although farm products are necessities of life, many farmers have relatively low incomes, so they should receive higher prices and incomes through public help.
- The "family farm" is a fundamental U.S. institution and should be nurtured as a way of life.
- Farmers are subject to extraordinary hazards—floods, droughts, and insects—that most other industries do not face. Without government help,

GLOBAL PERSPECTIVE 33.2

Agricultural Subsidies, Selected Nations

Farmers in various countries receive large percentages of their incomes as government subsidies.

Government Subsidies as a Percentage of Farm Production, 2001

Switzerland, Norway, South Korea, Japan, European Union, United States, Mexico, Canada, Turkey, Australia

Source: Organization for Economic Cooperation and Development, www.oecd.org.

farmers cannot fully insure themselves against these disasters.

- While farmers face purely competitive markets for their outputs, they buy inputs of fertilizer, farm machinery, and gasoline from industries that have considerable market power. Whereas those industries are able to control their prices, farmers are at the "mercy of the market" in selling their output. The supporters of subsidies argue that agriculture warrants public aid in order to offset the disadvantageous terms of trade faced by farmers.

Background: The Parity Concept

The *Agricultural Adjustment Act of 1933* established the **parity concept** as a cornerstone of agricultural policy. The rationale of the parity concept can be stated in both real and nominal terms. In real terms, parity says that year after year for a fixed output of farm products, a farmer should be able to acquire a specific total amount of other goods and services. A particular real output should always result in the same real income: "If a farmer could take a bushel of corn to town in 1912 and sell it for enough money to buy a shirt, he should be able to sell a bushel of corn today and buy a shirt." In nominal terms, the parity concept suggests that the relationship between the prices

FIGURE 33.6

Prices paid and received by farmers, 1910–2002.   Over the past five decades the prices paid by farmers have increased by more than prices received. As a result, the parity ratio—the ratio of prices received to prices paid—has substantially declined.

Source: U.S. Department of Agriculture, National Agricultural Statistics Service, www.usda.gov/nass.

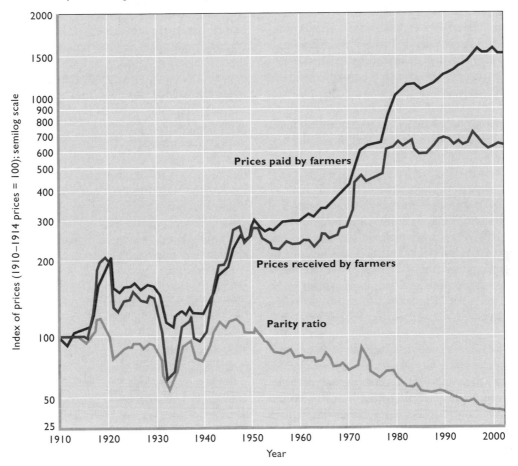

received by farmers for their output and the prices they must pay for goods and services should remain constant. The parity concept implies that if the price of shirts tripled over some time period, then the price of corn should have tripled too. Such a situation is said to represent 100 percent of parity.

Figure 33.6 indicates why farmers would benefit from having the prices of their products based on 100 percent of parity. It shows the prices paid and received by farmers from 1910 to 2002 relative to prices in the 1910–1914 base period. By 2002 prices paid had increased 16-fold, while prices received had increased only 7-fold compared with the base period.

The **parity ratio** graphed in Figure 33.6 is the ratio of prices received to prices paid, expressed as a percentage.

That is:

$$\text{Parity ratio} = \frac{\text{prices received by farmers}}{\text{prices paid by farmers}}$$

In 2002 the parity ratio was 38 percent, indicating that prices received in 2002 could buy 38 percent as much as prices received in the 1910–1914 period. So farm policy calling for 100 percent of parity would require substantially higher prices for farm products.

Economics of Price Supports

The concept of parity provides the rationale for government price floors on farm products. In agriculture those minimum prices are called **price supports.** We have

FIGURE 33.7

Effective price supports result in farm surpluses. The market demand D and supply S of a farm product yield equilibrium price P_e and quantity Q_e. An above-equilibrium price support P_s results in consumption of quantity Q_c, production of quantity Q_s, and a surplus of quantity Q_sQ_c. The blue rectangle represents a transfer of money from taxpayers to farmers.

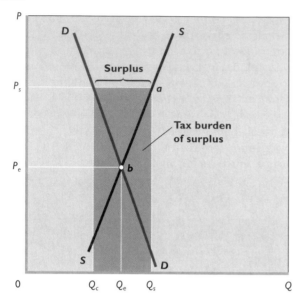

shown that, in the long run, the market prices received by farmers have not kept up with the prices paid by them. One way to achieve parity, or some percentage thereof, is to have the government establish above-equilibrium price supports for farm products.

Many different price-support programs have been tried, but they all tend to have similar effects, some of which are subtle and negative. Suppose in Figure 33.7 that the equilibrium price is P_e and the price support is P_s. Then the major effects would be as follows.

Surplus Output The most obvious result is a product surplus. Consumers are willing to purchase only Q_c units at the supported price, while farmers supply Q_s units. What about the Q_sQ_c surplus that results? The government must buy it to make the above-equilibrium price support effective. As you will see, this surplus farm output means that there is an overallocation of resources to agriculture.

Gain to Farmers Farmers benefit from price supports. In Figure 33.7, gross farm revenue rises from the

free-market level represented by area $0P_ebQ_e$ to the larger, supported level shown by area $0P_saQ_s$.

Loss to Consumers Consumers lose; they pay a higher price (P_s rather than P_e) and consume less (Q_c rather than Q_e) of the product. In some instances differences between the market price and the supported price are substantial. For example, the U.S.-supported price of a pound of sugar is about two times the world market price, and a quart of fluid milk is estimated to cost consumers twice as much as it would without government programs. Moreover, the burden of higher food prices falls disproportionately on the poor because they spend a larger part of their incomes on food.

Resource Overallocation Society loses because price supports create allocative inefficiency by encouraging an overallocation of resources to agriculture. A price floor (P_s) attracts more resources to the agricultural sector than would the free-market price (P_e). Viewed through the pure-competition model, the market supply curve in Figure 33.7 represents the marginal costs of all farmers producing this product at the various output levels. An efficient allocation of resources occurs at point b, where the market price P_e is equal to marginal cost. So the output Q_e reflects that efficient allocation of resources.

In contrast, the output Q_s associated with the price support P_s represents an overallocation of resources; for all units of output between Q_e and Q_s, marginal costs (measured on curve S) exceed the prices people are willing to pay for those units (measured on curve D). Simply stated, the marginal cost of the extra production exceeds its marginal benefit to society. Society incurs an *efficiency loss* from the price-support system.

Other Social Losses Society at large loses in three other ways.

First, taxpayers pay higher taxes to finance the government's purchase of the surplus. This added tax burden is equal to the surplus output Q_sQ_c multiplied by its price P_s, as shown by the blue area in Figure 33.7. Recall, too, that the mere collection of taxes imposes an efficiency loss (Figure 31.5). Also, the cost of storing surplus farm output adds to this tax burden.

Second, government's intervention in agriculture entails administrative costs. Thousands of government workers are needed to administer U.S. price supports and other farm programs.

Third, the *rent-seeking activity* involved—the pursuit of political support to maintain price supports—is costly and socially wasteful. Farm groups spend considerable sums to sustain political support for price floors and other programs that enhance farm incomes.

Environmental Costs

We know from Figure 33.7 that price supports encourage additional production. Although some of that extra output may come from the use of additional land, much of it comes from heavier use of fertilizer and pesticides. Those pesticides and fertilizers may pollute the environment (for example, groundwater) and create residues in food that pose health risks to farmworkers and consumers. Research shows a positive relationship between the level of price-support subsidies and the use of agrochemicals.

Moreover, farm policy may cause environmental problems in less obvious ways. First, farmers benefit from price supports only when they use their land consistently for a specific crop such as corn or wheat. That creates a disincentive to practice crop rotation, which is a nonchemical technique for controlling pests. Farm policy thus encourages the substitution of chemicals for other forms of pest control.

Second, we know from the concept of derived demand that an increase in the price of a product will increase the demand for relevant inputs. In particular, price supports for farm products increase the demand for land. And the land that farmers bring into farm production is often environmentally sensitive "marginal" land such as steeply sloped, highly erodable land or wetlands that provide wildlife habitat. Similarly, price supports result in the use of more water for irrigation, and the resulting runoff may contribute to soil erosion.

International Costs

Actually, the costs of farm price supports go beyond those indicated by Figure 33.7. Price supports generate economic distortions that cross national boundaries. For example, price supports make the U.S. agricultural market attractive to foreign producers. But inflows of foreign agricultural products would serve to increase supplies in the United States, aggravating the problem of U.S. surpluses. To prevent that from happening, the United States is likely to impose import barriers in the form of tariffs or quotas. Those barriers tend to restrict the output of more efficient foreign producers while encouraging more output from less efficient U.S. producers. The result is a less efficient use of world agricultural resources. This chapter's Last Word suggests that this is indeed the case for sugar.

Similarly, as the United States and other industrially advanced countries with similar agricultural programs

dump surplus farm products on world markets, the prices of such products are depressed. Developing countries are often heavily dependent on world commodity markets for their incomes. So they are particularly hurt because their export earnings are reduced. Thus, U.S. subsidies for rice production have imposed significant costs on Thailand, a major rice exporter. Similarly, U.S. cotton programs have adversely affected Egypt, Mexico, and other cotton-exporting nations. **(Key Question 8)**

Reduction of Surpluses

Figure 33.7 suggests that programs designed to reduce market supply (shift S leftward) or increase market demand (shift D rightward) would help boost the market price toward the supported price P_s. Further, such programs would reduce or eliminate farm surpluses. The U.S. government has tried both supply and demand approaches to reduce or eliminate surpluses.

Restricting Supply

Until recently, public policy focused mainly on restricting farm output. In particular, **acreage allotments** accompanied price supports. In return for guaranteed prices for their crops, farmers had to agree to limit the number of acres they planted in that crop. The U.S. Department of Agriculture first set the price support and then estimated the amount of the product consumers would buy at the supported price. It then translated that amount into the total number of planted acres necessary to provide it. The total acreage was apportioned among states, counties, and ultimately individual farmers.

These supply-restricting programs were only partially successful. They did not eliminate surpluses, mainly because acreage reduction did not result in a proportionate decline in production. Some farmers retired their worst land and kept their best land in production. They also cultivated their tilled acres more intensively. Superior seed, more and better fertilizer and insecticides, and improved farm equipment were used to enhance output per acre. And nonparticipating farmers expanded their planted acreage in anticipation of overall higher prices. Nevertheless, the net effect of acreage allotment undoubtedly was a reduction of farm surpluses and their associated costs to taxpayers.

Bolstering Demand

Government has tried several ways to increase demand for U.S. agricultural products.

New Uses

Both government and private industry have spent large sums on research to create new uses for agricultural goods. The production of "gasohol," which is a blend of gasoline and alcohol (ethanol) made from grain, is one such attempt to increase the demand for farm output. A less significant example is the use of soybeans to replace wax in producing crayons. Most experts conclude that such endeavors have been only modestly successful in bolstering the demand for farm products.

Domestic and Foreign Demand   The government has also created a variety of programs to stimulate domestic consumption of farm products. For example, the objective of the food-stamp program is not only to reduce hunger but also to bolster the demand for food. Similarly, the Food for Peace program has enabled developing countries to buy U.S. surplus farm products with their own currencies, rather than having to use dollars. The Federal government spends millions of dollars each year to advertise and promote global sales of U.S. farm products. Furthermore, U.S. negotiators have pressed hard in international trade negotiations to persuade foreign nations to reduce trade barriers to the importing of farm products. The government's supply-restricting and demand-increasing efforts helped reduce the amount of surplus production, but they did not succeed in eliminating surpluses.

QUICK REVIEW 33.2

- The parity concept suggests that farmers should obtain a constant ratio of the prices they receive for their farm products and the prices they pay for goods and services in general.
- Price supports are government-imposed price floors (minimum prices) on selected farm products.
- Price supports cause surplus production (which the government must buy and store); raise farm income; increase food prices to consumers; and cause an overallocation of resources to agriculture.
- Domestic price supports encourage nations to erect trade barriers against imported farm products and to dump surplus farm products on world markets.

Criticisms and Politics

After decades of experience with government price-support programs, it became apparent in the 1990s that farm policy was not working well. Major criticisms of farm subsidies emerged, as did more skeptical analysis of the politics of those subsidies.

Criticisms of the Price-Support System

Let's first examine the criticisms of the price-support system. As you will see, they were quite severe.

Symptoms, Not Causes   The price-support strategy in agriculture was designed to treat the symptoms, not the causes of the farm problem. The root cause of the long-run farm problem was misallocation of resources between agriculture and the rest of the economy. Historically, the problem had been one of too many farmers. The effect of that misallocation was relatively low farm prices and low farm income. But the price and income supports encouraged people to stay in farming rather than move to nonfarm occupations. That is, the price and income orientation of the farm program slowed the reallocation of resources necessary to resolve the long-run farm problem.

Misguided Subsidies   Because price supports were on a per-bushel basis, the subsidy system benefited those farmers who needed subsidies the least. If the goal of farm policy was to raise low farm incomes, it followed that any program of Federal aid should have been aimed at farmers with the lowest incomes. But the poor, low-output farmer did not produce and sell enough in the market to get much aid from price supports. Instead, the large, prosperous farmer reaped the benefits because of sizable output. On equity grounds, direct income payments to struggling farmers are highly preferable to indirect price-support subsidies that go primarily to large-scale, prosperous farmers. Better yet, say many economists, would be transition and retraining support for farmers willing to move out of farming and into other occupations and businesses in greater demand.

A related point concerns land values. The price and income benefits that the price-support system provided increased the value of farmland. By making crops more valuable, price supports made the land itself more valuable. That was helpful to farmers who owned the land they farmed but not to farmers who rented land. Farmers rented about 40 percent of their farmland, mostly from well-to-do nonfarm landlords. So price supports became a subsidy to people who were not actively engaged in farming.

Policy Contradictions   Because farm policy had many objectives, it often led to contradictions. Whereas most subsidized research was aimed at increasing farm productivity and the supply of farm products, acreage-allotment programs required that farmers take land out of production in order to reduce supply. Price supports for crops meant increased feed costs for ranchers and farmers and high consumer prices for animal products. Tobacco farmers were subsidized even though tobacco consumption was causing serious health problems. The U.S. sugar program raised prices for domestic producers by imposing import quotas that conflicted with free-trade policies. Conservation programs called for setting aside land for wildlife habitat, while price supports provided incentives to bring such acreage into production.

All these criticisms helped spawn policy reform. Nevertheless, as we will see, those reforms turned out to be less substantive than originally conceived. Nearly all these criticisms are as valid for current farm policy as they were for the price-support program.

The Politics of Farm Policy

In view of these criticisms, why did the United States continue its price-support program for 60 years and why does it still continue that program for sugar, milk, and tobacco? Why do farm subsidies in the billions of dollars still occur?

Public Choice Theory Revisited   Public choice theory (Chapter 31) helps answer these questions. Recall that rent-seeking behavior occurs when a group (a labor union, firms in a specific industry, or farmers producing a particular crop) uses political means to transfer income or wealth to itself at the expense of another group or of society as a whole. And recall that the special-interest effect involves a program or policy from which a small group receives large benefits at the expense of a much larger group whose members individually suffer small losses. Both rent-seeking behavior and the special-interest effect help explain the politics of farm subsidies.

Suppose a certain group of farmers, say, peanut or sugar producers, organize and establish a well-financed political action committee (PAC). The PAC's job is to promote government programs that will transfer income to the group (this is rent-seeking behavior). The PAC vigorously lobbies U.S. senators and representatives to enact or to continue price supports and import quotas for peanuts or sugar. The PAC does this in part by making political contributions to sympathetic legislators. Although peanut production is heavily concentrated in a few states such as Georgia, Alabama, and Texas, the peanut PAC will also make contributions to legislators from other states in order to gain support.

But how can a small interest group like peanut or sugar growers successfully lobby to increase its own income at the expense of society as a whole? Because, even though the total cost of the group's programs might be considerable, the cost imposed on each individual taxpayer is small (this is the special-interest effect). Taxpayers are likely to be uninformed about and indifferent to such programs, since they have little at stake. Unless you grow sugar beets or peanuts, you probably have no idea how much these programs cost you as an individual taxpayer and consumer and therefore do not object when your legislator votes for, say, a sugar-support program. Thus, there is little or no lobbying to counter the PAC's efforts.

Political logrolling, the trading of votes on policies and programs, also works to perpetuate certain programs: Senator Foghorn agrees to vote for a program that benefits Senator Moribund's constituents, and Moribund returns the favor. Example: Many members of Congress who represent low-income urban areas vote in favor of farm subsidies. In return, representatives of agricultural areas support such programs as food stamps, which provide subsidized food for the poor. The result is a rural-urban coalition through which representatives from both areas provide benefits for their constituents and enhance their reelection chances. Such coalitions help explain why farm subsidies persist and why the food-stamp program was, until recently, regularly expanded over the years.

Large agribusinesses that supply inputs to agriculture also lend political support to farm subsidies because subsidies increase the amounts of agrochemicals and farm machinery that farmers are able to buy. And, needless to say, most of the thousands of government employees whose jobs depend on farm programs are highly supportive. So, too, are owners of farmland.

Public choice theory also tells us that politicians are likely to favor programs that have hidden costs. As we have seen, that is often true of farm programs. Our discussion of Figure 33.7 indicated that price supports involve not simply a transfer of money from taxpayer to farmer but costs that are hidden as higher food prices, storage costs for surplus output, costs of administering farm programs, and costs associated with both domestic and international misallocations of resources. Because those costs are largely indirect and hidden, farm programs are much more acceptable to politicians and the public than they would be if all costs were explicit.

Changing Politics   In spite of rent seeking, special interests, and logrolling, a combination of factors has somewhat altered the politics of farm subsidies.

Declining Political Support   As the farm population has declined, agriculture's political power has weakened.

The farm population was about 25 percent of the general population in the 1930s, when many U.S. farm programs were established; now it is less than 2 percent. Urban congressional representatives now constitute a 9-to-1 majority over their rural colleagues. An increasing number of legislators are critically examining farm programs for their effects on consumers' grocery bills as well as on farm incomes. Also, more farmers themselves are coming to resent the intrusion of the Federal government into their farming decisions. Many rural-state congressional members now support free-market agriculture.

World Trade Considerations The United States has taken the lead to reduce barriers to world trade in agricultural products. That has also contributed to the more critical attitude toward farm subsidies, particularly price supports. The nations of the European Union (EU) and many other nations provide support for agricultural prices. And, to maintain their high domestic prices, they restrict imports of foreign farm products by imposing tariffs and quotas. They then try to rid themselves of their domestic surpluses by subsidizing exports into world markets.

The effects on the United States are that (1) trade barriers hinder U.S. farmers from selling to EU nations and (2) subsidized exports from those nations depress world prices for agricultural products, making world markets less attractive to U.S. farmers.

Perhaps most importantly, farm programs such as those maintained by the EU and the United States distort both world agricultural trade and the international allocation of agricultural resources. Encouraged by artificially high prices, farmers in industrially advanced nations produce more food and fiber than they would otherwise. The resulting surpluses flow into world markets, where they depress prices. This means that farmers in countries with no farm programs—many of them developing countries—face artificially low prices for their exports, and that signals them to produce less. Overall, the result is a shift in production away from what would occur on the basis of comparative advantage. As an example, price supports cause U.S. agricultural resources to be used for sugar production, even though sugar can be produced at perhaps half the cost in the Caribbean countries and Australia.

Recognizing these distortions, in 1994 the 128 nations then belonging to the World Trade Organization (WTO) agreed to reduce farm price-support programs by 20 percent by the year 2000 and to reduce tariffs and quotas on imported farm products by 15 percent. The United States made such a strong case against price supports in these

discussions that its stance undoubtedly altered the domestic debate on whether supports should be continued within this country.

Recent Reform

In the mid-1990s there was a common feeling among economists and political leaders that the goals and techniques of farm policy needed to be reexamined and revised. Moreover, crop prices were relatively high at the time and Congress wanted to reduce large Federal budget deficits.

Freedom to Farm Act of 1996

In 1996 Congress radically revamped 60 years of U.S. farm policy by passing the **Freedom to Farm Act.** The law ended price supports and acreage allotments for wheat, corn, barley, oats, sorghum, rye, cotton, and rice. Farmers were allowed to respond to changing crop prices by planting as much or as little of these crops as they chose. Also, they were free to plant crops of their choice. If the price of, say, oats increased, farmers could plant more oats and less barley. Markets, not government programs, were to determine the kinds and amounts of crops grown.

To ease the transition away from price supports, the Freedom to Farm Act granted declining annual transition payments through 2002. The $37 billion of total scheduled payments through 2002 was based on the production levels of the crops each farmer previously had grown under the price-support system. So a previous wheat farmer, for example, would receive cash payments for 7 years regardless of the current price of wheat or amount of wheat presently grown.

But this ambitious plan to wean American agriculture from subsidies unraveled in 1998 and 1999, when sharply reduced export demand and strong crop production in the United States depressed the prices of many farm products. Congress responded by supplementing the direct payments with large "emergency aid" payments to farmers. Agricultural subsidies for 1999–2002 averaged $20 billion annually—even more than they were before passage of the Freedom to Farm Act.

The Farm Act of 2002

In 2002 Congress passed the **Farm Act of 2002,** which continues the "freedom to plant" and "direct-payment" approaches of the 1996 farm law but incorporates an automatic system of "emergency aid." This 6-year $118 billion farm bill also extends the direct-payment system of the 1996 law to peanuts, soybeans, and other oilseeds. The law represents a substantial retreat from the free-market intent of the 1996 law. It provides three basic forms of commodity subsidies.

Direct Payments

The **direct payments** are similar to the transition payments paid under the Freedom to Farm Act. The cash payments are fixed for each crop based or a farmer's past production and are unaffected by current crop prices or current production. Farmers are free to plant as much or as little of any particular crop as they want and still receive these payments. Unlike the 1996 law, direct payments do not decline from year to year. They are a permanent part of the subsidy program.

Countercyclical Payments

A new component of farm policy ties a separate set of subsidies to the difference between market prices of specified farm products and a target price set for each crop. Like direct payments, these **countercyclical payments (CCP)** are based on previous crops grown and are received regardless of the current crop planted. For example, the target price for corn in the years 2004–2007 is $2.63 per bushel. If corn is at or exceeds $2.63 in one of those years, the farmer who qualifies will receive no CCP. But if the price is below $2.63, the farmer will receive CCP payments geared to the size of the price gap. The CCP system returns a form of price supports to a prominent role in farm policy, but it bases those supports on past crops grown, not current crops planted.

Marketing Loans

Finally, the 2002 Farm Act contains a marketing loan program under which farmers can receive a loan (on a per-unit-of-output basis) from a government lender. If the crop price at harvest is higher than the price specified in the loan (the loan price), farm-ers can repay their loans, with interest. If the crop price is lower than the loan price, farmers can forfeit their harvested crops to the lender and be free of their loans. In this second case, farmers receive a subsidy because the proceeds from the loan exceed the revenues from the sale of the crop in the market.

The Farm Act of 2002 makes it clear that the political clout of the farm lobby, although weaker than in earlier periods, remains very strong. All three components of the 2002 Farm Act help reduce the risk of price and income variability for farmers and raise farm incomes. But the act does not address the fundamental problem of subsidies. However structured, large subsidies slow the exodus of resources from agriculture and maintain high production levels. That means low crop prices and low market incomes for farmers. Those low prices and incomes, in turn, provide the rationale for continued government subsidies!

QUICK REVIEW 33.3

- Farm policy in the United States has been heavily criticized for delaying the shift of resources away from farming, directing most subsidies to wealthier farmers, and being fraught with policy contradictions.
- The persistence of farm subsidies can largely be explained in terms of rent-seeking behavior, the special-interest effect, political logrolling, and other aspects of public choice theory.
- The Freedom to Farm Act of 1996 eliminated price supports and acreage allotments for many of the nation's crops, while continuing direct subsidies to farmers for 7 years.
- The 2002 Farm Act runs through 2007 and provides three types of farm subsidies: direct payments, countercyclical payments, and marketing loans.

The Sugar Program Is a Sweet Deal for Domestic Sugar Producers, but It Imposes Heavy Costs on Domestic Consumers, Foreign Producers, and the American Economy.

The continuing U.S. sugar program uses price supports and import quotas to guarantee a minimum price of sugar for domestic sugar producers. The program has significant effects, both domestically and internationally.

Domestic Costs   Price supports and import quotas have boosted the domestic price of sugar to twice the world price. The estimated aggregate cost to domestic consumers is about $1.9 billion per year. Furthermore, the effect of artificially high sugar prices is regressive, because low-income households spend a larger percentage of their incomes on food than do high-income households. On the other hand, each sugar producer receives from subsidies alone an amount estimated to be twice the nation's average family income. In one recent year, a single producer received an estimated $30 million in benefits. Many sugar producers obtain more than $1 million each year in benefits.

Import Quotas   As a consequence of high U.S. domestic price supports, foreign sugar producers have a strong incentive to sell their output in the United States. But an influx of lower-priced foreign sugar into the U.S. domestic market would undermine U.S. price supports. The government therefore has imposed import quotas on foreign sugar. It decides how much sugar can be imported at a zero or very low tariff rate, and then it charges a prohibitively high tariff for any quantities above that amount. As the gap between U.S.-supported prices and world prices has widened, imports have declined as a percentage of sugar consumed in the United States. In 1975, about 30 percent of the sugar consumed in the United States was imported; currently about 16 percent comes from abroad. Domestic policy regarding the U.S. sugar industry largely dictates the nation's international trade policy with respect to sugar.

Developing Countries   The loss of the U.S. market has had several harmful effects on sugar-exporting developing countries

such as the Philippines, Brazil, and several Central American countries.

First, exclusion from the U.S. market has significantly reduced their export revenues—by an amount estimated to be many billions of dollars per year. That decline in export revenues is important, because many of the sugar-producing countries depend on such revenues to pay interest and principal on large debts owed to the United States and other industrially advanced nations.

Second, barred by quotas from sale in the U.S. market, the sugar produced by the developing countries has been added to world markets, where the increased supply has depressed the world price of sugar.

Third, domestic price supports have caused U.S. sugar production to expand to the extent that the United States may soon change from a sugar-importing to a sugar-exporting nation. That is, the U.S. sugar program may soon be a source of new competition for the sugar producers of the developing countries. Sugar price supports in the European Union have already turned that group of nations into sugar exporters.

U.S. Efficiency Loss   The Government Accounting Office estimates that the sugar program benefits sugar producers by about $1 billion annually but costs U.S. consumers about $1.9 billion each year. The excess of losses over gains is therefore $900 million annually. This efficiency loss results from the overallocation of U.S. resources to growing and processing sugar beets and sugar cane.

Global Resource Misallocation   Both domestically and globally, the sugar price-support programs of the United States and other industrially advanced economies have distorted the worldwide allocation of agricultural resources. Price supports have caused a shift of resources to sugar production by less efficient U.S. producers, and U.S. import quotas and consequent low world sugar prices have caused more efficient foreign producers to restrict their production. Thus high-cost producers are producing more sugar and low-cost producers are producing less, resulting in the inefficient use of the world's agricultural resources.

SUMMARY

1. In the short run, the highly inelastic demand for farm products transforms small changes in output and small shifts in demand into large changes in prices and income.

2. Over the long run, rapid technological advance, together with a highly inelastic and relatively slow-growing demand for agricultural output, has made agriculture a declining industry in the United States and dictated that resources exit the industry.

3. Historically, farm policy has been centered on price and based on the parity concept, which suggests that the relationship between prices received and paid by farmers should be constant over time.

4. The use of price floors or price supports has a number of economic effects: (a) It causes surplus production; (b) it increases the incomes of farmers; (c) it causes higher consumer prices for farm products; (d) it creates an overallocation of resources to agriculture; (e) it obliges society to pay higher taxes to finance the purchase and storage of surplus output; (f) it increases pollution because of the greater use of agrochemicals and vulnerable land; and (g) it forces other nations to bear the costs associated with import barriers and depressed world agricultural prices.

5. With only limited success, the Federal government has pursued programs to reduce agricultural supply and increase agricultural demand as a way to reduce the surpluses associated with price supports.

6. Economists have criticized U.S. farm policy for (a) confusing symptoms (low farm incomes) with causes (excess capacity), (b) providing the largest subsidies to high-income farmers, and (c) creating contradictions among specific farm programs.

7. The persistence of agricultural subsidies can be explained by public choice theory and, in particular, as rent-seeking behavior; the special-interest effect; and political logrolling.

8. Political backing for price supports and acreage allotments has eroded for several reasons: (a) The number of U.S. farmers, and thus their political clout, has declined relative to the number of urban consumers of farm products; and (b) successful efforts by the United States to get other nations to reduce their farm subsidies have altered the domestic debate on the desirability of U.S. subsidies.

9. The Freedom to Farm Act of 1996 ended price supports and acreage allotments for wheat, corn, barley, oats, sorghum, rye, cotton, and rice. The law established declining annual transition payments through the year 2002, but those payments were no longer tied to crop prices or the current crop produced.

10. When crop prices plummeted in 1998 and 1999, Congress supplemented the transition payments of the Freedom to Farm Act with large amounts of emergency aid. Total subsidies to agriculture averaged $20 billion annually in the years 1999–2002.

11. The Farm Act of 2002, which extends through 2007, retreated from the free-market goal of the Freedom to Farm Act. The 2002 law provides farmers with *direct payments* (based on previous crops planted), *countercyclical payments* (based on the differences between market prices and targeted prices), and *marketing loans* (based on a specified crop price and an option to either pay back the loan or forfeit the crop to the government lender).

TERMS AND CONCEPTS

short-run farm problem	parity concept	acreage allotments	direct payments
long-run farm problem	parity ratio	Freedom to Farm Act	countercyclical payments (CCP)
agribusiness	price supports	Farm Act of 2002	

STUDY QUESTIONS

1. *Key Question* Carefully evaluate: "The supply and demand for agricultural products are such that small changes in agricultural supply result in drastic changes in prices. However, large changes in farm prices have modest effects on agricultural output." (Hint: A brief review of the distinction between supply and quantity supplied may be helpful.) Do exports increase or reduce the instability of demand for farm products? Explain.

2. What relationship, if any, can you detect between the facts that farmers' fixed costs of production are large and the supply of most agricultural products is generally inelastic? Be specific in your answer.

3. *Key Question* Explain how each of the following contributes to the farm problem:
   a. The inelasticity of demand for farm products.
   b. The rapid technological progress in farming.

   c. The modest long-run growth in demand for farm com-
       modities.

   d. The volatility of export demand.

4. The key to efficient resource allocation is shifting resources
   from low-productivity to high-productivity uses. In view of
   the high and expanding physical productivity of agricultural
   resources, explain why many economists want to divert
   additional resources from farming to achieve allocative
   efficiency.

5. Explain and evaluate: "Industry complains of the higher
   taxes it must pay to finance subsidies to agriculture. Yet the
   trend of agricultural prices has been downward while industrial prices have been moving upward, suggesting that
   on balance agriculture is actually subsidizing industry."

6. "Because consumers as a group must ultimately pay the total income received by farmers, it makes no real difference
   whether the income is paid through free farm markets or
   through price supports supplemented by subsidies financed
   out of tax revenue." Do you agree?

7. If in a given year the indexes of prices received and paid by
   farmers were 120 and 165 respectively, what would the parity ratio be? Explain the meaning of that ratio.

8. *Key Question* Explain the economic effects of price supports. Explicitly include environmental and global impacts
   in your answer. On what grounds do economists contend
   that price supports cause a misallocation of resources?

9. Use supply and demand curves to depict equilibrium price
   and output in a competitive market for some farm product.
   Then show how an above-equilibrium price floor (price
   support) would cause a surplus in this market. Demonstrate
   in your graph how government could reduce the surplus
   through a policy that (*a*) changes supply or (*b*) changes demand. Identify each of the following actual government
   policies as primarily affecting the supply of or the demand
   for a particular farm product: acreage allotments; food-
   stamp program; Food for Peace program; a government
   buyout of dairy herds; export promotion.

10. Do you agree with each of the following statements? Explain
    why or why not.

    a. The problem with U.S. agriculture is that there are too
        many farmers. That is not the fault of farmers but the
        fault of government programs.

    b. The Federal government ought to buy up all U.S. farm
        surpluses and give them away to developing nations.

    c. All industries would like government price supports if
        they could get them; agriculture obtained price sup-
        ports only because of its strong political clout.

11. What are the effects of farm subsidies such as those of the
    United States and the European Union on (*a*) domestic
    agricultural prices, (*b*) world agricultural prices, and (*c*) the
    international allocation of agricultural resources?

12. Use public choice theory to explain the persistence of farm
    subsidies in the face of major criticisms of those subsidies.
    If the special-interest effect is so strong, what factors made
    it possible in 1996 for the government to end price sup-
    ports and acreage allotments for several crops?

13. What was the major intent of the Freedom to Farm Act of
    1996? Do you agree with the intent? Why or why not? Did
    the law succeed in reducing overall farm subsidies? Why or
    why not?

14. How do direct subsidies, countercyclical payments, and
    marketing loan subsidies differ under the Farm Act of 2002?
    In what way do countercyclical payments and marketing
    loans help solve the short-run farm problem? In what way
    do direct subsidies perpetuate the long-run farm problem
    of too many resources in agriculture?

15. *(Last Word)* Who benefits and who loses from the U.S.
    sugar subsidy program?

16. *Web-Based Question: Agricultural prices—what's up,
    what's down?* The USDA, at www.usda.gov/nass/aggraphs/
    agprices.htm, provides up-to-date color charts of current
    data for agricultural prices received by farmers. Check the
    prices received for cattle, corn, cotton, hogs, milk, soy-
    beans, and wheat and describe in general terms the price
    trend for each over the period shown in the chart. Why is
    it essential to know output levels, as well as prices, in eval-
    uating how individual farmers have fared in the market over
    that period?

17. *Web-Based Question: Farm size and farm sales revenue*
    Go to www.usda.gov/nass/aggraphs/landinfarms.htm, which
    provides information on farm size and farm revenue. Which
    of these three states had the smallest and largest average
    farm sizes: California, Florida, or Texas? What was the
    national average size of farms with sales revenue of less
    than $10,000 in the latest year? More than $100,000?
    What percentage of farms had $100,000 or more of
    sales? What percentage of land was in farms earning
    $100,000 or more?

34 | *Income Inequality and Poverty*

Evidence that suggests wide income disparity in the United States is easy to find. In 2001 movie producer George Lucas earned $200 million, television personality Oprah Winfrey earned $150 million, and author Tom Clancy made $48 million. In contrast, the salary of the president of the United States is $400,000, and the typical schoolteacher earns $45,000. A full-time minimum-wage worker at a fast-food restaurant makes about $10,000. Cash welfare payments to a mother with two children average $5000.

In 2001 about 32.9 million Americans—or 11.7 percent of the population—lived in poverty. An estimated 500,000 people were homeless in that year. The richest fifth of American families received about 48 percent of total income, while the poorest fifth received only 4 percent.

What are the sources of income inequality? Is income inequality rising or falling? Is the United States making progress against poverty? What are the major income-maintenance programs in the United States? Has welfare reform succeeded? These are some of the questions we will answer in this chapter.

Facts about Income Inequality

Average family income in the United States is among the highest in the world; in 2001, it was $66,863 per family. But that average tells us nothing about income inequality. To learn about that, we must examine how income is distributed around the average.

Distribution of Personal Income by Income Category

One way to measure **income inequality** is to look at the percentages of families in a series of income categories. Table 34.1 shows that about 21 percent of all families had annual before-tax incomes of less than $25,000 in 2001,

TABLE 34.1

The Distribution of U.S. Personal Income by Families, 2001

(1) Personal Income Category	(2) Percentage of All Families in This Category
Under $10,000	5.3
$10,000–$14,999	4.3
$15,000–$24,999	11.3
$25,000–$34,999	11.9
$35,000–$49,999	15.7
$50,000–$74,999	20.8
$75,000–$99,999	13.1
$100,000–$199,999	14.6
$200,000 and above	3.0
	100.0

Source: Bureau of the Census, www.census.gov/.

TABLE 34.2

The Quintile Distribution of U.S. Personal Income by Families, 2001

(1) Quintile	(2) Percentage of Total Income	(3) Upper Income Limit
Lowest 20 percent	4.2	$24,000
Second 20 percent	9.7	41,127
Third 20 percent	15.4	62,500
Fourth 20 percent	22.9	94,150
Highest 20 percent	47.7	No limit
Total	100.0	

Source: Bureau of the Census, www.census.gov/. Numbers do not add to 100 percent due to rounding.

while another 18 percent had annual incomes of $100,000 or more. The data in the table suggest considerable inequality of family income in the United States.[1]

Distribution of Personal Income by Quintiles (Fifths)

A second way to measure income inequality is to divide the total number of income receivers into five numerically equal groups, or *quintiles,* and examine the percentage of total personal (before-tax) income received by each quintile. We do this in Table 34.2, where we also provide the upper income limit for each quintile. Any amount of income more than those listed in column 3 would place a family into the next-higher quintile.

The Lorenz Curve and Gini Ratio

We can display the quintile distribution of personal income through a **Lorenz curve.** In Figure 34.1, we plot the cumulative percentage of families on the horizontal axis and the percentage of income they obtain on the vertical axis. The diagonal line 0*e* represents a *perfectly equal distribution of income* because each point along that line indicates that a particular percentage of families receive the

same percentage of income. In other words, points representing 20 percent of all families receiving 20 percent of total income, 40 percent receiving 40 percent, 60 percent receiving 60 percent, and so on, all lie on the diagonal line.

By plotting the quintile data from Table 34.2, we obtain the Lorenz curve for 2001. Observe from point *a* that the bottom 20 percent of all families received 4.2 percent

FIGURE 34.1

The Lorenz curve and Gini ratio. The Lorenz curve is a convenient way to show the degree of income inequality. The area between the diagonal (the line of perfect equality) and the Lorenz curve represents the degree of inequality in the U.S. distribution of total income. This inequality is measured numerically by the Gini ratio—area A (shown in gold) divided by area A + B (the gold + gray area).

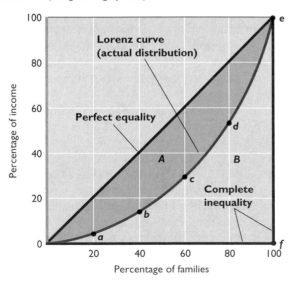

[1]The Census Bureau defines "families" as a group of two or more persons related by birth, marriage, or adoption and residing together. The bureau also gathers data for "households"—one or more persons occupying a housing unit. The distribution of personal income among households is slightly more unequal than the distribution among families.

of the income; the bottom 40 percent received 13.9 percent (= 4.2 + 9.7), as shown by point *b*; and so forth. The gold area between the diagonal line and the Lorenz curve is determined by the extent that the Lorenz curve sags away from the diagonal and indicates the degree of income inequality. If the actual income distribution were perfectly equal, the Lorenz curve and the diagonal would coincide and the gold area would disappear.

At the opposite extreme is complete inequality, where all families but one have zero income. In that case the Lorenz curve would coincide with the horizontal axis from 0 to point *f* (at 0 percent of income) and then would move immediately up from *f* to point *e* along the vertical axis (indicating that a single family has 100 percent of the total income). The entire area below the diagonal line (area 0*ef*) would indicate this extreme degree of inequality. So the farther the Lorenz curve sags away from the diagonal, the greater is the degree of income inequality.

The visual measurement of income inequality described by the Lorenz curve can easily be transformed into the **Gini ratio**—a numerical measure of the overall dispersion of income:

$$\text{Gini ratio} = \frac{\text{area between Lorenz curve and diagonal}}{\text{total area below the diagonal}}$$

$$= \frac{A \text{ (gold area)}}{A + B \text{ (gold + gray area)}}$$

For the distribution of family income shown in Figure 34.1, the Gini ratio is 0.435. As the area between the Lorenz curve and the diagonal gets larger, the Gini ratio rises to reflect greater inequality. (Test your understanding of this idea by confirming that the Gini coefficient for complete income equality is zero and for complete inequality is 1.)

Because Gini ratios are numerical, they are easier to use than Lorenz curves for comparing the income distributions of different ethnic groups and countries. For example, in 2001 the Gini ratio of U.S. family income for blacks was 0.447; for Hispanics, 0.432; and for whites, 0.426. Gini ratios of household income for various nations range from 0.707 to 0.025. Just a few examples: Nicaragua, 0.603; Mexico, 0.519; France, 0.327; Sweden, 0.250; and Japan, 0.249. **(Key Question 2)**

Income Mobility: The Time Dimension

The income data used so far have a major limitation: The income accounting period of 1 year is too short to be very meaningful. Because the Census Bureau data portray the distribution of income in only a single year, they may conceal a more equal distribution over a few years, a decade, or even a lifetime. If Brad earns $1000 in year 1 and $100,000 in year 2, while Jenny earns $100,000 in year 1 and only $1000 in year 2, do we have income inequality? The answer depends on the period of measurement. Annual data would reveal great income inequality, but there would be complete equality over the 2-year period.

This point is important because evidence suggests considerable "churning around" in the distribution of income over time. For most income receivers, income starts at a relatively low level, reaches a peak during middle age, and then declines. It follows that if all people receive exactly the same stream of income over their lifetimes, considerable income inequality would still exist in any specific year because of age differences. In any single year, the young and the old would receive low incomes while the middle-aged receive high incomes.

If we change from a "snapshot" view of income distribution in a single year to a "time exposure" portraying incomes over much longer periods, we find considerable movement of income receivers among income classes. This correctly suggests that income is more equally distributed over a 5-, 10-, or 20-year period than in a single year. Such movement of individuals or families from one income quintile to another over time is called **income mobility.**

A Federal Reserve Bank of Dallas study traced the movement of individuals from their quintile locations in 1975 to their quintile locations in 1991 and found that 95 percent of the people in the lowest income quintile in 1975 had moved to a higher quintile by 1991. Almost 30 percent of the lowest quintile had jumped to the richest quintile during that period. Undoubtedly this group included many people who were in college in 1975 but who graduated and became, say, high-income doctors, lawyers, and accountants by 1991. Nearly two-thirds of the people in the middle quintile changed to another quintile between 1975 and 1991. For the highest income quintile in 1975, about 37 percent had fallen to a lower quintile by 1991. Although the Federal Reserve study has not been updated, economists doubt that income mobility has appreciably changed over the past decade.

In short, there is significant individual and family income mobility over time; for many people, "low income" and "high income" are not permanent conditions. Also, the longer the time period considered, the more equal the distribution of income becomes.

Effect of Government Redistribution

The income data in Tables 34.1 and 34.2 include wages, salaries, dividends, and interest. They also include all cash

FIGURE 34.2

The impact of taxes and transfers on U.S. income inequality.   The distribution of personal income is significantly more equal after taxes and transfers are taken into account than before. Transfers account for most of the lessening of inequality and provide most of the income received by the lowest quintile of families.

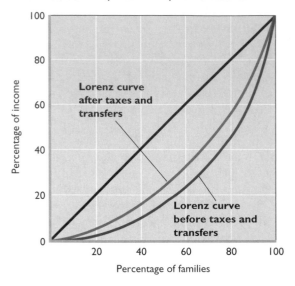

| | Percentage of Total Income Received, 2001 | |
| | (1) | (2) |
Quintile	Before Taxes and Transfers	After Taxes and Transfers
Lowest 20 percent	0.9	4.5
Second 20 percent	6.9	10.3
Third 20 percent	13.7	15.6
Fourth 20 percent	22.8	22.6
Highest 20 percent	55.6	47.0

Source: Bureau of the Census, www.census.gov/. The data include all money income from private sources, including realized capital gains and employer-provided health insurance. The "after taxes and transfers" data include the value of noncash transfers as well as cash transfers. Numbers may not add to 100 percent due to rounding.

transfer payments such as Social Security, unemployment compensation benefits, and welfare assistance to needy families. The data are before-tax data and therefore do not take into account the effects of personal income and payroll (Social Security) taxes that are levied directly on income receivers. Nor do they include in-kind or **noncash transfers,** which provide specific goods or services rather than cash. Noncash transfers include such things as Medicare, Medicaid, housing subsidies, subsidized school lunches, and food stamps. Such transfers are "income-like," since they enable recipients to "purchase" goods and services.

One economic function of government is to redistribute income, if society so desires. Figure 34.2 and its table[2] reveal that government significantly redistributes income from higher- to lower-income households through taxes and transfers. Note that the U.S. distribution of household income before taxes and transfers are taken into account (dark blue Lorenz curve) is substantially less equal than the distribution after taxes and transfers (light blue Lorenz curve). Without government redistribution, the lowest 20 percent of households in 2001 would

have received only 0.9 percent of total income. *With* redistribution, they received 4.5 percent, or five times as much.

Which contributes more to redistribution, government taxes or government transfers? The answer is transfers. Because the U.S. tax system is only modestly progressive, after-tax data would reveal only about 20 percent less inequality. Roughly 80 percent of the reduction in income inequality is attributable to transfer payments, which account for more than 75 percent of the income of the lowest quintile. Together with growth of job opportunities, transfer payments have been the most important means of alleviating poverty in the United States.

Causes of Income Inequality

There are several causes of income inequality in the United States. In general, the market system is an impersonal mechanism that embodies no conscience concerning what is an "equitable" or "just" distribution of income. It is permissive of a high degree of income inequality because it rewards individuals based on the contribution their resources make in producing society's output.

More specifically, the factors that contribute to income inequality are the following.

---

[2]The "before" data in this table differ from the data in Table 34.2 because the latter include cash transfers. Also, the data in Table 34.2 are for families, whereas the data in Figure 34.2 are for all households. Finally, the data in Figure 34.2 are based on a broader concept of income than are the data in Table 34.2.

Ability

People have different mental, physical, and aesthetic talents. Some have inherited the exceptional mental qualities that are essential to such high-paying occupations as medicine, corporate leadership, and law. Others are blessed with the physical capacity and coordination to become highly paid professional athletes. A few have the talent to become great artists or musicians or have the beauty to become top fashion models. Others have very weak mental endowments and may work in low-paying occupations or may be incapable of earning any income at all. The intelligence and skills of most people fall somewhere in between.

Education and Training

Native ability alone rarely produces high income; people must develop and refine their capabilities through education and training. Individuals differ significantly in the amount of education and training they obtain and thus in their capacity to earn income. Such differences may be a matter of choice: Chin enters the labor force after graduating from high school, while Rodriguez takes a job only after earning a college degree. Other differences may be involuntary: Chin and her parents may simply be unable to finance a college education.

People also receive varying degrees of on-the-job training, which also contributes to income inequality. Some workers learn valuable new skills each year on the job and therefore experience significant income growth over time; others receive little or no on-the-job training and earn no more at age 50 they than they did at age 30. Moreover, firms tend to select for advanced on-the-job training the workers who have the most formal education. That added training magnifies the education-based income differences between less educated and better-educated individuals.

Discrimination

Discrimination in education, hiring, training, and promotion undoubtedly contributes to income inequality in the United States, although the degree is uncertain. If discrimination restricts racial and ethnic minorities (or women) to low-paying occupations, the supply of labor will be great relative to demand in those occupations. So wages and incomes will be low. Conversely, discrimination reduces the competition that whites (or men) face in the occupations in which they are predominant. Thus, labor supply is artificially limited relative to demand in those occupations, with the result that wages and incomes are high.

Preferences and Risks

Incomes also differ because of differences in preferences for market work relative to leisure, market work relative to work in the household, and types of market work. People who choose to stay home with children, work part-time, or retire early usually have less income than those who make the opposite choices. Those who are willing to take arduous, unpleasant jobs (for example, underground mining or heavy construction), to work long hours with great intensity, or to "moonlight" will tend to earn more.

Individuals also differ in their willingness to assume risk. We refer here not only to the race driver or the professional boxer but also to the entrepreneur. Although many entrepreneurs fail, many of those who develop successful new products or services realize very substantial incomes. That contributes to income inequality.

Unequal Distribution of Wealth

Income is a *flow*; it represents a stream of wage and salary earnings, along with rent, interest, and profits, as depicted in Chapter 2's circular flow diagram. In contrast, wealth is a *stock*, reflecting at a particular moment the financial and real assets an individual has accumulated over time. A retired person may have very little income and yet own a home, mutual fund shares, and a pension plan that add up to considerable wealth. A new college graduate may be earning a substantial income as an accountant, middle manager, or engineer but has yet to accumulate significant wealth.

As you will discover in this chapter's Last Word, the ownership of wealth in the United States is more unequal than the distribution of income. This inequality of wealth leads to inequality in rent, interest, and dividends, which in turn contributes to income inequality. Those who own more machinery, real estate, farmland, stocks and bonds, and savings accounts obviously receive greater income from that ownership than people with less or no such wealth.

Market Power

The ability to "rig the market" on one's own behalf also contributes to income inequality. For example, in *resource* markets certain unions and professional groups have adopted policies that limit the supply of their services, thereby boosting the incomes of those "on the inside." Also, legislation that requires occupational licensing for, say, doctors, dentists, and lawyers can bestow market power that favors the licensed groups. In *product* markets, "rigging the market" means gaining or enhancing monopoly power, which results in greater profit and thus greater income to the firms' owners.

Luck, Connections, and Misfortune

Other forces also play a role in producing income inequality. Luck and "being in the right place at the right time" have helped individuals stumble into fortunes. Discovering oil on a ranch, owning land along a proposed freeway interchange, and hiring the right press agent have accounted for some high incomes. Personal contacts and political connections are other potential routes to attaining high income.

In contrast, economic misfortunes such as prolonged illness, serious accident, death of the family breadwinner, or unemployment may plunge a family into the low range of income. The burden of such misfortune is borne very unevenly by the population and thus contributes to income inequality. **(Key Question 5)**

QUICK REVIEW 34.1

• Data reveal considerable income inequality in the United States; in 2001 the richest fifth of all families received 47.7 percent of before-tax income, and the poorest fifth received 4.2 percent.

• The Lorenz curve depicts income inequality graphically by comparing percentages of total families and percentages of total income. The Gini ratio is a measure of the overall dispersion of income and is found by dividing the area between the diagonal and the Lorenz curve by the total area below the diagonal.

• The distribution of income is less unequal over longer time periods.

• Government taxes and transfers significantly reduce income inequality by redistributing income from higher-income groups to lower-income groups; the bulk of this redistribution results from transfer payments.

• Differences in ability, education and training, tastes for market work versus nonmarket activities, property ownership, and market power—along with discrimination and luck—help explain income inequality.

Trends in Income Inequality

Over a period of years economic growth has raised incomes in the United States: In *absolute* dollar amounts, the entire distribution of income has been moving upward. But incomes may move up in *absolute* terms while leaving

the *relative* distribution of income less equal, more equal, or unchanged. Table 34.3 shows the relative distribution of personal income over time. Recall that personal income is "before tax" and includes cash transfers but not noncash transfers. Let's see how this income distribution in the United States has changed over three periods: 1929 to 1947, 1947 to 1969, and 1969 to 2001.

The 1929–1947 Period Comparison of the income distribution data for 1929 and 1947 suggests a significant reduction in income inequality over those years. The percentage of personal income going to the top quintile declined, and the percentages received by the other four quintiles increased. Many of the forces at work during the Second World War contributed to this decline in inequality. Wartime prosperity eliminated many of the low incomes caused by the severe unemployment of the 1930s, reduced wage and salary differentials and boosted depressed farm incomes through sharp increases in farm prices. Those forces also temporarily diminished discrimination in employment and were accompanied by a decline in property incomes as a share of the national income.

The 1947–1969 Period Many of the forces contributing to greater equality during the Second World War became less influential after the war. Between 1947 and 1969, the income distribution continued its trend toward less inequality, but at a much slower pace. The income share of the lowest income group rose by .6 of a percentage point between 1947 and 1969, while that of the wealthiest quintile fell by 2.4 percentage points.

The 1969–2001 Period The distribution of income by quintiles has become more unequal since 1969. In 2001 the lowest 20 percent of families received only 4.2 percent of total before-tax income, compared with 5.6 percent in 1969. Meanwhile, the income share received by the highest 20 percent rose from 40.6 to 47.7 percent.

Global Perspective 34.1 compares income inequality in the United States (here by individuals, not by families) with that in several other nations. Income inequality tends to be highest in developing nations.

Causes of Growing Inequality

Economists suggest several major explanations for the growing U.S. income inequality of the past three decades.

Greater Demand for Highly Skilled Workers

Perhaps the most significant contributor to the growing income inequality has been an increasing demand by

TABLE 34.3

Percentage of Total Before-Tax Income Received by Each One-Fifth, and by the Top 5 Percent, of Families, Selected Years

Quintile	1929	1935–1936	1947	1955	1969	1985	2001
Lowest 20 percent ⎫		4.1	5.0	4.8	5.6	4.8	4.2
Second 20 percent ⎭	12.5	9.2	11.8	12.2	12.4	10.9	9.7
Third 20 percent	13.8	14.1	17.0	17.7	17.7	16.9	15.4
Fourth 20 percent	19.3	20.9	23.1	23.7	23.7	24.3	22.9
Highest 20 percent	54.4	51.7	43.0	41.6	40.6	43.1	47.7
Total	100.0	100.0	100.0	100.0	100.0	100.0	100.0
Top 5 percent	30.0	25.6	17.2	16.8	15.6	16.1	21.0

Source: Bureau of the Census, www.census.gov/. Numbers may not add to 100 percent due to rounding.

many firms for workers who are highly skilled and well-educated. Moreover, several industries requiring highly skilled workers have either recently emerged or expanded greatly, such as the computer software, business consulting, biotechnology, health care, and Internet industries. Because highly skilled workers remain relatively scarce, their wages have been bid up. Consequently, the wage differences between them and less skilled workers have increased.

Between 1980 and 2001 the wage difference between college graduates and high school graduates rose from 28 to 48 percent for women and from 22 to 43 percent for

men. And the so-called *90-10 ratio*—earnings at the 90th percentile of the wage and salary distribution compared to earnings at the 10th percentile—rose from 3.6 in 1980 to 4.3 in 2001.[3]

The rising demand for skill has also shown up in rapidly rising pay for chief executive officers (CEOs), sizable increases in income from stock options, substantial increases in income for professional athletes and entertainers, and huge fortunes for successful entrepreneurs. This growth of "superstar" pay has also contributed to rising income inequality.

Demographic Changes   The entrance of large numbers of less experienced and less skilled "baby boomers" into the labor force during the 1970s and 1980s may have contributed to greater income inequality in those two decades. Because younger workers tend to earn less income than older workers, their growing numbers contributed to income inequality. There has also been a growing tendency for men and women with high earnings potential to marry each other, thus increasing family income among the highest income quintiles. Finally, the number of families headed by single or divorced women has increased greatly. That trend has increased income inequality because such families lack a second major wage earner and also because the poverty rate for female-headed households is very high.

International Trade, Immigration, and Decline in Unionism   Other factors are probably at work as well. Stronger international competition from imports has reduced the demand for and employment of less skilled (but

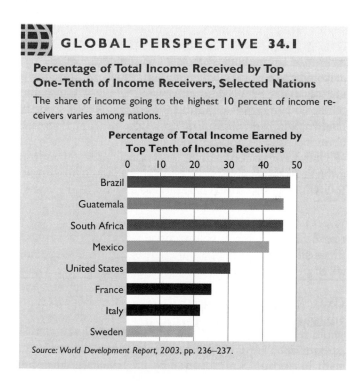

GLOBAL PERSPECTIVE 34.1

Percentage of Total Income Received by Top One-Tenth of Income Receivers, Selected Nations

The share of income going to the highest 10 percent of income receivers varies among nations.

Source: World Development Report, 2003, pp. 236–237.

---

[3]Economic Policy Institute, www.epinet.org. The college wage premiums are adjusted for differences in earnings based on race, ethnicity, marital status, and region.

highly paid) workers in such industries as the automobile and steel industries. The decline in such jobs has reduced the average wage for less skilled workers. It also has swelled the ranks of workers in already low-paying industries, placing further downward pressure on wages there.

Similarly, the transfer of jobs to lower-wage workers in developing countries has exerted downward wage pressure on less skilled workers in the United States. Also, an upsurge in immigration of unskilled workers has increased the number of low-income families in the United States. Finally, the decline in unionism in the United States has undoubtedly contributed to wage inequality, since unions tend to equalize pay within firms and industries.

Two cautions: First, when we note growing income inequality, we are not saying that the "rich are getting richer and the poor are getting poorer" in terms of absolute income. Both the rich and the poor are experiencing rises in real income. Rather, what has happened is that, while incomes have risen in all quintiles, income growth has been fastest in the top quintile. Second, increased income inequality is not solely a U.S. phenomenon. The recent rise of inequality has also occurred in several other industrially advanced nations.

The Lorenz curve can be used to contrast the distribution of income at different points in time. If we also plotted Table 34.3's data for 1947 and 1969 as Lorenz curves in Figure 34.1, we would find that the curve shifted toward the diagonal between 1947 and 1969 and then shifted back away from the diagonal between 1969 and 2001. That means the Gini ratio fell and then rose.

Equality versus Efficiency

The main policy issue concerning income inequality is how much is necessary and justified. While there is no general agreement on the justifiable amount, we can gain insight by exploring the cases for and against greater equality.

The Case for Equality: Maximizing Total Utility

The basic argument for an equal distribution of income is that income equality maximizes the total consumer satisfaction (utility) from any particular level of output and income. The rationale for this argument is shown in Figure 34.3, in which we assume that the money incomes of two individuals, Anderson and Brooks, are subject to diminishing marginal utility. In any time period, income receivers

spend the first dollars received on the products they value most—products whose marginal utility is high. As their most pressing wants become satisfied, consumers then spend additional dollars of income on less important, lower-marginal-utility goods. The identical diminishing-marginal-utility-from-income curves (MU_A and MU_B in the figure) reflect the assumption that Anderson and Brooks have the same capacity to derive utility from income.

Now suppose that there is $10,000 worth of income (output) to be distributed between Anderson and Brooks. According to proponents of income equality, the optimal distribution is an equal distribution, which causes the marginal utility of the last dollar spent to be the same for both persons. We can prove this by demonstrating that if the income distribution is initially unequal, then distributing income more equally can increase the combined utility of the two individuals.

Suppose that the $10,000 of income initially is distributed unequally, with Anderson getting $2500 and Brooks $7500. The marginal utility, a, from the last dollar received by Anderson is high, and the marginal utility, b, from Brooks' last dollar of income is low. If a single dollar of income is shifted from Brooks to Anderson—that is, toward greater equality—then Anderson's utility increases by a and Brooks' utility decreases by b. The combined utility then increases by a minus b (Anderson's large gain minus Brooks' small loss). The transfer of another dollar from Brooks to Anderson again increases their combined utility, this time by a slightly smaller amount. Continued transfer of dollars from Brooks to Anderson increases their combined utility until the income is evenly distributed and both receive $5000. At that time their marginal utilities from the last dollar of income are equal (at a' and b'), and any further income redistribution beyond the $2500 already transferred would begin to create inequality and decrease their combined utility.

The area under the MU curve and to the left of the individual's particular level of income represents the total utility of that income. Therefore, as a result of the transfer of the $2500, Anderson has gained utility represented by area G below curve MU_A, and Brooks has lost utility represented by area L below curve MU_B. Area G is obviously greater than area L, so income equality yields greater combined total utility than income inequality does.

The Case for Inequality: Incentives and Efficiency

Although the logic of the argument for equality is sound, critics attack its fundamental assumption that there is

FIGURE 34.3

The utility-maximizing distribution of income. With identical marginal-utility-of-income curves MU$_A$ and MU$_B$, Anderson and Brooks will maximize their combined utility when any amount of income (say, $10,000) is equally distributed. If income is unequally distributed (say, $2500 to Anderson and $7500 to Brooks), the marginal utility derived from the last dollar will be greater for Anderson than for Brooks, and a redistribution toward equality will result in a net increase in total utility. The utility gained by equalizing income at $5000 each, shown by area G below curve MU$_A$ in panel (a), exceeds the utility lost, indicated by area L below curve MU$_B$ in (b).

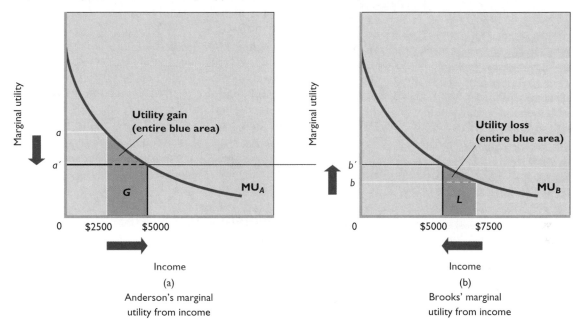

(a)
Anderson's marginal
utility from income

(b)
Brooks' marginal
utility from income

some fixed amount of output produced and therefore income to be distributed. Critics of income equality argue *that the way in which income is distributed is an important determinant of the amount of output or income that is produced and is available for distribution.*

Suppose once again in Figure 34.3 that Anderson earns $2500 and Brooks earns $7500. In moving toward equality, society (the government) must tax away some of Brooks' income and transfer it to Anderson. This tax and transfer process diminishes the income rewards of high-income Brooks and raises the income rewards of low-income Anderson; in so doing, it reduces the incentives of both to earn high incomes. Why should high-income Brooks work hard, save and invest, or undertake entrepreneurial risks when the rewards from such activities will be reduced by taxation? And why should low-income Anderson be motivated to increase his income through market activities when the government stands ready to transfer income to him? Taxes are a reduction in the rewards from increased productive effort; redistribution through transfers is a reward for diminished effort.

In the extreme, imagine a situation in which the government levies a 100 percent tax on income and distributes the tax revenue equally to its citizenry. Why would anyone work hard? Why would anyone work at all? Why would anyone assume business risk? Or why would anyone save (forgo current consumption) in order to invest? The economic incentives to "get ahead" will have been removed, greatly reducing society's total production and income. That is, the way income is distributed affects the size of that income. The basic argument for income inequality is that inequality is essential to maintain incentives to produce output and income—to get the output produced and income generated year after year.

The Equality-Efficiency Tradeoff

At the essence of the income equality-inequality debate is a fundamental tradeoff between equality and efficiency. In this **equality-efficiency tradeoff,** greater income equality (achieved through redistribution of income) comes at the opportunity cost of reduced production and income.

And greater production and income (through reduced redistribution) comes at the expense of less equality of income. The tradeoff obligates society to choose how much redistribution it wants, in view of the costs. If society decides it wants to redistribute income, it needs to determine methods that minimize the adverse effects on economic efficiency.

The Economics of Poverty

We now turn from the larger issue of income distribution to the more specific issue of very low income, or "poverty." A society with a high degree of income inequality can have either a high, moderate, or low amount of poverty. We need to learn about the extent of poverty in the United States, the characteristics of the poor, and the programs designed to reduce poverty.

Definition of Poverty

Poverty is a condition in which a person or a family does not have the means to satisfy basic needs for food, clothing, shelter, and transportation. The means include currently earned income, transfer payments, past savings, and property owned. The basic needs have many determinants, including family size and the health and age of its members.

The Federal government has established a minimum income level below which a person or a family is "in poverty." In 2001 an unattached individual receiving less than $9039 per year was said to be living in poverty. For a family of four, the poverty line was $18,104; for a family of six, it was $24,195. Applying these definitions to income data in the United States, we find for 2001 that 11.7 percent of the population—about 32.9 million people—lived in poverty.

Incidence of Poverty

Unfortunately for purposes of public policy, the poor are heterogeneous: They can be found in all parts of the nation; they are whites and nonwhites, rural and urban, young and old. But as Figure 34.4 indicates, poverty is far from randomly distributed. For example, the **poverty rate** (the percentage of the population living in poverty) for blacks is above the national average, as is the rate for Hispanics, while the rate for whites is below the average. In 2001, the poverty rates for blacks and Hispanics were 22.7 and 21.4 percent, respectively; the rate for whites was 9.9 percent.

Figure 34.5 shows that the incidence of poverty is extremely high among female-headed families, foreign-born people who are not citizens, and children under 18 years of age. Marriage is associated with a low poverty rate, and, thanks to the Social Security system, the incidence of poverty among the elderly is less than that for the population as a whole.

The high poverty rate for children is especially disturbing, because poverty tends to breed poverty. Poor children are at greater risk for a range of long-term problems, including poor health and inadequate education, crime, drug use, and teenage pregnancy. Many of today's impoverished children will reach adulthood unhealthy and illiterate and unable to earn above-poverty incomes.

Although in general there is considerable movement out of poverty, poverty is much more long-lasting among some groups than among others. In particular, black and Hispanic families, families headed by women, persons

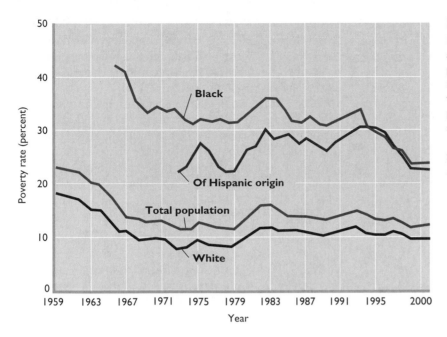

FIGURE 34.4

Poverty rates: for total population and by race and ethnicity, 1959–2001. Over the 1959–2001 period, poverty rates for blacks and Hispanics were much higher than the rate for the total population, while the rate for whites was below that for the total population. Although the national poverty rate declined sharply between 1959 and 1969, it stabilized in the 1970s only to increase significantly in the early 1980s. Since 1993, it has substantially declined.

Source: Bureau of the Census, www.census.gov/.

with little education and few labor market skills, and people who are dysfunctional because of drug use, alcoholism, or mental illness are more likely than others to remain in poverty.

Poverty Trends

As Figure 34.4 shows, the total poverty rate fell significantly between 1959 and 1969, stabilized at 11 to 13 percent over the next decade, and then rose in the early 1980s. In 1993 the rate was 15.1 percent, the highest since 1983. Between 1993 and 2000 the rate turned downward,

falling to 11.3 percent in 2000. Because of recession, the rate rose to 11.7 percent in 2001.

The "Invisible" Poor

The facts and figures on the extent and character of poverty may be difficult to accept. After all, the United States is an affluent society. The troubling statistics on poverty fit with our everyday assumptions of abundance mainly because much U.S. poverty is hidden; it is largely invisible.

There are three reasons for that invisibility. First, research has shown that as many as one-half of those in

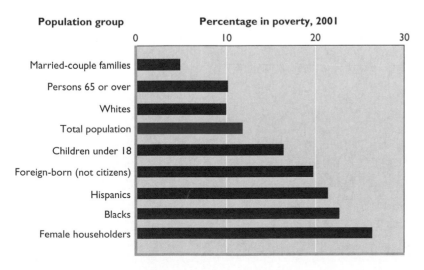

FIGURE 34.5

The distribution of poverty among selected population groups, 2001. Poverty is disproportionately borne by minorities, children, foreign-born residents who are not citizens, and families headed by women. People who are employed full-time, have a college degree, or are married tend to have low poverty rates.

Source: Bureau of the Census, www.census.gov/.

poverty are poor for only 1 or 2 years before climbing out of poverty. Many of those people are not visible as permanently downtrodden and needy. Second, the "permanently poor" are sometimes isolated geographically. Poverty persists in depressed areas of large cities and is not readily visible from the freeway. Similarly, rural poverty and the chronically depressed areas of Appalachia, the deep south, and the Indian reservations of the southwest are also off the beaten paths. Third, the poor are politically invisible. In general, they do not belong to advocacy organizations such as business groups (Chambers of Commerce), workers groups (unions and professional groups), or groups of senior citizens (such as the American Association of Retired People).

The Income-Maintenance System

The reduction of poverty is a widely accepted goal of public policy, and a number of income-maintenance programs have been devised to reduce it, the most important of which are listed in Table 34.4. Despite recent attempts to slow the upward trend in spending on such programs, they still involve enormous expenditures and large numbers of beneficiaries.

The U.S. income-maintenance system consists of two kinds of programs: (1) social insurance and (2) public assistance or "welfare." Both are known as **entitlement programs,** because all eligible persons are assured (entitled to) the benefits set forth in the programs.

Social Insurance Programs

Social insurance programs partially replace earnings that have been lost due to retirement, disability, or temporary unemployment; they also provide health insurance for the elderly. The main social insurance programs are "Social Security" (technically, Old Age, Survivors, and Disability Health Insurance, or OASDHI), unemployment compensation, and Medicare. Benefits are viewed as

TABLE 34.4

Characteristics of Major Income-Maintenance Programs

Program	Basis of Eligibility	Source of Funds	Form of Aid	Expenditures,* Billions	Beneficiaries, Millions
Social Insurance Programs					
Old Age, Survivors, and Disability Health Insurance (OASDHI)	Age, disability, or death of parent or spouse; individual earnings	Federal payroll taxes on employers and employees	Cash	$432	46
Medicare	Age or disability	Federal payroll tax on employers and employees	Subsidized health insurance	219	40
Unemployment compensation	Unemployment	State and Federal payroll taxes on employers	Cash	32	10
Public Assistance Programs					
Supplemental Security Income (SSI)	Age or disability; income	Federal revenues	Cash	35	7
Temporary Assistance for Needy Families (TANF)	Certain families with children; income	Federal-state-local revenues	Cash and services	14	5
Food stamps	Income	Federal revenues	Vouchers	20	18
Medicaid	Persons eligible for TANF or SSI and medically indigent	Federal-state-local revenues	Subsidized medical services	207	42
Earned-income tax credit (EITC)	Low-wage working families	Federal revenues	Refundable tax credit, cash	55	26

*Expenditures by Federal, state, and local governments; excludes administrative expenses.

Source: Statistical Abstract of the United States, 2002, www.census.gov/; other government sources. Latest data.

earned rights and do not carry the stigma of public charity. These programs are financed primarily out of Federal payroll taxes. In these programs the entire population shares the risk of an individual's losing income because of retirement, unemployment, disability, or illness. Workers (and employers) pay a part of wages into a government fund while they are working. The workers are then entitled to benefits when they retire or when a specified misfortune occurs.

OASDHI and Medicare

OASDHI is a gigantic social insurance program financed by compulsory payroll taxes levied on both employers and employees. Generically known as Social Security, the program replaces earnings lost because of a worker's retirement, disability, or death. Workers may retire at age 65 and receive full benefits or at age 62 with reduced benefits. When a worker dies, benefits accrue to his or her survivors. Special provisions provide benefits for disabled workers.

Currently, Social Security covers over 90 percent of the workforce; some 46 million people receive OASDHI benefits averaging about $874 per month. Those benefits are financed with a payroll tax of 15.3 percent, with both the worker and the employer paying 7.65 percent on the first $87,000 of earnings (in 2003). The 7.65 percent tax is comprised of 6.2 percent for Social Security and 1.45 percent for Medicare. Self-employed workers pay a tax of 15.3 percent.

Medicare, which was added to OASDHI in 1965, provides hospital insurance for the elderly and disabled and is financed out of the payroll tax. This overall 2.9 percent tax is paid on all work income. Medicare also makes available a low-cost voluntary insurance program that helps pay doctor fees.

Unemployment Compensation

All 50 states sponsor unemployment insurance programs. **Unemployment compensation** is financed by a modest payroll tax, paid by employers, which varies by state and by the size of the firm's payroll. Any insured worker who becomes unemployed can, after a short waiting period (usually 1 week), become eligible for benefit payments. The program covers almost all wage and salary workers. The size of payments and the number of weeks they are made available vary considerably from state to state. Generally, benefits approximate 33 percent of a worker's wages up to a certain maximum payment. Benefits averaged about $238 weekly in 2001. The number of beneficiaries and the level of total disbursements vary with economic conditions.

Public Assistance Programs

Public assistance programs (welfare) provide benefits for those who are unable to earn income because of permanent handicaps or have no or very low income and also have dependent children. These programs are financed out of general tax revenues and are regarded as public charity. They include "means tests" which require that individuals and families demonstrate low incomes in order to qualify for aid. The Federal government finances about two-thirds of the welfare program expenditures, and the rest is paid for by the states.

Many needy persons who do not qualify for social insurance programs are assisted through the Federal government's **Supplemental Security Income (SSI)** program. The purpose of SSI is to establish a uniform, nationwide minimum income for the aged, blind, and disabled who are unable to work and who do not qualify for OASDHI aid. Over half the states provide additional income supplements to the aged, blind, and disabled.

The **Temporary Assistance for Needy Families (TANF)** program is state-administered but is partly financed with Federal grants. The program provides cash assistance to families with children and also seeks to reduce welfare dependency by promoting job preparation and work. TANF's predecessor was the Aid for Families with Dependent Children (AFDC) program. But unlike that program, TANF has work requirements and limits on the length of time a family can receive welfare payments. In 2001 about 5 million people (including children) received TANF assistance.

The **food-stamp program** is designed to provide all low-income Americans with a "nutritionally adequate diet." Under the program, eligible households receive monthly allotments of coupons that are redeemable for food. The amount of food stamps received varies inversely with a family's earned income.

Medicaid helps finance the medical expenses of individuals participating in the SSI and the TANF programs.

The **earned-income tax credit (EITC)** is a tax credit for low-income working families, with or without children. The credit reduces the Federal income taxes such families owe or provides them with a cash payment if the credit exceeds their tax liability. The purpose of the credit is to offset Social Security taxes paid by low-wage earners and thus keep the Federal government from "taxing families into poverty." In essence, EITC is a wage subsidy from the Federal government that works out to be as much as $2 per hour for the lowest-paid workers with families. Under the program many people owe no income tax and get direct checks from the Federal government once a year. Some 26 million recipients qualified for the EITC in 2001, and the total cost of the program was about $55 billion.

There are also several welfare programs that are not listed in Table 34.4. Most provide help in the form of noncash transfers. Head Start provides education, nutrition, and social services to economically disadvantaged 3- and 4-year-olds. Housing assistance in the form of rent subsidies and funds for construction is available to low-income families. Pell grants provide assistance to undergraduate students from low-income families.

QUICK REVIEW 34.2

- The basic argument for income equality is that it maximizes total utility by equalizing the marginal utility of the last dollar of income received by all people.
- The basic argument for income inequality is that it is necessary as an economic incentive for production.
- By government standards, 32.9 million people in the United States, or 11.7 percent of the population, lived in poverty in 2001.
- The U.S. income-maintenance system includes both social insurance programs and public assistance (welfare) programs.

Welfare: Goals and Conflicts

An ideal public assistance (welfare) program should achieve three goals. First, the program should be effective in getting individuals and families out of poverty. Second, it should provide adequate incentives for able-bodied,

nonretired people to work. Third, its cost should be "reasonable." Unfortunately, these three goals conflict with one another, causing tradeoffs and necessitating compromises. To understand why, consider the three hypothetical welfare plans shown in Table 34.5.

Common Features

We first examine the two common elements in these three plans (and in real-world public assistance plans). First, there is a *minimum annual income* that the government will provide if the family has no earned income. Second, there is a *benefit-reduction rate*, which is the rate at which benefits are reduced or "lost" as a result of earned income.

Consider plan 1. The minimum annual income provided by the government is $8000, and the benefit-reduction rate is 50 percent. If a family earns no income, it will receive cash transfer payments totaling $8000. If it earns $4000, it will lose $2000 of transfer payments ($4000 of earnings × 50 percent benefit-reduction rate); its total income will then be $10,000 (= $4000 of earnings + $6000 of transfer payments). If it earns $8000, its transfer payments will fall to $4000, and so on. Note that at an income of $16,000, transfer payments are zero. The level of earned income at which the transfer payments disappear is called the *break-even income*.

We might criticize plan 1 on the grounds that a 50 percent benefit-reduction rate is too high and therefore does not provide sufficient incentives to work. As earned income increases, the loss of transfer payments constitutes a "tax" on earnings. Some people may choose not to work when they lose 50 cents of each extra dollar earned. Thus in plan 2 the $8000 minimum income is retained, but the benefit-reduction rate is reduced to 25 percent. But note that the break-even level of income increases to $32,000,

---

TABLE 34.5

Tradeoffs among Goals: Three Public Assistance Plans

Plan 1 ($8000 Minimum Income and 50% Benefit-Reduction Rate)			Plan 2 ($8000 Minimum Income and 25% Benefit-Reduction Rate)			Plan 3 ($12,000 Minimum Income and 50% Benefit-Reduction Rate)		
Earned Income	Transfer Payment	Total Income	Earned Income	Transfer Payment	Total Income	Earned Income	Transfer Payment	Total Income
$ 0	$8000	$ 8,000	$ 0	$8000	$ 8,000	$ 0	$12,000	$12,000
4,000	6000	10,000	8,000	6000	14,000	8,000	8,000	16,000
8,000	4000	12,000	16,000	4000	20,000	16,000	4,000	20,000
12,000	2000	14,000	24,000	2000	26,000	24,000*	0	24,000
16,000*	0	16,000	32,000*	0	32,000			

*Indicates break-even income. Determined by dividing the minimum income by the benefit-reduction rate.

so many more families would now qualify for transfer payments. Furthermore, a family with any earned income under $32,000 will receive a larger total transfer payment. For both reasons, a reduction of the benefit-loss rate to enhance work incentives will raise the cost of the income-maintenance plan.

After examining plans 1 and 2, we might argue that the $8000 minimum annual income is too low—it does not get families out of poverty. Plan 3 raises the minimum income to $12,000 and retains the 50 percent benefit-reduction rate of plan 1. While plan 3 does a better job of raising the incomes of the poor, it too yields a higher break-even income than plan 1 and therefore will be more costly. Also, if the $12,000 income guarantee of plan 3 were coupled with plan 2's 25 percent benefit-reduction rate to strengthen work incentives, the break-even income level would shoot up to $48,000 and add even more to the costs of the public assistance program.

Conflicts among Goals

Clearly, then, the goals of eliminating poverty, maintaining work incentives, and holding down program costs are in conflict.

Plan 1, with a low minimum income and a high benefit-reduction rate, keeps cost down. But the low minimum income means that this plan is not very effective in eliminating poverty, and the high benefit-reduction rate weakens work incentives.

In comparison, plan 2 has a lower benefit-reduction rate and therefore stronger work incentives. But it is more costly, because it sets a higher break-even income and therefore pays benefits to more families.

Compared with plan 1, plan 3 has a higher minimum income and is more effective in eliminating poverty. While work incentives are the same as those in plan 1, the higher guaranteed income in plan 3 makes the plan more costly. **(Key Question 11)**

Welfare Reform

The tradeoffs just mentioned shed light on the nation's relatively recent reform of the welfare system. The Personal Responsibility Act of 1996 resulted from a growing sense that welfare spending was not ending poverty. While the number of people receiving welfare benefits under the Aid to Families with Dependent Children (AFDC) program rose substantially in the 1980s and early 1990s, the number of people in poverty went up, instead of down. There was concern that the AFDC program was creating dependency on the government and thus robbing individuals and family members of motivation and dignity.

Temporary Assistance to Needy Families

The welfare reform of 1996 ended the Federal government's six-decade-old guarantee of cash assistance for poor families. Instead, the Federal government now pays each state a lump sum of Federal money each year to operate its own welfare and work programs. These lump-sum payments are called Temporary Assistance for Needy Families (TANF) funds. But the TANF reform did much more. It:

- Set a lifetime limit of 5 years on receiving TANF benefits and required able-bodied adults to work after receiving assistance for 2 years.
- Ended food-stamp eligibility for able-bodied persons age 18 to 50 (with no dependents) who are not working or engaged in job training programs.
- Tightened the definition of "disabled children" as it applies for eligibility of low-income families for Supplemental Security Income (SSI) assistance.
- Established a 5-year waiting period on public assistance for new legal immigrants who have not become citizens.

Assessment of TANF

Supporters of TANF believe that it already has played a key role in helping to end a "culture of welfare" in which dropping out of school, having a child, and going on welfare were allegedly becoming a normal way of life for part of the welfare population. They cite large declines in the welfare rolls as evidence of the law's effectiveness. In 1996 there were 12.6 million welfare recipients, including children, or 4.8 percent of the U.S. population. By the end of 2002 those totals had declined to 5.2 million and 2 percent of the population. Economists attribute about half the decline to welfare reform and the other half to the strong demand for labor and the low unemployment accompanying the economic expansion in the last half of the 1990s.

The recession of 2001 and the slack labor market in 2002 slowed the decline of welfare recipients but did not reverse the downward trend. Whether the slow economy will eventually create a major increase in welfare recipients remains to be seen. But, that uncertainty aside, economists judge the positive results of the 1996 welfare reform as strong confirmation of two economic principles: Economic growth and high levels of employment are powerful antipoverty forces, and welfare program incentives (and disincentives) clearly matter.

In 2003 the Federal Reserve Reported Its Latest Findings on Family Wealth (= Net Worth = Assets *Minus* Liabilities) in the United States. Between 1989 and 2001 Family Wealth Rose Rapidly and Became More Unequal.

The Federal Reserve conducts a Survey of Consumer Finances in the United States every 3 years, through which it determines median family wealth, average family wealth, and the distribution of wealth. *Median family wealth* is the wealth received by the family at the midpoint of the distribution; *average family wealth* is simply total wealth divided by the number of families. As shown in Table 1, median and average family wealth, adjusted for inflation, was considerably higher in 2001 than in 1989. That is, the value of family assets rose more rapidly than the value of liabilities, increasing net worth—or wealth. Between 1989 and 2001, median and average wealth rose by 33 percent and 55 percent, respectively. In general, American families are wealthier than they were before.

Table 2 looks at the distribution of family wealth for various percentile groups and reveals that the distribution of wealth is highly unequal. In 2001 the wealthiest 10 percent of families owned 70 percent of the total wealth and the top 1 percent owned 33 percent. The bottom 90 percent held only 30 percent of the total wealth.

Moreover, the general trend is toward greater inequality of wealth. The lowest 90 percent of the families owned 33 percent of total U.S. wealth in 1989, but that percentage fell to 30 percent in 2001. The share of wealth owned by the top 1 percent of American families increased from 30 percent in 1989 to 33 percent in 2001 (although it is down from its peak of 35 percent in 1995).

So from a normative standpoint, Tables 1 and 2 present a "mixed-news" combination. The welcome news is that median and average wealth in the United States rose substantially between 1989 and 2001. The discouraging news is that such wealth grew less rapidly for the typical American family than for the top 10 percent of American families over the entire period.

Tables 1 and 2 raise many interesting questions: Will the growing inequality of wealth continue? If so, what are the implications for the future character of the American society? Should government do more, or less, in the future to try to redistribute wealth? Would new government policies to redistribute wealth endanger or slow the creation of wealth and the growth of income for average Americans? The Federal estate tax is currently scheduled to phase out in 2012 and then return to high levels. Should the phase-out be made permanent?

Sources: Ana M. Aizcorbe, Arthur B. Kennickell, and Kevin B. Moore, "Recent Changes in U.S. Family Finances: Evidence from the 1998 and 2001 Surveys of Consumer Finances," *Federal Reserve Bulletin,* January 2003, pp. 1–32; Arthur B. Kennickell, "A Rolling Tide: Changes in the Distribution of Wealth in the United States, 1989–2001," Survey of Consumer Finances working paper, March 2003.

TABLE 1

Median and Average Family Wealth, Survey Years, 1989–2001 (in 2001 Dollars)

Year	Median	Average*
1989	$64,600	$255,400
1992	61,300	230,500
1995	66,400	244,800
1998	78,000	307,400
2001	86,100	395,500

*The averages greatly exceed the medians because the averages are boosted by the multibillion-dollar wealth of a relatively few families.

TABLE 2

Percentage of Total Family Wealth Held by Different Percentile Groups, Survey Years, 1989–2001

	Percentile of Wealth Distribution		
Year	Bottom 90%	Top 10%	Top 1%
1989	32.6%	67.4%	30.3%
1992	32.8	67.2	30.2
1995	32.2	67.8	34.6
1998	31.4	68.6	33.9
2001	30.2	69.8	32.7

SUMMARY

1. The distribution of income in the United States reflects considerable inequality. The richest 20 percent of families receive 47.7 percent of total income, while the poorest 20 percent receive 4.2 percent.

2. The Lorenz curve shows the percentage of total income received by each percentage of families. The extent of the gap between the Lorenz curve and a line of total equality illustrates the degree of income inequality.

3. The Gini ratio measures the overall dispersion of the income distribution and is found by dividing the area between the diagonal and Lorenz curve by the entire area below the diagonal. Higher Gini ratios signify greater degrees of income inequality.

4. Recognizing that the positions of individual families in the distribution of income change over time and incorporating the effects of noncash transfers and taxes would reveal less income inequality than do standard census data. Government transfers (cash and noncash) greatly lessen the degree of income inequality; taxes also reduce inequality, but not nearly as much as transfers.

5. Causes of income inequality include differences in abilities, in education and training, and in job tastes, along with discrimination, inequality in the distribution of wealth, and an unequal distribution of market power.

6. Census data show that income inequality declined significantly between 1929 and the end of the Second World War but has increased since 1969. The major cause of the recent increases in income inequality is a rising demand for highly skilled workers, which has boosted their earnings significantly.

7. The basic argument for income equality is that it maximizes consumer satisfaction (total utility) from a particular level of total income. The main argument for income inequality is that it provides the incentives to work, invest, and assume risk and is necessary for the production of output, which, in turn, creates income that is then available for distribution.

8. Current statistics reveal that 11.7 percent of the U.S. population lives in poverty. Poverty rates are particularly high for female-headed families, young children, blacks, and Hispanics.

9. The present income-maintenance program in the United States consists of social insurance programs (OASDHI, Medicare, and unemployment compensation) and public assistance programs (SSI, TANF, food stamps, Medicaid, and earned-income tax credit).

10. Public assistance programs (welfare) are difficult to design because their goals of reducing poverty, maintaining work incentives, and holding down program costs are often in conflict with one another.

11. In 1996 Congress established the Temporary Assistance for Needy Families (TANF) program, which shifted responsibility for welfare from the Federal government to the states. Among its provisions are work requirements for adults receiving welfare and a 5-year lifelong limit on welfare benefits.

12. A strong economy and TANF reduced the U.S. welfare rolls by more than one-half between 1996 and 2002.

TERMS AND CONCEPTS

income inequality	entitlement programs	public assistance programs	food-stamp program
Lorenz curve	social insurance programs	Supplemental Security Income (SSI)	Medicaid
Gini ratio	OASDHI		earned-income tax credit (EITC)
income mobility	Medicare	Temporary Assistance for Needy Families (TANF)	
noncash transfers	unemployment compensation		
equality-efficiency tradeoff			
poverty rate			

STUDY QUESTIONS

1. Use quintiles to briefly summarize the degree of income inequality in the United States. How and to what extent does government reduce income inequality?

2. *Key Question* Assume that Al, Beth, Carol, David, and Ed receive incomes of $500, $250, $125, $75, and $50, respectively. Construct and interpret a Lorenz curve for this five-person economy. What percentage of total income is received by the richest quintile and by the poorest quintile?

3. How does the Gini ratio relate to the Lorenz curve? Why can't the Gini ratio exceed 1? What is implied about the direction of income inequality if the Gini ratio declines from

0.42 to 0.35? How would one show that change of inequality in the Lorenz diagram?

4. Why is the lifetime distribution of income more equal than the distribution in any specific year?

5. *Key Question* Briefly discuss the major causes of income inequality. With respect to income inequality, is there any difference between inheriting property and inheriting a high IQ? Explain.

6. What factors have contributed to increased income inequality since 1969?

7. Should a nation's income be distributed to its members according to their contributions to the production of that total income or according to the members' needs? Should society attempt to equalize income or economic opportunities? Are the issues of equity and equality in the distribution of income synonymous? To what degree, if any, is income inequality equitable?

8. Analyze in detail: "There need be no tradeoff between equality and efficiency. An 'efficient' economy that yields an income distribution that many regard as unfair may cause those with meager incomes to become discouraged and stop trying. So efficiency may be undermined. A fairer distribution of rewards may generate a higher average productive effort on the part of the population, thereby enhancing efficiency. If people think they are playing a fair economic game and this belief causes them to try harder, an economy with an equitable income distribution may be efficient as well."[4]

9. Comment on or explain:
   a. Endowing everyone with equal income will make for very unequal enjoyment and satisfaction.
   b. Equality is a "superior good"; the richer we become, the more of it we can afford.
   c. The mob goes in search of bread, and the means it employs is generally to wreck the bakeries.
   d. Some freedoms may be more important in the long run than freedom from want on the part of every individual.
   e. Capitalism and democracy are really a most improbable mixture. Maybe that is why they need each other—to put some rationality into equality and some humanity into efficiency.
   f. The incentives created by the attempt to bring about a more equal distribution of income are in conflict with the incentives needed to generate increased income.

10. What are the essential differences between social insurance and public assistance programs? Why is Medicare a social insurance program whereas Medicaid is a public assistance program? Why is the earned-income tax credit considered to be a public assistance program?

11. *Key Question* The following table contains three hypothetical public assistance plans:

Plan 1		
Earned Income	Transfer Payment	Total Income
$ 0	$4,000	$4,000
2,000	3,000	5,000
4,000	2,000	6,000
6,000	1,000	7,000

Plan 2		
Earned Income	Transfer Payment	Total Income
$ 0	$4,000	$ 4,000
4,000	3,000	7,000
8,000	2,000	10,000
12,000	1,000	13,000

Plan 3		
Earned Income	Transfer Payment	Total Income
$ 0	$8,000	$ 8,000
4,000	6,000	10,000
8,000	4,000	12,000
12,000	2,000	14,000

   a. Determine the minimum income, the benefit-reduction rate, and the break-even income for each plan.
   b. Which plan is the most costly? The least costly? Which plan is the most effective in reducing poverty? The least effective? Which plan contains the strongest disincentive to work? The weakest disincentive to work?
   c. Use your answers in part *b* to explain the following statement: "The dilemma of public assistance is that you cannot bring families up to the poverty level and simultaneously preserve work incentives (without work requirements) and minimize program costs."

12. What major criticisms of the U.S. welfare system led to its reform in 1996 (via the Personal Responsibility Act)? How did this reform try to address those criticisms? Do you agree with the general thrust of the reform and with its emphasis on work requirements and time limits on welfare benefits? Has the reform reduced U.S. welfare rolls or increased them?

13. *(Last Word)* Go to Table 1 in the Last Word and compute the ratio of average wealth to median wealth for each of the 5 years. What trend do you find? What is your explanation for the trend? The Federal estate tax redistributes wealth in two ways: by encouraging charitable giving, which reduces the taxable estate, and by heavily taxing extraordinarily

---

[4]Paraphrased from Andrew Schotter, *Free Market Economics* (New York: St. Martin's Press, 1985), pp. 30–31.

large estates and using the proceeds to fund government programs. Do you favor repealing the estate tax? Explain.

14. ***Web-Based Question: How much family income does it take to be in the richest 5 percent?*** Go to the U.S. Census Bureau website, www.census.gov, and select Income (under People), Historical Income Tables (CPS), and Income Inequality. What is the lower limit of family (not household) income for the richest 5 percent of families in the most recent year listed? Do the historical data in the table suggest the poor are getting poorer and the rich are getting richer in absolute terms? Return to the tables on inequality and determine what has happened to the relative income share of the richest 5 percent of families over the last 10 years listed.

15. ***Web-Based Question: Is poverty on the rise or on the decline?*** Go to the U.S. Census Bureau website, www.census.gov, and select Poverty (under People). Use the data provided to answer the following questions:

   a. Is the number of people living below the official government poverty level higher or lower than it was in the preceding year? Than it was a decade earlier?

   b. Is the poverty rate (in percent) higher or lower than it was in the preceding year for the general population, children under 18, blacks, Asians, Pacific Islanders, and whites?

   c. How many states had increases in the poverty rate compared to the preceding year?

Labor Market Institutions and Issues: Unionism, Discrimination, Immigration

In this chapter we examine three separate topics: unionism, discrimination, and immigration. All are significant facets of the U.S. labor market, but otherwise they are largely unrelated.

- In the first part of the chapter we look at labor unions. We see who belongs to unions, examine collective bargaining, and discuss the reasons for the recent decline of unionism. Then we assess the effect of unions on wages, efficiency, and productivity.

- We then turn to labor market discrimination and discuss the types and costs of discrimination, economic theories of discrimination, and current antidiscrimination policies.

- In the last part of the chapter we examine immigration: the inflow of people to the United States from abroad. Our focus is on the extent and effects of both legal and illegal immigration.

Unionism in America

In 2002 about 16 million U.S. workers—13.2 percent of employed wage and salary workers—belonged to unions. (Global Perspective 35.1 compares this percentage with those of several other nations.) Some 13 million of the 16 million U.S. union members belong to one of many unions that are loosely and voluntarily affiliated with the **American Federation of Labor and the Congress of Industrial Organizations (AFL-CIO).** Examples of AFL-CIO unions are the Teamsters, United Autoworkers, Communications Workers, and Carpenters. Another 3 million union members belong to **independent unions**

that are not affiliated with the AFL-CIO. Among those unions are the National Education Association, the Nurses' Union, and the United Mine Workers.

Business Unionism

In the United States, unions generally have adhered to a philosophy of **business unionism:** unionism that is concerned with the short-run economic objectives of higher pay, better benefits, shorter hours, and improved working conditions. These unions have not pushed for long-run idealistic objectives aimed at significantly modifying or overthrowing the capitalist system. Nor have

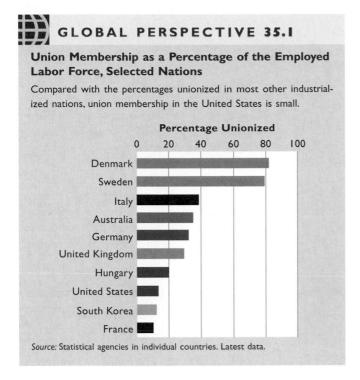

GLOBAL PERSPECTIVE 35.1

Union Membership as a Percentage of the Employed Labor Force, Selected Nations

Compared with the percentages unionized in most other industrialized nations, union membership in the United States is small.

Percentage Unionized

Denmark
Sweden
Italy
Australia
Germany
United Kingdom
Hungary
United States
South Korea
France

Source: Statistical agencies in individual countries. Latest data.

Union Membership

The likelihood that any particular worker will be a union member depends mainly on the industry in which the worker works and his or her occupation. Figure 35.1a shows that the rate of unionization (percentage of workers unionized) is high in government, transportation, construction, and manufacturing. The rate of unionization is very low in agriculture; finance, insurance, and real estate; retail trade; and services. Figure 35.1b shows that unionism also varies greatly by occupation. Protective service workers, transportation workers, craft workers, and machine operators have high rates of unionization; sales workers and managers have very low rates.

Because disproportionately more men than women work in the industries and occupations with high unionization rates, men are more likely to be union members than women. Specifically, 15 percent of male wage and salary workers belong to unions compared with 12 percent of women. For the same reason, blacks have higher unionization rates than whites: 17 percent compared with 13 percent. The unionization rate for Hispanics is 11 percent. Unionism in the United States is largely an urban phenomenon. Six heavily urbanized, heavily industrialized states (New York, California, Pennsylvania, Illinois, Ohio, and Michigan) account for approximately half of all union members.

The Decline of Unionism

Since the mid-1950s, union membership has not kept pace with the growth of the labor force. While 25 percent

union members organized into a distinct political party, such as the "labor parties" of several European nations. Unionism's political philosophy has been to reward its friends and punish its enemies at the polls, regardless of political party.

FIGURE 35.1

Union membership as a percentage of employed wage and salary workers, selected industries and occupations, 2002.

In percentage terms, union membership varies greatly by (a) industry and (b) occupation.

Source: Bureau of Labor Statistics, www.bls.gov.

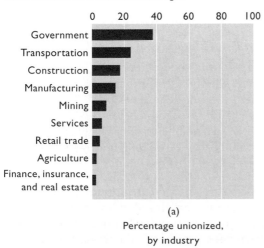

(a)
Percentage unionized,
by industry

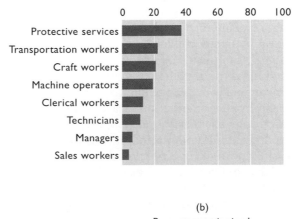

(b)
Percentage unionized,
by occupation

of employed wage and salary workers belonged to unions in the mid-1950s, today only 13.2 percent are union members. Over recent years, even the absolute number of union members has declined significantly. More than 22 million workers were unionized in 1980 but only about 16 million in 2002.

What explains the decline in unionization, relatively and absolutely?

Structural Changes
According to the **structural-change hypothesis,** changes unfavorable to the expansion of union membership have occurred in both the economy and the labor force.

Employment has shifted away from traditionally unionized industries. For example, U.S. domestic employment has moved away from manufactured goods (where unions have been strong) and toward services (where unions have been weak). Also, consumer demand in some cases has shifted toward foreign manufactured goods and away from goods produced by union labor in the United States. Increased foreign competition in several highly unionized manufacturing industries such as automobile and steel has reduced unionized workforces and, therefore, union membership. And within manufacturing, production has shifted from highly unionized "old-economy" firms to software production, computer manufacturing, and other "high-tech" industries in which unionization is virtually nonexistent.

Another factor in the decline in unionism is that an unusually high proportion of the increase in employment in recent decades has been concentrated among women, youths, and part-time workers. These groups are allegedly difficult to organize into unions, because they are less strongly attached to the labor force. Furthermore, the long-term trend of industry to shift from the northeast and midwest, where unionism is "a way of life," to "hard-to-organize" areas of the south and southwest has reduced the growth of union membership.

An ironic possibility is that the relative decline of unionism may in part reflect the success that unions have achieved in gaining a sizable wage advantage over nonunion workers in the United States. Confronted with high union wages, employers may have substituted machinery for workers, subcontracted more work to nonunion suppliers, opened nonunion plants in less industrialized areas, or shifted production of components to low-wage nations. All these actions reduce the employment of union workers and thus the level of union membership.

The success of unions in raising wages may have also raised the prices of union-produced goods relative to the prices of goods produced by nonunion workers. If so, we would expect output and employment in lower-cost nonunion firms and industries to increase at the expense of output and employment in higher-cost union firms and industries.

Managerial Opposition
Another view of the decline of unionism is that intensified managerial opposition to unions has deterred union growth. According to this **managerial-opposition hypothesis,** the wage advantage that union workers enjoy causes union firms to be less profitable than nonunion firms. The managements of both nonunionized and unionized firms have therefore undertaken policies to oppose or dissuade unionization. One managerial strategy has been to employ labor-management consultants who specialize in mounting aggressive antiunion drives to dissuade workers from unionizing or, alternatively, to persuade union workers to decertify (officially vote out) their union. Also, confronted with strikes by union workers, management has increasingly hired permanent strikebreakers to take the place of striking workers, in the expectation that these nonunion workers will later vote to eliminate the union. A conciliatory strategy by management has been to improve working conditions and personnel policies. When management treats workers with dignity and respect, workers feel less need to join unions.

Collective Bargaining

Despite the decline of unionism, **collective bargaining** (the negotiation of labor contracts) remains an important feature of labor-management relations. The goal of collective bargaining is to establish a "work agreement" between the firm and the union.

The Work Agreement

Collective bargaining agreements (contracts) assume many forms. Some contracts are brief, taking up only 2 or 3 pages; others are lengthy and highly detailed, requiring 200 or 300 pages of print. Some agreements involve only a local union and a single plant; others set wages, hours, and working conditions for entire industries.

Typically, however, collective bargaining agreements cover several topics.

Union Status and Managerial Prerogatives
As for *union status*, the closed shop affords the union the greatest security. In a **closed shop,** a worker must be (or must become) a member of the union before being hired.

Under Federal labor law, such shops are illegal in industries other than transportation and construction.

In contrast, a **union shop** permits the employer to hire nonunion workers but provides that these workers must join the union within a specified period, say 30 days, or relinquish their jobs. An **agency shop** requires that nonunion workers pay union dues or donate an equivalent amount to charity. Union and agency shops are legal, except in the 22 states that expressly prohibit them through so-called **right-to-work laws.**

In the **open shop,** an employer may hire either union or nonunion workers. Those who are nonunion are not obligated to join the union or to pay union dues; they may continue on their jobs indefinitely as nonunion workers. Nevertheless, the wages, hours, and working conditions set forth in the work agreement apply to the nonunion workers as well as to the union workers.

The management side of the union-status issue is *managerial prerogatives.* Most work agreements contain clauses outlining certain decisions that are reserved solely for management. These prerogatives usually cover such matters as the size and location of plants, the products to be manufactured, and the types of equipment and materials to be used in production and in production scheduling.

Wages and Hours The focal point of almost all bargaining agreements is wages and hours. Both labor and management press for the advantage in wage bargaining. The arguments that unions use most frequently in demanding (and, by the firm, in resisting) wage boosts are (1) "what others are getting," (2) the employer's ability to pay, based on its profitability, (3) increases in the cost of living, and (4) increases in labor productivity. In some cases, unions achieve success in tying wages to the cost of living through **cost-of-living adjustment (COLA)** clauses.

Hours of work, voluntary versus mandatory overtime, holiday and vacation provisions, profit sharing, health plans, and pension benefits are other contract issues that must be addressed in the bargaining process.

Seniority and Job Protection The uncertainty of employment in a market economy, along with the fear of antiunion discrimination on the part of employers, has made workers and their unions "job-conscious." The explicit and detailed provisions covering job opportunities that most agreements contain reflect this concern. Unions stress seniority (length of service) as the basis for worker promotion and for layoff and recall. They want the worker with the longest continuous service to have the first chance at relevant promotions, to be the last one laid off, and to be the first one recalled from layoff.

In recent years, unions have become increasingly sensitive to losing jobs to nonunion subcontractors and to overseas workers. Unions sometimes seek limits on the firm's ability to subcontract out work or to relocate production facilities overseas.

Grievance Procedures Even the most detailed and comprehensive work agreement cannot spell out all the specific issues and problems that might occur during its life. For example, suppose that Nelson gets reassigned to a less pleasant job. Was this reassignment for legitimate business reasons or, as Nelson suspects, because of a personality conflict with a particular manager? Labor contracts contain *grievance procedures* to resolve such matters.

The Bargaining Process

The date for the beginning of collective bargaining on a new contract is usually specified in the existing contract and is typically 60 days before the current one expires. The union normally takes the initiative, presenting its *demands* in the form of specific wage, fringe-benefit, and other adjustments to the present union-management contract. The firm counters with an offer relating to these and other contract provisions. It is not unusual for the original union demand and the first offer by the firm to be far apart, not only because of the parties' conflicting interests but also because the parties know they are obligated by law to bargain in good faith. The initial "large-demand–low-offer situation" leaves plenty of room for compromise during the negotiations.

The negotiating then begins in earnest on items in dispute. Hanging over the negotiations is the *deadline,* which occurs the moment the present contract expires. At that time there is a possibility of a **strike**—a "work stoppage" by the union—if it thinks its demands are not being satisfactorily met. But there is also the possibility that at the deadline the firm may engage in a **lockout,** in which it forbids the workers to return to work until a new contract is signed. In this setting of uncertainty prior to the deadline, both parties feel pressure to find mutually acceptable terms.

Although bluster and bickering often occur in collective bargaining, labor and management display a remarkable capacity for compromise and agreement. Typically they reach a compromise solution that is written into a new contract. Nevertheless, strikes and lockouts occasionally do occur. When they happen, workers lose income and firms lose profit. To stem their losses, both parties usually look for and eventually find ways to settle the labor dispute and get the workers back to work.

Bargaining, strikes, and lockouts occur within a framework of Federal labor law, specifically the **National Labor Relations Act (NLRA).** This act was first passed as the Wagner Act of 1935 and later amended by the Taft-Hartley Act of 1947 and the Landrum-Griffin Act of 1959. The act sets forth the dos and don'ts of union and management labor practices. For example, while union members can picket in front of a firm's business, they cannot block access to the business by customers, coworkers, or strikebreakers hired by the firm. Another example: Firms cannot refuse to meet and talk with the union's designated representatives.

Either unions or management can file charges of unfair labor practices under the labor law. The **National Labor Relations Board (NLRB)** has the authority to investigate such charges and to issue cease-and-desist orders in the event of violation. (The board also conducts worker elections to decide which specific union, if any, a group of workers might want to have represent them.)

QUICK REVIEW 35.1

- About 13 million of the 16 million union workers in the United States are members of the AFL-CIO, with the rest belonging to independent unions. About 13.2 percent of U.S. wage and salary workers belong to unions.
- The rate of unionization varies greatly by industry and occupation (see Figure 35.1).
- The decline of unionism in recent decades has been attributed to (a) changes in the structures of the economy and the labor force and (b) growing managerial opposition to unions.
- Collective bargaining determines the terms of work agreements, which typically cover (a) union status and managerial prerogatives, (b) wages, hours, and working conditions, (c) control over job opportunities, and (d) grievance procedures.

Economic Effects of Unions

What effects do unions have on the economy? Do unions raise wages? Do they increase or diminish economic efficiency?

The Union Wage Advantage

The three union models in Chapter 28 (see Figures 28.5, 28.6, and 28.7 and the accompanying discussions) all imply that unions are capable of raising wages. Has unionization really done so?

Empirical research overwhelmingly suggests that unions do raise the wages of their members relative to those of comparable nonunion workers, although the size of the union wage advantage varies according to occupation, industry, race, and gender. The consensus estimate is that the overall union wage advantage averages about 15 percent. On the other hand, unions have had little impact on the average level of real wages received by U.S. workers taken as a whole.

These two conclusions (higher union pay, no overall impact) may seem inconsistent, but they are not. The higher union wages apply to only a relatively small part of the labor force. Moreover, these wages may come at the expense of lower wages for some nonunion workers. As you will see (in Figure 35.2), higher wages in unionized labor markets may cause employers to hire fewer workers. The workers who are left unemployed may seek employment in nonunion labor markets. The resulting increase in the supply of labor in the nonunion labor markets reduces wage rates there. So the net result may be no change in the average level of wages.

The long-run relationship between productivity and the average level of real wages shown in Figure 28.1 suggests that unions have little power to raise the average real wage over long periods of time. But Figure 28.1 is an average relationship; it is therefore compatible with the idea that certain groups of (union) workers get higher relative wages while other (nonunion) workers simultaneously get lower real wages.

Efficiency and Productivity

Do labor unions increase or decrease efficiency and productivity? There is much disagreement on this question, but we can consider some of the ways in which unions might affect efficiency, both negatively and positively.

Negative View   There are three ways in which unions might exert a negative impact on productivity and efficiency.

Losses via Featherbedding and Work Rules   Some unions undoubtedly have diminished efficiency by engaging in "make-work" or "featherbedding" practices and resisting the introduction of output-increasing machinery and equipment. These productivity-reducing practices often arise in periods of technological change. For example, in 2002 the ILWU (dockworkers' union) obtained a contract provision guaranteeing 40-hour-per-week jobs for ILWU clerical personnel for the remaining years of their careers at west coast ports. Many of those workers will not be needed because the ports are rapidly moving toward computerized systems for tracking cargo. The new scanning systems will require far fewer workers than the older "paperwork" systems.

More generally, unions might reduce efficiency by establishing work rules and practices that impede putting the most productive workers in particular jobs. Under seniority rules, for example, workers may be promoted for their employment tenure rather than for their ability to perform the available job with the greatest efficiency. Also, unions might restrict the kinds of tasks workers may perform. Contract provisions may prohibit sheet-metal workers or bricklayers from doing the simple carpentry work often associated with their jobs. Observance of such rules means, in this instance, that firms must hire unneeded and underused carpenters. Finally, critics of unions contend that union contracts often chip away at managerial prerogatives to establish work schedules, determine production targets, introduce new technology, and make other decisions contributing to productive efficiency.

Losses via Strikes

A second way unions may impair efficiency is through calling a strike. If union and management reach an impasse in their negotiations, a strike may result and the firm's production may cease for the strike's duration. If so, the firm will forgo sales and profit; workers will sacrifice income; and the economy could lose output.

Statistics on U.S. strike activity suggest that strikes are rare and the associated aggregate economic losses are less than might be expected. In 2002 only 19 strikes occurred that involved 1000 or more employees, down from 29 a year earlier. Furthermore, many strikes lasted only a few days. Between 1995 and 2002, the average amount of work time lost each year because of strikes was .02 percent of total estimated work time. That was the equivalent of 4 hours per U.S. worker per year, which is less than 5 minutes per worker per week.

However, the economic costs associated with strikes may be greater or less than is suggested by the amount of work time lost. The costs may be greater if strikes disrupt production in nonstruck firms that either provide inputs to or buy goods and services from the struck firm. Example: An extended strike in the auto industry might reduce output and cause layoffs in firms producing, say, glass, tires, paints, and fabrics used in producing cars. It may also reduce sales and cause layoffs in auto dealerships.

On the other hand, the costs of strikes may be less than is implied by the work time lost by strikers if nonstruck firms increase their output to offset the loss of production by struck firms. While the output of General Motors declines when its workers strike, auto buyers may

shift their demand to Ford, Honda, or Toyota, which will respond by increasing their employment and output. Thus, although GM and its employees are hurt by a strike, society as a whole may experience little or no decline in employment, real output, and income.

Losses via Labor Misallocation

A more subtle way that unions might adversely affect efficiency is through the union wage advantage itself. Figure 35.2 shows (for simplicity) identical labor demand curves for a unionized sector and a nonunionized sector of the market for some particular kind of labor. We assume that there is pure competition in both the product market and all resource markets.

If there were no union in either sector initially, the wage rate that would result from the competitive hiring of labor would be W_n, while N_1 workers would be hired in each sector. Now suppose workers form a union in sector 1 and succeed in increasing the wage rate from W_n to W_u. As a consequence, N_1N_2 workers lose their jobs in the union sector. Assume that they all move to nonunion sector 2, where they are employed. This increase in labor supply (not shown) in the nonunion sector increases the quantity of labor supplied there from N_1 to N_3, reducing the wage rate from W_n to W_s.

Recall that the labor demand curves reflect the marginal revenue products (MRPs) of workers or, in other words, the contribution that each additional worker makes to domestic output. This means that area $A + B + C$ in the union sector represents the sum of the MRPs—the total contribution to domestic output—of the workers displaced by the wage increase achieved by the union. The reemployment of these workers in nonunion sector 2 results in an increase in domestic output, indicated by area $D + E$. Because area $A + B + C$ exceeds area $D + E$, there is a net loss of domestic output. More precisely, because $A = D$ and $C = E$, the net loss attributable to the union wage advantage is represented by area B. Since the same amount of employed labor is now producing a smaller output, labor is being misallocated and inefficiently used.

From a slightly different perspective, after the shift of N_1N_2 workers from the union sector to the nonunion sector has occurred, workers will be paid a wage rate equal to their MRPs in both sectors. But the workers who shifted sectors will be working at lower-MRP jobs after the shift. An economy always obtains a larger domestic output when labor is reallocated from a low-MRP use to a high-MRP use. But here the opposite has occurred. And assuming the union can maintain the W_u wage rate in its sector, a reallocation of labor from sector 2 to sector 1 will never occur.

FIGURE 35.2

The effects of the union wage advantage on the allocation of labor.   The higher wage W_u that the union receives in sector 1 causes the displacement of N_1N_2 workers. The reemployment of these workers in sector 2 increases employment from N_1 to N_3 and reduces the wage rate there from W_n to W_s. The associated loss of output in the union sector is area $A + B + C$, while the gain in the nonunion sector is only $D + E$. The net loss of output is area B. This loss of output suggests that the union wage advantage has resulted in a misallocation of labor and a decline in economic efficiency.

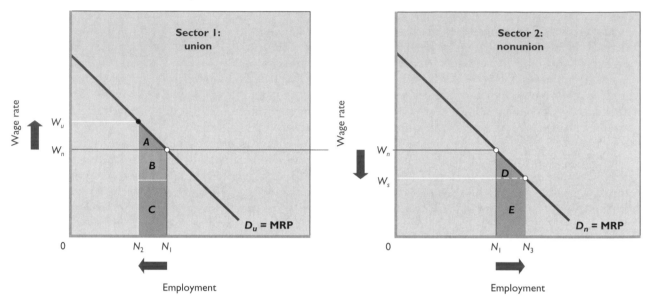

Attempts to estimate the output loss associated with union wage gains, however, suggest that the loss is small: perhaps .2 to .4 percent (or one-fifth of 1 percent to two-fifths of 1 percent) of U.S. GDP. In 2002 this cost would be about $21 billion to $42 billion, or $72 to $144 per person. **(Key Question 4)**

Positive View   Other economists take the position that, on balance, unions make a positive contribution to efficiency and productivity.

Longer-Run Positive Impacts: The Shock Effect
A wage increase won by a union may have a *shock effect* on affected firms, causing them in the long run to substitute capital for labor and in the very long run to implement productivity-increasing technologies. When faced with higher production costs due to the union wage increase, employers will be motivated to reduce costs by using more machinery and by seeking improved production techniques that use less of both labor and capital per unit of output. In fact, if the product market is reasonably competitive, a unionized firm with labor costs 10 to 15 percent higher than those of nonunionized competitors will not survive over long periods unless productivity can be raised. Hence, union wage pressure may generate man-

agerial actions that increase worker productivity and justify the higher union wages. If so, the overall economy benefits.

Reduced Worker Turnover   Unions may also contribute to raising productivity within firms through reduced worker turnover and improved worker security. A union functions as a *collective voice* for its members by taking their side in resolving disputes and improving working conditions.

If a group of workers are dissatisfied with their conditions of employment, they can respond in either of two ways: through the "exit mechanism" or through the "voice mechanism." With the **exit mechanism,** workers react to undesirable employers and working conditions by leaving their present jobs in search of better ones; they rely on the labor market. The use of this mechanism obviously increases worker turnover, the rate at which workers quit jobs and must be replaced.

With the **voice mechanism** workers communicate with the employer in an effort to improve working conditions and resolve worker grievances. It might be risky for individual workers to express their dissatisfaction to employers, because employers might retaliate by firing them as "troublemakers." But a union can provide workers with a collective voice to communicate problems and grievances to management and to press for satisfactory resolutions.

Unions may help reduce worker turnover in two ways:

- Unions provide the voice mechanism as a substitute for the exit mechanism. They use communication to correct job dissatisfactions that otherwise would be "resolved" by workers through the exit mechanism of changing jobs.
- The union wage advantage is a deterrent to job change. Higher wages make unionized firms more attractive places to work.

Compared with the rates at nonunion firms, the quit rate (resignation rate) for union workers is 31 to 65 percent lower, depending on the industry. A lower quit rate increases efficiency by giving a firm a more experienced, and thus a more productive, workforce. Also, having fewer resignations reduces the firm's recruitment, screening, and hiring costs. Finally, reduced turnover makes employers more willing to invest in the training (and therefore the productivity) of their workers. If a worker quits or "exits" at the end of, say, a year's training, the employer will get no return from providing that training. But lower turnover increases the likelihood that the employer will receive a return on the training it provides, thereby increasing its willingness to upgrade its workforce.

Increased Informal Training   Much productivity-increasing training is transmitted informally. Workers who are more skilled may share their experience with less skilled workers on the job, during lunch, or during coffee breaks. However, a skilled senior worker may want to conceal his or her knowledge from less skilled junior workers, who might become competitors for the skilled worker's job. Because of union insistence on the use of seniority in such matters as promotion and layoff, worker security is enhanced and this problem is overcome. With that security, senior workers are more willing to pass on their job knowledge and skills to new or subordinate workers. Such informal training enhances the quality and productivity of the firm's workforce.

Mixed Research Findings   Although many studies have tried to measure the effect of unionization on productivity, their results are inconclusive. For every study that finds that unions have a positive effect on productivity, another study using different methodology or data concludes that they have a negative effect. At present there simply is no generally accepted conclusion regarding the overall impact of unions on productivity.

QUICK REVIEW 35.2

- Union wages average about 15 percent higher than comparable nonunion wages.
- Union work rules, strikes, and the misallocation of labor associated with the union wage advantage are ways by which unions may reduce efficiency.
- Unions may enhance productivity by causing a shock effect, by reducing worker turnover, and by providing the worker security that is a prerequisite to informal on-the-job training.

Labor Market Discrimination

Broadly defined, **labor market discrimination** occurs when equivalent labor resources are paid or treated differently even though their productive contributions are equal. Table 35.1 shows various economic disparities by race, ethnicity, and gender. These statistical differences result from a combination of nondiscriminatory and discriminatory factors. For example, studies indicate that about one-half the differences in earnings between men and women and whites and blacks can be explained by such nondiscriminatory factors as differences in education, age, training, industry and occupation, union membership, location, work experience, continuity of work, and health. (Of course, some of these factors may be influenced by discrimination.) The other half is an unexplained difference, the bulk of which economists attribute to discrimination.

In labor market discrimination, certain groups of people are accorded inferior treatment with respect to hiring, occupational access, education and training, promotion, wage rates, or working conditions even though they have the same abilities, education and training, and experience as the more preferred groups. People who practice discrimination are said to exhibit a prejudice or bias against the targets of their discrimination.

Types of Discrimination

Labor market discrimination may take several forms:

- **Wage discrimination** occurs when women or members of minorities are paid less than white males for doing the same work. This kind of discrimination is declining because of its explicitness and the fact that it clearly violates Federal law. But wage discrimination can be subtle and difficult to detect. For example,

TABLE 35.1

Selected Economic Disparities by Gender, Race, and Ethnicity, 2001

Selected Measures	Blacks	Hispanics	Whites
Earnings and Income			
Median weekly earnings:			
Men	$ 518	$ 438	$ 694
Women	$ 451	$ 385	$ 521
Median income of families	$33,598	$34,490	$61,647
Percent of families in poverty	21.4	22.7	9.9
Labor-Force Participation and Employment			
Labor-force participation rate:			
Men	68.5	79.8	75.1
Women	62.9	56.8	59.7
Unemployment rate:			
Men	9.3	6.0	4.3
Women	8.1	7.4	4.1
Education			
Percent of population with at least 4 years of high school:*			
Men	79.5	55.5	88.6
Women	78.8	58.0	88.6
Percent of population with at least 4 years of college:			
Men	16.0	8.2	30.4
Women	18.2	13.3	36.9
Occupational Distribution (Percent of Group's Total Employment)			
Managerial and professional occupations:			
Men and women	22.6	14.6	31.9
Service occupations:			
Men and women	21.5	20.4	12.4

*Population 25 years or older.

Source: Bureau of Labor Statistics, www.bls.gov/; Census Bureau, www.census.gov/.

women and minorities sometimes find that their job classifications carry lower pay than job classifications held by white males, even though they are performing essentially the same tasks.

- **Employment discrimination** takes place when women or minority workers receive inferior treatment in hiring, promotions, assignments, temporary layoffs, and permanent discharges. This type of discrimination also encompasses sexual and racial harassment—demeaning treatment in the workplace by coworkers or administrators.
- **Occupational discrimination** occurs when women or minority workers are arbitrarily restricted or prohibited from entering the more desirable, higher-paying occupations. Businesswomen have found it difficult to break through the "glass ceiling" that prevents them from moving up to executive ranks. Blacks and Hispanics in executive and sales positions are relatively few. In addition, skilled and unionized work such as electrical work, bricklaying, and plumbing do not have high minority representation.
- **Human capital discrimination** occurs when women or members of minorities do not have the same access to productivity-enhancing investments in education and training as white males. Example: The lower average educational attainment (Table 35.1) of blacks and Hispanics has reduced their opportunities in the labor market.

Costs of Discrimination

Discrimination imposes costs on those who are discriminated against. The groups that discriminate get the good jobs and the better pay that are withheld from the targets of their discrimination. But discrimination does more than simply transfer benefits from women, blacks, and Hispanics to men and whites. Where it exists, discrimination actually diminishes the economy's output and income; like any other artificial barrier to free competition, it decreases economic efficiency and reduces production. By arbitrarily blocking certain qualified groups of people from high-productivity (and thus high-wage) jobs, discrimination prevents them from making their maximum contribution to the society's output, income, and well-being.

The effects of discrimination can be depicted as a point inside the economy's production possibilities curve, such as point D in Figure 35.3. At such a point, the economy obtains some combination of capital and consumption goods—here, $K_d + C_d$—which is less desirable than combinations represented by points such as X, Y, or Z on the curve. By preventing the economy from achieving productive efficiency, discrimination reduces the nation's real output and income.

FIGURE 35.3

Discrimination and production possibilities.   Discrimination represents a failure to achieve productive efficiency. The cost of discrimination to society is the sacrificed output associated with a point such as D inside the nation's production possibilities curve, compared with points such as X, Y, and Z on the curve.

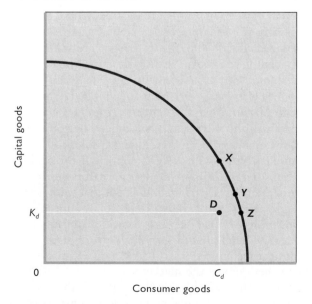

Economic Analysis of Discrimination

Prejudice reflects complex, multifaceted, and deeply ingrained beliefs and attitudes. Thus, economics can contribute some insights into discrimination but no detailed explanations. With this caution in mind, let's look more deeply into the economics of discrimination.

Taste-for-Discrimination Model

The **taste-for-discrimination model** examines prejudice by using the emotion-free language of demand theory. It views discrimination as resulting from a preference or taste for which the discriminator is willing to pay. The model assumes that, for whatever reason, prejudiced people experience a subjective or psychic cost—a disutility—whenever they must interact with those they are biased against. Consequently, they are willing to pay a certain "price" to avoid interactions with the nonpreferred group. The size of this price depends directly on the degree of prejudice.

35.1
Taste for discrimination model

The taste-for-discrimination model is general, since it can be applied to race, gender, age, and religion. But our discussion focuses on employer discrimination, in which employers discriminate against nonpreferred workers. For concreteness, we will look at a white employer discriminating against black workers.

Discrimination Coefficient   A prejudiced white employer behaves as if employing black workers would add a cost. The amount of this cost—this disutility—is reflected in a **discrimination coefficient,** d, measured in monetary units. Because the employer is not prejudiced against whites, the cost of employing a white worker is the white wage rate, W_w. However, the employer's perceived "cost" of employing a black worker is the black worker's wage rate, W_b, *plus* the cost d involved in the employer's prejudice, or $W_b + d$.

The prejudiced white employer will have no preference between black and white workers when the total cost per worker is the same, that is, when $W_w = W_b + d$. Suppose the market wage rate for whites is $10 and the monetary value of the disutility the employer attaches to hiring blacks is $2 (that is, $d = 2). This employer will be indifferent between hiring blacks and whites only when the black wage rate is $8, since at this wage the perceived cost of hiring either a white or a black worker is $10:

$10 white wage = $8 black wage + $2 discrimination coefficient

It follows that our prejudiced white employer will hire blacks only if their wage rate is sufficiently below that of whites. By "sufficiently" we mean at least the amount of the discrimination coefficient.

The greater a white employer's taste for discrimination as reflected in the value of d, the larger the difference between white wages and the lower wages at which blacks will be hired. A "color-blind" employer whose d is $0 will hire equally productive blacks and whites impartially if their wages are the same. A blatantly prejudiced white employer whose d is infinity would refuse to hire blacks even if the black wage were zero.

Most prejudiced white employers will not refuse to hire blacks under all conditions. They will, in fact, *prefer* to hire blacks if the actual white-black wage difference in the market exceeds the value of d. In our example, if whites can be hired at $10 and equally productive blacks at only $7.50, the biased white employer will hire blacks. That employer is willing to pay a wage difference of up to $2 per hour for whites to satisfy his or her bias, but no more. At the $2.50 actual difference, the employer will hire blacks.

Conversely, if whites can be hired at $10 and blacks at $8.50, whites will be hired. Again, the biased employer is willing to pay a wage difference of up to $2 for whites; a $1.50 actual difference means that hiring whites is a "bargain" for this employer.

Prejudice and the Market Black-White Wage Ratio

For a particular supply of black workers, the actual black-white wage ratio—the ratio determined in the labor market—will depend on the collective prejudice of white employers. To see why, consider Figure 35.4, which shows a labor market for *black* workers. Initially, suppose the relevant labor demand curve is D_1, so the equilibrium *black* wage is $8 and the equilibrium level of black employment is 16 million. If we assume that the *white* wage (not shown) is $10, then the initial black-white wage ratio is .80 (= $8/$10).

Now assume that prejudice against black workers increases—that is, the collective d of white employers rises. An increase in d means an increase in the perceived cost of black labor at each black wage rate, and that reduces the demand for black labor, say, from D_1 to D_2. The black wage rate falls from $8 to $6 in the market, and the level of black employment declines from 16 million to 12 million. The increase in white employer prejudice reduces the black wage rate and thus the actual black-white wage ratio. If the white wage rate remains at $10, the new black-white ratio is .6 (= $6/$10).

Conversely, suppose social attitudes change such that white employers become less biased and their discrimination coefficient as a group declines. This decreases the

FIGURE 35.4

The black wage and employment level in the taste-for-discrimination model. An increase in prejudice by white employers as reflected in higher discrimination coefficients would decrease the demand for black workers, here from D_1 to D_2, and reduce the black wage rate and level of black employment. Not shown, this drop in the black wage rate would lower the black-white wage ratio. In contrast, if prejudice were reduced such that discrimination coefficients of employers declined, the demand for black labor would increase, as from D_1 to D_3, boosting the black wage rate and level of employment. The higher black wage rate would increase the black-white wage ratio.

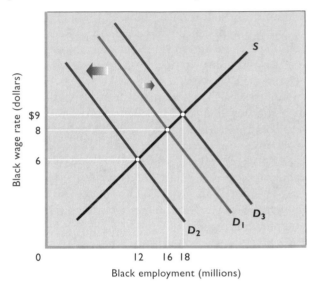

perceived cost of black labor at each black wage rate, so the demand for black labor increases, as from D_1 to D_3. In this case, the black wage rate rises to $9, and employment of black workers increases to 18 million. The decrease in white employer prejudice increases the black wage rate and thus the actual black-white wage ratio. If the white wage remains at $10, the new black-white wage ratio is .9 (= $9/$10).

Competition and Discrimination

The taste-for-discrimination model suggests that competition will reduce discrimination in the very long run, as follows: The actual black-white wage difference for equally productive workers—say, $2—allows nondiscriminators to hire blacks for less than whites. Firms that hire black workers will therefore have lower actual wage costs per unit of output and lower average total costs than will the firms that discriminate. These lower costs will allow nondiscriminators to underprice discriminating competitors, eventually driving them out of the market.

But critics of this implication of the taste-for-discrimination model say that it overlooks entry barriers to new firms and point out that progress in eliminating racial discrimination has been modest. Discrimination based on race has persisted in the United States and other market economies decade after decade. To explain why, economists have proposed alternative models. **(Key Question 7)**

Statistical Discrimination

A second theory of discrimination centers on the concept of **statistical discrimination,** in which *people are judged on the basis of the average characteristics of the group to which they belong, rather than on their own personal characteristics or productivity.* For example, insurance rates for teenage males are higher than those for teenage females. The difference is based on factual evidence indicating that, on average, young males are more likely than young females to be in accidents. But many young men are actually less accident-prone than the average young woman, and those men are discriminated against by having to pay higher insurance rates. The uniqueness of the theory of statistical discrimination is its suggestion that discriminatory outcomes are possible even where there is no prejudice.

Labor Market Example
How does statistical discrimination show itself in labor markets? Employers with job openings want to hire the most productive workers available. They have their personnel department collect information concerning each job applicant, including age, education, and prior work experience. They may supplement that information with preemployment tests, which they feel are helpful indicators of potential job performance. But it is very expensive to collect detailed information about job applicants, and it is difficult to predict job performance on the basis of limited data. Consequently, some employers looking for inexpensive information may consider the *average* characteristics of women and minorities in determining whom to hire. They are in fact practicing statistical discrimination when they do so. They are using gender, race, or ethnic background as a crude indicator of production-related attributes.

Example: Suppose an employer who plans to invest heavily in training a worker knows that on average women are less likely to be career-oriented than men, more likely to quit work in order to care for young children, and more likely to refuse geographic transfers. Thus, on average, the return on the employer's investment in training is likely to be less when choosing a woman than when choosing a man. All else equal, when choosing between two job applicants, one a woman and the other a man, this employer is likely to hire the man.

Note what is happening here. Average characteristics for a *group* are being applied to *individual* members of that group. The employer is falsely assuming that *each and every* woman worker has the same employment tendencies as the *average* woman. Such stereotyping means that numerous women who are career-oriented, who plan to work after having children, and who are flexible as to geographic transfers will be discriminated against.

Profitable, Undesirable, but Not Malicious
The firm that practices statistical discrimination is not being malicious in its hiring behavior (although it may be violating antidiscrimination laws). The decisions it makes will be rational and profitable because *on average* its hiring decisions are likely to be correct. Nevertheless, many people suffer because of statistical discrimination, since it blocks the economic betterment of capable people. And since it is profitable, statistical discrimination tends to persist.

Occupational Segregation: The Crowding Model

The practice of **occupational segregation**—*the crowding of women, blacks, and certain ethnic groups into less desirable, lower-paying occupations*—is still apparent in the U.S. economy. Statistics indicate that women are disproportionately concentrated in a limited number of occupations such as teaching, nursing, and secretarial and clerical jobs. Blacks and Hispanics are crowded into low-paying jobs such as those of laundry workers, cleaners and household aides, hospital orderlies, agricultural workers, and other manual laborers.

Let's look at a model of occupational segregation, using women and men as an example.

The Model
The character and income consequences of occupational discrimination are revealed through a labor supply and demand model. We make the following assumptions:
- The labor force is equally divided between men and women workers. Let's say there are 6 million male and 6 million female workers.
- The economy comprises three occupations, X, Y, and Z, with identical labor demand curves, as shown in Figure 35.5.
- Men and women have the same labor-force characteristics; each of the three occupations could be filled equally well by men or by women.

Effects of Crowding
Suppose that, as a consequence of discrimination, the 6 million women are excluded from occupations X and Y and crowded into occupation Z, where they earn wage W. The men distribute themselves equally among occupations X and Y, meaning that

FIGURE 35.5

The economics of occupational segregation.   By crowding women into one occupation, men enjoy high wage rates of M in occupations X and Y, while women receive low wages of W in occupation Z. The elimination of discrimination will equalize wage rates at B and result in a net increase in the nation's output.

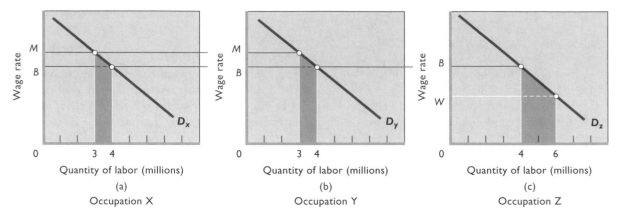

| (a) | (b) | (c) |
| Occupation X | Occupation Y | Occupation Z |

3 million male workers are in each occupation and have a common wage of M. (If we assume that there are no barriers to mobility between X and Y, any initially different distribution of males between X and Y would result in a wage differential between the two occupations. That would prompt labor shifts from the low- to the high-wage occupation until an equal distribution occurred.)

Because women are crowded into occupation Z, labor supply (not shown) is larger and their wage rate W is much lower than M. Because of the discrimination, this is an equilibrium situation that will persist as long as the crowding occurs. The occupational barrier means women cannot move into occupations X and Y in pursuit of a higher wage.

The result is a loss of output for society. To see why, recall again that labor demand reflects labor's marginal revenue product, which is labor's contribution to domestic output. Thus, the blue areas for occupations X and Y in Figure 35.5 show the decrease in domestic output—the market value of the marginal output—caused by subtracting 1 million women from each of these occupations. Similarly, the green area for occupation Z shows the increase in domestic output caused by moving 2 million women into occupation Z. Although society would gain the added output represented by the green area in occupation Z, it would lose the output represented by the sum of the two blue areas in occupations X and Y. That output loss exceeds the output gain, producing a net output loss for society.

Eliminating Occupational Segregation   Now assume that through legislation or sweeping changes in social attitudes, discrimination disappears. Women, attracted by higher wage rates, shift from occupation Z to X and Y; 1 million women move into X and another 1 million move into Y. Now there are 4 million workers in Z, and occupational segregation is eliminated. At that point there are 4 million workers in each occupation, and wage rates in all three occupations are equal, here at B. That wage equality eliminates the incentive for further reallocations of labor.

The new, nondiscriminatory equilibrium clearly benefits women, who now receive higher wages; it hurts men, who now receive lower wages. But women were initially harmed and men benefited through discrimination; removing discrimination corrects that situation.

Society also gains. The elimination of occupational segregation reverses the net output loss just discussed. Adding 1 million women to each of occupations X and Y in Figure 35.5 increases domestic output by the sum of the two blue areas. The decrease in domestic output caused by losing 2 million women from occupation Z is shown by the green area. The sum of the two increases in domestic output in X and Y exceeds the decrease in domestic output in Z. With the end of the discrimination, 2 million women workers have moved from occupation Z, where their contribution to domestic output (their MRP) is low, to higher-paying occupations X and Y, where their contribution to domestic output is high. Thus society gains a more efficient allocation of resources from the removal of occupational discrimination. (In terms of Figure 35.3, society moves from a point inside its production possibilities curve to a point closer to, or on, the curve.)

Example: The easing of occupational barriers has led to a surge of women gaining advanced degrees in some high-paying professions. In recent years, for instance, the percentage of law degrees and medical degrees awarded to women has exceeded 40 percent, compared with less than 10 percent in 1970. **(Key Question 9)**

QUICK REVIEW 35.3

- Discrimination reduces domestic output and occurs when workers who have the same abilities, education, training, and experience as other workers receive inferior treatment with respect to hiring, occupational access, promotion, or wages.

- Nondiscriminatory factors explain about one-half of the gender and racial earnings gaps; most of the remaining one-half is thought to reflect discrimination.

- The taste-for-discrimination model sees discrimination as representing a preference or "taste" for which the discriminator is willing to pay.

- The theory of statistical discrimination says that employers often wrongly judge individuals on the basis of average group characteristics rather than on personal characteristics, thus harming those discriminated against.

- The crowding model of discrimination suggests that when women and minorities are systematically excluded from high-paying occupations and crowded into low-paying ones, their wages and society's domestic output are reduced.

Antidiscrimination Policies and Issues

The government has several ways of dealing with discrimination. One indirect policy is to promote a strong, growing economy. An expanding demand for products increases the demand for all workers. When the economy is at or near full employment, prejudiced employers must pay higher and higher wages to entice preferred workers away from other employers. Many, perhaps most, such employers are likely to decide that their taste for discrimination is not worth the cost. Tight labor markets also help overcome stereotyping. Once women and minorities obtain good jobs in tight labor markets, they have an opportunity to show they can do the work as well as white males.

A second indirect antidiscrimination policy is to improve the education and training opportunities of women and minorities. For example, upgrading the quantity and quality of schooling received by blacks and Hispanics will make them more competitive with whites for higher-paying positions.

The third way of reducing discrimination is through direct government intervention. As summarized in Table 35.2, the U.S. government has outlawed certain practices in hiring, promotion, and compensation and has required that government contractors take affirmative action to hire more women and minorities.

The Affirmative Action Controversy

Consider the last item in Table 35.2. **Affirmative action** consists of special efforts by employers to increase employment and promotion opportunities for groups that have suffered past discrimination and continue to experience discrimination. Saying that affirmative action has

---

TABLE 35.2

Major Antidiscrimination Laws and Policies in the United States

Equal Pay Act of 1963   Makes it illegal to pay men and women different wage rates if they "do equal work on jobs, the performance of which requires equal skill, effort, and responsibility, and which are performed under similar working conditions."

Title VII of the Civil Rights Act of 1964   Makes it unlawful for any employer "to refuse to hire or to discharge any individual, or otherwise to discriminate against any individual with respect to compensation, terms, conditions, or privileges of employment, because of such individual's race, color, religion, sex, or national origin."

Affirmative action requirement   Presidential executive orders issued in 1965 and 1968 outlaw discriminatory practices of businesses and other institutions holding government contracts. The 1968 order also states that the "contractor will take *affirmative action* to ensure that applicants are employed, and that employees are treated during employment, without regard to their race, color, religion, sex, or national origin." This affirmative action was to apply to employment, upgrading, demotion, and transfer; recruitment and recruitment advertising; layoff and termination; rates of pay and other forms of compensation; and selection for training, including apprenticeships.

stirred controversy is an understatement. There are strong arguments for and against this approach to remedying discrimination.

In Support of Affirmative Action

Those who support affirmative action say that historically women and minorities have been forced to carry the extra burden of discrimination in their attempt to achieve economic success. Thus, they find themselves far behind white males, who have been preferred workers. Merely removing the discrimination burden does nothing to close the present socioeconomic gap. Aggressive action to hire women and minorities, not just equal opportunity, is necessary to counter the inherent bias in favor of white men if women and minorities are to catch up.

Supporters of affirmative action argue that job discrimination is so pervasive that it will persist for decades if society is content to accept only marginal antidiscriminatory changes in employment practices. Moreover, such changes are hampered by the fact that white males have achieved on-the-job seniority, which protects them from layoffs and places the burden of unemployment disproportionately on women and minorities. And women and minorities have been discriminated against in acquiring human capital: the education and job training needed to compete on equal terms with white males. Discrimination has supposedly become so highly institutionalized that extraordinary countermeasures are required.

Those who accept this line of reasoning endorse affirmative action and even preferential treatment as appropriate means for hastening the elimination of discrimination. In this view, affirmative action is not only a path toward social equity but also a good national strategy for enhancing efficiency and economic growth, since it brings formerly excluded groups directly into the productive economic mainstream.

Opposing View

Those who oppose affirmative action claim that it often goes beyond aggressive recruitment to become preferential treatment. In this view, affirmative action has sometimes prodded employers to hire less qualified women and minority workers. So economic efficiency is impaired. They also insist that preferential treatment is simply **reverse discrimination.** Preferential treatment and discrimination, they say, are simply two views of the same thing: To show preference for A is to discriminate against B.

Some opponents of affirmative action go further, contending that policies that give preferential treatment to disadvantaged groups have actually worked to the long-term detriment of those groups. Such policies, they say,

have had two effects, both negative: First, majority workers who have themselves been passed over for jobs or promotions resent those who are given special treatment. Second, others may mistakenly stereotype the highly qualified women and minority members of the workforce, who have no need of preferential treatment, as "affirmative action hires." In this highly controversial view, continuing racial tension not only reflects the long legacy of discrimination but also the well-meant but ill-conceived affirmative action policy designed to end it.

Recent Developments

Affirmative action has recently come under harsh legal and political attack. A series of important Supreme Court decisions in 1986 and 1987 upheld the constitutionality of affirmative action programs, but subsequent decisions have undermined some of those programs. For example, in 1989 the Court declared illegal a program by the city of Richmond, Virginia, that was designed to provide a specified proportion of the city's construction work to minority-owned firms; the Court argued that the program constituted reverse discrimination. Another 1989 ruling permitted white firefighters in Birmingham, Alabama, to challenge an existing affirmative action program on grounds that the program denied them promotions in favor of less qualified blacks. That ruling triggered a number of reverse-discrimination lawsuits throughout the country. Other Court rulings have made it necessary for minorities to prove that job discrimination exists in a particular firm, not just in the overall industry or economy.

In mid-1995 the Court ruled that race-based preferences in Federal programs could be allowed only if the programs are "narrowly tailored" to remedy identifiable past discrimination in a particular firm or government entity. A Federal circuit court of appeals ruled later that year that public universities in Texas, Mississippi, and Louisiana may not justify affirmative action programs by citing the benefits of racial diversity. Later that year, the Supreme Court let this ruling stand.

On the political scene, in 1996 Congress debated legislation intended to restrict affirmative action, and the Clinton administration halted several Federal minority programs designed to give preference to minorities in Federal contracting. In 1996 Californians voted in favor of a state constitutional amendment ending all state programs that give gender or racial preferences in government hiring and contracting, as well as in public education. A year later, Washington state also passed a law that ended affirmative action in the public sector.

Immigration

Immigration has long been a focus of controversy. Should more or fewer people be allowed to migrate to the United States? How should the problem of illegal entrants be handled?

Number of Immigrants

The annual flow of **legal immigrants** (who have permission to reside in the United States) was roughly 250,000 in the 1950s, 320,000 in the 1960s, and 500,000 to 600,000 during the 1970s and 1980s. In the 1990s, immigration averaged about 850,000 per year. About one-third of annual U.S. population growth in recent years has resulted from immigration. (Global Perspective 35.2 shows the countries of origin of U.S. legal immigrants in 2001.)

Such data are imperfect, however, because they do not include **illegal immigrants,** those who arrive without permission. The Census Bureau estimates that the net inflow of illegal immigrants (illegal aliens) is now about 100,000 per year, most coming from Mexico, the Caribbean, and Central America.

Economics of Immigration

Figure 35.6 provides some insight into the economic effects of immigration. In Figure 35.6a, D_u is the demand for labor in the United States; in Figure 35.6b, D_m is the demand for labor in Mexico. The demand for labor is greater in the United States, presumably because the nation has more capital and more advanced technologies that enhance the productivity of labor. (Recall from Chapter 27 that the labor demand curve is based on the marginal revenue productivity of labor.) Conversely, since machinery and equipment are presumably scarce in Mexico and technology less sophisticated, labor demand there is weak. We also assume that the before-migration labor forces of the

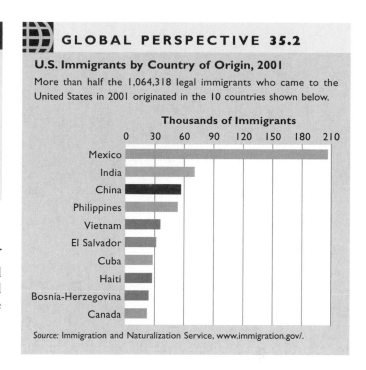

GLOBAL PERSPECTIVE 35.2

U.S. Immigrants by Country of Origin, 2001

More than half the 1,064,318 legal immigrants who came to the United States in 2001 originated in the 10 countries shown below.

Source: Immigration and Naturalization Service, www.immigration.gov/.

United States and Mexico are c and C, respectively, and that both countries are at full employment.

Wage Rates and World Output   If we further assume that migration (1) has no cost, (2) occurs solely in response to wage differentials, and (3) is unimpeded by law in either country, then workers will migrate from Mexico to the United States until wage rates in the two countries are equal at W_e. At that level, CF (equals cf) workers will have migrated from Mexico to the United States. Although the U.S. wage level will fall from W_u to W_e, domestic output (the sum of the marginal revenue products of the entire workforce) will increase from $0abc$ to $0adf$. In Mexico, the wage rate will rise from W_m to W_e, but domestic output will decline there from $0ABC$ to $0ADF$. Because the gain in domestic output $cbdf$ in the United States exceeds the output loss $FDBC$ in Mexico, the world's output has increased.

We can conclude that the elimination of barriers to the international flow of labor tends to increase worldwide economic efficiency. The world gains because the freedom to migrate enables people to move to countries where they can make larger contributions to world production. Migration involves an efficiency gain. It enables the world to produce a larger real output with a given amount of resources.

Income Shares   Our model also suggests that the flow of immigrants will enhance business income (or capitalist

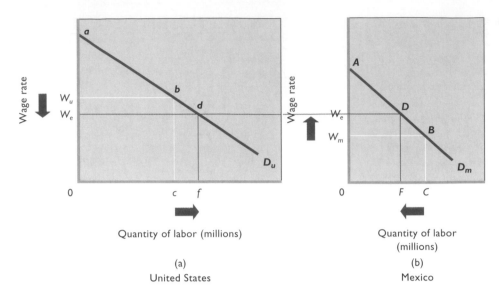

income) in the United States and reduce it in Mexico. As just noted, before-immigration domestic output in the United States is represented by area $0abc$. The total wage bill is $0W_u bc$—the wage rate multiplied by the number of workers. The remaining triangular area $W_u ab$ represents business income before immigration. The same reasoning applies to Mexico, where $W_m AB$ is before-immigration business income.

Unimpeded immigration increases business income from $W_u ab$ to $W_e ad$ in the United States and reduces it from $W_m AB$ to $W_e AD$ in Mexico. U.S. businesses benefit from immigration; Mexican businesses are hurt by emigration. This is what we would expect intuitively; the United States is gaining "cheap" labor, and Mexico is losing "cheap" labor. This conclusion is consistent with the historical fact that U.S. employers have often actively recruited immigrants.

35.1 Immigration

Complications and Modifications

Our model includes some simplifying assumptions and overlooks a relevant factor. We now relax some of the assumptions and introduce the omitted factor to see how our conclusions are affected.

Costs of Migration   We assumed that international movement of workers is without personal cost, but obviously it is not. There are both the explicit, out-of-pocket costs of physically moving a worker and his or her possessions and the implicit opportunity cost of lost income while the worker is moving and becoming established in the new country. Still more subtle costs are involved in adapting to a new culture, language, climate, and so forth. All such costs must be estimated by the potential immigrant and weighed against the expected benefits of higher wages in the new country. A person who estimates that benefits exceed costs will migrate; a person who sees costs as exceeding benefits will stay put.

In terms of Figure 35.6, the existence of migration costs means that the flow of labor from Mexico to the United States will stop short of that needed to close the wage differential entirely. Wages will remain somewhat higher in the United States than in Mexico; the wage difference will not cause further migration and close up the wage gap because the marginal benefit of the higher wage will not cover the marginal cost of migration. Thus, the world production gain from migration will be reduced, since wages will not equalize.

Remittances and Backflows   Most migration is permanent; workers who acquire skills in the receiving country tend not to return home. However, some migrants view their moves as temporary. They move to a more highly developed country, accumulate some wealth or education through hard work and frugality, and return home to establish their own enterprises. During their time in the new country, migrants frequently make sizable remittances to their families at home. That causes a redistribution of the net gain from migration between the countries involved. In Figure 35.6, remittances by Mexican workers in the United States to their relatives in Mexico would cause the gain in U.S. domestic output to be less than shown and the loss to Mexican domestic output also to be less than shown.

Actual backflows—the return of migrants to their home country—might also alter gains and losses through time. For example, if some Mexican workers who migrated to the United States acquired substantial labor market or managerial skills and then returned home, their enhanced human capital might make a substantial contribution to economic development in Mexico.

Full Employment versus Unemployment Our model assumes full employment in the sending and receiving countries. Mexican workers presumably leave low-paying jobs to take (more or less immediately) higher-paying jobs in the United States. However, in many cases the factor that "pushes" immigrants from their homelands is not low wages but chronic unemployment and underemployment. Many developing countries are overpopulated and have surplus labor; workers are either unemployed or so grossly underemployed that their marginal revenue product is zero.

If we allow for this possibility, then Mexico actually gains (not loses) by having such workers emigrate. The unemployed workers are making no contribution to Mexico's domestic output and must be sustained by transfers from the rest of the labor force. The remaining Mexican labor force will be better off by the amount of the transfers after the unemployed workers have migrated to the United States. Conversely, if the Mexican immigrant workers are unable to find jobs in the United States and are sustained through transfers from employed U.S. workers, then the after-tax income of working Americans will decline.

Fiscal Impacts What effects do immigrants have on tax revenues and government spending in the receiving country? Are immigrants contributors to output, or do they go on welfare and become a drain on the national treasury?

Prior to the 1970s, the immigrant population was less likely to receive public assistance than people born in the United States. Migrants were typically young, single men with significant education and job training. Thus they were readily employable and were net contributors. Illegal immigrants avoided the welfare system for fear of detection and deportation.

But since the 1970s the situation has reversed, and immigrants now use the welfare system proportionately more than natives. The main factor in the turnabout is the changing mix of immigrants, which today includes relatively fewer skilled workers and more unskilled workers. In fact, prior to its overhaul in 1996, critics of the U.S. welfare system claimed it was drawing unskilled (and

often illegal) workers to the United States from some of the world's poorest nations. Indeed, immigrants made up more than 10 percent of Supplemental Security Income (SSI) rolls in 1998, compared with only 3.3 percent a decade earlier. As a result of this trend, the 1996 welfare reform (Personal Responsibility Act) denied welfare benefits to new immigrants for their first 5 years in the United States. **(Key Question 12)**

Immigration: Two Views

As we have noted, the traditional perception of immigration is that it consists of young, ambitious workers seeking opportunity in the United States. They are destined for success because of the courage and determination they exhibit in leaving their cultural roots to improve their lives. These energetic workers increase the supply of goods and services with their labor and simultaneously increase the demand for goods and services with their incomes and spending. In short, immigration is an engine of economic progress.

The counterview is that immigration is a socioeconomic drag on the receiving country. Immigrants compete with domestic workers for scarce jobs, pull down the average level of real wages, and burden the U.S. welfare system.

Both these views are somewhat simplistic. Immigration can either benefit or harm the receiving nation, depending on the number of immigrants; their education, skills, and work ethic; and the rate at which they can be absorbed into the economy without disruption. From a strictly economic perspective, nations seeking to maximize net benefits from immigration should expand immigration until its marginal benefits equal its marginal costs. The MB = MC conceptual framework explicitly recognizes that there can be too few immigrants, just as there can be too many. Moreover, it recognizes that from a strictly economic standpoint, not all immigrants are alike. The immigration of, say, a highly educated scientist has a different impact on the economy than does the immigration of a long-term welfare recipient.

QUICK REVIEW 35.5

- All else equal, immigration reduces wages, increases domestic output, and increases business income in the receiving nation; it has the opposite effects in the sending nation.
- Assessing the impacts of immigration is complicated by such factors as unemployment, backflows and remittances, and fiscal effects.

Have "Blind" Musical Auditions, in Which "Screens" Are Used to Hide the Identity of Candidates, Affected the Success of Women in Obtaining Positions in Major Symphony Orchestras?

There have long been allegations of discrimination against women in the hiring process in some occupations. But such discrimination is usually difficult to demonstrate. Economists Claudia Goldin and Cecilia Rouse spotted a unique opportunity for testing such discrimination as it relates to major symphony orchestras. In the past, orchestras relied on their musical directors to extend invitations to candidates, audition them, and handpick new members. Concerned with the potential for hiring bias, in the 1970s and 1980s orchestras altered the process in two ways. First, orchestra members were included as judges, and, second, orchestras began open competitions using "blind" auditions with a physical "screen" (usually a room divider) to conceal the identity of the candidates. (These blind auditions, however, did not extend to the final competition in most orchestras.) Did the change in procedures increase the probability of women being hired?

To answer this question, Goldin and Rouse gained access to orchestral management files to examine auditions for eight major orchestras. These records contained the names of all candidates and identified those who advanced to the next round, including the ultimate winner of the competition. The researchers then looked for women in the sample who had "competed" in auditions both before and after the introduction of the blind screening.

There was a strong suspicion of bias against women in hiring musicians for the nation's finest orchestras. These positions are highly desirous, not only because they are prestigious but also because they offer high pay (often more than $75,000 annually). In 1970 only 5 percent of the members of the top five orchestras in the United States were women, and many music directors publicly suggested that women players, in general, have less musical talent.

The change to screens provided direct evidence of past discrimination. The screens increased by 50 percent the probability that a woman would be advanced from the preliminary rounds. The screens also greatly increased the likelihood that a woman would be selected in the final round. Without the screens about 10 percent of all hires were women, but with the screens about 35 percent were women. Today, about 25 percent of the members of top symphony orchestras are women, in contrast to the 5 percent in 1970. The screens explain from 25 to 45 percent of the increases in the proportion of women in the orchestras studied.

Was the past discrimination in hiring an example of statistical discrimination based on, say, a presumption of greater turnover by women or more leaves for medical (including maternity) or other reasons? To answer that question, Goldin and Rouse examined information on turnover and leaves of orchestra members for the period 1960–1996. They found that neither differed by gender, so leaves and turnover should not have influenced hiring decisions.

Instead, the discrimination in hiring seemed to reflect a taste for discrimination by musical directors. Male musical directors apparently had a positive discrimination coefficient d. At the fixed (union-determined) wage, they simply preferred male musicians, at women's expense.

Source: Claudia Goldin and Cecilia Rouse, "Orchestrating Impartiality: The Impact of 'Blind' Auditions on Female Musicians," *American Economic Review*, September 2000, pp. 715–741.

SUMMARY

1. Currently there are about 16 million union workers in the United States, with most of them belonging to the loose federation called the AFL-CIO. Unionism has declined relatively in the United States since the mid-1950s. Some economists attribute this decline to changes in the composition of domestic output and in the demographic structure of the labor force. Others contend that employers, recognizing that unions reduce profitability, have more aggressively sought to dissuade workers from becoming union members.

2. Labor and management "live together" under the terms of collective bargaining agreements. Those agreements cover (a) union status and managerial prerogatives; (b) wages, hours, and working conditions; (c) seniority and job control; and (d) a grievance procedure.

3. There is disagreement about whether unions increase or decrease efficiency and productivity. The negative view cites (a) inefficiencies associated with featherbedding and union-imposed work rules, (b) loss of output through strikes, and (c) the misallocation of labor caused by the union wage advantage. The positive view holds that (a) through the shock effect, union wage pressure spurs technological advance and mechanization of the production process; (b) as collective-voice institutions, unions contribute to rising productivity by reducing labor turnover; and (c) the enhanced security of union workers increases their willingness to teach their skills to less experienced workers.

4. Discrimination relating to the labor market occurs when women or minorities having the same abilities, education, training, and experience as men or white workers are given inferior treatment with respect to hiring, occupational choice, education and training, promotion, and wage rates. Forms of discrimination include wage discrimination, employment discrimination, occupational discrimination, and human capital discrimination. Discrimination redistributes national income and, by creating inefficiencies, diminishes its size.

5. In the taste-for-discrimination model, some white employers have a preference for discrimination, measured by a discrimination coefficient *d*. Prejudiced white employers will hire black workers only if their wages are at least *d* dollars

below those of whites. The model indicates that declines in the discrimination coefficients of white employers will increase the demand for black workers, raising the black wage rate and the ratio of black wages to white wages. It also suggests that competition may eliminate discrimination in the long run.

6. Statistical discrimination occurs when employers base employment decisions about *individuals* on the average characteristics of *groups* of workers. That can lead to discrimination against individuals even in the absence of prejudice.

7. The crowding model of occupational segregation indicates how white males gain higher earnings at the expense of women and minorities who are confined to a limited number of occupations. The model shows that discrimination also causes a net loss of domestic output.

8. Government antidiscrimination legislation and policies that involve direct government intervention include the Equal Pay Act of 1963, Title VII of the Civil Rights Act of 1964, and executive orders applicable to Federal contractors. The executive orders included requirements that these firms enact affirmative action programs to benefit women and certain minority groups.

9. Those who support affirmative action say it is needed to help women and minorities compensate for decades of discrimination. Opponents say affirmative action causes economic inefficiency and reverse discrimination. Recent Supreme Court decisions have limited the use of affirmative action programs to situations where past discrimination is clearly identifiable.

10. Supply and demand analysis suggests that the movement of migrants from a poor country to a rich country (a) increases domestic output in the rich country, (b) reduces the average wage in the rich country, and (c) increases business income in the rich country. The opposite effects occur in the poor country, but the world as a whole realizes a larger total output.

11. The outcomes of immigration predicted by simple supply and demand analysis become more complicated upon consideration of (a) the costs of moving, (b) the possibility of remittances and backflows, (c) the level of unemployment in each country, and (d) the fiscal impact on the taxpayers of each country.

TERMS AND CONCEPTS

American Federation of Labor and Congress of Industrial Organizations (AFL-CIO)

independent unions

business unionism

structural-change hypothesis

managerial-opposition hypothesis

collective bargaining

closed shop

union shop

agency shop

right-to-work laws

open shop

cost-of-living adjustment (COLA)

strike

lockout

National Labor Relations Act (NLRA)

National Labor Relations Board (NLRB)

exit mechanism

voice mechanism

labor market discrimination

wage discrimination

employment discrimination

occupational discrimination

human capital discrimination

taste-for-discrimination model

discrimination coefficient

statistical discrimination

occupational segregation

affirmative action

reverse discrimination

legal immigrants

illegal immigrants

STUDY QUESTIONS

1. Other things equal, who is more likely to be a union member: Stephen, who works as a salesperson at a furniture store, or Susan, who works as a machinist for an aircraft manufacturer? Explain.

2. Contrast the structural-change and managerial-opposition hypotheses as they relate to the decline in unionism. Which view do you think is more convincing?

3. Suppose that you are president of a newly established local union about to bargain with an employer for the first time. List the basic areas you want covered in the work agreement. Why might you begin with a larger wage demand than you actually are willing to accept?

4. *Key Question* What is the estimated size of the union wage advantage? How might this advantage diminish the efficiency with which labor resources are allocated?

5. Explain the logic of each of the following statements:
   a. By constraining the decisions of management, unions reduce efficiency and productivity growth.
   b. As collective-voice institutions, unions increase productivity by reducing worker turnover, inducing managerial efficiency, and enhancing worker security.

6. Explain how discrimination reduces domestic output and income. Demonstrate that loss using production possibilities analysis.

7. *Key Question* The labor demand and supply data in the following table relate to a single occupation. Use them to answer the questions that follow. Base your answers on the taste-for-discrimination model.

Quantity of Hispanic Labor Demanded, Thousands	Hispanic Wage Rate	Quantity of Hispanic Labor Supplied, Thousands
24	$16	52
30	14	44
35	12	35
42	10	28
48	8	20

a. Plot the labor demand and supply curves for Hispanic workers in this occupation.

b. What are the equilibrium Hispanic wage rate and quantity of Hispanic employment?

c. Suppose the white wage rate in this occupation is $16. What is the Hispanic-to-white wage ratio?

d. Suppose a particular employer has a discrimination coefficient d of $5 per hour. Will that employer hire Hispanic or white workers at the Hispanic-white wage ratio indicated in part c? Explain.

e. Suppose employers as a group become less prejudiced against Hispanics and demand 14 more units of Hispanic labor at each Hispanic wage rate in the table. What are the new equilibrium Hispanic wage rate and level of Hispanic employment? Does the Hispanic-white wage ratio rise or fall? Explain.

f. Suppose Hispanics as a group increase their labor services in that occupation, collectively offering 14 more units of labor at each Hispanic wage rate. Disregarding the changes indicated in part e, what are the new equilibrium Hispanic wage rate and level of Hispanic employment? Does the Hispanic-white wage ratio rise, or does it fall?

8. Males under the age of 25 must pay far higher auto insurance premiums than females in this age group. How does this fact relate to statistical discrimination? Statistical discrimination implies that discrimination can persist indefinitely, while the taste-for-discrimination model suggests that competition might reduce discrimination in the long run. Explain the difference.

9. *Key Question* Use a demand and supply model to explain the impact of occupational segregation or "crowding" on the relative wage rates and earnings of men and women. Who gains and who loses from the elimination of occupational segregation? Is there a net gain or a net loss to society? Explain.

10. "Current affirmative action programs are based on the belief that to overcome discrimination, we must practice discrimination. That perverse logic has created a system that undermines the fundamental values it was intended to protect." Do you agree? Why or why not?

11. Suppose Ann and Becky are applicants to your university and that they have identical admission qualifications (SAT

scores, high school GPA, etc.). Ann, who is black, grew up in a public housing development; Becky, who is white, grew up in a wealthy suburb. You can admit only one of the two. Which would you admit and why? Now suppose that Ann is white and Becky is black, all else equal. Does that change your selection? Why or why not?

12. *Key Question* Use graphical analysis to show the gains and losses resulting from the migration of population from a low-income country to a high-income country. Explain how your conclusions are affected by (*a*) unemployment, (*b*) remittances to the home country, (*c*) backflows of migrants to their home country, and (*d*) the personal characteristics of the migrants. If the migrants are highly skilled workers, is there any justification for the sending country to levy a "brain drain" tax on emigrants?

13. If a person favors the free movement of labor within the United States, is it then inconsistent to also favor restrictions on the international movement of labor? Why or why not?

14. Evaluate: "If the United States deported, say, 1 million illegal immigrants, the number of unemployed workers in the United States would decline by 1 million."

15. *(Last Word)* What two types of discrimination are represented by the discrimination evidenced in this chapter's Last Word?

16. *Web-Based Question: Union membership—falling or rising?* Go to the Bureau of Labor Statistics website, www.bls.gov, and select A-Z Index and then Workstoppages for historical data on strikes. What has been the trend concerning the number of strikes involving more than 1000 workers over the past 20 years? Use the A-Z Index to update the text's data on union membership. For the latest year, determine (*a*) the overall unionization rate for wage and salary workers, (*b*) the unionization rates for men and women wage and salary workers, and (*c*) the unionization rates for black, white, and Hispanic wage and salary workers. Have the unionization rates gone up, down, or stayed constant compared to the data reported in this chapter?

17. *Web-Based Question: The EEOC—what is it and what does it do?* Go to the website of the Equal Employment Opportunity Commission (EEOC), at www.eeoc.gov, to determine its role in enforcing the antidiscrimination laws. What specific laws does it enforce? List five of its most recent actions.

36 | *The Economics of Health Care*

Rarely can you read a newspaper or look at a television news program without encountering a story about the high costs of health care in the United States, seriously ill people who have no health insurance, or government health insurance programs that threaten to drain Federal and state budgets. Some news stories document disputes between employers and workers over sharing the cost of health insurance or cite instances of insurance companies dictating the medical care that doctors can provide. We even learn of companies that break their promises to provide health insurance to retirees and of lawsuits challenging such actions. Moreover, difficult ethical questions concerning "extreme care" for the acutely or terminally ill arise from time to time.

Health care accounts for 14 percent of U.S. GDP, making it worthy of specific study. Further, the tools of microeconomic analysis are particularly helpful in understanding the U.S. health care system, major health care issues, and actual and proposed reforms.

The Health Care Industry

Since the boundaries of the health care industry are not definite, it is difficult to define the industry. In general, it includes services provided in hospitals, nursing homes, laboratories, and physicians' and dentists' offices. It also includes prescription and nonprescription drugs, artificial limbs, and eyeglasses. Note, however, that many goods and services that may affect health are not included, for example, low-fat foods, vitamins, and health club services.

Health care is one of the largest U.S. industries, employing about 9 million people, including about 700,000 practicing physicians, or 255 doctors per 100,000 of population. There are about 5800 hospitals containing

984,000 beds. Americans make more than 824 million visits to office-based physicians each year.

Twin Problems: Costs and Access

Two highly publicized problems are related to the U.S. health care system:

- The cost of health care has risen rapidly in response to higher prices and an increase in the quantity of services provided. (Spending on health care involves both "prices" and "quantities" and is often loosely referred to as "health care costs.") The price of medical care has increased faster than the overall price level, for example, rising by 3.5 percent in 1999, 4.1 percent in 2000, 4.6 percent in 2001, and 4.7 percent in 2002. Health care spending grew by 8.7 percent in 2001 and is projected to grow at an average annual rate of 7.3 percent over the present decade.

- Forty-one million Americans do not have health insurance coverage, and many Americans have limited, or no, access to health care.

Efforts to reform health care have focused on controlling costs and making it accessible to everyone. Those two goals are related, since high and rising prices make health care services unaffordable to a significant portion of the U.S. population. In fact, a dual system of health care may be evolving in the United States. Those with insurance or other financial means receive the world's best medical treatment, but many people, because of their inability to pay, do not seek out even the most basic treatment.

High and Rising Health Care Costs

We need to examine several aspects of health care spending and health care costs.

Health Care Spending

Health care spending in the United States is high and rising in both absolute terms and as a percentage of domestic output.

Total Spending on Health Care   Figure 36.1a gives an overview of the major types of U.S. health care spending ($1.42 trillion in 2001). It shows that 33 cents of each health care dollar is spent on hospitals, while 22 cents goes to physicians and 22 cents for other health care services (dental, vision, and home care).

Figure 36.1b shows the sources of funds for health care spending. It reveals that nearly four-fifths of health care spending is financed by insurance. Public insurance (Medicaid, Medicare, and insurance for veterans, current military personnel, and government employees) is the source of 43 cents of each dollar spent. Private insurance accounts for 35 cents. So public and private insurance combined provide 78 cents of each dollar spent. The remaining 22 cents comes directly out of the health care consumer's pocket. It is paid mainly as insurance **deductibles** (that is, the insured pays the first $250 or $500 of each year's health care costs before the insurer begins paying) or **copayments** (that is, the insured pays, say, 20 percent of all health care costs and the insurance company pays 80 percent).

Recall that Medicare is a nationwide Federal health care program available to Social Security beneficiaries and persons with disabilities. One part of Medicare is a hospital insurance program that, after a deductible of $840 (in 2003), covers all reasonable costs for the first 60 days of inpatient care per "benefit period" and lesser amounts (on a cost-sharing basis) for additional days. Coverage is also provided for posthospital nursing services, home

---

FIGURE 36.1

Health care expenditures and finance.   (a) Most health care expenditures are for hospitals and the services of physicians and other skilled professionals. (b) Public and private insurance pay for nearly four-fifths of health care.

Source: Centers for Medicare and Medicaid Services, cms.hhs.gov/. Data are for 2001.

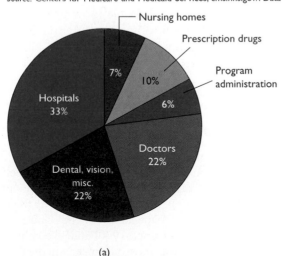

(a)
Health care expenditures

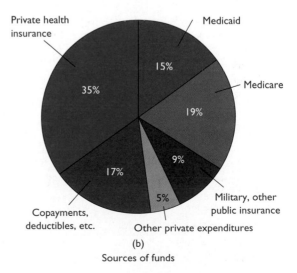

(b)
Sources of funds

health care, and hospice care for the terminally ill. The second part of Medicare, a medical insurance program (for physicians' services, laboratory and other diagnostic tests, and outpatient hospital services), is voluntary but is heavily subsidized by government. The $58.70 monthly premiums (in 2003) that participants pay cover about one-fourth of the cost of the benefits provided.

Medicaid provides payment for medical benefits to certain low-income people, including the elderly, the blind, persons with disabilities, children, and adults with dependent children. Those who qualify for Temporary Aid for Needy Families (TANF) and the Supplemental Security Income (SSI) program are automatically eligible for Medicaid. Nevertheless, Medicaid covers less than half of those living in poverty. The Federal government and the states share the cost of Medicaid. On average, the states fund 43 percent and the Federal government 57 percent of each Medicaid dollar spent.

Overall, about 22 percent of each dollar spent on health care is financed by direct out-of-pocket payments by individuals. The fact that most U.S. health care is paid for by private insurance companies or the government is an important contributor to rising health care costs.

Percentage of GDP Figure 36.2 shows how U.S. health care spending has been increasing as a percentage

FIGURE 36.2

U.S. health care expenditures as a percentage of GDP. U.S. health care spending as a percentage of GDP has greatly increased since 1960 and is projected to rise still more.
Source: Centers for Medicare and Medicaid Services, cms.hhs.gov/.

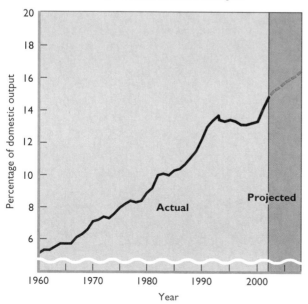

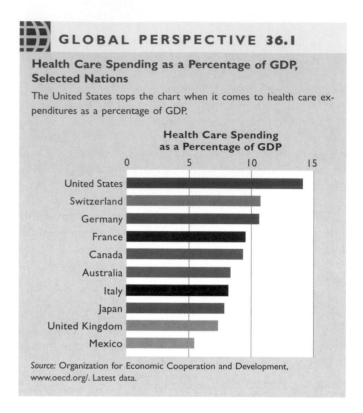

GLOBAL PERSPECTIVE 36.1

Health Care Spending as a Percentage of GDP, Selected Nations

The United States tops the chart when it comes to health care expenditures as a percentage of GDP.

Source: Organization for Economic Cooperation and Development, www.oecd.org/. Latest data.

of GDP. Health care spending absorbed 5.1 percent of GDP in 1960 but rose to 14.1 percent by 2001. Government agencies project that national health care expenditures will reach 16.4 percent of GDP by 2008.

International Comparisons Global Perspective 36.1 reveals that among the industrialized nations, health care spending as a percentage of GDP is highest in the United States. It is reasonable to assume that health care spending varies positively with output and incomes, but that doesn't account for the higher U.S. health expenditures as a percentage of GDP. For whatever reason, the United States is "in a league of its own" as to its proportion of output devoted to health care.

Quality of Care: Are We Healthier?

It is difficult to compare the quality of health care from country to country. Yet there is general agreement that medical care (although not health and not "preventive treatment") in the United States is probably the best in the world. Average life expectancy in the United States has increased by 6 years since 1970, and U.S. physicians and hospitals employ the most advanced medical equipment and technologies. Also, more than half the world's medical research funding is done in the United States. As a result, the incidence of disease has been declining and the quality of treatment has been improving. Polio has been virtually eliminated, ulcers are successfully treated without surgery, angioplasty and coronary bypass surgery greatly benefit those with heart disease, sophisticated body scanners are increasingly available diagnostic tools, and organ transplants and prosthetic joint replacements are more and more common.

That is the good news. But there is other news as well. Despite new screening and treatment technologies, the breast cancer mortality rate has shown little change. Tuberculosis, a virtually forgotten disease, has reappeared. The AIDS epidemic has claimed more than 486,000 American lives. More generally, some experts say that high levels of health care spending have not produced significantly better health and well-being. U.S. health care expenditures are the highest in the world absolutely, as a proportion of GDP, and on a per capita basis. Yet many other nations rank higher than the United States in world life expectancy, maternal mortality, and in infant mortality.

Economic Implications of Rising Costs

The most visible economic effects of rising health care costs are higher health insurance premiums to employers and higher out-of-pocket costs to workers. But rising health care costs have other economic effects as well.

Reduced Access to Care   Higher health care costs and insurance premiums reduce access to health care. Some employers reduce or eliminate health insurance as part of their pay packages and some uninsured workers go without private health insurance. Consequently, the number of uninsured grows. We will consider this issue in detail momentarily.

Labor Market Effects   Surging health care costs have two main effects on labor markets:

- *Slower wage growth*   First, gains in workers' total compensation (wage plus fringe benefits, including health insurance paid for by employers) generally match gains in productivity. When health care costs (and thus insurance prices) rise more rapidly than productivity, firms wanting to maintain the existing level of health care benefits for their workers must reduce the growth of the wage portion of the total compensation package. Thus, in the long run, workers bear the burden of rising health care costs in the form of slower-growing wages.

- *Use of part-time and temporary workers*   The high cost of employer-provided health insurance has led some employers to restructure their workforces: Full-time workers with health insurance benefits are employed in smaller numbers, and uninsured part-time or temporary workers are employed in greater numbers. Similarly, a large, prosperous employer with a generous health care plan might reduce its health insurance expense by discharging its insured lower-wage workers—janitors, gardeners, and cafeteria staff—and replacing them with outside independent contractors who provide no health insurance to their employees.

Impact on Government Budgets   The budgets of Federal, state, and local governments are negatively affected by spiraling and sometimes unpredictable health care expenditures. In the past two decades, spending for health care through Medicare and Medicaid has been by far the fastest-growing segment of the Federal budget. To cover those rising expenditures, the government must either raise taxes or reduce the portion of the budget used for national defense, education, environmental programs, scientific research, and other spending categories.

The states are also finding it difficult to cover their share of the Medicaid bill. Most of them have been forced to raise their tax rates and search for new sources of revenue, and many of them have had to reduce spending on nonhealth programs such as infrastructure maintenance, welfare, and education. Local governments face similar budget strains in trying to finance public health services, hospitals, and clinics.

The Basic Problem

Increased spending on computers or houses would be a sign of prosperity, not a cause for alarm, because society is obtaining more of each. What is different about increased spending on health care? Maybe nothing, say some economists. William Nordhaus of Yale, for example, has recently estimated that the economic value of increases in longevity over the last 100 years nearly equals the total value of the additional GDP during that period. But, while recognizing the tremendous benefits of health care, most economists contend that health care expenditures are inefficiently large because they arise partly from peculiarities in the market for health care. We will see that this possibility arises from the way health care is financed, the asymmetry of information between consumers and providers, and the interaction of health care insurance with technological progress in the industry.

The production of health care requires scarce resources such as capital in the form of hospitals and diagnostic equipment and the highly skilled labor of physicians, technicians, and nurses. Some people suggest that the total production and consumption of health care in the United States are so large that health care, at the margin, is worth less than the alternative goods and services these resources could otherwise have produced. That is, the United States may be consuming health care beyond the MB = MC point that defines efficiency. If there is an overallocation of resources to health care, society incurs a real economic loss. Resources used excessively in health care could be used more productively to build new factories, support research and development, construct new bridges and roads, support education, improve the environment, or provide more consumer goods.

Limited Access

The other health care problem is limited access. Even though there may be an overallocation of resources to health care, not all Americans can obtain the health care they need. In 2001 about 41 million Americans, or roughly 15 percent of the population, had no health insurance for the entire year. About 75 million people were uninsured at some point in 2001 or 2002. As health care costs (and therefore health care insurance premiums) continue to rise, the number of uninsured could grow.

Who are the medically uninsured? As incomes rise, so does the probability of being insured. So it is no surprise that the uninsured are concentrated among the poor. Medicaid is designed to provide health care for the poor who are on welfare. But many poor people work at low- or minimum-wage jobs without health care benefits, earning "too much" to qualify for Medicaid yet not enough to afford private health insurance. About half of the uninsured have a family head who works full-time. Many single-parent families, African Americans, and Hispanics are uninsured simply because they are more likely to be poor.

Curiously, those with excellent health and those with the poorest health also tend to be uninsured. Many young people with excellent health simply choose not to buy health insurance. The chronically ill find it very difficult and too costly to obtain insurance because of the likelihood that they will incur substantial health care costs in the future. Because private health insurance is most frequently obtained through an employer, the unemployed are also likely to lack insurance.

Workers for smaller firms are also less likely to have health insurance. The main reason is that administrative expenses for a small firm may be 30 to 40 percent of insurance premiums, as opposed to only 10 percent for a large firm. Also, corporations can deduct health insurance premiums from income to obtain substantial tax savings. Small unincorporated businesses can deduct only part of their health insurance expenses.

Low-wage workers are also less likely to be insured. Earlier we noted that in the long run employers pass on the increasing expense of health care insurance to workers as lower wages. This option is not available to employers who are paying the minimum wage. Thus as health care insurance premiums rise, employers cut or eliminate this benefit from the compensation package for their minimum- and low-wage workers. As a result, these workers are typically uninsured.

Although many of the uninsured forgo health care, some do not. A few are able to pay for it out of pocket. Others may wait until their illness reaches a critical stage and then go to a hospital for admittance or to be treated in the emergency room. These methods of treatment are inappropriate and unnecessarily costly. It is estimated that hospitals provide $20 billion to $25 billion of uncompensated ("free") health care per year. The hospitals then try to shift these costs to those who have insurance or who can pay out of pocket. **(Key Question 2)**

QUICK REVIEW 36.1

- Health care spending in the United States has been increasing absolutely and as a percentage of gross domestic output.

- Rising health care costs have caused (a) more people to find health insurance unaffordable; (b) adverse labor market effects, including slower real-wage growth and increased use of part-time and temporary workers; and (c) restriction of nonhealth spending by governments.

- The basic problem with rising health care spending is that it may reflect an overallocation of resources to the health care industry.

- Approximately 15 percent of all Americans have no health insurance and, hence, no (or limited) access to health care.

Why the Rapid Rise in Costs?

The rising prices, quantities, and costs of health care services are the result of the demand for health care increasing much more rapidly than supply. We will examine the reasons for this in some detail. But first it will be helpful to understand certain characteristics of the health care market.

Peculiarities of the Health Care Market

We know that purely competitive markets achieve both allocative and productive efficiency: The most desired products are produced in the least costly way. We also have found that many imperfectly competitive markets, perhaps aided by regulation or the threat of antitrust action, provide outcomes generally accepted as efficient. What, then, are the special features of the health care market that have contributed to rising prices and thus escalating costs to buyers?

- *Ethical and equity considerations* Ethical questions inevitably intervene in markets when decisions involve the quality of life, or literally life or death. Although we might not consider it immoral or unfair if a person cannot buy a Mercedes or a personal computer, society regards it as unjust for people to be denied access to basic health care or even to the best available health care. In general, society regards health care as an "entitlement" or a "right" and is reluctant to ration it solely by price and income.

- *Asymmetric information* Health care buyers typically have little or no understanding of complex diagnostic and treatment procedures, while the physicians who are the health care sellers of those procedures possess detailed information. This creates the unusual situation in which the doctor (supplier) as the agent of the patient (consumer) tells the patient what health care services he or she should consume. We will say more about this shortly.

- *Spillover benefits* The medical care market often generates positive externalities (spillover benefits). For example, an immunization against polio, smallpox, or measles benefits the immediate purchaser, but it also benefits society because it reduces the risk that other members of society will be infected with a highly contagious disease. Similarly, a healthy labor force is more productive, contributing to the general prosperity and well-being of society.

- *Third-party payments: insurance* Because nearly four-fifths of all health care expenses are paid through public or private insurance, health care consumers pay much lower out-of-pocket "prices" than they would otherwise. Those lower prices are a distortion that results in "excess" consumption of health care services.

The Increasing Demand for Health Care

With these four features in mind, let's consider some factors that have increased the demand for health care over time.

Rising Incomes: The Role of Elasticities Because health care is a normal good, increases in domestic income have caused increases in the demand for health care. While there is some disagreement as to the exact income elasticity of demand for health care, several studies for industrially advanced countries suggest that the income elasticity coefficient is about 1. This means that per capita health care spending rises approximately in proportion to increases in per capita income. For example, a 3 percent increase in income will generate a 3 percent increase in health care expenditures. There is some evidence that income elasticity may be higher in the United States, perhaps as high as 1.5.

Estimates of the price elasticity of demand for health care imply that it is quite inelastic, with this coefficient being as low as .2. This means that the quantity of health care consumed declines relatively little as price increases. For example, a 10 percent increase in price would reduce quantity demanded by only 2 percent. An important consequence is that total health care spending will increase as the price of health care rises.

The relative insensitivity of health care spending to price changes results from four factors. First, people consider health care a necessity, not a luxury. There are few, if any, good substitutes for medical care in treating injuries and infections and alleviating various ailments. Second, medical treatment is often provided in an emergency situation in which price considerations are secondary or irrelevant. Third, most consumers prefer a long-term relationship with their doctors and therefore do not "shop around" when health care prices rise. Fourth, most patients have insurance and are therefore not directly affected by the price of health care. If insured patients pay, for example, only 20 percent of their health care expenses, they are less concerned with price increases or price differences between hospitals and between doctors than they would be if they paid 100 percent themselves. **(Key Question 7)**

An Aging Population The U.S. population is aging. People 65 years of age and older constituted approximately 9 percent of the population in 1960 but 12.4 percent by 2000. Projections for the year 2030 indicate 20 percent of the population will be 65 or over.

This aging of the population affects the demand for health care because older people encounter more frequent and more prolonged spells of illness. Specifically, those 65 and older consume about three and one-half times as much health care as those between 19 and 64. In turn, people over 84 consume almost two and one-half times as much health care as those in the 65 to 69 age group.

Health care expenditures are often extraordinarily high in the last year of one's life.

Looking ahead, in 2011 the 76 million people born between 1946 and 1964 will begin turning 65. We can expect that fact to create a substantial surge in the demand for health care.

Unhealthy Lifestyles Substance abuse helps drive up health care costs. The abuse of alcohol, tobacco, and illicit drugs damages health and is therefore an important component of the demand for health care services. Alcohol is a major cause of injury-producing traffic accidents and liver disease. Tobacco use markedly increases the probability of cancer, heart disease, bronchitis, and emphysema. Illicit drugs are a major contributor to violent crime, health problems in infants, and the spread of AIDS. In addition, illicit-drug users make hundreds of thousands of costly visits to hospital emergency rooms each year. And overeating and lack of exercise contribute to heart disease, diabetes, and many other ailments.

The Role of Doctors Physicians may increase the demand for health care in several ways.

Supplier-Induced Demand As we mentioned before, doctors, the suppliers of medical services, have much more information about those services than consumers, who are the demanders. While a patient might be well informed about food products or more complex products such as cameras, he or she is not likely to be well informed about diagnostic tests such as magnetic resonance imaging or medical procedures such as joint replacements. Because of this asymmetric information (informational imbalance) the supplier, not the demander, decides what types and amounts of health care are to be consumed. This situation creates a possibility of "supplier-induced demand."

This possibility becomes especially relevant when doctors are paid on a **fee-for-service** basis, that is, paid separately for each service they perform. In light of the asymmetric information and fee-for-service arrangement, doctors have an opportunity and an incentive to suggest more health care services than are absolutely necessary (just as an auto repair shop has an opportunity and an incentive to recommend replacement of parts that are worn but still working).

More surgery is performed in the United States, where many doctors are paid a fee for each operation, than in foreign countries, where doctors are often paid annual salaries unrelated to the number of operations they perform. Furthermore, doctors who own X-ray or ultrasound machines do four times as many tests as doctors who refer their patients to radiologists. More generally, studies suggest that up to one-third of common medical tests and procedures are either inappropriate or of questionable value.

The seller's control over consumption decisions has another result: It eliminates much of the power buyers might have in controlling the growth of health care prices and spending.

Defensive Medicine "Become a doctor and support a lawyer," says a bumper sticker. The number of medical malpractice lawsuits admittedly is high. Today, every patient represents not only a need for medical care but also a possible malpractice suit. As a result, physicians tend to practice **defensive medicine.** That is, they recommend more tests and procedures than are warranted medically or economically in order to protect themselves against malpractice suits.

Medical Ethics Medical ethics may drive up the demand for health care in two ways. First, doctors are ethically committed to use "best-practice" techniques in serving their patients. This often means the use of costly medical procedures that may be of only slight benefit to patients.

Second, public values seem to support the medical ethic that human life should be sustained as long as possible. This makes it difficult to confront the notion that health care is provided with scarce resources and therefore must be rationed like any other good. Can society afford to provide $5000-per-day intensive care to a comatose patient unlikely to be restored to reasonable health? Public priorities seem to indicate that such care should be provided, and those values again increase the demand for health care.

Role of Health Insurance

As we noted in Figure 36.1, 78 percent of health care spending is done not by health care consumers through direct out-of-pocket payments but by private health insurance companies or by the government through Medicare and Medicaid.

Individuals and families are faced with potentially devastating monetary losses from a variety of hazards. Your house may burn down; you may be in an auto accident; or you may suffer a serious illness. An insurance program is a means of protection against the huge monetary losses that can result from such hazards. A number of people agree to pay certain amounts (premiums) periodically in return for the guarantee that they will be compensated if they should incur a particular misfortune.

Insurance is a means of paying a relatively small known cost for protection against an uncertain and much larger cost. While health insurance is therefore highly beneficial, it also contributes to rising costs and possible overconsumption of health care.

The Moral Hazard Problem

The moral hazard problem is the tendency of one party to an agreement to alter her or his behavior in a way that is costly to the other party. Health care insurance can change behavior in two ways. First, some insured people may be less careful about their health, taking fewer steps to prevent accident or illness. Second, insured individuals have greater incentives to use health care more intensively than they would if they did not have insurance. Let's consider both aspects of moral hazard.

Less Prevention

Health insurance may increase the demand for health care by encouraging behaviors that require more health care. Although most people with health care insurance are probably as careful about their health as are those without insurance, some may be more inclined to smoke, avoid exercise, and eat unhealthful foods, knowing they have insurance. Similarly, some individuals may take up ski jumping or rodeo bull riding if they have insurance covering the costs of orthopedic surgeons. And if their insurance covers rehabilitation programs, some people may be more inclined to experiment with alcohol or drugs.

Overconsumption

Insured people go to doctors more often and request more diagnostic tests and more complex treatments than they would if they were uninsured because, with health insurance, the price or opportunity cost of consuming health care is minimal. For example, many individuals with private insurance pay a fixed premium for coverage, and beyond that, aside from a modest deductible, their health care is "free." This situation differs from most markets, in which the price to the consumer reflects the full opportunity cost of each unit of the good or service. In all markets, price provides a direct economic incentive to restrict use of the product. The minimal direct price to the insured consumer of health care, in contrast, creates an incentive to overuse the health care system. Of course, the penalty for overuse will ultimately show up in higher insurance premiums, but all policyholders will share those premiums. The cost increase for the individual health consumer will be relatively small.

Also, the availability of insurance removes the consumer's budget constraint (spending limitation) when he or she decides to consume health care. Recall from Chapter 21 that budget constraints limit the purchases of most products. But insured patients face minimal or no out-of-pocket expenditures at the time they purchase health care. Because affordability is not the issue, health care may be overconsumed.

Government Tax Subsidy

Federal tax policy toward employer-financed health insurance works as a **tax subsidy** that strengthens the demand for health care services. Specifically, employees do not pay Federal income or payroll tax (Social Security) on the value of the health insurance they receive as an employee benefit. Employees thus request and receive more of their total compensation as nontaxed health care benefits and less in taxed wages and salaries.

The government rationale for this tax treatment is that positive spillover benefits are associated with having a healthy, productive workforce. So it is appropriate to encourage health insurance for workers. The tax break does enable more of the population to have health insurance, but it also contributes to greater consumption of health care. Combined with other factors, the tax break may result in an overconsumption of health care.

To illustrate: If the marginal tax rate is, say, 28 percent, $1 worth of health insurance is equivalent to 72 cents in after-tax pay. Because the worker can get more insurance for $1 than for 72 cents, the exclusion of health insurance from taxation increases purchases of health insurance, thus increasing the demand for health care. In essence, the 28-cent difference acts as a government subsidy to health care. A recent estimate suggests that this subsidy costs the Federal government $120 billion per year in forgone tax revenue and boosts private health insurance spending by about one-third. Actual health care spending may be 10 to 20 percent higher than otherwise because of the subsidy.

Graphical Portrayal

A simple demand and supply model illustrates the effect of health insurance on the health care market. Figure 36.3a depicts a competitive market for health care services; curve D shows the demand for health care services if all consumers are uninsured, and S represents the supply of health care. At market price P_u the equilibrium quantity of health care is Q_u.

Recall from the theory of competitive markets that output Q_u results in allocative efficiency, which means there is no better alternative use for the resources allocated to producing that level of health care. To see what we mean by "no better use," we must realize that:

- As we move down along demand curve D, each succeeding point indicates, via the price it represents, the

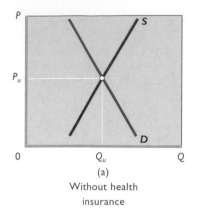

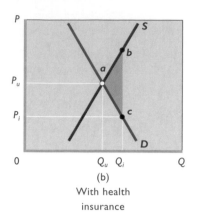

FIGURE 36.3

Insurance and the overallocation of resources to health care. (a) Without health insurance, the optimal amount of health care consumed is Q_u, where the marginal benefit and marginal cost of health care are equal. (b) The availability of private and public insurance reduces the direct price of health care from P_u to P_i, resulting in its overconsumption (Q_i rather than Q_u) and an overallocation of resources to the health care industry. Area abc represents the efficiency loss from that overallocation.

marginal benefit that consumers receive from that unit.

- The supply curve is the producers' marginal-cost curve. As we move up along the supply curve, each succeeding point indicates the marginal cost of that unit of health care.

- For each unit produced up to the equilibrium quantity Q_u, marginal benefit exceeds marginal cost (because points on D are above those on S). At Q_u marginal benefit equals marginal cost, designating allocative efficiency. No matter what else those resources could have produced, the greatest net benefit to society is obtained by using those resources to produce Q_u units of health care.

But allocative efficiency occurs only when we pay in full for a product, as is assumed in Figure 36.3a. What happens when we introduce health insurance that covers, say, one-half of all health care costs? In Figure 36.3b, with health insurance paying half the price, the consumer in effect is confronted with price P_i ($= \frac{1}{2}P_u$). The health care consumer reacts by purchasing Q_i units rather than just Q_u. This is economically inefficient because between Q_u and Q_i each unit's marginal cost to society (on curve S) exceeds its marginal benefit (on curve D). Each unit of health care between Q_u and Q_i reflects an overallocation of resources to health care. The total efficiency loss is represented by area abc. Because health insurance typically covers 80, not just 50, percent of health care costs, the efficiency loss in Figure 36.3b understates the actual efficiency loss to society. On the other hand, this loss may not be as large as the 80 percent figure would imply, because of the positive spillovers associated with health care.[1]

Figure 36.3b implies that there is a tradeoff between efficiency and equity. Standards of fairness or equity in the United States lead people to believe that all citizens should have access to basic health care, which is why government created social insurance in the form of Medicare and Medicaid. Also, it helps explain the Federal tax subsidy to private health insurance, which again makes health care more accessible. The problem, as Figure 36.3b shows, is that the greater the availability of insurance (and thus the more equitable society makes access to health care), the greater the overallocation of resources to the health care industry. This overallocation would be even greater if health care were provided completely "free" under a program of national health insurance. Consumers would purchase health care as long as the marginal benefit to themselves as individuals was positive, regardless of the true cost to society. **(Key Question 10)**

Supply Factors in Rising Health Care Prices

Supply factors have also played a role in rising health care prices. Specifically, the supply of health care services has increased, but more slowly than demand. A combination of factors has produced this relatively slow growth of supply.

Supply of Physicians
The supply of physicians in the United States has increased over the years; in 1975 there were 169 physicians per 100,000 people; by 2001 there were 255. But this increase in supply has not kept up with the increase in the demand for physicians' services. As a result, physicians' fees and incomes have increased more rapidly than average prices and incomes for the economy as a whole.

Conventional wisdom has been that physician groups, for example, the American Medical Association, have

---

[1]Technical footnote: There is no shortage at price P_i in Figure 36.3b. Insurance reduces the direct cost of health care to the insured, so in effect the supply curve shifts rightward (not shown) and intersects demand at point c.

purposely kept admissions to medical schools, and therefore the supply of doctors, artificially low. But that is too simplistic. A rapidly rising cost of medical education seems to be the main cause of the relatively slow growth of doctor supply. Medical training requires 4 years of college, 4 years of medical school, an internship, and perhaps 3 or 4 years of training in a medical specialty. The opportunity cost of this education has increased, because the salaries of similarly capable people have soared in other professions. The direct expenses have also increased, largely due to the increasingly sophisticated levels of medical care and therefore of medical training.

High and rising education and training costs have necessitated high and rising doctors' fees to ensure an adequate return on this sort of investment in human capital. Physicians' incomes are indeed high, averaging about $200,000 in 2001, but so too are the costs of obtaining the skills necessary to become a physician. Data show that while doctors have high rates of return on their educational expenses, those returns are below the returns for lawyers and holders of masters of business administration degrees.

Slow Productivity Growth Productivity growth in an industry tends to reduce costs and increase supply. In the health care industry, such productivity growth has been modest. One reason is that health care is a service, and it is generally more difficult to increase productivity for services than for goods. It is relatively easy to increase productivity in manufacturing by mechanizing the production process. With more and better machinery, the same number of workers can produce greater output. But services often are a different matter. It is not easy, for example, to mechanize haircuts, child care, and pizza delivery. How do you significantly increase the productivity of physicians, nurses, and home care providers?

Also, competition for patients among many providers of health care has not been sufficiently brisk to force them to look for ways to reduce cost by increasing productivity. When buying most goods, customers typically shop around for the lowest price. This shopping requires that sellers keep their prices low and look to productivity increases to maintain or expand their profits. But patients rarely shop for the lowest prices when seeking medical care. In fact, a patient may feel uncomfortable about being operated on by a physician who charges the lowest price. Moreover, if insurance pays for the surgery, there is no reason to consider price at all. The point is that unusual features of the market for health care limit competitive pricing and thus reduce incentives to achieve cost saving via advances in productivity.

Changes in Medical Technology Some technological advances in medicine have lowered costs. For example, the development of vaccines for polio, smallpox, and measles has greatly reduced health care expenditures for the treatment of those diseases. And reduced lengths of stays in hospitals have lowered the costs of medical care.

But many medical technologies developed since the Second World War have significantly increased the cost of medical care either by increasing prices or by extending procedures to a greater number of people. For example, because they give more accurate information, advanced body scanners costing up to $1000 per scan are often used in place of X rays that cost less than $100 for each scan. Desiring to offer the highest quality of service, hospitals want to use the very latest equipment and procedures. These newer, more expensive treatments are surely more effective than older ones. But doctors and hospital administrators both realize that the fixed high cost of such equipment means it must be used extensively to lower the cost per patient.

As another example, organ transplants are extremely costly. Before the development of this technology, a person with a serious liver malfunction died. Now a liver transplant can cost $200,000 or more, with subsequent medical attention costing $10,000 to $20,000 per year for the rest of the patient's life.

Finally, consider new prescription medications. Pharmaceutical companies have developed very expensive drugs that often replace less expensive ones and are prescribed for a much wider range of physical and mental illnesses. Although these remarkable new medications greatly improve health care, they also contribute to rising health care costs.

The historical willingness of private and public insurance to pay for new treatments without regard to price and number of patients has contributed to the incentive to develop and use new technologies. Insurers, in effect, have encouraged research into and development of health care technologies, regardless of their cost. Recently, when insurance companies resisted paying for new expensive treatments such as bone marrow transplants, public outcries led them to change their minds. So expanding insurance coverage leads to new, often more expensive medical technologies, which in turn lead to a demand for a wider definition of what should be covered by insurance.

Relative Importance

According to most analysts, the demand and supply factors we have discussed vary in their impact on escalating health

CONSIDER THIS . . .

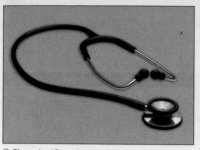

© Photodisc/Getty Images

What's Cold, Clammy, and Out of Date?

Medical technology often improves health care but adds to its cost. *The Wall Street Journal* reports that the era of the stethoscope is slowly giving way to a new hand-held ultrasound machine that enables the physician to visibly check a patient's heart and lungs. The new devices—produced by SonoSite and General Electric—capture images of the vital organs and thus allow for enhanced, albeit more expensive, physical exams. Stethoscopes cost between $50 and $200. Portable ultrasound machines range in price from $12,500 to $55,000. Physical exams, of course, are usually fully covered by private and government health insurance. Welcome to the world of modern technology, improved health care, and rising health care costs!

Source: Based on Amy Dockser Marcus, "What's Cold, Clammy, and Out of Date?" *The Wall Street Journal (On-Line)*, Dec. 4, 2002.

care costs. As we noted, the income elasticity of demand for health care is estimated to be +1 to +1.5, meaning that increased income brings with it proportionate or more-than-proportionate increases in health care spending. But rising income does not alone explain the rocketing increase in health care spending as a percentage of total domestic output (income). Furthermore, government studies estimate that the aging population accounts for less than 10 percent of the current increase in per capita health care spending.

Most experts attribute the relative rise in health care spending to (1) advances in medical technology, combined with (2) the medical ethic of providing the best treatment available, (3) private and public health insurance, and (4) fee-for-service physicians' payments by health insurance firms. Through technological progress, great strides have been made in the diagnosis, treatment, and prevention of illness. But the third-party (insurance) payment system provides little incentive to limit the development or use of such technologies, because it has no mechanism to force an equating of marginal costs and marginal benefits. And the "best treatment available" ethic, together with the fee-for-service payment system, ensures that any new technology with a positive marginal benefit will get used and be billed for, regardless of the marginal cost to society.

Reform of the Health Care System

What, if anything, can be done to ensure access for more Americans to the health care system? And how might health care costs be contained? Reform of the health care system to achieve these two goals will be difficult. First, there is a tradeoff between the two objectives: Greater access to the system will mean rising costs. Second, health care reform is complex because expectations (for example, access to the "best" medical care), tradition (the "right" to choose one's doctor), and the goals of self-interest groups (private insurers, health maintenance organizations, drug companies, physicians, and hospitals) all come into play.

This latter point is especially significant. The numerous affected interest groups will not passively accept rearrangement of costs and benefits in an industry that accounts for one-seventh of total U.S. spending. Physicians, hospitals, health insurers, health maintenance organizations, and drug companies seek to prevent price controls on their services and products. Older people—represented by AARP—want government to pay a larger portion of long-term (nursing-home) health care. Health insurance companies hope their business will not be curtailed by reforms. Labor unions advocate a generous basic-benefits package and oppose taxation of employer-financed health insurance. Drug companies want prescription drugs covered under Medicare. Psychiatrists, physical therapists, acupuncturists, and chiropractors want their services included in any new proposal. Trial lawyers want existing malpractice laws left alone. Small businesses strongly oppose any law requiring all companies to provide health insurance for their employees. The beer, liquor, and tobacco industries do not want additional "sin" taxes levied on them to help finance any reform proposal.

Universal Access

How can health care insurance, and thus health care, be made available to all U.S. citizens? Let's briefly consider three reform concepts.

"Play or Pay"   Because much of the nation's health insurance is paid by employers, one way is to expand that coverage using a **play-or-pay** approach. All employers would be required to either provide a basic health insurance program for their workers and their dependents ("play") or pay a special payroll tax to finance health insurance for uninsured workers ("pay"). Some form of publicly sponsored health care plan would cover people who are not in the labor force and thus uninsured.

Such plans, however, probably would lead to lower real wages. Also, unemployment might increase in firms currently paying wages at or near the minimum wage.

Tax Credits and Vouchers   Another approach, using tax credits and vouchers, would help the poor pay for health insurance. The Federal government would provide a tax credit, for example, of $1500 for a single person and $4000 for a family of four, to low-income individuals and families for use in purchasing health insurance. The size of the tax credit would diminish as the recipient's income rises. Those whose incomes are so low as to be exempt from the income tax would be issued a voucher for purchasing health insurance. This proposal is essentially a tax subsidy designed to make insurance more affordable to low-income people.

National Health Insurance   The most far-reaching and controversial reform concept is to establish a system of **national health insurance (NHI)** along the lines of the present Canadian system. The Federal government would provide a basic package of health care to every citizen at no direct charge or at a low cost-sharing level. The system would be financed out of tax revenues rather than out of insurance premiums.

NHI is not the same as socialized medicine. Under NHI the government would not own health care facilities such as hospitals, clinics, and nursing homes. Nor would health care practitioners such as doctors, nurses, and technicians be government employees. Under NHI the government would simply sponsor and finance basic health care for all citizens. Although the role of private health insurers would be reduced under NHI, they could provide health insurance for any medical procedures that were not covered in the basic NHI health care package.

Arguments for NHI   Proponents say that NHI is the simplest and most direct way of providing universal access to health care:

- It allows patients to choose their own physicians.
- It would reduce administrative costs. The present system, it is argued, is administratively chaotic and expensive because hundreds of private health care insurers are involved, each with its own procedures and claim forms. Administration costs in the Canadian system are less than 5 percent of total health care costs compared with almost 17 percent in the United States.
- It would separate health care availability from employment and therefore would eliminate the hiring of part-time and temporary workers as a way to avoid providing health care insurance.
- It would allow the government to use its single-insurer market power to contain costs. The government could apply its buying power to mandate fees for various medical procedures and thus control physician and hospital costs. Hospitals would operate on budgets set by the government.

Arguments Against NHI   Opponents of NHI provide weighty counterarguments:

- Government-determined price ceilings on physicians' services are not likely to control costs. Doctors can protect their incomes from fixed fees by manipulating the amount of care they provide a patient. Suppose the maximum fee for an office visit is $30. Doctors might spread a given number of diagnostic tests over three or four office visits, although all the tests could be done in one visit. Or a doctor might require an office visit to explain test results instead of phoning the patient. Similar arguments apply to government regulation of hospital charges.
- In the Canadian system patients often have waits of weeks, months, or even years for certain diagnostic procedures and surgeries. This is the result of the Canadian government's effort to control expenditures by restricting hospitals' capital spending. To illustrate, there are only one-fifth as many magnetic resonance imaging machines per million people in Canada as in the United States. This results in a waiting list for use of MRIs in Canada. NHI might strongly conflict with U.S. expectations of medical care "on demand."
- Doctors can mount "strikes" against low payments from the government, as they have done is several areas of Canada. Such disruptions in medical care rarely happen in the United States.
- The Federal government has a very poor record of containing costs. Despite its considerable buying power, the Department of Defense, for example, has a long history of cost overruns and mismanagement. And, as you have seen, spending has spiraled upward under the government's Medicare and Medicaid

programs. Also recall (Figure 36.3b) that insurance is a critical factor in the overconsumption of health care. Under NHI a completely "free" basic health care package would prompt consumers to "purchase" health care as long as marginal benefits were positive, regardless of the true cost to society.

- Subtle and perhaps undesirable redistribution effects would result under NHI. Under private health insurance, a particular health care insurance package costs the same regardless of the insured's income. This makes the cost of insurance resemble a regressive tax, since low-income workers pay a larger percentage of their incomes for the insurance than do high-income insurees. If NHI were financed out of personal income tax revenues, this financing would be progressive. Under NHI those with low incomes would receive health insurance and pay little or none of the cost. While some might view this as desirable, others believe that income redistribution in the United States has been overdone and that further redistribution through NHI would be unfair. Depending on the type of tax and its size, employers and workers in industries such as automobile and steel might receive windfalls in the form of higher profits and wages when NHI replaced their health insurance programs. Employers and workers in small retail establishments and fast-food restaurants, where health insurance is typically absent, might not realize such gains.

Cost Containment: Altering Incentives

Can the United States control the growth of health care costs, prices, and spending by reducing incentives to overconsume health care?

Deductibles and Copayments
Insurance companies have reacted to rising health care costs by imposing sizable deductibles and copayments on those they insure. Instead of covering all of an insuree's medical costs, a policy might now specify that the insuree pay the first $250 or $500 of each year's health care costs (the deductible) and 15 or 20 percent of all additional costs (the copayment). The deductible and copayment are intended to alleviate the overuse problem by creating a direct payment and therefore an opportunity cost to the health care consumer. The deductible has the added advantage of reducing the administrative costs of insurance companies in processing many small claims.

Managed Care
Managed-care organizations (or systems) are those in which medical services are controlled or coordinated by insurance companies or health care organizations in order to reduce health care expenditures.

In 2001 about 65 percent of all U.S. workers received health care through such "managed care." These organizations are of two main types.

Some insurance companies have set up **preferred provider organizations (PPOs),** which require that hospitals and physicians accept discounted prices for their services as a condition for being included in the insurance plan. The policyholder receives a list of participating hospitals and doctors and is given, say, 80 to 100 percent reimbursement of health care costs when treated by PPO physicians and hospitals. If a patient chooses a doctor or hospital outside the PPO, the insurance company reimburses only 60 to 70 percent. In return for being included as a PPO provider, doctors and hospitals agree to rates set by the insurance company for each service. Because these fees are less than those usually charged, PPOs reduce health insurance premiums and health care expenditures.

Many Americans now receive their medical care from **health maintenance organizations (HMOs),** which provide health care services to a specific group of enrollees in exchange for a set annual fee per enrollee. HMOs employ their own physicians and contract for specialized services with outside providers and hospitals. They then contract with firms or government units to provide medical care for their workers, who thereby become HMO members. Because HMOs have fixed annual revenue, they may lose money if they provide "too much" care. So they have an incentive to hold down costs. They also have an incentive to provide preventive care in order to reduce the far larger expense of corrective care.

Both PPOs and HMOs are managed-care organizations because medical use and spending are "managed" by close monitoring of physicians' and hospitals' behavior; the purpose is to eliminate unnecessary diagnostic tests and remedial treatments. Doctors in managed-care organizations might not order an MRI scan or an ultrasound test or suggest surgery because their work is monitored and because they may have a fixed budget. In contrast, an independent fee-for-service physician may face little or no control and have a financial incentive to order the test or do the surgery. Doctors and hospitals in a managed-care organization often share in an "incentive pool" of funds when they meet their cost-control goals.

The advantages of managed-care plans are that they provide health care at lower prices than traditional insurance and emphasize preventive medicine. The disadvantages are that the patient usually is restricted to physicians employed by or under contract with the managed-care plan. Also, some say that the focus on reducing costs has gone too far, resulting in denial of highly expensive, but effective, treatment. This has led to a call for passage of a "patients' bill of rights" to regulate the practices of managed-care providers and establish a process of appealing HMO decisions. We will return to this topic shortly.

Medicare and DRG In 1983 the Federal government altered the way it makes payments for hospital services received by Medicare patients. Rather than automatically paying all costs related to a patient's treatment and length of hospital stay, Medicare submitted payments based on a **diagnosis-related-group (DRG) system.** Under DRG a hospital receives a fixed payment for treating each patient; that payment is an amount associated with the one of several hundred carefully detailed diagnostic categories that best characterize the patient's condition and needs.

DRG-system payments obviously give hospitals the incentive to restrict the amount of resources used in treating patients. It is no surprise that under DRG the length of hospital stays has fallen sharply and more patients are treated on an outpatient basis. Critics, however, argue that this is evidence of diminished quality of medical care.

Recent Laws and Proposals

Although Congress has rejected major reforms of the health care system, it has made some noteworthy changes and is currently discussing further reforms:

- *Portability and accountability* A 1996 law ensures that workers with group health insurance can continue to buy insurance when they change jobs or become self-employed, even if they have major health problems. It also prohibits group insurance plans from dropping coverage of a sick employee or of a business that has a sick employee.

- *Medical savings accounts* The 1996 law also introduced, on a trial basis, medical savings accounts (MSAs) for small businesses, the self-employed, and the uninsured. Consumers can make tax-deductible contributions into these accounts, which include a catastrophic health insurance plan for large medical expenses. Earnings on the funds in the account are tax-free, and the money in the account can be used to pay routine medical expenses. Unused funds continue to grow each year. Withdrawals for nonmedical reasons are permitted but are taxed as income.

- *Patients' bill of rights* In 2000 the U.S. Senate and House of Representatives passed different versions of a "patients' bill of rights" law that would regulate HMOs and establish protections for patients. Both versions would include guaranteed access to emergency and specialty care, set up a rapid review process of decisions to deny medical procedures, and enable patients or family members to sue HMOs for actions leading to injury or death.

As of late 2003, however, the compromise between the Senate and House versions of the bill had not been reached. Still to be settled are several issues, including whether lawsuit awards for "pain and suffering" (as distinct from economic loss) should be unlimited and left to juries, as in the Senate bill, or be capped at $500,000, as in the House bill.

- *Limits on malpractice awards* Closely related are recent congressional efforts to cap the "pain and suffering" awards on all medical malpractice lawsuits against physicians (at, say, $250,000 or $500,000). Those who support malpractice caps say that patients should receive full compensation for economic losses but not be made wealthy through huge jury awards. They contend that capping the awards will reduce medical malpractice premiums and therefore lower health care costs. Opponents of caps counter that large "pain and suffering" awards deter medical malpractice. If so, such awards improve the overall quality of the health care system.

- *Prescription-drug coverage* Medicare currently (2003) does not pay for prescription drugs, but such coverage is gaining popularity in Congress. Prescription drugs have become a more integral part of health care, and their expense is claiming a larger part of the income of older Americans. Also, politicians are keenly aware of the growing number of elder Americans and their adult children who would welcome prescription-drug coverage.

   The debate on this issue centers on how best to provide coverage. Should coverage extend to all people regardless of income? If so, according to experts, Medicare expenditures would rise from 2.3 percent of GDP in 2000 to 6.5 percent of GDP in 2030 rather than to 4.4 percent. Or should government provide "free" or inexpensive prescription-drug coverage *only* to lower-income Medicare beneficiaries, while making similar coverage available for purchase (at cost) by higher-income seniors?

- *Medicare reform* In 2003 the Bush administration proposed that prescription-drug coverage be provided in conjunction with Medicare reform. The idea would be to allow those eligible for Medicare to select either a basic managed-care medical plan with prescription-drug coverage or other, more expensive plans in which they would pay supplemental premiums for more extensive coverage. The proposal has provoked considerable debate and it remains to be seen if prescription-drug coverage will be linked to Medicare reform.

(We recommend that you update the status of the aforementioned unresolved issues through a quick Internet search.)

A Market Might Eliminate the Present Shortage of Human Organs for Transplant. But There Are Many Serious Objections to Turning Human Body Parts into Commodities for Purchase and Sale.

Advances in medical technology make it possible for surgeons to replace some human body parts with donated "used parts," much like a backyard mechanic might replace a worn-out alternator in an automobile with one from a junked vehicle. It has become increasingly commonplace in medicine to transplant kidneys, lungs, livers, eye corneas, pancreases, and hearts from deceased individuals to those whose organs have failed or are failing. But surgeons and many of their patients face a growing problem: There are shortages of donated organs available for transplant. Not everyone who needs a transplant can get one. In 2003, there were 81,000 Americans on the waiting list for transplants. Indeed, an inadequate supply of donated organs causes an estimated 4000 deaths in the United States each year.

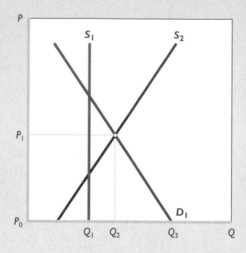

Why Shortages? Seldom, if ever, do we hear of shortages of used auto parts such as alternators, batteries, transmissions, or water pumps. What is different about organs for transplant? One difference is that there is a market for used auto parts but not for human organs. To understand this situation, observe the demand curve D_1 and supply curve S_1 in the accompanying figure. The downward slope of the demand curve tells us that if there were a market for human organs, the quantity of organs demanded would be greater at lower prices than at higher prices. Perfectly inelastic supply curve S_1 represents the fixed quantity of human organs now donated via consent before death. Because the price of these donated organs is in effect zero, quantity demanded Q_3 exceeds quantity supplied Q_1. The shortage of $Q_3 - Q_1$ is rationed through a waiting list of those in medical need of transplants. Many people die while still on the waiting list.

Use of a Market A market for human organs would increase the incentive to donate organs. Such a market might work like this: An individual might specify in a legal document that he or she is willing to sell one or more usable human organs upon death or near-death. The person could specify where the money from the sale would go, for example, to family, a church, an educational institution, or a charity. Firms would then emerge to purchase organs and resell them where needed for profit. Under such a system, the supply curve of usable organs would take on the normal upward slope of typical supply curves. The higher the

SUMMARY

1. The U.S. health care industry comprises 9 million workers (including about 700,000 practicing physicians) and 5800 hospitals.

2. Health care spending has increased both absolutely and as a percentage of GDP.

3. Rising health care costs and prices have (a) reduced access to the health care system, (b) contributed to slower real wage growth and expanded the employment of part-time and temporary workers, and (c) caused governments to restrict spending on nonhealth programs and to raise taxes.

4. The core of the health care problem is an alleged overallocation of resources to the health care industry.

5. About 41 million Americans, or 15 percent of the population, do not have health insurance. The uninsured are concentrated among the poor, the chronically ill, the unemployed, the young, those employed by small firms, and low-wage workers.

6. Special characteristics of the health care market include (a) the belief that health care is a "right," (b) an imbalance

of information between consumers and suppliers, (c) the presence of spillover benefits, and (d) the payment of most health care expenses by private or public insurance.

7. While rising incomes, an aging population, and substance abuse have all contributed to an increasing demand for health care, the role of doctors is also significant. Because of asymmetric information, physicians influence the demand for their own services. The fee-for-service payment system, combined with defensive medicine to protect against malpractice suits, also increases demand for health care.

8. The moral hazard problem arising from health insurance takes two forms: (a) People may be less careful of their health, and (b) there is an incentive to overconsume health care.

9. The exemption of employer-paid health insurance from the Federal income tax subsidizes health care.

10. Slow productivity growth in the health care industry and, more important, cost-increasing advances in health care technology have restricted the expansion of the supply of medical care and have boosted prices.

expected price of an organ, the greater the number of people willing to have their organs sold at death. Suppose that the supply curve is S_2 in the figure. At the equilibrium price P_1, the number of organs made available for transplant (Q_2) would equal the number purchased for transplant (also Q_2). In this generalized case, the shortage of organs would be eliminated and, of particular importance, the number of organs available for transplanting would rise from Q_1 to Q_2. This means more lives would be saved and enhanced than is the case under the present donor system.

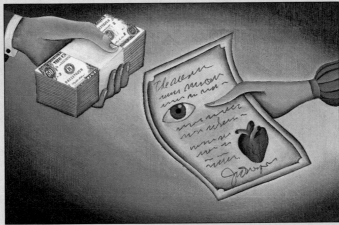

Objections In view of this positive outcome, why is there no such market for human organs? Critics of market-based solutions have two main objections. The first is a moral objection: Critics feel that turning human organs into commodities commercializes human beings and diminishes the special nature of human life. They say there is something unseemly about selling and buying body organs as if they were bushels of wheat or ounces of gold. (There is, however, a market for blood!) Moreover, critics note that the market would ration the available organs (as represented by Q_2 in the figure) to people who either can afford them (at P_1) or have health insurance for transplants.

Second, a health-cost objection suggests that a market for body organs would greatly increase the cost of health care. Rather than obtaining freely donated (although "too few") body organs, patients or their insurance companies would have to pay market prices for them, further increasing the cost of medical care. Moreover, as transplant procedures are further perfected, the demand for transplants is expected to increase significantly. Rapid increases in demand relative to supply would boost the prices of human organs and thus further contribute to the problem of escalating health care costs.

Supporters of market-based solutions to organ shortages point out that the laws against selling organs are simply driving the market underground. Worldwide, an estimated $1 billion-per-year illegal market in human organs has emerged. As in other illegal markets, the unscrupulous tend to thrive. Those who support legalization say that it would be greatly preferable to legalize and regulate the market for transplantable human organs.

11. Reforms designed to increase access to the health care system include (a) "play-or-pay" proposals designed to increase employer-sponsored health insurance, (b) tax credits and vouchers to help low-income families afford health care, and (c) national health insurance.

12. Insurance companies have introduced deductibles and copayments in an attempt to contain health care prices and spending.

13. Managed-care organizations—preferred provider organizations (PPOs) and health maintenance organizations (HMOs)—attempt to control their enrolled members' use of health care in order to contain health care costs.

14. Changes to the health care system in 1996 (a) ensure paid access to continuing health insurance to workers who change jobs or become self-employed, (b) prohibit insurance firms from dropping coverage of workers or businesses that have high medical claims, and (c) establish medical savings accounts (on a trial basis).

15. Current (2003) policy issues include (a) "patients' bill of rights" legislation, (b) limits on "pain and suffering" awards in medical malpractice suits, (c) prescription drug coverage under Medicare, and (d) reforms of Medicare to provide a choice of varying types of insurance coverage.

TERMS AND CONCEPTS

deductibles

copayments

fee for service

defensive medicine

tax subsidy

"play or pay"

national health insurance (NHI)

preferred provider organizations (PPOs)

health maintenance organizations (HMOs)

diagnosis-related-group (DRG) system

STUDY QUESTIONS

1. Why would increased spending as a percentage of GDP on, say, household appliances or education in a particular economy be regarded as economically desirable? Why, then, is there so much concern about rising expenditures as a percentage of GDP on health care?

2. *Key Question* What are the "twin problems" of the health care industry as viewed by society? How are they related?

3. Briefly describe the main features of Medicare and Medicaid, indicating how each is financed.

4. What are the implications of rapidly rising health care prices and spending for (*a*) the growth of real-wage rates and (*b*) government budgets? Explain.

5. Who are the main groups without health insurance?

6. List the special characteristics of the U.S. health care market and specify how each affects health care problems.

7. *Key Question* What are the estimated income and price elasticities of demand for health care? How does each relate to rising health care costs?

8. Briefly discuss the demand and supply factors that contribute to rising health costs. Specify how (*a*) asymmetric information, (*b*) fee-for-service payments, (*c*) defensive medicine, and (*d*) medical ethics might cause health care costs to rise.

9. "Health care expenditures have been rising principally because of the technological transformation of medical care." Do you agree? Explain.

10. *Key Question* Using the concepts in Chapter 21's discussion of consumer behavior, explain how health care insurance results in an overallocation of resources to the health care industry. Use a demand and supply diagram to specify the resulting efficiency loss.

11. How is the moral hazard problem relevant to the health care market?

12. What is the rationale for exempting a firm's contribution to its workers' health insurance from taxation as worker income? What is the impact of this exemption on allocative efficiency in the health care industry?

13. Comment on or explain:
    a. Providing health insurance to achieve equity goals creates a tradeoff with the efficient allocation of resources to the health care industry.
    b. Improved health habits are desirable but would not necessarily reduce health care costs. For example, the deaths of many smokers are caused by sudden and lethal heart attacks and are therefore medically inexpensive.

c. If the government were to require employer-sponsored health insurance for all workers, the likely result would be an increase in the unemployment of low-wage workers.

14. Briefly describe (*a*) "play or pay," (*b*) tax credits and vouchers, and (*c*) national health insurance as means of increasing access to health care. What are the major criticisms of national health insurance?

15. What are (*a*) preferred provider organizations and (*b*) health maintenance organizations? In your answer, explain how each is designed to alleviate the overconsumption of health care.

16. Do you think prescription drugs should be covered under Medicare? Are you willing to pay a higher Social Security/Medicare tax to pay for this added benefit? Do you think the prescription-drug benefit should go to everyone covered by Medicare, including those who can easily afford to pay for prescription drugs out of pocket?

17. Which of the following groups do you think would favor limits on "pain and suffering" awards in suits against HMOs and doctors: health insurance companies, advocacy groups for patients' rights, physicians, trial lawyers? Explain.

18. *(Last Word) Web-Based Question: How long is the waiting list for transplants today?* The United Network for Organ Sharing, www.unos.org, provides a daily update of the number of candidates waiting for organ transplants. What is the current overall number? Select Go to Data and in the "At a Glance" section find the summary of data relating to waiting lists for specific organs. For what transplant organ is the waiting list the longest? The shortest? Do you think these waiting lists would be shorter or longer if there were a market for transplant organs? Explain. Do you favor the establishment of such a market? Why or why not?

19. *Web-Based Question: Health expenditures per capita—going up or down?* Go to the website of the Centers for Medicare and Medicaid, www.cms.hhs.gov, and use the search line to find information on *health expenditures per capita* for the United States. What was the level of such expenditures in 1990? In 2000? For the most recent year shown? Is the level of expenditures per capita projected to rise or to fall over the next 5 years? Find information on *health expenditures as a percentage of GDP*. Contrast the percentage for the latest year shown with the percentage projected for the most distant future year shown. Is the health care problem going away?

Part X | International Economics and the World Economy

37 | *International Trade*

The WTO, Trade deficits, dumping. Exchange rates, the EU, the G8 nations. The IMF, official reserves, currency interventions. This is some of the language of international economics, the subject of Part 10. To understand the increasingly integrated world economy, we need to learn more about this language and the ideas that it conveys.

In this chapter we build on Chapter 6 by providing both a deeper analysis of the benefits of international trade and a fuller appraisal of the arguments for protectionism. Then in Chapter 38 we examine exchange rates and the balance of payments. Two "bonus" Internet chapters at this book's website examine the special problems of developing economies and the transition economies of Russia and China. (Please see the website at: www.mcconnell16.com.)

Some Key Facts

In Chapter 6 we dealt with a number of facts about international trade. Let's briefly review them and add a few more:

- Exports of goods and services make up about 11 percent of total U.S. output. That percentage is much lower than the percentage in many other nations. Examples: Netherlands, 62 percent; Canada, 41 percent; New Zealand, 33 percent; and the United Kingdom, 26 percent.
- The United States leads the world in the volume of exports and imports, as measured in dollars. Currently, the United States provides about one-eighth of the world's exports. Germany, Japan, France, and the United Kingdom follow in the list of the top five exporters by dollar volume.

- Since 1975, U.S. exports have doubled as a percentage of GDP.
- In 2002 the United States imported $484 billion more goods than it exported. But in that year U.S. exports of services exceeded imports of services by $49 billion. So the combined trade deficit of goods and services was $435 billion.
- The principal commodities among U.S. exports are chemicals, semiconductors, consumer durables, and computers. The principal imports are automobiles, petroleum, computers, and household appliances.
- Like other advanced industrial nations, the United States imports some of the same categories of goods that it exports. Examples: automobiles, computers, chemicals, semiconductors, and telecommunications equipment.

GLOBAL PERSPECTIVE 37.1

Shares of World Exports, Selected Nations

The United States has the largest share of world exports, followed by Germany and Japan. The seven largest export nations account for nearly 50 percent of world exports.

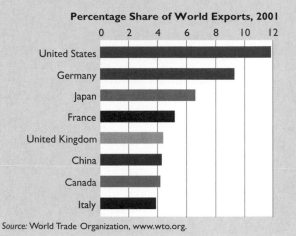

Percentage Share of World Exports, 2001

Source: World Trade Organization, www.wto.org.

- Most of U.S. export and import trade takes place with other industrially advanced nations, specifically Canada, nations of western Europe, and Japan.
- Although the United States, Japan, and western European nations dominate world trade (Global Perspective 37.1), several other nations have increased their roles significantly. China has become a major international trader, with $266 billion of exports in 2002. Other Asian economies—including South Korea, Taiwan, and Singapore—are also active in international trade. Their combined exports exceed those of France, Britain, or Italy. The North American Free Trade Agreement has expanded international trade between Canada, Mexico, and the United States.
- International trade (and finance) link world economies (review Figure 6.1, page 92.) Through trade, changes in economic conditions in one place on the globe can quickly affect other places. Examples: In 1998 economic problems in the southeast Asian countries of South Korea, Indonesia, Malaysia, and the Philippines reduced demand for Japanese imports and negatively affected Japan's economy. In early 2003, hikes in world oil prices threatened to slow economic growth in Europe and the United States.
- International trade and finance is often at the center of economic policy. Examples: The U.S. Congress often grapples with international trade issues such as trade

relations with China. The World Trade Organization (WTO) and the International Monetary Fund (IMF) regularly meet to establish rules relating to international trade and finance. Such meetings often attract protestors who oppose global capitalism.

With these facts in mind, we now look more closely at the economics of international trade.

The Economic Basis for Trade

Chapter 6 revealed that international trade enables nations to specialize their production, enhance their resource productivity, and acquire more goods and services. Sovereign nations, like individuals and the regions of a nation, can gain by specializing in the products they can produce with greatest relative efficiency and by trading for the goods they cannot produce as efficiently. A more complete answer to the question "Why do nations trade?" hinges on three facts:

- The distribution of natural, human, and capital resources among nations is uneven; nations differ in their endowments of economic resources.
- Efficient production of various goods requires different technologies or combinations of resources.
- Products are differentiated as to quality and other nonprice attributes. A few or many people may prefer certain imported goods to similar goods made domestically.

To recognize the character and interaction of these three facts, think of Japan, for example, which has a large, well-educated labor force and abundant, and therefore inexpensive, skilled labor. As a result, Japan can produce efficiently (at low cost) a variety of **labor-intensive goods** such as digital cameras, portable CD players, video game players, and DVD players whose design and production require much skilled labor.

In contrast, Australia has vast amounts of land and can inexpensively produce such **land-intensive goods** as wheat, wool, and meat. Brazil has the soil, tropical climate, rainfall, and ready supply of unskilled labor that are needed for the efficient, low-cost production of coffee.

Industrially advanced economies with relatively large amounts of capital can inexpensively produce goods whose production requires much capital, including such **capital-intensive goods** as automobiles, agricultural equipment, machinery, and chemicals.

All nations, regardless of their labor, land, or capital intensity, can find special niches for individual products that are in demand worldwide because of their special qualities. Examples: fashions from Italy, luxury automobiles from Germany, software from the United States, and watches from Switzerland.

The distribution of resources, technology, and product distinctiveness among nations, however, is not forever fixed. When that distribution changes, the relative efficiency and success with which nations produce and sell goods also changes. For example, in the past few decades South Korea has upgraded the quality of its labor force and has greatly expanded its stock of capital. Although South Korea was primarily an exporter of agricultural products and raw materials a half-century ago, it now exports large quantities of manufactured goods. Similarly, the new technologies that gave us synthetic fibers and synthetic rubber drastically altered the resource mix needed to produce these goods and changed the relative efficiency of nations in manufacturing them.

As national economies evolve, the size and quality of their labor forces may change, the volume and composition of their capital stocks may shift, new technologies may develop, and even the quality of land and the quantity of natural resources may be altered. As such changes occur, the relative efficiency with which a nation can produce specific goods will also change.

Comparative Advantage: Graphical Analysis

37.1
Comparative
advantage

Implicit in what we have been saying is the principle of comparative advantage, described through production possibilities tables in Chapter 6. We look again at that idea, now using graphical analysis.

Two Isolated Nations

Suppose the world economy is composed of just two nations: the United States and Brazil. Each nation can produce both wheat and coffee, but at different levels of economic efficiency. Suppose the U.S. and Brazilian domestic production possibilities curves for coffee and wheat are as shown in Figure 37.1a and 37.1b. Note especially two characteristics of these production possibilities curves:

• **Constant costs** The "curves" are drawn as straight lines, in contrast to the concave-to-the-origin production possibilities frontiers we examined in Chapter 2. This means that we have replaced the law of increasing opportunity costs with the assumption of constant costs. This substitution simplifies our discussion but does not impair the validity of our analysis and conclusions. Later we will consider the effects of increasing opportunity costs.

• **Different costs** The production possibilities curves of the United States and Brazil reflect different resource mixes and differing levels of technological progress. Specifically, they tell us that the opportunity costs of producing wheat and coffee differ between the two nations.

United States In Figure 37.1a, with full employment, the United States will operate on its production possibilities curve. On that curve, it can increase its output of wheat from 0 tons to 30 tons by forgoing 30 tons of coffee output. This means that the slope of the production possibilities curve is −1 (= −30 coffee/+30 wheat), implying that 1 ton of coffee must be sacrificed for each

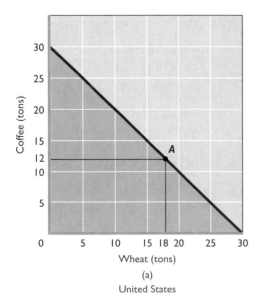

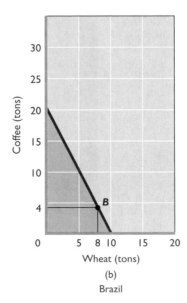

FIGURE 37.1

Production possibilities for the United States and Brazil. The two production possibilities curves show the combinations of coffee and wheat that (a) the United States and (b) Brazil can produce domestically. The curves for both countries are straight lines because we are assuming constant opportunity costs. The different cost ratios, 1 coffee ≡ 1 wheat for the United States, and 2 coffee ≡ 1 wheat for Brazil, are reflected in the different slopes of the two lines.

(a)
United States

(b)
Brazil

extra ton of wheat. In the United States the domestic exchange ratio or **cost ratio** for the two products is 1 ton of coffee for 1 ton of wheat, or $1C \equiv 1W$. Said differently, the United States can "exchange" a ton of coffee for a ton of wheat. Our constant-cost assumption means that this exchange or opportunity-cost equation prevails for all possible moves from one point to another along the U.S. production possibilities curve.

Brazil   Brazil's production possibilities curve in Figure 37.1b represents a different full-employment opportunity-cost ratio. In Brazil, 20 tons of coffee must be given up to get 10 tons of wheat. The slope of the production possibilities curve is $-2 \ (= -20 \text{ coffee}/+10 \text{ wheat})$. This means that in Brazil the opportunity-cost ratio for the two goods is 2 tons of coffee for 1 ton of wheat, or $2C \equiv 1W$.

Self-Sufficiency Output Mix   If the United States and Brazil are isolated and are to be self-sufficient, then each country must choose some output mix on its production possibilities curve. It will choose the mix that provides the greatest total utility, or satisfaction. Assume that point A in Figure 37.1a is the optimal mix in the United States; that is, society deems the combination of 18 tons of wheat and 12 tons of coffee preferable to any other combination of the goods available along the production possibilities curve. Suppose Brazil's optimal product mix is 8 tons of wheat and 4 tons of coffee, indicated by point B in Figure 37.1b. These choices are reflected in column 1 of Table 37.1.

Specializing Based on Comparative Advantage

We can determine the products in which the United States and Brazil should specialize as follows: The **principle of comparative advantage** says that total output will be greatest when each good is produced by the nation that has the lowest domestic opportunity cost for that good. In our two-nation illustration, the United States has the lower domestic opportunity cost for wheat; the United States need forgo only 1 ton of coffee to produce 1 ton of wheat, whereas Brazil must forgo 2 tons of coffee for 1 ton of wheat. The United States has a comparative (cost) advantage in wheat and should specialize in wheat production. The "world" (that is, the United States and Brazil) in our example would clearly not be economizing in the use of its resources if a high-cost producer (Brazil) produced a specific product (wheat) when a low-cost producer (the United States) could have produced it. Having Brazil produce wheat would mean that the world economy would have to give up more coffee than is necessary to obtain a ton of wheat.

Brazil has the lower domestic opportunity cost for coffee; it must sacrifice only $\frac{1}{2}$ ton of wheat in producing 1 ton of coffee, while the United States must forgo 1 ton of wheat in producing a ton of coffee. Brazil has a comparative advantage in coffee and should specialize in coffee production. Again, the world would not be employing its resources economically if coffee were produced by a high-cost producer (the United States) rather than by a low-cost producer (Brazil). If the United States produced coffee, the world would be giving up more wheat than necessary to obtain each ton of coffee. Economizing requires that any particular good be produced by the nation having the lowest domestic opportunity cost, or the comparative advantage for that good. The United States should produce wheat, and Brazil should produce coffee.

In column 2 of Table 37.1 we verify that specialized production enables the world to get more output from its fixed amount of resources. By specializing completely in wheat, the United States can produce 30 tons of wheat and no coffee. Brazil, by specializing completely in coffee,

TABLE 37.1

International Specialization According to Comparative Advantage and the Gains from Trade

Country	(1) Outputs before Specialization	(2) Outputs after Specialization	(3) Amounts Exported (−) and Imported (+)	(4) Outputs Available after Trade	(5) Gains from Specialization and Trade (4) − (1)
United States	18 wheat	30 wheat	−10 wheat	20 wheat	2 wheat
	12 coffee	0 coffee	+15 coffee	15 coffee	3 coffee
Brazil	8 wheat	0 wheat	+10 wheat	10 wheat	2 wheat
	4 coffee	20 coffee	−15 coffee	5 coffee	1 coffee

can produce 20 tons of coffee and no wheat. The world ends up with 4 more tons of wheat (30 tons compared with 26) *and* 4 more tons of coffee (20 tons compared with 16) than it would if there were self-sufficiency or unspecialized production.

Terms of Trade

But consumers of each nation want both wheat *and* coffee. They can have both if the two nations trade the two products. But what will be the **terms of trade?** At what exchange ratio will the United States and Brazil trade wheat and coffee?

Because $1W \equiv 1C$ in the United States, the United States must get *more than* 1 ton of coffee for each ton of wheat exported; otherwise, it will not benefit from exporting wheat in exchange for Brazilian coffee. The United States must get a better "price" (more coffee) for its wheat in the world market than it can get domestically; otherwise, there is no gain from trade and it will not occur.

Similarly, because $1W \equiv 2C$ in Brazil, Brazil must get 1 ton of wheat by exporting some amount *less than* 2 tons of coffee. Brazil must be able to pay a lower "price" for wheat in the world market than it must pay domestically, or else it will not want to trade. The international exchange ratio or terms of trade must lie somewhere between

$$1W \equiv 1C \text{ (United States' cost conditions)}$$

and

$$1W \equiv 2C \text{ (Brazil's cost conditions)}$$

But where between these limits will the world exchange ratio fall? The United States will prefer a rate close to $1W \equiv 2C$, say, $1W \equiv 1\frac{3}{4}C$. The United States wants to get as much coffee as possible for each ton of wheat it exports. Similarly, Brazil wants a rate near $1W \equiv 1C$, say, $1W \equiv 1\frac{1}{4}C$. Brazil wants to export as little coffee as possible for each ton of wheat it receives in exchange. The exchange ratio or terms of trade determine how the gains from international specialization and trade are divided between the two nations.

The actual exchange ratio depends on world supply and demand for the two products. If overall world demand for coffee is weak relative to its supply and if the demand for wheat is strong relative to its supply, the price of coffee will be lower and the price of wheat higher. The exchange ratio will settle nearer the $1W \equiv 2C$ figure the United States prefers. If overall world demand for coffee is great relative to its supply and if the demand for wheat

is weak relative to its supply, the ratio will settle nearer the $1W \equiv 1C$ level favorable to Brazil. (We discuss equilibrium world prices later in this chapter.)

Gains from Trade

Suppose the international terms of trade are $1W \equiv 1\frac{1}{2}C$. The possibility of trading on these terms permits each nation to supplement its domestic production possibilities curve with a **trading possibilities line** (or curve), as shown in **Figure 37.2 (Key Graph).** Just as a production possibilities curve shows the amounts of these products a full-employment economy can obtain by shifting resources from one to the other, a trading possibilities line shows the amounts of two products a nation can obtain by specializing in one product and trading for the other. The trading possibilities lines in Figure 37.2 reflect the assumption that both nations specialize on the basis of comparative advantage: The United States specializes completely in wheat (at point W in Figure 37.2a), and Brazil specializes completely in coffee (at point c in Figure 37.2b).

Improved Options Now the United States is not constrained by its domestic production possibilities line, which requires it to give up 1 ton of wheat for every ton of coffee it wants as it moves up its domestic production possibilities line from, say, point W. Instead, the United States, through trade with Brazil, can get $1\frac{1}{2}$ tons of coffee for every ton of wheat it exports to Brazil, as long as Brazil has coffee to export. Trading possibilities line WC' thus represents the $1W \equiv 1\frac{1}{2}C$ trading ratio.

Similarly, Brazil, starting at, say, point c, no longer has to move down its domestic production possibilities curve, giving up 2 tons of coffee for each ton of wheat it wants. It can now export just $1\frac{1}{2}$ tons of coffee for each ton of wheat it wants by moving down its trading possibilities line cw'.

Specialization and trade create a new exchange ratio between wheat and coffee, reflected in each nation's trading possibilities line. This exchange ratio is superior for both nations to the unspecialized exchange ratio embodied in their production possibilities curves. By specializing in wheat and trading for Brazil's coffee, the United States can obtain more than 1 ton of coffee for 1 ton of wheat. By specializing in coffee and trading for U.S. wheat, Brazil can get 1 ton of wheat for less than 2 tons of coffee. In both cases, self-sufficiency is undesirable.

Added Output By specializing on the basis of comparative advantage and by trading for goods that are

KEY GRAPH

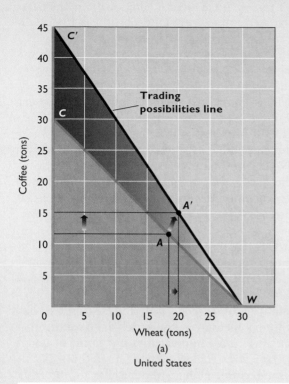

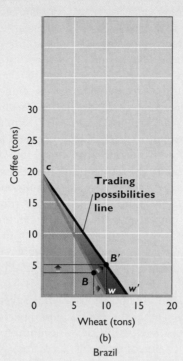

FIGURE 37.2

Trading possibility lines and the gains from trade. As a result of specialization and trade, both the United States and Brazil can have higher levels of output than the levels attainable on their domestic production possibilities curves. (a) The United States can move from point A on its domestic production possibilities curve to, say, A' on its trading possibilities line. (b) Brazil can move from B to B'.

QUICK QUIZ 37.2

1. The production possiblities curves in graphs (a) and (b) imply:
    a. increasing domestic opportunity costs.
    b. decreasing domestic opportunity costs.
    c. constant domestic opportunity costs.
    d. first decreasing, then increasing, domestic opportunity costs.

2. Before specialization, the domestic opportunity cost of producing 1 unit of wheat is:
    a. 1 unit of coffee in both the United States and Brazil.
    b. 1 unit of coffee in the United States and 2 units of coffee in Brazil.
    c. 2 units of coffee in the United States and 1 unit of coffee in Brazil.
    d. 1 unit of coffee in the United States and $\frac{1}{2}$ unit of coffee in Brazil.

3. After specialization and international trade, the world output of wheat and coffee is:
    a. 20 tons of wheat and 20 tons of coffee.
    b. 45 tons of wheat and 15 tons of coffee.
    c. 30 tons of wheat and 20 tons of coffee.
    d. 10 tons of wheat and 30 tons of coffee.

4. After specialization and international trade:
    a. the United States can obtain units of coffee at less cost than it could before trade.
    b. Brazil can obtain more than 20 tons of coffee, if it so chooses.
    c. the United States no longer has a comparative advantage in producing wheat.
    d. Brazil can benefit by prohibiting coffee imports from the United States.

Answers: 1. c; 2. b; 3. c; 4. a

produced in the nation with greater domestic efficiency, the United States and Brazil can realize combinations of wheat and coffee beyond their production possibilities curves. *Specialization according to comparative advantage results in a more efficient allocation of world resources, and larger outputs of both products are therefore available to both nations.*

Suppose that at the $1W \equiv 1\frac{1}{2}C$ terms of trade, the United States exports 10 tons of wheat to Brazil and in

return Brazil exports 15 tons of coffee to the United States. How do the new quantities of wheat and coffee available to the two nations compare with the optimal product mixes that existed before specialization and trade? Point *A* in Figure 37.2a reminds us that the United States chose 18 tons of wheat and 12 tons of coffee originally. But by producing 30 tons of wheat and no coffee and by trading 10 tons of wheat for 15 tons of coffee, the United

States can obtain 20 tons of wheat and 15 tons of coffee. This new, superior combination of wheat and coffee is indicated by point A' in Figure 37.2a. Compared with the no-trade amounts of 18 tons of wheat and 12 tons of coffee, the United States' **gains from trade** are 2 tons of wheat and 3 tons of coffee.

Similarly, recall that Brazil's optimal product mix was 4 tons of coffee and 8 tons of wheat (point B) before specialization and trade. Now, after specializing in coffee and trading, Brazil can have 5 tons of coffee and 10 tons of wheat. It accomplishes that by producing 20 tons of coffee and no wheat and exporting 15 tons of its coffee in exchange for 10 tons of American wheat. This new position is indicated by point B' in Figure 37.2b. Brazil's gains from trade are 1 ton of coffee and 2 tons of wheat.

As a result of specialization and trade, both countries have more of both products. Table 37.1, which summarizes the transactions and outcomes, merits careful study.

The fact that points A' and B' are economic positions superior to A and B is enormously important. We know that a nation can expand its production possibilities boundary by (1) expanding the quantity and improving the quality of its resources or (2) realizing technological progress. We have now established that international trade can enable a nation to circumvent the output constraint illustrated by its production possibilities curve. The outcome of international specialization and trade is equivalent to having more and better resources or discovering improved production techniques.

Trade with Increasing Costs

To explain the basic principles underlying international trade, we simplified our analysis in several ways. For example, we limited discussion to two products and two nations. But multiproduct and multinational analysis yields the same conclusions. We also assumed constant opportunity costs (linear production possibilities curves), which is a more substantive simplification. Let's consider the effect of allowing increasing opportunity costs (concave-to-the-origin production possibilities curves) to enter the picture.

Suppose that the United States and Brazil initially are at positions on their concave production possibilities curves where their domestic cost ratios are $1W \equiv 1C$ and $1W \equiv 2C$, as they were in our constant-cost analysis. As before, comparative advantage indicates that the United States should specialize in wheat and Brazil in coffee. But now, as the United States begins to expand wheat production, its cost of wheat will rise; it will have to sacrifice

more than 1 ton of coffee to get 1 additional ton of wheat. Resources are no longer perfectly substitutable between alternative uses, as the constant-cost assumption implied. Resources less and less suitable to wheat production must be allocated to the U.S. wheat industry in expanding wheat output, and that means increasing costs—the sacrifice of larger and larger amounts of coffee for each additional ton of wheat.

Similarly, Brazil, starting from its $1W \equiv 2C$ cost ratio position, expands coffee production. But as it does, it will find that its $1W \equiv 2C$ cost ratio begins to rise. Sacrificing a ton of wheat will free resources that are capable of producing only something less than 2 tons of coffee, because those transferred resources are less suitable to coffee production.

As the U.S. cost ratio falls from $1W \equiv 1C$ and the Brazilian ratio rises from $1W \equiv 2C$, a point will be reached where the cost ratios are equal in the two nations, perhaps at $1W \equiv 1\frac{3}{4}C$. At this point the underlying basis for further specialization and trade—differing cost ratios—has disappeared, and further specialization is therefore uneconomical. And, most importantly, this point of equal cost ratios may be reached while the United States is still producing some coffee along with its wheat and Brazil is producing some wheat along with its coffee. The primary effect of increasing opportunity costs is less-than-complete specialization. For this reason we often find domestically produced products competing directly against identical or similar imported products within a particular economy. **(Key Question 4)**

The Case for Free Trade

The case for free trade reduces to one compelling argument: *Through free trade based on the principle of comparative advantage, the world economy can achieve a more efficient allocation of resources and a higher level of material well-being than it can without free trade.*

Since the resource mixes and technological knowledge of the world's nations are all somewhat different, each nation can produce particular commodities at different real costs. Each nation should produce goods for which its domestic opportunity costs are lower than the domestic opportunity costs of other nations and exchange those goods for products for which its domestic opportunity costs are high relative to those of other nations. If each nation does this, the world will realize the advantages of geographic and human specialization. The world and each free-trading nation can obtain a larger real income from the fixed supplies of resources available to it. Government trade barriers lessen or eliminate gains from specialization. If nations cannot trade freely, they must shift resources from efficient (low-cost) to inefficient (high-cost) uses in order to satisfy their diverse wants.

One side benefit of free trade is that it promotes competition and deters monopoly. The increased competition from foreign firms forces domestic firms to find and use the lowest-cost production techniques. It also compels them to be innovative with respect to both product quality and production methods, thereby contributing to economic growth. And free trade gives consumers a wider range of product choices. The reasons to favor free trade are the same as the reasons to endorse competition.

A second side benefit of free trade is that it links national interests and breaks down national animosities. Confronted with political disagreements, trading partners tend to negotiate rather than make war.

QUICK REVIEW 37.1

- International trade is increasingly important to the United States and other nations of the world; the percentage of total output traded has increased since the Second World War.

- International trade enables nations to specialize, increase productivity, and increase output available for consumption.

- Comparative advantage means total world output will be greatest when each good is produced by the nation that has the lowest domestic opportunity cost.

- Specialization is less than complete among nations because opportunity costs normally rise as any given nation produces more of a particular good.

Supply and Demand Analysis of Exports and Imports

Supply and demand analysis reveals how equilibrium prices and quantities of exports and imports are determined. The amount of a good or a service a nation will export or import depends on differences between the equilibrium world price and the equilibrium domestic price. The interaction of *world* supply and demand determines the equilibrium **world price**—the price that equates the quantities supplied and demanded globally. *Domestic* supply and demand determine the equilibrium **domestic price**—the price that would prevail in a closed economy that does not engage in international trade. The domestic price equates quantity supplied and quantity demanded domestically.

In the absence of trade, the domestic prices in a closed economy may or may not equal the world equilibrium prices. When economies are opened for international trade, differences between world and domestic prices encourage exports or imports. To see how, consider the international effects of such price differences in a simple two-nation world, consisting of the United States and Canada, that are both producing aluminum. We assume there are no trade barriers, such as tariffs and quotas, and no international transportation costs.

Supply and Demand in the United States

Figure 37.3a shows the domestic supply curve S_d and the domestic demand curve D_d for aluminum in the United States, which for now is a closed economy. The intersection of S_d and D_d determines the equilibrium domestic price of $1 per pound and the equilibrium domestic quantity of 100 million pounds. Domestic suppliers produce 100 million pounds and sell them all at $1 a pound. So there are no domestic surpluses or shortages of aluminum.

But what if the U.S. economy were opened to trade and the world price of aluminum were above or below this $1 domestic price?

U.S. Export Supply If the aluminum price in the rest of the world (that is, Canada) exceeds $1, U.S. firms will produce more than 100 million pounds and will export the excess domestic output. First, consider a world price of $1.25. We see from the supply curve S_d that U.S. aluminum firms will produce 125 million pounds of aluminum at that price. The demand curve D_d tells us that the United States will purchase only 75 million pounds at $1.25. The outcome is a domestic surplus of 50 million pounds of aluminum. U.S. producers will export those 50 million pounds at the $1.25 world price.

What if the world price were $1.50? The supply curve shows that U.S. firms will produce 150 million pounds of aluminum, while the demand curve tells us that U.S. consumers will buy only 50 million pounds. So U.S. producers will export the domestic surplus of 100 million pounds.

Toward the top of Figure 37.3b we plot the domestic surpluses—the U.S. exports—that occur at world prices above the $1 domestic equilibrium price. When the world and domestic prices are equal (= $1), the quantity of

FIGURE 37.3

U.S. export supply and import demand. (a) Domestic supply S_d and demand D_d set the domestic equilibrium price of aluminum at $1 per pound. At world prices above $1 there are domestic surpluses of aluminum. At prices below $1 there are domestic shortages. (b) Surpluses are exported (top curve), and shortages are met by importing aluminum (lower curve). The export supply curve shows the direct relationship between world prices and U.S. exports; the import demand curve portrays the inverse relationship between world prices and U.S. imports.

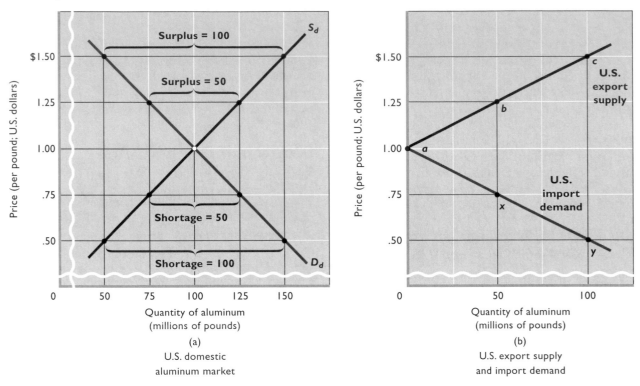

(a)
U.S. domestic
aluminum market

(b)
U.S. export supply
and import demand

exports supplied is zero (point *a*). There is no surplus of domestic output to export. But when the world price is $1.25, U.S. firms export 50 million pounds of surplus aluminum (point *b*). At a $1.50 world price, the domestic surplus of 100 million pounds is exported (point *c*).

The U.S. **export supply curve,** found by connecting points *a*, *b*, and *c*, shows the amount of aluminum U.S. producers will export at each world price above $1. This curve *slopes upward*, indicating a direct or positive relationship between the world price and the amount of U.S. exports. *As world prices increase relative to domestic prices, U.S. exports rise.*

U.S. Import Demand

If the world price is below the domestic $1 price, the United States will import aluminum. Consider a $.75 world price. The supply curve in Figure 37.3a reveals that at that price U.S. firms produce only 75 million pounds of aluminum. But the demand curve shows that the United States wants to buy 125 million pounds at that price. The result is a

domestic shortage of 50 million pounds. To satisfy that shortage, the United States will import 50 million pounds of aluminum.

At an even lower world price, $.50, U.S. producers will supply only 50 million pounds. Because U.S. consumers want to buy 150 million pounds at that price, there is a domestic shortage of 100 million pounds. Imports will flow to the United States to make up the difference. That is, at a $.50 world price U.S. firms will supply 50 million pounds and 100 million pounds will be imported.

In Figure 37.3b we plot the U.S. **import demand curve** from these data. This *downsloping curve* shows the amounts of aluminum that will be imported at world prices below the $1 U.S. domestic price. The relationship between world prices and imported amounts is inverse or negative. At a world price of $1, domestic output will satisfy U.S. demand; imports will be zero (point *a*). But at $.75 the United States will import 50 million pounds of aluminum (point *x*); at $.50, the United States will import 100 million pounds (point *y*). Connecting points *a*, *x*, and *y* yields the *downsloping* U.S. import demand curve. *It reveals that as world prices fall relative to U.S. domestic prices, U.S. imports increase.*

Supply and Demand in Canada

We repeat our analysis in Figure 37.4, this time from the viewpoint of Canada. (We have converted Canadian dollar prices to U.S. dollar prices via the exchange rate.) Note that the domestic supply curve S_d and the domestic demand curve D_d for aluminum in Canada yield a domestic price of $.75, which is $.25 lower than the $1 U.S. domestic price.

The analysis proceeds exactly as above except that the domestic price is now the Canadian price. If the world price is $.75, Canadians will neither export nor import aluminum (giving us point *q* in Figure 37.4b). At world prices above $.75, Canadian firms will produce more aluminum than Canadian consumers will buy. Canadian firms will export the surplus. At a $1 world price, Figure 37.4a tells us that Canada will have and export a domestic surplus of 50 million pounds (yielding point *r*). At

$1.25, it will have and will export a domestic surplus of 100 million pounds (point *s*). Connecting these points yields the upsloping Canadian export supply curve, which reflects the domestic surpluses (and hence the exports) that occur when the world price exceeds the $.75 Canadian domestic price.

At world prices below $.75, domestic shortages occur in Canada. At a $.50 world price, Figure 37.4a shows that Canadian consumers want to buy 125 million pounds of aluminum but Canadian firms will produce only 75 million pounds. The shortage will bring 50 million pounds of imports to Canada (point *t* in Figure 37.4b). The Canadian import demand curve in that figure shows the Canadian imports that will occur at all world aluminum prices below the $.75 Canadian domestic price.

Equilibrium World Price, Exports, and Imports

We now have the tools for determining the **equilibrium world price** of aluminum and the equilibrium world levels of exports and imports when the world is opened to

FIGURE 37.4

Canadian export supply and import demand. (a) At world prices above the $.75 domestic price, production in Canada exceeds domestic consumption. At world prices below $.75, domestic shortages occur. (b) Surpluses result in exports, and shortages result in imports. The Canadian export supply curve and import demand curve depict the relationships between world prices and exports or imports.

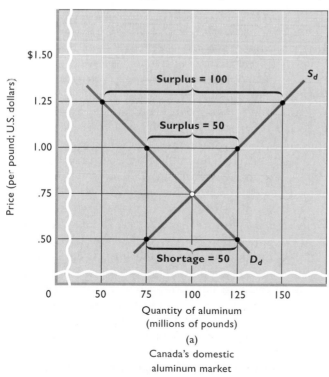

(a)
Canada's domestic
aluminum market

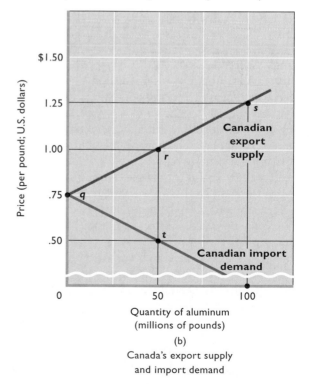

(b)
Canada's export supply
and import demand

FIGURE 37.5

Equilibrium world price and quantity of exports and imports. In a two-nation world, the equilibrium world price (= $.88) is determined by the intersection of one nation's export supply curve and the other nation's import demand curve. This intersection also decides the equilibrium volume of exports and imports. Here, Canada exports 25 million pounds of aluminum to the United States.

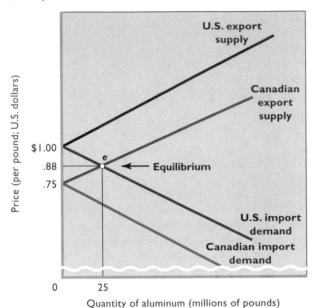

Quantity of aluminum (millions of pounds)

trade. Figure 37.5 combines the U.S. export supply curve and import demand curve in Figure 37.3b and the Canadian export supply curve and import demand curve in Figure 37.4b. The two U.S. curves proceed rightward from the $1 U.S. domestic price; the two Canadian curves proceed rightward from the $.75 Canadian domestic price.

International equilibrium occurs in this two-nation model where one nation's import demand curve intersects another nation's export supply curve. In this case the U.S. import demand curve intersects Canada's export supply curve at *e*. There, the world price of aluminum is $.88. The Canadian export supply curve indicates that Canada will export 25 million pounds of aluminum at this price. Also at this price the United States will import 25 million pounds from Canada, indicated by the U.S. import demand curve. The $.88 world price equates the quantity of imports demanded and the quantity of exports supplied (25 million pounds). Thus there will be world trade of 25 million pounds of aluminum at $.88 per pound.

Note that after trade, the single $.88 world price will prevail in both Canada and the United States. Only one

price for a standardized commodity can persist in a highly competitive world market. With trade, all consumers can buy a pound of aluminum for $.88, and all producers can sell it for that price. This world price means that Canadians will pay more for aluminum with trade ($.88) than without it ($.75). The increased Canadian output caused by trade raises Canadian per-unit production costs and therefore raises the price of aluminum in Canada. The United States, however, pays less for aluminum with trade ($.88) than without it ($1). The U.S. gain comes from Canada's comparative cost advantage in producing aluminum.

Why would Canada willingly send 25 million pounds of its aluminum output to the United States for U.S. consumption? After all, producing this output uses up scarce Canadian resources and drives up the price of aluminum for Canadians. Canadians are willing to export aluminum to the United States because Canadians gain the means—the U.S. dollars—to import other goods, say, computer software, from the United States. Canadian exports enable Canadians to acquire imports that have greater value to Canadians than the exported aluminum. Canadian exports to the United States finance Canadian imports from the United States. **(Key Question 6)**

Trade Barriers

No matter how compelling the case for free trade, barriers to free trade *do* exist. Let's expand Chapter 6's discussion of trade barriers.

Excise taxes on imported goods are called **tariffs;** they may be imposed to obtain revenue or to protect domestic firms. A **revenue tariff** is usually applied to a product that is not being produced domestically, for example, tin, coffee, or bananas in the case of the United States. Rates on revenue tariffs are modest; their purpose is to provide the Federal government with revenue. A **protective tariff** is designed to shield domestic producers from foreign competition. Although protective tariffs are usually not high enough to stop the importation of foreign goods, they put foreign producers at a competitive disadvantage in selling in domestic markets.

An **import quota** specifies the maximum amount of a commodity that may be imported in any period. Import quotas can more effectively retard international commerce than tariffs. A product might be imported in large quantities despite high tariffs; low import quotas completely prohibit imports once quotas have been filled.

A **nontariff barrier (NTB)** is a licensing requirement that specifies unreasonable standards pertaining to product quality and safety, or unnecessary bureaucratic red tape that is used to restrict imports. Japan and the European countries frequently require that their domestic importers of foreign goods obtain licenses. By restricting the issuance of licenses, imports can be restricted. The United Kingdom uses this barrier to bar the importation of coal.

A **voluntary export restriction (VER)** is a trade barrier by which foreign firms "voluntarily" limit the amount of their exports to a particular country. VERs, which have the effect of import quotas, are agreed to by exporters in the hope of avoiding more stringent trade barriers. In the late 1990s, for example, Canadian producers of softwood lumber (fir, spruce, cedar, pine) agreed to a VER on exports to the United States under the threat of a permanently higher U.S. tariff. Later in this chapter we will consider the arguments and appeals that are made to justify protection.

37.1
Mercantilism

Economic Impact of Tariffs

Once again we turn to supply and demand analysis—now to examine the economic effects of protective tariffs. Curves D_d and S_d in Figure 37.6 show domestic demand and supply for a product in which a nation, say, the United States, has a comparative disadvantage—for example, digital versatile disk (DVD) players. (Disregard curve $S_d + Q$ for now.) Without world trade, the domestic price and output would be P_d and q, respectively.

Assume now that the domestic economy is opened to world trade and that the Japanese, who have a comparative advantage in DVD players, begin to sell their players in the United States. We assume that with free trade the domestic price cannot differ from the world price, which here is P_w. At P_w domestic consumption is d and domestic production is a. The horizontal distance between the domestic supply and demand curves at P_w represents imports of ad. Thus far, our analysis is similar to the analysis of world prices in Figure 37.3.

Direct Effects Suppose now that the United States imposes a tariff on each imported DVD player. The tariff, which raises the price of imported players from P_w to P_t, has four effects:

- **Decline in consumption** Consumption of DVD players in the United States declines from d to c as the higher price moves buyers up and to the left along their demand curve. The tariff prompts consumers to buy fewer players, and reallocate a portion of their

FIGURE 37.6

The economic effects of a protective tariff or an import quota. A tariff that increases the price of a good from P_w to P_t will reduce domestic consumption from d to c. Domestic producers will be able to sell more output (b rather than a) at a higher price (P_t rather than P_w). Foreign exporters are injured because they sell less output (bc rather than ad). The orange area indicates the amount of tariff paid by domestic consumers. An import quota of bc units has the same effect as the tariff, with one exception: The amount represented by the orange area will go to foreign producers rather than to the domestic government.

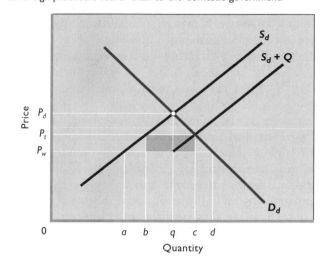

expenditures to less desired substitute products. U.S. consumers are clearly injured by the tariff, since they pay P_wP_t more for each of the c units they buy at price P_t.

- **Increased domestic production** U.S. producers—who are not subject to the tariff—receive the higher price P_t per unit. Because this new price is higher than the pretariff world price P_w, the domestic DVD-player industry moves up and to the right along its supply curve S_d, increasing domestic output from a to b. Domestic producers thus enjoy both a higher price and expanded sales; this explains why domestic producers lobby for protective tariffs. But from a social point of view, the greater domestic production from a to b means that the tariff permits domestic producers of players to bid resources away from other, more efficient, U.S. industries.

- **Decline in imports** Japanese producers are hurt. Although the sales price of each player is higher by P_wP_t, that amount accrues to the U.S. government, not to Japanese producers. The after-tariff world price, or the per-unit revenue to Japanese producers, remains at P_w, but the volume of U.S. imports (Japanese exports) falls from ad to bc.

- *Tariff revenue* The orange rectangle represents the amount of revenue the tariff yields. Total revenue from the tariff is determined by multiplying the tariff, $P_w P_t$ per unit, by the number of players imported, bc. This tariff revenue is a transfer of income from consumers to government and does not represent any net change in the nation's economic well-being. The result is that government gains this portion of what consumers lose by paying more for DVD players.

Indirect Effect Tariffs have a subtle effect beyond what our supply and demand diagram can show. Because Japan sells fewer DVD players in the United States, it earns fewer dollars and so must buy fewer U.S. exports. U.S. export industries must then cut production and release resources. These are highly efficient industries, as we know from their comparative advantage and their ability to sell goods in world markets.

Tariffs directly promote the expansion of inefficient industries that do not have a comparative advantage; they also indirectly cause the contraction of relatively efficient industries that do have a comparative advantage. Put bluntly, tariffs cause resources to be shifted in the wrong direction—and that is not surprising. We know that specialization and world trade lead to more efficient use of world resources and greater world output. But protective tariffs reduce world trade. Therefore, tariffs also reduce efficiency and the world's real output.

Economic Impact of Quotas

We noted earlier that an import quota is a legal limit placed on the amount of some product that can be imported in a given year. Quotas have the same economic impact as a tariff, with one big difference: While tariffs generate revenue for the domestic government, a quota transfers that revenue to foreign producers.

Suppose in Figure 37.6 that, instead of imposing a tariff, the United States prohibits any imports of Japanese DVD players in excess of bc units. In other words, an import quota of bc players is imposed on Japan. We deliberately chose the size of this quota to be the same amount as imports would be under a $P_w P_t$ tariff so that we can compare "equivalent" situations. As a consequence of the quota, the supply of players is $S_d + Q$ in the United States. This supply consists of the domestic supply plus the fixed amount bc ($= Q$) that importers will provide at each domestic price. The supply curve $S_d + Q$ does not extend below price P_w, because Japanese producers would not export players to the United States at any price below P_w; instead, they would sell them to other countries at the world market price of P_w.

Most of the economic results are the same as those with a tariff. Prices of DVD players are higher (P_t instead of P_w) because imports have been reduced from ad to bc. Domestic consumption of DVD players is down from d to c. U.S. producers enjoy both a higher price (P_t rather than P_w) and increased sales (b rather than a).

The difference is that the price increase of $P_w P_t$ paid by U.S. consumers on imports of bc—the orange area—no longer goes to the U.S. Treasury as tariff (tax) revenue but flows to the Japanese firms that have acquired the rights to sell DVD players in the United States. For consumers in the United States, a tariff produces a better economic outcome than a quota, other things being the same. A tariff generates government revenue that can be used to cut other taxes or to finance public goods and services that benefit the United States. In contrast, the higher price created by quotas results in additional revenue for foreign producers. **(Key Question 7)**

Net Costs of Tariffs and Quotas

Figure 37.6 shows that tariffs and quotas impose costs on domestic consumers but provide gains to domestic producers and, in the case of tariffs, revenue to the Federal government. The consumer costs of trade restrictions are calculated by determining the effect the restrictions have on consumer prices. Protection raises the price of a product in three ways: (1) The price of the imported product goes up; (2) the higher price of imports causes some consumers to shift their purchases to higher-priced domestically produced goods; and (3) the prices of domestically produced goods rise because import competition has declined.

Study after study finds that the costs to consumers substantially exceed the gains to producers and government. A sizable net cost or efficiency loss to society arises from trade protection. Furthermore, industries employ large amounts of economic resources to influence Congress to pass and retain protectionist laws. Because these rent-seeking efforts divert resources away from more socially desirable purposes, trade restrictions impose that cost on society.

Conclusion: The gains that U.S. trade barriers create for protected industries and their workers come at the expense of much greater losses for the entire economy. The result is economic inefficiency.

Impact on Income Distribution

Tariffs and quotas affect low-income families proportionately more than high-income families. Because they act much like sales or excise taxes, these trade restrictions are highly regressive. That is, the "overcharge" associated with trade protection falls as a percentage of income as income increases. For example, a family with an annual income of $10,000 may pay an overcharge of $100 per year because of the trade restrictions on apparel, while a family with an income of $100,000 may pay a $500 overcharge. As a percentage of income, the lower-income family pays 1 percent (= $100 of overcharge/$10,000 of income); the higher-income family, only .5 percent (= $500/$100,000).

The Case for Protection: A Critical Review

Despite the logic of specialization and trade, there are still protectionists in some union halls, corporate boardrooms, and the halls of Congress. What arguments do protectionists make to justify trade barriers? How valid are those arguments?

Military Self-Sufficiency Argument

The argument here is not economic but political-military: Protective tariffs are needed to preserve or strengthen industries that produce the materials essential for national defense. In an uncertain world, the political-military objectives (self-sufficiency) sometimes must take precedence over economic goals (efficiency in the use of world resources).

Unfortunately, it is difficult to measure and compare the benefit of increased national security against the cost of economic inefficiency when protective tariffs are imposed. The economist can only point out that there are economic costs when a nation levies tariffs to increase military self-sufficiency.

All people in the United States would agree that it is not a good idea to rely on hostile nations for necessary military equipment, yet the self-sufficiency argument is open to serious abuse. Nearly every industry can claim that it makes direct or indirect contributions to national security and hence deserves protection from imports.

Are there not better ways than tariffs to provide needed strength in strategic industries? When it is achieved through tariffs, this self-sufficiency increases the domestic prices of the products of the protected industry. Thus only those consumers who buy the industry's products shoulder the cost of greater military security. A direct subsidy to strategic industries, financed out of general tax revenues, would distribute those costs more equitably.

Increased Domestic Employment Argument

Arguing for a tariff to "save U.S. jobs" becomes fashionable as an economy encounters a recession. In an economy that engages in international trade, exports involve spending on domestic output and imports reflect spending to obtain part of another nation's output. So, in this argument, reducing imports will divert spending on another nation's output to spending on domestic output. Thus domestic output and employment will rise. But this argument has several shortcomings:

- *Job creation from imports*   While imports may eliminate some U.S. jobs, they create others. Imports may have eliminated the jobs of some U.S. steel and textile workers in recent years, but other workers have gained jobs unloading ships and selling imported cars and imported electronic equipment. Import restrictions alter the composition of employment, but they may have little or no effect on the volume of employment.

- *Fallacy of composition*   All nations cannot simultaneously succeed in restricting imports while maintaining their exports; what is true for one nation is not true for all nations. The exports of one nation must be the imports of another nation. To the extent that one country is able to expand its economy through an excess of exports over imports, the resulting excess of imports over exports worsens another economy's unemployment problem. It is no wonder that tariffs and import quotas meant to achieve domestic full employment are called "beggar my neighbor" policies: They achieve short-run domestic goals by making trading partners poorer.

- *Possibility of retaliation*   Nations adversely affected by tariffs and quotas are likely to retaliate, causing a "trade-barrier war" that will choke off trade and make all nations worse off. The Smoot-Hawley Tariff Act of 1930, which imposed the highest tariffs ever enacted in the United States, backfired miserably. Rather than raising U.S. output, those tariffs only produced retaliatory restrictions by affected nations. That trade war caused a further contraction of international trade and lowered the income and employment levels of all nations.

- *Long-run feedbacks*   In the long run, forcing an excess of exports over imports cannot succeed in raising domestic employment. It is through U.S. imports that foreign nations earn dollars for buying U.S. exports. In the long run a nation must import in order to export. The long-run impact of tariffs is not an increase in domestic employment but, at best, a reallocation of workers away from export industries and to protected domestic industries. This shift implies a less efficient allocation of resources.

Diversification-for-Stability Argument

Highly specialized economies such as Saudi Arabia (based on oil) and Cuba (based on sugar) are dependent on international markets for their income. In these economies, wars, international political developments, recessions abroad, and random fluctuations in world supply and demand for one or two particular goods can cause deep declines in export revenues and therefore in domestic income. Tariff and quota protection are allegedly needed in

CONSIDER THIS . . .

Shooting Yourself in the Foot

© Grant V. Faint/Getty Images

In the lore of the Wild West, a gunslinger on occasion would accidentally pull the trigger on his pistol while retrieving it from its holster, shooting himself in the foot. Since then, the phrase "shooting yourself in the foot" implies doing damage to yourself rather than the intended party.

That is precisely how economist Paul Krugman sees a trade war:

A trade war in which countries restrict each other's exports in pursuit of some illusory advantage is not much like a real war. On the one hand, nobody gets killed. On the other, unlike real wars, it is almost impossible for anyone to win, since the main losers when a country imposes barriers to trade are not foreign exporters but domestic residents. In effect, a trade war is a conflict in which each country uses most of its ammunition to shoot itself in the foot.*

The same analysis is applicable to trade boycotts between major trading partners. Such a boycott was encouraged by some American commentators against French imports because of the opposition of France to the U.S.- and British-led war in Iraq. But the decline of exports to the United States would leave the French with fewer U.S. dollars to buy American exports. So the unintended effect would be a decline in U.S. exports to France and reduced employment in U.S. export industries. Moreover, such a trade boycott, if effective, might lead French consumers to retaliate against American imports. As with a "tariff war," a "boycott war" typically harms oneself as much as the other party.

*Paul Krugman, *Peddling Prosperity* (New York: Norton, 1994), p. 287.

such nations to enable greater industrial diversification. That way, these economies will not be so dependent on exporting one or two products to obtain the other goods they need. Such goods will be available domestically, thereby providing greater domestic stability.

There is some truth in this diversification-for-stability argument. There are also two serious shortcomings:

- The argument has little or no relevance to the United States and other advanced economies.
- The economic costs of diversification may be great; for example, one-crop economies may be highly inefficient at manufacturing.

Infant Industry Argument

The infant industry argument contends that protective tariffs are needed to allow new domestic industries to establish themselves. Temporarily shielding young domestic firms from the severe competition of more mature and more efficient foreign firms will give infant industries a chance to develop and become efficient producers.

This argument for protection rests on an alleged exception to the case for free trade. The exception is that young industries have not had, and if they face mature foreign competition will never have, the chance to make the long-run adjustments needed for larger scale and greater efficiency in production. In this view, tariff protection for such infant industries will correct a misallocation of world resources perpetuated by historically different levels of economic development between domestic and foreign industries.

Counterarguments There are some logical problems with the infant industry argument:

- In the developing nations it is difficult to determine which industries are the infants that are capable of achieving economic maturity and therefore deserving protection.
- Protective tariffs may persist even after industrial maturity has been realized.
- Most economists feel that if infant industries are to be subsidized, there are better means than tariffs for doing so. Direct subsidies, for example, have the advantage of making explicit which industries are being aided and to what degree.

Strategic Trade Policy In recent years the infant industry argument has taken a modified form in advanced economies. Now proponents contend that government should use trade barriers to reduce the risk of investing in product development by domestic firms, particularly where advanced technology is involved. Firms protected from foreign competition can grow more rapidly and achieve greater economies of scale than unprotected foreign competitors. The protected firms can eventually dominate world markets because of their lower costs. Supposedly, dominance of world markets will enable the domestic firms to return high profits to the home nation. These profits will exceed the domestic sacrifices caused by trade barriers. Also, advances in high-technology industries are deemed beneficial, because the advances achieved in one domestic industry often can be transferred to other domestic industries.

Japan and South Korea, in particular, have been accused of using this form of **strategic trade policy.** The problem with this strategy and therefore with this argument for tariffs is that the nations put at a disadvantage by strategic trade policies tend to retaliate with tariffs of their own. The outcome may be higher tariffs worldwide, reduction of world trade, and the loss of potential gains from technological advances.

Protection-against-Dumping Argument

This argument contends that tariffs are needed to protect domestic firms from "dumping" by foreign producers. **Dumping** is the selling of excess goods in a foreign market at a price below cost. Economists cite two plausible reasons for this behavior. First, firms may use dumping abroad to drive out domestic competitors there, thus obtaining monopoly power and monopoly prices and profits for the importing firm. The long-term economic profits resulting from this strategy may more than offset the earlier losses that accompany the below-cost sales.

Second, dumping may be a form of price discrimination, which is charging different prices to different customers even though costs are the same. The foreign seller may find it can maximize its profit by charging a high price in its monopolized domestic market while unloading its surplus output at a lower price in the United States. The surplus output may be needed so that the firm can obtain the overall per-unit cost saving associated with large-scale production. The higher profit in the home market more than makes up for the losses incurred on sales abroad.

Because dumping is a legitimate concern, many nations prohibit it. For example, where dumping is shown to injure U.S. firms, the Federal government imposes tariffs called "antidumping duties" on the specific goods. But there are relatively few documented cases of dumping each year, and those few cases do not justify widespread, permanent tariffs.

In fact, foreign producers argue that the United States uses dumping allegations and antidumping duties to restrict legitimate trade. Some foreign firms clearly can produce certain goods at substantially less per-unit cost than U.S. competitors. So what may seem to be dumping actually is comparative advantage at work. If antidumping laws are abused, they might increase the price of imports and restrict competition in the U.S. market. Such reduced competition might enable U.S. firms to raise prices at consumers' expense. And even where true dumping does occur, U.S. consumers gain from the lower-priced product, at least in the short run, much as they gain from a price war among U.S. producers.

Cheap Foreign Labor Argument

The cheap foreign labor argument says that domestic firms and workers must be shielded from the ruinous competition of countries where wages are low. If protection is not provided, cheap imports will flood U.S. markets and the prices of U.S. goods—along with the wages of U.S. workers—will be pulled down. That is, the domestic living standards in the United States will be reduced.

This argument can be rebutted at several levels. The logic of the argument suggests that it is not mutually beneficial for rich and poor persons to trade with one another. However, that is not the case. A low-income farmworker may pick lettuce or tomatoes for a rich landowner, and both may benefit from the transaction. And U.S. consumers gain when they buy a Taiwanese-made pocket radio for $12 as opposed to a similar U.S.-made radio selling for $20.

Also, recall that gains from trade are based on comparative advantage, not on absolute advantage. Look back at Figure 37.1, and suppose that the United States and Brazil have labor forces of exactly the same size. Noting the positions of the production possibilities curves, observe that U.S. labor can produce more of either good. Thus, it is more productive. Because of this greater productivity, we can expect wages and living standards to be higher for U.S. labor. Brazil's less productive labor will receive lower wages.

The cheap foreign labor argument suggests that, to maintain our standard of living, the United States should not trade with low-wage Brazil. Suppose it does not trade with Brazil. Will wages and living standards rise in the United States as a result? No. To obtain coffee, the United States will have to reallocate a portion of its labor from its efficient wheat industry to its inefficient coffee industry. As a result, the average productivity of U.S. labor will fall, as will real wages and living standards. The labor forces of both countries will have diminished standards of living because without specialization and trade they will have less output available to them. Compare column 4 with column 1 in Table 37.1

Various Protest Groups Have Angrily Targeted the World Trade Organization (WTO). What Is the Source of All the Noise and Commotion?

The WTO became known to the general public in November 1999, when tens of thousands of people took part in sometimes violent demonstrations in Seattle. Since then, international WTO meetings have drawn large numbers of angry demonstrators. The groups involved include some labor unions (which fear loss of jobs and labor protections), environmental groups (which oppose environmental degradation), socialists (who dislike capitalism and multinational corporations), and a few anarchists (who detest government authority of any kind). Dispersed within the crowds are other, smaller groups such as European farmers who fear the WTO will threaten their livelihoods by reducing agricultural tariffs and farm subsidies.

The most substantive WTO issues involve labor protections and environmental standards. Labor unions in industrially advanced countries (IACs) would like the international trade rules to include such labor standards as collective bargaining rights, minimum wages, workplace safety standards, and prohibitions of child labor. Such rules are fully consistent with the long-standing values and objectives of unions. But there is a hitch. Imposing labor standards on low-income developing countries (DVCs) would raise labor and production costs in those nations. The higher costs in the DVCs would raise the relative price of DVC goods and make them less competitive with goods produced in the IACs (which already meet the labor standards). So the trade rules would increase the demands for products and workers in the IACs and reduce them in the DVCs. Union workers in the IACs would benefit; consumers in the IACs and workers in the DVCs would be harmed. The trade standards would contribute to poverty in the world's poorest nations.

Not surprisingly, the DVCs say "thanks, but no thanks" to the protesters' pleas for labor standards. Instead, they want the IACs to reduce or eliminate tariffs on goods imported from the developing countries. That would expand the demand for DVC products and workers, boosting DVC wages. As living standards in the DVCs rise, those countries then can afford to devote more of their annual productivity advances to improved working conditions.

The 145-nation WTO points out that its mandate is to liberalize trade through multilateral negotiation, not to set labor standards for each nation. That should be left to the countries themselves. Economists suggest that protesters channel their efforts to supporting activities of the International Labour Organization (ILO), which strives to improve wages and working conditions worldwide. Demonstrators might also help local groups bring political pressure on individual nations to improve their labor protections as their standards of living rise. If nations with minimal labor protections are ruled by dictators, then demonstrators may want to support international and domestic efforts to reform those political systems.

---

or points *A′* and *B′* with *A* and *B* in Figure 37.2 to confirm this point.

A Summing Up

The many arguments for protection are not weighty. Under proper conditions, the infant industry argument stands as a valid exception, justifiable on economic grounds. And on political-military grounds, the self-sufficiency argument can be used to validate some protection. But both arguments are open to severe overuse, and both neglect other ways of promoting industrial development and military self-sufficiency. Most of the other arguments are emotional appeals—half-truths and fallacies. They see only the immediate, direct consequences of protective tariffs, but ignore the fact that in the long run a nation must import in order to export.

There is also compelling historical evidence suggesting that free trade has led to prosperity and growth and that protectionism has had the opposite effects. Here are several examples:

- The U.S. Constitution forbids individual states from levying tariffs, and that makes the United States itself a huge free-trade area. Economic historians cite this as a positive factor in the economic development of the United States.

- The creation of the Common Market in Europe after the Second World War eliminated tariffs among member nations. Economists agree that the creation of this free-trade area, now the European Union, was a major ingredient in western European prosperity.

- The trend toward tariff reduction since the mid-1930s stimulated expansion of the world economy after the Second World War.

- The high tariffs imposed by the Smoot-Hawley Act of 1930 and the retaliation that they engendered worsened the Great Depression of the 1930s.

- In general, developing countries that have relied on import restrictions to protect their domestic industries have had slow growth compared to those that have pursued more open economic policies.

Environmental standards are the second substantive WTO issue. Critics are concerned that trade liberalization will encourage more activities that degrade sensitive forests, fisheries, and mining lands and contribute to air, water, and solid-waste pollution. Critics would like the WTO to establish trade rules that set minimum environmental standards for the member nations. The WTO nations respond that environmental standards are outside the mandate of the WTO and must be established by the individual nations via their own political processes.

Moreover, imposing such standards on DVCs may simply provide competitive cost advantages to companies in the IACs. As with labor standards, that will simply slow economic growth and prolong poverty in the DVCs. Studies show that economic growth and rising living standards are strongly associated with greater environmental protections. In the early phases of their development, low-income developing nations typically

choose to trade off some environmental damage to achieve higher real wages. But studies show that the tradeoff is usually reversed once standards of living rise beyond threshold levels.

Labor standards and environmental protections are worthy objectives. But impeding efforts to liberalize trade may be an ineffective—even detrimental—way to achieve them. Reductions in tariffs and impediments to investment increase productivity, output, and incomes worldwide. The higher living standards enable developing and developed nations alike to "buy" more protections for labor and the environment. Strong, sustained economic growth results not only in more goods and services but also in more socially desirable and environmentally sensitive production methods.

The World Trade Organization

As indicated in Chapter 6, the inefficiencies of trade protectionism have led nations to seek various ways to reduce tariffs and quotas. In the Uruguay Round agreement (1994), 120 of the world's nations formed the **World Trade Organization (WTO)** and agreed to several trade liberalizations to be fully implemented by 2005. The liberalizations include (1) reductions in tariffs worldwide; (2) new rules to promote trade in services; (3) reductions in agricultural subsidies that have distorted the global pattern of trade in agricultural goods; (4) new protections for intellectual property (copyrights, patents, trademarks); and (5) the phasing out of quotas on textiles and apparel, replacing them with gradually declining tariffs. The WTO estimates that the world's GDP for 2005 will be $6 trillion greater (or 8 percent higher) because of the trade liberalizations.

The 1994 agreement created the WTO to oversee the provisions of the agreement, resolve any disputes under the trade rules, and meet periodically to consider further trade liberalization. By late 2001 some 145 nations belonged to the WTO and they met in Doha, Qatar, to initiate the current round of negotiations to liberalize trade and investment. The Doha Round is scheduled to take place in various locations around the world and is expected to last several years.

As a symbol of trade liberalization and global capitalism, the WTO has become a target of a variety of protest groups. This chapter's Last Word examines some of the reasons for the protests, and we strongly urge you to read it.

SUMMARY

1. The United States leads the world in the volume of international trade. Since 1975 U.S. exports and imports have more than doubled as a percentage of GDP. Other major trading nations are Germany, Japan, the western European nations, and the Asian economies of China, South Korea, Taiwan, and Singapore.

2. World trade is based on three considerations: the uneven distribution of economic resources among nations, the fact that efficient production of various goods requires particular techniques or combinations of resources, and the differentiated products produced among nations.

3. Mutually advantageous specialization and trade are possible between any two nations if they have different domestic opportunity-cost ratios for any two products. By specializing on the basis of comparative advantage, nations can obtain larger real incomes with fixed amounts of resources. The terms of trade determine how this increase in world output is shared by the trading nations. Increasing (rather than constant) opportunity costs limit specialization and trade.

4. A nation's export supply curve shows the quantities of a product the nation will export at world prices that exceed the domestic price (the price in a closed, no-international-trade economy). A nation's import demand curve reveals the quantities of a product it will import at world prices below the domestic price.

5. In a two-nation model, the equilibrium world price and the equilibrium quantities of exports and imports occur where one nation's export supply curve intersects the other nation's import demand curve.

6. Trade barriers take the form of protective tariffs, quotas, nontariff barriers, and "voluntary" export restrictions. Supply and demand analysis reveals that protective tariffs and quotas increase the prices and reduce the quantities demanded of the affected goods. Sales by foreign exporters diminish; domestic producers, however, gain higher prices and enlarged sales. Consumer losses from trade restrictions greatly exceed producer and government gains, creating an efficiency loss to society.

7. The strongest arguments for protection are the infant industry and military self-sufficiency arguments. Most other arguments for protection are half-truths, emotional appeals, or fallacies that emphasize the immediate effects of trade barriers while ignoring long-run consequences. Numerous historical examples suggest that free trade promotes economic growth; protectionism does not.

8. In 2003 the World Trade Organization (WTO) consisted of 145 member nations. The WTO oversees trade agreements among the members, resolves disputes over the rules, and periodically meets to discuss and negotiate further trade liberalization. In 2001 the WTO initiated a new round of trade negotiations in Doha, Qatar. The Doha Round (named after its place of initiation) will occur over the next several years.

9. As a symbol of global capitalism, the WTO has become a target of considerable protest. The controversy surrounding the WTO is the subject of this chapter's Last Word. Most economists are concerned that tying trade liberalization to a host of other issues such as environmental and labor standards will greatly delay or block further trade liberalization. Such liberalization is one of the main sources of higher living standards worldwide.

TERMS AND CONCEPTS

labor-intensive goods

land-intensive goods

capital-intensive goods

cost ratio

principle of comparative advantage

terms of trade

trading possibilities line

gains from trade

world price

domestic price

export supply curve

import demand curve

equilibrium world price

tariffs

revenue tariff

protective tariff

import quota

nontariff barrier (NTB)

voluntary export restriction (VER)

strategic trade policy

dumping

World Trade Organization (WTO)

STUDY QUESTIONS

1. Quantitatively, how important is international trade to the United States relative to other nations?

2. Distinguish among land-, labor-, and capital-intensive commodities, citing one nontextbook example of each. What role do these distinctions play in explaining international trade? What role do distinctive products, unrelated to cost advantages, play in international trade?

3. Suppose nation A can produce 80 units of X by using all its resources to produce X or 60 units of Y by devoting all its resources to Y. Comparable figures for nation B are 60 units of X and 60 units of Y. Assuming constant costs, in which product should each nation specialize? Why? What are the limits of the terms of trade?

4. *Key Question* Below are hypothetical production possibilities tables for New Zealand and Spain. Each country can produce apples and plums.

New Zealand's Production Possibilities Table
(Millions of Bushels)

Product	Production Alternatives			
	A	**B**	**C**	**D**
Apples	0	20	40	60
Plums	15	10	5	0

Spain's Production Possibilities Table
(Millions of Bushels)

Product	Production Alternatives			
	R	**S**	**T**	**U**
Apples	0	20	40	60
Plums	60	40	20	0

Plot the production possibilities data for each of the two countries separately. Referring to your graphs, answer the following:
   a. What is each country's cost ratio of producing plums and apples.
   b. Which nation should specialize in which product?
   c. Show the trading possibilities lines for each nation if the actual terms of trade are 1 plum for 2 apples. (Plot these lines on your graph.)
   d. Suppose the optimum product mixes before specialization and trade were alternative B in New Zealand and alternative S in Spain. What would be the gains from specialization and trade?

5. "The United States can produce X more efficiently than can Great Britain. Yet we import X from Great Britain." Explain.

6. *Key Question* Refer to Figure 3.5, page 49. Assume that the graph depicts the U.S. domestic market for corn. How many bushels of corn, if any, will the United States export or import at a world price of $1, $2, $3, $4, and $5? Use this information to construct the U.S. export supply curve and import demand curve for corn. Suppose the only other corn-producing nation is France, where the domestic price is $4. Which country will export corn; which will import it?

7. *Key Question* Draw a domestic supply and demand diagram for a product in which the United States does not have a comparative advantage. What impact do foreign imports have on domestic price and quantity? On your diagram show a protective tariff that eliminates approximately one-half of the assumed imports. What are the price-quantity effects of this tariff on (*a*) domestic consumers, (*b*) domestic producers, and (*c*) foreign exporters? How would the effects of a quota that creates the same amount of imports differ?

8. "The potentially valid arguments for tariff protection are also the most easily abused." What are those arguments? Why are they susceptible to abuse? Evaluate the use of artificial trade barriers, such as tariffs and import quotas, as a means of achieving and maintaining full employment.

9. Evaluate the following statements:
   a. Protective tariffs reduce both the imports and the exports of the nation that levies tariffs.
   b. The extensive application of protective tariffs destroys the ability of the international market system to allocate resources efficiently.
   c. Unemployment in some industries can often be reduced through tariff protection, but by the same token inefficiency typically increases.
   d. Foreign firms that "dump" their products onto the U.S. market are in effect providing bargains to the country's citizens.
   e. In view of the rapidity with which technological advance is dispersed around the world, free trade will inevitably yield structural maladjustments, unemployment, and balance-of-payments problems for industrially advanced nations.
   f. Free trade can improve the composition and efficiency of domestic output. Competition from Volkswagen, Toyota, and Honda forced Detroit to make a compact car, and foreign imports of bottled water forced American firms to offer that product.
   g. In the long run, foreign trade is neutral with respect to total employment.

10. Suppose Japan agreed to a voluntary export restriction (VER) that reduced U.S. imports of Japanese steel by 10 percent. What would be the likely short-run effects of that VER on the U.S. and Japanese steel industries? If this restriction were permanent, what would be its long-run effects in the two nations on (*a*) the allocation of resources,

(*b*) the volume of employment, (*c*) the price level, and (*d*) the standard of living?

11. What is the WTO and how does it relate to international trade? How many nations belong to the WTO? (Update the number given in this book at www.wto.org.) What did the Uruguay Round (1994) of WTO trade negotiations accomplish? What is the name of the current WTO round of trade negotiations?

12. *(Last Word)* What are the main concerns of the WTO protesters? What problems, if any, arise when too many extraneous issues are tied to efforts to liberalize trade?

13. *Web-Based Question: Trade liberalization—the WTO* Go to the website of the World Trade Organization (www.wto.org/) to retrieve the latest news from the WTO. List and summarize three recent news items relating to the WTO.

14. *Web-Based Question: The U.S. International Trade Commission—what is it and what does it do?* Go to www.usitc.gov to determine the duties of the U.S. International Trade Commission (USITC). How does this organization differ from the World Trade Organization (question 13)? Go to the "Information Center" and find News Releases. Identify and briefly describe three USITC "determinations" relating to charges of unfair international trade practices that harm U.S. producers.

38 | *Exchange Rates, the Balance of Payments, and Trade Deficits*

If you take a U.S. dollar to the bank and ask to exchange it for U.S. currency, you will get a puzzled look. If you persist, you may get a dollar's worth of change: One U.S. dollar can buy exactly one U.S. dollar. But on June 5, 2003, for example, 1 U.S. dollar could buy 1,428,571 Turkish lira, 1.50 Australian dollars, .60 British pounds, 1.34 Canadian dollars, .84 European euros, 117.61 Japanese yen, or 10.56 Mexican pesos. What explains this seemingly haphazard array of exchange rates?

In Chapter 37 we examined comparative advantage as the underlying economic basis of world trade and discussed the effects of barriers to free trade. Now we introduce the monetary or financial aspects of international trade: How are currencies of different nations exchanged when import and export transactions occur? What is meant by a "favorable" or an "unfavorable" balance of payments? What is the difference between flexible exchange rates and fixed exchange rates? What are the causes and consequences of the large U.S. trade deficits?

Financing International Trade

One factor that makes international trade different from domestic trade is the involvement of different national currencies. When a U.S. firm exports goods to a Mexican firm, the U.S. exporter wants to be paid in dollars. But the Mexican importer possesses pesos. The importer must exchange pesos for dollars before the U.S. export transaction can occur.

This problem is resolved in foreign exchange markets, in which dollars can purchase Mexican pesos, European euros, South Korean won, British pounds, Japanese yen, or any other currency, and vice versa. Sponsored by major banks in New York, London, Zurich, Tokyo, and elsewhere, foreign exchange markets facilitate exports and imports.

U.S. Export Transaction

Suppose a U.S. exporter agrees to sell $300,000 of computers to a British firm. Assume, for simplicity, that the rate of exchange—the rate at which pounds can be exchanged for, or converted into, dollars, and vice versa—is $2 for £1 (the actual exchange rate is about $1.50 = 1 pound). This means the British importer must pay the equivalent of £150,000 to the U.S. exporter to obtain the $300,000 worth of computers. Also assume that all buyers of pounds and dollars are in the United States and Great Britain. Let's follow the steps in the transaction:

- To pay for the computers, the British buyer draws a check for £150,000 on its checking account in a London bank and sends it to the U.S. exporter.
- But the U.S. exporting firm must pay its bills in dollars, not pounds. So the exporter sells the £150,000 check on the London bank to its bank in, say, New York City, which is a dealer in foreign exchange. The bank adds $300,000 to the U.S. exporter's checking account for the £150,000 check.
- The New York bank deposits the £150,000 in a correspondent London bank for future sale to some U.S. buyer who needs pounds.

Note this important point: *U.S. exports create a foreign demand for dollars, and the fulfillment of that demand increases the supply of foreign currencies (pounds, in this case) owned by U.S. banks and available to U.S. buyers.*

Why would the New York bank be willing to buy pounds for dollars? As just indicated, the New York bank is a dealer in foreign exchange; it is in the business of buying (for a fee) and selling (also for a fee) one currency for another.

U.S. Import Transaction

Let's now examine how the New York bank would sell pounds for dollars to finance a U.S. import (British export) transaction. Suppose a U.S. retail firm wants to import £150,000 of compact discs produced in Britain by a hot new musical group. Again, let's track the steps in the transaction:

- The U.S. importer purchases £150,000 at the $2 = £1 exchange rate by writing a check for $300,000 on its New York bank. Because the British exporting firm wants to be paid in pounds rather than dollars, the U.S. importer must exchange dollars for pounds, which it does by going to the New York bank and purchasing £150,000 for $300,000. (Perhaps the U.S. importer purchases the same £150,000 that the New York bank acquired from the U.S. exporter.)
- The U.S. importer sends its newly purchased check for £150,000 to the British firm, which deposits it in the London bank.

Here we see that *U.S. imports create a domestic demand for foreign currencies (pounds, in this case), and the fulfillment of that demand reduces the supplies of foreign currencies (again, pounds) held by U.S. banks and available to U.S. consumers.*

The combined export and import transactions bring one more point into focus. U.S. exports (the computers) make available, or "earn," a supply of foreign currencies for U.S. banks, and U.S. imports (the compact discs) create a demand for those currencies. In a broad sense, any nation's exports finance or "pay for" its imports. Exports provide the foreign currencies needed to pay for imports.

Postscript: Although our examples are confined to exporting and importing goods, demand for and supplies of pounds also arise from transactions involving services and the payment of interest and dividends on foreign investments. The United States demands pounds not only to buy imports but also to buy insurance and transportation services from the British, to vacation in London, to pay dividends and interest on British investments in the United States, and to make new financial and real investments in Britain. **(Key Question 2)**

The Balance of Payments

A nation's **balance of payments** is the sum of all the transactions that take place between its residents and the residents of all foreign nations. Those transactions include exports and imports of goods, exports and imports of services, tourist expenditures, interest and dividends received or paid abroad, and purchases and sales of financial or real assets abroad. The U.S. Commerce Department's Bureau of Economic Analysis compiles the balance-of-payments statement each year. *The statement shows all the payments a nation receives from foreign countries and all the payments it makes to them.*

Table 38.1 is a simplified balance-of-payments statement for the United States in 2002. Let's take a close look at this accounting statement to see what it reveals about U.S. international trade and finance. To help our explanation, we divide the single balance-of-payments account into three components: the *current account*, the *capital account*, and the *official reserves account*.

Current Account

The top portion of Table 38.1 summarizes U.S. trade in currently produced goods and services and is called the **current account.** Items 1 and 2 show U.S. exports and imports of goods (merchandise) in 2002. U.S. exports have a *plus* (+) sign because they are a *credit;* they earn and make available foreign exchange in the United States. As you saw in the preceding section, any export-type transaction that obligates foreigners to make "inpayments" to

TABLE 38.1

The U.S. Balance of Payments, 2002 (in Billions)

Current account		
(1) U.S. goods exports	$+ 683	
(2) U.S. goods imports	−1167	
(3) *Balance on goods*		$−484
(4) U.S. exports of services.	+ 289	
(5) U.S. imports of services	− 240	
(6) *Balance on services*.		+ 49
(7) *Balance on goods and services*		−436
(8) Net investment income.	− 12	
(9) Net transfers	− 56	
(10) **Balance on current account**		−504
Capital account		
(11) Foreign purchases of assets in the United States. . . .	+645*	
(12) U.S. purchases of assets abroad	− 145*	
(13) **Balance on capital account**		+500
Official reserves account		
(14) **Official reserves**		+ 4
		$ 0

*Includes one-half of a $29 billion statistical discrepancy that is listed in the capital account.

Source: U.S. Department of Commerce, Bureau of Economic Analysis, www.bea.gov/. Preliminary 2002 data.

the United States generates supplies of foreign currencies in the U.S. banks.

U.S. imports have a *minus* (−) sign because they are a *debit;* they reduce the stock of foreign currencies in the United States. Our earlier discussion of trade financing indicated that U.S. imports obligate the United States to make "outpayments" to the rest of the world that reduce available supplies of foreign currencies held by U.S. banks.

Balance on Goods Items 1 and 2 in Table 38.1 reveal that in 2002 U.S. goods exports of $683 billion did not earn enough foreign currencies to finance U.S. goods imports of $1167 billion. A country's *balance of trade on goods* is the difference between its exports and its imports of goods. If exports exceed imports, the result is a surplus on the balance of goods. If imports exceed exports, there is a trade deficit on the balance of goods. We note in item 3 that in 2002 the United States incurred a trade deficit on goods of $484 billion.

Balance on Services The United States exports not only goods, such as airplanes and computer software, but also services, such as insurance, consulting, travel, and brokerage services, to residents of foreign nations. Item 4 in Table 38.1 shows that these service "exports" totaled $289 billion in 2002 and are a credit (thus the + sign). Item 5 indicates that the United States "imports" similar

services from foreigners; those service imports were $240 billion in 2002 and are a debit (thus the − sign). So the balance on services (item 6) in 2002 was $49 billion.

The **balance on goods and services** shown as item 7 is the difference between U.S. exports of goods and services (items 1 and 4) and U.S. imports of goods and services (items 2 and 5). In 2002, U.S. imports of goods and services exceeded U.S. exports of goods and services by $436 billion. So a **trade deficit** (or "unfavorable balance of trade") occurred. In contrast, a **trade surplus** (or "favorable balance of trade") occurs when exports of goods and services exceed imports of goods and services. (Global Perspective 38.1 shows U.S. trade deficits and surpluses with selected nations.)

Balance on Current Account Item 8, *net investment income*, represents the difference between (1) the interest and dividend payments foreigners paid the United States for the use of exported U.S. capital and (2) the interest and dividends the United States paid for the use of foreign capital invested in the United States. Observe that in 2002 U.S. net investment income was a negative $12 billion worth of foreign currencies.

Item 9 shows net transfers, both public and private, between the United States and the rest of the world. Included here is foreign aid, pensions paid to U.S. citizens living abroad, and remittances by immigrants to relatives

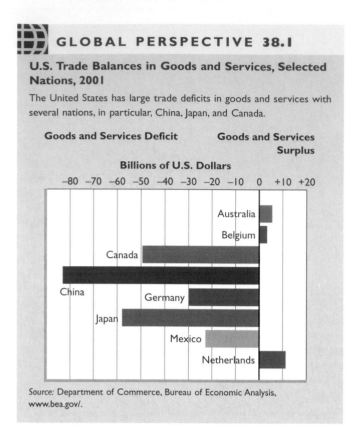

GLOBAL PERSPECTIVE 38.1

U.S. Trade Balances in Goods and Services, Selected Nations, 2001

The United States has large trade deficits in goods and services with several nations, in particular, China, Japan, and Canada.

Source: Department of Commerce, Bureau of Economic Analysis, www.bea.gov/.

abroad. These $56 billion of transfers are net U.S. outpayments that decrease available supplies of foreign exchange. They are, in a sense, the exporting of goodwill and the importing of "thank-you notes."

By adding all transactions in the current account, we obtain the **balance on current account** shown in item 10. In 2002 the United States had a current account deficit of $504 billion. This means that the U.S. current account transactions (items 2, 5, 8, and 9) created outpayments of foreign currencies from the United States greater than the inpayments of foreign currencies to the United States.

Capital Account

The second account within the overall balance-of-payments account is the **capital account,** which summarizes the purchase or sale of real or financial assets and the corresponding flows of monetary payments that accompany them. For example, a foreign firm may buy a real asset, say, an office building in the United States, or a financial asset, for instance, a U.S. government security. Both kinds of transaction involve the "export" of the ownership of U.S. assets from the United States in return for

inpayments of foreign currency. As indicated in line 11, these "exports" of ownership of assets are designated *foreign purchases of assets in the United States.* They have a + sign because, like exports of U.S. goods and services, they represent inpayments of foreign currencies.

Conversely, a U.S. firm may buy, say, a hotel chain (real asset) in a foreign country or some of the common stock (financial asset) of a foreign firm. Both transactions involve the "import" of the ownership of the real or financial assets to the United States and are paid for by outpayments of foreign currencies. These "imports" are designated *U.S. purchases of assets abroad* and, as shown in line 12, have a − sign; like U.S. imports of goods and services, they represent outpayments of foreign currencies from the United States.

Items 11 and 12 combined yield a **balance on capital account** of $500 billion for 2002 (line 13). In 2002 the United States "exported" $645 billion of ownership of its real and financial assets and "imported" $145 billion. This capital account surplus brought in $500 billion of foreign currencies to the United States.

Official Reserves Account

The third account in the overall balance of payments is the official reserves account. The central banks of nations hold quantities of foreign currencies called **official reserves.** These reserves can be drawn on to make up any net deficit in the combined current and capital accounts (much as you would draw on your savings to pay for a special purchase). In 2002 the United States had a $4 billion deficit in the combined current and capital accounts (line 10 plus line 13). This balance in the U.S. international payments required that the U.S. government deplete its official reserves of foreign currencies by $4 billion (item 14). The + sign indicates that this drawing down and exporting of reserves is a credit—an inpayment from official reserves that was needed to balance the overall balance-of-payments account.

In some years, the current and capital accounts balances are positive, meaning that the United States earned more foreign currencies than it needed. The surplus would create outpayments, not to other countries, but to the stock of official reserves. As such, item 14 would have a − sign because it is a debit.

The three components of the balance of payments (the current account, the capital account, and the official reserves account) must together equal zero. Every unit of foreign exchange used (as reflected in a minus outpayment or debit transaction) must have a source (a plus inpayment or credit transaction).

Payments Deficits and Surpluses

Although the balance of payments must always sum to zero, economists and political officials speak of **balance-of-payments deficits and surpluses;** they are referring to imbalances between the current and capital accounts (line 10 minus line 13) that cause a drawing down or a building up of foreign currencies. A drawing down of official reserves (to create a positive official reserves entry in Table 38.1) measures a nation's balance-of-payments deficit; a building up of official reserves (which is shown as a negative official reserves entry) measures a nation's balance-of-payments surplus.

A balance-of-payments deficit is not necessarily bad, nor is a balance-of-payments surplus necessarily good. Both simply happen. However, any nation's official reserves are limited. Persistent payments deficits, which must be financed by drawing down those reserves, would ultimately deplete the reserves. That nation would have to adopt policies to correct its balance of payments. Such policies might require painful macroeconomic adjustments, trade barriers and similar restrictions, or a major depreciation of its currency. For this reason, nations seek to achieve payments balance, at least over several-year periods.

The United States had official reserves of $80 billion in 2002, so the depletion of $4 billion of reserves in that year was not of major concern. But the United States has been running historically large current account deficits in recent years. Those deficits need to be financed by equally large surpluses in the capital account. We need to examine the causes and consequences of recent trade deficits but will defer that discussion until later in this chapter. **(Key Question 3)**

QUICK REVIEW 38.1

- U.S. exports create a foreign demand for dollars, and fulfillment of that demand increases the domestic supply of foreign currencies; U.S. imports create a domestic demand for foreign currencies, and fulfillment of that demand reduces the supplies of foreign currency held by U.S. banks.

- The current account balance is a nation's exports of goods and services less its imports of goods and services plus its net investment income and net transfers.

- The capital account balance is a nation's sale of real and financial assets to people living abroad less its purchases of real and financial assets from foreigners.

- A balance-of-payments deficit occurs when the sum of the balances on current and capital accounts is negative; a balance-of-payments surplus arises when the sum of the balances on current and capital accounts is positive.

Flexible Exchange Rates

Both the size and the persistence of a nation's balance-of-payments deficits and surpluses and the adjustments it must make to correct those imbalances depend on the system of exchange rates being used. There are two "pure" types of exchange-rate systems:

- A **flexible-** or **floating-exchange-rate system** through which demand and supply determine exchange rates and in which no government intervention occurs.

- A **fixed-exchange-rate system** through which governments determine exchange rates and make necessary adjustments in their economies to maintain those rates.

We begin by looking at flexible exchange rates. Let's examine the rate, or price, at which U.S. dollars might be exchanged for British pounds. In **Figure 38.1 (Key Graph)** we show demand D_1 and supply S_1 of pounds in the currency market.

38.1
Flexible
exchange
rates

The *demand-for-pounds* curve is downward-sloping because all British goods and services will be cheaper to the United States if pounds become less expensive to the United States. That is, at lower dollar prices for pounds, the United States can get more pounds and therefore more British goods and services per dollar. To buy those cheaper British goods, U.S. consumers will increase the quantity of pounds they demand.

The *supply-of-pounds* curve is upward-sloping because the British will purchase more U.S. goods when the dollar price of pounds rises (that is, as the pound price of dollars falls). When the British buy more U.S. goods, they supply a greater quantity of pounds to the foreign exchange market. In other words, they must exchange pounds for dollars to purchase U.S. goods. So, when the dollar price of pounds rises, the quantity of pounds supplied goes up.

The intersection of the supply curve and the demand curve will determine the dollar price of pounds. Here, that price (exchange rate) is $2 for £1.

Depreciation and Appreciation

An exchange rate determined by market forces can, and often does, change daily like stock and bond prices. When the dollar price of pounds *rises*, for example, from $2 = £1 to $3 = £1, the dollar has *depreciated* relative to the pound (and the pound has appreciated relative to the dollar). When a currency depreciates, more units of it (dollars) are needed to buy a single unit of some other currency (a pound).

KEY GRAPH

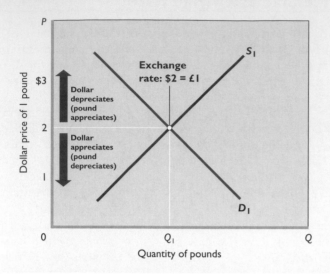

P

Exchange
rate: $2 = £1

$3

Dollar
depreciates
(pound
appreciates)

2

Dollar
appreciates
(pound
depreciates)

1

Dollar price of 1 pound

S_1

D_1

0   Q_1 Q

Quantity of pounds

FIGURE 38.1

The market for foreign currency (pounds). The intersection of the demand-for-pounds curve D_1 and the supply-of-pounds curve S_1 determines the equilibrium dollar price of pounds, here, $2. That means that the exchange rate is $2 = £1. The upward blue arrow is a reminder that a higher dollar price of pounds (say, $3 = £1, caused by a shift in either the demand or the supply curve) means that the dollar has depreciated (the pound has appreciated). The downward blue arrow tells us that a lower dollar price of pounds (say, $1 = £1, again caused by a shift in either the demand or the supply curve) means that the dollar has appreciated (the pound has depreciated).

QUICK QUIZ 38.1

1. Which of the following statements is true?
   a. The quantity of pounds demanded falls when the dollar appreciates.
   b. The quantity of pounds supplied declines as the dollar price of the pound rises.
   c. At the equilibrium exchange rate, the pound price of $1 is $\frac{1}{2}$ pound.
   d. The dollar appreciates if the demand for pounds increases.

2. At the price of $2 for 1 pound in this figure:
   a. the dollar-pound exchange rate is unstable.
   b. the quantity of pounds supplied equals the quantity demanded.
   c. the dollar price of 1 pound equals the pound price of $1.
   d. U.S. goods exports to Britain must equal U.S. goods imports from Britain.

3. Other things equal, a leftward shift of the demand curve in this figure:
   a. would depreciate the dollar.

   b. would create a shortage of pounds at the previous price of $2 for 1 pound.
   c. might be caused by a major recession in the United States.
   d. might be caused by a significant rise of real interest rates in Britain.

4. Other things equal, a rightward shift of the supply curve in this figure would:
   a. depreciate the dollar and might be caused by a significant rise of real interest rates in Britain.
   b. depreciate the dollar and might be caused by a significant fall of real interest rates in Britain.
   c. appreciate the dollar and might be caused by a significant rise of real interest rates in the United States.
   d. appreciate the dollar and might be caused by a significant fall of interest rates in the United States.

Answers: 1. c; 2. b; 3. c; 4. c

When the dollar price of pounds *falls*, for example, from $2 = £1 to $1 = £1, the dollar has *appreciated* relative to the pound. When a currency appreciates, fewer units of it (dollars) are needed to buy a single unit of some other currency (pounds).

In our U.S.-Britain illustrations, depreciation of the dollar means an appreciation of the pound, and vice versa. When the dollar price of a pound jumps from $2 = £1 to $3 = £1, the pound has appreciated relative to the dollar because it takes fewer pounds to buy $1. At $2 = £1, it took £$\frac{1}{2}$ to buy $1; at $3 = £1, it takes only £$\frac{1}{3}$ to buy $1. Conversely, when the dollar appreciated relative to the

pound, the pound depreciated relative to the dollar. More pounds were needed to buy a dollar.

Determinants of Exchange Rates

What factors would cause a nation's currency to appreciate or depreciate in the market for foreign exchange? Here are three generalizations:

- If the demand for a nation's currency increases (all else equal), that currency will appreciate; if the demand declines, that currency will depreciate.

- If the supply of a nation's currency increases, that currency will depreciate; if the supply decreases, that currency will appreciate.
- If a nation's currency appreciates, some foreign currency depreciates relative to it.

With these generalizations in mind, let's examine the determinants of exchange rates—the factors that shift the demand or supply curve for a certain currency.

Changes in Tastes Any change in consumer tastes or preferences for the products of a foreign country may alter the demand for that nation's currency and change its exchange rate. If technological advances in U.S. wireless phones make them more attractive to British consumers and businesses, then the British will supply more pounds in the exchange market in order to purchase more U.S. wireless phones. The supply-of-pounds curve will shift to the right, causing the pound to depreciate and the dollar to appreciate.

In contrast, the U.S. demand-for-pounds curve will shift to the right if British woolen apparel becomes more fashionable in the United States. So the pound will appreciate and the dollar will depreciate.

Relative Income Changes A nation's currency is likely to depreciate if its growth of national income is more rapid than that of other countries. Here's why: A country's imports vary directly with its income level. As total income rises in the United States, people there buy both more domestic goods and more foreign goods. If the U.S. economy is expanding rapidly and the British economy is stagnant, U.S. imports of British goods, and therefore U.S. demands for pounds, will increase. The dollar price of pounds will rise, so the dollar will depreciate.

Relative Price-Level Changes Changes in the relative price levels of two nations may change the demand and supply of currencies and alter the exchange rate between the two nations' currencies.

The **purchasing-power-parity theory** holds that exchange rates equate the purchasing power of various currencies. That is, the exchange rates among national currencies adjust to match the ratios of the nations' price levels: If a certain market basket of goods costs $10,000 in the United States and £5,000 in Great Britain, according to this theory the exchange rate will be $2 = £1. That way, a dollar spent on goods sold in Britain, Japan, Turkey, and other nations will have equal purchasing power.

In practice, however, exchange rates depart from purchasing power parity, even over long periods. Nevertheless, changes in relative price levels are a determinant of

---

CONSIDER THIS . . .

© Felicia Martinez/PhotoEdit

The Big Mac Index

The purchasing-power-parity (PPP) theory says that exchange rates will adjust such that a given broad market basket of goods and services will cost the same in all countries. If the market basket costs $1000 in the United States and 100,000 yen in Japan, then the exchange rate will be $1 = ¥100 (= 1000/100,000). If instead the exchange rate is $1 = ¥110, we can expect the dollar to depreciate and the yen to appreciate such that the exchange rate moves to the purchasing-power-parity rate of $1 = ¥100. Similarly, if the exchange rate is $1 = ¥90, we can expect the dollar to appreciate and the yen to depreciate.

Instead of using a market basket of goods and services, *The Economist* magazine has offered a light-hearted test of the purchasing-power-parity theory through its *Big Mac index*. It uses the exchange rates of 100 countries to convert the domestic currency price of a Big Mac into U.S. dollar prices. If the converted dollar price in, say, Britain exceeds the dollar price in the United States, the *Economist* concludes (with a wink) that the pound is overvalued relative to the dollar. On the other hand, if the adjusted dollar price of a Big Mac in Britain is less than the dollar price in the United States, then the pound is undervalued relative to the dollar.

The *Economist* finds wide divergences in actual dollar prices across the globe and thus little support for the purchasing-power-parity theory. Yet it humorously trumpets any predictive success it can muster (or is that "mustard"?):

> Some readers find our Big Mac index hard to swallow. This year (1999), however, has been one to relish. When the euro was launched at the start of the year most forecasters expected it to rise. The Big Mac index, however, suggested the euro was overvalued against the dollar—and indeed it has fallen [13 percent]. . . . Our correspondents have once again been munching their way around the globe . . . [and] experience suggests that investors ignore burgernomics at their peril.*

Maybe so—bad puns and all. Economist Robert Cumby examined the Big Mac index for 14 countries for 10 years.[†] Among his findings:

- A 10 percent undervaluation, according to the Big Mac standard, in one year is associated with a 3.5 percent appreciation of that currency over the following year.
- When the U.S. dollar price of a Big Mac is high in a country, the relative local currency price of a Big Mac in that country generally declines during the following year.

Hmm. Not bad.

*"Big MacCurrencies," *The Economist*, Apr. 3, 1999; "Mcparity," *The Economist*, Dec. 11, 1999.

[†]Robert Cumby, "Forecasting Exchange Rates and Relative Prices with the Hamburger Standard: Is What You Want What You Get with Mcparity?" National Bureau of Economic Research, January 1997.

exchange rates. If, for example, the domestic price level rises rapidly in the United States and remains constant in Great Britain, U.S. consumers will seek out low-priced British goods, increasing the demand for pounds. The British will purchase fewer U.S. goods, reducing the supply of pounds. This combination of demand and supply changes will cause the pound to appreciate and the dollar to depreciate.

Relative Interest Rates Changes in relative interest rates between two countries may alter their exchange rate. Suppose that real interest rates rise in the United States but stay constant in Great Britain. British citizens will then find the United States an attractive place in which to make financial investments. To undertake these investments, they will have to supply pounds in the foreign exchange market to obtain dollars. The increase in the supply of pounds results in depreciation of the pound and appreciation of the dollar.

Speculation Currency speculators are people who buy and sell currencies with an eye toward reselling or repurchasing them at a profit. Suppose speculators expect the U.S. economy to (1) grow more rapidly than the British economy and (2) experience a more rapid

rise in its price level than will Britain. These expectations translate into an anticipation that the pound will appreciate and the dollar will depreciate. Speculators who are holding dollars will therefore try to convert them into pounds. This effort will increase the demand for pounds and cause the dollar price of pounds to rise (that is, cause the dollar to depreciate). A self-fulfilling prophecy occurs: The pound appreciates and the dollar depreciates because speculators act on the belief that these changes will in fact take place. In this way, speculation can cause changes in exchange rates. (We deal with currency speculation in more detail in this chapter's Last Word.)

Table 38.2 has more illustrations of the determinants of exchange rates; the table is worth careful study.

Flexible Rates and the Balance of Payments

Proponents of flexible exchange rates say they have an important feature: They automatically adjust and eventually eliminate balance-of-payments deficits or surpluses. We can explain this idea through Figure 38.2, in which S_1 and D_1 are the supply and demand curves for pounds from

TABLE 38.2

Determinants of Exchange Rates: Factors That Change the Demand for or the Supply of a Particular Currency and Thus Alter the Exchange Rate

Determinant	Examples
Change in tastes	Japanese autos decline in popularity in the United States (Japanese yen depreciates; U.S. dollar appreciates).
	European tourists flock to the United States (U.S. dollar appreciates; European euro depreciates).
Change in relative incomes	England encounters a recession, reducing its imports, while U.S. real output and real income surge, increasing U.S. imports (British pound appreciates; U.S. dollar depreciates).
Change in relative prices	Switzerland experiences a 3% inflation rate compared to Canada's 10% rate (Swiss franc appreciates; Canadian dollar depreciates).
Change in relative real interest rates	The Federal Reserve drives up interest rates in the United States, while the Bank of England takes no such action (U.S. dollar appreciates; British pound depreciates).
Speculation	Currency traders believe South Korea will have much greater inflation than Taiwan (South Korean won depreciates; Taiwan dollar appreciates).
	Currency traders think Finland's interest rates will plummet relative to Denmark's rates (Finland's markka depreciates; Denmark's krone appreciates).

FIGURE 38.2

Adjustments under flexible exchange rates and fixed exchange rates. Under flexible exchange rates, a shift in the demand for pounds from D_1 to D_2, other things equal, would cause a U.S. balance-of-payments deficit *ab*. That deficit would be corrected by a change in the exchange rate from $2 = £1 to $3 = £1. Under fixed exchange rates, the United States would cover the shortage of pounds *ab* by using international monetary reserves, restricting trade, implementing exchange controls, or enacting a contractionary stabilization policy.

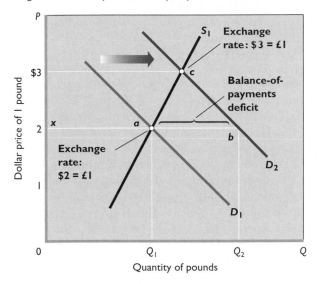

Figure 38.1. The equilibrium exchange rate of $2 = £1 means that there is no balance-of-payments deficit or surplus between the United States and Britain. At that exchange rate, the quantity of pounds demanded by U.S. consumers to import British goods, buy British transportation and insurance services, and pay interest and dividends on British investments in the United States equals the amount of pounds supplied by the British in buying U.S. exports, purchasing services from the United States, and making interest and dividend payments on U.S. investments in Britain. The United States would have no need to either draw down or build up its official reserves to balance its payments.

Suppose tastes change and U.S. consumers buy more British automobiles; the U.S. price level increases relative to Britain's; or interest rates fall in the United States compared to those in Britain. Any or all of these changes will increase the U.S. demand for British pounds, for example, from D_1 to D_2 in Figure 38.2.

If the exchange rate remains at the initial $2 = £1, a U.S. balance-of-payments deficit will occur in the amount of *ab*. At the $2 = £1 rate, U.S. consumers will demand the quantity of pounds shown by point *b* but

Britain will supply only the amount shown by *a*. There will be a shortage of pounds. But this shortage will not last because this is a competitive market. Instead, the dollar price of pounds will rise (the dollar will depreciate) until the balance-of-payments deficit is eliminated. That occurs at the new equilibrium exchange rate of $3 = £1, where the quantities of pounds demanded and supplied are again equal.

To explain why this occurred, we reemphasize that the exchange rate links all domestic (U.S.) prices with all foreign (British) prices. The dollar price of a foreign good is found by multiplying the foreign price by the exchange rate (in dollars per unit of the foreign currency). At an exchange rate of $2 = £1, a British automobile priced at £15,000 will cost a U.S. consumer $30,000 (= 15,000 × $2).

A change in the exchange rate alters the prices of all British goods to U.S. consumers and all U.S. goods to British buyers. The shift in the exchange rate (here from $2 = £1 to $3 = £1) changes the relative attractiveness of U.S. imports and exports and restores equilibrium in the U.S. (and British) balance of payments. From the U.S. view, as the dollar price of pounds changes from $2 to $3, the British auto priced at £15,000, which formerly cost a U.S. consumer $30,000, now costs $45,000 (= 15,000 × $3). Other British goods will also cost U.S. consumers more, and U.S. imports of British goods will decline. A movement from point *b* toward point *c* in Figure 38.2 graphically illustrates this concept.

From Britain's standpoint, the exchange rate (the pound price of dollars) has fallen (from £$\frac{1}{2}$ to £$\frac{1}{3}$ for $1). The international value of the pound has appreciated. The British previously got only $2 for £1; now they get $3 for £1. U.S. goods are therefore cheaper to the British, and U.S. exports to Britain will rise. In Figure 38.2, this is shown by a movement from point *a* toward point *c*.

The two adjustments—a decrease in U.S. imports from Britain and an increase in U.S. exports to Britain—are just what are needed to correct the U.S. balance-of-payments deficit. These changes end when, at point *c*, the quantities of British pounds demanded and supplied are equal. **(Key Questions 6 and 9)**

Disadvantages of Flexible Exchange Rates

Even though flexible exchange rates automatically work to eliminate payment imbalances, they may cause several significant problems.

Uncertainty and Diminished Trade The risks and uncertainties associated with flexible exchange rates may discourage the flow of trade. Suppose a U.S. automobile dealer contracts to purchase 10 British cars for £150,000. At the current exchange rate of, say, $2 for £1, the U.S. importer expects to pay $300,000 for these automobiles. But if during the 3-month delivery period the rate of exchange shifts to $3 for £1, the £150,000 payment contracted by the U.S. importer will be $450,000.

That increase in the dollar price of pounds may thus turn the U.S. importer's anticipated profit into substantial loss. Aware of the possibility of an adverse change in the exchange rate, the U.S. importer may not be willing to assume the risks involved. The U.S. firm may confine its operations to domestic automobiles, so international trade in this product will not occur.

The same thing can happen with investments. Assume that when the exchange rate is $3 to £1, a U.S. firm invests $30,000 (or £10,000) in a British enterprise. It estimates a return of 10 percent; that is, it anticipates annual earnings of $3000 or £1000. Suppose these expectations prove correct in that the British firm earns £1000 in the first year on the £10,000 investment. But suppose that during the year, the value of the dollar appreciates to $2 = £1. The absolute return is now only $2000 (rather than $3000), and the rate of return falls from the anticipated 10 percent to only $6\frac{2}{3}$ percent (= $2000/$30,000). Investment is risky in any case. The added risk of changing exchange rates may persuade the U.S. investor not to venture overseas.[1]

Terms-of-Trade Changes A decline in the international value of its currency will worsen a nation's terms of trade. For example, an increase in the dollar price of a pound will mean that the United States must export more goods and services to finance a specific level of imports from Britain.

Instability Flexible exchange rates may destabilize the domestic economy because wide fluctuations stimulate and then depress industries producing exported goods. If the U.S. economy is operating at full employment and its currency depreciates, as in our illustration, the results will be inflationary, for two reasons. (1) Foreign demand for U.S. goods may rise, increasing total spending and pulling

up U.S. prices. Also, the prices of all U.S. imports will increase. (2) Conversely, appreciation of the dollar will lower U.S. exports and increase imports, possibly causing unemployment.

Flexible or floating exchange rates may also complicate the use of domestic stabilization policies in seeking full employment and price stability. This is especially true for nations whose exports and imports are large relative to their total domestic output.

Fixed Exchange Rates

To circumvent the disadvantages of flexible exchange rates, at times nations have fixed or "pegged" their exchange rates. For our analysis of fixed exchange rates, we assume that the United States and Britain agree to maintain a $2 = £1 exchange rate.

The problem is that such a government agreement cannot keep from changing the demand for and the supply of pounds. With the rate fixed, a shift in demand or supply will threaten the fixed-exchange-rate system, and government must intervene to ensure that the exchange rate is maintained.

In Figure 38.2, suppose the U.S. demand for pounds increases from D_1 to D_2 and a U.S. payment deficit *ab* arises. Now, the new equilibrium exchange rate ($3 = £1) is above the fixed exchange rate ($2 = £1). How can the United States prevent the shortage of pounds from driving the exchange rate up to the new equilibrium level? How can it maintain the fixed exchange rate? The answer is by altering market demand or market supply or both so that they will intersect at the $2 = £1 rate. There are several ways to do this.

Use of Reserves

One way to maintain a fixed exchange rate is to manipulate the market through the use of official reserves. Such manipulations are called **currency interventions.** By selling part of its reserves of pounds, the U.S. government could increase the supply of pounds, shifting supply curve S_1 to the right so that it intersects D_2 at *b* in Figure 38.2 and thereby maintains the exchange rate at $2 = £1.

How do official reserves originate? Perhaps a balance-of-payments surplus occurred in the past. The U.S. government would have purchased that surplus. That is, at some earlier time the U.S. government may have spent dollars to buy the surplus pounds that were threatening to reduce the exchange rate to below the $2 = £1 fixed rate.

---

[1]You will see in this chapter's Last Word, however, that a trader can circumvent part of the risk of unfavorable exchange-rate fluctuations by "hedging" in the "futures market" or "forward market" for foreign exchange.

Those purchases would have bolstered the U.S. official reserves of pounds.

Nations have also used gold as "international money" to obtain official reserves. In our example, the U.S. government could sell some of its gold to Britain to obtain pounds. It could then sell pounds for dollars. That would shift the supply-of-pounds curve to the right, and the $2 = £1 exchange rate could be maintained.

It is critical that the amount of reserves and gold be enough to accomplish the required increase in the supply of pounds. There is no problem if deficits and surpluses occur more or less randomly and are of similar size. Then, last year's balance-of-payments surplus with Britain will increase the U.S. reserve of pounds, and that reserve can be used to "finance" this year's deficit. But if the United States encounters persistent and sizable deficits for an extended period, it may exhaust its reserves, and thus be forced to abandon fixed exchange rates. Or, at the least, a nation whose reserves are inadequate must use less appealing options to maintain exchange rates. Let's consider some of those options.

Trade Policies

To maintain fixed exchange rates, a nation can try to control the flow of trade and finance directly. The United States could try to maintain the $2 = £1 exchange rate in the face of a shortage of pounds by discouraging imports (thereby reducing the demand for pounds) and encouraging exports (thus increasing the supply of pounds). Imports could be reduced by means of new tariffs or import quotas; special taxes could be levied on the interest and dividends U.S. financial investors receive from foreign investments. Also, the U.S. government could subsidize certain U.S. exports to increase the supply of pounds.

The fundamental problem is that these policies reduce the volume of world trade and change its makeup from what is economically desirable. When nations impose tariffs, quotas, and the like, they lose some of the economic benefits of a free flow of world trade. That loss should not be underestimated: Trade barriers by one nation lead to retaliatory responses from other nations, multiplying the loss.

Exchange Controls and Rationing

Another option is to adopt exchange controls and rationing. Under **exchange controls** the U.S. government could handle the problem of a pound shortage by requiring that all pounds obtained by U.S. exporters be sold to the Federal government. Then the government would allocate or ration this short supply of pounds (represented by xa in Figure 38.2) among various U.S. importers, who actually demand the quantity xb. In effect, this policy would restrict the value of U.S. imports to the amount of foreign exchange earned by U.S. exports. Assuming balance in the capital account, there would then be no balance-of-payments deficit. U.S. demand for British imports with the value ab would simply not be fulfilled.

There are major objections to exchange controls:

- **Distorted trade** Like tariffs, quotas, and export subsidies (trade controls), exchange controls would distort the pattern of international trade away from the pattern suggested by comparative advantage.

- **Favoritism** The process of rationing scarce foreign exchange might lead to government favoritism toward selected importers (big contributors to reelection campaigns, for example).

- **Restricted choice** Controls would limit freedom of consumer choice. The U.S. consumers who prefer Volkswagens might have to buy Chevrolets. The business opportunities for some U.S. importers might be impaired if the government were to limit imports.

- **Black markets** Enforcement problems are likely under exchange controls. U.S. importers might want foreign exchange badly enough to pay more than the $2 = £1 official rate, setting the stage for black-market dealings between importers and illegal sellers of foreign exchange.

Domestic Macroeconomic Adjustments

A final way to maintain a fixed exchange rate would be to use domestic stabilization policies (monetary policy and fiscal policy) to eliminate the shortage of foreign currency. Tax hikes, reductions in government spending, and a high-interest-rate policy would reduce total spending in the U.S. economy and, consequently, domestic income. Because the volume of imports varies directly with domestic income, demand for British goods, and therefore for pounds, would be restrained.

If these "contractionary" policies served to reduce the domestic price level relative to Britain's, U.S. buyers of consumer and capital goods would divert their demands from British goods to U.S. goods, reducing the demand for pounds. Moreover, the high-interest-rate policy would lift U.S. interest rates relative to those in Britain.

Lower prices on U.S. goods and higher U.S. interest rates would increase British imports of U.S. goods and would increase British financial investment in the United

States. Both developments would increase the supply of pounds. The combination of a decrease in the demand for and an increase in the supply of pounds would reduce or eliminate the original U.S. balance-of-payments deficit. In Figure 38.2 the new supply and demand curves would intersect at some new equilibrium point on line *ab*, where the exchange rate remains at $2 = £1.

Maintaining fixed exchange rates by such means is hardly appealing. The "price" of exchange-rate stability for the United States would be a decline in output, employment, and price levels—in other words, a recession. Eliminating a balance-of-payments deficit and achieving domestic stability are both important national economic goals, but to sacrifice stability to balance payments would be to let the tail wag the dog.

QUICK REVIEW 38.2

- In a system in which exchange rates are flexible (meaning that they are free to float), the rates are determined by the demand for and supply of individual national currencies in the foreign exchange market.
- Determinants of flexible exchange rates (factors that shift currency supply and demand curves) include changes in (a) tastes, (b) relative national incomes, (c) relative price levels, (d) real interest rates, and (e) speculation.
- Under a system of fixed exchange rates, nations set their exchange rates and then maintain them by buying or selling reserves of currencies, establishing trade barriers, employing exchange controls, or incurring inflation or recession.

International Exchange-Rate Systems

In recent times the world's nations have used three different exchange-rate systems: a fixed-rate system, a modified fixed-rate system, and a modified flexible-rate system.

The Gold Standard: Fixed Exchange Rates

Between 1879 and 1934 the major nations of the world adhered to a fixed-rate system called the **gold standard.** Under this system, each nation must:
- Define its currency in terms of a quantity of gold.
- Maintain a fixed relationship between its stock of gold and its money supply.
- Allow gold to be freely exported and imported.

If each nation defines its currency in terms of gold, the various national currencies will have fixed relationships to one another. For example, if the United States defines $1 as worth 25 grains of gold, and Britain defines £1 as worth 50 grains of gold, then a British pound is worth 2 × 25 grains, or $2. This exchange rate was fixed under the gold standard. The exchange rate did not change in response to changes in currency demand and supply.

Gold Flows If we ignore the costs of packing, insuring, and shipping gold between countries, under the gold standard the rate of exchange would not vary from this $2 = £1 rate. No one in the United States would pay more than $2 = £1 because 50 grains of gold could always be bought for $2 in the United States and sold for £1 in Britain. Nor would the British pay more than £1 for $2. Why should they when they could buy 50 grains of gold in Britain for £1 and sell it in the United States for $2?

Under the gold standard, the potential free flow of gold between nations resulted in fixed exchange rates.

Domestic Macroeconomic Adjustments When currency demand or supply changes, the gold standard requires domestic macroeconomic adjustments to maintain the fixed exchange rate. To see why, suppose that U.S. tastes change such that U.S. consumers want to buy more British goods. The resulting increase in the demand for pounds creates a shortage of pounds in the United States (recall Figure 38.2), implying a U.S. balance-of-payments deficit.

What will happen? Remember that the rules of the gold standard prohibit the exchange rate from moving from the fixed $2 = £1 rate. The rate cannot move to, say, a new equilibrium at $3 = £1 to correct the imbalance. Instead, gold will flow from the United States to Britain to correct the payments imbalance.

But recall that the gold standard requires that participants maintain a fixed relationship between their domestic money supplies and their quantities of gold. The flow of gold from the United States to Britain will require a reduction of the money supply in the United States. Other things equal, that will reduce total spending in the United States and lower U.S. real domestic output, employment, income, and, perhaps, prices. Also, the decline in the money supply will boost U.S. interest rates.

The opposite will occur in Britain. The inflow of gold will increase the money supply, and this will increase total spending in Britain. Domestic output, employment, income, and, perhaps, prices will rise. The British interest rate will fall.

Declining U.S. incomes and prices will reduce the U.S. demand for British goods and therefore reduce the U.S. demand for pounds. Lower interest rates in Britain will make it less attractive for U.S. investors to make financial investments there, also lessening the demand for pounds. For all these reasons, the demand for pounds in the United States will decline. In Britain, higher incomes, prices, and interest rates will make U.S. imports and U.S. financial investments more attractive. In buying these imports and making these financial investments, British citizens will supply more pounds in the exchange market.

In short, domestic macroeconomic adjustments in the United States and Britain, triggered by the international flow of gold, will produce new demand and supply conditions for pounds such that the $2 = £1 exchange rate is maintained. After all the adjustments are made, the United States will not have a payments deficit and Britain will not have a payments surplus.

So the gold standard has the advantage of maintaining stable exchange rates and correcting balance-of-payments deficits and surpluses automatically. However, its critical drawback is that nations must accept domestic adjustments in such distasteful forms as unemployment and falling incomes, on the one hand, or inflation, on the other hand. Under the gold standard, a nation's money supply is altered by changes in supply and demand in currency markets, and nations cannot establish their own monetary policy in their own national interest. If the United States, for example, were to experience declining output and income, the loss of gold under the gold standard would reduce the U.S. money supply. That would increase interest rates, retard borrowing and spending, and produce further declines in output and income.

Collapse of the Gold Standard

The gold standard collapsed under the weight of the worldwide Depression of the 1930s. As domestic output and employment fell worldwide, the restoration of prosperity became the primary goal of afflicted nations. They responded by enacting protectionist measures to reduce imports. The idea was to get their economies moving again by promoting consumption of domestically produced goods. To make their exports less expensive abroad, many nations redefined their currencies at lower levels in terms of gold. For example, a country that had previously defined the value of its currency at 1 unit = 25 ounces of gold might redefine it as 1 unit = 10 ounces of gold. Such redefining is an example of **devaluation**—a deliberate action by government to reduce the international value of its currency. A series of such devaluations in the 1930s meant that exchange rates were no longer fixed. That violated a major tenet of the gold standard, and the system broke down.

The Bretton Woods System

The Great Depression and the Second World War left world trade and the world monetary system in shambles. To lay the groundwork for a new international monetary system, in 1944 major nations held an international conference at Bretton Woods, New Hampshire. The conference produced a commitment to a modified fixed-exchange-rate system called an *adjustable-peg system*, or, simply, the **Bretton Woods system.** The new system sought to capture the advantages of the old gold standard (fixed exchange rate) while avoiding its disadvantages (painful domestic macroeconomic adjustments).

Furthermore, the conference created the **International Monetary Fund (IMF)** to make the new exchange-rate system feasible and workable. The new international monetary system managed through the IMF prevailed with modifications until 1971. (The IMF still plays a basic role in international finance; in recent years it has performed a major role in providing loans to developing countries, nations experiencing financial crises, and nations making the transition from communism to capitalism.)

IMF and Pegged Exchange Rates

How did the adjustable-peg system of exchange rates work? First, as with the gold standard, each IMF member had to define its currency in terms of gold (or dollars), thus establishing rates of exchange between its currency and the currencies of all other members. In addition, each nation was obligated to keep its exchange rate stable with respect to every other currency. To do so, nations would have to use their official currency reserves to intervene in foreign exchange markets.

Assume again that the U.S. dollar and the British pound were "pegged" to each other at $2 = £1. And suppose again that the demand for pounds temporarily increases so that a shortage of pounds occurs in the United States (the United States has a balance-of-payments deficit). How can the United States keep its pledge to maintain a $2 = £1 exchange rate when the new equilibrium rate is, say, $3 = £1? As we noted previously, the United States can supply additional pounds to the exchange market, increasing the supply of pounds such that the equilibrium exchange rate falls back to $2 = £1.

Under the Bretton Woods system there were three main sources of the needed pounds:

- *Official reserves*   The United States might currently possess pounds in its official reserves as the result of past actions against a payments surplus.
- *Gold sales*   The U.S. government might sell some of its gold to Britain for pounds. The proceeds would then be offered in the exchange market to augment the supply of pounds.
- *IMF borrowing*   The needed pounds might be borrowed from the IMF. Nations participating in the Bretton Woods system were required to make contributions to the IMF based on the size of their national income, population, and volume of trade. If necessary, the United States could borrow pounds on a short-term basis from the IMF by supplying its own currency as collateral.

Fundamental Imbalances: Adjusting the Peg

The Bretton Woods system recognized that from time to time a nation may be confronted with persistent and sizable balance-of-payments problems that cannot be corrected through the means listed above. In such cases, the nation would eventually run out of official reserves and be unable to maintain its fixed-exchange-rate system. The Bretton Woods remedy was correction by devaluation, that is, by an "orderly" reduction of the nation's pegged exchange rate. Also, the IMF allowed each member nation to alter the value of its currency by 10 percent, on its own, to correct a so-called fundamental (persistent and continuing) balance-of-payments deficit. Larger exchange-rate changes required the permission of the Fund's board of directors.

By requiring approval of significant rate changes, the Fund guarded against arbitrary and competitive currency devaluations by nations seeking only to boost output in their own countries at the expense of other countries. In our example, devaluation of the dollar would increase U.S. exports and lower U.S. imports, correcting its persistent payments deficit.

Demise of the Bretton Woods System

Under this adjustable-peg system, nations came to accept gold and the dollar as international reserves. The acceptability of gold as an international medium of exchange derived from its earlier use under the gold standard. Other nations accepted the dollar as international money because the United States had accumulated large quantities of gold, and between 1934 and 1971 it maintained a policy of buying gold from, and selling gold to, foreign governments at a fixed price of $35 per ounce. The dollar was convertible into gold on demand, so the dollar came to be regarded as a substitute for gold, or "as good as gold." And since the discovery of new gold was limited, the growing volume of dollars helped provide a medium of exchange for the expanding world trade.

But a major problem arose. The United States had persistent payments deficits throughout the 1950s and 1960s. Those deficits were financed in part by U.S. gold reserves but mostly by payment of U.S. dollars. As the amount of dollars held by foreigners soared and the U.S. gold reserves dwindled, other nations began to question whether the dollar was really "as good as gold." The ability of the United States to continue to convert dollars into gold at $35 per ounce became increasingly doubtful, as did the role of dollars as international monetary reserves. Thus the dilemma was: To maintain the dollar as a reserve medium, the U.S. payments deficit had to be eliminated. But elimination of the payments deficit would remove the source of additional dollar reserves and thus limit the growth of international trade and finance.

The problem culminated in 1971 when the United States ended its 37-year-old policy of exchanging gold for dollars at $35 per ounce. It severed the link between gold and the international value of the dollar, thereby "floating" the dollar and letting market forces determine its value. The floating of the dollar withdrew U.S. support from the Bretton Woods system of fixed exchange rates and, in effect, ended the system.

The Current System: The Managed Float

The current international exchange-rate system (1971–present) is an "almost" flexible system called **managed floating exchange rates.** Exchange rates among major currencies are free to float to their equilibrium market levels, but nations occasionally use currency interventions in the foreign exchange market to stabilize or alter market exchange rates.

Normally, the major trading nations allow their exchange rates to float up or down to equilibrium levels based on supply and demand in the foreign exchange market. They recognize that changing economic conditions among nations require continuing changes in equilibrium exchange rates to avoid persistent payments deficits or surpluses. They rely on freely operating foreign exchange markets to accomplish the necessary adjustments. The result has been considerably more volatile exchange rates than those during the Bretton Woods era.

But nations also recognize that certain trends in the movement of equilibrium exchange rates may be at odds with national or international objectives. On occasion, nations therefore intervene in the foreign exchange market by buying or selling large amounts of specific currencies. This way, they can "manage" or stabilize exchange rates by influencing currency demand and supply.

The leaders of the *G8 nations* (Canada, France, Germany, Italy, Japan, Russia, United Kingdom, and United States) meet regularly to discuss economic issues and try to coordinate economic policies. At times they have collectively intervened to try to stabilize currencies. For example, in 2000 they sold dollars and bought euros in an effort to stabilize the falling value of the euro relative to the dollar. In the previous year the euro (€) had depreciated from €1 = $1.17 to €1 = $.87.

The current exchange-rate system is thus an "almost" flexible exchange-rate system. The "almost" refers mainly to the periodic currency interventions by governments; it also refers to the fact that the actual system is more complicated than described. While the major currencies such as dollars, euros, pounds, and yen fluctuate in response to changing supply and demand, some developing nations peg their currencies to the dollar and allow their currencies to fluctuate with it against other currencies. Also, some nations peg the value of their currencies to a "basket" or group of other currencies.

How well has the managed float worked? It has both proponents and critics.

In Support of the Managed Float
Proponents of the managed-float system argue that is has functioned far better than many experts anticipated. Skeptics had predicted that fluctuating exchange rates would reduce world trade and finance. But in real terms world trade under the managed float has grown tremendously over the past several decades. Moreover, as supporters are quick to point out, currency crises such as those in Mexico and southeast Asia in the last half of the 1990s were not the result of the floating-exchange-rate system itself. Rather, the abrupt currency devaluations and depreciations resulted from internal problems in those nations, in conjunction with the nations' tendency to peg their currencies to the dollar or to a basket of currencies. In some cases, flexible exchange rates would have made these adjustments far more gradual.

Proponents also point out that the managed float has weathered severe economic turbulence that might have caused a fixed-rate system to break down. Such events as extraordinary oil price increases in 1973–1974 and again in 1981–1983, inflationary recessions in several nations in the mid-1970s, major national recessions in the early 1980s, and large U.S. budget deficits in the 1980s and the first half of the 1990s all caused substantial imbalances in international trade and finance. Flexible rates enabled the system to adjust to those events, whereas the same events would have put unbearable pressures on a fixed-rate system.

Concerns with the Managed Float
There is still much sentiment in favor of greater exchange-rate stability. Those favoring more stable exchange rates see problems with the current system. They argue that the excessive volatility of exchange rates under the managed float threatens the prosperity of economies that rely heavily on exports. Several financial crises in individual nations (for example, Mexico, South Korea, Indonesia, Thailand, Russia, and Brazil) have resulted from abrupt changes in exchange rates. These crises have led to massive "bailouts" of those economies via IMF loans. The IMF bailouts, in turn, may encourage nations to undertake risky and inappropriate economic policies since they know that, if need be, the IMF will come to the rescue. Moreover, some exchange-rate volatility has occurred even when underlying economic and financial conditions were relatively stable, suggesting that speculation plays too large a role in determining exchange rates.

Perhaps more importantly, assert the critics, the managed float has not eliminated trade imbalances, as flexible rates are supposed to do. Thus, the United States has run persistent trade deficits for many years, while Japan has run persistent surpluses. Changes in exchange rates between dollars and yen have not yet corrected these imbalances, as is supposed to be the case under flexible exchange rates.

Skeptics say the managed float is basically a "nonsystem"; the guidelines concerning what each nation may or may not do with its exchange rates are not specific enough to keep the system working in the long run. Nations inevitably will be tempted to intervene in the foreign exchange market, not merely to smooth out short-term fluctuations in exchange rates but to prop up their currency if it is chronically weak or to manipulate the exchange rate to achieve domestic stabilization goals.

So what are we to conclude? Flexible exchange rates have not worked perfectly, but they have not failed miserably. Thus far they have survived, and no doubt have eased, several major shocks to the international trading system. Meanwhile, the "managed" part of the float has given nations some sense of control over their collective economic destinies. On balance, most economists favor continuation of the present system of "almost" flexible exchange rates.

Recent U.S. Trade Deficits

As indicated in Figure 38.3a, the United States has experienced large and persistent trade deficits over the past several years. These deficits climbed steadily between 1995 and 2000, fell slightly in the recessionary year 2001, and rose again in 2002. In 2002 the trade deficit on goods was $484 billion and the trade deficit on goods and services was $436 billion. The current account deficit (Figure 38.3b) reached a record $504 billion in 2002. Large trade deficits are expected to continue for many years.

Causes of the Trade Deficits

There are several reasons for these large trade deficits. First, between 1995 and 2000 the U.S. economy grew more rapidly than the economies of several of its major trading partners. That strong growth of U.S. income enabled Americans to buy more imported goods. In contrast, Japan, Canada, and some European nations either suffered recession or experienced slow income growth. So their purchases of U.S. exports did not keep pace with the growing U.S. imports. Large trade deficits with Japan were particularly noteworthy throughout the 1990s.

Second, large trade deficits with China emerged, reaching $83 billion in 2002. This is even greater than the U.S. trade imbalance with Japan ($58 billion in 2002). The United States is China's largest export market, and although China has increased its imports from the United States, its standard of living has not yet increased enough

FIGURE 38.3

U.S. trade deficits, 1994–2002.   (a) The United States experienced large deficits in *goods* and in *goods and services* between 1994 and 2002. (b) The U.S. current account, generally reflecting the goods and services deficit, was also in substantial deficit. These trade deficits are expected to continue throughout the current decade.

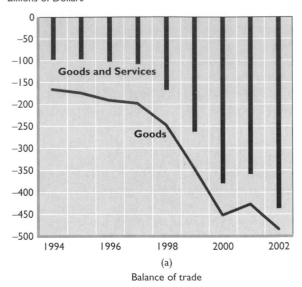

(a)
Balance of trade

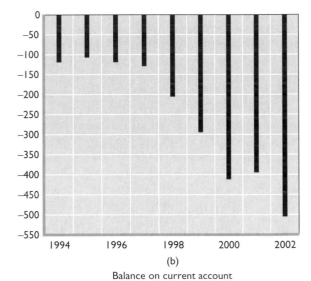

(b)
Balance on current account

for its citizens to afford large quantities of U.S. goods and services.

Finally, a declining U.S. saving rate (= saving/total income) has also contributed to U.S. trade deficits. In the 1990s, the saving rate declined while the investment rate (= investment/total income) remained stable or even increased. The gap was met through foreign purchases of U.S. real and financial assets, creating a large capital account surplus. Because foreign savers were willingly financing a larger part of U.S. investment, Americans were able to save less than otherwise and consume more. Part of that added consumption spending was on imported goods. That is, the capital account surplus may be one cause of the trade deficits, not just a result of those deficits.

The U.S. recession of 2001 temporarily lowered income and reduced U.S. imports and trade deficits. But the general trend toward higher trade deficits quickly reemerged in 2002.

Implications of U.S. Trade Deficits

There is disagreement on whether the large trade deficits should concern the United States. Most economists see both benefits and costs to trade deficits.

Increased Current Consumption At the time a trade deficit or a current account deficit is occurring, American consumers benefit. A trade deficit means that the United States is receiving more goods and services as imports from abroad than it is sending out as exports. Taken alone, a trade deficit allows the United States to consume outside its production possibilities curve. It augments the domestic standard of living. But there is a catch: The gain in present consumption may come at the expense of reduced future consumption.

Increased U.S. Indebtedness A trade deficit is considered "unfavorable" because it must be financed by borrowing from the rest of the world, selling off assets, or dipping into foreign currency reserves. Recall that current account deficits are financed primarily by net inpayments of foreign currencies to the United States. When U.S. exports are insufficient to finance U.S. imports, the United States increases both its debt to people abroad and the value of foreign claims against assets in the United States. Financing of the U.S. trade deficit has resulted in a larger foreign accumulation of claims against U.S. financial and real assets than the U.S. claim against foreign assets. Today, the United States is the world's largest debtor nation. In 2001 foreigners owned $2.3 billion more of U.S. assets (corporations, land, stocks, bonds, loan notes) than U.S. citizens and institutions owned in foreign assets.

If the United States wants to regain ownership of these domestic assets, at some future time it will have to export more than it imports. At that time, domestic consumption will be lower because the United States will need to send more of its output abroad than it receives as imports. Therefore, the current consumption gains delivered by U.S. current account deficits may mean permanent debt, permanent foreign ownership, or large sacrifices of future consumption.

We say "may mean" above because the foreign lending to U.S. firms and foreign investment in the United States increases the U.S. capital stock. U.S. production capacity therefore might increase more rapidly than otherwise because of a large surplus on the capital account. Faster increases in production capacity and real GDP enhance the economy's ability to service foreign debt and buy back real capital, if that is desired.

In short, U.S. trade deficits are a mixed blessing. Their long-term impacts are largely unknown.

Are Speculators a Negative or a Positive Influence in Currency Markets and International Trade?

Most people buy foreign currency to facilitate the purchase of goods or services from another country. A U.S. importer buys Japanese yen to purchase Japanese autos. A Hong Kong financial investor purchases Australian dollars to invest in the Australian stock market. But there is another group of participants in the currency market—speculators—that buys and sells foreign currencies in the hope of reselling or rebuying them later at a profit.

Contributing to Exchange-Rate Fluctuations Speculators were much in the news in late 1997 and 1998 when they were widely accused of driving down the values of the South Korean won, Thailand baht, Malaysian ringgit, and Indonesian rupiah. The value of these currencies fell by as much as 50 percent within 1 month, and speculators undoubtedly contributed to the swiftness of those declines. The expectation of currency depreciation (or appreciation) can be self-fulfilling. If speculators, for example, expect the Indonesian rupiah to be devalued or to depreciate, they quickly sell rupiah and buy currencies that they think will increase in relative value. The sharp increase in the supply of rupiah indeed reduces its value; this reduction then may trigger further selling of rupiah in expectation of further declines in its value.

But changed economic realities, not speculation, are normally the underlying causes of changes in currency values. That was largely the case with the southeast Asian countries in which actual and threatened bankruptcies in the financial and manufacturing sectors undermined confidence in the strength of the currencies. Anticipating the eventual declines in currency values, speculators simply hastened those declines. That is, the declines in value probably would have occurred with or without speculators.

Moreover, on a daily basis, speculation clearly has positive effects in foreign exchange markets.

Smoothing Out Short-Term Fluctuations in Currency Prices When temporarily weak demand or strong supply reduces a currency's value, speculators quickly buy the currency, adding to its demand and strengthening its value. When temporarily strong demand or weak supply increases a currency's value, speculators sell the currency. That selling increases the supply of the currency and reduces its value. In this way speculators smooth out supply and demand, and thus exchange rates, over short time periods. This day-to-day exchange-rate stabilization aids international trade.

Absorbing Risk Speculators also absorb risk that others do not want to bear. Because of potential adverse changes in exchange rates, international transactions are riskier than domestic transactions. Suppose AnyTime, a hypothetical retailer, signs a contract with a Swiss manufacturer to buy 10,000 Swatch watches to be delivered in 3 months. The stipulated price is 75 Swiss francs per watch, which in dollars is $50 per watch at the present exchange rate of, say, $1 = 1.5 francs. AnyTime's total bill for the 10,000 watches will be $500,000 (= 750,000 francs).

SUMMARY

1. U.S. exports create a foreign demand for dollars and make a supply of foreign exchange available to the United States. Conversely, U.S. imports create a demand for foreign exchange and make a supply of dollars available to foreigners. Generally, a nation's exports earn the foreign currencies needed to pay for its imports.

2. The balance of payments records all international trade and financial transactions taking place between a given nation and the rest of the world. The balance on goods and services (the trade balance) compares exports and imports of both goods and services. The current account balance includes not only goods and services transactions but also net investment income and net transfers.

3. A deficit in the current account may be offset by a surplus in the capital account. Conversely, a surplus in the current account may be offset by a deficit in the capital account. A balance-of-payments deficit occurs when the sum of the current and capital accounts is negative. Such a deficit is financed with official reserves. A balance-of-payments surplus occurs when the sum of the current and capital accounts is positive. A payments surplus results in an increase in official reserves. The desirability of a balance-of-payments deficit or surplus depends on its size and its persistence.

4. Flexible or floating exchange rates between international currencies are determined by the demand for and supply of those currencies. Under flexible rates a currency will depreciate or appreciate as a result of changes in tastes, relative income changes, relative price changes, relative changes in real interest rates, and speculation.

5. The maintenance of fixed exchange rates requires adequate reserves to accommodate periodic payments deficits. If reserves are inadequate, nations must invoke protectionist trade policies, engage in exchange controls, or endure undesirable domestic macroeconomic adjustments.

6. The gold standard, a fixed-rate system, provided exchange-rate stability until its disintegration during the 1930s. Under this system, gold flows between nations precipitated sometimes painful changes in price, income, and employment levels in bringing about international equilibrium.

But if the Swiss franc were to appreciate, say, to $1 = 1 franc, the dollar price per watch would rise from $50 to $75 and AnyTime would owe $750,000 for the watches (= 750,000 francs). AnyTime may reduce the risk of such an unfavorable exchange-rate fluctuation by hedging in the futures market. Hedging is an action by a buyer or a seller to protect against a change in future prices. The futures market is a market in which currencies are bought and sold at prices fixed now, for delivery at a specified date in the future.

AnyTime can purchase the needed 750,000 francs at the current $1 = 1.5 francs exchange rate, but with delivery in 3 months when the Swiss watches are delivered. And here is where speculators come in. For a price determined in the futures market, they agree to deliver the 750,000 francs to AnyTime in 3 months at the $1 = 1.5 francs exchange rate, regardless of the exchange rate then. The speculators need not own francs when the agreement is made. If the Swiss franc depreciates to, say, $1 = 2 francs in this period, the speculators profit. They can buy the 750,000 francs stipulated in the contract for $375,000, pocket-

ing the difference between that amount and the $500,000 AnyTime has agreed to pay for the 750,000 francs. If the Swiss franc appreciates, the speculators, but not AnyTime, suffer a loss.

The amount AnyTime must pay for this "exchange-rate insurance" will depend on how the market views the likelihood of the franc depreciating, appreciating, or staying constant over the 3-month period. As in all competitive markets, supply and demand determine the price of the futures contract.

The futures market thus eliminates much of the exchange-rate risk associated with buying foreign goods for future delivery. Without it, AnyTime might have decided against importing Swiss watches. But the futures market and currency speculators greatly increase the likelihood that the transaction will occur. Operating through the futures market, speculation promotes international trade.

In short, although speculators in currency markets occasionally contribute to swings in exchange rates, on a day-to-day basis they play a positive role in currency markets.

7. Under the Bretton Woods system, exchange rates were pegged to one another and were stable. Participating nations were obligated to maintain these rates by using stabilization funds, gold, or loans from the IMF. Persistent or "fundamental" payments deficits could be resolved by IMF-sanctioned currency devaluations.

8. Since 1971 the world's major nations have used a system of managed floating exchange rates. Market forces generally set rates, although governments intervene with varying frequency to alter their exchange rates.

9. Between 1994 and 2002, the United States had large and rising trade deficits, which are projected to last well into the future. Causes of the trade deficits include (a) more rapid income growth in the United States than in Japan, Canada, and some European nations, resulting in expanding U.S. imports relative to exports, (b) the emergence of a large trade deficit with China, and (c) a large surplus in the capital account that enabled Americans to reduce their saving and buy more imports.

10. U.S. trade deficits have produced current increases in the living standards of U.S. consumers. The accompanying surpluses on the capital account have increased U.S. debt to the rest of the world and increased foreign ownership of assets in the United States. This greater foreign investment in the United States, however, has undoubtedly increased U.S. production possibilities.

TERMS AND CONCEPTS

balance of payments

current account

balance on goods and
    services

trade deficit

trade surplus

balance on current account

capital account

balance on capital account

official reserves

balance-of-payments deficits
    and surpluses

flexible- or floating-
    exchange-rate system

fixed-exchange-rate system

purchasing-power-parity theory	exchange controls	Bretton Woods system	managed floating exchange rates
currency interventions	gold standard	International Monetary Fund (IMF)	
	devaluation		

STUDY QUESTIONS

1. Explain how a U.S. automobile importer might finance a shipment of Toyotas from Japan. Trace the steps as to how a U.S. export of machinery to Italy might be financed. Explain: "U.S. exports earn supplies of foreign currencies that Americans can use to finance imports."

2. *Key Question* Indicate whether each of the following creates a demand for or a supply of European euros in foreign exchange markets:
   a. A U.S. airline firm purchases several Airbus planes assembled in France.
   b. A German automobile firm decides to build an assembly plant in South Carolina.
   c. A U.S. college student decides to spend a year studying at the Sorbonne in Paris.
   d. An Italian manufacturer ships machinery from one Italian port to another on a Liberian freighter.
   e. The U.S. economy grows faster than the French economy.
   f. A U.S. government bond held by a Spanish citizen matures, and the loan amount is paid back to that person.
   g. It is widely believed that the euro will depreciate in the near future.

3. *Key Question* Alpha's balance-of-payments data for 2003 are shown below. All figures are in billions of dollars. What are (*a*) the balance of trade, (*b*) the balance on goods and services, (*c*) the balance on current account, and (*d*) the balance on capital account? Does Alpha have a balance-of-payments deficit or surplus? Explain.

Goods exports	+$40	Net transfers	+$10
Goods imports	− 30	Foreign purchases	
Service exports	+ 15	of assets in the	
Service imports	− 10	United States	+ 10
Net investment		U.S. purchases	
income	− 5	of assets abroad	− 40
		Official reserves	+ 10

4. "A rise in the dollar price of yen necessarily means a fall in the yen price of dollars." Do you agree? Illustrate and elaborate: "The critical thing about exchange rates is that they provide a direct link between the prices of goods and services produced in all trading nations of the world." Explain the purchasing-power-parity theory of exchange rates.

5. Suppose that a Swiss watchmaker imports watch components from Sweden and exports watches to the United States. Also suppose the dollar depreciates, and the Swedish krona appreciates, relative to the Swiss franc. Speculate as to how each would hurt the Swiss watchmaker.

6. *Key Question* Explain why the U.S. demand for Mexican pesos is downward-sloping and the supply of pesos to Americans is upward-sloping. Assuming a system of flexible exchange rates between Mexico and the United States, indicate whether each of the following would cause the Mexican peso to appreciate or depreciate:
   a. The United States unilaterally reduces tariffs on Mexican products.
   b. Mexico encounters severe inflation.
   c. Deteriorating political relations reduce American tourism in Mexico.
   d. The U.S. economy moves into a severe recession.
   e. The United States engages in a high-interest-rate monetary policy.
   f. Mexican products become more fashionable to U.S. consumers.
   g. The Mexican government encourages U.S. firms to invest in Mexican oil fields.
   h. The rate of productivity growth in the United States diminishes sharply.

7. Explain why you agree or disagree with the following statements:
   a. A country that grows faster than its major trading partners can expect the international value of its currency to depreciate.
   b. A nation whose interest rate is rising more rapidly than interest rates in other nations can expect the international value of its currency to appreciate.
   c. A country's currency will appreciate if its inflation rate is less than that of the rest of the world.

8. "Exports pay for imports. Yet in 2002 the nations of the world exported about $436 billion more worth of goods and services to the United States than they imported from the United States." Resolve the apparent inconsistency of these two statements.

9. *Key Question* Diagram a market in which the equilibrium dollar price of 1 unit of fictitious currency zee (Z) is $5 (the exchange rate is $5 = Z1). Then show on your diagram a decline in the demand for zee.

   a. Referring to your diagram, discuss the adjustment options the United States would have in maintaining the exchange rate at $5 = Z1 under a fixed-exchange-rate system.

   b. How would the U.S. balance-of-payments surplus that is created (by the decline in demand) get resolved under a system of flexible exchange rates?

10. Compare and contrast the Bretton Woods system of exchange rates with that of the gold standard. What caused the collapse of the gold standard? What caused the demise of the Bretton Woods system?

11. Describe what is meant by the term "managed float." Did the managed-float system precede or follow the adjustable-peg system? Explain.

12. What have been the major causes of the large U.S. trade deficits since 1995? What are the major benefits and costs associated with trade deficits? Explain: "A trade deficit means that a nation is receiving more goods and services from abroad than it is sending abroad." How can that be called "unfavorable"?

13. *(Last Word)* Suppose Winter Sports—a hypothetical French retailer of snowboards—wants to order 5000 snowboards made in the United States. The price per board is $200, the present exchange rate is 1 euro = $1, and payment is due in dollars when the boards are delivered in 3 months. Use a numerical example to explain why exchange-rate risk might make the French retailer hesitant to place the order. How might speculators absorb some of Winter Sports' risk?

14. *Web-Based Question: The U.S. balance on goods and services—what are the latest figures?* The U.S. Census Bureau reports the latest data on U.S. trade in goods and services at its website, www.census.gov/indicator/www/ustrade.html. In the latest month, did the trade balance in goods and services improve (that is, yield a smaller deficit or a larger surplus) or deteriorate? Was the relative trade strength of the United States compared to the rest of the world in goods or in services? Which product groups had the largest increases in exports? Which had the largest increases in imports?

15. *Web-Based Question: The yen-dollar exchange rate* The Federal Reserve Board of Governors provides exchange rates for various currencies for the last decade at www.federalreserve.gov/releases (Foreign Exchange Rates; Historical bilateral rates). Has the dollar appreciated, depreciated, or remained constant relative to the Canadian dollar, the European euro, the Japanese yen, the Swedish krona, and the Swiss franc since 2000?

39 WEB

The Economics of Developing Countries

Chapter 39 Web is a bonus chapter found at the book's website, www.mcconnell16.com. It extends the analysis of Part 10, "International Economics and the World Economy," and may or may not be assigned by your instructor.

Chapter 39W Contents

40 WEB

Transition Economies: Russia and China

Chapter 40 Web is a bonus chapter found at the book's website, www.mcconnell16.com. It extends the analysis of Part 10, "International Economics and the World Economy," and may or may not be assigned by your instructor.

Chapter 40W Contents

GLOSSARY

Note: Terms set in *italic* type are defined separately in this glossary.

ability-to-pay principle The idea that those who have greater *income* (or *wealth*) should pay a greater proportion of it as taxes than those who have less income (or wealth).

abstraction Elimination of irrelevant and noneconomic facts to obtain an *economic principle*.

acreage allotment program A pre-1996 government program that determined the total number of acres to be used in producing (reduced amounts of) various food and fiber products and allocated these acres among individual farmers. These farmers had to limit their plantings to the allotted number of acres to obtain *price supports* for their crops.

actual investment The amount that *firms* do invest; equal to *planned investment* plus *unplanned investment*.

actual reserves The funds that a bank has on deposit at the *Federal Reserve Bank* of its district (plus its *vault cash*).

adjustable pegs The device used in the *Bretton Woods system* to alter *exchange rates* in an orderly way to eliminate persistent payments deficits and surpluses. Each nation defined its monetary unit in terms of (pegged it to) gold or the dollar, kept the *rate of exchange* for its money stable in the short run, and adjusted its rate in the long run when faced with international payments disequilibrium.

adverse selection problem A problem arising when information known to one party to a contract or agreement is not known to the other party, causing the latter to incur major costs. Example: Individuals who have the poorest health are most likely to buy health insurance.

advertising A seller's activities in communicating its message about its product to potential buyers.

affirmative action Policies and programs that establish targets of increased employment and promotion for women and minorities.

AFL-CIO An acronym for the American Federation of Labor–Congress of Industrial Organizations; the largest federation of *labor unions* in the United States.

agency shop A place of employment where the employer may hire either *labor union* members or nonmembers but where those who do not join the union must either pay union dues or donate an equivalent amount of money to a charity.

aggregate demand A schedule or curve that shows the total quantity of goods and services demanded (purchased) at different *price levels*.

aggregate demand–aggregate supply model The macroeconomic model that uses *aggregate demand* and *aggregate supply* to determine and explain the *price level* and the real *domestic output*.

aggregate expenditures The total amount spent for final goods and services in an economy.

aggregate expenditures–domestic output approach Determination of the equilibrium *gross domestic product* by finding the real GDP at which *aggregate expenditures* equal *domestic output*.

aggregate expenditures schedule A schedule or curve showing the total amount spent for final goods and services at different levels of *real GDP*.

aggregate supply A schedule or curve showing the total quantity of goods and services supplied (produced) at different *price levels*.

aggregate supply shocks Sudden, large changes in resource costs that shift an economy's aggregate supply curve.

aggregation The combining of individual units or data into one unit or number. For example, all prices of individual goods and services are combined into a *price level* or all units of output are aggregated into *real gross domestic product*.

Alcoa case A 1945 case in which the courts ruled that the possession of monopoly power, no matter how reasonably that power had been used, was a violation of the antitrust laws; temporarily overturned the *rule of reason* applied in the *U.S. Steel case*.

allocative efficiency The apportionment of resources among firms and industries to obtain the production of the products most wanted by society (consumers); the output of each product at which its *marginal cost* and *price* or *marginal benefit* are equal.

annually balanced budget A budget in which government expenditures and tax collections are equal each year.

anticipated inflation Increases in the price level (*inflation*) that occur at the expected rate.

antitrust laws Legislation (including the *Sherman Act* and *Clayton Act*) that prohibits anticompetitive business activities such as *price fixing*, bid rigging, monopolization, and *tying contracts*.

antitrust policy The use of the *antitrust laws* to promote *competition* and economic efficiency.

appreciation (of the dollar) An increase in the value of the dollar relative to the currency of another nation, so a dollar buys a larger amount of the foreign currency and thus of foreign goods.

asset Anything of monetary value owned by a firm or individual.

asset demand for money The amount of *money* people want to hold as a *store of value;* this amount varies inversely with the *interest rate*.

asymmetric information A situation where one party to a market transaction has much more information about a product or service than the other. The result may be an under- or overallocation of resources.

G

average fixed cost A firm's total *fixed cost* divided by output (the quantity of product produced).

average product The total output produced per unit of a *resource* employed (*total product* divided by the quantity of that employed resource).

average propensity to consume Fraction (or percentage) of *disposable income* that households plan to spend for consumer goods and services; consumption divided by *disposable income*.

average propensity to save Fraction (or percentage) of *disposable income* that households save; *saving* divided by *disposable income*.

average revenue Total revenue from the sale of a product divided by the quantity of the product sold (demanded); equal to the price at which the product is sold when all units of the product are sold at the same price.

average tax rate Total tax paid divided by total (taxable) income, as a percentage.

average total cost A firm's *total cost* divided by output (the quantity of product produced); equal to *average fixed cost* plus *average variable cost*.

average variable cost A firm's total *variable cost* divided by output (the quantity of product produced).

backflows The return of workers to the countries from which they originally migrated.

balance of payments (See *international balance of payments*.)

balance-of-payments deficit The amount by which the sum of the *balance on current account* and the *balance on capital account* is negative in a year.

balance-of-payments surplus The amount by which the sum of the *balance on current account* and the *balance on capital account* is positive in a year.

balance on capital account The foreign purchases of assets in the United States less American purchases of assets abroad in a year.

balance on current account The exports of goods and services of a nation less its imports of goods and services plus its *net investment income* and *net transfers* in a year.

balance on goods and services The exports of goods and services of a nation less its imports of goods and services in a year.

balance sheet A statement of the *assets*, *liabilities*, and *net worth* of a firm or individual at some given time.

bank deposits The deposits that individuals or firms have at banks (or thrifts) or that banks have at the *Federal Reserve Banks*.

bankers' bank A bank that accepts the deposits of and makes loans to *depository institutions*; in the United States, a *Federal Reserve Bank*.

bank reserves The deposits of commercial banks and thrifts at *Federal Reserve Banks* plus bank and thrift *vault cash*.

barrier to entry Anything that artificially prevents the entry of firms into an industry.

barter The exchange of one good or service for another good or service.

base year The year with which other years are compared when an index is constructed; for example, the base year for a *price index*.

benefit-reduction rate The percentage by which subsidy benefits in a *public assistance program* are reduced as earned income rises.

benefits-received principle The idea that those who receive the benefits of goods and services provided by government should pay the taxes required to finance them.

bilateral monopoly A market in which there is a single seller *(monopoly)* and a single buyer *(monopsony)*.

Board of Governors The seven-member group that supervises and controls the money and banking system of the United States; the Board of Governors of the Federal Reserve System; the Federal Reserve Board.

bond A financial device through which a borrower (a firm or government) is obligated to pay the principal and interest on a loan at a specific date in the future.

brain drain (Web chapter) The emigration of highly educated, highly skilled workers from a country.

break-even income The level of *disposable income* at which *households* plan to consume (spend) all their income and to save none of it; also, in an income transfer program, the level of earned income at which subsidy payments become zero.

break-even output Any output at which a (competitive) firm's *total cost* and *total revenue* are equal; an output at which a firm has neither an *economic profit* nor a loss, at which it earns only a normal profit.

Bretton Woods system The international monetary system developed after the Second World War in which *adjustable pegs* were employed, the *International Monetary Fund* helped stabilize foreign exchange rates, and gold and the dollar were used as *international monetary reserves*.

budget constraint The limit that the size of a consumer's income (and the prices that must be paid for goods and services) imposes on the ability of that consumer to obtain goods and services.

budget deficit The amount by which the expenditures of the Federal government exceed its revenues in any year.

budget line A line that shows the different combinations of two products a consumer can purchase with a specific money income, given the products' prices.

budget surplus The amount by which the revenues of the Federal government exceed its expenditures in any year.

built-in stabilizer A mechanism that increases government's budget deficit (or reduces its surplus) during a recession and increases government's budget surplus (or reduces its deficit) during inflation without any action by policymakers. The tax system is one such mechanism.

Bureau of Economic Analysis (BEA)   An agency of the U.S. Department of Commerce that compiles the national income and product accounts.

business cycle   Recurring increases and decreases in the level of economic activity over periods of years; consists of peak, recession, trough, and recovery phases.

business firm   (See *firm*.)

business unionism   Labor unionism that concerns itself with such practical and short-run objectives as higher wages, shorter hours, and improved working conditions.

capital   Human-made resources (buildings, machinery, and equipment) used to produce goods and services; goods that do not directly satisfy human wants; also called capital goods.

capital account   The section of a nation's *international balance-of-payments* statement that records the foreign purchases of assets in the United States (creating monetary inflows) and U.S. purchases of assets abroad (creating monetary outflows).

capital account deficit   A negative *balance on capital account*.

capital account surplus   A positive *balance on capital account*.

capital flight   (Web chapter) The transfer of savings from *developing countries* to industrially advanced countries to avoid government expropriation, taxation, and high rates of inflation or to realize better investment opportunities.

capital gain   The gain realized when securities or properties are sold for a price greater than the price paid for them.

capital goods   (See *capital*.)

capital-intensive commodity   A product that requires a relatively large amount of *capital* to be produced.

capitalism   An economic system in which property resources are privately owned and markets and prices are used to direct and coordinate economic activities.

capital-saving technological advance   (Web chapter) An improvement in *technology* that permits a greater quantity of a product to be produced with a specific amount of *capital* (or permits the same amount of the product to be produced with a smaller amount of capital).

capital stock   The total available *capital* in a nation.

capital-using technological advance   (Web chapter) An improvement in *technology* that requires the use of a greater amount of *capital* to produce a specific quantity of a product.

cartel   A formal agreement among firms (or countries) in an industry to set the price of a product and establish the outputs of the individual firms (or countries) or to divide the market for the product geographically.

causation   A relationship in which the occurrence of one or more events brings about another event.

CEA   (See *Council of Economic Advisers*.)

cease-and-desist order   An order from a court or government agency to a corporation or individual to stop engaging in a specified practice.

ceiling price   (See *price ceiling*.)

Celler-Kefauver Act   The Federal act of 1950 that amended the *Clayton Act* by prohibiting the acquisition of the assets of one firm by another firm when the effect would be less competition.

central bank   A bank whose chief function is the control of the nation's *money supply*; in the United States, the Federal Reserve System.

central economic planning   Government determination of the objectives of the economy and how resources will be directed to attain those goals.

ceteris paribus **assumption**   (See *other-things-equal assumption*.)

change in demand   A change in the *quantity demanded* of a good or service at every price; a shift of the *demand curve* to the left or right.

change in supply   A change in the *quantity supplied* of a good or service at every price; a shift of the *supply curve* to the left or right.

checkable deposit   Any deposit in a *commercial bank* or *thrift institution* against which a check may be written.

checkable-deposit multiplier   (See *monetary multiplier*.)

check clearing   The process by which funds are transferred from the checking accounts of the writers of checks to the checking accounts of the recipients of the checks.

checking account   A *checkable deposit* in a *commercial bank* or *thrift institution*.

circular flow model   The flow of resources from *households* to *firms* and of products from firms to households. These flows are accompanied by reverse flows of money from firms to households and from households to firms.

Civil Rights Act of 1964   Federal law that, in Title VII, outlaws *discrimination* based on race, color, religion, gender, or national origin in hiring, promoting, and compensating workers.

classical economics   The macroeconomic generalizations accepted by most economists before the 1930s that led to the conclusion that a capitalistic economy was self-regulating and therefore would usually employ its resources fully.

Clayton Act   The Federal antitrust act of 1914 that strengthened the *Sherman Act* by making it illegal for firms to engage in certain specified practices.

closed economy   An economy that neither exports nor imports goods and services.

closed shop   A place of employment where only workers who are already members of a labor union may be hired.

Coase theorem   The idea, first stated by economist Ronald Coase, that *spillover* problems may be resolved through private negotiations of the affected parties.

coincidence of wants   A situation in which the good or service that one trader desires to obtain is the same as that which another trader desires to give up and an item that the second trader wishes to acquire is the same as that which the first trader desires to surrender.

COLA (See *cost-of-living adjustment*.)

collective bargaining The negotiation of labor contracts between *labor unions* and *firms* or government entities.

collective voice The function a *labor union* performs for its members as a group when it communicates their problems and grievances to management and presses management for a satisfactory resolution.

collusion A situation in which firms act together and in agreement (collude) to fix prices, divide a market, or otherwise restrict competition.

command system A method of organizing an economy in which property resources are publicly owned and government uses *central economic planning* to direct and coordinate economic activities; command economy.

commercial bank A firm that engages in the business of banking (accepts deposits, offers checking accounts, and makes loans).

commercial banking system All *commercial banks* and *thrift institutions* as a group.

communism (See *command system*.)

comparative advantage A lower relative or comparative cost than that of another producer.

compensating differences Differences in the *wages* received by workers in different jobs to compensate for nonmonetary differences in the jobs.

compensation to employees *Wages* and salaries plus wage and salary supplements paid by employers to workers.

competition The presence in a market of independent buyers and sellers competing with one another and the freedom of buyers and sellers to enter and leave the market.

competitive industry's short-run supply curve The horizontal summation of the short-run supply curves of the *firms* in a purely competitive industry (see *pure competition*); a curve that shows the total quantities offered for sale at various prices by the firms in an industry in the short run.

competitive labor market A resource market in which a large number of (noncolluding) firms demand a particular type of labor supplied by a large number of nonunion workers.

complementary goods Products and services that are used together. When the price of one falls, the demand for the other increases (and conversely).

concentration ratio The percentage of the total sales of an industry made by the four (or some other number) largest sellers in the industry.

conglomerate merger The merger of a *firm* in one *industry* with a firm in another industry (with a firm that is neither a supplier, customer, nor competitor).

conglomerates Firms that produce goods and services in two or more separate industries.

constant-cost industry An industry in which expansion by the entry of new firms has no effect on the prices firms in the industry must pay for resources and thus no effect on production costs.

consumer goods Products and services that satisfy human wants directly.

Consumer Price Index (CPI) An index that measures the prices of a fixed "market basket" of some 300 goods and services bought by a "typical" consumer.

consumer sovereignty Determination by consumers of the types and quantities of goods and services that will be produced with the scarce resources of the economy; consumers' direction of production through their dollar votes.

consumer surplus The difference between the maximum price a consumer is (or consumers are) willing to pay for an additional unit of a product and its market price; the triangular area below the demand curve and above the market price.

consumption of fixed capital An estimate of the amount of *capital* worn out or used up (consumed) in producing the *gross domestic product*; also called depreciation.

consumption schedule A schedule showing the amounts *households* plan to spend for *consumer goods* at different levels of *disposable income*.

contractionary fiscal policy A decrease in *government purchases* for goods and services, an increase *in net taxes*, or some combination of the two, for the purpose of decreasing *aggregate demand* and thus controlling inflation.

coordination failure A situation in which people do not reach a mutually beneficial outcome because they lack some way to jointly coordinate their actions; a possible cause of macroeconomic instability.

copayment The percentage of (say, health care) costs that an insured individual pays while the insurer pays the remainder.

copyright A legal protection provided to developers and publishers of books, computer software, videos, and musical compositions against the copying of their works by others.

corporate income tax A tax levied on the net income (accounting profit) of corporations.

corporation A legal entity ("person") chartered by a state or the Federal government that is distinct and separate from the individuals who own it.

correlation A systematic and dependable association between two sets of data (two kinds of events); does not necessarily indicate causation.

cost-benefit analysis A comparison of the *marginal costs* of a government project or program with the *marginal benefits* to decide whether or not to employ resources in that project or program and to what extent.

cost-of-living adjustment (COLA) An automatic increase in the incomes (wages) of workers when inflation occurs; guaranteed by a collective bargaining contract between firms and workers.

cost-push inflation Increases in the price level (inflation) resulting from an increase in resource costs (for example, raw-material prices) and hence in *per-unit production costs*; inflation caused by reductions in *aggregate supply*.

cost ratio   An equality showing the number of units of two products that can be produced with the same resources; the cost ratio 1 corn ≡ 3 olives shows that the resources required to produce 3 units of olives must be shifted to corn production to produce a unit of corn.

Council of Economic Advisers (CEA)   A group of three persons that advises and assists the president of the United States on economic matters (including the preparation of the annual *Economic Report of the President*).

countercyclical payments   Cash *subsidies* paid to farmers when market prices for certain crops drop below targeted prices. Payments are based on previous production and are received regardless of the current crop grown.

craft union   A labor union that limits its membership to workers with a particular skill (craft).

creative destruction   The hypothesis that the creation of new products and production methods simultaneously destroys the market power of existing monopolies.

credit   An accounting item that increases the value of an asset (such as the foreign money owned by the residents of a nation).

credit union   An association of persons who have a common tie (such as being employees of the same firm or members of the same labor union) that sells shares to (accepts deposits from) its members and makes loans to them.

cross elasticity of demand   The ratio of the percentage change in *quantity demanded* of one good to the percentage change in the price of some other good. A positive coefficient indicates the two products are *substitute goods;* a negative coefficient indicates they are *complementary goods.*

crowding model of occupational discrimination   A model of labor markets suggesting that *occupational discrimination* has kept many women and minorities out of high-paying occupations and forced them into a limited number of low-paying occupations.

crowding-out effect   A rise in interest rates and a resulting decrease in *planned investment* caused by the Federal government's increased borrowing in the money market.

currency   Coins and paper money.

currency appreciation   (See *exchange-rate appreciation*.)

currency depreciation   (See *exchange-rate depreciation*.)

currency intervention   A government's buying and selling of its own currency or foreign currencies to alter international exchange rates.

current account   The section in a nation's *international balance of payments* that records its exports and imports of goods and services, its net *investment income*, and its *net transfers*.

cyclical deficit   A Federal *budget deficit* that is caused by a recession and the consequent decline in tax revenues.

cyclically balanced budget   The equality of government expenditures and net tax collections over the course of a *business cycle;* deficits incurred during periods of recession are offset by surpluses obtained during periods of prosperity (inflation).

cyclical unemployment   A type of *unemployment* caused by insufficient total spending (or by insufficient *aggregate demand*).

debit   An accounting item that decreases the value of an asset (such as the foreign money owned by the residents of a nation).

declining industry   An industry in which *economic profits* are negative (losses are incurred) and that will, therefore, decrease its output as firms leave it.

decreasing-cost industry   An industry in which expansion through the entry of firms lowers the prices that firms in the industry must pay for resources and therefore decreases their production costs.

deductible   The dollar sum of (for example, health care) costs that an insured individual must pay before the insurer begins to pay.

deflating   Finding the *real gross domestic product* by decreasing the dollar value of the GDP for a year in which prices were higher than in the *base year*.

deflation   A decline in the economy's *price level*.

demand   A schedule showing the amounts of a good or service that buyers (or a buyer) wish to purchase at various prices during some time period.

demand curve   A curve illustrating *demand*.

demand factor (in growth)   The increase in the level of *aggregate demand* that brings about the *economic growth* made possible by an increase in the production potential of the economy.

demand management   The use of *fiscal policy* and *monetary policy* to increase or decrease *aggregate demand*.

demand-pull inflation   Increases in the price level (inflation) resulting from an excess of demand over output at the existing price level, caused by an increase in *aggregate demand*.

dependent variable   A variable that changes as a consequence of a change in some other (independent) variable; the "effect" or outcome.

depository institutions   Firms that accept deposits of *money* from the public (businesses and persons); *commercial banks, savings and loan associations, mutual savings banks*, and *credit unions*.

depreciation   (See *consumption of fixed capital*.)

depreciation (of the dollar)   A decrease in the value of the dollar relative to another currency, so a dollar buys a smaller amount of the foreign currency and therefore of foreign goods.

derived demand   The demand for a resource that depends on the demand for the products it helps to produce.

determinants of aggregate demand   Factors such as consumption spending, *investment*, government spending, and *net exports* that, if they change, shift the aggregate demand curve.

determinants of aggregate supply   Factors such as input prices, *productivity*, and the legal-institutional environment that, if they change, shift the aggregate supply curve.

determinants of demand   Factors other than price that determine the quantities demanded of a good or service.

determinants of supply Factors other than price that determine the quantities supplied of a good or service.

devaluation A decrease in the governmentally defined value of a currency.

developing countries Many countries of Africa, Asia, and Latin America that are characterized by lack of capital goods, use of nonadvanced technologies, low literacy rates, high unemployment, rapid population growth, and labor forces heavily committed to agriculture.

differentiated oligopoly An *oligopoly* in which the firms produce a *differentiated product*.

differentiated product A product that differs physically or in some other way from the similar products produced by other firms; a product such that buyers are not indifferent to the seller when the price charged by all sellers is the same.

diffusion The spread of an *innovation* through its widespread imitation.

dilemma of regulation The tradeoff faced by a *regulatory agency* in setting the maximum legal price a monopolist may charge: The *socially optimal price* is below *average total cost* (and either bankrupts the *firm* or requires that it be subsidized), while the higher, *fair-return price* does not produce *allocative efficiency*.

diminishing marginal returns (See *law of diminishing returns*.)

direct foreign investment (Web chapter) The building of new factories (or the purchase of existing capital) in a particular nation by corporations of other nations.

direct payments Cash subsidies paid to farmers based on past production levels; unaffected by current crop prices and current production.

direct relationship The relationship between two variables that change in the same direction, for example, product price and quantity supplied.

discount rate The interest rate that the *Federal Reserve Banks* charge on the loans they make to *commercial banks* and *thrift institutions*.

discouraged workers Employees who have left the *labor force* because they have not been able to find employment.

discretionary fiscal policy Deliberate changes in taxes (tax rates) and government spending by Congress to promote full employment, price stability, and economic growth.

discrimination The practice of according individuals or groups inferior treatment in hiring, occupational access, education and training, promotion, wage rates, or working conditions even though they have the same abilities, education and skills, and work experience as other workers.

discrimination coefficient A measure of the cost or disutility of prejudice; the monetary amount an employer is willing to pay to hire a preferred worker rather than a nonpreferred worker.

diseconomies of scale Increases in the *average total cost* of producing a product as the *firm* expands the size of its *plant* (its output) in the *long run*.

disinflation A reduction in the rate of *inflation*.

disposable income *Personal income* less personal taxes; income available for *personal consumption expenditures* and *personal saving*.

dissaving Spending for consumer goods and services in excess of *disposable income*; the amount by which *personal consumption expenditures* exceed disposable income.

dividends Payments by a corporation of all or part of its profit to its stockholders (the corporate owners).

division of labor The separation of the work required to produce a product into a number of different tasks that are performed by different workers; *specialization* of workers.

Doha Round The latest, uncompleted (as of 2003) sequence of trade negotiations by members of the *World Trade Organization*; named after Doha, Qatar, where the set of negotiations began.

dollar votes The "votes" that consumers and entrepreneurs cast for the production of consumer and capital goods, respectively, when they purchase those goods in product and resource markets.

domestic capital formation The process of adding to a nation's stock of *capital* by saving and investing part of its own domestic output.

domestic output *Gross* (or net) *domestic product*; the total output of final goods and services produced in the economy.

domestic price The price of a good or service within a country, determined by domestic demand and supply.

double taxation The taxation of both corporate net income (profits) and the *dividends* paid from this net income when they become the personal income of households.

dumping The sale of products below cost in a foreign country or below the prices charged at home.

DuPont cellophane case The antitrust case brought against DuPont in which the U.S. Supreme Court ruled (in 1956) that while DuPont had a monopoly in the narrowly defined market for cellophane, it did not monopolize the more broadly defined market for flexible packaging materials. It was thus not guilty of violating the *Sherman Act*.

durable good A consumer good with an expected life (use) of 3 or more years.

earned-income tax credit A refundable Federal tax credit for low-income working people designed to reduce poverty and encourage labor-force participation.

earnings The money income received by a worker; equal to the *wage* (rate) multiplied by the amount of time worked.

easy money policy Federal Reserve System actions to increase the *money supply* to lower interest rates and expand *real GDP*.

economic analysis The process of deriving *economic principles* from relevant economic facts.

economic concentration A description or measure of the degree to which an industry is dominated by one or a handful of firms or is characterized by many firms. (See *concentration ratio*.)

economic cost   A payment that must be made to obtain and retain the services of a *resource;* the income a firm must provide to a resource supplier to attract the resource away from an alternative use; equal to the quantity of other products that cannot be produced when resources are instead used to make a particular product.

economic efficiency   The use of the minimum necessary resources to obtain the socially optimal amounts of goods and services; entails both *productive efficiency* and *allocative efficiency.*

economic growth   (1) An outward shift in the *production possibilities curve* that results from an increase in resource supplies or quality or an improvement in *technology;* (2) an increase of real output (*gross domestic product*) or real output per capita.

economic law   An *economic principle* that has been tested and retested and has stood the test of time.

economic model   A simplified picture of economic reality; an abstract generalization.

economic perspective   A viewpoint that envisions individuals and institutions making rational decisions by comparing the marginal benefits and marginal costs associated with their actions.

economic policy   A course of action intended to correct or avoid a problem.

economic principle   A widely accepted generalization about the economic behavior of individuals or institutions.

economic profit   The *total revenue* of a firm less its *economic costs* (which include both *explicit costs* and *implicit costs*); also called "pure profit" and "above-normal profit."

economic regulation   (See *industrial regulation* and *social regulation.*)

economic rent   The price paid for the use of land and other natural resources, the supply of which is fixed (*perfectly inelastic*).

economic resources   The *land, labor, capital,* and *entrepreneurial ability* that are used in the production of goods and services; productive agents; factors of production.

economics   The social science dealing with the use of scarce resources to obtain the maximum satisfaction of society's virtually unlimited economic wants.

economic system   A particular set of institutional arrangements and a coordinating mechanism for solving the economizing problem; a method of organizing an economy, of which the *market system* and the *command system* are the two general types.

economic theory   A statement of a cause-effect relationship; when accepted by all economists, an *economic principle.*

economies of scale   Reductions in the *average total cost* of producing a product as the firm expands the size of plant (its output) in the *long run;* the economies of mass production.

economizing problem   The choices necessitated because society's economic wants for goods and services are unlimited but the resources available to satisfy these wants are limited (scarce).

efficiency factors (in growth)   The capacity of an economy to combine resources effectively to achieve growth of real output that the *supply factors* (of growth) make possible.

efficiency loss   (Web chapter) Reductions in combined consumer and producer surplus caused by an underallocation or overallocation of resources to the production of a good or service.

efficiency loss of a tax   The loss of net benefits to society because a tax reduces the production and consumption of a taxed good below the level of allocative efficiency.

efficiency wage   A wage that minimizes wage costs per unit of output by encouraging greater effort or reducing turnover.

efficient allocation of resources   That allocation of an economy's resources among the production of different products that leads to the maximum satisfaction of consumers' wants, thus producing the socially optimal mix of output with society's scarce resources.

elastic demand   Product or resource demand whose *price elasticity* is greater than 1. This means the resulting change in *quantity demanded* is greater than the percentage change in *price.*

elasticity coefficient   The number obtained when the percentage change in *quantity demanded* (or supplied) is divided by the percentage change in the *price* of the commodity.

elasticity formula   (See *price elasticity of demand.*)

elastic supply   Product or resource supply whose price elasticity is greater than 1. This means the resulting change in quantity supplied is greater than the percentage change in price.

Employment Act of 1946   Federal legislation that committed the Federal government to the maintenance of economic stability (a high level of employment, a stable price level, and economic growth); established the *Council of Economic Advisers* and the *Joint Economic Committee;* and required an annual economic report by the president to Congress.

employment discrimination   Inferior treatment in hiring, promotions, work assignments, and such for a particular group of employees.

employment rate   The percentage of the *labor force* employed at any time.

entitlement programs   Government programs such as *social insurance, food stamps, Medicare,* and *Medicaid* that guarantee particular levels of transfer payments or noncash benefits to all who fit the programs' criteria.

entrepreneurial ability   The human resource that combines the other resources to produce a product, makes nonroutine decisions, innovates, and bears risks.

equality-versus-efficiency tradeoff   The decrease in *economic efficiency* that may accompany a decrease in *income inequality;* the presumption that some income inequality is required to achieve economic efficiency.

Equal Pay Act of 1963   Federal government legislation making it illegal to pay men and women different wage rates if they do equal work on jobs that require equal skill, effort, and responsibility and that are performed under similar working conditions.

equation of exchange $MV = PQ$, in which M is the supply of money, V is the *velocity* of money, P is the *price level*, and Q is the physical volume of *final goods and services* produced.

equilibrium price The *price* in a competitive market at which the *quantity demanded* and the *quantity supplied* are equal, there is neither a shortage nor a surplus, and there is no tendency for price to rise or fall.

equilibrium price level The price level at which the aggregate demand curve intersects the aggregate supply curve.

equilibrium quantity (1) The quantity demanded and supplied at the equilibrium price in a competitive market; (2) the profit-maximizing output of a firm.

equilibrium real domestic output The *gross domestic product* at which the total quantity of final goods and services purchased (*aggregate expenditures*) is equal to the total quantity of final goods and services produced (the real domestic output); the real domestic output at which the aggregate demand curve intersects the aggregate supply curve.

euro The common currency unit used by 12 European nations (as of 2003) in the Euro zone, which consists of Austria, Belgium, Finland, France, Germany, Greece, Ireland, Italy, Luxembourg, the Netherlands, Portugal, and Spain.

European Union (EU) An association of 25 European nations including 10 nations to be added in 2004 that has eliminated tariffs and quotas among them, established common tariffs for imported goods from outside the member nations, eliminated barriers to the free movement of capital, and created other common economic policies.

excess capacity Plant resources that are underused when imperfectly competitive firms produce less output than that associated with achieving minimum average total cost.

excess reserves The amount by which a bank's or thrift's *actual reserves* exceed its *required reserves;* actual reserves minus required reserves.

exchange control (See *foreign exchange control.*)

exchange rate The *rate of exchange* of one nation's currency for another nation's currency.

exchange-rate appreciation An increase in the value of a nation's currency in foreign exchange markets; an increase in the *rate of exchange* for foreign currencies.

exchange-rate depreciation A decrease in the value of a nation's currency in foreign exchange markets; a decrease in the *rate of exchange* for foreign currencies.

exchange-rate determinant Any factor other than the *rate of exchange* that determines a currency's demand and supply in the *foreign exchange market.*

excise tax A tax levied on the production of a specific product or on the quantity of the product purchased.

exclusive unionism The practice of a *labor union* of restricting the supply of skilled union labor to increase the wages received by union members; the policies typically employed by a *craft union.*

exhaustive expenditure An expenditure by government resulting directly in the employment of *economic resources* and in the absorption by government of the goods and services those resources produce; a *government purchase.*

exit mechanism The process of leaving a job and searching for another one as a means of improving one's working conditions.

expanding industry An industry whose firms earn *economic profits* and for which an increase in output occurs as new firms enter the industry.

expansionary fiscal policy An increase in *government purchases* of goods and services, a decrease in *net taxes,* or some combination of the two for the purpose of increasing *aggregate demand* and expanding real output.

expectations The anticipations of consumers, firms, and others about future economic conditions.

expected rate of return The increase in profit a firm anticipates it will obtain by purchasing capital (or engaging in research and development); expressed as a percentage of the total cost of the investment (or R&D) activity.

expenditures approach The method that adds all expenditures made for *final goods and services* to measure the *gross domestic product.*

expenditures-output approach (See *aggregate expenditures–domestic output approach.*)

explicit cost The monetary payment a *firm* must make to an outsider to obtain a *resource.*

exports Goods and services produced in a nation and sold to buyers in other nations.

export subsidies Government payments to domestic producers to enable them to reduce the *price* of a good or service to foreign buyers.

export supply curve An upward-sloping curve that shows the amount of a product that domestic firms will export at each *world price* that is above the *domestic price.*

export transaction A sale of a good or service that increases the amount of foreign currency flowing to a nation's citizens, firms, and government.

external benefit (See *spillover benefit.*)

external cost (See *spillover cost.*)

external debt Private or public debt owed to foreign citizens, firms, and institutions.

externality (See *spillover.*)

face value The dollar or cents value placed on a U.S. coin or piece of paper money.

factors of production *Economic resources: land, capital, labor, and entrepreneurial ability.*

fair-return price The price of a product that enables its producer to obtain a *normal profit* and that is equal to the *average total cost* of producing it.

fallacy of composition The false notion that what is true for the individual (or part) is necessarily true for the group (or whole).

Farm Act of 2002 Farm legislation that continued the "freedom to plant" and direct subsidies of the *Freedom to Farm Act* of 1996 but added an automatic, countercyclical system of emergency farm aid.

farm problem The fact that technological advance, coupled with a price-inelastic and relatively constant demand, has made agriculture a *declining industry;* also, the tendency for farm income to fluctuate sharply from year to year.

FDIC (See *Federal Deposit Insurance Corporation.*)

Federal Deposit Insurance Corporation (FDIC) The federally chartered corporation that insures deposit liabilities (up to $100,000 per account) of *commercial banks* and *thrift institutions* (excluding *credit unions,* whose deposits are insured by the *National Credit Union Administration*).

Federal funds rate The interest rate banks and other depository institutions charge one another on overnight loans made out of their *excess reserves.*

Federal government The government of the United States, as distinct from the state and local governments.

Federal Open Market Committee (FOMC) The 12-member group that determines the purchase and sale policies of the *Federal Reserve Banks* in the market for U.S. government securities.

Federal Reserve Banks The 12 banks chartered by the U.S. government to control the *money supply* and perform other functions. (See *central bank, quasi-public bank,* and *bankers' bank.*)

Federal Reserve Note Paper money issued by the *Federal Reserve Banks.*

Federal Trade Commission (FTC) The commission of five members established by the *Federal Trade Commission Act* of 1914 to investigate unfair competitive practices of firms, to hold hearings on the complaints of such practices, and to issue *cease-and-desist orders* when firms were found to engage in such practices.

Federal Trade Commission Act The Federal act of 1914 that established the *Federal Trade Commission.*

fiat money Anything that is *money* because government has decreed it to be money.

final goods and services Goods and services that have been purchased for final use and not for resale or further processing or manufacturing.

financial capital (See *money capital.*)

firm An organization that employs resources to produce a good or service for profit and owns and operates one or more *plants.*

fiscal policy Changes in government spending and tax collections designed to achieve a full-employment and noninflationary domestic output; also called *discretionary fiscal policy.*

fixed cost Any cost that in total does not change when the *firm* changes its output; the cost of *fixed resources.*

fixed exchange rate A *rate of exchange* that is set in some way and therefore prevented from rising or falling with changes in currency supply and demand.

fixed resource Any resource whose quantity cannot be changed by a firm in the *short run.*

flexible exchange rate A *rate of exchange* determined by the international demand for and supply of a nation's money; a rate free to rise or fall (to float).

floating exchange rate (See *flexible exchange rate.*)

food-stamp program A program permitting low-income persons to purchase for less than their retail value, or to obtain without cost, coupons that can be exchanged for food items at retail stores.

foreign competition (See *import competition.*)

foreign exchange control The control a government may exercise over the quantity of foreign currency demanded by its citizens and firms and over the *rates of exchange* in order to limit its *outpayments* to its *inpayments* (to eliminate a *payments deficit*).

foreign exchange market A market in which the money (currency) of one nation can be used to purchase (can be exchanged for) the money of another nation.

foreign exchange rate (See *rate of exchange.*)

foreign purchase effect The inverse relationship between the *net exports* of an economy and its price level relative to foreign price levels.

45° line A line along which the value of *GDP* (measured horizontally) is equal to the value of *aggregate expenditures* (measured vertically).

Four Fundamental Questions (of economics) The four questions that every economy must answer: what to produce, how to produce it, how to divide the total output, and how to ensure economic flexibility.

fractional reserve A *reserve requirement* that is less than 100 percent of the checkable-deposit liabilities of a *commercial bank* or *thrift institution.*

freedom of choice The freedom of owners of property resources to employ or dispose of them as they see fit, of workers to enter any line of work for which they are qualified, and of consumers to spend their incomes in a manner that they think is appropriate.

freedom of enterprise The freedom of *firms* to obtain economic resources, to use those resources to produce products of the firm's own choosing, and to sell their products in markets of their choice.

Freedom to Farm Act A law passed in 1996 that revamped 60 years of U.S. farm policy by ending *price supports* and *acreage allotments* for wheat, corn, barley, oats, sorghum, rye, cotton, and rice.

free-rider problem The inability of potential providers of an economically desirable good or service to obtain payment from those who benefit, because of *nonexcludability.*

free trade The absence of artificial (government-imposed) barriers to trade among individuals and firms in different nations.

frictional unemployment A type of unemployment caused by workers voluntarily changing jobs and by temporary layoffs; unemployed workers between jobs.

fringe benefits The rewards other than *wages* that employees receive from their employers and that include pensions, medical and dental insurance, paid vacations, and sick leaves.

full employment (1) The use of all available resources to produce want-satisfying goods and services; (2) the situation in which the *unemployment rate* is equal to the *full-employment unemployment rate* and there is *frictional* and *structural* but no *cyclical unemployment* (and the *real GDP* of the economy equals *potential output*).

full-employment budget A comparison of the government expenditures and tax collections that would occur if the economy operated at *full employment* throughout the year.

full-employment unemployment rate The *unemployment rate* at which there is no *cyclical unemployment* of the *labor force*; equal to between 4 and 5 percent in the United States because some *frictional* and *structural unemployment* is unavoidable.

full production Employment of available resources so that the maximum amount of (or total value of) goods and services is produced; occurs when both *productive efficiency* and *allocative efficiency* are realized.

functional distribution of income The manner in which *national income* is divided among the functions performed to earn it (or the kinds of resources provided to earn it); the division of national income into wages and salaries, proprietors' income, corporate profits, interest, and rent.

functional finance The use of *fiscal policy* to achieve a noninflationary full-employment *gross domestic product* without regard to the effect on the *public debt*.

gains from trade The extra output that trading partners obtain through specialization of production and exchange of goods and services.

game theory A means of analyzing the pricing behavior of oligopolists that uses the theory of strategy associated with games such as chess and bridge.

GDP (See *gross domestic product*.)

GDP gap Actual *gross domestic product* minus potential output; may be either a positive amount (a *positive GDP gap*) or a negative amount (a *negative GDP gap*).

GDP price index A *price index* for all the goods and services that make up the *gross domestic product*; the price index used to adjust *nominal gross domestic product* to *real gross domestic product*.

G8 nations A group of eight major nations (Canada, France, Germany, Italy, Japan, Russia, United Kingdom, and United States) whose leaders meet regularly to discuss common economic problems and try to coordinate economic policies.

General Agreement on Tariffs and Trade (GATT) The international agreement reached in 1947 in which 23 nations agreed to give equal and nondiscriminatory treatment to one another, to reduce tariff rates by multinational negotiations, and to eliminate *import quotas*. It now includes most nations and has become the *World Trade Organization*.

generalization Statement of the nature of the relationship between two or more sets of facts.

Gini ratio A numerical measure of the overall dispersion of income among households, families, or individuals; found graphically by dividing the area between the diagonal line and the *Lorenz curve* by the entire area below the diagonal line.

gold standard A historical system of fixed exchange rates in which nations defined their currencies in terms of gold, maintained a fixed relationship between their stocks of gold and their money supplies, and allowed gold to be freely exported and imported.

government failure Inefficiencies in resource allocation caused by problems in the operation of the public sector (government), specifically, rent-seeking pressure by special-interest groups, shortsighted political behavior, limited and bundled choices, and bureaucratic inefficiencies.

government purchases Expenditures by government for goods and services that government consumes in providing public goods and for public (or social) capital that has a long lifetime; the expenditures of all governments in the economy for those *final goods and services*.

government transfer payment The disbursement of money (or goods and services) by government for which government receives no currently produced good or service in return.

grievance procedure The method used by a *labor union* and a *firm* to settle disputes that arise during the life of the collective bargaining agreement between them.

gross domestic product (GDP) The total market value of all *final goods and services* produced annually within the boundaries of the United States, whether by U.S. or foreign-supplied resources.

gross private domestic investment Expenditures for newly produced *capital goods* (such as machinery, equipment, tools, and buildings) and for additions to inventories.

guiding function of prices The ability of price changes to bring about changes in the quantities of products and resources demanded and supplied.

health maintenance organizations (HMOs) Health care providers that contract with employers, insurance companies, labor unions, or government units to provide health care for their workers or others who are insured.

Herfindahl index A measure of the concentration and competitiveness of an industry; calculated as the sum of the squared percentage market shares of the individual firms in the industry.

homogeneous oligopoly An *oligopoly* in which the firms produce a *standardized product*.

horizontal merger The merger into a single *firm* of two firms producing the same product and selling it in the same geographic market.

household An economic unit (of one or more persons) that provides the economy with resources and uses the income received to purchase goods and services that satisfy economic wants.

human capital The accumulation of prior investments in education, training, health, and other factors that increase productivity.

human capital discrimination The denial of equal access to productivity-enhancing education and training to members of particular groups.

human capital investment Any expenditure undertaken to improve the education, skills, health, or mobility of workers, with an expectation of greater productivity and thus a positive return on the investment.

hyperinflation A very rapid rise in the price level; an extremely high rate of inflation.

hypothesis A tentative explanation of cause and effect that requires testing.

illegal immigrant A person who enters a country unlawfully for the purpose of residing there.

IMF (See *International Monetary Fund*.)

immobility The inability or unwillingness of a worker to move from one geographic area or occupation to another or from a lower-paying job to a higher-paying job.

imperfect competition All market structures except *pure competition*; includes *monopoly*, *monopolistic competition*, and *oligopoly*.

implicit cost The monetary income a *firm* sacrifices when it uses a resource it owns rather than supplying the resource in the market; equal to what the resource could have earned in the best-paying alternative employment; includes a *normal profit*.

import competition The competition that domestic firms encounter from the products and services of foreign producers.

import demand curve A downsloping curve showing the amount of a product that an economy will import at each *world price* below the *domestic price*.

import quota A limit imposed by a nation on the quantity (or total value) of a good that may be imported during some period of time.

imports Spending by individuals, *firms*, and governments for goods and services produced in foreign nations.

import transaction The purchase of a good or service that decreases the amount of foreign money held by citizens, firms, and governments of a nation.

incentive function of price The inducement that an increase in the price of a commodity gives to sellers to make more of it

available (and conversely for a decrease in price), and the inducement that an increase in price offers to buyers to purchase smaller quantities (and conversely for a decrease in price).

incentive pay plan A compensation structure that ties worker pay directly to performance. Such plans include piece rates, bonuses, *stock options*, commissions, and *profit sharing*.

inclusive unionism The practice of a labor union of including as members all workers employed in an industry.

income A flow of dollars (or purchasing power) per unit of time derived from the use of human or property resources.

income approach The method that adds all the income generated by the production of *final goods and services* to measure the *gross domestic product*.

income effect A change in the quantity demanded of a product that results from the change in *real income (purchasing power)* caused by a change in the product's price.

income elasticity of demand The ratio of the percentage change in the *quantity demanded* of a good to a percentage change in consumer income; measures the responsiveness of consumer purchases to income changes.

income inequality The unequal distribution of an economy's total income among households or families.

income-maintenance system A group of government programs designed to eliminate poverty and reduce inequality in the distribution of income.

increase in demand An increase in the *quantity demanded* of a good or service at every price; a shift of the *demand curve* to the right.

increase in supply An increase in the *quantity supplied* of a good or service at every price; a shift of the *supply curve* to the right.

increasing-cost industry An *industry* in which expansion through the entry of new firms raises the prices *firms* in the industry must pay for resources and therefore increases their production costs.

increasing marginal returns An increase in the *marginal product* of a resource as successive units of the resource are employed.

increasing returns An increase in a firm's output by a larger percentage than the percentage increase in its inputs.

independent goods Products or services for which there is little or no relationship between the price of one and the demand for the other. When the price of one rises or falls, the demand for the other tends to remain constant.

independent unions U.S. unions that are not affiliated with the *AFL-CIO*.

independent variable The variable causing a change in some other (dependent) variable.

indifference curve A curve showing the different combinations of two products that yield the same satisfaction or *utility* to a consumer.

indifference map A set of *indifference curves*, each representing a different level of *utility*, that together show the preferences of a consumer.

indirect business taxes Such taxes as *sales*, *excise*, and business *property taxes*, license fees, and *tariffs* that firms treat as costs of producing a product and pass on (in whole or in part) to buyers by charging higher prices.

individual demand The demand schedule or *demand curve* of a single buyer.

individual supply The supply schedule or *supply curve* of a single seller.

industrially advanced countries High-income countries such as the United States, Canada, Japan, and the nations of western Europe that have highly developed *market economies* based on large stocks of technologically advanced capital goods and skilled labor forces.

industrial regulation The older and more traditional type of regulation in which government is concerned with the prices charged and the services provided to the public in specific industries, in contrast to *social regulation*.

industrial union A *labor union* that accepts as members all workers employed in a particular industry (or by a particular firm).

industry A group of (one or more) *firms* that produce identical or similar products.

inelastic demand Product or resource demand for which the *elasticity coefficient* for price is less than 1. This means the resulting percentage change in *quantity demanded* is less than the percentage change in *price*.

inelastic supply Product or resource supply for which the price elasticity coefficient is less than 1. The percentage change in *quantity supplied* is less than the percentage change in *price*.

inferior good A good or service whose consumption declines as income rises (and conversely), price remaining constant.

inflating Determining *real gross domestic product* by increasing the dollar value of the *nominal gross domestic product* produced in a year in which prices are lower than those in a *base year*.

inflation A rise in the general level of prices in an economy.

inflationary expectations The belief of workers, firms, and consumers that substantial inflation will occur in the future.

inflationary gap The amount by which the *aggregate expenditures schedule* must shift downward to decrease the *nominal GDP* to its full-employment noninflationary level.

inflation premium The component of the *nominal interest rate* that reflects anticipated inflation.

information technology New and more efficient methods of delivering and receiving information through use of computers, fax machines, wireless phones, and the Internet.

infrastructure The capital goods usually provided by the *public sector* for the use of its citizens and firms (for example, highways, bridges, transit systems, wastewater treatment facilities, municipal water systems, and airports).

injection An addition of spending to the income-expenditure stream: *investment*, *government purchases*, and *net exports*.

injunction A court order directing a person or organization not to perform a certain act because the act would do irreparable damage to some other person or persons; a restraining order.

in-kind transfer The distribution by government of goods and services to individuals for which the government receives no currently produced good or service in return; a *government transfer payment* made in goods or services rather than in money; also called a noncash transfer.

innovation The first commercially successful introduction of a new product, the use of a new method of production, or the creation of a new form of business organization.

inpayments The receipts of domestic or foreign money that individuals, firms, and governments of one nation obtain from the sale of goods and services abroad, as investment income and remittances, and from foreign purchases of its assets.

insider-outsider theory The hypothesis that nominal wages are inflexible downward because firms are aware that workers ("insiders") who retain employment during recession may refuse to work cooperatively with previously unemployed workers ("outsiders") who offer to work for less than the current wage.

insurable risk An event that would result in a loss but whose frequency of occurrence can be estimated with considerable accuracy. Insurance companies are willing to sell insurance against such losses.

interest The payment made for the use of money (of borrowed funds).

interest income Payments of income to those who supply the economy with *capital*.

interest rate The annual rate at which interest is paid; a percentage of the borrowed amount.

interest-rate effect The tendency for increases in the *price level* to increase the demand for money, raise interest rates, and, as a result, reduce total spending and real output in the economy (and the reverse for price-level decreases).

interindustry competition The competition for sales between the products of one industry and the products of another industry.

interlocking directorate A situation where one or more members of the board of directors of a *corporation* are also on the board of directors of a competing corporation; illegal under the *Clayton Act*.

intermediate goods Products that are purchased for resale or further processing or manufacturing.

internally held public debt *Public debt* owed to citizens, firms, and institutions of the same nation that issued the debt.

international balance of payments A summary of all the transactions that took place between the individuals, firms, and government units of one nation and those of all other nations during a year.

international balance-of-payments deficit   (See *balance-of-payments deficit*.)

international balance-of-payments surplus   (See *balance-of-payments surplus*.)

international gold standard   (See *gold standard*.)

International Monetary Fund (IMF)   The international association of nations that was formed after the Second World War to make loans of foreign monies to nations with temporary *payments deficits* and, until the early 1970s, to administer the *adjustable pegs*. It now mainly makes loans to nations facing possible defaults on private and government loans.

international monetary reserves   The foreign currencies and other assets such as gold that a nation can use to settle a *balance-of-payments deficit*.

international value of the dollar   The price that must be paid in foreign currency (money) to obtain one U.S. dollar.

intrinsic value   The market value of the metal within a coin.

invention   The first discovery of a product or process through the use of imagination, ingenious thinking, and experimentation and the first proof that it will work.

inventories   Goods that have been produced but remain unsold.

inverse relationship   The relationship between two variables that change in opposite directions, for example, product price and quantity demanded.

inverted-U theory   A theory saying that, other things equal, *R&D* expenditures as a percentage of sales rise with industry concentration, reach a peak at a four-firm *concentration ratio* of about 50 percent, and then fall as concentration further increases.

investment   Spending for the production and accumulation of *capital* and additions to inventories.

investment demand curve   A curve that shows the amounts of *investment* demanded by an economy at a series of *real interest rates*.

investment goods   Same as *capital* or capital goods.

investment in human capital   (See *human capital investment*.)

investment schedule   A curve or schedule that shows the amounts firms plan to invest at various possible values of *real gross domestic product*.

invisible hand   The tendency of firms and resource suppliers that seek to further their own self-interests in competitive markets to also promote the interest of society.

Joint Economic Committee (JEC)   Committee of senators and representatives that investigates economic problems of national interest.

Keynesian economics   The macroeconomic generalizations that lead to the conclusion that a capitalistic economy is characterized by macroeconomic instability and that *fiscal policy* and *monetary policy* can be used to promote *full employment*, *price-level stability*, and *economic growth*.

Keynesianism   The philosophical, ideological, and analytical views pertaining to *Keynesian economics*.

kinked-demand curve   The demand curve for a noncollusive oligopolist, which is based on the assumption that rivals will match a price decrease and will ignore a price increase.

labor   People's physical and mental talents and efforts that are used to help produce goods and services.

labor force   Persons 16 years of age and older who are not in institutions and who are employed or are unemployed and seeking work.

labor-force participation rate   The percentage of the working-age population that is actually in the *labor force*.

labor-intensive commodity   A product requiring a relatively large amount of *labor* to be produced.

labor productivity   Total output divided by the quantity of labor employed to produce it; the *average product* of labor or output per hour of work.

labor theory of value   (Web chapter) The Marxian idea that the economic value of any commodity is determined solely by the amount of labor that is required to produce it.

labor union   A group of workers organized to advance the interests of the group (to increase wages, shorten the hours worked, improve working conditions, and so on).

Laffer Curve   A curve relating government tax rates and tax revenues and on which a particular tax rate (between zero and 100 percent) maximizes tax revenues.

laissez-faire capitalism   (See *capitalism*.)

land   Natural resources ("free gifts of nature") used to produce goods and services.

land-intensive commodity   A product requiring a relatively large amount of *land* to be produced.

law of demand   The principle that, other things equal, an increase in a product's price will reduce the quantity of it demanded, and conversely for a decrease in price.

law of diminishing marginal utility   The principle that as a consumer increases the consumption of a good or service, the *marginal utility* obtained from each additional unit of the good or service decreases.

law of diminishing returns   The principle that as successive increments of a variable resource are added to a fixed resource, the *marginal product* of the variable resource will eventually decrease.

law of increasing opportunity costs   The principle that as the production of a good increases, the *opportunity cost* of producing an additional unit rises.

law of supply   The principle that, other things equal, an increase in the price of a product will increase the quantity of it supplied, and conversely for a price decrease.

leakage   (1) A withdrawal of potential spending from the income-expenditures stream via *saving*, tax payments, or *imports*;

(2) a withdrawal that reduces the lending potential of the banking system.

learning by doing Achieving greater *productivity* and lower *average total cost* through gains in knowledge and skill that accompany repetition of a task; a source of *economies of scale*.

least-cost combination of resources The quantity of each resource a firm must employ in order to produce a particular output at the lowest total cost; the combination at which the ratio of the *marginal product* of a resource to its *marginal resource cost* (to its *price* if the resource is employed in a competitive market) is the same for the last dollar spent on each of the resources employed.

legal cartel theory of regulation The hypothesis that some industries seek regulation or want to maintain regulation so that they may form or maintain a legal *cartel*.

legal immigrant A person who lawfully enters a country for the purpose of residing there.

legal tender A legal designation of a nation's official currency (bills and coins). Payment of debts must be accepted in this monetary unit, but creditors can specify the form of payment, for example, "cash only" or "check or credit card only."

lending potential of an individual commercial bank The amount by which a single bank can safely increase the *money supply* by making new loans to (or buying securities from) the public; equal to the bank's excess reserves.

lending potential of the banking system The amount by which the banking system can increase the *money supply* by making new loans to (or buying securities from) the public; equal to the *excess reserves* of the banking system multiplied by the *monetary multiplier*.

liability A debt with a monetary value; an amount owed by a firm or an individual.

limited liability Restriction of the maximum loss to a predetermined amount for the owners (stockholders) of a *corporation*. The maximum loss is the amount they paid for their shares of stock.

limited-liability company An unincorporated business whose owners are protected by *limited liability*.

liquidity The ease with which an asset can be converted quickly into cash with little or no loss of purchasing power. Money is said to be perfectly liquid, whereas other assets have a lesser degree of liquidity.

loanable funds *Money* available for lending and borrowing.

loanable funds theory of interest The concept that the supply of and demand for *loanable funds* determine the equilibrium rate of interest.

lockout An action by a firm that forbids workers to return to work until a new collective bargaining contract is signed; a means of imposing costs (lost wages) on union workers in a collective bargaining dispute.

logrolling The trading of votes by legislators to secure favorable outcomes on decisions concerning the provision of *public goods* and *quasi-public goods*.

long run (1) In *microeconomics*, a period of time long enough to enable producers of a product to change the quantities of all the resources they employ; period in which all resources and costs are variable and no resources or costs are fixed. (2) In *macroeconomics*, a period sufficiently long for *nominal wages* and other input prices to change in response to a change in the nation's *price level*.

long-run aggregate supply curve The aggregate supply curve associated with a time period in which input prices (especially *nominal wages*) are fully responsive to changes in the *price level*.

long-run competitive equilibrium The price at which firms in *pure competition* neither obtain *economic profit* nor suffer losses in the *long run* and the total quantity demanded and supplied are equal; a price equal to the minimum long-run *average total cost* of producing the product.

long-run farm problem The tendency for agriculture to be a declining industry as technological progress increases supply relative to an inelastic and slowly increasing demand.

long-run supply A schedule or curve showing the prices at which a purely competitive industry will make various quantities of the product available in the *long run*.

Lorenz curve A curve showing the distribution of income in an economy. The cumulated percentage of families (income receivers) is measured along the horizontal axis and cumulated percentage of income is measured along the vertical axis.

lump-sum tax A tax that is a constant amount (the tax revenue of government is the same) at all levels of GDP.

M1 The most narrowly defined *money supply*, equal to *currency* in the hands of the public and the *checkable deposits* of commercial banks and thrift institutions.

M2 A more broadly defined *money supply*, equal to *M1* plus *noncheckable savings accounts* (including *money market deposit accounts*), small *time deposits* (deposits of less than $100,000), and individual *money market mutual fund* balances.

M3 A very broadly defined *money supply*, equal to *M2* plus large *time deposits* (deposits of $100,000 or more).

macroeconomics The part of economics concerned with the economy as a whole; with such major aggregates as the household, business, and government sectors; and with measures of the total economy.

managed floating exchange rate An *exchange rate* that is allowed to change (float) as a result of changes in currency supply and demand but at times is altered (managed) by governments via their buying and selling of particular currencies.

managerial-opposition hypothesis An explanation that attributes the relative decline of unionism in the United States to the increased and more aggressive opposition of management to unions.

managerial prerogatives The decisions that management of the firm has the sole right to make; often enumerated in the labor contract (work agreement) between a *labor union* and a *firm*.

marginal analysis The comparison of marginal ("extra" or "additional") benefits and marginal costs, usually for decision making.

marginal benefit The extra (additional) benefit of consuming 1 more unit of some good or service; the change in total benefit when 1 more unit is consumed.

marginal cost The extra (additional) cost of producing 1 more unit of output; equal to the change in *total cost* divided by the change in output (and, in the short run, to the change in total *variable cost* divided by the change in output).

marginal product The additional output produced when 1 additional unit of a resource is employed (the quantity of all other resources employed remaining constant); equal to the change in total product divided by the change in the quantity of a resource employed.

marginal productivity theory of income distribution The contention that the distribution of income is equitable when each unit of each resource receives a money payment equal to its marginal contribution to the firm's revenue (its *marginal revenue product*).

marginal propensity to consume The fraction of any change in *disposable income* spent for *consumer goods;* equal to the change in consumption divided by the change in disposable income.

marginal propensity to save The fraction of any change in *disposable income* that households save; equal to the change in *saving* divided by the change in disposable income.

marginal rate of substitution The rate at which a consumer is prepared to substitute one good for another (from a given combination of goods) and remain equally satisfied (have the same *total utility*); equal to the slope of a consumer's *indifference curve* at each point on the curve.

marginal resource cost The amount the total cost of employing a *resource* increases when a firm employs 1 additional unit of the resource (the quantity of all other resources employed remaining constant); equal to the change in the *total cost* of the resource divided by the change in the quantity of the resource employed.

marginal revenue The change in *total revenue* that results from the sale of 1 additional unit of a firm's product; equal to the change in total revenue divided by the change in the quantity of the product sold.

marginal-revenue–marginal-cost approach A method of determining the total output where *economic profit* is a maximum (or losses are a minimum) by comparing the *marginal revenue* and the *marginal cost* of each additional unit of output.

marginal revenue product The change in a firm's *total revenue* when it employs 1 additional unit of a resource (the quantity of all other resources employed remaining constant); equal to the change in total revenue divided by the change in the quantity of the resource employed.

marginal tax rate The tax rate paid on each additional dollar of income.

marginal utility The extra *utility* a consumer obtains from the consumption of 1 additional unit of a good or service; equal to the change in total utility divided by the change in the quantity consumed.

market Any institution or mechanism that brings together buyers (demanders) and sellers (suppliers) of a particular good or service.

market demand (See *total demand*.)

market economy An economy in which only the private decisions of consumers, resource suppliers, and firms determine how resources are allocated; the *market system*.

market failure The inability of a market to bring about the allocation of resources that best satisfies the wants of society; in particular, the overallocation or underallocation of resources to the production of a particular good or service because of *spillovers* or informational problems or because markets do not provide desired *public goods*.

market for externality rights A market in which firms can buy rights to discharge pollutants. The price of such rights is determined by the demand for the right to discharge pollutants and a *perfectly inelastic supply* of such rights (the latter determined by the quantity of discharges that the environment can assimilate).

market period A period in which producers of a product are unable to change the quantity produced in response to a change in its price and in which there is a *perfectly inelastic supply*.

market system All the product and resource markets of a *market economy* and the relationships among them; a method that allows the prices determined in those markets to allocate the economy's scarce resources and to communicate and coordinate the decisions made by consumers, firms, and resource suppliers.

median-voter model The theory that under majority rule the median (middle) voter will be in the dominant position to determine the outcome of an election.

Medicaid A Federal program that helps finance the medical expenses of individuals covered by the *Supplemental Security Income (SSI)* and *Temporary Assistance for Needy Families (TANF)* programs.

Medicare A Federal program that is financed by *payroll taxes* and provides for (1) compulsory hospital insurance for senior citizens and (2) low-cost voluntary insurance to help older Americans pay physicians' fees.

medium of exchange Any item sellers generally accept and buyers generally use to pay for a good or service; *money;* a convenient means of exchanging goods and services without engaging in *barter*.

merger The combination of two (or more) firms into a single firm.

microeconomics The part of economics concerned with such individual units as *industries*, *firms*, and *households* and with individual markets, specific goods and services, and product and resource prices.

Microsoft case A 2002 antitrust case in which Microsoft was found guilty of violating the *Sherman Act* by engaging in a series of unlawful activities designed to maintain its monopoly in operating systems for personal computers; as a remedy the company was prohibited from engaging in a set of specific anticompetitive business practices.

minimum efficient scale The lowest level of output at which a firm can minimize long-run *average total cost*.

minimum wage The lowest *wage* employers may legally pay for an hour of work.

monetarism The macroeconomic view that the main cause of changes in aggregate output and the price level is fluctuations in the *money supply*; espoused by advocates of a *monetary rule*.

monetary multiplier The multiple of its *excess reserves* by which the banking system can expand *checkable deposits* and thus the *money supply* by making new loans (or buying securities); equal to 1 divided by the *reserve requirement*.

monetary policy A central bank's changing of the *money supply* to influence interest rates and assist the economy in achieving price stability, full employment, and economic growth.

monetary rule The rule suggested by *monetarism*. As traditionally formulated, the rule says that the *money supply* should be expanded each year at the same annual rate as the potential rate of growth of the *real gross domestic product*; the supply of money should be increased steadily between 3 and 5 percent per year. (Also see *Taylor rule*.)

money Any item that is generally acceptable to sellers in exchange for goods and services.

money capital Money available to purchase *capital*; simply *money*, as defined by economists.

money income (See *nominal income*.)

money market The market in which the demand for and the supply of money determine the *interest rate* (or the level of interest rates) in the economy.

money market deposit accounts (MMDAs) Interest-earning accounts at banks and *thrift institutions*, which pool the funds of depositors to buy various short-term securities.

money market mutual funds (MMMFs) Interest-bearing accounts offered by investment companies, which pool depositors' funds for the purchase of short-term securities. Depositors may write checks in minimum amounts or more against their accounts.

money supply Narrowly defined, *M*1; more broadly defined, *M*2 and *M*3.

monopolistic competition A market structure in which many firms sell a *differentiated product*, into which entry is relatively easy, in which the firm has some control over its product price, and in which there is considerable *nonprice competition*.

monopoly A market structure in which the number of sellers is so small that each seller is able to influence the total supply and the price of the good or service. (Also see *pure monopoly*.)

monopsony A market structure in which there is only a single buyer of a good, service, or resource.

moral hazard problem The possibility that individuals or institutions will change their behavior as the result of a contract or agreement. Example: A bank whose deposits are insured against loss may make riskier loans and investments.

most-favored-nation (MFN) status An agreement by the United States to allow some other nation's *exports* into the United States at the lowest tariff level levied by the United States, then or at any later time.

MR = MC rule The principle that a firm will maximize its profit (or minimize its losses) by producing the output at which *marginal revenue* and *marginal cost* are equal, provided product price is equal to or greater than *average variable cost*.

MRP = MRC rule The principle that to maximize profit (or minimize losses), a firm should employ the quantity of a resource at which its *marginal revenue product* (MRP) is equal to its *marginal resource cost* (MRC), the latter being the wage rate in pure competition.

multinational corporations Firms that own production facilities in two or more countries and produce and sell their products globally.

multiple counting Wrongly including the value of *intermediate goods* in the *gross domestic product*; counting the same good or service more than once.

multiplier The ratio of a change in the equilibrium GDP to the change in *investment* or in any other component of *aggregate expenditures* or *aggregate demand*; the number by which a change in any component of aggregate expenditures or aggregate demand must be multiplied to find the resulting change in the equilibrium GDP.

multiplier effect The effect on equilibrium GDP of a change in *aggregate expenditures* or *aggregate demand* (caused by a change in the *consumption schedule, investment,* government expenditures, or *net exports*).

mutual interdependence A situation in which a change in price strategy (or in some other strategy) by one firm will affect the sales and profits of another firm (or other firms). Any firm that makes such a change can expect the other rivals to react to the change.

national bank A *commercial bank* authorized to operate by the U.S. government.

National Credit Union Administration (NCUA) The federally chartered agency that insures deposit liabilities (up to $100,000 per account) in *credit unions*.

national health insurance (NHI) A proposed program in which the Federal government would provide a basic package of health care to all citizens at no direct charge or at a low cost-sharing level. Financing would be out of general tax revenues.

national income Total income earned by resource suppliers for their contributions to *gross domestic product*; equal to the gross domestic product minus *nonincome charges*, minus *net foreign factor income*.

national income accounting   The techniques used to measure the overall production of the economy and other related variables for the nation as a whole.

National Labor Relations Act (Wagner Act of 1935)   As amended, the basic labor-relations law in the United States; defines the legal rights of unions and management and identifies unfair union and management labor practices; established the *National Labor Relations Board.*

National Labor Relations Board (NLRB)   The board established by the *National Labor Relations Act* of 1935 to investigate unfair labor practices, issue *cease-and-desist orders,* and conduct elections among employees to determine if they wish to be represented by a *labor union.*

natural monopoly   An industry in which *economies of scale* are so great that a single firm can produce the product at a lower average total cost than would be possible if more than one firm produced the product.

natural rate of unemployment   The *full-employment unemployment rate;* the unemployment rate occurring when there is no cyclical unemployment and the economy is achieving its potential output; the unemployment rate at which actual inflation equals expected inflation.

near-money   Financial assets, the most important of which are *noncheckable savings accounts, time deposits,* and U.S. short-term securities and savings bonds, which are not a medium of exchange but can be readily converted into money.

negative GDP gap   A situation in which actual *gross domestic product* is less than *potential output.*

negative relationship   (See *inverse relationship.*)

net domestic product   *Gross domestic product* less the part of the year's output that is needed to replace the *capital goods* worn out in producing the output; the nation's total output available for consumption or additions to the *capital stock.*

net export effect   The idea that the impact of a change in *monetary policy* or *fiscal policy* will be strengthened or weakened by the consequent change in *net exports.* The change in net exports occurs because of changes in real interest rates, which affect exchange rates.

net exports   *Exports* minus *imports.*

net foreign factor income   Payments by a nation of resource income to the rest of the world minus receipts of resource income from the rest of the world.

net investment income   The interest and dividend income received by the residents of a nation from residents of other nations less the interest and dividend payments made by the residents of that nation to the residents of other nations.

net private domestic investment   *Gross private domestic investment* less *consumption of fixed capital;* the addition to the nation's stock of *capital* during a year.

net taxes   The taxes collected by government less *government transfer payments.*

net transfers   The personal and government transfer payments made by one nation to residents of foreign nations less the personal and government transfer payments received from residents of foreign nations.

network effects   Increases in the value of a product to each user, including existing users, as the total number of users rises.

net worth   The total *assets* less the total *liabilities* of a firm or an individual; for a firm, the claims of the owners against the firm's total assets; for an individual, his or her wealth.

new classical economics   The theory that, although unanticipated price-level changes may create macroeconomic instability in the short run, the economy is stable at the full-employment level of domestic output in the long run because prices and wages adjust automatically to correct movements away from the full-employment, noninflationary output.

New Economy   The label attached by some economists and the popular press to the U.S. economy since 1995. The main characteristics are accelerated *productivity growth* and *economic growth,* caused by rapid technological advance and the emergence of the global economy.

NLRB   (See *National Labor Relations Board.*)

nominal gross domestic product (GDP)   The *GDP* measured in terms of the price level at the time of measurement (unadjusted for *inflation*).

nominal income   The number of dollars received by an individual or group for its resources during some period of time.

nominal interest rate   The interest rate expressed in terms of annual amounts currently charged for interest and not adjusted for inflation.

nominal wage   The amount of money received by a worker per unit of time (hour, day, etc.); money wage.

noncash transfer   A *government transfer payment* in the form of goods and services rather than money, for example, food stamps, housing assistance, and job training; also called in-kind transfers.

noncollusive oligopoly   An *oligopoly* in which the firms do not act together and in agreement to determine the price of the product and the output that each firm will produce.

noncompeting groups   Collections of workers in the economy who do not compete with each other for employment because the skill and training of the workers in one group are substantially different from those of the workers in other groups.

nondiscretionary fiscal policy   (See *built-in stabilizer.*)

nondurable good   A *consumer good* with an expected life (use) of less than 3 years.

nonexcludability   The inability to keep nonpayers (free riders) from obtaining benefits from a certain good; a *public good* characteristic.

nonexhaustive expenditure   An expenditure by government that does not result directly in the employment of economic resources or the production of goods and services; see *government transfer payment.*

nonincome charges   *Consumption of fixed capital* and *indirect business taxes;* amounts subtracted from *GDP* (along with *net foreign factor income*) in determining *national income.*

nonincome determinants of consumption and saving   All influences on consumption and saving other than the level of *GDP.*

noninterest determinants of investment   All influences on the level of investment spending other than the *interest rate.*

noninvestment transaction   An expenditure for stocks, bonds, or secondhand *capital goods.*

nonmarket transactions   The production of goods and services excluded in the measurement of the *gross domestic product* because they are not bought and sold.

nonprice competition   Competition based on distinguishing one's product by means of *product differentiation* and then *advertising* the distinguished product to consumers.

nonpriced goods   (Web chapter) Goods or resources that are not priced in markets because they are owned in common by society and available for the taking on public lands.

nonproduction transaction   The purchase and sale of any item that is not a currently produced good or service.

nonrivalry   The idea that one person's benefit from a certain good does not reduce the benefit available to others; a *public good* characteristic.

nontariff barriers   All barriers other than *protective tariffs* that nations erect to impede international trade, including *import quotas,* licensing requirements, unreasonable product-quality standards, unnecessary bureaucratic detail in customs procedures, and so on.

normal good   A good or service whose consumption increases when income increases and falls when income decreases, price remaining constant.

normal profit   The payment made by a firm to obtain and retain *entrepreneurial ability;* the minimum income entrepreneurial ability must receive to induce it to perform entrepreneurial functions for a firm.

normative economics   The part of economics involving value judgments about what the economy should be like; focused on which economic goals and policies should be implemented; policy economics.

North American Free Trade Agreement (NAFTA)   A 1993 agreement establishing, over a 15-year period, a free-trade zone composed of Canada, Mexico, and the United States.

OASDHI   (See *Old Age, Survivors, and Disability Health Insurance.*)

occupational discrimination   The arbitrary restriction of particular groups from entering the more desirable, higher-paying occupations.

occupational licensure   The laws of state or local governments that require that a worker satisfy certain specified requirements and obtain a license from a licensing board before engaging in a particular occupation.

occupational segregation   The crowding of women or minorities into less desirable, lower-paying occupations.

official reserves   Foreign currencies owned by the central bank of a nation.

Okun's law   The generalization that any 1-percentage-point rise in the *unemployment rate* above the *full-employment unemployment rate* will increase the GDP gap by 2 percent of the *potential output* (GDP) of the economy.

Old Age, Survivors, and Disability Health Insurance (OASDHI)   The social program in the United States financed by Federal *payroll taxes* on employers and employees and designed to replace the *earnings* lost when workers retire, die, or become unable to work.

oligopoly   A market structure in which a few firms sell either a *standardized* or *differentiated product,* into which entry is difficult, in which the firm has limited control over product price because of *mutual interdependence* (except when there is collusion among firms), and in which there is typically *nonprice competition.*

OPEC   (See *Organization of Petroleum Exporting Countries.*)

open economy   An economy that exports and imports goods and services.

open-market operations   The buying and selling of U.S. government securities by the *Federal Reserve Banks* for purposes of carrying out *monetary policy.*

open shop   A place of employment in which the employer may hire nonunion workers and the workers need not become members of a *labor union.*

opportunity cost   The amount of other products that must be forgone or sacrificed to produce a unit of a product.

Organization of Petroleum Exporting Countries (OPEC)   A cartel of 11 oil-producing countries (Algeria, Indonesia, Iran, Iraq, Kuwait, Libya, Nigeria, Qatar, Saudi Arabia, Venezuela, and the UAE) that controls the quantity and price of crude oil exported by its members and that accounts for 60 percent of the world's export of oil.

other-things-equal assumption   The assumption that factors other than those being considered are held constant.

outpayments   The expenditures of domestic or foreign currency that the individuals, firms, and governments of one nation make to purchase goods and services, for remittances, to pay investment income, and for purchases of foreign assets.

output effect   The situation in which an increase in the price of one input will increase a firm's production costs and reduce its level of output, thus reducing the demand for other inputs; conversely for a decrease in the price of the input.

paper money   Pieces of paper used as a *medium of exchange;* in the United States, *Federal Reserve Notes.*

paradox of voting   A situation where paired-choice voting by majority rule fails to provide a consistent ranking of society's preferences for *public goods* or services.

parity concept   The idea that year after year a specific output of a farm product should enable a farmer to acquire a constant amount of nonagricultural goods and services.

parity ratio   The ratio of the price received by farmers from the sale of an agricultural commodity to the prices of other goods paid by them; usually expressed as a percentage; used as a rationale for *price supports*.

partnership   An unincorporated firm owned and operated by two or more persons.

patent   An exclusive right given to inventors to produce and sell a new product or machine for 20 years from the time of patent application.

payments deficit   (See *balance-of-payments deficit*.)

payments surplus   (See *balance-of-payments surplus*.)

payroll tax   A tax levied on employers of labor equal to a percentage of all or part of the wages and salaries paid by them and on employees equal to a percentage of all or part of the wages and salaries received by them.

$P = MC$ rule   The principle that a purely competitive firm will maximize its profit or minimize its loss by producing that output at which the *price* of the product is equal to *marginal cost*, provided that price is equal to or greater than *average variable cost* in the short run and equal to or greater than *average total cost* in the long run.

per capita GDP   *Gross domestic product* (GDP) per person; the average GDP of a population.

per capita income   A nation's total income per person; the average income of a population.

perfectly elastic demand   Product or resource demand in which *quantity demanded* can be of any amount at a particular product *price*; graphs as a horizontal *demand curve*.

perfectly elastic supply   Product or resource supply in which *quantity supplied* can be of any amount at a particular product or resource *price*; graphs as a horizontal *supply curve*.

perfectly inelastic demand   Product or resource demand in which *price* can be of any amount at a particular quantity of the product or resource demanded; *quantity demanded* does not respond to a change in price; graphs as a vertical *demand curve*.

perfectly inelastic supply   Product or resource supply in which *price* can be of any amount at a particular quantity of the product or resource demanded; *quantity supplied* does not respond to a change in price; graphs as a vertical *supply curve*.

per se violations   Collusive actions, such as attempts by firms to fix prices or divide a market, that are violations of the *antitrust laws*, even if the actions themselves are unsuccessful.

personal consumption expenditures   The expenditures of *households* for *durable* and *nondurable consumer goods* and *services*.

personal distribution of income   The manner in which the economy's *personal* or *disposable income* is divided among different income classes or different households or families.

personal income   The earned and unearned income available to resource suppliers and others before the payment of personal taxes.

personal income tax   A tax levied on the taxable income of individuals, households, and unincorporated firms.

Personal Responsibility Act   A 1996 law that eliminated the Federal government's six-decade-long guarantee of cash assistance for poor families, whether adults in the family work or not; sets a limit of 5 years on receiving *Temporary Assistance for Needy Families (TANF)* benefits and requires that able-bodied adults work after 2 years to continue to receive public assistance.

personal saving   The *personal income* of households less personal taxes and *personal consumption expenditures; disposable income* not spent for *consumer goods*.

per-unit production cost   The average production cost of a particular level of output; total input cost divided by units of output.

Phillips Curve   A curve showing the relationship between the *unemployment rate* (on the horizontal axis) and the annual rate of increase in the *price level* (on the vertical axis).

planned investment   The amount that *firms* plan or intend to invest.

plant   A physical establishment that performs one or more functions in the production, fabrication, and distribution of goods and services.

"play or pay"   A means of expanding health insurance coverage by requiring that employers either provide insurance for their workers or pay a special *payroll tax* to finance insurance for noncovered workers.

policy economics   The formulation of courses of action to bring about desired economic outcomes or to prevent undesired occurrences.

political business cycle   The alleged tendency of Congress to destabilize the economy by reducing taxes and increasing government expenditures before elections and to raise taxes and lower expenditures after elections.

positive economics   The analysis of facts or data to establish scientific generalizations about economic behavior.

positive GDP gap   A situation in which actual *gross domestic product* exceeds *potential output*.

positive relationship   A direct relationship between two variables.

post hoc, ergo propter hoc fallacy   The false belief that when one event precedes another, the first event must have caused the second event.

potential competition   The new competitors that may be induced to enter an industry if firms now in that industry are receiving large *economic profits*.

potential output   The real output *(GDP)* an economy can produce when it fully employs its available resources.

poverty   A situation in which the basic needs of an individual or family exceed the means to satisfy them.

poverty rate   The percentage of the population with incomes below the official poverty income levels that are established by the Federal government.

preferred provider organization (PPO) An arrangement in which doctors and hospitals agree to provide health care to insured individuals at rates negotiated with an insurer.

price The amount of money needed to buy a particular good, service, or resource.

price ceiling A legally established maximum price for a good or service.

price discrimination The selling of a product to different buyers at different prices when the price differences are not justified by differences in cost.

price elasticity of demand The ratio of the percentage change in *quantity demanded* of a product or resource to the percentage change in its *price;* a measure of the responsiveness of buyers to a change in the price of a product or resource.

price elasticity of supply The ratio of the percentage change in *quantity supplied* of a product or resource to the percentage change in its *price;* a measure of the responsiveness of producers to a change in the price of a product or resource.

price fixing The conspiring by two or more firms to set the price of their products; an illegal practice under the *Sherman Act*.

price floor A legally determined price above the *equilibrium price*.

price index An index number that shows how the weighted-average price of a "market basket" of goods changes over time.

price leadership An informal method that firms in an *oligopoly* may employ to set the price of their product: One firm (the leader) is the first to announce a change in price, and the other firms (the followers) soon announce identical or similar changes.

price level The weighted average of the prices of all the final goods and services produced in an economy.

price-level stability A steadiness of the price level from one period to the next; zero or low annual inflation; also called "price stability."

price-level surprises Unanticipated changes in the price level.

price maker A seller (or buyer) of a product or resource that is able to affect the product or resource price by changing the amount it sells (or buys).

price support A minimum price that government allows sellers to receive for a good or service; a legally established or maintained minimum price.

price taker A seller (or buyer) of a product or resource that is unable to affect the price at which a product or resource sells by changing the amount it sells (or buys).

price war Successive and continued decreases in the prices charged by firms in an oligopolistic industry. Each firm lowers its price below rivals' prices, hoping to increase its sales and revenues at its rivals' expense.

prime interest rate The benchmark *interest rate* that banks use as a reference point for a wide range of loans to businesses and individuals.

principal-agent problem A conflict of interest that occurs when agents (workers or managers) pursue their own objectives to the detriment of the principals' (stockholders') goals.

private good A good or service that is individually consumed and that can be profitably provided by privately owned firms because they can exclude nonpayers from receiving the benefits.

private property The right of private persons and firms to obtain, own, control, employ, dispose of, and bequeath *land, capital,* and other property.

private sector The *households* and business *firms* of the economy.

process innovation The development and use of new or improved production or distribution methods.

producer surplus (Web chapter) The difference between the actual price a producer receives (or producers receive) and the minimum acceptable price; the triangular area above the supply curve and below the market price.

product differentiation A strategy in which one firm's product is distinguished from competing products by means of its design, related services, quality, location, or other attributes (except price).

product innovation The development and sale of a new or improved product (or service).

production possibilities curve A curve showing the different combinations of two goods or services that can be produced in a *full-employment, full-production* economy where the available supplies of resources and technology are fixed.

productive efficiency The production of a good in the least costly way; occurs when production takes place at the output at which *average total cost* is a minimum and *marginal product* per dollar's worth of input is the same for all inputs.

productivity A measure of average output or real output per unit of input. For example, the productivity of labor is determined by dividing real output by hours of work.

productivity growth The percentage change in *productivity* from one period to another.

product market A market in which products are sold by *firms* and bought by *households*.

profit The return to the resource *entrepreneurial ability* (see *normal profit*); *total revenue* minus *total cost* (see *economic profit*).

profit-maximizing combination of resources The quantity of each resource a firm must employ to maximize its profit or minimize its loss; the combination in which the *marginal revenue product* of each resource is equal to its *marginal resource cost* (to its *price* if the resource is employed in a competitive market).

profit-sharing plan A compensation device through which workers receive part of their pay in the form of a share of their employer's profit (if any).

progressive tax A tax whose *average tax rate* increases as the taxpayer's income increases and decreases as the taxpayer's income decreases.

property tax A tax on the value of property (*capital, land, stocks* and *bonds,* and other *assets*) owned by *firms* and *households.*

proportional tax A tax whose *average tax rate* remains constant as the taxpayer's income increases or decreases.

proprietor's income The net income of the owners of unincorporated firms (proprietorships and partnerships).

protective tariff A *tariff* designed to shield domestic producers of a good or service from the competition of foreign producers.

public assistance programs Government programs that pay benefits to those who are unable to earn income (because of permanent disabilities or because they have very low income and dependent children); financed by general tax revenues and viewed as public charity (rather than earned rights).

public choice theory The economic analysis of government decision making, politics, and elections.

public debt The total amount owed by the Federal government to the owners of government securities; equal to the sum of past government *budget deficits* less government *budget surpluses.*

public good A good or service that is characterized by *nonrivalry* and *nonexcludability;* a good or service with these characteristics provided by government.

public interest theory of regulation The presumption that the purpose of the regulation of an *industry* is to protect the public (consumers) from abuse of the power possessed by *natural monopolies.*

public investments Government expenditures on public capital (such as roads, highways, bridges, mass-transit systems, and electric power facilities) and on *human capital* (such as education, training, and health).

public sector The part of the economy that contains all government entities; government.

public utility A firm that produces an essential good or service, has obtained from a government the right to be the sole supplier of the good or service in the area, and is regulated by that government to prevent the abuse of its monopoly power.

purchasing power The amount of goods and services that a monetary unit of income can buy.

purchasing power parity The idea that exchange rates between nations equate the purchasing power of various currencies. Exchange rates between any two nations adjust to reflect the price-level differences between the countries.

pure competition A market structure in which a very large number of firms sells a *standardized product,* into which entry is very easy, in which the individual seller has no control over the product price, and in which there is no nonprice competition; a market characterized by a very large number of buyers and sellers.

pure monopoly A market structure in which one firm sells a unique product, into which entry is blocked, in which the single firm has considerable control over product price, and in which *nonprice competition* may or may not be found.

pure profit (See *economic profit.*)

pure rate of interest An essentially risk-free, long-term interest rate that is free of the influence of market imperfections.

quantity demanded The amount of a good or service that buyers (or a buyer) desire to purchase at a particular price during some period.

quantity supplied The amount of a good or service that producers (or a producer) offer to sell at a particular price during some period.

quasi-public bank A bank that is privately owned but governmentally (publicly) controlled; each of the U.S. *Federal Reserve Banks.*

quasi-public good A good or service to which excludability could apply but that has such a large *spillover benefit* that government sponsors its production to prevent an underallocation of resources.

R&D Research and development activities undertaken to bring about *technological advance.*

rate of exchange The price paid in one's own money to acquire 1 unit of a foreign currency; the rate at which the money of one nation is exchanged for the money of another nation.

rate of return The gain in net revenue divided by the cost of an investment or an *R&D* expenditure; expressed as a percentage.

rational behavior Human behavior based on comparison of marginal costs and marginal benefits; behavior designed to maximize total utility.

rational expectations theory The hypothesis that firms and households expect monetary and fiscal policies to have certain effects on the economy and (in pursuit of their own self-interests) take actions that make these policies ineffective.

rationing function of prices The ability of market forces in competitive markets to equalize *quantity demanded* and *quantity supplied* and to eliminate shortages and surpluses via changes in prices.

real-balances effect The tendency for increases in the *price level* to lower the real value (or purchasing power) of financial assets with fixed money value and, as a result, to reduce total spending and real output, and conversely for decreases in the price level.

real-business-cycle theory A theory that *business cycles* result from changes in technology and resource availability, which affect *productivity* and thus increase or decrease long-run aggregate supply.

real capital (See *capital.*)

real GDP (See *real gross domestic product.*)

real gross domestic product (GDP) *Gross domestic product* adjusted for inflation; gross domestic product in a year divided by the GDP *price index* for that year, the index expressed as a decimal.

real income   The amount of goods and services that can be purchased with *nominal income* during some period of time; nominal income adjusted for inflation.

real interest rate   The interest rate expressed in dollars of constant value (adjusted for *inflation*) and equal to the *nominal interest rate* less the expected rate of inflation.

real wage   The amount of goods and services a worker can purchase with his or her *nominal wage;* the purchasing power of the nominal wage.

recession   A period of declining real GDP, accompanied by lower real income and higher unemployment.

recessionary gap   The amount by which the *aggregate expenditures schedule* must shift upward to increase the real *GDP* to its full-employment, noninflationary level.

Reciprocal Trade Agreements Act   A 1934 Federal law that authorized the president to negotiate up to 50 percent lower tariffs with foreign nations that agreed to reduce their tariffs on U.S. goods. (Such agreements incorporated the *most-favored-nation* clause.)

refinancing the public debt   Paying owners of maturing government securities with money obtained by selling new securities or with new securities.

regressive tax   A tax whose *average tax rate* decreases as the taxpayer's income increases and increases as the taxpayer's income decreases.

regulatory agency   An agency, commission, or board established by the Federal government or a state government to control the prices charged and the services offered by a *natural monopoly.*

rental income   The payments (income) received by those who supply *land* to the economy.

rent-seeking behavior   The actions by persons, firms, or unions to gain special benefits from government at the taxpayers' or someone else's expense.

required reserves   The funds that banks and thrifts must deposit with the *Federal Reserve Bank* (or hold as *vault cash*) to meet the legal *reserve requirement;* a fixed percentage of the bank's or thrift's checkable deposits.

reserve requirement   The specified minimum percentage of its checkable deposits that a bank or thrift must keep on deposit at the Federal Reserve Bank in its district or hold as *vault cash.*

resource   A natural, human, or manufactured item that helps produce goods and services; a productive agent or factor of production.

resource market   A market in which *households* sell and *firms* buy resources or the services of resources.

retiring the public debt   Reducing the size of the *public debt* by purchasing U.S. government securities or by not reissuing maturing securities.

revenue tariff   A *tariff* designed to produce income for the Federal government.

reverse discrimination   The view that the preferential treatment associated with *affirmative action* efforts constitutes discrimination against other groups.

right-to-work law   A state law (in about 22 states) that makes it illegal to require that a worker join a *labor union* in order to retain his or her job; laws that make *union shops* and *agency shops* illegal.

roundabout production   The construction and use of *capital* to aid in the production of *consumer goods.*

rule of reason   The rule stated and applied in the *U.S. Steel case* that only combinations and contracts unreasonably restraining trade are subject to actions under the antitrust laws and that size and possession of monopoly power are not illegal.

rule of 70   A method for determining the number of years it will take for some measure to double, given its annual percentage increase. Example: To determine the number of years it will take for the *price level* to double, divide 70 by the annual rate of *inflation.*

sales tax   A tax levied on the cost (at retail) of a broad group of products.

saving   Disposable income not spent for consumer goods; equal to *disposable income* minus *personal consumption expenditures.*

savings and loan association (S&L)   A firm that accepts deposits primarily from small individual savers and lends primarily to individuals to finance purchases such as autos and homes; now nearly indistinguishable from a *commercial bank.*

saving schedule   A schedule that shows the amounts *households* plan to save (plan not to spend for *consumer goods*), at different levels of *disposable income.*

savings deposit   A deposit that is interest-bearing and that the depositor can normally withdraw at any time.

savings institution   (See *thrift institution.*)

Say's law   The largely discredited macroeconomic generalization that the production of goods and services (supply) creates an equal *demand* for those goods and services.

scarce resources   The limited quantities of *land, capital, labor,* and *entrepreneurial ability* that are never sufficient to satisfy people's virtually unlimited economic wants.

scientific method   The procedure for the systematic pursuit of knowledge involving the observation of facts and the formulation and testing of hypotheses to obtain theories, principles, and laws.

seasonal variations   Increases and decreases in the level of economic activity within a single year, caused by a change in the season.

secular trend   A long-term tendency; a change in some variable over a very long period of years.

self-interest   That which each firm, property owner, worker, and consumer believes is best for itself and seeks to obtain.

seniority   The length of time a worker has been employed absolutely or relative to other workers; may be used to determine which workers will be laid off when there is insufficient work for them all and who will be rehired when more work becomes available.

separation of ownership and control   The fact that different groups of people own a *corporation* (the stockholders) and manage it (the directors and officers).

service   An (intangible) act or use for which a consumer, firm, or government is willing to pay.

Sherman Act   The Federal antitrust act of 1890 that makes monopoly and conspiracies to restrain trade criminal offenses.

shirking   Workers' neglecting or evading work to increase their *utility* or well-being.

shortage   The amount by which the *quantity demanded* of a product exceeds the *quantity supplied* at a particular (below-equilibrium) price.

short run   (1) In microeconomics, a period of time in which producers are able to change the quantities of some but not all of the resources they employ; a period in which some resources (usually plant) are fixed and some are variable. (2) In macroeconomics, a period in which nominal wages and other input prices do not change in response to a change in the price level.

short-run aggregate supply curve   An aggregate supply curve relevant to a time period in which input prices (particularly *nominal wages*) do not change in response to changes in the *price level*.

short-run competitive equilibrium   The price at which the total quantity of a product supplied in the *short run* in a purely competitive industry equals the total quantity of the product demanded and that is equal to or greater than *average variable cost*.

short-run farm problem   The sharp year-to-year changes in the prices of agricultural products and in the incomes of farmers.

short-run supply curve   A supply curve that shows the quantity of a product a firm in a purely competitive industry will offer to sell at various prices in the *short run;* the portion of the firm's short-run marginal cost curve that lies above its *average-variable-cost* curve.

shutdown case   The circumstance in which a firm would experience a loss greater than its total *fixed cost* if it were to produce any output greater than zero; alternatively, a situation in which a firm would cease to operate when the *price* at which it can sell its product is less than its *average variable cost*.

simple multiplier   The *multiplier* in any economy in which government collects no *net taxes*, there are no *imports*, and *investment* is independent of the level of income; equal to 1 divided by the *marginal propensity to save*.

slope of a line   The ratio of the vertical change (the rise or fall) to the horizontal change (the run) between any two points on a line. The slope of an upward-sloping line is positive, reflecting a direct relationship between two variables; the slope of a downward-sloping line is negative, reflecting an inverse relationship between two variables.

Smoot-Hawley Tariff Act   Legislation passed in 1930 that established very high tariffs. Its objective was to reduce imports and stimulate the domestic economy, but it resulted only in retaliatory tariffs by other nations.

social insurance programs   Programs that replace the earnings lost when people retire or are temporarily unemployed, that are financed by payroll taxes, and that are viewed as earned rights (rather than charity).

socially optimal price   The price of a product that results in the most efficient allocation of an economy's resources and that is equal to the *marginal cost* of the product.

social regulation   Regulation in which government is concerned with the conditions under which goods and services are produced, their physical characteristics, and the impact of their production on society; in contrast to *industrial regulation.*

Social Security program   (See *Old Age, Survivors, and Disability Health Insurance.*)

Social Security trust fund   A Federal fund that saves excessive Social Security tax revenues received in one year to meet Social Security benefit obligations that exceed Social Security tax revenues in some subsequent year.

sole proprietorship   An unincorporated *firm* owned and operated by one person.

special economic zones   (Web chapter) Regions of China open to foreign investment, private ownership, and relatively free international trade.

special-interest effect   Any result of government promotion of the interests (goals) of a small group at the expense of a much larger group.

specialization   The use of the resources of an individual, a firm, a region, or a nation to concentrate production on one or a small number of goods and services.

speculation   The activity of buying or selling with the motive of later reselling or rebuying for profit.

spillover   A benefit or cost from production or consumption, accruing without compensation to nonbuyers and nonsellers of the product (see *spillover benefit* and *spillover cost*).

spillover benefit   A benefit obtained without compensation by third parties from the production or consumption of sellers or buyers. Example: A beekeeper benefits when a neighboring farmer plants clover.

spillover cost   A cost imposed without compensation on third parties by the production or consumption of sellers or buyers. Example: A manufacturer dumps toxic chemicals into a river, killing the fish sought by sport fishers.

SSI   (See *Supplemental Security Income.*)

stagflation   Inflation accompanied by stagnation in the rate of growth of output and an increase in unemployment in the economy; simultaneous increases in the *price level* and the *unemployment rate*.

standardized product A product whose buyers are indifferent to the seller from whom they purchase it as long as the price charged by all sellers is the same; a product all units of which are identical and thus are perfect substitutes for each other.

Standard Oil case A 1911 antitrust case in which Standard Oil was found guilty of violating the *Sherman Act* by illegally monopolizing the petroleum industry. As a remedy the company was divided into several competing firms.

startup (firm) A new firm focused on creating and introducing a particular new product or employing a specific new production or distribution method.

state bank A *commercial bank* authorized by a state government to engage in the business of banking.

state-owned enterprises (Web chapter) Businesses that are owned by the government; the major type of enterprises in Russia and China before their transitions to the market system.

statistical discrimination The practice of judging an individual on the basis of the average characteristic of the group to which he or she belongs rather than on his or her own personal characteristics.

stock (corporate) An ownership share in a corporation.

stock options Contracts that enable executives or other key employees to buy shares of their employers' stock at fixed, lower prices when the stock prices rise.

store of value An *asset* set aside for future use; one of the three functions of *money*.

strategic behavior Self-interested economic actions that take into account the expected reactions of others.

strategic trade policy The use of trade barriers to reduce the risk inherent in product development by domestic firms, particularly that involving advanced technology.

strike The withholding of labor services by an organized group of workers (a *labor union*).

structural-change hypothesis The explanation that ascribes the decline of unionism in the United States to changes in the structure of the economy and of the labor force.

structural unemployment Unemployment of workers whose skills are not demanded by employers, who lack sufficient skill to obtain employment, or who cannot easily move to locations where jobs are available.

subsidy A payment of funds (or goods and services) by a government, firm, or household for which it receives no good or service in return. When made by a government, it is a *government transfer payment*.

substitute goods Products or services that can be used in place of each other. When the price of one falls, the demand for the other product falls; conversely, when the price of one product rises, the demand for the other product rises.

substitution effect (1) A change in the quantity demanded of a *consumer good* that results from a change in its relative expensiveness caused by a change in the product's price; (2) the effect of a change in the price of a *resource* on the quantity of the resource employed by a firm, assuming no change in its output.

sunk cost A cost that has been incurred and cannot be recovered.

Supplemental Security Income (SSI) A federally financed and administered program that provides a uniform nationwide minimum income for the aged, blind, and disabled who do not qualify for benefits under the *Old Age, Survivors, and Disability Health Insurance* or *unemployment insurance* program in the United States.

supply A schedule showing the amounts of a good or service that sellers (or a seller) will offer at various prices during some period.

supply curve A curve illustrating *supply*.

supply factor (in growth) An increase in the availability of a resource, an improvement in its quality, or an expansion of technological knowledge that makes it possible for an economy to produce a greater output of goods and services.

supply-side economics A view of macroeconomics that emphasizes the role of costs and *aggregate supply* in explaining *inflation*, *unemployment*, and *economic growth*.

surplus The amount by which the *quantity supplied* of a product exceeds the *quantity demanded* at a specific (above-equilibrium) price.

surplus payment A payment to a resource that is not required to ensure its availability in the production process; for example, land rent.

surplus value (Web chapter) The amount by which a worker's daily output in dollar terms exceeds his or her daily wage; the amount of the worker's output appropriated by capitalists as profit; a Marxian term.

tacit collusion Any method used by an oligopolist to set prices and outputs that does not involve outright (or overt) *collusion*. *Price leadership* is a frequent example.

TANF (See *Temporary Assistance for Needy Families*.)

tariff A tax imposed by a nation on an imported good.

taste-for-discrimination model A theory that views discrimination as a preference for which an employer is willing to pay.

tax An involuntary payment of money (or goods and services) to a government by a *household* or *firm* for which the household or firm receives no good or service directly in return.

tax incidence The person or group that ends up paying a tax.

tax subsidy A grant in the form of reduced taxes through favorable tax treatment. For example, employer-paid health insurance is exempt from Federal income and payroll taxes.

tax-transfer disincentives Decreases in the incentives to work, save, invest, innovate, and take risks that allegedly result from high *marginal tax rates* and *transfer payments*.

Taylor rule A modern monetary rule proposed by economist John Taylor that would stipulate exactly how much the Federal

Reserve should change interest rates in response to divergences of real GDP from potential GDP and divergences of actual rates of inflation from a target rate of inflation.

technological advance   New and better goods and services and new and better ways of producing or distributing them.

technology   The body of knowledge and techniques that can be used to combine *economic resources* to produce goods and services.

Temporary Assistance for Needy Families (TANF)   A state-administered and partly federally funded program in the United States that provides financial aid to poor families; the basic welfare program for low-income families in the United States; contains time limits and work requirements.

terms of trade   The rate at which units of one product can be exchanged for units of another product; the price of a good or service; the amount of one good or service that must be given up to obtain 1 unit of another good or service.

theoretical economics   The process of deriving and applying economic theories and principles.

theory of human capital   The generalization that *wage differentials* are the result of differences in the amount of *human capital investment* and that the incomes of lower-paid workers are raised by increasing the amount of such investment.

thrift institution   A *savings and loan association, mutual savings bank,* or *credit union.*

tight money policy   Federal Reserve System actions that contract, or restrict, the growth of the nation's *money supply* for the purpose of reducing or eliminating inflation.

till money   (See *vault cash.*)

time deposit   An interest-earning deposit in a *commercial bank* or *thrift institution* that the depositor can withdraw without penalty after the end of a specified period.

token money   Coins having a *face value* greater than their *intrinsic value.*

total cost   The sum of *fixed cost* and *variable cost.*

total demand   The demand schedule or the *demand curve* of all buyers of a good or service; also called market demand.

total demand for money   The sum of the *transactions demand for money* and the *asset demand for money.*

total product   The total output of a particular good or service produced by a firm (or a group of firms or the entire economy).

total revenue   The total number of dollars received by a firm (or firms) from the sale of a product; equal to the total expenditures for the product produced by the firm (or firms); equal to the quantity sold (demanded) multiplied by the price at which it is sold.

total-revenue test   A test to determine elasticity of *demand* between any two prices: Demand is elastic if *total revenue* moves in the opposite direction from price; it is inelastic when it moves in the same direction as price; and it is of unitary elasticity when it does not change when price changes.

total spending   The total amount that buyers of goods and services spend or plan to spend; also called *aggregate expenditures.*

total supply   The supply schedule or the *supply curve* of all sellers of a good or service; also called market supply.

total utility   The total amount of satisfaction derived from the consumption of a single product or a combination of products.

township and village enterprises   (Web chapter) Privately owned rural manufacturing firms in China.

trade balance   The export of goods (or goods and services) of a nation less its imports of goods (or goods and services).

trade bloc   A group of nations that lower or abolish trade barriers among members. Examples include the *European Union* and the nations of the *North American Free Trade Agreement.*

trade controls   *Tariffs, export subsidies, import quotas,* and other means a nation may employ to reduce *imports* and expand *exports.*

trade deficit   The amount by which a nation's *imports* of goods (or goods and services) exceed its *exports* of goods (or goods and services).

trademark   A legal protection that gives the originators of a product an exclusive right to use the brand name.

tradeoff   The sacrifice of some or all of one economic goal, good, or service to achieve some other goal, good, or service.

trade surplus   The amount by which a nation's *exports* of goods (or goods and services) exceed its *imports* of goods (or goods and services).

trading possibilities line   A line that shows the different combinations of two products that an economy is able to obtain (consume) when it specializes in the production of one product and trades (exports) it to obtain the other product.

transactions demand for money   The amount of money people want to hold for use as a *medium of exchange* (to make payments); varies directly with the *nominal GDP.*

transfer payment   A payment of *money* (or goods and services) by a government to a *household* or *firm* for which the payer receives no good or service directly in return.

tying contract   A requirement imposed by a seller that a buyer purchase another (or other) of its products as a condition for buying a desired product; a practice forbidden by the *Clayton Act.*

unanticipated inflation   Increases in the price level (*inflation*) at a rate greater than expected.

underemployment   (1) The failure to produce the maximum amount of goods and services that can be produced from the resources employed; the failure to achieve *full production;* (2) a situation in which workers are employed in positions requiring less education and skill than they have.

undistributed corporate profits   After-tax corporate profits not distributed as dividends to stockholders; corporate or business saving; also called retained earnings.

unemployment   The failure to use all available *economic resources* to produce desired goods and services; the failure of the economy to fully employ its *labor force*.

unemployment compensation   (See *unemployment insurance*).

unemployment insurance   The social insurance program that in the United States is financed by state *payroll taxes* on employers and makes income available to workers who become unemployed and are unable to find jobs.

unemployment rate   The percentage of the *labor force* unemployed at any time.

uninsurable risk   An event that would result in a loss and whose occurrence is uncontrollable and unpredictable. Insurance companies are not willing to sell insurance against such a loss.

union shop   A place of employment where the employer may hire either *labor union* members or nonmembers but where nonmembers must become members within a specified period of time or lose their jobs.

unit elasticity   Demand or supply for which the *elasticity coefficient* is equal to 1; means that the percentage change in the quantity demanded or supplied is equal to the percentage change in price.

unit labor cost   Labor cost per unit of output; total labor cost divided by total output; also equal to the *nominal wage* rate divided by the *average product* of labor.

unit of account   A standard unit in which prices can be stated and the value of goods and services can be compared; one of the three functions of *money*.

unlimited liability   Absence of any limits on the maximum amount that an individual (usually a business owner) may become legally required to pay.

unlimited wants   The insatiable desire of consumers for goods and services that will give them satisfaction or *utility*.

unplanned changes in inventories   Changes in inventories that firms did not anticipate; changes in inventories that occur because of unexpected increases or decreases of aggregate spending (of *aggregate expenditures*).

unplanned investment   Actual investment less *planned investment*; increases or decreases in the *inventories* of firms resulting from production greater than sales.

urban collectives   (Web chapter) Chinese enterprises jointly owned by their managers and their workforces and located in urban areas.

Uruguay Round   A 1995 trade agreement (to be fully implemented by 2005) that established the *World Trade Organization (WTO)*, liberalized trade in goods and services, provided added protection to intellectual property (for example, *patents* and *copyrights*), and reduced farm subsidies.

U.S. Steel case   The antitrust action brought by the Federal government against the U.S. Steel Corporation in which the courts ruled (in 1920) that only unreasonable restraints of trade were illegal and that size and the possession of monopoly power were not violations of the antitrust laws.

usury laws   State laws that specify the maximum legal interest rate at which loans can be made.

utility   The want-satisfying power of a good or service; the satisfaction or pleasure a consumer obtains from the consumption of a good or service (or from the consumption of a collection of goods and services).

utility-maximizing rule   The principle that to obtain the greatest *utility*, the consumer should allocate *money income* so that the last dollar spent on each good or service yields the same marginal utility.

value added   The value of the product sold by a *firm* less the value of the products (materials) purchased and used by the firm to produce the product.

value-added tax   A tax imposed on the difference between the value of the product sold by a firm and the value of the goods purchased from other firms to produce the product; used in several European countries.

value judgment   Opinion of what is desirable or undesirable; belief regarding what ought or ought not to be (regarding what is right or just and wrong or unjust).

value of money   The quantity of goods and services for which a unit of money (a dollar) can be exchanged; the purchasing power of a unit of money; the reciprocal of the *price level*.

variable cost   A cost that in total increases when the firm increases its output and decreases when the firm reduces its output.

VAT   (See *value-added tax*.)

vault cash   The *currency* a bank has in its vault and cash drawers.

velocity   The number of times per year that the average dollar in the *money supply* is spent for *final goods and services*; nominal GDP divided by the money supply.

vertical integration   A group of *plants* engaged in different stages of the production of a final product and owned by a single *firm*.

vertical intercept   The point at which a line meets the vertical axis of a graph.

vertical merger   The merger of one or more *firms* engaged in different stages of the production of a final product.

very long run   A period in which *technology* can change and in which *firms* can introduce new products.

vicious circle of poverty   (Web chapter) A problem common in some *developing countries* in which their low per capita incomes are an obstacle to realizing the levels of saving and investment requisite to acceptable rates of economic growth.

voice mechanism   Communication by workers through their union to resolve grievances with an employer.

voluntary export restrictions   Voluntary limitations by countries or firms of their exports to a particular foreign nation to avoid enactment of formal trade barriers by that nation.

wage   The price paid for the use or services of *labor* per unit of time (per hour, per day, and so on).

wage differential   The difference between the *wage* received by one worker or group of workers and that received by another worker or group of workers.

wage discrimination   The payment of a lower wage to members of a less preferred group than that paid to members of a more preferred group for the same work.

wage rate   (See *wage*.)

wages   The income of those who supply the economy with *labor*.

wealth   Anything that has value because it produces income or could produce income. Wealth is a stock; income is a flow. Assets less liabilities; net worth.

wealth effect   The tendency for people to increase their consumption spending when the value of their financial and real assets rises and to decrease their consumption spending when the value of those assets falls.

welfare programs   (See *public assistance programs*.)

Wheeler-Lea Act   The Federal act of 1938 that amended the *Federal Trade Commission Act* by prohibiting and giving the commission power to investigate unfair and deceptive acts or practices of commerce (such as false and misleading advertising and the misrepresentation of products).

"will to develop"   (Web chapter) The state of wanting economic growth strongly enough to change from old to new ways of doing things.

World Bank   (Web chapter) A bank that lends (and guarantees loans) to developing nations to assist them in increasing their *capital stock* and thus in achieving *economic growth;* formally, the International Bank for Reconstruction and Development.

world price   The international market price of a good or service, determined by world demand and supply.

World Trade Organization (WTO)   An organization of 145 nations (as of 2003) that oversees the provisions of the current world trade agreement, resolves trade disputes stemming from it, and holds forums for further rounds of trade negotiations.

WTO   (See *World Trade Organization*.)

X-inefficiency   The failure to produce any specific output at the lowest average (and total) cost possible.

National income and related statistics for selected years, 1978–2002

National income statistics in rows 1–17 are in billions of current dollars. Details may not add to totals because of rounding.

			1978	1979	1980	1981	1982	1983	1984	1985	1986	1987
THE SUM OF	1	Personal consumption expenditures	1,430.4	1,596.3	1,762.9	1,944.2	2,079.3	2,286.4	2,498.4	2,712.6	2,895.2	3,105.3
	2	Gross private domestic investment	436.0	490.6	477.9	570.8	516.1	564.2	735.5	736.3	747.2	781.5
	3	Government purchases	455.6	503.5	569.7	631.4	684.4	735.9	800.8	878.3	942.3	997.9
	4	Net exports	−26.1	−24.0	−14.9	−15.0	−20.5	−51.7	−102.0	−114.2	−131.9	−142.3
EQUALS	5	Gross domestic product	2,295.9	2,566.4	2,795.6	3,131.3	3,259.2	3,534.9	3,932.7	4,213.0	4,452.9	4,742.5
LESS	6	Consumption of fixed capital	261.5	300.4	345.3	394.8	436.4	456.1	482.3	516.5	551.6	586.1
EQUALS	7	Net domestic product	2,034.4	2,266.0	2,450.3	2,736.5	2,822.8	3,078.8	3,450.4	3,696.5	3,901.3	4,156.4
LESS	8	Net foreign factor income earned in the U.S.	−22.1	−32.9	−35.3	−34.7	−36.5	−36.9	−35.3	−25.3	−15.5	−13.7
LESS	9	Indirect business taxes*	196.3	223.3	242.6	274.1	256.3	319.2	323.4	341.4	391.0	366.7
EQUALS	10	National income	1,860.2	2,075.6	2,243.0	2,497.1	2,603.0	2,796.5	3,162.3	3,380.4	3,525.8	3,803.4
LESS	11	Social Security contributions	131.3	152.7	166.2	195.7	208.9	226.0	257.5	281.4	303.4	323.1
LESS	12	Corporate income taxes	83.5	88.0	84.8	81.1	63.1	77.2	94.0	96.5	106.5	127.1
LESS	13	Undistributed corporate profits	82.9	77.0	49.6	64.1	61.9	93.2	124.7	128.3	88.0	107.3
PLUS	14	Transfer payments*	285.8	323.6	381.5	443.2	499.3	546.8	588.7	640.8	684.5	716.6
EQUALS	15	Personal income	1,848.3	2,081.5	2,323.9	2,599.4	2,768.4	2,946.9	3,274.8	3,515.0	3,712.4	3,962.5
LESS	16	Personal taxes	233.5	273.3	304.1	351.5	361.6	360.9	387.2	428.5	449.9	503.0
EQUALS	17	Disposable income	1,614.8	1,808.2	2,019.8	2,247.9	2,406.8	2,586.0	2,887.6	3,086.5	3,262.5	3,459.5

RELATED STATISTICS

		1978	1979	1980	1981	1982	1983	1984	1985	1986	1987
18	Real gross domestic product (in billions of 1996 dollars)	4,760.6	4,912.1	4,900.9	5,021.0	4,919.3	5,132.3	5,505.2	5,717.1	5,912.4	6,113.3
19	Percent change in real GDP	5.5	3.2	−0.2	2.5	−2.0	4.3	7.3	3.8	3.4	3.4
20	Real disposable income per capita (in 1996 dollars)	15,845	16,120	16,063	16,265	16,328	16,673	17,799	18,229	18,641	18,870
21	Consumer price index (1982–84 = 100)	65.2	72.6	82.4	90.9	96.5	99.6	103.9	107.6	109.6	113.6
22	Rate of inflation (%)	7.6	11.3	13.5	10.3	6.2	3.2	4.3	3.6	1.9	3.6
23	Index of industrial production (1997 = 100)	63.4	65.3	63.5	64.3	60.9	62.5	68.1	68.8	69.5	72.8
24	Supply of money, M1 (in billions of dollars)	356.9	381.4	408.1	436.2	474.3	520.8	551.2	619.1	724.0	749.6
25	Prime interest rate (%)	9.06	12.67	15.27	18.87	14.86	10.79	12.04	9.93	8.33	8.21
26	Population (in millions)	222.6	225.1	227.7	230.0	232.2	234.3	236.3	238.5	240.7	242.8
27	Civilian labor force (in millions)	102.3	105.0	106.9	108.7	110.2	111.6	113.5	115.5	117.8	119.9
28	Unemployment (in millions)	6.2	6.1	7.6	8.3	10.7	10.7	8.5	8.3	8.2	7.4
29	Unemployment rate as % of civilian labor force	6.1	5.8	7.1	7.6	9.7	9.6	7.5	7.2	7.0	6.2
30	Index of productivity (1992 = 100)	80.7	80.7	80.4	82.0	81.7	84.6	87.0	88.7	91.4	91.9
31	Annual change in productivity (%)	1.1	0.0	−0.3	1.9	−0.4	3.6	2.8	2.0	3.0	0.5
32	Trade balance on current account (in billions of dollars)	−15.1	−0.3	2.3	5.0	−5.5	−38.7	−94.3	−118.2	−147.2	−160.7
33	Public debt (in billions of dollars)	776.6	829.5	909.1	994.8	1,137.3	1,371.7	1,564.7	1,817.5	2,120.6	2,346.1

*Includes a statistical discrepancy.